THE

GOSPEL ACCORDING TO S. LUKE

REV. ALFRED PLUMMER, M.A., D.D.

PRINTED IN GREAT BRITAIN BY
T. AND A. CONSTABLE LIMITED
FOR
T. & T. CLARK LIMITED, EDINBURGH

ISBN 0 567 05023 8

First Edition . . *1896*
Fifth Edition . . *1922*
Latest Impression . *1975*

The
International Critical Commentary
on the Holy Scriptures of the Old and New Testaments.

PLANNED AND FOR YEARS EDITED BY

THE REV. ALFRED PLUMMER, M.A., D.D.

PROFESSOR SAMUEL ROLLES DRIVER, D.D., D.LITT.

PROFESSOR CHARLES AUGUSTUS BRIGGS, D.D., D.LITT.

THE INTERNATIONAL CRITICAL COMMENTARY

A CRITICAL AND EXEGETICAL COMMENTARY

ON THE

GOSPEL ACCORDING TO S. LUKE

BY THE

REV. ALFRED PLUMMER, M.A., D.D.

LATE MASTER OF UNIVERSITY COLLEGE, DURHAM

FORMERLY FELLOW AND SENIOR TUTOR OF TRINITY COLLEGE, OXFORD

FIFTH EDITION

EDINBURGH

T. & T. CLARK, 38 GEORGE STREET

PREFACE TO THE FIRST EDITION

THIS volume has no such ambitious aim as that of being a final commentary on the Gospel according to S. Luke. The day is probably still far distant when any such commentary can be written. One of the difficulties with which the present commentator has had to contend is the impossibility of keeping abreast of all that is constantly appearing respecting the Synoptic Gospels as a whole and this or that detail in them. And the Third Gospel abounds in details which have elicited special treatment at the hands of a variety of scholars. Every quarter, indeed almost every month, brings its list of new books, some of which the writer wishes that he could have seen before his own words were printed. But to wait is but to prolong, if not to increase, one's difficulties: it is waiting *dum defluat amnis.* Notes written and rewritten three or four times must be fixed in some form at last, if they are ever to be published. And these notes are now offered to those who care to use them, not as the last word on any one subject, but simply as one more stage in the long process of eliciting from the inexhaustible storehouse of the Gospel narrative some of those things which it is intended to convey to us. They will have done their work if they help someone who is far better equipped entirely to supersede them.

The writer of this volume is well aware of some of its shortcomings. There are omissions which have been knowingly tolerated for one or other of two adequate reasons. (1) This series is to include a *Commentary on the Synopsis of the Four Gospels* by the Rev. Dr. Sanday, Lady Margaret Professor of Divinity, Oxford, and his distinguished pupil, the Rev. W. C. Allen, Fellow and Lecturer of Exeter College. Various questions, especially as regards the relations of the Third Gospel to the First and Second, which have been but slightly touched or entirely passed over in this volume, can be more suitably treated, and will be much more efficiently treated, by those who are to comment on the Synopsis. (2) Economy of space has had to be considered and rigorously enforced. It has been thought undesirable to allow more than one volume to any one book in the New Testament: and therefore subjects, which might with propriety be discussed at some length in a work on the Gospel of S. Luke, have of necessity been handled very briefly or left entirely untouched. Indeed, as editor of those New Testament volumes which are written by British scholars, the present writer has been obliged to strike out a good deal of what he had written as contributor to this series. And it has been with a view to economize space that the paraphrastic summaries, which are so very valuable a feature in the commentary on *Romans*, have been altogether omitted, as being a luxury rather than a necessity in a commentary on one of the Synoptic Gospels. For the same reason separate headings to sections and to special notes have been used very sparingly. The sub-sections have no separate headings, but are preceded by an introductory paragraph, the first sentence of which is equivalent to a heading.

The fact of the same person being both contributor and editor has, in the case of this volume, produced shortcomings of another kind. Two heads are better than one, and two pairs of eyes are better than one. Unintentional and unnecessary omissions might have been avoided, and questionable or erroneous statements might have been amended, if the writer had had the advantage of another's supervision. Even in the humble but important work of detecting misprints the gain of having a different reviser is great. Only those who have had the experience know how easy it is for the same eye to pass the same mistakes again and again.

If this commentary has any special features, they will perhaps be found in the illustrations taken from Jewish writings, in the abundance of references to the Septuagint and to the Acts and other books of the New Testament, in the frequent quotations of renderings in the Latin Versions, and in the attention which has been paid, both in the Introduction and throughout the Notes, to the marks of S. Luke's style.

The illustrations from Jewish writings have been supplied, not because the writer has made any special study of them, but because it is becoming recognized that the pseudepigraphical writings of the Jews and early Jewish Christians are now among the most promising helps towards understanding the New Testament; and because these writings have of late years become much more accessible than formerly, notably by the excellent editions of the *Book of Enoch* by Mr. Charles, of the *Psalms of Solomon* by Professor Ryle and Dr. James, and of the *Fourth Book of Ezra* by the late Professor Bensly and Dr. James.[1]

A very eminent scholar has said that the best commentary on the New Testament is a good Concordance; and another venerable scholar is reported to have said that the best commentary on the New Testament is the Vulgate. There is truth in both these sayings: and, with regard to the second of them, if the Vulgate by itself is helpful, *à fortiori* the Vulgate side by side with the Latin Versions which preceded it is likely to be helpful. An effort has

[1] For general information on these Jewish writings see Schürer, *Hist. of the Jewish People in the Time of Jesus Christ*, Edinburgh, 1886, Div. II. vol. iii.; W. J. Deane, *Pseudepigrapha*, Edinburgh, 1891; J. Winter und A. Wünsche, *Die jüdische Literatur seit Abschluss des Kanons*, Trier: Part III. has just appeared.

been made to render those who use this commentary to a large extent independent of a Concordance, and to some extent independent of the invaluable edition of the Vulgate now being produced by the Bishop of Salisbury and Mr. White. Great trouble has been taken with the numerous references to the Septuagint, the books of the New Testament, and other writings. The large majority of them have been verified at least twice. But the difficulty of excluding error in such things is so great that the writer cannot suppose that he has succeeded in doing so. It is possible that a few references have accidentally escaped verification. A very few have been knowingly admitted without it, because the reference seemed to be of value, the source was trustworthy, and verification was not easy.

Reasons are stated in the Introduction for regarding a study of S. Luke's style as a matter of great interest and importance; and it is hoped that the analysis given of it there will be found useful. A minute acquaintance with it tells us something about the writer of the Third Gospel. It proves to us that he is identical with the writer of the Acts, and that the whole of both these books comes from his hand. And it justifies us in accepting the unswerving tradition of the first eight or nine centuries, that the writer of these two books was Luke the beloved physician.

Dogma in the polemical sense is excluded from the plan of these commentaries. It is not the business of the commentator to advocate this or that belief. But dogma in the historical sense must of necessity be conspicuous in a commentary on any one of the Gospels. It is a primary duty of a commentator to ascertain the convictions of the writer whose statements he undertakes to explain. This is specially true of the Third Gospel, whose author tells us that he wrote for the very purpose of exhibiting the historical basis of the Christian faith (i. 1–4). The Evangelist assures Theophilus, and with him all other Christians, that he knows, upon first-hand and carefully investigated evidence, that at a definite point in the history of the world, not far removed from his own time, a Prophet of God once more appeared in Israel to herald the coming of the Christ (iii. 1–6), and that his appearance was immediately followed by that of the Christ Himself (iii. 23, iv. 14, 15), whose Ministry, Passion, Death, and Resurrection he then narrates in detail. On all these points the student is again and again met by the question, What does the Evangelist mean? And, although about this or that word or sentence there may often be room for discussion, about the meaning of the Gospel as a whole there is no doubt. If we ask what were "the things wherein" Theophilus "was instructed" and of "the certainty" concerning which he is assured, the answer is not difficult. We may take the Old Roman Creed as a convenient summary of it.

Πιστεύω εἰς Θεὸν πατέρα παντοκράτορα (i. 37, iii. 8, xi. 2–4, xii. 32, etc.). Καὶ εἰς Χριστὸν Ἰησοῦν, υἱὸν αὐτοῦ τὸν μονογενῆ (i. 31, ii. 21, 49, ix. 35, x. 21, 22, xxii. 29, 70, xxiii. [33] 46: comp. iv. 41, viii. 28), τὸν κύριον ἡμῶν (i. 43, ii. 11, vii. 13, x. 1, xi. 39, xii. 42, xvii. 5, 6, xix. 8, 31, xxii. 61, xxiv. 3, 34) τὸν γεννηθέντα ἐκ πνεύματος ἁγίου καὶ Μαρίας τῆς παρθένου (i. 31–35, 43, ii. 6, 7), τὸν ἐπὶ Ποντίου Πιλάτου σταυρωθέντα καὶ ταφέντα (xxii., xxiii.), τῇ τρίτῃ ἡμέρᾳ ἀναστάντα ἐκ νεκρῶν (xxiv. 1–49), ἀναβάντα εἰς τοὺς οὐρανούς (xxiv. 50–53), καθήμενον ἐν δεξιᾷ τοῦ πατρός (xxii. 69), ὅθεν ἔρχεται κρῖναι ζῶντας καὶ νεκρούς (comp. ix. 26, xii. 35–48, xviii. 8). Καὶ εἰς πνεῦμα ἅγιον (i. 15, 35, 41, 67, ii. 26, iv. 1, 14, xi. 13, xii. 10, 12)· ἁγίαν ἐκκλησίαν (comp. i. 74, 75, ix. 1–6, x. 1–16, xxiv. 49)· ἄφεσιν ἁμαρτιῶν (i. 77, iii. 3, xxiv. 47)· σαρκὸς ἀνάστασιν (xiv. 14, xx. 27–40).

The Evangelist's own convictions on most of these points are manifest; and we need not doubt that they include the principal things in which Theophilus had been instructed, and which the writer of the Gospel solemnly affirms to be well established. Whether in our eyes they are well established depends upon the estimate which we form of his testimony. Is he a truth-loving and competent witness? Does the picture which he draws agree with what can be known from other authorities? Could he or his informants have invented the words and works which he attributes to Jesus Christ? A patient and fair student of the Third Gospel will not be at a loss for an answer.

ALFRED PLUMMER.

University College, Durham,
Feast of S. Luke, 1896.

PREFACE TO THE SECOND EDITION

THE correction of many misprints and other small errors has been greatly facilitated by the generous help of several correspondents, and by the invaluable *Concordance to the Greek Testament*, according to the texts of WH., Tischendorf, and R.V., by Moulton and Geden, an indispensable aid, which had not been published when the first edition of this volume appeared. But to no one is the writer more indebted than to the Rev. John Richard Pullan, who has bestowed upon the work of a stranger an amount of attention which one would not venture to solicit from an old friend.

This edition has also been improved by many small insertions, chiefly of references to books, which have either appeared, or have come to the writer's knowledge, since the first edition was published. First amongst these in importance is vol. i. of the new *Dictionary of the Bible*, edited by Dr. Hastings, which should be in the hands of every Biblical student. Three articles in particular may be mentioned, both on account of their excellence, and also of their helpfulness to the student of the Third Gospel: these are the articles on "Angels" (for this Gospel might be called the Gospel of the Angels, so often does it mention these glorious beings); on the "Chronology of the New Testament"; and on the "Acts of the Apostles." To this must be added the new edition of A. S. Lewis' translation of the *Sinaitic Syriac Palimpsest;* the editions of *The Assumption of Moses* and *The Apocalypse of Baruch*, by R. H. Charles; and of *The Book of the Secrets of Enoch*, by Morfill and Charles; *Das Kindheitsevangelium*, by A. Resch; *Bibelstudien* and *Neue Bibelstudien*, by G. A. Deissmann, both of which contain valuable illustrations of Biblical Greek from papyri; *Grammatik des NT. Griechisch*, by F. Blass; and the instructive but eccentric *Historical Greek Grammar*, by A. N. Jannaris. The interesting work on the *Philology of the Gospels*, by F. Blass, is chiefly occupied with the Gospel of S. Luke, and should be read side by side with the sections of the Introduction to this volume which treat of the same topics. The writer has only to add, that nothing which he has read since he wrote the Introduction has shaken his convictions as to the authorship, date, or integrity of this Gospel.

A. P.

University College, Durham,
Whitsuntide, 1898.

PREFACE TO THE THIRD EDITION

THIS edition is marked by the correction of some errors that had escaped notice, and by the addition of numerous references and short notes. Since the second edition was published, three volumes have appeared which the student of the Third Gospel cannot afford to neglect. These are the *Horae Synopticae* of the Rev. Sir John C. Hawkins, *The Gospel according to S. Luke in Greek*, edited by the Rev. Arthur Wright, and vol. ii. of the *Dictionary of the Bible*, edited by Dr. Hastings. In the last of these, the article on "Jesus Christ" is a masterpiece of critical acumen and lucidity combined with reverential treatment. The present writer desires to express his obligations to all three volumes. Mr. Wright suggests in his preface that his own work should be used in conjunction with this commentary; and those who use the commentary will certainly profit greatly if they follow his suggestion.

A. P.

University College, Durham,
Whitsuntide, 1900.

CONTENTS

INTRODUCTION.

§ 1. THE AUTHOR.

As in the case of the other Gospels, the author is not named in the book itself. But two things may be regarded as practically certain, and a third as highly probable in itself and much more probable than any other hypothesis. (i.) The author of the Third Gospel is the author of the Acts. (ii.) The author of the Acts was a companion of S. Paul. (iii.) This companion was S. Luke.

(i.) *The Author of the Third Gospel is the Author of the Acts.*

This position is so generally admitted by critics of all schools that not much time need be spent in discussing it. Both books are dedicated to Theophilus. The later book refers to the former. The language and style and arrangement of the two books are so similar, and this similarity is found to exist in such a multitude of details (many of which are very minute), that the hypothesis of careful imitation by a different writer is absolutely excluded. The idea of minute literary analysis with a view to discover peculiarities and preferences in language was an idea foreign to the writers of the first two centuries; and no known writer of that age gives evidence of the immense skill which would be necessary in order to employ the results of such an analysis for the production of an elaborate imitation. To suppose that the author of the Acts carefully imitated the Third Gospel, in order that his work might be attributed to the Evangelist, or that the Evangelist carefully imitated the Acts, in order that his Gospel might be attributed to the author of the Acts, is to postulate a literary miracle. Such an idea would not have occurred to any one; and if it had, he would not have been able to execute it with such triumphant success as is conspicuous here. Any one who will underline in a few chapters of the Third Gospel the phrases, words, and constructions which are specially frequent in the book, and then underline the same phrases, words, and constructions wherever they occur in the Acts, will soon have a strong conviction respecting the identity of authorship. The converse process will lead to a similar result. Moreover, the expressions which can be marked in this way by no means exhaust the points of similarity between the two books. There are parallels of *description*; *e.g.* about angelic appearances (comp. Lk. i. 11 with Acts xii. 7; Lk. i. 38 with Acts i. 11 and x. 7; Lk. ii. 9 and xxiv. 4 with Acts i. 10 and x. 30); and about other matters (comp. Lk. i. 39 with Acts i. 15; Lk. ii. 39 with Acts xiii. 29; Lk. iii. 8 with Acts xxvi. 20; Lk. xx. 1 with Acts iv. 1; Lk. xxi. 18 with Acts xxvii. 34; Lk. xxi. 35 with Acts xvii. 26; Lk. xxiii. 2 with Acts xxiv. 2–5; Lk. xxiii. 5 with Acts x. 37; Lk. xxiv. 27 with Acts viii. 35).[1] And there are parallels of *arrangement*. The main portion of the Gospel has three marked divisions: The Ministry *in Galilee* (iii. 1–ix. 50), *between Galilee and Jerusalem* (ix. 51–xix. 28), and *in Jerusalem* (xix. 29–xxiv. 11). And the main portion of the Acts has three marked divisions: *Hebraic* (ii.–v.), *Transitional* (vi.–xii.), and *Gentile* (xiii.–xxviii.). In the one case the movement is from Galilee through Samaria, etc. to Jerusalem: in the other from Jerusalem through Samaria, etc. to Rome. And in both cases there is an introduction connecting the main narrative with what precedes.

(ii.) *The Author of Acts was a Companion of S. Paul.*

A full discussion of this statement belongs to the commentary on the Acts rather than to the present volume: but the main points in the evidence must be noted here. It is perhaps no exaggeration to say that nothing in biblical criticism is more certain than this statement.

There are the "we" sections in which the writer uses the first person plural in describing journeys of S. Paul. This "we" is found in Codex Bezae as early as xi. 28 at Antioch, and may represent a true tradition without being the original reading.[2] It appears certainly xvi. 10 at Troas[3] and continues to Philippi (xvi. 17).[4] Several years later it reappears at Philippi (xx. 5)[5] and continues to Jerusalem (xxi. 18).[6] Finally, it reappears at the departure for Italy (xxvii. 1)[7] and continues to Rome (xxviii. 16).[8]

[1] J. Friedrich, *Das Lukasevangelium und die Apostelgeschichte Werke desselben Verfassers*, Halle a.S., 1890. The value of this useful pamphlet is somewhat lessened by want of care in sifting the readings. The argument as a whole stands; but the statistics on which it is based are often not exact.

[2] For *ἀναστὰς δὲ εἶς ἐξ αὐτῶν* D has *συνεστραμμένων δὲ ἡμῶν ἔφη εἶς ἐξ αὐτῶν*, *revertentibus autem nobis ait unus ex ipsis*. This reading is also found in Augustine (*De Serm. Dom.* ii. 57 [xvii.]).

[3] *ἐζητήσαμεν ἐξελθεῖν.* [4] *ἡμῖν ἔκραζεν.* [5] *ἔμενον ἡμᾶς.*

[6] *εἰσῄει ὁ Παῦλος σὺν ἡμῖν.* [7] *τοῦ ἀποπλεῖν ἡμᾶς.* [8] *εἰσήλθαμεν εἰς Ῥώμην.*

The "we" necessarily implies companionship, and may possibly represent a diary kept at the time. That the "we" sections are by the same hand as the rest of the book is shown by the simple and natural way in which they fit into the narrative, by the references in them to other parts of the narrative, and by the marked identity of style. The expressions which are so characteristic of this writer run right through the whole book. They are as frequent inside as outside the "we" sections, and no change of style can be noted between them and the rest of the treatise. The change of person is intelligible and truthlike, distinguishing the times when the writer was with the Apostle from the times when he was not: but there is otherwise no change of language. To these points must be added the fact that the author of the Acts is evidently a person of considerable literary powers, and the probability that a companion of S. Paul who possessed such powers would employ them in producing such a narrative as the Acts. See Hastings, *D.B.* i. p. 29.

(iii.) *The Companion of S. Paul who wrote the Acts and the Third Gospel was S. Luke.*

Of the companions of S. Paul whose names are known to us no one is so probable as S. Luke; and the voice of the first eight centuries pronounces strongly for him and for no one else as the author of these two writings.

If antiquity were silent on the subject, no more reasonable conjecture could be made than "Luke the beloved physician." He fulfils the conditions. Luke was the Apostle's companion during both the Roman imprisonments (Col. iv. 14; Philem. 24; 2 Tim. iv. 11), and may well have been his companion at other times. That he is not mentioned in the earlier groups of Epistles is no objection; for none of them coincide with the "we" sections in the Acts. Moreover, the argument from medical language, although sometimes exaggerated, is solid and helpful. Both in the Acts and in the Third Gospel there are expressions which are distinctly medical; and there is also a good deal of language which is perhaps more common in medical writers than elsewhere. This feature does not amount to proof that the author was a physician; still less can it prove that, if the author was a physician, he must have been Luke. The Apostle might have had another medical companion besides the beloved physician. But, seeing that there is abundance of evidence that Luke was the writer of these two documents, the medical colour which is discernible here and there in the language of each of them is a valuable confirmation of the evidence which assigns the authorship of both to Luke.

For the voice of antiquity is not silent on the subject; and we are not left to conjecture. There is no need to argue whether Timothy, or Titus, or Silas, or some unnamed companion of the Apostle is more likely than S. Luke to have written these two books. The evidence, which is both abundant and strong, is wholly in favour of Luke. Until we reach the blundering statement in Photius near the end of the ninth century, there is no hint that any one ever thought of any person but Luke as the author of either treatise. Photius has this statement: "Some say that the writer of the Acts was Clement of Rome, others Barnabas, and others again Luke the Evangelist; but Luke himself decides the question, for at the beginning of his preface he mentions that another treatise containing the acts of the Lord had been composed by him" (*Amphil.* Qu. 123). Here he seems to be transferring to the Acts conjectures which had been made respecting the Epistle to the Hebrews. But at any rate the statement shows that the Third Gospel was regarded as unquestionably by Luke.

The Pauline authorship of Romans and Galatians is now commonly regarded as certain, and the critic who questions it is held to stultify himself. But is not the external evidence for the Lucan authorship of the Third Gospel and the Acts equally strong? If these are not named by any writer earlier than Irenæus, neither are those Epistles. And the silence of the Apostolic Fathers respecting the Third Gospel and the Acts is even more intelligible than their silence respecting Galatians and Romans, because the two former, being addressed to Theophilus, were in the first instance of the nature of private writings, and because, as regards the Gospel narrative, the oral tradition still sufficed. But from Irenæus onwards the evidence in all these cases is full and unwavering, and it comes from all quarters of the Christian world. And in considering this third point, the first point must be kept steadily in view, viz. the certainty that the Third Gospel and the Acts were written by one and the same person. Consequently all the evidence for either book singly is available for the other book. Every writer who attributes the Third Gospel to Luke thereby attributes the Acts to Luke and *vice versâ*, whether he know anything about the second book or not. Thus in favour of Luke as the author of the Third Gospel we have three classes of witnesses viz. those who state that Luke wrote the Third Gospel, those who state that Luke wrote the Acts, and those who state that he wrote both treatises. Their combined testimony is very strong indeed; and there is nothing against it. At the opening of his commentary on the Acts, Chrysostom says that many in his day were ignorant of the authorship and even of the existence of the book (Migne, lx. 13). But that statement creates no difficulty. Many could be found at the present day, even among educated Christians, who could not name the author of the Acts. And we have seen that the late and confused statement in Photius, whatever it may mean respecting the Acts, testifies to the universal conviction that the Third Gospel was written by Luke.

But we obtain a very imperfect idea of the early evidence in favour of the Third Gospel when we content ourselves with the statement that it is not attributed to Luke by any one before Irenæus and the Muratorian Fragment, which may be a little earlier than the work of Irenæus, but is probably a little later. We must consider the evidence of the existence of this Gospel previous to Irenæus; and also the manner in which he himself and those who immediately follow him speak of it as the work of S. Luke.

That Justin Martyr used the Third Gospel (or an authority which was practically identical with it) cannot be doubted. He gives a variety of particulars which are found in that Gospel alone; *e.g.* Elizabeth as the mother of the Baptist, the sending of Gabriel to Mary, the census under Quirinius, there being no room in the inn, His ministry beginning when Jesus was thirty years old, His being sent by Pilate to Herod, His last cry, "Father, into Thy hands I commend My spirit" (1 *Apol.* xxxiv.; *Try.* lxxviii., lxxxviii., c., ciii., cv., cvi.). Moreover, Justin uses expressions respecting the Agony, the Resurrection, and the Ascension which show that the Third Gospel is in his mind.

That his pupil Tatian possessed this Gospel is proved by the Diatessaron. See Hemphill, *Diatessaron of Tatian*, pp. 3 ff.

Celsus also knew the Third Gospel, for he knew that one of the genealogies made Jesus to be descended from the first man (Orig. *Con. Cels.* ii. 32).

The Clementine Homilies contain similarities which are probably allusions (iii. 63, 65, xi. 20, 23, xvii. 5, xviii. 16, xix. 2).

The Third Gospel was known to Basilides and Valentinus, and was commented upon by Heracleon (Clem. Alex. *Strom.* iv. 9, p. 596, ed. Potter).

Marcion adopted this Gospel as the basis for what he called the "Gospel of the Lord" or "Gospel of Christ." He omitted a good deal as being inconsistent with his own teaching, but he does not appear to have added anything.[1] See § 7; also Wsctt., *Int. to Gospels*, App. D; Sanday, *Gospels in the Second Century*, App.

In the Epistle of the Churches of Lyons and Vienne to the Churches in Asia there is a quotation of Lk. i. 6 (Eus. *H.E.* v. 1. 9).

[1] What Pseudo-Tert. says of Cerdo is perhaps a mere transfer to Cerdo of what is known of Marcion.

These instances, which are by no means exhaustive, may suffice as evidence for the early existence of the Third Gospel. It remains to notice the way in which Irenæus and his later contemporaries speak of the book. Irenæus, who represents the traditions of Asia Minor and Rome and Gaul in the second half of the second century, quotes it many times and quotes from nearly every chapter, especially from those which are wholly or in the main peculiar to this Gospel, *e.g.* i., ii., ix.–xix., xxiv. In a very remarkable passage he collects together many of the things which this Gospel alone narrates and definitely assigns them to Luke: "Now if any one reject Luke, as if he did not know the truth, he will manifestly be casting out the Gospel of which he claims to be a disciple. For very many and specially necessary elements of the Gospel we know through him, as the generation of John, the history of Zacharias, the coming of the angel to Mary," etc. etc. (iii. 14. 3. Comp. iii. 10. 1, 22. 4, 12. 12, 14. 4, etc.). It will be observed that he does not contemplate the possibility of any one denying that Luke was the author. Those who may reject it will do so as thinking that Luke's authority is inadequate; but the authorship is unquestioned.

Clement of Alexandria (A.D. 190–202) had had teachers from Greece, Egypt, Assyria, Palestine, and had received the tradition handed down from father to son from the Apostles (*Strom.* i. 1, p. 322, ed. Potter). He quotes the Gospel very frequently, and from many parts of it. He definitely assigns it to Luke (*Strom.* i. 21, p. 407, ed. Potter).

Tertullian (A.D. 190–220) speaks for the African Church. He not only quotes the Gospel frequently in his other works, but in his treatise against Marcion he works through the Gospel from ch. iv. to the end, often calling it Luke's.

The Muratorian Fragment (A.D. 170–200) perhaps represents Rome. The first line of the mutilated Catalogue probably refers to S. Mark; but the next seven unquestionably refer to S. Luke, who is twice mentioned and is spoken of as *medicus*. (See Lft. on *Supernatural Religion*, p. 189.)

It would be waste of time to cite more evidence. It is manifest that in all parts of the Christian world the Third Gospel had been recognized as authoritative before the middle of the second century, and that it was universally believed to be the work of S. Luke. No one speaks doubtfully on the point. The possibility of questioning its value is mentioned; but not of questioning its authorship. In the literature of that period it would not be easy to find a stronger case. The authorship of the four great Epistles of S. Paul is scarcely more certain. In all these cases, as soon as we have sufficient material for arriving at a conclusion, the evidence is found to be all on one side and to be decisive. And exactly the same result is obtained when the question is examined as to the authorship of the Acts, as Bishop Lightfoot has shown (art. "Acts" in *D.B.*[2]). Both the direct and the indirect argument for the Lucan authorship is very strong.

With this large body of historical evidence in favour of S. Luke before us, confirmed as it is by the medical expressions in both books, it is idle to search for another companion of S. Paul who might have been the author. Timothy, Sopater, Aristarchus, Secundus, Gaius, Tychicus, and Trophimus are all excluded by Acts xx. 4, 5. And it is not easy to make Silas fit into the "we" sections. Titus is possible: he can be included in the "we" and the "us" without contradiction or difficulty. But what is gained by this suggestion? Is a solution which is supported by no evidence to be preferred to an intrinsically more probable solution, which is supported by a great deal of evidence, and by evidence which is as early as we can reasonably expect?

Those who neglect this evidence are bound to explain its existence. Irenæus, Clement, and Tertullian, to say nothing of other authorities, treat the Lucan authorship as a certainty. So far as their knowledge extends, Luke is everywhere regarded as the writer. How did this belief grow up and spread, if it was not true? There is nothing in either treatise to suggest Luke, and he is not prominent enough in Scripture to make him universally acceptable as a conjecture. Those who wanted apostolic authority for their own views would have made their views more conspicuous in these books, and would have assigned the books to a person of higher position and influence than the beloved physician, *e.g.* to Timothy or Titus, if not to an Apostle. As Renan says, "There is no very strong reason for supposing that Luke was not the author of the Gospel which bears his name. Luke was not yet sufficiently famous for any one to make use of his name, to give authority to a book" (*Les Évangiles*, ch. xiii. p. 252, Eng. tr. p. 132). "The placing of a celebrated name at the head of a work . . . was in no way repugnant to the custom of the times. But to place at the head of a document a false name and an obscure one withal, that is inconceivable. . . . Luke had no place in tradition, in legend, in history" (*Les Apôtres*, p. xvii., Eng. tr. p. 11).[1] See Ramsay in the *Expositor*, Jan. 1898.

[1] Even Jülicher still talks of "the silence of Papias" as an objection (*Einl. in das N.T.* § 27, 3, Leipzig, 1894). In the case of a writer of whose work only a few fragments are extant, how can we know what was not mentioned in the much larger portions which have perished? The probabilities, in the absence of evidence, are that Papias did write of Luke. But we are not quite without evidence. In the "Hexaemeron" of Anastasius of Sinai is a passage in which Papias is mentioned as an ancient interpreter, and in which Lk. x. 18 is quoted in illustration of an interpretation. Possibly the illustration is borrowed from Papias. Lft. *Supernatural Religion*, pp. 186, 200. Hilgenfeld thinks

§ 2. S. LUKE THE EVANGELIST.

The name Lucas is probably an abbreviation of Lucanus, but possibly of Lucilius, or Lucius, or Lucianus. There is, however, no *proof* that Lucanus was shortened into Lucas.[1] Nevertheless some of the oldest Latin MSS. (*e.g. Corbeiensis* and *Vercellensis*) have *secundum Lucanum* as the title of the Third Gospel. Lucas, like Apollos, Artemas, Demas, Hermas, and Nymphas, is a form not found in classical literature, whereas Lucanus is common in inscriptions. Lobeck has noticed that these contracted proper names in -ᾶς are common in the case of slaves (*Patholog. Proleg.* p. 506). Slaves were sometimes physicians, and S. Luke may have been a freedman. Antistius, the surgeon of Julius Cæsar, and Antonius Musa, the physician of Augustus, were freedmen.

That Lucas=Lucanus is probable.[2] But that Lucanus=Silvanus, because *lucus=silva*, and that therefore Luke and Silas are the same person (Van Vloten), looks like a caricature of critical ingenuity. Equally grotesque is the idea that Luke is the Aristion of Papias (Eus. *H. E.* iii. 39. 4, 6), because ἀριστεύειν=*lucere* (Lange).

Only in three places is Lk. *named* in Scripture; and it is worth noting that in all three of them the other Evangelist who is not an Apostle is named with him (Col. iv. 10, 14; Philem. 24; 2 Tim. iv. 11). These passages tell us that "the physician, the beloved one" (ὁ ἰατρὸς ὁ ἀγαπητός),[3] was with S. Paul during the first Roman imprisonment, when the Epistles to the Colossians and to Philemon were written, and also during the second imprisonment, when 2 Timothy was written. Besides telling us that Luke was a physician very dear to the Apostle, they also tell us that he was his "fellow-worker" in spreading the Gospel. But apparently he was not his "fellow-prisoner." In Col. iv. 10 Aristarchus is called συναιχμάλωτος, and in Philem. 23 Epaphras is called such; but Lk. in neither place.

Almost all critics are agreed that in Col. iv. 14 Luke is

that the preface to Papias shows that he was acquainted with the preface to Luke. Salmon is disposed to agree with him (*Intr.* p. 90, ed. 5).

[1] The argument from the Greek form (that Λευκανός, not Λουκανός, is the equivalent of Lucanus) is inconclusive. After about A.D. 50 forms in Λουκ- begin to take the place of forms in Λευκ-.

[2] Comp. Annas for Ananus; Apollos for Apollonius (Codex Bezae, Acts xviii. 24); Artemas for Artemidorus (Tit. iii. 12; Mart. v. 40); Cleopas for Cleopatros; Demas for Demetrius, Demarchus for Demaratus, Nymphas for Nymphodorus, Zenas for Zenodorus, and possibly Hermas for Hermodorus. For other examples see Win. xvi. 5, p. 127; Lft. on Col. iv. 15; Chandler, *Grk. Accent.* § 34.

[3] Marcion omitted these words, perhaps because he thought that an Evangelist ought not to devote himself to anything so contemptible as the human body (*Texte und Unters.* viii. 4, p. 40)

separated from "those of the circumcision," and therefore was a Gentile Christian.[1] Hofmann, Tiele, and Wittichen have not succeeded in persuading many persons that the passage does not necessarily imply this. Whether he was a Jewish proselyte before he was a Christian must remain uncertain: his knowledge of Jewish affairs and his frequent Hebraisms are no proof. That he was originally a heathen may be regarded as certain. He is the only one of the Evangelists who was of Gentile origin; and, with the exception of his companion S. Paul, and possibly of Apollos, he was the only one among the first preachers of the Gospel who had had scientific training.

If Luke was a Gentile, he cannot be identified with Lucius, who sends a salutation from Corinth to Rome (Rom. xvi. 21). This Lucius was Paul's kinsman, and therefore a Jew. The identification of Luke with Lucius of Cyrene (Acts xiii. 1) is less impossible. But there is no evidence, and we do not even know that Lucas was ever used as an abbreviation of Lucius. In *Apost. Const.* vi. 18. 5 Luke is distinguished from Lucius. Nor can he be identified with Silas or Silvanus, who was evidently a Jew (Acts xv. 22). Nor can a Gentile have been one of the Seventy, a tradition which seems to have been adopted by those who made Lk. x. 1–7 the Gospel for S. Luke's Day. The tradition probably is based solely on the fact that Luke alone records the Mission of the Seventy (Epiph. *Hær.* ii. 51. 11, Migne, xli. 908). The same reason is fatal to Theophylact's attractive guess, which still finds advocates, that Lk. was the unnamed companion of Cleopas in the walk to Emmaus (xxiv. 13), who was doubtless a Jew (*vv.* 27, 32). The conjecture that Luke was one of the Greek proselytes who applied to Philip to be introduced to Christ shortly before His Passion (Jn. xii. 20) is another conjecture which is less impossible, but is without evidence. In common with some of the preceding guesses it is open to the objection that Luke, in the preface to his Gospel, separates himself from those "who from the beginning were eyewitnesses and ministers of the word" (i. 2). The Seventy, these Greeks, and the companion of Cleopas were eye-witnesses, and Lk. was not. In the two latter cases it is possible to evade this objection by saying that Luke means that he was not an eye-witness *from the beginning*, although at the end of Christ's ministry he became such. But this is not satisfactory. He claims to be believed because of the accuracy of his researches among the best

[1] Of the six who send greetings, the first three (Aristarchus, Mark, Jesus Justus) are doubly bracketed together: (1) as οἱ ὄντες ἐκ περιτομῆς, (2) as μόνοι συνεργοὶ εἰς τὴν βασιλείαν τοῦ Θεοῦ, *i.e.* the only Jewish converts in Rome who loyally supported S. Paul. The second three (Epaphras, Luke, Demas) are not bracketed together. In Philem. 23 Epaphras is συναιχμάλωτος, and Mark, Aristarchus, Demas, and Luke are οἱ συνεργοί μου, while Justus is not mentioned.

authorities. Had he himself been an eye-witness of any portion, would he not have let us know this? Why did he not use the first person, as in the "we" sections in the Acts? He belongs to the second generation of Christians, not to the first.

It is, however, possible that Chrysostom and the Collect for S. Luke's Day are right in identifying "the brother whose praise in the Gospel is spread through all the Churches" (2 Cor. viii. 18) with S. Luke. But the conjectures respecting this unnamed brother are endless; and no more can be affirmed than that Luke is a reasonable conjecture.

The attempt to show that the writer of the Third Gospel and the Acts is a Jew is a failure; and the suggestion that he is S. Paul is absurd. See below (§ 5) for evidence that our Evangelist is a Gentile writing for Gentiles.

Besides the three passages in the Pauline Epistles and the preface to the Gospel, there are three passages of Scripture which tell us something about S. Luke, viz. the "we" sections. The first of these (Acts xvi. 10–17) tells us that during the second missionary journey Luke accompanied Paul from Troas to Philippi (A.D. 51 or 52), and thus brings the physician to the Apostle about the time when his distressing malady (2 Cor. xii. 7) prostrated him in Galatia, and thereby led to the conversion of the Galatians (Gal. iv. 13–15). Even without this coincidence we might believe that the relation of doctor to patient had something to do with drawing Luke to the afflicted Apostle, and that in calling him "the physician, the beloved one," the Apostle is not distinguishing him from some other Luke, but indicating the way in which the Evangelist earned his gratitude. The second section (xx. 5–xxi. 18) tells us that about six years later (A.D. 58), during the third missionary journey, Luke was again at Philippi[1] with Paul, and went with him to Jerusalem to confer with James and the elders. And the third (xxvii. 1–xxviii. 16) shows that he was with him during the voyage and shipwreck until the arrival in Rome.

With these meagre notices of him in the N.T. our knowledge of Luke ends. We see him only when he is at the side of his *magister* and *illuminator* (Tertull. *Adv. Marcion.* iv. 2) S. Paul. That he was with the Apostle at other times also we can hardly doubt,—*inseparabilis fuit a Paulo*, says Irenæus: but how often he was with him, and in each case for how long a time, we have no means of knowing. Tertullian perhaps means us to understand that Luke was converted to the Gospel by Paul, and this is in itself probable enough. And it is not improbable that it was at Tarsus,

[1] Renan conjectures that Luke was a native of Philippi. Ramsay takes the same view, suggesting that the Macedonian whom S. Paul saw in a vision (Acts xvi. 9) was Luke himself, whom he had just met for the first time at Troas (*S. Paul the Traveller*, p. 202).

where there was a school of philosophy and literature rivalling those of Alexandria and Athens (Strabo, xiv. 5. 13), that they first met. Luke may have studied medicine at Tarsus. Nowhere else in Asia Minor could he obtain so good an education: φιλοσοφίαν καὶ τ. ἄλλην παιδείαν ἐγκύκλιον ἅπασαν (*l.c.*). Our earliest authorities appear to know little or nothing beyond what can be found in Scripture or inferred from it (Iren. i. 1. 1, 10. 1, 14. 1–4, 15. 1, 22. 3; *Canon Murator. sub init.*; Clem. Alex. *Strom.* v. 12 *sub fin.*; Tert. *Adv. Marcion.* iv. 2). Nor can much that is very trustworthy be gleaned from later writers. The statement of Eusebius (*H. E.* iii. 4. 7) and of Jerome (*De vir. ill.* vii.), which may possibly be derived from Julius Africanus (Harnack, *Texte und Unters.* viii. 4, p. 39), and is followed by Theophylact, Euthymius Zigabenus, and Nicephorus, that Luke was by family of Antioch in Syria, is perhaps only an inference from the Acts Λουκᾶς δὲ τὸ μὲν γένος ὢν τῶν ἀπ' Ἀντιοχείας (Eus.) need not mean more than that Luke had a family connexion with Antioch; but it hardly "amounts to an assertion that Luke was not an Antiochian." Jerome says expressly *Lucas medicus Antiochensis*. This is probable in itself and is confirmed by the Acts. Of only one of the deacons are we told to which locality he belonged, "Nicolas a proselyte of *Antioch*" (vi. 5)[1]: and we see elsewhere that the writer was well acquainted with Antioch and took an interest in it (xi. 19–27, xiii. 1, xiv. 19, 21, 26, xv. 22, 23, 30, 35, xviii. 22).

Epiphanius states that Luke "preached in Dalmatia and Gallia, in Italy and Macedonia, but first in Gallia, as Paul says of some of his companions, in his Epistles, *Crescens in Gallia*, for we are not to read *in Galatia*, as some erroneously think, but *in Gallia*" (*Hær.* ii. 51. 11, Migne, xli. 908); and Oecumenius says that Luke went from Rome to preach in Africa. Jerome believes that his bones were translated to Constantinople,[2] and others give Achaia or Bithynia as the place of his death. Gregory Nazianzen, in giving an off-hand list of primitive martyrs—Stephen, Peter, Andrew, etc.—places Luke among them (*Orat. adv. Jul.* i. 79). None of these statements are of any value.

The legend which makes Luke a painter is much more ancient than is sometimes represented. Nicephorus Callistus (*H. E.* ii. 43) in the fourteenth century is by no means the earliest authority for it. Omitting Simeon Metaphrastes (*c.* A.D. 1100) as doubtful, the Menology of the Emperor Basil II., drawn up A.D. 980, represents

[1] It has been noted that of eight narratives of the Russian campaign of 1812, three English, three French, and two Scotch, only the last (Alison and Scott) state that the Russian General Barclay de Tolly was of Scotch extraction.

[2] His words are: *Sepultus est Constantinopoli* [vixit octoginta et quatuor annos, uxorem non habens] *ad quam urbem vicesimo Constantii anno ossa ejus cum reliquiis Andreæ apostoli translata sunt* [de Achaia]. The words in brackets are not genuine, but are sometimes quoted as such. The first insertion is made in more than one place in *De vir. ill.* vii.

S. Luke as painting the portrait of the Virgin. The oldest witness, however, is Theodorus Lector, reader in the Church of Constantinople in the sixth century. Some place him as late as the eighth century; but the name is common, and between A.D. 500 and 800 there may have been many readers of that name at Constantinople. He says that the Empress Eudoxia found at Jerusalem a picture of the Θεομήτωρ painted by Luke *the Apostle*, and sent it to Constantinople as a present to her daughter Pulcheria, wife of Theodosius II. (*Collectan.* i. 7, Migne, *Patr. Gr.* lxxxvi. 165). In 1204 this picture was brought to Venice. In the Church of S. Maria Maggiore at Rome, in the Capella Paolina, is a very ancient picture of the Virgin ascribed to S. Luke. It can be traced back to A.D. 847, and may be still older.[1] But although no such legend seems to be known to Augustine, for he says, *neque novimus faciem virginis Mariæ* (*De Trin.* viii. 5. 7), yet it is many centuries older than Nicephorus (Kraus, *Real-Enc. d. Christ. Alt.* ii. p. 344, which quotes Glükselig, *Christus-Archäol.* 101; Grimouard de S. Laurent, *Guide de l'art chrét.* iii. 15–20). And the legend has a strong element of truth. It points to the great influence which Luke has had upon Christian art, of which in a real sense he may be called the founder. The Shepherd with the Lost Sheep on His shoulders, one of the earliest representations of Christ, comes from Lk. xv (Tert. *De Pud.* vii. and x.): and both medieval and modern artists have been specially fond of representing those scenes which are described by S. Luke alone: the Annunciation, the Visit of Mary to Elizabeth, the Shepherds, the Manger, the Presentation in the Temple, Symeon and Anna, Christ with the Doctors, the Woman at the Supper of Simon the Pharisee, Christ weeping over Jerusalem, the Walk to Emmaus, the Good Samaritan, the Prodigal Son. Many other scenes which are favourites with painters might be added from the Acts. See below, § 6. i. d.

The four symbolical creatures mentioned in Ezek. i. and Rev. iv., the Man, the Lion, the Ox, and the Eagle, are variously explained by different writers from Irenæus (iii. 11. 8) downwards. But all agree in assigning the Ox or Calf to S. Luke. "This sacerdotal animal implies Atonement and Propitiation; and this exactly corresponds with what is supposed to be the character of St. Luke's Gospel, as one which more especially conveys mercy to the Penitent. . . . It begins with the Priest, dwelling on the Priestly family of the Baptist; and ends with the Victim, in our Lord's death" (Isaac Williams, *On the Study of the Gospels*, Pt. I. sect. vi.).

[1] For an interesting account of this famous picture, and of others attributed to the Evangelist, see *The Madonna of St. Luke*, by H. I. Bolton, Putnam, 1895.

§ 3. THE SOURCES OF THE GOSPEL.

The idea of a special revelation to the Evangelist is excluded by the prologue to the Gospel: his narrative is the result of careful enquiry in the best quarters. But (*a*) which "eye-witnesses and ministers of the word" were his principal informants, (*b*) whether their information was mostly oral or documentary, (*c*) whether it was mostly in Aramaic or in Greek, are questions about which he is silent. Internal evidence, however, will carry us some way in finding an answer to them.

(*a*) During a large portion of the time in which he was being prepared, and was consciously preparing himself, for writing a Gospel, he was constantly with S. Paul; and we may be sure that it was among S. Paul's companions and acquaintances that Luke obtained much of his information. It is probable that in this way he became acquainted with some of the Twelve, with other disciples of Christ, and with His Mother and brethren. He certainly was acquainted with S. Mark, who was perhaps already preparing material for his own Gospel when he and S. Luke were with the Apostle in Rome (Col. iv. 10, 14; Philem. 24). S. Paul himself could tell Luke only that which he himself received (1 Cor. xv. 3); but he could help him to first-hand information. While the Apostle was detained in custody at Cæsarea, Luke would be able to do a good deal of investigation, and as a physician he would perhaps have access to people of position who could help him.

(*b*) In discussing the question whether the information was given chiefly in an oral or a documentary form, we must remember that the difference between oral tradition and a document is not great, when the oral tradition has become stereotyped by frequent repetition. A document cannot have much influence on a writer who already knows its contents by heart. Luke tells us that many documents were already in existence, when he decided to write; and it is improbable that he made no use of these. Some of his sources were certainly documents, *e.g.* the genealogy (iii. 23–38): and we need not doubt that the first two chapters are made up of written narratives, of which we can see the conclusions at i. 80, ii. 40, and ii. 52. The early narrative (itself perhaps not primary), of which all three Synoptists make use, and which constitutes the main portion of S. Mark's Gospel, was probably already in writing when Lk. made use of it. S. Luke may have had the Second Gospel itself, pretty nearly in the form in which we have it, and may include the author of it among the πολλοί (i. 1). But some phenomena are rather against this. Luke omits (vi. 5) "the sabbath was made for man, and not man for the sabbath" (Mk. ii. 27). He omits the whole of Mk. vi. 45–viii. 9, which contains the digression into the borders of Tyre and Sidon and the incident with the Syrophenician woman, which is also in Matthew (xv. 21–28). And all this would have been full of interest to Luke's Gentile readers. That he had our First Gospel is much less probable. There is so much that he would have been likely to appropriate if he had known it, that the omission is most easily explained by assuming that he did not know it. He omits the visit of the Gentile Magi (Mt. ii. 1–15). At xx. 17 he omits "Therefore I say to you, The kingdom of God shall be taken away from you, and *shall be given to a nation bringing forth the fruits thereof*" (Mt. xxi. 43). At xxi. 12–16 he omits "And this gospel of the kingdom *shall be preached in the whole world* for a testimony unto *all the nations*" (Mt. xxiv. 14; comp. Mk. xiii. 10). Comp. the omission of Mt. xvii. 6, 7 at Lk. ix. 35, of Mt. xvii. 19, 20 at Lk. ix. 43, of Cæsarea Philippi (Mt. xvi. 13; Mk. viii. 27) at Lk. ix. 18; and see p. xli. Both to S. Luke and his readers such things would have been most significant. Again, would Luke have left the differences between his own Gospel and that of Matthew as they are, if he had been aware of them? Contrast Mt. ii. 14, 15 with Lk. ii. 39, Mt. xxviii. 7, 10, 16 with Lk. xxiv. 49; and generally mark the differences between the narratives of the Nativity and of the Resurrection in these two Gospels, the divergences in the two genealogies, the "eight days" (Lk.) and the "six days" (Mt. and Mk.) at the Transfiguration, and the perplexing phenomena in the Sermon on the Mount. These points lead us to the conclusion that Lk. was not *familiar* with our First Gospel, even if he knew it at all. But, besides the early narrative, which seems to have been nearly coextensive with our Second Gospel, Matthew and Luke used the same collection, or two similar collections, of "Oracles" or "Sayings of the Lord"; and hence the large amount of matter, chiefly discourses, which is common to Matthew and Luke, but is not found in Mark. This collection, however, can hardly have been a single document, for the common material is used very differently by the two Evangelists, especially as regards arrangement.[1] A *Book* of "Oracles" must not be hastily assumed.

In addition to these two main sources, (1) the narrative of events, which he shares with Matthew and Mark, and (2) the collection of discourses, which he shares with Matthew; and besides (3) the smaller documents about the Infancy incorporated in the first two chapters, which are peculiar to himself,—Luke

[1] There are a few passages which are common to Mark and Luke, but are not found in Matthew: the Demoniac (Mk. i. 23-28 = Lk. iv. 33-37); the Journey in Galilee (Mk. i. 35-39 = Lk. iv. 42-44); the Request of the Demoniac (Mk. v. 18 = Lk. viii. 38); the Complaint of John against the Caster out of Demons (Mk. ix. 38 = Lk. ix. 49); the Spices brought to the Tomb (Mk. xvi. 1 = Lk. xxiv. 1). Are these the result of the time when S. Mark and S. Luke were together (Col. iv. 10, 14; Philem. 24)?

evidently had (4) large sources of information respecting the Ministry, which are also peculiar to himself. These are specially prominent in chapters ix. to xix. and in xxiv. But it must not be forgotten that the matter which S. Luke alone gives us extends over the whole range of Christ's life, so far as we have any record of it. It is possible that some of these sources were oral, and it is probable that one of them was connected with the court of Herod (iii. 1, 19, viii. 3, ix 7–9, xiii. 31, xxiii. 7–12; Acts xiii. 1). But we shall probably not be wrong if we conjecture that most of this material was in writing before Luke made use of it.

It is, however, begging the question to talk of an "*Ebionitic* source." First, is there any Ebionism in S. Luke? And secondly, does what is called Ebionism in him come from a portion of his materials, or wholly from himself? That Luke is profoundly impressed by the contrasts between wealth and poverty, and that, like S. James, he has great sympathy with the suffering poor and a great horror of the temptations which beset all the rich and to which many succumb, is true enough. But this is not Ebionism. He nowhere teaches that wealth is sinful, or that rich men must give away all their wealth, or that the wealthy may be spoiled by the poor. In the parable of Dives and Lazarus, which is supposed to be specially Ebionitic, the rich Abraham is in bliss with the beggar, and Lazarus neither denounces on earth the superfluity of Dives, nor triumphs in Hades over the reversal of positions. The strongest saying of Christ against wealth, "It is easier for a camel to go through a needle's eye, than for a rich man to enter into the Kingdom of God" is in Matthew (xix. 24) and Mark (x. 25) as well as in Luke (xviii. 25). So also is the story of Peter and Andrew, James and John leaving their means of life and following Christ (Mt. iv. 18–22; Mk. i. 16–20; Lk. v. 1–11). So also is the story of Matthew or Levi leaving his lucrative calling to follow Christ (Mt. ix. 9; Mk. ii. 14; Lk. v. 27, 28). In both these cases Luke expressly states that they forsook *all* (v. 11, 28), which, however, is sufficiently clear from the other narratives. In the story about Zacchæus, which is peculiar to Luke, this head tax-collector retains half his great wealth, and there is no hint that he ought to have surrendered the whole of it. Elsewhere we find touches in the other Gospels which are not in Luke, but which would no doubt have been considered Ebionitic, if they had been found in Luke and not in the others. Thus, in the description of the Baptist, it is Matthew (iii. 4) and Mark (i. 6) who tell us of John's ascetic clothing and food, about which Luke is silent. In the parable of the Sower it is the others (Mt. xiii. 22; Mk. iv. 19) who speak of "*the deceitfulness* of riches," while Luke (viii. 14) has simply "riches." It is they who record (Mt. xix. 29; Mk. x. 29) that Christ spoke of the blessedness of leaving relations and *pro-*

perty (ἀγρούς) for His sake, where Luke (xviii. 29) omits ἀγρούς. He alone preserves Christ's declaration that he who sits at meat is superior to him who serves (xxii. 27), and there is no hint that to have servants is wrong. While the others tell us that Joseph of Arimathæa was a man of rank (Mk. xv. 43) and wealth (Mt. xxvii. 57), Luke is much more explicit than they are about his goodness and rectitude (xxiii. 50, 51), which does not look like prejudice against the rich. And it is Luke alone who tells us of the women, presumably well-to-do, who "ministered unto them of their substance" (viii. 3). To which may perhaps be added the fact that in the quotation from Ps. cvii. 10 in Lk. i. 79 those "fast bound in poverty" (πτωχείᾳ) are omitted. Throughout the Third Gospel there is a protest against worldliness; but there is no protest against wealth. And there is no evidence that the protest against worldliness is due to some particular source from which he drew, and from which the others did not draw. Rather it is something in the writer himself, being apparent in the Acts, as well as in the Gospel; and it shows itself, sometimes in what he selects from his materials, sometimes in the way in which he treats it. As Jülicher says, *Man hat von dem ebionitischen charakter dieses Evang. gesprochen und nach den judischen Einflussen oder Quellen gesucht: sehr mit Unrecht. . . . Von tendenziöser Ebionitisirung des Evangeliums kann bei ihm nicht die Rede sein* (*Einl.* § 27, p. 206). Hastings, *D.C.G.* i. p. 506.

(*c*) Frequent Hebraisms indicate that a great deal of Luke's material was originally in Aramaic. These features are specially common in the first two chapters. In translating Aramaic sources Luke would have ample opportunity for exhibiting his own predilection for certain words, phrases, and constructions. If the materials were already in Greek when Luke made use of them, then he could and did somewhat alter the wording in appropriating them. But it will generally be found that wherever the expressions which are characteristic of him are less frequent than usual, there we have come upon material which is common to him and the others, and which he has adopted without much alteration. Thus the parable of the Sower (viii. 4–15) has few marks of his style (ἐν μέσῳ, ver. 7; ὁ λόγος τοῦ Θεοῦ, ver. 11; δέχονται and ἀφίστανται, ver. 13) which are not also in Mt. (τοῦ σπεῖραι, ver. 5) or in both (ἐν τῷ σπείρειν, ver. 5). But absence or scarcity of Luke's characteristics is most common in those reports of discourses which are common to him and Matthew: *e.g.* iii. 7–9, 17 = Mt. iii. 7–10, 12; vii. 6–9 = Mt. viii. 8–10; ix. 57, 58 = Mt. viii. 19, 20; vii. 22–28 = Mt. xi. 4–11; vii. 31–35 = Mt. xi. 16–19. This last passage is one of those which were excised by Marcion. As we might expect, there is much more variation between the Gospels in narrating the same facts than in reporting the same sayings;

and the greater the variation, the greater the room for marks of individual style. But we cannot doubt that an immense amount of what Luke has in common with Matthew, or with both him and Mark, was already in a Greek form before he adopted it. It is incredible that two or three independent translations should agree quite or almost word for word.

It is very interesting to notice how, in narratives common to all three, individual characteristics appear: *e.g.* viii. 22–56 = Mk. iv. 35–41, v. 1–43 = Mt. viii. 23–34, ix. 18–25. These narratives swarm with marks of Luke's style, although he keeps closely to the common material (see below, § 6. ii.). Thus he has εἶπεν πρὸς αὐτούς, ἐπιστάτα, δέομαι σου, ἐξελθεῖν ἀπό, ἱκανός, ἐδεῖτο αὐτοῦ, σύν, ὑπόστρεφε, παρὰ τοὺς πόδας, παραχρῆμα, etc., where Mark has λέγει αὐτοῖς, διδάσκαλε, ὁρκίζω σε, ἐξελθεῖν ἐκ, μέγας, παρεκάλει αὐτόν, μετά, ὕπαγε, πρὸς τοὺς πόδας, εὐθύς, etc. Moreover Luke has ἐν τῷ *c. infin.*, καὶ οὗτος, καὶ αὐτός, ὑπάρχειν, πᾶς or ἅπας, μονογενής, etc., where the others have nothing. The following examples will repay examination: iv. 38–41 = Mk. i. 29–34 = Mt. viii. 14–17; v. 12–16 = Mk. i. 40–45 = Mt. viii. 1–4; v. 17–26 = Mk. ii. 1–12 = Mt. ix. 1–8; ix. 10–17 = Mk. vi. 30–44 = Mt. xiv. 13–21; ix. 38–40 = Mk. ix. 17, 18 = Mt. xvii. 15, 16; and many others. It is quite evident that in appropriating material Luke works it over with his own touches, and sometimes almost works it up afresh; and this is specially true of the narrative portion of the Gospel.

It is impossible to reach any certain conclusion as to the amount of material which he had at his disposal. Some suppose that this was very large, and that he has given us only a small portion of it, selected according to the object which he is supposed to have had in view, polemical, apologetic, conciliatory, or historical. Others think that his aim at completeness is too conspicuous to allow us to suppose that he rejected anything which he believed to be authentic. Both these views are probably exaggerations. No doubt there are cases in which he *deliberately* omits what he knew well and did not question. And the reason for omission may have been either that he had recorded something very similar, or that the incident would be less likely to interest or edify Gentile readers. No doubt there are other cases in which the most natural explanation of the omission is *ignorance*: he does not record because he does not know. We know of a small amount which Mark alone records; of a considerable amount which Matthew alone records; of a very considerable amount which John alone records; and of an enormous amount (Jn. xxi. 25) which no one records. To suppose that Luke knew the great part of this, and yet passed it over, is an improbable hypothesis. And to suppose that he knew scarcely any of it, is also improbable. But a definite estimate cannot be made.

The statement that *Luke avoids duplicates on principle* has been made and accepted too hastily. It is quite possible that he has deliberately omitted some things, because of their similarity to others which he has recorded. It is possible that he has omitted the feeding of the 4000, because he has recorded the feeding of the 5000; and the anointing by Mary of Bethany, because of the anointing by the sinner; and the healing of the Syrophenician's daughter at a distance, because of the centurion's servant at a distance; and the cursing of the barren fig-tree, because of the parable of the same; and the mocking by Pilate's soldiers, because of the mocking by Herod's soldiers. But in many, or even most, of these cases some other motive may have caused the omission. On the other hand, we must look at the doublets and triplets which he has admitted. If he made it a rule to exclude duplicates, the exceptions are more numerous than the examples, and they extend all through the Gospel.

The Mother of the Christ has a song (i. 46 ff.), and the father of the Baptist has a song (68 ff.). The venerable Simeon welcomes the infant Christ in the temple (ii. 28), and so does the venerable Anna (38). Levi the publican is converted and entertains Jesus (v. 27 ff.), and Zacchæus the publican also (xix. 1 ff.). The mission of the Twelve (ix. 1) is followed by the mission of the Seventy (x. 1). True disciples are equal to Christ's relations (viii. 21), and to His Mother (xi. 28). Twice there is a dispute as to who is the greatest (ix. 46, xxii. 24). Not content with the doublets which he has in common with Mt. (viii. 19–22, ix. 16, 17, xxiv. 40, 41), he adds a third instance (ix. 61, 62, v. 39, xvii. 36?); or where Mt. has only one example (xxiv. 37–39), he gives two (xvii. 26–29). So also in the miracles. We have the widow's son raised (vii. 14), and also Jairus' daughter (viii. 54), where no other Evangelist gives more than one example. There are two instances of cleansing lepers (v. 13, xvii. 14); two of forgiving sins (v. 20, vii. 48); three healings on the sabbath (vi. 6, xiii. 10, xiv. 1); four castings out of demons (iv. 35, viii. 29, ix. 42, xi. 14). Similar repetition is found in the parables. The Rash Builder is followed by the Rash King (xiv. 28–32), the Lost Sheep by the Lost Coin (xv. 1–10); and the Friend at Midnight (xi. 5) does not involve the omission of the Unrighteous Judge (xviii. 1). The exceptions to the supposed principle are still more numerous in the shorter sayings of Christ: viii. 16 = xi. 33; viii. 17 = xii. 2; viii. 18 = xix. 26; ix. 23 = xiv. 27; ix. 24 = xvii. 33; ix. 26 = xii. 9; x. 25 = xviii. 18; xi. 43 = xx. 46; xii. 11, 12 = xxi. 14, 15; xiv. 11 = xviii. 14; xix. 44 = xxi. 6; and comp. xvii. 31 with xxi. 21, and xxi. 23 with xxiii. 29. These instances, which are not exhaustive, suffice to show that the Evangelist cannot have had any very strong objection to recording duplicate instances of similar incidents and sayings. Could more duplicates be found in any other Gospel?

For recent (since 1885) discussions of the Synoptic problem see Badham, *The Formation of the Gospels*, 1891; Blair, *The Apostolic Gospel*, 1896; Jolley, *The Synoptic Problem*, 1893; Salmon, *Historical Introduction to the Books of the N.T.*, 5th ed. 1891; Wright, *The Composition of the Gospels*, 1890; *Synopsis of the Gospels in Greek*, 1896; Holsten, *Die synopt. Evang. nach Form ihres Inhalts dargestellt*, 1886; Holtzmann, *Einleitung in das N.T.* 1892; Jülicher, *Einl. in das N.T.* 1894; Nösgen, *Geschichte Jesu Christi*, being Part I. of *Gesch. der N.T. Offenbarung*, 1891; H. H. Wendt. *Die Lehre und das Leben Jesu*, 1885–1890. Other literature is mentioned on p. lxxxv.

See especially Sanday in *Book by Book*, 1893, p. 345 ff.; in *Dict. of the Bible*, 2nd ed. 1893, supplement to the article on "Gospels," pp. 1217–1243; and in the *Expositor*, 4th series, Feb. to June, 1891.

§ 4. TIME AND PLACE.

(i.) It is a disappointment that Bishop Lightfoot's admirable article on the Acts (*D.B.*[2] i. pp. 25–43) does not discuss the *Date*. The Bishop told the present writer that he regarded the question of date as the province of the writer of the article on S. Luke, an article which has not yet been rewritten. The want has, however, been to a large extent supplied in the *Bampton Lectures* for 1893 (Lect. vi.), and we may safely accept this guidance.

The main theories respecting the date of the Third Gospel contend respectively for a time in or near the years A.D. 100, A.D. 80, and A.D. 63.

(*a*) The strongest argument used by those who advocate a date near the close of the first century or early in the second[1] is the hypothesis that the author of the Third Gospel and of the Acts had read the *Antiquities* of Josephus, a work published about A.D. 94. But this hypothesis, if not absolutely untenable, is highly improbable. The coincidences between Luke and Josephus are not greater than might accidentally occur in persons writing independently about the same facts; while the divergences are so great as to render copying improbable. At any rate Josephus must not be used both ways. If the resemblances are made to prove that Luke copied Josephus, then the discrepancies should not be employed to prove that Luke's statements are erroneous. If Luke had a correct narrative to guide him, why did he diverge from it only to make blunders? It is much more reasonable to suppose that where Luke differs from the *Antiquities* he had independent knowledge, and that he had never read Josephus. Moreover, where the statements of either can be tested, it is Luke who is commonly found to be accurate, whereas Josephus is often

[1] Among these are Baur, Davidson, Hilgenfeld, Jacobsen, Pfleiderer, Overbeck, Schwegler, Scholten, Volkmar, Weizsäcker, Wittichen, and Zeller. The more moderate of these suggest A.D. 95–105, the more extreme A.D. 120–135.

convicted of exaggeration and error. See the authorities cited by Lft. *D.B.*[2] p. 39; by Holtzmann, *Einl. in d. N.T.* p. 374, 1892, and by Schanz, *Comm. über d. Evang. d. h. Lukas*, p. 16, 1883.

The relation of Luke to Josephus has recently been rediscussed; on the one side by Clemen (*Die Chronologie der paulin. Briefe*, Halle, 1893) and Krenkel (*Josephus und Lukas; der schriftstellerische Einfluss des jüdischen Geschichtschreibers auf den christlichen*, Leipzig, 1894), who regard the use of Josephus by Luke as certain; on the other by Belser (*Theol. Quartalschrift*, Tübingen, 1895, 1896), who justly criticizes the arguments of these writers and especially of Krenkel.[1] It is childish to point out that Luke, like Josephus, uses such words as ἀποστέλλειν, ἀφικνεῖσθαι, αὐξάνειν, παιδίον, πέμπειν, πύλη, κ.τ.λ., in their usual sense: and such phrases as προέκοπτεν τῇ σοφίᾳ καὶ ἡλικίᾳ (Lk. ii. 52) and ἐξίσταντο πάντες οἱ ἀκούοντες αὐτοῦ ἐπὶ τῇ συνέσει καὶ ταῖς ἀποκρίσεσιν αὐτοῦ (ii. 47) are not strikingly similar to εἰς μεγάλην παιδείας προὔκοπτον ἐπίδοσιν, μνήμῃ τε καὶ συνέσει δοκῶν διαφέρειν (Jos. *Vita*, 2) and θαύμασας τὴν ἀπόκρισιν αὐτοῦ σοφὴν οὕτω γενομένην (*Ant.* xii. 4. 9). Far more striking resemblances may be found in writings which are indisputably independent. Luke alone in N.T. calls the Sea of Galilee ἡ λίμνη Γεννησαρέτ. Could he not call it a *lake* without being prompted? Josephus also calls it a λίμνη, but his designations all differ from Luke's: Γεννησὰρ ἡ λίμνη, ἡ λ. Γεννησάρ, λ. ἡ Γεννησαρῖτις, ἡ Γεννησαρῖτις λ. (*B. J.* ii. 20. 6, iii. 10. 7; *Ant.* xviii. 2. 1; *Vita*, 65), and other variations. Luke has προσέπεσεν τοῖς γόνασιν Ἰησοῦ (v. 8), and Josephus has τοῖς γόνασιν αὐτοῦ προσπέσοντες (*Ant.* xix. 3. 4). But Josephus more often writes προσπίπτειν τινι πρὸς τὰ γόνατα, and the more frequent phrase would more probably have been borrowed. Comp. συνεχομένη πυρετῷ μεγάλῳ (Lk. iv. 38) with τεταρταίῳ πυρετῷ συσχεθεὶς (*Ant.* xiii. 15. 5); μὴ μετεωρίζεσθε (xii. 29) with *Ant.* xvi. 4. 6, *sub fin.* (where, however, νενεωτέριστο is the more probable reading); ἄφαντος ἐγένετο ἀπ' αὐτῶν (xxiv. 31) with ἀφανὴς ἐγένετο (*Ant.* xx. 8. 6). In these and many other cases the hypothesis of copying is wholly uncalled for. The expressions are not very uncommon. Some of them perhaps are the result of both Luke and Josephus being familiar with LXX. Others are words or constructions which are the common material of various Greek writers. Indeed, as Belser has shown, a fair case may be made out to show the influence of Thucydides on Luke. In a word, the theory that Luke had read Josephus "rests on little more than the fact that both writers relate or allude to the same events, though the differences between them are really more marked than the resemblances" (Sanday, *Bampton Lectures*, 1893, p. 278). As Schürer and Salmon put it, if Luke had read Josephus, he must very quickly have forgotten all that he read in him. See Hastings, *D.B.* i. p. 30.

In itself, the late date A.D. 100 is not incredible, even for those who are convinced that the writer is Luke, and that he never read Josephus. Luke may have been quite a young man, well under thirty, when he first joined S. Paul, A.D. 50–52; and he may have been living and writing at the beginning of the second century. But the late date has nothing to recommend it; and we may believe that both his writings would have assumed a different form, had they been written as late as this. Would not ὁ Χριστός, which is still a title and means "the Messiah" (ii. 26, iii. 15, iv. 41, ix. 20, xx. 41, xxii. 67, xxiii. 35, 39, xxiv. 26, 46), have become a

[1] F. Bole, *Flavius Josephus über Christus und die Christen in den Jüdischen Alterthümern*, Brixen, 1896, defends the disputed passage about Christ (xviii. 3. 3) rather than the independence of S. Luke.

proper name, as in the Epistles? Would not ὁ Κύριος, as a designation of Jesus Christ, have been still more frequent? It is not found in Matthew or Mark (excepting in the disputed appendix); but it is the invariable designation in the *Gospel of Peter*. In Luke (vii. 13, x. 1, xi. 39, xii. 42, xiii. 15, xvii. 5, 6, xviii. 6, xix. 8, xxii. 61, xxiv. 34) and in John this use is beginning, but it is still exceptional. Above all, would xxi. 32 have stood as it does, at a date when "this generation" had "passed away" without seeing the Second Advent? Moreover, the historical atmosphere of the Acts is not that of A.D. 95–135. In the Acts the Jews are the persecutors of the Christians; at this late date the Jews were being persecuted themselves. Lastly, *what would have induced a companion of S. Paul, whether Luke or not, to wait so long before publishing the results of his researches?* Opportunities of contact with those who had been eye-witnesses would have been rapidly vanishing during the last twenty years.

(*b*) The intermediate date of A.D. 75–80 has very much more to recommend it.[1] It avoids the difficulties just mentioned. It accounts for the occasional but not yet constant use of ὁ Κύριος to designate Jesus. It accounts for the omission of the very significant hint, "let him that readeth understand" (Mk. xiii. 14; Mt. xxiv. 15). When the first two Gospels (or the materials common to both) were compiled, the predicted dangers had not yet come but were near; and each of these Evangelists warns his readers to be on the alert. When the Third Gospel was written, these dangers were past. It accounts for the greater definiteness of the prophecies respecting the destruction of Jerusalem as given by Luke (xix. 43, 44, xxi. 10–24), when compared with the records of them in Mark (xiii. 14–19) and Matthew (xxiv. 15–22). After the destruction had taken place the tradition of the prediction might be influenced by what was known to have happened; and this without any conscious tampering with the report of the prophecy. The possibility of this influence must be admitted, and with it a possibility of a date subsequent to A.D. 70 for the Gospel and the Acts. Twice in the Gospel (viii. 51, ix. 28), as in the Acts (i. 13), Luke places John before his elder brother James, which Mt. and Mk. never do; and this may indicate that Luke wrote after John had become the better known of the two. Above all, *such a date allows sufficient time for the "many" to "draw up narratives" respecting the acts and sayings of Christ.*

[1] Some year between A.D. 70 and 95 is advocated by Beyschlag, Bleek, Cook, Credner, De Wette, Ewald, Güder, Holtzmann?, Jülicher, Keim?, Köstlin, Lechler, Lekebusch, Mangold, Ramsay, Renan, Reuss, Sanday, Schenkel, Trip, Tobler, Weiss, and others. And the more trustworthy of these, *e.g.* Ramsay, Sanday, and Weiss, are disposed to make A.D. 80 the latest date that can reasonably be assigned to the Gospel, or even to the Acts.

(*c*) The early date of about A.D. 63 still finds advocates;[1] and no doubt there is something to be said for it. Quite the *simplest* explanation of the fact that S. Paul's death is not recorded in the Acts is that it had not taken place. If that explanation is correct the Third Gospel cannot be placed much later than A.D. 63. Again, the writer of the Acts can hardly have been familiar with the Epistles to the Corinthians and the Galatians: otherwise he would have inserted some things and explained others (Salmon, *Hist. Int. to N.T.* p. 319, ed. 5). How long might Luke have been without seeing these Epistles? Easily till A.D. 63; but less easily till A.D. 80. Once more, when Luke records the prophecy of Agabus respecting the famine, he mentions that it was fulfilled (Acts xi. 28). When he records the prophecy of Christ respecting the destruction of Jerusalem (xxi. 5–36), he does not mention that it was fulfilled. The *simplest* explanation is that the destruction had not yet taken place. And, if it be said that the prediction of it has been retouched in Luke's record in order to make it more distinctly in accordance with facts, we must notice that the words, "Let them that are in Judæa *flee to the mountains*," are in all three reports. The actual flight seems to have been, not to the mountains, but to Pella in north Peræa; and yet "to the mountains" is still retained by Luke (xxi. 21). Eusebius says that there was a "revelation" before the war, warning the Christians not only to leave the city, but to dwell in a town called Pella (*H. E.* iii. 5. 3). This "revelation" is evidently an adaptation of Christ's prophecy; and here we reasonably suspect that the detail about Pella has been added after the event. But there is nothing of it in Luke's report.

Nevertheless, the reasons stated above, and especially those derived from the prologue to the Gospel, make the intermediate date the most probable of the three. It combines the advantages of the other two dates and avoids the difficulties of both. It may be doubted whether any of the Gospels, as we have them, was written as early as A.D. 63; and if the Third Gospel is placed after the death of S. Paul, one main reason for placing it before A.D. 70 is gone.

(ii.) As to the *Place* in which Luke wrote his Gospel we have no evidence that is of much value. The Gospel itself gives no sure clue. The peculiarities of its diction point to a centre in which Hellenistic influences prevailed; and the way in which places in Palestine are mentioned have been thought to indicate that the Gospel was written outside Palestine (i. 26, ii. 4, iv. 31, viii. 26, xxiii. 51, xxiv. 13). The first of these considerations does not lead to anything very definite, and the

[1] Among them are Alford, Ebrard, Farrar, Gloag, Godet, Grau, Guerike, Hahn, Hitzig, Hofmann, Hug, Keil, Lange, Lumby, Nösgen, Oosterzee, Resch, Riehm, Schaff, Schanz (67–70), Thiersch, Tholuck, Wieseler, and now Blass. Harnack has changed from (*b*) to (*c*).

second has little or no weight. The fact that the Gospel was written for readers outside Palestine, who were not familiar with the country, accounts for all the topographical expressions. We do not know what evidence Jerome had for the statement which he makes in the preface to his commentary on S. Matthew: *Tertius Lucas medicus, natione Syrus Antiochensis* (*cujus laus in Evangelio*), *qui et discipulus apostoli Pauli*, in Achaiæ Bœotiæque partibus volumen condidit (2 Cor. viii.), *quædam altius repetens, et ut ipse in procemio confitetur, audita magis, quam visa describens* (Migne, xxvi. 18), where some MSS. have *Bithyniæ* for *Bœotiæ*. Some MSS. of the Peshitto give Alexandria as the place of composition, which looks like confusion with Mark. Modern guesses vary much: Rome (Holtzmann, Hug, Keim, Lekebusch, Zeller), Cæsarea (Michaelis, Schott, Thiersch, Tholuck), Asia Minor (Hilgenfeld, Overbeck), Ephesus (Köstlin), and Corinth (Godet). There is no evidence for or against any of them.

§ 5. OBJECT AND PLAN.

(i.) The immediate *Object* is told us in the preface. It was written to give Theophilus increased confidence in the faith which he had adopted, by supplying him with further information respecting its historical basis. That Theophilus is a real person, and not a symbolical personage representing devout Christians in general,[1] is scarcely doubtful, although Bishop Lightfoot, with characteristic caution, has warned us not to be too confident of this. A real person is intrinsically more probable. The name was a very common one,—fairly frequent among Jews, and very frequent among Gentiles. It is thus quite unlike such obviously made up names as Sophron and Neologus in a modern book, or Philotheus, to whom Ken dedicates his *Manual of Prayer* for Winchester scholars. Moreover, the epithet κράτιστε is far more likely to have been given to a real person than to a fictitious one. It does not however necessarily imply high rank or authority (Acts xxiii. 26, xxiv. 3, xxvi. 25), and we must be content to be in ignorance as to who Theophilus was and where he lived. But the tone of the Gospel leads us to regard him as a representative *Gentile* convert, who was anxious to know a good deal more than the few fundamental facts which were taught to catechumens. The topographical statements mentioned above, and such remarks as "the

[1] The idea that Theophilus may symbolize the true disciple is as old as Origen (*Hom.* i. *in Luc.*), and is adopted by Ambrose: *scriptum est evangelium ad Theophilum, hoc est ad eum quem Deus diligit* (*Comm. in Luc.* i. 3). Epiphanius regards the name's denoting πᾶς ἄνθρωπος Θεὸν ἀγαπῶν as a possible alternative (*Hær.* ii. 1. 51, Migne, xli. 900).

feast of unleavened bread which is called the passover" (xxii. 1), would not have been required for a Jewish convert.

But, although Theophilus was almost certainly an actual person well known to Luke, we need not suppose that the Evangelist had only this one reader in view when he wrote. It is evident that he writes for the instruction and encouragement of all Gentile converts, and possibly Greek-speaking converts in particular. Theophilus is to be the patron of the book with a view to its introduction to a larger circle of readers. Perhaps Luke hoped that Theophilus would have it copied and disseminated, as he probably did.

Among the many indications that the book is written by a Gentile for Gentiles are the substitution of Greek for Hebrew names, ὁ Ζηλωτής for ὁ Καναναῖος (vi. 15; Acts i. 13), and Κρανίον for Γολγοθᾶ (xxiii. 33); his never using Ῥαββεί as a form of address, but either διδάσκαλε or ἐπιστάτα;[1] his comparatively sparing use of ἀμήν (seven times as against thirty in Matthew), for which he sometimes substitutes ἀληθῶς (ix. 27, xii. 44, xxi. 3) or ἐπ' ἀληθείας (iv. 25, xxii. 59); his use of νομικός for γραμματεύς (vii. 30, x. 25, xi. 45, 46, 52, xiv. 3); his adding ἀκάθαρτον as an epithet to δαιμόνιον (iv. 33), for Gentiles believed in good δαιμόνια, whereas to a Jew all δαιμόνια were evil; his avoiding μετεμορφώθη (Mk. ix. 2; Mt. xvii. 2) in his account of the Transfiguration (ix. 29), a word which might have suggested the metamorphoses of heathen deities; his notice of the Roman Emperor (ii. 1), and using his reign as a date (iii. 1); his tracing the Saviour's descent to Adam, the parent of Gentile as well as Jew (iii. 38). Although full honour is shown to the Mosaic Law as binding on Jews (ii. 21, 27, 39, v. 14, x. 26, xvi. 17, 29–31, xvii. 14, xviii. 20), yet there is not much appeal to it as of interest to his readers. Luke has no parallels to Mt. v. 17, 19, 20, 21, 27, 31, 33, xii. 5–7, 17–20, xv. 1–20. The quotations from the Old Testament are few as compared with Matthew, and they are found mostly in the sayings of Christ (iv. 4, 8, 12, 18, 19, 26, vi. 4, vii. 27, viii. 10, xiii. 19, 28, 29, 35, xviii. 20, xix. 46, xx. 17, 37, 42, 43, xxi. 10, 24, 26, 27, 35, xxii. 37, 69, xxiii. 30, 46) or of others (i. 15, 17, 37, 46–55, 68–79, ii. 30, 31, 32, iv. 10, 11, x. 27, xx. 28). Very little is said about the fulfilment of prophecy, which would not greatly interest Gentile readers (iii. 4, iv. 21, xxi. 22, xxii. 37, xxiv. 44); and of these five instances, all but the first occur in sayings of Christ addressed to Jews. Many of the quotations noted above are mere

[1] The following Hebrew or Aramaic words, which occur in the other Gospels, are not found in Luke: Ἀββᾶ (Mk.), Βοανηργές (Mk.), Γαββαθᾶ (Jn.), Ἑβραϊστί (Jn.), Ἐμμανουήλ (Mt.), ἐφφαθά (Mk.), Κορβᾶν (Mk.), Κορβανάς (Mt.), Μεσσίας (Jn.), ὡσαννά (Mt. Mk. Jn.), together with the sayings, ταλειθὰ κοῦμι (Mk.) and ἐλωΐ. ἐλωΐ. κ.τ.λ. (Mt. Mk.).

reproductions, more or less conscious, of the words of Scripture; but the following are definitely given as citations: ii. 23, 24, iii. 4, iv. 4, 8, 10, 11, 12, 18, 19, vii. 27, x. 27, xviii. 20, xix. 46, xx. 17, 28, 37, 42, 43, xxii. 37 Excepting vii. 27, they may all have come from LXX.[1] And vii. 27 does not agree with either the Hebrew or LXX of Mal. iii. 1, and is no evidence that the Evangelist knew Hebrew. But, excepting ἐγώ, it agrees *verbatim* with Mt. xi. 10, and we need not doubt that both Evangelists used the same source and copied it exactly. Add to these his command of the Greek language and his use of "Judæa" for the land of the Jews, *i.e.* the whole of Palestine (i. 5, iv. 44?, vii. 17, xxiii. 5; Acts ii. 9, x. 37, xi. 1, 29). This combination of non-Jewish features would be extraordinary in a treatise written by a Jew or for Jews. It is thoroughly intelligible in one written by a Gentile for Gentiles.

In his desire to give further instruction to Theophilus and many others like him, it is evident that Luke aims at *fulness*. He desires to make his Gospel as *complete* as possible. This is clearly indicated in the prologue. He has "traced up the course of *all* things accurately *from the first*" (ἄνωθεν πᾶσιν), in order that Theophilus may "know *in full detail*" (ἐπιγνῷς) the historic foundations of the faith. And it is equally clearly seen in the Gospel itself. Luke begins at the very beginning, far earlier than any other Evangelist; not merely with the birth of the Christ, but with the promise of the birth of the Forerunner. And he goes on to the very end: not merely to the Resurrection but to the Ascension. Moreover his Gospel contains an immense proportion of material which is peculiar to himself. According to one calculation, if the contents of the Synoptic Gospels are divided into 172 sections, of these 172 Luke has 127 ($\frac{3}{4}$), Matthew 114 ($\frac{2}{3}$), and Mark 84 ($\frac{1}{2}$); and of these 172 Luke has 48 which are peculiar to himself ($\frac{2}{7}$), Matthew has 22 ($\frac{1}{8}$), and Mark has 5 ($\frac{1}{37}$). According to another calculation, if the total be divided into 124 sections, of these Lk. has 93, Matthew 78, and Mark 67; and of these 124 Luke has 38 peculiar to himself, Matthew 17, and Mark 2.[2] The portions of the Gospel narrative which Luke alone has preserved for us are among the most beautiful treasures which we possess, and we owe them in a great measure to his desire to make his collection as full as possible.

[1] Jerome (*Comm. in Is.* vi. 9, Migne, xxiv. 100) says, *Evangelistam Lucam tradunt veteres Ecclesiæ tractatores medicinæ artis fuisse scientissimum, et magis Græcas litteras scisse quam Hebræas. Unde et sermo ejus, tam in Evangelio quam in Actibus Apostolorum, id est in utroque volumine comptior est, et secularem redolet eloquentiam, magisque testimoniis Græcis utitur quam Hebræis.*

[2] Six miracles are peculiar to Luke, three to Matthew, and two to Mark. Eighteen parables are peculiar to Luke, ten to Matthew, and one to Mark. See p. xli. For other interesting statistics respecting the relations between the Synoptists see Westcott, *Intr. to Gospels*, pp. 194 ff.

It is becoming more and more generally admitted that the old view of the purpose of Gospel and Acts is not far off the truth. It was Luke's intention to write history, and not polemical or apologetic treatises. It was his aim to show all Christians, and especially Gentile Christians, on how firm a basis of fact their belief was founded. The Saviour had come, and He had come to save the whole human race. The work of the Christ and the work of His Apostles proved this conclusively. In the Gospel we see the Christ winning salvation for the whole world; in the Acts we see His Apostles carrying the good tidings of this salvation to the whole world. Luke did not write to depreciate the Twelve in the interests of S. Paul; nor to vindicate S. Paul against the attacks of Judaizing opponents; nor yet to reconcile the Judaizers with the disciples of S. Paul. A Gospel which omits the severe rebuke incurred by Peter (Mt. xvi. 23; Mk. viii. 33), the ambitious request of James and John (Mt. xx. 21; Mk. x. 37), the boastful declaration of loyalty made by all the Twelve (Mt. xxvi. 35; Mk. xiv. 31), and the subsequent flight of all (Mt. xxvi. 56; Mk. xiv. 50); which promises to the Twelve their judgment-thrones (xxii. 30), and trusts them with the conversion of "all the nations" (xxiv. 47), cannot be regarded as hostile to the Twelve. And why address a vindication of Paul to a representative Gentile? Lastly, how could Judaizers be conciliated by such stern judgments on Judaism as Luke has recorded? See, for instance, the following passages, all of them from what is peculiar to Luke: iv. 28, 29, x. 10, 11, 31, 32, xi. 39, 40, xii. 47, xiii. 1–5, 15, xvi. 15, xvii. 18, xviii. 10–14, xxiii. 28–31; Acts ii. 23, v. 30, vii. 51–53, etc. It is well that these theories as to the purpose of the Evangelist have been propounded: the examination of them is most instructive. But they do not stand the test of careful investigation. S. Luke remains unconvicted of the charge of writing party pamphlets under the cover of fictitious history.

(ii.) The *Plan* of the Gospel is probably not elaborated. In the preface Luke says that he means to write "in order" (καθεξῆς), and this most naturally means in chronological order. Omitting the first two chapters and the last chapter in each case, the main features of the First and Third Gospels agree; and in outline their structure agrees to a large extent with that of the Second.[1] Luke perhaps took the tradition which underlies all three Gospels as his chief guide, and inserted into it what he had gathered from other sources. In arranging the additional material he followed chronology, where he had any chronological clue; and where he

[1] As regards order, in the first half the Second and Third Gospels commonly agree, while the First varies. In the second half the First and Second commonly agree, while the Third varies. Matthew's additions to the common material are mostly in the first half; Luke's are mostly in the second.

had none (which perhaps was often the case), he placed similar incidents or sayings in juxtaposition.

But a satisfactory solution of the perplexing phenomena has not yet been found: for what explains one portion of them with enticing clearness cannot be made to harmonize with another portion. We may assert with some confidence that Luke generally aims at chronological order, and that on the whole he attains it; but that he sometimes prefers a different order, and that he often, being ignorant himself, leaves us also in ignorance as to chronology. Perhaps also some of his chronological arrangements are not correct.

The chronological sequence of the Acts cannot be doubted; and this is strong confirmation of the view that the Gospel is meant to be chronological in arrangement. Comp. the use of καθεξῆς viii. 1; Acts iii. 24, xi. 4, xviii. 23.

That the whole Gospel is elaborately arranged to illustrate the development and connexion of certain theological ideas does not harmonize with the impression which it everywhere gives of transparent simplicity. That there was connexion and development in the life and work of Christ need not be doubted; and the narrative which reports that life and work in its true order will illustrate the connexion and development. But that is a very different thing from the supposition that Luke first formed a scheme, and then arranged his materials to illustrate it. So far as there is "organic structure and dogmatic connexion" in the Third Gospel, it is due to the materials rather than to the Evangelist. Attempts to trace this supposed dogmatic connexion are instructive in two ways. They suggest a certain number of connexions, which (whether intended or not) are illuminative. They also show, by their extraordinary divergences, how far we are from anything conclusive in this direction. The student who compares the schemes worked out by Ebrard (*Gosp. Hist.* I. i. 1, § 20, 21), McClellan (*N.T.* pp. 427 ff.), Oosterzee (*Lange's Comm.* Int. § 4), and Westcott (*Int. to Gospels*, ch. vii. note G) will gather various suggestive ideas, but will also doubt whether anything like any one of them was in the mind of the Evangelist.

The analysis which follows is obtained by separating the different sections and grouping them under different heads. There is seldom any doubt as to where one section ends and another begins; and the grouping of the sections is avowedly tentative. But most analyses recognize a break between chapters ii. and iii., at or about ix. 51 and xix. 28, and between chapters xxi. and xxii. If we add the preface, we have six divisions to which the numerous sections may be assigned. In the two main central divisions, which together occupy nearly seventeen chapters, some subsidiary grouping has been attempted, but without confidence in its correctness. It may, however, be conducive to clearness, even if nothing of the kind is intended by S. Luke.[1] The mark § indicates that this portion is found in Luke alone; ° that it is common to Luke and Mark; † that it is common to Luke and Matthew; * that it is common to all three.

[1] The divisions and subdivisions of the Gospel in the text of WH. are most instructive. Note whether paragraphs and sentences have spaces between them or not, and whether sentences begin with a capital letter or not. The analysis of the Gospel by Sanday in *Book by Book*, pp. 402–404 (Isbister, 1893), will be found very helpful.

There is a presumption that what is peculiar to Luke comes from some source that was not used by Mark or Matthew; and this presumption is in some cases a strong one; *e.g.* the Examination of Christ before Herod, or the Walk to Emmaus; but all that we know is that Luke has preserved something which they have not. Again there is a presumption that what is given by Luke and Matthew, but omitted by Mark, comes from some source not employed by the latter; and this presumption is somewhat stronger when what is given by them, but omitted by him, is not narrative but discourse; *e.g.* the Parable of the Lost Sheep. Yet the book of "Oracles," known to Matthew and Luke, but not known to Mark, is nothing more than a convenient hypothesis for which a good deal may be said. And it would be rash to affirm that the few (p. xxiv) sections which are found in Mark and Luke, but not in Matthew, such as the Widow's Mite, come from some source unknown to Matthew. The frequency of the mark § gives some idea of what we should have lost had S. Luke not been moved to write. And it must be remembered that in the sections which are common to him and either or both of the others he often gives touches of his own which are of the greatest value. Attention is frequently called to these in the notes. They should be contrasted with the additions made to the Canonical Gospels in the apocryphal gospels.

I. i. 1–4. § THE PREFACE. THE SOURCES AND OBJECT OF THE GOSPEL.

II. i. 5–ii. 52. § THE GOSPEL OF THE INFANCY.

1. The Annunciation of the Birth of the Forerunner (5–25).
2. The Annunciation of the Birth of the Saviour (26–38).
3. The Visit of the Mother of the Saviour to the Mother of the Forerunner (39–56).
4. The Birth of the Forerunner (57–80)
5. The Birth of the Saviour (ii. 1–20).
6. The Circumcision and Presentation of the Saviour (21–40).
7. The Boyhood of the Saviour (41–52).

III. iii. 1–ix. 50. THE MINISTRY, MAINLY IN GALILEE.

i. *The External Preparation for the Ministry; The Preaching of the Baptist* (iii. 1–22).

1. § The Date (1, 2).
2. * The New Prophet, his Preaching, Prophecy, and Death (3–20).
3. * He baptizes the Christ (21, 22).
   § The Genealogy of the Christ (23–38).

ii. *The Internal Preparation for the Ministry; * The Temptation* (iv. 1–13).

iii. *The Ministry in Galilee* (iv. 14–ix. 50).

1. Visit to Nazareth; °At Capernaum an unclean Demon cast out (iv. 14–44).
2. §* The Miraculous Draught and the Call of Simon, * Two Healings which provoke Controversy; * The Call of Levi; * Two Sabbath Incidents which provoke Controversy (v. 1–vi. 11).

3. * The Nomination of the Twelve; † The Sermon "on the Level Place"; † The Centurion's Servant; § The Widow's Son at Nain: † The Message from the Baptist; § The Anointing by the Sinner; § The Ministering Women; * The Parable of the Sower; * The Relations of Jesus; * The Stilling of the Tempest; * The Gerasene Demoniac; * The Woman with the Issue and the Daughter of Jairus (vi. 12–viii. 56).
4. * The Mission of the Twelve; * The Feeding of the Five Thousand; * Peter's Confession and the First Prediction of the Passion; * The Transfiguration; * The Demoniac Boy; * The Second Prediction of the Passion; * Who is the greatest? * Not against us is for us (ix. 1–50).

IV. ix. 51–xix. 28. THE JOURNEYINGS TOWARDS JERUSALEM: MINISTRY OUTSIDE GALILEE.

i. *The departure from Galilee and First Period of the Journey* (ix. 51–xiii. 35).

1. § The Samaritan Village; †§ Three Aspirants to Discipleship; § The Seventy: The Lawyer's Questions and § the Good Samaritan; § Mary and Martha (ix. 51–x. 42).
2. § Prayer; * Casting out Demons by Beelzebub; § True Blessedness; * The Demand for a Sign: § Denunciation of Pharisaism; † Exhortation to Sincerity; § The Avaricious Brother; § The Rich Fool; God's Providential Care; § The Signs of the Times (xi. 1–xii. 59).
3. § Three Exhortations to Repentance; § The Woman with a Spirit of Infirmity; * The Mustard Seed; † The Leaven; The Number of the Saved; § The Message to Antipas and † the Lament over Jerusalem (xiii. 1–35).

ii. *The Second Period of the Journey* (xiv. 1–xvii. 10).

1. § The Dropsical Man; § Guests and Hosts; § The Great Supper; § The Conditions of Discipleship; † The Lost Sheep; § The Lost Coin; § The Lost Son (xiv. 1–xv. 32).
2. § The Unrighteous Steward; §† Short Sayings; § The Rich Man and Lazarus; Four Sayings on * Offences, § Forgiveness, † Faith, § Works (xvi. 1–xvii. 10).

iii. *The Third Period of the Journey* (xvii. 11–xix. 28).

1. § The Ten Lepers; §* The coming of the Kingdom; § The Unrighteous Judge; § The Pharisee and the Publican (xvii. 11–xviii. 14).

2. * Little Children; * The Rich Young Ruler; * The Third Prediction of the Passion; * The Blind Man at Jericho; § Zacchæus; § The Pounds (xviii. 15–xix. 28).

V. xix. 29–xxi. 38. LAST DAYS OF PUBLIC TEACHING: MINISTRY IN JERUSALEM.

1. * The Triumphal Procession and § Predictive Lamentation; * The Cleansing of the Temple (xix. 29–48).
2. The Day of Questions. * Christ's Authority and John's Baptism; * The Wicked Husbandmen; * Tribute; * The Woman with Seven Husbands; * David's Son and Lord; * The Scribes; ° The Widow's Mite; *§ Apocalyptic Discourse (xx. 1–xxi. 38).

VI. xxii.–xxiv. THE PASSION AND THE RESURRECTION.

i. *The Passion* (xxii. 1–xxiii. 56).

1. * The Treachery of Judas (xxii. 1–6).
2. * The Paschal Supper and Institution of the Eucharist; * The Strife about Priority; § The New Conditions (xxii. 7–38).
3. *§ The Agony; * The Arrest; * Peter's Denials; The Ecclesiastical Trial; * The Civil Trial; § Jesus sent to Herod; * Sentence; * Simon of Cyrene; § The Daughters of Jerusalem; * The Crucifixion; § The Two Robbers; * The Death (xxii. 39–xxiii. 49).
4. * The Burial (xxiii. 50–56).

ii. *The Resurrection and the Ascension* (xxiv.).

1. *§ The Women at the Tomb (1–11).
2. § [Peter at the Tomb (12).]
3. § The Walk to Emmaus (13–32).
4. § The Appearance to the Eleven (33–43)
5. § Christ's Farewell Instructions (44–49).
6. § The Departure (50–53).

Note that each of the three divisions of the Ministry begins with scenes which are typical of Christ's rejection by His people: the Ministry in Galilee with the attempt on His life at Nazareth (iv. 28–30); the Ministry outside Galilee with the refusal of Samaritans to entertain Him (ix. 51–56); and that in Jerusalem with the Lament over the city (xix. 41–44). In the first and last case the tragic rejection is heightened by being preceded by a momentary welcome.

It will be useful to collect for separate consideration the Miracles and the Parables which are recorded by S. Luke.

MIRACLES.	PARABLES.
* Unclean Demon cast out.	§ Two Debtors.
* Peter's Wife's Mother healed.	* Sower.
§ Miraculous Draught of Fish.	§ Good Samaritan.
* Leper cleansed.	§ Friend at midnight.
* Palsied healed.	§ Rich Fool.
* Withered Hand restored.	§ Watchful Servants.
† Centurion's Servant healed.	§ Barren Fig-tree.
§ Widow's Son raised.	* Mustard Seed.
* Tempest stilled.	† Leaven.
* Gerasene Demoniac.	§ Chief Seats.
* Woman with the Issue.	§ Great Supper.
* Jairus' Daughter raised.	§ Rash Builder.
* Five Thousand fed.	§ Rash King.
* Demoniac Boy.	† Lost Sheep.
† Dumb Demon cast out.	§ Lost Coin.
§ Spirit of Infirmity.	§ Lost Son.
§ Dropsical Man.	§ Unrighteous Steward.
§ Ten Lepers cleansed.	§ Dives and Lazarus.
* Blind Man at Jericho.	§ Unprofitable Servants.
§ Malchus' ear.	§ Unrighteous Judge.
	§ Pharisee and Publican.
	§ Pounds.
	* Wicked Husbandmen.

Thus, out of twenty miracles recorded by Luke, six are peculiar to him; while, out of twenty-three parables, all but five are peculiar to him. And he omits only eleven, ten peculiar to Matthew, and one peculiar to Mark (iv. 26–29). Whence did Luke obtain the eighteen parables which he alone records? And whence did Matthew obtain the ten parables which he alone records? If the "Oracles" contained them all, why does each Evangelist omit so many? If S. Luke knew our Matthew, why does he omit all these ten, especially the Two Sons (Mt. xxi. 28–32), which points to the obedience of the Gentiles (see p. xxiv). In illustration of the fact that the material common to all three Gospels consists mainly of narratives rather than discourses, it should be noticed that most of the twenty miracles in Luke are in the other two also, whereas only three of the twenty-three parables in Luke are also in Matthew and Mark. It is specially worthy of note that the eleven miracles recorded by all three occur in the same order in each of the Gospels; and the same is true of the three parables which are common to all three. Moreover, if we add to these the three miraculous occurrences which attest the Divinity of Christ, these also are in the same order in each. The Descent of the Spirit with the Voice from Heaven at the Baptism precedes all. The Transfiguration is placed between the feeding of the 5000 and the healing of the demoniac boy. The Resurrection closes all. Evidently the order had already been fixed in the material which all three Evangelists employ.

§ 6. CHARACTERISTICS, STYLE, AND LANGUAGE.

(i.) It has already been pointed out (p. xxxv) that Luke aims at fulness and completeness. (*a*) *Comprehensiveness* is a characteristic of his Gospel. His Gospel is the nearest approach to a biography; and his object seems to have been to give his readers as full a picture as he could of the life of Jesus Christ, in all the portions of it—infancy, boyhood, manhood—respecting which he had information.

But there is a comprehensiveness of a more important kind which is equally characteristic of him: and for the sake of a different epithet we may say that the Gospel of S. Luke is in a special sense the *universal* Gospel. All four Evangelists tell us that the good tidings are sent to "all the nations" (Mt. xxviii. 19; Mk. xiii. 10; Lk. xxiv. 47) independently of birth (Jn. i. 12, 13). But no one teaches this so fully and persistently as S. Luke. He gives us, not so much the Messiah of the O.T., as the Saviour of all mankind and the Satisfier of all human needs. Again and again he shows us that forgiveness and salvation are offered to all, and offered freely, independently of privileges of birth or legal observances. Righteousness of heart is the passport to the Kingdom of God, and this is open to everyone; to the Samaritan (ix. 51–56, x. 30–37, xvii. 11–19) and the Gentile (ii. 32, iii. 6, 38, iv. 25–27, vii. 9, x. 1, xiii. 29, xxi. 24, xxiv. 47) as well as to the Jew (i. 33, 54, 68–79, ii. 10); to publicans, sinners, and outcasts (iii. 12, 13, v. 27–32, vii. 37–50, xv. 1, 2, 11–32, xviii. 9–14, xix. 2–10, xxiii. 43) as well as to the respectable (vii. 36, xi. 37, xiv. 1); to the poor (i. 53, ii. 7, 8, 24, iv. 18, vi. 20, 21, vii. 22, xiv. 13, 21, xvi. 20, 23) as well as to the rich (xix. 2, xxiii. 50). And hence Dante calls S. Luke "the writer of the story of the gentleness of Christ," *scriba mansuetudinis Christi* (*De Monarchiâ*, i. 16 [18], ed. Witte, 1874, p. 33; Church, p. 210). It cannot be mere accident that the parables of the Good Samaritan, the Prodigal Son, the Great Supper, the Pharisee and the Publican, the rebukes to intolerance, and the incidents of the sinner in the house of Simon, and of the penitent robber are peculiar to this Gospel. Nor yet that it omits Mt. vii. 6, x. 5, 6, xx. 16, xxii. 14, which might be regarded as hostile to the Gentiles. S. Luke at the opening of the ministry shows this universal character of it by continuing the great prophecy from Is. xl. 3 ff. (which all four Evangelists quote) till he reaches the words "All flesh shall see the salvation of God" (iii. 6). And at the close of it he alone records the gracious declaration that "the Son of Man is come to seek and to save that which was lost" (xix. 10; interpolated Mt. xviii. 11).[1]

It is a detail, but an important one, in the universality of the Third Gospel, that it is in an especial sense the Gospel for *women* Jew and Gentile alike looked down on women.[2] But all through this Gospel they are allowed a prominent place, and many types

[1] Comp. also the close of the Acts, esp. xxviii. 28; and the πᾶς (Lk. xvi. 16), which is not in Mt. (xi. 12).

[2] In the Jewish liturgy the men thank God that they have not been made women.

of womanhood are placed before us: Elizabeth, the Virgin Mary, the prophetess Anna, the widow at Nain, the nameless sinner in the house of Simon, Mary Magdalene, Joanna, Susanna, the woman with the issue, Martha and Mary, the widow with the two mites, the "daughters of Jerusalem," and the women at the tomb. A Gospel with this marked antipathy to exclusiveness and intolerance appropriately carries the pedigree of the Saviour past David and Abraham to the parent of the whole human race (iii. 38). It is possible that Luke simply copied the genealogy as he found it, or that his extending it to Adam is part of his love of completeness; but the thought of the father of all mankind is likely to have been present also.

It is this all-embracing love and forgiveness, as proclaimed in the Third Gospel, which is meant, or ought to be meant, when it is spoken of as the "*Gospel of S. Paul.*" The *tone* of the Gospel is Pauline. It exhibits the liberal and spiritual nature of Christianity. It advocates *faith* and *repentance* apart from the works of the Law, and tells abundantly of God's *grace* and *mercy* and the work of the *Holy Spirit*. In the Pauline Epistles these topics and expressions are constant.

The word πίστις, which occurs eight times in Mt., five in Mk., and not at all in Jn., is found eleven times in Lk. and sixteen in the Acts: μετάνοια, twice in Mt., once in Mk., not in Jn., occurs five times in Lk. and six in Acts: χάρις, thrice in Jn., not Mt. or Mk., is frequent both in Lk. and Acts: ἔλεος, thrice in Mt., not in Mk. or Jn., occurs six times in Lk. but not in Acts: ἄφεσις ἁμαρτιῶν, once in Mt., twice in Mk., not in Jn., is found thrice in Lk. and five times in Acts; and the expression "Holy Spirit," which is found five times in Mt., four in Mk., four in Jn., occurs twelve times in Lk. and forty-one in Acts. See on i. 15.

It is characteristic that τίνα μισθὸν ἔχετε (Mt. v. 46) becomes ποία ὑμῖν χάρις ἐστιν (Lk. vi. 32); and ἔσεσθε ὑμεῖς τέλειοι, ὡς ὁ πατὴρ ὑμῶν ὁ οὐράνιος τέλειός ἐστιν (Mt. v. 48) becomes γίνεσθε οἰκτίρμονες, καθὼς ὁ πατὴρ ὑμῶν οἰκτίρμων ἐστιν (Lk. vi. 36). Note also the incidents recorded iv. 25–27 and x. 1–16, and the office of the Holy Spirit as indicated i. 15, 35, 41, 67, ii. 25, 26, 27, iv. 1, x. 21, xi. 13, all of which are peculiar to Lk.

But it is misleading in this respect to compare the Second Gospel with the Third. From very early times the one has been called the Petrine Gospel, and the other the Pauline. S. Mark is said to give us the teaching of S. Peter, S. Luke the teaching of S. Paul. The statements are true, but in very different senses. Mark derived his materials from Peter. Luke exhibits the spirit of Paul: and no doubt to a large extent he derived this spirit from the Apostle. But he got his material from eye-witnesses. Mark was the *interpreter* of Peter, as Irenæus (iii. 1. 1, 10. 6) and Tertullian (*Adv. Marcion.* iv. 5) aptly call him: he made known to others what Peter had said. Paul was the *illuminator* of Luke (Tert. iv. 2): he enlightened him as to the essential character of the Gospel.

Luke, as his "fellow-worker," would teach what the Apostle taught, and would learn to give prominence to those elements in the Gospel narrative of which he made most frequent use. Then at last "Luke, the companion of Paul, recorded in a book the Gospel preached by him" (Iren. iii. 1. 1).

Jülicher sums up the case justly when he says that Luke has adopted from Paul no more than the whole Catholic Church has adopted, viz. the universality of salvation and the boundlessness of Divine grace: and it is precisely in these two points that Paul has been a clear-sighted and logical interpreter of Jesus Christ (*Einl.* § 27, p. 204). See also Knowling, *The Witness of the Epistles*, p. 328, and the authorities there quoted.

Holtzmann, followed by Davidson (*Introd. to N.T.* ii. p. 17) and Schaff (*Apostolic Christianity*, ii. p. 667), gives various instances of parallelism between the Third Gospel and the Pauline Epistles. Resch (*Aussercanonische Paralleltexte*, p. 121, Leipzig, 1893), while ignoring some of Holtzmann's examples, adds others; but some of his are not very convincing, or depend upon doubtful readings. The following are worth considering:—

S. Luke.	S. Paul.
iv. 32. ἐν ἐξουσίᾳ ἦν ὁ λόγος αὐτοῦ.	1 Cor. ii. 4. ὁ λόγος μου . . . ἐν ἀποδείξει πνεύματος καὶ δυνάμεως.
vi. 36. ὁ πατὴρ ὑμῶν οἰκτίρμων ἐστίν.	2 Cor. i. 3. ὁ πατὴρ τῶν οἰκτιρμῶν.
vi. 39. μήτι δύναται τυφλὸς τυφλὸν ὁδηγεῖν;	Rom. ii. 19. πέποιθας σεαυτὸν ὁδηγὸν εἶναι τυφλῶν.
vi. 48. ἔθηκεν θεμέλιον.	1 Cor. iii. 10. θεμέλιον ἔθηκα.
vii. 8. ἄνθρωπός εἰμι ὑπὸ ἐξουσίαν τασσόμενος.	Rom. xiii. 1. ἐξουσίαις ὑπερεχούσαις ὑποτασσέσθω.
viii. 12. πιστεύσαντες σωθῶσιν.	1 Cor. i. 21. σῶσαι τοὺς πιστεύοντας. Rom. i. 16. εἰς σωτηρίαν παντὶ τ. πιστεύοντι.
viii. 13. μετὰ χαρᾶς δέχονται τ. λόγον.	1 Thes. i. 6. δεξάμενοι τ. λόγον . . . μετὰ χαρᾶς.
x. 7. ἄξιος γὰρ ὁ ἐργάτης τοῦ μισθοῦ αὐτοῦ.	1 Tim. v. 18. ἄξιος ὁ ἐργάτης τοῦ μισθοῦ αὐτοῦ.
x. 8. ἐσθίετε τὰ παρατιθέμενα ὑμῖν.	1 Cor. x. 27. πᾶν τὸ παρατιθέμενον ὑμῖν ἐσθίετε.
x. 16. ὁ ἀθετῶν ὑμᾶς ἐμὲ ἀθετεῖ· ὁ δὲ ἐμὲ ἀθετῶν ἀθετεῖ τὸν ἀποστείλαντά με.	1 Thes. iv. 8. ὁ ἀθετῶν οὐκ ἄνθρωπον ἀθετεῖ ἀλλὰ τὸν Θεόν.
x. 20. τὰ ὀνόματα ὑμῶν ἐνγέγραπται ἐν τοῖς οὐρανοῖς.	Phil. iv. 3. ὧν τὰ ὀνόματα ἐν βίβλῳ ζωῆς (Ps. lxix. 28).
xi. 7. μή μοι κόπους πάρεχε.	Gal. vi. 17. κόπους μοι μηδεὶς παρεχέτω.
xi. 29. ἡ γενεὰ αὕτη . . . σημεῖον ζητεῖ.	1 Cor. i. 22. Ἰουδαῖοι σημεῖα αἰτοῦσιν.
xi. 41. καὶ ἰδοὺ πάντα καθαρὰ ὑμῖν ἐστίν.	Tit. i. 15. πάντα καθαρὰ τοῖς καθαροῖς.
xii. 35. ἔστωσαν ὑμῶν αἱ ὀσφύες περιεζωσμέναι.	Eph. vi. 14. στῆτε οὖν περιζωσάμενοι τὴν ὀσφὺν ὑμῶν (Is. xi. 5).
xii. 42. τίς ἄρα ἐστὶν ὁ πιστὸς οἰκονόμος;	1 Cor. iv. 2. ζητεῖται ἐν τοῖς οἰκονόμοις ἵνα πιστός τις εὑρεθῇ.
xiii. 27. ἀπόστητε ἀπ' ἐμοῦ πάντες ἐργάται ἀδικίας (Ps. vi. 8).	2 Tim. ii. 19. ἀποστήτω ἀπὸ ἀδικίας πᾶς ὁ ὀνομάζων τὸ ὄνομα κυρίου.
xviii. 1. δεῖν πάντοτε προσεύχεσθαι αὐτούς.	Col. i. 3. πάντοτε προσευχόμενοι. 2 Thes. i. 11. προσευχόμεθα πάντοτε.

καὶ μὴ ἐνκακεῖν.	Gal. vi. 9. μὴ ἐνκακῶμεν.
xx. 16. μὴ γένοιτο.	Rom. ix. 14, xi. 11; Gal. iii. 21
xx. 22, 25. ἔξεστιν ἡμᾶς Καίσαρι φόρον δοῦναι ἢ οὔ; ἀπόδοτε τὰ Καίσαρος Καίσαρι.	Rom. xiii. 7. ἀπόδοτε πᾶσιν τὰς ὀφειλάς, τῷ τὸν φόρον τὸν φόρον.
xx. 35. οἱ δὲ καταξιωθέντες τοῦ αἰῶνος ἐκείνου τυχεῖν.	2 Thes. i. 5. εἰς τὸ καταξιωθῆναι ὑμᾶς τῆς βασιλείας τοῦ Θεοῦ.
xx. 38. πάντες γὰρ αὐτῷ ζῶσιν.	Rom. vi. 11. ζῶντας τῷ Θεῷ. Gal. ii. 19. ἵνα Θεῷ ζήσω.
xxi. 23. ἔσται γὰρ . . . ὀργὴ τῷ λαῷ τούτῳ.	1 Thes. ii. 16. ἔφθασεν δὲ ἐπ' αὐτοὺς ἡ ὀργὴ εἰς τέλος.
xxi. 24. ἄχρι οὗ πληρωθῶσιν καιροὶ ἐθνῶν.	Rom. xi. 25. ἄχρι οὗ τὸ πλήρωμα τῶν ἐθνῶν εἰσέλθῃ.
xxi. 34. μή ποτε βαρηθῶσιν αἱ καρδίαι ὑμῶν ἐν κρεπάλῃ καὶ μέθῃ . . . καὶ ἐπιστῇ ἐφ' ὑμᾶς ἐφνίδιος ἡ ἡμέρα ἐκείνη ὡς παγίς.	1 Thes. v. 3–5. τότε αἰφνίδιος αὐτοῖς ἐπίσταται ὄλεθρος . . . ὑμεῖς δὲ οὐκ ἐστὲ ἐν σκότει, ἵνα ἡ ἡμέρα ὑμᾶς ὡς κλέπτης [κλέπτας] καταλάβῃ.
xxi. 36. ἀγρυπνεῖτε δὲ ἐν παντὶ καιρῷ δεόμενοι.	Eph. vi. 18. προσευχόμενοι ἐν παντὶ καιρῷ . . . καὶ ἀγρυπνοῦντες.
xxii. 53. ἡ ἐξουσία τοῦ σκότους.	Col. i. 13. ἐκ τῆς ἐξουσίας τοῦ σκότους.

It is not creditable to modern scholarship that the foolish opinion, quoted by Eusebius with a φασὶ δέ (*H. E.* iii. 4. 8) and by Jerome with *quidam suspicantur* (*De vir. illus.* vii.), that wherever S. Paul speaks of "my Gospel" (Rom. ii. 16, xvi. 25; 2 Tim. ii. 8) he means the Gospel of S. Luke, still finds advocates. And the supposition that the Third Gospel is actually quoted 1 Tim. v. 18 is incredible. The words λέγει ἡ γραφή refer to the first sentence only, which comes from Deut. xxv. 4. What follows, "the labourer is worthy of his hire," is a popular saying, adopted first by Christ (Lk. x. 7; Mt. x. 10) and then by S. Paul. Had S. Paul quoted the saying as an utterance of Christ, he would not have said λέγει ἡ γραφή. He would have used some such expression as μνημονεύειν τῶν λόγων τοῦ κυρίου Ἰησοῦ ὅτι αὐτὸς λέγει (Acts xx. 35), or παραγγέλλει ὁ κύριος (1 Cor. vii. 10, 12), or μεμνημένοι τῶν λόγων τοῦ κυρίου Ἰησοῦ, οὓς ἐλάλησεν (Clem. Rom. *Cor.* xiii. 1; comp. xlvi. 7), or simply εἶπεν ὁ κύριος (Polyc. vii. 2). Comp. 1 Thes. iv. 15; 1 Cor. ix. 14, xi. 23.

(*b*) More than any of the other Evangelists S. Luke brings before his readers the subject of *Prayer*; and that in two ways, (1) by the example of Christ, and (2) by direct instruction. All three Synoptists record that Christ prayed in Gethsemane (Mt. xxvi. 39; Mk. xiv. 35; Lk. xxii. 41); Mark (i. 35) mentions His retirement for prayer after healing multitudes at Capernaum, where Luke (iv. 42) merely mentions the retirement: and Matthew (xiv. 23) and Mark (vi. 46) relate His retirement for prayer after the feeding of the 5000, where Luke (ix. 17) relates neither. But on seven occasions Luke is alone in recording that Jesus prayed: at His Baptism (iii. 21); before His first collision with the hierarchy (v. 16); before choosing the Twelve (vi. 12); before the first prediction of the Passion (ix. 18); at the Transfiguration (ix. 29); before teaching the Lord's Prayer (xi. 1); and on the Cross (xxiii. [34], 46). Moreover, Luke alone relates the declaration of Jesus that He had made supplication for Peter, and His charge to the Twelve, "Pray that ye enter not into temptation" (xxii. 32, 40)

It was out of the fulness of His own experience that Jesus said, "Ask, and it shall be given you" (xi. 9). Again, Luke alone records the parables which enjoin persistence in prayer, the Friend at Midnight (xi. 5–13) and the Unrighteous Judge (xviii. 1–8); and to the charge to "watch" (Mt. xxv. 13; Mk. xiii. 33) he adds "at every season, making supplication, that ye may prevail," etc. (xxi. 36). In the parable of the Pharisee and the Publican the difference between real and unreal prayer is illustrated (xviii 11–13).

(*c*) The Third Gospel is also remarkable for the prominence which it gives to *Praise and Thanksgiving*. It begins and ends with worship in the temple (i. 9, xxiv. 53). Luke alone has preserved for us those hymns which centuries ago passed from his Gospel into the daily worship of the Church: the *Gloria in Excelsis*, or Song of the Angels (ii. 14); the *Magnificat*, or Song of the blessed Virgin Mary (i. 46–55); the *Benedictus*, or Song of Zacharias (i. 68–79); and the *Nunc Dimittis*, or Song of Symeon (ii. 29–32). Far more often than in any other Gospel are we told that those who received special benefits "glorified God" (δοξάζειν τὸν Θεόν) for them (ii. 20, v. 25, 26, vii. 16, xiii. 13, xvii. 15, xviii. 43). Comp. Mt. ix. 8, xv. 31; Mk. ii. 12. The expression "praising God" (αἰνεῖν τὸν Θεόν) is almost peculiar to Luke in N.T. (ii. 13, 20, xix. 37, xxiv. 53?; Acts ii. 47, iii. 8, 9). "Blessing God" (εὐλογεῖν τὸν Θεόν) is almost peculiar to Luke (i. 64, ii. 28, xxiv. 53?): elsewhere only Jas. iii. 9. "Give praise (αἶνον διδόναι) to God" occurs Luke xviii. 43 only. So also χαίρειν, which occurs eight times in Matthew and Mark, occurs nineteen times in Luke and Acts; χαρά seven times in Matthew and Mark, thirteen times in Luke and Acts.

(*d*) The Gospel of S. Luke is rightly styled "the most *literary* of the Gospels" (Renan, *Les Évangiles*, ch. xiii.). "S. Luke has more literary ambition than his fellows" (Sanday, *Book by Book*, p. 401). He possesses the art of composition. He knows not only how to tell a tale truthfully, but how to tell it with effect. He can feel contrasts and harmonies, and reproduce them for his readers. The way in which he tells the stories of the widow's son at Nain, the sinner in Simon's house, Martha and Mary at Bethany, and the walk to Emmaus, is quite exquisite. And one might go on giving other illustrations of his power, until one had mentioned nearly the whole Gospel. The sixth century was not far from the truth when it called him a painter, and said that he had painted the portrait of the Virgin. There is no picture of her so complete as his. How lifelike are his sketches of Zacharias, Anna, Zacchæus, Herod Antipas! And with how few touches is each done! As a rule Luke puts in fewer descriptive details than Mark. In his description of the Baptist he omits the strange attire and food (Mk. i. 6; Mt. iii. 4). In the healing of Simon's wife's mother he omits the taking of her hand (Mk. i. 31; Mt. viii. 15). In that of the palsied he omits the crowding at the door (Mk. ii. 2). And there are plenty of such cases. But at other times we have an illuminating addition which is all his own (iii. 15, 21, iv. 13, 15, 40, 42, v. 1, 12, 15, 16, vi. 12, viii. 47, etc.). His contrasts are not confined to personal traits, such as the unbelieving priest and the believing maiden (i. 18, 38), the self-abasing woman and the self-satisfied Pharisee (vii. 37 ff.), the thankless Jews and the thankful Samaritan (xvii. 17), the practical Martha and the contemplative Mary (x. 38–42), the hostile hierarchy and the attentive people (xix. 47, 48), and the like; the fundamental antithesis between Christ's work and Satan's[1] (iv. 13, x. 17–20, xiii. 16, xxii. 3, 31, 53), often exhibited in the opposition of the scribes and Pharisees to His work (xi. 52, xii. 1, xiii. 14, 31, xv. 2, xvi. 14, xix. 39, 47, xx. 20), is brought out with special clearness. The development of the hostility of the Pharisees is one of the main threads in the narrative. It is this rare combination of descriptive power with simplicity and dignity, this insight into the lights and shadows of character and the conflict between spiritual forces, which makes this Gospel much more than a fulfilment of its original purpose (i. 4). There is no rhetoric, no polemics, no sectarian bitterness. It is by turns joyous and sad; but even where it is most tragic it is almost always serene.[2] As the fine literary taste of Renan affirms, it is the most beautiful book in the world.

(*e*) S. Luke is the only Evangelist who writes *history* as distinct from memoirs. He aims at writing "in order," which probably means in chronological order (i. 5, 26, 36, 56, 59, ii. 42, iii. 23, ix. 28, 37, 51, xxii. 1, 7), and he alone connects his narrative with the history of Syria and of the Roman Empire (ii. 1, iii. 1). The sixfold date (iii. 1) is specially remarkable: and it is possible that both it and ii. 1 were inserted as finishing touches to the narrative. The words ἔτος ($\frac{26}{23}$) and μήν ($\frac{10}{8}$) occur more often in his writings than in the rest of N.T.: and this fact points to a special fondness for exactitude as regards time. Where he gives no date,—probably because he found none in his authorities,—he frequently lets us know what incidents are connected together although he does not know in what year or time of year to place the group (iv. 1, 38, 40, vii. 1, 18, 24, viii. 1, x. 1, 21, xi. 37, xii. 1, xiii. 1, 31, xix. 11, 28, 41, xxii. 66, xxiv. 13). He is very much

[1] Both in Mark (i. 21–28) and in Luke (iv. 31–37) the miracle of healing the demoniac in the synagogue at Capernaum is perhaps placed first as being typical of Christ's whole work. But there is no evidence of any special "demonology" in Luke. With the doubtful exception of the "spirit of infirmity" (xiii. 10) there is no miracle of casting out demons which he alone records.

[2] A marked exception is the violent scene so graphically described xi. 53, 54.

less definite than Josephus or Tacitus; but that is only what we ought to expect. He had not their opportunities of consulting public records, and he was much less interested in chronology than they were. Yet it has been noticed that the *Agricola* of Tacitus contains no chronology until the last chapter is reached. The value of Christ's words and works was quite independent of dates. Such remarks as he makes xvi. 14, xviii. 1, 9, xix. 11 throw far more light upon what follows than an exact note of time would have done. Here and there he seems to be giving us his own estimate of the situation, as an historian or biographer might do (ii. 50, iii. 15, viii. 30, xx. 20, xxii. 3, xxiii. 12): and the notes, whether they come from himself or his sources, are helpful. If chronology even in his Gospel is meagre, yet there is a continuity and development which may be taken as evidence of the true historic spirit.[1] He follows the Saviour through the stages, not only of His ministry, but of His physical and moral growth (ii. 40, 42, 51, 52, iii. 23, iv. 13, xxii. 28, 53). He traces the course of the ministry from Nazareth to Capernaum and other towns of Galilee, from Galilee to Samaria and Peræa, from Peræa to Jerusalem, just as in the Acts he marks the progress of the Gospel, as represented successively by Stephen, Philip, Peter, and Paul, from Jerusalem to Antioch, from Antioch to Ephesus and Greece, and finally to Rome.

(*f*) But along with these literary and historical features it has a marked *domestic tone*. In this Gospel we see most about Christ in His social intercourse with men. The meal in the house of Simon, in that of Martha and Mary, in that of a Pharisee, when the Pharisees were denounced, in that of a leading Pharisee on a sabbath, when the dropsical man was healed, His sojourn with Zacchæus, His walk to Emmaus and the supper there, are all peculiar to Luke's narrative, together with a number of parables, which have the same quiet and homely setting. The Good Samaritan in the inn, the Friend at Midnight, the Woman with the Leaven, the Master of the house rising and shutting the door, the Woman sweeping for the Lost Coin, the Father welcoming the Lost Son, all have this touch of familiar domesticity. And perhaps it is to this love of homely scenes that we may trace the fact that whereas Mk. (iv. 31) has the mustard-seed sown "on the earth," and Mt. (xiii. 31) makes a man sow it "in his field," Lk. (xiii. 19) tells us that a man sowed it "in his *own garden*." Birks, *Hor. Ev.*

(ii.) When we consider the *style and language* of S. Luke, we are struck by two apparently opposite features,—his great *com-*

[1] Ramsay regards Luke as a historical writer of the highest order, one who "commands excellent means of knowledge . . . and brings to the treatment of his subject genius, literary skill, and sympathetic historical insight" (*S. Paul the Traveller*, pp. 2, 3, 20, 21, Hodder, 1895).

mand of Greek and his very un-Greek *use of Hebrew phrases and constructions.* These two features produce a result which is so peculiar, that any one acquainted with them in detail would at once recognize as his any page torn out of either of his writings. This peculiarity impresses us less than that which distinguishes the writings of S. John, and which is felt even in a translation; but it is much more easily analysed. It lies in the diction rather than in the manner, and its elements can readily be tabulated. But for this very reason a good deal of it is lost in translation, in which peculiarities of construction cannot always be reproduced. In any version the difference between S. Mark and S. John is felt by the ordinary reader. The most careful version would fail to show to an attentive student more than a good portion of the differences between S. Mark and S. Luke.

The author of the Third Gospel and of the Acts is the most *versatile* of all the N.T. writers. He can be as Hebraistic as the LXX, and as free from Hebraisms as Plutarch. And, in the main, whether intentionally or not, he is Hebraistic in describing Hebrew society, and Greek in describing Greek society. It is impossible to determine how much of the Hebraistic style is due to the sources which he is employing, how much is voluntarily adopted by himself as suitable to the subject which he is treating. That Aramaic materials which he translated, or Greek materials which had come from an Aramaic source, influenced his language considerably, need not be doubted; for it is where he had no such materials that his Greek shows least sign of such influences. In the second half of the Acts, where he writes of his own experiences, and is independent of information that has come from an Aramaic source, he writes in good late Greek. But then it is precisely here that he is describing scenes far away from Jerusalem in an Hellenistic or Gentile atmosphere. So that it is quite possible that to some extent he is a free agent in this matter, and is not merely exhibiting the influence under which he is writing at the moment. No doubt it is true that, where he has used materials which directly or indirectly are Aramaic, there his style is Hebraistic; but it may also be true that he has there *allowed* his style to be Hebraistic, because he felt that such a style was appropriate to the subject-matter.

He has enabled us to judge of the two styles by placing two highly characteristic specimens of each in immediate juxtaposition. In the Acts the change from the more Hebrew portion to the more Greek portion takes place gradually, just as in the narrative there is a change from a Hebrew period (i.–v.), through a transitional period (vi.–xii.), to a Gentile period (xiii.–xxviii.).[1] But in the

[1] Compare in this respect the letter of Lysias (xxiii. 26–30) and the speech of Tertullus (xxiv. 2–9) with the speeches of Peter (ii. 14–39, iii. 12–26).

Gospel the remarkably elegant and idiomatic Greek of the Preface is suddenly changed to the intensely Hebraistic Greek of the opening narrative. It is like going from a chapter in Xenophon to a chapter in the LXX.[1] And he never returns to the style of the Preface. In the Gospel itself it is simply a question of more or less Hebrew elements. They are strongest in the first two chapters, but they never entirely cease; and they are specially common at the beginning of narratives, *e.g.* v. 1, 12, 17, vi. 1, 6, 12, viii. 22, ix. 18, 51, etc. It will generally be found that the parallel passages are, in the opening words, less Hebraistic than Luke. In construction, even Matthew, a Jew writing for Jews, sometimes exhibits fewer Hebraisms than this versatile Gentile, who writes for Gentiles. Comp. Lk. ix. 28, 29, 33, 38, 39 with Mt. xvii. 1, 2, 4, 15; Lk. xiii. 30 with Mt. xix. 30; Lk. xviii. 35 with Mt. xx. 29; Lk. xx. 1 with Mt. xxi. 23.

From this strong Hebraistic tinge in his language some (Tiele, Hofmann, Hahn) have drawn the unnecessary and improbable conclusion that the Evangelist was a Jew; while others, from the fact that some of the Hebraisms and many other expressions which occur in the Third Gospel and the Acts are found also in the Pauline Epistles, have drawn the quite impossible conclusion that this hypothetical Jew was none other than S. Paul himself. To mention nothing else, the "we" sections in the Acts are fatal to the latter theory. In writing of himself and his companions, what could induce the Apostle to change backwards and forwards between "they" and "we"? As to the former theory, good reasons have been given above for attributing both books to a Gentile and to S. Luke, who (as S. Paul clearly implies in Col. iv. 11–14) was a Gentile. The Hebraistic colour in the Evangelist's language, and the elements common to his diction and that of the Pauline Epistles, can be easily explained, and more satisfactorily explained, without an hypothesis which imports more difficulties than it solves. The Hebraisms in Luke come partly from his sources, partly from his knowledge of the LXX, and partly from his intercourse with S. Paul, who often in his presence discussed the O.T. with Jews in language which must often have been charged with Hebraisms. The expressions which are common to the two Lucan documents and the Pauline Epistles are partly mere accidents of language, and partly the result of companionship between the two writers. Two such men could not have been together so often without influencing one another's language.

S. Luke's *command of Greek* is abundantly shown both in the *freedom of his constructions* and also in the *richness of his vocabulary.*

[1] There are some who attribute the strongly Hebraistic tone of the first two chapters to a conscious and deliberate imitation of the LXX rather than to the influence of Aramaic sources.

(*a*) The *freedom of his constructions* is seen not infrequently even in his Hebraisms. Two instances will suffice. (1) His frequent use of ἐγένετο is often purely Hebraistic (i. 8, 9), sometimes less so (vi. 1), sometimes hardly Hebraistic at all (Acts ix. 3, xxi. 1). This will be found worked out in detail in a detached note at the end of ch. i. (2) His frequent use of periphrastic tenses, *i.e.* the substantive verb with a present or perfect participle instead of the simple tense, exhibits a similar variety.

The use of ἦν with pres. or perf. part. as a periphrasis for imperf. or pluperf. indic. is of Aramaic origin in many cases and is frequent in the Gospels,—most frequent in Luke; but it is not always easy to say whether it is a Hebraism or a use that might very well stand in classical Greek. For ἦν with pres. part. see i. 10, 21, 22, ii. 33, 51, iv. 20, 31, 38, 44, v. 16, 17, 29, vi. 12, viii. 40, ix. 53, xi. 14, xiii. 10, 11, xiv. 1, xv. 1, xix. 47, [xxi. 37], xxiii. 8, xxiv. 13, 32. Most of these are probably due to Hebrew or Aramaic influence; but many would be admissible in classical Greek, and may be used to imply continuance of the action. In i. 21, 22, ii. 51, iv. 31, xv. 1, xix. 47, xxiii. 8, xxiv. 13, 32 the simple imperf. follows immediately in the next clause or sentence. That such cases as ii. 33, iv. 20, ix. 53, xi. 14, xiii. 10, 11, xiv. 1 are Hebraistic need hardly be doubted. So also where ἦν with perf. part. is used for the pluperf. (i. 7, ii. 26, iv. 16, 17, v. 17, ix. 32, 45, xviii. 34), i. 7 and ix. 32 with most of the others are probably Hebraistic, but v. 17 almost certainly is not. Anyhow, Luke shows that he is able to give an Hellenic turn to his Hebraisms, so that they would less offend a Greek ear. Much the same might be said of his use of καί to introduce the apodosis, which may be quite classical (ii. 21), but may also be Hebraistic, especially where ἰδού is added (vii. 12, xxiv. 4), or αὐτός (v. 1, 17, viii. 1, 22, ix. 51, etc.): or of his frequent use of ἐν τῷ with the infinitive (i. 8, 21, ii. 6, 43, v. 1, etc.).

Simcox, *Lang. of N.T.* pp. 131–134, has tabulated the use of periphrastic imperf. and pluperf. See also his remarks on Luke's Hebraisms, *Writers of N.T.* pp. 19–22.

But Luke's freedom of construction is conspicuous in other respects. Although he sometimes co-ordinates clauses, joining them, Hebrew fashion, with a simple καί (i. 13, 14, 31–33, xvi. 19, etc.), yet he is able to vary his sentences with relatives, participles, dependent clauses, genitive absolutes, and the like, almost to any extent. We find this even in the most Hebraistic parts of the Gospel (i. 20, 26, 27, ii. 4, 21, 22, 26, 36, 37, 42, 43); but still more in other parts: see especially vii. 36–50. He is the only N.T. writer who uses the optative in indirect questions, both without ἄν (i. 29, iii. 15, viii. 9, xxii. 23; Acts xvii. 11, xxi. 33, xxv. 20) and with it (vi. 11, xv. 26; Acts v. 24, x. 17), sometimes preceded by the article (i. 62, ix. 46). In xviii. 36 the ἄν is doubtful. The elegant and idiomatic attraction of the relative is very common in Luke (i. 4, v. 9, ix. 36, xii. 46, xv. 16, xxiii. 41; Acts i. 22, ii. 22, iii. 21, 25, etc.), especially after πᾶς (ii. 20, iii. 19, ix. 43, xix. 37, xxiv. 25; Acts i. 1, x. 39, xiii. 39, xxii. 10), whereas it occurs only twice in Matthew (xviii. 19, xxiv. 50) and once in Mark (vii. 13). His more frequent use of τε is another instance of more idiomatic Greek (ii. 16, xii. 45, xv. 2, xxi. 11 (*bis*), xxii. 66, xxiii. 12, xxiv. 20): only once in Mark and four times in Matthew. Sometimes we find the harsh Greek of Matthew or Mark improved in the parallel passage in Luke: *e.g.* τῶν θελόντων ἐν στολαῖς περιπατεῖν καὶ ἀσπασποὺς ἐν ταῖς ἀγοραῖς (Mk. xii. 38) has an awkwardness which Luke avoids by inserting φιλούντων before ἀσπασμούς (xx. 46). Or again, ἀλλὰ εἴπωμεν Ἐξ ἀνθρώπων—ἐφοβοῦντο τὸν ὄχλον· ἅπαντες γὰρ εἶχον τὸν Ἰωάνην ὄντως ὅτι προφήτης ἦν (Mk. xi. 32) is smoothed in more details than one in Luke: ἐὰν δὲ εἴπωμεν Ἐξ ἀνθρώπων, ὁ λαὸς ἅπας καταλιθάσει ἡμᾶς· πεπεισμένος γάρ ἐστιν Ἰωάνην προφήτην εἶναι (xx. 6). Compare καὶ πρωὶ ἔννυχα λίαν, which perhaps is a provincialism (Mk. i. 35), with γενομένης δὲ ἡμέρας (Lk. iv. 42). In the verses which follow, Luke's diction is smoother than Mark's. Compare also Lk. v. 29, 30 with Mk. ii. 15, 16 and Mt. ix. 10, 11; Lk. v. 36 with Mk. ii. 21 and Mt. ix. 16; Lk. vi. 11 with Mk. iii. 6 and Mt. xii. 14. The superior freedom and fulness of Luke's narrative of the message of the Baptist (vii. 18-21), as compared with that of Matthew (xi. 2, 3), is very marked.

(*b*) But Luke's command of Greek is seen also in the *richness of his vocabulary*. The number of words which occur in his two writings and nowhere else in N.T. is estimated at 750 or (including doubtful[1] cases) 851; of which 26 occur in quotations from LXX. In the Gospel the words peculiar to Luke are 312; of which 52 are doubtful, and 11 occur in quotations. Some of these are found nowhere else in Greek literature. He is very fond of compound verbs, especially with διά or ἐπί, or with two prepositions, as ἐπανάγειν, ἐπεισέρχεσθαι, ἀντιπαρέρχεσθαι, συγκατατιθέναι, προσαναβαίνειν. He may have coined some of them for himself. The following are among the most remarkable words and expressions which occur either in both his writings and nowhere else in N.T., or in his Gospel and nowhere else in N.T. No account is here taken of the large number, which are peculiar to the Acts.

Those in thick type are found in LXX. Those with an asterisk are shown by Hobart to be frequent in medical writers. Many of these might be frequent in any writers. But the number of less common words, which are peculiar to Luke in N.T., and are fairly common in medical writers, is remarkable; and those of them which are not found in LXX are specially to be noted.

Thirty times in G. and A. **ἐγένετο δέ** (not Jn. x. 22).
Nine times in G. and A. ἡμέρα γίνεται : nine in G. **μνᾶ**.
Eight times in G. **ἐν αὐτῇ τῇ** (ἡμέρᾳ, **ὥρᾳ**, οἰκίᾳ).
Seven times in G. and A. **ἀποδέχεσθαι**, *συνβάλλειν, ἐν ταῖς ἡμέραις ταύταις.
Six times in G. and A. **καθότι**, **πονηρός** as an epithet of πνεῦμα: six in G. **ἐπιστάτα**, λέγειν παράβολήν.
Five times in G. and A. **ἑξῆς**, καθεξῆς, καθ' ὅλης τῆς, **προσέχετε ἑαυτοῖς**, **ὁ στρατηγός** or **οἱ στρ. τοῦ ἱεροῦ**, **ὁ ὕψιστος** or **ὕψιστος** (of God): five in G. **ἀνακρίνειν** (in the legal sense), καὶ οὗτος, καὶ ὡς, **λίμνη**, ἐν μιᾷ τῶν.
Four times in G. and A. **ἅπτειν**, διαπορεῖν, **ἐπαίρειν τὴν φωνήν**, **ἐπιφωνεῖν**, **καθιέναι**, ***ὀδυνᾶσθαι**, ***ὁμιλεῖν**, ***συναρπάζειν**, αἴτιον, **ἐναντίον**, **εὐλαβής**, **κράτιστος**, *παραλελυμένος (in the medical sense of "palsied"): four in G. ***κατακλίνειν**, **βαλλάντιον**, **φάτνη**, **ὡς ἤγγισεν**.
Three times in G. and A. **ἀναζητεῖν**, **ἀξιουν** *c. infin.*, **διελθεῖν ἕως**, **διιστάναι**, **ἐπιβιβάζειν**, ***ἐπιχειρεῖν**, **συμπληροῦν**, **αὐτῇ τῇ ὥρᾳ**, **ἀπ' αἰῶνος**, **τὰ δέσμα**, **δούλη**, **ἔναντι**, **ἑσπέρα**, **θάμβος**, **βουλὴ τοῦ Θεοῦ**, ***ἴασις**, πολίτης, **τῇ ἡμέρα τῶν σαββάτων**, ***συγγένεια**, τὰ ὑπάρχοντα αὐτῷ, **χεὶρ κυρίου**: three in G. **θεραπεύειν ἀπό**, **σκάπτειν**, **σκιρτᾷν**, **κατὰ τὸ ἔθος**, **σιτευτός**, τῃ ἡμέρᾳ τοῦ σαββάτου, **ἐν μιᾳ τῶν ἡμερῶν**.

[1] Owing to the various readings it may be doubted either (1) whether the word is used by Luke, or (2) whether it is not used by some other writer. In the lists on pp. lii, liii, the lower number has generally been preferred in doubtful cases.

Twice in G. and A. ἀναδεικνύναι, ἀνακαθίζειν, * ἀνασπᾶν, ἀναφαίνειν, * ἀνευρίσκειν, ἀντειπεῖν, ἀπογραφή, * ἀποτινάσσειν, * διατηρεῖν, * διισχυρίζεσθαι, * διοδεύειν, * ἐνεδρεύειν, ἐπιδεῖν, * εὐτόνως, τῇ ἐχομένῃ, ἄχρι καιροῦ, * κατακλείειν, κατακολουθεῖν, κλάσις, κλίνει ἡ ἡμέρα, * κλινίδιον, ὀρινός, * παραβιάζεσθαι, περιλάμπειν, πορεύου εἰς εἰρήνην, * προβάλλειν, προπορεύεσθαι, * προσδοκία, * προυπάρχειν, στρατιά, συνεῖναι, τραυματίζειν, τραχύς, χρεοφιλέτης : twice in G. ἄγρα, * ἀνάπειρος, * ἀντιπαρέρχεσθαι, ἀστράπτειν, ἄτερ, * αὐστηρός, βουνός, γελᾶν, διαγογγύζειν, διαλαλεῖν, * δοχή, ἐκμυκτηρίζειν, ἐκτελεῖν, ἐπαιτεῖν, * ἐπανέρχεσθαι, ἐφημερία, ζεῦγος, ἡγεμονεύειν, οὐσία, ἡ παῖς, πράκτωρ, πρεσβεία, προφέρειν, * σπαργανοῦν, συκοφαντεῖν, * ὑποχωρεῖν.

It is not worth while to make a complete list of the words (over 200 in number) which occur *once* in the Third Gospel and nowhere else in N.T. The following will give a good idea of their character :—

ἀγραυλεῖν, ἀθροίζειν, ἀλλογενής, ἀμπελουργός, ἀνάδειξις, * ἀνάλημψις, * ἀναφωνεῖν, * ἀντιβάλλειν, ἀπαρτισμός, ἀπελπίζειν, * ἀποκλείειν, ἀποστοματίζειν, * ἀποψύχειν, ἀρχιτελώνης, * αὐτόπτης, * ἀφρός, * βελόνη, * βολή, βρώσιμος, * γῆρας, * διαβάλλειν, διαγρηγορεῖν, * διαλείπειν, διαμερισμός, διανεύειν, * διανόημα, * διανυκτερεύειν, * διαπραγματεύεσθαι, * διασείειν, * διαχωρίζειν, * διήγησις, * ἔγκυος, * ἐθίζειν, * ἐκκρέμασθαι, * ἐκχωρεῖν, * ἑλκοῦν, * ἐμβάλλειν, ἐνδέχεται, ἐπαθροίζειν, ἐπειδήπερ, ἐπεισέρχεσθαι, τὸ ἐπιβάλλον, * ἐπιμελῶς, ἐπιπορεύεσθαι, ἐπισιτισμός, * ἐπισχύειν, * ἐπιχεῖν, * εὐφορεῖν, * ἡμιθανής, * θεωρία, * θυμιᾶν, * ἰκμάς, ἰσάγγελος, * κατάβασις, * καταδεῖν, καταλιθάζειν, καταπλεῖν, * καταψύχειν, κεράτιον, κλισία, κρεπάλη, κρυπτή, λαμπρῶς, * λῆρος, * λυσιτελεῖ, * μετεωρίζειν, μεριστής, * ὁδεύειν, ὄμβρος, * ὀπτός, * ὀφρύς, παμπληθεί, πανδοχεῖον, πανδοχεύς, * παράδοξος, παρακαλύπτειν, * παρατήρησις, περικρύπτειν, περιοικεῖν, περισπᾶν, πήγανον, * πιέζειν, * πινακίδιον, * πλημμύρα, * πραγματεύεσθαι, προμελετᾶν, * προσαναβαίνειν, προσδαπανᾶν, προσεργαζέσθαι, * προσψαύειν, * πτύσσειν, * ῥῆγμα, * σάλος, σίκερα, σινιάζειν, σιτομέτριον, * συκάμινος, συκομορέα, συνκατατιθέναι, * συνκυρία, * συνπίπτειν, * συνφύειν, * τελεσφορεῖν, τετραπλόος, * τραῦμα, * ὑγρός, * ὑδρωπικός, * ὑποστρωννύναι, * φόβηθρον, φρονίμως, * χάσμα, * ὠόν.

But the words which are peculiar to Luke in N.T. are by no means even the chief of the marks of his style. Still more striking are those expressions and constructions which he uses frequently, or more frequently than any other writer. Many of these occur more often in S. Luke's writings than in all the rest of N.T. A collection of them is rendered much more useful by being to some extent classified; and the following lists have been made with a view to illustrating the affinities between the diction of S. Luke and of S. Paul and that of the Epistle to the Hebrews both jointly with the Pauline Epistles and also by itself. In this survey the Pastoral Epistles have been kept distinct from the main groups of the Pauline Epistles, in order to show their harmony with the diction of the Apostle's beloved companion. Words peculiar to Luke and to the Pastoral Epistles are not improbably Pauline. Words which are found in other Pauline Epistles as well as in the Pastoral Epistles and in Luke's writings are still more safely regarded as Pauline.

Eight classes have been made; and in them the very great variety of the words included,—many of them quite classical or of classical formation,—illustrate the richness of S. Luke's vocabulary and his command of the Greek language. (1) Expressions peculiar to S. Luke and S. Paul in N.T. (2) Peculiar to S. Luke and S. Paul and the Epistle to the Hebrews. (3) Peculiar to S. Luke and the Epistle to the Hebrews. (4) Not found in any other Gospel and more frequent in S. Luke than in the rest of N.T. (5) Found in one or more of the other Gospels, but more frequent in S. Luke than in the rest of N.T. (6) Due to Hebrew influence. (7) Miscellaneous expressions and constructions which are specially frequent in his writings. (8) Expressions probably or possibly medical. In the first of these classes the second list contains expressions peculiar to the writers in question, although not *frequent* in Luke. The figures state the number of times which the word occurs in that book or group; and in fractions the upper figures indicates the number of times that the word occurs in the writings of Luke, the lower figure the number of times which it occurs elsewhere: *e.g.* in class 3 the fraction $\frac{2}{1}$ means twice in Luke's writings and once in Hebrews; and in classes 4 and 5 the fraction $\frac{7}{4}$ means seven times in Luke's writings and four times in the other books of N.T. Where various readings render the exact proportions doubtful a "*c.*" is placed in front of the fraction; *e.g. c.* $\frac{7}{3}$. In classes 1 and 2, when a reference to chapter and verse is given, this is the only instance of the use of the word in that book or group.

(1) *Expressions peculiar to S. Luke and S. Paul in N.T.*

	S. Luke.		S. Paul.	
	Gosp.	Acts.	Main.	Past.
ἀνθ' ὧν . . .	3	xii. 23	2 Th. ii. 10	
ἀπολογεῖσθαι . . .	2	6	2	
ἀπὸ τοῦ νῦν . . .	5	xviii. 6	2 Cor. v. 16	
*ἀτενίζειν . . .	2	10	2	
*ἄτοπος . . .	xxiii. 41	2	2 Th. iii. 2	
διαπορεύεσθαι? . .	3	xvi. 4	Rom. xv. 24	
ἐγκαλεῖν . . .		6	Rom. viii. 33	
τὸ εἰρημένον . .	ii. 24	2	Rom. iv. 18	
ἐξαποστέλλειν . .	4	7	2	
ἐργασία . . .	xii. 58	4	Eph. iv. 19	
ἐφιστάναι . . .	7	11	1 Th. v. 3	2
*ἡσυχάζειν . . .	2	2	1 Th. iv. 11	
ἰδοὺ γάρ . . .	5	ix. 11	2 Cor. vii. 11	
κακοῦργος . . .	3			2 Tim. ii. 9
καταγγέλλειν . .		11	7	
κατάγειν . . .	v. 11	7	Rom. x. 6	
καταντᾶν . . .		9	4	

	S. LUKE.		S. PAUL.	
	Gosp.	Acts.	Main.	Past.
καταξιωθῆναι . .	xx. 35	v. 41	2 Th. i. 5	
ὁ λόγος τ. κυρίου . .		6	1 Th. i. 8	
οἰκονομία . . .	3		5	? 1 Tim. i. 4
τὰ περί . . .	3	11	5	
συνειδέναι, -ιδεῖν . .		3	1 Cor. iv. 4	
ψαλμός . . .	2	2	3	

All the above are proportionately common in S. Luke's writings; but there are many more which illustrate the affinities between the two writers; *e.g.*

	Gosp.	Acts.	Main.	Past.
ἄδηλος . . .	xi. 44		1 Cor. xiv. 8	
αἰφνίδιος . . .	xxi. 34		1 Th. v. 3	
αἰχμαλωτίζειν . .	xxi. 24		2	2 Tim. iii. 6
ἀνάγνωσις . . .		xiii. 15	2 Cor. iii. 14	1 Tim. iv. 13
ἀνάθεμα . . .		xxiii. 14	5	
ἀνακρίνειν . . .	xxiii. 14	5	10	
ἀναλίσκειν . . .	ix. 54		2 ?	
ἀναλύειν . . .	xii. 36		Phil. i. 23	
*ἀναπέμπειν . . .	3	? xxv. 21	Philem. 12	
ἀναστατοῦν . . .		2	Gal. v. 12	
ἀνατίθεσθαι . . .		xxv. 14	Gal. ii. 2	
*ἄνεσις . . .		xxiv. 23	4	
ἀνόητος . . .	xxiv. 25		3	2
ἄνοια . . .	vi. 11			2 Tim. iii. 9
ἀνταπόδομα . .	xiv. 12		Rom. xi. 9	
ἀνταποκρίνεσθαι . .	xiv. 6		Rom. ix. 20	
ἀντικεῖσθαι . . .	2		4	2
ἀντιλαμβάνεσθαι . .	i. 54	xx. 35		1 Tim. vi. 2
ἀπειθής . . .	i. 17	xxvi. 19	Rom. i. 30	3
ἀπειλή . . .		2	Eph. vi. 9	
ἀποδεικνύναι . .		2	2	
ἀποβολή . . .		xxvii. 22	Rom. xi. 15	
*ἀπολούεσθαι . .		xxii. 16	1 Cor. vi. 11	
ἀποστολή . . .		i. 25	3	
ἀπρόσκοπος . . .		xxiv. 16	2	
ἀπωθεῖσθαι . . .		3	2	1 Tim. i. 19
ἆρα; or ἄρα; . .	xviii. 8	viii. 30	Gal. ii. 17	
ἀροτριᾶν . . .	xvii. 7		1 Cor. ix. 10	
*ἀσφάλεια . . .	i. 4	v. 23	1 Th. v. 3	
*ἄτοπος . . .	xxiii. 41	2	2 Th. iii. 2	
ἀχάριστος . . .	vi. 35			2 Tim. iii. 2
βάρβαρος . . .		2	4	
βιωτικός . . .	xxi. 34		2	
βυθίζειν . . .	v. 7			1 Tim. vi. 9
δέησιν ποιεῖσθαι . .	v. 31		Phil. i. 4	1 Tim. ii. 1
δεκτός . . .	2	x. 35	2	

	S. Luke.		S. Paul.	
	Gosp.	Acts.	Main.	Past.
διαγγέλλειν . . .	ix. 60	xxi. 26	Rom. ix. 17	
διαιρεῖν . . .	xv. 12		1 Cor. xii. 11	
διαταγή . . .		vii. 53	Rom. xiii. 2	
διερμηνεύειν . .	xxiv. 27	ix. 36	4	
δόγμα	ii. 1	2	2	
δρόμος . . .		2		2 Tim. iv. 7
δυνάστης . . .	i. 52	viii. 27		1 Tim. vi. 15
εἰ δὲ καί . . .	xi. 18		4	
ἐμφανής . . .		x. 40	Rom. x. 20	
ἔνδοξος . . .	2		2	
ἐνδύεσθαι . . .	xxiv. 49		14	
ἐνκακεῖν . . .	xviii. 1		5	
ἔννομος . . .		xix. 39	1 Cor. ix. 21	
ἐξαρτίζειν . . .		xxi. 5		2 Tim. iii. 17
ἐξουθενεῖν . . .	2	iv. 11	8	
ἐξουσία τ. σκότους .	xxii. 53		Col. i. 13	
ἐξουσιάζειν . . .	xxii. 25		3	
ἐπαινεῖν . . .	xvi. 8		4	
ἐπαναπαύεσθαι . .	x. 6		Rom. ii. 17	
ἐπέχειν . . .	xiv. 7	2	Phil. ii. 16	1 Tim. iv. 16
ἐπιείκεια . . .		xxiv. 4	2 Cor. x. 1	
ἐπιμελεῖσθαι . .	2			1 Tim. iii. 5
ἐπίστασις . . .		xxiv. 12	2 Cor. xi. 28	
ἐπιφαίνειν . . .	i. 79	xxvii. 20		2
εὐαγγελιστής . .		xxi. 8	Eph. iv. 11	2 Tim. iv. 5
εὐγενής . . .	xix. 12	xvii. 11	1 Cor. i. 26	
εὐσεβεῖν . . .		xvii. 23		1 Tim. v. 4
ζέειν τ. πνεύματι . .		xviii. 25	Rom. xii. 11	
ζημία		2	2	
ζωγρεῖν . . .	v. 10			2 Tim. ii. 26
*ζωογονεῖν . . .	xvii. 33	vii. 19		1 Tim. vi. 13
θέατρον . . .		2	1 Cor. iv. 9	
καθήκειν . . .		xxii. 22	Rom. i. 28	
κατευθύνειν . . .	i. 79		2	
κινδυνεύειν . . .	viii. 23	2	1 Cor. xv. 30	
κραταιοῦσθαι . .	2		2	
κυριεύειν . . .	xxii. 25		5	1 Tim. vi. 15
λείπειν = fail . .	xviii. 22			2
μαρτύρεσθαι . . .		2	3	
μεθιστάναι -ειν . .	xvi. 4	2	2	
μεθύσκεσθαι . .	xii. 45		2	
μερίς	x. 42	2	2	
μεταδιδόναι . . .	iii. 11		4	
νομοδιδάσκαλος . .	v. 17	v. 34		1 Tim. i. 7
νοσφίζεσθαι . . .		2		Tit. ii. 10
νουθετεῖν . . .		xx. 31	7	
ξενία		xxviii. 23	Philem. 22	
ξυρᾶσθαι . . .		xxi. 24	2	

	S. Luke.		S. Paul.	
	Gosp.	Acts.	Main.	Past.
ὁμοθυμαδόν		10	Rom. xv. 6	
ὀπτασία	2	xxvi. 19	2 Cor. xii. 1	
ὁσιότης	i. 75		Eph. iv. 24	
ὀψώνιον	iii. 14		3	
παγίς	xxi. 34		Rom. xi. 9	3
πανοπλία	xi. 22		2	
πανουργία	xx. 23		4	
πάντως	iv. 23	3	5	
παραγγελία		2	1 Th. iv. 2	2
παρασκευάζειν		x. 10	3	
παραχειμάζειν		2	1 Cor. xvi. 6	Tit. iii. 12
*παροξύνεσθαι		xvii. 16	1 Cor. xiii. 5	
παρρησιάζεσθαι		7	2	
πατριά	ii. 4	iii. 25	Eph. iii. 15	
πειθαρχεῖν		3		Tit. iii. 1
περίεργος		xix. 19		1 Tim. v. 13
περιποιεῖσθαι	xvii. 33	xx. 28		1 Tim. iii. 13
ἐπὶ πλεῖον		3		2
πληροφορεῖν	i. 1		3	2
πολιτεία		xxii. 28	Eph. ii. 12	
πολιτεύεσθαι		xxiii. 1	Phil. i. 27	
πορθεῖν		ix. 21	2	
πρεσβυτέριον	xxii. 66	xxii. 5		1 Tim. iv. 14
πρεσβύτης	i. 18		Philem. 9	Tit. ii. 2
προδότης	vi. 16	vii. 52		2 Tim. iii. 4
προειπεῖν		i. 16	2	
προθυμία		xvii. 11	4	
προϊδεῖν		ii. 31	Gal. iii. 8	
προκόπτειν	ii. 52		2	3
πρόνοια		xxiv. 2	Rom. xiii. 14	
προορίζειν		iv. 28	5	
προπετής		xix. 36		2 Tim. iii. 4
κατὰ πρόσωπον	ii. 31	2	2	
ῥαβδίζειν		xvi. 22	2 Cor. xi. 25	
σέβασμα		xvii. 23	2 Th. ii. 4	
σκοπεῖν	xi. 35		5	
στοιχεῖν		xxi. 24	4	
συγκαθίζειν	xxii. 55		Eph. ii. 6	
συγκλείειν	v. 6		3	
συγχαίρειν	3		4	
συμβιβάζειν		3	4	
συναντιλαμβάνειν	x. 40		Rom. viii. 26	
σύνδεσμος		viii. 23	3	
συνέκδημος		xix. 29	2 Cor. viii. 19	
συνεσθίειν	xv. 2	2	2	
συνευδοκεῖν	xi. 48	2	3	
συνοχή	xxi. 25		2 Cor. ii. 4	
συστέλλειν		v. 6	1 Cor. vii. 29	

	S. LUKE.		S. PAUL.	
	Gosp.	Acts.	Main.	Past.
σωματικός . . .	iii. 22			I Tim. iv. 8
τὸ σωτήριον . . .	2	xxviii. 28	Eph. vi. 17	
σωφροσύνη . . .		xxvi. 25		2
τετράποδα . . .		2	Rom. i. 23	
*τήρησις . . .		2	I Cor. vii. 19	
δοῦναι τόπον . .	xiv. 9		2	
ὕβρις		2	2 Cor. xii. 10	
ὑπήκοος . . .		vii. 39	2	
ὑπωπιάζειν . . .	xviii. 5		I Cor. ix. 27	
ὑστέρημα . . .	xxi. 4		8	
φάσκειν . . .		2	Rom. i. 22	
φιλανθρωπία . .		xxviii. 2		Tit. iii. 4
φιλάργυρος . . .	xvi. 14			2 Tim. iii. 2
φόρος	2		2	
φρόνησις . . .	i. 17		Eph. i. 8	
χαρίζεσθαι . . .	3	4	15	
χαριτοῦν . . .	i. 28		Eph. i. 6	
χειροτονεῖν . . .		xiv. 23	2 Cor. viii. 19	
χρῆσθαι . . .		2	7	2

(2) *Expressions peculiar to S. Luke and S. Paul and the Epistle to the Hebrews.*

	Gosp.	Acts.	Main.	Past.	Heb.
ἄμεμπτος .	i. 6		3		viii. 7
ἀναγκαῖος .		2	4	Tit. iii. 14	viii. 3
ἀνάμνησις .	[xxii. 19]		2		x. 3
ἀνταποδιδόναι	2		4		x. 30
ἀξιοῦν . .	vii. 7	2	2 Th. i. 11	I Tim. v. 17	2
ἀποκεῖσθαι .	xix. 20		Col. i. 5	2 Tim. iv. 8	ix. 27
ἀπολύτρωσις .	xxi. 28		7		2
ἀσφαλής .		3	Phil. iii. 1		vi. 19
ἀφιστάν .	4	6	2 Cor. xii. 8	2	iii. 12
βουλή . .	2	7	2		vi. 17
διαμαρτύρεσθαι	xvi. 28	9	I Th. iv. 6	3	ii. 6
δι' ἣν αἰτίαν .	viii. 47	3		3	ii. 11
ἐκφέρειν ? .	xv. 22	4		I Tim. vi. 7	vi. 8
ἐκφεύγειν .	xxi. 36	2	3		2
ἐνδυναμοῦν .		ix. 22	3	3	? xi. 34
ἐντυγχάνειν .		xxv. 24	3		vii. 25
ἐπίθεσις .		viii. 18		2	vi. 2
καταργεῖν .	xiii. 7		24	2 Tim. i. 10	ii. 14
λειτουργεῖν .		xiii. 2	Rom. xv. 27		x. 11

	Gosp.	Acts.	Main.	Past.	Heb.
λειτουργία .	i. 23		3		2
μεταλαμβάνειν		4		2 Tim. ii. 6	2
νυνί . .		2	18?		2?
*ὁρίζειν . .	xxii. 22	5	Rom. i. 4		iv. 7
παραιτεῖσθαι?	3	xxv. 11		4	3
παράκλησις .	2	4	19	1 Tim. iv. 13	3
περιαιρεῖν .		2	2 Cor. iii. 16		x. 11
περιέρχεσθαι .		2		1 Tim. v. 13	xi. 37
σκληρύνειν .		xix. 9	Rom. ix. 18		4
τάξις . .	i. 8		2		6
τυγχάνειν .	xx. 35	5	3	2 Tim. ii. 10	2
*ὑποστέλλειν .		2	Gal. ii. 12		x. 38
χρίειν . .	iv. 18	2	2 Cor. i. 21		i. 9

(3) *Expressions peculiar to S. Luke's Writings and to the Epistle to the Hebrews.*

ἀναδέχεσθαι $\frac{1}{1}$, ἀναθεωρεῖν $\frac{1}{1}$, ἀναστάσεως τυγχάνειν $\frac{1}{1}$, *ἀνορθοῦν $\frac{2}{1}$, ἀνώτερον $\frac{1}{1}$, *ἀπαλλάσσειν $\frac{2}{1}$, ἀπογράφεσθαι $\frac{3}{1}$, ἀρχηγός $\frac{2}{2}$, ἀσάλευτος $\frac{1}{1}$, ἀστεῖος $\frac{1}{1}$, ἄστρον $\frac{3}{1}$, *βοήθεια $\frac{1}{1}$, διατίθεσθαι $\frac{3}{4}$, μετ' εἰρήνης $\frac{1}{1}$, εἰσιέναι $\frac{3}{1}$, ἐκλείπειν $\frac{3}{1}$, *ἐνοχλεῖν $\frac{1}{1}$, ἔντρομος $\frac{2}{1}$, ἐπιστέλλειν $\frac{2}{1}$, ἐσώτερος $\frac{1}{1}$, *εὔθετος $\frac{2}{1}$, ἱερατεία $\frac{1}{1}$, ἱλάσκεσθαι $\frac{1}{1}$, καταπαύειν $\frac{1}{3}$, καταφεύγειν $\frac{1}{1}$, κεφάλαιον $\frac{1}{1}$, λύτρωσις $\frac{2}{1}$, μέτοχοι $\frac{1}{5}$, ὀρθός $\frac{1}{1}$, παλαιοῦν $\frac{1}{3}$, εἰς τὸ παντελές $\frac{1}{1}$, *παραλύεσθαι $\frac{4}{1}$, παροικεῖν $\frac{1}{1}$, *παροξυσμός $\frac{1}{1}$, πατριάρχης $\frac{3}{1}$, περικεῖσθαί τι $\frac{1}{1}$, πόρρωθεν $\frac{1}{1}$, συναντᾶν $\frac{4}{2}$, σχεδόν $\frac{2}{1}$, τελείωσις $\frac{1}{1}$, ὕπαρξις $\frac{1}{1}$. Excepting ἀναθεωρεῖν, ἀναστάσεως τυγχάνειν, ἀνώτερον, ἐσώτερος, and εἰς τὸ παντελές, all the above are in LXX.

(4) *Expressions not found in the other Gospels and more frequent in S. Luke's Writings than in all the rest of N.T.*

ἀγαλλίασις $\frac{3}{2}$, αἰνεῖν $\frac{6}{2}$, *ἀναπέμπειν $\frac{4}{1}$, ἀνθ' ὧν $\frac{4}{1}$, ἀπολογεῖσθαι $\frac{8}{2}$, ἀσφάλεια $\frac{2}{1}$, *ἀτενίζειν $\frac{12}{2}$, *ἄτοπος $\frac{3}{1}$, ἀφιστάναι $\frac{10}{4}$, βουλή $\frac{9}{3}$, βρέφος $\frac{6}{2}$, διαμαρτύρεσθαι $\frac{10}{5}$, διαπορεύεσθαι $\frac{4}{1}$, ἐγκαλεῖν $\frac{6}{1}$, ἔμφοβος $\frac{5}{1}$, ἐξαποστέλλειν $\frac{10}{2}$, ἐπέρχεσθαι $\frac{7}{2}$, *ἐργασία $\frac{5}{1}$, ἐσθής $\frac{4}{3}$, εὐαγγελίζεσθαι $\frac{23}{21}$, ἐφιστάναι $\frac{18}{3}$, *ἡσυχάζειν $\frac{4}{1}$, κατάγειν $\frac{8}{1}$, καταντᾶν $\frac{9}{4}$, *κατέρχεσθαι c. $\frac{14}{1}$, ὁ λόγος τοῦ κυρίου $\frac{6}{1}$, μεθιστάναι $\frac{3}{2}$, μερίς $\frac{3}{2}$, μήν $\frac{10}{8}$, ἀπὸ τοῦ νῦν $\frac{6}{1}$, ὀπτασία $\frac{3}{1}$, *ὁρίζειν $\frac{6}{2}$, παύεσθαι $\frac{9}{6}$, τὰ περί $\frac{14}{8}$, πρεσβυτέριον $\frac{2}{1}$, προέρχεσθαι c. $\frac{5}{1}$, *προσάγειν c. $\frac{3}{1}$, πυκνός $\frac{2}{1}$, σιγᾶν $\frac{8}{4}$, σπεύδειν $\frac{5}{1}$, *στεῖρα $\frac{3}{1}$, συναντᾶν $\frac{4}{2}$, ὑπάρχειν (excluding τὰ ὑπάρχοντα) $\frac{32}{15}$, *ὑποδέχεσθαι $\frac{3}{1}$, *ὑπολαμβάνειν $\frac{4}{1}$, ὑποστρέφειν $\frac{33}{3}$: and several others which occur twice in Luke and once elsewhere. All of these occur in LXX, except ἀναπέμπειν.

(5) *Expressions found in one or more of the other Gospels, but more frequent in S. Luke's Writings than in all the rest of N.T.*

ἄγειν c. $\frac{41}{27}$, *ἀκριβῶς, -έστερον $\frac{6}{3}$, ἐπ' ἀληθείας $\frac{5}{2}$, ἀμφότεροι $\frac{8}{6}$, ἀνάγειν $\frac{21}{3}$, *ἀναιρεῖν $\frac{21}{3}$, ἀνιστάναι c. $\frac{60}{22}$, ἀντιλέγειν $\frac{5}{4}$, ἀπαγγέλλειν c. $\frac{26}{18}$, ἀποτάσσειν $\frac{4}{2}$, αὔριον $\frac{8}{6}$, καὶ αὐτός $\frac{32}{26}$, ἄφεσις ἁμαρτιῶν $\frac{8}{3}$, βοᾶν c. $\frac{8}{5}$, γίνεται φωνή c. $\frac{8}{6}$, δεῖσθαι $\frac{15}{7}$, διαμερίζειν $\frac{8}{3}$, διανοίγειν $\frac{7}{1}$, διαστρέφειν $\frac{5}{2}$, διασώζειν $\frac{6}{2}$, διατάσσειν $\frac{9}{7}$, διέρχεσθαι c. $\frac{32}{12}$, διηγεῖσθαι $\frac{5}{3}$, δοῦναι $\frac{13}{8}$, ἐᾶν $\frac{9}{2}$, ἐγγίζειν $\frac{24}{17}$, ἔθος $\frac{10}{2}$, εἰ δὲ μήγε $\frac{5}{3}$, εἷς ἕκαστος $\frac{8}{7}$, εἰσάγειν $\frac{9}{2}$, εἰσφέρειν $\frac{5}{3}$, ἑκατοντάρχης $\frac{17}{4}$, ἔκστασις $\frac{5}{2}$, ἐλεημοσύνη $\frac{10}{3}$, ἐμπιμπλάναι, ἐμπλήθειν $\frac{3}{2}$, ἐνθάδε $\frac{6}{2}$, ἐξάγειν $\frac{9}{3}$, ἐξαίφνης $\frac{4}{1}$, ἐξαυτῆς $\frac{4}{2}$, ἐξηγεῖσθαι $\frac{5}{1}$, ἐξιστάναι $\frac{11}{6}$, ἐπιλαμβάνεσθαι $\frac{12}{7}$, ἐπιπίπτειν c. $\frac{8}{3}$, ἐπισκέπτεσθαι $\frac{7}{4}$, ἔτος $\frac{26}{23}$, ἐν ταῖς ἡμέραις $\frac{23}{12}$, καθ' ἡμέραν $\frac{12}{6}$, θαυμάζειν ἐπί $\frac{5}{1}$, *ἰᾶσθαι $\frac{15}{11}$, ἰδοὺ γάρ $\frac{6}{1}$, ἱκανός c. $\frac{27}{12}$, ἱματισμός $\frac{3}{2}$, καθαιρεῖν $\frac{6}{3}$, κατάλυμα $\frac{2}{1}$, κατανοεῖν $\frac{8}{6}$, καταφιλεῖν $\frac{4}{2}$, κολλᾶσθαι $\frac{7}{5}$, κονιορτός $\frac{4}{1}$, κρεμᾶν $\frac{4}{3}$, κτᾶσθαι $\frac{5}{2}$, κωλύειν $\frac{12}{11}$, πᾶς ὁ λαός $\frac{14}{2}$, μεγαλύνειν $\frac{5}{3}$, *μεσονύκτιον $\frac{3}{1}$, μνῆμα $\frac{5}{4}$, νομίζειν $\frac{9}{6}$, νομικός $\frac{6}{3}$, ἡ οἰκουμένη $\frac{8}{7}$, ὀνόματι $\frac{28}{2}$, ὀρθῶς $\frac{3}{1}$, πανταχοῦ $\frac{5}{3}$, εἰπεῖν or λέγειν παραβολήν $\frac{14}{1}$, παραγίνεσθαι c. $\frac{29}{9}$, *παρατηρεῖν $\frac{4}{2}$, παραχρῆμα $\frac{16}{2}$, περίχωρος $\frac{6}{3}$, πήρα $\frac{4}{2}$, πληθεῖν $\frac{22}{2}$, *πλῆθος $\frac{25}{7}$, πλήν $\frac{19}{13}$, *πλήρης $\frac{10}{6}$, προσδοκᾶν $\frac{11}{5}$, προστιθέναι $\frac{13}{5}$, προσφωνεῖν $\frac{6}{1}$, ῥύμη $\frac{3}{1}$, σαλεύειν $\frac{8}{7}$, στάσις $\frac{7}{2}$, διὰ στόματος $\frac{6}{1}$, στρέφεσθαι $\frac{9}{7}$, συγκαλεῖν $\frac{7}{1}$, συλλαλεῖν $\frac{4}{2}$, *συλλαμβάνειν $\frac{11}{5}$, συμπορεύεσθαι $\frac{3}{1}$, σύν c. $\frac{75}{53}$, συνέρχεσθαι $\frac{19}{13}$, *συνέχειν $\frac{9}{3}$, συντιθέναι $\frac{2}{1}$, τάσσειν c. $\frac{6}{4}$, τετράρχης $\frac{3}{1}$, τίς ἐξ ὑμῶν $\frac{5}{1}$, ὃν τρόπον $\frac{5}{4}$, ὑβρίζειν $\frac{3}{2}$, τὰ ὑπάρχοντα $\frac{9}{5}$, ὑποδεικνύναι $\frac{5}{1}$, ὕψιστος $\frac{9}{4}$, χαλᾶν $\frac{5}{2}$, ὡσεί c. $\frac{18}{10}$. Excepting ἀκριβέστερον, ἄφεσις ἁμαρτιῶν, ἐξαυτῆς, ὀνόματι, τετράρχης, and τίς ἐξ ὑμῶν, all the above are found in LXX.

To these may be added a few which are specially frequent in Luke's writings, although not in excess of the rest of N.T. taken together: ἄρχεσθαι $\frac{41}{43}$, ἄχρι c. $\frac{20}{29}$, δέχεσθαι $\frac{25}{28}$, ἐπιτάσσειν $\frac{5}{5}$, ὁ λόγος τοῦ Θεοῦ $\frac{16}{16}$, λύχνος $\frac{6}{8}$, παραγγέλλειν $\frac{14}{16}$, προσπίπτειν $\frac{4}{4}$, προσδέχεσθαι $\frac{5}{7}$, σχίζειν $\frac{5}{6}$, τρέφειν $\frac{4}{5}$, τροφή $\frac{8}{8}$, χάρις twenty-five times in Lk. and Acts, not in Mt. or Mk., and only thrice in Jn.

Phrases which indicate the *expression of emotion* are unusually common, and belong to the picturesqueness of Luke's style; *e.g.* φόβος μέγας $\frac{4}{1}$, χαρὰ μεγάλη or πολλή $\frac{4}{1}$, φωνὴ μεγάλη $\frac{13}{24}$.

Equally remarkable is his fondness for ἀνήρ, where others have ἄνθρωπος or εἷς or nothing. Thus, vi. 8 τῷ ἀνδρί, Mt. and Mk. τῷ ἀνθρώπῳ; viii. 27 ἀνήρ τις, Mk. ἄνθρωπος; ix. 38 ἀνήρ, Mt. ἄνθρωπος, Mk. εἷς; xxiii. 50 ἀνήρ, Mt. ἄνθρωπος, Mk. nothing. Comp. v. 8, 12, 18, viii. 38, ix. 30, xxii. 63: and the word is very much more frequent in Lk. than in all the other Gospels together.

The expression παῖς αὐτοῦ or σου in the sense of "God's servant" is peculiar to Lk. in N.T. (i. 54, 69; Acts iii. 13, 26, iv. 25, 27, 30), with the exception of Mt. xii. 18, which is a quotation from Is. xlii. 1.

(6) *Expressions frequent in S. Luke's Writings and probably due to Hebrew Influence.*

The frequent use of ἐγένετο is discussed at the end of ch. i. Add to this Luke's fondness for ἐνώπιον, which does not occur in Mt. or Mk. and only once in Jn. (xx. 30). It is found more than thirty times in Lk. and Acts, especially in the phrase ἐνώπιον τοῦ Θεοῦ (i. 19, 75, xii. 6, xvi. 15) or κυρίου (i. 15). With this compare πρὸ προσώπου τινός (vii. 27, ix. 52, x. 1) and κατὰ πρόσωπόν τινος (ii. 31). The frequent use of ἰδού (i. 38, ii. 34, 48, vii. 25, 27, 34, etc.) and καὶ ἰδού (i. 20, 31, 36, ii. 25, v. 12, vii. 12, 37, etc.); of ῥῆμα for the *matter* of what is spoken (i. 65, ii. 15, 19, 51); of οἶκος in the sense of "family" (i. 27, 33, 69, ii. 4, x. 5, xix. 9); of εἷς in the sense of τις (v. 12, 17, viii. 22, xiii. 10, xx. 1) or of πρῶτος (xxiv. 1); of ὕψιστος for "the Most High" (i. 32, 35, 76, vi. 35), illustrates the same kind of influence. So also do such expressions as ποιεῖν ἔλεος μετά (i. 72, x. 37) and μεγαλύνειν ἔλεος μετά (i. 58); ποιεῖν κράτος (i. 51); ἐκ κοιλίας μητρός (i. 15); combinations with ἐν τῇ καρδίᾳ or ἐν ταῖς κ., such as διαλογίζεσθαι (iii. 15, v. 22; comp. xxiv. 38), διατηρεῖν (ii. 51), θέσθαι (i. 66, xxi. 14), συνβάλλειν (ii. 19); ἐν ταῖς ἡμέραις (i. 5, 39, ii. 1, iv. 2, 25, v. 35, etc.); τῇ ἡμέρᾳ τοῦ σαββάτου (xiii. 14, 16, xiv. 5); with perhaps διὰ στόματος (i. 70), where both the expression and the omission of the article seem to be Hebraistic: in LXX we commonly have, however, ἐν τῷ στόματι or ἐκ τοῦ στόματος. Nearly all these expressions are found in the Acts also, in some cases very often. The frequent use of periphrastic tenses has been pointed out above (p. li) as being due in many cases to Hebraistic influence. The same may be said of the attributive or characterizing genitive, which is specially common in Luke (iv. 22, xvi. 8, 9, xviii. 6; comp. x. 6, xx. 34, 36); and of the frequent use of καὶ αὐτός (ii. 28, v. 1, 17, viii. 1, 22, xvii. 11, xix. 2), καὶ αὐτή (ii. 37), and καὶ αὐτοί (xiv. 1, xxiv. 14) after ἐγένετο, καὶ ἰδού, and the like. Phrases like δοξάζειν τὸν Θεόν (v. 25, 26, vii. 16, xiii. 13, xvii. 15, xviii. 43, xxiii. 47), ὁ λόγος τοῦ Θεοῦ (v. 1, viii. 11, 21, xi. 28), and ἐπαίρειν τὴν φωνήν (xi. 27) may be placed under the same head; and they all of them occur several times in the Acts.

In common with other N.T. writers S. Luke uses several Hebrew words, which may be mentioned here, although they are not specially common in his writings: ἀμήν (iv. 24, xii. 37, xviii. 17, etc.), βεεζεβούλ (xi. 15, 18, 19), γέεννα (xii. 5), πάσχα (ii. 41, xxii. 1, 7, 8, 11, 13, 15), σάββατον (iv. 16, 31, vi. 1, 2, 5, 6, 7, 9, etc.), σατανᾶς (x. 18, xi. 18, xiii. 16, etc.). Three others occur once in his Gospel and nowhere else in N.T.; βάτος (xvi. 6), κόρος (xvi. 7), σίκερα (i. 15). Other words, although Greek in origin, are used by him, as by other N.T. writers, in a sense which is due to Hebrew influence; ἄγγελος (i. 11, 13, 18, etc.), γραμματεύς (v. 21, 30, vi. 7, ix. 22, etc.), διάβολος (iv. 2–13, viii. 12), ἔθνη (ii. 32, xviii. 32, xxi. 24 *bis*, etc.), εἰρήνη (i. 79, ii. 29, vii. 50, etc.), κύριος (i. 6, 9, 11, 15, etc.); and ἐφημερία (i. 5, 8) is a Greek word specially formed to express a Hebrew idea.

(7) *Miscellaneous Expressions and Constructions which are specially frequent in S. Luke's Writings.*

In his use of the *article* he has several favourite constructions. He is very fond of ἐν τῷ followed by a present infinitive to express time *during* which (i. 8, 21, ii. 6, 43, v. 1, 12, viii. 5, 42, etc.) or by an aorist infinitive to express time *after* which (ii. 27, iii. 21, ix. 34, 36, xi. 37, etc.); also of τοῦ with an infinitive to express purpose or result (i. 73, ii. 27, v. 7, xii. 42, etc.). He frequently employs τό to introduce a whole clause, especially interrogations, much as we use inverted commas (i. 62, ix. 46, xix. 48, xxii. 2, 4, 23, 24, 37).

In the case of certain *verbs* he has a preference for special constructions. After verbs of speaking, answering, and the like he very often has πρός and the accusative instead of the simple dative. Thus, we have εἰπεῖν πρός (i. 13, 18, 28, 34, 61, ii. 34, 48, 49, etc.), λαλεῖν πρός (i. 19, 55, ii. 15, 18, 20, xii. 3, etc.), λέγειν πρός (iv. 21, v. 36, vii. 24, viii. 25, ix. 23, etc.), ἀποκρίνεσθαι πρός (iv. 4, vi. 3, xiv. 5?), γογγύζειν πρός (v. 30), συνζητεῖν πρός (xxii. 23), συνλαλεῖν πρός (iv. 36). It often happens that where Mt. or Mk. has the dative, Luke has the accusative with πρός (Mt. ix. 11; Mk. ii. 16; Lk. v. 30). Whereas others prefer ἐξέρχεσθαι ἐκ, he has ἐξέρχεσθαι ἀπό (iv. 35, 41, v. 8, viii. 2, 29, 33, 35, 38, ix. 5, etc.), and for θαυμάζειν τι he prefers θαυμάζειν ἐπί τινι (ii. 33, iv. 22, ix. 43, xx. 26). For θεραπεύειν νόσους he sometimes has θεραπεύειν ἀπὸ νόσων (v. 15, vii. 21, viii. 2). He is fond of the infinitive after διὰ τό (ii. 4, viii. 6, ix. 7, xi. 8, xviii. 5, etc.), μετὰ τό (xii. 5, xxii. 20), and πρὸ τοῦ (ii. 21, xxii. 15). The quite classical ἔχειν τι is common (vii. 42, ix. 58, xi. 6, xii. 17, 50, xiv. 14). His use of the optative has been mentioned above (p. li).

Participles with the article often take the place of substantives (ii. 27, iv. 16, viii. 34, xxii. 22, xxiv. 14). They are frequently added to verbs in a picturesque and classical manner: ἀναστάντες ἐξέβαλον (iv. 29), καθίσας ἐδίδασκεν (v. 3), σταθεὶς ἐκέλευσεν (xviii. 40), στραφεὶς ἐπετίμησεν (ix. 55), etc. They are sometimes strung together without a conjunction (ii. 36, iv. 35, v. 11, 19, 25, etc.).

S. Luke is very fond of πᾶς, and especially of the stronger form ἅπας. It is not always easy to determine which is the right reading; but ἅπας is certainly very common (iii. 21, iv. 6, v. 26, viii. 37, ix. 15, xix. 37, 48, xxiii. 1; also in Acts). Elsewhere in N.T. ἅπας is rare. Not unfrequently Luke has πᾶς or ἅπας where the others have nothing (iii. 15, 16, 21, iv. 37, v. 11, 28, vi. 10, 17, 19, 30, vii. 35, etc.). πᾶς ὁ λαός and ἅπας ὁ λ. are very freq.

In the use of certain *prepositions* he has some characteristic expressions: εἰς τὰ ὦτα (i. 44, ix. 44) and εἰς τὰς ἀκοάς (vii. 1), ἐν τοῖς ὠσίν (iv. 21) and ἐν μέσῳ (ii. 46, viii. 7, x. 3, xxi. 21, xxii. 27, 55,

xxiv. 36); κατὰ τὸ ἔθος (i. 9, ii. 42, xxii. 39), τὸ εἰθισμένον (ii. 27), τὸ εἰωθός (iv. 16), τὸ εἰρημένον (ii. 24), and τὸ ὡρισμένον (xxii. 22); παρὰ τοὺς πόδας (vii. 38, viii. 35, 41, xvii. 16), whereas Mark has πρὸς τ. πόδας (v. 22, vii. 25). Luke is very fond of σύν, which is rather rare in the other Gospels but is *very* frequent in both of Luke's writings. Sometimes he has σύν where the others have μετά (viii. 38, 51, xxii. 14, 56) or καί (xx. 1) or nothing (v. 19).

The *pronouns* αὐτός (see below) and οὗτος are specially common. The latter is added to a numeral, τρίτην ταύτην ἡμέραν (xxiv. 21), to make it more definite. τίς ἐξ ὑμῶν; is almost peculiar to him (xi. 5, xii. 25, xiv. 28, xv. 4, xvii. 7), and so also is τίς ἐστιν οὗτος ὅς; (v. 21, vii. 49). The indefinite τις with nouns is freq.

In using *conjunctions* he is very fond of combining δέ with καί, a combination which occurs twenty-six times in his Gospel (ii. 4, iii. 9, 12, iv. 41, v. 10, 36, vi. 6, ix. 61, etc.) and seven in the Acts. It is rare in the other Gospels. His Hebraistic use of καὶ αὐτός, αὐτή or αὐτοί, and of καὶ ἰδού, to introduce the apodosis to ἐγένετο and the like, has been pointed out above (p. lxi). But Luke is also fond of καὶ αὐτός at the beginning of sentences or independent clauses (i. 17, 22, iii. 23, iv. 15, v. 37, vi. 20, xv. 14, etc.), and of καὶ οὗτος, which is peculiar to him (i. 36, viii. 41?, xvi. 1, xx. 28). In quoting sayings he most frequently uses δέ, and εἶπεν δέ occurs forty-six times in the Gospel and fourteen in the Acts. It is not found in Mt. or Mk., and perhaps only once in Jn. (xii. 6 [viii. 11,] ix. 37?): they prefer ὁ δὲ εἶπεν, or καὶ λέγει, κ.τ.λ. Luke also has ἔλεγεν δέ nine times in the Gospel; it occurs twice in Mk., once in Jn., and never in Mt. Five times he begins a sentence with καὶ ὡς (temporal), which is not found elsewhere in N.T. (xv. 25, xix. 41, xxii. 66, xxiii. 26; Acts i. 10). The interrogative εἰ is found eighteen times in Gospel and Acts (vi. 7, 9, xiii. 23, xiv. 28, 31, xxii. 49, 67, etc.), εἰ δὲ μήγε five times, and εἰ ἄρα twice. All of these are comparatively rare elsewhere.

The idiomatic *attraction of the relative* is very common in both books (i. 4, ii. 20, iii. 19, v. 9, ix. 36, 43, xii. 46, xv. 16, xix. 37, etc.): it is rare in Mt. and Mk., and is not common in Jn.

After τοῦτο he has ὅτι in Gospel and Acts (x. 11, xii. 39, etc.); Mt. and Mk. never; Jn. only after διὰ τοῦτο.

He is fond of *combinations of cognate words*, *e.g.* φυλάσσοντες φυλακάς (ii. 8), ἐφοβήθησαν φόβον μέγαν (ii. 9), βαπτισθέντες τὸ βάπτισμα (vii. 29), ἡ ἀστραπὴ ἀστράπτουσα (xvii. 24). Some of these are Hebraistic, especially such as ἐπιθυμίᾳ ἐπεθύμησα (xxii. 15).

(8) *Expressions probably or possibly medical.*

It was perhaps not until 1841 that attention was called to the existence of *medical phraseology* in the writings of S. Luke. In the

Gentleman's Magazine for June 1841 a paper appeared on the subject, and the words ἀχλύς (Acts xiii. 11), κραιπάλη (Lk. xxi. 34), παραλελυμένος (v. 18, 24; Acts viii. 7, ix. 33), παροξυσμός (Acts xv. 39), συνεχομένη πυρετῷ μεγάλῳ (Lk. iv. 38), and ὑδρωπικός (xiv. 2) were given as instances of technical medical language. Since then Dr. Plumptre and others have touched on the subject; and in 1882 Dr. Hobart published his work on *The Medical Language of St. Luke*, Dublin and London. He has collected over 400 words from the Gospel and the Acts, which in the main are either peculiar to Luke or are used by him more often than by other N.T. writers, and which are also used (and often very frequently) by Greek medical writers. He gives abundant quotations from such writers, that we may see for ourselves; and the work was well worth doing. But there can be no doubt that the number of words in the Gospel and the Acts which are due to the Evangelist's professional training is something very much less than this. It may be doubted whether there are a hundred such words. But even if there are twenty-five, the fact is a considerable confirmation of the ancient and universal tradition that "Luke the beloved physician" is the author of both these books. Of Dr Hobart's long list of words more than eighty per cent. are found in LXX, mostly in books known to S. Luke, and sometimes occurring very frequently in them. In all such cases it is more reasonable to suppose that Luke's use of the word is due to his knowledge of LXX, rather than to his professional training. In the case of some words, both of these causes may have been at work. In the case of others, the medical training, and not familiarity with LXX, *may* be the cause. But in most cases the probability is the other way. Unless the expression is known to be distinctly a medical one, if it occurs in books of LXX which were known to Luke, it is probable that his acquaintance with the expression in LXX is the explanation of his use of it. If the expression is also found in profane authors, the chances that medical training had anything to do with Lk.'s use of it become very remote. It is unreasonable to class as in any sense medical such words as ἀθροίζειν, ἀκοή, ἀναιρεῖν, ἀναλαμβάνειν, ἀνορθοῦν, ἀπαιτεῖν, ἀπαλλάσσειν, ἀπολύειν, ἀπορεῖν, ἀσφάλεια, ἄφεσις, etc. etc. All of these are frequent in LXX, and some of them in profane authors also.

Nevertheless, when Dr. Hobart's list has been well sifted, there still remains a considerable number of words, the occurrence or frequency of which in S. Luke's writings may very possibly be due to the fact of his being a physician. The argument is a cumulative one. Any two or three instances of coincidence with medical writers may be explained as mere coincidences: but the large number of coincidences renders this explanation unsatisfactory for all of them; especially where the word is either rare in LXX, or not found there at all.

The instances given in the *Gentleman's Magazine* require a word of comment. Galen in treating of the diseases of the eye gives ἀχλύς as one of them, and repeatedly uses the word, which occurs nowhere else in N.T. or LXX. Perhaps κραιπάλη, which in bibl. Grk. is found Lk. xxi. 34 only, is a similar instance. It occurs more than once in Aristophanes, but is frequent in medical writers of the nausea which follows excess. In παραλελυμένος we have a stronger instance. Whereas the other Evangelists use παραλυτικός, Luke in harmony with medical usage has παραλελυμένος, as also has Aristotle, a physician's son (*Eth. Nic.* i. 13. 15). But this use may come from LXX, as in Heb. xii. 12. That παροξυσμός is a medical term is indisputable; but as early as Demosthenes it is found in the sense of exasperation, as also in LXX (Deut. xxix. 28; Jer. xxxix. [xxxii.] 37). The instance in Lk. iv. 38 is perhaps a double one: for συνεχομένη is possibly, and πυρετῷ μεγάλῳ probably, a medical expression. Moreover, here Mt. and Mk. have merely πυρέσσουσα, and in Acts xxviii. 8 we have the parallel πυρετοῖς καὶ δυσεντερίῳ συνεχόμενον. In ὑδρωπικός we have a word peculiar to Luke in bibl. Grk. and perhaps of purely medical origin.

By adopting doubtful or erroneous readings Hobart makes other instances double, *e.g.* ἐπέπεσεν for ἔπεσεν (Acts xiii. 11), βαρυνθῶσιν for βαρηθῶσιν (Lk. xxi. 34). Again, whether or no ἀναπτύσσειν has any medical flavour, Lk. iv. 17 must not be quoted in connexion with it, for there the true reading is ἀνοίξας.

To the examples given in the *Gentleman's Magazine* may perhaps be added such instances as δακτύλῳ προσψαύειν (xi. 46), where Mt. has δακτύλῳ κινῆσαι: διὰ τρήματος βελόνης (xviii. 25), where Mk. has διὰ τρυμαλιᾶς ῥαφίδος: ἔστη ἡ ῥύσις τοῦ αἵματος (viii. 44), where Mk. has ἐξηράνθη ἡ πηγὴ τ. αἵματος: ἐστερεώθησαν αἱ βάσεις αὐτοῦ καὶ τὰ σφυδρά (Acts iii. 7); and more doubtfully ὀθόνην τέσσαρσιν ἀρχαῖς καθιέμενον (Acts x. 11) and ἀνεκάθισεν (vii. 15; Acts ix. 40).

Luke alone relates what may be called the surgical miracle of the healing of Malchus' ear (xxii. 51). And perhaps the marked way in which he distinguishes demoniacal possession from disease (vi. 18, xiii. 32; Acts xix. 12) may be put down to medical training. His exactness in stating how long the person healed had been afflicted (xiii. 11; Acts ix. 33) and the age of the person healed (viii. 42; Acts iv. 22) is a feature of the same kind. For other possible instances see notes on iv. 35, v. 12, vii. 10.

The coincidences between the preface of the Gospel and the opening words of some medical treatises are remarkable (see small print, pp. 5, 6). And it is worth noting that Luke alone records Christ's quotation of the proverb, Ἰατρέ, θεράπευσον σεαυτόν

(iv. 23); and that almost the last words that he records in the Acts are S. Paul's quotation from Is. vi., which ends *καὶ ἰάσομαι αὐτούς* (xxviii. 26, 27).

The following table will illustrate some characteristics of S. Luke's diction as compared with that of the other Synoptists:—

S. MATTHEW.	S. MARK.	S. LUKE.
iii. 10. ἤδη δέ.		iii. 9. ἤδη δὲ καί.
iii. 16. πνεῦμα Θεοῦ.	i. 10. τὸ πνεῦμα.	iii. 22. τὸ πν. τὸ ἅγιον.
iii. 17. φωνὴ ἐκ τ. οὐρανῶν.	i. 11. φωνὴ ἐκ τ. οὐρανῶν.	iii. 22. φωνὴν ἐξ οὐρανοῦ γενέσθαι.
iv. 1. ἀνήχθη.	i. 12. τὸ πν. αὐτὸν ἐκβάλλει.	iv. i. ὑπέστρεψεν.
iv. 5, 8. παραλαμβάνει.		iv. 5, 9. ἤγαγεν, ἀναγαγών.
iv. 12. ἀνεχώρησεν.	i. 14. ἦλθεν.	iv. 14. ὑπέστρεψεν.
iv. 18. τὴν θάλασσαν.	i. 16. τὴν θάλασσαν.	v. 1. τὴν λίμνην.
iv. 20. ἀφέντες τὰ δίκτυα.	i. 18. ἀφέντες τὰ δίκτυα.	v. 11. ἀφέντες πάντα.
viii. 2. λεπρὸς προσελθὼν προσεκύνει αὐτῷ.	i. 40. λεπρὸς παρακαλῶν αὐτὸν καὶ γονυπετῶν.	v. 12. ἀνὴρ πλήρης λέπρας πεσὼν ἐπὶ πρόσωπον ἐδεήθη αὐτοῦ.
viii. 4. καὶ λέγει ὁ Ἰησοῦς.	i. 44. καὶ λέγει.	v. 14. καὶ αὐτὸς παρήγγειλεν.
ix. 2. προσέφερον αὐτῷ παραλυτικόν.	ii. 3. φέροντες πρὸς αὐτὸν παραλυτικόν.	v. 18. ἄνδρες φέροντες . . . παραλελυμένος.
ix. 7. ἐγερθείς.	ii. 12. ἠγέρθη καὶ εὐθύς.	v. 25. παραχρῆμα ἀναστὰς ἐνώπιον αὐτῶν.
ix. 8. ἐφοβήθησαν.	ii. 12. ἐξίστασθαι.	v. 26. ἐπλήσθησαν φόβου.
ix. 9. Μαθθαῖον λεγόμενον.	ii. 14. Λευείν.	v. 27. ὀνόματι Λευείν.
xii. 50. τὸ θέλημα τ. πατρός μου.	iii. 35. τὸ θέλημα τ. Θεοῦ.	viii. 21. τὸν λόγον τ. Θεοῦ.
xiii. 7. ἐπὶ τὰς ἀκάνθας.	iv. 7. εἰς τὰς ἀκάνθας.	viii. 7. ἐν μέσῳ τ. ἀκανθῶν.
xiii. 19. τ. λόγον τ. βασιλείας.	iv. 14. τὸν λόγον.	viii. 11. ὁ λόγος τ. Θεοῦ.
xiii. 20. λαμβάνων.	iv. 16. λαμβάνουσιν.	viii. 13. δέχονται.
xiii. 21. σκανδαλίζεται.	iv. 17. σκανδαλίζονται.	viii. 13. ἀφίστανται.
v. 15. καίουσιν λύχνον.		viii. 16. λύχνον ἅψας.
viii. 21. κύριε.	iv. 38. διδάσκαλε.	viii. 24. ἐπιστάτα.
	v. 7. ὁρκίζω σε.	viii. 28. δέομαί σου.
viii. 30. ἀγέλη χοίρων πολλῶν.	v. 11. ἀγέλη χοίρων μεγάλη.	viii. 32. ἀγέλη χοίρων ἱκανῶν.
ix. 18. ἰδοὺ ἄρχων [εἷς] προσελθὼν προσκύνει αὐτῷ.	v. 22. ἔρχεται εἷς τῶν ἀρχισυναγώγων καὶ πίπτει πρὸς τοὺς πόδας αὐτοῦ.	viii. 41. καὶ ἰδοὺ ἦλθεν ἀνὴρ καὶ οὗτος ἄρχων τῆς συναγωγῆς ὑπῆρχεν· καὶ πεσὼν παρὰ τοὺς πόδας Ἰησοῦ.
ix. 18. ἐτελεύτησεν.	v. 23. ἐσχάτως ἔχει.	viii. 42. καὶ αὐτὴ ἀπέθνησκεν.
	v. 29. εὐθὺς ἐξηράνθη ἡ πηγή.	viii. 44. παραχρῆμα ἔστη ἡ ῥύσις.
x. 14. ἐξερχόμενοι ἔξω.	vi. 11. ἐκπορευόμενοι ἐκεῖθεν.	ix. 5. ἐξερχόμενοι ἀπό.
xvi. 15. λέγει.	viii. 29. ἐπηρώτα.	ix. 20. εἶπεν δέ.

S. Matthew.	S. Mark.	S. Luke.
xvi. 20. ἐπετίμησεν.	viii. 30. ἐπετίμησεν.	ix. 21. ἐπιτιμήσας παρήγγειλεν.
xvi. 28. ἀμὴν λέγω ὑμῖν.	ix. 1. ἀμὴν λέγω ὑμῖν.	ix. 27. λέγω ὑμῖν ἀληθῶς.
xvii. 4. κύριε.	ix. 5. Ῥαββεί.	ix. 33. ἐπιστάτα.
xvii. 16. προσήνεγκα.	ix. 18. εἶπα.	ix. 40. ἐδεήθην.
xvii. 18. ἐθεραπεύθη ὁ παῖς.	ix. 27. ἀνέστη.	ix. 42. ἰάσατο τὸν παῖδα.
xix. 13. παιδία.	x. 13. παιδία.	xviii. 15. τὰ βρέφη.
xxii. 18. γνοὺς τὴν πονηρίαν.	xii. 15. εἰδὼς τὴν ὑπόκρισιν.	xx. 23. κατανοήσας τὴν πανουργίαν.
xxvi. 20. μετὰ τ. δώδεκα μαθητῶν.	xiv. 17. μετὰ τῶν δώδεκα.	xxii. 14. οἱ ἀπόστολοι σὺν αὐτῷ.
xxvi. 27. λαβών.	xiv. 23. λαβών.	xxii. 17. δεξάμενος.
xxvi. 29. οὐ μὴ ἀπ᾿ ἄρτι.	xiv. 25. οὐκέτι οὐ μή.	xxii. 18. οὐ μὴ ἀπὸ τοῦ νῦν.
xxvi. 41. γρηγορεῖτε καὶ προσεύχεσθε.	xiv. 38. γρηγορεῖτε καὶ προσεύχεσθε.	xxii. 46. ἀναστάντες προσεύχεσθε.
xxvi. 64. ἀπ ἄρτι.		xxii. 69. ἀπὸ τοῦ νῦν.
xxvii. 2. ἀπήγαγον καὶ παρέδωκαν Πειλάτῳ.	xv. 1. ἀπήνεγκαν καὶ παρέδωκαν Πειλάτῳ.	xxiii. 1. ἀναστὰν ἅπαν τὸ πλῆθος αὐτῶν ἤγαγον αὐτὸν ἐπὶ τ. Πειλᾶτον.
xxvii. 13. λέγει.	xv. 4. ἐπηρώτα.	xxiii. 9. ἐπηρώτα ἐν λόγοις ἱκανοῖς.
xxvii. 57. ἄνθρωπος πλούσιος, τοὔνομα Ἰωσήφ.	xv. 43. Ἰωσὴφ εὐσχήμων βουλευτής.	xxiii. 50. καὶ ἰδοὺ ἀνὴρ ὀνόματι Ἰ., βουλευτὴς ὑπάρχων.
xxviii. 8. ἀπελθοῦσαι . . . ἔδραμον ἀπαγγεῖλαι τοῖς μαθηταῖς αὐτοῦ.	xvi. 8. ἐξελθοῦσαι . . . οὐδενὶ οὐδὲν εἶπαν.	xxiv. 9. ὑποστρέψασαι . . . ἀπήγγειλαν ταῦτα πάντα τοῖς ἕνδεκα καὶ πᾶσιν τοῖς λοιποῖς.

These are only specimens taken from a large number of instances, and selected for their brevity and the ease with which they admit of comparison. The student who has mastered the main features of Luke's style will be able to find many more for himself.

§ 7. THE INTEGRITY OF THE THIRD GOSPEL.

This question may be regarded as naturally following the discussion of S. Luke's peculiarities and characteristics, for it is by a knowledge of these that we are able to solve it. The question has been keenly debated during the last forty years, and may now be said to be settled, mainly through the exertions of Volkmar, Hilgenfeld, and Sanday. Dr. Sanday's article in the *Fortnightly Review*, June 1875, in answer to *Supernatural Religion*, was pronounced by Bishop Lightfoot to be "able and (as it seems to me) unanswerable" (On *Sup. Rel.* p. 186). This article was incorporated in *The Gospels in the Second Century*, Macmillan, 1876, now unfortunately out of print, and it remains unanswered. It is now conceded on all sides[1] that Marcion's Gospel does not represent the original S. Luke, and that our Third Gospel has not been largely augmented and interpolated, especially by the addition of the first three chapters and the last seven verses; but that Marcion's Gospel is an abridgment of our S. Luke, which therefore was current before Marcion began to teach in Rome in or before A.D. 140. The statements of early Christian writers (not to be accepted as conclusive without examination) have been strongly confirmed, and it is right to speak of Marcion's Gospel as a "mutilated" or "amputated" edition of S. Luke.

Irenæus says of Marcion: *id quod est secundum Lucam evangelium circumcidens* (i. 27. 2, iii. 12. 7); and again: *Marcion et qui ab eo sunt, ad intercidendas conversi sunt Scripturas, quasdam quidem in totum non cognoscentes, secundum Lucam autem evangelium et epistolas Pauli decurtantes, hæc sola legitima esse dicunt, quæ ipsi minoraverunt* (iii. 12. 12). Similarly Tertullian: *Quis tam comesor mus Ponticus quam qui evangelia corrosit?* (*Adv. Marcion.* i. 1). *Marcion evangelio suo nullum adscribit auctorem. . . . ex iis commentatoribus quos habemus Lucam videtur Marcion elegisse quem cæderet* (*ibid.* iv. 2). Epiphanius also: ὁ μὲν γὰρ χαρακτὴρ τοῦ κατὰ Λουκᾶν σημαίνει τὸ εὐαγγέλιον· ὡς δὲ ἠκρωτηρίασται μήτε ἀρχὴν ἔχων, μήτε μέσα, μήτε τέλος, ἱματίου βεβρωμένου ὑπὸ πολλῶν σητῶν ἐπέχει τὸν τρόπον (*Hær.* i. 3. 11, Migne, xli. 709). Epiphanius speaks of additions, τὰ δὲ προστίθησιν: but these were very trifling, perhaps only some two or three dozen words.

The evidence of Tertullian and Epiphanius as to the contents of Marcion's Gospel is quite independent, and it can be checked to some extent by that of Irenæus. Their agreement is remarkable, and we can determine with something like certainty and exactness the parts of the Third Gospel which Marcion omitted; not at all because he doubted their authenticity, but because he disliked their contents. They contradicted his doctrine, or did not harmonize well with it, or in some other way displeased him. In this arbitrary manner he discarded i. ii. and iii. excepting iii. 1, with which his Gospel began. Omitting iii. 2–iv. 13, 17–20, 24, he went on continuously to xi. 28. His subsequent omissions were xi. 29–32, 49–51, xiii. 1–9, 29–35, xv. 11–32, xvii. 5–10, xviii. 31–34, xix. 29–48, xx. 9–18, 37, 38, xxi. 1–4, 18, 21, 22, xxii. 16–18, 28–30, 35–38, 49–51, xxiv. 47–53. Perhaps he also omitted vii. 29–35; and he transposed iv. 27 to xvii. 18.

It should be observed that not only does Marcion's Gospel

[1] An exception must be made of the author of *The Four Gospels as Historical Records*, Norgate, 1895, pp. 93–95. The work is retrograde, and rakes together criticisms and positions which have been rendered impotent and untenable. One is tempted to apply to it the author's own words (respecting a volume of very real merit and ability, which has rendered signal service to the cause of truth), that it "may be said, without much injustice, to beg every question with which it deals" (p. 491).

contain nearly all the sections which are peculiar to Luke, but it contains them in the same order. Where Luke inserts something into the common tradition, Marcion has the insertion; where Luke omits, Marcion omits also. This applies in particular to "the great intercalation" (ix. 51–xviii. 14) as well as to smaller insertions; and this minute agreement, step by step, between Marcion and Luke renders the hypothesis of their independence incredible. The only possible alternatives are that Marcion has expurgated our Third Gospel, or that our Third Gospel is an expansion of Marcion's; and it can be demonstrated that the second of these is untenable.

(1) In most cases we can see *why* Marcion omitted what his Gospel did not contain. He denied Christ's human birth; therefore the whole narrative of the Nativity and the genealogy must be struck out. The Baptism, Temptation, and Ascension involved anthropomorphic views which he would dislike. All allusions to the O.T. as savouring of the kingdom of the Demiurge must be struck out. And so on. In this way most of the omissions are quite intelligible. The announcement of the Passion (xviii. 31–34) and the triumphal entry into Jerusalem, etc. (xix. 29–48), were probably disliked as being fulfilments of O.T. prophecy. It is less easy to see Marcion's objection to the Prodigal Son (xv. 11–32) and the massacre of Galileans, etc. (xiii. 1–9); but our knowledge of his strange tenets is imperfect, and these passages probably conflicted with some of them. But such changes as "all the righteous" for "Abraham and Isaac and Jacob and all the prophets" (xiii. 28), or "the Lord's words" for "the law" (xvi. 17), or "those whom the god of that world shall account worthy" for "they that are accounted worthy to attain to that world" (xx. 35), are thoroughly intelligible. Others which his critics supposed to be wilful depravations of the text are mere differences of reading found in other authorities; *e.g.* the omission of αἰώνιον (x. 25) and of ἢ μεριστήν (xii. 14); and the insertion of καὶ καταλύοντα τὸν νόμον καὶ τοὺς προφήτας (xxiii. 2).

(2) But the chief evidence (in itself amounting to something like demonstration) that Marcion abridged our S. Luke, rather than the Evangelist expanded Marcion, is found in the peculiarities and characteristics of Luke's style and diction. These run through our Gospel from end to end, and on the average are as frequent in the portions which Marcion omitted as in the rest. In the first two chapters they are perhaps somewhat more frequent than elsewhere. It is quite incredible that the supposed interpolator made a minute analysis of the style and diction of Marcion's Gospel, practised himself in it, and then added those portions of our Gospel which Marcion did not include in his Gospel: and that he accomplished this feat without raising a suspicion. Such a feat in

that age would have been a literary miracle. Only those who have worked through the passages expunged by Marcion, carefully marking what is peculiar to Luke or characteristic of him, can estimate the full force of this argument. But the analysis of a few verses will be instructive.

The dotted lines indicate that the expression is found more often in Luke's writings than in the rest of N.T., and the fraction indicates the proportion: *e.g.* the $\frac{6}{3}$ with καθεῖλεν means that καθαιρεῖν occurs six times in Lk. and Acts, and three elsewhere in the rest of N.T. The plain lines indicate that the expression is peculiar to Luke in N.T., and the figure states the number of times in which it occurs in his writings: *e.g.* κατὰ τὸ ἔθος occurs thrice in Lk. and Acts, and nowhere else in N.T.

Καθεῖλεν $\frac{6}{3}$ δυνάστας ἀπὸ θρόνων, καὶ ὕψωσεν ταπεινούς, πεινῶντας ἐνέπλησεν $\frac{22}{2}$ ἀγαθῶν, καὶ πλουτοῦντας ἐξαπέστειλεν $\frac{10}{2}$ κενούς. ἀντελάβετο Ἰσραὴλ παιδὸς $\frac{7}{1}$ αὐτοῦ, μνησθῆναι ἐλέους (καθὼς ἐλάλησεν πρὸς τοὺς πατέρας ἡμῶν) τῷ Ἀβραὰμ καὶ τῷ σπέρματι αὐτοῦ εἰς τὸν αἰῶνα. Ἔμεινεν δὲ Μαριὰμ σὺν $\frac{75}{53}$ αὐτῇ ὡς μῆνας $\frac{10}{8}$ τρεῖς, καὶ ὑπέστρεψεν $\frac{33}{3}$ εἰς τὸν οἶκον αὐτῆς (i. 52–56).

Καὶ ἐπορεύοντο οἱ γονεῖς αὐτοῦ κατ᾽ ἔτος $\frac{26}{23}$ εἰς Ἰερουσαλὴμ τῇ ἑορτῇ τοῦ πάσχα. καὶ ὅτε ἐγένετο ἐτῶν $\frac{26}{23}$ δώδεκα, ἀναβαινόντων αὐτῶν κατὰ τὸ ἔθος 3 τῆς ἑορτῆς, καὶ τελειωσάντων τὰς ἡμέρας, ἐν τῷ ὑποστρέφειν $\frac{33}{3}$ αὐτοὺς ὑπέμεινεν Ἰησοῦς ὁ παῖς ἐν Ἰερουσαλήμ· καὶ οὐκ ἔγνωσαν οἱ γονεῖς αὐτοῦ· νομίσαντες $\frac{9}{6}$ δὲ αὐτὸν ἐν τῇ συνοδίᾳ εἶναι ἦλθον ἡμέρας ὁδόν, καὶ ἀνεζήτουν 3 αὐτὸν ἐν τοῖς συγγενέσι καὶ τοῖς 2 γνωστοῖς· $\frac{12}{3}$ καὶ μὴ εὑρόντες ὑπέστρεψαν $\frac{33}{3}$ εἰς Ἰερουσαλήμ, ἀναζητοῦντες 3 αὐτόν. καὶ ἐγένετο μεθ᾽ ἡμέρας τρεῖς, εὗρον αὐτὸν ἐν τῷ ἱερῷ, καθεζόμενον ἐν μέσῳ τῶν διδασκάλων, καὶ ἀκούοντα αὐτῶν, καὶ ἐπερωτῶντα αὐτούς· ἐξίσταντο $\frac{11}{6}$ δὲ πάντες οἱ ἀκούοντες αὐτοῦ ἐπὶ τῇ συνέσει καὶ ταῖς ἀποκρίσεσιν αὐτοῦ (ii. 41–47).

§ 8. THE TEXT.

The authorities quoted for the various readings are taken from different sources, of which Tischendorf's *Nov. Test. Græc.* vol. i. ed. 8, Lipsiæ, 1869, and Sanday's *App. ad Nov. Test. Steph.*, Oxonii, 1889, are the chief. The Patristic evidence has been in many cases verified. Gregory's *Prolegomena* to Tischendorf, Lipsiæ, 1884–94, and Miller's edition of Scrivener's *Introduction to the Criticism of N.T.*, Bell, 1894, must be consulted by those who desire more complete information respecting the authorities.

(1) Greek Manuscripts.

Primary uncials.

ℵ Cod. Sinaiticus, sæc. iv. Brought by Tischendorf from the Convent of St. Catherine on Mt. Sinai; now at St. Petersburg. Contains the whole Gospel complete.

Its correctors are

ℵ[a] contemporary, or nearly so, and representing a second MS. of high value;

ℵ[b] attributed by Tischendorf to sæc. vi.;

ℵ[c] attributed to the beginning of sæc. vii. Two hands of about this date are sometimes distinguished as ℵ[ca] and ℵ[cb].

A. Cod. Alexandrinus, sæc. v. Once in the Patriarchal Library at Alexandria; sent by Cyril Lucar as a present to Charles I. in 1628, and now in the British Museum. Complete.

B. Cod. Vaticanus, sæc. iv. In the Vatican Library certainly since 1533[1] (Batiffol, *La Vaticane de Paul iii, etc.*, p. 86). Complete.

The corrector B² is nearly of the same date and used a good copy, though not quite so good as the original. Some six centuries later the faded characters were retraced, and a few new readings introduced by B³.

C. Cod. Ephraemi Rescriptus, sæc. v. In the National Library at Paris. Contains the following portions of the Gospel: i. 2–ii. 5, ii. 42–iii. 21, iv. 25–vi. 4, vi. 37–vii. 16 or 17, viii. 28–xii. 3, xix. 42–xx. 27, xxi. 21–xxii. 19, xxiii. 25–xxiv. 7, xxiv. 46–53.

These four MSS. are parts of what were once complete Bibles, and are designated by the same letter throughout the LXX and N.T.

D. Cod. Bezae, sæc. vi. Given by Beza to the University Library at Cambridge 1581. Greek and Latin. Contains the whole Gospel.

L. Cod. Regius Parisiensis, sæc. viii. National Library at Paris. Contains the whole Gospel.

R. Cod. Nitriensis Rescriptus, sæc. viii. Brought from a convent in the Nitrian desert about 1847, and now in the British Museum. Contains i. 1–13, i. 69–ii. 4, 16–27, iv. 38–v. 5, v. 25–vi. 8, 18–36, 39, vi. 49–vii. 22, 44, 46, 47, viii. 5–15, viii. 25–ix. 1, 12–43, x. 3–16, xi. 5–27, xii. 4–15, 40–52, xiii. 26–xiv. 1, xiv. 12–xv. 1, xv. 13–xvi. 16, xvii. 21–xviii. 10, xviii. 22–xx. 20, xx. 33–47, xxi. 12–xxii. 15, 42–56, xxii. 71–xxiii. 11, 38–51. By a second hand xv. 19–21.

T Cod. Borgianus, sæc. v. In the Library of the Propaganda at Rome. Greek and Egyptian. Contains xxii. 20–xxiii. 20.

X. Cod. Monacensis, sæc. ix. In the University Library at Munich. Contains i. 1–37, ii. 19–iii. 38, iv. 21–x. 37, xi. 1–xviii. 43, xx. 46–xxiv. 53.

Δ. Cod. Sangallensis, sæc. ix. In the monastery of St. Gall in Switzerland. Greek and Latin. Contains the whole Gospel.

Ξ. Cod. Zacynthius Rescriptus, sæc. viii. In the Library of the Brit. and For. Bible Soc. in London. Contains i. 1–9, 19–23, 27, 28, 30–32, 36–66, i. 77–ii. 19, 21, 22, 33–39, iii. 5–8, 11–20, iv. 1, 2, 6–20, 32–43, v. 17–36, vi. 21–vii. 6, 11–37, 39–47, viii. 4–21, 25–35, 43–50, ix. 1–28, 32, 33, 35, ix. 41–x. 18, 21–40, xi. 1, 2, 3, 4, 24–30, 31, 32, 33.

If these uncials were placed in order of merit for the textual criticism of the Gospel, we should have as *facile princeps* B, with א as equally easily second. Then T, Ξ, L, C, R. The Western element which sometimes disturbs the text of B is almost entirely absent from the Gospels.

Secondary Uncials.

E. Cod. Basileensis, sæc. viii. In the Public Library at Basle. Contains the whole Gospel, except iii. 4–15 and xxiv. 47–53.

F. Cod. Boreeli, sæc. ix. In the Public Library at Utrecht. Contains considerable portions of the Gospel.

G. Cod. Harleianus, sæc. ix. In the British Museum. Contains considerable portions.

K. Cod. Cyprius, sæc. ix. In the National Library at Paris. Contains the whole Gospel.

M. Cod. Campianus, sæc. ix. In the National Library at Paris. Contains the whole Gospel.

S. Cod. Vaticanus, sæc. x. In the Vatican. The earliest *dated* MS. of the Greek Testament. Contains the whole Gospel.

U. Cod. Nanianus, sæc. x. In the Library of St. Mark's, Venice. Contains the whole Gospel.

Only six uncial MSS., א B K M S U, afford complete copies of all four Gospels.

(2) Versions.

The Versions quoted are the following :

- The Latin (Latt.).
  - The Vetus Latina (Lat. Vet.).
  - The Vulgate (Vulg.).
- The Egyptian (Aegyptt.).
  - The Bohairic (Boh.).
  - The Sahidic (Sah.).
- The Syriac (Syrr.).
  - The Curetonian (Cur.).
  - The Sinaitic (Sin.)
  - The Peshitto (Pesh.).

The Harclean (Harcl.).
The Palestinian (Hier.).
The Armenian (Arm.).
The Ethiopic (Aeth.).
The Gothic (Goth.).

We are not yet in a position to determine the relation of the recently discovered Sinaitic Syriac (Syr-Sin.) to the other Syriac Versions and to other representatives of primitive texts: and it would be rash for one who is ignorant of Syriac to attempt a solution of this problem. But the readings of Syr-Sin., as given in the translation by Mrs. Lewis, are frequently quoted in the notes, so that the reader may judge to what extent they support the text adopted in this commentary.

It should be noticed that four of the seven instances of *Conflate Readings*, cited by WH. (ii. pp. 99–104) as proof of the comparative lateness of the traditional text, are found in this Gospel (ix. 10, xi. 54, xii. 18, xxiv. 53). Mr. Miller, in his new edition of Scrivener's *Introduction to the Criticism of the N.T.* (Bell, 1894), denies the cogency of the proof; but the only case with which he attempts to deal, and that inadequately (ii. pp. 292, 293), is Lk. xxiv. 53. See the *Classical Review*, June 1896, p. 264.

§ 9. LITERARY HISTORY.

It is not easy to determine where the literary history of the Third Gospel begins. The existence of the oral tradition side by side with it during the first century of its existence, and the existence of many other documents (i. 1) previous to it, which may have resembled it, or portions of it, very closely, are facts which render certainty impossible as to quotations which bear considerable resemblance to our Gospel. They may come from this Gospel; but they may also have another source. Again, there are possibilities or probabilities which have to be taken into account. We do not know how soon Harmonies of two, or three, or four Gospels were constructed. The Third Gospel itself is a combination of documents; and there is nothing improbable in the supposition that before Tatian constructed his *Diatessaron* others had made combinations of Matthew and Luke, or of all three Synoptic Gospels (Sanday, *Bampton Lectures*, p. 302). Some early quotations of the Gospel narrative look as if they may have come either from material which the Evangelists used, or from a compound of their works, rather than from any one of them as they have come down to us. On the other hand the difficulty of exact quotation must be remembered. MSS. were not abundant, and even those who possessed them found a difficulty in "verifying their references," when rolls were used and not pages, and when neither verses nor even chapters were numbered or divided. In quoting from memory similar passages of different Gospels would easily become mixed; all the more so, if the writers who quote were in the habit of giving oral instruction in the Gospel narrative; for in giving such instruction they would be in the habit of constructing a compound text out of the words which they chanced to remember from any two or three Gospels. What they wanted to convey was the substance of "the Gospel," and not the exact wording of the Gospel according to Matthew, or Mark, or Luke.

There is nothing in the Epistle of Barnabas which warrants us in believing that the writer knew the Third Gospel: and the coincidence of κοινωνήσεις ἐν πᾶσιν τῷ πλησίον σου, καὶ οὐκ ἐρεῖς ἴδια εἶναι (xix. 8) with Acts iv. 32 is too slight to be relied upon. Comp. *Didaché* iv. 8. Indeed it is not impossible that this Epistle was written before our Gospel (A.D. 70–80). In the Epistle of Clement, which doubtless is later than the Gospel (A.D. 95, 96), we have the perplexing phenomena alluded to above.

Mt. v. 7, vii. 1, 2.	Clem. Rom. *Cor.* xiii. 2.	Lk. vi. 36–38.
μακάριοι οἱ ἐλεήμονες, ὅτι **αὐτοὶ ἐλεηθήσονται.**	οὕτως γὰρ **εἶπεν**· ἐλεᾶτε, ἵνα ἐλεηθῆτε· ἀφίετε, ἵνα ἀφεθῇ ὑμῖν· ὡς ποιεῖτε, οὕτω ποιηθήσεται ὑμῖν· ὡς δίδοτε, οὕτως δοθήσεται ὑμῖν· ὡς κρίνετε, οὕτως κριθήσεσθε· ὡς χρηστεύεσθε, οὕτως χρηστευθήσεται ὑμῖν· ᾧ μέτρῳ μετρεῖτε, ἐν αὐτῷ μετρηθήσεται ὑμῖν.	γίνεσθε **οἰκτίρμονες καθ**ὼς ὁ πατὴρ ὑμῶν **οἰκ**τίρμων ἐστίν· **καὶ μὴ** κρίνετε, **καὶ οὐ μὴ κριθῆτε**· **καὶ** μὴ καταδικάζετε, **καὶ οὐ** μὴ καταδικασθῆτε. ἀπολύετε, καὶ ἀπολυθήσεσθε· δίδοτε, καὶ δοθήσεται ὑμῖν . . . ᾧ γὰρ μέτρῳ μετρεῖτε **ἀντιμετρη**θήσεται [or **μετρηθήσεται**] ὑμῖν.
μὴ κρίνετε, ἵνα μὴ κριθῆτε· **ἐν** ᾧ γὰρ κρίματι **κρίνετε** κριθήσεσθε, καὶ **ἐν** ᾧ **μέτρῳ** μετρεῖτε **μετρηθήσεται ὑμῖν.**		

This quotation is found in the Epistle of Polycarp (ii. 3) in this form: μνημονεύοντες δὲ ὧν εἶπεν ὁ κύριος διδάσκων· μὴ κρίνετε, ἵνα μὴ κριθῆτε· ἀφίετε, καὶ ἀφεθήσται ὑμῖν· ἐλεᾶτε, ἵνα ἐλεηθῆτε· ᾧ μέτρῳ μετρεῖτε, ἀντιμετρηθήσεται ὑμῖν. And Clement of Alexandria (*Strom.* ii. 18, p. 476, ed. Potter) has it exactly as Clement of Rome, with the exception of ἀντιμετρηθήσεται for μετρηθήσεται: but he is perhaps quoting his namesake. If not, then the probability that both are quoting a source different from any of our Gospels becomes much greater (Resch, *Agrapha*, pp. 96, 97).

MT. xviii. 6, 7, xxvi. 24.	CLEM. ROM. *Cor.* xlvi. 8.	LK. xvii. 1, 2, xxii. 22.
ὃς δ' ἂν σκανδαλίσῃ ἕνα τῶν μικρῶν τούτων, τῶν πιστευόντων εἰς ἐμέ, συμφέρει αὐτῷ ἵνα κρεμασθῇ μύλος ὀνικὸς περὶ τ. τράχηλον αὐτοῦ καὶ καταποντισθῇ ἐν τῷ πελάγει τῆς θαλάσσης. οὐαὶ τῷ κόσμῳ. . . . οὐαὶ δὲ τῷ ἀνθρώπῳ ἐκείνῳ δι' οὗ ὁ υἱὸς τοῦ ἀνθρώπου παραδίδοται· καλὸν ἦν αὐτῷ εἰ οὐκ ἐγεννήθη ὁ ἄνθρωπος ἐκεῖνος.	εἶπεν γάρ· οὐαὶ τῷ ἀνθρώπῳ ἐκείνῳ· καλὸν ἦν αὐτῷ εἰ οὐκ ἐγεννήθη, ἢ ἕνα τῶν ἐκλεκτῶν μου σκανδαλίσαι· κρεῖττον ἦν αὐτῷ περιτεθῆναι μύλον καὶ καταποντισθῆναι εἰς τὴν θάλασσαν, ἢ ἕνα τῶν ἐκλεκτῶν μου διαστρέψαι.	ἀνένδεκτόν ἐστιν τοῦ τὰ σκάνδαλα μὴ ἐλθεῖν, πλὴν οὐαὶ δι' οὗ ἔρχεται· λυσιτελεῖ αὐτῷ εἰ λίθος μυλικὸς περίκειται περὶ τὸν τράχηλον αὐτοῦ καὶ ἔρριπται εἰς τὴν θάλασσαν, ἢ ἵνα σκανδαλίσῃ τῶν μικρῶν τούτων ἕνα. οὐαὶ τῷ ἀνθρώπῳ ἐκείνῳ δι' οὗ παραδίδοται.

Here again Clement of Alexandria (*Strom.* iii. 18, p. 561) quotes exactly as Clement of Rome, with the exception of μή for οὐκ after εἰ, and the omission of τήν before θαλάσσαν. In Clem. Rom. *Cor.* lix. 3 we have a composite quotation (Is. xiii. 11; Ps. xxxiii. 10; Job v. 11, etc.), which may possibly have been influenced by Lk. i. 52, 53, xiv. 11, xviii. 14; but nothing can be built on this possibility. We must be content to leave it doubtful whether Clement of Rome knew our Gospel according to Luke; and the same must be said of Polycarp (see above) and of Ignatius. In *Eph.* xiv. we have φανερὸν τὸ δένδρον ἀπὸ τοῦ καρποῦ αὐτοῦ, which recalls ἐκ γὰρ τοῦ καρποῦ τὸ δένδρον γινώσκεται (Mt. xii. 33) and ἕκαστον γὰρ δένδρον ἐκ τοῦ ἰδίου καρποῦ γινώσκεται (Lk. vi. 44). *Smyr.* iii. we have the very remarkable passage which perplexed Origen, Eusebius, and Jerome as to its source: ὅτε πρὸς τοὺς περὶ Πέτρον ἦλθεν, ἔφη αὐτοῖς· Λάβετε, ψηλαφήσατέ με, καὶ ἴδετε ὅτι οὐκ εἰμὶ δαιμόνιον ἀσώματον. This may be a condensation of Lk. xxiv. 36–39, or may come from oral tradition or a lost document. Of other possibilities, τὸ πῦρ τὸ ἄσβεστον (*Eph.* xvi.) recalls Mk. ix. 43 rather than Lk. iii. 17: καλοὺς μαθητὰς ἐὰν φιλῇς, χάρις σοι οὐκ ἔστιν (*Polyc.* ii.) is not very close to Lk. vi. 32: ἡδοναὶ τοῦ βίου (*Rom.* vii.) is found Lk. viii. 14, but is a common phrase: and other slight resemblances (*e.g.* *Magn.* x.) may as easily come from other Gospels or from tradition.

We are on surer ground when we come to the *Didaché* and the *Gospel of Peter*, the dates of which remain to be determined, but which may be placed between A.D. 75 and 125. In the former we find further evidence of a combination of passages from Matthew and Luke, of which we have seen traces in Clement of Rome, and which suggests the possibility of a primitive Harmony of these two documents.

Mt. xxv. 13.	Didaché xvi. 1.	Lk. xii. 35.
γρηγορεῖτε οὖν, ὅτι οὐκ οἴδατε τὴν ἡμέραν οὐδὲ τὴν ὥραν.	γρηγορεῖτε ὑπὲρ τῆς ζωῆς ὑμῶν· οἱ λύχνοι ὑμῶν μὴ σβεσθήσωσαν, καὶ αἱ ὀσφύες ὑμῶν μὴ ἐκλυέσθωσαν, ἀλλὰ γίνεσθε ἕτοιμοι· οὐ γὰρ οἴδατε τὴν ὥραν ἐν ᾗ ὁ κύριος ἡμῶν ἔρχεται.	ἔστωσαν ὑμῶν αἱ ὀσφύες περιεζωσμέναι καὶ οἱ λύχνοι καιόμενοι, καὶ ὑμεῖς ὅμοιοι ἀνθρώποις προσδεχομένοις τὸν κύριον ἑαυτῶν.

Here the acquaintance with our Gospel is highly probable, for of the Evangelists Luke alone has the plural of λύχνος and of ὀσφύς. In giving the substance of the Sermon on the Mount, the *Didaché* again seems to compound the two Gospels.

Mt. vii., v.	Didaché i. 2–5.	Lk. vi.
12 πάντα οὖν ὅσα ἐὰν θέλητε ἵνα ποιῶσιν ὑμῖν οἱ ἄνθρωποι, οὕτως καὶ ὑμεῖς ποιεῖτε αὐτοῖς. 44 ἀγαπᾶτε τοὺς ἐχθροὺς ὑμῶν καὶ προσεύχεσθε ὑπὲρ τῶν διωκόντων ὑμᾶς. 46 ἐὰν γὰρ ἀγαπήσητε τοὺς ἀγαπῶντας ὑμᾶς, τίνα μισθὸν ἔχετε; . . . 47 . . . οὐχὶ καὶ οἱ ἐθνικοὶ τὸ αὐτὸ ποιοῦσιν; 39 ὅστις σε ῥαπίζει εἰς τὴν δεξιὰν σιαγόνα, στρέψον αὐτῷ καὶ τὴν ἄλλην. 41 ὅστις σε ἀγγαρεύσει μίλιον ἕν, ὕπαγε μετ' αὐτοῦ δύο. 40 τῷ θέλοντί σοι κριθῆναι καὶ τὸν χιτῶνά σου λαβεῖν, ἀφὲς αὐτῷ καὶ τὸ ἱμάτιον. 42 τῷ αἰτοῦντί σε δός, καὶ τὸν θέλοντα ἀπὸ σοῦ δανίσασθαι μὴ ἀποστραφῇς.	πάντα δὲ ὅσα ἐὰν θελήσῃς μὴ γίνεσθαί σοι, καὶ σὺ ἄλλῳ μὴ ποίει . . . εὐλογεῖτε τοὺς καταρωμένους ὑμῖν καὶ προσεύχεσθε ὑπὲρ τῶν ἐχθρῶν ὑμῶν, νηστεύετε δὲ ὑπὲρ τῶν διωκόντων ὑμᾶς· ποία γὰρ χάρις, ἐὰν ἀγαπᾶτε τοὺς ἀγαπῶντας ὑμᾶς; οὐχὶ καὶ τὰ ἔθνη τὸ αὐτὸ ποιοῦσιν; ὑμεῖς δὲ ἀγαπᾶτε τοὺς μισοῦντας ὑμᾶς καὶ οὐχ ἕξετε ἐχθρόν . . . ἐάν τις σοι δῷ ῥάπισμα εἰς τὴν δεξιὰν σιαγόνα, στρέψ' αὐτῷ καὶ τὴν ἄλλην, καὶ ἔσῃ τέλειος· ἐὰν ἀγγαρεύσῃ σέ τις μίλιον ἕν, ὕπαγε μετ' αὐτοῦ δύο· ἐὰν ἄρῃ τις τὸ ἱμάτιόν σου, δὸς αὐτῷ καὶ τὸν χιτῶνα· ἐὰν λάβῃ τις ἀπὸ σοῦ τὸ σόν, μὴ ἀπαίτει· οὐδὲ γὰρ δύνασαι. παντὶ τῷ αἰτοῦντί σε δίδου, καὶ μὴ ἀπαίτει.	31 καθὼς θέλετε ἵνα ποιῶσιν ὑμῖν οἱ ἄνθρωποι, ποιεῖτε αὐτοῖς ὁμοίως. 28 εὐλογεῖτε τοὺς καταρωμένους ὑμᾶς, προσεύχεσθε περὶ τῶν ἐπηρεαζόντων ὑμᾶς. 27 ἀλλὰ ἀγαπᾶτε τοὺς ἐχθροὺς ὑμῶν. 32 καὶ εἰ ἀγαπᾶτε τοὺς ἀγαπῶντας ὑμᾶς, ποία ὑμῖν χάρις ἐστίν; καὶ γὰρ οἱ ἁμαρτωλοὶ τοὺς ἀγαπῶντας αὐτοὺς ἀγαπῶσιν. 35 πλὴν ἀγαπᾶτε τοὺς ἐχθροὺς ὑμῶν . . . καὶ ἔσται ὁ μισθὸς ὑμῶν πολύς. 29 τῷ τύπτοντί σε ἐπὶ τὴν σιαγόνα πάρεχε καὶ τὴν ἄλλην, καὶ ἀπὸ τοῦ αἴροντός σου τὸ ἱμάτιον καὶ τὸν χιτῶνα μὴ κωλύσῃς. 30 παντὶ αἰτοῦντί σε δίδου, καὶ ἀπὸ τοῦ αἴροντος τὰ σὰ μὴ ἀπαίτει.

Expressions which are peculiar to each form of the Sermon are here so abundant that we conclude that this doctrine of the Two Ways has been influenced by both forms. But the order in which the several precepts are put together is so different from both Gospels, that the editor can scarcely have had either Gospel before him. Very possibly the order and wording have been disturbed by oral instruction in Christian morality given to catechumens (Sanday, *Bamptons*, p. 302). But the evidence of acquaintance with the Third Gospel is strong; and it is somewhat strengthened by the fact that in the *Didaché* Christ is called the "Servant (παῖς) of God" (ix. 2, 3, x. 2, 3), a use of παῖς which in N.T. is almost confined to Luke (Acts iii. 13, 26, iv. 27, 30; comp. iv. 25; Lk. i. 54, 69). But this use is common in LXX, and may easily be derived from Isaiah or the Psalms rather than from the Acts. Nevertheless there is other evidence of the influence of the Acts on the *Didaché*, and scarcely any evidence of the influence of Isaiah or of the Psalms: indeed the references to the O.T. are remarkably few. And this not only makes it quite possible that the use of ὁ παῖς σου comes from the Acts, but also still further strengthens the conviction that the *Didaché* is indebted to the writings of S. Luke. Comp. συγκοινωνήσεις δὲ πάντα τῷ ἀδελφῷ σου καὶ οὐκ ἐρεῖς ἴδια εἶναι (*Did.* iv. 8) with οὐδὲ εἷς τι τῶν ὑπαρχόντων αὐτῷ ἔλεγεν ἴδιον εἶναι, ἀλλ' ἦν αὐτοῖς πάντα κοινά (Acts iv. 32). Bryennios and Wünsche see traces of Lk. ix. 1–6 and x. 4–21 in *Did.* xi.; but this chapter might easily have stood as it does if Luke had never written. Yet there is enough in what has been quoted above to establish the fact of the influence of Luke on the *Didaché*.

It is generally admitted that the fragment of the *Gospel of Peter* suffices to show that the writer of that apocryphal narrative was acquainted with all four of the Canonical Gospels. But it will be worth while to quote some of the expressions and statements which have a marked resemblance to Luke in particular.

Gospel of Peter.	Lk. xxiii., xxiv.
4. Πειλᾶτος πέμψας πρὸς Ἡρώδην.	7. Πειλᾶτος . . . ἀνέπεμψεν αὐτὸν πρὸς Ἡρῴδην.
5. καὶ σάββατον ἐπιφώσκει.	54. καὶ σάββατον ἐπέφωσκεν.
10. ἤνεγκον δύο κακούργους.	32. ἤγοντο δὲ καὶ ἕτεροι κακοῦργοι δύο.
13. εἷς δέ τις τῶν κακούργων ἐκείνων ὠνείδισεν αὐτούς, λέγων· ἡμεῖς διὰ τὰ κακὰ ἃ ἐποιήσαμεν οὕτω πεπόνθαμεν, οὗτος δὲ σωτὴρ γενόμενος τῶν ἀνθρώπων τί ἠδίκησεν ἡμᾶς;	39. εἷς δὲ τῶν κρεμασθέντων κακούργων ἐβλασφήμει αὐτόν. . . . 41. ἄξια γὰρ ὧν ἐπράξαμεν ἀπολαμβάνομεν· οὗτος δὲ οὐδὲν ἄτοπον ἔπραξεν.
15. ὁ ἥλιος ἔδυ.	45. τοῦ ἡλίου ἐκλείποντος.
28. ὁ λαὸς ἅπας γογγύζει καὶ κόπτεται τὰ στήθη.	48. πάντες οἱ συνπαραγενόμενοι ὄχλοι . . . τύπτοντες τὰ στήθη.
34. πρωΐας δὲ ἐπιφώσκοντος τοῦ σαββάτου.	54. καὶ σάββατον ἐπέφωσκεν.
36. δύο ἄνδρας κατελθόντας ἐκεῖθεν πολὺ φέγγος ἔχοντας.	4. ἄνδρες δύο ἐπέστησαν αὐταῖς ἐν ἐσθῆτι ἀστραπτούσῃ.
50. ὄρθρου δὲ τῆς κυριακῆς . . . ἐπὶ τῷ μνήματι.	1. τῇ δὲ μιᾷ τῶν σαββάτων ὄρθρου βαθέως ἐπὶ τὸ μνῆμα ἦλθαν φέρουσαι ἃ ἡτοίμασαν ἀρώματα.
54. ἃ φέρομεν εἰς μνημοσύνην αὐτοῦ.	

These resemblances, which are too close and too numerous to be accidental, are further emphasized when the parallel narratives are compared. S. Luke alone mentions the sending to Herod. He alone uses the expression σάββατον ἐπέφωσκεν (contrast Mt. xxviii. 1). He alone calls the two robbers κακοῦργοι. He alone tells us that *one* of the robbers reviled, and that one contrasted the justice of their fate with the innocence of Jesus. He alone mentions the sun in connexion with the darkness. He alone speaks of *all* the multitudes of spectators, and of their beating their breasts. He alone calls the two Angels at the tomb ἄνδρες (Mt. and Mk. mention only one), and calls the tomb μνῆμα; and he alone uses φέρειν of the women bringing the spices. There are other passages in which the *Gospel of Peter* resembles Luke with one or more of the other Gospels; but what has been quoted above is sufficient to show that the writer of the apocryphal gospel was influenced by S. Luke's narrative. It must be remembered that these ten coincidences are found within the compass of fifty-five verses, and that they are not exhaustive. The inscription on the cross, οὗτός ἐστιν ὁ βασιλεὺς τοῦ Ἰσραήλ (11), is closer to that given by S. Luke, ὁ β. τῶν Ἰουδαίων οὗτος (xxiii. 38), than to any of the other forms; and perhaps the words of the robber, σωτὴρ γενόμενος (see above, 13), are suggested by σῶσον σεαυτὸν καὶ ἡμᾶς (xxiii. 39). The use of μεσημβρία for "midday" (15) is found in N.T. nowhere but Acts xxii. 6. The cry of the Jews after Christ's death, ἴδετε ὅτι πόσον δίκαιός ἐστιν (28), looks like an adaptation of the centurion's confession, ὄντως ὁ ἄνθρωπος οὗτος δίκαιος ἦν (xxiii. 47); and perhaps ἐξηγήσαντο πάντα ἅπερ εἶδον (45) is an echo of ἐξηγοῦντο τὰ ἐν τῇ ὁδῷ (xxiv. 35). And, as already pointed out (§ 1), Pseudo-Peter always speaks of Jesus Christ as ὁ κύριος, a use which begins to be common in the Third Gospel.

The evidence of another interesting document of about the same date is worth quoting. The *Testaments of the XII. Patriarchs* is a Greek translation of a Hebrew original. It was gradually Christianized, and reached its present form *c.* A.D. 70–135. It shows marked traces of a knowledge of the Synoptic traditions and of S. Luke's Gospel in particular. Some of the coincidences given below are probably the result of independent citation of the O.T. But the citation may have been suggested to the later writer by acquaintance with it in the Gospel narrative.

TEST. XII. PATR.	S. LUKE.
οἶνον καὶ σίκερα οὐκ ἔπιον (Reuben i.).	οἶνον καὶ σίκερα οὐ μὴ πίῃ (i. 15; Num. vi. 3).
ἔγνων ὅτι δικαίως πάσχω (Sim. iv.).	καὶ ἡμεῖς μὲν δικαίως (xxiii. 41).
ἔσεσθε εὑρίσκοντες χάριν ἐνώπιον Θεοῦ καὶ ἀνθρώπων (Sim. v.).	Ἰησοῦς προέκοπτεν . . . χάριτι παρὰ Θεῷ καὶ ἀνθρώποις (ii. 52; 1 Sam. ii. 26).

ὁ Θεὸς σῶμα λαβὼν καὶ συνεσθίων ἀνθρώποις ἔσωσεν αὐτούς (Sim. vi.).	συνεσθίει αὐτοῖς (xv. 2) comp. συνεφάγομεν καὶ συνεπίομεν αὐτῷ (Acts x. 41).
ἀνεῴχθησαν οἱ οὐρανοὶ (Levi ii., xviii.).	ἀνεῳχθῆναι τὸν οὐρανὸν (iii. 21 ; Is. lxiv. 1).
περὶ τοῦ μέλλοντος λυτροῦσθαι τὸν Ισραήλ (*Ibid.*).	αὐτός ἐστιν ὁ μέλλων λυτροῦσθαι τὸν Ἰσραήλ (xxiv. 21).
ἕως ἐπισκέψηται Κύριος πάντα τὰ ἔθνη ἐν σπλάγχνοις υἱοῦ αὐτοῦ ἕως αἰῶνος (Levi iv.).	διὰ σπλάγχνα ἐλέους Θεοῦ ἡμῶν ἐν οἷς ἐπισκέψεται ἡμᾶς ἀνατολὴ ἐξ ὕψους (i. 78).
συνετήρουν τοὺς λόγους τούτους ἐν τῇ καρδίᾳ μου (Levi vi.).	συνετήρει τὰ ῥήματα ταῦτα . . . ἐν τῇ καρδίᾳ αὐτῆς (ii. 19 ; comp. ii. 51).
καίγε ἔκρυψα τοῦτο ἐν τῇ καρδίᾳ μου, καὶ οὐκ ἀνήγγειλα αὐτὸ παντὶ ἀνθρώπῳ (Levi viii.).	καὶ αὐτοὶ ἐσίγησαν καὶ οὐδενὶ ἀπήγγειλαν ἐν ἐκείναις ταῖς ἡμέραις οὐδὲν ὧν ἑώρακαν (ix. 36).
δύναμις Ὑψίστου (Levi xvi.).	δύναμις Ὑψίστου (i. 35).
ἐπέπεσεν ἐπ' αὐτοὺς τρόμος (Judah iii.).	φόβος ἐπέπεσεν ἐπ' αὐτόν (i. 12 ; comp. Acts xix. 17).
ποιεῖν πάντα τὰ δικαιώματα Κυρίου καὶ ὑπακούειν ἐντολὰς Θεοῦ (Judah xiii.).	πορευόμενοι ἐν πάσαις ταῖς ἐντολαῖς καὶ δικαιώμασιν τοῦ κυρίου (i. 6).
ἀνοιγήσονται ἐπ' αὐτὸν οἱ οὐρανοί, ἐκχέαι πνεῦμα, εὐλογίαν Πατρὸς ἁγίου (Judah xxiv.).	ἀνεῳχθῆναι τὸν οὐρανὸν καὶ καταβῆναι τὸ πνεῦμα τὸ ἅγιον (iii. 21, 22).
οἱ ἐν πτωχείᾳ διὰ κύριον πλουτισθήσονται, καὶ οἱ ἐν πενίᾳ χορτασθήσονται, καὶ οἱ ἐν ἀσθενείᾳ ἰσχύσουσι (Judah xxv.).	μακάριοι οἱ πτωχοί, ὅτι ὑμετέρα ἐστὶν ἡ βασιλεία τοῦ Θεοῦ. μακάριοι οἱ πεινῶντες νῦν, ὅτι χορτασθήσεσθε (vi. 20, 21 ; Mt. v. 3–6).
ἐπιστρέψει καρδίας ἀπειθεῖς πρὸς Κύριον (Dan v.).	ἐπιστρέψαι καρδίας πατέρων ἐπὶ τέκνα· καὶ ἀπειθεῖς ἐν φρονήσει δικαίων (i. 17 ; Mal. iv. 5).
καὶ ἐὰν ὁμολογήσας μετανοήσῃ ἄφες αὐτῷ (Gad vi.).	καὶ ἐὰν μετανοήσῃ, ἄφες αὐτῷ (xvii. 3).
καὶ αὐτὸς ἐλθὼν ὡς ἄνθρωπος, ἐσθίων καὶ πίνων μετὰ τῶν ἀνθρώπων (Asher vii.). See above, Sim. vi.	ἐλήλυθεν ὁ υἱὸς τοῦ ἀνθρώπου ἔσθων καὶ πίνων (vii. 34 ; Mt. xi. 19).

Besides these verbal coincidences there are many coincidences in thought, especially respecting the admission of the Gentiles to the Kingdom through the Messiah, who is the Saviour of all, Jew and Gentile alike. "The Lord shall raise up from Levi a Priest, and from Judah a King, God and man. He shall save all the nations and the race of Israel" (Simeon vii.). "A King shall rise from Judah and shall make a new priesthood . . . unto all the nations" (Levi viii.). Comp. Judah xxiv.; Zebulon ix.; Dan vi.; Naphtali iv., viii.; Asher vii.; Benjamin ix. Moreover, there are passages which are very similar in meaning, although not in wording, to passages in Luke: comp. the end of Joseph xvii. with Lk. xvii. 27, and the beginning of Joseph xviii. with Lk. vi. 28.

It is hardly necessary to trace the history of the Third Gospel in detail any further. It has been shown already (pp. xv–xvii) that Justin Martyr, Tatian, Celsus, the writer of the Clementine Homilies, Basilides, Valentinus, Marcion, and the Churches of Lyons and Vienne, knew the Third Gospel, and that Irenæus, the

Muratorian Canon, Tertullian, Clement of Alexandria, and others definitely assign it to S. Luke. In the second half of the second century this Gospel is recognized as authentic and authoritative; and it is impossible to show that it had not been thus recognized at a very much earlier date.

The order of the Gospels has not always been the same. But, just as in the interpretation of the four symbolical creatures, the calf has uniformly been taken as indicating S. Luke, so in the arrangement of the Gospels his has almost invariably been placed third. The order with which we are familiar is the common order in most MSS. and Versions: but in D 594, *a b c d e f ff_2 i q r* and the Gothic Version, and in the *Apostolic Constitutions*, what is called the Western order (Matthew, John, Luke, Mark) prevails. The obvious reason for it is to have the two Apostles together and before the other two Evangelists. In a few authorities other arrangements are found. X and the Latin *k* have John, Luke, Mark, Matthew, while 90 has John, Luke, Matthew, Mark, and 399 John, Luke, Matthew. The Curetonian Syriac has Matthew, Mark, John, Luke.

§ 10. COMMENTARIES.

A good and full list of commentaries on the Gospels is given by Dr. W. P. Dickson in the English translation of Meyer's *Commentary on S. Matthew*, i. pp. xxiii–xliii and of commentaries on S. Mark and S. Luke in that of Meyer's *Commentary on S. Mark and S. Luke*, i. pp. xiii–xvi. It will suffice to name a few of the chief works mentioned by him, especially those which have been in constant use during the writing of this commentary, and to add a few others which have appeared since Dr. Dickson published his lists (1877, 1880), or for other reasons were omitted by him.[1] Of necessity the selection here given in many cases corresponds with that in the volume on Romans by Dr. Sanday and Mr. Headlam; and the reader is referred to that (pp. xcix–cix) for excellent remarks on the characteristics of the different commentaries, which need not be repeated here.

1. Greek Writers

Origen (Orig.); † 253. *Homiliæ in Lucam* in *Origenis Opp.* ed. Delarue, iii. 932; Lommatzsch, v. 85; Migne, xiii. 1801, 1902. These thirty-nine short Homilies are an early work, and have been preserved in the Latin translation made by Jerome. A few fragments of the original Greek survive in the *Philocalia* (ed.

[1] See also *Introduction to the Synoptic Gospels* by Dr. P. J. Gloag, T. & T. Clark, 1895, and the literature quoted p. 209.

J. A. Robinson, Camb. 1893) and elsewhere. The genuineness of these Homilies has been disputed, but is not doubtful. A summary of the contents of each is given in Westcott's article ORIGENES, *D. Chr. Biog.* iv. 113. The first twenty are on Lk. i., ii., and the next thirteen on Lk. iii., iv., leaving the main portion of the Gospel almost untouched. Besides these there are fragments of notes in the original Greek, which have been preserved in Venice MS. (28, 394); Migne, xviii. 311–370. They extend over chapters i.–xx.

EUSEBIUS of Cæsarea (Eus.); † before 341. Εἰς τὸ κατὰ Λουκᾶν εὐαγγέλιον in Migne, xxiv. 529. Only fragments remain: on Lk. i. 5, 18, 19, 32, 35, 38, ii. 32, iv. 18, vi. 18, 20, vii. 29, 30, viii. 31, 43, ix. 1, 3, 4, 7, 26, 28, 34, x. 6, 8, xi. 21, xii. 11, 22, 34, 36, 37, 42, 45, xiii. 20, 35, xiv. 18, xvii. 3, 23, 25–31, 34, 37, xviii. 2, xix. 12, 13, 17, xx. 2, 3, xxi. 25, 26, 28–32, 36, xxii. 30, 57, xxiv. 4.

CYRIL of Alexandria (Cyr. Alex.); † 444. Ἐξήγησις εἰς τὸ κατὰ Λουκᾶν εὐαγγέλιον in Migne, lxxii. 475. Only portions of the original Greek are extant, but a Syriac version of the whole has been edited by Dr. R. Payne Smith, who has also translated this version into English (Oxford, 1859). The Syriac version shows that many Greek fragments previously regarded as part of the commentary are from other writings of Cyril, or even from other writings which are not his. The Greek fragments which coïncide with the Syriac prove that the latter is a faithful translation. The commentary is homiletic in form.

THEOPHYLACT (Theoph.), archbishop of Bulgaria (1071–1078); † after 1118. Migne, cxxiii.

EUTHYMIUS ZIGABENUS (Euthym.); † after 1118. Migne, cxxix. 853.

These two almost contemporaneous commentaries are among the best of their kind. They draw much from earlier writers, but do not follow slavishly, and are far superior to mediæval Latin commentaries. The terseness of Euthymius is not unlike that of Bengel.

2. LATIN WRITERS.

AMBROSE (Ambr.); † 397. *Expositio Evang. sec. Lucam*; Migne, xv. 1525. Ambrose follows Philo and Origen in seeking for spiritual or mystical meanings under the natural or historical sense, and these are sometimes very far-fetched: *in verbis ludit, in sententiis dormitat* (Jerome, *Prol. in Hom. Orig. in Luc.*).

EUCHERIUS; † 449 or 450. *Liber instructionum in Lucæ Evang.*; Migne, l. 799.

ARNOBIUS JUNIOR; † after 460. *Annotationes ad quædam Evangeliorum loca*; Migne, liii. 570, 578.

f

PATERIUS of Brescia; friend of Gregory the Great. He collected from the writings of Gregory an *Expositio Vet. et Nov. Test.*, of which Book III. is a catena of Passages on S. Luke; Migne, lxxix. 1057. In the eleventh century the monk ALULF made a similar collection; Migne, lxxix. 1199.

None of these works are very helpful as regards exegesis. Eucherius and Arnobius do not repay perusal. The extracts from Gregory are mainly from the *Moralia* or commentary on Job, full of allegorical interpretation.

BEDE, the Venerable; †735. *In Lucam Exp. Libri VI.*; Migne, xcii. 307; Giles, xi., xii.; ed. Colon. 1612, v. 217. The character of the work may be given in his own words: "I have made it my business, for the use of me and mine, briefly to compile out of works of the venerable Fathers, and to interpret according to their meaning (adding somewhat of my own) these following pieces"—and he gives a list of his writings (*H. E. sub fin.* See also the *Prol. in Marc.*). This commentary is far superior to those just mentioned, and is an oasis in a desert.

SEDULIUS SCOTUS; † *c.* 830. A mere compiler, often from Origen; Migne, ciii. 27. WALAFRID STRABUS of Reichenau; † 849. *Glossa ordinaria*, a compilation with some original matter; Migne, cxiv. 243, 893. It became very famous. We may pass over with bare mention CHRISTIANUS DRUTHMARUS; *c.* 850; Migne, cvi. 1503: BRUNO ASTENSIS; *c.* 1125; Migne, clxv. 33: and PETRUS COMESTOR; *c.* 1180; Migne, cxcviii. 1537.

THOMAS AQUINAS, Doctor Angelicus; †1274. *Expositio continua* or *Catena aurea in Evangelia*, a mosaic of quotations (to be accepted with caution) from over eighty Christian writers, from Ignatius to Euthymius, so arranged as to form a summary of patristic theological teaching. *Opp.* ed. Venet. iv. 5; translated Oxford, 1845.

ALBERTUS MAGNUS of Ratisbon; †1280.

3. REFORMATION AND POST-REFORMATION WRITERS.

ERASMUS, Desiderius; †1536. *Adnotationes in N.T.*, 1516; *Paraphrases*, 1522.

BUTZER OR BUCER, Martin; †1551. *In sacra quatuor Evangelia Enarrationes*, 1551.

CALVIN, John; †1564. *In harmoniam ex Matt. Marc. et Luc. compositam Commentarii*, 1553; Brunsvigæ, 1868; translated by the Calvin Trans. Society, 1842; strong and independent.

BEZA, Theodore; †1605. *Adnotationes in N.T.*, 1565, 1594.

GROTIUS (Huig van Groot); †1645. *Adnotationes in N.T.*, 1644. Arminian; an early attempt to apply philological principles (learned from J. J. Scaliger) and classical illustrations to the Bible; still useful.

HAMMOND, Henry; † 1660. Canon of Christ Church, Oxford; "the Father of English Commentators." *Paraphrase and Annotations of the N.T.*, 1653, 1845; "reveals genuine exegetical tact and learning." Biblical paraphrase is of English origin.

One or two Roman Catholic commentators in this period require mention.

CAJETAN, Cardinal (Jacob de Vio); † 1534; a Dominican. *In quatuor Evang. et Acta Apost. Commentarii*, 1543. Under pressure from Luther (1518) he became considerably emancipated from patristic and scholastic influence.

MALDONATUS, Joannes (Maldon.); † 1583; a Spanish Jesuit. *Commentarii in quatuor Evangelia* 1596; ed. Sansen, 1840; ed. K. Martin (condensed) 1850. Admirable of its kind: he rarely shirks a difficulty, and is often sagacious in his exposition. An English translation by G. J. Davie is being published by Hodges.

CORNELIUS A LAPIDE (van Stein); † 1637; a Jesuit. *Comm. in quatuor Evang.*, 1638. Part of a commentary on almost the whole Bible. A voluminous compilation, including much allegory and legend; devout and often edifying, but sometimes puerile. English translation of the Comm. on S. Luke, Hodges, 1887.

ESCOBAR Y MENDOSA, Antonio; † 1669; a Spanish Jesuit, whose casuistry was gibbeted by Pascal. *In Evangelia sanctorum et temporis commentarii*, 1637.

Two great names in the eighteenth century serve well as a transition from the writers of the two preceding centuries to the present age.

BENGEL, Johann Albrecht (Beng.); † 1751. *Gnomon N.T.*, 1742. A masterpiece, rivalling Euthymius Zigabenus in terseness, and excelling him in originality and insight. English translation, Clark, 1857.

WETSTEIN, Johann Jacob (Wetst.), † 1754. *Nov. Test. Græcum*, 1751, 1752. A monument of criticism and learning. Wetstein was a leader in the field of textual criticism, and the stores of learning collected in his notes have been of the greatest service to all subsequent students of N.T.

4. MODERN WRITERS.

SCHLEIERMACHER, Fried. Dan. Ernst; † 1834; *Ueber die Schriften des Lukas*, 1817. Translated anonymously by Thirlwall, 1825.

BORNEMANN, Fried. August.; † 1850. *Scholia in Lucæ Evangelium*, 1830

De Wette, Wilh. Mart. L.; †1849. *Kurze Erklärung der Evangelien des Lukas und Markus*, 1839. Free, precise, and compact.

Meyer, Hein. Aug. Wilh.; †1873. *Kritisch exegetischer Kommentar uber das N.T. Markus und Lukas*, 1846. Excellent. A good English translation of the fifth edition was published by T. & T. Clark, 1880. Grammar is sometimes ridden to death; but this is still one of the best commentaries for English readers. The German revisions of Meyer by Bernhard and Johannes Weiss, 1885, etc., are superior, especially as regards the text.

Oosterzee, Jan Jacob van; †1882. In Lange's *Theologische-homiletisches Bibelwerk*, 1857–1876, he commented on S. Luke. English translation published by T. & T. Clark, 1864. The notes are in three sections throughout; critical, doctrinal, and homiletic.

Hahn, G. L., Professor of Theology at Breslau. *Das Evangelium des Lukas*, 1892, 1894. Two substantial volumes, full of useful material, but grievously perverse in questions of textual criticism.

Schanz, Paul. *Das Evangelium des heiligen Lucas*, 1883. Probably much the best Roman Catholic commentary.

Lasserre, Henri. *Les Saints Évangiles*, 1886, 1887. A French translation of the Gospels with brief notes. Uncritical, but interesting. It received the *imprimatur* of the Archbishop of Paris and the praise of Leo xiii., ran through twenty-five editions in two years, and then through the influence of the Jesuits was suppressed.

Godet, Fréderic, Professor at Neuchatel. *Commentaire sur l'Évangile de S. Luc*, 1871, 1872, 1888. Equal to Meyer in exegesis, but weak in textual criticism. The edition of 1888 is greatly to be preferred. An English translation of the second edition was published by T. & T. Clark, 1879.

Alford, Henry; †1871. *Greek Testament*, vol. i. 1849, 5th ed. 1863. Sensible and clear.

Wordsworth, Christopher, Bishop of Lincoln; †1885. *Greek Testament*, vol. i. 1856, 5th ed. 1866. Scholarly and devout, supplying the patristic element wanting in Alford, but otherwise inferior; weak in textual criticism.

McClellan, John Brown. *The New Testament*, a new translation, from a revised text, with analyses, copious references and illustrations, chronological and analytical harmony, notes and dissertations, vol. i. 1875; unfortunately the only one published. Contains some grotesque renderings and perverse arguments, with a great deal of valuable matter.

Plumptre, Edward Hayes; †1891. The Synoptic Gospels in Bishop Ellicott's *Commentary for English Readers*, Cassell, 1878. Popular and suggestive, with a tendency to excessive ingenuity.

Jones, William Basil, Bishop of St. David's, and Cook, Frederic Charles, Canon of Exeter; St. Luke in the *Speaker's Commentary*, 1878. Inadequate.

Carr, Arthur, *Notes on the Greek Testament, St. Luke*, 1875. A scholarly handbook.

Farrar, Fred. William, Dean of Canterbury. St. Luke in the *Cambridge Greek Testament*, 1884 and later. More full, but less precise, than Carr.

Sadler, Michael Ferrebee: †1895. *Gospel acc. to St. Luke*, 1886. Dogmatic and practical rather than critical: somewhat capricious in textual criticism.

Bond, John. WH. text of St. Luke with introduction and notes, 1890. Brief to a fault, but useful.

Campbell, Colin. *Critical Studies in St. Luke's Gospel*, 1890. Fails to establish a special demonology and Ebionite tendency, but contains many useful remarks.

Bernard, Thomas Dehany. *The Songs of the Holy Nativity*, 1895. Did not come to the knowledge of the present writer until the commentary on chapters i. and ii. was in print.[1]

Bruce, Alexander Balmain. The Synoptic Gospels in the *Expositor's Greek Testament*, Hodder & Stoughton, 1897. T. R. with introduction and notes; modelled on Alford.

Blass, Fredericus. *Evangelium secundum Lucam sive Lucæ ad Theophilum Liber Prior, secundam Formam quæ videtur Romanam*, Trubner, 1897. Western text with introduction and critical notes.

Index II. contains the names of many other writers whose works are of great use to the student of this Gospel.

[1] A similar fact caused the omission at p. xxix of some recent discussions of the Synoptic problem: *e.g.* The Abbé Loisy, Essays in *L'Enseignement Biblique*, 1892, *Revue des Religions*, 1894, and *Revue Biblique*, 1896 (see the *Guardian*, August 1896, p. 1317); W. Arnold Stevens and E. De Witt Burton *A Harmony of the Gospels for Historical Study*, Boston, 1896.

ABBREVIATIONS.

Ecclesiastical Writers.

Ambr.	Ambrose.
Aug.	Augustine.
Bas.	Basil.
Chrys.	Chrysostom.
Clem. Alex.	Clement of Alexandria.
Clem. Hom.	Clementine Homilies.
Clem. Recogn.	Clementine Recognitions.
Clem. Rom.	Clement of Rome.
Cypr.	Cyprian.
Cyr. Alex.	Cyril of Alexandria.
Cyr. Hier.	Cyril of Jerusalem.
Dion. Alex.	Dionysius of Alexandria.
Epiph.	Epiphanius.
Eus.	Eusebius.
Euthym.	Euthymius Zigabenus.
Greg. Naz.	Gregory of Nazianzum.
Greg. Nys.	Gregory of Nyssa.
Herm.	Hermas.
Hippol.	Hippolytus.
Ign.	Ignatius.
Iren.	Irenæus.
Iren-lat.	Latin Version of Irenæus.
Jer. (Hieron.)	Jerome.
Jos.	Josephus.
Just. M.	Justin Martyr.
Orig.	Origen.
Orig-lat.	Latin Version of Origen.
Tert.	Tertullian.
Theoph.	Theophylact.

Versions.

Aegyptt.	Egyptian.
Boh.	Bohairic.
Sah.	Sahidic.

Aeth.	Ethiopic.
Arm.	Armenian.
Goth.	Gothic.
Latt.	Latin.
Lat. Vet.	Vetus Latina.
Vulg.	Vulgate.
Cod. Am.	Codex Amiatinus.
Syrr.	Syriac.
Cur.	Curetonian.
Sin.	Sinaitic.
Pesh.	Peshitto.
Harcl.	Harclean.
Hier.	Jerusalem.
Cov.	Coverdale.
Gen.	Geneva.
Luth.	Luther.
Rhem.	Rheims (or Douay).
Tyn.	Tyndale.
Wic.	Wiclif.
AV.	Authorized Version.
RV.	Revised Version.

Editors.

TR.	Textus Receptus.
Tisch.	Tischendorf.
Treg.	Tregelles.
WH.	Westcott and Hort.
Alf.	Alford.
Beng.	Bengel.
De W.	De Wette.
Grot.	Grotius.
Maldon.	Maldonatus.
Mey.	Meyer.
Nösg.	Nösgen.
Wetst.	Wetstein.
Wordsw.	Wordsworth (Chr.).

Miscellaneous.

Burton	Burton, *N.T. Moods and Tenses.*
C. I. G.	*Corpus Inscriptionum Græcarum.*
Didon, *J. C.*	Père Didon, *Jésus Christ.*
L. J.	*Leben Jesu.*
V. de J.	*Vie de Jésus.*

Lft. *Epp.*	J. B. Lightfoot,[1] *Notes on Epistles of S. Paul.*
Wsctt.	Westcott.
Edersh. *L. & T.*	Edersheim, *Life and Times of Jesus the Messiah.*
Hist. of J. N.	*History of the Jewish Nation.*
Rob. *Res. in Pal.*	Robinson, *Researches in Palestine.*
Schürer, *J. P. in T. of J. C.*	Schürer, *Jewish People in the Times of Jesus Christ.*
Scriv. *Int.*	Scrivener, *Introduction to the Criticism of the New Testament.*
Stanley, *Sin. & Pal.*	Stanley, *Sinai and Palestine*
Trench, *Mir.*	Trench, *Miracles.*
Par.	" *Parables.*
Syn.	" *New Testament Synonyms.*
Tristram, *Nat. Hist. of B.*	Tristram, *Natural History of the Bible.*
D. B.[1] or *D. B.*[2]	Smith's *Dictionary of the Bible*, 1st or 2nd edition.
D. Chr. Ant.	Smith's *Dictionary of Christian Antiquities.*
Kraus, *Real-Enc. d. Chr. Alt.*	Kraus, *Real-Encyklopädie der Christlichen Alterthümer.*
Herzog, *PRE.*[1] or *PRE.*[2]	Herzog's *Protestantische Real-Encyklopädie*, 1st or 2nd edition.
Crem. *Lex.*	Cremer, *Lexicon of New Testament Greek.*
L. & S. *Lex.*	Liddell and Scott, *Lexicon.*
Greg. *Proleg.*	Gregory, *Prolegomena ad Tischendorfii ed. N.T.*
Win.	Winer, *Grammar of N.T. Greek* (the page refers to Moulton's edition).
om.	omit.
ins.	insert.

N.B.—The text commented upon is that of Westcott and Hort. The very few instances in which the editor is inclined to dissent from this text are noted as they occur.

[1] The name of John Lightfoot is not abbreviated in this volume.

THE

GOSPEL ACCORDING TO S. LUKE.

THE TITLE OF THE GOSPEL.

THE title cannot be any part of the original autograph. It is found in different forms in ancient authorities, the earliest being the simplest: κατὰ Λουκᾶν (ℵ B F), εὐαγγέλιον κατὰ Λουκᾶν (A C D Ξ), τὸ κατὰ Λουκᾶν εὐαγγέλιον or τὸ κατὰ Λουκᾶν ἅγιον εὐαγγέλιον (cursives).

The **κατά** neither affirms nor denies *authorship*: it implies *conformity to a type*. But, inasmuch as all four Gospels have the κατά, these uniform titles must be interpreted according to the belief of those who gave the titles, viz. the Christians of the first four centuries; and it was their belief that each Evangelist composed the Gospel which bears his name. Had the κατά meant no more than "drawn up according to the teaching of," then this Gospel would have been called κατὰ Παῦλον, and the second Gospel would have been called κατὰ Πέτρον; for it was the general tradition that Mark wrote according to the teaching of Peter, and Luke (in a different sense) according to the teaching of Paul. The κατά, however, is not a mere substitute for the genitive of authorship, but indicates that *the same subject has been treated by others*. Thus, ἡ παλαιὰ διαθήκη κατὰ τοὺς ἑβδομήκοντα points to the existence of other translations, just as Ὅμηρος κατὰ Ἀρίσταρκον or κατὰ Ἀριστοφάνην points to the existence of other editions. That the κατά does not exclude authorship is shown by such expressions as ἡ κατὰ Μωϋσέα πεντάτευχος (Epiphanius) and ἡ καθ' Ἡρόδοτον ἱστορία (Diodorus): comp. ἐν τοῖς ὑπομνηματισμοῖς τοῖς κατὰ τὸν Νεεμίαν (2 Mac. ii. 13). Strictly speaking, there is only one Gospel, εὐαγγέλιον Θεοῦ, the Gospel of God concerning His Son (Rom. i. 1); but it has been given to us in four shapes, εὐαγγέλιον τετράμορφον (Iren. *Hær.* iii. 11. 8), and the κατά indicates the shape in which the writer named composed it.

I. 1–4. THE PROLOGUE OR PREFACE.

The classical style of this opening, and its similarity to the prefaces of Herodotus, Thucydides, and Polybius, hardly amount to proof that Lk. was well read in classical literature, and consciously imitated Greek historians; but there is nothing improbable in this supposition. Among the words which are classical rather than biblical should be noticed ἐπειδήπερ, ἐπιχειρεῖν, ἀνατάσσεσθαι, διήγησις, καθεξῆς. The construction also is classical, and in no way Hebraistic. We have clauses idiomatically interlaced, not simply co-ordinated. The modest position claimed by the writer is evidence of his honesty. A forger would have claimed to be an eye-witness, and would have made no apology for writing. Ewald remarks that "in its utter simplicity, modesty, and brevity, it is the model of a preface to an historical work." Its grammatical construction should be compared with that of the preface to the synodical epistle in Acts xv. 24, 25: Ἐπειδὴ ἠκούσαμεν . . . ἔδοξεν ἡμῖν.

This prologue contains all that we really *know* respecting the composition of early narratives of the life of Christ, and it is the test by which theories as to the origin of our Gospels must be judged. No hypothesis is likely to be right which does not harmonize with what is told us here. Moreover, it shows that an inspired writer felt that he was bound to use research and care in order to secure accuracy.

1. Ἐπειδήπερ. A stately compound, suitable for a solemn opening: freq. in class. Grk., but not found in LXX, or elsewhere in N.T. *Quoniam quidem*, "For as much as," *Weil denn einmal.*

πολλοί. The context seems to imply that these, like Lk., were not eye-witnesses. That at once would exclude Mt., whose Gospel Lk. does not appear to have known. It is doubtful whether Mk. is included in the πολλοί. The writers of extant apocryphal gospels cannot be meant, for these are all of later origin. Probably all the documents here alluded to were driven out of existence by the manifest superiority of the four Canonical Gospels. The **ἐπεχείρησαν** cannot imply censure, as some of the Fathers thought, for Lk. brackets himself with these writers (ἔδοξε κἀμοί); what they attempted he may attempt. The word occurs 2 Mac. ii. 29, vii. 19; Acts ix. 29, xix. 13; and is freq. in class. Grk. in the sense of "put the hand to, take in hand, attempt." The notion of *unlawful* or *unsuccessful* attempting is sometimes implied by the context: it is not contained in the word. Luther renders *unterwunden haben*, "have ventured." Lk. must have regarded these attempts as *insufficient*, or he would not have added another. Meyer quotes Ulpian, p. 159 (in Valckenaer), ἐπειδήπερ περὶ τούτου πολλοὶ ἐπεχείρησαν ἀπολογήσασθαι. It is doubtful whether ἐπιχειρ. necessarily implies a *great* undertaking.

ἀνατάξασθαι διήγησιν. "To draw up again in order a narrative"; *i.e.* to arrange afresh so as to show the sequence of events. The verb is a rare one, and occurs elsewhere only Plut. *Moral* p. 969 C, *De sollert. animal.* xii. (Reiske, x. p. 36), in the sense of "practise, go over again in order," Iren. iii. 21. 2, and as *v.l.* Eccles. ii. 20. The subst. implies something more than mere notes or anecdotes; "a leading through to the end" (*durchführen*), "a narrative" (Ecclus. vi. 35, ix. 15; 2 Mac. ii. 32, vi. 17; Plat. *Rep.* 392 D; Arist. *Rhet.* iii. 16. 1).

Versions vary greatly: *ordinare narrationem* (Latt.), *componere narrationem* (Beza), *stellen die Rede* (Luth.), "ordeyne the telling" (Wic.), "compyle a treates" (Tyn.), "set forth the words" (Cov.), "set forth the declaracion" (Cran.), "write the historie" (Gen.), "compile a narration" (Rhem.), "set forth in order a declaration" (AV.), "draw up a narrative" (RV.), *composer une narration suivie* (Godet), *coordonner en corps de récit* (Lasserre), "restore from memory a narrative" (Blass).

τῶν πεπληροφορημένων. "Of the things which have been carried through to the end, of the matters which have been accomplished, fully established." Here again English Versions differ much; but "surely known" (Tyn.), "surely to be believed" (Cran.), "surely believed" (AV.), cannot be justified. The verb when used of *persons* may mean "persuade fully, convince," and in pass. "be fully persuaded" (Rom. iv. 21, xiv. 5); but of *things* it means "fulfil" (2 Tim. iv. 5, 17). Here we may render "accomplished." Others less well render "fully proved." See Lightfoot on Col. iv. 12. The ἐν ἡμῖν probably means "among us Christians." Christendom is the sphere in which these facts have had their full accomplishment. The ἡμῖν in ver. 2 shows that contemporaries are not meant. If these things were handed down to Lk., then he was not contemporary with them. The verse is evidence that the accomplished facts were already fully established and widely known, for they had already been narrated by many. See Westcott, *Intr. to Gosp.* p. 190, 7th ed.

2. καθὼς παρέδοσαν ἡμῖν. "*Even* as they delivered them to us." The difference between ὡς, "as," and καθώς, "just as," should be marked in translation: the correspondence was exact. Lk. implies that he himself was among those who *received* the tradition. Like the πολλοί, he can only arrange afresh what has been handed down, working at second hand, not as an eye-witness. He gives no hint as to whether the facts were handed down orally or in writing. The difference between the πολλοί and these αὐτόπται is not that the πολλοί wrote their narratives while the αὐτόπται did not, but that the αὐτόπται were primary authorities, which the πολλοί were not.

ὑπηρέται γενόμενοι τοῦ λόγου. They not only had personal knowledge of the facts (αὐτόπται), they also had practical experience of the effects. They had preached and taught, and had thus learned what elements in the Gospel were of most efficacy for the winning and saving of souls. That τοῦ λόγου belongs to ὑπηρέται only, not to αὐτόπται, and means "the doctrine," *i.e.* the Gospel (Acts vi. 4, viii. 4, xiv. 25, xvi. 6, xvii. 11), is manifest from the context. Origen and Athanasius are wrong in making τοῦ λόγου mean the personal Word, the Son of God, a use which is peculiar to Jn. The ἀπ' ἀρχῆς refers to the beginning of Christ's ministry (Jn. xv. 27, xvi. 4). For ὑπηρέτης see on iv. 20 and comp. Acts xiii. 5.

3. ἔδοξε κἀμοί. This is the main sentence, the apodosis of ἐπειδήπερ πολλοὶ ἐπεχείρησαν. It neither implies nor excludes inspiration: the ἔδοξε may or may not have been inspired. The wish to include inspiration caused the addition in some Latin MSS. of *et spiritui sancto* (Acts xv. 28), which makes what follows to be incongruous. With ἔδοξε comp. the Muratorian Fragment: *Lucas iste medicus . . . nomine suo ex opinione conscripsit—Dominum tamen nec ipse vidit in carne—et idem, prout assequi potuit, ita et a nativitate Joannis incepit dicere.* The κἀμοί shows that Lk. does not blame the πολλοί: he desires to imitate and supplement them. It is their attempts that encourage him to write. What they have done he may do, and perhaps he may be able to improve upon their work. This is his first reason for writing a narrative. See Blass, *NT. Gram.* p. 274.

παρηκολουθηκότι. This is his second reason for writing, making the argument *à fortiori.* He has had special advantages and qualifications; and therefore what was allowed to others may be still more allowed to him. These qualifications are fourfold, and are told off with precision. In the literal sense of "following a person closely so as to be always beside him," παρακολουθεῖν does not occur in N.T. Here it does not mean that Lk. was contemporaneous with the events, but that he had brought himself abreast of them by careful investigation. Comp. the famous passage in Dem. *De Cor.* cap. liii. p. 285 (344), παρηκολουθηκότα τοῖς πράγμασιν ἐξ ἀρχῆς: also *De Fal. Leg.* p. 423.

ἄνωθεν. This is the *first* of the four qualifications: he has gone back to the very beginning, viz. the promise of the birth of the Forerunner. "From the first" is the meaning of ἄνωθεν here, not "thoroughly," *radicitus*, as in Acts xxvi. 5, which would make ἄνωθεν almost the same as πᾶσιν. Vulg. has *a principio*, and *d* has *desusum* (comp. the French *dessus*). It is the πᾶσιν which implies thoroughness; and this is the *second* point. He has begun at the beginning, and he has investigated everything. The Syriac makes πᾶσιν masc., but there is little doubt that it is neut., and refers to πραγμάτων in ver. 1.

ἀκριβῶς. This is the *third* point. He has done all this "accurately." There is no idle boast in any one of the three points. No other Gospel gives us this early history about the Baptist and the Christ. No other is throughout so full, for of 170 sections contained in the synoptic narrative 48 are peculiar to Lk. And, in spite of the severest scrutiny, his accuracy can very rarely be impugned. We cannot be sure whether he means to imply that ἀκριβῶς was not true of the πολλοί, but we may be sure that none of them could claim all three of these points. In any case we have an inspired historian telling us in his inspired writings that he is giving us the results of careful investigation. From this it seems to follow that an inspired historian may fail in accuracy if his investigation is defective.

καθεξῆς. This is the *fourth* point, resulting from the other three. He does not propose to give a mere collection of anecdotes and detached sayings, but an orderly narrative systematically arranged. Chronological order is not necessarily implied in *καθεξῆς*, but merely arrangement of some kind. Nevertheless, he probably has chronological order chiefly in view. In N.T. the word is peculiar to Lk. (viii. 1; Acts iii. 24, xi. 4, xviii. 23), as is also the more classical ἑξῆς (vii. 11, ix. 37, etc.); but ἐφεξῆς does not occur.

κράτιστε Θεόφιλε. The epithet *κράτιστος*, often given to persons of rank (Acts xxiii. 26, xxiv. 3, xxvi. 25), is strongly in favour of the view that Theophilus was a real person. The name Theophilus was common both among Jews (=Jedidiah) and among Gentiles. But it was a name likely to be used to represent any pious reader. See Lft. on "Acts," *D.B.*[2] pp. 25, 26. The word *κράτιστος* occurs in N.T. only here and in the Acts, where it is evidently a purely official epithet, for the persons to whom it is applied are of bad character. See Deissmann, *Bibelstudien*, p. 19, for the name.

4. ἵνα ἐπιγνῷς περὶ ὧν κατηχήθης λόγων τὴν ἀσφάλειαν. "In order that thou mightest fully know the certainty concerning the words wherein thou wast instructed." The *λόγοι* are not the *πράγματα* or historic facts, but the details of the *λόγος* or Gospel (ver. 2), which "ministers of the word" had communicated to Theophilus. The compound *ἐπιγνῷς* indicates additional and more thorough knowledge. It is very freq. in Lk. and Paul: see esp. Rom. i. 28, 32; 1 Cor. xiii. 12; Lft. on Col. i. 9; Trench, *Syn.* lxxv. In N.T. *κατηχεῖν*, "to sound down into the ears, teach orally," is found only in Lk. and Paul. The position of *τὴν ἀσφάλειαν* gives it solemn emphasis. Theophilus shall know that the faith which he has embraced has an impregnable historical foundation. Hastings, *D.C.G.* ii. p. 726.

The idiomatic attraction, *περὶ ὧν κατηχήθης λόγων*, is best resolved into *περὶ τῶν λόγων οὓς κατηχήθης*, not *περὶ τῶν λόγων περὶ ὧν κατηχήθης*. Only of *persons* does *περί τινος* stand after *κατηχεῖν* (Acts xxi. 21, 24): of *things* we have the acc. (Acts xviii. 25; Gal. vi. 6). These attractions are very freq. in Lk. See Blass, *Gr.* p. 170.

On the superficial resemblance between this preface and Jos. *Con. Apion.* i. 9, 10, see Godet, i. pp. 92, 93, 3ème ed. 1888. The resemblance hardly amounts to remarkable coincidence, and such similarities are common in literature. It is more interesting to compare this preface with that of the medical writer Dioscorides. The opening words of Dioscorides' treatise, *περὶ ὕλης ἰατρικῆς*, run thus: *Πολλῶν οὐ μόνον ἀρχαίων, ἀλλὰ καὶ νέων συνταξαμένων* περὶ τῆς τῶν φαρμάκων σκευασίας τε καὶ δυνάμεως καὶ δοκιμασίας, φίλτατε Ἀρεῖε, πειράσομαί σοι παραστῆσαι μὴ κενὴν μηδὲ ἄλογον ὁρμὴν ἐσχηκέναι πρὸς τήνδε τὴν πραγματείαν. The date of Dioscorides Pedacius is uncertain; but, as Pliny does not mention him, he is commonly assigned to the first or second century A.D. He is said to have been a native of Anazarbus in Cilicia, about fifty miles from Tarsus; and in that case he would almost certainly obtain his medical knowledge in the great school at Tarsus. That he and S. Luke may have been there at the same time with S. Paul, seems to be a not impossible conjecture. The treatise περὶ ἀρχαίης ἰητρικῆς, commonly attributed to Hippocrates (*c.* 460–350 B.C.), begins: Ὁκόσοι ἐπεχείρησαν περὶ ἰητρικῆς λέγειν ἢ γράφειν, κ.τ.λ.

I. 5–II. 52. THE GOSPEL OF THE INFANCY.

These chapters have often been attacked as unhistorical. That Marcion omitted them from his mutilated edition of this Gospel is of no moment. He did not do so upon critical grounds, but because their contents did not harmonize with his doctrine. It is more to the point to urge that these early narratives lack apostolic authority; that they cover ground which popular imagination, in the absence of history, would be sure to fill; that they abound in angelic appearances and other marvels; that their form is often highly poetical; and that it is sometimes difficult to reconcile them with the narrative of Mt. or with known facts of history. To this it may be replied that reserve would keep Christ's Mother from making known these details at first. Even Apostles may have been ignorant of them, or unwilling to make them known until the comparatively late period at which Lk. wrote. The dignity, beauty, and spirituality of these narratives is strong evidence of their authenticity, especially when contrasted with the silly, grotesque, and even immoral details in the apocryphal gospels. They abound in historic features, and are eminently true to life. Their independence of Mt. is evident, and both accounts bear the stamp of truthfulness, which is not destroyed by possible discrepancies in a few minor points. That Lk. is ever at variance with other historians, has still to be proved; and the merit of greater accuracy may still be with him, even if such variance exists.

This Gospel of the Infancy is made up of seven narratives, in two parallel groups of three, followed by a supplement, which connects these two groups with the main body of the Gospel.

I. 1. The Annunciation of the Birth of the Forerunner (5–25); 2. The Annunciation of the Birth of the Saviour (26–38); 3. The Visit of the Mother of the Saviour to the Mother of the Forerunner (39–56).

II. 4. The Birth of the Forerunner (57–80); 5. The Birth of the Saviour (ii. 1–20); 6. The Circumcision and Presentation of the Saviour (ii. 21–40).

III. 7. The Boyhood of the Saviour (ii. 41–52).

On the two accounts of our Lord's infancy see Resch, *Das Kindheitsevangelium*, pp. 10 ff., 1897; Gore, *Dissertations on Subjects connected with the Incarnation*, pp. 12 ff.: Murray, 1895.

I. 5–25. *The Annunciation of the Birth of the Forerunner.*

"When John the Baptist appeared, not the oldest man in Palestine could remember to have spoken even in his earliest childhood with any man who had seen a prophet. . . . In these circumstances it was *an occurrence of the first magnitude, more important far than war or revolution*, when a new prophet actually appeared" (*Ecce Homo*, ch. i.). The miracles recorded are in keeping with this. God was making a new departure in dealing with His people. We need not, therefore, be startled if a highly exceptional situation is accompanied by highly exceptional facts. After more than three centuries of silence, Jehovah again speaks by prophecies and signs to Israel. But there is no violent rupture with the past in making this new departure. The announcement of the rise of a new Prophet is made in the temple at Jerusalem, to a priest of the old covenant, who is to be the Prophet's father. It is strong evidence of the historic truth of the narrative that no miracles are prophesied of the new Prophet, and that after his appearance his disciples attribute none to him.

5. **Ἐγένετο ἐν ταῖς ἡμέραις.** The elegant idiomatic Greek of the preface comes abruptly to an end. Although the marks of Lk.'s style are as abundant here as in any part of the Gospel, yet the form of the narrative is strongly Hebraistic; so much so that one may be confident that he is translating from an Aramaic document These first two chapters seem to consist of a series of such documents, each with a distinct conclusion (i. 80, ii. 40, ii. 52). If they are historical, the Virgin Mary must have been the source of much that is contained in these first two chapters; and she may have been the writer of documents used by Lk. In any case, we have here the earliest documentary evidence respecting the origins of Christianity which has come down to us,—evidence which may justly be called contemporary. Both ἐγένετο and ἐν ταῖς ἡμέραις are Hebraistic (see on ver. 39); but there is no need to understand ἦν or any other verb after ἐγένετο, "It came to pass that there was." Rather, "There arose, came into notice," or simply "There was." See on iv. 36, and comp. Mk. i. 4; Jn. i. 6.

Ἡρῴδου βασιλέως τῆς Ἰουδαίας. Herod "the Great," a title not given to him by his contemporaries, who during his last years suffered greatly from his cruelty. It is in these last years that the narrative of Lk. begins. The Herods were Idumæans by birth,[1] though Jews by religion, and were dependent upon the Romans for their sovereignty. As Tacitus says: *Regnum ab Antonio Herodi datum victor Augustus auxit* (*Hist.* v. 9. 3).

The name Ἡρῴδης is contracted from Ἡρωΐδης, and should have iota subscript, which is well supported by early inscriptions. Later inscriptions and coins omit the iota. In the *Codex Ambrosianus* of Josephus the name is written with iota adscript, Ηρωιδης (*Ant.* xi –xx.). See the numerous instances from inscriptions cited by Schürer in the *Theol. Litztg.* 1892, No. 21, col. 516. The τοῦ inserted before βασιλέως in A and other texts is in accordance with classical usage. But in LXX the art. is commonly omitted in such cases, because in Hebrew, as in English, "Saul, king of Israel," "George, king of England," is the common idiom (Gen. xiv. 1, 2, 18, xx. 2, xxvi. 1, etc. etc.). See Simcox, *Lang. of N.T.* p. 47.

βασιλέως τῆς Ἰουδαίας. This was the title conferred on him by the Senate at the request of Antony, Messala, and Atratinus (Jos. *Ant.* xiv. 14. 4). Judæa here may mean "the land of the Jews, Palestine" (vii. 17, xxiii. 5; Acts ii. 9, x. 37, xi. 1, 29). Besides Judæa in the narrower sense, Herod's dominions included Samaria, Galilee, a great deal of Peræa, and Cœle-Syria. For the abundant literature on the Herods see *D.B.*[2] i. p. 1341; Herzog, *PRE.*[2] vi. p. 47; Schürer, *Jewish People in the T. of J. C.* i. 1, p. 400.

ἱερεύς τις ὀνόματι Ζαχαρίας. In the *Protevangelium of James* (viii.), Zacharias is called high priest; and this has been adopted by later writers, who have supposed that the incident narrated by Lk. took place on the Day of Atonement in the Holy of Holies. But the high priest would not have been called ἱερεύς τις, and it could not have been by *lot* (ἔλαχε) that he offered incense on the Day of Atonement. Priestly descent was much esteemed. The name means "Remembered by Jehovah." For ὀνόματι see on v. 27.

ἐξ ἐφημερίας Ἀβιά. The word ἐφημερία has two meanings: 1. "service for a term of days" (Neh. xiii. 30; 1 Chron. xxv. 8; 2 Chron. xiii. 10); 2. "a course of priests who were on duty for a term of days," viz. for a week (1 Chron. xxiii. 6, xxviii. 13; 1 Esdr. i. 2, 15). These courses were also called διαιρέσεις, and by Josephus πατριαί and ἐφημερίδες (*Ant.* vii. 14. 7; *Vita*, i.). Abijah was descended from Eleazar, and gave his name to the eighth of the twenty-four courses into which David divided the priests (1 Chron. xxiv. 10; 2 Chron. viii. 14). Of these twenty-four only the courses of Jedaiah, Immer, Pashur, and Harim returned from captivity (Ezra ii. 36–39); but these four were divided again into twenty-

[1] *Tempus quoque Herodis alienigenæ videlicet regis etiam ipsum Domenico attestatur adventui. Prædictum namque fuerat, quia non deficiet princeps ex Juda, donec veniat qui mittendus erat* (Bede). See Farrar, *The Herods*, ch. vi., vii.

four with the old names. So that Zacharias did not belong to the original course of Abijah, for that did not return from exile. Each course was on duty twice during the year; but we know far too little about the details of the arrangement to derive any sure chronology from the statements made by Lk. See on ii. 7.

Wieseler places the vision of Zacharias early in October A.U.C. 748 or B.C. 6 (*Chron. Syn.* ii. 2, Eng. tr. p. 123). With this result Edersheim agrees (*L. and T.* i. p. 135), as also does Andrews (*L. of our Lord*, p. 52, ed. 1892). Lewin prefers May 16th, B.C. 7 (*Fasti Sacri*, 836). Caspari is for July 18th, B.C. 3, but remarks "how little reliance is to be placed upon conclusions of this kind" (*Chron. Einl.* § 42, Eng. tr. p. 57). For the courses of priests, see Herzog, *PRE.*[2] art. *Priestertum im A.T.*; Schürer, *Jewish People in the T. of J. C.* ii. 1, pp. 216–220.

γυνὴ αὐτῷ ἐκ τῶν θυγατέρων Ἀαρών. "He had a wife," not "his wife was" (AV.). Lk. follows LXX in omitting the art. with the gen. after *θυγάτηρ*: comp. xiii. 16 and the quotations Mt. xxi. 5 and Jn. xii. 15, and contrast Mt. xiv. 6. To be a priest and married to a priest's daughter was a double distinction. It was a common summary of an excellent woman, "She deserves to marry a priest." In the fullest sense John was of priestly birth. See Wetst.: *Sacrosancta præcursoris nobilitas non solum a parentibus, sed etiam a progenitoribus gloriosa descendit* (Bede). Aaron's wife was Elisabeth = Elisheba = "God is my oath."

6. δίκαιοι. Once a term of high praise, and meaning righteousness in the fullest sense (Ezek. xviii. 5, 9, 11, 19, 20, 22, 24, 26); but it had come to mean little more than careful observance of legal duties. The addition of the Hebraistic **ἐναντίον τοῦ Θεοῦ** (Acts viii. 21; Gen. vi. 8, 11, 13, vii. 1, x. 9) gives *δίκαιοι* its full meaning: Zacharias and Elisabeth were saints of the O.T. type. Symeon is called *δίκαιος* (ii. 25), and Joseph (Mt. i. 19). Comp. *δίκαιον εἶναί μ' ὁ νόμος ἥ φύσις θ' ἅμα παρεῖχε τῷ Θεῷ* (Eur. *Ion.* 643). The Gospel was to restore to *δίκαιος* its original spiritual meaning. See detached note on *the word* **δίκαιος** *and its cognates*, Rom. i. 17. For **ἀμφότεροι** see on v. 7.

πορευόμενοι ἐν πάσαις ταῖς ἐντολαῖς καὶ δικαιώμασιν τ. κ. Another Hebraism (Deut. xxviii. 9; 1 Sam. viii. 3, 5; 1 Kings iii. 14, etc.). The distinction often drawn, that **ἐντολαί** are moral, while **δικαιώματα** are ceremonial, is baseless; the difference is, that the latter is the vaguer term. Here, although they differ in gender, they have only one article and adjective, *because they are so similar in meaning*. Comp. Col. ii. 22; Rev. v. 12; and see Win. xix. 3 c, p. 157. The two words are found combined Gen. xxvi. 5 and Deut. iv. 40. For **δικαιώματα**, "things declared right, ordinances," comp. Rom. ii. 26 and Heb. ix. 1, and see note in *Sp. Comm.* on 1 Cor. v. 6 as to the force of the termination *-μα*. The genitive here, as in Rom. ii. 26 and viii. 4, expresses the authority from which the ordinance springs. The ἄμεμπτοι anticipates what follows, and, of course, does not mean that they were sinless. No one is sinless; but the conduct of some is free from reproach. Comp. Phil. iii. 6. See the quotation Eus. *H.E.* v. 1. 9.

7. καὶ οὐκ ἦν αὐτοῖς τέκνον. This calamity is grievous to all Orientals, and specially grievous to Jews, each of whom is ambitious of being among the progenitors of the Messiah. It was commonly believed to be a punishment for sin (Lev. xx. 20, 21; Jer. xxii. 30). The story of Glaucus, who tempted the oracle at Delphi, and "at the present time has not a single descendant" (Hdt. vi. 86. 16), indicates a similar belief among the Greeks. Zacharias and Elisabeth had the sorrow of being childless, as Anna of being husbandless, and all three had their consolation. Comp. the births of Samson and Samuel, both of whom were Nazirites, and of Isaac.

καθότι. Peculiar to Lk. "Because that" (xix. 9; Acts ii. 24, xvii. 31), or "according as" (Acts ii. 45, iv. 35). In class. Grk. editors commonly write *καθ' ὅ τι*. The clause *καὶ ἀμφότεροι . . . ἦσαν* does not depend upon *καθότι*, which would be illogical, but is a separate statement. Their age would not explain why they had had no children, but why they were not likely to have any. "They had no child, because that Elisabeth was barren; and they were both advanced in years," so that they had no hope of children.

προβεβηκότες ἐν ταῖς ἡμέραις αὐτῶν. Hebraistic: in class. Grk we should rather have had *τῇ ἡλικίᾳ*. In LXX we have *προβεβ. ἡμέραις*, or *ἡμερῶν*, or *τῶν ἡμερῶν* (1 Kings i. 1; Gen. xxiv. 1; Josh. xiii. 1). Levites were superannuated at about sixty, but a priest served as long as he was able.

8. Ἐγένετο . . . ἔλαχε. On the various constructions with *ἐγένετο* in Lk. see detached note at the end of this chapter; and on **ἐν τῷ ἱερατεύειν αὐτόν**, "while he was officiating as priest," which is another very favourite construction with Lk., see on iii. 21. The verb *ἱερατεύειν* is freq. in LXX, but occurs nowhere else in N.T. It is not found earlier than LXX, but is not rare in later Greek. See Kennedy, *Sources of N. T. Grk.* p. 119. The phrase **κατὰ τὸ ἔθος** is peculiar to Lk. in N.T. (ii. 42, xxii. 39), but occurs in Theod. Bel 15; and *ἔθος* occurs ten times in his writings, and only twice elsewhere (Jn. xix. 40; Heb. x. 25). Comp. *κατὰ τὸ εἰθισμένον* (ii. 27) and *κατὰ τὸ εἰωθὸς* (iv. 16; Acts xvii. 2). It is for the sake of those who were unfamiliar with the usages of the temple that he says that it was "according to the custom of the priest's service" that it was decided by lot which priest should offer incense. To take *κατὰ τὸ ἔθος τῆς ἱερατίας* with what precedes robs it of all point; it is tautology to say that he was officiating as priest according to the custom of the priest's service. But the number of cases in which Lk. has a clause or word which is grammatically amphibolous is very large; *vv.* 25, 27, ii. 22, where see note. The word *ἱερατεία* occurs in N.T. only here and Heb. vii. 5. "In relation to *ἱερωσύνη* (Heb. vii. 11, 12, 24) it expresses the actual service of the priests, and not the office of priesthood" (Wsctt. on Heb. vii. 5).

ἔλαχε τοῦ θυμιᾶσαι. The casting of lots took place twice a day, at the morning and the evening offering of incense. In the morning the drawing lots for offering the incense was the third and chief of a series of drawings, four in all; in the evening it was the only one. We do not know whether this was morning or evening. No priest might have this honour twice; and the number of priests was so great that many never offered the incense. The fortunate lot was a ψῆφος λευκή, to which there is a possible reference Rev. ii. 17. The priest who obtained it chose two others to help him; but, when they had done their part, they retired, leaving him alone in the Holy Place. For the very elaborate details see Edersh. *The Temple, its Ministry and Services*, pp. 129–142.

The gen. τοῦ θυμιᾶσαι is probably governed by ἔλαχε, which in class. Grk. commonly has a gen. when it means "became possessed of," and an acc. when it means "obtained by lot" (Acts i. 17; comp. 2 Pet. i. 1). In 1 Sam. xiv. 47 we have Σαοὺλ ἔλαχε [*al. l.* κατακληροῦται] τοῦ βασιλεύειν ἐπὶ Ἰσραήλ. The εἰσελθὼν εἰς τὸν ναόν must be taken with θυμιᾶσαι, not with ἔλαχε: "he obtained by lot to go in and burn incense," not "after entering into the ναός he obtained by lot to burn incense." The lots were cast *before* he entered the Holy Place, which was the front part of the ναός.

10. πᾶν τὸ πλῆθος ἦν τοῦ λαοῦ προσευχόμενον. Cod. Am. has the same order, *omnis multitudo erat populi orans*. The position of τοῦ λαοῦ is against taking ἦν with προσευχόμενον as the analytical tense instead of the imperf., a constr. of which Lk. is very fond (*vv.* 20, 21, 22, ii. 33, iv. 17, 31, 38, 44, etc.); ἦν may mean "was there," or "there was," and τοῦ λαοῦ be epexegetic of τὸ πλῆθος. But certainty is unattainable and unimportant. We need not infer from πᾶν τὸ πλῆθος that there was a great multitude. As compared with the solitary priest in the ναός, all the worshippers outside were a πλῆθος. The word is a favourite one with Lk., who uses it twenty-five times against seven in the rest of N.T. It is remarkable that prayer is not expressly mentioned in the Law as part of public worship, except in connexion with the offering of the first-fruits (Deut. xxvi. 15). But comp. 1 Kings viii. 33–48, 2 Chron. vi. 14–42; Is. lvi. 7. The people were inside the ἱερόν, although outside (ἔξω) the ναός, and the other priests would be between them and the ναός. Syr-Sin. omits **ἔξω.**

11. ὤφθη δὲ αὐτῷ ἄγγελος Κυρίου. It was the most solemn moment of his life, when he stood alone in that sacred spot to offer the pure and ideal symbol of the imperfect prayer which he and those outside were offering. The unique circumstances contributed to make him conscious of that unseen world which is around all of us (2 Kings vi. 17; comp. Lk. xv. 7, 10). For ὤφθη see on xxii. 43; and for an analysis of the psychological facts see Lange, *L. of Christ*, bk. ii. pt. ii. § 2; Eng. tr. i. 264. But must we not choose between admitting an objective appearance and rejecting the whole as a myth? To explain it as a "false perception" or optical delusion, *i.e.* a purely subjective result of psychological causes, seems to be not admissible. In that case Zacharias, like Lord Herbert of Cherbury,[1] would have accepted the sign which he supposed that he had received. To believe in the reality of a subjective appearance and not believe its testimony is a contradiction. Moreover, the psychological explanation leaves the dumbness to be explained. Again, we have similar appearances ver. 26, ii. 9, 13, xxii. 43, xxiv. 4. Can we accept here an explanation which is very difficult (ii. 9, 13) or inadmissible (xxiv. 4) elsewhere? Are all these cases of false perception? See Paley, *Evidences of Christianity*, prop. ii. ch. i.; Mill, *Pantheistic Principles*, ii. 1. 4, p. 123, 2nd ed. 1861; Edersh. *L. & T.* i. p. 142, ii. p. 751.

ἐκ δεξιῶν τοῦ θυσιαστηρίου. The place of honour. It was "the right side of the altar," not of Zacharias, who was facing it. Comp. Acts vii. 55, 56. The right side was the south side, and the Angel would be between the altar and the golden candlestick. On the left, or north side, of the altar was the table with the shewbread.

12. φόβος ἐπέπεσεν ἐπ' αὐτόν. Fear is natural when man becomes suddenly conscious of contact with the unseen: *Humanæ fragilitatis est spiritualis creaturæ visione turbari* (Bede). Comp. ii. 9, ix. 34; Judg. vi. 22, xiii. 22; Job iv. 15, etc. For the phrase comp. Acts xix. 17; Exod. xv. 16; Judith xv. 2. In class. Grk. the dat. is more usual: Thuc. iii. 87. 1; Xen. *Anab.* ii. 2. 19; Eur. *Andr.* 1042.

13. εἶπεν δὲ πρὸς αὐτόν. Both εἶπεν δέ and εἶπεν πρός are very freq. in Lk., who prefers εἶπεν δέ to καὶ εἶπεν even at the beginning of narratives, and uses πρὸς αὐτόν, αὐτούς, κ.τ.λ. in preference to αὐτῷ, αὐτοῖς, κ.τ.λ., after verbs of speaking, answering, etc., to an extent which is quite remarkable (*vv.* 18, 19, 34, 55, 61, 73, ii. 15, 18, 20, 34, 48, 49, etc. etc.). This πρός is so strong a mark of his style that it should be distinguished in translation: εἶπεν πρὸς αὐτόν, "He said *unto* him," and εἶπεν αὐτῷ, "He said *to* him." But not even RV. does this. See pp. lxii, lxiii.

Μὴ φοβοῦ. This gracious charge is specially common in Lk. (ver. 30, ii. 10, viii. 50, xii. 4, 7, 32; Acts xviii. 9, xxvii. 24). Bengel says of it, *Primum alloquium cœleste in aurora N.T. per Lucam amœnissime descripta.* Comp. Gen. xv. 1; Josh. viii. 1; Is. xliii. 1, 5, xliv. 2; Jer. xlvi. 27, 28; Dan. x. 12.

διότι. "Because," as generally in N.T. Comp. ii. 7, xxi. 28. It never means "therefore"; not Rom. i. 19 nor 1 Thes. ii. 18.

εἰσηκούσθη ἡ δέησίς σου. "Thy supplication was heard," at the time when it was offered. The pass. is used both of the petition (Acts x. 31; Ecclus. li. 11) and of the petitioner (Mt. vi. 7; Heb. v. 7). The word δέησις implies *personal need*; it is a "special petition for the supply of want" (Lft. on Phil. iv. 6; Trench, *Syn.* li.). Unlike προσευχή, it may be used of petitions to men. The word

[1] *Life*, written by himself, *sub fin.*, pp. 171 ff. ed. 1792, pp. 241 ff., ed. 1824

favours, but by no means proves, the view that the prayer of Zacharias was for a son. And the context at first seems to confirm this. But would Zacharias have made his private wishes the main subject of his prayer at so unique an opportunity? Would he have prayed for what he regarded as impossible? As Bede remarks, *Nemo orat quod se accepturum desperat.* Having prayed for it as possible, would he have refused to believe an Angel who told him that the petition was granted? It is much more probable that he and the people were praying for the redemption of Israel,—for the coming of the Messiah's kingdom; and it is this supplication which was heard. To make δέησις refer to habitual supplication, and not to the prayer offered with the incense, seems unnatural.

What Didon points out (p. 298) in quite a different connexion seems to have point here. It was an axiom with the Rabbins that a prayer in which there was no mention of the kingdom of God was no prayer at all (*Babyl.*, *Beracoth*, fol. 40, 2); and in the ritual of the temple the response of the people to the prayers of the priests was, "Blessed be the name of the glory of the Kingdom of God for ever" (*Babyl.*, *Taanith*, fol. 16, 2): *Jésus Christ*, ed. 1891. See also Edersh. *The Temple*, p. 127.

καὶ ἡ γυνή σου Ἐλεισάβετ γεννήσει υἱόν σοι. Not ἡ γυνὴ γάρ. "*For* thy wife shall bear thee a son" would have made it clear that the son was the answer to the δέησις. But "*and* thy wife shall bear thee a son" may mean that this is an *additional* boon, which (as ver. 17 shows) is to prepare the way for the blessing prayed for and granted. Thus, like Solomon, Zacharias receives the higher blessing for which he prayed, and also the lower blessing for which he did not pray.

Γεννάω is generally used of the father (Mt. i. 1–16; Acts vii. 8, 29; Gen. v. 3–30, xi. 10–28, etc.); but sometimes of the mother (ver. 57, xxiii. 29; Jn. xvi. 21). The best authorities give Ἰωάνης, with only one ν (WH. ii. App. p. 159). In LXX we have Ἰωάνης (2 Chron. xxviii. 12); Ἰωάναν 2 Chron. xvii. 15; Neh. xii. 13); Ἰωνάν (Neh. vi. 18); Ἰωνά (2 Kings xxv. 23; comp. Jn. xxi. 15–17). All these forms are abbreviations of Jehohanan, "Jehovah's gift," or "God is gracious." Gotthold is a German name of similar meaning. It was a Rabbinical saying that the names of six were given before they were born—Isaac, Ishmael, Moses, Solomon, Josiah, and Messiah.

14. πολλοὶ ἐπὶ τῇ γενέσει αὐτοῦ χαρήσονται. With the πολλοί here contrast παντὶ τῷ λαῷ in ii. 10. The joy at the appearance of a Prophet after centuries of need was immense, although not universal. The Pharisees did not dare to say that John was not a Prophet (Mt. xxi. 26); and Herod, until driven to it, did not dare to put him to death (Mt. xiv. 5). The word ἀγαλλίασις means "extreme joy, exultation." It is not class., but is freq. in LXX. Elsewhere in N.T. only ver. 44; Acts ii. 46; Jude 24; Heb. i. 9 (from Ps. xliv. 8).

In class. Grk. χαίρειν more often has the simple dat., but ἐπί is usual in N.T. (xiii. 17; Acts xv. 31; Mt. xviii. 13, etc.). It marks the *basis* of the joy. The reading γεννήσει (G X Γ) for γενέσει (ℵ A B C D) probably comes from γεννήσει in ver. 13.

15. ἔσται γὰρ μέγας ἐνώπιον [τοῦ] Κυρίου. For he shall be great in the truest sense of the term. Whatsoever a character man has before God, of that character he really is.

The adj. ἐνώπιος is found in Theocr. (xxii. 152) and in LXX, but ἐνώπιον as a prep. seems to be confined to LXX and N.T. It is not in Mt. or Mk., but is specially freq. in Lk. (*vv.* 17, 19, 75, iv. 7, v. 18, 25, etc.), as also in Rev. The phrase ἐνώπιον τοῦ κυρίου or Θεοῦ is a Hebraism (xii. 6, xvi. 15; Acts iv. 19, vii. 46, x. 31, 33; Judg. xi. 11; 1 Sam. x. 19; 2 Sam. v. 3, vi. 5). The preposition retains this meaning in modern Greek.

οἶνον καὶ σίκερα οὐ μὴ πίῃ. He is to drink neither wine nor any intoxicating liquor other than wine. The same Hebrew word is rendered sometimes σίκερα, sometimes μέθυσμα, and sometimes σίκερα μέθυσμα (Lev. x. 9; Num. vi. 3; Judg. xiii. 4, 7, 14). Wiclif here has "ne wine ne syder." See *D.B.*[2] art. "Drink, Strong." John is to be a Nazirite, not only for a time, as was usual, but for all his life, as Samson and Samuel. This is not disproved by the omission of the command not to cut his hair (Edersh. *The Temple*, p. 322). Eusebius (*Præp. Evang.* vi. 10. 8) has gen. σίκερος, and σικέρατος is also quoted; but σίκερα is usually undeclined.

πνεύματος ἁγίου πλησθήσεται. This is in obvious contrast to οἶνον καὶ σίκερα. In place of the physical excitement of strong drink he is to have the supernatural inspiration of the Holy Spirit. The whole phrase is peculiar to Lk. (*vv.* 41, 67; Acts ii. 4, iv. 8, 31, ix. 17, xiii. 9); and the two elements of it are specially characteristic of him. Excepting Mt. xxii. 10, xxvii. 48, the verb πίμπλημι occurs only in Lk., who uses it twenty-two times. Mt. has the expression "Holy Spirit" five times, Mk. and Jn. each four times. Lk. has it fifty-three times, of which twelve are in the Gospel. He uses three forms: πνεῦμα ἅγιον (i. 15, 35, 41, 67, [ii. 25,] iii. 16, iv. 1, xi. 13); τὸ ἅγιον πνεῦμα (xii. 10, 12); and τὸ πνεῦμα τὸ ἅγιον (ii. 26, iii. 22). According to Schoettgen (i. p 255), "to be filled with the Holy Spirit is" *locutio Judæis familiaris.* He gives one example. Comp. the contrast in Eph. v. 18.

ἔτι ἐκ κοιλίας μητρὸς αὐτοῦ. A Hebraism (Ps. xxii. 11, lxxi. 6; Is. xlix. 1, 5: comp. Judg. xiii. 5, 7, xvi. 17; Job xxxi. 18, etc.); instead of the more classical ἐκ γενετῆς, with or without εὐθύς (Hom. *Il.* xxiv. 535, *Od.* xviii. 6; Arist. *Eth. Nic.* vi. 13. 1, vii. 14. 4, viii. 12. 6). For the ἔτι comp. ἔτι ἐκ βρέφεος, ἔτι ἀπ' ἀρχῆς ἔτι καὶ ἐκ παρόντων, where ἔτι seems to mean "even." The expression does not imply that John was filled with the Spirit before he was born (ver. 41). In LXX κοιλία is often used of the womb (see esp. Jer. i. 5); but this is very rare in class. Grk.

16, 17. The two personal characteristics just stated—subjection of the flesh and sovereignty of the spirit—will manifest themselves in two external effects,—a great religious revival and the preparation for the Messianic kingdom. The first of these was the recognized work of every Prophet. Israel, through sin, was constantly being alienated from God; and it was one of the chief functions of a Prophet to convert the people to God again (Jer. iii. 7, 10, 14, xviii. 8; Ezek. iii. 19; Dan. ix. 13).

καὶ αὐτός. The personal pronouns are much more used in N.T. than in class. Grk., esp. in the oblique cases. But even in the nom. the pronoun is sometimes inserted, although there is little or no emphasis. Lk. is very fond of beginning sentences with *καὶ αὐτός*, even where *αὐτός* can hardly mean "he on his part," as distinct from others (iii. 23, v. 14, 17, vi. 20, etc.). In *προελεύσεται* we have another mark of Lk.'s style. Excepting Mk. vi. 33 and 2 Cor. ix. 5, the verb is peculiar to Lk. in N.T. (xxii. 47; Acts xii. 10, xx. 5?, 13).

ἐνώπιον αὐτοῦ. "Before God," who comes to His people in the person of the Messiah (Is. xl. 1–11; Mal. iii. 1–5). It is unlikely that *αὐτοῦ* means the Messiah, who has not yet been mentioned. There is no analogy with αὐτὸς ἔφα, *ipse dixit*, where the pronoun refers to some one so well known that there is no need to mention him by name. For **ἐνώπιον** see on ver. 15; and for **δύναμις**, on iv. 14, 36. Elijah is mentioned, not as a worker of miracles, for "John did no sign" (Jn. x. 41), but as a preacher of repentance: it was in this that the Baptist had his spirit and power. For Rabbinic traditions respecting Elijah as the Forerunner see Edersh. *L. & T.* ii. p. 706. Comp. Justin, *Try.* xlix.

The omission of the articles before *πνεύματι* and *δυνάμει* is probably due to the influence of an Aramaic original, in which the gen. which follows would justify the omission. Proper names in *-ας* pure commonly have gen. in *-ου* (Mt. i. 6, iii. 3); but here Ἠλεία is the true reading.

ἐπιστρέψαι καρδίας πατέρων ἐπὶ τέκνα. The literal interpretation here makes good sense, and perhaps, on the whole, it is the best. In the moral degradation of the people even parental affection had languished: comp. Ecclus. xlviii. 10. Genuine reform strengthens family ties; whatever weakens them is no true reform. Or the meaning may be that the patriarchs will no longer be ashamed of their offspring: comp. Is. lxiii. 16. In any case, **ἀπειθεῖς** is not to be referred to **τέκνα**. It is not the disobedience of children to parents that is meant, but that of the Jews to God.

The Vulg. renders *ἀπειθεῖς* by *incredibiles*, for which some MSS. have *incredulos*: comp. *dissociabilis*, *penetrabilis* for adjectives in *-bilis* with this force. Lat. Vet. varies: *ineruditos* (*f*), *non consentientes* (*d*), *contumaces* (*e*).

ἐν φρονήσει δικαίων. The prep. of rest after a verb of motion expresses the result of the motion (vii. 17; Mt. xiv. 3): "Turn them *so as to be* in the wisdom of the just." For *φρόνησις* see Lft. on Col. i. 9: the word occurs only here and Eph. i. 8 in N.T. De Wette, Bleek, and others maintain that φρόνησις here means simply "disposition," *Gesinnung*. In what follows it is better to make ἑτοιμάσαι dependent upon ἐπιστρέψαι, not co-ordinate with it. The preparation is the consequence of the conversion, and the final object of the προελεύσεται: *ne Dominus populum imparatum majestate sua obterat* (Beng.).

18. Κατὰ τί γνώσομαι τοῦτο; The very question asked by Abraham (Gen. xv. 8): "In accordance with what shall I obtain knowledge of this?" *i.e.* What shall be in harmony with it, so as to be a sign of it? Comp. the cases of Gideon (Judg. vi. 36–39) and of Hezekiah (2 Kings xx. 8), who asked for signs; also of Moses (Exod. iv. 2–6) and of Ahaz (Is. vii. 11), to whom signs were given unasked. The spirit in which such requests are made may vary much, although the form of request may be the same; and the fact that Zacharias had all these instances to instruct him made his unbelief the less excusable. By his ἐγὼ γάρ εἰμι, κ.τ.λ., he almost implies that the Angel must have forgotten the fact.

19. ἀποκριθεὶς ὁ ἄγγελος εἶπεν. In Attic ἀποκρίνομαι, in Homeric and Ionic ὑποκρίνομαι, is used in the sense of "answering." In N.T. ὑποκρίνομαι occurs only once (xx. 20), and there of "acting a part," not "answering": comp. 2 Mac. v. 25. But ἀποκριθείς for the class. ἀποκρινάμενος (which is rare in N.T.) marks the decay of the middle voice. In bibl. Grk. the middle voice is dying; in mod. Grk. it is dead. Machon, a comic poet about B.C. 250, is perhaps the earliest writer who uses ἀπεκρίθην like ἀπεκρινάμην in the sense of "replied, answered." In LXX, as in N.T., ἀπεκρινάμην is rare (Judg. v. 29 [A]; 1 Kings ii. 1; 1 Chron. x. 13). See Veitch, *Greek Verbs*, p. 78.

19. Ἐγώ εἰμι Γαβριήλ. Gabriel answers his ἐγώ εἰμι with another. "Thou art old, and not likely to have children, but I am one whose word is to be believed": ἀγγέλῳ ἀπιστεῖς, καὶ τῷ ἀποστείλαντι (Eus.). The names of two heavenly beings are given us in Scripture, Gabriel (Dan. viii. 16, ix. 21) and Michael (Dan. x. 13, 21, xii. 1; Jude 9; Rev. xii. 7); other names were given in the later Jewish tradition. It is one thing to admit that such names are of foreign origin, quite another to assert that the belief which they represent is an importation. Gabriel, the "Man of God," seems to be the representative of angelic ministry to man; Michael, "Who is like God," the representative of angelic opposition to Satan. In Scripture Gabriel is the angel of mercy, Michael the angel of judgment. In Jewish legend the reverse is the case, proving that the Bible does not borrow Jewish fables. In the Targums Gabriel destroys Sennacherib's army; in the O.T. he instructs and comforts Daniel. The Rabbis said that Michael flies in one flight, Gabriel in two, Elijah in four, and Death in eight; *i.e.* mercy is swifter than judgment, and judgment is swifter than destruction. See Hastings, *D.B.* i. p. 97; *D.C.G.* i. p. 55.

ὁ παρεστηκὼς ἐνώπιον τοῦ Θεοῦ. See on ver. 15. Gabriel is "the angel of His presence" (Is. lxiii. 9; comp. Mt. xviii. 10). "Standing before" implies ministering. In LXX the regular phrase is παραστῆναι ἐνώπιον (Job i. 6, which is a close parallel to this; 1 Kings xvii. 1, xviii. 15; 2 Kings iii. 14, v. 16). It is also used of service to a king (1 Kings x. 8). But when Gehazi "stood before his master," we have παρειστήκει πρὸς τὸν κύριον αὐτοῦ (2 Kings v. 25).

Only here and ix. 27 does Lk. use the unsyncopated form of the perf. part. of ἵστημι and its compounds. Elsewhere he prefers ἑστώς to ἑστηκώς (i. 11, v. 1, 2, xviii. 13; Acts iv. 14, vii. 55, etc.). In Mt. xxvii. 47 and Mk. ix. 1 and xi. 5, ἑστηκότων is the right reading. In Jn. the unsyncopated form is common.

ἀπεστάλην λαλῆσαι πρὸς σὲ καὶ εὐαγγελίσασθαί σοι ταῦτα. This reminds Zacharias of the extraordinary favour shown to him, and so coldly welcomed by him. It is the first use in the Gospel narrative of the word which was henceforward to be so current, and to mean so much. In LXX it is used of any good tidings (2 Sam. i. 20; 1 Chron. x. 9), but especially of communications respecting the Messiah (Is. xl. 9, lii. 7, lx. 6, lxi. 1). See on ii. 10 and iii. 18.

20. καὶ ἰδοὺ ἔσῃ σιωπῶν καὶ μὴ δυνάμενος λαλῆσαι. The ἰδού is Hebraistic, but is not rare in class. Grk. It introduces something new with emphasis. *Signum poscenti datur congruum, quamvis non optatum* (Beng.). The analytical form of the fut. marks the duration of the silence (comp. v. 10, vi. 40?, xvii. 35?, xxi. 17); and μὴ δυνάμενος, κ.τ.λ., is added to show that the silence is not a voluntary act, but the sign which was asked for (comp. Dan. x. 15). Thus his wrong request is granted in a way which is at once a judgment and a blessing; for the unbelief is cured by the punishment. For σιωπάω of dumbness comp. 4 Mac. x. 18.

We have here one of many parallels in expression between Gospel and Acts. Comp. this with Acts xiii. 11; i. 39 with Acts i. 15; i. 66 with Acts xi. 21; ii. 9 with Acts xii. 7; xv. 20 with Acts xx. 37; xxi. 18 with Acts xxvii. 34; xxiv. 19 with Acts vii. 22.

In N.T. μή with the participle is the common constr., and in mod. Grk. it is the invariable use. In Lk. there is only one instance of οὐ with a participle (vi. 42). See Win. lv. 5. β, pp. 607–610; Lft. *Epp. of St. Paul*, p. 39, 1895. The combination of the negative with the positive statement of the same thing, although found in class. Grk., is more common in Heb. literature. In Acts xiii. 11 we have ἔσῃ τυφλὸς μὴ βλέπων; comp. Jn. i. 3, 20, iii. 16, x. 5, 18, xviii. 20, xx. 27; Rev. ii. 13, iii. 9; Ps. lxxxix. 30, 31, 48; 2 Sam. xiv. 5; Is. xxxviii. 1, etc.

ἄχρι ἧς ἡμέρας. Gal. iii. 19 is the only certain exception to the rule that ἄχρι, not ἄχρις, usually precedes vowels in N.T. Comp. xvii. 27, xxi. 24, and see on xvi. 16. For the attraction, comp. Acts i. 2; Mt. xxiv. 38. Attractions are specially freq. in Lk. See on iii. 10; also Blass, *Gr.* pp. 169, 214.

ἀνθ᾽ ὧν. Only in this phrase does ἀντί suffer elision in N.T. It is equivalent to ἀντὶ τούτων ὅτι, "for that, because" (xix. 44; Acts xii. 23; 2 Thes. ii. 10; Lev. xxvi. 43; 2 Kings xxii. 17; Ezek. v. 11). It is found in class. Grk. (Soph. *Ant.* 1068; Aristoph. *Plut.* 434).

οἵτινες. Stronger than the simple relative: "which are of such a character that." Comp. ii. 10, vii. 37, 39, viii. 3, 15. Almost always in nom.

εἰς τὸν καιρὸν αὐτῶν. That which takes place in a time may be regarded as entering into that time: the words go on to their fulfilment. Comp. *εἰς τὸ μέλλον* (xiii. 9) and *εἰς τὸ μεταξὺ σάββατον* (Acts xiii. 42).

21. ἦν ὁ λαὸς προσδοκῶν. As in ver. 20, the analytical tense marks the duration of the action. Zacharias was longer than was customary; and the Talmud states that the priests were accustomed to return soon to prevent anxiety. It was feared that in so sacred a place they might incur God's displeasure, and be slain (Lev. xvi. 13). Hence **ἐθαύμαζον ἐν τῷ χρονίζειν**, "They were wondering *while* he tarried." Comp. ver. 8, and see on iii. 21. The common rendering, "*at* his tarrying," or "because he tarried," *quod tardaret*, is improbable even if possible. This would have been otherwise expressed: *ἐθαύμαζον ἐπί* (ii. 33, iv. 22, ix. 43, etc.), which D reads here; or *διά* (Mk. vi. 6; Jn. vii. 21?); or *ὅτι* (xi. 38; Jn. iii. 7, iv. 27); or *περί* (ii. 18).

22. οὐκ ἐδύνατο λαλῆσαι αὐτοῖς. He ought to pronounce the benediction (Num. vi. 24-26) from the steps, either alone or with other priests. His look and his inability to speak told them at once that something extraordinary had taken place; and the sacred circumstances would suggest a supernatural appearance, even if his signs did not make this clear to them.

The compound **ἐπέγνωσαν** implies clear recognition and full knowledge (v. 22, xxiv. 16, 31); and the late form **ὀπτασίαν** (for *ὄψιν*) is commonly used of supernatural sights (xxiv. 23; Acts xxvi. 19; 2 Cor. xii. 1; Dan. ix. 23, x. 1, 7, 8, 16). For **καὶ αὐτός**, "he on his part," as distinct from the congregation, see on ver. 17, and Win. xxii. 4. b, p. 187. The periphrastic tense **ἦν διανεύων** again calls attention to the continued action. The verb is found here only in N.T., but occurs twice in LXX (Ps. xxxiv. 19; Ecclus. xxvii. 22). In **διέμεινε κωφός** both the compound and the tense emphasize the fact that it was no mere temporary seizure (xxii. 28; Gal. ii. 5; 2 Pet. iii. 4).

23. ὡς ἐπλήσθησαν αἱ ἡμέραι τῆς λειτουργίας αὐτοῦ. When the week for which the course of Abijah was on duty for public service was at an end. See on *vv.* 15 and 57. In class. Grk. **λειτουργία** (**λεώς**, *ἔργον*) is freq. of public service undertaken by a citizen at his own expense. In bibl. Grk. it is used of priestly service in the worship of God (Heb. viii. 6, ix. 21; Num. viii. 22, xvi. 9, xviii. 4; 2 Chron. xxxi. 2), and also of service to the needy (2 Cor. ix. 12; Phil. ii. 30). See Deissmann, *Bible Studies*, p. 140.

ἀπῆλθεν εἰς τὸν οἶκον αὐτοῦ. This was not in Jerusalem, in the Ophel quarter, where many of the priests resided, but in an unnamed town in the hill-country south of Jerusalem (ver. 39). It is probable that most of the priests who did not live in the city itself resided in the towns and villages in the neighbourhood. Convenience would suggest that they should live inside Judæa. In Neh. xi. 10-19 we have 1192 priests in Jerusalem; in 1 Chron. ix.

13 we have 1760. Later authorities speak of 24,000; but such figures are very untrustworthy. The whole question of the residences of the priests is an obscure one, and Josh. xxi. must not be quoted as evidence for more than a projected arrangement. That it was carried into effect and *maintained*, or that it was revived after the Exile, is a great deal more than we know. Schürer, *Jewish People in the T. of J. C.* ii. 1, p. 229.

24. συνέλαβεν. The word occurs eleven times in Lk. against five times elsewhere. He alone uses it in the sense of conceiving offspring, and only in these first two chapters (*vv.* 31, 36, ii. 21). This sense is common in medical writers and in Aristotle. Hobart remarks that the number of words referring to pregnancy and barrenness used by Lk. is almost as great as that used by Hippocrates: ἐν γαστρὶ ἔχειν (xxi. 23), ἔγκυος (ii. 5), στεῖρα (i. 7), ἄτεκνος (xx. 28). And, excepting ἐν γαστρὶ ἔχειν, all of these are peculiar to himself in N.T. (*Med. Lang. of Lk.* p. 91).

περιέκρυβεν ἑαυτὴν μῆνας πέντε. The reflexive pronoun brings out more forcibly than the middle voice would have done that the act was entirely her own (Acts xxiii. 14; 1 Cor. xi. 31; 1 Jn. i. 8); and the compound verb implies *all round*, *complete* concealment. Her motive can only be conjectured; but the enigmatical conduct and remark are evidence of historic truth, for they would not be likely to be invented. The five months are the first five months; and at the end of them it would be evident that she had ceased to be ἡ στεῖρα (ver. 36). During these five months she did not wish to risk hearing a reproach, which had ceased to be true, but which she would not care to dispute. She withdrew, therefore, until all must know that the reproach had been removed.

The form ἔκρυβον is late: in class. Grk. ἔκρυψα is used. But a present κρύβω is found, of which this might be the imperfect.

It can hardly be accidental that μήν is scarcely ever used in N.T. in a literal sense by any writer except Lk., who has it five times in his Gospel and five times in the Acts. The chronological details involved in this frequent use are the results of the careful investigation of which he writes in the preface. The other passages are Gal. iv. 10; Jas. v. 17, and six times in Revelation. So also ἔτος occurs fifteen times in Lk. and six in Mt. Mk. and Jn.

25. ἐπεῖδεν ἀφελεῖν ὄνειδός μου ἐν ἀνθρώποις. The object of ἐπεῖδεν is neither ἐμέ understood (as all English Versions except Wic. and Rhem.) nor τὸ ὄνειδός μου (Hofmann), but ἀφελεῖν: "watched to take away, taken care to remove." The constr. seems to be unique; but comp. Acts xv. 14. Alford and Holtzmann translate "hath deigned, condescended to remove"; but can ἐπεῖδεν mean that? Elsewhere in N.T. it occurs only Acts iv. 29; but in class. Grk. it is specially used of the gods regarding human affairs (Aesch. *Suppl.* 1. 1031; *Sept.* 485). Hdt. i. 124. 2 is not rightly quoted as parallel. Omitting ἐπεῖδεν, Rachel makes the same remark: Ἀφεῖλεν ὁ Θεός μου τὸ ὄνειδος (Gen. xxx. 23; comp. Ps. cxiii. 9; Is. iv. 1); but the different position of the μου is worth noting. In ἐν ἀνθρώποις we have another amphibolous expression (see on ver. 8). It may be taken with ἀφελεῖν, but more probably it belongs to τὸ ὄνειδός μου (ver. 36).

26–38. *The Annunciation of the Birth of the Saviour.*[1]

The birth of the Baptist is parallel to the birth of Isaac; that of the Messiah to the creation of Adam. Jesus is the second Adam. But once more there is no violent breach with the past. Even in its revolutions Providence is conservative. Just as the Prophet who is to renovate Israel is taken from the old priesthood, so the Christ who is to redeem the human race is not created out of nothing, but "born of a woman."

26. εἰς πόλιν τῆς Γαλιλαίας ᾗ ὄνομα Ναζαρέτ. The description perhaps implies that Lk. is writing for those who are not familiar with the geography of Palestine. There is no reason for believing that he himself was unfamiliar with it. Comp. ver. 39, iv. 31, vii. 11, viii. 26, ix. 10, xvii. 11, xix. 29, 37, 41.

Galilee is one of many geographical names which have gradually extended their range. It was originally a little "circuit" of territory round Kadesh-Naphtali containing the towns given by Solomon to Hiram (1 Kings ix. 11). This was called the "circuit of the Gentiles," because the inhabitants were strangers (1 Mac. v. 15, Γαλ. ἀλλοφύλων). But it grew, until in the time of Christ it included the territory of Naphtali, Asher, Zebulon, and Issachar (*D.B.*[2] i. p. 1117). For a description of this region see Jos. *B. J.* iii. 3. 1–3. *Nazareth* is mentioned neither in O.T. nor in Josephus, but it was probably not a new town in our Lord's time. The site is an attractive one, in a basin among the south ridges of Lebanon. The sheltered valley is very fruitful, and abounds in flowers. From the hill behind the town the view over Lebanon, Hermon, Carmel, the Mediterranean, Gilead, Tabor, Gilboa, the plain of Esdraelon, and the mountains of Samaria, is very celebrated (Renan, *Vie de J.* p. 27). It would seem as if Mt. (ii. 23) was not aware that Nazareth was the original home of Joseph and Mary.

---

[1] "It has been argued that the different modes in which God is recorded to have communicated with men, in St. Matthew by dreams and in St. Luke by Angels, show the extent of the subjective influence of the writer's mind upon the narrative. But surely those are right who see in this difference the use of various means adapted to the peculiar state of the recipient. Moreover, as St. Matthew recognizes the ministry of Angels (xxviii. 2), so St. Luke relates Visions (Acts x. 9–16, xvi. 9, xviii. 9, 10). . . . It is to be noticed that the contents of the divine messages (Matt. i. 20, 21; Luke i. 30–33) are related conversely to the general character of the Gospels, as a consequence of the difference of character in those to whom they are addressed. The promise of Redemption is made to Joseph; of a glorious Kingdom to the Virgin" (Wsctt. *Int. to Gospels*, p. 317, 7th ed.). See Hastings, *D.B.* i. p. 93.

The form of the name of the town varies much, between Nazareth, Nazaret, Nazara, and Nazarath. Keim has twice contended strongly for Nazara (*J. of Naz.*, Eng. tr. ii. p. 16, iv. p. 108); but he has not persuaded many of the correctness of his conclusions. WH. consider that "the evidence when tabulated presents little ambiguity" (ii. App. p. 160). Ναζαράθ is found frequently (eight out of eleven times) in Codex Δ, but hardly anywhere else. Ναζαρά is used once by Mt. (iv. 13), and perhaps once by Lk. (iv. 16). Ναζαρέθ occurs once in Mt. (xxi. 11) and once in Acts (x. 38). Everywhere else (Mt. ii. 23; Mk. i. 9; Lk. i. 26, ii. 4, 39, 51; Jn. i. 46, 47) we have certainly or probably Ναζαρέτ. Thus Mt. uses the three possible forms equally; Lk. all three with a decided preference for Nazaret; while Mk. and Jn. use Nazaret only. This appears to be fairly conclusive for Nazaret. Yet Scrivener holds that "regarding the orthography of this word no reasonable certainty is to be attained" (*Int. to Crit. of N.T.* ii. p. 316); and Alford seems to be of a similar opinion (i. *Prolegom.* p. 97). Weiss thinks that Nazara may have been the original form, but that it had already become unusual when the Gospels were written. The modern town is called *En Nazirah*, and is shunned by Jews. Its population of 5000 is mainly Christian, with a few Mahometans.

27. ἐμνηστευμένην. This is the N.T. form of the word (ii. 5): in LXX we have *μεμνηστευμ.* (Deut. xxii. 23). The interval between betrothal and marriage was commonly a year, during which the bride lived with her friends. But her property was vested in her future husband, and unfaithfulness on her part was punished, like adultery, with death (Deut. xxii. 23, 24). The case of the woman taken in adultery was probably a case of this kind.

ἐξ οἴκου Δαυείδ. It is unnecessary, and indeed impossible, to decide whether these words go with *ἀνδρί*, or with *παρθένον*, or with both. The last is the least probable, but Chrysostom and Wieseler support it. From *vv.* 32 and 69 we may with probability infer that Lk. regards Mary as descended from David. In ii. 4 he states this of Joseph. Independently of the present verse, therefore, we may infer that, just as John was of priestly descent both by Zacharias and Elisabeth, so Jesus was of royal descent both by Mary and Joseph. The title "Son of David" was publicly given to Jesus and never disputed (Mt. i. 1, ix. 27, xii. 23, xv. 22, xx. 30, 31; Mk. x. 47, 48; Lk. xviii. 38, 39). In the *Test. XII. Patr.* Christ is said to be descended from *Levi* and Judah (*Simeon* vii.); and the same idea is found in a fragment of Irenæus (*Frag.* xvii., Stieren, p. 836). It was no doubt based, as Schleiermacher bases it (*St. Luke*, Eng. tr. p. 28), on the fact that Elisabeth, who was of Levi, was related to Mary (see on ver. 36). The repetition involved in **τῆς παρθένου** is in favour of taking *ἐξ οἴκου Δαυείδ* with *ἀνδρί*: otherwise we should have expected *αὐτῆς*. But this is not conclusive.

28. Χαῖρε, κεχαριτωμένη.[1] Note the alliteration and the con-

[1] The *Ave Maria* as a liturgical address to the Virgin consists of three parts, two of which are scriptural and one not. The first two parts, "Hail, Mary, full of grace; the Lord is with thee," and "Blessed art thou among

nexion between χαῖρε and χάρις. The *gratia plena* of the Vulg. is too indefinite. It is right, if it means "full of grace, *which thou hast received*"; wrong, if it means "full of grace, *which thou hast to bestow*." From Eph. i. 6 and the analogy of verbs in -όω, κεχαριτωμένη must mean "endued with grace" (Ecclus. xviii. 17). *Non ut mater gratiæ, sed ut filia gratiæ* (Beng.). What follows explains κεχαριτωμένη, for with μετὰ σοῦ we understand ἐστι, not ἔστω (comp. Judg. vi. 12). It is because the Lord is with her that she is endued with grace. Tyn., Cov., and Cran., no less than Wic. and Rhem., have "full of grace"; Genev. has "freely beloved." See Resch, *Kindheitsev.* p. 78.

The familiar εὐλογημένη σὺ ἐν γυναιξίν, although well attested (A C D X Γ Δ Π, Latt. Syrr. Aeth. Goth., Tert. Eus.), probably is an interpolation borrowed from ver. 42: ℵ B L, Aegyptt. Arm. omit.

29. Here also ἰδοῦσα (A), for which some Latin texts have *cum audisset*, is an interpolation borrowed perhaps from ver. 12. It is not stated that Mary saw Gabriel. The pronominal use of the article (ἡ δέ) is rare in N.T. (Acts i. 6; Mt. ii. 5, 9). It is confined to phrases with μέν and δέ, and mostly to nom. masc. and fem.

διεταράχθη. Here only in N.T. It is stronger than ἐταράχθη in ver. 12. Neither Zacharias nor Mary are accustomed to visions or voices: they are troubled by them. There is no evidence of hysterical excitement or hallucination in either case. The **διελογίζετο**, "reckoned up different reasons," is in itself against this. The verb is confined to the Synoptic Gospels (v. 21, 22; Mk. ii. 6, 8): Jn. xi. 50 the true reading is λογίζεσθε.

ποταπός. In N.T. this adj. never has the local signification, "from what country or nation?" *cujas*? (Aesch. *Cho.* 575; Soph. *O.C.* 1160). It is synonymous with ποῖος, a use which is found in Demosthenes; and it always implies astonishment, with or without admiration (vii. 39; Mt. viii. 27; Mk. xiii. 1; 2 Pet. iii. 11; 1 Jn. iii. 1). In LXX it does not occur. The original form is ποδαπός, and may come from ποῦ ἀπό; but -δαπος is perhaps a mere termination.

εἴη. It is only in Lk. in N.T. that we find the opt. in indirect questions. In him it is freq. both without ἄν (iii. 15, viii. 9, xxii. 23; Acts xvii. 11, xxi. 33, xxv. 20) and with ἄν (vi. 11; Acts v. 24, x. 17). In Acts viii. 31 we have opt. with ἄν in a direct question. Simcox, *Lang. of N.T.* p. 112; Win. xli. 4. c, p. 374.

30. Μὴ φοβοῦ, Μαριάμ, εὗρες γὰρ χάριν παρὰ τῷ Θεῷ. See on

women, and blessed is the fruit of thy womb" (ver. 42), are first found in the *Liber Antiphonianus* attributed to Gregory the Great; and they were authorized as a formula to be taught with the Creed and the Lord's Prayer, *c.* A.D. 1198. The third part, "Holy Mary, Mother of God, pray for us sinners now and at the hour of death," was added in the fifteenth century, and was authorized by Pope Pius v. in 1568.

ver. 13. The εὗρες χάριν π. τ. Θ. explains κεχαριτωμένη. The phrase is Hebraic: Νῶε εὗρεν χάριν ἐναντίον Κυρίου τοῦ Θεοῦ (Gen. vi. 8; comp. xviii. 3, xxxix. 4). See on iv. 22.

συλλήμψῃ. For the word see on ver. 24, and for the form comp. ii. 21, xx. 47; Acts i. 8, ii. 38, xxiii. 27; Jn. v. 43, xvi. 14, 24. In Ionic we have fut. λάμψομαι. Veitch, p. 359; Win. v. 4 f, p. 54.

ἐν γαστρὶ καὶ τέξῃ υἱόν, καὶ καλέσεις τὸ ὄνομα. The same wording is found Gen. xvi. 11 of Ishmael, and Is. vii. 14 of Immanuel. Comp. Gen. xvii. 19 of Isaac, and Mt. i. 21 of Jesus. In all cases the καλέσεις is not a continuation of the prophecy, but a command, as in most of the Ten Commandments (Mt. v. 21, 27, 33; comp. Lk. iv. 12; Acts xxiii. 5, etc.). Win. xliii. 5. c, p. 396. The name Ἰησοῦς was revealed independently to Joseph also (Mt. i. 21). It appears in the various forms of Oshea, Hoshea, Jehoshua, Joshua, Jeshua, and Jesus. Its meaning is "Jehovah is help," or "God the Saviour." See Pearson, *On the Creed*, art. ii. *sub init.* p. 131, ed. 1849. See also Resch, *Kindheitsev.* pp. 80, 95.

32. οὗτος ἔσται μέγας. As in ver. 15, this is forthwith explained; and the greatness of Jesus is very different from the greatness of John. The title **υἱὸς Ὑψίστου** expresses some very close relation between Jesus and Jehovah, but not the Divine Sonship in the Trinity; comp. vi. 35. On the same principle as Θεός and Κύριος, Ὕψιστος is anarthrous: there can be only one Highest (Ecclus. vii. 15, xvii. 26, xix. 17, xxiv. 2, 23, xxix. 11, etc.). The **κληθήσεται** is not a mere substitute for ἔσται: He not only shall be the Son of God, but shall be recognized as such. In the *Acta Pauli et Theclæ* we have Μακάριοι οἱ σοφίαν λαβόντες Ἰησοῦ Χριστοῦ, ὅτι αὐτοὶ υἱοὶ ὑψίστου κληθήσονται (Tischendorf, p. 239). For **τὸν θρόνον Δαυείδ** comp. 2 Sam. vii. 12, 13; Is. ix. 6, 7, xvi. 5.

Δαυείδ τοῦ πατρὸς αὐτοῦ. This is thought to imply the Davidic descent of Mary; but the inference is not quite certain. Jesus was the heir of Joseph, as both genealogies imply. Comp. Ps. cxxxii. 11; Hos. iii. 5. There is abundant evidence of the belief that the Messiah would spring from David: Mk. xii. 35, x. 47, xi. 10; Lk. xviii. 38, xx. 41; 4 Ezra xii. 32 (Syr. Arab. Arm.); *Ps. Sol.* xvii. 23, 24; Talmud and Targums. See on Rom. i. 3.

33. βασιλεύσει . . . εἰς τοὺς αἰῶνας. Comp. "But of the Son he saith, God is Thy throne for ever and ever" (Heb. i. 8, where see Wsctt.); also Dan. ii. 44, vii. 14; Jn. xii. 34; Rev. xi. 15. The eternity of Christ's kingdom is assured by the fact that it is to be absorbed in the kingdom of the Father (1 Cor. xv. 24–28). These magnificent promises could hardly have been invented by a writer who was a witness of the condition of the Jews during the half century which followed the destruction of Jerusalem. Indeed, we may perhaps go further and say that "it breathes the spirit of the Messianic hope before it had received the rude and crushing blow in the rejection of the Messiah" (Gore, *Dissertations*, p. 16). Comp. *vv.* 17, 54, 55, 68–71, ii. 38.

The constr. *βασιλεύειν ἐπί c. acc.* is not classical. **We have it again xix.** 14, 27.

34. Πῶς ἔσται τοῦτο. She does not ask for *proof*, as Zacharias did (ver. 18); and only in the form of the words does she ask as to the mode of accomplishment. Her utterance is little more than an involuntary expression of amazement: *non dubitantis sed admirantis* (Grotius). In contrasting her with Zacharias, Ambrose says, *Hæc jam de negotio tractat; ille adhuc de nuntio dubitat.* It is clear that she does not doubt the fact promised, nor for a moment suppose that her child is to be the child of Joseph.

ἐπεὶ ἄνδρα οὐ γινώσκω. Comp. Gen. xix. 8; Judg. xi. 39; Num. xxxi. 17. The words are the avowal of a maiden conscious of her own purity; and they are drawn from her by the strange declaration that she is to have a son before she is married. It is very unnatural to understand the words as a vow of perpetual virginity, or as stating that such a vow has already been taken, or is about to be taken. It is difficult to reconcile *οὐκ ἐγίνωσκεν* (imperf., not aor.) *αὐτὴν ἕως* (Mt. i. 25) with any such vow.[1]

35. Πνεῦμα ἅγιον ἐπελεύσεται ἐπὶ σέ. It may be doubted whether the article is omitted "because Holy Spirit is here a proper name"; rather because it is regarded impersonally as the creative power of God. Comp. *καὶ πνεῦμα Θεοῦ ἐπεφέρετο ἐπάνω τοῦ ὕδατος* (Gen. i. 2): the two passages are very parallel. See on ver. 15. Both *πνεῦμα* and *ἅγιον* have special point. It is spirit and not flesh, what is holy and not what is sinful, that is to produce this effect in her. With *ἐπελεύσεται ἐπὶ σέ* comp. Acts i. 8. Excepting Eph. ii. 7 and Jas. v. 1, the verb is peculiar to Lk. (xi. 22, xxi. 26; Acts i. 8, viii. 24, xiii. 40, xiv. 19).

δύναμις Ὑψίστου ἐπισκιάσει σοι. For **δύναμις** see on iv. 14; for **ἐπισκιάσει** comp. the account of the Transfiguration (ix. 34), and for the dat. comp. the account of Peter's shadow (Acts v. 15). It is the idea of the Shechinah which is suggested here (Exod. xl. 38). The cloud of glory signified the Divine presence and power, and it is under such influence that Mary is to become a mother.

διό. This illative particle is rare in the Gospels (vii. 7; Mt. xxvii. 8); not in Mk. or Jn.

τὸ γεννώμενον ἅγιον κληθήσεται υἱὸς Θεοῦ. "The holy thing which shall be born shall be called the Son of God," or, "That which

[1] H. Lasserre renders *puisque je n'ai nul rapport avec mon mari*, and explains that *ἀνήρ signifie* mari, epoux; *et la phrase marque la voeu de virginité conjugale fait par Marie* (pp. 265, 564, ed. 1887). It is impossible that **ἄνδρα**, without either article or possessive pronoun, can mean "my husband."

shall be born shall be called holy, the Son of God." The latter of these two renderings seems to be preferable. Comp. ἅγιον τῷ κυρίῳ κληθήσεται (ii. 22); Ναζωραῖος κληθήσεται (Mt. ii. 23); υἱοὶ Θεοῦ κληθήσονται (v. 9); ἐλάχιστος κληθήσεται and μέγας κλ. (v. 19). In all cases the appellation *precedes* the verb. The unborn child is called ἅγιον as being free from all taint of sin. *De hoc Sancto idem angelus est locutus*, Dan. ix. 24 (Beng.). The ἐκ σοῦ, which many authorities insert after γεννώμενον, is probably an ancient gloss, derived perhaps from Mt. i. 16: ℵ A B C[3] D and most versions omit.

The title "Son of God," like "Son of Man," was a recognized designation of the Messiah. In *Enoch*, and often in 4 Ezra, the Almighty speaks of the Messiah as His Son. Christ seldom used it of Himself (Mt. xxvii. 43; Jn. x. 36). But we have it in the voice from heaven (iii. 22, ix. 35); in Peter's confession (Mt. xvi. 16); in the centurion's exclamation (Mk. xv. 39); in the devil's challenge (iv. 3, 9); in the cries of demoniacs (Mk. iii. 11, v. 7). Very early the Christian Church chose it as a concise statement of the divine nature of Christ. See on Rom. i. 4, and Swete, *Apost. Creed*, p. 24. For ἅγιον see on Rom. i. 7. The radical meaning is "set apart for God, consecrated."

36. καὶ ἰδοὺ Ἐλεισάβετ ἡ συγγενίς σου. Comp. ver. 20. Mary, who did not ask for one, receives a more gracious sign than Zacharias, who demanded it. The relationship between her and Elisabeth is unknown.

"Cousin," started by Wiclif, and continued until RV. substituted "kinswoman," has now become too definite in meaning. The kinship has led artists to represent the two children as being playmates; but Jn. i. 31 seems to be against such companionship. It has also led to the conjecture that Jesus was descended from both Levi and Judah (see on ver. 27). But Levites might marry with other tribes; and therefore Elisabeth, who was descended from Aaron, might easily be related to one who was descended from David. This verse is not evidence that Mary was not of the house of David.

The late form συγγενίς (comp. εὐγενίς), and the Ion. dat. γήρει for γήρᾳ (Gen. xv. 15, xxi. 7, xxv. 8), should be noticed; also that οὗτος being the subject, the noun has no article. Comp. xxi. 22. The combination καὶ οὗτος is peculiar to Lk. (viii. 41?, xvi. 1, xx. 28). The relative ages of Jesus and of John are fixed by this statement.

We may take καλουμένῃ as imperf. part., "*Used* to be called." This reproach would cease when she reappeared at the end of the five months (ver. 24). καλούμενος with appellations is freq. in Lk.

37. οὐκ ἀδυνατήσει παρὰ τοῦ Θεοῦ πᾶν ῥῆμα. The negative and the verb are to be closely combined and taken as the predicate of πᾶν ῥῆμα. We must not take οὐκ without πᾶν. This is plain from Gen. xviii. 14: μὴ ἀδυνατεῖ παρὰ τῷ Θεῷ ῥῆμα; *i.e.* "Hath God said, and can He not do it?" or, Is anything which God has promised impossible? RV. here has "be void of power" for ἀδυνατεῖν; but it is doubtful whether the verb ever has this signification. Of things, it means "to be impossible" (Mt. xvii. 20); and of persons, "to be unable"; in which case, like δυνατεῖν (Rom. xiv. 4; 2 Cor. ix. 8), it is followed by the infin. That "be impossible" is the meaning, both here and Gen. xviii. 14, is probable from Job xlii. 2 οἶδα ὅτι πάντα δύνασαι, ἀδυνατεῖ δέ σοι οὐθέν; and from Zech. viii. 6, where ἀδυνατήσει is used of a thing being too hard for man but not too hard for God; and from Jer. xxxii. 17, where both Aquila and Symmachus have οὐκ ἀδυνατήσει for οὐ μὴ ἀποκρυβῇ of LXX. We render, therefore, "From God no word shall be impossible." The idiom οὐ . . . πᾶς, in the sense of "all . . . not," *i.e.* "none," is probably Hebraic. Comp. Mt. xxiv. 22. It is less common in N.T. than in LXX (Exod. xii. 16, 43, xx. 16; Dan. ii. 10, etc.), Win. xxvi. 1, p. 214; Blass, *Gr.* p. 174.

38. Ἰδού ἡ δούλη Κυρίου. That ἰδού is not a verb, but an exclamation, is manifest from the verbless nominative which follows it. Comp. v. 12, 18. "Handmaid" or "servant" is hardly adequate to δούλη. It is rather "bondmaid" or "slave." In an age in which almost all servants were slaves, the idea which is represented by our word "servant" could scarcely arise. In N.T. the fem. δούλη occurs only here, ver. 48, and Acts ii. 18, the last being a quotation.

γένοιτό μοι κατὰ τὸ ῥῆμά σου. This is neither a prayer that what has been foretold may take place, nor an expression of joy at the prospect. Rather it is an expression of *submission*,—"God's will be done": πίναξ εἰμι γράφομενος· ὃ βούλεται ὁ γραφεύς, γραφέτω (Eus.). Mary must have known how her social position and her relations with Joseph would be affected by her being with child before her marriage. There are some who maintain that the revelation made to Joseph (Mt. i. 18–23) is inconsistent with what Lk. records here; for would not Mary have told him of the angelic message? We may reasonably answer that she would not do so. Her own inclination would be towards reserve (ii. 51); and what likelihood was there that he would believe so amazing a story? She would prefer to leave the issue with regard to Joseph in God's hands. Hastings, *D.C.G.* art. "Annunciation."

ἀπῆλθεν ἀπ' αὐτῆς ὁ ἄγγελος. *Ut peracta legatione.* Comp. Acts xii. 10; Judg. vi. 21.

On the whole of this exquisite narrative Godet justly remarks: "*Quelle dignité, quelle pureté, quelle simplicité, quelle délicatesse dans tout ce dialogue! Pas un mot de trop, pas un de trop peu. Une telle narration n'a pu émaner que de la sphère sainte dans laquelle le fait lui-même avait eu lieu*" (i. p. 128, 3ème ed. 1888). Contrast the attempts in the apocryphal gospels, the writers of which had our Gospels to imitate, and yet committed such gross offences against taste, decency, and even morality. What would their inventions have been if they had had no historical Gospels to guide them?

Dr. Swete has shown that the doctrine of the Miraculous Conception was from the earliest times part of the Creed. Beginning with Justin Martyr (*Apol.* i. 21, 31, 32, 33, 63; *Try.* 23, 48, 100), he traces back through Aristides (J. R. Harris, p. 24; Hennecke, p. 9; Barnes, *Canon. and Uncanon. Gospp.* p. 13), Ignatius (Eph. xix.; Trall. ix.; Smyr. i.), the Valentinians, and Basilides, to S. Luke, to whom these Gnostics appealed. The silence of S. Mark is of no weight; his record does not profess to go farther back than the ministry of the Baptist. In the Third Gospel we reach not merely the date of the Gospel (A.D. 75–80), but the date of the early traditions incorporated in these first chapters, traditions preserved (possibly in writing) at Jerusalem, and derived from Mary herself.

The testimony of the First Gospel is perhaps even earlier in origin, and is certainly independent. It probably originated with Joseph, as the other with Mary (Gore, *Bampton Lectures*, p. 78; *Dissertations on Subjects connected with the Incarnation*, pp. 12–40). Greatly as the two narratives differ, both bear witness to the virgin birth (Swete, *The Apostles' Creed*, ch. iv.).

39–56. *The Visit of the Mother of the Saviour to the Mother of the Forerunner.*

This narrative grows naturally out of the two which precede it in this group. The two women, who through Divine interposition are about to become mothers, meet and confer with one another. Not that a desire to talk about her marvellous experience prompts Mary to go, but because the Angel had suggested it (ver. 36). That Joseph's intention of putting her away caused the journey, is an unnecessary conjecture.

It is not easy to see why the Song of Elisabeth is not given in metrical form either in WH. or in RV. It seems to have the characteristics of Hebrew poetry in a marked degree, if not in so full a manner as the *Magnificat*, *Benedictus*, and *Nunc Dimittis*. It consists of two strophes of four lines each, thus—

Εὐλογημένη σὺ ἐν γυναιξίν,
καὶ εὐλογημένος ὁ καρπὸς τῆς κοιλίας σου.
καὶ πόθεν μοι τοῦτο
ἵνα ἔλθῃ ἡ μήτηρ τοῦ κυρίου μου πρὸς ἐμέ;

ἰδοὺ γὰρ ὡς ἐγένετο ἡ φωνὴ τοῦ ἀσπασμοῦ σου εἰς τὰ ὦτά μου,
ἐσκίρτησεν ἐν ἀγαλλιάσει τὸ βρέφος ἐν τῇ κοιλίᾳ μου.
καὶ μακαρία ἡ πιστεύσασα ὅτι ἔσται τελείωσις
τοῖς λαλημένοις αὐτῇ παρὰ Κυρίου.

On all four songs see a paper on "Messianic Psalms of the N.T.," by B. B. Warfield, *Expositor*, 3rd series, ii. pp. 301, 321 ff.

39. Ἀναστᾶσα. A very favourite word with Lk., who has it about sixty times against about twenty-two times in the rest of N.T. It occurs hundreds of times in LXX. Of preparation for a journey it is specially common (xv. 18, 20; Acts x. 20, xxii. 10, etc.). Lk. is also fond of such phrases as ἐν ταῖς ἡμέραις ταύταις, or ἐν ταῖς ἡμέραις τινος (ver. 5, ii. 1, iv. 2, 25, v. 35, vi. 12, ix. 36, etc.; Acts i. 15, ii. 18, v. 37, vi. 1, vii. 41, etc.). They are not found in Jn., and occur only four times in Mt., and the same in Mk. Here "in those days" means soon after the Annunciation. As the projected journey was one of several days, it would require time to arrange it and find an escort. See small print note on ver. 20.

ἐπορεύθη εἰς τὴν ὀρινήν. There is no trace of Ὀρεινή as a proper name; ἡ ὀρινή means the mountainous part of Judah as distinct from the plain (ver. 65; Gen. xiv. 10; Num. xiii. 29; Josh. ix. 1, x. 40; comp. Judith 1. 6, ii. 22, iv. 7). It is worth noting that in this narrative, which is from an independent source, Lk. twice uses ἡ ὀρινή. Elsewhere, when he is on the same ground as Mt. and Mk., he uses, as they do, τὸ ὄρος (vi. 12, viii. 32, ix. 28, 37). None of them use either ὄρος or τὰ ὄρη. Lft. *On a Fresh Revision of N.T.* pp. 124, 186, 3rd ed. 1891. For the shortening of ὀρεινή to ὀρινή see WH. ii. App. p. 154. Grotius rightly remarks on **μετὰ σπουδῆς**, *ne negligeret signum quod augendæ ipsius fiduciæ Deus assignaverat.* Comp. Mk. vi. 25; Exod. xii. 11; Wisd. xix. 2.

εἰς πόλιν Ἰούδα. Lk. does not give the name, probably because he did not know it. It may have been Hebron, just as it may have been any town in the mountainous part of Judah, and Hebron was chief among the cities allotted to the priests. But if Lk. had *meant* Hebron, he would either have named it or have written τὴν πόλιν in the sense of the chief priestly dwelling. But it is very doubtful whether the arrangement by which certain cities were allotted to the priests was carried into effect; and, if so, whether it continued. Certainly priests often lived elsewhere. Eli lived at Shiloh, Samuel at Ramathaim-Zophim, Mattathias at Modin. None of these had been allotted to the priests. See on ver. 23.

That Ἰούδα is the name of the town, and represents Juttah (Ἰτάν or Ἰεττά or Τανύ), which was in the mountain region of Judah (Josh. xv. 55), and had been allotted to the priests (Josh. xxi. 16), is possible. Reland (1714) was perhaps the first to advocate this. Robinson found a village called *Yuttah* in that region (*Res. in Pal.* ii. p. 206), and the identification is attractive. But the best authorities seem to regard it as precarious. A tradition, earlier than the Crusades, makes *Ain Karim* to be the birthplace of John the Baptist. Didon (*Jésus Christ*, App. D) contends for this, appealing to V. Guérin, *Description de la Palestine*, i. p. 83, and Fr. Liévin, *Guide de la Palestine*, ii. But it is best to regard the place as an unknown town of Judah. In any case, the spelling "Juda" (AV.) is indefensible; comp. iii. 33.

41. ἐγένετο . . . ἐσκίρτησεν. See detached note at the end of the chapter. It is improbable that in her salutation Mary told Elisabeth of the angelic visit. The salutation caused the movement of the unborn child, and Elisabeth is inspired to interpret this sign aright. Grotius states that the verb is a medical word for the movement of children in the womb, but he gives no instances. It is used Gen. xxv. 22 of the unborn Esau and Jacob, and Ps. cxiii. 4, 6 of the mountains skipping like rams. In class. Grk. it is used of the skipping both of animals and of men. For **ἐπλήσθη πνεύματος ἁγίου** see on ver. 15. **ὡς** = "when" is very freq. in Lk.

42. ἀνεφώνησεν. 1 Chron. xv. 28, xvi. 4, 5, 42; 2 Chron.

v. 13; here only in N.T. Lk. frequently records strong expressions of emotion, adding μεγάλη to κραυγή, φωνή, χαρά, etc. (ii. 10, iv. 33, viii. 28, xvii. 15, xix. 37, xxiii. 23, 46, xxiv. 52). It is perhaps because κραυγή seemed less appropriate to express a cry of joy that it has been altered (A C D) to the more usual φωνή. But it is convincingly attested (ℵ B L Ξ). It means any cry of strong feeling, whether surprise (Mt. xxv. 6), anger (Eph. iv. 31), or distress (Heb. v. 7). Comp. *Apoc. Baruch*, liv. 10.

Εὐλογημένη σὺ ἐν γυναιξίν. A Hebraistic periphrasis for the superlative, "Among women thou art the one who is specially blessed." Mary has a claim to this title κατ' ἐξοχήν. Comp. vii. 28. Somewhat similar expressions occur in class. Grk., esp. in poetry: ὦ φίλα γυναικῶν (Eur. *Alc.* 460); ὦ σχέτλι' ἀνδρῶν (Aristoph. *Ran.* 1048). In N.T. εὐλογημένος is used of men, εὐλογητός of God: see on ver. 68. With **εὐλογημένος ὁ καρπὸς τῆς κοιλίας σου** comp. εὐλογημένα τὰ ἔκγονα τῆς κ. σου (Deut. xxviii. 4) and καρπὸν κοιλίας (Gen. xxx. 2; Lam. ii. 20). See small print on ver. 15.

43. καὶ πόθεν μοι τοῦτο. We understand γέγονεν: comp. Mk. xii. 37. *Modestiæ filii præludens qui olim Christo erat dicturus*, σὺ ἔρχῃ πρός με; (Grotius). It is by inspiration (ver. 41) that Elisabeth knows that she who greets her is ἡ μήτηρ τοῦ κυρίου, *i.e.* of the Messiah (Ps. cx. 1). The expression "Mother of God" is not found in Scripture.[1]

In ἵνα ἔλθῃ we have a weakening of the original force of ἵνα, which begins with the Alexandrine writers as an alternative for the infinitive, and has become universal in modern Greek. Godet would keep the telic force by arbitrarily substituting "What have I done?" for "Whence is this to me?" "What have I done in order that?" etc. Comp. the Lucan constr., τοῦτο ὅτι (x. 11, xii. 39; Acts xxiv. 14). See Blass, *Gr.* p. 224.

44. Ἰδοὺ γὰρ ὡς ἐγένετο ἡ φωνὴ τοῦ ἀσπασμοῦ σου. On this γάρ Bengel bases the strange notion that the conception of the Christ takes place at the salutation: γάρ *rationem experimens, cur hoc ipso temporis puncto Elisabet primum "Matrem Domini sui" proclamet Mariam. . . . Nunc Dominus, et respectu matris et progenitorum, et respectu locorum, ubi conceptus æque ac natus est, ex Juda est ortus.* It is a mark of the delicacy and dignity of the narrative that the time is not stated; but ver. 38 is more probable than ver. 40. Excepting 2 Cor. vii. 11, ἰδοὺ γάρ is peculiar to Lk. (ver. 48, ii. 10, vi. 23, xvii. 21; Acts ix. 11). For **ἐγένετο ἡ φωνή** see on iii. 22 and ix. 35, 36.

45. μακαρία ἡ πιστεύσασα ὅτι. Latin texts, both of Lat. Vet. and of Vulg., vary much between *beata quæ credidit quoniam* and *beata quæ credidisti quoniam.* English Versions are equally varied, even Wic. and Rhem. being different. "Blessed is *she* that

[1] P. Didon inaccurately renders this, *Comment se fait-il que la mère de mon Dieu vienne à moi* (p. 111).

believed" is probably right. This is the first beatitude in the Gospel; and it is also the last: *μακάριοι οἱ μὴ ἰδόντες καὶ πιστεύσαντες* (Jn. xx. 29). In Mk. *μακάριος* does not occur; and in Jn. only xiii. 17 and xx. 29. It is specially common in Lk.

This verse is one of many places in N.T. in which *ὅτι* may be either "that" or "because": see on vii. 16. There can be little doubt that Luther, Erasmus, Beza, and all Latin and English Versions are right in taking the latter sense here. The *ὅτι* introduces the reason why the belief is blessed and not the contents (Syr. Sin.) of the belief. There is no need to state what Mary believed. Elisabeth adds her faith to Mary's, and declares that, amazing as the promise is, it will assuredly be fulfilled. Only a small portion of what had been promised (31–33) had as yet been accomplished; and hence the **ἔσται τελείωσις,** "There shall be a bringing to perfection, an accomplishment" (Heb. vii. 11). Comp. *ἐξελεύσομαι εἰς τελείωσιν τῶν λόγων ὧν ἐλαλήσατε μετ' ἐμοῦ* (Judith x. 9).

46–56. *The Magnificat or Song of Mary.*

This beautiful lyric is neither a reply to Elisabeth nor an address to God. It is rather a meditation; an expression of personal emotions and experiences. It is more calm and majestic than the utterance of Elisabeth. The exultation is as great, but it is more under control. The introductory **εἶπεν**, as contrasted with *ἀνεφώνησεν κραυγῇ μεγάλῃ* (ver. 42), points to this. The hymn is modelled upon the O.T. Psalms, especially the Song of Hannah (1 Sam. ii. 1–10); but its superiority to the latter in moral and spiritual elevation is very manifest. From childhood the Jews knew many of the O.T. lyrics by heart; and, just as our own poor, who know no literature but the Bible, easily fall into biblical language in times of special joy or sorrow, so Mary would naturally fall back on the familiar expressions of Jewish Scripture in this moment of intense exultation. The exact relation between her hymn and these familiar expressions can be best seen when the two are placed side by side in a table.

THE MAGNIFICAT.	THE OLD TESTAMENT.
Μεγαλύνει ἡ ψυχή μου τὸν κύριον καὶ ἠγαλλίασεν τὸ πνεῦμά μου ἐπὶ τῷ Θεῷ τῷ σωτῆρί μου·	[1] *Ἐστερεώθη ἡ καρδία μου ἐν Κυρίῳ, ὑψώθη κέρας μου ἐν Θεῷ μου.*
ὅτι ἐπέβλεψεν ἐπὶ τὴν ταπείνωσιν τῆς δούλης αὐτοῦ	[2] *ἐὰν ἐπιβλέπων ἐπιβλέψῃς τὴν ταπείνωσιν τῆς δούλης σου—*
ἰδοὺ γὰρ ἀπὸ τοῦ νῦν μακαριοῦσίν με πᾶσαι αἱ γενεαί.	[3] *Μακαρία ἐγώ, ὅτι μακαρίζουσίν με πᾶσαι αἱ γυναῖκες.*
ὅτι ἐποίησέν μοι μεγάλα ὁ δυνατός,	[4] *ὅστις ἐποίησεν ἐν σοὶ τὰ μεγάλα—*
καὶ ἅγιον τὸ ὄνομα αὐτοῦ,	[5] *ἅγιον καὶ φοβερὸν τὸ ὄνομα αὐτοῦ.*
καὶ τὸ ἔλεος αὐτοῦ εἰς γενεὰς καὶ γενεάς τοῖς φοβουμένοις αὐτόν.	[6] *τὸ δὲ ἔλεος τοῦ κυρίου ἀπὸ τοῦ αἰῶνος καὶ ἕως τοῦ αἰῶνος ἐπὶ τοὺς φοβουμένους αὐτόν.*

[1] 1 Sam. ii. 1. [2] 1 Sam. i. 11. [3] Gen. xxx. 13.
[4] Deut. x. 21. [5] Ps. cxi. 9. [6] Ps. ciii. 17.

Ἐποίησεν κράτος ἐν βραχίονι αὐτοῦ·	[1] σὺ ἐταπείνωσας ὡς τραυματίαν ὑπερήφανον, καὶ ἐν τῷ βραχίονι τῆς δυνάμεώς σου διεσκόρπισας τοὺς ἐχθρούς σου.
διεσκόρπισεν ὑπερηφάνους διανοίᾳ καρδίας αὐτῶν. καθεῖλεν δυνάστας ἀπὸ θρόνων καὶ ὕψωσεν ταπεινούς, πεινῶντας ἐνέπλησεν ἀγαθῶν καὶ πλουτοῦντας ἐξαπέστειλεν κενούς.	[2] ἐξαποστέλλων ἱερεῖς αἰχμαλώτους δυνάστας δὲ γῆς κατέστρεψεν. [3] τὸν ποιοῦντα ταπεινοὺς εἰς ὕψος, καὶ ἀπολωλότας ἐξεγείροντα. [4] Κύριος πτωχίζει καὶ πλουτίζει ταπεινοῖ καὶ ἀνυψοῖ. [5] ψυχὴν πεινῶσαν ἐνέπλησεν ἀγαθῶν.
Ἀντελάβετο Ἰσραὴλ παιδὸς αὐτοῦ,	[6] Σὺ δέ, Ἰσραήλ, παῖς μου, οὗ ἀντελαβόμην—
μνησθῆναι ἐλέους,	[7] ἐμνήσθη τοῦ ἐλέους αὐτοῦ τῷ Ἰακώβ.
καθὼς ἐλάλησεν πρὸς τοὺς πατέρας ἡμῶν τῷ Ἀβραὰμ καὶ τῷ σπέρματι αὐτοῦ εἰς τὸν αἰῶνα.	[8] δώσει εἰς ἀλήθειαν τῷ Ἰακώβ, ἔλεον τῷ Ἀβραάμ, καθότι ὤμοσας τοῖς πατράσιν ἡμῶν κατὰ τὰς ἡμέρας τὰς ἔμπροσθεν. [9] τῷ Δαυεὶδ καὶ τῷ σπέρματι αὐτοῦ ἕως αἰῶνος.

The hymn falls into four strophes, 46–48, 49 and 50, 51–53, 54 and 55.[10]

46. Μεγαλύνει ἡ ψυχή μου τὸν κύριον. The verb is used in the literal sense of "enlarge," Mt. xxiii. 5: comp. Lk. i. 58. More often, as here, in the derived sense of "esteem great, extol, magnify" (Acts v. 13, x. 46, xix. 17). So also in class. Grk. Weiss goes too far when he contends that "distinctions drawn between ψυχή and πνεῦμα have absolutely no foundation in N.T. usage" (*sind gänzlich unbegründet*); but it is evident that no distinction is to be made here. The ψυχή and the πνεῦμα are the immaterial part of man's nature as opposed to the body or the flesh. It is in her inner, higher life, in her real self, that Mary blesses God in jubilation. If a distinction were made here, we ought to have μεγαλύνει τὸ πνεῦμά μου and ἠγαλλίασεν ἡ ψυχή μου, for the πνεῦμα is the seat of the religious life, the ψυχή of the emotions. See Lft. *Notes on the Epp. of S. Paul*, p. 88, 1895, and the literature there quoted, esp. Olshausen, *Opusc.* p. 157.

47. ἠγαλλίασεν. A word formed by Hellenists from ἀγάλλομαι, and freq. in LXX (Ps. xv. 9, xlvii. 12, lxix. 5; Is. xxxv. 2; Jer. xlix. 4). The act. is rare; perhaps only here and Rev. xix. 7; but as *v.l.* 1 Pet. i. 8. The aor. may refer to the occasion of the angelic visit. But it is the Greek idiom to use the aor. in many cases in which we use the perf., and then it is misleading to translate the Grk. aor. by the Eng. aor. Moreover, in late Grk.

---

[1] Ps. lxxxix. 11. [2] Job xii. 19. [3] Job v. 11.
[4] 1 Sam. ii. 7. [5] Ps. cvii. 9. [6] Is. xli. 8.
[7] Ps. xcviii. 3. [8] Mic. vii. 20. [9] 2 Sam. xxii. 51.

[10] On the structure of Hebrew poetry, see Driver, *Literature of the O.T.* pp. 338–345, T. & T. Clark, 1891.

On the use of the *Magnificat*, first at Lauds in the Gallican Church, from A.D. 507, and then at Vespers on Saturday in the Sarum Breviary, see Blunt, *Annotated Prayer-Book*.

the distinction between aor. and perf. had become less sharp. Simcox, *Lang. of N.T.* pp. 103–106; Lagarde, *Mittheilungen*, iii. 374.

τῷ Θεῷ τῷ σωτῆρί μου. He is the Saviour of Mary as well as of her fellows. She probably included the notion of external and political deliverance, but not to the exclusion of spiritual salvation. For the expression comp. 1 Tim. i. 1, ii. 3; Tit. i. 3, ii. 10, iii. 4; Jude 25; Ps. xxiii. 5, cvi. 21. In the *Ps. Sol.* we have Ἀλήθεια τῶν δικαίων παρὰ Θεοῦ σωτῆρος αὐτῶν (iii. 7); and ἡμεῖς δὲ ἐλπιοῦμεν ἐπὶ Θεὸν τὸν σωτῆρα ἡμῶν (xvii. 3). Comp. *Ps. Sol.* viii. 39, xvi. 4.

48. ὅτι ἐπέβλεψεν ἐπὶ τὴν ταπείνωσιν τῆς δούλης αὐτοῦ. Comp. Hannah's prayer for a child 1 Sam. i. 11. In spite of her humble position as a carpenter's bride, Mary had been chosen for the highest honour that a human being could receive. For ταπείνωσις comp. Acts viii. 33 (from Is. liii. 8) and Phil. iii. 21; and for ἰδεῖν τὴν ταπείνωσιν comp. 2 Kings xiv. 26 and Ps. xxv. 18. This use of ἐπιβλέπειν ἐπί is freq. in LXX (Ps. xxv. 16, lxix. 16, cii. 19, cxix. 132, etc.); see esp. 1 Sam. ix. 16.

ἰδοὺ γὰρ ἀπὸ τοῦ νῦν μακαριοῦσίν με πᾶσαι αἱ γενεαί. For ἰδοὺ γάρ see on ver. 44, and for ἀπὸ τοῦ νῦν see on v. 10. Elisabeth had begun this μακαρίζειν, and we have another instance in the woman from the crowd (xi. 27). Note the wide difference between the scope of Mary's prophecy, μακαριοῦσιν πᾶσαι αἱ γενεαί, and Leah's statement of fact, μακαρίζουσίν με πᾶσαι αἱ γυναῖκες (Gen. xxx. 13). See Resch, *Kindheitsev.* p. 104.

The Latin renderings of ἀπὸ τοῦ νῦν are interesting: *ex hoc* (Vulg.), *a modo* (d), *a nunc* (Cod. Gall.).

49. ὅτι ἐποίησέν μοι μεγάλα ὁ δυνατός. Here the second strophe begins. The reading μεγαλεῖα may come from Acts ii. 11: comp. ἃ ἐποίησας μεγαλεῖα (Ps. lxx. 19). With ὁ δυνατός comp. δύναμις Ὑψίστου (ver. 35) and Κύριος κραταιὸς καὶ δυνατός (Ps. xxiii. 8). In LXX δυνατός is very common, but almost invariably of men. After both δυνατός and αὐτοῦ we should place a colon. The clause καὶ ἅγιον τὸ ὄνομα αὐτοῦ is a separate sentence, neither dependent upon the preceding ὅτι, nor very closely connected with what follows.

50. καὶ τὸ ἔλεος αὐτοῦ εἰς γενεὰς καὶ γενεὰς τοῖς φοβουμένοις αὐτόν. Comp. *Ps. Sol.* x. 4, καὶ τὸ ἔλεος Κυρίου ἐπὶ τοὺς ἀγαπῶντας αὐτὸν ἐν ἀληθείᾳ, καὶ μνησθήσεται Κύριος τῶν δούλων αὐτοῦ ἐν ἐλέει: also xiii. 11, ἐπὶ δὲ τοὺς ὁσίους τὸ ἔλεος κυρίου, καὶ ἐπὶ τοὺς φοβουμένους αὐτὸν τὸ ἔλεος αὐτοῦ. With εἰς γενεὰς κ. γ. comp. εἰς γενεὰς γενεῶν (Is. xxxiv. 17), εἰς γενεὰν καὶ γενεάν (Ps. lxxxix. 2), and κατὰ γενεὰν καὶ γενεάν (1 Mac. ii. 61). "Fearing God" is the O.T. description of piety. Nearly the whole verse comes from Ps. ciii. 17. Syr-Sin. for καὶ γενεάς has "and on the tribe."

51. Ἐποίησεν κράτος ἐν βραχίονι αὐτοῦ, διεσκόρπισεν, κ.τ.λ. Beginning of the third strophe. The six aorists in it are variously explained

1. They tell of things which the Divine power and holiness and mercy (*vv.* 49, 50) have already accomplished in the past. 2. According to the common prophetic usage, they speak of the future as already past, and tell of the effects to be produced by the Messiah as if they had been produced. 3. They are gnomic, and express God's normal acts. We may set aside this last. It is very doubtful whether the aor. is ever used of what is normal or habitual (Win. xl. 5. b, 1, p. 346). Of the other two explanations, the second is to be preferred. It is more likely that Mary is thinking of the far-reaching effects of the blessing conferred upon herself than of past events unconnected with that blessing. In either case the six aorists must be translated by the English perfect. They show that in this strophe, as in the second, we have a triplet. There it was God's power, holiness, and mercy. Here it is the contrasts between proud and humble, high and low, rich and poor.

Both **ἐποίησεν κράτος** and **ἐν βραχίονι αὐτοῦ** are Hebraisms. For the former comp. *δεξιὰ Κυρίου ἐποίησεν δύναμιν* (Ps. cxviii. 15). For *βραχίων* to express Divine power comp. Acts xiii. 17; Jn. xii. 38 (from Is. liii. 1); Ps. xliv. 3, xcviii. 1, etc. The phrase *ἐν χειρὶ κραταιᾷ καὶ ἐν βραχίονι ὑψηλῷ* is freq. in LXX (Deut. iv. 34, v. 15, vi. 21, xxvi. 8). This use of *ἐν* is in the main Hebraistic (xxii. 49; Rev. vi. 8; Judg. xv. 15, xx. 16; 1 Kings xii. 18; Judith vi. 12, viii. 33). Win. xlviii. 3. d, p. 485.

ὑπερηφάνους διανοίᾳ καρδίας αὐτῶν. The dat. limits *ὑπερηφάνους*: they are proud and overweening in thought. In N.T. *ὑπερήφανος* is never "conspicuous above" others, but always in a bad sense, "looking down on" others (Jas. iv. 6; 1 Pet. v. 5; Rom. i. 30; 2 Tim. iii. 2. It is freq. in LXX. Comp. *Ps. Sol.* ii. 35, *κοιμίζων ὑπερηφάνους εἰς ἀπώλειαν αἰώνιον ἐν ἀτιμίᾳ*; also iv. 28. See Wsctt. on 1 Jn. ii. 16, and Trench, *Syn.* xxix.

52. καθεῖλεν δυνάστας ἀπὸ θρόνων καὶ ὕψωσεν ταπεινούς. "He hath put down potentates from thrones." "Potentates" rather than "princes" (RV.), or "the mighty" (AV.), because of 1 Tim. vi. 15. Comp. *δυνάσται Φαραώ* (Gen. l. 4). In Acts viii. 27 it is an adj. It is probable that *ταπεινούς* here means primarily the oppressed poor as opposed to tyrannical rulers. See Hatch, *Biblical Greek*, pp. 73-77. Besides the parallels given in the table (p. 31) comp. *ἀναλαμβάνων πρᾳεῖς ὁ κύριος, ταπεινῶν δὲ ἁμαρτωλοὺς ἕως τῆς γῆς* (Ps. cxlvii. 6); *θρόνους ἀρχόντων καθεῖλεν ὁ κύριος, καὶ ἐκάθισεν πρᾳεῖς ἀντ' αὐτῶν* (Ecclus. x. 14); also Lk. xiv. 11, xviii. 14; Jas. i. 9, 10. In Clem. Rom. *Cor.* lix. 3 we have what looks like a paraphrase, but may easily come from O.T. Comp. *Enoch* xlvi. 5.

53. πεινῶντας ἐνέπλησεν ἀγαθῶν. Both material and spiritual goods may be included. Comp. *πλήρεις ἄρτων ἠλαττώθησαν, καὶ ἀσθενοῦντες παρῆκαν γῆν* (1 Sam. ii. 5); also *Ps. Sol.* v. 10-12, x. 7.

54. Ἀντελάβετο Ἰσραὴλ παιδὸς αὐτοῦ. The fourth strophe. The regular biblical meaning of *ἀντιλαμβάνομαι* is "lay hold of in order to *support* or *succour*" (Acts xx. 35; Ecclus. ii. 6); hence *ἀντίληψις* is "succour, help" (1 Cor. xii. 28; Ps. xxi. 20, lxxxiii. 8), and *ἀντιλήπτωρ* is "helper" (Ps. xviii. 3, liv. 6). There is no doubt that *παιδὸς αὐτοῦ* means "His servant," not "His son." The children of God are called *τέκνα* or *υἱοί*, but not *παῖδες*. We have *παῖς* in the sense of God's servant used of Israel or Jacob (Is. xli. 8, 9, xlii. 1, xliv. 1, 2, 21, xlv. 4); of David (Lk. i. 69;

Acts iv. 25; Ps. xvii. 1; Is. xxxvii. 35); and of Christ (Acts iii. 13, 26, iv. 27, 30). Comp. *Ps. Sol.* xii. 7, xvii. 23; *Didaché*, ix. 2, 3, x. 2, 3.

μνησθῆναι ἐλέους. "So as to remember mercy," *i.e.* to prove that He had not forgotten, as they might have supposed. Comp. *Ps Sol.* x. 4, *καὶ μνησθήσεται Κύριος τῶν δούλων αὐτοῦ ἐν ἐλέει.*

55. καθὼς ἐλάλησεν πρός. "Even as He spake unto": see on *vv.* 2 and 13. This clause is not a parenthesis, but explains the extent of the remembrance of mercy. RV. is the first English Version to make plain that **τῷ Ἀβραάμ, κ.τ.λ.**, depends upon *μνησθῆναι* and not upon *ἐλάλησεν* by rendering *πρός* "unto" and the dat. "toward." To make this still more plain, "As He spake unto our fathers" is put into a parenthesis, which is not necessary. The Genevan is utterly wrong, "(Even as He promised to our fathers, *to wit*, to Abraham and his sede) for ever." It is improbable that Lk. would use both *πρός* and the simple dat. after *ἐλάλησεν* in the same sentence; or that he means to say that God spoke to Abraham's seed for ever. The phrase **εἰς τὸν αἰῶνα** is common in the Psalms, together with *εἰς τὸν αἰῶνα τοῦ αἰῶνος* (Heb. i. 8) and *εἰς αἰῶνα αἰῶνος*. It means "unto the age," *i.e.* the age *κατ' ἐξοχήν*, the age of the Messiah. The belief that whatever is allowed to see that age will continue to exist in that age, makes *εἰς τὸν αἰῶνα* equivalent to "for ever." This strophe, like ver. 72, harmonizes with the doctrine that Abraham is still alive (xx. 38), and is influenced by what takes place in the development of God's kingdom on earth (Jn. viii. 56; comp. Heb. xii. 1; Is. xxix. 22, 23).

For *εἰς τὸν αἰῶνα* ACFMS here have *ἕως αἰῶνος* (1 Chron. xvii. 16; Ezek. xxv. 15?), which does not occur in N.T.

56. Ἔμεινεν δὲ Μαριὰμ σὺν αὐτῇ. Lk. greatly prefers *σύν* to *μετά*. He uses *σύν* much more often than all N.T. writers put together. In his Gospel we find him using *σύν* where the parallel passage in Mt. or Mk. has *μετά* or *καί*; *e.g.* viii. 38, 51, xx. 1, xxii. 14, 56. We have *σύν* three times in these first two chapters; here, ii. 5 and 13. It is not likely that an interpolator would have caught all these minute details in Lk.'s style: see Introd. § 6.

ὡς μῆνας τρεῖς. This, when compared with *μὴν ἕκτος* (ver. 36), leads us to suppose that Mary waited until the birth of John the Baptist. She would hardly have left when that was imminent. Lk. mentions her return before mentioning the birth in order to complete one narrative before beginning another; just as he mentions the imprisonment of the Baptist before the Baptism of the Christ in order to finish his account of John's ministry before beginning to narrate the ministry of Jesus (iii. 20, 21). That Mary is not named in *vv.* 57, 58 is no evidence that she was not present. It would be unnatural to say that one of the household heard of the event; and, in fact, οἱ συγγενεῖς would include her whether it is intended to do so or not. Origen, Ambrose, Bede, and others believe that she remained until the birth of John. For the patristic arguments for and against see Corn. à Lap. Lk. leaves us in doubt, probably because his authority left him in doubt; but Didon goes too far in saying that Lk. insinuates that she was not present.[1]

For this use of ὡς comp. viii. 42 (not ii. 37); Acts i. 15, v. 7, 36. Lk. more often uses ὡσεί in this sense (iii. 23, ix. 14, 28, xxii. 41, 59, xxiii. 44; Acts ii. 41, etc.). In ὑπέστρεψεν we have another very favourite word which runs through both Gospel and Acts. It is found elsewhere only Mk. xiv. 40; Gal. i. 17; Heb. vii. 1; 2 Pet. ii. 21.

Meyer rightly remarks that "the historical character of the Visitation of Mary stands or falls with that of the Annunciation." The arguments against it are very inconclusive. 1. That it does not harmonize with Joseph's dream in Mt. i. 20; which has been shown to be incorrect. 2. That there is no trace elsewhere of great intimacy between the two families; which proves absolutely nothing. 3. That the obvious purpose of the narrative is to glorify Jesus, in making the unborn Baptist acknowledge Him as the Messiah; which is mere assertion. 4. That the poetic splendour of the narrative lifts it out of the historical sphere; which implies that what is expressed with great poetic beauty cannot be historically true,—a canon which would be fatal to a great deal of historical material. We may assert of this narrative, as of that of the Annunciation, that no one in the first or second century could have imagined either. Least of all could any one have given us the *Magnificat*,—"the most magnificent cry of Joy that has ever issued from a human breast." Nothing that has come down to us of that age leads us to suppose that any writer could have composed these accounts without historic truth to guide him, any more than an architect of that age could have produced Milan cathedral. Comp. the *Protevangelium of James* xii.–xiv.; the *Pseudo-Matthew* ix.–xii.; the *Hist. of Joseph the Carpenter* iii.–vi.

57–80. *The Birth and Circumcision of the Forerunner.*

57. ἐπλήσθη ὁ χρόνος τοῦ τεκεῖν αὐτήν. Expressions about time or days being fulfilled are found chiefly in these two chapters in N.T. (ver. 23, ii. 6, 21, 22). They are Hebraistic: *e.g.* ἐπληρώθησαν αἱ ἡμέραι τοῦ τεκεῖν αὐτήν (Gen. xxv. 24; comp. xxix. 21; Lev. xii. 4, 6; Num. vi. 5, etc.). And τοῦ τεκεῖν is gen. after ὁ χρόνος.

[1] Didon has some excellent remarks on the poetical portion of this narrative. *La poésie est le langage des impressions véhémentes et des idées sublimes. Chez les Juifs, comme chez tous les peuples d'Orient, elle jaillait d'inspiration. Tout âme est poète, la joie ou la douleur la fait chanter. Si jamais un coeur a dû faire explosion dans quelque hymne inspirée, c'est bien celui de la jeune fille élue de Dieu pour être la mère du Messie.*

Elle emprunte à l'histoire biblique des femmes qui, avant elle, ont tressailli dans leur maternité, comme Liah et la mère de Samuel des expressions qu' elle élargit et transfigure. Les hymnes nationaux qui célèbrent la gloire de son peuple, la miséricorde, la puissance, la sagesse et la fidélité de Dieu, reviennent sur ses lèvres habituées à les chanter (*Jésus Christ*, p. 112, ed. 1891). The whole passage is worth consulting.

ἐμεγάλυνεν Κύριος τὸ ἔλεος αὐτοῦ μετ' αὐτῆς. The verb is not used in the same sense as in ver. 46, nor yet quite literally as in Mt. xxiii. 5, but rather "made conspicuous," *i.e.* bestowed conspicuous mercy. Comp. ἐμεγάλυνας τὴν δικαιοσύνην σου (Gen. xix. 19). The μετ' αὐτῆς does not mean that she co-operates with God, but that He thus deals with her. Comp. ver. 72, x. 37, and εἴδετε ἃ ἐμεγάλυνεν μεθ' ὑμῶν (1 Sam. xii. 24). In **συνέχαιρον αὐτῇ** we have the first beginning of the fulfilment of ver. 14. It means "rejoiced with her" (xv. 6, 9; 1 Cor. xii. 26), rather than "congratulated her" (Phil. ii. 17).

59. ἦλθαν περιτεμεῖν τὸ παιδίον. The nom. must be understood from the context, *amici ad eam rem advocati*, viz. some of those mentioned ver. 58. Circumcision might be performed anywhere and by any Jew, even by a woman (Exod. iv. 25).

On the mixture of first and second aorist in such forms as ἦλθαν, ἔπεσα, εἴδαμεν, ἀνεῖλαν, etc., see Win. xiii. 1. a, p. 86; WH. ii. App. p. 164; and comp. ver. 61, ii. 16, v. 7, 26, vi. 17, vii. 24, xi. 2, 52, xxii. 52; Acts ii. 23, xii. 7, xvi. 37, xxii. 7, etc.

ἐκάλουν αὐτὸ ἐπὶ τῷ ὀνόματι τοῦ πατρὸς αὐτοῦ. Not merely "they wished to call," but "they began to call, were calling"; comp. v. 6; Acts vii. 26; Mt. iii. 14. The custom of combining the naming with circumcision perhaps arose from Abram being changed to Abraham when circumcision was instituted. Naming after the father was common among the Jews (Jos. *Vita*, 1; *Ant.* xiv. 1. 3). For the ἐπί comp. ἐκλήθη ἐπ' ὀνόματι αὐτῶν (Neh. vii. 63).

60. κληθήσεται Ἰωάνης. It is quite gratuitous to suppose that the name had been divinely revealed to her, or that she chose it herself to express the boon which God had bestowed upon her. Zacharias would naturally tell her in writing what had taken place in the temple. With **καλεῖται τῷ ὀνόματι** comp. xix. 2.

62. ἐνένευον. Here only in N.T., but we have νεύω similarly used Acts xxiv. 10 and Jn. xiii. 24. Comp. ἐννεύει ὀφθαλμῷ, σημαίνει δὲ ποδί, διδάσκει δὲ ἐννεύμασιν δακτύλων (Prov. vi. 13), and ὁ ἐννεύων ὀφθαλμοῖς μετὰ δόλου (Prov. x. 10). Some infer that Zacharias was deaf as well as dumb; and this is often the meaning of κωφός (ver. 22), viz. "*blunted* in speech or hearing, or both" (vii. 22). But the question is not worth the amount of discussion which it has received.

τὸ τί ἂν θέλοι. The art. turns the whole clause into a substantive. "They communicated by signs *the question*, what he," etc. Comp. Rom. viii. 26; 1 Thes. iv. 1; Mt. xix. 18. The τό serves the purpose of marks of quotation.

This use of τό with a sentence, and especially with a question, is common in Lk. (ix. 46, xix. 48, xxii. 2, 4, 23, 24, 37; Acts iv. 21, xxii. 30). Note the ἄν: "what he would *perhaps* wish, might wish." We have exactly the same use of ἄν Jn. xiii. 24?; comp. Lk. vi. 11; Acts v. 24, xxi. 33?. Win. xlii. 4, p. 386; Blass, *Gr.* p. 215.

63. αἰτήσας πινακίδιον. *Postulans pugillarem* (Vulg.), *cum petisset tabulam* (d). Of course by means of signs, ἐννεύμασιν δακτύλων. One is inclined to conjecture that Lk. or his authority accidentally put the ἐννεύειν in the wrong place. Signs must have been used here, and they are not mentioned. They need not have been used ver. 62, and they are mentioned. The πινακίδιον would probably be a tablet covered with wax: *loquitur in stylo, auditur in cera* (Tert. *De idol.* xxiii.).

All four forms, πίναξ, πινακίς, πινάκιον, and πινακίδιον, are used of writing-tablets, and πινακίδα is *v.l.* (D) here. But elsewhere in N.T. πίναξ is a "dish" or "platter" (xi. 39; Mt. xiv. 8, 11; Mk. vi. 25, 28). Note the Hebraistic particularity in ἔγραψεν λέγων, and comp. 2 Kings x. 6; 1 Mac. x. 17, xi. 57. This is the first mention of writing in N.T.

Ἰωάνης ἐστὶν ὄνομα αὐτοῦ. Not ἔσται, but ἐστίν: *habet vocabulum suum quod agnovimus, non quod elegimus* (Bede); *quasi dicat nullam superesse consultationem in re quam Deus jam definiisset* (Grotius); *non tam jubet, quam jussum divinum indicat* (Beng.). The **ἐθαύμασαν πάντες** may be used on either side of the question of his deafness. They wondered at his agreeing with Elisabeth, although he had not heard her choice of name; or, they wondered at his agreeing with her, although he had heard the discussion.

64. ἀνεῴχθη δὲ τὸ στόμα αὐτοῦ παραχρῆμα. The prophecy which he had refused to believe was now accomplished, and the sign which had been granted to him as a punishment is withdrawn. That the first use of his recovered speech was to continue blessing God (ἐλάλει εὐλογῶν), rather than to complain, is evidence that the punishment had proved a blessing to him. The addition of **καὶ ἡ γλῶσσα αὐτοῦ** involves a zeugma, such as is common in all languages: comp. 1 Cor. iii. 2; 1 Tim. iv. 3; Win. lxvi. 1. e, p. 777. The Complutensian Bible, on the authority of two cursives (140, 251), inserts διηρθρώθη after ἡ γλῶσσα αὐτοῦ: see on ii. 22. For **παραχρῆμα** see on v. 25 and comp. iv. 39. We are left in doubt as to whether **ἐλάλει εὐλογῶν** refers to the *Benedictus* or to some εὐλογία which preceded it. The use of ἐπροφήτευσεν and not εὐλόγησεν in ver. 67 does not prove that two distinct acts of thanksgiving are to be understood. Here Syr-Sin. has "They marvelled all."

65. ἐγένετο ἐπὶ πάντας φόβος. See on iv. 36. Zacharias (ver. 12) and Mary (ver. 30) had had the same feeling when conscious of the nearness of the spiritual world. A writer of fiction would have been more likely to dwell upon the joy which the wonderful birth of the future Prophet produced; all the more so as such joy had been predicted (ver. 14). The **αὐτούς** means Zacharias and Elisabeth.

διελαλεῖτο πάντα τὰ ῥήματα ταῦτα. This need not be confined to what was *said* at the circumcision of John. It is probably the Hebraistic use of ῥήματα for the *things* which are the subject-matter of narration. Comp. ii. 19, 51, where RV. has "sayings" in the text and "things" in the margin; and Acts v. 32, where it has "things" in the text and "sayings" in the margin. Comp. LXX Gen. xv. 1, xxii. 1, 16, xxxix. 7, xl. 1, xlviii. 1, and esp. xxiv. 66, πάντα τὰ ῥήματα ἃ ἐποίησεν. The verb διαλαλεῖν occurs only here and vi. 11: not in LXX, but in Sym. several times in the Psalms. Syr-Sin. omits πάντα τὰ ῥήματα.

66. ἔθεντο πάντες οἱ ἀκούσαντες ἐν τῇ καρδίᾳ αὐτῶν. Comp. ii. 19. We find all three prepositions with this phrase, ἐν, ἐπί, and εἰς: ἔθετο Δαυεὶδ τὰ ῥήματα ἐν τῇ καρδίᾳ αὐτοῦ (1 Sam. xxi. 12); ἔθετο Δανιὴλ ἐπὶ τὴν καρδίαν αὐτοῦ (Dan. i. 8); τίθεσθε εἰς τὴν καρδίαν ὑμῶν (Mal. ii. 2). Lk. is fond of constructions with ἐν τῇ κ. or ἐν ταῖς κ. (ii. 19, iii. 15, v. 22, xxi. 14; comp. ii. 51, xxiv. 38). In Hom. we have both θεῖναί τι and θέσθαι τι, either ἐν φρεσί or ἐν στήθεσσι. Note that, not only is πᾶς or ἅπας a favourite word with Lk., but either form combined with a participle of ἀκούω is also freq. and characteristic (ii. 18, 47, iv. 28, vi. 47, vii. 29, xx. 45; Acts v. 5, 11, ix. 21, x. 44, xxvi. 29; comp. Acts iv. 4, xviii. 8). See on vi. 30.

Τί ἄρα τὸ παιδίον τοῦτο ἔσται; Not τίς; the neut. makes the question more indefinite and comprehensive: comp. τί ἄρα ὁ Πέτρος ἐγένετο (Acts xii. 18). The ἄρα, *igitur*, means "in these circumstances"; viii. 25, xii. 42, xxii. 23.

καὶ γὰρ χεὶρ Κυρίου ἦν μετ' αὐτοῦ. "For besides all that," *i.e.* in addition to the marvels which attended his birth. This is a remark of the Evangelist, who is wont now and then to interpose in this manner: comp. ii. 50, iii. 15, vii. 39, xvi. 14, xx. 20, xxiii. 12. The recognition that John was under special Divine influence caused the question, τί ἄρα ἔσται; to be often repeated in after times. Here, as in Acts xi. 21, χεὶρ Κυρίου is followed by μετά, and the meaning is that the Divine power interposes to guide and bless. See small print on i. 20 for other parallels between Gospel and Acts. Where the preposition which follows is ἐπί, the Divine interposition is generally one of punishment (Acts xiii. 11; Judg. ii. 15; 1 Sam. v. 3, 6, vii. 13; Exod. vii. 4, 5). But this is by no means always the case (2 Kings iii. 15; Ezra vii. 6, viii. 22, 31), least of all where χείρ has the epithet ἀγαθή (Ezra vii. 9, 28, viii. 18). In N.T. χεὶρ Κυρίου is peculiar to Lk. (Acts xi. 21, xiii. 11; comp. iv. 28, 30).

67-79. The *Benedictus* or Song of Zacharias may be the εὐλογία mentioned in ver. 64.[1] To omit it there, in order to continue the narrative without interruption, and to give it as a solemn conclusion, would be a natural arrangement. As the *Magnificat* is modelled on the psalms, so the *Benedictus* is modelled on the

[1] Like most of the canticles, the *Benedictus* was originally said at Lauds: and it is still said at Lauds, in the Roman Church daily, in the Greek Church on special occasions. See footnote on p. 67.

prophecies, and it has been called "the last prophecy of the Old Dispensation and the first in the New." And while the tone of the *Magnificat* is regal, that of the *Benedictus* is sacerdotal. The one is as appropriate to the daughter of David as the other to the son of Aaron. The relation between new and old may again be seen in a table.

The Benedictus.	The Old Testament.
Εὐλογητὸς Κύριος ὁ Θεὸς τοῦ Ἰσραήλ,	[1] Εὐλογητὸς Κύριος ὁ Θεὸς Ἰσραήλ.
ὅτι ἐπεσκέψατο καὶ ἐποίησεν λύτρωσιν τῷ λαῷ αὐτοῦ,	[2] λύτρωσιν ἀπέστειλεν τῷ λαῷ αὐτοῦ.
καὶ ἤγειρεν κέρας σωτηρίας ἡμῖν	[3] ἐκεῖ ἐξανατελῶ κέρας τῷ Δαυείδ.
ἐν οἴκῳ Δαυεὶδ παιδὸς αὐτοῦ,	[4] ἀνατελεῖ κέρας παντὶ τῷ οἴκῳ Ἰσραήλ.
	[5] ὑψώσει κέρας Χριστοῦ αὐτοῦ.
καθὼς ἐλάλησεν διὰ στόματος τῶν ἁγίων ἀπ' αἰῶνος προφητῶν αὐτοῦ	
σωτηρίαν ἐξ ἐχθρῶν ἡμῶν καὶ ἐκ χειρὸς πάντων τῶν μισούντων ἡμᾶς,	[6] ἔσωσεν αὐτοὺς ἐκ χειρῶν μισούντων καὶ ἐλυτρώσατο αὐτοὺς ἐκ χειρὸς ἐχθροῦ.
ποιῆσαι ἔλεος μετὰ τῶν πατέρων ἡμῶν	[7] δώσει εἰς ἀλήθειαν τῷ Ἰακώβ, ἔλεον τῷ Ἀβραάμ, καθότι ὤμοσας τοῖς πατράσιν ἡμῶν.
καὶ μνησθῆναι διαθήκης ἁγίας αὐτοῦ,	[8] ἐμνήσθη τῆς διαθήκης αὐτοῦ.
ὅρκον ὃν ὤμοσεν πρὸς Ἀβραὰμ τὸν πατέρα ἡμῶν,	[9] ἐμνήσθη ὁ Θεὸς τῆς διαθήκης αὐτοῦ τῆς πρὸς Ἀβραάμ, καὶ Ἰσαάκ, καὶ Ἰακώβ.
τοῦ δοῦναι ἡμῖν ἀφόβως ἐκ χειρὸς ἐχθρῶν ῥυσθέντας λατρεύειν αὐτῷ ἐν ὁσιότητι	[10] ὅπως στήσω τὸν ὅρκον μου, ὃν ὤμοσα τοῖς πατράσιν ὑμῶν, τοῦ δοῦναι αὐτοῖς γῆν ῥέουσαν γάλα καὶ μέλι.
καὶ δικαιοσύνῃ ἐνώπιον αὐτοῦ πάσαις ταῖς ἡμέραις ἡμῶν.	[11] ἐμνήσθη εἰς τὸν αἰῶνα διαθήκης αὐτοῦ λόγου οὗ ἐνετείλατο εἰς χιλίας γενεάς, ὃν διέθετο τῷ Ἀβραάμ, καὶ τοῦ ὅρκου αὐτοῦ τῷ Ἰσαάκ.
Καὶ σὺ δέ, παιδίον, προφήτης Ὑψίστου κληθήσῃ, προπορεύσῃ γὰρ ἐνώπιον Κυρίου	[12] Ἐγὼ ἐξαποστέλλω τὸν ἄγγελόν μου καὶ ἐπιβλέψεται ὁδὸν πρὸ προσώπου μου.
ἑτοιμάσαι ὁδοὺς αὐτοῦ,	[13] ἑτοιμάσατε τὴν ὁδὸν Κυρίου.
τοῦ δοῦναι γνῶσιν σωτηρίας τῷ λαῷ αὐτοῦ ἐν ἀφέσει ἁμαρτιῶν αὐτῶν διὰ σπλάγχνα ἐλέους Θεοῦ ἡμῶν, ἐν οἷς ἐπισκέψεται ἡμᾶς ἀνατολὴ ἐξ ὕψους,	[14] καθημένους ἐν σκότει.
ἐπιφᾶναι τοῖς ἐν σκότει καὶ σκιᾷ θανάτου καθημένοις	[15] οἱ κατοικοῦντες ἐν χώρᾳ καὶ σκιᾳ θανάτου φῶς λάμψει ἐφ' ὑμᾶς.
τοῦ κατευθῦναι τοὺς πόδας ἡμῶν εἰς ὁδὸν εἰρήνης.	[16] καθημένους ἐν σκότει καὶ σκιᾳ θανάτου.

There is a manifest break at the end of ver. 75. The first of these two portions thus separated may be divided into three

[1] Ps. xli. 14, lxxii. 18, cvi. 48. [2] Ps. cxi. 9. [3] Ps. cxxxii. 17. [4] Ezek. xxix. 21. [5] 1 Sam. ii. 10. [6] Ps. cvi. 10. [7] Mic. vii. 20. [8] Ps. cvi. 45. [9] Exod. ii. 24. [10] Jer. xi. 5. [11] Ps. cv. 8, 9. [12] Mal. iii. 1. [13] Is. xl. 3. [14] Is. xlii. 7. [15] Is. ix. 1. [16] Ps. cvii. 10.

strophes (68, 69; 70–72; 73–75), and the second into two (76, 77; 78, 79).

67. ἐπλήσθη πνεύματος ἁγίου καὶ ἐπροφήτευσεν. See on ver. 15. The prophesying must not be confined to the prediction of the future; it is the delivery of the Divine message; speaking under God's influence, and in His Name. Zacharias sees in his son the earnest and guarantee of the deliverance of Israel.

In some texts *ἐπροφήτευσεν* has been altered into the more regular *προεφήτευσεν*, but everywhere in N.T. (even Jude 14) the augment should precede the prep. in this compound. This is intelligible, seeing that there is no simple verb *φητεύω*. Comp. Num. xi. 25, 26; Ecclus. xlviii. 13, and the similar forms *ἤφιεν* and *ἤνοιξεν*. Win. xii. 5, p. 84.

68. Εὐλογητὸς Κύριος ὁ Θεὸς τοῦ Ἰσραήλ. Not *ἐστίν* but *εἴη* is to be supplied. The line is *verbatim* as Ps. xli. 14, lxxii. 18, cvi. 48, excepting that in LXX *τοῦ* is omitted. In N.T. *εὐλογητός* is used of God, but never of men: see on ver. 42. In LXX there are a few exceptions: Deut. vii. 14; Ruth ii. 20; 1 Sam. xv. 13, xxv. 33.

ἐπεσκέψατο καὶ ἐποίησεν λύτρωσιν τῷ λαῷ αὐτοῦ. Here, as in Ecclus. xxxii. 17, an acc. is to be supplied after *ἐπεσκέψατο*; there *τὸν ταπεινόν*, here *τὸν λαόν*. See on vii. 16. Excepting Heb. ii. 6, where it is a quotation from Ps. viii. 5, this verb is used in the Hebrew sense (Exod. iv. 31) of Divine visitation by Lk. alone in N.T. Comp. *Ps. Sol.* iii. 14. No doubt *λύτρωσιν* has reference to political redemption (ver. 71), but accompanied by and based upon a moral and spiritual reformation (*vv.* 75, 77). Comp. Ps. cxxix. 7.

69. καὶ ἤγειρεν κέρας σωτηρίας ἡμῖν. For this use of *ἐγείρω* comp. *ἤγειρεν Κύριος σωτῆρα τῷ Ἰσραήλ* (Judg. iii. 9, 15). In Ezek. xxix. 21 and Ps. cxxxii. 17 the verb used is *ἀνατέλλω* or *ἐξανατέλλω* (see table). The metaphor of the horn is very freq. in O.T. (1 Sam. ii. 10; 2 Sam. xxii. 3; Ps. lxxv. 5, 6, 11, etc.), and is taken neither from the horns of the altar, nor from the peaks of helmets or head-dresses, but from the horns of animals, especially bulls. It represents, therefore, primarily, neither safety nor dignity, but strength. The wild-ox, wrongly called "unicorn" in AV., was proverbial for strength (Num. xxiv. 8; Job xxxix. 9–11; Deut. xxxiii. 17). In Horace we have *addis cornua pauperi*, and in Ovid *tum pauper cornua sumit*. In Ps. xviii. 3 God is called a *κέρας σωτηρίας*. See below on ver. 71. For **παιδὸς αὐτοῦ** see on ver. 54. "In the house of His servant David" is all the more true if Mary was of the house of David. But the fact that Jesus was the heir of Joseph is sufficient, and this verse is no proof of Mary's descent from David.

70. Second strophe. Like ver. 55, this is not a parenthesis, but determines the preceding statement more exactly. As a priest,

Zacharias would be familiar with O.T. prophecies. Even if the τῶν before ἀπ' αἰῶνος (A C D) were genuine, it would be unlikely that τῶν ἁγίων means "the saints" in app. with τῶν ἀπ' αἰῶνος προφητῶν. Lk. is fond of the epithet ἅγιος (ver. 72, ix. 26; Acts iii. 21, x. 22, xxi. 28). He is also fond of the periphrasis διὰ στόματος (Acts i. 16, iii. 18, 21, iv. 25): comp. 2 Chron. xxxvi. 22. And the expression ἀπ' αἰῶνος is peculiar to him in N.T. (Acts iii. 21, xv. 18). It is used vaguely for "of old time." Here it does not mean that there have been Prophets "since the world began." Comp. οἱ γίγαντες οἱ ἀπ' αἰῶνος (Gen. vi. 4), and καταβροντᾷ καὶ καταφέγγει τοὺς ἀπ' αἰῶνος ῥήτορας (Longin. xxxiv.), and adverbially (Hes. *Theog.* 609).

71. σωτηρίαν ἐξ ἐχθρῶν ἡμῶν. This is in app. with κέρας σωτηρίας and epexegetic of it. That the ἐχθρῶν ἡμῶν and τῶν μισούντων ἡμᾶς are identical is clear from Ps. xviii. 18 and cvi. 10 (see table). The heathen are meant. Gentile domination prevents the progress of God's kingdom, and the Messiah will put an end to this hindrance. Comp. Exod. xviii. 10.

Neither σωτηρία (*vv.* 69, 77, xix. 9; Acts iv. 12, etc.) nor τὸ σωτήριον (ii. 30, iii. 6; Acts xxviii. 28) occur in Mt. or Mk. The former occurs once in Jn. (iv. 22). Both are common in LXX. The primary meaning is preservation from bodily harm (Gen. xxvi. 31; 2 Sam. xix. 2), especially of the great occasions on which God had preserved Israel (Exod. xiv. 13, xv. 2; 2 Chron. xx. 17); and hence of the deliverance to be wrought by the Messiah (Is. xlix. 6, 8), which is the meaning here. Comp. τοῦ κυρίου ἡ σωτηρία ἐπ' οἶκον Ἰσραὴλ εἰς εὐφροσύνην αἰώνιον (*Ps. Sol.* x. 9; and very similarly xii. 7). As the idea of the Messianic salvation became enlarged and purified, the word which so often expressed it came gradually to mean much the same as "eternal life." See on Rom. i. 16.

72. ποιῆσαι ἔλεος μετά, κ.τ.λ. This is the purpose of ἤγειρεν κέρας. The phrase is freq. in LXX (Gen. xxiv. 12; Judg. i. 24, viii. 35; Ruth i. 8; 1 Sam. xx. 8, etc.). Comp. μετ' αὐτῆς, ver. 58. "In delivering us God purposed to deal mercifully with our fathers." This seems to imply that the fathers are conscious of what takes place: comp. *vv.* 54, 55. Besides the passages given in the table, comp. Lev. xxvi. 42, and see Wsctt. on Heb. ix. 15, 16.

73. ὅρκον ὃν ὤμοσεν πρὸς Ἀβραάμ. Third strophe. The oath is recorded Gen. xxii. 16–18: comp. *Ep. of Barnabas*, xiv. 1.

It is best to take ὅρκον in app. with διαθήκης, but attracted in case to ὅν: comp. *vv.* 4, 20, and see on iii. 19. It is true that in LXX μνησθῆναι is found with an acc. (Exod. xx. 8; Gen. ix. 16). But would Lk. give it first a gen. and then an acc. in the same sentence? For the attraction of the antecedent to the relative comp. xx. 17 and perhaps Acts x. 36.

ὤμοσεν πρός Ἀ. So also in Hom. (*Od.* xiv. 331, xix. 288): but see on ver. 13.

74. τοῦ δοῦναι ἡμῖν. This is probably to be taken after ὅρκον as the contents and purpose of the oath; and the promise that "thy seed shall possess the gate of his enemies" (Gen. xxii. 17) is in favour of this. But it is possible to take τοῦ δοῦναι as epexegetic of ver. 72; or again, as the purpose of ἤγειρεν κέρας, and therefore parallel to ver. 72. This last is not likely, because there is no τοῦ with ποιῆσαι. This τοῦ *c. infin.* of the purpose or result is a favourite constr. with Lk. (*vv.* 77, 79, ii. 24, where see reff.). It marks the later stage of the language, in which aim and purpose become confused with result. Perhaps the gen. of the aim may be explained on the analogy of the part. gen. after verbs of hitting or missing.

ἐκ χειρὸς ἐχθρῶν. It does not follow from ὁσιότητι καὶ δικαιοσύνῃ that spiritual enemies are meant. The tyranny of heathen conquerors was a hindrance to holiness. In addition to the parallel passages quoted in the table, comp. Ps. xviii. 18, ῥύσεταί με ἐξ ἐχθρῶν μου δυνατῶν καὶ ἐκ τῶν μισούντων με.

For the acc. ῥυσθέντας after ἡμῖν comp. σοὶ δὲ συγγνώμη λέγειν τάδ' ἐστί, μὴ πάσχουσαν ὡς ἐγὼ κακῶς (Eur. *Med.* 814).

75. λατρεύειν αὐτῷ. Comp. λατρεύσετε τῷ Θεῷ ἐν τῷ ὄρει τούτῳ (Exod. iii. 12). We must take ἐνώπιον αὐτοῦ with λατρεύειν αὐτῷ. The service of the redeemed and delivered people is to be a *priestly* service, like that of Zacharias (ver. 8). For ἐνώπιον see on ver. 15, and for λατρεύειν on iv. 8. The combination ὁσιότης καὶ δικαιοσύνη becomes common; but perhaps the earliest instance is Wisd. ix. 3. We have it Eph. iv. 24 and Clem. Rom. xlviii.: comp. Tit. i. 8 and 1 Thes. ii. 10.

76. Καὶ σὺ δέ, παιδίον. Here the second part of the hymn, and the distinctively predictive portion of it, begins. The Prophet turns from the bounty of Jehovah in sending the Messiah to the work of the Forerunner. "*But* thou also, child," or "Yea and thou, child" (RV.). Neither the καί nor the δέ must be neglected. There is combination, but there is also contrast. Not "*my* child": the personal relation is lost in the high calling. The κληθήσῃ has the same force as in ver. 32: not only "shalt be," but "shalt be acknowledged as being."

προπορεύσῃ γὰρ ἐνώπιον Κυρίου. Comp. Κύριος ὁ Θεός σου ὁ προπορευόμενος πρὸ προσώπου σου, καθὰ ἐλάλησεν Κύριος (Deut. xxxi. 3). Here Κυρίου means Jehovah, not the Christ, as is clear from *vv.* 16, 17.

77. τοῦ δοῦναι γνῶσιν σωτηρίας τῷ λαῷ αὐτοῦ. This is the aim and end of the work of the Forerunner. In construction it comes after ἑτοιμάσαι ὁδοὺς αὐτοῦ. We may take ἐν ἀφέσει ἁμαρτιῶν αὐτῶν with either δοῦναι, or γνῶσιν, or σωτηρίας. The last is best. John did not grant remission of sins; and to make "*knowledge* of salvation" consist in remission of sins, yields no very clear sense. But that *salvation* is found in remission of sins makes excellent sense (Acts v. 31). The Messiah brings the σωτηρία (*vv.* 69, 71): the Forerunner gives the knowledge of it *to* the people, as consisting, not in a political deliverance from the dominion of Rome, but in a spiritual deliverance from the dominion of sin. This is the first mention of the "remission of sins" in the Gospel narrative.

78. διὰ σπλάγχνα ἐλέους Θεοῦ ἡμῶν. The concluding strophe, referring to the whole of the preceding sentence, or (if we take a single word) to προπορεύσῃ. It is *because* of God's tender mercy that the child will be able to fulfil his high calling and to do all this. Comp. *Test. XII. Patr.* Levi iv., ἕως ἐπισκέψηται Κύριος πάντα τὰ ἔθνη **ἐν σπλάγχνοις** υἱοῦ αὐτοῦ ἕως αἰῶνος: also Levi vii. and viii.

Originally the σπλάγχνα were the "inward parts," esp. the upper portions, the heart, lungs, and liver (*viscera thoracis*), as distinct from the ἔντερα or bowels (*viscera abdominis*). The Greeks made the σπλάγχνα the seat of the emotions, anger, anxiety, pity, etc. By the Jews these feelings were placed in the ἔντερα; and hence in LXX we have not only σπλάγχνα (which may include the ἔντερα), but also κοιλία and ἔγκατα used for the affections. Moreover in Hebr. literature these words more often represent compassion or love, whereas σπλάγχνα in class. Grk. is more often used of wrath (Aristoph. *Ran.* 844, 1006; Eur. *Alc.* 1009). "Heart" is the nearest English equivalent for σπλάγχνα (RV. Col. iii. 12; Philem. 12, 20). See Lft. on Phil. i. 8. "Because of our God's heart of mercy," *i.e.* merciful heart, is the meaning here. For this descriptive or characterizing gen. comp. Jas. i. 25, ii. 4; Jude 18. Some would make γνῶσιν σωτηρίας an instance of it, "saving knowledge," *i.e.* that brings salvation. But this is not necessary. For **ἐν οἷς** see on ἐν βραχίονι, ver. 51. For **ἐπισκέψεται**[1] comp. vii. 17; Ecclus. xlvi. 14; Judith viii. 33; and see on ver. 68.

ἀνατολὴ ἐξ ὕψους. "Rising from on high." The word is used of the rising of the *sun* (Rev. vii. 2, xvi. 12; Hom. *Od.* xii. 4) and of *stars* (Æsch. *P.V.* 457; Eur. *Phœn.* 504). Here the rising of the heavenly body is put for the heavenly body itself. Comp. the use of ἀνατέλλω in Is. lx. 1 and Mal. iv. 2. Because sun, moon, and stars do not rise *from* on high, some join ἐξ ὕψους with ἐπισκέψεται, which is admissible. But, as ἀνατολή means the sun or star itself, whose light comes from on high, this is not necessary. Seeing that ἀνατέλλω is used of the rising or sprouting of *plants*, and that the Messiah is sometimes called "the Branch" (Jer. xxiii. 5, xxxiii. 15; Zech. iii. 8, vi. 12), and that in LXX this is expressed by ἀνατολή, some would adopt that meaning here. But ἐξ ὕψους, ἐπιφᾶναι, and κατευθῦναι are conclusive against it. These expressions agree well with a rising sun or star, but not with a sprouting branch.

79. ἐπιφᾶναι τοῖς ἐν σκότει καὶ σκιᾷ θανάτου καθημένοις. For ἐπιφᾶναι comp. Acts xxvii. 20, and for the form Ps. xxx. 17, cxvii. 27. In 3 Mac. vi. 4 we have Σὺ Φαραὼ . . . ἀπώλεσας, Φέγγος ἐπιφάνας ἐλέους Ἰσραὴλ γένει. Note that the καθημένους ἐν σκότει of Is. xlii. 7 and the σκίᾳ θανάτου of Is. ix. 1 are combined here as in Ps. cvii. 10 (see table). Those who hold that these hymns are

[1] This is the reading of ℵ B Syr. Arm. Goth. Boh. and virtually of L, which has ἐπεσκέψαιται. Godet defends ἐπεσκέψατο, because Zacharias would not suddenly turn from the past to the future; but this thought would lead tc the corruption of the more difficult reading.

written in the interests of Ebionism have to explain why πεπεδημένους ἐν πτωχείᾳ (Ps. cvii. 10) is omitted.

τοῦ κατευθῦναι τοὺς πόδας ἡμῶν εἰς ὁδὸν εἰρήνης. For the constr. comp. *vv.* 74, 77. Those who sat in darkness did not use their feet: the light enables them to do so, and to use them profitably. The ἡμῶν shows that Jews as well as Gentiles are regarded as being in darkness until the Messianic dawn. "The way of peace" is the way that leads to peace, especially peace between God and His people (Ps. xxix. 11, lxxxv. 9, cxix. 165; Jer. xiv. 13). It was one of the many blessings which the Messiah was to bring (ii. 14, x. 5, xxiv. 36). See on Rom. i. 7 and comp. ὁδὸν σωτηρίας (Acts xvi. 17).

80. Τὸ δὲ παιδίον ηὔξανε καὶ ἐκραταιοῦτο πνεύματι. The verse forms a set conclusion to the narrative, as if here one of the Aramaic documents used by Lk. came to an end. Comp. ii. 40, 52; Judg. xiii. 24, 25; 1 Sam. ii. 26. In LXX αὐξάνω is never, as here, intrans. Thus αὐξανῶ σε σφόδρα (Gen. xvii. 6); ηὐξήθη τὸ παιδίον (Gen. xxi. 8). In N.T. it is used of physical growth (ii. 40, xii. 27, xiii. 19), and of the spread of the Gospel (Acts vi. 7, xii. 24, xix. 20). With ἐκραταιοῦτο πνεύματι comp. Eph. iii. 16; and for the dat. Rom. iv. 20? and 1 Cor. xiv. 20.

ἦν ἐν ταῖς ἐρήμοις. The wilderness of Judæa, west of the Dead Sea, is no doubt meant. But the name is not given, because the point is, not that he lived in any particular desert, but that he lived in desert places and not in towns or villages. He lived a solitary life. Hence nothing is said about his being "in favour with men"; for he avoided men until his ἀνάδειξις brought him disciples. This fact answers the question whether John was influenced by the Essenes, communities of whom lived in the wilderness of Judæa. We have no reason to believe that he came in contact with them. Excepting the ascetic life, and a yearning for something better than obsolete Judaism, there was little resemblance between their principles and his. He preached the Kingdom of God; they preached isolation. They abandoned society; he strove to reform it. See Godet *in loco* and *D.B.*[2] art. "Essenes." Lk. alone uses the plur. αἱ ἔρημοι (v. 16, viii. 29).

ἕως ἡμέρας ἀναδείξεως αὐτοῦ πρὸς τὸν Ἰσραήλ. John probably went up to Jerusalem for the feasts, and on those occasions he and the Messiah may have met, but without John's recognizing Him as such. Here only in N.T. does ἀνάδειξις occur. In Ecclus. xliii. 6 we have ἀνάδειξιν χρόνων as a function of the moon. In Plut. the word is used of the proclaiming or inauguration of those who are appointed to office (*Mar.* viii.; *C. Grac.* xii.). It is also used of the dedication of a temple (Strabo, viii. 5. 23, p. 381). Comp. ἀνέδειξεν of the appointment of the Seventy (x. 1). It was John himself who proclaimed the inauguration of his office by manifesting himself to the people at God's command (iii. 2).

Note on the Use of ἐγένετο.

More than any other Evangelist Lk. makes use of the Hebr. formula, ἐγένετο δέ or καὶ ἐγένετο. But with it he uses a variety of constructions, some of which are modelled on the classical use of συνέβη, which Lk. himself employs Acts xxi. 35. The following types are worth noting.

(α) The ἐγένετο and that which came to pass are placed side by side as parallel statements in the indicative mood without a conjunction.

i. 8. ἐγένετο δὲ ἐν τῷ ἱερατεύειν αὐτὸν . . . ἔλαχε τοῦ θυμιᾶσαι.
i. 23. καὶ ἐγένετο ὡς ἐπλήσθησαν αἱ ἡμέραι τῆς λειτουργίας αὐτοῦ, ἀπῆλθεν.
i. 41. καὶ ἐγένετο ὡς ἤκουσεν τὸν ἀσπασμὸν τῆς Μ. ἡ Ἐ., ἐσκίρτησεν τὸ βρέφος.
ii. 1. ἐγένετο δὲ ἐν ταῖς ἡμέραις ἐκείναις ἐξῆλθεν δόγμα.

Of the same type are i. 59, ii. 6, 15, 46, vii. 11, ix. 18, 28, 29, 33, 37, xi. 1, 14, 27, xvii. 14, xviii. 35, xix. 29, xx. 1, xxiv. 30, 51. In viii. 40, ix. 57, x. 38 the ἐγένετο δέ is probably spurious. In the Acts this type does not occur.

(β) The ἐγένετο and that which came to pass are coupled together by καί, which may be regarded as (1) uniting two co-ordinate statements; or (2) epexegetic, "It came to pass, *namely*"; or (3) introducing the apodosis, as often in class. Grk., "It came to pass *that*."

v. 1. ἐγένετο δὲ ἐν τῷ τὸν ὄχλον ἐπικεῖσθαι αὐτῷ . . . καὶ αὐτὸς ἦν ἑστώς.
v. 17. καὶ ἐγένετο ἐν μιᾷ τῶν ἡμερῶν καὶ αὐτὸς ἦν διδάσκων.
viii. 1. καὶ ἐγένετο ἐν τῷ καθεξῆς καὶ αὐτὸς διώδευεν.
viii. 22. ἐγένετο δὲ ἐν μιᾷ τῶν ἡμερῶν καὶ αὐτὸς ἐνέβη εἰς πλοῖον.

Of the same type are v. 12, ix. 51, xiv. 1, xvii. 11, xix. 15, xxiv. 4; Acts v. 7. It will be observed that in nearly all cases the καί is followed by αὐτός or αὐτοί. In v. 12 and xxiv. 4 it is followed by the Hebraistic ἰδού, and in xix. 15 we have simply καὶ εἶπεν.

(γ) That which takes place is put in the infinitive mood, and this depends upon ἐγένετο.

iii. 21. ἐγένετο δέ ἐν τῷ βαπτισθῆναι ἅπαντα τὸν λαὸν . . . ἀνεῳχθῆναι τὸν οὐρανόν.
vi. 1. ἐγένετο δὲ ἐν σαββάτῳ διαπορεύεσθαι αὐτὸν διὰ σπορίμων.
vi. 12. ἐγένετο δὲ ἐν ταῖς ἡμέραις ταύταις ἐξελθεῖν αὐτὸν εἰς τὸ ὄρος.
xvi. 22. ἐγένετο δὲ ἀποθανεῖν τὸν πτωχόν.

This type of construction is common in the Acts: iv. 5, ix. 32, 37, 43, xi. 26, xiv. 1, xvi. 16, xix. 1, xxii. 6, 17, xxviii. 8, 17.

(δ) In the Acts we have several other forms still more closely assimilated to classical constructions, the ἐγένετο being placed later in the sentence, or being preceded by ὡς or ὅτε.

ix. 3. ἐν δὲ τῷ πορεύεσθαι ἐγένετο αὐτὸν ἐγγίζειν τῇ Δαμασκῷ.
xxi. 1. ὡς δὲ ἐγένετο ἀναχθῆναι ἡμᾶς . . . ἤλθομεν εἰς τὴν Κῶ.
xxi. 5. ὅτε δὲ ἐγένετο ἐξαρτίσαι ἡμᾶς τὰς ἡμέρας, ἐξέλθοντες ἐπορευόμεθα.
x. 25. ὡς δὲ ἐγένετο τοῦ εἰσελθεῖν τὸν Πέτρον, . . . προσεκύνησεν.

In these last three instances we are far removed from the Hebraistic types (α) and (β). The last is very peculiar; but comp. xxvii. 1 and the exact parallel in *Acta Barnab. Apocryp.* vii. quoted by Lumby, ὡς δὲ ἐγένετο τοῦ τελέσαι αὐτοὺς διδάσκοντας.

We have obtained in this analysis the following results. Of the two Hebraistic types, (α) is very common in the first two chapters of the Gospel, where Lk. is specially under the influence of Hebrew thought and literature, and is probably translating from the Aramaic; but (α) is not found at all in the Acts, and (β) occurs there only once. On the other hand, of the more classical types, (γ) is much less common in the Gospel than in the Acts, while the forms grouped under (δ) do not occur in the Gospel at all. All which is quite what we might have expected. In the Acts there is much less room for Hebrew influences than there is in the Gospel; and thus the more classical forms of construction become there the prevailing types.

II. 1–20. *The Birth of the Saviour, its Proclamation by the Angels, and its Verification by the Shepherds.*

The second of the narratives in the second group (i. 57–ii. 40) in the Gospel of the Infancy (i. 5–ii. 52). It corresponds to the Annunciation (i. 26–38) in the first group. Like the sections which precede and which follow, it has a clearly marked conclusion. And these conclusions have in some cases a very marked resemblance. Comp. ii. 20 with i. 56, and ii. 40 and 52 with i. 80. This similarity of form points to the use of material from one and the same source, and carefully arranged according to the subject-matter. This source would be some member of the Holy Family (see on i. 5). The marks of Lk.'s style, accompanied by Hebraistic forms of expression, still continue; and we infer, as before, that he is translating from an Aramaic document. The section has three marked divisions: the Birth (1–7), the Angelic Proclamation (8–14), and the Verification (15–20). The connexion with what precedes is obvious. We have just been told how the promise to Zacharias was fulfilled; and we are now to be told how the promise to Mary was fulfilled.

1–7. The Birth of the Saviour at Bethlehem at the Time of the Enrolment. The extreme simplicity of the narrative is in very marked contrast with the momentous character of the event thus narrated. We have a similar contrast between matter and form in the opening verses of S. John's Gospel. The difference between the evangelical account and modern Lives of Christ is here very remarkable. The tasteless and unedifying elaborations of the apocryphal gospels should also be compared.[1]

1–3. How Bethlehem came to be the Birthplace of Jesus Christ, although Nazareth was the Home of His Parents. This explanation has exposed Lk. to an immense amount of criticism, which has been expressed and sifted in a manner that has produced a voluminous literature. In addition to the commentaries, some

[1] "Such marvellous associations have clung for centuries to these verses, that it is hard to realise how absolutely naked they are of all ornament. We are obliged to read them again and again to assure ourselves that they really do set forth what we call the great miracle of the world. If, on the other hand, the Evangelist was possessed by the conviction that he was not recording a miracle which had interrupted the course of history and deranged the order of human life, but was telling of a divine act which explained the course of history and restored the order of human life, one can very well account for his calmness" (F. D. Maurice, *Lectures on S. Luke*, p. 28, ed. 1879).

of the following may be consulted, and from Schürer and Herzog further information about the literature may be obtained.

S. J. Andrews, *Life of our Lord*, pp. 71–81, T. & T. Clark, 1892; T. Lewin, *Fasti Sacri*, 955, Longmans, 1865; J. B. McClellan, *The New Testament of our Lord and Saviour*, i. pp. 392–399, Macmillan, 1875; C. F. Nösgen, *Geschichte Jesu Christi*, pp. 172–174, Beck, 1891; *E. Schürer, *Jewish People in the Time of Jesus Christ*, i. 2, pp. 105–143, T. & T. Clark, 1890; B. Weiss, *Leben Jesu*, i. 2. 4, Berlin, 1882; Eng. tr. pp. 250–252; K. Wieseler, *Chronological Synopsis of the Four Gospels*, pp. 66–106, 129–135, Deighton, 1864; O. Zöckler, *Handbuch der Theologischen Wissenschaften*, i. 2, pp. 188–190, Beck, 1889; A. W. Zumpt, *Das Geburtsjahr Christi* (reviewed by Woolsey in the *Bibliotheca Sacra*, 1870), Leipzig, 1869; *D.B.*[2] art. "Cyrenius"; Herzog, *PRE.*[2] xiii. art. "Schatzung"; P. Schaff, *History of the Church*, i. pp. 121–125, T. & T. Clark, 1883; Ramsay, *Was Christ Born at Bethlehem?* 1899; Hastings, *D.B.* art. Chronology of N.T.

1. Ἐγένετο δὲ ἐν ταῖς ἡμέραις ἐκείναις ἐξῆλθεν δόγμα παρὰ Καίσαρος Αὐγούστου ἀπογράφεσθαι πᾶσαν τὴν οἰκουμένην. For the constr. see detached note at the end of ch. i.; and for ἐν ταῖς ἡμέραις ἐκείναις see on i. 5 and 39. The time of the birth of John is roughly indicated. Even in class. Grk. the first meaning of **δόγμα**, as "opinion, philosophic tenet," is not very common (Plat. *Rep.* 538 C); it is more often a "public decree, ordinance." This is always the meaning in N.T., whether an ordinance of the Roman Emperor (Acts xvii. 7), or of the Apostles (Acts xvi. 4; comp. Ign. *Mag.* xiii.; *Didaché*, xi. 3), or of the Mosaic Law (Col. ii. 14; Eph. ii. 15; comp. 3 Mac. i. 3; Jos. *Ant.* xv. 5. 3). For **ἐξῆλθεν δόγμα** comp. Dan. ii. 13 (Theod.). In Daniel δόγμα is freq. of a royal decree (iii. 10, iv. 3, vi. 9, 10). See Lft. on Col. ii. 14.

ἀπογράφεσθαι. Probably passive, *ut describeretur* (Vulg.), not middle, as in ver. 3. The present is here used of the continuous enrolment of the multitudes; the aorist in ver. 5 of the act of one person. The verb refers to the *writing off*, copying, or entering the names, professions, fortunes, and families of subjects in the *public register*, generally with a view to *taxation* (ἀποτίμησις or τίμημα). It is a more general word than ἀποτιμάω, which implies assessment as well as enrolment. But it is manifest that the ἀπογραφή here and in Acts v. 37 included assessment. The Jews were exempt from military service; and enrolment for that purpose cannot be intended. In the provinces the census was mainly for purposes of taxation.

πᾶσαν τὴν οἰκουμένην. "The whole inhabited world," *i.e.* the Roman Empire, *orbis terrarum*. Perhaps in a loose way the expression might be used of the provinces only. But both the πᾶσαν and the context exclude the limitation to Palestine, a meaning which the expression never has, not even in Jos. *Ant.* viii. 3. 4. See on iv. 5 and xxi. 26. In inscriptions Roman Emperors are called κύριοι τῆς οἰκουμένης. The verse implies *a decree for a general census throughout the empire.*

It must be confessed that *no direct evidence of any such decree exists* beyond this statement by Lk., and the repetitions of it by Christian writers. But a variety of items have been collected, which tend to show that a Roman census in Judæa at this time, in accordance with some general instructions given by Augustus, is not improbable.

1. The *rationarium* or *rationes imperii*, which was a sort of balance-sheet published periodically by the emperor (Suet. *Aug.* xxviii.; *Cal.* xvi.). 2. The *libellus* or *breviarium totius imperii*, which Augustus deposited with his will (Tac. *Ann.* i. 11. 5, 6; Suet. *Aug.* ci.). 3. The *index rerum gestarum* to be inscribed on his tomb, which was the original of the *Marmor Ancyranum.* But these only indicate the orderly administration of the empire. A general census would have been useful in producing such things; but that does not prove that it took place. Two passages in Dion Cassius are cited; but one of these (liv. 35) refers to a registration of the emperor's private property, and the other (lv. 13) to a census of Roman citizens. If Augustus made a general survey of the empire, of which there is evidence from the *commentarii* of Agrippa mentioned by Pliny (*Nat. Hist.* iii. 2. 17), this also would have been conveniently combined with a general census, although it does not show that such a census was ordered. Of some of the provinces we *know* that *no* census was held in them during the reign of Augustus. But it is probable that in the majority of them a census took place; and the statement of so accurate a writer as Lk., although unsupported by direct evidence, may be accepted as substantially true: viz. that in the process of reducing the empire to order, Augustus had required that a census should be held throughout most of it. So that Lk. groups the various instances under one expression, just as in Acts xi. 28 he speaks of the famines, which took place in different parts of the empire in the time of Claudius, as a famine ἐφ' ὅλην οἰκουμένην. Of the Christian witnesses none is of much account. Riess seems to be almost alone in contending that Orosius (*Hist. Rom.* vi. 22. 6) had any authority other than Lk. Cassiodorus (*Variarum Epp.* iii. 52) does not mention a census of persons at all clearly; but if *orbis Romanus agris divisus censuque descriptus est* means such a census, he may be referring to Lk. ii. 1. The obscure statement of Isidore of Spain (*Etymologiarum*, v. 26. 4; *Opera*, iii. 229, ed. Arevallo) may either be derived from Lk. or refer to another period. What Suidas states (*Lex. s.v.* ἀπογραφή) partly comes from Lk. and partly is improbable. At the best, all this testimony is from 400 to 1000 years after the event, and cannot be rated highly. The passages are given in full by Schürer (*Jewish People in the T. of J. C.* i. 2, pp. 116, 117). But it is urged that a Roman census, even if held elsewhere, could not have been made in Palestine during the time of Herod the Great, because Palestine was not yet a Roman province. In A.D. 6, 7, when Quirinius certainly did undertake a Roman census in Judæa, such a proceeding was quite in order. Josephus shows that in taxation Herod acted independently (*Ant.* xv. 10. 4, xvi. 2. 5, xvii. 2. 1, 11. 2; comp. xvii. 8. 4). That Herod paid tribute to Rome is not certain; but, if so, he would pay it out of taxes raised by himself. The Romans would not assess his subjects for the tribute which he had to pay. Josephus, whose treatment of the last years of Herod is very full, does not mention any Roman census at that time. On the contrary, he implies that, even after the death of Herod, so long as Palestine was ruled by its own princes, there was no Roman taxation; and he states that

the census undertaken by Quirinius A.D. 7 excited intense opposition, presumably as being an innovation (*Ant.* xviii. 1. 1, 2. 1).

In meeting this objection, let us admit with Schürer and Zumpt that the case of the Clitæ(?) is not parallel. Tacitus (*Ann.* vi. 41. 1) does not say that the Romans held a census in the dominions of Archelaus, but that Archelaus wished to have a census after the Roman fashion. Nevertheless, the objection that Augustus would not interfere with Herod's subjects in the matter of taxation is untenable. When Palestine was divided among Herod's three sons, Augustus ordered that the taxes of the Samaritans should be reduced by one-fourth, because they had not taken part in the revolt against Varus (*Ant.* xvii. 11. 4; *B. J.* ii. 6. 3); and this was before Palestine became a Roman province. If he could do that, he could require information as to taxation throughout Palestine; and the obsequious Herod would not attempt to resist.[1] The value of such information would be great. It would show whether the tribute paid (if tribute was paid) was adequate; and it would enable Augustus to decide how to deal with Palestine in the future. If he knew that Herod's health was failing, he would be anxious to get the information before Herod's death; and thus the census would take place just at the time indicated by Lk., viz. in the last months of the reign of Herod. For "Clitæ" we should read *Kietai*; Ramsay, *Expositor*, April, 1897.

2. αὕτη ἀπογραφὴ πρώτη ἐγένετο. This may be accepted as certainly the true reading;[2] and the meaning of it is not really doubtful. "This took place as a first enrolment, when Q. was governor of Syria." The object of the remark is to distinguish the census which took Joseph and Mary to Bethlehem from the one undertaken by Q. in A.D. 6, 7, at which time Q. *was* governor of Syria. But was he governor B.C. 4, when Herod died? It is very difficult to establish this.

From B.C. 9 to 6 Sentius Saturninus was governor; from B.C. 6 to 4 Quinctilius Varus. Then all is uncertain until A.D. 6, when P. Sulpicius Quirinius becomes governor and holds the census mentioned Acts v. 37 and also by Josephus (*Ant.* xviii. 1. 1, 2. 1). It is quite possible, as Zumpt and others have shown, that Quirinius was governor of Syria during part of the interval between B.C. 4 and A.D. 6, and that his first term of office was B.C. 3, 2. But it seems to be impossible to find room for him between B.C. 9 and the death of Herod; and, unless we can do that, Lk. is not saved from an error in chronology. Tertullian states that the census was held by Sentius Saturninus (*Adv. Marc.* iv. 19); and if that is correct we may suppose that it was begun by him and continued by his successor. On the other hand, Justin Martyr three times states that Jesus Christ was born ἐπὶ Κυρηνίου, and in one place states that this can be officially ascertained ἐκ τῶν ἀπογραφῶν τῶν γενομένων (*Apol.* i. 34, 46; *Dial.* lxxviii.).

[1] See the treatment to which Herod had to submit in the matter of Syllæus (Jos. *Ant.* xvi. 9. 3, 4).

[2] B (supported by 81, 131, 203) has αὕτη ἀπογραφὴ πρώτη ἐγένετο.
ℵ has the impossible αὐτὴν ἀπογραφὴν ἐγένετο πρώτη.
D (supported by Orig-Lat.) has αὕτη ἐγένετο ἀπογραφὴ πρώτη.
Thus all three are against the ἡ before ἀπογραφή inserted in A C L R Ξ.

We must be content to leave the difficulty unsolved. But it is monstrous to argue that because Lk. has (possibly) made a mistake as to Quirinius being governor at this time, therefore the whole story about the census and Joseph's journey to Bethlehem is a fiction. Even if there was no census at this time, business connected with enrolment might take Joseph to Bethlehem, and Lk. would be correct as to his main facts. That Lk. has confused this census with the one in A.D. 6, 7, which he himself mentions Acts v. 37, is not credible. We are warranted in maintaining (1) that a Roman census in Judæa at this time, in accordance with instructions given by Augustus, is not improbable; and (2) that some official connexion of Quirinius with Syria and the holding of this census is not impossible. The accuracy of Lk. is such that we ought to require very strong evidence before rejecting any statement of his as an unquestionable blunder. But it is far better to admit the possibility of error than to attempt to evade this by either altering the text or giving forced interpretations of it.

The following methods of tampering with the *text* have been suggested: to regard πρώτη as a corruption of πρώτῳ ἔτει through the intermediate πρωτει (Linwood); to insert πρὸ τῆς after ἐγένετο (Michaelis); to substitute for Κυρηνίου either Κυιντιλίου (Huetius), or Κρονίου = Saturnini (Heumann), or Σατουρνίνου (Valesius); to omit the whole verse as a gloss (Beza, Pfaff, Valckenaer). All these are monstrous. The only points which can be allowed to be doubtful in the text are the accentuation of αὕτη and the spelling of Κυρηνίου, to which may perhaps be added the insertion of the article.

Among the various *interpretations* may be mentioned—

(1) Giving πρῶτος a comparative force, as in Jn. i. 15, 30: "This taxing took place before Quirinius was governor of Syria" (Huschke, Ewald, Caspari); or, as ἐσχάτη τῶν υἱῶν ἡ μήτηρ ἐτελεύτησε (2 Mac. vii. 41) means "The mother died last of all, and later than her sons," this may mean, "This took place as the first enrolment, and before Q. was governor of S." (Wieseler). But none of these passages are parallel: the addition of ἡγεμονεύοντος is fatal. When πρῶτος is comparative it is followed by a simple noun or pronoun. It is incredible that Lk., if he had meant this, should have expressed it so clumsily.

(2) Emphasizing ἐγένετο, as in Acts xi. 28: "This taxing took effect, was carried out, when Q. was governor of S." (Gumpach, etc.); *i.e.* the decree was issued in Herod's time, and executed ten or twelve years later by Q. This makes nonsense of the narrative. Why did Joseph go to Bethlehem to be enrolled, if no enrolment took place then? There would be some point in saying that the census was *finished*, brought to a close, under Q., after having been begun by Herod; but ἐγένετο cannot possibly mean that.

(3) Reading and accentuating αὐτὴ ἡ ἀπογραφή: "The raising of the tax itself (as distinct from the enrolment and assessment) first took place when Q.," etc. "Augustus ordered a census and it took place, but no money was raised until the time of Q." (Ebrard). This involves giving to ἀπογραφή in ver. 2 a totally different meaning from ἀπογράφεσθαι in ver. 1 and ἀπογράψασθαι in ver. 5; which is impossible.

(4) With αὐτὴ ἡ ἀπογραφή, as before: "The census itself called the first took place when Q.," etc. The better known census under Q. was commonly regarded as the first Roman census in Judæa: Lk. reminds his readers that there had really been an earlier one (Godet). This is very forced, requires the insertion of the article, which is almost certainly an interpolation, and assumes

that the census of A.D. 6, 7 was generally known as "the *first* census." From Acts v. 37 it appears that it was known as "*the* census": no previous or subsequent enrolment was taken into account. In his earlier edition Godet omitted the ἡ: in the third (1888) he says that this interpretation requires the article (i. p. 170).

McClellan quotes in illustration of the construction: *αἰτία δὲ αὕτη πρώτη ἐγένετο τοῦ πολέμου* (Thuc. i. 55. 3); *αὕτη τῶν περὶ Θήβας ἐγένετο ἀρχὴ καὶ κατάστασις πρώτη* (Dem. 291. 10); *πρώτη μὲν μήνυσις ἐγένετο αὕτη κατὰ τούτων τῶν ἀνδρῶν* (Andoc. iii. 5); *αὕτη πρώτη δημοτελὴς κρίσις ἐγένετο ἀρετῆς πρὸς πλοῦτον* (Aristid. i. 124); and adds the curious remark that "the Holy Spirit would have us note that the Saviour of the World was registered in the *first census* of the World!"

ἡγεμονεύοντος τῆς Συρίας Κυρηνίου. Like *ἡγεμών* (xx. 20, xxi. 12, etc.) and *ἡγεμονία* (iii. 1), the verb is generic, and may express the office of any ruler, whether emperor, proprætor, procurator, etc. It does not tell us that Quirinius was *legatus* in B.C. 4 as he was in A.D. 6. And it should be noted that Justin (see above) states that Quirinius was *procurator* (*ἐπίτροπος*) at the time of this census (*Apol.* i. 34); and that in the only other place in which Lk. uses this verb he uses it of a *procurator* (iii. 1). This gives weight to the suggestion that, although Varus was *legatus* of Syria at the time of the enrolment, yet Quirinius may have held some office in virtue of which he undertook this census. Lk. is probably not giving a mere date. He implies that Quirinius was in some way connected with the enrolment. For what is known about P. Sulpicius Quirinius see Tac. *Ann.* ii 30. 4, iii. 22. 1, 2, 23. 1, and esp. 48; Suet. *Tib.* xlix. Dion Cassius (liv. 48) calls him simply *Πόπλιος Σουλπίκιος*. But he was not really a member of the old patrician *gens Sulpicia*. The familiar word Quirinus (*Κυρῖνος*) induced copyists and editors to substitute Quirinus for Quirinius.

B has *Κυρείνου*, but there is no doubt that the name is Quirinius and not Quirinus. This is shown, as Furneaux points out in a note on Tac. *Ann.* ii. 30. 4, by the MS. readings in Tacitus; by the Greek forms *Κυρίνιος* (Strabo, 12, 6, 5, 569) and *Κυρήνιος* (here and Jos. *Ant.* xviii. 1. 1), and by Latin inscriptions (Orell. 3693, etc.). Quirinius is one of the earliest instances of a person bearing two gentile names.

3. καὶ ἐπορεύοντο πάντες ἀπογράφεσθαι, ἕκαστος εἰς τὴν ἑαυτοῦ πόλιν. The *καί* looks back to ver. 1, ver. 2 being a parenthesis. The *πάντες* means all those in Palestine who did not reside at the seat of their family. A purely Roman census would have required nothing of the kind. If Herod conducted the census for the Romans, Jewish customs would be followed. So long as Augustus obtained the necessary information, the manner of obtaining it was immaterial. Where does Lk. place the death of Herod?

4. Ἀνέβη δὲ καὶ Ἰωσὴφ ἀπὸ τῆς Γαλιλαίας ἐκ πόλεως Ναζαρέτ For **ἀνέβη** comp. ver. 42, xviii. 31, xix. 28; Acts xi. 2; and for

δὲ καί see on iii. 9. Note the change of prep. from *ἀπό* to *ἐκ*. But *ἀπό* is used of towns (x. 30; Acts viii. 26, xiii. 14, xx. 17, etc.), and *ἐκ* of districts (xxiii. 55; Acts vii. 4, etc.); so that there is no special point in the change, although it should be preserved in translation. Comp. Jn. i. 45 and xi. 1; also the *ἐκ* of Lk. xxi. 18 with the *ἀπό* of Acts xxvii. 34.

εἰς πόλιν Δαυείδ. That Bethlehem was David's birthplace and original home is in accordance with 1 Sam. xvii. 12 ff. and xvii. 58; but both passages are wanting in LXX. In O.T. "the city of David" always means the fortress of Zion, formerly the stronghold of the Jebusites (2 Sam. v. 7, 9; 1 Chron. xi. 5, 7), and in LXX *πόλις* in this phrase commonly has the article. Bethlehem is about six miles from Jerusalem. Note that Lk. does not connect Christ's birth at Bethlehem with prophecy.

ἥτις καλεῖται Βηθλεέμ. In late Greek *ὅστις* is sometimes scarcely distinguishable from *ὅς*: comp. Acts xvii. 10. But in ix. 30 (as in Acts xxiii. 14, xxviii. 18, and Eph. i. 23, which are sometimes cited as instances of *ὅστις* = *ὅς*) there may be special point in *ὅστις*. Even here it may "denote an attribute which is the essential property of the antecedent," and may possibly refer to the meaning of Bethlehem. Comp. *πόλιν κτίσας ταύτην, ἥτις νῦν Μέμφις καλεῖται* (Hdt. ii. 99. 7).

Βηθλεέμ. "House of Bread"; one of the most ancient towns in Palestine. It is remarkable that David did nothing for Bethlehem, although he retained affection for it (2 Sam. xxiii. 15); and that Jesus seems never to have visited it again. In Jn. vii. 42 it is called a *κώμη*, and no special interest seems to have attached to the place for many years after the birth of Christ. Hadrian planted a grove of Adonis there, which continued to exist from A.D. 135 to 315. About 330 Constantine built the present church. *D.B.*[2] art. "Bethlehem." The modern name is *Beit Lahm*; and, as at Nazareth, the population is almost entirely Christian.

οἴκου κ. πατριᾶς. Both words are rather indefinite, and either may include the other. Here *οἶκος* seems to be the more comprehensive; otherwise *καὶ πατριᾶς* would be superfluous. Usually *πατριά* is the wider term. That a village carpenter should be able to prove his descent from David is not improbable. The two grandsons of S. Jude, who were taken before Domitian as descendants of David, were labourers (Eus. *H. E.* iii. 20. 1–8).

5. ἀπογράψασθαι. "To get himself enrolled." The aorist of his single act, the present (ver. 3) of a series of such acts. Both are middle, while *ἀπογράφεσθαι* in ver. 1 is probably passive. We must not take *σὺν Μαριάμ* with *ἀπογράψασθαι*: it belongs to *ἀνέβη*. It is essential to the narrative that she should go up with him; it is not so that she should be enrolled with him. In a Roman census women paid the poll-tax, but were not obliged to come in person. That Mary had property in Bethlehem is a conjecture which is almost disproved by her resourcelessness in the place. And if it was necessary for her to come, because she also was of David's line, would not Lk. have written διὰ τὸ εἶναι αὐτοὺς ἐξ οἴκου κ. π. Δ.? This reading is found in Syr-Sin.: "because they were both of the house of D." It is futile to argue that a woman in her condition would not have gone unless she was compelled: therefore Lk. represents her as being compelled: therefore he has made a mistake. She would be anxious at all risks not to be separated from Joseph. Lk. does not even imply that her presence was obligatory; and, if he had said that it was, we do not know enough about the matter to say whether he would have been wrong. Had there been a law which required her to remain at home, then Lk. might be suspected of an error. For σύν see on i. 56.

τῇ ἐμνηστευμένῃ αὐτῷ, οὔσῃ ἐγκύῳ. The γυναικί of A, Vulg. Syr. and Aeth. is a gloss, but a correct one. Had she been only his betrothed (i. 27; Mt. i. 18), their travelling together would have been impossible. But by omitting γυναικί Lk. intimates what Mt. states i. 25. Syr-Sin. and some Latin texts have "wife" without "espoused." The οὔσῃ introduces, not a mere fact, but the reason for what has just been stated; he took her with him, "*because* she was with child." After what is related Mt. i. 19 he would not leave her at this crisis. See on i. 24.

6, 7. The Birth of the Saviour at Bethlehem. The *Gospel of Pseudo-Matthew* (xiii.) represents the birth as taking place before Bethlehem is reached. So also apparently the *Protevangelium of James* (xvii.), which limits the decree of Augustus to those who lived at Bethlehem! For ἐπλήσθησαν see on i. 15 and 57.

7. τὸν υἱὸν αὐτῆς τὸν πρωτότοκον. The expression might certainly be used without implying that there had been subsequent children. But it implies the possibility of subsequent children, and when Luke wrote this possibility had been decided. Would he have used such an expression if it was then known that Mary had never had another child? He might have avoided all ambiguity by writing μονογενῆ, as he does vii. 12, viii. 42, ix. 38. In considering this question the imperf. ἐγίνωσκεν (Mt. i. 25) has not received sufficient attention. See Mayor, *Ep. of St. James*, pp. xix–xxii.

ἐσπαργάνωσεν αὐτόν. It has been inferred from her being able to do this that the birth was miraculously painless (τὴν ἀνώδινον κύησιν, Euthym.), of which there is no hint. For the verb comp. ὁμίχλῃ αὐτὴν ἐσπαργάνωσα, "I made thick darkness a swaddling band for it" (Job xxxviii. 9).

ἐν φάτνῃ. The traditional rendering "in a manger" is right; not "a stall" either here or in xiii. 15. The animals were out at pasture, and the manger was not being used. Justin (*Try.* lxxviii.) and some of the apocryphal gospels say that it was in a cave, which is not improbable. In Origen's time the cave was shown, and the manger also (*Con. Cels.* i. 51). One suspects that the cave *may* be a supposed prophecy turned into history, like the vine in xix. 31. Is. xxxiii. 16 (οὗτος οἰκήσει ἐν ὑψηλῷ σπηλαίῳ πέτρας ὀχυρᾶς) was supposed to point to birth in a cave, and then the cave may have been imagined in order to fit it, just as the colt is represented as "tied *to a vine*," in order to make Gen. xlix. 11 a prediction of Lk. xix. 30–33 (Justin, *Apol.* i. 32).

οὐκ ἦν αὐτοῖς τόπος ἐν τῷ καταλύματι. Most of the Jews then residing in Palestine were of Judah or Benjamin, and all towns and villages of Judah would be very full. No inhospitality is implied. It is a little doubtful whether the familiar translation "in the inn" is correct. In x. 34 "inn" is πανδοχεῖον, and in xxii. 11 κατάλυμα is not "inn." It is possible that Joseph had relied upon the hospitality of some friend in Bethlehem, whose "guest-chamber," however, was already full when he and Mary arrived. See on xxii. 11. But κατάλυμα in LXX represents five different Heb. words, so that it must have been elastic in meaning. All that it implies is a place where burdens are loosed and let down for a rest. In Polybius it occurs twice in the plural: of the general's quarters (ii. 36. 1), and of reception rooms for envoys (xxxii. 19. 2). It has been suggested that the "inn" was the *Geruth Chimham* or "lodging-place of Chimham" (Jer. xli. 17), the [son] of Barzillai (2 Sam. xix. 37, 38), "which was *by* Bethlehem," and convenient for those who would "go to enter into Egypt." See Stanley, *Sin. & Pal.* pp. 163, 529. Justin says that the cave was σύνεγγυς τῆς κώμης, which agrees with "by Bethlehem." The Mandra of Josephus (*Ant.* x. 9. 5) was perhaps the same place as *Geruth Chimham*. Syr-Sin. omits "in the inn."

8–14. The Angelic Proclamation to the Shepherds: πτωχοὶ εὐαγγελίζονται (vii. 22). It was in these pastures that David spent his youth and fought the lion and the bear (1 Sam. xvii. 34, 35). "A passage in the Mishnah (Shek. vii. 4; comp. Baba K. vii. 7, 80 *a*) leads to the conclusion that the flocks which pastured there were destined for Temple-sacrifices, and accordingly, that the shepherds who watched over them were not ordinary shepherds. The latter were under the ban of Rabbinism on account of their necessary isolation from religious ordinances and their manner of life, which rendered strict religious observance unlikely, if not absolutely impossible. The same Mischnic passage also leads us to infer that these flocks lay out *all the year round*, since they are spoken of as in the fields thirty days before the Passover—that is, in the month of February, when in Palestine the average rainfall is nearly greatest" (Edersh. *L. & T.* i. pp. 186, 187). For details of the life of a shepherd see *D.B.* art. "Shepherds," and Herzog, *PRE.*[2] art. "*Viehzucht und Hirtenleben.*"

8. ἀγραυλοῦντες. Making the ἀγρός their αὐλή, and so "spending their life in the open air": a late and rare word, whereas ἄγραυλος is class. This statement is by no means conclusive against December as the time of the year. The season may have been a mild one; it is not certain that all sheep were brought under cover at night during the winter months.

It is of the flocks in the *wilderness*, far from towns or villages, that the often quoted saying was true, that they were taken out in March and brought home in November. These shepherds may have returned from the wilderness, and if so, the time would be between November and March. But the data for determining the time of year are so very insufficient, that after minute calculation of them all we are left in our original uncertainty. Among those who have made a special study of the question we have advocates for almost every month in the year. The earliest attempts to fix the day of which we have knowledge are those mentioned (and apparently condemned as profane curiosity) by Clement of Alexandria (*Strom.* i. 21 *sub fin.*). In his time some took April 21, others April 22, and others May 20, to be the day. What was unknown in his time is not likely to have been discovered afterwards respecting such a detail. December 25th cannot be traced higher than the fourth century, and it seems to have been adopted first in the West. We must be content to remain in ignorance as to the date of the birth of Christ. See on ἐφημερίας i. 5; *D. of Chr. Ant.* art. "Christmas"; Andrews, *L. of our Lord*, pp. 12–21, ed. 1892.

φυλάσσοντες φυλακάς. The plural refers to their watching in turns rather than in different places. The phrase occurs Num. viii. 26; Xen. *Anab.* ii. 6. 10; but in LXX **τὰς** φυλακὰς φυλ. is more common; Num. iii. 7, 8, 28, 32, 38, etc. Comp. Plat. *Phædr.* 240 E; *Laws*, 758 D. The fondness of Lk. for such combinations of cognate words is seen again ver. 9, vii. 29, xvii. 24, xxii. 15, and several times in the Acts. See on xi. 46 and xxiii. 46. We may take τῆς νυκτός after φυλακάς, "night-watches," or as gen. of time, "by night." See Blass, *Gr.* p. 199.

9. ἄγγελος Κυρίου ἐπέστη αὐτοῖς. The notion of coming *suddenly* is not inherent in the verb, but is often derived from the context: see on ver. 38.[1] In N.T. the verb is almost peculiar to Lk., and almost always in 2nd aor. In class. Grk. also it is used of the appearance of heavenly beings, dreams, visions, etc. Hom. *Il.* x. 496, xxiii. 106; Hdt. i. 34. 2, vii. 14. 1. Comp. Lk. xxiv. 4; Acts xii. 7, xxiii. 11.

δόξα Κυρίου. The heavenly brightness which is a sign of the presence of God or of heavenly beings, 2 Cor. iii. 18: comp. Lk. ix. 31, 32. In O.T. of the Shechinah, Exod. xvi. 7, 10, xxiv. 17,

[1] In Vulg. it is very variously translated: *e.g. stare juxta* (here), *supervenire* (ii. 38, xxi. 34), *stare* (iv. 39, x. 40, xxiv. 4), *convenire* (xx. 1), *concurrere* (Acts vi. 12), *adstare* (Acts x. 17, xi. 11, xii. 7), *adsistere* (Acts xvii. 5, xxiii. 11), *imminere* (Acts xxviii. 2).

xl. 34; Lev. ix. 6, 23; Num. xii. 8, etc. This glory, according to the Jews, was wanting in the second temple.

10. ὁ ἄγγελος. The art. is used of that which has been mentioned before without the art. Comp. τὸ βρέφος and τῇ φάτνῃ in ver. 16.

Μὴ φοβεῖσθε. Comp. i. 13, 30, v. 10; Mt. xiv. 27, xxviii. 5, 10.[1] For ἰδοὺ γάρ see on i. 44.

εὐαγγελίζομαι ὑμῖν χαρὰν μεγάλην. The verb is very freq. in Lk. and Paul, but is elsewhere rare; not in the other Gospels excepting Mt. xi. 5, which is a quotation. See on i. 19.

The act. occurs Rev. x. 7, xiv. 6; the pass. Lk. vii. 22, xvi. 16; Gal. i. 11; Heb. iv. 2, 6; 1 Pet. i. 25, iv. 6; the mid. is freq. with various constructions. As here, dat. of pers. and acc. of thing, i. 19, iv. 43; Acts viii. 35; acc. of thing only, viii. 1; Acts v. 42, viii. 4, 12?; acc. of person, iii. 18; Acts viii. 25, 40; acc. of person and of thing, Acts xiii. 32.

ἥτις ἔσται παντὶ τῷ λαῷ. "Which shall have the special character of being for all the people." The ἥτις has manifest point here (see on ver. 4); and the art. before λαῷ should be preserved. A joy so extensive may well banish fear. Comp. τῷ λαῷ, i. 68, 77, and τὸν λαόν, vii. 16. In both these verses (9, 10) we have instances of Lk. recording intensity of emotion: comp. i. 42, viii. 37, xxiv. 52; Acts v. 5, 11, xv. 3. Dat. after εἰμί is freq. in Lk.

11. ἐτέχθη ὑμῖν σήμερον σωτήρ. To the shepherds, as a part, and perhaps a specially despised part, of the people of Israel. Here first in N.T. is σωτήρ used of Christ, and here only in Lk. Not in Mt. or Mk., and only once in Jn. (iv. 42): twice in Acts (v. 31, xiii. 23), and freq. in Tit. and 2 Pet. The 1st aor. of τίκτω, both act. and pass., is rare: see Veitch.

Χριστὸς κύριος. The combination occurs nowhere else in N.T., and the precise meaning is uncertain. Either "Messiah, Lord," or "Anointed Lord," or "the Messiah, the Lord," or "an anointed one, a Lord." It occurs once in LXX as a manifest mistranslation. Lam. iv. 20, "The breath of our nostrils, the anointed of the Lord," is rendered πνεῦμα προσώπου ἡμῶν Χριστὸς κύριος. If this is not a corrupt reading, we may perhaps infer that the expression Χριστὸς κύριος was familiar to the translator. It occurs in the *Ps. Sol.*, where it is said of the Messiah καὶ οὐκ ἔστιν ἀδικία ἐν ταῖς ἡμέραις αὐτοῦ ἐν μέσῳ αὐτῶν, ὅτι πάντες ἅγιοι, καὶ βασιλεὺς αὐτῶν Χριστὸς κύριος (xvii. 36: comp. the title of xviii.). But this may easily be another mistranslation, perhaps based on

[1] "This Gospel of Luke is scarce begun, we are yet but a little way in the second chapter, and we have already three *noli timeres* in it, and all, as here, at the coming of an Angel (i. 13, 30, ii. 10). . . . What was it? It was not the fear of an evil conscience; they were about no harm. . . . It is a plain sign our nature is fallen from her original; Heaven and we are not in the terms we should be, not the best of us all" (Bishop Andrewes, *Serm. V. On the Nativity*).

that in Lam. iv. 20. Comp. *εἶπεν ὁ κύριος τῷ κυρίῳ μου* (Ps. cx. 1), and *ἐπεκαλεσάμην Κύριον πατέρα κυρίου μου* (Ecclus. li. 10). See Ryle and James, *Ps. of Sol.* pp. 141–143. The addition of **ἐν πόλει Δαυείδ** here indicates that this *σωτήρ* is the King of Israel promised in the Prophets: see on ver. 4.

12. καὶ τοῦτο ὑμῖν τὸ σημεῖον. B Ξ omit the *τό*. Sign for what? By which to prove that what is announced is true, rather than by which to find the Child. It was all-important that they should be convinced as to the first point; about the other there would be no great difficulty.—**εὑρήσετε βρέφος.** "Ye shall find *a* babe," "not *the* babe," as most English Versions and Luther; Wiclif has "a yunge child." This is the first mention of it; in ver. 16 the art. is right. In N.T., as in class. Grk., *βρέφος* is more often a newly-born child (xviii. 15; Acts vii. 19; 2 Tim. iii. 15; 1 Pet. ii. 2) than an unborn child (Lk. i. 41, 44); in LXX it is always the former (1 Mac. i. 61; 2 Mac. vi. 10; 3 Mac. v. 49; 4 Mac. iv. 25), unless Ecclus. xix. 11 be an exception. Aquila follows the same usage (Ps. viii. 3, xvi. 14; Is. lxv. 20).—**ἐσπαργανωμένον καὶ κείμενον ἐν φάτνῃ.** Both points are part of the sign. The first participle is no more an adjective than the second. No art. with *φάτνῃ*: the shepherds have not heard of it before.

13. ἐξέφνης.[1] The fact that this is expressly stated here confirms the view that suddenness is not necessarily included in *ἐπέστη* (ver. 9). For **σὺν τῷ ἀγγέλῳ** see on i. 56.—**στρατιᾶς.** *Magna appellatio. Hic* exercitus *tamen* pacem *laudat* (Beng.). The genitive is partitive: "*a* multitude (no art.) forming part of the host." Comp. 1 Kings xxii. 19; 2 Chron. xviii. 18; Ps. ciii. 21; Josh. v. 15).—**αἰνούντων.** *Constr. ad sensum.* The whole host of heaven was praising God, not merely that portion of it which was visible to the shepherds. The verb is a favourite with Lk. (ver. 20, xix. 37, xxiv. 53?; Acts ii. 47, iii. 8, 9). Elsewhere only Rom. xv. 11 (from Ps. cxvii. 1) and Rev. xix. 5; very freq. in LXX.

14. Δόξα . . . εὐδοκίας. The hymn consists of two members connected by a conjunction; and the three parts of the one member exactly correspond with the three parts of the other member.

GLORY to God *in the highest*,
And *on earth* PEACE among men of His good will.

Δόξα balances *εἰρήνη*, *ἐν ὑψίστοις* balances *ἐπὶ γῆς*, *Θεῷ* balances *ἐν ἀνθρώποις εὐδοκίας*. This exact correlation between the parts is lost in the common triple arrangement; which has the further awkwardness of having the second member introduced by a con-

[1] The word is thus written in the best texts here and ix. 39: comp. *ἐφνίδιος*, xxi. 34; *κερέαν*, xvi. 17; *κρεπάλη*, xxi. 34 (WH. App. pp. 150, 151). In class. Grk. *οὐράνιος* is of three terminations; but the true reading here may be *οὐρανοῦ* (B D).

junction,[1] while the third is not, and of making the second and third members tautological. "On earth peace" is very much the same as "Good will amongst men." Yet Scrivener thinks that "in the first and second lines heaven and earth are contrasted; the third refers to both those preceding, and *alleges the efficient cause which has brought God glory and earth peace*" (*Int. to Crit. of N.T.* ii. p. 344); which seems to be very forced. The construction ἐν ἀνθρώποις εὐδοκίας is difficult; but one of the best of modern Greek scholars has said that it "may be translated 'among men of His counsel for good' or 'of His gracious purpose.' This rendering seems to be in harmony with the preceding context and with the teaching of Scripture in general" (T. S. Evans, *Contemp. Rev.*, Dec. 1881, p. 1003). WH. take a similar view. They prefer, among possible meanings, "in (among and within) accepted mankind," and point out that "the Divine 'favour' (Ps. xxx. 5, 7, lxxxv. 1, lxxxix. 17, cvi. 4) or 'good pleasure,' declared for the Head of the race at the Baptism (iii. 22), was already contemplated by the Angels as resting on the race itself in virtue of His birth" (ii. App. p. 56, where the whole discussion should be studied). H. suggests that the first of the two clauses should end with ἐπὶ γῆς rather than Θεῷ, and that we should arrange thus: "Glory to God in the highest and on earth; Peace among men of His good pleasure." With the construction of this first clause he compares vii. 17 and Acts xxvi. 23: "Glory to God *not only* in heaven, *but now also* on earth." "In this arrangement 'glory' and 'peace' stand severally at the head of the two clauses as twin fruits of the Incarnation, that which redounds to 'God' and that which enters into 'men.'" This division of the clauses, previously commended by Olshausen, makes the stichometry as even as in the familiar triplet, but it has not found many supporters. It destroys the exact correspondence between the parts of the two clauses, the first clause having three or four parts, and the second only two. W. here leaves H. to plead alone.

εὐδοκίας. The word has three meanings: (1) "design, desire," as Ecclus. xi. 17; Rom. x. 1; (2) "satisfaction, contentment," as Ecclus. xxxv. 14; 2 Thes. i. 11; (3) "benevolence, goodwill," as Ps. cvi. 4; Lk. ii. 14. Both it and εὐδοκεῖν are specially used of the favour with which God regards His elect, as Ps. cxlvi. 12; Lk. iii. 22. The meaning here is "favour, goodwill, good pleasure"; and ἄνθρωποι εὐδοκίας are "men whom the Divine favour has blessed." See Lft. on Phil. i. 15. Field (*Otium Norv.* iii. p. 37) urges that, according to Græco-biblical usage, this would be, not ἄνθρωποι εὐδοκίας, but ἄνδρες εὐδοκίας, and he appeals to nine examples in LXX. But two-thirds of them are not in point, being singulars, and having reference to a definite *adult male* and not to

[1] Syr-Sin. inserts a second "and" before "goodwill to man."

human beings in general. These are 2 Sam. xvi. 7, xviii. 20; Ps. lxxx. 18; Jer. xv. 10; *ibid.* Aq.; Dan. x. 11. There remain ἄνδρες βουλῆς μου, Ps. cxix. 24, Aq.; οἱ ἄνδρες τῆς διαθήκης σου, Obad. 7; ἄνδρες εἰρηνικοί σου, Obad. 7. This last is again not parallel, as being accompanied by an adj. and not a gen. Substitute ἄνδρες αἱμάτων, Ps. cxxxviii. 19. Of these instances, all *necessarily* refer to adult males, excepting Aq. in Ps. cxix. 24, and this more naturally does so, for "counsellors" are generally thought of as male. But, allowing that the usual expression would have been ἀνδράσιν εὐδοκίας, this might well have been avoided here in order to emphasize the fact that all, male and female, young and old, are included. Even in the case of an individual S. Paul writes ὁ ἄνθρωπος τῆς ἀνομίας (2 Thes. ii. 3), so that the combination is at any rate possible. See on Rom. x. 1.

The reading is a well-known problem, but the best textual critics are unanimous for εὐδοκίας. The internal evidence is very evenly balanced, as regards both transcriptional and intrinsic probabilities, which are well stated and estimated in WH. (ii. App. pp. 55, 56). The external evidence is very decidedly in favour of the apparently more difficult reading εὐδοκίας. Roughly speaking, we have all the best MSS. (excepting C, which is here defective), with all Latin authorities, against the inferior MSS., with nearly all versions, except the Latin, and nearly all the Greek writers who quote the text. Syr-Sin. has "*and goodwill* to men."

For εὐδοκίας, ℵ* A B D, Latt. (Vet. Vulg.) Goth. Iren-Lat. Orig-Lat. and the Lat. *Gloria in excelsis.*

For εὐδοκία, L P Γ Δ Λ Ξ, etc., Syrr. (Pesh. Sin. Harcl.) Boh. Arm. Aeth. Orig. Eus. Bas. Greg-Naz. Cyr-Hier. Did. Epiph. Cyr-Alex.

"The agreement, not only of ℵ with B, but of D and all the Latins with both, and of A with them all, supported by Origen in at least one work, and that in a certified text, affords a peculiarly strong presumption in favour of εὐδοκίας. If this reading is wrong, it must be Western; and no other reading in the New Testament open to suspicion as Western is so comprehensively attested by the earliest and best uncials" (WH. p. 54). The vehemence with which Scrivener argues against εὐδοκίας is quite out of place.

15–20. The Verification by the Shepherds.

15. ἐλάλουν πρὸς ἀλλήλους Διέλθωμεν δή. "They repeatedly said unto one another, Come then let us go over," or "Let us at once go across." The compound verb refers to the intervening country (Acts ix. 38, xi. 19, xviii. 27), and the δή makes the exhortation urgent. Lk. is fond of διέρχεσθαι, which occurs thirty times in his writings and less than ten elsewhere in N.T. In LXX it is very freq. Note ὡς = "when."

τὸ ῥῆμα τοῦτο. This need not be limited to the *saying* of the Angel. It is rather the thing of which he spoke: see on i. 65. In class. Grk. λόγος is used in a similar manner; *e.g.* Hdt. i. 21. 2. *Videamus hoc verbum quod factum est* (Vulg.).

16. ἦλθαν σπεύσαντες καὶ ἀνεῦραν. For these mixed forms of the aor. see on i. 59. Lk. alone in N.T. uses σπεύδειν in its class. intrans. sense (xix.

5, 6; Acts xx. 16, xxii. 18). In 2 Pet. iii. 12 it is trans. as in Is. xvi. 5. Lk. alone uses ἀνευρίσκειν (Acts xxi. 4), but the mid. occurs 4 Mac. iii. 14: 2nd aor. in all three cases. The compound implies a *search* in order to find. In his Gospel Lk. never uses τε without καί (xii. 45, xv. 2, xxi. 11, etc.). Here both βρέφος and φάτνῃ, having been mentioned before, have the article.

17. ἐγνώρισαν. "They made known," not merely to Mary and Joseph, but to the inhabitants of Bethlehem generally. Both in N.T. and LXX γνωρίζω is commonly trans.; but in Phil. i. 22 and Job xxxiv. 25, as usually in class. Grk., it is intrans. Vulg. makes it intrans. here: *cognoverunt de verbo quod dictum erat illis de puero hoc.* But ver. 18 makes this very improbable.

18. πάντες οἱ ἀκούσαντες. See on i. 66. This probably includes subsequent hearers, just as ver. 19 includes a time subsequent to the departure of the shepherds. The constr. ἐθαύμασαν περί is unusual. But in English "about," which is common after "perplexed," might easily be transferred to such a word as "astonished."

19. ἡ δὲ Μαρία πάντα συνετήρει τὰ ῥήματα ταῦτα. "*But* Mary" could have no such astonishment; neither did she publish her impressions. The revelations to Joseph and herself precluded both. Note the change from momentary wonder (aor.) to sustained reticence (imperf.): also that πάντα is put before the verb with emphasis. Comp. Dan. vii. 28; Ecclus. xxxix. 2.—**συνβάλλουσα ἐν τῇ καρδίᾳ αὐτῆς.** *Conferens in corde suo.* From whom could Lk. learn this? The verb is peculiar to him (xiv. 31; Acts iv. 15; xvii. 18, xviii. 27, xx. 14). See small print note on i. 66.

20. δοξάζοντες καὶ αἰνοῦντες. The latter is the more definite word. The former is one of the many words which have acquired a deeper meaning in bibl. Grk. Just as δόξα in bibl. Grk. never (except 4 Mac. v. 18) has the class. meaning of "opinion," but rather "praise" or "glory," so δοξάζω in bibl. Grk. never means "form an opinion about," but "praise" or "glorify." It is used of the honour done by man to man (1 Sam. xv. 30), by man to God (Exod. xv. 2), and by God to man (Ps. xci. 15). It is also used of God glorifying Christ (Acts iii. 13), a use specially common in Jn. (viii. 54, xi. 4, etc.), and of Christ gloryfying God (xvii. 4). See on Rom. i. 21. For the combination comp. αἰνετὸν καὶ δεδοξασμένον (Dan. iii. 26, 55). For αἰνεῖν see on ver. 13.

πᾶσιν οἷς. For the attraction see on iii. 19. If ἤκουσαν refers to the angelic announcement, then καθώς refers to εἶδον only. But ἤκουσαν καὶ εἶδον may sum up their experiences at Bethlehem, which were a full confirmation (καθώς = "even as, just as") of what the Angel had said. Syr-Sin. omits καὶ αἰνοῦντες and πᾶσιν.

Schleiermacher points out that, if this narrative had been a mere poetical composition, we should have had the hymn of the shepherds recorded and more extensive hymns assigned to the Angels (*S. Luke*, Eng. tr. p. 31). He regards the shepherds as the probable source of the narrative; "for that which to them was most material and obvious, the nocturnal vision in the fields, is the only circumstance treated in detail" (p. 33). But any narrator would give the vision, and could hardly give it more briefly without material loss. The brevity of it, especially when contrasted with the apocryphal gospels, is strong guarantee for its truth. How tempting to describe the search for the Babe and the conversation between the parents and the shepherds! Of the myth-hypothesis Weiss rightly says that "it labours in vain to explain the part played here by the shepherds by means of the pastoral tales of the ancients, and is driven to drag in, awkwardly enough, the legends of Cyrus and Romulus" (*Leben Jesu*, i. 2. 4, note, Eng. tr. p. 255). As for the old rationalism, which explained the angelic vision by *ignis fatuus* or other phosphoric phenomena, which travellers have said to be common in those parts; "the more frequent such phenomena, the more familiar must shepherds above all men, accustomed to pass their nights the whole summer long in the open air, have been with them, and the less likely to consider them as a sign from heaven pointing at a particular event" (Schleierm. p. 36).

21–40. *The Circumcision and the Presentation in the Temple.*

This forms the third and last section in the second group of narratives (i. 57–ii. 40) in the Gospel of the Infancy (i. 5–ii. 52). It corresponds to the Visitation (i. 39–56) in the first group. Its very marked conclusion has close resemblance to i. 80 and ii. 52 See introductory note to *vv.* 1–20 (p. 46). The absence of parallel passages in the other Gospels shows that at first this portion of the Gospel narrative was less well known. An oral tradition respecting the childhood of the Christ (when hardly anyone suspected that He was the Christ) would be much less likely to arise or become prevalent than an oral tradition respecting the ministry and crucifixion. We can once more trace a threefold division, viz. a longer narrative between two very short ones: the Circumcision (21), the Presentation in the Temple (22–38), and the Return to Home Life at Nazareth (39, 40).

21. The Circumcision. The verse contains an unusual number of marks of Lk.'s style. 1. Καὶ ὅτε (*vv.* 22, 42, vi. 13, xxii. 14, xxiii. 33); 2. πλήθειν (twenty-two times in Lk. and Acts, and thrice elsewhere in N.T.); see on i. 57; 3. τοῦ *c. infin.* to express aim or purpose (i. 74, 77, 79, ii. 24, iv. 10, v. 7, viii. 5, etc.); see on i. 74; 4. καί introducing the apodosis (v. 1, 12, 17, vii. 12, ix. 51, etc.); 5. συλλαμβάνειν (eleven times in Lk. and Acts, and five times elsewhere). See on v. 1.

21. τοῦ περιτεμεῖν αὐτόν. There being no art. with ἡμέραι (contrast ver. 22), we cannot, as in ver. 6 and i. 57, make the gen. depend on αἱ ἡμέραι or ὁ χρόνος. The ὀκτώ does not take the place of the art. As Jesus was sent "in the likeness of sinful flesh" (Rom. viii. 3), and "it behoved Him in all things to be made like unto His brethren" (Heb. ii. 17), He underwent circumcision. He was "born under the law" (Gal. iv. 4), and fulfilled the law as a loyal son of Abraham. Had He not done so, οὐκ ἂν ὅλως παρεδέχθη διδάσκων, ἀλλ' ἀπεπέμφθη ἂν ὡς ἀλλόφυλος

(Euthym.) His circumcision was a first step in His obedience to the will of God, and a first shedding of the redeeming blood. It was one of those things which became Him, in order "to fulfil all righteousness" (Mt. iii. 15). The contrast with the circumcision of the Baptist is marked. Here there is no family gathering of rejoicing neighbours and kinsfolk. Joseph and Mary are strangers in a village far from home. Hastings, *D.C.G.* i. p. 331.

The reading τὸ παιδίον (D E G H) for αὐτόν (ℵ A B R Ξ and versions) probably arose from this being the beginning of a lection, "Him" being changed to "the child" (AV.) for greater clearness. The same kind of thing has been done at the beginning of many of the Gospels in the Book of Common Prayer, "Jesus" being substituted for "He" or "Him": *e.g.* the Gospels for the 6th, 9th, 11th, 12th, 16th, 18th, 19th, and 22nd Sundays after Trinity.

καὶ ἐκλήθη. The καί is almost our "then" and the German *da*: but it may be left untranslated. It introduces the apodosis, as often in Grk., and esp. in Lk. This is simpler than to explain it as a mixture of two constructions, "*When* eight days were fulfilled . . . He was called" and "Eight days were fulfilled . . . *and* He was called" (Win. liii. 3. f, p. 546, lxv. 3. c, p. 756). Comp. Acts i. 10. "He was *also* called" is not likely to be right. The Vulgate and Luther are right. *Et postquam consummati sunt dies octo ut circumcideretur vocatum est nomen ejus Jesus. Und da acht Tage um waren, dass das Kind beschnitten würde, da ward sein Name genannt Jesus.* This passage, with that about John the Baptist (i. 59), is the chief biblical evidence that naming was connected with circumcision: comp. Gen. xvii. 5, 10. Among the Romans the naming of girls took place on the eighth day: of boys on the ninth. The purification accompanied it; and hence the name *dies lustricus*. Tertullian uses *nominalia* of the naming festival (*Idol.* xvi. 1). Among the Greeks the naming festival was on the tenth day; δεκάτην ἑστιᾶν or θύειν.

συλλημφθῆναι This and corresponding forms, such as λήμψομαι, προσωπολημψία, and the like, are abundantly attested in good MSS. both of LXX and of N.T See on i. 31. κοιλία = "womb" is specially freq. in Lk.

22–38. The Purification and the Presentation in the Temple. Here also we have a triplet. The Ceremony (22–24); Symeon and the Nunc Dimittis (25–35); and Anna the Prophetess (36–38). Symeon and Anna, like Zacharias and Elisabeth, with those spoken of in ver. 38, are evidence that Judaism was still a living religion to those who made the most of their opportunities.

22. αἱ ἡμέραι τοῦ κ. Lev. xii. 6. Lk. is fond of these periphrases, which are mostly Hebraistic. Comp. ἡ ἡμέρα τῶν σαββάτων (iv. 16), or τοῦ σαββάτου (xiii. 14, 16, xiv. 5), ἡ ἡμέρα τῶν ἀζύμων (xxii. 7), and the like.

τοῦ καθαρισμοῦ αὐτῶν. "Of *their* purification." The Jewish law (Lev. xii.) did not include the child in the purification. This fact, and the feeling that least of all could Jesus need purifying, produced the corrupt reading αὐτῆς, followed in AV.

No uncial and perhaps only one cursive (76) supports the reading αὐτῆς, which spread from the Complutensian Polyglott Bible (1514) to a number of editions. It is a remarkable instance of a reading which had almost no authority becoming widely adopted. It now has the support of Syr-Sin. The Complutensian insertion of διηρθρώθη after ἡ γλῶσσα αὐτοῦ in i. 64 was less successful, although that has the support of two cursives (140, 251). D here has the strange reading αὐτοῦ, which looks like a slip rather than a correction. No one would alter αὐτῶν to αὐτοῦ. The Vulgate also has *purgationis ejus*, but some Lat. MSS. have *eorum*. The αὐτῆς might come from LXX of Lev. xii. 6, ὅταν ἀναπληρωθῶσιν αἱ ἡμέραι καθάρσεως αὐτῆς. Note that Lk. uses καθαρισμός and not κάθαρσις, which is a medical term for menstruation, and which Gentile readers might misunderstand.

The meaning of αὐτῶν is not clear. Edersheim and Van Hengel interpret it of the Jews; Godet, Meyer, and Weiss of Mary and Joseph. The latter is justified by the context: "When the days of *their* purification were fulfilled . . . *they* brought Him." Contact with an unclean person involved uncleanness. Purification after childbirth seems to have been closely connected with purification after menstruation; the rites were similar. Herzog, *PRE.*[2] art. *Reinigungen*. After the birth of a son the mother was unclean for seven days, then remained at home for thirty-three days, and on the fortieth day after the birth made her offerings.

κατὰ τὸν νόμον Μωυσέως. These words must be taken with what precedes, for the law did not require them to bring Him to Jerusalem (Lev. xii. 1–8). We have already had several places in ch. i. (*vv.* 8, 25, 27) in which there are amphibolous words or phrases: comp. viii. 39, ix. 17, 18, 57, x. 18, xi. 39, xii. 1, xvii. 22, xviii. 31, xix. 37, xxi. 36, etc.

The trisyllabic form Μωϋσῆς is to be preferred to Μωσῆς. The name is said to be derived from two Egyptian words, *mo* = "water," and *ugai* = "to be preserved." Hence the LXX, a version made in Egypt, and the best MSS. of the N.T., which in the main represent the text of the N.T. that was current in Egypt, keep nearest to the Egyptian form of the name by preserving the υ. Josephus also has Μωυσῆς. But Μωσῆς is closer to the Hebrew form of the name, and is the form most commonly used by Greek and Latin writers. Win. v. 8, p. 47.

ἀνήγαγον. One of Lk.'s favourite words (iv. 5, viii. 22, and often in Acts). It is here used of bringing Him *up to the capital*, like ἀναβαινόντων in ver. 43. In the literal sense they went *down*; for Bethlehem stands higher than Jerusalem. This journey is the first visit of the Christ to His own city.

Ἱεροσόλυμα. In both his writings Lk. much more often uses the Jewish form Ἰερουσαλήμ (*vv.* 25, 38, 41, 43, 45, etc.), which Mt. uses only once (xxiii. 37), and Mk. perhaps not at all (? xi. 1). Jn. uses the Greek form in his Gospel, and the Jewish form in the Apocalypse. The Jewish form is used wherever the name is not a geographical term, but has a specially religious signification (Gal. iv. 25; Heb. xii. 22). The Greek form is neut. plur. In Mt. ii. 3 it may be fem.; but perhaps πᾶσα ἡ πόλις was in the writer's mind. Neither form should have the aspirate, which a "false association with ἱερός" has produced (WH. ii. 313; App. p. 160). This visit to Jerusalem probably preceded the arrival of the Magi, after which Joseph and Mary would hardly have ventured to bring Him to the city. If this is correct, we must abandon the traditional view that the Epiphany took place on the thirteenth day after the Nativity. There is no improbability in Joseph's going back to Bethlehem for a while before returning to Nazareth. See Andrews, *Life of our Lord*, p. 92, ed. 1892; Swete, *The Apostles' Creed*, p. 50, ed. 1894.

In any case the independence of Mt. and Lk. is manifest, for we do not know how to harmonize the accounts. Lk. seems to imply that "the law of Moses" was kept in all particulars; and if so, the purification did not take place before the fortieth day. Mt. implies that the flight into Egypt took place immediately after the visit of the Magi (ii. 14). As Bethlehem is so close to Jerusalem, Herod would not wait long for the return of the Magi before taking action. We adopt, therefore, as a tentative order the Presentation on the fortieth day, Return to Bethlehem, Visit of the Magi, Flight into Egypt, without any return to Nazareth.

παραστῆσαι τῷ κυρίῳ. The Heb. verb in Ex. xiii. 12 means "cause to pass over." It is elsewhere used of parents causing their children to pass through the fire in offering them to Moloch, but is not then translated by παρίστημι (Deut. xviii. 10; 2 Kings xvi. 3, xvii. 17, xxiii. 10, etc.). For παραστῆσαι of offering to God comp. Rom. xii. 1. This παραστῆσαι τῷ κυρίῳ is quite distinct from the purification, which concerned the mother, whereas the presentation concerned the son. It is evident that the presentation is the main fact here. Not, "she came to offer a sacrifice," but "they brought Him up to present Him to the Lord," is the principal statement. The latter rite points back to the primitive priesthood of all firstborn sons. Their functions had been transferred to the tribe of Levi (Num. iii. 12); but every male firstborn had to be redeemed from service in the sanctuary by a payment of five shekels (Num. xviii. 15, 16), as an acknowledgment that the rights of Jehovah had not lapsed. This sum would be about twelve shillings according to the present worth of that amount of silver, but in purchasing power would be nearly double that.

23. The quotation (which is not a parenthesis) is a combination of Ex. xiii. 2 with Ex. xiii. 12 and is not exact with either: **κληθήσεται ἅγ.** perhaps comes from Ex. xii. 16; comp. Lk. i. 35. For **πᾶν ἄρσεν** see Gen. vii. 23;

Ex. i. 22. The **διανοῖγον μήτραν** seems to be fatal to patristic speculations respecting Mary's having given birth to the Christ *clauso utero*, and therefore painlessly: see on ver. 7.

Excepting Mk. vii. 34, *διανοίγω* is peculiar to Lk. (xxiv. 31, 45; Acts vii. 56, xvi. 14, xvii. 3); freq. in LXX (Gen. iii. 5, 7; Exod. xiii. 15; Num. iii. 12, etc.).

24. τοῦ δοῦναι θυσίαν. See on i. 74, and to the reff. there given add v. 7, viii. 5, ix. 51, xii. 42, xxi. 22, xxii. 6, 31, xxiv. 16, 25, 29, 45. This is Mary's offering for her own purification: it has nothing to do with the ransom of the firstborn. The record of the offerings is considerable guarantee for the truth of the history. A legend would very probably have emphasized the miraculous birth by saying that the virgin mother was divinely instructed *not* to bring the customary offerings, which in her case would not be required.

ζεῦγος τρυγόνων. The offering of the poor. It has been argued that this is evidence that the Magi had not yet come. But their gifts, even if they had already offered them, would not have raised Mary's condition from poverty to riches. Only well-to-do people offered a lamb and a pigeon. Neither here nor elsewhere in N.T. have we any evidence that our Lord or His parents were among the abjectly poor.

"The pigeon and turtle-dove were the only birds enjoined to be offered in sacrifice by the law of Moses. In almost every case they were permitted as a substitute for those who were too poor to provide a kid or a lamb. . . . But while the turtle-dove is a migrant, and can only be obtained from spring to autumn, the wild pigeons remain throughout the year; and not only so—they have young at all times. Consequently, at any time of the year when the turtle-dove was unattainable, young pigeons might be procured. There is also a force in the adjective 'young'; for while the old turtle-dove could be trapped, it was hopeless to secure the old pigeon" (Tristram, *Nat. Hist. of the B.* pp. 211, 213).

25–35. The Benediction of Symeon. He and Anna are representatives of the holiness which, in a time of great spiritual deadness, still survived among the men and women of Israel. They are instances of that "spontaneous priesthood" which sometimes springs up, and often among the lower orders, when the regular clergy have become corrupt and secularized. To identify Symeon with any other Symeon is precarious, the name being exceedingly common. He is introduced rather as an unknown person (*ἄνθρωπος ἦν*). It is sometimes said that Symeon, son of Hillel and father of Gamaliel, would hardly have been old enough; he was president of the Sanhedrin A.D. 13. But ver. 29 does not necessarily imply that Symeon is very old. What we know of the Sanhedrin at this period, however, does not lead us to expect to find saints among its presidents. In the *Gospel of Nicodemus* he is called *sacerdos magnus*, and it is his two sons who are raised from the dead by Christ, and reveal what they have seen in Hades (*Pars altera*, A. i.).

25. **ἐν Ἰερουσαλήμ.** It is remarkable that with one exception (Rom. xv. 26) this expression is used in N.T. by no one but Lk., who has it very often (ver. 43, ix. 31; Acts i. 8, ii. 5, vi. 7, ix. 13, 21, x. 39, xiii. 27, xvi. 4, xxi. 11). In LXX it is common. See Deissmann, *Bible Studies*, p. 316.

εὐλαβής. The word is peculiar to Lk. in N.T. (Acts ii. 5, viii. 2, xxii. 12): lit. "taking hold well," and so "cautious." Lat. *timoratus* (Vulg.), *timens* (e), *metuens* (d), *timens deum* (r). Plutarch uses εὐλάβεια in the sense of "carefulness about religious duties, piety"; but εὐλαβής is not thus used in class. Grk. We find the combination of these same two adjectives, δίκαιος and εὐλαβής, twice in Plato's sketch of the ideal statesman. He ought to have both moderation and courage; and of moderation the two chief elements are *justice* and *circumspection*. If he is merely courageous, he will be wanting in τὸ δίκαιον καὶ εὐλαβές (*Polit.* 311 B). See also Philo, *Quis rer. div. hær.* vi., of the εὐλάβεια of Abraham. The meaning of the combination here is that Symeon was conscientious, especially in matters of religion.

προσδεχόμενος (see on xxiii. 51) **παράκλησιν.** 1. "Appeal for help"; 2. "encouragement"; 3. "consolation." The last is the meaning here. Those who "sit in darkness and the shadow of death" (i. 79) need *consolation*; and the salvation which the Messiah was to bring was specially called such by the Jews Comp. "Comfort ye, comfort ye, My people" (Is. xl. 1, xlix. 13, li. 3, lxi. 2, lxvi. 13). There was a belief that a time of great troubles (*dolores Messiæ*) would precede the coming of the Christ. Hence the Messiah Himself was spoken of as "the Consoler," or "the Consolation." Comp. Joseph of Arimathæa, "who was waiting for the kingdom of God" (xxiii. 51; Mk. xv. 43); and with this "waiting" or "looking" of Symeon and Joseph comp. Jacob's death-song, Gen. xlix. 18.

πνεῦμα ἦν ἅγιον. This is the order of the words in the best authorities; and the separation of ἅγιον from πνεῦμα by ἦν accentuates the difference between this expression and that in the next verse. Here the meaning is, "an influence which was holy was upon him"; i. 15, 35, 41, 67 are not parallel. See on i. 15. The accusative, ἐπ' αὐτόν, indicates the *coming*, rather than the resting, of the holy influence; the prophetic *impulse*.

26. **κεχρηματισμένον.** The act. = 1. "transact business" (χρῆμα); 2. "give a divine response" to one who consults an oracle; 3. "give a divine admonition, teach from heaven" (Jer. xxv. 30, xxxiii. 2; Job xl. 8). The pass. is used both of the admonition divinely given, as here, and of the person divinely admonished (Mt. ii. 12, 22; Acts x. 22; Heb. viii. 5, xi. 7). It is gratuitous to conjecture that it was in a dream that the Holy Spirit made this known to Symeon. Comp. Acts xi. 26; Rom. vii. 3.

μὴ ἰδεῖν θ. πρὶν ἢ ἂν ἴδῃ. This is the only example in N.T. of πρίν with the subj. (Win. xli. 3. b, p. 371); and, if the reading is correct, the only instance of πρὶν ἄν: but perhaps either ἤ or ἄν should be omitted. The repetition of "see" is doubtless intentional. In many languages "see" is used of any kind of experience (Acts ii. 27, 31, xiii. 35–37, etc.).

τὸν Χριστὸν Κυρίου. "The Anointed of the Lord"; Him whom God has sent as the Messiah. Comp. τὸν Χρ. τοῦ Θεοῦ (ix. 20), and also 1 Sam. xxiv. 7.

27. ἐν τῷ πνεύματι. Not "in a state of ecstasy" (Rev. i. 10), but "under the influence of the Spirit," who had told him of the blessing in store for him. By τὸ ἱερόν is probably meant the Court of the Women.—ἐν τῷ εἰσαγαγεῖν. "After they had brought in": see on iii. 21. The verb is a favourite with Lk. (xiv. 21, xxii. 54, and six times in Acts): elsewhere only Jn. xviii. 16; Heb. i. 6.

τοὺς γονεῖς. We cannot infer from this that either here or ver. 41 Luke is using an authority that was ignorant of the supernatural birth of Jesus. It is more reasonable to suppose that the whole of this "Gospel of the Infancy" comes from one source, viz. the house of Mary, and that in these passages the narrator employs the usual expression. Joseph (iv. 22) and Mary were commonly called His parents: comp. ver. 33.—It is possible to take περὶ αὐτοῦ after νόμου or after εἰθισμένον; but more probably it belongs to τοῦ ποιῆσαι. For κατὰ τὸ εἰθισμένον see on i. 8.

28. καὶ αὐτός. First the parents, and then *he* holds the child in his arms; the καί being either "also" (he as well as they), or simply introducing the apodosis after ἐν τῷ εἰσαγαγεῖν. Each side acts its proper part. The parents bring Him in accordance with the Divine Law, and Symeon welcomes Him in accordance with the Divine impulse. Symeon is sometimes called Θεοδόχος. See on viii. 13.

Latin renderings of ἀγκάλας vary: *ulnas* (Vulg.), *manus* (c e f), *amplexum* (a), *alas* (d). The last is a late use of *ala*.

29–32. The *Nunc Dimittis*. In its suppressed rapture and vivid intensity this canticle equals the most beautiful of the Psalms. Since the fifth century it has been used in the evening services of the Church (*Apost. Const.* vii. 48[1]), and has often been the hymn of dying saints. It is the sweetest and most solemn of all the canticles. See Bacon's Essay on Death.

Symeon represents himself as a servant or watchman released from duty, because that for which he was commanded to watch has appeared. Comp. the opening of the *Agamemnon* of Æschylus,

[1] Most of the canticles from O.T. and N.T. were said at Lauds both in East and West. But the *Magnificat* was transferred in the West to Vespers, and the *Nunc Dimittis* seems to have been always used in the evening, in the East at Vespers, in the West at Compline. Kraus, *Real.-Enc. d. Chr. Alt.* ii. p. 506; Bingham, *Orig.* vi. 47.

where the sentinel rejoices at his release from the long watch for the fire signal respecting the capture of Troy.

29. νῦν. "*Now* that I have at last seen the long-looked for Messiah": the νῦν stands first with emphasis.

ἀπολύεις τ. δοῦλόν σ., δέσποτα. All three words show that the figure is that of the manumission of a slave, or of his release from a long task. Death is the instrument of release. Ἀπολύω is used of the deaths of Abraham (Gen. xv. 2), of Aaron (Num. xx. 29), of Tobit (Tob. iii. 6), of a martyr (2 Mac. vii. 9): comp. Soph. *Ant.* 1268, and many examples in Wetst. Δεσπότης is the "master of a *slave*," and the Greeks sometimes refused the title to any but the gods in reference to themselves (Eur. *Hippol.* 88). In Scripture it is not often used of God: Acts iv. 24; Rev. vi. 10; perhaps Jude 4, which, however, like 2 Pet. ii. 1, may refer to Christ. Comp. Job v. 8; Wisd. vi. 7, viii. 3; Ecclus. xxxvi. 1; 3 Mac. ii. 2; Philo, *Quis rer. div. hær.* vi.; and see Trench, *Syn.* xxviii. In using the word Symeon acknowledges God's absolute right to dispose of him, either in retaining or dispensing with his service.

κατὰ τὸ ῥῆμά σου. The Divine command communicated to him (ver. 26). Note the exact correspondence between his hymn and the previous promise: ἀπολύεις = ἰδεῖν θάνατον, εἶδον = ἴδῃ, τὸ σωτήριόν σου = τὸν Χριστὸν Κυρίου.—**ἐν εἰρήνῃ.** With emphasis, answering to the emphatic **νῦν**: the beginning and the end of the verse correspond. It is the peace of completeness, of work finished and hopes fulfilled. Comp. "Thou shalt go to thy fathers in peace" (Gen. xv. 15).

30. **ὅτι.** Introduces the cause of the perfect peace.—**εἶδον οἱ ὀφθαλμοί μου.** Hebraistic fulness of expression: comp. Job xix. 27, xlii. 5. His hands also had handled (1 Jn. i. 1); but he mentions sight rather than handling, because sight was specially promised (ver. 26). This verse probably suggested the worthless tradition that Symeon was blind, and received his sight as the Messiah approached him.

τὸ σωτήριον. "The Messianic salvation," and scarcely to be distinguished from τὴν σωτηρίαν. Comp. iii. 6; Acts xxviii. 28; Ps. xcviii. 3; Is. xl. 5; Clem. Rom. *Cor.* xxxvi. 1. In LXX it is freq., sometimes in the sense of "safety," sometimes of "peace-offering." Win. xxxiv. 2, p. 294. That Symeon says so little about the Child, and nothing about the wonders which attended His birth (of which he had probably not heard), is a mark of genuineness. Fiction would have made him dwell on these things.

31, 32. The second strophe of the canticle. Having stated what the appearance of the Messiah has been to himself, Symeon now states what the Messiah will be to the world.

31. **ἡτοίμασας.** When used of God, the verb almost = "ordain." Comp. Mt. xx. 23, xxv. 34; Mk. x. 40; 1 Cor. ii. 9; Heb. xi. 16.

where, as here, the word is used of ordaining blessings. It is used only once of punishment (Mt. xxv. 41).

κατὰ πρόσωπον πάντων τῶν λαῶν. This includes both Jews and Gentiles, as the next verse shows, and is in harmony with the universal character of this Gospel: comp. Is. xix. 24, 25, xlii. 6, xlix. 6, lx. 3, and especially lii. 10, ἀποκαλύψει Κύριος τὸν βραχίονα αὐτοῦ τὸν ἅγιον ἐνώπιον πάντων τῶν ἐθνῶν, καὶ ὄψονται πάντα τὰ ἄκρα τῆς γῆς τὴν σωτηρίαν τὴν παρὰ τοῦ Θεοῦ ἡμῶν. Both in LXX and N.T. κατὰ πρόσωπον is common; it occurs several times in Polybius. Comp. *Test. XII. Patr.* Benj. xi.

32. The σωτήριον is analysed into light and glory, and "the peoples" into heathen and Jews,—that "profound dualism which dominates the biblical history of humanity from Genesis to Revelation" (Godet). The passage is a combination of Ps. xcviii. 2, ἐναντίον τῶν ἐθνῶν ἀπεκάλυψε τὴν δικαιοσύνην αὐτοῦ, with Is. xlix. 6, δέδωκά σε εἰς φῶς ἐθνῶν, and φῶς and δόξαν are in apposition with τὸ σωτήριον. But some take both as depending on ἡτοίμασας, and others take δόξαν after εἰς co-ordinately with ἀποκάλυψιν. This last is Luther's: *ein Licht zu erleuchten die Heiden und zum Preis deines Volkes*; but it is very improbable. Comp. Jn. i. 7, xii. 35, 46.

ἀποκάλυψιν ἐθνῶν. Either 1. "revelation *to belong to* the Gentiles"; or 2. "*instruction of* the Gentiles"; or 3. "*unveiling of* the Gentiles," *i.e.* for removing the gross darkness which covers them (Is. xxv. 7, lx. 2); or 4. (taking ἐθνῶν after φῶς) "a light of the Gentiles unto revelation" (Is. xl. 5). The first is best, "a light with a view to revelation which shall belong to the Gentiles," making ἐθνῶν a poss. gen. Does ἀποκάλυψις ever mean "instruction"? [1] And to represent the heathen as revealed by the light seems to be an inversion: revealed *to whom*? *D.C.G.* ii. p. 253.

Elsewhere in N.T. the gen. after ἀποκάλυψις is either the person who reveals (2 Cor. xii. 1; Rev. i. 1), or the thing revealed (Rom. ii. 5; 1 Pet. iv. 13); but the poss. gen. is quite possible. The word is eminently Pauline (Crem. *Lex.* p. 343). It may be doubted whether the glory of Israel (Rom. ix. 4) is mentioned after the enlightening of the Gentiles in order to indicate that Israel obtained its full glory after and through the enlightenment of the Gentiles; for the heathen accepted the salvation which the Jews refused, and from the heathen it came back to Israel (Bede, Beng.).

The strain of confidence and joy which pervades the canticle is strong evidence of the historical character of the narrative. The condition of the Jewish nation at the close of the first century or beginning of the second is certainly not reflected in it: *c'est le pur accent primitif* (Godet). And Schleiermacher remarks that "it is a circumstance too natural for a poetical fiction" that Symeon takes no notice of the parents until they show surprise, but is lost in an enthusiastic address to God. See small print on i. 56.

33-35. Symeon's Address to the Virgin. "The foreboding of suffering to Mary, so indefinitely expressed, bears no mark of *post*

[1] Grotius admits without commending this rendering, and quotes Ps. cxix. 18, ἀποκάλυψον τοὺς ὀφθαλμούς μου.

actum invention. But the inspired idea of Messiah in the pious old man obviously connected the sufferings which He was to endure in His strife against the corrupt people with those which were foretold of Him in Is. liii." (Neander, *Leben Jesus Christi*, § 18, Eng. tr. p. 27). The change from the unmixed joy and glory of the angelic announcements and of the evangelic hymns is very marked. Here for the first time in the narrative we have an intimation of future suffering.

33. ἦν. When the sing. verb was written, only the first of the persons mentioned was in the writer's mind: such irregularities are common (Mt. xvii. 3, xxii. 40).—**θαυμάζοντες ἐπί.** Excepting Mk. xii. 17, this construction is peculiar in N.T. to Lk. (iv. 22, ix. 43, xx. 26; Acts iii. 12). It is quite class. and freq. in LXX (Judith x. 7, 19, 23, xi. 20; Job xli. 1; Eccles. v. 7; Is. lii. 15). The objection of Strauss, that this wonder of the parents is inconsistent with the angelic annunciation, is pointless. Symeon's declaration about the Gentiles goes far beyond the Angel's promise, and it was marvellous that Symeon should know anything about the Child's nature and destiny.

34. κεῖται. "Is appointed," Phil. i. 16; 1 Thes. iii. 3; Josh. iv. 6; not "is lying" here in thine arms.

εἰς πτῶσιν. In accordance with Is. viii. 14, where the same double destiny is expressed. The coming of the Messiah necessarily involves a *crisis*, a separation, or judgment (*κρίσις*). Some welcome the Light; others "love the darkness rather than the Light, because their works are evil" (Jn. iii. 19), and are by their own conduct condemned. Judas despairs, Peter repents; one robber blasphemes, the other confesses (2 Cor. ii. 16). Hence the *πτῶσις* of many is an inevitable *result* of the manifestation of the Christ. Yet the *purpose* is not *πτῶσις*, but *ἀνάστασις* and *σωτηρία* (Rom. xi. 11, 12). Elsewhere in N.T. **ἀνάστασις** means the resurrection of the dead; in bibl. Grk. it is never transitive. Some understand the metaphor as that of a stone lying (*κεῖται*), against which some stumble and fall (Mt. xxi. 44; Acts iv. 11; Rom. ix. 33; 1 Pet. ii. 6), while others use it as a means to rise. But the latter half of the figure is less appropriate.

σημεῖον. A manifest token, a phenomenon impossible to ignore, by means of which something else is known. A person may be a *σημεῖον*, as Christ is said to be here, and Jonah in xi. 30.—**ἀντιλεγόμενον.** "Which *is* spoken against." This is the *πτῶσις*, that men recognize, and yet reject and oppose, the *σημεῖον*; an opposition which reached a climax in the crucifixion (Heb. xii. 3). For the passive comp. Acts xxviii. 22.

35. From **καὶ σοῦ** to **ῥομφαία** is not a parenthesis; there is nothing in the construction to indicate that it is one, and a statement of such moment to the person addressed would hardly be introduced parenthetically. It is the inevitable result of the **ἀντιλογία**: the Mother's heart is pierced by the rejection and crucifixion of her Son.—**αὐτῆς.**[1] In opposition to **οὗτος.—τὴν ψυχήν.** The seat of the affections and human emotions.—**ῥομφαία.** (1) A long Thracian pike; (2) a large sword, greater than *μάχαιρα* (xxii. 36, 38, 49, 52) or *ξίφος*. Such a weapon better signifies *extreme anguish* than *doubt*, the interpretation which Origen, Bleek, and Reuss prefer, as if she would be tempted to join in the *ἀντιλέγειν*. In that case we should expect *τὸ πνεῦμα* for *τ. ψυχήν*. The word is frequent in LXX and Rev. (i. 16, ii. 12, 16, vi. 8, xix. 15, 21). Syr-Sin. and Diatess-Tat. have "spear."

ὅπως ἄν. This depends upon the whole statement from Ἰδού to *ῥομφαία*, not on the last clause only; on *κεῖται*, not on *διελεύσεται*. It was the Divine purpose that the manifestation of the Messiah should cause the crisis just described; men must decide either to join or to oppose Him. The *ἄν* indicates that in every case the appearance of the Christ produces this result: thoughts, hitherto secret, become known through acceptance or rejection of the Christ.

Acts iii. 19, 20 should be compared. There, as here, we have *εἰς* (?) followed by *ὅπως ἄν*. In N.T. *ὅπως ἄν* is rare; elsewhere only in quotations from LXX (Acts xv. 17 from Amos ix. 12; Rom. iii. 4 from Ps. li. 6).

ἐκ π. καρδιῶν. "*Forth* from many hearts," where they have been concealed; or "Forth from the hearts of many." For **διαλογισμοί** see on v. 22.

36–38. Anna the Prophetess. That the Evangelist obtained this narrative "directly or indirectly from the lips of this Anna who is so accurately described," is less probable than that the source for all this chapter is one and the same, viz. some member of the Holy Family, and probably Mary herself.

36. ἦν. Either "was *present*," as in Mk. xv. 40, in which case *ἦν* in the sense of "was" has to be understood with what follows; or simply "there was," which is better. Thus all runs in logical order. First the existence of Anna is stated, then her life and character, and finally her presence on this occasion. Symeon comes to the temple under the influence of the Spirit; Anna (Hannah) dwells there continually. The sight of the Messiah makes him at once long for death; it seems to give her renewed vigour of life. Is this subtle distinction of character the creation of a writer of fiction? We find fiction at work in the tradition that Mary had been brought up in the temple under the tutelage of Anna. There is nothing here to indicate that Anna had ever seen Mary previously. *D.C.G.* i. p. 70.

[1] It is not easy to decide whether the *δέ* after *σοῦ* is genuine or not. Om. B L Ξ, Vulg. Boh. Aeth. Arm. Ins. ℵ A D, Syrr., Orig. If it be admitted, comp. i. 76; and render *καὶ . . . δὲ . . .* in the same way in both passages: "Yea and." For *διελεύσεται* see on ver. 15.

Neither in ver. 36 (καὶ ἦν) nor in ver. 37 (καὶ αὐτή) does καί = "also" in ref. to ver. 25. The meaning is not "There was Symeon, the holy and aged man; *also* Anna, the holy and aged woman." Throughout the section καί = "and."

προφῆτις. She was known as such before this occasion. Like Miriam, Deborah, Huldah, and the daughters of Philip, Anna was a woman divinely inspired to make known God's will to others. That her genealogy is given because prophetesses are rare, is doubtful. But Lk.'s accuracy appears in such details, which a forger would have avoided for fear of mistakes. Although the ten tribes were lost, some families possessed private genealogies. For the word προφῆτις comp. Rev. ii. 20; Exod. xv. 20; Judg. iv. 4; 2 Chron. xxxiv. 22; Is. viii. 3.

For the omission of the art. after θυγάτηρ see on i. 5.—Φανουήλ = "Face of God," Peniel or Penuel (Gen. xxxii. 31, 32); in LXX εἶδος Θεοῦ.—Ἀσήρ, 2 Chron. xxx. 11.

αὕτη προβεβηκυῖα, κ.τ.λ. "She was advanced in many days, having lived with a husband seven years from her virginity, and herself a widow even for eighty-four years." From αὕτη προβεβ. to τεσσάρων is a parenthesis in which ἦν is to be understood: ζήσασα explains προβεβηκυῖα, and αὐτή balances μετὰ ἀνδρός. She was of great age, *because* she had lived[1] seven years as a wife and eighty-four years *by herself* (Rom. vii. 25) as a widow. The ἕως draws attention to the great length of her widowhood; "up to as much as" (Mt. xviii. 21, 22). That she should be considerably over a hundred years old is not incredible. But the eighty-four may be intended to include the seven years and the time before her marriage. In any case the clumsy arrangement of taking all three verses (36–38) as one sentence, and making αὕτη the nom. to ἀνθωμολογεῖτο, should be avoided. That she had never, in spite of her early widowhood, married again, was held to be very honourable to her: comp. 1 Tim. v. 3, 5. *Monogamia apud ethnicos in summo honore est* (Tertul. *de. Exh. Cast.* xiii.: comp. *de Monog.* xvi.; *ad Uxor.* i. 7). See quotations in Wetst. on 1 Tim. iii. 2, and Whiston's note on Jos. *Ant.* xviii. 6. 6. Syr-Sin. has "seven *days.*"

37. οὐκ ἀφίστατο τοῦ ἱεροῦ. See on viii. 13. This is to be understood, like xxiv. 53, of constant attendance, rather than of actual residence within the temple precincts, although the latter may have been possible. She never missed a service, and between the services she spent most of her time in the temple. In spite of her age she kept more than the customary fasts (comp. v. 33), perhaps more than the Mondays and Thursdays (see on xviii. 12), and spent an unusual amount of time in prayer.

[1] The first aorist of ζῆν is late Greek. It occurs Acts xxvi. 5; Rom. xiv. 9; Rev. ii. 8, xx. 4. Attic writers use ἐβίων, which is not found in N.T.

λατρεύουσα. Freq. in Lk., Paul, and Heb. See on iv. 8. Not in Mk. or Jn. Mt. iv. 10 from Deut. vi. 13.—**νύκτα κ. ἡμέραν.** Comp. Acts xxvi. 7. This is the usual order: Mk. iv. 27, v. 5; Acts xx. 31; 1 Thes. ii. 9, iii. 10; 2 Thes. iii. 8; 1 Tim. v. 5; 2 Tim. i. 3. But the other is also common: xviii. 7; Acts ix. 24; Rev. iv. 8, etc.; and in O.T. is more common. It may be doubted whether the order makes any difference of meaning: see Ellicott on 1 Tim. v. 5, and comp. Hom. *Od.* ii. 345; *Il.* xxiv. 73, v. 490; Plat. *Theaet.* 151 A.

38. αὐτῇ τῇ ὥρᾳ. "That very hour" (RV.): see on x. 7, 21. AV. exaggerates with "that instant," as does Beza with *eo ipso momento*, and also Gen. with "at the same instant."—**ἐπιστᾶσα.** "Coming up" and "standing by," rather than "coming suddenly" (Gen. and Rhem.), although the word often has this meaning from the context. Comp. xxi. 34, x. 40, xx. 1; Acts iv. 1, vi. 12, xxii. 13, xxiii. 27; and see on ver. 9.—**ἀνθωμολογεῖτο.** The ἀντί does not refer to Symeon, meaning that "she *in turn* gave thanks"; but to the making *a return*, which is involved in all thanksgiving: Ps. lxxviii. 13; Ezra iii. 11; 3 Mac. vi. 33; *Test. XII. Patr.* Judah i.

ἐλάλει. Not on that occasion, but afterwards, "she was habitually speaking." When she met Mary and Joseph she could not speak πᾶσιν τοῖς προσδεχομένοις, for they were not present. Grammatically **περὶ αὐτοῦ** may refer to τῷ Θεῷ, but it evidently refers to the Child. Godet divides the people into three sections: the Pharisees, who expected a political deliverer; the Sadducees, who expected nothing; and the blessed few, who expected the spiritual deliverance or consolation (ver. 25) of Jerusalem. Bengel argues from πᾶσιν *erant igitur non pauci*, which does not follow, especially when we consider Lk.'s fondness for the word.

λύτρωσιν Ἰερουσαλήμ. This, without ἐν, is certainly the true reading (ℵ B, many Versions and Fathers), "redemption *of* Jerusalem." Comp. Is. xl. 2. Fiction would probably have given Anna also a hymn. Against the hypothesis that this narrative is "a poetical and symbolical representation," Schleiermacher asks, "Why should the author, along with Symeon, have introduced Anna, who is not made even to answer any poetical purpose?"

39. ἐτέλεσαν. "Brought to a close, accomplished"; especially of executing what has been *prescribed*: xii. 50, xviii. 31, xxii. 37; Acts xiii. 29; Rom. ii. 27; Jas. ii. 8. See Jn. xix. 28, which illustrates the difference between τελέω and τελειόω. Syr-Sin. here inserts "Joseph and Mary" as nom. to "accomplished." Why not "His father and His mother" (ver. 33) or "His parents" (ver. 43), if that text was framed to discredit the virgin birth?

Ναζαρέτ. Lk. appears to know nothing of the visit of the Magi. It would have suited his theme of the *universality* of the Gospel so well, that he would hardly have omitted it, if he had known it. In that case he was not familiar with our First Gospel From Mt. ii. 11 we infer that the Holy Family, after the Purification, returned to Bethlehem and there occupied a house (τὴν *οἰκίαν*). The parents may have thought that the Son of David, born in Bethlehem, ought to be brought up there. Thence they fly to Egypt, a flight not mentioned in the authority used by Lk.

40. The conclusion of a separate narrative: comp. i. 80. Contrast the reticence of this verse (which is all that we know respecting the next eleven years) with the unworthy inventions of the apocryphal gospels. Hastings, *D.C.G.* art. "Boyhood of Jesus."

ηὔξανεν κ. ἐκραταιοῦτο. Of bodily development in size and strength; for *πνεύματι* is an insertion from i. 80.—**πληρούμενον.** Pres. part. "Being filled" day by day. The **σοφία** is to be regarded as wisdom in the highest and fullest sense. The intellectual, moral, and spiritual growth of the Child, like the physical, was *real.* His was a perfect humanity developing perfectly, unimpeded by hereditary or acquired defects. It was the first instance of such a growth in history. For the first time a human infant was realizing the ideal of humanity. See Martensen, *Christian Dogmatics*, § 139.

χάρις Θεοῦ ἦν ἐπ' αὐτό. See on iv. 22 and comp. Acts iv. 33.

It was near the beginning of this interval that the Jews sent an embassy of fifty to follow Archelaus to Rome, to protest against his accession, and to petition that Judæa might be annexed to Syria (Jos. *B. J.* ii. 6. 1; *Ant.* xvii. 11. 1), of which fact we perhaps have a trace in the parable of the Pounds (xix. 14). And it was near the end of this interval that another embassy went to complain of Archelaus to Augustus: and he was then deposed, and banished to Vienne in Gaul (*Ant.* xvii. 13. 2; *B. J.* ii. 7. 3). Lewin, *Fasti Sacri*, 877, 944, 1011, 1026.

41–52. *The Boyhood of the Messiah.*

His Visit to Jerusalem and the Temple, and His first recorded Words. Here again, as in the Circumcision, the Purification, and the Presentation, the idea of *fidelity to the Law* is very conspicuous. Hort, *Judaistic Christianity*, Lect. ii., Macmillan, 1894.

41. κατ' ἔτος. The expression occurs here only in N.T. Combined with the imperf. it expresses the habitual annual practice of Joseph and Mary. At the Passover, Pentecost, and Tabernacles every male had to go up to Jerusalem (Ex. xxiii. 14–17, xxxiv. 23; Deut. xvi. 16). But since the Dispersion this law could not be kept; yet most Palestinian Jews tried to go at least once a year. About women the Law says nothing, but Hillel prescribed that they also should go up to the Passover. Mary, like Hannah (1 Sam. i. 7), probably went out of natural piety, and not in obedience to Hillel's rule.

τῇ ἑορτῇ. "*For* the feast," or, more probably, "*at* the feast": dat. of time, as in viii. 29, xii. 20, xiii. 14, 15, 16; Acts vii. 8, xii. 21, xxi. 26, xxii. 13, xxvii. 23. In class. Grk. *τῇ ἑορτῇ* without *ἐν* is rare: Win. xxxi. 5, p. 269. The phrase *ἡ ἑορτὴ τοῦ πάσχα* occurs again Jn. xiii. 1 only; not in

LXX. The fact that γονεῖς has not been changed here, even in those MSS. in which *vv.* 27 and 43 have been corrupted, is some evidence that the corruption was not made for dogmatic reasons. The love of amplification or of definiteness might suffice.

42. ἐτῶν δώδεκα. At the age of twelve a young Jew became "a son of the Law," and began to keep its enactments respecting feasts, fasts, and the like. The mention of the age implies that since the Presentation Jesus had not been up to Jerusalem.—**ἀναβαινόντων.** Imperf. part. "On their usual going up."—**κατὰ τὸ ἔθος.** See small print on i. 9; also Deissmann, *Bible Studies*, p. 251.

43. καὶ τελειωσάντων. Note the change of tense. "And after they had fulfilled." There is nothing ungrammatical in the combination of an aor. with an imperf. part. But the reading ἀναβάντων is an obvious correction to avoid apparent awkwardness.—**τὰς ἡμέρας.** The prescribed seven days (Ex. xii. 15, 16; Lev. xxiii. 6–8; Deut. xvi. 3), or the customary two days, for many pilgrims left after the principal sacrifices were over.

ὑπέμεινεν. Contains an idea of persistence and perseverance, and hence is used of remaining after others have gone: comp. Acts xvii. 14. The attraction of Divine things held Him fast in spite of the departure of His parents. It would be His first experience of the temple services, and especially of the slaying of the Paschal lamb.—**ὁ παῖς.** "The Boy," to distinguish from τὸ παιδίον: see on ver. 52.—**οὐκ ἔγνωσαν.** This shows what confidence they had in Him, and how little they were accustomed to watch Him. That it shows neglect on their part is a groundless assertion. They were accustomed to His obedience and prudence, and He had never caused them anxiety. See Hase, *Geschichte Jesu*, § 28, p. 276, ed. 1891.

44. τῇ συνοδίᾳ. "The caravan." The inhabitants of a village, or of several neighbouring villages, formed themselves into a caravan, and travelled together. The Nazareth caravan was so long that it took a whole day to look through it. The caravans went up singing psalms, especially the "songs of degrees" (Ps. cxx.–cxxxiv.): but they would come back with less solemnity. It was probably when the caravan halted for the night that He was missed. At the present day the women commonly start first, and the men follow; the little children being with the mothers, and the older with either. If this was the case then, Mary might fancy that He was with Joseph, and Joseph that He was with Mary. Tristram, *Eastern Customs in Bible Lands*, p. 56.

ἡμέρας ὁδόν. In LXX ὁδὸν ἡμέρας (Num. xi. 31; 1 Kings xix. 4). Comp. πορείαν ἡμέρας μιᾶς (Jon. iii. 4).

The compound ἀνεζήτουν expresses thoroughness (Acts xi. 25; Job iii. 4, x. 6; 2 Mac. xiii. 21).

συγγενεῦσιν. A barbarous form of dat. plur. found also Mk. vi. 4 and 1 Mac. x. 89. For γνωστοῖς see on xxiii. 49.

45. μὴ εὑρόντες. "Because they did not find": see on iii. 9.—ὑπέστρεψαν ἀναζητοῦντες. The turning back was a single act, the seeking continued a long time. Comp. Mk. viii. 11, x. 2. In such cases the pres. part. is not virtually fut., as if it meant "in order to seek." The seeking was present directly the turning back took place. Win. xlv. 1. b, p. 429. For ὑπέστρεψαν see small print on i. 56, and for ἐγένετο see detached note after ch. i.

46. ἡμέρας τρεῖς. These are reckoned in three ways. (1) One day out, at the end of which the Child is missed; one day back; and on the third the finding. This is probably correct. (2) One day's search on the journey back; one day's search in Jerusalem; and on the third the finding. (3) Two days' search in Jerusalem, and then the finding. This is improbable. Jerusalem was not a large place, and less than a day would probably suffice. We may understand that on all three days Jesus was in the temple with the doctors. Godet conjectures that He there had an experience similar to that of Jacob at Bethel (Gen. xxviii. 10–22): "God became more intimately *His* God, *His* Father." There is no evidence.

ἐν τῷ ἱερῷ. Not in a synagogue, if there was one in the temple enclosure, but probably on the terrace, where members of the Sanhedrin gave public instruction on sabbaths and festivals. If this is correct, His parents had left on the third day, and the Passover was still going on. If all had been over, this public teaching would have ceased.

καθεζόμενον. As a learner, not as a teacher. St. Paul sat "at the feet of Gamaliel" (Acts xxii. 3). Jesus probably sat on the ground, while the Rabbis sat on benches or stood.—ἐν μέσῳ. See on viii. 7. Not *dignitatis causâ* (Beng.) or as *doctor doctorum* (Calov.), but because there were teachers on each side, possibly in a semicircle. The point is that He was not hidden, but where He could easily be found. For a list of distinguished persons who *may* have been present, see Farrar, *L. of Christ*, i. ch. vi., from Sepp, *Leben Jesu*, i. § 17. Of biblical personages, Symeon, Gamaliel, Annas, Caiaphas, Nicodemus, and Joseph of Arimathea are possibilities.

ἀκούοντα αὐτῶν καὶ ἐπερωτῶντα αὐτούς. Note that the hearing is placed first, indicating that He was there as a learner; and it was as such that He questioned them. It was the usual mode of instruction that the pupil should ask as well as answer questions. A holy thirst for knowledge, especially of sacred things, would prompt His inquiries. The *Arabic Gospel of the Infancy* represents Him as instructing them in the statutes of the Law and the mysteries of the Prophets, as well as in astronomy, medicine, physics, and metaphysics (l.–lii.). See on iii. 10.

47. ἐξίσταντο. A strong word expressing great amazement:

viii. 56; Acts ii. 7, 12, viii. 13, ix. 21. For *ἐπί* comp. Wisd. v. 2 and the *ἐπί* which Lk. commonly uses after *θαυμάζειν* (see on ver. 33); and for **πάντες οἱ ἀκούοντες** see on i. 66.—**συνέσει.** "Intelligence"; an application of the *σοφία* with which He was ever being filled (ver. 40): see Lft. on Col. i. 9.—**ἀποκρίσεσιν.** His replies would show His wonderful intellectual and spiritual development. The vanity of Josephus (*Vita*, 2) and of Bellarmine (*Vita*, pp. 28–30, ed. Döllinger und Reusch, Bonn, 1887) leads them to record similar amazement respecting themselves.

48. ἰδόντες. Return to the original subject, *οἱ γονεῖς.*—**ἐξεπλάγησαν.** Another strong expression: ix. 43; Acts xiii. 12. They were astonished at finding Him there, and thus occupied, apparently without thought of them.

ἡ μήτηρ αὐτοῦ. It was most natural that she should be the first to speak. Her reproachful question perhaps contains in it a vein of self-reproach. She and Joseph had appeared to be negligent.

ζητοῦμεν. "Are seeking": the pain of the anxiety has not yet quite ceased. For **καὶ ἐγώ** see on xvi. 9.

ℵ B read *ζητοῦμεν*, which WH. adopt. Almost all other editors follow almost all other authorities in reading *ἐζητοῦμεν*.

ὀδυνώμενοι. "In great anguish" of mind, as in Acts xx. 38 and Zech. xii. 10; of body and mind, xvi. 24, 25; comp. Rom. ix. 2; 1 Tim. vi. 10. The *ῥομφαία* (ver. 35) has already begun its work. Anguish cannot be reasonable. But they might have been sure that the Child who was to be the Messiah could not be lost. This agrees with ver. 50.

49. τί ὅτι ἐζητεῖτέ με; Not a reproof, but an expression of surprise: comp. Mk. ii. 16. He is not surprised at their coming back for Him, but at their not knowing where to find Him.

Here also ℵ has the pres. *ζητεῖτε.*

ἐν τοῖς τοῦ πατρός μου. "Engaged in My Father's business" is a possible translation: comp. *τὰ τοῦ Θεοῦ* (Mt. xvi. 23; Mk. viii. 33); *τὰ τοῦ Κυρίου* (1 Cor. vii. 32, 34). But "in My Father's house" is probably right, as in Gen. xli. 51. Irenæus (*Hær.* v. 36. 2) paraphrases the *ἐν τῇ οἰκίᾳ* of Jn. xiv. 2 by *ἐν τοῖς*: comp. *ἐν τοῖς Ἀμάν* (Esth. vii. 9); *ἐν τοῖς αὐτοῦ* (Job xviii. 19); *τὰ Λύκωνος* (*Theoc.* ii. 76). Other illustrations in Wetst. Arm. and Diatess-Tat. have *in domo patris mei.* The words indicate His surprise that His parents did not know *where* to find Him. His Father's business could have been done elsewhere. There is a gentle but decisive correction of His Mother's words, "Thy *father* and I," in the reply, "Where should a child be (*δεῖ*), but in his father's house? and My Father is God." For the **δεῖ** see on iv. 43. It is notable that the first recorded words of the Messiah are an expression of His Divine

Sonship as man; and His question implies that they knew it, or ought to know it. But there is nothing which implies that He had just received a revelation of this relationship. These first recorded words are the kernel of the whole narrative, and the cause of its having been preserved. They must mean more than that Jesus is a son of Abraham, and therefore has God as His Father. His parents would easily have understood so simple a statement as that.

50. οὐ συνῆκαν τὸ ῥῆμα. *Ergo non ex illis hoc didicerat* (Beng.). There is nothing inconsistent in this. They learnt only gradually what His Messiahship involved, and this is one stage in the process. From the point of view of her subsequent knowledge, Mary recognized that at this stage she and Joseph had not understood. This verse, especially when combined with the next, shows clearly who was the source of Lk.'s information.[1] Comp. ix. 45 and xviii. 34.

51. ἦν ὑποτασσόμενος. This sums up the condition of the Messiah during the next seventeen years. The analytical tense gives prominence to the continuance of the subjection: comp. i. 18, 20, 21. For *ὑποτάσσειν* comp. x. 17, 20.

αὐτοῖς. The last mention of Joseph. He was almost certainly dead before Christ's public ministry began; but this statement of continued subjection to him and Mary probably covers some years. The main object of the statement, however, may be to remove the impression that in His reply (ver. 49) Jesus resents, or henceforward repudiates, their authority over Him. Comp. Ign. *Magn.* xiii.

διετήρει. Expresses careful and continual keeping. Gen. xxxvii. 11 is a close parallel: comp. Acts xv. 29. We must not confine **πάντα τὰ ῥήματα** to *vv.* 48, 49; the phrase is probably used in the Hebraistic sense of "things spoken of." Comp. i. 65, ii. 19; Acts v. 32: but in all these cases "sayings" is more possible than here. Still more so in Dan. vii. 28: *τὸ ῥῆμα ἐν τῇ καρδίᾳ μου διετήρησα* [? *συνετήρησα*]. Syr-Sin. omits "in her heart."

52. The verse is very similar to 1 Sam. ii. 26, of which it is perhaps a quotation. See Athan. *Con. Arian.* iii. 51, p. 203, ed. Bright; Card. Newman, *Select Treatises of S. Athan.* i. p. 419; Wace & Schaff, p. 421; Pearson, *On the Creed*, art. iii. p. 160.

Ἰησοῦς. The growth is very clearly marked throughout: *τὸ βρέφος* (ver. 16); *τὸ παιδίον* (ver. 40); *Ἰησοῦς ὁ παῖς* (ver. 43), *Ἰησοῦς* (ver. 52). *Non statim plena statura, ut Protoplasti, apparuit: sed omnes ætatis gradus sanctificavit. Senectus eum non decebat* (Beng.). Schaff, *The Person of Christ*, pp. 10–17, Nisbet, 1880.

[1] "This fine tender picture, in which neither truth to nature, nor the beauty which that implies, is violated in a single line, . . . cannot have been devised by human hands, which, when left to themselves, were always betrayed into coarseness and exaggeration, as shown by the apocryphal gospels" (Keim, *Jes. of Naz.*, Eng tr. ii. p. 137).

προέκοπτεν. Here only in the Gospels, and elsewhere in N.T. only in S. Paul (Rom. xiii. 12; Gal. i. 14; 2 Tim. ii. 16, iii. 9, 13). The metaphor probably comes from pioneers *cutting in front*; but some refer it to *lengthening by hammering*. Hence the meaning of "promote": but more often it is intransitive, as always in N.T. Actual growth is expressed by the word, and to explain it of progressive *manifestation* is inadequate. Hooker, *Eccl. Pol.* bk. v. 53. 1–3.

σοφίᾳ. Not "knowledge" but "wisdom," which includes knowledge: it is used of the wisdom of the Egyptians (Acts vii. 22). Jesus was capable of growth in learning; *e.g.* He increased in learning through experience in suffering: ἔμαθεν ἀφ' ὧν ἔπαθεν (Heb. v. 8, where see Westcott's notes).

ἡλικίᾳ. Not "age," which is probably the meaning xii. 25 and Mt. vi. 27, but would be rather an empty truism here. Rather, "stature," as in xix. 3: *justam proceritatem nactus est ac decoram* (Beng.). His intellectual and moral growth (σοφία), as well as His physical growth (ἡλικία), was perfect. The προέκοπτε ἡλικίᾳ corresponds to ἐμεγαλύνετο (in some copies ἐπορεύετο μεγαλυνόμενον) in 1 Sam. ii. 26. See Martensen, *Chr. Dogm.* § 142.

χάριτι. "Goodwill, favour, loving-kindness" (ver. 40, i. 30; Acts iv. 33, vii. 10): see on iv. 22. That He *advanced* in favour with God plainly indicates that there was moral and spiritual growth. At each stage He was perfect for that stage, but the perfection of a child is inferior to the perfection of a man; it is the difference between perfect innocence and perfect holiness. He was *perfectly* (τελέως) man, as set forth in the Council of Constantinople (A.D. 381) against Apollinaris, who held that in Jesus the Divine Logos was a substitute for a human soul. In that case an increase in σοφία and in χάρις παρὰ Θεῷ would have been inconceivable, as Pearson points out (*On the Creed*, art. iii. p. 160; comp. E. Harold Browne, *Exp. of the XXXIX. Articles*, iv. 2. 4).

καὶ ἀνθρώποις. Nothing of the kind is said of John (i. 66, 80); his sternness and his retirement into the desert prevented it. But an absolutely perfect human being living among men could not fail to be attractive until His public ministry brought Him into collision with their prejudices and sins.[1] Comp. what Josephus says of the development of Moses (*Ant.* ii. 9. 6); also the promise made in Prov. iii. 4 to him who keeps mercy and truth: "so shalt

[1] Pearson in a long note gives the chief items of evidence as to the primitive belief that Is. liii. 2, 3 was to be understood literally of the personal appearance of Jesus as "a personage no way amiable; an aspect, indeed, rather uncomely." . . . "But what the aspect of His outward appearance was, because the Scriptures are silent, we cannot now know" (*On the Creed*, art. ii. pp. 87, 88).

Lange has some good remarks on the "master-stroke of Divine wisdom" which caused Jesus to be brought up at Nazareth (*L. of Christ*, Eng. tr. i. pp. 317, 324).

thou find favour and good understanding in the sight of God and man"—ἐνώπιον Κυρίου καὶ ἀνθρώπων.

For answers to the objections urged by Strauss against the historical character of this narrative see Hase, *Gesch. Jesu*, § 28, p. 280, ed. 1891.

III. 1–IX. 50. THE MINISTRY.

III. 1–22. *The External Preparation for the Ministry of the Christ: the Ministry of John the Baptist*, Mt. iii. 1–12; Mk. i. 1–8; Jn. i. 15–28.

Hic quasi scena N.T. panditur is Bengel's illuminative remark. "It was the glory of John the Baptist to have revived the function of the prophet" (*Ecce Homo*, p. 2); and it is difficult for us to realize what that meant. A nation, which from Samuel to Malachi had scarcely ever been without a living oracle of God, had for three or four centuries never heard the voice of a Prophet. It seemed as if Jehovah had withdrawn from His people. The breaking of this oppressive silence by the voice of the Baptist caused a thrill through the whole Jewish population throughout the world. Lk. shows his appreciation of the magnitude of the crisis by the sixfold attempt to give it an exact date. Of the four Evangelists he is the only one to whom the title of historian in the full sense of the term can be given; and of Christian writers he is the first who tries to fit the Gospel history into the history of the world. It is with a similar wish to do justice to a crisis that Thucydides gives a sixfold date of the entry of the Thebans into Platæa, by which the thirty years' truce was manifestly broken and the Peloponnesian War begun (ii. 2; comp. v. 20).

The section is carefully arranged. First the Date (1, 2); then a Description of the new Prophet (3–6); then an account of his Preaching and its Effects (7–17); and an Explanation as to how it came to an End (18–20). He baptizes the Christ (21, 22).

1, 2. The Date. The event that is thus elaborately dated is the appearance of the new Prophet, not the beginning of Christ's ministry. See below on the conclusion of ver. 2. Ellicott considers it the date of the captivity of the Baptist. This had been advocated by Wieseler in his *Synopsis* (ii. ch. ii. Eng. tr. p. 178), but he abandoned it in his *Beiträge*. Others would make it refer to Christ's baptism, which may have followed closely upon John's first appearance as a preacher (Caspari, *Chron. Einl.* § 33, Eng. tr. p. 41). But the interval between the beginning of John's ministry and his baptizing Jesus cannot be determined Some estimate it at one month, others at six months, because John was six months older than Jesus (Lewin, *Fasti Sacri*, 1171). Weiss (*Leben Jesu*, I. ii. 8, Eng. tr. i. p. 316) shows that the interval was not more than six months. The appearance of one who seemed to be a Prophet soon attracted immense attention; and when large numbers accepted his doctrine and baptism, it became imperative that the hierarchy should make inquiry as to his authority and claims. But it appears from Jn. i. 19–28 that the first investigation made by the Sanhedrin was about the time when the Baptist met Jesus. In neither case can year or time of year be determined. *If* Jesus was born towards the end, John about the middle, of 749 (B.C. 5), then John might begin to preach about the middle of 779, and Jesus be baptized early in 780 (A.D. 27).

It is little or no confirmation of this result that both the Greek and the Roman Churches celebrate the Baptism of Christ on Jan. 6th. Originally, the Nativity, the Visit of the Magi, and the Baptism were all celebrated on Jan. 6th. When Dec. 25th was adopted as the date of the Nativity, the Roman Church continued to celebrate the Baptism with the Epiphany to the Gentiles on Jan. 6th, while the Greek Church transferred the latter along with the Nativity to Dec. 25th, commemorating the Baptism alone on Jan. 6th. The fact that both the Eastern and the Western Church have concurred in celebrating the Baptism on Jan. 6th seems at first sight to be imposing testimony. But there is little doubt that all trustworthy evidence had perished before any of these dates were selected.[1]

Instead of the elaborate dates given in these first two verses, Mt. (iii. 1) has simply Ἐν δὲ ταῖς ἡμέραις ἐκείναις, while Mk. (i. 4) has nothing. Comp. the somewhat similar dating of the erection of Solomon's temple (1 Kings vi. 1). Beng. says of this date, *Epocha ecclesiæ omnium maxima. Hic quasi scena N.T. panditur. Ne nativitatis quidem, aut mortis, resurrectionis, ascensionis christi tempus tam præcise definitur.*

1. Ἐν ἔτει δὲ πεντεκαιδεκάτῳ τῆς ἡγεμονίας Τιβερίου Καίσαρος. He naturally begins with the Roman Empire, and then takes the local governors, civil and ecclesiastical. "Now in the 15th year of the reign of Tiberius Cæsar," or "of Tiberius as Cæsar." Is the 15th year to be counted from the death of Augustus, Aug. 19th, A.U.C. 767, A.D. 14? or from the time when he was associated with Augustus as joint ruler at the end of 764 or beginning of 765, A.D. 11 or 12? It is impossible to determine this with certainty. Good authorities (Zumpt, Wieseler, Weiss) plead for the latter reckoning, which makes the Gospel chronology as a whole run more smoothly; but it is intrinsically less probable,

[1] For the chief *data* respecting the limits of our Lord's life see Lft. *Biblical Essays*, p. 58, note; and on Lk.'s chronology in these verses see Ewald, *Hist. of Israel*, vi., Eng. tr. p. 149, and Lange. *L. of C.* bk. ii. pt. iii. § 1, i. p. 342.

and *seems* to be inconsistent with the statements of Tacitus and Suetonius. See Hastings, *D.B.* i. p. 405.

The main points are these. 1. Tiberius was not joint *Emperor* with Augustus; he was associated with him only in respect of the provinces and armies: *ut provincias cum Augusto communiter administraret, simulque censum ageret* (Suet. *Tib.* xxi.); *ut æquum ei jus in omnibus provinciis exercitibusque esset* (Vell. Paterc. ii. 121); *filius, collega imperii, consors tribuniciæ protestatis adsumitur, omnisque per exercitus ostentatur* (Tac. *Ann.* i. 3. 3; comp. i. 11. 2 and iii. 56. 2). 2. It is clear from Tacitus (*Ann.* i. 5-7) that, when Augustus died, *Tiberius was not regarded by himself or by others as already Emperor.* Suetonius confirms this by saying that Tiberius, while manifestly getting the imperial power into his hands, for a time refused the offer of it (*Tib.* xxiv.). 3. No instance is known of reckoning the reign of Tiberius from his association with Augustus. The coins of Antioch, Lk.'s own city, which helped to convert Wieseler from the one view to the other by seeming to date the reign of Tiberius from the association, are not admitted by Eckhel to be genuine. On the other hand, there are coins of Antioch which date the reign of Tiberius from the death of Augustus. It remains, therefore, that, although to reckon from the association was a possible method, especially in the provinces, for there Tiberius had been really a consort of Augustus, yet it is more probable that Lk. reckons in the usual way from the death of the predecessor (see Wieseler, *Chron. Synop.* ii. ch. ii.; Keim, *Jesus of Naz.* ii. pp. 381, 382; Lewin, *Fasti Sacri*, 1044; Sanday, *Fourth Gospel*, p. 65). Fifteen years from the death of Augustus would be A.D. 29, at which time our Lord would probably be 32 years of age, which sufficiently agrees with Lk.'s "about 30" (ver. 23). *If* the earlier date is admissible, the agreement becomes exact.

ἡγεμονίας. Quite a vague term, and applicable to the rule of emperor, king, *legatus*, or *procurator*, as is shown by Jos. *Ant.* xviii. 4. 2, and by the use of ἡγεμών in N.T.: xx. 20, xxi. 12; Acts xxiii. 24, 26, 33, etc. Wieseler is alone in seeing in this word (instead of μοναρχία), and in καῖσαρ (instead of Σεβαστός), evidence that the co-regency of Tiberius is meant (*Beiträge z. richtigen Würdigung d. Evan.* 1869, pp. 191–194). From the Emperor Lk. passes to the local governor under him.

ἡγεμονεύοντος. The more exact ἐπιτροπεύοντος of D and other authorities is an obvious correction to mark his office with precision: ἐπίτροπος = *procurator.* Pilate succeeded Valerius Gratus A.D. 25, and was recalled A.D. 36 or 37 by Tiberius, who died, March A.D. 37, before Pilate reached Rome. Having mentioned the Roman officials, Lk. next gives the local national rulers.

τετραρχοῦντος. The word occurs nowhere else in N.T., but is used by Josephus of Philip, tetrarch of Trachonitis (*B. J.* iii. 10. 7). The title tetrarch was at first used literally of the governor of a fourth; *e.g.* of one of the four provinces of Thessaly (Eur. *Alc.* 1154), or one of the fourths into which each of the three divisions of Galatia were divided (Strabo, 430, 540, 560, 567). But afterwards it came to mean the governor of any division, as a third or a half, or of any small country; any ruler not a βασιλεύς (Hor

Sat. i. 3. 12). Such seems to be the meaning here; but it may be used in its literal sense, Pilate's province representing the fourth tetrarchy, viz. the dominions of Archelaus.

In d we have the singular rendering: *in anno quintodecimo ducatus Tiberi Cæsaris procurante Pontio Pilato Judææ, quaterducatus Galilææ Herode.*

Ἡρῴδου. Antipas, son of Herod the Great and Malthace the Samaritan. See small print on i. 5 for the iota subscript. Two inscriptions have been found, one at Cos and one at Delos, which almost certainly refer to him as tetrarch, and son of Herod the king (Schürer, *Jewish People in the T. of J. C.* I. vol. ii. p. 17). His coins have the title tetrarch, and, like those of his father, bear no image. Herod Philip was the first to have any portrait on the coins of a Jewish prince. He had the images of Augustus and Tiberius put upon his coins. As his dominions were wholly heathen, this would cause little scandal. He even went so far as to put the temple of Augustus at Panias on his coins. Herod Antipas was made tetrarch of Peræa and Galilee, B.C. 4 (Jos. *Ant.* xvii. 11. 4; *B. J.* ii. 6. 3). As he ruled this district until A.D. 39 or 40, the whole of Christ's life falls within his reign, and nearly the whole of Christ's ministry took place within his dominions. For his character see on xiii. 32. He was by courtesy allowed the title of *βασιλεύς* (Mk. vi. 14); and as Agrippa had obtained this by right, Antipas and Herodias went to Rome, A.D. 39, to try and get the courtesy title made a real one by Caligula. The attempt led to his banishment, the details of which are uncertain, for Josephus makes inconsistent statements. Either he was banished at Baiæ, A.D. 39, to *Lugdunum* (*Ant.* xviii. 7. 2), or he had a second audience with Caligula *at* Lugdunum, A.D. 40, and was banished to *Spain* (*B. J.* ii. 9. 6). The latter is probably correct (Lewin, *Fasti Sacri*, 1561). But see Farrar, *Herods*, p. 178.

Φιλίππου. Herod Philip, son of Herod the Great and Cleopatra. He reigned for nearly 37 years, B.C. 4 to A.D. 33, when he died at Julias, which he had built and named in honour of the infamous Julia, d. of Augustus and wife of Tiberius. He was the builder of Cæsarea Philippi (*B. J.* ii. 9. 1), and was the best of the Herods (*Ant.* xviii. 4. 6). He married his niece Salome soon after she had danced for the head of the Baptist, *c.* A.D. 31 (*Ant.* xviii. 5. 4). Trachonitis (*τραχών = τραχὺς καὶ πετρώδης τόπος*) derived its name from the rugged character of the country. It lay N.E. of Galilee in the direction of Damascus, and its inhabitants were skilled archers and very often banditti (*Ant.* xv. 10. 1). The expression *τῆς Ἰτ. καὶ Τρ. χώρας*, "the *region* of Ituræa and Trachonitis," seems to indicate that more than these two is included; probably Auranitis and Batanæa. *Ἰτυραία*, both here and perhaps everywhere, is an adjective. Farrar, p. 164.

Λυσανίου τῆς Ἀβιληνῆς τετρ. Not merely Strauss, Gfrörer, B. Bauer, and Hilgenfeld, but even Keim and Holtzmann, attribute to Lk. the gross chronological blunder of supposing that Lysanias, son of Ptolemy, who ruled this region previous to B.C. 36, when he was killed by M. Antony, is still reigning 60 years after his death. Such a mistake is very improbable; and the only difficulty about Lk.'s statement is that we have no indisputable evidence of this tetrarch Lysanias. *D.C.G.* art. "Lysanias."

But 1. Lysanias, son of Ptolemy, was styled *king* and not tetrarch, and the seat of his kingdom was *Chalcis* in Cœle-Syria, not Abila in Abilene. 2. It is pure assumption that no one of his name ever ruled in these parts afterwards. 3. Josephus (*Ant.* xix. 5. 1) speaks of "Abila of Lysanias," and (xx. 7. 1) of a tetrarchy of Lysanias (comp. *B. J.* ii. 11. 5, 12. 8); and as the son of Ptolemy was not called tetrarch, nor was connected with Abila, and, moreover, reigned for only 5 or 6 years, it is improbable that "Abila of Lysanias" was called after him. Therefore these passages in Josephus confirm rather than oppose Lk. 4. A medal found by Pococke designates Lysanias "*tetrarch* and high priest." If this refers to either, it is more likely to refer to Lk.'s Lysanias. 5. Two inscriptions exist, one of which proves that Lysanias, the son of Ptolemy, *left children*; the other, that at the time when Tiberius was associated with Augustus there was a "*tetrarch* Lysanias" (Boeckh, *Corp. inscr. Gr.* 4523, 4521). See Davidson, *Intr. to N.T.* i. pp. 214–221, 1st ed.; Rawlinson, *Bampton Lectures for* 1859, p. 203; Wieseler in Herzog,[2] i. pp. 87–89; and the reff. in Thayer's Grimm under Λυσανίας.

2. ἐπὶ ἀρχιερέως Ἅννα καὶ Καιάφα. Lk. now passes to the ecclesiastical rulers. The singular is probably not accidental, and certainly not ironical. "Under the high priest Annas-Caiaphas," which means that between them they discharged the duties, or that each of them in different senses was regarded high priest, Annas *de jure* (Acts iv. 6) and Caiaphas *de facto* (Jn. xi. 49).

Annas had held office A.D. 7–14, when he had been deposed by Valerius Gratus, the predecessor of Pilate, who set up in succession Ismael, Eleazar (son of Annas), Simon, and Joseph surnamed Caiaphas, who held office A.D. 18–36, when he was deposed by Vitellius. Four more sons of Annas succeeded Caiaphas, the last of whom (another Annas) put to death James the "brother of the Lord" and the first bishop of Jerusalem. It is manifest that Annas retained very great influence, and sometimes acted as high priest. "Annas the high priest was there, and Caiaphas, and John, and Alexander, and as many as were of the kindred of the high priest" (Acts iv. 6). Perhaps, so far as it was safe to do so, he was encouraged to ignore the Roman appointments and to continue in office during the high priesthoods of his successors. This would be especially easy when his own son-in-law or son happened to be the Roman nominee.[1] There were no less than twenty-eight high priests from the time of Herod the Great to the capture of Jerusalem by Titus (Jos. *Ant.* xx. 10).

ἐγένετο ῥῆμα Θεοῦ ἐπὶ Ἰωάνην. It is clear from this that what Lk. is anxious to date with precision is not any event in the life of the Messiah, but *the appearance of the new Prophet*, who was

[1] Josephus says that David appointed Zadok high priest μετ' Ἀβιαθάρου, φίλος γὰρ ἦν αὐτῷ (*Ant.* vii. 5. 4). See Lft. *Biblical Essays*, p. 163.

to be the Messiah's herald, and who was by some mistaken for the Messiah. John's preaching and baptizing is an epoch with Lk. (Acts i. 22, x. 37, xiii. 24). As distinct from ὁ λόγος τοῦ Θεοῦ, which means the Gospel message as a whole (see on viii. 11), ῥῆμα Θεοῦ means some particular utterance (Mt. iv. 4; comp. Lk. xxii. 61). The phrase γίνεσθαι ῥῆμα Κυρίου (not Θεοῦ) is freq. in LXX (Gen. xv. 1; 1 Sam. xv. 10; 2 Sam. vii. 4; 1 Kings xvii. 2, 8, xviii. 1, xx. 28, etc.); also γίνεσθαι λόγον Κυρίου (2 Sam. xxiv. 11; 1 Kings vi. 11, xii. 22, xiii. 20, xvi. 1, etc.). It is the O.T. formula to express Divine inspiration. In such cases the phrase is almost always followed by πρός: but in 1 Chron. xxii. 8 (?) and Jer. i. 1 we have ἐπί. Jer. i. 1 is a close parallel to this: τὸ ῥῆμα τοῦ Θεοῦ ὃ ἐγένετο ἐπὶ Ἱερεμίαν. The phrase occurs nowhere else in N.T.

Ἰωάνην τὸν Ζαχαρίου υἱόν. Lk. alone describes the Baptist thus. No other N.T. writer mentions Zacharias.—**ἐν τῇ ἐρήμῳ.** The one mentioned as his abode (i. 80). Both AV. and RV. rather obscure this by using "deserts" in i. 80 and "wilderness" here. Mt. calls it "the wilderness of Judæa" (iii. 1). It is the Jeshimon of 1 Sam. xxiii. 19. See *D.B.*[2] art. "Arabah," and Stanley, *Sin. & Pal.* p. 310.

3–6. Description of the New Prophet. Lk. omits the statements about his dress and food (Mt. iii. 4; Mk. i. 6), and also the going out of the people of Jerusalem and Judæa to him (Mt. iii. 5; Mk. i. 5). The famous account of the Baptist in Jos. *Ant.* xviii. 5. 2 should be compared. It may have been altered by Christian scribes, but its divergence from the Gospel narrative as to the motive for imprisoning and killing John, is in favour of its originality.[1] See Hastings, *D.B.* i. p. 240.

3. πᾶσαν περίχωρον τοῦ Ἰορδάνου. The same as "the *plain* of Jordan," which is thus rendered in LXX Gen. xiii. 10, 11; by τῷ περιχώρῳ τοῦ Ἰ., 2 Chron. iv. 17; and by τῷ περιοίκῳ τοῦ Ἰ., 1 Kings vii. 46. The expression covers a considerable portion of the Jordan valley at least as far north as Succoth (2 Chron. iv. 17). The Baptist, therefore, moved north from the limestone desert on the W. shore of the Dead Sea, and perhaps went almost the whole length of the valley to the confines of the Sea of Galilee. For "Bethany (Beth-Anijah = 'House of Shipping') beyond Jordan" must have been near Galilee (Jn. i. 28), and is supposed by Conder to be the same as Bashan (*Handbook of the Bible*, pp. 315, 320). See, however, *D.B.*[2] art. "Bethabara." John was sometimes on one bank and sometimes on the other, for we read of his working in Peræa (Jn. x. 40). His selection of the valley of the

[1] "This part of John's ministry, viz. his work as a reformer, Josephus has brought out prominently; while he has entirely failed to notice the indelible stamp of the Baptist's labours left upon the history of the Theocracy" (Neander, *L.J.C.* § 34).

Jordan as his sphere of work was partly determined by the need of water for immersion. Stanley, *Sin. & Pal.* p. 312.

κηρύσσων . . . ἁμαρτιῶν. *Verbatim* as Mk. i. 4. Nowhere in N.T. has *κηρύσσειν* its primary meaning of "act as a herald"; but either "proclaim openly" (viii. 39, xii. 3; Mk. i. 45, etc.) or "preach the Gospel" (Mt. xi. 1; Mk. iii. 14; Rom. x. 14, 15, etc.). To "preach baptism" is to preach the necessity or value of baptism; and "repentance baptism" (*βάπτισμα μετανοίας*) is baptism connected with repentance as being an external symbol of the inward change (Acts xiii. 24, xix. 4). The repentance precedes the baptism, which seals it and reminds the baptized of his new obligations. To submit to this baptism was to confess that one was a sinner, and to pledge oneself to a new life. The "change of mind"[1] (*μετάνοια*) has reference both to past deeds and to future purposes, and is the result of a realization of their true moral significance (Wsctt. on Heb. vi. 1, 6, xii. 17). This inward change is specially insisted upon in the account of John's preaching in Jos. *Ant.* xviii. 5. 2. The word is rare in Mt. (iii. 8, 11) and Mk. (i. 4), and does not occur in Jn. It is freq. in Lk. (ver. 8, v. 32, xv. 7, xxiv. 47; Acts v. 31, xi. 18, etc.). We find it in Jos. *Ant.* xiii. 11. 3 of Aristobulus after the murder of his brother; in Plut. *Pericles*, x., of the Athenians after the banishment of Cimon; and in Thuc. iii. 36. 3 of the Athenians after the sentence on Mitylene. See *American Ch. Rev.* No. 134, pp. 143 ff. John's "repentance baptism" was **εἰς ἄφεσιν ἁμαρτιῶν.** This was its *purpose*, assuring the penitent of forgiveness, and of deliverance from the burden, penalty, and bondage of sin (Trench, *Syn.* xxxiii.; Crem. *Lex.* p. 297: comp. Lk. i. 77; Acts ii. 38; Heb. x. 18).

4. ἐν βίβλῳ λόγων. With the exception of Phil. iv. 3, *ἐν βίβλῳ* is peculiar to Lk. (xx. 42; Acts i. 20, vii. 42). The form *βίβλος* is usual where the meaning is a writing or document, *βύβλος* where the plant or papyrus as writing material is intended (Hdt. ii. 96. 3, v. 58. 3). For *λόγοι* in the sense of the "utterances of a teacher or prophet" comp. Acts xx. 35; Amos i. 1.

φωνὴ βοῶντος . . . τὰς τρίβους αὐτοῦ. From Mt. iii. 3 and Mk. i. 3 we see that, in the tradition of which all three make use, these words were quoted as applying to the Baptist. This is therefore a primitive interpretation; and we learn from Jn. i. 23 that it originated with the Baptist himself. John was a *φωνή* making known the *Λόγος*. "The whole man was a sermon." The message was more than the messenger, and hence the messenger is regarded

[1] Lactantius, in writing *de Pœnitentia* prefers *resipiscentia* as a better, although still inadequate, rendering. *Is enim quem facti sui pœnitet, errorem suum pristinum intelligit; ideoque Græci melius et significantius μετάνοιαν dicunt, quam nos latine possumus* resipiscentiam *dicere. Resipiscit enim ac mentem suam quasi ab insania recipit*, etc. (*Div. Inst.* vi. 24. 6).

as mainly a voice. Jn. has εὐθύνατε for εὐθείας ποιεῖτε (i. 23), and this looks as if he were translating direct from the Hebrew, which has one word and not two. The quotation in the other three is identical, and (with the substitution of αὐτοῦ for τοῦ Θεοῦ [ἡμῶν]) verbatim as LXX. Lk. quotes Is. xl. 4, 5 as well as xl. 3, and here slightly varies from LXX, having εὐθείας for εὐθεῖαν, and αἱ τραχεῖαι εἰς ὁδοὺς λείας for ἡ τραχεῖα εἰς πεδία.[1]

ἐν τῇ ἐρήμῳ. It is possible to take these words with ἑτοιμάσατε rather than with φωνὴ βοῶντος: but here, as in Mt. and Mk., the latter arrangement is more natural—*vox clamantis in deserto.* Barnabas (ix. 3) connects them with βοῶντος. It is evident from the scenery which is mentioned that it is in a desert that the road for the coming King has to be made. The details symbolize the moral obstacles which have to be removed by the repentance baptism of John, in order to prepare the people for the reception of the Messiah, or (as some prefer) of Jehovah (Is. xxxv. 8–10). That Lk. means the Messiah is shown by the substitution of αὐτοῦ for τοῦ Θεοῦ: and that this interpretation is in accordance with the primitive tradition is shown by the fact that all three Gospels have this substitution. Just as Oriental monarchs, when making a royal progress, send a courier before them to exhort the population to prepare roads, so the Messiah sends His herald to exhort His own people (Jn. i. 11) to prepare their hearts for His coming.

5. φάραγξ. "A valley shut in by precipices, a ravine"; here only in N.T., but found in LXX (Judith ii. 8) and in class. Grk. (Thuc. ii. 67. 4). It is perhaps from the same root as φαράω = "plough" and *foro* = "bore."

βουνός. Herodotus seems to imply that this is a Cyrenaic word (iv. 199. 2): but it is freq. in later writers and in LXX. Comp. xxiii. 30, and for the sense Zech. iv. 7; Is. xl. 4.

ἔσται τὰ σκολιὰ εἰς, κ.τ.λ. "The crooked *places* shall become straight *ways*, and the rough *ways* smooth ways": *i.e.* roads shall be made where there were none before, and bad roads shall be made good roads. Comp. the account of Vespasian's march into Galilee, especially the work of the pioneers (Jos. *B. J.* iii. 6. 2).

6. πᾶσα σάρξ. Everywhere in N.T. this expression seems to refer to the human race only; so even Mt. xxiv. 22; Mk. xiii. 20; 1 Pet. i. 24; comp. Acts ii. 17; Rom. iii. 20. Fallen man, man in his frailty and need of help, is meant. In LXX it often includes the brutes: Gen. vi. 19, vii. 15, 16, 21, viii. 17, ix. 11,

[1] Ewald says of the prophecy of which these verses form the introduction, that "it is not only the most comprehensive, but also, in respect of its real prophetic subject-matter, the weightiest piece of that time, and altogether one of the most important portions of the O.T., and one of the richest in influence for all future time. . . . It is especially the thought of the passing away of the old time, and the flourishing of the new, which is the life of the piece" (*Prophets of O.T.*, Eng. tr. iv. pp. 244, 254; comp. pp. 257, 259).

15, 16, 17; Ps. cxxxvi. 25; Jer. xxxii. 27, xlv. 5. The phrase is one of many which occur frequently in Is. xl.–lxvi., but not at all in the earlier chapters (Driver, *Isaiah*, p. 197).

τὸ σωτήριον. It was obviously for the sake of this declaration that Lk. continued the quotation thus far. That "the salvation of God" is to be made known to the whole human race is the main theme of his Gospel.

7–17. John's Preaching and its Effects. This section gives us *the burden of his preaching* (Ἔλεγεν, imperf.) in accordance (οὖν) with the character which has just been indicated. The herald who has to see that hearts are prepared for the Messiah must be stern with hypocrites and with hardened sinners, because the impenitent cannot escape punishment (7–9); must supply different treatment for different classes (10–14; comp. ver. 5); and must declare the certainty of his Master's coming and of its consequences (15–17).

7. Ἔλεγεν οὖν. "He used to say, therefore": being the predicted Forerunner, his utterances were of this character. We need not regard this as a report of what was said on any one occasion, but as a summary of what he was in the habit of saying during his ministry to the multitudes who came out of the towns and villages (ἐκπορευομένοις) into the wilderness to hear the Prophet and gain something from him. Mt. (iii. 7) represents this severe rebuke as addressed to the Pharisees and Sadducees; which confirms the view that Lk. is here giving us the *substance* of the preaching rather than what John said on some particular day. What he said to some was also said to all; and as the salvation offered was universal, so also was the sin. This is thoroughly characteristic of Lk.

βαπτισθῆναι. As a *substitute* for repentance, or as some magical rite, which would confer a benefit on them independently of their moral condition. Their desire for his baptism showed their belief in him as a Prophet; otherwise the baptism would have been valueless (Jn. i. 25; comp. Zech. xiii. 1; Ezek. xxxvi. 25). Hence the indignation of John's disciples when they heard of Jesus baptizing, a rite which they regarded as their master's prerogative (Jn. iii. 26). The title ὁ βαπτιστής or ὁ βαπτίζων shows that his baptism was regarded as something exceptional and not an ordinary purification (Jos. *Ant.* xviii. 5. 2). Its exceptional character consisted in (1) its application to the whole nation, which had become polluted; (2) its being a preparation for the more perfect baptism of the Messiah. It is only when baptism is administered by immersion that its full significance is seen.

Βαπτίζω is intensive from βάπτω, like βαλλίζω from βάλλω: βάπτω, "I dip"; βαπτίζω, "I immerse." Γεννήματα is "offspring" of animals or men (Ecclus. x. 18); "fruits" of the earth or of plants (Deut. xxviii. 4, 11, 18, 42, 5; Mt. xxvi. 29; Mk. xiv. 25; Lk. xxii. 18); "rewards" of righteousness (Hos. x. 12; 2 Cor. ix. 10).

Γεννήματα ἐχιδνῶν. *Genimina* (Vulg.) or *generatio* (b ff2 l q r) or *progenies* (a c d e f) *viperarum*. In Mt. this is addressed to the *Pharisees*, first by John and afterwards by Jesus (iii. 7, xii. 34, xxiii. 33). It indicates another parentage than that of Abraham (Jn. viii. 44), and is perhaps purposely used in opposition to their trust in their descent: comp. Aesch. *Cho.* 249; Soph. *Ant.* 531. John's metaphors, like those of the prophecy (ver. 5), are from the wilderness;—vipers, stones, and barren trees. It is from this stern, but fresh and undesecrated region, and not from the "Holy," but polluted City, that the regenerating movement proceeds (Is. xli. 18). These serpent-like characters are the *σκολιά* that must be made straight. Comp. Ps. lviii. 4, cxl. 3.

ὑπέδειξεν. "Suggested" by showing to eye or ear: vi. 47, xii. 5; Acts ix. 16, xx. 35; elsewhere in N.T. only Mt. iii. 7.

τῆς μελλούσης ὀργῆς. It is possible that this refers primarily to the national judgments involved in the destruction of Jerusalem and the banishment of the Jews (xxi. 23; 1 Mac. i. 64); but the penalties to be inflicted at the last day are probably included (Rom. i. 18, ii. 5, 8, iii. 5, v. 9). The Jews believed that the judgments of God, especially in connexion with the coming of the Messiah, as threatened by the Prophets (Joel ii. 31; Mal. iii. 2, iv. 1; Is. xiii. 9), were to be executed on the *heathen*. The Baptist proclaims that there is no such distinction. Salvation is for all who prepare their hearts to receive the Messiah; judgment, for all who harden their hearts and reject Him. Birth is of no avail.

8. ποιήσατε οὖν καρποὺς ἀξίους τ. μ. "If you desire to escape this wrath and to welcome the Messiah (*οὖν*), repent, and act *at once* (aor. imperat.) as those who repent." Comp. xx. 24; Acts iii. 4, vii. 33, ix. 11, xvi. 9, xxi. 39, xxii. 13; and see Win. xliii. 3. a, p. 393. Mt. has *καρπόν* (iii. 8), which treats the series of acts as a collective result. Comp. S. Paul's summary of his own preaching, esp. *ἄξια τῆς μετανοίας ἔργα πράσσοντας* (Acts xxvi. 20).

It was a Rabbinical saying, "If Israel would repent only one day, the Son of David would come forthwith"; and again, "If Israel would observe only one sabbath according to the ordinance, forthwith would the Son of David come"; and, "All the stages are passed, and all depends solely on repentance and good works."

The phrase *ποιεῖν καρπόν* is not necessarily a Hebraism (Gen. i. 11, 12): it occurs [Arist.] *De Plant.* i. 4, p. 819, ii. 10, p. 829. Comp. Jas. iii. 12: Mk. iv. 32.

μὴ ἄρξησθε. "Do not even begin to have this thought in your minds." *Omnem excusationis etiam conatum præcidit* (Beng.). If there are any passages in which *ἄρχομαι* with an infin. is a mere periphrasis for the simple verb (xx. 9), this is not one of them. See Win. lxv. 7. d, p. 767; Grim-Thay. p. 79; Fritzsche on Mt. xvi. 21, p. 539.—**λέγειν ἐν ἑαυτοῖς.** "To say within yourselves" rather than "among yourselves." Comp. vii. 49 and λέγετε ἐν ταῖς καρδίαις ὑμῶν (Ps. iv. 5). For the perennial boast about their descent from Abraham comp. Jn. viii. 33, 53; Jas. ii. 21; 2 Esdr. vi. 56–58; Jos. *Ant.* iii. 5. 3; *B. J.* v. 9. 4; Wetst. on Mt. iii. 9.

ἐκ τῶν λίθων τούτων. There is a play upon words between "children" (*banim*) and "stones" (*abanim*). It was God who made Abraham to be the rock whence the Jews were hewn (Is. li. 1, 2); and out of the most unpromising material He can make genuine children of Abraham (Rom. iv., ix. 6, 7, xi. 13–24; Gal. iv. 21–31). The verb **ἐγεῖραι** is applicable to both stones and children.

9. ἤδη. "Although you do not at all expect it." The image of the axe is in harmony with that of the fruits (ver. 8). In the East trees are valued mainly for their fruit; and trees which produce none are usually cut down. "And even now also the axe is laid unto the root."

The **πρός** after **κεῖται** may be explained either, "is brought to the root and lies there"; or, "lies directed towards the root." In either case the meaning is that judgment is not only inevitable, but will come speedily: hence the presents, **ἐκκόπτεται** and **βάλλεται.**

The δὲ καί (in Mt. simply δέ) is Lk.'s favourite method of giving emphasis; ver. 12, ii. 4, iv. 41, v. 10, 36, ix. 61, x. 32, xi. 18, xii. 54, 57, xiv. 12, xvi. 1, 22, xviii. 9, xix. 19, xx. 12. For μή with a participle, expressing a reason or condition, comp. ii. 45, vii. 30, xi. 24, xii. 47, xxiv. 23; Acts ix. 26, xvii. 6, xxi. 34, xxvii. 7; and see Win. lv. 5 (β), p. 607. For ἐκκόπτειν, "to cut off," of felling trees, comp. xiii. 7, 9; Hdt. ix. 97. 1. See notes on vi. 43.

10–14. John's Different Treatment of Different Classes. Peculiar to Lk., but probably from the same source as the preceding verses. It shows that, in levelling the mountains and raising the valleys, etc. (ver. 5), he did not insist upon any extraordinary penances or "counsels of perfection." Each class is to forsake its besetting sin, and all are to do their duty to their neighbour. The stern warnings of the Baptist made the rulers leave in disgust without seeking baptism at his hands (vii. 30; Mt. xxi. 25); but they made the multitude anxious to comply with the conditions for avoiding the threatened judgment.

10. ἐπηρώτων. "Continually put this question." The notion of *repetition* comes from the imperf. and not, as in ἐπαιτεῖν (xvi. 3, xviii. 35), from the ἐπί, which in ἐπερωτᾷν indicates the *direction* of the inquiry; Plato, *Soph.* 249 E, 250. Comp. ἐπεδόθη in iv. 17.

Τί οὖν ποιήσωμεν; "What then, if the severe things which thou sayest are true, must we do?" For the *conjunctivus deliberativus* comp. xxiii. 31; Mt. xxvi. 54, Mk. xii. 14; Jn. xii. 27; and see Win. xli. 4. b, p. 356; Matth. 515. 2; Arnold's *Madvig*, p. 99; Green, p. 150.

11. δύο χιτῶνας. The **χιτών was the under and less necessary**

garment, distinguished from the upper and almost indispensable ἱμάτιον; vi. 29; Acts ix. 39; Mt. v. 40; Jn. xix. 23. When two of these χιτῶνες were worn at once, the under one or shirt would be the Hebrew *cetoneth*, the upper would be the Hebrew *meil*, which was longer than the *cetoneth*. It was common for travellers to wear two (Jos. *Ant.* xvii. 5. 7); but Christ forbade the disciples to do so (ix. 3; Mt. x. 10). It is not implied here that the two are being worn simultaneously. See Trench, *Syn.* l.; Conder, *Handb. of B.* p. 195; *D.B.*[2] art. "Dress"; Schaff's *Herzog*, art. "Clothing and Ornaments of the Hebrews." If the owner of two shirts is to "give a *share*" (μεταδότω), he will give one shirt. Comp. Rom. i. 11, xii. 8; and contrast Peter's reply to the same question Acts ii. 37, 38. With regard to βρώματα, nothing is said or implied about having superfluity or abundance. He who has any food is to share it with the starving. Comp. 1 Thes. ii. 8.

This verse is one of those cited to support the view that Lk. is Ebionite in his sympathies, a view maintained uncompromisingly by Renan (*Les Évangiles*, ch. xiii.; *V. de J.* chs. x., xi.), and by Campbell (*Critical Studies in St. Luke*, p. 193). For the answer see Bishop Alexander (*Leading Ideas of the Gospel*, p. 170). Here it is to be noticed that it is Mt. and Mk. who record, while Lk. omits, the poor clothing and poor food of the Baptist himself; and that it is Mt. who represents his sternest words as being addressed to the wealthy Pharisees and Sadducees, while Lk. directs them against the multitudes generally.

12. τελῶναι. From τέλη (Mt. xvii. 25; Rom. xiii. 7) and ὠνέομαι; so that *etymologically* τελῶναι = *publicani*, "those who *bought* or farmed the taxes" under the Roman government. But in *usage* τελῶναι = *portitores*, "those who collected the taxes" for the *publicani*. This usage is common elsewhere, and invariable in N.T. Sometimes, and perhaps often, there was an intermediate agent between the τελῶναι and the *publicani*, *e.g.* ἀρχιτελώνης or *magister* (xix. 2).

These "tax-collectors" were detested everywhere, because of their oppressiveness and fraud, and were classed with the vilest of mankind: μοιχοὶ καὶ πορνοβοσκοὶ καὶ τελῶναι καὶ κόλακες καὶ συκοφάνται, καὶ τοιοῦτος ὅμιλος τῶν πάντα κυκώντων ἐν τῷ βίῳ (Lucian. *Necyomant.* xi.; comp. Aristoph. *Equit.* 248; Theophr. *Charac.* vi.; Grotius, *in loco*; Wetst. on Mt. v. 46). The Jews especially abhorred them as bloodsuckers for a heathen conqueror. For a Jew to enter such a service was the most utter degradation. He was excommunicated, and his whole family was regarded as disgraced. But the Romans allowed the Herods to retain some powers of taxation; and therefore not all tax-collectors in Palestine were in the service of Rome. Yet the characteristic faults of the profession prevailed, whether the money was collected in the name of Cæsar or of Herod; and what these were is indicated by the Baptist's answer. See Lightfoot, *Opera*, i. pp. 324, 325; Herzog, *PRE.*[2] art. *Zoll*; Edersh. *L. & T.* i. p. 515.

13. Διδάσκαλε. *Publicani majore ceteris reverentia utuntur* (Beng.). Syr-Sin. omits the word.

πλέον παρά. For παρά after comparatives comp. Heb. i. 4, iii. 3, ix. 23,

xi. 4, xii. 24; Hdt. vii. 103. 6; Thuc. i. 23. 4, iv. 6. 1. The effect is to intensify the notion of excess: so also ὑπέρ, xvi. 8; Heb. iv. 12.

τὸ διατεταγμένον. "That which stands prescribed" (perf.); a favourite word with Lk.: viii. 55; xvii. 9, 10; Acts vii. 44, xviii. 2, xx. 13, xxiii. 31, xxiv. 23. Comp. dis*ponere*, ver*ordnen*. It is from the general meaning of "transacting business" that **πράσσειν** acquires the special sense of "exacting tribute, extorting money": comp. xix. 23. This use is found from Herodotus onwards: Hdt. iii. 58. 4; Æsch. *Cho.* 311; *Pers.* 476; *Eum.* 624; Xen. *Anab.* vii. 6. 17: comp. πράκτωρ, εἰσπράσσειν, ἐκπράσσειν, and many illustrations in Wetst. *Agere* is similarly used: *publicum quadragesimæ in Asia egit* (Suet. *Vesp.* i.); but what follows is of interest as showing how rare an honourable *publicanus* was: *manebantque imagines in civitatibus ei positæ sub hoc titulo* ΚΑΛΩΣ ΤΕΛΩΝΗΣΑΝΤΙ. This is said of Sabinus, father of Vespasian. After farming the *quadragesima* tax in Asia he was a money-lender among the Helvetii. It is to be noticed that the Baptist does not condemn the calling of a tax-collector as unlawful for a Jew. He assumes that these τελῶναι will continue to act as such.

14. στρατευόμενοι. "Men on service, on military duty"; *militantes* rather than *milites* (Vulg.). In 2 Tim. ii. 4, οὐδεὶς στρατευόμενος is rightly rendered *nemo militans*. Who these "men on service" were cannot be determined; but they were Jewish soldiers and not Roman, and not on service in the war between Antipas and his father-in-law Aretas about the former's repudiation of the latter's daughter in order to make room for Herodias. That war took place after the Baptist's death (Jos. *Ant.* xviii. 5. 2), two or three years later than this, and probably A.D. 32 (Lewin, *Fasti Sacri*, 1171, 1412). These στρατευόμενοι were possibly *gendarmerie*, soldiers acting as police, perhaps in support of the tax-collectors. Such persons, as some modern nations know to their cost, have great opportunities for bullying and delation. By their καὶ ἡμεῖς they seem to connect themselves with the τελῶναι, either as knowing that they also were unpopular, or as expecting a similar answer from John.

Μηδένα διασείσητε. Like *concutio*, διασείω is used of intimidation, especially of intimidating to extort money (3 Mac. vii. 21). Eusebius uses it of the extortions of Paul of Samosata (*H. E.* vii. 30. 7); where, however, the true reading may be ἐκσείει. In this sense σείω also is used (Aristoph. *Equit.* 840; *Pax*, 639); and it is interesting to see that Antipho couples σείω with συκοφαντῶ. Φιλοκράτης οὑτοσὶ ἑτέρους τῶν ὑπευθεύνων ἔσειε καὶ ἐσυκοφάντει (*Orat.* vi. p. 146, l. 22).[1] This last passage, combined with the verse

[1] In the *Passio S. Perpetuæ*, iii., the martyr suffers much στρατιωτῶν συκοφαντίαις πλείσταις, and this is represented in the Latin by *concussuræ militum*. Comp. Tert. *De Fuga in Pers.* xii., xiii.

before us, renders it probable that συκοφάντης, a "fig-shower," is not one who *gives information* to the police about the *exportation* of figs, but one who *shows* figs by *shaking* the tree; *i.e.* who makes the rich yield money by intimidating them. Nowhere is συκοφάντης found in the sense of "informer," nor yet of "sycophant." It always denotes a "false accuser," especially with a view to obtaining money; Arist. *Ach.* 559, 825, 828. Hatch quotes from Brunet de Presle, *Notices et textes du Musée du Louvre*, a letter of B.C. 145 from Dioscorides, a chief officer of finance, to his subordinate Dorion: **περὶ δὲ διασεισμῶν καὶ παραλειῶν ἐνίων δὲ καὶ συκοφαντεῖσθαι προσφερομένων βουλόμεθα ὑμᾶς μὴ διαλανθάνειν,** κ.τ.λ., "in the matter of fictitious legal proceedings and plunderings, some persons being, moreover, alleged to be even made the victims of false accusations," etc. (*Bibl. Grk.* p. 91). Comp. Lev. xix. 11; Job xxxv. 9. Hesychius explains συκοφάντης as ψευδοκατήγορος.

ὀψωνίοις. From ὄψον, "cooked food" to be eaten with bread, and ὠνέομαι, "I buy": hence "rations, allowance, pay" of a soldier; 1 Cor. ix. 7; 1 Mac. iii. 28, xiv. 32; 1 Esdr. iv. 56; and freq. in Polybius. John does not tell these men on service that theirs is an unlawful calling. Nor did the early Christians condemn the life of a soldier: see quotations in Grotius and J. B Mozley, *University Sermons*, Serm. v.

15–17. The certainty of the Messiah's Coming and the Consequences of the Coming. Mt. iii. 11, 12. The explanatory opening (ver. 15) is peculiar to Lk. The substance of ver. 16 is common to all three; but here Lk. inserts the characteristic π ᾶ σ ι ν. In ver. 17 he and Mt. are together, while Mk. is silent. Lk. shows more clearly than the other two how intense was the excitement which the Baptist's preaching caused.

15. Προσδοκῶντος. What were they expecting? The result of all this strange preaching, and especially the Messianic judgment. Would it be put in execution by John himself? For this absolute use of προσδοκάω comp. Acts xxvii. 33. Excepting Mt. xi. 3, xxiv. 50, 2 Pet. iii. 12–14, the verb is peculiar to Lk. (i. 21, vii. 19, 20, viii. 40, xii. 46; Acts iii. 5, etc.). Syr-Sin. omits.

The Vulg. here has the strange rendering *existimante*; although in i. 21, vii. 19, 20, viii. 40 προσδοκάω is rendered *expecto*, and in xii. 46 *spero*. Cod. Brix. has *sperante* here. See on xix. 43 and xxi. 23, 25 for other slips in Jerome's work. Here d has an attempt to reproduce the gen. abs. in Latin: *et cogitantium omnium*. Comp. ix. 43, xix. 11, xxi. 5, xxiv. 36, 41.

μή ποτε αὐτός. "If haply he himself were the Christ." Their thinking this possible, although "John did no sign," and had none of the insignia of royalty, not even descent from David, is remarkable. *Non ita crassam adhuc ideam de Christo habebant, nam*

Johannes nil splendoris externi habebat et tamen talia de eo cogitabant (Beng.). That this question had been raised is shown by Jn. i. 20. The Baptist would not have declared "I am not the Christ," unless he had been asked whether he was the Messiah, or had heard the people discussing the point.

For the constr. comp. *μή ποτε δῴη αὐτοῖς ὁ Θεὸς μετάνοιαν* (2 Tim. ii. 25). The opt. in indirect questions is freq. in Lk. both without *ἄν* (i. 29, viii. 9, Acts xvii. 11, xxi. 33) and also with *ἄν* (i. 62, vi. 11, xv. 26; Acts v. 24, x. 17).

16. πᾶσιν. Showing how universal the excitement on this point was. Neither Mt. (iii. 11) nor Mk. (i. 7) has the *πᾶσιν* of which Luke is so fond: comp. vi. 30, vii. 35, ix. 43, xi. 4, xii. 10.

The aor. mid. *ἀπεκρίνατο* is rare in N.T. (xxiii. 9; Acts iii. 12; Mt. xxvii. 12; Mk. xiv. 61; Jn. v. 17, 19); also in LXX (Judg. v. 29; 1 Kings ii. 1; 1 Chron. x. 13; Ezek. ix. 11). In bibl. Grk. the pass. forms prevail: see small print on i. 19.

Ἐγὼ μὲν ὕδατι. Both with emphasis: "*I* with *water*."

ὁ ἰσχυρότερος. *Valebat Johannes, sed Christus multo plus* (Beng.). The art. marks him as one who ought to be well known.

λῦσαι τὸν ἱμάντα τῶν ὑποδημάτων. More graphic than Mt.'s *τὰ ὑποδ. βαστάσαι*, but less so than Mk.'s *κύψας λῦσαι τὸν ἱμ. τῶν ὑποδ. αὐτοῦ*. Both AV. and RV. mark the difference between *ὑπόδημα*, "that which is bound under" the foot, and *σανδάλιον*, dim. of *σάνδαλον*, by rendering the former "shoe" (x. 4, xv. 22, xxii. 35; Acts vii. 33, xiii. 25) and the other "sandal" (Mk. vi. 9; Acts xii. 8). The Vulg. has *calceamenta* for *ὑποδήματα*, and *sandalia* or *caligæ* for *σανδάλια*. In LXX the two words seem to be used indiscriminately (Josh. ix. 5, 13); but *ὑποδ.* is much the more common, and it is doubtful whether the Jews before the Captivity wore shoes or *manalim* (Deut. xxxiii. 25) as distinct from sandals. Comp. *οἱ ἱμάντες τῶν ὑποδημάτων αὐτῶν* (Is. v. 27). To unfasten shoes or sandals, when a man returned home, or to bring them to him when he went out, was the office of a slave (See Wetst. on Mt. iii. 11). John is not worthy to be the bond-servant of the Christ. The **αὐτοῦ** is not so entirely redundant as in some other passages: "whose latchet of his shoes."[1]

αὐτός. In emphatic contrast to the speaker.

ἐν πνεύματι ἁγίῳ. See on i. 15. That the *ἐν* with *πνεύματι ἁγίῳ* and its absence from *ὕδατι* marks a distinction of any great moment, either here or Acts i. 5, must be doubted; for in Mt. iii. 11 *both* expressions have the *ἐν*, and in Mk. i. 8 *neither*. The simple dat. marks the instrument or matter *with* which the baptism

[1] Comp. Mk. vii. 25; 1 Pet. ii. 24; Rev. iii. 8, vii. 2, 9, xiii. 8, xx. 8. Such pleonasms are Hebraistic, and are specially common in LXX (Gen. i. 11; Exod. xxxv. 29, etc.); Win. xxii. 4 (b), p. 184.

is effected; the ἐν marks the element *in* which it takes place (Jn. i. 31). See Hastings, *D.B.* i. p. 244.

καὶ πυρί. This remarkable addition is wanting in Mk. Various explanations of it are suggested. (1) That the *fiery tongues at Pentecost* are meant, is improbable. Were any of those who received the Spirit at Pentecost among the Baptist's hearers on this occasion? Moreover, in Acts i. 5 καὶ πυρί is not added. (2) That it distinguishes two baptisms, the penitent with the Spirit, and the impenitent with *penal fire*, is very improbable. The *same* persons (ὑμᾶς) are to be baptized with the Spirit *and* with fire. In ver. 17 the good and the bad are separated, but not here. This sentence must not be made parallel to what follows, for the winnowing-shovel is not baptism. (3) More probably the πυρί refers to the illuminating, kindling, and *purifying power* of the grace given by the Messiah's baptism. *Spiritus sanctus, quo Christus baptizat*, igneam *vim habet: atque ea vis ignea etiam conspicua fuit oculis hominum* (Beng.): comp. Mal. iii. 2. (4) Or, the *fiery trials* which await the disciple who accepts Christ's baptism may be meant: comp. xii. 50; Mk. x. 38, 39. The passage is one of many, the exact meaning of which must remain doubtful; but the purifying of the believer rather than the punishment of the unbeliever seems to be intended.

17. πτύον. The "winnowing-shovel" (*pala lignea*; Vulg. *ventilabrum*), with which the threshed corn was thrown up into the wind (πτύω = "spit").[1] This is a further description of the Messiah,—He whose πτύον is ready for use. Note the impressive repetition of αὐτοῦ after τῇ χειρί, τὴν ἅλωνα, and τὴν ἀποθήκην.[2]

τὴν ἅλωνα. The threshing-floor itself, and not its contents. It is by removing the contents—corn to the barn, and refuse to the fire—that the floor is thoroughly cleansed. Christ's threshing-floor is the world; or, in a more restricted sense, the Holy Land. See Meyer on Mt. iii. 12.

ἀσβέστῳ. Comp. Mk. ix. 43; Lev. vi. 12, 13; Is. xxxiv. 8–10, lxvi. 24; Jer. vii. 20; Ezek. xx. 47, 48. In Homer it is a freq. epithet of γέλως, κλέος, βοή, μένος, and once of φλόξ (*Il.* xvi. 123). As an epithet of πῦρ it is opposed to μαλθακόν and μακρόν. See

[1] The wooden shovel, *pala lignea* (Cato, *R. R.* vi. 45. 151), *ventilabrum* (Varro, *R. R.* i. 52), seems to have been more primitive than the *vannus*, which was a basket, shaped like the blade of a large shovel. The πτύον was a shovel rather than a basket. In Tertullian (*Præscrip.* iii.) palam *in manu portat ad purgandam aream suam* is probably the true reading: but some MSS. have *ventilabrum* for *palam*.

[2] The form διακαθᾶραι is worth noting: in later Greek ἐκάθᾱρα for ἐκάθηρα is not uncommon. Mt. here has διακαθαριεῖ, but classical writers prefer διακαθαίρειν to διακαθαρίζειν.—For the details of Oriental threshing see Herzog, *PRE.*[2] art. *Ackerbau*; *D.B.*[2] art. "Agriculture." For ἄχυρα comp. Job xxi. 18, and Hdt. iv. 72. 2; the sing. is less common (Jer. xxiii. 28).

Heinichen on Eus. *H. E.* vi. 41. 15 and viii. 12. 1. It is therefore a fierce fire which cannot be extinguished, rather than an endless fire that will never go out, that seems to be indicated: and this is just such a fire as τὸ ἄχυρον (the refuse left after threshing and winnowing) would make. But ἄσβεστος is sometimes used of a fire that never goes out, as that of Apollo at Delphi or of Vesta at Rome (Dion. Hal. cxciv. 8). For **κατακαίειν** comp. Mt. xiii. 30, 40; also Ex. iii. 2, where it is distinguished from **καίειν**: it implies utter consumption.

18–20. § Explanation of the Abrupt Termination of the Baptist's Ministry. This is given here by anticipation in order to complete the narrative. Comp. the conclusions to previous narratives: i. 66, 80, ii. 40, 52.

18. Πολλὰ μὲν οὖν καὶ ἕτερα. The comprehensive πολλὰ καὶ ἕτερα confirms the view taken above (ver. 7) that this narrative (7–18) gives a summary of John's teaching rather than a report of what was said on any one occasion. The ἕτερα means "of a different kind" (Gal. i. 6, 7), and intimates that the preaching of the Baptist was not always of the character just indicated.

The cases in which μὲν οὖν occurs must be distinguished. 1. Where, as here, μέν is followed by a corresponding δέ, and we have nothing more than the distributive μὲν . . . δὲ . . . combined with οὖν (Acts viii. 4, 25, xi. 19, xii. 5, xiv. 3, xv. 3, 30, etc.). 2. Where no δέ follows, and μέν confirms what is said, while οὖν marks an inference or transition, *quidem igitur* (Acts i. 6, ii. 41, v. 41, xiii. 4, xvii. 30; Heb. vii. 11, viii. 4, etc.). Win. liii. 8. a, p. 556.

παρακαλῶν εὐηγγελίζετο . . . ἐλεγχόμενος. These words give the three chief functions of the Baptist: to exhort all, to preach good tidings to the penitent, to reprove the impenitent. It is quite unnecessary to take τὸν λαόν with παρακαλῶν, and the order of the words is against such a combination.

In late Greek the acc. of the *person to whom* the announcement is made is freq. after εὐαγγελίζεσθαι (Acts xiv. 15, xvi. 10; Gal. i. 9; 1 Pet. i. 12; comp. Acts viii. 25, 40, xiv. 21): and hence in the pass. we have πτωχοὶ εὐαγγελίζονται. The acc. of the *message* announced is also common (viii. 1; Acts v. 42, viii. 4, 12?, x. 36, xi. 20). Where both person and message are combined, the person addressed is in the dat. (i. 19, ii. 10, iv. 43; Acts viii. 35; comp. Lk. iv. 18; Acts xvii. 18; Rom. i. 15, etc.): but in Acts xiii. 32 we have double acc. Here the Lat. texts vary between *evangelizabat populum* (Cod. Am.) and *evang. populo* (Cod. Brix.).

19. Ἡρῴδης. Antipas, as in ver. 1. The insertion of the name Φιλίππου after γυναικός comes from Mk. and Mt. (A C K X and some versions). This Philip must be carefully distinguished from the tetrarch Philip, with whom Jerome confuses him. He was the son of Mariamne, on account of whose treachery he had been disinherited by Herod the Great; and he lived as a private individual at Jerusalem (Jos. *B. J.* i. 30. 7). Josephus calls both Antipas and also this Philip simply "Herod" (*Ant.* xviii. 5. 4). Herodias became the evil genius of the man who seduced her from his brother. It was her ambition which brought about the downfall of Antipas. Lk. alone tells us that John rebuked Antipas for his wicked life (καὶ περὶ πάντων) as well as for his incestuous marriage. Obviously ἐλεγχόμενος means "rebuked, reproved" (1 Tim. v. 20; 2 Tim. iv. 2), and not "convicted" or "convinced" (Jn. viii. 46, xvi. 8). In the former sense ἐλέγχειν is stronger than ἐπιτιμᾶν: see Trench, *Syn.* iv.

Once more (see on ver. 1) we have a remarkable rendering in **d**: *Herodes autem quaterducatus cum argueretur ab eo*, etc.

Note the characteristic and idiomatic attraction (πάντων ὧν), and comp. ii. 20, v. 9, ix. 43, xii. 46, xv. 16, xix. 37, xxiv. 25; Acts iii. 21, x. 39, xiii. 39, xxii. 10, xxvi. 2.

20. προσέθηκεν καὶ τοῦτο ἐπὶ πᾶσιν, κατέκλεισεν, κ.τ.λ. "He added this also on the top of all—he shut up John in prison"; *i.e.* he added this to all the other πονηρά of which he had been guilty. Farrar, *Herods*, p. 171.

Josephus, in the famous passage which confirms and supplements the Gospel narrative respecting the Baptist (*Ant.* xviii. 5. 2), says that Antipas put him in prison because of his immense influence with the people. They seemed to be ready to do whatever he told them; and he might tell them to revolt. This may easily have been an additional reason for imprisoning him: it is no contradiction of the Evangelists. What Josephus states is what Antipas publicly alleged as his reason for arresting John: of course he would not give his private reasons. The prison in which the Baptist was confined was in the fortress of Machærus at the N.E. corner of the Dead Sea. Seetzen discovered the site in 1807 above the valley of the Zerka, and dungeons can still be traced among the ruins. Tristram visited it in 1872 (*Discoveries on the East Side of the Dead Sea*, ch. xiv.). It was hither that the daughter of Aretas fled on her way back to her father, when she discovered that Antipas meant to discard her for Herodias. Machærus was then in her father's dominions; but Antipas probably seized it immediately afterwards (Jos. *Ant.* xviii. 5. 1, 2).

The expression προσέθηκεν τοῦτο, κατέκλεισεν must not be confounded with the Hebraisms προσέθετο πέμψαι (xx. 11, 12), προσέθετο συλλαβεῖν (Acts xii. 3). It is true that in LXX the act. as well as the mid. is used in this manner: προσέθηκε τεκεῖν (Gen. iv. 2); προσέθηκε λαλῆσαι (Gen. xviii. 29): see also Exod. x. 28; Deut. iii. 26; and for the mid. Exod. xiv. 13. But in this Hebraistic use of προστίθημι for "go on and do" the second verb is always in the infin. (Win. liv. 5, p. 588). Here there is no Hebraism, and therefore no sign that Lk. is using an Aramaic source.

Κατακλείειν is classical, but occurs in N.T. only here and Acts xxvi. 10; in both cases of imprisoning. It is freq. in medical writers, and Galen uses it of imprisonment (Hobart, *Med. Lang. of Lk.* pp. 66, 67). Mt. xiv. 3 we have ἀπέθετο, and Mk. vi. 17, ἔδησεν, of Herod's putting John into prison.

21, 22. *Jesus is baptized by John.*—It is remarkable, that although the careers of the Forerunner and of the Messiah are so closely connected, and so similar as regards prediction of birth, retirement, ministry, and early end, yet, so far as we know, they come into actual contact only at one brief period, when the Forerunner baptized the Christ. Once some of John's disciples raised the question of fasting, and Jesus answered it (v. 33; Mt. ix. 14), and once John sent some of his disciples to Jesus to question Him as to His Messiahship (vii. 19–23; Mt. xi. 2–19); but there is no meeting between Christ and the Baptist. Lk., having completed his brief account of the Forerunner and his work, begins his main subject, viz. the Messiah and His work. This involves a return to the point at which the Forerunner met the Messiah, and performed on Him the rite which prepared Him for His work, by publicly uniting Him with the people whom He came to save, and proclaiming Him before them.

21. ἐν τῷ βαπτισθῆναι ἅπαντα τὸν λαόν. "*After* all the people had been baptized"; *cum baptizatus esset omnis populus* (Cod. Brix.): not, "*while* they were being baptized"; *cum baptizaretur* (Cod. Am.). The latter would be ἐν τῷ with the *pres.* infin.

Both constructions are very freq. in Lk. Contrast the aorists in ii. 27, ix. 36, xi. 37, xiv. 1, xix. 15, xxiv. 30, Acts xi. 15 with the presents in v. 1, 12, viii. 5, 42, ix. 18, 29, 33, 51, x. 35, 38, xi. 1. 27, xvii. 11, 14, xxiv. 4, 15, 51; Acts viii. 6, xix. 1. Lk. is also fond of the stronger form ἅπας, which is rare in N.T. outside his writings. Readings are often confused, but ἅπας is well attested v. 26, viii. 37, ix. 15, xix. 37, 48, xxiii. 1; Acts ii. 44, iv. 31, v. 16, x. 8, xi. 10, xvi. 3, 28, xxv. 24; and may be right in other places.

That there were great multitudes present when John baptized the Christ is not stated; nor is it probable. Had Lk. written ἐν τῷ βαπτίζεσθαι, this would have implied the presence of many other candidates for baptism; but it was not until "*after* every one of the people had been baptized" that the baptism of Jesus took place. Possibly Jesus waited until He could be alone with John. In any case, those who had long been waiting for their turn would go home soon after they had accomplished their purpose. It was some time after this that John said to the people, "He that cometh after me . . . is standing in the midst of you, and *ye know Him not*" (Jn. i. 26). They could hardly have been so ignorant of Him, if large multitudes had been present when John baptized Him.

καὶ Ἰησοῦ βαπτισθέντος. It is remarkable that this, which seems to us to be the main fact, should be expressed thus incidentally by a participle. It is as if the baptism of all the people were regarded as carrying with it the baptism of Jesus almost as a necessary complement: "After they had been baptized, and when He had been baptized and was praying." But perhaps the purpose of Lk. is to narrate the baptism, not so much for its own sake as an instance of Christ's conformity to what was required of the people, as for the sake of the Divine recognition and authentication which Jesus then received.

Jerome has preserved this fragment of the *Gospel acc. to the Hebrews*: "Lo, the mother of the Lord and His brethren said to Him, John the Baptist baptizeth for remission of sins: let us go and be baptized by him. But He said to them, Wherein have I sinned that I should go and be baptized by him? except perchance this very thing which I have said is ignorance" (*Adv. Pelag.* iii. 1). The *Tractatus de Rebaptismate* says that the *Pauli Prædicatio* represented "Christ, the only man who was altogether without fault, both making confession respecting His own sin, and driven almost against His will by His mother Mary to accept the baptism of John: also that when He was baptized fire was seen on the water, which is not written in any Gospel" (xvii.; Hartel's *Cyprian*, ii. p. 90). The fire in the water is mentioned in Justin (*Try.* lxxxviii.), but not as recorded by the Apostles; and also in the *Gospel acc. to the Hebrews.*

καὶ προσευχομένου. Lk. alone mentions this. On his Gospel as emphasizing the duty of prayer see Introd. § 6. Mt. and Mk. say that Jesus saw the Spirit descending; Jn. says that the Baptist saw it; Lk. that it took place (ἐγένετο) along with the opening of the heaven and the coming of the voice. Mk. says simply τὸ πνεῦμα; Mt. has πνεῦμα Θεοῦ; Lk. τὸ πνεῦμα τὸ ἅγιον. See on i. 15.

The constr. of ἐγένετο with acc. and infin. is on the analogy of the class. constr. of συνέβη: it is freq. in Lk. See note, p. 45. The form ἀνεῳχθῆναι is anomalous, as if assimilated to ἀνεῷχθαι: comp. Jn. ix. 10, 14; Rev. iv. 1, vi. 1.

22. σωματικῷ εἴδει ὡς περιστεράν. "In a bodily form" is peculiar to Lk. Nothing is gained by admitting something visible and rejecting the dove. Comp. the symbolical visions of Jehovah granted to Moses and other Prophets. We dare not assert that the Spirit cannot reveal Himself to human sight, or that in so doing He cannot employ the form of a dove or of tongues of fire. The tongues were appropriate when the Spirit was given "by measure" to many. The dove was appropriate when the Spirit was given in His fulness to one. It is not true that the dove was an ancient Jewish symbol for the Spirit. In Jewish symbolism the dove is Israel. The descent of the Spirit was not, as some Gnostics taught, the moment of the Incarnation: it made no change in the nature of Christ. But it may have illuminated Him so as to complete His growing consciousness of His relations to God and to man (ii. 52). It served two purposes: (1) to make Him known to the Baptist, who thenceforward had Divine authority for making Him known to the world (Jn. i. 32, 33); and (2) to mark the official beginning of the ministry, like the anointing of a king. As at the Transfiguration, Christ is miraculously glorified before setting out to suffer, a voice from heaven bears witness to Him, and "the goodly fellowship of the Prophets" waits on His glory.

The phrase φωνὴν γενέσθαι is freq. in Lk. (i. 44, ix. 35, 36; Acts ii. 6, vii. 31, x. 13, xix. 34). Elsewhere only Mk. i. 11, ix. 7; Jn. xii. 30; Rev. viii. 5. Comp. ἔρχεται φωνή, Jn. xii. 28; ἐξέρχεται φωνή, Rev. xvi. 17, xix. 5.

Σύ. *Responsio ad preces*, ver. 21 (Beng.). The Σύ shows that the voice conveyed a message to the Christ as well as to the Baptist. Mk. also has Σὺ εἶ: in Mt. iii. 17 we have Οὗτός ἐστιν. *Diversitas locutionum adhuc etiam utilis est, ne uno modo dictum minus intelligatur* (Aug.). In the narrative of the Transfiguration all three have **Οὗτός ἐστιν.**

The reference seems to be to Ps. ii. 7; and here D and other important witnesses have Υἱός μου εἶ σύ, ἐγὼ σήμερον γεγέννηκά σε. Augustine says that this was the reading of some MSS., "although it is *stated* not to be found in the more ancient MSS." (*De Cons. Evang.* ii. 14: comp. *Enchir. ad Laurent.* xlix.). Justin has it in his accounts of the Baptism (*Try.* lxxxviii., ciii.). In Mt. it is possible to take ὁ ἀγαπητός with what follows: "The beloved in whom I am well pleased"; but this is impossible here and in Mk. i. 11, and therefore improbable in Mt. The repetition of the article presents the epithet as a separate fact: "Thou art My Son, My beloved one." Comp. μοῦνος ἐὼν ἀγαπητός (Hom. *Od.* ii. 365). It is remarkable that St. John never uses ἀγαπητός of Christ: neither in the Fourth Gospel nor in the Apocalypse does the word occur in any connexion.

εὐδόκησα. "I *am* well pleased": the timeless aorist. Comp. Jn. xiii. 3. The verb is an exception to the rule that, except where a verb is compounded with a prep., the verbal termination is not retained, but one from a noun of the same root is substituted: *e.g.* ἀδυνατεῖν, εὐεργετεῖν, not ἀδύνασθαι, εὐεργάζεσθαι. Comp. καραδοκεῖν and δυσθνήσκειν, which are similar exceptions, Win. xvi. 5, p. 125.

The voice does not proclaim Jesus as the Messiah, as a legend would probably have represented. No such proclamation was needed either by Jesus or by the Baptist. The descent of the Spirit had told John that Jesus was the Christ (Jn. i. 33). This voice from heaven, as afterwards at the Transfiguration (ix. 35), and again shortly before the Passion (Jn. xii. 28), followed closely upon Christ's prayer, and may be regarded as the answer to it. His humanity was capable of needing the strength which the heavenly assurance gave. To call this voice from heaven the *Bath-Kol* of the Rabbis, or to treat it as analogous to it, is misleading. The Rabbinic *Bath-Kol*, or "Daughter-voice," is regarded as an echo of the voice of God: and the Jews liked to believe that it had been granted to them after the gift of prophecy had ceased. The utterances attributed to it are in some cases so frivolous or profane, that the more intelligent Rabbis denounced it as a superstition.

It has been pointed out that Lk. appears to treat the baptism of Jesus by John as a matter of course. Mt. tells us that the Baptist at first protested against it; and many writers have felt that it requires explanation. Setting aside the profane suggestions that Jesus was not sinless, and therefore needed "repentance baptism for remission of sins," or that He was in collusion with John, we may note four leading hypotheses. 1. He wished to do honour to John. 2. He desired to elicit from John a declaration of His Messiahship. 3. He thereby gave a solemn sign that He had done with home life, and was beginning His public ministry. 4. He thereby consecrated Himself for His work.—This last seems to be nearest to the truth. The other three would be more probable if we were expressly told that multitudes of spectators were present; whereas the reverse seems to be implied. John's baptism was preparatory to the kingdom of the Messiah. For everyone else it was a baptism of repentance. The Messiah, who needed no repentance, could yet accept the preparation. In each case it marked the beginning of a new life. It consecrated the people for the reception of salvation. It consecrated the Christ for the bestowing of it (Neander, *L. J. C.* § 42 (5), Eng. tr. p. 68). But besides this it was a "fulfilment of righteousness," a complying with the requirements of the Law. Although pure Himself, through His connexion with an unclean people He was Levitically unclean. "On the principles of O.T. righteousness His baptism was required" (Lange, *L. of C.* i. p. 355).

In the Fathers and liturgies we find the thought that by being baptized Himself Jesus elevated an external rite into a sacrament, and consecrated the element of water for perpetual use. *Baptizatus est ergo Dominus non mundari volens, sed mundare aquas* (Ambr. on Lk. iii. 21, 23). "By the Baptisme of thy wel beloved sonne Jesus Christe, thou dydest sanctifie the fludde Jordan, and al other waters to this misticall washing away of synne" (First Prayer-Book of Edw. VI. 1549, Public Baptism); which follows the Gregorian address, "By the Baptism of Thine Only-begotten Son hast been pleased to sanctify the streams of water" (Bright, *Ancient Collects*, p. 161).

There is no contradiction between John's "Comest Thou to me?" (Mt. iii. 14) and "I knew Him not" (Jn. i. 31, 33). As a Prophet John recognized the sinlessness of Jesus, just as Elisha recognized the avarice and untruthfulness of Gehazi, or the treachery and cruelty of Hazael (2 Kings v. 26, viii. 10–12); but until the Spirit descended upon Him, he did not know that He was the Messiah (Weiss, *Leben Jesu*, I. ii. 9, Eng. tr. i. p. 320). John had three main functions: to predict the coming of the Messiah; to prepare the people for it; and to point out the Messiah when He came. When these were accomplished, his work was nearly complete.

23–38. *The Genealogy of Jesus Christ.* Comp. Mt. i. 1–17. The literature is very abundant: the following are among the principal authorities, from which a selection may be made, and the names of other authorities obtained.

Lord A. Hervey, *The Genealogies of our Lord and Saviour*, Macmillan, 1853; J. B. McClellan, *The New Testament of our Lord and Saviour*, i. pp. 408–422, Macmillan, 1875; W. H. Mill, *Observations on the Application of Pantheistic Principles to the Theory and Historic Criticism of the Gospel*, pp. 147–218; *D.B.*[2] art. "Genealogy"; *D. of Chr. Biog.* art. "Africanus"; Schaff's *Herzog*, art. "Genealogy"; Commentaries of Mansel (*Speaker*), Meyer, Schaff, on Mt. i.; of Farrar, Godet, M. R. Riddle, on Lk. iii.

Why does Lk. insert the genealogy here instead of at the beginning of his Gospel? It would be only a slight exaggeration to say that this *is* the beginning of his Gospel, for the first three chapters are only introductory. The use of ἀρχόμενος here implies that the Evangelist is now making a fresh start. Two of the three introductory chapters are the history of the Forerunner, which Lk. completes in the third chapter before beginning his account of the work of the Messiah. Not until Jesus has been anointed by the Spirit does the history of the Messiah, *i.e.* the Anointed One, begin; and His genealogy then becomes of importance. In a similar way the pedigree of Moses is placed, not just before or just after the account of his birth (Exod. ii. 1, 2), where not even the names of his parents are given, but just after his public appearance before Pharaoh as the spokesman of Jehovah and the leader of Israel (Exod. vi. 14–27).

The statement of Julius Africanus, that Herod the Great caused the genealogies of ancient Jewish families to be destroyed, in order to conceal the defects of his own pedigree (Eus. *H. E.* i. 7. 13), is of no moment. If he ever gave such an order, it would of necessity be very imperfectly executed. The rebuilding of the temple would give him the opportunity of burning the genealogies of the priests, which were preserved in the temple archives, but pedigrees in the possession of private families would be carefully concealed. Josephus was able to give his own genealogy, as he "found it described in the *public* records"—ἐν ταῖς δημοσίαις δέλτοις ἀναγεγραμμένην (*Vita*, 1); and he tells us what great care was taken to preserve the pedigrees of the priests, not merely in Judæa, but in Egypt, and Babylon, and "whithersoever our priests are scattered" (*Apion.* i. 7). It is therefore an empty objection to say that Lk. *could* not have obtained this genealogy from any authentic source, for all such sources had been destroyed by Herod. It is clear from Josephus that, if Herod made the attempt, he did not succeed in destroying even all public records. Jews are very tenacious of their genealogies; and a decree to destroy such things would be evaded in every possible way. The importance of the evidence of Africanus lies in his claim to have obtained information from members of the family, who gloried in preserving the memory of their noble extraction; and *in his referring both pedigrees as a matter of course to Joseph.* It is not probable that Joseph was the only surviving descendant of David who was known to be such. But it is likely enough that all such persons were in humble positions, like Joseph himself, and thus escaped the notice and jealousy of Herod. Throughout his reign he took no precaution against Davidic claimants; and had he been told that a village carpenter was the representative of David's house, he would possibly have treated him as Domitian is said to have treated the grandsons of Judas the brother of the Lord—with supercilious indifference (Eus. *H. E.* iii. 20).

23. αὐτός. "He Himself," to whom these miraculous signs had reference: comp. i. 22; Mt. iii. 4. The AV. translation of the whole clause, αὐτὸς ἦν Ἰησοῦς ἀρχόμενος ὡσεὶ ἐτῶν τριάκοντα, "Jesus Himself began to be about thirty years of age," is impossible. It is probably due to the influence of Beza: *incipiebat esse quasi annorum triginta.* But Cranmer led the way in this error in the Bible of 1539, and the later versions followed. Purvey is vague, like the Vulgate: "was bigynnynge as of thritti year,"—*erat incipiens quasi annorum triginta.* Tyndale is right: "was about thirty yere of age when He beganne"; *i.e.* when He began His ministry in the solemn way just recorded. Comp. the use of ἀρξάμενος in Acts i. 22. In both cases διδάσκειν may be understood, but is not necessary. In Mk. iv. 1 we have the full expression, ἤρξατο διδάσκειν, which is represented in the parallel, Mt. xiii. 1, by ἐκάθητο. Professor Marshall has shown that ἤρξατο and ἐκάθητο may be equivalents for one and the same Aramaic verb (*Expositor*, April 1891): see on v. 21.

It is obvious that this verse renders little help to chronology. "About thirty" may be anything from twenty-eight to thirty-two,—to give no wider margin. It is certain that our era is at least four years too late, for it begins with A.U.C. 754. Herod the Great died just before the Passover A.U.C. 750, which is therefore the latest year possible for the Nativity. If we reckon the "fifteenth year" of ver. 1 from the death of Augustus, Jesus was probably thirty-two at the time of His Baptism.

ὢν υἱός, ὡς ἐνομίζετο, Ἰωσὴφ τοῦ Ἡλεί. This is the right punctuation: "being the son (as was supposed) of Joseph the son of Heli." It is altogether unnatural to place the comma *after* Ἰωσήφ and not before it: "being the son (as was supposed of Joseph) of Heli"; *i.e.* being supposed to be the son of Joseph, but being really the grandson of Heli. It is not credible that υἱός can mean both son and grandson in the same sentence. J. Lightfoot proposed that "Jesus" (viz. υἱός, not υἱοῦ) should be understood throughout; "Jesus (as was supposed) the son of Joseph, and so the son of Heli, and so the son of Matthat," etc. (*Hor. Heb.* on Lk. iii. 23). But this is not probable: see on τοῦ Θεοῦ (ver. 38).

It is evident from the *wording* that Lk. is here giving *the genealogy of Joseph and not of Mary*. It would have been quite out of harmony with either Jewish ideas or Gentile ideas to derive the birthright of Jesus from His mother. In the eye of the law Jesus was the heir of Joseph; and therefore it is Joseph's descent which is of importance. Mary may have been the daughter of Heli; but, if she was, Lk. ignores the fact. The difference between the two genealogies was from very early times felt to be a difficulty, as is seen from the letter of Julius Africanus to Aristides, *c.* A.D. 220 (Eus. *H. E.* i. 7; Routh, *Rel. Sacr.* ii. p. 228); and it is probable that so obvious a solution, as that one was the pedigree of Joseph and the other the pedigree of Mary, would have been very soon advocated, if there had been any reason (excepting the difficulty) for adopting it. But this solution is not advocated by anyone until Annius of Viterbo propounded it, *c.* A.D. 1490. Yet see Victorinus (?) on Rev. iv. 7 (Migne v. 324).

The main facts of the two genealogies are these. From Adam to Abraham Lk. is alone. From Abraham to David, Lk. and Mt. agree. From David to Joseph they differ, excepting in the names of Zorobabel and his father Salathiel. The various attempts which have been made at reconciling the divergences, although in no case convincingly successful, are yet sufficient to show that reconciliation is not impossible. Nevertheless, the possibility that we have here divergent attempts of Jewish pedigree-makers may be admitted; for divergent theories, corresponding to the two genealogies, existed at the time. In addition to the authorities named above, the monographs of Hottinger, Surenhusius, and Voss may be consulted. See also the parallel tables in Resch, *Kindheitsev.* p. 188.

27. τοῦ Ζοροβάβελ τοῦ Σαλαθιήλ. It is highly improbable that these are different persons from the Zerubbabel and the Shealtiel of Mt. i. 12. That at the same period of Jewish history there should be two fathers bearing the rare name Salathiel or Shealtiel, each with a son bearing the rare name Zerubbabel, and that both of these unusually-named fathers should come in different ways into the genealogy of the Messiah, is scarcely credible, although this hypothesis has been adopted by both Hottinger and Voss. Zerubbabel (= "Dispersed in Babylon," or "Begotten in Babylon") was head of the tribe of Judah at the time of the return from the Babylonish Captivity in the first year of Cyrus; and he was therefore an obvious person to include in the pedigree of the Messiah. Hence he was called the *Rhesa* or Prince of the Captivity. In 1 Chron. iii. 19 he is given as the son of Pedaiah and nephew of Shealtiel: and this is probably correct. But he became the heir of Shealtiel because the latter had no sons. In Mt. i. 12 and 1 Chron. iii. 17, Shealtiel is the son of Jechoniah, king of Judah; whereas Lk. makes him the son of Neri. Jeconiah is called Coniah, Jer. xxii. 24, and Jehoiachin, lii. 31; 2 Kings xxiv. 6; 2 Chron. xxxvi. 8, 9; and all three names mean "The Lord will establish." From Jer. xxii. 30 we learn that he had no children; and therefore the line of David *through Solomon* became extinct in him. The three pedigrees indicate that an heir for the childless Jeconiah was found in Shealtiel the son of Neri, who was of the house of David *through Nathan*. Thus the junction of the two lines of descent in Shealtiel[1] and Zerubbabel is fully explained. Shealtiel was the son of Neri of Nathan's line, and also the heir of Jeconiah of Solomon's line; and having no sons himself, he had his nephew Zerubbabel as adopted son and heir. Rhesa, who appears in Lk., but neither in Mt. nor in 1 Chron., is probably not a name at all, but a title, which some Jewish copyist mistook for a name. "Zerubbabel Rhesa," or "Zerubbabel the Prince," has been made into "Zerubbabel (begat) Rhesa." This correction brings Lk. into harmony with both Mt. and 1 Chron. For (1) the Greek Ἰωανάς represents the Hebrew Hananiah (1 Chron. iii. 19), a generation which is omitted by Mt.; and (2) Lk.'s Ἰούδα is the same as Mt.'s Ἀβιούδ (Jud-a = Ab-jud). Again, Ἰούδα or Ἀβιούδ may be identified with Hodaviah (1 Chron. iii. 24); for this name is interchanged with Judah, as is seen by a comparison of Ezra iii. 9 and Neh. xi. 9 with Ezra ii. 40 and 1 Chron. ix. 7.

36. Σαλὰ τοῦ Καινὰμ τοῦ Ἀρφαξάδ. In LXX this Cainan appears as the father of Sala or Shelah, and son of Arphaxad, in the genealogy of Shem (Gen. x. 24, xi. 12; 1 Chron. i. 18). But the name is not found in any Hebrew MS., or in any other version made from the Hebrew. In LXX it *may* be an insertion, for no one earlier than Augustine mentions the name. D omits it here, while ℵ B L have the form Καινάμ for Καινάν. But the hypothesis that interpolation here has led to interpolation in LXX cannot be maintained upon critical principles.

38. Ἀδάμ. That Lk. should take the genealogy beyond David and Abraham to the father of the whole human race, is entirely in harmony with the Pauline universality of his Gospel. To the Jew it was all-important to know that the Messiah was of the stock of Abraham and of the house of David. Mt. therefore places this fact

[1] Both forms of the name, Shealtiel and Salathiel, are found in Haggai and elsewhere in O.T.; but in the Apocrypha and N.T. the form used is Salathiel ("I have asked God").

in the forefront of his Gospel. Lk., writing to all alike, shows that the Messiah is akin to the Gentile as well as to the Jew, and that all mankind can claim Him as a brother.[1]

But why does Lk. add that Adam was the son of God? Certainly not in order to show the Divine Sonship of the Messiah, which would place Him in this respect on a level with all mankind. More probably it is added for the sake of Gentile readers, to remind them of the Divine origin of the human race,—an origin which they share with the Messiah. It is a correction of the myths respecting the origin of man, which were current among the heathen. *Scriptura, etiam quod ad humani generis ortum pertinet, figit satiatque cognitionem nostram; eam qui spernunt aut ignorant, pendent errantque inter tempora antemundana et postmundana* (Beng.). It is very forced and unnatural to take τοῦ Θεοῦ as the gen. of ὁ Θεός, and make this gen. depend upon ὢν υἱός at the beginning of the genealogy, as if Jesus and not Adam was styled the "son of God." Thus the whole pedigree from ὡς ἐνομίζετο to Ἀδάμ would be a gigantic parenthesis between ὢν υἱός and τοῦ Θεοῦ. The τοῦ throughout belongs to the word *in front* of it, as is clear from the fact that Ἰωσήφ, the first name, has no τοῦ before it. Each τοῦ means "who was of," *i.e.* either "the son of" or "the heir of." Both AV. and RV. give the sense correctly.

IV. 1-13. *The Internal Preparation for the Ministry of the Christ: the Temptation in the Wilderness*, Mt. iv. 1–11; Mk. i. 12, 13.

R. C. Trench, *Studies in the Gospels*, pp. 1-65, Macmillan, 1867; B. Weiss, *Leben Jesu*, I. ii. 10, Berlin, 1882; Eng. tr. i. pp. 319–354; H. Latham, *Pastor Pastorum*, pp. 112–146, Bell, 1890; P. Schaff, *Person of Christ*, pp. 32, 153, Nisbet, 1880; A. M. Fairbairn, *Expositor*, first series, vol. iii. pp. 321–342, Hodder, 1876; P. Didon, *Jésus Christ*, ch. iii. pp. 208–226, Plon, 1891.

Many futile and irreverent questions have been raised respecting this mysterious subject; futile, because it is impossible to answer them, excepting by empty conjectures; and irreverent, because they are prompted by curiosity rather than by a desire for illumination. Had the answers to them been necessary for our spiritual welfare, the answers would have been placed within our reach. Among such questions are such as these: Did Satan

[1] "In the one case we see a royal Infant born by a legal title to a glorious inheritance; and in the other a ministering Saviour who bears the natural sum of human sorrow" (Wsctt. *Int. to the Gospels*, 7th ed. p. 316). The whole passage should be read.

assume a human form, and change his form with each change of temptation, or did he remain invisible? Did he know who Jesus was, or was he trying to discover this? Did he know, until he was named, that Jesus knew who he was? Where was the spot from which he showed all the kingdoms of the world?

Three points are insisted upon in the Epistle to the Hebrews (ii. 18, iv. 15), and beyond them we need not go. 1. The temptations were real. 2. Jesus remained absolutely unstained by them. 3. One purpose of the temptations was to assure us of His sympathy when we are tempted. The second point limits the first and intensifies the third. The sinlessness of Jesus excluded all those temptations which spring from previous sin; for there was no taint in Him to become the *source* of temptation. But the fact that the solicitations came wholly from without, and were not born from within, does not prevent that which was offered to Him being regarded as desirable. The force of a temptation depends, not upon the sin involved in what is proposed, but upon the advantage connected with it. And a righteous man, whose will never falters for a moment, may feel the attractiveness of the advantage more keenly than the weak man who succumbs; for the latter probably gave way before he recognized the whole of the attractiveness; or his nature may be less capable of such recognition. In this way the sinlessness of Jesus augments His capacity for sympathy: for in every case He felt the *full* force of temptation.[1]

It is obvious that the substance of the narrative could have had only one source. No one has succeeded in suggesting any probable alternative. There is no Old Testament parallel, of which this could be an adaptation. Nor is there any prophecy that the Messiah would have to endure temptation, of which this might be a fictitious fulfilment. And we may be sure that, if the whole had been baseless invention, the temptations would have been of a more commonplace, and probably of a grosser kind. No Jewish or Christian legend is at all like this. It is from Christ Himself that the narrative comes; and He probably gave it to the disciples in much the same form as that in which we have it here.

[1] "Sympathy with the sinner in his trial does not depend on the experience of sin, but on the experience of the strength of the temptation to sin, which only the sinless can know in its full intensity. He who falls yields before the last strain" (Wsctt. on Heb. ii. 18). See Neander, *L. J. C.* §§ 46, 47, pp. 77, 78.

1. πλήρης πνεύματος ἁγίου. These words connect the Temptation closely with the Baptism.[1] It was under the influence of the Spirit, which had just descended upon Him, that He went, in obedience to God's will, into the wilderness. All three accounts mark this connexion; and it explains the meaning of the narrative. Jesus had been endowed with supernatural power; and He was tempted to make use of it in furthering His own interests without regard to the Father's will. And here ἀνήχθη . . . πειρασθῆναι (Mt. iv. 1) must not be understood as meaning that Christ went into the wilderness to *court* temptation. That would be too like yielding to the temptation which He resisted (*vv.* 9–12). He went into the desert in obedience to the Spirit's promptings. That He should be *tempted* there was the Divine purpose respecting Him, to prepare Him for His work. *D.C.G.* ii. p. 714.

Neither Mt. nor Mk. has ἅγιον as an epithet of πνεῦμα here (see on i. 15); and neither of them has Lk.'s favourite ὑπέστρεψεν.

ἤγετο ἐν τῷ πνεύματι ἐν τῇ ἐρήμῳ. "He was led *in* (not *into*) the wilderness," *i.e.* in His wanderings there, as in His progress thither, He was under Divine influence and guidance. The imperf. indicates continued action. Tradition, which is not likely to be of any value, places this wilderness close to Jericho. Some region farther north is more probable. The **ἡμέρας τεσσεράκοντα** may be taken either with ἤγετο (RV.) or with πειραζόμενος (AV.). As the temptation by Satan was simultaneous (pres. part.) with the leading by the Spirit, the sense will be the same, whichever arrangement be adopted. In Mk. also the words are amphibolous, and may be taken either with ἦν ἐν τῇ ἐρήμῳ or with πειραζόμενος. If we had only the account in Mt. we might have supposed that the temptations did not begin until the close of the forty days. The three recorded may have come at the end of the time, as seems to be implied with regard to the first of them. Or they may be given as representative of the struggles which continued throughout the whole period.

2. πειραζόμενος. The word is here used in its commonest sense of "try or test," with a *sinister* motive. In N.T. it has three uses: 1. "try or *attempt*" to do (Acts ix. 26, xvi. 7, xxiv. 6); 2. "try or *test*," with a *good* motive (Jn. vi. 6; 2 Cor. xiii. 5; Rev. ii. 2), especially of God's sending trials (1 Cor. x. 13; Heb. xi. 17;

[1] *Le baptême et la tentation se succèdent l'un à l'autre dans la réalité de l'histoire, comme dans le récit des Evangélistes. Ces deux faits inséparables, qui s'éclairent en s'opposant dans un contraste vigoreux, sont le vrai prélude de la vie du Christ. L'un est la manifestation de l'Esprit de Dieu, l'autre, celle de l'esprit du mal; l'un nous montre la filiation divine de Jésus, l'autre, sa nature humaine vouée à la lutte et à l'épreuve; l'un nous révèle la force infinie avec laquelle il agira, l'autre, l'obstacle qu'il saura renverser; l'un nous enseigne sa intime, l'autre, la loi de son action* (Didon, p. 225).

Rev. iii. 10); 3. "try or *test*," with a *bad* motive, in order to produce perplexity or failure (xi. 16; Mt. xix. 3; [Jn.] viii. 6), especially of tempting to sin (1 Cor. vii. 5; 1 Thes. iii. 5; Jas. i. 13). It is thus of much wider meaning than δοκιμάζειν (xii. 56, xiv. 19), which has only the second of these meanings. Trench, *Syn.* lxxiv.; Cremer, *Lex.* p. 494.

ὑπὸ τοῦ διαβόλου. All three use ὑπό of the agency of Satan He is not a mere instrument. Comp. 2 Cor. ii. 11; Acts x. 38. In N.T. διάβολος with the art. always means Satan, "the calumniator," κατ' ἐξοχήν. In Mt., Jn., Acts, Eph., 1 and 2 Tim., Heb., James, Jude, 1 Pet., and Rev. this use is invariable. It is possible that ὁ διάβολος was originally a translation of Satan = "the adversary." In LXX ἐνδιαβάλλειν sometimes means "meet, oppose" (Num. xxii. 22, 32), and διάβολος means "adversary" (1 Mac. i. 36). In Job (i. 6–12, ii. 1–7) and Zech. (iii. 1–3) ὁ διάβολος is used as in N.T. for Satan, as the accuser or slanderer of God to man and of man to God. In this scene he endeavours to misrepresent God, and to induce Jesus to adopt a false view of His relation to God.

The existence of such a being is sometimes denied, but on purely *à priori* grounds. To science the question is an open one, and does not admit of demonstration either way. But the teaching of Christ and His Apostles is clear and explicit; and only three explanations are possible. Either (1) they accommodated their language to a gross superstition, knowing it to be such; or (2) they shared this superstition, not knowing it to be such; or (3) the doctrine is not a superstition, but they taught the actual truth. As Keim rightly says, one cannot possibly regard all the sayings of Jesus on this subject as later interpolations, and "Jesus plainly designated His contention with the empire of Satan as a personal one" (*Jes. of Naz.*, Eng. tr. ii. pp. 318, 325). See Gore, *Dissertations on Subjects connected with the Incarnation*, pp. 23–27.

οὐκ ἔφαγεν οὐδέν. This does not agree well with the supposition that Jesus partook of the scanty food which might be found in the wilderness. The νηστεύσας of Mt. seems to imply the deliberate fasting which was customary in times of solemn retirement for purposes of devotion. But this does not exclude the possibility that the mental and spiritual strain was so great that for a time there was no craving for food. In any case the want of food would at last bring prostration of body and mind; and then the violence of temptation would be specially felt. Both Mt. and Lk. appear to mean that it was not until near the end of the forty days that the pangs of hunger were endured. For **συντελεῖσθαι** of days being completed comp. Acts xxi. 27; Job i. 5; Tobit x. 7.[1]

[1] The fasts of Moses and Elijah were of similar duration (Deut. ix. 9; 1 K. xix. 8). The number forty in Scripture is connected with suffering. The

3. εἶπεν. Mt. adds προσελθών, which is a very favourite expression of his. It does not necessarily imply corporal presence, although Mt. himself may have understood it in that sense. Jesus says of the approaching struggle in Gethsemane, "The prince of the world *cometh*" (Jn. xiv. 30). Nowhere in Scripture is Satan said to have appeared in a visible form: Zech. iii. 1 is a vision. And nothing in this narrative requires us to believe that Satan was visible on this occasion.

Εἰ υἱὸς εἶ τοῦ Θεοῦ. Both Mt. and Lk. have υἱός τ. Θ. without the article, the reference being to the relationship to God, rather than to the office of the Messiah. The emphatic word is υἱός. The allusion to the voice from heaven (iii. 22) is manifest, but is not likely to have occurred to a writer of fiction, who would more probably have written, "If Thou art *the Christ*." The "if" does not necessarily imply any doubt in Satan, although Augustine takes it so;[1] but it is perhaps meant to inspire doubt in Jesus: "Hath God said, Thou art My beloved Son, and yet forbidden Thee to give Thyself bread?" Comp. "Yea, hath God said, Ye shall not eat of any tree of the garden?" (Gen. iii. 1). The suggestion seems to be that He is *to work a miracle in order to prove the truth of God's express declaration*, and that He may doubt His relation to God, if God does not allow the miracle.

This seems better than to regard the first temptation as a *temptation of the flesh*. If the food had been there, would it have been sinful for Jesus to partake of it? Again, it is sometimes said that it was a temptation *to use His supernatural power to supply His own necessities*. Among "the Laws of the Working of Signs" we are told was one to the effect that "Our Lord will not use His special powers to provide for His personal wants or those of His immediate followers."[2] This law perhaps does not hold, except so far as it coincides with the principle that no miracle is wrought where the given end can be obtained without miracle. Some of Christ's escapes from His enemies seem to have been miraculous. Was not that "providing for a personal want"? His rejoining His disciples by walking on the sea might be classed under the same head. The boat coming suddenly to land might be called "providing for the wants of His immediate followers." Had He habitually supplied His personal wants by miracle, then He would have ceased to share the lot of mankind. But it would be rash to say that it would have been sinful for Him to supply Himself with food miraculously, when food was necessary for His work and could not be obtained by ordinary means. It is safer to regard this as a temptation to satisfy Himself of the truth of God's word by a test of His own.

Deluge lasted forty days and nights (Gen. vii. 4, 12). The Israelites wandered for forty years (Num. xiv. 33, xxxii. 13). Egypt is to lie waste forty years (Ezek. xxix. 11). Ezekiel is to bear the iniquity of the house of Judah (*i.e.* the penalty for that iniquity) forty days, each day representing a year (iv. 6). Offenders received forty stripes as a maximum (Deut. xxv. 3). A mother was unclean for forty days after childbirth (Lev. xii. 1–4). Perhaps we are to understand that the fast of the Ninevites lasted forty days.

[1] *Dubitavit de illo dæmonum princeps, eumque tentavit, an Christus esset explorans* (*De Civ. Dei*, ix. 21).

[2] Latham, *Pastor Pastorum*, p. 113.

The singular τῷ λίθῳ τούτῳ is more graphic than the οἱ λίθοι οὗτοι of Mt. A single loaf is all that He need produce. The similarity between lumps of stone and loaves of bread perhaps explains why this material, so common in the wilderness, was selected for change into food.

For the use of ἵνα after εἰπέ (x. 40, xix. 15, etc.) see Win. xliv. 8, pp. 420-424; B. Weiss on Mt. iv. 3; Simcox, *Lang. of N.T.* p. 177; Green, *Gr. of N.T.* p. 170. It is a weakening of the telic force of ἵνα rather than a mere substitute for the infinitive. See Blass, *Gr.* pp. 217 ff.

4. Christ does not reply to the "if" by affirming that He is the Son of God; nor does He explain why the Son of God does not accept the devil's challenge. He gives an answer which holds good for any child of God in similar temptation.[1] The reply is a pointed refutation, however, of the special suggestion to Himself, ὁ ἄνθρωπος having direct reference to υἱὸς τ. Θεοῦ. Satan suggests that God's Son would surely be allowed to provide food for Himself. Jesus replies that God can sustain, not only His Son, but any human being, with or without food, and can make other things besides bread to be food. Comp. "My meat is to do the will of Him that sent Me" (Jn. iv. 34). The reply is *verbatim* as LXX of Deut. viii. 3. As all His replies come from this book, we may conjecture that Jesus had recently been reading it or meditating on it. The repeated use of a book which is so full of the trials of Israel in the wilderness may suggest a parallel between the forty days and the forty years. The direct reference is to the manna.

The addition of the remainder of the quotation in A D and other authorities comes from Mt. It differs in wording in the texts which insert it. If it were genuine here, its absence from the best authorities would be most extraordinary. The insertion of ὁ διάβολος and of εἰς ὄρος ὑψηλόν in ver. 5, and the substitution of τοῦ κόσμου for τῆς οἰκουμένης, are corruptions of the same kind.

5. Lk. places second the temptation which Mt. places last. The reasons given for preferring one order to the other are subjective and unconvincing. Perhaps neither Evangelist professes to give any chronological order. Temptations may be intermingled. It is very doubtful whether the τότε with which Mt. introduces the temptation which he places second, and the πάλιν with which he introduces his third, are intended to specify sequence in time. Many Lat. MSS. (G b c f l q r) here place *vv.* 5–8 after *vv.* 9–11. Lk. omits the command to Satan to depart;[2] and we have no means of knowing which temptation it *immediately* followed. Mt. naturally connects it with the one which he places last.

ἀναγαγών. See on ii. 22. The word does not require us to

[1] Trench quotes from Ambrose: *Non enim quasi Deus utitur potestate (quid enim mihi proderat), sed quasi homo commune sibi arcessit auxilium.*

[2] It is worth noting that A.V., which follows those texts that insert Ὕπαγε ὀπίσω μου, Σατανᾶ in ver. 8, renders the words "Get thee behind Me, Satan" there, and "Get thee hence, Satan" in Mt.

believe that Satan had control of Christ's person and transferred Him bodily from the desert to a mountain-top. From no mountain could "all the kingdoms of the world" be visible, least of all "in a moment of time." If Satan on the mountain could present to Christ's mind kingdoms which were not visible to the eye, he could do so in the desert. We may suppose that he transferred Jesus *in thought* to a mountain-top, whence He could in thought see all. For "all the kingdoms of the world" comp. Ezra i. 2, where we have τῆς γῆς for "of the world": in Mt. τοῦ κόσμου, which D substitutes here.

τῆς οἰκουμένης. A favourite expression with Lk. (ii. 1, xxi. 26; Acts xi. 28, xvii. 6, 31, xix. 27, xxiv. 5): elsewhere only six times, of which one is a quotation (Rom. x. 18 from Ps. xix. 5). It describes the world as *a place of settled government*, "the civilized world." To a Greek it might mean the Greek world as distinct from barbarian regions (Hdt. iv. 110. 4; comp. Dem. *De Cor.* p. 242). Later it meant "the Roman Empire," *orbis terrarum*, as in ii. 1 (Philo, *Leg. ad Cai.* 25). In inscriptions the Roman Emperor is ὁ κύριος τῆς οἰκουμένης. Finally, it meant "the whole inhabited earth," as here and xxi. 26 (Rev. xvi. 14; Heb. i. 6; Jos. *Ant.* viii. 13. 4: *B. J.* vii. 3. 3). In Heb. ii. 5 it is used of the world to come as an ordered system: see Wsctt. Lk. omits καὶ τὴν δόξαν αὐτῶν here, but adds it in Satan's offer.

ἐν στιγμῇ χρόνου. *Puncto temporis*: comp. ἐν ῥιπῇ ὀφθαλμοῦ (1 Cor. xv. 52). Not in Mt. Comp. Is. xxix. 5; 2 Mac. ix. 11. It intimates that the kingdoms were represented, not in a series of pageants, but simultaneously: *acuta tentatio* (Beng.). To take ἐν στιγμῇ χρ. with ἀναγαγών is not a probable arrangement. With στιγμή (στίζειν = "to prick") comp. *stimulus*, "stick," and "sting."

6. Σοὶ δώσω . . . ὅτι ἐμοὶ παραδέδοται. Both pronouns are emphatic: "To *Thee* I will give . . . because to *me* it hath been delivered."

The αὐτῶν after τὴν δόξαν is a *constructio ad sensum*, referring to the kingdoms understood in τὴν ἐξουσίαν ταύτην, "this authority and jurisdiction." In παραδέδοται we have the common use of the perf. to express permanent and present result of past action; "it has been given over" and remains in my possession: comp. γέγραπται (4, 8, 10) and εἴρηται (12).

Satan does not say by whom it has been given over; and two answers are possible: 1. by God's permission; 2. by man's sin. But the latter does not exclude the former; and in any case *confitetur tentator, se non esse conditorem* (Beng.). That it refers to a Divine gift previous to his revolt against God, is a gratuitous conjecture. Christ Himself speaks of Satan as "the ruler of this world" (Jn. xii. 31, xiv. 30, xvi. 11). In the Rabbinical writings "Lord of this world" is a common name for Satan, as ruler of the heathen, in opposition to God, the Head of the Jewish theocracy. The devil is the ruler of the unbelieving and sinful; but he mixes truth with falsehood when he claims to have dominion over all the material glory of the world. Comp. Eph. ii. 2; 2 Cor

iv. 4; Rev. xiii. 2. In ᾧ ἂν θέλω the mixture of falsehood seems to be still greater. Even of those who are under the dominion of Satan it is only in a limited sense true that he can dispose of them as he pleases. But the subtlety of the temptation lies partly in the fact that it appeals to what is in a very real sense true. Satan intimates that the enormous influence which he possesses over human affairs may be obtained for the promotion of the Messiah's Kingdom. Thus all the pain and suffering, which otherwise lay before the Saviour of the world, might be evaded.[1]

7. ἐὰν προσκυνήσῃς. Mt. adds πεσών, which, like προσελθών, indicates that he may have believed that Satan was visible, although this is not certain. Even actual prostration is possible to an invisible being, and "fall down and worship" is a natural figure for entire submission or intense admiration. In the East, prostration is an acknowledgment of *authority*, not necessarily of *personal merit*. The temptation, therefore, seems to be that of *admitting Satan's authority* and accepting promotion from him.

ἐνώπιον ἐμοῦ. Lk.'s favourite expression (i. 15, 17, 19, 75, etc.). The usual constr. after προσκυνεῖν is the acc. (ver. 8; Mt. iv. 10; Rev. ix. 20, xiii. 12, xiv. 9, 11) or the dat. (Acts vii. 43; Jn. iv. 21, 23; Rev. iv. 10, vii. 11): but Rev. xv. 4 as here.

ἔσται σοῦ πᾶσα. "The ἐξουσία which has been delivered to me I am willing to delegate or transfer": *magna superbia* (Beng.). The acceptance of it would be equivalent to προσκύνησις. Just as in the first case the lawful desire for food was made an occasion of temptation, so here the lawful desire of power, a desire specially lawful in the Messiah. Everything depends upon why and how the food and the power are obtained. Christ was born to be a king; but His Kingdom is not of this world (Jn. xviii. 36, 37), and the prince of this world has nothing in Him (Jn. xiv. 30). He rejects the Jewish idea of the Messiah as an earthly potentate, and thus condemns Himself to rejection by His own people. He rejects Satan as an ally, and thereby has him as an implacable enemy. The end does not sanctify the means.

8. προσκυνήσεις. Mt. also has this word in harmony with Satan's προσκυνήσῃς; but in LXX of Deut. vi. 13 we have φοβηθήσῃ: see on vii. 27.—**λατρεύσεις.** Lit. "serve for hire" (λάτρις = "hireling"). In class. Grk. it is used of the service of slaves and of freemen, whether rendered to men or to God: in N.T. always of religious service, but sometimes of the worship of idols (Acts vii. 42; Rom. i. 25). Trench, *Syn.* xxxv. *Propositum erat Domino humilitate diabolum vincere, non potentia* (Jerome).

9. τὸ πτερύγιον τοῦ ἱεροῦ. It is impossible to determine what

[1] In this connexion a remark of Père Didon is worth quoting. Of the traditional scene of the Temptation he says that there Christ *avait sous les yeux ce chemin de Jéricho à Jérusalem qu'il devait suivre, un jour, avec ses disciples, pour aller à la mort* (*Jésus Christ* ch. iii. p. 209).

this means. The article points to its being something well known by this name. The three points conjectured are: 1. the top of the Royal Porch, whence one looked into an abyss (Jos. *Ant.* xv. 11. 5); 2. the top of Solomon's Porch; 3. the roof of the ναός. It was from τὸ πτερύγιον τοῦ ἱεροῦ that James the Just was thrown, according to Hegesippus (Eus. *H. E.* ii. 23. 11, 16). Had any part of the ναός been intended, we should perhaps have had τ. ναοῦ rather than τ. ἱεροῦ.

Εἰ υἱὸς εἶ τοῦ Θεοῦ. The repetition of this preamble is evidence that this temptation is in part the same as the first (ver. 3). In both cases Jesus is to "tempt" (ver. 12) God, to challenge Him to prove His Fatherhood by a test of His Son's own choosing. But, whereas in the first case Christ was to be rescued from an *existing* danger by a miracle, here He is to *court* needless danger in order to be rescued by a miracle. It may be that this is also a partial repetition of the second temptation. If the suggestion is that He should throw Himself down into the courts of the temple, so that the priests and the people might see His miraculous descent, and be convinced of His Messiahship, then this is once more a temptation to take a short cut to success, and, by doing violence to men's wills, avoid all the pain and suffering involved in the work of redemption.[1] If this is correct, then this temptation is *a combination of the other two.* It is difficult to see what point there is in mentioning the temple, if presumptuously seeking peril was the only element in the temptation. The precipices of the wilderness would have served for that. The **βάλε σεαυτόν** expresses more definitely than the mid. would have done that the act is to be entirely His own. Not "Fall," nor "Spring," but "Cast Thyself"; *dejice teipsum.* Comp. ἑαυτοὺς πλανῶμεν (1 Jn. i. 8).

10. The fact that after τ. **διαφυλάξαι σε** Satan omits ἐν πάσαις ταῖς ὁδοῖς σου is in favour of the view that presumptuous rushing into danger is part of the temptation. To fling oneself down from a height is not going "in one's ways," but out of them. The disobedient Prophet was slain by the lion, the obedient Daniel was preserved in the lions' den. But we are not sure that the omission of the words has this significance.

11. ἐπὶ χειρῶν. "*On* their hands," implying great carefulness. The **πρὸς λίθον** has no special reference either to the temple or the rocks below: stones abound in most places, and lie in the way of those who stumble.

12. Εἴρηται. In Mt. Πάλιν γέγραπται. Jesus had appealed to Scripture; Satan does the same; and then Jesus shows that isolated texts may be misleading. They may be understood in a sense plainly at variance with some other passage. Satan had

[1] See Edersh. *L. & T.* i. p. 304; Latham, *Pastor Pastorum*, p. 140.

suggested that it was impossible to put too much trust in God. Christ points out that testing God is not trusting Him.

The verb ἐκπειράζειν is wholly biblical (x. 25; Mt. iv. 7; Ps. lxxvii. 18). In the Heb. it is "*Ye* shall not tempt": but in LXX we have the sing. as here.

13. **πάντα πειρασμόν.** "Every kind of temptation": a further indication that He was tempted throughout the forty days, and that what is recorded is merely an illustration of what took place. The enemy tried all his weapons, and was at all points defeated. Comp. πᾶσα ἁμαρτία καὶ βλασφημία, "all manner of sin and blasphemy" (Mt. xii. 31); πᾶν δένδρον, "every kind of tree (Mt. iii. 10); ὁ μὲν πάσης ἡδονῆς ἀπολαύων καὶ μηδεμιᾶς ἀπεχόμενος ἀκόλαστος, "he who enjoys every kind of pleasure," etc. (Arist. *Eth. Nic.* ii. 2. 7).

ἄχρι καιροῦ. "Until a convenient season." This rendering gives the proper meaning both of ἄχρι and of καιρός: comp. Acts xiii. 11, xxiv. 25; Lk. xxi. 24. It is Satan's expectation that on some future occasion he will have an opportunity of better success; and an opportunity came when Judas was allowed to deliver the Christ into the hands of His enemies. That this was such an occasion seems to be indicated by Christ's own declarations: "The prince of this world cometh; and he hath nothing in Me" (Jn. xiv. 30); and "This is your hour and the power of darkness" (Lk. xxii. 53). Satan was not visible in a bodily shape then, and probably not on this earlier occasion. It is Peter who on one occasion became a visible tempter (Mt. xvi. 23; Mk. viii. 33). Not that we are to suppose, however, that Satan entirely desisted from attacks between the beginning and end of Christ's ministry: "Ye are they which have continued with Me in My temptations," rather implies the contrary (xxii. 28); but the evil one seems to have accumulated attacks at the beginning and the end. In the wilderness he employed the attractiveness of painless glory and success; in the garden he tried the dread of suffering and failure. All human temptation takes place through the instrumentality of pleasure or pain. Comp. xxii. 3.

Luke says nothing about the ministration of Angels which followed the temptation, as recorded by both Mt. and Mk., not because he doubts such facts, for he repeatedly records them (i. 11, 26, ii. 9, xxii. 43; Acts v. 19, viii. 26, xii. 7, xxvii. 23), but probably because his source said nothing about them. Mk. seems to mean that Angels were ministering to Jesus during the whole of the forty days: his three imperfects (ἦν . . . ἦν . . . διηκόνουν) are co-ordinate.

The Temptation is not a dream, nor a vision, nor a myth, nor a parable, translated into history by those who heard and misunderstood it, but an historical fact. It was part of the Messiah's preparation for His work. In His baptism He received strength. In His temptation He practised the use of it. Moreover, He thus as man acquired experience (Heb. v. 8) of the possibilities of evil, and of the violent and subtle ways in which His work could be ruined.

Only from Himself could the disciples have learned the history of this struggle. Among other things it taught them the value of the Jewish Scriptures. With these for their guide they could overcome the evil one, as He had done: no special illumination was necessary (xvi. 29, 31).

IV. 14–IX. 50. *The Ministry in Galilee.*

Lk., like Mt. and Mk., omits the early ministry in Judæa; but we shall find that his narrative, like theirs, implies it. All three of them connect the beginning of the Galilean ministry with the Baptism and the Temptation; while Mt. and Mk. make the imprisonment of the Baptist to be the occasion of Christ's departure from Judæa into Galilee (Mt. iv. 12; Mk. i. 14). But they neither assert nor imply that John was imprisoned soon after the Temptation; nor do they explain why the arrest of John by Herod Antipas should make Christ take refuge in this same Herod's dominions. It is from the Fourth Gospel that we learn that there was a considerable interval between the Temptation and John's imprisonment, and that during it Jesus went into Galilee and returned to Judæa again (ii. 13). From it also we learn that the occasion of the second departure into Galilee was the jealousy of the Pharisees, who had been told that Jesus was making and baptizing more disciples even than the Baptist. Much as they disliked and feared the revolutionary influence of John, they feared that of Jesus still more. John declared that he was not the Christ, he "did no sign," and he upheld the Law. Whereas Jesus had been pointed out as the Messiah; He worked miracles, and He disregarded, not only traditions which were held to be equal to the Law (Jn. iv. 9), but even the Law itself in the matter of the Sabbath (Jn. v. 9, 10). Thus we see that it was not to escape the persecution of Herod, but to escape that of the Pharisees, who had delivered the Baptist into the hands of Herod, that Jesus retired a second time from Judæa into Galilee. It was "after that John was *delivered up*" (Mk. i. 14), and "when He *heard* that John was *delivered up*" (Mt. iv. 12), that Christ retired into Galilee. In neither case was it Herod's action, but the action of those who delivered John into the hands of Herod, that led to Christ's change of sphere. And in this way what is recorded in the Fourth Gospel explains the obscurities of the other three.

There is a slight apparent difference between the first two Gospels and the third. The three Evangelists agree in noticing only one return from Judæa to Galilee, and possibly each knows of only one. But whereas Mt. and Mk. seem to point to the second return, for they connect it with the delivering up of the Baptist, Lk. seems rather to point to the first return, for he connects it with "the power of the Spirit," an expression which suggests a reference to that power which Jesus had received at the Baptism and exercised in the Temptation. It is quite possible, however, that the expression refers to the power with which He had worked miracles and taught in Galilee and Judæa; in which case all three Gospels treat of the second return to Galilee.

Not very much plan is discernible in this portion of the Gospel; and it may be doubted whether the divisions made by commentators correspond with any arrangement which the writer had in his mind. But even artificial schemes help to a clearer apprehension of the whole; and the arrangement suggested by Godet is, at any rate, useful for this purpose. He takes *the Development in the Position of Christ's Disciples* as the principle of his divisions.

1. iv. 14–44. To the Call of the first Disciples.
2. v. 1–vi. 11. To the Nomination of the Twelve.
3 vi. 12–viii. 56. To the first Mission of the Twelve.
4. ix. 1–50. To the Departure for Jerusalem.

These divisions are clearly marked out in the text of WH., a space being left at the end of each.

IV. 14–44. *The Ministry in Galilee to the Call of the first Disciples. The Visits to Nazareth and Capernaum.*

14, 15. Comp. Mt. iv. 12; Mk. i. 14. These two verses are introductory, and point out three characteristics of this period of Christ's activity. 1. He worked in the power of the Spirit. 2. His fame spread far and wide. 3. The synagogues were the scenes of His preaching (comp. ver. 44).

14. ἐν τῇ δυνάμει τοῦ πνεύματος. This is perhaps to remind us that since His first departure from Galilee He has been endowed with the Holy Spirit and has received new powers (iii. 22, iv. 1, 18). Bengel's *post victoriam corroboratus* connects it too exclusively with the Temptation. Unless, with De Wette, we take καὶ φήμη ἐξῆλθεν as anticipating what follows, the statement implies much preaching and perhaps some miracles, of which Lk. has said nothing; for Jesus is famous directly He returns. The power of the Spirit had already been exhibited in Him. Jn. says that "the Galileans received Him, having seen all the things that He did in Jerusalem at the feast" (iv. 45). But it is not likely that they had heard of the wonders which attended the Birth, or of those which attended the Baptism.

There are various marks of Lk.'s style. 1. ὑπέστρεψεν, for which Mt. has ἀνεχώρησεν and Mk. ἦλθεν. Comp. ver. 1, where Lk. has ὑπέστρεψεν, while Mt. has ἀνήχθη. 2. δύναμις of Divine power. Comp. i. 35, and see on iv. 36. 3. καθ' ὅλης in this sense. Comp. xxiii. 5; Acts ix. 31, 42, x. 37;

it is peculiar to Lk. See Simcox, *Lang. of N.T.* p. 148. 4. ἡ περίχωρος, *sc.* γῆ, is an expression of which Lk. is fond (iii. 3, iv. 37, vii. 17, viii. 37; Acts xiv. 6); not in Jn., and only twice in Mt. (iii. 5, xiv. 35) and once in Mk. (i. 28; not vi. 55).

15. καὶ αὐτὸς ἐδίδασκεν. Lk. is so fond of this mode of transition that αὐτός possibly has no special significance; if it has, it is "He Himself," as distinct from the rumour respecting Him. The imperf. points to His habitual practice at this time, and seems to deprive what follows of all chronological connexion. All the Gospels mention His teaching in synagogues, and give instances of His doing so during the early part of His ministry (Mt. iv. 23, ix. 35, xii. 9, xiii. 54; Mk. i. 21, 39, iii. 1, vi. 2; Lk. iv. 44, vi. 6; Jn. vi. 59). Towards the close of it, when the hostility of the teachers became more pronounced, there is less mention of this practice: perhaps He then taught elsewhere, in order to avoid needless collision. It should be noticed that here, as elsewhere, it is the *teaching* rather than the *worship* in the synagogues that is prominent. Synagogues were primarily places of instruction (xiii. 10; Jn. xviii. 20; Acts xiii. 27, xv. 21, etc.), and it was as such that Augustus encouraged them. Morality of a high kind was taught there, and morality is on the side of order.

ἐν ταῖς συναγωγαῖς αὐτῶν. This means in the synagogues of the Galileans. Galilee at this time was very populous. Josephus no doubt exaggerates when he says that the smallest villages had fifteen thousand inhabitants (*B. J.* iii. 3. 2), and that there were over two hundred towns and villages. But in any case there were many Galileans. Among them there was more freshness and less formalism than among the inhabitants of Judæa. Here the Pharisees and the hierarchy had less influence, and therefore Galilee was a more hopeful field in which to seek the first elements of a Church. On the other hand, it was necessary to break down the prejudices of those who had known Him in His youth, and had seen in Him no signs of His being the Messiah that they were expecting: and the fame of the miracles which He had wrought in Judæa was likely to contribute towards this. Thus the Judæan ministry prepared the way for the more promising ministry in Galilee. We have no means of estimating the number of Galilean synagogues; but the fact that such a place as Capernaum had either none, or only a poor one, until a Roman centurion was moved to provide one ("himself built us *our* synagogue," vii. 5), is some evidence that by no means every village or even every small town possessed one. The remains of ancient synagogues exist at several places in Galilee; *Tell-Hum*, *Irbid* (the Arbela of 1 Mac. ix. 2), *Jisch* (Giscala), *Meiron* (Mero), *Kasyoun*, *Nabartein*, and *Kefr-Bereim*. But it is doubtful whether any of these are older than the second or third century.

The origin of synagogues is to be sought in the Babylonish captivity; and they greatly increased in number after the destruction of the temple. The fact that Jewish legend derives the institution of synagogues from Moses, shows how essential the Jews considered it to be. The statement that there were at one time 480 synagogues in Jerusalem is also legendary; but 480 may be a symbolical number. One has only to remember the size of Jerusalem to see the absurdity of 480 places of public instruction in it. But large towns sometimes had several synagogues, either for different nationalities (Acts vi. 9; see Lumby and Blass) or different handicrafts.[1]

δοξαζόμενος ὑπὸ πάντων. Because of the power of His preaching, especially when contrasted with the lifeless repetitions and senseless trivialities of ordinary teachers.

16–30. The Visit to Nazareth. Comp. Mt. xiii. 53–58; Mk. vi. 1–6. It remains doubtful whether Lk. here refers to the same visit as that recorded by Mt. and Mk. If it is the same, he perhaps has purposely transposed it to the opening of the ministry, as being typical of the issue of Christ's ministry. He was rejected by His own people. Similarly the non-Galilean ministry opens with a rejection (ix. 51–56). In any case, the form of the narrative is peculiar to Lk., showing that he here has some special source. We are not to understand that the Galilean ministry began at Nazareth. More probably Christ waited until the reports of what He had said and done in other parts of Galilee prepared the way for His return to Nazareth as a teacher.

16. οὗ ἦν [ἀνα]τεθραμμένος. This tells us rather more than ii. 51: it implies, moreover, that for some time past Nazareth had ceased to be His home. But the addition of "where He had been brought up" explains what follows. It had been "His custom" during His early life at Nazareth to attend the synagogue every sabbath. It is best to confine *κατὰ τὸ εἰωθός* to the clause in which it is embedded, and not carry it on to *ἀνέστη ἀναγνῶναι*: it was possibly the first time that He had stood up to read at Nazareth. But the phrase may refer to what had been His custom elsewhere since He began His ministry; or it may be written from the Evangelist's point of view of what was afterwards His custom. We may therefore choose between these explanations. 1. He had previously been in the habit of attending the synagogue at Nazareth, and on this occasion stood up to read. 2. He had previously been in the habit of reading at Nazareth. 3. He had lately been in the habit of reading elsewhere, and now does so at Nazareth. 4. This was an early example of what became His custom. In no case must the sermon be included in the custom. That this was His first sermon at Nazareth is implied by the whole context.

[1] On synagogues see Edersh. *L. & T.* i. pp. 430–450, *Hist. of Jewish Nation*, pp. 100–129, ed. 1896; Schürer, *Jewish People in the T. of J. C.* ii. 2, pp. 52–89; Hausrath, *N.T. Times*, i. pp. 84–93; Plumptre in *D.B.*; Leyrer in Herzog, *PRE.*[1]; Strack in Herzog, *PRE.*[2]; and other authorities in Schürer.

In D both *τεθραμμένος* and *αὐτῷ* after *εἰωθὸς* are omitted, and the text runs, *ἐλθὼν δὲ εἰς Ναζαρὲδ ὅπου ἦν κατὰ τὸ εἰωθὸς ἐν τῇ ἡμέρᾳ τῶν σαββάτων εἰς τὴν συναγωγήν*; but in the Latin the former word is restored, ***veniens autem in Nazared ubi erat nutricatus introibit secundum consuetudinem in sabbato in synagogam.*** The omissions are perhaps due to Marcionite influence. According to Marcion, Christ came direct from heaven into the synagogue, *de cœlo in synagogam* (see p. 131); and therefore all trace of His previous life in Nazareth must be obliterated. He was not reared there, and was not accustomed to visit the synagogue there. Only a custom of attending the synagogue existed. See Rendel Harris, *Study of Codex Bezæ*, p. 232, in *Texts and Studies*, ii. 1. Comp. the insertions ix. 54, 55, which may be due to the same influence.

The phrase *κατὰ τὸ εἰωθός* occurs in LXX Num. xxiv. 1; Sus. 13. It is characteristic of Lk. See on *κατὰ τὸ ἔθος*, i. 8. With the dat. *κατὰ τὸ εἰωθός* occurs only here and Acts xvii. 2; and *τῇ ἡμέρᾳ τῶν σαββάτων* occurs only here, Acts xiii. 14, and xvi. 13: but comp. Lk. xiii. 14, 16 and xiv. 5. It is a periphrasis for *ἐν τοῖς σαβ.*, or *ἐν τῷ σαβ.*, or *τοῖς σαβ.*, or *τῷ σαβ.*

ἀνέστη ἀναγνῶναι. Standing to read was the usual practice, excepting when the Book of Esther was read at the Feast of Purim: then the reader might sit. Christ's standing up indicated that He had been asked to read, or was ready to do so. This is the only occasion on which we are told that Jesus read.

The lectern was close to the front seats, where those who were most likely to be called upon to read commonly sat. A lesson from the *Thorah* or Law was read first, and then one from the Prophets. After the lesson had been read in Hebrew it was interpreted into Aramaic (Neh. viii. 8), or into Greek in places where Greek was commonly spoken. This was done verse by verse in the Law; but in the Prophets three verses might be taken at once, and in this case Jesus seems to have taken two verses. Then followed the exposition or sermon. The reader, interpreter, and preacher might be one, two, or three persons. Here Christ was both reader and preacher; and possibly He interpreted as well.[1] Although there were officers with fixed duties attached to each synagogue, yet there was no one specially appointed either to read, or interpret, or preach, or pray. Any member of the congregation might discharge these duties; and probably those who were competent discharged them in turn at the invitation of the *ἀρχισυνάγωγος* (Acts xiii. 15. Comp. Philo in Eus. *Præp. Evang.* viii. 7, p. 360 A, and *Quod omnis probus liber* xii.). Hence it was always easy for Jesus to address the congregation. When He became famous as a teacher He would often be invited to do so.[2] And during His early years He may have read without interpreting or expounding; for even those under age were sometimes allowed to read in the synagogues. We cannot infer from His being able to read that He Himself possessed the Scriptures. In N.T. *ἀναγινώσκω* is used in no other sense than that of *reading*; lit. recognizing

---

[1] We have no right to infer from this incident that the Hebrew Bible could still be understood by the people. Nothing is said about interpretation; but we cannot assume that it did not take place. Mk. xv. 34 is evidence of some knowledge of O.T. in Aramaic. See *Classical Review*, May 1894, p. 216, against Kautzsch, *Grammatik des biblischen Aramäischen*, p. 19.

[2] Comp. Ἀναστὰς δέ τις τῶν ἐμπειροτάτων ὑφηγεῖται τἄριστα καὶ συνοίσοντα, οἷς ἅπας ὁ βίος ἐπιδώσει πρὸς τὸ βέλτιον (Philo, *De Septenario*, vi.). See also the fragments of Philo in Eus. *Præp. Evang.* viii. 7. 12, 13, and viii. 12. 10, ed. Gaisford. These three passages give us Philo's account of the synagogue services.

again the written characters; of reading *aloud*, Acts xiii. 27, xv. 21; 2 Cor. iii. 15; Col. iv. 16; 1 Thes. v. 27.

17. ἐπεδόθη. "Was handed" to Him, "was given over by handing": comp. ἐπεζήτουν (ver. 42). It does not mean "was handed to Him *in addition*," implying that something else had been handed to Him previously. This meaning is not common, and is not found elsewhere in N.T. The reading of the *Parascha*, or section from the Law, had probably preceded, and had been read possibly by someone else. This was the *Haphthara*, or prophetic section (Acts xiii. 15). That Is. lxi. 1, 2 was the lesson appointed for the day is quite uncertain. We do not even know whether there was at that time any cycle of prophetical lessons, nor whether it would be strictly adhered to, if there was such. Apparently Isaiah was handed to Him without His asking for it; but that also is uncertain. The cycle of lessons now in use is of much later origin; and therefore to employ the Jewish lectionary in order to determine the day on which this took place is futile. On the other hand, there is no evidence that "Jesus takes the section which He lights upon as soon as it is unrolled"; for εὗρε quite as easily may mean the opposite;—that He intentionally found a passage which had been previously selected.

The more definite ἀναπτύξας (ℵ D) is probably a correction of ἀνοίξας (A B L and most versions). The former occurs nowhere in N.T., while the latter is very common: see esp. Rev. v. 2, 3, 4, 5, x. 2, 8, xx. 12. Fond as Lk. is of analytical tenses, ἦν γεγραμμένον occurs nowhere else in his writings: ἔστι γεγραμ. is common in Jn. (ii. 17, vi. 31, 45, x. 34, xii. 14, 16).

18. The quotation is given by the Evangelist somewhat freely from LXX, probably from memory and under the influence of other passages of Scripture. To argue that the Evangelist cannot be S. Luke, because S. Luke was a Gentile, and therefore would not know the LXX, is absurd. S. Luke was not only a constant companion of S. Paul, but a fellow-worker with him in dealing with both Jews and Gentiles. He could not have done this without becoming familiar with the LXX.

Down to ἀπέσταλκέν με inclusive the quotation agrees with LXX. After that the text of LXX runs thus: ἰάσασθαι τοὺς συντετριμμένους τὴν καρδίαν, κηρύξαι αἰχμαλώτοις ἄφεσιν καὶ τυφλοῖς ἀνάβλεψιν, καλέσαι ἐνιαυτὸν Κυρίου δεκτόν. In many authorities the clause ἰάσασθαι τοὺς συντετριμμένους τὴν καρδίαν has been inserted into the text of Lk. in order to make the quotation more full and more in harmony with O.T. We have similar insertions Mt. xv. 8; Acts vii. 37; Rom. xiii. 9; Heb. xii. 20, and perhaps ii. 7.[1]

[1] Scrivener, *Int. to Crit. of N.T.* i. pp. 12, 13, 4th ed.

The evidence against the clause ἰάσασθαι . . . τὴν καρδίαν here (in ℵ A Q of LXX τῇ καρδίᾳ) is decisive. It is omitted by ℵ B D L Ξ, 13–69, 33, most MSS. of

In the original the Prophet puts into the mouth of Jehovah's ideal Servant a gracious message to those in captivity, promising them release and a return to the restored Jerusalem, the joy of which is compared to the joy of the year of jubilee. It is obvious that both figures, the return from exile and the release at the jubilee, admirably express Christ's work of redemption.

Πνεῦμα Κυρίου ἐπ' ἐμέ. In applying these words to Himself the Christ looks back to His baptism. He is more than a Prophet; He is "the Son, the Beloved One," of Jehovah (iii. 21, 22).

With ἐπ' ἐμέ (ἐστι) comp. ἦν ἐπ' αὐτόν (ii. 25).—*οὗ εἵνεκεν.* Not "wherefore," as in Acts xix. 32, which here would spoil the sense, but "because," a meaning which οὕνεκεν often has in class. Grk. Vulg. has *propter quod.* Comp. Gen. xviii. 5, xix. 8, xxii. 16, xxxviii. 26; Num. x. 31, xiv. 43, etc. The Ionic form εἵνεκεν is found xviii. 29; Acts xxviii. 20; 2 Cor. iii. 10: but ἕνεκεν is the commonest form (2 Cor. vii. 12), and ἕνεκα also occurs before consonants (vi. 22; Acts xxvi. 21).

ἔχρισέν με. The Christ was anointed with the Spirit, as Prophets and priests were anointed with oil (1 Kings xix. 16; Ex. xxviii. 41, xxx. 30). Unlike πένης (2 Cor. ix. 9), **πτωχός** "always had a bad meaning until it was ennobled by the Gospels" (vi. 20, vii. 22; 2 Cor. vi. 10; Jas. ii. 5). It suggests abject poverty (πτώσσω = "I crouch"). See Hatch, *Bibl. Grk.* pp. 76, 77.

ἀπέσταλκέν με. Change from aor. to perf. "He anointed Me (once for all); He hath sent Me (and I am here)": comp. 1 Cor. xv. 4. We have had ἀποστέλλω of the mission of Gabriel (i. 19, 26); here and ver. 43 we have it of the mission of the Christ; vii. 27 of the Forerunner; ix. 2 of the Twelve. Whereas πέμπω is quite general and implies no special relation between sender and sent, ἀποστέλλω adds the idea of a delegated authority making the person sent to be the envoy or representative of the sender. But πέμπω also is used of the mission of the Christ (xx. 13), of Prophets (ver. 26, xx. 11, 12), and of the Apostles (Jn. xiii. 20, xx. 21). Strictly speaking, **αἰχμαλώτοις** means "prisoners *of war*" (αἰχμή and ἁλωτός): freq. in class. Grk. but here only in N.T. The cognate αἰχμαλωτίζω occurs xxi. 24; 2 Cor. x. 5; 2 Tim. iii. 6; αἰχμαλωσία, Eph. iv. 8. Neither this metaphor nor that of **τυφλοῖς ἀνάβλεψιν** harmonizes very well with the year of jubilee, to which Godet would restrict the whole passage. Both might apply to captives in exile, some of whom had been blinded by their captors, or by long confinement in a dungeon.

ἀποστεῖλαι τεθραυσμένους ἐν ἀφέσει. These words come from another part of Isaiah (lviii. 6), and are perhaps inserted through a slip of memory. Jesus was reading, not quoting without book; and therefore we cannot suppose that He inserted the clause.

Lat. Vet. and best MSS. of Vulg., most MSS. of Boh. Aeth. Arm. Syr-Sin., Orig. Eus. etc., all the best editors and RV. See Sanday, *App. ad N.T.* p. 117.

Lightfoot says that it was lawful to skip from one passage to another in reading the Prophets, but not in reading the Law (*Hor. Heb.* on Lk. iv. 17). That might explain the omission of a few verses, but not the going *back* three chapters. The insertion comes from the Evangelist, who is probably quoting from memory, and perhaps regards the unconsciously combined passages as a sort of "programme of the ministry." The strong expression **τεθραυσμένους** is here applied to those who are shattered in fortune and broken in spirit.

For the pregnant construction, "send so as to be in," comp. i. 17. The asyndeton throughout, first between ἔχρισεν and ἀπέσταλκεν, and then between the three infinitives which depend upon ἀπέσταλκεν, is impressive.

19. ἐνιαυτὸν Κυρίου δεκτόν. The age of the Messiah, which is Jehovah's time for bestowing great blessings on His people. Comp. καιρὸς δεκτός (2 Cor. vi. 2; Is. xlix. 8): δεκτός is not found in class. Grk. It is strange that Clement of Alexandria and Origen, who are commonly so ready to turn fact into figure, here turn an expression which is manifestly figurative into a literal statement of fact, and limit Christ's ministry to a period of twelve months (comp. *Clem. Hom.* xvii. 19). Keim and other modern writers have made the same limit; but the three Passovers distinguished by S. John (ii. 13, vi. 4, xi. 55) are quite fatal to it.[1] It is, however, an equally faulty exegesis to find the three years (*i.e.* two years and a fraction) of Christ's ministry in the three years of Lk. xiii. 6–9 or the three days of xiii. 31–33. The first of these is obviously a parabolic saying not to be understood literally; and the other probably is such. The suggestion that the three servants sent to the wicked husbandmen mean the three years of the ministry is almost grotesque. See Nösgen, *Gesch. Jesu Christi*, Kap. viii., München, 1890.

20. The vivid description of what followed the reading of the lesson points to an eye-witness as the source of the narrative. But the "closed" of AV. and RV. gives a wrong impression of the first incident: it leads one to think of a modern book with leaves. The Rhemish has "folded"; but "rolled up" would be a better rendering of **πτύξας.** The long strip of parchment, or less probably papyrus (2 Jn. 12), would be wound upon a roller, or possibly upon two rollers, one at each end of the strip. Hence the name *megillah* (*volumen*), from *gâlal*, "to roll." Such a book was in Greek sometimes called κεφαλίς (Ezr. vi. 2; Ezek. iii. 1–3) or κεφαλὶς βιβλίου (Heb. x. 7; Ps. xxxix. 8; Ezek. ii. 9): and it is said that κεφαλίς originally meant the knob (*cornu* or *umbilicus*) at the end of the roller; but no instance of this use of κεφαλίς appears to be known (Wsctt. on Heb. x. 7).

ἀποδοὺς τῷ ὑπηρέτῃ. The ἀπο- implies that it was the minister or

[1] On the uncertainty respecting the length of the ministry, and the conjectures respecting it made by early Christians, see Iren. *Hær.* ii. 22; Eus. *H. E.* i. 10; Sanday in the *Expositor*, 1st series, xi. p. 16.

chazzan who had handed Him the book who received it *back* again. The τῷ may have the same meaning, just as τὸ βιβλίον means the book which had been given to Him. But τῷ ὑπηρέτῃ more probably means the minister usually found in a synagogue. It was among the duties of the *chazzan* to take the Scriptures from the ark and put them away again (Surenhusius, *Mishna*, ii. 246, iii. 266). He taught the children to read, and inflicted the scourgings (Mt. x. 17). A Roman epitaph to a Jew who held this office is quoted by Schürer, II. ii. p. 66—

Φλαβιος Ιουλιανος υπηρετης
Φλαβια Ιουλιανη θυγατηρ πατρι
Εν ειρηνη η κοιμησις σου.

The *chazzan* of the synagogue became the deacon or sub-deacon of the Christian Church.

A ὑπηρέτης is lit. "an under-rower" (ἐρέσσω). The word may be used of almost any kind of attendant or servant (Acts v. 22, 26, xiii. 5; Mt. xxvi. 58; Mk. xiv. 54, 65; Jn. vii. 32, 45; 1 Cor. iv. 1). For the two participles, πτύξας . . . ἀποδούς, without καί, comp. Acts xii. 4, 25.

ἐκάθισεν. This was the usual attitude for expounding or preaching, and in the synagogues there was commonly a raised seat for the purpose. On other occasions we find Christ sitting to teach (v. 3; Mt. v. 1; Mk. iv. 1; [Jn. viii. 2]); and the disciples do the same (Acts xvi. 13).

ἦσαν ἀτενίζοντες. "Were fixed intently." Their intense interest was caused by His reputation as a teacher and as a worker of miracles, as well as by His having been brought up amongst them; perhaps also by His look and manner of reading. That He had selected an unexpected passage, or had omitted the usual lesson from the Law, and that this surprised them, is pure conjecture. Comp. Acts vi. 15, where the same verb is used of the whole Sanhedrin riveting their eyes upon Stephen. It is a favourite word with Lk., who uses it a dozen times: elsewhere in N.T. only 2 Cor. iii. 7, 13. It occurs in LXX (1 Es. vi. 28; 3 Mac. ii. 26), in Aq. (Job vii. 8), and in Jos. (*B.J.* v. 12. 3). The analytical tense marks the continuance of the action.

21. ἤρξατο δὲ λέγειν. The ἤρξατο is not pleonastic: it points to the solemnity of the moment when His words broke the silence of universal expectation: comp. vii. 24, xi. 29, xii. 1, xiv. 18. What follows may be regarded as a summary of what was said. It gives us the main subject of His discourse. We are led to suppose that He said much more; perhaps interpreting to them in detail the things concerning Himself (xxiv. 27). The conversation with Nicodemus is similarly condensed by S. John (iii. 1–21). Even without this narrative we should know from vii. 22 and Mt.

xi. 5 that Christ interpreted Is. lxi. 1 ff. of Himself. The whole of the O.T. was to Him a prophecy respecting His life and work. And this applies not only to prophetic utterances, but also to rites and institutions, as well as to historical events, which were so ordered as to be a forecast of the salvation and judgment which He was to bring.[1] This verse sums up His sermon.

ἡ γραφὴ αὕτη. "This *passage* of Scripture" (Mk. xii. 10; Jn. vii. 42, etc.): for Scripture as a whole the plural is used (xxiv. 27, 32, 45; Mt. xxi. 42, xxii. 29, xxvi. 54, 56; Mk. xii. 24, etc.). His interpretation of the prophecy was at the same time a fulfilment of it; for the voice of Him of whom the Prophet wrote was sounding in their ears. Hence it is that he affirms πεπλήρωται ἐν τοῖς ὠσὶν ὑμῶν. As Renan says, *Il ne prêchait pas ses opinions, il se prêchait luimême.*

22. ἐμαρτύρουν αὐτῷ. "They bore witness to Him," not that what He said about Himself, but that what rumour had said respecting His power as a teacher, was true. They praised Him in an empty-hearted way. What they remembered of Him led them to think that the reports about Him were exaggerations; but they were willing to admit that this was not the case. Comp. xi. 48. This "bearing witness" almost of necessity implies that Jesus had said a great deal more than is recorded here. What follows shows that they did not believe the teaching which so startled and impressed them, any more than those whose attention was riveted on Stephen, before he began to address them, were disposed to accept his teaching. The cases are very similar. Hence *ἐθαύμαζον* expresses amazement rather than admiration. For *θαυμάζειν ἐπί* see small print on ii. 33.

τοῖς λόγοις τῆς χάριτος. Characterizing genitive or genitive of quality; freq. in writings influenced by Hebrew, "which employs this construction, not merely through poverty in adjectives, but also through the vividness of phraseology which belongs to Oriental languages" (Win. xxxiv. 3. b, p. 297). Comp. *οἰκονόμος τῆς ἀδικίας* (xvi. 8); *κριτὴς τῆς ἀδικίας* (xviii. 6); *ἀκροατὴς ἐπιλησμονῆς* (Jas. i. 25); *κριταὶ διαλογισμῶν πονηρῶν* (Jas. ii. 4); and perhaps the difficult *τροπῆς ἀποσκίασμα* (Jas. i. 17). The meaning here is "winning words." The very first meaning of *χάρις* (*χαίρω*) is "comeliness, winsomeness" (Hom. *Od.*

---

[1] "Jesus acknowledged the Old Testament in its full extent and its perfect sacredness. *The Scripture cannot be broken,* He says (Jn. x. 35), and forthwith draws His argument from the wording of it. Of course He can only have meant by this the Scripture in the form in which it was handed down, and He must have regarded it exactly as His age did (comp. xi. 51). Any kind of superior knowledge in these matters would merely have made Him incapable of placing Himself on a level with His hearers respecting the use of Scripture, or would have compelled Him to employ a far-reaching accommodation, the very idea of which involves internal untruthfulness. All, therefore, that is narrated in Scripture He accepted absolutely as actual history, and He regarded the several books as composed by the men to whom they were ascribed by tradition" (B. Weiss, *Leben Jesu,* I. iii. 5, Eng. tr. ii. pp. 62, 63).

viii. 175; Eccles. x. 12; Ps. xliv. 3; Ecclus. xxi. 16, xxxvii. 21; Col. iv. 6): and in all these passages it is the winsomeness of *language* that is specially signified. From this objective attractiveness it easily passes to subjective "favour, kindness, goodwill," esp. from a superior to an inferior (Acts ii. 47; Gen. xviii. 3, xxxii. 5, xxxiii. 8, etc.); and hence, in particular, of finding "favour" with God (i. 30; Acts vii. 46; Exod. xxxiii. 12, 13, 16, etc.). From the sense of God's favour generally (ii. 40, 52; Jn. i. 14, 16) we come to the specially theological sense of "God's favour to sinners, the free gift of His grace" (Acts xiv. 3, xx. 24, 32; and the Pauline Epp. *passim*). Lastly, it sometimes means the "gratitude" which this favour produces in the recipient (vi. 32–34, xvii. 9; 1 Cor. x. 30). The word does not occur in Mt. or Mk. See Sanday on Rom. i. 5, and Blass on Acts ii. 47 and iv. 33.

Origen evidently had this passage in his mind when he wrote: "For a proof that *grace was poured on His lips* (Ps. xliv. 3, ἐξεχύθη ἡ χάρις ἐν χείλεσίν σου) is this, that although the period of His teaching was short,—for He taught somewhere about a year and a few months,—the world has been filled with His teaching" (*De Prin.* iv. 1. 5). But the words so calculated to win did not win the congregation. They were "fulfilled in their ears," but not in their hearts.[1] A doubt at once arose in their minds as to the congruity of such words with one whom they had known all His life as the "son of Joseph" the carpenter. Here οὗτος has a contemptuous turn, as often (v. 21, vii. 39, 49, xv. 2, xxii. 56, 59, etc.): yet the Vulg. in none of these places has *iste*, but *hic*. "Is not this person Joseph's son? What does he mean by using such language?" Just as a single sentence is given as a summary of His discourse, so a single question is given as a summary of their scepticism.

While the οὗτος and υἱός is in all three, the question as a whole differs. Mk. has Οὐχ οὗτός ἐστιν ὁ τέκτων, ὁ υἱὸς τῆς Μαρίας; (vi. 3). Mt. has Οὐχ οὗτός ἐστιν ὁ τοῦ τέκτονος υἱός; (xiii. 55). Lk. Οὐχὶ υἱός ἐστιν Ἰωσὴφ οὗτος; And while the others mention Christ's brothers and sisters in close connexion with His mother, Lk. mentions none of them. Lk. and Jn. seem to prefer the expression "son of Joseph" (Lk. iii. 23, iv. 22; Jn. i. 45, vi. 42). Renan thinks that *Marc ne connaît pas Joseph* (*V. de J.* p. 71). But it may be that, as he does not record the virgin birth of Christ, he avoids the expression "son of Joseph" or "the carpenter's son," which those who have recorded the virgin birth could use without risk of being misunderstood.

23. Πάντως ἐρεῖτέ μοι τὴν παραβολὴν ταύτην. "At all events, assuredly, ye will say," etc.: πάντως is used in strong affirmations (Acts xxi. 22, xxviii. 4; 1 Cor. ix. 10). Excepting Heb. ix. 9 and xi. 19, παραβολή occurs only in the Synoptic Gospels: in Jn. x. 6 and xvi. 25, 29, as in 2 Pet. ii. 22, the word used is παροιμία. It need not be doubted that the notion of placing *beside* for the sake of *comparison*, rather than that of merely putting forth, lies at the root of παραβολή. From the notion of (1) "throwing beside" come the further notions of (2) "exposing" and (3) "comparing," all three of which are common meanings of παραβάλλειν. While the adj. παράβολος represents the derived notion on the one side, the subst. παραβολή represents that on the other side. A παραβολή, therefore, is "an utterance which involves a comparison." Hence various meanings: 1. a complete parable or allegory (viii. 4, xiii. 6,

[1] Comp. Augustine's description of his indifference to the preaching of Ambrose, although charmed with his winning style: *Rerum incuriosus et contemptor adstabam et delectabar suavitate sermonis* (*In Ezek.* xxxiii. 32).

etc.); 2. a single figurative saying, proverb, or illustration (here; v. 36, vi. 39); 3. a saying of deeper meaning, which becomes intelligible through comparison, in which sense it is sometimes joined with σκοτεινὸς λόγος (Prov. i. 6), πρόβλημα (Ps. xlix. 5, lxxviii. 2), and the like. In the teaching of Christ παραβολή is commonly used in the first sense, and is a means of making known the mysteries of the kingdom in a mixed audience; for it conceals from the unworthy what it reveals to the worthy (viii. 9, 10). See Crem. *Lex.* pp. 124, 657; Hatch, *Bibl. Grk.*, p. 70; Hase, *Gesch. Jesu*, § 63, p. 535, ed. 1891; Didon, *Jésus Christ*, ch. vi. p. 391, ed. 1891; Latham, *Pastor Pastorum*, ch. x.

Ἰατρέ, θεράπευσον σεαυτόν. "Heal thine own lameness" is the Hebrew form of the proverb. Similar sayings exist in other literatures: *e.g.* a fragment of Euripides, ἄλλων ἰατρός, αὐτὸς ἕλκεσι βρύων; Ser. Sulpicius to Cicero, *Neque imitare malos medicos, qui in alienis morbis profitentur tenere se medicinæ scientiam, ipsi se curare non possunt* (Cic. *Epp. ad diversos*, iv. 5). Hobart quotes from Galen, ἐχρῆν οὖν αὐτὸν ἑαυτοῦ πρῶτον ἰᾶσθαι τὸ σύμπτωμα καὶ οὕτως ἐπιχειρεῖν ἑτέρους θεραπεύειν. Comp. Aesch. *P. V.* 469; Ov. *Metam.* vii. 561; and the other examples in Lightfoot and Wetst. It is remarkable that this saying of Christ is preserved only by the beloved physician. Its meaning is disputed. Some take the words which follow to be the explanation of it: "Heal the ills of thine own town." Thus Corn. à Lap., "Cure Thine own people and Thine own country, which should be as dear to Thee as Thyself." Similarly Beng. Alf. Sadler and others. It is thus made to mean much the same as "Charity begins at home." But ἰατρέ and σεαυτόν ought to be interpreted of the same person or group; not one of a person and the other of his neighbours. "Prophet, heal Thine own countrymen" is not parallel to "Physician, heal *Thyself*." The saying plainly refers to the passage just read from Isaiah; and although Lk. omits the words "to heal the brokenhearted," yet Christ must have read them, and He had probably explained them. He professed to be the fulfilment of them, and to be healing the miseries of mankind. The people are supposed to tell Him to better His own condition before bettering that of others. He must make His own position more secure, and give evidence of His high mission before asserting it. He must work convincing miracles, such as He is *said* to have worked elsewhere. Comp. σῶσον σεαυτὸν καὶ ἡμᾶς (xxiii. 39). Comp. also *Logion* vi.

ὅσα ἠκούσαμεν. They do not say ὅσα ἐποίησας, wishing to leave it open whether the report may not be untrue. We learn from Jn. ii. 12 that after the miracle at Cana, Jesus was at Capernaum for a short time; and we know also that there were many unrecorded miracles. It is probably to reports of some of these that reference is here made. For the constr. comp. Acts vii. 12 and xxiv. 10.

εἰς τὴν Καφαρναούμ. See on ver. 31. The readings vary between εἰς τὴν Καφ. (א B), εἰς Καφ. (D L), ἐν τῇ Καφ. (X), and ἐν Καφ. (A K). The substitution of ἐν for εἰς, and the omission of the article between a preposition and a proper name, are obvious corrections by a later hand. The εἰς is not "put for ἐν." It may be doubted whether these two prepositions are ever interchanged. Rather εἰς is used because of the idea of motion contained in "come to pass." It is scarcely possible that εἰς contains the notion of "to the advantage of," and indicates the petty jealousy of the people of Nazareth. We have the same constr. i. 44; Acts xxviii. 6 (comp. Lk. xi. 7); and in no case is there any idea of advantage. That the jealousy was a fact, and that the people of Nazareth were inclined to discount or discredit all that seemed to tell in favour of prosperous Capernaum, is probable; but there is no hint of this in the εἰς. What is said to have happened *to* Capernaum ought to happen *here*. Comp. the Cornish use of "to" for "at." In N.T. ὧδε is never "thus," but either "hither" (ix. 41, xiv. 21, xix. 27) or "here" (ix. 33, xxii. 38). The ἐν τῇ πατρίδι σου is epexegetic of ὧδε, and means "Thy native town," not the whole of Israel: comp. Mk. vi. 5; Mt. xiii. 58.

24. Εἶπεν δέ. When these words occur between two utterances of Christ, they seem to indicate that there is an interval between what precedes and what follows. The report of what was said on this occasion is evidently very condensed. Comp. vi. 39, xii. 16, xv. 11, xvii. 1, 22, xviii. 9, and see on i. 8. The δέ is "but" (Cov.) rather than "and" (all other English Versions); *ait autem* (Vulg.). "But, instead of gratifying them, He said" There are various proverbial sayings which declare that those who are close to what is great do not appreciate the greatness. Jesus declares that He is no exception to this rule, and implies that He will work no miracles to free Himself from its operation. In the wilderness He had resisted a similar suggestion that He should work a miracle of display, a mere τέρας (*vv.* 9–11). In this matter Nazareth is a type of the whole nation, which rejected Him because He did not conform to their own ideas of the Messiah. Their test resembles that of the hierarchy, "He is the King of Israel; let Him now come down from the cross, and we will believe on Him" (Mt. xxvii. 42). For εἶπεν δέ see p. lxiii.

25. "But I am like the Prophets, not only in the treatment which I receive from My own people, but also in My principles of action. For they also bestowed their miraculous benefits upon outsiders, although there were many of their own people who would have been very glad of such blessings." Christ is here appealing to their knowledge of Scripture, not to any facts outside the O.T. *Testatur hoc Dominus ex luce omniscientiæ suæ* is not a legitimate inference. Arguments drawn from what was known to Him, but not known to them, would not be likely to influence His audience. Note ὡς = "when."

ἐπ' ἀληθείας. "On a basis of truth": comp. Mk. xii. 14. We have similar adverbial expressions in ἐπ' ἴσης (*sc.* μοίρας), ἐπὶ σχολῆς, ἐπὶ καιροῦ, ἐπ' ἀδείας.

ἐπὶ ἔτη τρία καὶ μῆνας ἕξ. Jesus, like His brother James (Jas. v. 17), follows Jewish tradition as to the duration of the famine. In 1 Kings xviii. 1 we are told that the rain came in the third year, which would make the drought about *two* years and a half. But ever since the persecution under Antiochus Epiphanes, three years and a half (=42 months=1260 days) had become the traditional duration of times of great calamity (Dan. vii. 25, xii. 7; Rev. xi. 2, 3, xii. 6, 14, xiii. 5). The Jews would regard "in the third year" as covering three years, and would argue that the famine must have continued for some time after the rain came.

For ἐπί *c. acc.* of duration of time ("over," *i.e.* "during"), comp. Acts xiii. 31, xix. 10; Hdt. iii. 59. 2, vi. 101. 3; Thuc. ii. 25. 4. Heb. xi. 30 is different. In accordance with common usage λιμός is here masc.; but in xv. 14 and Acts xi. 28 it is fem. acc. to what is called Doric usage, as in the Megarean of Aristoph. *Acharn.* 743. But this usage occurs elsewhere in late Greek. It perhaps passed from the Doric into the Κοινὴ Διάλεκτος: for examples see Wetst. and L. and S. *Lex.* In LXX perhaps only 1 Kings xviii. 2.

ἐπὶ πᾶσαν τὴν γῆν. Here, as in Jas. v. 17, only the land of Israel need be understood; but it is possible that in each case we have a popular hyperbole, and that the whole world is meant. Lk. xxi. 23 and Rom. ix. 28 are not quite parallel, for there the context plainly limits the meaning. Lk. xxiii. 44 is another doubtful case, and there AV. has "earth" and RV. "land." Both have "land" here.

26. The translation of εἰ μή in this and the following clauses by "but only" (RV.), *sed* (Beza), or *sed tantum*, is justifiable, because "save" (AV.) and *nisi* (Vulg.) seem to involve an absurdity which was not apparent to a Greek. It is not, however, correct to say that in such cases εἰ μή is put for ἀλλά, any more than in Mt. xx. 23 or Mk. iv. 22 it would be correct to say that ἀλλά is put for εἰ μή. Here and in Mt. xii. 4 (comp. Rom. xiv. 14; 1 Cor. vii. 17; Gal. i. 7, ii. 16) "the question is not whether εἰ μή retains its exceptive force, for this it seems always to do, but whether the exception refers to the whole clause or to the verb alone" (Lft. on Gal. i. 19): comp. Rev. xxi. 27.—In εἰς Σάρεπτα, κ.τ.λ., we perhaps have a quotation from LXX of 1 Kings xvii. 9. There, as here, the readings vary between Σιδῶνος and Σιδωνίας (*sc.* γῆς or χώρας). Here the latter is right, meaning the *territory* of Sidon, in which Sarepta lay. Zarephath (in Syriac *Tsarfah*, in Greek Σάρεφθα, Σάρεπτα, and Σέφθα) is probably represented by the modern *Sŭrafend* on the coast road between Tyre and Sidon.

27. ἐπὶ Ἐλισαίου. For this use of ἐπί with a proper name to give a date, "in the time of," comp. iii. 2; Acts xi. 28; 1 Mac. xiii. 42, xiv. 27; 2 Mac. xv. 22. The spelling Ἐλισσαῖος is not well attested (WH. ii. App. p. 159). For some of the "many lepers" comp. 2 Kings vii. 3, where we have four at the gate of Samaria. In N.T. Σύρος is the only form of the adj. that is found, viz. here and perhaps Mk. vii. 26; but Σύρος, Σύριος, and Συριακός occur elsewhere (Hdt. ii. 104. 6; Aesch. *Pers.* 83; Theophr. *C. P.* ii. 17. 3).

28. ἐπλήσθησαν πάντες θυμοῦ. See on i. 66. They see the point of His illustrations; He has been comparing them to those Jews who were judged less worthy of Divine benefits than the heathen. It is this that infuriates them, just as it infuriated the Jews at Jerusalem to be told by S. Paul that the heathen would receive the blessings which they despised (Acts xiii. 46, 50, xxii. 21, 22). Yet to this day the position remains the same; and Gentiles enjoy the Divine privileges of which the Jews have deprived themselves. His comparing Himself to such Prophets as Elijah and Elisha would add to the wrath of the Nazarenes. On the other hand, these early instances of God's special blessings being conferred upon heathen would have peculiar interest for Lk.

29. ἕως ὀφρύος τοῦ ὄρους. Tradition makes the scene of this attempt to be a precipice, varying from 80 to 300 feet in height, which exists some distance off to the S.E. of the town; and we read that "they cast Him *out* of the town and led Him *as far as* the brow," etc. But modern writers think that a much smaller precipice close at hand is the spot. Van der Velde conjectures that it has crumbled away; Conder, that it is hidden under some of the houses. Stanley says that Nazareth "is built 'upon,' that is, on the side of, 'a mountain'; but the 'brow' is not beneath, but over the town, and such a cliff as is here implied is to be found, as all modern travellers describe, in the abrupt face of the limestone rock, about 30 or 40 feet high, overhanging the Maronite Convent at the S.W. corner of the town" (*Sin. & Pal.* p. 367). So also Robinson (*Res. in Pal.* ii. pp. 325, 330), Hacket (*D.B.* ii. p. 470), and Schulz in Herzog (*PRE.*[2] x. p. 447). The ἐφ' οὗ, of course, refers to τοῦ ὄρους, not to ὀφρύος. Both AV. and RV. have "*the* brow of the hill whereon," which might easily be misunderstood. The town is on the hill, but not on the brow of it: the brow is above the modern village. Nowhere else in N.T. does ὀφρύς occur. Comp. Hom. *Il.* xx. 151; and ὀφρυόεις, *Il.* xxii. 411, and Hdt. v. 92. 10, with other instances in Wetst. *Supercilium* is similarly used: Virg. *Georg.* i. 108; Liv. xxvii. 18, xxxiv. 29.

ὥστε κατακρημνίσαι. The ὥστε is not needed (i. 22; Mt. ii. 2, xx. 28; Acts v. 31); but it expresses more clearly the result which was intended. Comp. xx. 20, where, as here, ὥστε has been altered in some texts into the simpler εἰς τό, a constr. which Lk. does not employ elsewhere. In ix. 52 the true reading is perhaps ὡς; but in Mt. x. 1, xxiv. 24, xxvii. 1 there is no doubt about the ὥστε. For κατακρημνίζω (here only in N.T.) comp. 2 Chron. xxv. 12; 2 Mac. xii. 15, xiv. 43; 4 Mac. iv. 25; Jos. *Ant.* vi. 6. 2, ix. 9. 1.

The whole attempt to put Jesus to death was perhaps an instance of the form of punishment which the Jews called the "rebel's beating," which was somewhat analogous to Lynch Law. The "rebel's beating" was administered by the people, without trial and on the spot, when anyone was caught in what seemed to be a flagrant violation of some law or tradition. Comp. the attempts to stone Jesus (Jn. viii. 59, x. 31). We have a similar attempt upon S. Paul's life (Acts xxi. 31, 32). In S. Stephen's case a formal trial seems to have ended in the "rebel's beating" (Edersh. *The Temple*, p. 43).

30. αὐτὸς δὲ διελθὼν διὰ μέσου αὐτῶν ἐπορεύετο. "But He (in contrast to this attempt), after passing through the midst of them, went His way." The addition of διὰ μέσου is for emphasis, and seems to imply that there was something miraculous in His passing through the very midst of those who were intending to slay Him, and seemed to have Him entirely in their power. They had asked for a miracle, and this was the miracle granted to them. Those who think that it was His determined look or personal majesty which saved Him, have to explain why this did not prevent them from casting Him out of the synagogue.[1] It seems better with Meyer and ancient commentators to understand a miracle dependent on the will of Jesus: comp. Jn. xviii. 6; Dan. vi. 22. Jn. viii. 59 is different: then Jesus hid Himself before escaping. For **διελθών** see on ii. 15.

ἐπορεύετο. Here used in its common signification of going on towards a goal: "He went His way" to Capernaum. And, so far as we know, He did not return to Nazareth. It had become a typical example of "His own people receiving Him not" (Jn. i. 11); and apparently it had no other opportunity (but see Edersh. *L. & T.* i. ch. xxvii.). If Mk. vi. 1–6 and Mt. xiii. 53–58 refer to a different occasion, it probably preceded this. After the attempt on His life He would not be likely to return; and, if He did return, they could hardly, after this experience of Him, ask, "Whence has this man this wisdom?" or be astonished at His teaching.

Meyer (on Mt. xiii. 53), Wieseler (*Chron. Syn.* iii. 2, Eng. tr. p. 258), Godet (*l.c.*, Eng. tr. i. p. 240), Tischendorf (*Synop. Evan.* §§ 29, 54), and others distinguish the two occasions. If with Caspari (*Chron. Int.* § 100) we identify them, then Lk. is the more full and vivid, for the others omit the text of the discourse and the attempt to kill Him. In this case Strauss may be right in supposing that Lk. has placed the incident at the beginning of the ministry, although it took place later, because he saw how typical it was of the ministry as a whole (*Leben Jesu*, p. 121, 1864). That it was this attempt on His life which made Christ change His abode from Nazareth to Capernaum is contradicted by ver. 16. "Where He had been brought up" implies that He had ceased to reside there: and from ver. 23 we infer that Capernaum had already become His headquarters. Thither His Mother and brethren had also moved, while His sisters remained at Nazareth (Mt. xiii. 56; Mk. vi. 3), very probably because they had married there.

31–44. The Stay at Capernaum: chiefly a Record of Miracles of Healing. See Wsctt. *Characteristics of the Gospel Miracles*, Macmillan, 1859; *Introduction to the Study of the Gospels*, App. E: "A Classification of the Gospel Miracles," Macmillan, 1888.

31–37. The Healing of a Demoniac in the Synagogue at Caper-

[1] Even Godet is among these. *La majesté de sa personne et la fermeté de son regard imposèrent à ces furieux. L'historie raconte plusieurs traits semblables* (i. p. 327, 3ème ed.). Better Didon: *Une force divine le gardait* (p. 312, ed. 1891). See Hase, *Gesch. Jesu*, p. 445, ed. 1891.

naum. Mk. i. 21–28. Both Lk. and Mk. place this first among Christ's miracles; whereas Mt. puts the healing of a leper first (viii. 2–4). Marcion began his mutilated edition of Lk. at this point with the words 'Ο ΘΕΟ'Σ κατῆλθεν εἰς Καφαρναούμ. The earlier portion, which teaches the humanity of Christ, he omitted, excepting the first clause of iii. 1 (Tert. *Adv. Marc.* iv. 7. 1).

31. κατῆλθεν. Nazareth is on higher ground than Capernaum, which was on the shore of the lake; and therefore "went down" or "came down" is the probable meaning. But it is possible that here and Acts xviii. 5 it means "returned," as often in class. Grk. (Hdt. iv. 4. 2, v. 30. 4; Thuc. viii. 68. 3). Excepting Jas. iii. 15, the verb occurs in N.T. only in Lk. (ix. 37 and twelve times in Acts).

Καφαρναούμ. This is the correct spelling, Caphar-Nahum, of which Καπερναούμ is a Syrian corruption (WH. ii. App. p. 160). It was the chief Jewish town, as Tiberias was the chief Roman town, of the neighbourhood. It was therefore a good centre, especially as traders from all parts frequently met there (Mk. ii. 15, iii. 20, 32, etc.). It is not mentioned in O.T., and perhaps was not founded till after the Exile. Josephus mentions it only once, viz. in his description of the lake (*B. J.* iii. 10. 7, 8), and then not as a town but as a πηγὴ γονιμωτάτη, which irrigates the neighbourhood: but there is no doubt that the Κεφαρνώμη, to which Josephus was carried, when he was thrown from his horse in a skirmish with Roman troops, is Capernaum (*Vita*, 72). The identification with the modern *Tell Hûm* (Nau, Pococke, Burckhardt, Renan,[1] Ritter, Rödiger, Ewald) is possible, but not certain. Many advocate the claims of *Khan Minyeh*, which is three miles to the south (Quaresmius, Keim, Robinson, Sepp, Stanley, Strauss, Wilson). For the chief arguments see Wilson in *D.B.*[2] i. p. 530, and in *Picturesque Palestine*, ii. p. 81; Schulz in Herzog, *RE.*[2] vii. p. 501; Keim, *Jes. of Naz.*, Eng. tr. ii. p. 369; Andrews, *Life of our Lord*, pp. 221–239, ed. 1892. The doubts about the site show how completely the woes pronounced upon the place (Mt. xi. 23) have been fulfilled. But in any case Jesus left the seclusion of the mountains for a busy mercantile centre by the lake.

πόλιν τῆς Γαλιλαίας. Lk. adds this, because this is the first time that he mentions Capernaum in his narrative. The explanation could not be made ver. 23. It is another small indication that he is writing for those who are not familiar with the geography of Palestine: comp. i. 26, ii. 4, viii. 26.

ἦν διδάσκων αὐτοὺς ἐν τοῖς σάββασιν. Some make *vv.* 31, 32 a general introduction, stating the habitual practice, of which *vv.* 33–37 gave a particular instance. In support of this they urge the analytical tense, ἦν διδάσκων, and the plur. τοῖς σάββασιν: "He used to teach them on the sabbath days." But in the parallel passage ἐδίδασκεν and ἦν διδάσκων are equivalent, and

[1] Of the *cinq petites villes dont l'humanité parlera eternellement autant que de Rome et d'Athènes*, Renan considers the identification of Magala (*Medjdel*) alone as certain. Of Capharnahum, Chorazin, Dalmanutha, and Bethsaida he says, *Il est douteux qu'on arrive jamais sur ce sol profondement dévasté, à fixer les places où l'humanité voudrait venir baiser l'empreinte de ses pieds* (*Vie de Jésus*, p. 142, ed. 1863).

apparently refer to one occasion only (note the εὐθύς, Mk. i. 22, 23): and τὰ σάββατα is often sing. in meaning (Mt. xxviii. 1; Col. ii. 16; Exod. xx. 10; Lev. xxiii. 32; Jos. *Ant.* i. 1. 1, iii. 6. 6, x. 1, Hor. *Sat.* i. 9. 69). Acts xvii. 2 is the only place in N.T. in which σάββατα is plur. in meaning, and there a numeral necessitates it, ἐπὶ σάββατα τρία; which, however, *may* mean "for three *weeks*," and not "for three *sabbaths*." Syr-Sin. here has "the sabbath days."

The Aramaic form of the word ends in a, the transliteration of which into Greek looked like a neut. plur. This idea was confirmed by the fact that Greek festivals are commonly neut. plur.: τὰ γενέσια, ἐγκαίνια, παναθήναια, κ.τ.λ. Hence σάββατα may either mean "a sabbath" or "sabbaths" or "a week." Here it is better to retain the sing. meaning, and refer the whole of 32–37 to one occasion. In N.T. σάββασιν is the usual form of the dat. plur., with σαββάτοις as *v.l.* in some authorities (in B twice, Mt. xii. 1, 12). In LXX σαββάτοις prevails. Josephus uses both.

32. ἐν ἐξουσίᾳ ἦν ὁ λόγος αὐτοῦ. This does not refer to the power which His words had over the demoniac, but to the authority with which they came home to the consciences of His hearers. The healing of the demoniac was not so much an example of this ἐξουσία as evidence that He had a Divine commission to exercise it. Lk. omits the comparison with the formal and ineffectual teaching of the scribes (Mk. i. 22; Mt. vii. 29).

The ἐν means "clothed in, invested with" (i. 17, iv. 36, xi. 15, 18, 19, 20, xx. 2, 8; 1 Cor. ii. 4; Eph. vi. 2; 2 Thes. ii. 9). This use of ἐν is freq. in late Grk. Green, *Gram. of N.T.* p. 206.

33. ἐν τῇ συναγωγῇ. "In *the* synagogue" in which He was teaching on that sabbath; which confirms the view that ver. 31 refers to a particular occasion. We have already been told that it was His practice to teach in the synagogues. But "in the synagogue" may mean in the only one which Capernaum possessed (vii. 5).

ἔχων πνεῦμα δαιμονίου ἀκαθάρτου. The phrase is unique, and the exact analysis of it is uncertain. The gen. may be of apposition (ii. 41, xxii. 1; Jn. ii. 21, xi. 13, xiii. 1), or of quality (see on ver. 22), or of possession, *i.e.* an influence which belonged to an unclean demon (Rev. xvi. 14). As to the Evangelists' use of the epithet ἀκάθαρτον, strange mistakes have been made. Wordsworth inaccurately says, "Both St. Mark and St. Luke, writing for Gentiles, add the word ἀκάθαρτον to δαιμόνιον, which St. Matthew, writing to Jews (for whom it was not necessary), *never* does." Alford in correcting him is himself inaccurate. He says, "The real fact is, that St. Mark uses the word δαιμόνιον thirteen times, and *never* adds the epithet ἀκάθαρτον to it (his word here is πνεῦμα only); St. Luke, eighteen times, and only adds it this once. So much for the accuracy of the data on which inferences of this kind are founded." Edersheim is still more inaccurate in his statement of the facts (*L. & T.* i. p. 479 n). Farrar has the strange misstatement that "the word 'unclean' is peculiar to St. Luke, who writes for Gentiles." It occurs in Mt., Paul, and Apoc., as well as Mk. The facts are these. Mt. uses δαιμόνιον ten times, and has ἀκάθαρτον twice as an epithet of πνεῦμα. Mk. has δαιμόνιον thirteen times, and ἀκάθαρτον eleven times as an epithet of πνεῦμα. Lk. in the Gospel has δαιμόνιον twenty-three times, with ἀκάθαρτον as an epithet, once of δαιμόνιον, and five times of πνεῦμα; and with πονηρόν twice as an epithet of πνεῦμα. In the Acts he has δαιμόνιον once; and uses ἀκάθαρτον twice, and πονηρόν four times, as an epithet of πνεῦμα. The fact, therefore, remains, that the two Evangelists who wrote for Gentiles (to whom demons or spirits were indifferent) add a distinctive epithet much more often than the one who wrote for Jews (who distinguished evil spirits from good). Moreover, both Mk. and Lk. add this epithet the very first time that they mention these beings (Mk. i. 23; Lk. iv. 33); whereas Mt. mentions them several times (vii. 22, viii. 16, ix. 33, 34) before he adds the ἀκάθαρτον (x. 1). In this passage Lk. and Mk. describe the fact of possession in opposite ways. Here the man has the unclean spirit. There he is in the unclean spirit's power, ἐν πνεύματι ἀκαθάρτῳ: with which we may compare the expression of Josephus, τοὺς ὑπὸ τῶν δαιμονίων λαμβανομένους (*Ant.* viii. 2. 5). Similarly, we say of a man that "he is out of his mind," or that "his mind is gone" out of him. That a man thus afflicted should be in the synagogue is surprising. He may have come in unobserved; or his malady may have been dormant so long as to have seemed to be cured. The presence of "the Holy One of God" provokes a crisis. For ἀνέκραξεν comp. Josh. vi. 5; 1 Sam. iv. 5; and for φωνῇ μεγάλῃ see on i. 42. *D.C.G.* art. "Demon."

34. Ἔα. Probably not the imperative of ἐάω, "Let alone, leave me in peace," but an interjection of anger or dismay; common in Attic poetry, but rare in prose (Aesch. *P. V.* 298, 688; Eur. *Hec.* 501; Plato, *Prot.* 314 D). Here only in N.T. Comp. Job iv. 19?, xv. 16, xix. 5, xxv. 6. Fritzsche on Mk. i. 24 (where the word is an interpolation) and L. and S. *Lex.* regard the imperative as the origin of the interjection, which does not seem probable.

τί ἡμῖν καὶ σοί; Not "What have we to contend about?" a meaning which the phrase has nowhere in N.T. and perhaps only once, if at all, in O.T. (2 Chron. xxxv. 21), but "What have we in common?" Comp. viii. 28; Mt. viii. 29; Mk. i. 24; Jn. ii. 4; Judg. xi. 12; 1 Kings xvii. 18; 2 Kings iii. 13; 2 Sam. xvi. 10; 1 Esdr. i. 26; Epict. *Diss.* i. 1. 16, i. 27. 13, ii. 9. 16.

Ἰησοῦ Ναζαρηνέ. This form of the adjective is found xxiv. 19; Mk. i. 24, x. 47, xiv. 67, xvi. 6; but not in Mt. or Jn. or Acts. Its appearance here is no proof that Lk. is borrowing from Mk. **Ναζωραῖος** occurs Lk. xviii.

37; Mt. ii. 23, xxvi. 71; Jn. xviii. 5, 7, xix. 19; Acts ii. 22, iii. 6, iv. 10, vi. 14, xxii. 8, xxvi. 9; but not in Mk. The adjective, esp. Ναζωραῖος, which is used in the title on the cross, sometimes has a tinge of contempt; and with the article it may be rendered "the Nazarene." Hence the early Christians were contemptuously called "the Nazarenes" (Acts xxiv. 5). Contrast ὁ ἀπὸ Ναζαρέτ (Mt. xxi. 11; Mk. i. 9; Jn. i. 46; Acts x. 38), which is a mere statement of fact. It is worth noting that this demoniac, who is a Jew, addresses Jesus as "of Nazareth," which the Gerasene, who was *possibly* a heathen, does not do (viii. 28).

ἦλθες ἀπολέσαι ἡμᾶς; The ἡμᾶς and the preceding ἡμῖν probably do not include the man, but rather other evil spirits. *Communem inter se causam habent dæmonia* (Beng.). It seems to be idle to speculate as to the meaning of ἀπολέσαι: apparently it is the same as εἰς τὴν ἄβυσσον ἀπελθεῖν (viii. 31).

οἶδά σε τίς εἶ, ὁ ἅγιος τοῦ Θεοῦ. In Mk. οἴδαμεν (?), which is more in harmony with ἡμῖν and ἡμᾶς. Godet remarks that ὁ ἅγιος τοῦ Θεοῦ explains the knowledge. It was instinctive, and therefore οἶδα is more suitable than γινώσκω. *L'antipathie n'est pas moins clairvoyante que la sympathie.* In the unique holiness of Jesus the evil spirit felt an essentially hostile power. The expression ὁ ἅγιος τοῦ Θεοῦ occurs in the parallel in Mk. and Jn. vi. 69; but nowhere else: comp. Acts iv. 27; 1 Jn. ii. 20; Rev. iii. 7. It may mean either "consecrated *to* God" or "consecrated *by* God." In a lower sense priests and Prophets are called ἅγιοι τοῦ Θεοῦ or Κυρίου (Ps. cvi. 16). It was not in flattery (*male adulans*, as Tertullian says) that the evil spirit thus addressed Him, but in horror. From the Holy One he could expect nothing but destruction (Jas. ii. 19; comp. Mt. viii. 29).

35. ἐπετίμησεν αὐτῷ. "He rebuked the demon" who had used the man as his mouth-piece. The verb is often used of rebuking *violence* (ver. 41, viii. 24, ix. 42; Mt. viii. 26, xvii. 18; Mk. iv. 39; Jude 9); yet must not on that account be rendered "restrain" (Fritzsche on Mt. viii. 26, p. 325).

In N.T. ἐπιτιμάω has no other meaning than "rebuke"; but in class. Grk. it means—1. "lay a value on, *rate*"; 2. "lay a penalty on, sentence"; 3. "chide, *rate*, rebuke." But while there is a real connexion between the first and third meanings of the Greek verb, in English we have a mere accident of language: "rate" = "value" is a different word from "rate" = "scold." Note that Christ required no faith from demoniacs.

Φιμώθητι. Lit. "Stop thy mouth with a φιμός, be muzzled": used literally 1 Cor. ix. 9; 1 Tim. v. 18; and as here, Mt. xxii. 12; Mk. i. 25, iv. 39; Jos. *B. J.* i. 22. 3. The peculiar infin. φιμοῖν occurs 1 Pet. ii. 15. Comp. ἀποδεκατοῖν (Heb. vii. 5); κατασκηνοῖν (Mt. xiii. 32; Mk. iv. 32). The verb is probably a vernacular word: it is not found between Aristoph. (*Nub.* 592) and LXX (Kennedy, *Sources of N.T. Grk.* p. 41).

καὶ ἐξελθε ἀπ' αὐτοῦ. This is the true reading. Other writers commonly have ἐξέρχομαι ἐκ; but Lk. prefers ἐξέρχομαι ἀπό (ver. 41, v. 8, viii. 2, 29, 33, 35, 38, ix. 5, xi. 24, etc.).

ῥίψαν αὐτὸν . . . μηδὲν βλάψαν αὐτόν. "Having thrown him" down in convulsions (σπαράξαν Mk.) . . . without (as one might have expected) having injured him at all." With οὐδὲν βλάψαν we should have had a mere statement of fact. But in N.T. we commonly have μή with participles: comp. xi. 24, xii. 47, and see Win. lv. 5. β, p. 607. For μηδὲν βλάψαν Mk. has φωνῆσαν φωνῇ μεγάλῃ. It was the convulsions and the loud cry which made the spectators suppose that the man had been injured. The malice of the demon made the healing of the man as painful as possible. Hobart classes both ῥίπτειν and βλάπτειν as medical words, the one being used of convulsions, the latter of injury to the system (*Med. Lang. of Lk.* p. 2).

36. ἐγένετο θάμβος. Mk. has ἐθαμβήθησαν; but Lk. is fond of these periphrases with γίνομαι (i. 65, vi. 49, viii. 17, xii. 40, xiii. 2, 4, xviii. 23, etc.): see on iii. 22. The word expresses amazement akin to terror, and the subst. is peculiar to Lk. (v. 9; Acts iii. 10). Just as Christ's doctrine amazed them in comparison with the formalism of the scribes, so His authority over demons in comparison with the attempts of the exorcists: all the more so, because a single word sufficed for Him, whereas the exorcists used incantations, charms, and much superstitious ceremonial (Tob. viii. 1–3; Jos. *Ant.* viii. 2. 5; Justin, *Apol.* ii. 6; *Try.* lxxxv.).

τίς ὁ λόγος οὗτος. Not, *Quid hoc rei est?* "What manner a thinge is this?" (Beza, Luth. Tyn. Cran. Grotius), but *Quod est hoc verbum?* "What is this word?" (Vulg. Wic. Rhem. RV.). It is doubtful whether in N.T. λόγος has the meaning of "event, occurrence, deed": but comp. i. 4 and Mk. i. 45. Whether λόγος is here to be confined to the command given to the demon, or includes the previous teaching (ver. 32), is uncertain. Mk. i. 27 is in favour of the latter. In this case we have an ambiguous ὅτι to deal with; and once more "because" or "for" is more probable than "that" (see on i. 45). But if "that" be adopted, ὁ λόγος has the more limited meaning: "What is this word, that with authority?" etc.

ἐν ἐξουσίᾳ καὶ δυνάμει. ἐξουσίᾳ, *cui non potest contradici*; δυνάμει, *cui non potest resisti* (Beng.). Mk. has κατ' ἐξουσίαν only. The beloved physician is fond of δύναμις, esp. in the sense of "inherent power of *healing*" (v. 17, vi. 19, viii. 46, ix. 1; Acts iii. 12, iv. 7, vi. 8). Mk. has it only once in this sense (v. 30), and Mt. not at all. The plural in the sense of "manifestations of power, miracles" (x. 13, xix. 37), is freq. in Mt. and Mk. See on Rom. i. 16.

37. ἐξεπορεύετο ἦχος περὶ αὐτοῦ. In these sections attention is often directed to the impression which Jesus made on His audiences (*vv.* 20, 22, 32, 36, v. 26), and to the fame which spread abroad respecting Him (*vv.* 14, 15, 37, 40, v. 15, 17). Ἦχος (ὁ) occurs only here, Acts ii. 2, and Heb. xii. 19. In xxi. 25, ἤχους may be gen. of either ἡ ἠχώ or τὸ ἦχος. But the existence of τὸ ἦχος is doubtful. The more classical word is ἡ ἠχή, of which ὁ ἦχος is a later form. Hobart classes it as a medical word, esp. for noises in the ears or the head (p. 64).

As already stated, this healing of a demoniac is recorded by Mk., but not by Mt. Ebrard and Holtzmann would have us believe that it is to compensate for this omission that Mt. gives two demoniacs among the Gadarenes, where Mk. and Lk. have only one.

In considering the question of *demoniacal possession* we must never lose sight of the indisputable fact, that our sources of information clearly, consistently, and repeatedly represent Christ as healing demoniacs by commanding demons to depart out of the afflicted persons. *The Synoptic Gospels uniformly state that Jesus went through the form of casting out demons.*

If the demons were there, and Christ expelled them and set their victims free, there is nothing to explain: the narrative is in harmony with the facts.

If the demons were not there, and demoniacal possession is a superstition, we must choose between three hypotheses.

1. Jesus did not employ this method of healing those who were believed to be possessed, but the Evangelists have erroneously attributed it to Him.

2. Jesus did employ this method and went through the form of casting out demons, although He knew that there were no demons there to be cast out.

3. Jesus did employ this method and went through the form of casting out demons, because in this matter He shared the erroneous belief of His contemporaries.

On the whole subject consult articles in *D.B.*², Schaff-Herzog, *Ency. Brit.* on "Demoniacs," "Demons," "Demonology"; Trench, *Miracles*, No. 5; Caldwell, *Contemp. Rev.* Feb. 1876, vol. xxvii. pp. 369 ff. No explanation is satisfactory which does not account for the uniform and repeated testimony of the Evangelists.

38, 39. The Healing of Peter's Mother-in-law. Mk. i. 30.

It is quite beyond doubt that the relationship expressed by πενθερά is either "wife's mother" or "husband's mother" (xii. 53; Mt. viii. 14, x. 35; Mk. i. 30; Ruth i. 14, ii. 11, 18, 19, 23; Mic. vii. 6; Dem. Plut. Lucian). So also πενθερός is either "wife's father" or "husband's father" (Jn. xviii. 13; Gen. xxxviii. 13, 25; Judg. i. 16; 1 Sam. iv. 19, 21). But for "wife's father" the more indefinite γαμβρός ("a relation by marriage") is freq. in LXX (Exod. iii. 1, iv. 18; Num. x. 29; Judg. iv. 11, xix. 4, 7, 9). In Greek there is a distinct term for "stepmother," viz. the very common word μητρυιά (Hom. Hes. Hdt. Æsch. Plat. Plut.); and if Lk. had intended to designate the second wife of Peter's father, he would have used this term. That he should have ignored a word in common use which would express his meaning, and employ another word which has quite a different meaning, is incredible. That Peter was married is clear from 1 Cor. ix. 5. Clement of Alexandria says that Peter's wife helped him in ministering to women,—an apostolic anticipation of Zenana missions (*Strom.* iii. 6, p. 536, ed. Potter). He also states that Peter and Philip had children, and that Philip gave his daughters in marriage (*ibid.* p. 535, ed. Potter, quoted Eus. *H. E.* iii. 30. 1); but he gives no names. It is remarkable that nothing is known of any children of any one Apostle. This is the first mention of Peter by Lk., who treats him as a person too well known to need introduction. For other miracles of mercy on the sabbath see on xiv. 1.

38. Ἀναστὰς δὲ ἀπὸ τῆς συναγωγῆς. This may refer to Christ's rising from His seat; but it is more natural to understand it of His leaving the synagogue. The verb is used where no sitting or lying is presupposed, and means no more than preparation for departure (i. 39, xv. 18, 20, xxiii. 1; Acts x. 20, xxii. 10): see on i. 39. Mk. has ἐξελθόντες, the plur. including Simon and Andrew, James and John. Neither Lk. nor Mt. mention the presence of disciples, but Peter, and perhaps Andrew, may be understood among those who ἠρώτησαν αὐτὸν περὶ αὐτῆς.

συνεχομένη πυρετῷ μεγάλῳ. Perhaps all three words are medical, and certainly συνέχομαι occurs three times as often in Lk. as in the rest of N.T. Galen states that fevers were distinguished as "great" and "slight," μεγάλοι and σμικροί (Hobart, p. 3). Comp. Plat. *Gorg.* 512 A. Note the analytical tense.

39. ἐπιστὰς ἐπάνω αὐτῆς ἐπετίμησεν. Instead of this both Mt. and Mk. state that He touched her hand. *Proximus accessus ostendebat, virtuti Jesu cedere morbum, neque ullum corpori ejus a morbo imminere periculum* (Beng.). The ἐπετίμησεν of ver. 35 does not show that the use of the same word here is meant to imply that the fever is regarded as a personal agent. But comp. xiii. 11, 16; Mk. ix. 17, 23. The ἀφῆκεν, which is in all three narratives, harmonizes with either view In any case this unusual mode of healing would interest and impress a physician; and Lk. alone notices the suddenness with which her strength returned. For παραχρῆμα see on v. 25. Syr-Sin. omits the standing over her.

διηκόνει αὐτοῖς. Mt. has αὐτῷ: the αὐτοῖς includes the disciples and others present. Her being able to minister to them proves the completeness of the cure. Recovery from fever is commonly attended by great weakness. And this seems to be fatal to the view of B. Weiss, that Christ's cures were "momentary effects produced by His touch, which, although the result was absolutely certain, yet merely began a healing process that was completed in a perfectly natural way." What is gained by such an hypothesis?

The Attic form of the imperf. of διακονέω is ἐδιακόνουν; but διηκόνουν is the reading of the MSS. in Eur. *Cycl.* 406 (Veitch, *s.v.*). Comp. viii. 3; Mt. iv. 11, viii. 15; Mk. i. 13, 31; Jn. xii. 2; 1 Pet. i. 12.

40, 41. Numerous Healings in the Evening. *Nous rencontrons ici un de ces moments dans la vie du Seigneur où la puissance miraculeuse se déployait avec une richesse particulière*: vi. 19" (Godet, i. p. 339). Comp. Mt. viii. 16, 17; Mk. i. 32–34. The healing of the demoniac (ver. 35), and of Peter's mother-in-law, had proved that He could heal diseases both of mind and body. All three note the two kinds of healing; but "the physician separates the two with special distinctness, and lends no support to the view that possession is merely a physical disorder."

40. Δύνοντος δὲ τοῦ ἡλίου. Mt. has Ὀψίας δὲ γενομένης, while Mk. has Ὀψίας δὲ γενομένης, ὅτε ἔδυσεν ὁ ἥλιος. We infer that here Mk. gives us the whole expression in the original tradition, of which all three make use; and that Mt. uses one half and Lk. the other half of it. See v. 13, xxii. 34, xxiii. 38, for similar cases. Some infer that Mk. has combined the phrases used by the other two, and therefore must have written last of the three. But an analysis of the passages which all three have in common shows that this is incredible. The literary skill required for combining two narratives, without adding much new material, would be immense; and Mk. does not possess it. It is much simpler to suppose that Mk. often gives the original tradition in full, and that the other two each give portions of it, and sometimes different portions. See E. A. Abbott, *Ency. Brit.* 9th ed. art. "Gospels," and Abbott and Rushbrooke, *The Common Tradition of the Syn. Gosp.* p. x.

Δύνοντος. "When the sun *was setting*," or "*ere* the sun *was set*," as the hymn gives it.[1] The eagerness of the people was such that the very moment the sabbath was over they began to move the sick: comp. Jn. v. 10. Note Lk.'s favourite ἅπαντες.

ἑνὶ ἑκάστῳ αὐτῶν τὰς χεῖρας ἐπιτιθείς. Lk. alone preserves this graphic detail, which emphasizes the laborious solicitude of the work. *Sic singuli penitius commoti sunt ad fidem* (Beng.). It does not apply to the demoniacs, who were healed λόγῳ, as Mt. states.

The action is a generally recognized symbol of *transmission*, especially in conferring a blessing (Gen. xlviii. 14; Lev. ix. 22, 23; Mk. x. 16). It is also used to symbolize the transmission of guilt (Lev. i. 4, iii. 2, viii. 14, xvi. 21, 22). The statement that "our Lord healed at first by laying on of hands, but gradually passed over to the exclusive use of the word of power, in order that He might not encourage the popular idea that there was a necessary connexion between the laying on of hands and the cure," is not confirmed by Scripture. The nobleman's son and the man at Bethesda were healed by a word (Jn. iv. 50, v. 8); Malchus, by a touch. There was no necessity to use either word or touch. He could heal by an act of will, and at a distance from His person (vii. 10, xvii. 14; Jn. iv. 50). But He more often used means, possibly to aid the faith of those who needed healing (xiii. 13, xiv. 4, Mt. viii. 3, ix. 29; Mk. vii. 33, viii. 23, 25; Jn. ix. 6: comp. Mk. v. 23, 28, 41, vii. 32, viii. 22). The fact that Jesus commonly used some action in healing made the Jews the more irate at His healing on the sabbath. Excepting Acts xvii. 25, θεραπεύω in N.T. is always "heal, cure," not merely "serve, take care of." Like *colere*, it is used of service both to God and to men; and like *curare*, it is both "to care for" and "to cure." The imperfects, ἐθεράπευεν and ἐξήρχετο, mark the continuance and repetition of the actions.

41. ἐξήρχετο δὲ καὶ δαιμόνια ἀπὸ πολλῶν. "But demons also"

[1] The form δύνω seems to be Ionic, but occurs once or twice in Attic prose (Veitch, *s.v.*). Except ἔδυσεν or ἔδυ in Mk. i. 32, the word does not occur again in N.T. It is freq. in LXX (Judg. xiv. 18; 2 Sam. ii. 24; 1 Kings xxii. 36; 2 Chron. xviii. 34, etc.). It means "sink into, enter," πόντον or the like being expressed or understood. Lk. never uses the unclassical ὀψία (ix. 12, xxii. 14, xxiii. 54, xxiv. 29), which occurs often in Mt. and Mk. and twice in Jn.

(as well as diseases) "came out of many." For δὲ καί see on III. 9, and for ἐξέρχεσθαι ἀπό see on ver. 35: both are characteristic of Lk. He alone mentions the κράζειν of the demons. There is not much difference between ὁ υἱὸς τοῦ Θεοῦ here and ὁ ἅγιος τοῦ Θεοῦ in ver. 34. In both cases it is the presence of Divine holiness which is felt and proclaimed. Phil. ii. 10 is here not to the point; for καταχθόνια there probably does not mean devils.

οὐκ εἴα αὐτὰ λαλεῖν, ὅτι. "He suffered them not to speak, because." Not, "suffered them not to say that"; which would require λέγειν. In N.T. λαλεῖν and λέγειν are never confused; not even Rom. xv. 18; 2 Cor. xi. 17; 1 Thes. i. 8. Excepting Mt. xxiv. 43 and 1 Cor. x. 13, ἐάω is peculiar to Lk. in N.T. (xxii. 51, Acts xiv. 16, xvi. 7, xix. 30, xxiii. 32, xxvii. 32, 40, xxviii. 4); and εἴων is the usual form of imperf.

Godet's suggestion, that the demons wished to compromise Jesus by exciting a dangerous enthusiasm among the people, or to create a belief that there was a bond of connexion between their work and His, is gratuitous. Their cries are more like involuntary exclamations of dismay. That Jesus should not allow them to make Him known was natural, although Strauss condemns it as inconsistent. *Nec tempus erat, nec hi præcones* (Beng. on Mk. iii. 12). "It was not meet that unclean demons should usurp the glory of the apostolic office" (Cyril Alex.). Jesus had rejected the offered assistance of the evil one in the wilderness, and could not desire to be proclaimed as the Messiah by his ministers. Moreover, while the national ideas respecting the Messiah remained so erroneous, the time for such proclamation had not yet come. Comp. Jn. vi. 15.

42, 43. The Multitude's Pursuit of Him. Comp. Mk. i. 35-39. Although Lk. has some features which Mk. has not, the latter's account is more like that of an eye-witness.

42. Γενομένης δὲ ἡμέρας. See on vi. 13. Mk. has the strong expression πρωῒ ἔννυχα λίαν. It was so early that it was still like night. This shows His anxiety to escape the multitude and secure time for refreshment of His spiritual nature by converse with God: Mk. adds κἀκεῖ προσηύχετο. Jesus had probably passed the night in Simon's house; and for οἱ ὄχλοι Mk has Σίμων καὶ οἱ μετ' αὐτοῦ, for as yet Jesus had no fixed disciples. Peter in telling Mk. of the incident would say, "*We* went after Him."

οἱ ὄχλοι ἐπεζήτουν αὐτόν. "The multitudes kept seeking for Him." The ἐπι- marks the direction of the search: comp. ἐπέδοθη (ver. 17). They wanted more of His teaching and of His miraculous cures. See on xi. 29. But neither this nor the πολλῶν in ver. 41 proves that there had not been time to heal all who came the previous evening. Would He have sent any empty away? Lk. is fond of recording the eagerness of the people to come to Christ (v. 1, 19, vi. 19, viii. 19, 40, xii. 1, xxi. 38: comp. xix. 3 and xxiii. 8).

ἦλθον ἕως αὐτοῦ, καὶ κατεῖχον αὐτὸν τοῦ μὴ πορεύεσθαι ἀπ' αὐτῶν.

They did not leave off seeking *until* they reached Him, and they *tried* to stay Him from going away from them.

This use of ἕως with a person is not classical: comp. ἕως ἡμῶν (Acts ix. 38) and ἕως τοῦ βασιλέως (1 Mac. iii. 26). Of place (iv. 29, x. 15) or of time (xxiii. 44) ἕως is common enough.

With κατεῖχον (imperf. of attempted or intended action) comp. ἐκάλουν (i. 59). The τοῦ μὴ πορεύεσθαι is not Lk.'s favourite construction to express purposes or result (see on i. 74), but the gen. after a verb of detention or prevention: comp. Rom. xv. 22. For the apparently superfluous negative comp. xxiv. 16; Acts x. 47, xiv. 18, xx. 27. Win. xliv. 4. b, p. 409; lxv. 2. β, p. 755. Blass, *Gr.* p. 250.

43. Καὶ ταῖς ἑτέραις πόλεσιν. Placed first for emphasis. "To *the* other cities also (as well as to Capernaum) I must preach the good tidings." It is a rebuke to them for wishing to monopolize Him. It is not a rebuke for interrupting His preaching by requiring Him to work miracles. There is no evidence that He ever regarded these works of mercy as an interruption of His ministry, or as an unworthy lowering of it. On the contrary, they were an essential part of it; not as evidence of His Messiahship, but as the natural work of the great Healer of body and soul. They were, moreover, an important element in His teaching, for His miracles were parables. As evidence they did not prove His Messiahship, and He did not greatly value the faith which was produced by them (Jn. ii. 23, 24). He Himself regarded them as merely auxiliary (Jn. xiv. 11). He warned His disciples that false Christs and false prophets would work miracles (Mk. xiii. 22), just as the O.T. had warned the Jews that a Prophet was not to be believed simply because he worked miracles (Deut. xiii. 1–3). And, as a matter of fact, Christ's miracles did not convince the Jews (Jn. xii. 37). Some thought that He was a Prophet (vii. 16, ix. 8, 19; Mt. xxi. 11; Jn. ix. 17), a view taken even by His disciples after the crucifixion (xxiv. 19); while others attributed His miracles to Satanic agency (Mt. xii. 24). On the other hand, the Baptist, although he wrought no miracles, was thought to be the Messiah (see on iii. 15). The saying here recorded does not mean, therefore, "You are mistaking My work. I came to preach the good tidings, not to do works of healing": but, "You are selfish in your desires. I came to preach the good tidings and to do works of healing to all, and not to a favoured few." For **εὐαγγελίσασθαι** see on ii. 10.

δεῖ. For the second time (ii. 49) Christ uses this word respecting His own conduct. Comp. ix. 22, xiii. 33, xvii. 25, xix. 5, xxii. 37, xxiv. 7, 26, 44. His work and His sufferings are ordered by Divine decree. The word is thus used of Christ throughout N.T. (Acts iii. 21, xvii. 3; 1 Cor. xv. 25).

τὴν βασιλείαν τοῦ Θεοῦ. This is Lk.'s first use of this frequent expression (vi. 20, vii. 28, viii. 1, 10, etc.), which Jn. employs twice (iii. 3, 5), Mt. four times (xii. 28, xix. 24, xxi. 31, 43), Mk. often. For its import see Ewald, *Hist. of Israel*, vi., Eng. tr. pp. 201–210; Schaff's *Herzog*, art. "Kingdom of God"; Edersh. *L. & T.* i. pp. 265–270. The ἐπὶ τοῦτο refers to the whole of what precedes: "For this end," viz. "to preach the good tidings everywhere in the land." For this use of ἐπί comp. xxiii. 48 and Mt. xxvi. 50. It is quite classical (Xen. *Anab.* ii. 5. 22, vii. 8. 4). For ἀπεστάλην see on ver. 18. The evidence for it (א B C D L X) as against ἀπέσταλμαι (A Q R) is overwhelming. Yet Godet says *on peut hésiter*. It refers to the mission from the Father, as does the ἐξῆλθον of Mk. But it is possible to give the latter the inadequate interpretation of leaving the house at Capernaum.

44. Καὶ ἦν κηρύσσων εἰς τὰς συναγωγὰς τῆς Ἰουδαίας. This statement forms a conclusion to the section (14–44); and the analytical tense indicates that what is stated continued for some time.

Both Lk. and Mk. have εἰς τὰς συναγωγάς, which in both cases has been altered into the easier ἐν ταῖς συναγωγαῖς. The εἰς may be explained as a pregn. constr., "He went into the synagogues and preached there" or as expressing the motion or direction of the preaching (Mk. iv. 15; Jn. viii. 26). Comp. ἐς τὸν δῆμον ταῦτα λέγωσιν (Thuc. v. 45. 1). It seems probable that the reading Ἰουδαίας (א B C L Q R) is the original one, which has been corrected to Γαλιλαίας (A D X Γ Δ Λ Π) on account of its difficulty. But, as in i. 5 and vii. 17, Judæa may here mean the whole country of the Jews, Palestine. Lk. often uses Ἰουδαία in this sense (xxiii. 5; Acts ii. 9, x. 37, xi. 1, 29, xxvi. 20; comp. Gal. i. 22). Classic writers use the term in much the same manner. Strabo means by it all the region from Lebanon southwards. Syr-Sin. has "of Judæa."

V. 1–VI. 11. *From the Call of the first Disciples to the Nomination of the Twelve.*

This section presents a symmetrical arrangement, which possibly is intentional. The call of a leading disciple (1–11) is followed by two healings which provoke controversy (12–16, 17–26); and then the call of another leading disciple (27–39) is followed by two incidents on the sabbath, which again provoke controversy (vi. 1–5, 6–11).

V. 1–11. The call of Simon. In Mt. iv. 18–22 and Mk. i. 16–20 the narrative is the call of Simon and Andrew, and of James and John. Here Andrew is not mentioned. And although all obey the call (ver. 11), yet Simon alone is addressed (*vv.* 4, 10). But the identity of this incident with that narrated by Mt. and Mk. can neither be affirmed nor denied with certainty. In Mt. and Mk. the disciples are fishing; here they are washing their nets before putting them away. The important point is that in all narratives those called are at work. Similarly, Levi is called from his business. It would seem as if none of the Twelve were called when idle.

1. Ἐγένετο δέ. See detached note at the end of ch. i. For **τὸν ὄχλον** see on xi. 29; for *ἐν τῷ τὸν ὄχλον ἐπικεῖσθαι* see on iii. 21; for **τὸν λόγον τοῦ Θεοῦ** see on viii. 11; for **καί** introducing the apodosis see on ii. 21; and for **καὶ αὐτός** see on ver. 14. All these points, with the analytical **ἦν ἑστώς** (i. 7, 10, 20, 21, etc.), are characteristic of Lk. Not often do we find so many marks of his style in so small a compass. Comp. viii. 22, 37, 40, 41. For the popular desire to behold Christ see on iv. 42. With **ἐπικεῖσθαι** comp. xxiii. 23; Acts xxvii. 20; 1 Cor. ix. 16; Heb. ix. 10; Jos. *Ant.* xx. 5. 3. It is used in a literal sense Jn. xi. 38, xxi. 9. Here it is mainly figurative, but it includes the notion of physical pressure. The *αὐτός* distinguishes Jesus from the *ὄχλος*: comp. iv. 15, 30.

παρὰ τὴν λίμνην Γεννησαρέτ. With characteristic accuracy Lk. never calls it a sea, while the others never call it a lake. Except in Rev. of the "lake of fire," *λίμνη* in N.T. is peculiar to Lk. When he uses *θάλασσα*, he means sea in the ordinary sense (xvii. 2, 6, xxi. 25; Acts iv. 24, etc.).

In **AV.** of 1611 both here and Mk. vi. 53 the name appears as "Genesareth," following the spelling of the Vulgate; but in Mt. xiv. 34 as "Genesaret." The printers have corrected this to "Gennesaret" in all three places. *Γεννησαρέτ* is the orthography of the best MSS. in all three places. Josephus writes both *λίμνη Γεννησαρῖτις* (*Ant.* xviii. 2. 1) and *λίμνη Γεννησάρ* (*B. J.* iii. 10. 7). 1 Mac. xi. 67 we have *τὸ ὕδωρ τοῦ Γεννησάρ*. But in O.T. the lake is called Θάλασσα Χενέρεθ (Num. xxxiv. 11?; Josh. xii. 3) from a town of that name near to it (Josh. xix. 35). Josephus contrasts its fertility with the barrenness of the lower lake in the Jordan valley (*B. J.* iv. 8. 2): the one is the "Sea of Life," the other the "Sea of Death." See Stanley's fine description of "the most sacred sheet of water that this earth contains" (*Sin. & Pal.* pp. 368–378); Farrar, *Life of Christ*, i. pp. 175–182; Conder, *D.B.*[2] art. "Gennesaret."

For *παρά c. acc.* after a verb of rest comp. xviii. 35; Acts x. 6, 32; Heb. xi. 12: Xen. *Anab.* iii. 5. 1, vii. 2. 11.

With *ἦν ἑστώς* (which is the apodosis of *ἐγένετο*), *καὶ εἶδεν* is to be joined: "It came to pass that He was standing, and He saw." It is very clumsy to make *καὶ αὐτὸς ἦν ἑστώς* parenthetical, and take *καὶ εἶδεν* as the apodosis of *ἐγένετο*.

2. οἱ δὲ ἁλεεῖς. "But the sea-folk" (*ἅλς*) or "fishermen." It is one of many Homeric words which seem to have gone out of use and then to have reappeared in late Greek. Fishing in the lake has now almost ceased. The Arabs dislike the water. The washing of the nets was preparatory to hanging them up to dry. As distinct from *νίπτω*, which is used of washing part of the human body, and λούω, which is used of washing the whole of it, **πλύνω** is used of washing inanimate objects (Rev. vii. 14, xxii. 14; Gen. xlix. 11; Exod. xix. 10). In Lev. xv. 11 all three words are used with exactly this difference of meaning. Trench, *Syn.* xlv.

τὰ δίκτυα. The most general term for nets of all kinds, of which ἀμφίβληστρον (Mt. iv. 18) and σαγήνη (Mt. xiii. 47) are special varieties. Trench, *Syn.* lxiv.; *D.B.* art. "Net."

3. ἐπαναγαγεῖν. The correct word for "putting off to sea" (2 Mac. xii. 4?; Xen. *Hellen.* vi. 2. 28): elsewhere in N.T. only Mt. xxi. 18 in the sense of "return." For the double preposition comp. ἐπανέρχομαι (x. 35, xix. 15) and ἐπαναπαύω (x. 6). Christ uses Peter's boat as a pulpit, whence to throw the net of the Gospel over His hearers. We have a similar scene Mk. iv. 1, and in both cases He sits to teach, as in the synagogue at Nazareth. Peter was probably steering, and therefore both before and after the sermon he is addressed as to the placing of the boat. But the letting down of the nets required more than one person, and hence the change to the plural (χαλάσατε). *Non statim promittit Dominus capturam: explorat prius obsequia Simonis* (Beng.).

5. Ἐπιστάτα. Lk. alone uses ἐπιστάτης (viii. 24, 45, ix. 33, 49, xvii 13), and always in addresses to Christ. He never uses Ῥαββεί, which is common in the other Gospels, esp. in Jn., but would not be so intelligible to Gentiles. The two words are not synonymous, ἐπιστάτης implying authority of any kind, and not merely that of a teacher. Here it is used of one who has a right to give orders.

δι᾽ ὅλης νυκτὸς κοπιάσαντες. Through the whole of the best time for fishing they had toiled fruitlessly. Only in bibl. Grk. has κοπιάω the meaning of "work with much effort, toil wearisomely" (xii. 27; Acts xx. 35; Mt. vi. 28; Josh. xxiv. 13, etc.). The original meaning is "become exhausted, grow weary" (Jn. iv. 6). Clem. Alex. quotes a letter of Epicurus, Μήτε νέος τις ὢν μελλέτω φιλοσοφεῖν, μήτε γέρων ὑπάρχων κοπιάτω φιλοσοφῶν (*Strom.* iv. 8, p. 594, ed. Potter).

ἐπὶ δὲ τῷ ῥήματί σου χαλάσω τὰ δίκτυα. "But relying upon Thy word I will have the nets let down." The "nevertheless" of AV. Cran. and Gen. is too strong: for that we should have πλήν (vi. 24, 35, etc.). For this use of ἐπί, "on the strength of," comp. ii. 20; Acts iv. 21. Win. xlviii. d, p. 491. The χαλάσατε and ποιήσαντες show that the χαλάσω includes the employment of others. Excepting Mk. ii. 4 and 2 Cor. xi. 33, χαλάω is peculiar to Lk. (*vv.* 4, 5; Acts ix. 25, xxvii. 17, 30). With the faith involved in χαλάσω τὰ δίκτυα we may compare κέλευσόν με ἐλθεῖν πρὸς σὲ ἐπὶ τὰ ὕδατα (Mt. xiv. 28).

6. συνέκλεισαν πλῆθος ἰχθύων πολύ. Not a miracle of creation, but at least of knowledge, even if Christ's will did not bring the fish to the spot. In no miracle before the Resurrection does Jesus create; and we have no sufficient reason for believing that the food provided at the second miraculous draught of fishes was created (Jn. xxi. 9–13). There is no exaggeration, as De Wette thinks, in διερήσετο or in βυθίζεσθαι (ver. 7). The nets "were breaking," *i.e.* beginning to break, when the help from the other boat prevented further mischief, and then both boats were overloaded. On the masses of fish to be seen in the lake see Tristram, *Nat. Hist. of the Bible*, p. 285, and *D.B.*[2] p. 1074: "The density of the shoals of fish in the Lake of Galilee can scarcely be conceived by those who have not witnessed them. They sometimes cover an acre or more on the surface in one dense mass."

The form ῥήσσω occurs in poetry (Hom. *Il.* xviii. 571, xxiv. 454) and late prose (Strab. xi. 14. 8). It is a collat. form of ῥήγνυμι (Veitch, *s.v.*, and Curtius, *Etym.* 511, 661): but see on ix. 42.

7. κατένευσαν τοῖς μετόχοις. Possibly because they were too far off for a call to be heard. The other boat was still close to the shore (ver. 2), for Simon alone had been told to put out into deep water. The verb is freq. in Hom., and occurs in Hdt. and Plato, generally in the sense of "nod assent, grant." Here only in N.T. Euthymius suggests that they were too agitated to call.

Here and Heb. i. 9 (from Ps. xliv. 8) we have μέτοχος as a subst. Comp. Heb. iii. 1, 14, vi. 4, xii. 8: and see T. S. Evans on 1 Cor. x. 16–18 in *Speaker's Com.* "As distinguished from κοινωνός (ver. 10; Heb. x. 33), which suggests the idea of personal fellowship, μέτοχος describes participation in some common blessing or privilege, or the like. The bond of union lies in that which is shared and not in the persons themselves" (Wsctt. on Heb. iii. 1). For **συλλαβέσθαι** in the sense of "assist" comp. Phil. iv. 3. In class. Grk. the act. is more common in this sense. For **ἦλθαν** see on i. 59.

ἔπλησαν ἀμφότερα τὰ πλοῖα ὥστε βυθίζεσθαι αὐτά. For ἔπλησαν see on i. 15; ἀμφότεροι is another favourite word (i. 6, 7, vi. 39, vii. 42; Acts viii. 38, xix. 16, xxiii. 8); not in Mk. or Jn. "They filled both the boats, so that they *began* to sink": comp. διερήσετο. The act is used 2 Mac. xii. 4 of the sinking of persons; by Polybius (ii. 10. 5) of the sinking of ships; and 1 Tim. vi. 9 of sending down to perdition. Nowhere else in N.T.

8. Σίμων Πέτρος προσέπεσεν τοῖς γόνασιν Ἰησοῦ. This is the only place in his Gospel in which Lk. gives Peter both names, and it is the first mention of the surname: see on vi. 14. Syr-Sin. omits Πέτρος.

The constr. προσπίπτειν τοῖς γον. is quite classical (Eur. *Or.* 1332; comp. Mk. vii. 25; Soph. *O. C.* 1606); often with dat. of pers. (viii. 28, 47; Acts xvi. 29; Mk. iii. 11, v. 33).

Ἔξελθε ἀπ' ἐμοῦ. Not "Leave my boat," which is too definite, but, "Go out of my vicinity, Depart from *me*." See on iv. 35.

It is quite erroneous to introduce here the notion that sailors believe it to be unlucky to have a criminal on board (Cic. *De Nat Deor.* iii. 37. 89; Hor. *Carm.* iii. 2. 26). In that case Peter, like Jonah, would have asked to be thrown into the sea. That the Twelve, before their call, were exceptionally wicked, ὑπὲρ πᾶσαν ἁμαρτίαν ἀνομωτέρους (Barn. v. 9), is unscriptural and incredible. But Origen seems to accept it (*Con. Cels.* i. 63; comp. Jerome, *Adv. Pelag.* iii. 2). See Schanz, *ad loc.* p. 198.

Peter does not regard himself as a criminal, but as a sinful man; and this miracle has brought home to him a new sense, both of his own sinfulness and of Christ's holiness. It is not that he fears that Christ's holiness is *dangerous* to a sinner (B. Weiss), but that the contrast between the two is felt to be so intense as to be intolerable. The presence of the sinless One is a reproach and a condemnation, rather than a peril; and therefore such cases as those of Gideon and Manoah (Judg. vi. 22, xiii. 22), cited by Grotius and De Wette, are not quite parallel. Job (xlii. 5, 6) is a better illustration; and Beng. compares the centurion (Mt. viii. 8). The objection that Peter had witnessed the healing of his wife's mother and other miracles, and therefore could not be so awestruck by this miracle, is baseless. It frequently happens that one experience touches the heart, after many that were similar to it have failed to do so. Perhaps, without being felt, they prepare the way. Moreover, this was a miracle in Peter's own craft, and therefore was likely to make a special impression on him; just as the healing of a disease, known to the profession as incurable, would specially impress a physician.

Κύριε. The change from ἐπιστάτα (see on ver. 5) is remarkable, and quite in harmony with the change of circumstances. It is the "Master" whose orders must be obeyed, the "Lord" whose holiness causes moral agony to the sinner (Dan. x. 16). Grotius, followed by Trench, points out that the dominion over all nature, including "the fish of the sea, and whatsoever passeth through the paths of the seas" (Ps. viii. 8), lost by Adam, is restored in Christ, the ideal man and the second Adam. But that Peter recognized this is more than we know. In what follows notice the characteristic πάντας and σύν.

9. ἐπὶ τῇ ἄγρᾳ τῶν ἰχθύων. This was the *basis* of their amazement: see small print on ii. 33, and comp. Acts xiv. 3 and Rom. v. 14. There is no need to make ἄγρα act. in ver. 4, "a catching," and pass. here, "the thing caught." "For a catch" in ver. 4; "at the catch of fish" here. If ὧν συνέλαβον (B D X, Goth.) is the true reading, both may be act. But if ᾗ συνέλαβον is right, then in both places ἄγρα is pass. In either case we have the idiomatic attraction of the relative which is so freq. in Lk. See small print on iii. 19. The word is common in poetry both act. and pass. Not in LXX, nor elsewhere in N.T. Note the change of meaning from συλλαβέσθαι in ver. 7 to συνέλαβον. The verb is freq. in Lk., but elsewhere rare in N.T.

10. Ἰάκωβον καὶ Ἰωάνην. The first mention of them by Lk.

In Mt. and Mk. they were in their boat, mending their nets, when Jesus called them; and Mt. adds that Zebedee was with them, which Mk. implies (i. 20). For κοινωνοί see on ver. 7. Are they the same as the *μέτοχοι*? It is possible that Peter had his *κοινωνοί* in his boat, while the *μέτοχοι* were in the other boat. In any case the difference of word should be preserved in translation. This Tyn. Cran. and Gen. effect, with "fellows" for *μέτοχοι* and "partners" for *κοινωνοί*. But Vulg. and Beza have *socii* for both; and RV. follows AV. with "partners" for both.

εἶπεν πρὸς τὸν Σίμωνα Ἰησοῦς. It is still Peter who is singled out for notice. Yet some critics affirm that it is the tendency of this Evangelist to depreciate Peter. For μὴ φοβοῦ see on i. 13: excepting Mk. v. 36 and Rev. i. 17, Lk. alone uses the expression without an accusative. Peter's sense of unworthiness was in itself a reason for courage. *Quo magis sibi displicebat hoc magis Domino placet* (Grotius).

ἀπὸ τοῦ νῦν. The present moment is a crisis in his life, of which he was reminded at the second miraculous draught of fishes, when the commission given to him now was restored to him after his fall. Excepting 2 Cor. v. 16 and [Jn. viii. 11], *ἀπὸ τοῦ νῦν* is peculiar to Lk. (i. 48, xii. 52, xxii. 18, 69; Acts xviii. 6). Comp. ἕως *τοῦ νῦν* (Mt. xxiv. 21; Mk. xiii. 19) and *ἄχρι τοῦ νῦν* (Rom. viii. 22; Phil. i. 5). Deissmann, *Bible Studies*, p. 253.

ἀνθρώπους ἔσῃ ζωγρῶν. Both substantive and verb have special point (*men* instead of fish; *for life* instead of for death); while the analytical tense marks the permanence of the new pursuit: comp. i. 20. This last is preserved in Rhem. "shalt be taking," following Vulg. *eris capiens*. Beza seems to be alone in giving the full force of *ζωγρῶν* (*ζωός* and *ἀγρεῖν*): *vivos capies homines*. But to add "alive" in English deprives "men" of the necessary emphasis.[1] The verb is used of sparing the lives of those taken in battle: *ζώγρει, Ἀτρέος υἱέ, σὺ δ' ἄξια δέξαι ἄποινα* (Hom. *Il.* vi. 46). Elsewhere in N.T. only 2 Tim. ii. 26, of the evil one. Comp. the exhortation of Socrates to Critobulus: *Ἀλλὰ θαρρῶν πειρῶ ἀγαθὸς γίγνεσθαι, καὶ τοιοῦτος γιγνόμενος θηρᾶν ἐπιχείρει τοὺς καλούς τε κἀγαθούς* (Xen. *Mem.* ii. 6. 28).

11. καταγαγόντες τὰ πλοῖα. Like *ἐπαναγαγεῖν* in ver. 3, this is a nautical expression; freq. in Acts (ix. 30, xxii. 30, xxiii. 15, 20, etc.). Comp. *ἀνάγειν*, viii. 22.

ἀφέντες πάντα ἠκολούθησαν αὐτῷ. Even the large draught of fishes does not detain them. They are sure that He who has given them such marvellous returns from their usual business will be ready to provide for them when, at His summons, they abandon

[1] Cod. Brix. has *hominum eritis captores*, including James and John, although *noli timere* precedes. D has *ποιήσω γὰρ ὑμᾶς ἁλιεῖς ἀνθρώπων* (from Mt. and Mk.) after the insertion *μὴ γίνεσθε ἁλιεῖς ἰχθύων*.

their business. The call was addressed to Peter (ver. 10), but the sons of Zebedee recognize that it concerns them also; and they leave and follow.

In this late Greek ἀφίημι is preferred to λείπω and its compounds, and ἀκολουθέω to ἕπομαι (which does not occur in N.T.) and its compounds.

The fact that other disciples besides Peter obeyed the call and followed Jesus, is the main reason for identifying this narrative with Mk. i. 16–20 and Mt. iv. 18-22. All three have the important word ἀφέντες, and Mt. and Lk. have ἠκολούθησαν αὐτῷ, for which Mk. has ἀπῆλθον ὀπίσω αὐτοῦ. But note that Lk. alone has his favourite πάντα after ἀφέντες (comp. vi. 30, vii. 35, ix. 43, xi. 4, xii. 10). Against these similarities, however, we have to set the differences, chief among which is the miraculous draught of fishes, which Mt. and Mk. omit. Could Peter have failed to include this in his narrative? And would Mk. have omitted it, if the Petrine tradition had contained it? It is easier to believe that some of the disciples were called more than once, and that their abandonment of their original mode of life was gradual: so that Mk. and Mt. may relate one occasion and Lk. another. Even after the Resurrection Peter speaks quite naturally of "going a fishing" (Jn. xxi. 3), as if it was still at least an occasional pursuit. But we must be content to remain in doubt as to the relation of this narrative to that of Mk. and Mt. See Weiss, *Leben Jesu*, I. iii. 4, Eng. tr. ii. pp. 54-59.

This uncertainty, however, need not be extended to the relation of this miracle to that recorded in Jn. xxi. 1-14. It cannot be accepted as probable that, in the source from which Lk. drew, "the narrative of the call of Peter has been confused with that of his reinstatement in the office which had been entrusted to him, and so the history of the miraculous draught of fishes which is connected with the one has been united with the other." The contrast between all the main features of the two miracles is too great to be explained by confused recollection. 1. There Jesus is not recognized at first; here He is known directly He approaches. 2. There He is on the shore; here He is in Peter's boat. 3. There Peter and John are together; here they seem to be in different boats. 4. There Peter leaves the capture of the fish to others; here he is chief actor in it. 5. There the net is not broken; here it is. 6. There the fish are caught close to the shore and brought to the shore; here they are caught in deep water and are taken into the boats. 7. There Peter rushes through the water to the Lord whom he had lately denied; here, though he had committed no such sin, he says, "Depart from me, for I am a sinful man, O Lord." There is nothing improbable in two miracles of a similar kind, one granted to emphasize and illustrate the call, the other the re-call, of the chief Apostle.

The way in which the Fathers allegorize the two miracles is well known, the first of the Church Militant, the second of the Church Triumphant. R. A. Lipsius would have it that the first is an allegory of quite another kind, the main point of which is the μέτοχοι in the other boat. He assumes that James and John are in Peter's boat, and explains thus. That Christ first teaches and then suddenly speaks of fishing, tells us that the fishing is symbolical. The fishing in deep water is the mission to the heathen, which Peter at first is unwilling (?) to undertake (comp. Acts x. 14). The marvellous draught after the night of fruitless toil is the conversion of many heathen after the failure of the mission to the Jews. This work is so great that Peter with the two other Apostles of the Jews are unequal to it, and have to call Paul, Barnabas, and others to help them. Peter then recognizes his former unwillingness (?) as a sin, and both he and the sons of Zebedee are amazed at the success of the mission to the heathen (Gal. ii. 9). Thus the rejection of Jesus by the people of Nazareth (iv. 29, 30), and His preaching "to the other cities also" (iv. 43), teach the same lesson as the miraculous draught; viz. the failure of the mission to the Jews and the success of the mission to the heathen (*Jahrb. für prot. Theol.* 1875, i. p. 189). The whole is exceedingly forced, and an examination of the details shows that they do not fit. If the common view is correct, that James and John were the *μέτοχοι* in the other boat, the whole structure falls to the ground. Had Lk. intended to convey the meaning read into the narrative by Lipsius, he would not have left the point on which the whole is based so open to misconception. Keim on the whole agrees with Lipsius, and dogmatically asserts that "the artificial narrative of Lk. must unhesitatingly be abandoned . . . It is full of subtle and ingenious invention . . . Its historical character collapses under the weight of so much that is artificial" (*Jes. of Naz.* iii. pp. 264, 265). Holtzmann also pronounces it to be "legendary and consciously allegorical" (*in loco*). Does Peter's apparently inconsistent conduct, beseeching Jesus to depart and yet abiding at His feet, look like invention?

12–16. The Healing of a Leper. Here we certainly have an incident which is recorded by all three Evangelists. The amount of verbal agreement is very great, and we may confidently affirm that all three make use of common material. Mt. (viii. 1–4) is the most brief, Mk. (i. 40–45) the most full; but Mt. is the only one who gives any note of time. He places the miracle just after Jesus had come down from delivering the Sermon on the Mount.

On the subject of Leprosy see H. V. Carter, *Leprosy and Elephantiasis*, 1874; Tilbury Fox, *Skin Diseases*, 1877; Kaposi, *Hautkrankheiten*, Wien, 1880; and the literature given at the end of art. *Aussatz* in Herzog; also in Hirsch, *Handb. d. Pathologie*, 1860.

12. Καὶ ἰδού. Hebraistic; in Mt. viii. 2, but not in Mk. i. 40: the *καί* is the apodosis to *ἐγένετο*, as in ver. 1. No verb follows the *ἰδού*, as if the presence of the leper were a surprise. Had the man disregarded the law in approaching the crowd? Or had the people come upon him suddenly, before he could avoid them? What follows shows a third possibility. Syr-Sin. omits *καὶ ἰδού*.

πλήρης λέπρας. This particular is given only by the beloved physician. His face and hands would be covered with ulcers and sores, so that everyone could see that the hideous disease was at a very advanced stage. This perhaps accounts for the man's venturing into the multitude, and for their not fleeing at his approach; for by a strange provision of the law, "if the leprosy break out abroad in the skin, and the leprosy cover all the skin of him that hath the plague, from his head even to his feet, . . . then the priest . . . shall pronounce him clean that hath the plague" (Lev. xiii. 12, 13).

ἐδεήθη αὐτοῦ. Excepting Mt. ix. 38, the verb is peculiar in N.T. to Lk. and Paul. It is especially freq. in Lk. (viii. 28, 38, ix. 38, 40, x. 2, etc.). In LXX it represents a variety of Hebrew words, and is very common. Here Mk. has *παρακαλῶν*.

ἐὰν θέλῃς, δύνασαί με καθαρίσαι. All three accounts have these words, and the reply to them, *Θέλω, καθαρίσθητι*, without variation. The *δύνασαι* is evidence of strong faith in the Divine power of Jesus; for leprosy was believed to be incurable by human means

It was "the stroke" of God, and could not be removed by the hand of man. But it is characteristic of the man's imperfect apprehension of Christ's character, that he has more trust in His power than in His goodness. He doubts the will to heal. He says καθαρίσαι rather than θεραπεῦσαι or ἰάσασθαι because of the pollution which leprosy involved (Lev. xiii. 45, 46). In O.T. "unclean" and "clean," not "sick" and "healed," are the terms used about the leper. The old rationalistic explanation, that καθαρίσαι means "to *pronounce* clean," and that the man was already cured, but wanted the great Rabbi of Nazareth to absolve him from the expensive and troublesome journey to Jerusalem, contradicts the plain statements of the Gospels. He was "full of leprosy" (Lk.); "immediately the leprosy departed from him" (Mk. Lk.). If καθαρίσαι means "to pronounce clean," then καθαρίσθητι means "be thou pronounced clean." Yet Jesus sends him to the priest (Lk. Mk. Mt.). Contrast the commands of Christ with the prayers of Moses, Elijah, and Elisha, when they healed. See Deissmann, *Bible Studies*, p. 216.

13. ἐκτείνας τὴν χεῖρα. All three have this Hebraistic amplification. In LXX the phrase commonly occurs in connexion with an act of punishment: Ex. vii. 5, 19, viii. 1, 2, ix. 22, 23, x. 12, 21, 22, xiv. 16, 21, 26, 27; Ezek. vi. 14, xiv. 9, xvi. 27, xxv. 7, 13, 16, xxxv. 3; Zeph. i. 4, ii. 13; Jer. vi. 12, xv. 6. In N.T. it rarely has this meaning. Jesus touched the leper on the same principle as that on which He healed on the sabbath: the ceremonial law gives place to the law of charity when the two come into collision. His touch aided the leper's faith.

ἡ λέπρα ἀπῆλθεν ἀπ' αὐτοῦ. Here again (see on iv. 40) Mk. has the whole expression, of which Lk. and Mt. each use a part. Mk. has ἀπῆλθεν ἀπ' αὐτοῦ ἡ λέπρα, καὶ ἐκαθαρίσθη, and Mt. has ἐκαθαρίσθη αὐτοῦ ἡ λέπρα. All three have εὐθέως or εὐθύς, showing that Jesus not merely prepared the way for a cure which nature accomplished, but healed the leper at once by His touch.

14. καὶ αὐτός. Lk.'s favourite form of connexion in narrative: *vv.* 1, 17, 37, i. 17, 22, ii. 28, iii. 23, iv. 15, vi. 20, etc.

παρήγγειλεν. The word is specially used of commanders, whose orders are passed along the line (παρά), and is freq. in Lk. (viii. 29, 56, ix. 21; Acts i. 4, iv. 18, v. 28, 40, x. 42, etc.); rare in Mt. (x. 5, xv. 35) and Mk. (vi. 8, viii. 6); not in Jn. All the others use ἐντέλλεσθαι, and Mt. κελεύειν, both of which are rare in Lk. Here Mt. and Mk. have λέγει.

μηδενὶ εἰπεῖν. The charge was given with emphasis (ὅρα μηδενὶ μηδὲν εἴπῃς) and sternness (ἐμβριμησάμενος), as Mk. tells us. The meaning of it is variously explained. To prevent (1) the *man* from having intercourse with others before being pronounced clean by proper authority; (2) the *man* from becoming proud through frequent telling of the amazing benefit bestowed upon him; (3) the *priests* from hearing of the miracle before the man arrived, and then deciding, out of hostility to Jesus, to deny the cure; (4) the *people* from becoming unhealthily excited about so great a miracle. Chrysostom and Euthymius suggest (5) that Christ was setting an example of humility, *διδάσκων τὸ ἀκόμπαστον καὶ ἀφιλότιμον*, in forbidding the leper to proclaim His good deeds. Least probable of all is the supposition (6) that "our Lord desired to avoid the Levitical rites for uncleanness which the unspiritual ceremonialism of the Pharisees might have tried to force upon Him" for having touched the leper. The first of these was probably the chief reason; but one or more of the others may be true also. The man would be likely to think that one who had been so miraculously cured was not bound by ordinary rules; and if he mixed freely with others before he was declared by competent authority to be clean, he would give a handle to Christ's enemies, who accused Him of breaking the law. In the Sermon on the Mount He had said, "Think not that I came to destroy the law or the prophets" (Mt. v. 17); which implies that this had been said of Him. The command *μηδενὶ μηδὲν εἴπῃς* is further evidence that Jesus did not regard miracles as His chief credentials. And there are many such commands (viii. 56; Mt. ix. 30, xii. 16; Mk. i. 34, iii. 12, v. 43, vii. 36, viii. 26).

ἀλλὰ ἀπελθὼν δεῖξον σεαυτὸν τῷ ἱερεῖ. Sudden changes to the *oratio directa* are common after *παραγγέλλω* and similar verbs (Acts i. 4, xxiii. 22; Mk. vi. 8, 9?; comp. Acts xvii. 3; Tobit viii. 21; Xen. *Anab.* i. 3. 16, 20). Win. lxiii. 2, p. 725.

τῷ ἱερεῖ. As in the original (Lev. xiii. 49), the sing. refers to the priest who was on duty at the time. Note the *καθώς*, "exactly as": the reference is to Lev. xiv. 4–10, which enjoins rather expensive offerings. Comp. Mt. i. 24. For the form *Μωυσῆς* see on ii. 22. This charge is in all three narratives almost in the same words. On its import see Hort, *Judaistic Christianity*, p. 30

καθαρισμοῦ. *Emundatio* (Vulg.), *mundatio* (f q) *purgatio* (a), *purificatio* (d).

εἰς μαρτύριον αὐτοῖς. This addition is in all three, and various xplanations have been suggested. That (1) the priests may be onvinced of My Divine power; (2) the priests may see that I do ot disregard the Law; (3) the people may be convinced that the cure is complete, and that the leper may be readmitted to society; (4) the people may see that I do not disregard the Law. It is the sacrifice which is the *μαρτύριον*, and therefore the second or fourth explanation is to be preferred. Both may be right.[1]

[1] "It is worthy of notice, that all the places where our Lord is stated to have met with lepers are in the central districts of Samaria and Galilee. . . . It

15. διήρχετο δὲ μᾶλλον ὁ λόγος περὶ αὐτοῦ. Lk. does not state, as Mk. does, that this was owing to the man's disobedience. Mt. omits both points. This use of *διέρχομαι* of the spreading of a report is quite classical (Thuc. vi. 46. 5; Xen. *Anab.* i. 4. 7). The word is a favourite one with Lk.; see on ii. 15. The *μᾶλλον* means "more than before, more than ever" (Jn. v. 18, xix. 8), or "all the more," because of the command not to tell (xviii. 39; Acts v. 14, ix. 22, xxii. 2).

συνήρχοντο ὄχλοι πολλοὶ ἀκούειν καὶ θεραπεύεσθαι ἀπὸ τῶν ἀσθενειῶν. For miracles mentioned as being numerous, but without details, comp. iv. 40, vi. 18, vii. 21. The constr. **θεραπεύεσθαι ἀπό** is peculiar to Lk. (vii. 21, viii. 2). The usual constr. with *θερ.* is the acc. (iv. 23, 40, ix. 1, etc.). For **ἀσθενειῶν** comp. viii. 2, xiii. 11, 12; Acts xxviii. 9; Heb. xi. 34, where we have a similar constr., *ἐδυναμώθησαν ἀπὸ ἀσθενείας.*

16. αὐτὸς δὲ ἦν ὑποχωρῶν ἐν ταῖς ἐρήμοις καὶ προσευχόμενος. The verse forms one of those resting-places with which Lk. frequently ends a narrative (i. 80, ii. 20, 40, 52, iii. 18–20, iv. 13, 15, 30, 44). "But He" on His part, in contrast to the multitudes who came to see Him, "was in retirement in the deserts, and in prayer." See on iii. 21. The analytical tense expresses what Jesus was engaged in while the multitudes were seeking Him. That they were unable to find Him is not implied here, and Mk. states the opposite. For the **αὐτός** comp. iv. 30, vi. 8, viii. 37, 54, xi. 17, 28, xxiii. 9; and for **ὑποχωρεῖν**, ix. 10. The verb occurs nowhere else in N.T., but is freq. in class. Grk. Lk. alone uses the plur. of *ἔρημος* (i. 80, viii. 29). See Bede, *ad loc.*

For *ἐν* after a verb of motion, to express the rest which is the result of the motion, comp. Mt. xiv. 3; Jn. iii. 35; 2 Cor. viii. 16. Such condensed constructions are not common, if found at all, in earlier writers. The converse use of *εἰς* after verbs of rest is more common (xi. 7, xxi. 37; Acts ii. 39, vii. 4, viii. 20, 23, 40, etc.). Win. l. 4. a, p. 514.

17–26. The Healing of a Paralytic. **Mt. ix. 1–8; Mk. ii. 1–12.** We again have a narrative which is narrated by all three Synoptists in a way which shows that they are using common material. Mt. is again the most brief. Mk. and Lk. agree in the details, but differ considerably in the wording. Different translations of the same Aramaic original, or of two very similar Aramaic originals, would account for these similarities and differences. The cast of the opening verse is very Hebraistic, as is shown by *ἐγένετο*, by *ἐν μιᾷ τῶν ἡμερῶν*, by *καὶ αὐτός*, and by *δύναμις Κυρίου ἦν εἰς.* See on iv. 36 and on viii. 22. The *ἐν μιᾷ τῶν ἡμερῶν* is an absolutely indefinite expression, which we have no right to limit. Mt. and Mk. give no date. The phrase *ἐν μιᾷ τῶν* is peculiar to Lk.

is just in this district that to this day we find the colonies of lepers most numerous" (Tristram, *Eastern Customs in Bible Lands*, p. 19).

17. Φαρισαῖοι. The first mention of them by Lk., who assumes that his readers know who the Pharisees were. This introduction of them stamps them as hostile to Christ; and we have here the first collision in Galilee between Jesus and the authorities at Jerusalem. On the Pharisees see Jos. *Ant.* xiii. 5. 9, 10. 6, xvii. 2. 4, xviii. 1. 2, 3; *B. J.* ii. 8. 14; Schürer, *Jewish People*, II. ii. § 26, p. 10; Hausrath, *N.T. Times*, i. p. 135; Keim, *Jes. of Naz.* i. p. 321; Edersh. *L. & T.* i. pp. 96, 97, 310–324.

νομοδιδάσκαλοι. The word is formed on the analogy of ἱεροδιδάσκαλος and χοροδιδάσκαλος, but is not classical. Elsewhere only Acts v. 34 and 1 Tim. i. 7. In all three cases teachers of the Jewish Law are meant, and the term is almost a synonym for οἱ γραμματεῖς in the N.T. sense. That they had come **ἐκ πάσης κώμης τῆς Γαλιλαίας καὶ Ἰουδαίας** is, of course, a popular hyperbolical expression, and illustrates Lk.'s fondness for πᾶς: comp. vi. 17.

δύναμις Κυρίου ἦν εἰς τὸ ἰᾶσθαι αὐτόν. "The power of Jehovah was present for Him to heal with"; *i.e.* for Jesus to employ in working miracles of healing. See on iv. 36 and comp. i. 35, xxiv. 49; Acts vi. 8. Hence miracles are often called δυνάμεις, or outcomes of the power of God. Trench, *Syn.* xci. The failure to see that αὐτόν is the subject, not the object, of ἰᾶσθαι produced the corrupt reading αὐτούς (A C D and versions). This corrupt reading produced the erroneous interpretation of Κυρίου as meaning Christ. Lk. often calls Christ "the Lord"; but in such cases Κύριος always has the article (vii. 13, x. 1, xi. 39, xii. 42, xiii. 15, xvii. 5, 6, xviii. 6, xix. 8, xxii. 61). Κύριος without the article means Jehovah (i. 11, ii. 9, iv. 18; Acts v. 19, viii. 26, 39, xii. 7). This verse shows us Jesus armed with Divine power and confronted by a large body of hostile spies and critics. What follows (*vv.* 19, 26) proves that there was also a multitude of curious spectators, who had not declared for either side, like the multitude round Elijah and the prophets of Baal on Carmel (1 Kings xviii. 21).

Except in quotations from LXX (Mt. xiii. 15; Jn. xii. 40) and one other passage (Jn. iv. 47), ἰᾶσθαι with act. signif. is peculiar to Lk. (vi. 19, ix. 2, 11, 42, xiv. 4, xxii. 51; Acts ix. 34, x. 38, etc.).

18. ὃς ἦν παραλελυμένος. "Here and wherever St. Luke mentions this disease, he employs the verb παραλύεσθαι, and never παραλυτικός. The other N.T. writers use the popular form παραλυτικός, and never use the verb, the apparent exception to this, Heb. xii. 12, being a quotation from the LXX, Is. xxxv. 3. St. Luke's use is in strict agreement with that of the medical writers" (Hobart, *Med. Lang. of St. Lk.* p. 6).

ἐζήτουν αὐτὸν εἰσενεγκεῖν. Into the house, although it has not yet been stated that Jesus was in a house. Mk. tells us that there were four bearers, and that the place was thronged even about the door. For ἐνώπιον see small print on i. 15.

19. For μή with a participle expressing a reason see small print on iii. 9. With ποίας understand ὁδοῦ and comp. ἐκείνης (xix. 4). Here we should have expected διά, which some inferior MSS. insert in both places. "By what *kind* of a way" emphasizes their perplexity. For the omission of ὁδός comp. iii. 5. Win. xxx. 11, lxiv. 5, pp. 258, 738. The classical τὴν ἄλλως illustrates this common ellipse. Blass, *Gr.* pp. 106, 137.

διὰ τὸν ὄχλον. "Because of the multitude"; not "through the multitude," a meaning of διά *c. acc.* which is found only in poetry and freq. in Hom. It was probably by means of outside steps that they "went up on to the top of the house." Oriental houses sometimes have such steps; and in any case ladders could be used. That the **δῶμα** was a dwelling-house is not stated. In bibl. Grk. it means a *roof* rather than a house (Deut. xxii. 8; Josh. ii. 6, 8), and in N.T. seems to imply a flat roof (xii. 3, xvii. 31; Acts x. 9; Mk. xiii. 15; Mt. x. 27, xxiv. 17). It may have been over a large hall on the ground floor. Even if Jesus was teaching in the upper room of a dwelling-house (and the Rabbis often taught there), the difficulty of getting on to the roof and removing a small portion of it would not be very great. Edersh. *Hist. of J. N.* p. 253.

διὰ τῶν κεράμων καθῆκαν. The verb is peculiar to Lk. in N.T. (Acts ix. 25, x. 11, xi. 5); freq. in class. Grk. Mk. has ἀπεστέγασαν τὴν στέγην ὅπου ἦν, καὶ ἐξορύξαντες χαλῶσιν. Perhaps Lk. thinks of Græco-roman houses, Mk. of Palestinian. We need not infer from ἐξορύξαντες that under the tiles was clay or mortar to be "dug out." But, if there was anything of the kind to be cut through and removed, this could easily be done without serious consequences to those who were in the crowded room below. Men who had so much at stake, and who had got thus far, would not desist through fear of sprinkling a few persons with rubbish. To make these difficulties, which are very unsubstantial, a reason for rejecting the whole narrative as a legend, is rather childish criticism. The constructor of a legend would not have made his details conspicuously incredible. The suggestion that Jesus was in a gallery outside the house, teaching the multitude in the open court below, is not helpful. In that case, why unroof the gallery? The sick man might have been let down to the front of it.[1]

σὺν τῷ κλινιδίῳ. Lk. alone has his favourite σύν. The substantive occurs here only. It is the dim. of κλίνη (viii. 16, xvii. 34), and perhaps means here a portion of the κλίνη mentioned in ver. 18. Not all of what had been used to bring him through the streets would be let down through the roof. Comp. κλινάριον (Acts v. 15). Double forms of diminutives are not uncommon;

[1] For another explanation see Tristram, *Eastern Customs*, pp. 34, 35.

e.g. γυναίκιον and γυναικάριον (2 Tim. iii. 6); παιδίον (i. 59, 66) and παιδάριον (Jn. vi. 9); πινάκιον and πινακίδιον (i. 63). Mk. has the inelegant κράβαττος, *grabatus* (Acts v. 15, ix. 33), for which the Greeks preferred σκίμπους or σκιμπόδιον.

20. ἰδὼν τὴν πίστιν αὐτῶν. The faith of the man and of those who brought him. All three accounts have the words; but Mt. omits the persevering energy which proved how strong their faith was. We need not assume that the paralytic himself did not share his friends' confidence.

For a full discussion of the *Meaning of "Faith" in the New Testament and in some Jewish Writings* see detached note on Rom. i. 17. Here it will suffice to point out its four main uses for (1) belief in God; (2) belief in His promises; (3) belief in Christ; (4) belief in some particular utterance or claim of God or of Christ. Of these four the last is the commonest use in the Synoptic Gospels, where it generally means belief in the power of Christ, or of God in Christ, to work miracles. The efficacy of Christ's power is commonly dependent upon the faith of those who are to be benefited by its exercise, as here. Comp. vii. 50, viii. 48, xvii. 19, xviii. 42. By an easy transition this faith in the power of God or of Christ to work miracles becomes used of the conviction that the believer himself has received power to work miracles. Comp. xvii. 6. In xviii. 8 the faith to be found on earth means faith in the Son of Man.

Ἄνθρωπε, ἀφέωνταί σοι αἱ ἁμαρτίαι σου. Mk. has τέκνον, and Mt. has θάρσει τέκνον. It is not likely that Lk., the writer of the Gospel of grace for all, has deliberately changed the more tender address, because it seemed to be unsuitable to one who must, as he thinks, have been a grievous sinner. Comp. xii. 14 and xxii. 58. And we affirm more than we know, if we say that this absolution was necessary for the man's cure, because otherwise he would not have believed that Jesus could heal him, and his faith was essential to the cure. He probably believed, and perhaps knew, that his malady was the direct consequence of his own sin (xiii. 2; Jn. v. 14, ix. 2; 1 Cor. xi. 30). But it does not follow from this that faith on his part was thus far absent.

Suidas seems to be right in regarding ἀφέωνται as a Doric form of the perf. indic. for ἀφεῖνται. But it was admitted rather freely, even by Attic writers. Comp. ἀνέωνται (Hdt. ii. 165. 1; but the reading is not certain) and εἴωθα from ἔθω (iv. 16). Win. xiv. 3. a, p. 96; Veitch, *s. v.* In Mt. and Mk. the true reading here is ἀφίενται: but ἀφέωνται occurs again vii. 47, 48; 1 John ii. 12, and probably Jn. xx. 23. Some have regarded it as a subjunctive: *remissa sunto.* Fritzsche (on Mt. ix. 2) pertinently asks, *Quo usu aut more subjunctivum in talibus locis absolute positum defendas?*

21. ἤρξαντο διαλογίζεσθαι. Not a mere periphrasis for διελογίσαντο: see on iv. 21. Hitherto they had found nothing in His words to excite criticism. Here they seemed to see the opportunity for which they had been watching, and their discussions forthwith began.[1] The **γραμματεῖς** are evidently the same as the

[1] It has been suggested that ἦσαν καθήμενοι (Mk. ii. 6) and ἤρξαντο (= ἦσαν ἀρχόμενοι) here are simply different translations of the Aramaic verb, which has

νομοδιδάσκαλοι in ver. 17. Neither Mt. nor Mk. mention the Pharisees here; and both of them imply that the criticisms were not uttered aloud: ἐν ἑαυτοῖς (Mt.), ἐν ταῖς καρδίαις (Mk.). Even here utterance is not stated, for λέγοντες may be used of thoughts (xii. 17; Mt. xxi. 25).

Τίς ἐστιν οὗτος ὃς λαλεῖ βλασφημίας; An accidental iambic line. We have another ver. 39, if εὐθέως be admitted as genuine. The οὗτος is contemptuous, as often (iv. 22, vii. 39, 49, ix. 9, xiv. 30, xv. 2, etc.). In N.T., as in class. Grk., βλασφημία has the two meanings of "evil speaking" (Col. iii. 8; Eph. iv. 31; 1 Tim. vi. 4; Jude 9: comp. Rom. iii. 8, xiv. 16) and "blasphemy" (Mt. xii. 31, xxvi. 65; Rev. xiii. 6). These cavillers assume that Jesus has claimed to have pardoned the man on His own authority, not merely to have said that He knew that his sins have been forgiven by God. And Jesus does not say that they are mistaken in this. He acts on His own authority in accordance with the will of the Father, doing on earth what the Father does in heaven (Jn. v. 19, 21). For ἀφιέναι of sins comp. Mt. xii. 31; Mk. iii. 28; Rom. iv. 7, etc.

22. ἐπιγνοὺς δὲ ὁ Ἰησοῦς τοὺς διαλογισμοὺς αὐτῶν. The compound verb implies thorough and accurate knowledge (1 Cor. xiii. 12; Rom. i. 32; Justin, *Try.* iii. p. 221 A). The subst. ἐπίγνωσις is used of "the knowledge of God and of Christ as being the perfection of knowledge: *e.g.* Prov. ii. 5; Hos. iv. 1, vi. 6; Eph. i. 17, iv. 13; 2 Pet. i. 2, 3, 8, ii. 20; Clem. Alex. *Pæd.* ii. 1, p. 173" (Lft. on Col. i. 9). Comp. the climax in *Apost. Const.* vii. 39. 1, γνῶσις, ἐπίγνωσις, πληροφορία. On both ἐπίγνωσις and διαλογισμούς see Hatch, *Bibl. Grk.* p. 8. The latter seems here to mean "thoughts" (ἐνθυμήσεις, Mt. ix. 4) rather than "discussions" (ix. 46). In LXX it is used of the counsels of God (Ps. xxxix. 6, xci. 6). It is, however, more often used in a bad sense (Ps. lv. 5, xciii. 11, cxlv. 4, etc.), and is specially freq. in Lk. (ii. 35, vi. 8, ix. 47, xxiv. 38). Not in Jn., and only once each in Mt. and Mk.

ἐν ταῖς καρδίαις ὑμῶν. This seems to imply that there had been no utterance. Christ read their thoughts. See on Rom. i. 21.

23. τί ἐστιν εὐκοπώτερον, εἰπεῖν . . . ἢ εἰπεῖν. It is in this verse and the next that the three accounts are most similar—almost *verbatim* the same. The challenge is a very practical one, and the point of it is in the εἰπεῖν. It is easier to *say*, "Thy sins are forgiven," because no one can prove that they are not forgiven. But the claim to heal with a word can be easily and quickly tested.

the very different meanings of "sitting at rest" and "beginning"; or possibly of two verbs which are identical in spelling (*Expositor*, April 1891, p. 285). See on iii. 23. But these possibilities seem to be too isolated and sporadic to be of great value in accounting for differences between the Gospels.

εὐκοπώτερον. Lit. "more capable of being done with easy labour" (εὐ, κόπος). In N.T. always in the comparative (xvi. 17, xviii. 25; Mk. x. 25; Mt. xix. 24); but εὔκοπον occurs 1 Mac. iii. 18; Ecclus. xxii. 15. It is found in Polyb., but not in class. Grk.—For τίς in the sense of "whether of two" like πότερος, as *quis* = *uter*, comp. xxii. 27; Mt. xxi. 31, xxiii. 17, xxvii. 17, 21; Xen. *Cyr.* iii. 1. 17.

24. ὁ υἱὸς τοῦ ἀνθρώπου. This remarkable phrase in all four Gospels is invariably used by Christ of Himself; upwards of eighty times in all. The Evangelists never use it of Him, and no one ever addresses Him by this title. Yet none of the four ever directs our attention to this strict limitation in the use of the phrase, so that their agreement must be regarded as undesigned, and as evidence of their accuracy. *D.C.G.* art. "Son of Man."

In O.T. we have "son of man" used in three different connexions, and it must be noted that in each case the rendering in LXX is υἱὸς ἀνθρώπου and not ὁ υἱὸς τοῦ ἀνθρώπου. In the *Psalms* it is used of the ideal man: viii. 4, lxxx. 16, cxliv. 3, cxlvi. 3. In *Ezekiel* it is the title by which the Prophet is addressed, ii. 1, 3, 6, 8, iii. 1, 3, 4, etc. etc.; upwards of eighty times in all. In *Daniel's* night visions (vii. 13, 14), "One like a son of man came with the clouds of heaven, and came to the Ancient of Days," and received a dominion which was universal and eternal. With this should be compared various passages in the *Book of Enoch*, of which this is specially noteworthy. "There I saw one who had a head of days, and His head was white like wool; and with Him was a Second, whose countenance was like the appearance of a man, and His countenance was full of grace, like one of the holy angels. And I asked one of the angels who were with me, and who showed me all the secrets, concerning this Son of Man, who He was, and whence He was, and why He goes with the Head of days. And he answered and said to me: This is the Son of Man who has justice, and justice dwells with Him; and all the treasures of secrecy He reveals, because the Lord of the spirits has chosen Him, and His portion overcomes all things before the Lord of the spirits in rectitude to eternity. And this Son of Man, whom thou hast seen, will arouse the kings and mighty from their couches, and the strong from their thrones, and will loosen the bands of the strong, and will break the teeth of the sinners" (xlvi.). This Son of Man is the Messiah. He is called "the Anointed" (xlviii. 11, li. 4), "the Righteous One" (xxxviii. 2, liii. 6), "the Elect One" (*passim*), and the Lord speaks of Him as "My Son" (cv. 2). That these Messianic passages in the Book of Enoch are of Christian origin is the opinion of a few critics, but it is difficult to maintain it. Everything distinctly Christian is absent. This Son of Man or Messiah is not the Word, is not God. That He has lived on the earth is nowhere intimated. Of the historical Jesus, the Crucifixion, the Resurrection, or the Ascension, there is not a hint; nor yet of baptism, or of the eucharist, or of the doctrine of the Trinity. Why should a Christian write just what any Jew might accept about the Messiah and no more? But if the whole of the Book of Enoch was written before the birth of Christ, then we have sufficient evidence to show that when Christ was teaching on earth "Son of Man" was already accepted by the Jews as one title, although not a common one, for the Messiah.[1] The idea of a weak and suffering Messiah was unwelcome to the Jews, and therefore a name

[1] *Le Livre d'Hénoch, en particulier, lequel était fort lu dans l'entourage de Jésus* (Judæ Epist. 14) *nous donne la clef de l'expression de "Fils de l'homme," et des idées qui s'y rattachaient* (Renan, *V. de J.* p. xi.). It is, of course, quite possible that the writer of the Book of Enoch took the idea from Daniel. For a discussion of the title see Dorner, *Person of Christ*, Eng. tr. I. i. p. 54.

which emphasized human weakness was not a favourite one. "But the very reason which induced them to avoid the title induced our Lord to take it. It expressed His Messiahship definitely enough for His purpose; but it expressed it in that veiled and suggestive way which characterised the whole of His teaching on His own person. At the same time, it conveyed to those who had ears to hear the whole secret of the Incarnation. That which the Jews shrank from and ignored He rather placed in the forefront of His mission" (Sanday in the *Expositor*, Jan. 1891, p. 30, art. "On the Title, 'Son of Man'").

ἐπὶ τῆς γῆς. In all three accounts there is room for doubt as to the words which this expression qualifies. Here either ἐξουσίαν ἔχει or ἀφιέναι ἁμαρτίας. In Mk. and Mt. it may qualify ὁ υἱὸς τοῦ ἀνθρώπου. It is best taken with ἐξουσίαν ἔχει. But the difference in meaning is not great.

εἶπεν τῷ παραλελυμένῳ. This is not the apodosis to ἵνα εἰδῆτε, but a parenthesis:[1] the apodosis to ἵνα εἰδῆτε is Σοὶ λέγω. Note the emphasis on σοί: "to *thee* I say the crucial words." Clement of Alexandria gives this address to the paralytic in singularly different language: ἀνάστα, φησὶ τῷ παρειμένῳ, τὸν σκίμποδα ἐφ' ὃν κατάκεισαι λαβὼν ἄπιθι οἴκαδε (*Pæd.* i. 2, p. 101, ed. Potter). Probably a paraphrase. For the pres. imperat. see Blass, *Gr.* p. 191.

25. παραχρῆμα ἀναστὰς ἐνώπιον. Every one of these words is characteristic of Lk. For παραχρῆμα Mk. has his equally characteristic εὐθύς, a feature which recurs Lk. viii. 44, 55, xviii. 43, xxii. 60. Lk. has παραχρῆμα ten times in the Gospel and six times in the Acts: elsewhere only Mt. xxi. 19, 20. For ἀναστάς Mt. has ἐγερθείς and Mk. ἠγέρθη καί: see on i. 39. For ἐνώπιον αὐτῶν Mk. has ἔμπροσθεν πάντων.

ἄρας ἐφ' ὃ κατέκειτο. *Il doit porter maintenant ce grabat qui l'a si longtemps porté* (Godet). The wording is peculiar to Lk., and is perhaps intended to suggest this inversion of relations. Lk. alone records that he glorified God. The phrase δοξάζειν τὸν Θεόν is specially common with him (ver. 26, vii. 16, xiii. 13, xvii. 15, xviii. 43, xxiii. 47; Acts iv. 21, xi. 18, xxi. 20): once in Mk., twice in Mt., once in Jn.

The reading ἐφ' ᾧ (R U Λ) is an obvious correction to a more usual construction. For the acc. after a verb of rest comp. xxi. 35; Mt. xiii. 2; Mk. iv. 38; Jn. xxi. 4; also Plato, *Sym.* 212 D, ἐπιστῆναι ἐπὶ τὰς θύρας.

26. ἔκστασις ἔλαβεν ἅπαντας. Mk. has πάντας, Mt. nothing. Lk. is fond of the stronger form. He alone records all three emotions—amazement, fear, and gratitude to God. The last is in all three. For ἔκστασις comp. Mk. v. 42, xvi. 8; Acts iii. 10; Gen. xxvii. 33; 1 Sam. xiv. 15; 2 Chron. xiv. 14. Mt., whose narrative

[1] That this parenthesis occurs in exactly the same place in all three proves that all three made use of a narrative, the form of which was already fixed, either in memory or in writing (Salmon, *Int. to N.T.* p. 121, 5th ed.). Comp. Lk. viii. 28, 29 with Mk. v. 7, 8, where we have similar agreement in arrangement.

is much the most brief, adds after ἐδόξασαν τὸν Θεόν, τὸν δόντα ἐξουσίαν τοιαύτην τοῖς ἀνθρώποις, which seems to refer to the preceding ἐξουσίαν ἔχει. He who is *the* Son of Man, the ideal representative of the race, had vindicated His claim to possess authority to forgive sins.

Εἴδαμεν παράδοξα σήμερον. The adj. occurs here only in N.T In LXX it is not rare (Judith xiii. 13; Wisd. v. 2; Ecclus. xliii. 25; 2 Mac. ix. 24; 4 Mac. ii. 13). It is used of the miracles of Jesus in the famous passage, of very doubtful origin, in Josephus: σοφὸς ἀνὴρ, εἴ γε ἄνδρα αὐτὸν λέγειν χρή· ἦν γὰρ παραδόξων ἔργων ποιητής (*Ant.* xviii. 3. 3). Whereas ἔνδοξα (xiii. 17) has reference to the δόξα or *glory* of the agent, παράδοξα refers to the δόξα or *opinion* of the spectators; but δόξα in the sense of "opinion" or "belief" is not found in N.T. For the mixed form of aor. εἴδαμεν see small print on i. 59, and comp. 1 Sam. x. 14 and 2 Sam. x. 14.

27-39. The Calling of Levi and the Discussion about Fasting. Mt. ix. 9–17; Mk. ii. 13–22. In all three narratives this section is connected closely with the healing of the paralytic; but Mt. places both incidents much later, viz. after the return from the country of the Gadarenes.

The common identification of Levi with Matthew is probably correct; but his father must not be identified with the father of James the Less. Matthew is probably a contraction of Mattathias = "Gift of God," and this name may have been given to Levi after His conversion, like that of Peter to Simon. Comp. Joseph Barsabbas, surnamed Justus (Acts i. 23). In Galilee it was common to have two names; and therefore both names may have been original. But if Levi was the earlier name, and was less well known among Christians, that would account for Mk. and Lk. using it, while Mt. equally naturally would let it be evident that a τελώνης had become, by Christ's mercy, the well-known Apostle. There can be no reasonable doubt that the three narratives refer to the same incident. And, as Levi is mentioned in no list of the Twelve, and Matthew is mentioned in all such lists, the identity of Levi the τελώνης with Mt. the τελώνης and Apostle need not be doubted. Such doubts, however, are ancient. They existed in the Gnostic commentator Heracleon (Clem. Alex. *Strom.* iv. 9, p. 595, ed. Potter), and were shared by Origen. They have been reproduced by Grotius (on Mt. ix. 9) and Michaelis; and more recently by Sieffert, Neander, Ewald, Keim, and Reuss. But a satisfactory solution, which is not contradicted by any evidence, is not to be rejected because it does not amount to demonstration.

27. ἐξῆλθεν. So also Mk., while Mt. has παράγων ἐκεῖθεν. Departure from the town, rather than from the house, is probably meant; and we therefore obtain no evidence as to the site of Capernaum. We may place Capernaum away from the lake, and yet suppose the τελώνιον to have been close to the shore. The customs collected there went to Herod Antipas, not to the imperial *fiscus* (Jos. *Ant.* xvii. 11. 4, 5; *B. J.* ii. 6. 3): see on xx. 25.

ἐθεάσατο τελώνην. "Looked attentively at, contemplated, a tax-collector," as if reading his character. The verb often implies *enjoyment* in beholding (vii. 24; Jn. i. 14, 32, 38; 1 Jn. i. 1). For the τελῶναι see on iii. 12. The Talmud distinguishes two classes of τελῶναι: the *Gabbai* or tax-gatherer (*e.g.* of income-tax or poll-tax), and the *Mokhes* or custom-house officer. The latter was specially hated, as having greater opportunities for vexatious exactions, especially from the poor. Levi was one of the latter. The great commercial route from Acre to Damascus, which continued until the crusades as the *via maris*, passed the lake at or near Capernaum, and gave employment to excisemen (Is. ix. 1).

ὀνόματι Λευείν. Mk. has Λευεὶν τὸν τοῦ Ἀλφαίου, and Mt. has Μαθθαῖον. The fondness of Lk. for ὀνόματι in introducing a name is here conspicuous. Mt. has λεγόμενον, and Mk. has neither. Comp. i. 5, x. 38, xvi. 20, xxiii. 50, and over twenty times in the Acts. Mt. and Mk. have ὀνόματι once each. Jn. says ὄνομα αὐτῷ (i. 6, iii. 1, xviii. 10).

καθήμενον ἐπὶ τὸ τελώνιον. Excepting in the parallel passages, τελώνιον does not occur in N.T. Nor is it common elsewhere. In Strabo, xvi. 1. 27, it seems to mean "customs, taxes," and some would render ἐπὶ τὸ τελώνιον, "to receive the customs." But it is more probable that it means the place where dues were collected, "the tol bothe" (Wic.) or "the custom-house" (Rhem.). Comp. the similarly formed δεκατώνιον, "the office of a collector of tenths." Very likely Levi was sitting outside the *portitorium*. He must have been visible from the outside: the ἐπί is "at," not "in."

28. καταλιπὼν πάντα. Lk alone mentions this.[1] Note the characteristic πάντα, and comp. ver. 11. The fact illustrates the doctrine, to which Lk. often bears witness, that riches are a peril and an impediment, and that the kingdom of God is specially preached to the poor. The statement is against the supposition (*D.B.* ii. p. 969) that Mt. returned to his business afterwards; and it is quite gratuitous to suppose that the statement is a mere reminiscence of ver. 11. In that case why has **ἀφιέναι** been changed to καταλείπειν? Syr-Sin. omits ἀναστάς.

There is a slight awkwardness in καταλιπών preceding ἀναστάς: the rising was the first act in the leaving all and in the following Christ. Both Mt. (?) and Lk. represent the following as habitual, ἠκολούθει. Mk. regards the single act on this occasion, ἠκολούθησεν. With the call, Ἀκολούθει μοι, comp. Jn. i. 44, and with the result comp. ver. 11 and Mt. iv. 19, 22. The two combined lead one to the view that this is a call to become an Apostle.

29. ἐποίησεν δοχὴν μεγάλην. "Made a great reception" (δέχομαι) or banquet. The word is peculiar to Lk., who has δοχὴν ποιεῖν again xiv. 13. The phrase occurs in LXX (Gen. xxi. 8, xxvi. 30; Esth. i. 3, v. 4, 8). Of course **ἐν τῇ οἰκίᾳ αὐτοῦ**

[1] *Ce seul mot suffit. La parole qui venait de guérir le lépreux, de rendre au paralysé le mouvement et de remettre les péchés, transforma soudainement un publicain en disciple* (Didon, *J. C.* ch. iii. p. 340).

means in Levi's house, which is not included in καταλιπὼν πάντα. He was not at his house when he left all. The πάντα refers to his whole mode of life, his business as a τελώνης.

It is strange that any one should understand the words either here or Mk. ii. 15 as meaning "in the house of Jesus." Had Jesus a house? If so, how improbable that Levi should hold a reception in it! If the narrator had meant this, must he not have given the name instead of αὐτοῦ, which would inevitably be misunderstood? Mt. has simply ἐν τῇ οἰκίᾳ, which possibly means "indoors," as opposed to the outdoor scene ἐπὶ τὸ τελώνιον. There is no evidence that Christ had a house at Capernaum. After the call of Simon and Andrew He is entertained in the house of Simon and Andrew (Mk. i. 16, 29); and after the call of Levi He is entertained in the house of Levi. The new disciple wishes his old friends to make the acquaintance of his new Master. *C'est son premier acte missionaire* (Godet).

ἦν ὄχλος πολὺς τελωνῶν καὶ ἄλλων οἳ ἦσαν μετ' αὐτῶν κατακείμενοι. This proves that the house was a large one, which the house of Jesus would not have been: and it also shows the character of the company, for only social outcasts would sit down at the same table with τελῶναι.

30. ἐγόγγυζον οἱ Φαρισαῖοι καὶ οἱ γραμματεῖς αὐτῶν. The αὐτῶν means "the scribes of the Pharisees," *i.e.* who belonged to that party. Some scribes were Sadducees. That this is the meaning is clear from Mk. ii. 16. It is pointless, and scarcely grammatical, to make αὐτῶν refer to the inhabitants of the place, who have not been mentioned. These scribes were probably not invited guests, but had entered during the meal, like the woman that was a sinner in the house of Simon. The *Sinaiticus* and other authorities omit αὐτῶν, doubtless because it was not clear what it meant.

For γογγύζω, which is not in Mk. or Mt., see Lft. on Phil. ii. 14, and Kennedy, *Sources of N.T. Grk.* p. 39. The Atticists preferred τονθορύζω. Both are probably onomatop.—Note that here, as in *vv.* 31, 33 and iv. 43, Lk. has πρός *c. acc.* after a verb of speaking, where Mk. (ii. 16–19) has the dat. See on i. 13.

Διὰ τί μετὰ τῶν τελωνῶν καὶ ἁμαρτωλῶν ἐσθίετε; The single article (so in all three) brackets them as one class. In Mt. and Mk. the disciples are not included in the charge (ἐσθίει, not ἐσθίετε); but they both mention that the disciples were sitting at table with Jesus and the τελῶναι, and therefore were open to the charge. Lk., on the other hand, does not mention that the disciples were sitting at table, but his ἐσθίετε implies it. With διὰ τί comp. Exod. v. 14.

31. In all three accounts Jesus ignores the insinuation against His disciples, and answers for Himself. He is responsible for the intercourse with tax-collectors and sinners. For **οἱ ὑγιαίνοντες** Mt. and Mk. have οἱ ἰσχύοντες. This looks like a deliberate change made by Lk. for the sake of a word which would more definitely express health as opposed to sickness. Like **παραλελυμένος** for παραλυτικός (*vv.* 18, 24) and ἰᾶσθαι for διασώζειν (vi. 19), these changes may be the result of Lk.'s medical training (Hobart, p. 67; Salmon, *Int. to N.T.* p. 129, 5th ed.). But would Lk. have made changes in a report of Christ's words? There would be no need to have scruples, for οἱ ἰσχύοντες is only a translation of the Aramaic, and Lk. might think that οἱ ὑγιαίνοντες was a better translation. Christ's reply is an *argumentum ad hominem*, partly ironical. On their own showing the Pharisees had no need of a teacher, while these outcasts were in the greatest need of one.

32. εἰς μετάνοιαν. These words are peculiar to Lk., but in some texts have been transferred to Mk. and Mt. Both μετάνοια and μετανοεῖν are freq. in Lk. See on xv. 7. Obviously those who are really δίκαιοι do not need to be called to repentance; but who are δίκαιοι? That is the question which Christ's reply suggests. If we had only Mk.'s account, we might suppose that what follows took place on some other occasion; but both Lk. and Mt. (τότε) connect it with the banquet in Matthew's house.

33. οἱ δὲ εἶπαν. The same who asked the previous question, viz. the Pharisees and their scribes (ver. 30). Mt. says that it was the disciples of John who came up and put this question. Mk. states that both the disciples of John and the Pharisees were keeping a fast at that very time, and joined in asking why Christ's disciples did not do so also. We know from Jn. iii. 26 how jealous the Baptist's disciples were of Christ, and therefore ready to criticize. Perhaps they were also jealous of the freedom from legal restraints which His disciples seemed to enjoy. They leave an opening for the reply, "*You* have no need to fast." The four words which follow νηστεύουσιν, viz. the words **πυκνὰ καὶ δεήσεις ποιοῦνται**, are peculiar to Lk. They imply that Christ's disciples habitually neglected the frequent fasts which the disciples of John and of the Pharisees kept. The fasts on Mondays and Thursdays are probably meant, which were not obligatory, but which some Pharisees observed (xviii. 12). Moses was believed to have gone up Mount Sinai on a Thursday and to have come down on a Monday. The Day of Atonement was the only fast of universal obligation. For **ποιεῖσθαι δεήσεις** comp. 1 Tim. ii. 1; it refers to prayers at fixed times according to rule. The disciples of Jesus seemed to have no rule respecting such things. A late tradition fixes the number of the Baptist's disciples as thirty, answering to the days of the month, as the Twelve are supposed to answer to the months of the year (*Clem. Hom.* ii. 23).—**καὶ πίνουσιν.** These words also are peculiar to Lk. in harmony with καὶ πίνετε in ver. 30.

34. Individuals were at liberty to choose their own days for fasting, but they must not select a sabbath or any of the great feasts. Christ suggests another exception, which very possibly was made by the Pharisees themselves. Is it possible to make the guests fast at a wedding? Mt. and Mk. omit the ποιεῖν: Can the wedding-guests fast? Would it not be morally impossible to have such a combination? To John's disciples this parable would come home with special force, for their master had called Jesus "the Bridegroom," and himself "the friend of the Bridegroom."

τοὺς υἱοὺς τοῦ νυμφῶνος. The common Hebraism to express those who are closely connected with the *νυμφών*: comp. x. 6, xvi. 8, xx. 36; Acts iv. 36; Mt. xxiii. 15; Jn. xii. 36, etc. In 1 Mac. iv. 2 *οἱ υἱοὶ τῆς ἄκρας* means the garrison of the citadel. But in LXX such expressions are not very common (1 Kings i. 52; 2 Sam. xii. 5; Gen. xi. 10). The word *νυμφών* seems scarcely to occur in class. Grk., but it is rightly formed (Tobit vi. 14, 17). Comp. *παρθενών, γυναικών, ἀνδρών, βοών, ἀμπελών, κ.τ.λ.*

35. ἐλεύσονται δὲ ἡμέραι. "But days will come," *i.e.* days very different from the joyous days of the wedding. It is best to take this clause separately. After it there is an aposiopesis, which is mournfully impressive; and then the sentence begins again.

καὶ ὅταν ἀπαρθῇ ἀπ' αὐτῶν ὁ νυμφίος. There is no *καί* in Mt. or Mk., and some texts omit it here, because of its apparent awkwardness. We may take the *καί* as beginning a fresh sentence, or as epexegetic of the preceding clause. "But days will come—and when the bridegroom shall be taken away," etc. Or, "But days will come, yea, days when the bridegroom," etc. The word *ἀπαρθῇ* is in all three, and nowhere else in N.T. It is common in class. Grk., esp. of the moving of fleets and armies.

τότε νηστεύσουσιν. "Then they will fast"—of their own accord. He does not say, "Then ye will be able to make them fast," which would be the exact antithesis of what goes before; and the change is significant. Compulsion will be as superfluous then as it would be outrageous now: comp. xvii. 22. This is the first intimation of His death and departure, after which fasting will be appropriate and voluntary. Its value consists in its being spontaneously adopted, not forcibly imposed. This point is further developed in the short parables which follow. Note the characteristic *ἐν ἐκείναις ταῖς ἡμέραις* (not in Mt. ix. 15), and see on ix. 36.

36. Ἔλεγεν δὲ καὶ παραβολὴν πρὸς αὐτούς. These introductory words are peculiar to Lk., and the phrase *λέγειν παραβολήν* is used by no one else (xii. 41, xiii. 6, xiv. 7, xviii. 1, xx. 9). For the characteristic **δὲ** *καί* see small print on iii. 9, and for **λέγειν πρός** see on i. 13. For pairs of parables see on ver. 37 and xiii. 18.

ἀπὸ ἱματίου καινοῦ σχίσας. This also is peculiar to Lk.'s narrative, and it heightens the effect of the parable. Both Mt. and Mk represent the patch as coming from an unused piece of cloth. To tear it from a new garment is an aggravation of the folly. A good garment is ruined in order to mend, and that very ineffectually, an old one. In all three we have *ἐπίβλημα* for patch; in Mt. and Mk. *πλήρωμα* also; and Mk. for *ἐπιβάλλει* has *ἐπιράπτει*. In Plutarch and Arrian *ἐπίβλημα* means "tapestry" for hangings. In the sense of "patch" it seems to occur only in Sym. Josh. ix. 11 (5). The Latin translations of ἐπίβλημα vary: *commissura* (Vulg.), *insumentum* (a), *immissura* (d).

εἰ δὲ μήγε (εἰ δὲ μή γε, Lach. Treg.). "But if he acts otherwise," *i.e.* if he commits this folly. *Ni caveat errorem* (Grotius). The formula is freq. in Lk. (ver. 37, x. 6, xiii. 9, xiv. 32), who never uses εἰ δὲ μή. Εἰ δὲ μή γε is stronger than εἰ δὲ μή, and follows both negative (xiv. 32; Mt. ix. 17; 2 Cor. xi. 16) and affirmative sentences (x. 6, xiii. 9; Mt. vi. 1). It is found in Plato (*Rep.* iv. 425 E): comp. Hdt. iv. 120. 4. See Fritzsche on Mt. vi. 1 and Meyer on 2 Cor. xi. 16.

καὶ τὸ καινὸν σχίσει. "Both he will rend the new garment"—in tearing the patch from it. AV. here goes wrong, although (except as regards the tense) all previous English Versions were right. Reading σχίζει with A and Vulg. *rumpit*, Wic. Tyn. Cran. and Rhem. have "*He* breaketh the new," while Cov. has "*He* renteth the new." Beza has "the *old* breaketh the new." Luther and AV. seem to be alone in taking τὸ καινόν as the nom., "Both the new maketh a rent." With σχίσει comp. Jn. xix. 24; Is. xxxvii. 1.

καὶ τὸ καινὸν . . . καὶ τῷ παλαιῷ. The double καί marks the double folly. RV. avoids the awkwardness of "*Both* he will rend . . *and* the piece," etc., by rendering, "He will rend . . . *and also* the piece," etc. The combination with καὶ τῷ παλαιῷ shows that τὸ καινόν is object and not subject.

As to the precise meaning, interpreters are not agreed, beyond the general truth that a new spirit requires a new form. But the piece torn from the new garment is probably exemption from fasting. To deprive Christ's disciples of this freedom, while He is with them, would be to spoil the system in which they are being trained. And to impose this exemption upon the disciples of John and the Pharisees, would also spoil the system in which they have been trained. In the one case fasting, in the other non-fasting, was the natural outcome of the environment. For a variety of interpretations see Godet, who in his third ed. has changed his own (1888).

37. This second parable carries on and develops the teaching of the first. We have similar pairs of parables in the Mustard-seed and the Leaven, the Treasure hid in the Field and the Pearl of great price, the Ten Virgins and the Talents, the Lost Sheep and the Lost Coin, the Unwise Builder and the Unwise King. In three respects this second parable differs from the first. (1) The piece of new cloth represents only a fragment of the new system; the new wine represents the whole of it. (2) The new garment and the old one are only marred; the new wine is lost and the old skins are destroyed. (3) Not only is the wrong method condemned, the right method is indicated (ἀλλὰ . . . βλητέον). The argument is *à fortiori*. If it is a mistake to take the natural out come from one system and force it upon an alien system, much more fatal will it be to try to force the whole of a new and growing system into the worn out forms of an old one. "I thank Thee, O Father, Lord of heaven and earth, that Thou didst hide these things from the wise and understanding, and didst reveal them unto babes" (x. 21). The scribes and Pharisees, wise in the letter of the law, and understanding their own cramping traditions, were incapable of receiving the free spirit of the Gospel. Young and fresh natures, free from prejudice and open to new light and new impressions, were needed to receive the new word and preserve it unchecked and untramelled for future generations. On the fitness of the twofold parable to the occasion Bengel remarks, *parabolam a veste, a vino: imprimis opportunam convivio.*

οὐδεὶς βάλλει οἶνον νέον εἰς ἀσκοὺς παλαιούς. For *βάλλειν* of pouring liquids comp. Jn. xiii. 5; Mt. xxvi. 12; Judg. vi. 19; Epictet. iv. 19. 12. Skin-bottles, *utres*, are still in use in the East, made of a single goat-skin (Hom. *Il.* iii. 247), from which the flesh and bones are drawn without ripping up the body. The neck of the animal becomes the neck of the bottle. Gen. xxi. 14, 15, 19; Ps. cxix. 83. Comp. Hdt. ii. 121. 20, iii. 9. 2; Hom. *Od.* v. 265. In Job xxxii. 19 it is said that even new skins are ready to burst when they are full of new wine: comp. xxxviii. 37. See Herzog, *PRE.*[2] art. *Schlauch*; Tristram, *Nat. Hist. of B.* p. 92.

38. οἶνον νέον εἰς ἀσκοὺς καινοὺς βλητέον. Here certainly, and perhaps here only in N.T., the difference between *νέος* and *καινός* must be marked in translation: "*New* wine must be put into *fresh* wine-skins." While *νέος* is new in reference to *time*, "young" as opposed to "aged," *καινός* is new in reference to *quality*, "fresh" as opposed to "worn out." Trench, *Syn.* lx.; Crem. *Lex.* p. 321. But "a fresh heaven and a fresh earth" (2 Pet. iii. 13; Rev. xxi. 1), and still more a "fresh Jerusalem" (Rev. iii. 12, xxi. 2), would be intolerable. No English version prior to RV. distinguishes here between *νέος* and *καινός*; and Vulg. has *novus* for both. None translates *ἀσκοί* "skins" or "wine-skins," but either "bottles" (Wic. Cran. Rhem. AV.) or "vessels" (Tyn. Cov. Gen.). The conclusion, *καὶ ἀμφότεροι συντηροῦνται*, is an interpolation from Mt. ix. 17 (ℵ B L and Aegyptt. omit).

39. This third parable is peculiar to Lk. While the first two show how fatal it would be to couple the new spirit of the Gospel with the worn out forms of Judaism, the third shows how natural it is that those who have been brought up under these forms should be unwilling to abandon them for something untried. The conversion of an outcast *τελώνης*, who has no such prejudices, may be easier than one whose life is bound up in the formalism of the past. Grotius, starting from Ecclus. ix. 15, *οἶνος νέος φίλος νέος· ἐὰν παλαιωθῇ, μετ' εὐφροσύνης πίεσαι αὐτόν*, interprets: *Significavit hoc* *proverbio Christus homines non subito ad austeriorem vitam pertrahendos, sed per gradus quosdam assuefaciendos esse*; which implies that Christ considered Jewish fasting the more excellent way, up to which His disciples must be gradually educated. Moreover, the *subito* on which this explanation turns is an interpolation: εὐθέως is not genuine (ℵ B C[1] L, Boh. Æth. Arm. omit). Wetstein quotes a multitude of passages to show that old wine was considered to be superior to new, and concludes; *Pharisæorum austeritas comparatur vino novo, Christi lenitas vino veteri*; which exactly inverts the parable. The comparative *merits* of the old and the new wine are not touched by the parable, but the *taste* for them. One who is accustomed to old will not *wish* for new: it does not attract him by look or fragrance. See Hort, *Judaistic Christianity*, p. 24.

λέγει γάρ· Ὁ παλαιὸς χρηστός ἐστιν. The reading of A C and Vulg. (χρηστότερος, *melius*) is a manifest corruption. The prejudiced person will not even try the new, or admit that it has *any* merits. He knows that the old is pleasant, and suits him; and that is enough: he is not going to change. *Pharisæis doctrina sua antiqua magis erat ad palatum, quam generosa doctrina Jesu, quam illi putabant esse novam* (Beng.), and which they would not even taste. Comp. Rom. vii. 6; 2 Cor. iii. 6. If we admit the undoubtedly spurious εὐθέως, we have another iambic line in this verse as in ver. 21: πιὼν παλαιὸν εὐθέως θέλει νέον. The whole verse is omitted in D and in most of the best MSS. of the old Latin; but WH. seem to be alone in placing it in brackets as of doubtful authority. On the three parables see Trench, *Studies in the Gospels*, pp. 168–183.

VI. 1–5. The first Incident on the Sabbath (see Maurice, *Lectures on St. Luke*, pp. 82, 83, ed. 1879). The Call of Peter was followed by two healings which provoked opposition to Christ: and now the Call of Levi is followed by two incidents on the sabbath, which lead to similar opposition. Mk. agrees with Lk. in placing these two immediately after the call of Levi; Mt. has them much later (xii. 1–14). On the connexion here see Schanz, *ad loc.*

1. ἐν σαββάτῳ δευτεροπρώτῳ. This passage is a well-known *crux* in textual criticism and exegesis. Is δευτεροπρώτῳ part of the true text? If so, what does it mean? The two questions to some extent overlap, but it is possible to treat them separately.

1. The external evidence is very much divided, but the balance is against the words being original.[1] The reading is Western and Syrian, and "has no other clearly pre-Syrian authority than that of D *a ff*." The internal evidence is also divided. On the one hand, "The very obscurity of the expression, which does not occur in the parallel Gospels or elsewhere, attests strongly to its genuineness" (Scriv.), for "there is no reason which can explain the insertion of this

[1] *ins.* A C D E H K M R S U V X Γ Δ Λ Π most cursives, Vulg. Syr-Harcl. Goth. Arm., Epiph. Chrys. Greg-Naz. Amb. Hieron. and perhaps Clem-Alex.

om. ℵ B L six or seven good cursives, Syrr. Boh. Aeth. That *evangelistaria* omit is not of much moment, as they often omit notes of time.

word, while the reason for omitting it is obvious" (Tisch.) On the other hand, "all known cases of probable omission on account of difficulty are limited to single documents or groups of restricted ancestry, bearing no resemblance to the attestation of text in either variety or excellence" (WH.). Moreover, if any sabbath had really borne this strange name, which is introduced without explanation as familiar to the readers, it would almost certainly have been found elsewhere, either in LXX, Philo, Josephus, or the Talmud. In the life of Eutychius (512–582) by his chaplain Eustathius *δευτεροπρώτη κυριακή* is used of the first Sunday after Easter, but the expression is obviously borrowed from this passage, and throws no light. In the whole of Greek literature, classical, Jewish, or Christian, no such word is found independently of this text. The often quoted *δευτεροδεκάτη*, "second tenth" (Hieron. *ad Ez.* xlv. 13), gives no help. The analogy of *δευτερογάμος*, *δευτεροτόκος*, *κ.τ.λ.*, suggests the meaning of "a sabbath which for a second time is first"; that of *δευτερέσχατος*, which Heliodorus (*apud* Soran. *Med. vet.*) uses for "last but one," suggests the meaning "first but one," *i.e.* "second of two firsts." But what sense, suitable to the passage, can be obtained from either of these? The more probable conclusion is that the word is spurious.

How then did it get into the text and become so widely diffused? The conjecture of Meyer is reasonable. An early copyist inserted *πρώτῳ* to explain *ἐν ἑτέρῳ σαββάτῳ* in ver. 6; this was corrected to *δευτέρῳ* because of iv. 31; and the next copyist, not understanding the correction, combined the two words. A few MSS. have the reading *δευτέρῳ πρώτῳ*, among them R (Cod. Nitriensis), a palimpsest of the sixth cent. in the British Museum. See Knight's Field.

2. If the word is genuine, what can be its meaning? Jerome put this question to Gregory Nazianzen, and the latter *eleganter lusit*, saying, *Docebo te super hac re in ecclesia* (Hieron. *Ep.* lii.). Of the numerous conjectures the following may be mentioned as not altogether incredible. (1) The first sabbath of the second year in a sabbatical cycle of seven years. This theory of Wieseler has won many adherents. (2) The first sabbath in Nisan. The Jewish civil year began in Tisri, while the ecclesiastical year began in Nisan; so that each year there were two first sabbaths, one according to civil, the other according to ecclesiastical reckoning: just as Advent Sunday and the first Sunday in January are each, from different points of view, the first Sunday in the year. It would be possible to call the second of the two "a second first Sunday." But would anyone use such language and expect to be understood? (3) The first sabbath of the second month. It is asserted that the story of David obtaining the shewbread would often be in the lesson for that sabbath. But the lectionary of the synagogues in the time of Christ is unknown. See on iv. 17. For other guesses see Godet, McClellan, and Meyer. Most editors omit or bracket it. Tisch. changed his decision several times, but finally replaced it in his eighth edition.

διαπορεύεσθαι αὐτὸν διὰ σπορίμων. Excepting Rom. xv. 24, the verb is peculiar to Lk. (xiii. 22, xviii. 36; Acts xvi. 4). In N.T. *σπόριμος* occurs only here and parallels. In Theophr. (*H. P.* vi. 5. 4) we have *ἡ σπορίμη, sc. γῆ*. In Gen. i. 29 it is applied to the seed, *πάντα χόρτον σπόριμον σπεῖρον σπέρμα*; so that, like *σπείρεσθαι*, it can be used either of the field or of the seed.

ἔτιλλον οἱ μαθηταὶ αὐτοῦ καὶ ἤσθιον τοὺς στάχυας. For this Mk. has *ἤρξαντο ὁδὸν ποιεῖν τίλλοντες τοὺς στάχυας*, which has been interpreted to mean "began to make a way by plucking the ears." But (1) all three imply that Jesus was walking in front of the disciples. What need was there for them to make a way? (2) How would plucking the *ears* make a path? (3) In LXX *ὁδὸν ποιεῖν* is used for *iter facere* (Judg. xvii. 8). All three mean that the disciples went along plucking the ears. This was allowed (Deut. xxiii. 25).

ψώχοντες ταῖς χερσίν. This and the *τίλλοντες* constituted the offence: it was unnecessary labour on the sabbath. According to Rabbinical notions, it was reaping, thrashing, winnowing, and preparing food all at once. Lk. alone mentions the rubbing, and the word *ψώχειν* seems to occur elsewhere only in the medical writer Nicander (*Theriaca*, 629). It is from the obsolete *ψώω*, a collat. form of *ψάω*. Comp. Hdt. iv. 75. 2. For the action described see Robinson, *Res. in Pal.* i. pp. 493, 499.

2. τινὲς δὲ τῶν φαρισαίων. As in v. 30, they are represented as addressing their question to the disciples. In Mk. ii. 24 and Mt xii. 2 the charge against the disciples is addressed to Christ, while in Mk. ii. 16 and Mt. ix. 11 the charge against Christ is addressed to the disciples. The **τοῖς σάββασιν** may mean either "on the sabbath days" (AV. and most English Versions) or "on the sabbath day" (RV.). Although Vulg. has *in sabbatis*, Wic. has "in the saboth"; Cov. also "upon the sabbath." See on iv. 31.

3. οὐδὲ τοῦτο ἀνέγνωτε ὃ ἐποίησεν Δαυείδ. "Have ye not read even this that David did?" Does your knowledge not extend even thus far? RV. follows AV. in translating *ὃ ἐποίησεν* as if it were the same as the *τί ἐποίησεν* of Mt. and Mk., "*what* David did."

καὶ οἱ μετ' αὐτοῦ. "The young men," whom David was to meet afterwards. He came to Nob alone (1 Sam. xxi. 1).

4. εἰσῆλθεν εἰς τὸν οἶκον τοῦ Θεοῦ. This is not stated in O.T., but may be inferred from his being seen by Doeg the Edomite, who was "detained before the Lord": *i.e.* he was in the tabernacle as a proselyte, perhaps to be purified, or to perform a vow.

τοὺς ἄρτους τῆς προθέσεως. Lit. "the loaves of the setting forth." These were the twelve loaves of wheaten bread placed before the Lord in the Holy Place every sabbath. The word "shewbread" first appears in Coverdale, probably from Luther's *Schaubrote*. Wic. follows the *panes propositionis* of Vulg. with "looves of proposisiounn," which is retained in Rhem. Tyn. has "loves of halowed breed." In O.T. we have also *ἄρτοι τοῦ προσώπου*, *i.e.* of the presence of God (1 Sam. xxi. 6; Neh. x. 33), or *ἄρτοι ἐνώπιοι* (Exod. xxv. 30), or *ἄρτοι τῆς προσφορᾶς* (1 Kings vii. 48), or again *οἱ ἄρτοι οἱ διαπαντός*, *i.e.* "the perpetual loaves" (Num. iv. 7). But the expression used here, Mt. xii. 4 and Mk. ii. 26, occurs Exod. xxxix. 36?, xl. 23; 1 Chron. ix. 32, xxiii. 29: comp. 2 Chron. iv. 19. For the origin of *ἡ πρόθεσις τῶν ἄρτων* (Heb. ix. 2) comp. 2 Chron. xiii. 11, xxix. 18. See Edersh. *The Temple*, pp. 152–157; Herzog, *PRE.*[2] art. *Schaubrote*.

καὶ ἔδωκεν τοῖς μετ' αὐτοῦ. This also is not stated in 1 Sam. xxi., but it is implied in David's asking for *five* loaves, and in Abimelech's asking whether the wallets of the young men were Levitically clean. For ἔξεστιν *c. acc. et inf.* see on xx. 22.

5. Κύριός ἐστιν τοῦ σαββάτου ὁ υἱὸς τοῦ ἀνθρώπου. In all three accounts Κύριος comes first with emphasis. The Son of Man controls the sabbath, not is controlled by it. This does not mean that He abrogates it (Mt. v. 17–20), but that He has power to cancel the literal observance of it in order to perform or permit what is in accordance with its spirit. Mk. gives the additional reason that "the sabbath was made for man, and not man for the sabbath," *i.e.* that it was given to be a blessing, not a burden. Even the Rabbis sometimes saw this; "The sabbath is handed over to you; not, ye are handed over to the sabbath" (Edersh. *L. & T.* ii. p. 58). Ritual must give way to charity. The Divine character of the Law is best vindicated by making it lovable; and the Pharisees had made it an iron taskmaster. And, if the sabbath gives way to man, much more to the Son of Man. In Jn. v. 17 Christ takes still higher ground. The Father knows no sabbath in working for man's good, and the Son has the same right and liberty. For ὁ υἱὸς τοῦ ἀνθρώπου see on v. 24. The point here is that Christ as the representative of man defends man's liberty.

Cod. D transfers ver. 5 to after ver. 10, and instead of it has the remarkable insertion: *τῇ αὐτῇ ἡμέρᾳ θεασάμενός τινα ἐργαζόμενον τῷ σαββάτῳ εἶπεν αὐτῷ· ἄνθρωπε, εἰ μὲν οἶδας τί ποιεῖς, μακάριος εἶ· εἰ δὲ μὴ οἶδας, ἐπικατάρατος καὶ παραβάτης εἶ τοῦ νόμου.* For *ἄνθρωπε* comp. xii. 14; *ἐπικατάρατος*, Gal. iii. 10; *παραβάτης νόμου*, Rom. ii. 25, 27; Jas. ii. 11. It is possible that the tradition here preserved in Cod. D is the source from which both S. Paul and S. James derive the phrase *παραβάτης νόμου*. In Rom. ii., where it occurs twice, we have the address *ἄνθρωπε* twice (*vv.* 1, 3). There is nothing incredible in Christ's having seen a man working (not necessarily in public) on the sabbath. The words attributed to Christ are so unlike the undignified, silly, and even immoral inventions in the apocryphal gospels that we may believe that this traditional story is true, although it is no part of the Canonical Gospels. D has other considerable insertions Mt. xx. 28 and Jn. vi. 56. See A. Resch, *Agrapha Aussercanonische Evangelienfragmente* (Leipzig, 1889) pp. 36, 189.

6–11. The Second Incident on the Sabbath. Mt. xii. 9 would lead us to suppose that it was the same sabbath (*μεταβὰς ἐκεῖθεν ἦλθεν*). Lk. definitely states that it was *ἐν ἑτέρῳ σαββάτῳ*, but not that it was "on the very next sabbath following." He alone mentions that Jesus taught in the synagogue on this occasion, and that the withered hand that was healed was the right one.

6. *Ἐγένετο δὲ . . . εἰσελθεῖν αὐτὸν . . . καὶ ἦν . . . καὶ ἦν.* The same Hebraistic constr. as in ver. 1, somewhat modified in accordance with classical usage: see note at the end of ch. i. We have *ξηροί* at the Pool of Bethesda (Jn. v. 3); but outside N.T. the word seems to mean, when applied to the human body, either "not wet" or "lean."

7. παρετηροῦντο δὲ αὐτὸν οἱ γραμματεῖς καὶ οἱ Φαρισαῖοι. Lk. alone tells us who the spies were. Mt. puts their inquisitiveness into words, "Is it lawful to heal on the sabbath day?" The verb signifies "watch narrowly," esp. with sinister intent, perhaps from looking sideways out of the corner of one's eyes, *ex obliquo et occulto.* As in Gal. iv. 10, the mid. gives the idea of *interested* observance. Mk. has *παρετήρουν*: comp. xx. 20; Sus. 12, 15, 16; Polyb. xvii. 3. 2; Aris. *Rhet.* ii. 6. 20; *Top.* viii. 11. 1.

εἰ ἐν τῷ σαββάτῳ θεραπεύει. The present has reference to His habitual practice, of which His conduct on this occasion would be evidence. But ℵ B with other authorities read *θεραπεύσει*, which is probably genuine in Mk. iii. 2, and may be genuine here. The future would limit the question to the case before them.

ἵνα εὕρωσιν κατηγορεῖν αὐτοῦ. According to what is probably the invariable rule in N.T. we have the subj. in spite of the past tense on which the final clause is dependent. The opt. for this purpose is obsolete; for *γνοῖ* (Mk. ix. 30) and similar forms are probably meant to be subj. Simcox, *Lang. of N.T.* p. 107.

8. αὐτὸς δὲ ᾔδει τοὺς διαλογισμοὺς αὐτῶν. "But He," in contrast to these spies (v. 16, viii. 37, 54) "knew their thoughts." For **διαλογισμός** comp. ii. 35, v. 22, ix. 46, xxiv. 38. It commonly means intellectual and inward questioning rather than actual dis puting: but see on v. 22 and comp. 1 Tim. ii. 8.

τῷ ἀνδρὶ τῷ ξηρὰν ἔχοντι τὴν χεῖρα. "To the man who had *his* hand withered," not "who had the withered hand." For *ἀνδρί* comp. v. 12: Mt. and Mk. have *ἀνθρώπῳ*.

Ἔγειρε καὶ στῆθι εἰς τὸ μέσον. Lk. alone has *καὶ στῆθι*. Christ's method is as open as that of His adversaries is secret. "Arise and stand *into* the midst"; *i.e.* "Come into the midst and stand there": comp. xi. 7; Acts viii. 40. Win. l. 4. b, p. 516. In what follows note Lk.'s favourite *ἀναστάς* (i. 39), which neither Mt. nor Mk. has here.

None of them records any words of the man; but Jerome in commenting on Mt. xii. 13 states, *in evangelio quo utuntur Nazareni et Ebionitæ . . . homo iste qui aridam habet manum cæmentarius scribitur, istiusmodi vocibus auxilium precans, Cæmentarius eram, manibus victum quæritans: precor te, Jesu, ut mihi restituas sanitatem, ne turpiter mendicem cibos.* See on xviii. 25.

9. Ἐπερωτῶ ὑμᾶς, εἰ. He answers the questioning in their hearts by a direct question which puts the matter in the true light. To refuse to do good is to do evil; and it could not be right to do evil on the sabbath.

The reading of TR., *ἐπερωτήσω ὑμᾶς τι*, is wrong in both variations; and has the disadvantage of being ambiguous, for *τι* may be indefinite or interrogative. "I will ask you something, Is it lawful?" etc. Or, "I will ask you what is lawful," etc.

ψυχὴν σῶσαι ἢ ἀπολέσαι. It was a principle of the Rabbinists that *periculum vitæ pellit sabbatum*; but the life must be that of a Jew. This canon was liberally interpreted; so that a large number of diseases might be attended to on the sabbath, as being dangerous. These modifications of the rigid rule were based on the principle that it was lawful to do good and avert evil on the sabbath; and to this Jesus appeals. If the Pharisees said, "This man's life is not in danger," the answer would have been easy, "You do not know that, any more than in the cases always allowed." The addition of ἢ ἀπολέσαι has special point, for this was what these objectors were doing. They did not consider that they were breaking the sabbath in plotting to destroy Jesus on this day (ver. 7). Were they to be allowed to destroy, while He was forbidden to save?

10. περιβλεψάμενος πάντας αὐτούς. Mk. adds, still more graphically, μετ' ὀργῆς, συλλυπούμενος ἐπὶ τῇ πωρώσει τῆς καρδίας αὐτῶν: but πάντας is peculiar to Lk. See on vii. 35 and ix. 43. Mt. omits the whole of this, but inserts the case of the sheep fallen into a pit. Lk. has a similar question about a son or ox fallen into a well, which was asked on another occasion (xiv. 5).

Ἔκτεινον τὴν χεῖρά σου. As His challenge to His enemies remained unanswered, He now makes trial of the man. The attempt to obey this command was evidence of his faith.

With the double augment in ἀπεκατεστάθη comp. ἐπροέταξα, ἐπροεφήτευον, ἐκατεσκεύασαν, ἐσυνεμαρτύρουν, ἠφώρισται, which occur in various writers. Exod. iv. 7, ἀπεκατέστη; Jer. xxiii. 8, ἀπεκατέστησεν; Ign. *Smyr.* xi., ἀπεκατεστάθη. Win. xii. 7. a, p. 84.

Cod. D here inserts ver. 5.

11. ἀνοίας. The phrensy or loss of reason which is caused by extreme excitement; *dementia* rather than *insipientia* (Vulg.) or *amentia* (Beza). Plato distinguishes two kinds of ἄνοια, τὸ μὲν μανίαν, τὸ δ' ἀμαθίαν (*Tim.* 86 B). It is the former which is intended here. Elsewhere 2 Tim. iii. 9; Prov. xxii. 15; Eccl. xi. 10; Wisd. xv. 18, xix. 3; 2 Mac. iv. 6, etc.

τί ἂν ποιήσαιεν. "What they should do," if they did anything. In Lk. the opt. is still freq. in indirect questions: see on iii. 15. Mk. says that the Pharisees forthwith took counsel with the Herodians how they might destroy Him (ἀπολέσωσιν). They would be glad of the assistance of the court party to accomplish this end. With their help Antipas might be induced to treat Jesus as he had treated the Baptist. Lk. nowhere mentions the Herodians.

The Aeolic form ποιήσειαν is not found in the best MSS. here. In Acts xvii. 27 ψηλαφήσειαν is probably genuine.

VI. 12–VIII. 56. *From the Nomination of the Twelve to their First Mission.*

In proportion as the work of Christ progresses the opposition between Him and the supporters of moribund Judaism is intensified.

12–16. The Nomination of the Twelve. Common to all three: comp. Mk. iii. 13–19; Mt. x. 2–4. *L'élection des Douze est le premier acte organisateur accompli par Jésus-Christ. Sauf les sacrements, c'est le seul. Car c'était ce collège, une fois constitué, qui devait un jour faire le reste* (Godet).

12. ἐν ταῖς ἡμέραις τ. See on i. 39. This expression, and **ἐγένετο** and **ἦν** with the participle, are characteristic of Lk., and are not found in the parallels in Mt. and Mk. For the constr. comp. *vv.* 1 and 6; for **προσεύξασθαι** see Introd. § 6. The momentous crisis of choosing the Twelve is at hand, and this vigil is the preparation for it.

διανυκτερεύων. Here only in N.T., but not rare elsewhere; Job ii. 9 (where LXX has much which is not in the extant Heb.); Jos. *Ant.* vi. 13. 9; *B. J.* i. 29. 2; Xen. *Hellen.* v. 4. 3. The analytical tense emphasizes the long continuance of the prayer.

τῇ προσευχῇ τοῦ Θεοῦ. The phrase occurs nowhere else. It means prayer which has God for its object: comp. ζῆλος Θεοῦ (Rom. x. 2); ὁ ζῆλος τοῦ οἴκου σου (Jn. ii. 17); πίστις Ἰησοῦ (Gal. iii. 22). Win. xxx. 1. a, p. 231.[1] That προσευχή here means an oratory or place of prayer is incredible: see on Acts xvi. 13. Lightfoot says that some Rabbis taught that God prays: "Let it be My will that My mercy overcome My wrath." But such trifling has no place here. Mk. xi. 22 and Jas. ii. 1 are perhaps parallel.

13. ἐγένετο ἡμέρα. The phrase is freq. in Lk. (iv. 42, xxii. 66; Acts xii. 18, xvi. 35, xxiii. 12, xxvii. 29, 33, 39).—**προσεφώνησεν.** "Called to Him, summoned." This is the more correct use of the word. Elsewhere in N.T. it means "address, call to"; and, excepting Mt. xi. 16, it is used only by Lk. (vii. 32, xiii. 12, xxiii. 20; Acts xxi. 40, xxii. 2).—**τοὺς μαθητάς.** These are the larger circle of disciples, out of whom He selected the Twelve. Comp. Jn. vi. 70; Mt. xix. 28; Rev. xxi. 14. That either the larger circle or the Twelve had spent the night with Him is neither stated nor implied.

ἐκλεξάμενος. This implies the telling over (λέγειν) in preference to others (ἐκ) for one's own advantage (mid.). The word is fatal

[1] Green compares ἐπ' εὐσεβείᾳ Θεοῦ (Jos. *Ant.* ii. 8. 1) and πρὸς ἱκετείαν τοῦ Θεοῦ (ii. 9. 3): and, for the art. before προσευχῇ "as an abstract or general term," Mt. xxi. 22; Acts i. 14; 1 Cor. vii. 5 (*Gram. of N.T.* p. 87).

to Lange's theory that Judas was forced upon our Lord by the importunity of the other Apostles (*L. of C.* ii. p. 179).

οὓς καὶ ἀποστόλους ὠνόμασεν. Not at the time possibly, but afterwards. The *καί* marks the naming as a separate act from the election. The word **ἀπόστολος** is used only once each by Mt. (x. 2), Mk. (vi. 30), and Jn. (xiii. 16); by Lk. six times in the Gospel (ix. 10, xi. 49, xvii. 5, xxii. 14, xxiv. 10) and often in the Acts. In the Gospels the Twelve are generally *called* the Twelve. The word occurs once in LXX, *ἐγώ εἰμι ἀπόστολος πρός σε σκληρός* (1 Kings xiv. 6); and once in N.T. it is used of Christ (Heb. iii. 1). See Lft. *Galatians*, pp. 92–101, 6th ed.; *D.B.*[2] art. "Apostle"; Harnack in *Texte u. Untersuch.* ii. 111 ff.; Sanday on Rom. i. 1. The theory that Lk. writes in order to depreciate the Twelve, does not harmonize with the solemn importance which he assigns to their election. And criticism is out of harmony with itself, when it adopts this theory, and then suggests that Lk. has invented this early election. See on xxii. 45. Mk. iii. 14 is doubtful.

14–16. In construction the twelve names are in apposition to *ἀποστόλους*, and the narrative is not resumed until ver. 17. The four lists of the Apostles preserved in the Synoptic Gospels and the Acts agree in two main features. 1. The names are arranged in three groups of four. 2. The same Apostles, Peter, Philip, and James of Alphæus, stand first in each group. Only in respect of one name is there material difference between the lists. In the third group Lk. both here and Acts i. 13 has Judas of James; for whom Mt. (x. 3) and Mk. (iii. 18) have Thaddæus or Lebbæus. In both places Thaddæus is probably correct, Lebbæus being due to an attempt to include Levi among the Apostles. Levi = Lebi or Lebbi, the Greek form of which might be *Λεββαῖος*, as *Θαδδαῖος* of Thaddi. Some MSS. read *Λεβαῖος*, which is still closer to Levi. See WH. ii. App. pp. 12, 24. The identification of Thaddæus with Judas of James solves the difficulty, and there is nothing against it excepting lack of direct evidence. No pairing of the Apostles is manifest in this list as in that of Mt. If the *καί* after *Θωμᾶν* be omitted, there is a break between the second and third group; but otherwise the list is a simple string of names. In the first six names Lk. agrees with the first three pairs of Mt. In the other six he places Matthew before Thomas (while Mt. places himself last in his group) and Simon Zelotes before Judas of James.

14. Σίμωνα ὃν καὶ ὠνόμασεν Πέτρον. The similarity to the preceding clause is marked. This certainly does not mean that Simon received the name of Peter on this occasion, and there is nothing to show that the Twelve received the name of Apostles on this occasion. But it should be noticed that henceforth Lk. always speaks of him as Peter (viii. 45, 51, ix. 20, 28, 32, 33, xii. 41, etc.) and not as Simon. In xxii. 31 and xxiv. 34 Lk. is quoting the words of others. Hitherto he has called him Simon (iv. 38, v. 3, 4, 5, 10) and once Simon Peter (v. 8), but never Peter. In the Acts he is never called Simon without the addition of the surname. The usage with regard to the names Saul and Paul is very similar. See papers by Dean Chadwick on "The Group of the Apostles" and on "Peter" in *Expositor*, 3rd series, vol. ix. pp. 100–114, 187–199, 1889; also Schanz, *ad loc.* p. 216.

Ἀνδρέαν. Only in his lists of the Apostles does Lk. mention Andrew. Mt. mentions him on one other occasion, and Mk. on three others (Mt. iv. 18; Mk. i. 16, 29, xiii. 3). Nearly all that we know about him comes from Jn. (i. 41, 44, vi. 8, xii. 22). Although one of the earliest disciples, he does not become one of the chosen three, although Mk. xiii. 3 seems to indicate special intimacy. For legends respecting him see Lipsius, *Apokryphen Apostelgeschichten u. Apostellegenden*, i. pp. 543–622; Tregelles, *Canon Muratorianus*, pp. 17, 34.

Ἰάκωβον καὶ Ἰωάνην. This is their order according to age, and it is observed in all three Gospels; in Acts i. 13 John precedes James. The fact that James was the first of the Twelve to be put to death is evidence that he was regarded as specially influential. James and John were probably first cousins of the Lord; for, according to the best interpretation of Jn. xix. 25, their mother Salome was the sister of the Virgin Mary. That the title of Boanerges was given to them "at the time of the appointment of the Twelve" (*D.B.*[2] i. p. 1509) is a baseless hypothesis. See Trench, *Studies in the Gospels*, pp. 138–146; Suicer, *Thesaurus*, *s.v.* *βροντή*. For legends see *D.B.*[2] i. p. 1511; Lipsius, iii. pp. 201–228, i. pp. 348–542.

Φίλιππον. All that we know of him comes from Jn. (i. 44–49, vi. 5–7, xii. 21, 22, xiv. 8, 9). There seems to have been some connexion between him and Andrew (Jn. i. 44, xii. 22); and both in Mk. iii. 18 and Acts i. 13 their names are placed together in the lists; but the nature of the connexion is unknown. Lipsius, iii. pp. 1–53.

Βαρθολομαῖον. The ancient and common identification with Nathanael is probable, but by no means certain. 1. As Bar-tholomew is only a patronymic, "son of Talmai," the bearer of it would be likely to have another name. 2. The Synoptists do not mention Nathanael; Jn. does not mention Bartholomew. 3. The Synoptists place Bartholomew next to Philip, and Philip brought Nathanael to Christ. 4. The companions of Nathanael who are named Jn. xxi. 2 are all of them Apostles. Lipsius, iii. pp. 54–108.

15. Μαθθαῖον καὶ Θωμᾶν. In all three these names are combined; but Mt. reverses the order, and after his own name adds ὁ τελώνης, which is found in none of the other lists. All that we know of Thomas is told us by Jn. (xi. 16, xiv. 5, xx. 24–29, xxi. 2). Lipsius, iii. pp. 109–141, i. pp. 225–347.

Ἰάκωβον Ἀλφαίου. His father is probably not the father of Levi (Mk. ii. 14), and James himself is certainly not the brother of the Lord (Mt. xiii. 55; Mk. vi. 3; Gal. i. 19) who was the first overseer of the Church of Jerusalem (Acts xii. 17, xv. 13; Gal. ii. 9, 12).

The brethren of the Lord did not believe on Him at this time (Jn. vii. 5), and none of them can have been among the Twelve. But the Apostle James the son of Alphæus is probably identical with James the Little (Mt. xxvii. 56; Mk. xv. 40; Jn. xix. 25), for Alphæus and Clopas may be two different Greek forms of the Aramaic Chalpai; but this is uncertain. See Mayor, *Ep. of S. James*, pp. i–xlvi; also *Expositor's Bible, S. James and S. Jude*, pp. 25–30 (Hodder, 1891). In all the catalogues James of Alphæus heads the third group of Apostles. Lipsius, iii. 229–238.

τὸν καλούμενον ζηλωτήν.[1] Lk. has this in both his lists, while Mt. and Mk. have ὁ Καναναῖος, which in some authorities has been corrupted into Κανανίτης. Neither of these forms can mean "Canaanite," for which the Greek is Χαναναῖος (Mt. xv. 22 and LXX), nor yet "of Cana," for which the Greek would be Καναῖος. Καναναῖος is the Aramaic *Kanan* in a Greek form (on the analogy of Φαρισαῖος from *Pharish* and Ἀσσιδαῖος from *Chasid*) and = ζηλωτής. Lipsius, iii. pp. 142–200. See on i. 36.

Rhem. leaves the word untranslated, *Cananæus*, and Wic. makes it unintelligible, "Canane." All the other English Versions make it a local adj., "of Cana," or "of Cane," or "of Canan," or "of Canaan," or "the Canaanite." The last error seems to begin with Cranmer in 1539. RV. is the first to make clear that "Kananæan" means "Zealot." Lft. *On Revision*, pp. 138, 139 (154, 155, 2nd ed.); Fritzsche on Mt. x. 4. The Zealots date from the time of the Maccabees as a class who attempted to force upon others their own rigorous interpretations of the Law. S. Paul speaks of himself as περισσοτέρως ζηλωτὴς ὑπάρχων τῶν πατρικῶν μου παραδόσεων (Gal. i. 14), *i.e.* he belonged to the extreme party of the Pharisees (Acts xxii. 3, xxiii. 6, xxvi. 5; Phil. iii. 5, 6). Large numbers of this party were among the first converts at Jerusalem (Acts xxi. 20). From these extremists had sprung the revolt under Judas of Galilee (Acts. v. 37; Jos. *Ant.* xviii. 1. 1, 6), and the *Sicarii*, who were the proximate cause of the destruction of Jerusalem (Jos. *B. J.* iv. 3. 9, 5. 1, 7. 2, vii. 8. 1, 10. 1, 11. 1). Milman, *Hist. of the Jews*, ii. pp. 191, 291, 299, 323, 4th ed. 1866; Ewald, *Hist. of Israel*, vii. 559 ff., Eng. tr.; Herzog, *PRE.*[2] art. "Zeloten." Whether the Apostle Simon was called ζηλωτής because he had once belonged to this party, or because of his personal character either before or after his call, must remain uncertain.

16. Ἰούδαν Ἰακώβου. That there were two Apostles of the name of Judas is clear from Jn. xiv. 22, although Mt. and Mk. mention only one; and the identification of their Thaddæus with the Judas not Iscariot of Jn. and with this Judas of James makes all run smoothly. Ἰούδας Ἰακώβου must be rendered "Judas the *son* of James," not "the *brother* of James," for which there is no justification. When Lk. means "brother" he inserts ἀδελφός (iii. 1, vi. 14; Acts xii. 2). Nonnus in his *Paraphrase* (Μεταβολή) of Jn. xiv. 22 has Ἰούδας υἱὸς Ἰακώβοιο. Ἰούδας ἀδελφὸς Ἰακώβου (Jude 1) is quite a different person, viz. the brother of James the

[1] This use of καλούμενος is very common in Lk. (vii. 11, viii. 2, ix. 10, x. 39, xxi. 37, xxii. 3, xxiii. 33), and still more so in Acts. Not in Mt. Mk. or Jn.

Lord's brother. Tyn. Cov. and Cran. rightly supply "sonne" here, and Luth. also has *sohn* The error begins with Beza's *fratrem*. Of this James, the father of Judas Thaddæus, nothing is known. Lk. adds the name of the father, because his arrangement places this Judas next to the traitor.

Ἰσκαριώθ. This epithet probably means "man of Kerioth," which was a place in Judah (Josh. xv. 25), or possibly in Moab (Jer. xlviii. 24). Jn. vi. 71 confirms this; for there and Jn. xiii. 26 the true reading gives "Judas son of Simon Iscariot"; and if the name is a local epithet, both father and son would be likely to have it. In this case Judas was the only Apostle who was not a Galilean, and this may have helped to isolate him. Other derivations of "Iscariot," which connect the word with "lying," or "strangling," or "apron," *i.e.* bag, or "date-trees" (καριωτίδες), are much less probable. We know nothing about Simon Iscariot. Farrar identifies him with Simon Zelotes, which is most improbable. Simon was one of the commonest of names. The MSS. vary between Ἰσκαριώθ, which is right here, and Ἰσκαριώτης, which is right xxii. 3. Here only is **προδότης** used of Judas: it occurs in the plur. Acts vii. 52; 2 Tim. iii. 4; and in the sing. 2 Mac. v. 15, x. 13. All English Versions go wrong about **ἐγένετο προδότης**. Nowhere in Scripture is Judas styled "*the* traitor," and ἐγένετο should be distinguished from ἦν: therefore, not "*was the* traitor," but "*became a* traitor," as the American Revisers proposed. Judas "turned traitor." The difficulty about the call of Judas is parallel to the powers bestowed upon a Napoleon. The treason of Judas shows that no position in the Church, however exalted, gives security against the most complete fall.

The *verb* used of the treachery of Judas is never προδιδόναι, but παραδιδόναι (xxii. 4, 6, 21, 22, 48; Mt. x. 4; Mk. iii. 19; Jn. vi. 64, 71). In class. Grk. προδιδόναι commonly has this meaning; παραδιδόναι rarely. Here the Lat. texts vary between *proditor* (Vulg.) and *traditor* (c f ff_2 r) and *qui tradidit eum* or *illum* (d e).

17–19. The Descent from the Mountain, and many Miracles of Healing. The parallel passages in Mk. iii. 7–12 and Mt. iv. 24, 25 are very different from Lk. and from one another in wording.

17. ἐπὶ τόπου πεδινοῦ. This *may* mean a level spot below the summit; but in connexion with καταβάς, and without qualification, it more naturally means level ground near the foot of the mountain. Hither it would be more likely that multitudes would come and bring their sick, than to a plateau high up the mountain.

The Latin texts vary: *in loco campestri* (Vulg.), *in loco campense* (a), *in l. lano* (f) *in l. pedeplano* (l.).

καὶ ὄχλος πολὺς μαθητῶν αὐτοῦ. Not a *nom. pendens*, but included in the preceding ἔστη: comp. the constr. viii. 1–3. He stood, and they stood. But the ἔστη is no evidence as to Christ's attitude during the discourse, because the healings intervene: iv. 20 shows that Lk. is aware of Christ's sitting to preach.

καὶ πλῆθος πολὺ τοῦ λαοῦ, κ.τ.λ. This is a third group. Christ and the Twelve form one group. The multitude of disciples in the wider sense form a second. And besides these there is a mixed throng from Judæa and the sea-coast: see on xi. 29.

ἰαθῆναι ἀπό. The prep. is not classical; but we say "to be cured *from*" (Mk. v. 29). In the perf., 1 aor. and 1 fut. pass. the dep. *ἰάομαι* is pass. in meaning (vii. 7, viii. 47, xvii. 15; not Acts iii. 11). Except in Lk., the verb is rare in N.T. writers.—There should be at least a colon at *τῶν νόσων αὐτῶν*: here the long sentence which began at ver. 13 ends.

18, 19. For similarly condensed accounts of groups of miracles comp. iv. 40, v. 15, vii. 21. We once more have an amphibolous expression: see on ii. 22. Here **ἀπὸ πνευμάτων ἀκαθάρτων** may be taken either with ἐνοχλούμενοι or with ἐθεραπεύοντο. From ver. 17 and vii. 21 we infer that the latter constr. is right: "They that were troubled with them were healed of unclean spirits." But in the other cases the gen. with ἀπό follows the verb; so that ἐνοχλούμενοι ἀπό may be right. The "and" before "were healed" in AV. is from a corrupt reading: not only Wic. and Rhem. with Vulg., but also Cov., omit the "and." For **πνευμάτων ἀκαθάρτων** see on iv. 33. Note πᾶς and πάντας here and πάσης in ver. 17. They are not found in Mk. iii. 7, 10: see on ver. 30. With **παρ' αὐτοῦ ἐξήρχετο** comp. Jn. xvi. 27. Lk. commonly writes ἐξέρχομαι ἀπό: see small print on iv. 35, and comp. viii. 46, which illustrates ἅπτεσθαι, δύναμις, and ἐξήρχετο. For **δύναμις** and **ἰᾶτο** see on iv. 36.

20–49. The Sermon ἐπὶ τόπου πεδινοῦ. *D.B.* v. art. "Sermon."

To call it "the Sermon on the Plain," following the AV. in ver. 17, is convenient, but scarcely justifiable. "The plain" has not been mentioned, and *τὸ πεδίον* does not occur in N.T. Moreover, it is by no means certain that this *τόπος πεδινός* was at the foot of the mount. And to talk of "the Sermon on the Plain" assumes, what cannot be proved, that the discourse here recorded is entirely distinct from "the Sermon on the Mount" (Mt. v. 1–vii. 29). The relations between the two discourses will never cease to be discussed, because the materials are insufficient for a final decision. The following are the chief hypotheses which have been suggested in order to explain the marked similarities and differences. 1. They are reports, at first or second hand, of two similar but different discourses, distinct in time, place, and circumstance (Auger, Greswell, Osiander, Patritius, Plumptre, Sadler; so also in the main Barradius, Basil, Doddridge, Toletus, Tostatus). 2. They are reports of two different discourses delivered on the same day, Mt. giving the esoteric address to the disciples on the mountain, Lk. the exoteric address to the mixed multitude below (Augustine, Lange). 3. They are recensions, with interpolations and omissions, of two independent reports of one and the same sermon (Schleiermacher). 4. They are recensions of the same report, to which Mt. adds material from other sources, and from which Lk. perhaps omits portions (B. Weiss). 5. Mt. gives a conflate arrangement of sayings which were uttered on various occasions, and some of these occasions are given by Lk. (Bleek, Calvin, Godet, Holtzmann, Keim, Kuinoel, Neander, Pott, Semler, Weizsäcker, Wieseler). 6. Both sermons are a conglomeration of detached sayings collected into an anthology of aphorisms (Strauss, and to some extent Baur). Besides the writers mentioned above under the last four heads, a multitude of commentators adopt the view that the main portions of the reports given by Mt. and Lk. represent one and the same discourse (Bengel, Bucer, Calovius, Caspari, Chemnitz, Chrysostom, De Wette, Ebrard, Edersheim, Ellicott, Ewald, Farrar, Fritzsche, Grotius, Hilgenfeld, Keim, Lewin, Luther, McClellan, Meyer, Milman, Olshausen, Oosterzee, Origen, Robinson, Schanz, Schneckenburger, Sieffert, Stroud, Tholuck, Tischendorf, Wordsworth).

Bad or inadequate arguments are used on both sides. It is a great deal too much to say with Schleiermacher that the fact that the portions common to both appear in the same order, with the same beginning and end, "*proves incontrovertibly* the identity of the discourse." Any preacher repeating a carefully prepared sermon would begin and end in the same way, and would put his points in the same order. And it is mere dogmatism without argument when Sadler asserts that "the Lord *must* have pronounced each [beatitude] which St. Matthew records, and yet it is equally plain that He *could* hardly have pronounced them according to St. Luke's form. He would not have said, Blessed are ye meek ones, Blessed are ye merciful ones, Blessed are ye peacemakers. The four given by St. Luke are the only ones which *could* well have been pronounced personally on the disciples; so that the beatitudes as given by St. Matthew and St. Luke respectively, *could* not have been altered forms of the same discourse." Much more reasonable is the position of Grotius, who believes that both record the same sermon: *sicut facti narrationes circumstantiis congruentes non temere ad res diversas referendæ sunt, ita sermones nihil vetat sæpius habitos eosdem aut similes, præsertim continentes vitæ totius præcepta, quæ non potuerunt nimium sæpe repeti* (on Lk. vi. 17). We know beyond all question that some of our Lord's words were uttered several times, and there is nothing antecedently improbable in the hypothesis that the words of this discourse, *quæ non potuerunt nimium sæpe repeti*, were delivered in one or other of these forms more than once. Nor does it follow that those portions which Lk. gives as having been uttered on other occasions were not also uttered as parts of a continuous discourse. A preacher naturally repeats fragments of his own sermons in giving catechetical instruction, and also gathers up detached items of instruction when composing a sermon. The fact that Lk. meant to record these other occasions may have been part of his reason for omitting the similar words in this discourse. Another consideration which may have determined his selection is the thought of what would best suit Gentile readers. But in any case the dictum of Grotius must be remembered, that the hypothesis of a repetition of verbally similar sayings may be used with much more freedom than the hypothesis of a repetition of circumstantially similar acts.

The conclusion arrived at by Sanday and P. Ewald is of this kind. The beatitudes originally stood in the *Logia* in a form similar to that in Mt. v. 3–12. Lk. used the *Logia*, but had also a document entirely independent of the *Logia*; and this contained a discourse, spoken originally on some other occasion, but yet so like the Sermon on the Mount as to be identified with it by Lk. The sermon in Luke is, therefore, a compound of the reports of two similar but different discourses; and in this compound the elements derived from the *Logia* are dominated by those derived from the independent document (*Expositor* for April 1891, p. 315). It seems, however, simpler to suppose that Lk. took the whole of his report from the document which contained this very similar, but different sermon. See Paul Feine, *Ueber das gegenseit. Verhältniss d. Texte der Bergpredigt bei Matthäus und Lukas* in the *Jahrb. für Protest. Theologie*, xi. 1.

The following tables will show the parallels between the two Evangelists :—

BETWEEN THE TWO SERMONS.

Lk. vi. 20, 21	Mt. v. 3, 4, 6.	Lk. vi. 37, 38	Mt. vii. 1, 2.
22, 23	11, 12.	41, 42	3-5.
27-30	39-42.	43-46	16-21.
31	vii. 12.	47-49	24-27.
32-36	v. 42-48.		

BETWEEN DETACHED SAYINGS IN LK. AND THE SERMON IN MT.

Lk. xiv. 34, 35	Mt. v. 13.	Lk. xi. 34-36	Mt. vi. 22-23.
viii. 16 and xi. 33	15.	xvi. 13	24.
xvi. 17	18.	xii. 22-31	25-34.
xii. 58, 59	25, 26.	xi. 9-13	vii. 7-11.
xvi. 18	32.	xiii. 24	13.
xi. 2-4	vi. 9-13.	25-27	22, 23.
xii. 33, 34	19, 21.		

BETWEEN THE SERMON IN LK. AND DETACHED SAYINGS IN MT.

Lk. vi. 39	Mt. xv. 14.	Lk. vi. 40	Mt. x. 24.

This last saying was frequently uttered. It is recorded twice by Jn. (xiii. 16, xv. 20), and the four records seem to refer to four different occasions; besides which we have a similar utterance Lk. xxii. 27.

These tables leave three verses of the sermon in Lk. without a parallel in Mt. (or any other Gospel), viz. the four woes corresponding to the four beatitudes, *vv.* 24-26. The portions of the sermon in Mt. which have no parallel in Lk. amount to forty-one verses, viz. Mt. v. 5, 7-10, 14, 16, 17, 19-24, 27-31, 33-38, 43, vi. 1-8, 14-18, vii. 6, 14, 15.

The plan of both discourses is the same. 1. The qualifications of those who can enter the kingdom (Lk. 20-26; Mt. v. 1-12); 2. The duties of those who have entered the kingdom (Lk. 27-45; Mt. v. 13-vii. 12); 3. The judgments which await the members of the kingdom (Lk. 46-49; Mt. vii. 13-27). Encouragement, requirement, warning; or invitation, principles, sanction;—these are the three gradations which may be traced in these discourses; and, as Stier remarks, the course of all preaching is herein reflected.

There is considerable unanimity as to the spot where the sermon was delivered (Stanley, *Sin & Pal.* pp. 368, 369; Caspari, *Chron. and Geograph. Int. to the L. of C.* § 108, p. 171; Robinson, *Pal.* ii. 370, iii. pp. 241, 485; Farrar, *L. of C.* i. p. 250, and on Lk. vi. 12; Keim, *Jes. of Naz.* ii. p. 289). On the other hand, Edersheim asserts that "the locality is for many reasons unsuitable"; but he gives no reasons (*L. & T.* i. p. 524; see also Thomson, *Land and Book*, ii. p. 118).

20-26. The Qualifications necessary for Admission to the Kingdom: the Happiness of those who possess them (20-23), and the Misery of those who possess them not (24-26). This contrast of Blessings and Woes at the beginning of the sermon corresponds with the contrast in the parable with which it ends.

THE BEATITUDES COMMON TO MT. AND LK. WITH THE CORRESPONDING WOES IN LK.

Μακάριοι	Μακάριοι	Οὐαί
1. οἱ πτωχοὶ τῷ πνεύματι, ὅτι αὐτῶν ἐστιν ἡ βασιλεία τῶν οὐρανῶν.	1. οἱ πτωχοί, ὅτι ὑμετέρα ἐστὶν ἡ βασιλεία τοῦ Θεοῦ.	1. ὑμῖν τοῖς πλουσίοις, ὅτι ἀπέχετε τὴν παράκλησιν ὑμῶν.
2. οἱ πενθοῦντες, ὅτι αὐτοὶ παρακληθήσονται.	3. οἱ κλαίοντες νῦν, ὅτι γελάσετε.	3. οἱ γελῶντες νῦν, ὅτι πενθήσετε καὶ κλαύσετε.
4. οἱ πεινῶντες καὶ διψῶντες τὴν δικαιοσύνην, ὅτι αὐτοὶ χορτασθήσονται.	2. οἱ πεινῶντες νῦν, ὅτι χορτασθήσεσθε.	2. ὑμῖν, οἱ ἐμπεπλησμένοι νῦν, ὅτι πεινάσετε.
8. ἐστε ὅταν ὀνειδίσωσιν ὑμᾶς καὶ διώξωσιν καὶ εἴπωσιν πᾶν πονηρὸν καθ' ὑμῶν ψευδόμενοι ἕνεκεν ἐμοῦ· χαίρετε καὶ ἀγαλλιᾶσθε, ὅτι ὁ μισθὸς ὑμῶν πολὺς ἐν τοῖς οὐρανοῖς· οὕτως γὰρ ἐδίωξαν τοὺς προφήτας τοὺς πρὸ ὑμῶν.	4. ἐστε ὅταν μισήσωσιν ὑμᾶς οἱ ἄνθρωποι, καὶ ὅταν ἀφορίσωσιν ὑμᾶς καὶ ὀνειδίσωσιν καὶ ἐκβάλωσιν τὸ ὄνομα ὑμῶν ὡς πονηρὸν ἕνεκα τοῦ υἱοῦ τοῦ ἀνθρώπου· χάρητε ἐν ἐκείνῃ τῇ ἡμέρᾳ καὶ σκιρτήσατε, ἰδοὺ γὰρ ὁ μισθὸς ὑμῶν πολὺς ἐν τῷ οὐρανῷ· κατὰ τὰ αὐτὰ γὰρ ἐποίουν τοῖς προφήταις οἱ πατέρες αὐτῶν.	4. ὅταν καλῶς ὑμᾶς εἴπωσιν πάντες οἱ ἄνθρωποι, κατὰ τὰ αὐτὰ γὰρ ἐποίουν τοῖς ψευδοπροφήταις οἱ πατέρες αὐτῶν.

VI. 20–23. Four Beatitudes; which correspond to the first, second, fourth, and eighth in Mt. v. 3–12; those relating to the meek, the merciful, the pure in heart, and the peacemakers being omitted. In the four that Lk. gives the more spiritual words which occur in Mt. are omitted, and the blessings are assigned to more external conditions. *Actual* poverty, sorrow, and hunger are declared to be blessed (as being opportunities for the exercise of internal virtues); and this doctrine is emphasized by the corresponding Woes pronounced upon wealth, jollity, and fulness of bread (as being sources of temptation). It is in the last Beatitude that there is least difference between the two. Even in Lk. unpopularity is not declared to be blessed, unless it is "for the Son of Man's sake"; and there is no Woe pronounced upon popularity for the Son of Man's sake. See Hastings, *D.B.* i. p. 261.

20. Καὶ αὐτὸς ἐπάρας τοὺς ὀφθαλμοὺς αὐτοῦ εἰς τοὺς μαθητάς. Lk.'s favourite mode of connexion in narrative: see on v. 14 and comp. viii. 1, 22, ix. 51, etc. With ἐπάρας τ. ὀφθ. comp. xviii. 13 and Jn. xvii. 1. We must not take εἰς with ἔλεγεν; Lk. would have written πρός, and *after* ἔλεγεν: contrast xxii. 65 and Mk. iii. 29. Mt. has προσῆλθαν αὐτῷ οἱ μαθηταὶ αὐτοῦ. **καὶ . . . ἐδίδασκεν αὐτούς.** The discourse in *both* cases is addressed to *the disciples*; there is nothing to indicate that the discourse *in Lk.* is addressed to mixed multitudes, including unbelieving Jews and heathen. These Beatitudes would not be true, if addressed to them. It is to the faithful Christian that poverty, hunger, sorrow, and unpopularity are real blessings; to others they may be mere sterile suffering. Whereas, even for the heathen, to be poor *in spirit* and to hunger and thirst *after righteousness* are blessed things. In Mt. the Beatitudes are in the third person and have a wider sweep.

μακάριοι οἱ. This is the common constr. both in LXX and N.T., the reason for the blessedness being expressed by a noun or participle which is the subject of the sentence (Ps. ii. 12, xl. 5, xli. 2, lxxxiv. 5, 6, 13, lxxxix. 16, etc.); but the reason is sometimes expressed by the relative with a finite verb (Ps. i. 1, xxxii. 1, 2; Lk. xiv. 15; Jas. i. 12), or by ὅτι (xiv. 14; 1 Pet. iv. 14), or by ἐάν (Jn. xiii. 17; 1 Cor. vii. 40).

οἱ πτωχοί. See on iv. 18. We have no right to supply τῷ πνεύματι from Mt. It is actual poverty that is here meant. Nor is it the meaning that actual poverty makes men "poor in spirit." Still less does it mean that in itself poverty is to all men a blessing. There is no Ebionite doctrine here. But "to *you*, My disciples, poverty is a blessing, because it preserves you in your dependence on God, and helps you to be truly His subjects": τὸ γὰρ ὑμετέρα δεικτικῶς πρὸς πάροντας ἐλέγετο (Eus.) Some of these disciples had made themselves poor by surrendering all in order to follow Christ. Comp. Ps. lxxii. 12, 13.

ὑμετέρα ἐστὶν ἡ βασιλεία. "Yours *is* the kingdom," not "will be." It is not a promise, as in the next Beatitudes, but the statement of a fact. But the Kingdom is not yet theirs in its fulness; and those elements which are not yet possessed are promised in the Beatitudes which follow.

21. οἱ πεινῶντες νῦν. "Those of you who are suffering from actual want in this life. Ye shall have compensation."

χορτασθήσεσθε. Originally the verb was confined to supplying animals with fodder (χόρτος), and if used of men implied a brutish kind of feeding (Plato, *Rep.* ix. p. 586). But in N.T. it is never used of cattle, and when it is used of men it has no degrading associations (ix. 17; Jn. vi. 26; Phil. iv. 12; Jas. ii. 16); not even xv. 16, if the word is genuine there, nor xvi. 21. Comp. τοὺς πτωχοὺς αὐτῆς χορτάσω ἄρτων (Ps. cxxxii. 15). In LXX χορτάζω and πίμπλημι are used to translate the same Hebrew word, sometimes in the same verse: ὅτι ἐχόρτασεν ψυχὴν κενήν, καὶ ψυχὴν πεινῶσαν ἐνέπλησεν ἀγαθῶν (Ps. cvii. 9). Here the filling refers to the spiritual abundance in the Kingdom of God. *In all four cases*, although the suffering endured is external and literal, yet *the compensating blessing is spiritual.*

οἱ κλαίοντες νῦν. Mt. has πενθοῦντες, which expresses the mourning, while κλαίοντες implies outward manifestation of grief in loud weeping, just as γελάσετε implied outward expression of mirth in laughter. Though common in LXX, γελάω occurs in N.T. only here and ver. 25.

22. ἀφορίσωσιν ὑμᾶς. "Mark you off from (ἀπό) by a boundary (ὅρος)." It is used both in a good sense (Acts xiii. 2; Rom. i. 1; Gal. i. 15) and also in a bad, as here. Comp. *καί μ' ἀπὸ γᾶς ὥρισε* (Eur. *Hec.* 940). Excommunication from the congregation as well as from social intercourse is here meant. The usual sentence was for thirty days, during which the excommunicated might not come within four cubits of any one. Comp. Jn. ix. 22, xii. 42, xvi. 2. Whether there was at this time a more severe form of excommunication is uncertain. Herzog, *PRE.*[2] art. *Bann bei den Hebräern*; Grotius on Lk. vi. 22; Lightfoot, *Hor. Heb.* on Jn. ix. 22.

ὀνειδίσωσιν. The object to be supplied may be either the preceding *ὑμᾶς* (so most English Versions) or the following *τὸ ὄνομα ὑμῶν* (Bede, Weiss). Vulg. supplies nothing; and Tyn. and Gen. have simply "and rayle" without an object. Neither AV. nor RV. has "you" in italics.

ἐκβάλωσιν τὸ ὄνομα ὑμῶν ὡς πονηρόν. "Throw your name contemptuously away, reject it with ignominy, as an evil thing." There is no idea of striking a name off the list as a mark of disgrace, *ex albo expungere*, a meaning which *ἐκβάλλειν* never has. It is used of hissing an actor off the stage and otherwise dismissing with contempt (Aristoph. *Eq.* 525; *Nub.* 1477; Soph. *O. C.* 631, 636; *O. T.* 849; Plato, *Crito*, 46 B). "Your name" means "the name by which you are known as My disciples," as Christians. "Christian" or "Nazarene" was a name of bad repute, which it was disgraceful, and even unlawful, to bear, for Christianity was not a *religio licita*. For *πονηρόν* as an epithet of *ὄνομα* comp. Deut. xxii. 19.

ἕνεκα τοῦ υἱοῦ τοῦ ἀνθρώπου. A vital qualification. The hatred and contempt must be undeserved, and be endured for Christ's sake; not merited by one's own misconduct.

23. σκιρτήσατε. Peculiar to Lk. See on i. 41 and comp. Mal. iv. 2.

κατὰ τὰ αὐτὰ γὰρ ἐποίουν τοῖς προφήταις. This implies that they are to receive "a prophet's reward" (Mt. x. 41), as in this world, so in the next.

For the dat. comp. *τοῖς μισοῦσιν ὑμᾶς* (ver. 27). In class. Gk. we should have had *τὰ αὐτὰ ἐποίουν τοὺς προφ.* Thus, *ἐγὼ δὲ ταῦτα τοῦτον ἐποίησα σὺν δίκῃ* (Hdt. i. 115. 3, iv. 166. 3: comp. Aristoph. *Nub.* 259; *Vesp.* 697). In later Gk. the dat. of relation becomes much more common.

οἱ πατέρες αὐτῶν. The gen. refers to *οἱ ἄνθρωποι* in ver. 22; "the fathers of them" who hate and abuse you.

24–26. Four Woes corresponding to the four Beatitudes. There is no evidence that these were not part of the original discourse. Assuming that Mt. and Lk. report the same discourse, Mt. may have omitted them. But they may have been spoken on some other occasion. Schleiermacher and Weiss would have it that they are mere glosses added by Lk. to emphasize and explain the preceding blessings. Cheyne thinks that some of them were suggested to Lk. by Is. lxv. 13–16. We have no right to assume that no persons were present to whom these words would be applicable. Even if there were none present, yet these Woes might have been uttered as warnings both to those who heard them and to others who would learn them from those who heard. Just as the Beatitudes express the qualifications of those who are to enter the Kingdom, so these show the qualities which exclude men from it. It is possible that some of the spies and adversaries from Judæa were among the audience, and thus Jesus warns them of their condition. When the discourse as placed by Mt. was spoken there was less opposition to Christ, and hence no Woes (*Pastor Pastorum*, p. 256).

24. πλήν. Curtius makes πλήν an adverbial form of πλέον, so that its radical meaning would be "more than, beyond" (*Gr. Etym.* 282); but Lft. (Phil. iii. 16) connects it with πέλας, in the meaning "besides, apart from this, only." For the accusatival form comp. δίκην, ἐπίκλην, *clam*, *coram*. It sometimes restricts, sometimes expands, what precedes. It is a favourite word with Lk., in the Gospel as an adv. (ver. 35, x. 11, 14, 20, xi. 41, xii. 31, xiii. 33, xvii. 1, xviii. 8, xix. 27, xxii. 21, 22, 42, xxiii. 28), in the Acts as a prep. (viii. 1, xv. 28, xxvii. 22). "But" is the only possible rendering here.

οὐαὶ ὑμῖν τοῖς πλουσίοις. As a matter of fact the opponents of Christ came mostly from the wealthy classes, like the oppressors of the first Christians (Jas. v. 1–6). See Renan, *L'Antechrist*, p. xii; Ewald, *Hist. of Israel*, vii. p. 451. But the cases of Nicodemus and Joseph of Arimathea show that the rich as such were not excluded from the kingdom.—**ἀπέχετε.** "Ye have to the full"; so that there is nothing more left to have. The poor consolation derived from the riches in which they trusted is all that they get: they have no treasure in heaven. Comp. Mt. vi. 2, 5, 16; Philem. 15; and see Lft. on Phil. iv. 18. This meaning is classical: comp. ἀπολαμβάνω, ἀπεργάζομαι. Deissmann, *Bible Studies*, p. 229. For **παράκλησιν** see on ii. 25, and comp. xvi. 25 of Lazarus.

25. οἱ ἐμπεπλησμένοι νῦν. "Sated with the good things of this life," like Dives (Ezek. xvi. 49). Grotius compares the epitaph, τόσσ' ἔχω ὅσσ' ἔπιον καὶ ἐδήτυα. It may be doubted whether the change of word from χορτάζεσθαι (ver. 21) indicates that *horum plenitudo non meretur nomen satietatis* (Beng.): comp. i. 53. In Lat. Vet. and Vulg. we have *saturor* both here and ver. 21.

πεινάσετε. This received a partial and literal fulfilment when Jerusalem was reduced to starvation in the siege: but the reference is rather to the loss of the spiritual food of the Kingdom. Comp. Is. lxv. 13. Hillel said, "The more flesh one hath the more worms, the more treasures the more care, the more maids the more unchastity, the more men-servants the more theft The more law the more life, the more schools the more wisdom, the more counsel the more insight, the more righteousness the more peace."

οἱ γελῶντες νῦν. "Who laugh for joy over your present prosperity," the loss of which will surely come and cause grief. But the worst loss will be that of spiritual joy hereafter (Is. lxv. 14).

26. ὅταν καλῶς εἴπωσιν ὑμᾶς. It is the wealthy who are commonly admired and praised by all who hope to win their favour. The praise of worldly men is no guarantee of merit: rather it shows that those who have won it do not rise above the world's standard (Jn. xv. 19; Jas. iv. 4). Plutarch says that Phocion, when his speech was received with universal applause, asked his friends whether he had inadvertently said anything wrong.

τοῖς ψευδοπροφήταις. Just as the persecuted disciples are the representatives of the true Prophets, so the wealthy hierarchy whom all men flatter are the representatives of the false (Jer. v. 31; comp. xxiii. 17; Is. xxx. 10; Mic. ii. 11).

Having stated who can and who cannot enter the Kingdom, Jesus goes on to make known the principles which regulate the Kingdom. See Hastings, *D.B.* i. p. 783.

27–45. Requirement: the Duties to be performed by those who are admitted to the Kingdom of God. This forms the main body of the discourse. Lk. omits the greater portion of what is reported in Mt. respecting Christ's relation to the Mosaic Law (v. 17–19), and His condemnation of existing methods of interpreting it (v. 20–48) and of fulfilling it (vi. 1–18). This discussion of Judaic principles and practices would not have much meaning for Lk.'s Gentile readers. The portion of it which he gives is stated without reference to Judaism. The main point in Mt. is the contrast between legal righteousness and true righteousness. In Lk. the main point is that true righteousness is love; but the opposition between formalism and the spirit of love is not urged. The opposition which is here marked is the more universal opposition between the spirit of selfishness and the spirit of love. There is a break in this main portion, which Lk. marks by making a fresh start, *Εἶπεν δὲ καὶ παραβολὴν αὐτοῖς*, but the second half (39–45) continues the subject of the working of the principle of love.

27. Ἀλλά. What is the contrast which this *ἀλλά* marks? The emphatic position of the *ὑμῖν* seems to show that the contrast is between those on whom the Woes have been pronounced and the faithful hearers now addressed. Others interpret, "But, although

I have denounced them, I do not allow you to hate them: you must love them." There is, however, no indication that the enemies who are to be loved are the wealthy who have just been denounced, and such a limitation of the meaning of enemies cannot be justified: comp. Mt. v. 44.

τοῖς ἀκούουσιν. "Who give ear and obey," τοῖς πειθομένοις (Euthym.). It is unnatural to take it literally as meaning "My audience," in contrast to the rich who have just been addressed *in their absence*. Representatives of the rich may have been present among the audience. Schanz interprets "who listen with attention."

There is on the whole a double climax in what follows,—the worse the treatment received, the better the return made; but it is not quite exact. One would expect that ἀγαπᾶτε would be coupled with τοὺς μισοῦντας. This is the first time that Lk. uses the word ἀγαπᾷν, which sums up the whole spirit of the Gospel: it is most frequent in the writings of Jn. "It should never be forgotten that ἀγάπη is a word born within the bosom of revealed religion: it occurs in the Septuagint; but there is no example of its use in any heathen writer whatever" (Trench, *Syn.* xii.). This is not true of ἀγαπᾷν and ἀγαπάζειν, which are common in class. Grk. But Christianity has ennobled the meaning of both ἀγαπᾷν and φιλεῖν, with their cognates: ἐρᾷν, which is scarcely Capable of such advancement, does not occur in N.T. See on xi. 42, the only place where ἀγάπη occurs in Lk. Deissmann, *Bible Studies*, p. 198.

τοὺς ἐχθρούς. For the combination with τοῖς μισοῦσιν comp. i. 71; Ps. xviii. 18, cvi. 10; and for the fourfold description of enmity comp. ver. 22. In Mt. v. 44 we have only enemies and persecutors according to the best texts; and as καλῶς ποιεῖτε τοὺς μισ. ὑμᾶς (note the acc.) is not genuine there, this is the only passage in which καλῶς ποιεῖν = "benefit, do good *to*": comp. καλῶς εἰπεῖν (ver. 26), and contrast Mt. xii. 12; Mk. vii. 37; Acts x. 33; 1 Cor. vii. 37, 38; Phil. iv. 14; Jas. ii. 8, 19; 2 Pet. i. 19; 3 Jn. 6.—**τοῖς μισοῦσιν.** For the dat. comp. τοῖς προφήταις (ver. 23) and τοῖς ψευδοπροφήταις (ver. 26). See the expansion of this principle Rom. xii. 17–21; 1 Thes. v. 15; 1 Pet. iii. 9. Comp. Exod. xxiii. 4; Job xxxi. 29; Prov. xvii. 5, xxiv. 17, xxv. 21. See detached note on *the relation of Rom.* xii.–xiv. *to the Gospels* at the end of Rom. xiii.

28. εὐλογεῖτε τοὺς καταρωμένους ὑμᾶς. In class. Grk. εὐλογεῖν means "praise, honour," whether gods or men: comp. i. 64, ii. 28; Jas. iii. 9. The meaning "invoke blessings upon" is confined to LXX and N.T. (Gen. xiv. 19, xxii. 17, xlviii. 9; Rom. xii. 14; Acts iii. 26).

In class. Grk. καταρᾶσθαι is followed by a dat. (Hom. Hdt. Xen. Dem.), as in Ep. Jer. 65: but in N.T. by an acc. (Mk. xi. 21; Jas. iii. 9); and the interpolation Mt. v. 44.—For προσεύχεσθε περί we might have expected πρ. ὑπέρ, and the MSS. here and elsewhere are divided between ὑπέρ and περί (Gal. i. 4; Col. i. 3; Rom. i. 8). But comp. Acts viii. 15; Heb. xiii. 18; Col. iv. 3. Win. xlvii. l. 2, p. 478.

τῶν ἐπηρεαζόντων ὑμᾶς. Aristotle defines ἐπηρεασμός as ἐμποδισμὸς ταῖς βουλήσεσιν, οὐχ ἵνα τι αὐτῷ, ἀλλ' ἵνα μὴ ἐκείνῳ (*Rhet.* ii. 2. 3). It is "spiteful treatment."

29, 30. Whereas *vv.* 27, 28 refer to the active ἀγάπη which returns good for evil, these refer rather to the passive μακροθυμία, which never retaliates. The four precepts here given are startling. It is impossible for either governments or individuals to keep them. A State which endeavoured to shape its policy in exact accordance with them would soon cease to exist; and if individuals acted in strict obedience to them society would be reduced to anarchy. Violence, robbery, and shameless exaction would be supreme. The inference is that *they are not precepts, but illustrations of principles.* They are in the form of rules; but as they *cannot* be kept as rules, we are *compelled* to look beyond the letter to the spirit which they embody. If Christ had given precepts which could be kept literally, we might easily have rested content with observing the letter, and have never penetrated to the spirit. What is the spirit? Among other things this:—that resistance of evil and refusal to part with our property must never be a *personal* matter: so far as *we* are concerned we must be willing to suffer still more and to surrender still more. It is right to withstand and even to punish those who injure us: but in order to correct them and protect society; not because of any personal *animus.* It is right also to withhold our possessions from those who without good reason ask for them; but in order to check idleness and effrontery; not because we are too fond of our possessions to part with them. *So far as our personal feeling goes,* we ought to be ready to offer the other cheek, and to give, without desire of recovery, whatever is demanded or taken from us. Love knows no limits but those which love itself imposes. When love resists or refuses, it is because compliance would be a violation of love, not because it would involve loss or suffering.

29. τῷ τύπτοντί σε ἐπὶ τὴν σιαγόνα. A violent blow with the fist seems to be meant rather than a contemptuous slap, for σιαγών means "jaw-bone" (Judg. xv. 15, 16; Ezek. xxix. 4; Mic. v. 1; Hos. xi. 4). In what follows also it is an act of violence that is meant; for in that case the upper and more valuable garment (ἱμάτιον) would be taken first. In Mt. v. 40 the spoiler adopts a legal method of spoliation (κριθῆναι), and takes the under and less indispensable garment (χιτῶνα) first. See on iii. 11 and comp. Jn. xix. 23.

Here only do we find τύπτειν ἐπί *c. acc.* In class. Grk. *c. gen.*, *e.g.* ἐπὶ κόρρης τύπτειν or πατάσσειν (Plato, *Gorg.* 486 C, 508 D, 527 A). Sometimes we have εἰς (Mt. xxvii. 30), which some MSS. read here and xviii. 13. Comp. Xen. *Cyr.* v. 4. 5. So also κωλύειν ἀπό is not common. Comp. οὐ μὴ κωλύσει τὸ μνημεῖον αὐτοῦ ἀπὸ σοῦ (Gen. xxiii. 6) and ἀπὸ σοῦ κωλύων (Xen. *Cyr.* i. 3. 11, iii. 3. 51). The more usual constr. both in N.T. and class. Grk. is either acc. and inf. (xxiii. 2; Acts xvi. 6, xxiv. 23) or acc. of pers. and gen. of thing (Acts xxvii. 43). Note that αἴρειν does not mean simply "take," which is λαμβάνειν, but either "take up" (v. 24, ix. 23) or "take away" (xix. 24, xxiii. 18).

30. παντὶ αἰτοῦντί σε δίδου. There is no παντί in Mt. v. 42, and this is one of many passages which illustrate Lk.'s fondness for πᾶς (ver. 17, vii. 35, ix. 43, xi. 4). The παντί has been differently understood. "No one is to be excluded, not even one's enemies" (Meyer, Weiss). *Omni petenti te tribue, non omnia petenti; ut id des, quod dare honeste et juste potes* (Aug.). Neither remark is quite right. Our being able to give *juste et honeste* depends not only on what is asked, but upon who asks it. Some things must not be conceded to any one. Others ought to be given to some petitioners, but not to all. In every case, however, we ought to be *willing* to part with what may be lawfully given to any. The wish to keep what we have got is not the right motive for refusing.

δίδου, καὶ ἀπὸ τοῦ αἴροντος τὰ σὰ μὴ ἀπαίτει. The pres. in all three cases implies continual action, making a practice of it. "Continually give, and from him who continues to take away thy goods do not continue to ask them again." For *αἴρειν* in the sense of "take as one's own, appropriate," comp. xi. 52, xix. 21; Mk. xv. 24. It does not imply that violence is used. But the *μὴ ἀπαίτει* implies that hitherto asking them back has been usual. The verb *ἀπαιτεῖν* is peculiar to Lk. in N.T. (xii. 20: comp. Wisd. xv. 8; Ecclus. xx. 15; Hdt. i. 3. 2). Prof. Marshall thinks that we have here another instance of different translation of the same Aramaic, and that Lk.'s *αἴροντος* and Mt.'s *δανείσασθαι* may represent the same word; also Lk.'s *ἀπαίτει* and Mt.'s *ἀποστραφῇς*. See on v. 21 and viii. 15. See Hastings, *D.B.* i. p. 68.

31. καὶ καθὼς θέλετε. The *καί* introduces the general principle which covers all these cases: "and in short, in a word." How would one wish to be treated oneself if one was an aggressor? How *ought* one to wish to be treated? But obviously the principle covers a great deal more than the treatment of aggressors and enemies. In Tobit iv. 15 we have, "Do that to no man which thou hatest"; but this purely negative precept, which was common with the Rabbis, falls immeasurably short of the positive command of Christ. Isocrates has *ἃ πάσχοντες ὑφ' ἑτέρων ὀργίζεσθε, ταῦτα τοῖς ἄλλοις μὴ ποιεῖτε*, and the Stoics said, *Quod tibi fieri non vis, alteri ne feceris*; and the same is found in Buddhism. In the *Διδαχή*, i. 2, and *Apost. Const.* vii. 2. 1, we have both the positive and the negative form. Cod. D, Iren. (iii. 12. 14), Cypr. (*Test.* iii. 119) and other authorities insert the negative form Acts xv. 29. How inadequate the so-called Rabbinical parallels to the Sermon on the Mount are, as collected by Wünsche and others, has been shown by Edersheim (*L. & T.* i. p. 531). Note the *καθώς*, "even as, precisely as": the conformity is to be exact. For **θέλειν ἵνα** comp. Mt. vii. 12; Mk. vi. 25, ix. 30, x. 35; Jn. xvii. 24, and see on iv. 3. The *καὶ ὑμεῖς* before *ποιεῖτε* is omitted by B and some Latin texts. "Do likewise" occurs only here, iii. 11, and x. 37.

32–35. Interested affection is of little account: Christian love is of necessity disinterested; unlike human love, it embraces what is repulsive and repellent.

32. ποία ὑμῖν χάρις. "What kind of thank, or favour, have you?" This may be understood either of the gratitude of the persons loved or of the favour of God. The latter is better, and is more clearly expressed by *τίνα μισθὸν ἔχετε;* (Mt. v. 46). Otherwise there does not seem to be much point in *οἱ ἁμαρτωλοί.* For *χάρις* of Divine favour comp. i. 30, ii. 40, 52; Acts vii. 46.

καὶ γάρ. "For even"; *nam etiam.* Comp. Mt. viii. 9; Mk. vii. 28?, x. 45; Jn. iv. 45; 1 Cor. xii. 14; and see Ellicott on 2 Thes. iii. 10; Meyer on 2 Cor. xiii. 4. Syr-Sin. omits the clause.

33. Here only is **ἀγαθοποιεῖν** found with an acc. after it. It does not occur in profane writers, and elsewhere in N.T. is absolute: *vv.* 9, 35; Mk. iii. 4; 1 Pet. ii. 15, 20, iii. 6, 17; 3 Jn. 11. But in 1 Pet. and 3 Jn. it is used of doing what is right as opposed to doing what is wrong, whereas in Lk. and Mt. it is used, as in LXX, of helping others as opposed to harming them: Num. x. 32; Jud. xvii. 13 (Cod. B *ἀγαθυνεῖ*); Zeph. i. 12. Hatch, *Bibl. Grk.* p. 7; but see Lft. on Clem. Rom. *Cor.* ii. p. 17.

For **ἁμαρτωλοί** Mt. has in the one case *τελῶναι* and in the other *ἐθνικοί.* Of course both "publicans" and "heathen" are here used in a moral sense, because of their usual bad character; and Weiss confidently asserts that Lk. is here interpreting, while Mt. gives the actual words used. But it is possible that Mt., writing as a Jew, has given the classes who to Jews were sinners *κατ' ἐξοχήν* instead of the general term.

34. This third illustration has no parallel in Mt., but see Mt. v. 42; and comp. Prov. xix. 17.

δανίσητε. The texts are divided between this form, *δανείσητε, δανείζητε,* and *δανείζετε.* In N.T. *δανίζω* is to be preferred to *δανείζω,* which is the class. form. The verb means to "lend upon *interest*," whereas *κίχρημι* indicates a friendly loan; and therefore *τὰ ἴσα* would include both interest and principal.

ἀπολάβωσιν. "Receive as their *due*, receive *back*," or perhaps "receive *in full*"; comp. *ἀπέχω* in ver. 24, and see Lft. on Gal. iv. 5; also Ellicott and Meyer. The phrase **ἀπολ. τὰ ἴσα** need not mean more than "receive equivalent services," but more probably it refers to repayment in full: comp. *ἐρανίζω* and *ἀντερανίζω.*

35. πλήν. See on ver. 24. "*But*, when this kind of interested affection has been rejected as worthless, what must be aimed at is this." Note the pres. imperat. throughout: "*Habitually* love, do good, and lend"; also that Christ does not change the word *δανίζετε*, nor intimate that it does not here have its usual meaning of lending on interest.

μηδὲν ἀπελπίζοντες. The meaning of this famous saying depends partly upon the reading, whether we read *μηδέν* or *μηδένα,*[1]

[1] The external evidence stands thus—
For *μηδὲν ἀπ.* A B L R X Γ Δ etc., Latt. Syr-Harcl.? Boh.
For *μηδένα ἀπ.* ℵ Ξ Π*, Syrr. Tisch. is almost alone among recent editors in preferring *μηδένα*; WH. and RV. place in the margin.

but mainly upon the interpretation of ἀπελπίζοντες. All English Versions previous to RV. adopt the common view that ἀπελπ. means "hoping for in return," a meaning which is without example, but which is supposed to be justified by the context, or rather by the corrupted context. Thus Field argues: "No doubt this use of the word is nowhere else to be met with; but the context is here too strong for philological *quibbles* (!). 'If ye lend to them παρ' ὧν 'ΕΛΠΙΖΕΤΕ 'ΑΠΟλαβεῖν, what thank have ye?' Then follows the precept: 'Lend μηδὲν 'ΑΠΕΛΠΙΖΟΝΤΕΣ,' which can by no possibility bear any other meaning than μηδὲν ἐλπίζοντες ἀπολαβεῖν" (*Otium Norv.* iii. p. 40). The argument would be precarious, even if the facts were as stated; but the true reading is παρ' ὧν ἐλπίζετε λαβεῖν (ℵ B L Ξ, Justin), and therefore the whole falls to the ground. The usual meaning of ἀπελπίζω, "I give up in despair," makes excellent sense; either "despairing of nothing," or "despairing of no one" (μηδένα). "Despairing of nothing" or "never despairing" may mean either "never doubting that God will requite you," or "never despairing about your money." The latter meaning is almost identical with "despairing of no one," *i.e.* "never doubting that your debtor will pay." But it has been suggested that μηδένα may be *neut. plur.*, on the authority of Steph. *Thesaur.* v. col. 962 [iii. col. 3645]. If this were correct, the two readings would have the same meaning. On the authority of a single passage in the *Anthologia Palatina* (ii. 114, p. 325, Brunck), Liddell and Scott give ἀπελπίζω a transitive meaning, "causing to despair"; but there ἄλλον ἀπελπίζων (of an astrologer who said that a person had only nine months to live) may mean "giving him up in despair": comp. Polyb. ii. 54. 7. Therefore we may safely abandon the common interpretation and render "giving up nothing in despair" or "never despairing." Comp. ἐπὶ φίλον ἐὰν σπάσῃς ῥομφαίαν, μὴ ἀπελπίσῃς (Ecclus. xxii. 21); ὁ δὲ ἀποκαλύψας μυστήρια ἀπήλπισε (xxvii. 21); τὰ κατ' αὐτὸν ἀπελπίσας (2 Mac. ix. 18), of Antiochus when stricken with an incurable disease. Galen often uses the verb of desperate cases in medicine; see Hobart, p. 118, and Wetst.[1]

D and many early Latin texts have *nihil desperantes*. See the valuable note in Wordsworth's Vulgate, p. 344. But he thinks it *possible* that Lk. may have written ἀπελπίζειν for ἐλπίζειν ἀπό on the analogy of ἀπεσθίειν for ἐσθίειν ἀπό and ἀπολαβεῖν for λαβεῖν ἀπό.

---

[1] What mischief the common interpretation (sanctioned by the Vulgate, ***nihil inde sperantes***) has wrought in Europe is strikingly shown by Döllinger (*Akademische Vorträge*, i. pp. 223 ff.; *Studies in European History*, pp. 224 ff.). On the strength of it Popes and councils have repeatedly condemned the taking of any interest whatever for loans. As loans could not be had without interest, and Christians were forbidden to take it, money-lending passed into the hands of the Jews, and added greatly to the unnatural detestation in which Jews were held. The paradox that Christians may not take interest has been revived by Ruskin. See Morfill and Charles, *Book of the Secrets of Enoch*, p. 58.

ἔσεσθε υἱοὶ Ὑψίστου. In Mt. v. 9 peacemakers are called *υἱοὶ Θεοῦ*. The moral likeness proves the parentage. Just as in *vv.* 32, 33 Lk. has the generic ἁμαρτωλοί where Mt. has the specific τελῶναι and ἐθνικοί, so here we have "*is kind towards* the unthankful and evil" instead of "*maketh His sun to rise on* the evil and the good, and *sendeth rain on* the just and the unjust" (Mt. v. 45). For Ὑψίστου comp. i. 32, 35, 76.

36, 37. A further development of the principle of Christian love. Having told His disciples to cherish no personal *animus* against those who injure them, He now warns them against judging others respecting any supposed misconduct. To pose as a general *censor morum* is unchristian. Censoriousness is a transgression of the royal law of love, and an invasion of the Divine prerogatives. Not only vengeance but judgment belongs to God. And judgment, when it is inevitable, must be charitable (ἀπολύετε), directed by a desire to acquit rather than to condemn. Comp. 1 Cor. xiii. 4; Jas. iv. 11, 12. Hillel said, "Judge not thy neighbour until thou comest into his place" (Ewald, *Hist. of Israel*, vi. p. 27). See on ver. 31.

The loose citations of these two verses by Clement of Rome (i. 13. 2) and Clement of Alexandria (*Strom.* ii. 18, p. 476, ed. Potter) are interesting. Both have the words ὡς χρηστεύεσθε, οὕτως χρηστευθήσεται ὑμῖν immediately before ᾧ μέτρῳ, κ.τ.λ. They represent γίνεσθε οἰκτίρμονες in Lk., for which Justin has γίνεσθε δὲ χρηστοὶ καὶ οἰκτίρμονες (*Try.* xcvi.; *Apol.* i. 15). Comp. *Clem. Hom.* iii. 57. It is probable that Clem. Alex. here quotes Clem. Rom. unconsciously.

38. The transition is easy from charity in judging others to benevolence in general. Comp. ver. 30 and iii. 11. God remains in debt to no man. "He giveth not by measure" (Jn. iii. 34), nor does He recompense by measure, unless man serves Him by measure. Disciples who serve in the spirit of love make no such calculations, and are amply repaid. We are here assured of this fact in an accumulation of metaphors, which form a climax. They are evidently taken from the measuring of corn, and Bengel is clearly wrong in interpreting ὑπερεκχυννόμενον of fluids: **εἰς τὸν κόλπον** is conclusive. The asyndeton is impressive.

The form ὑπερεκχυννόμενον seems to occur nowhere else, excepting as *v.l.* Joel ii. 24. The class. form is ὑπερεκχέω.

δώσουσιν εἰς τὸν κόλπον ὑμῶν. Who shall give? Not the persons benefited, but the instruments of God's bounty. The verb is almost impersonal, "there shall be given," δοθήσεται. Comp. αἰτοῦσιν (xii. 20) and αἰτήσουσιν (xii. 48). The **κόλπος** is the fold formed by a loose garment overhanging a girdle. This was often used as a pocket (Exod. iv. 6; Prov. vi. 27; and esp. Ps. lxxix. 12; Is. lxv. 6; Jer. xxxii. 18). Comp. Hdt. vi. 125. 5; Liv. xxi 18. 10; Hor. *Sat.* ii. 3. 172, and other illustrations in Wetst.

ᾧ γὰρ μέτρῳ μετρεῖτε. There is no inconsistency, as Weiss states (*stimmt immer nicht recht*), with what precedes; but he is right in condemning such interpretations as *τῷ αὐτῷ μέτρῳ, οὐ μὴν τοσούτῳ* (Theophyl.) and *eadem mensura in genere sed exuberans* (Grot.) as evasions. The loving spirit uses no measure in its services; and then God uses no measure in requiting. But the niggardly and grudging servant, who tries to do just the minimum, receives just the minimum in return. In Mk. iv. 24, 25 we have this saying with a different application.

39. The second half of the discourse begins here, and this is marked by a repetition of the introductory **Εἶπεν.** The connexion with what precedes perhaps is, that, before judging others, we must judge ourselves; otherwise we shall be blind leaders of the blind. This saying occurs in quite another connexion Mt. xv. 14. It may easily have been uttered several times, and it is a commonplace in literature. We are thus shown the manifold application of Christ's sayings, and the versatility of truth. See Wetst. on Mt. xv. 14. With the exception of Mk. xii. 12, the phrase **εἶπεν παραβολήν** is peculiar to Lk. (xii. 16, xv. 3, xviii. 9, xix. 11, xx. 19, xxi. 29).

εἰς βόθυνον. "Into a pit" rather than "into the ditch," which all English Versions prior to RV. have both here and Mt. xv. 14. In Mt. xii. 11 nearly all have "a pit." The word is a doublet of *βόθρος*, *puteus*, and is perhaps connected with *βαθύς*. Palestine is full of such things, open wells without walls, unfenced quarries, and the like. For *ὁδηγεῖν* comp. Acts viii. 31; Jn. xvi. 13; Ps xxiv. 5, lxxxv. 11, cxviii. 35; Wisd. ix. 11, x. 17.

40. This again is one of Christ's frequent sayings. Here the connexion seems to be that disciples will not get nearer to the truth than the teacher does, and therefore teachers must beware of being blind and uninstructed, especially with regard to knowledge of self. In xxii. 27 and in Jn. xiii. 16 the meaning is that disciples must not set themselves above their master. In Mt. x. 24 the point is that disciples must not expect better treatment than their master. So also in Jn. xv. 20, which was a different occasion.

κατηρτισμένος δὲ πᾶς ἔσται ὡς ὁ διδάσκαλος αὐτοῦ. The sentence may be taken in various ways. 1. Every well instructed disciple shall be as his master (AV.). 2. Every disciple, when he has been well instructed, shall be as his master. 3. Every disciple shall be as well instructed as his master (Tyn. Cran.). But *Perfectus autem omnis erit, si sit sicut magister ejus* (Vulg.), "Every one shall be perfect, if he be as his master" (Rhem.), *Wenn der Jünger ist wie sein Meister, so ist er vollkommen* (Luth.), is impossible. The meaning is that the disciple will not excel his master; at the best he will only equal him. And, if the master has faults, the disciple will be likely to copy them. Syr-Sin. omits.

For **καταρτίζω**, "make ἄρτιος, equip," comp. Mt. iv. 21; Mk. i. 19; 1 Thes. iii. 10; Gal. vi. 1; Heb. x. 5, xi. 3, xiii. 21. It is a surgical word, used of setting a bone or joint: for examples see Wetst. on Mt. iv. 21. There is no πᾶς in Mt. x. 24, 25: see on ver. 30.

41, 42. In order to avoid becoming a blind teacher, whose disciples will be no better than oneself, one must, before judging and attempting to correct others, correct oneself. Self-knowledge and self-reform are the necessary preparation of the reformer, without which his work is one of presumption rather than of love.

41. κάρφος. "Anything small and dry": in class. Grk. usually in plur. of chips, twigs, bits of wood, etc. Curtius connects it with σκαρφίον, "a splinter" (*Grk. Etym.* 683); but better with κάρφειν, "to dry up." In Gen. viii. 11 it is used of the olive twig brought by the dove. See Wetst. on Mt. vii. 3. The **δοκός** is the "bearing-beam, main beam," that which receives (δέχομαι) the other beams in a roof or floor. It is therefore as necessarily large as a κάρφος is small.

κατανοεῖς. "Fix thy mind upon." It expresses prolonged attention and observation. Careful consideration of one's own faults must precede attention to those of others. The verb is specially freq. in Lk. (xii. 24, 27, xx. 23; Acts xi. 6, xxvii. 39: comp. Heb. iii. 1, x. 24; Rom. iv. 19).

42. πῶς δύνασαι λέγειν. "With what face can you adopt this tone of smug patronage?" In Mt. vii. 4 the patronizing **'Αδελφέ** is wanting.

ἄφες ἐκβάλω. For the simple subj. after ἀφίημι comp. Mt. xxvii. 49; Mk. xv. 36. Epict. *Diss.* i. 9. 15, iii. 12. 15. In modern Greek it is the regular idiom. Win. xli. 4. b, p. 356.—In **οὐ βλέπων** we have the only instance in Lk. of οὐ with a participle: "When thou dost not look at, much less anxiously consider" (κατανοῶν): see small print on i. 20.

ὑποκριτά. The hypocrisy consists in his pretending to be so pained by the presence of trifling evil that he is constrained to endeavour to remove it Comp. xiii. 15. That he conceals his own sins is not stated; to some extent he is not aware of them. The **τότε** means "then, and not till then"; and the **διαβλέψεις** is neither imperative nor concessive, but the simple future. When self-reformation has taken place, then it will be possible to see how to reform others. Note the change from βλέπειν to διαβλέπειν; not merely look at, but "see clearly." In class. Grk. διαβλέπω means "look fixedly," as in deep thought. Plato notes it as a habit of Socrates (*Phædo*, 86 D).

43. οὐ γάρ ἐστιν. Codex D and some versions omit the γάρ, the connexion with the preceding not being observed. The connexion is close. A good Christian cannot but have good results in the work of converting others, and a bad Christian cannot have such, for his bad life will more than counteract his efforts to reclaim others.

The etymological connexion between καρπὸς (*carpo*, *Herbst*, harvest) and κάρφος is by no means certain. But if it is a fact, it has no place here. The phrase ποιεῖν καρπὸν is not classical, but a Hebraism (iii. 9, viii. 8, xiii. 9; Gen. i. 11, 12; Ps. cvii. 37). By σαπρόν (σήπω) is meant (1) what is "rotten, putrid," and (2) what is "worthless." See Wetst. on Mt. vii. 18. A rotten tree would produce no fruit; and fishes just caught would not be putrid (Mt. xiii. 48). In both places the secondary meaning is required.

44. The unreformed can no more reform others than thorns and briars can produce figs and grapes. It is by their fruits that each comes to be known (γινώσκεται). The identification of the many Hebrew words which denote thorny shrubs is a hopeless task. Neither the originals nor their Greek representatives can be satisfactorily determined (Groser, *Trees and Plants of the Bible*, p. 172). Elsewhere in N.T. βάτος is used of the burning bush (xx. 37; Acts vii. 30, 35; Mk. xii. 26; Exod. iii. 2, 3, 4): in Hom. it is a "thorn-bush, bramble" (*Od.* xxiv. 230). The verb τρυγάω is specially used of the vintage (Rev. xiv. 18, 19; Lev. xix. 10, xxv. 5, 11; Deut. xxiv. 21). Comp. the similar sayings Jas. iii. 11, 12, which are probably echoes of Christ's teaching as remembered by the Lord's brother.

45. This forms a link with the next section. When men are natural, heart and mouth act in concert. But otherwise the mouth sometimes professes what the heart does not feel.

46–49. The Judgments which await the Members of the Kingdom. The Sanction or Warning. Mt. vii. 13–27. This is sometimes called the Epilogue or the Peroration: but it is not a mere summing up. It sets forth the consequences of following, and the consequences of not following, what has been enjoined.

46. The question here asked may be addressed to all disciples, none of whom are perfect. The inconsistency of calling Him Lord and yet failing in obedience to Him was found even in Apostles. What follows shows that the question applies to the whole of Christian conduct. Of the four parables in the latter half of the sermon, the first two (the blind leading the blind; the mote and the beam) have special reference to the work of correcting others; the third (the good and bad trees) may be either special or general; while the fourth (the wise and foolish builders) is quite general. With Κύριε comp. xiii. 25; Mt. xxv. 11, 12; Jas. i. 22, 26.

47. For **πᾶς ὁ ἐρχόμενος** see small print on i. 66, and for **ὑποδείξω** see on iii. 7 and Fritzsche on Mt. iii. 7.

48. ἔσκαψεν καὶ ἐβάθυνεν καὶ ἔθηκεν θεμέλιον. "He dug and went deep (not a hendiadys for 'dug deep') and laid a foundation." The whole of this graphic description is peculiar to Lk.

Robinson stayed in a new house at Nazareth, the owner of which had dug down for thirty feet in order to build upon rock (*Res. in Pal.* ii. p. 338). The parables in Mt. and Lk. are so far identical that in both the two builders desire to have their houses near a water-course, water in Palestine being very precious. In Mt. they build on different places, the one on the rock and the other on the sand, such as is often found in large level tracts by a dry water-course. Nothing is said about the wise builder digging through the sand till he comes to rock. Each finds what seems to him a good site ready to hand.

πλημμύρης. "A flood," whether from a river or a sea: and hence a flood of troubles and the like. See Jos. *Ant.* ii. 10. 2 and examples in Wetst. Here only in N.T., and in LXX only Job xl. 18 (23).

οὐκ ἴσχυσεν. "Had not strength to." The expression is a favourite one with Lk. (viii. 43, xiii. 24, xiv. 6, 29, xvi. 3, xx. 26; Acts vi. 10, xv. 10, xix. 16, 20, xxv. 7, xxvii. 16). For σαλεῦσαι comp. vii. 24, xxi. 26; Acts ii. 25 fr. Ps. xv. 8, iv. 31: freq. in LXX.

διὰ τὸ καλῶς οἰκοδομῆσθαι αὐτήν. This is certainly the true reading (א B L Ξ 33 157, Boh. Syr-Harcl. marg.). The common reading, τεθεμελίωτο γὰρ ἐπὶ τὴν πέτραν (A C D X etc.; Latt. Syrr. Goth. Arm.), is obviously taken from Mt. The Ethiopic combines the two readings. Syr-Sin. omits.

49. ᾗ προσέρηξεν ὁ ποταμός. Lk. gives only the main incident, the river, created by the rain, smiting the house. But Mt. is much more graphic: κατέβη ἡ βροχὴ καὶ ἦλθον οἱ ποταμοὶ καὶ ἔπνευσαν οἱ ἄνεμοι καὶ προσέκοψαν τῇ οἰκίᾳ ἐκείνῃ.

συνέπεσεν. "It fell in," *i.e.* the whole fell together in a heap: much more expressive than ἔπεσεν, which some texts (A C) here borrow from Mt.

ἐγένετο τὸ ῥῆγμα. To harmonize with προσέρηξεν. This use of ῥῆγμα for "ruin" (so first in Rhem.) seems to be without example. In class. Grk. it is used of bodily fractures or ruptures, and also of clothes; so also in 1 Kings xi. 30, 31; 2 Kings ii. 12. But Amos vi. 11 of rents in a building, πατάξει τὸν οἶκον τὸν μέγαν θλάσμασιν, καὶ τὸν οἶκον τὸν μικρὸν ῥάγμασιν. Hobart contrasts the βροχή, προσέκοψαν, ἔπεσεν, and πτῶσις of Mt. with the πλήμμυρα, προσέρρηξεν, συνέπεσεν, and ῥῆγμα of Lk., and contends that the latter four belong to medical phraseology (pp. 55, 56).

The μέγα, like μεγάλη in Mt., comes last with emphasis. Divine instruction, intended for building up, must, if neglected, produce disastrous ruin. The κεῖται εἰς πτῶσιν (ii. 34) is fulfilled. The audience are left with the crash of the unreal disciple's house sounding in their ears.

Similar Rabbinical sayings are quoted, but as coming from persons who lived after A.D. 100, by which time Christ's teaching had filtered into both Jewish and pagan thought. "Whosesoever wisdom is above his works, to what is he like? To a tree whose branches are many and its roots few. Then the wind cometh and rooteth it up and turneth it over. And, whosesoever works are above his wisdom, to what is he like? To a tree whose branches are few and its roots many. Though all the winds come upon it, they move it not from its place" (*Mishna*, *Pirqe aboth*, III. xxvii.). And again, "To whom is he like, that with many merits uniteth great wisdom? To him who first layeth granite blocks and then bricks. Though ever so mighty floods wash round the building, yet they cannot make it give way. But to whom is he like, who knoweth much and fulfilleth little? To him who layeth the foundation with bricks, which are disturbed by the least water (*Aboth R. Nathan*, xxiii.). See Edersh. *L. & T.* i. p. 540; Nicholson on Mt. vii. 24.

VII. 1. The division of the chapters is misleading. This verse forms the conclusion of the preceding narrative quite in Lk.'s manner. Comp. iv. 30, 37, 44, v. 11, 16, 26, vi. 11, etc. It is not the introduction to what follows, for Jesus must have been in Capernaum some time before the centurion heard about Him. Lk. says nothing about the impression which the discourse made upon the people (Mt. vii. 28), or about their following Him (Mt. viii. 1).

Ἐπειδὴ ἐπλήρωσεν πάντα τὰ ῥήματα αὐτοῦ. This is the only place in N.T. in which ἐπειδή is used in the temporal sense of "after that, when now." Hence Ἐπεὶ δέ is found in many texts. K has Ἐπειδὴ δέ, while D has Καὶ ἐγένετο ὅτε. In the causal sense of "since, seeing that," ἐπειδή occurs only in Lk. and Paul (xi. 6; Acts xiii. 46, xiv. 12, xv. 24; 1 Cor. i. 21, 22, xiv. 16, xv. 21). See Ellicott on Phil. ii. 26. For ἐπλήρωσε, "completed," so that no more remained to be said, comp. Acts xii. 25, xiii. 25, xiv. 26, xix. 21.

εἰς τὰς ἀκοὰς τοῦ λαοῦ. The εἰς marks the direction of what was said: comp. i. 44, iv. 44; Acts xi. 22, xvii. 20. Both in bibl. Grk. and in class. Grk. ἀκοή has three senses. 1. "The thing heard, report" (1 Sam. ii. 24; 1 Kings ii. 28; Jn. xii. 38; Rom. x. 16). 2. "The sense of hearing" (2 Sam. xxii. 45; Job xlii. 5; 1 Cor. xii. 17; 2 Pet. ii. 8). 3. "The ear" (Mk. vii. 35; Heb. v. 11; 2 Mac. xv. 39).

2–10. The healing of the Centurion's Servant at Capernaum. Mt. viii. 5–13. Mt. places the healing of the leper (Lk. v. 12–14) between the Sermon on the Mount and the healing of the centurion's slave. This centurion was a heathen by birth (ver. 9), and was probably in the service of Antipas. He had become in some degree attracted to Judaism (ver. 5), and was an illustration of the great truth which Lk. delights to exhibit, that Gentile and Jew alike share in the blessings of the kingdom. The *anima naturaliter Christiana* of the man is seen in his affection for his slave.

2. ἤμελλεν τελευτᾷν. "Was on the point of dying," and would have done so but for this intervention (Acts xii. 6, xvi. 27, etc.). Burton, § 73. For **ἔντιμος**, "held in honour, held dear," comp. xiv. 8; Phil. ii. 29; 1 Pet. ii. 4, 6; Is. xxviii. 16. The fact explains why this deputation of elders came.

3. ἀπέστειλεν πρὸς αὐτὸν πρεσβυτέρους. These elders (no article) would be leading citizens; but they need not be identified with the ἀρχισυνάγωγοι (viii. 49, xiii. 14; Acts xiii. 15, xviii. 8, 17), as Godet formerly advocated. The compound **διασώζειν**, "to bring safe through," is almost peculiar to Lk. in N.T. (Acts xxiii. 24, xxvii. 43, 44, xxviii. 1, 4; Mt. xiv. 36; 1 Pet. iii. 20).

4. οἱ δὲ παραγενόμενοι. A favourite verb (ver. 20, viii. 19, xi. 6, xii. 51, xiv. 21, xix. 16, xxii. 52; and about twenty times in Acts): elsewhere in N.T. eight or nine times, but very freq. in LXX.

ἄξιός ἐστιν ᾧ παρέξῃ τοῦτο. "He is worthy that Thou shouldest do this for him"; 2 sing. fut. mid. The reading *παρέξει* (G Γ Δ) is 3 sing. fut. act. and must not be taken as analogous to the exceptional forms *οἴει*, *ὄψει*, and *βούλει*. But beyond doubt *παρέξῃ* (א A B C D R Ξ etc.) is the correct reading.

5. ἀγαπᾷ γὰρ τὸ ἔθνος ἡμῶν. This would hardly be said of one who was actually a proselyte. He had learned to admire and respect the pure worship of the Jews and to feel affection for the people who practised it. This would be all the more likely if he were in the service of the Herods rather than that of heathen Rome. See Hastings, *D.B.* i. p. 366.

τὴν συναγωγὴν αὐτὸς ᾠκοδόμησεν ἡμῖν. "At his own expense he built us *our* synagogue," the one which we have; not "*a* synagogue" (AV.). Had Capernaum only one synagogue?

If *Tell Hûm* represents Capernaum, and if the ruins of the synagogue there are from a building of this date, they show with what liberality this centurion had carried out his pious work. But it is doubtful whether the excellent work exhibited in these ruins is quite so early as the first century. The centurions appear in a favourable light in N.T. (xxiii. 47; Acts x. 22, xxii. 26, xxiii. 17, 23, 24, xxiv. 23, xxvii. 43). Roman organization produced, and was maintained by, excellent individuals, who were a blessing to others and themselves. As Philo says, after praising Petronius the governor of Syria, *τοῖς δὲ ἀγαθοῖς ἀγαθὰς ὑπηχεῖν ἔοικε γνώμας ὁ Θεὸς δι᾽ ὧν ὠφελοῦντες ὠφεληθήσονται* (*Leg. ad Caium*, p. 1027, ed. Gelen.). Augustus had recognized the value of synagogues in maintaining order and morality. Hastings, *D.C.G.* art. "Capernaum."

6. οὐ μακράν. Comp. Acts xvii. 27. The expression is peculiar to Lk., who is fond of *οὐ* with an adj. or adv. to express his meaning. Comp. *οὐ πολλοί* (xv. 13; Acts i. 5), *οὐ πολύ* (Acts xxvii. 14), *οὐκ ὀλίγος* (Acts xii. 18, xiv. 28, xv. 2, xvii. 4, 12, xix. 23, 24, xxvii. 20), *οὐκ ὁ τυχών* (Acts xix. 11, xxviii. 2), *οὐκ ἄσημος* (Acts xxi. 39), *οὐ μετρίως* (Acts xx. 12).

ἔπεμψεν φίλους. Comp. xv. 6, Acts x. 24. Mt. says nothing about either of these deputations, but puts the message of both into the mouth of the centurion himself, who comes in person. In Lk. the man's humility and faith prevail over his anxiety as soon as he sees that the first deputation has succeeded, and that the great Rabbi and Prophet is really coming to him. Therefore he sends the second deputation to say that he is not worthy of a visit, and that the visit is not necessary.

Κύριε, μὴ σκύλλου. "Lord, cease to trouble Thyself." The verb is a marked instance of the tendency of words to become weaker in meaning: *σκύλλω* (*σκῦλον*, xi. 22) is 1. "flay"; 2. "mangle"; 3. "vex, annoy" (viii. 49; Mk. v. 35; Mt. ix. 36). See *Expositor*, 1st series, 1876, iv. pp. 30, 31. What follows seems to show that the centurion was not a proselyte. The house of a Gentile was polluting to a Jew; and therefore *οὐ γὰρ ἱκανός εἰμι, κ.τ.λ.*, is quite in point if he was still a heathen. But it is rather strong language if he had ceased to be a heathen. For *ἵνα* after *ἱκανός* see Burton, § 216.

7. εἰπὲ λόγῳ, καὶ ἰαθήτω ὁ παῖς μου. Lit. "Say with a word, and let my servant be healed." The word is to be the instrument with which the healing is to take place, instead of Jesus' coming in person: comp. Acts ii. 40 and Gal. vi. 11. There is no doubt that *ὁ παῖς μου* means "my servant." This use is found in N.T. (xii. 45, xv. 26; Mt. viii. 6, 8, 13), and is very freq. in LXX and in class. Grk.

It has been contended that in Mt. viii. 6, 8, 13 *παῖς* must mean "son," because the centurion calls his servant *δοῦλος* in ver. 9: as if it were improbable that a person in the same conversation should speak sometimes of his "servant" and sometimes of his "boy." In both narratives *παῖς* and *δοῦλος* are used as synonyms; and it is gratuitous to suppose that in using *δοῦλος* Lk. has misinterpreted the *παῖς* in the source which he employed. Comp. xv. 22, 26. Here *ὁ παῖς μου* is more affectionate than *ὁ δοῦλός μου* would have been.

8. ἐγὼ ἄνθρωπός εἰμι ὑπὸ ἐξουσίαν τασσόμενος. The *εἰμι* must not be united with *τασσόμενος* and made the equivalent of *τάσσομαι*: *τασσόμενος* is adjectival. Thus, "For I am a man who is habitually (pres. part.) placed under authority." But, "For I am an ordinary person (*ἄνθρωπος*), *and* a person in a dependent position" is rather an exaggeration of the Greek. Comp. *ὑπὸ τὴν τοῦ βασιλέως ἐξουσίαν πεσεῖν* (2 Mac. iii. 6). The *καὶ γάρ* shows the intimate connexion with what precedes, *εἰπὲ λόγῳ καὶ ἰαθήτω*: see on vi. 32. "I know from personal experience what a word from one in authority can do. A word from my superiors secures my obedience, and a word from me secures the obedience of my subordinates. Thou, who art under no man, and hast authority over unseen powers, hast only to say a word and the sickness is healed." Perhaps *ἄνθρωπος* hints that Jesus is superhuman. Evidently *ὑπὸ ἐξουσίαν τασσόμενος* means that, if an inferior can give effective orders, much more can a superior do so. It is the certainty of the result *without personal presence* that is the point.

9. ὁ Ἰησοῦς ἐθαύμασεν αὐτόν. This is stated in both narratives. Comp. Mk. vi. 6. Those who are unwilling to admit any limitations in Christ's knowledge have to explain how wonder is compatible with omniscience. One limitation is clearly told us by Himself (Mk. xiii. 32); so that the only question is how far such limitations extend. See on ii. 46, 52, and xvii. 14. Note the solemn Λέγω ὑμῖν, and comp. ver. 28, x. 12, 24, xi. 8, 9, 51, etc.

οὐδὲ ἐν τῷ Ἰσραὴλ τοσαύτην πίστιν εὗρον. This again points to the centurion being still a heathen. Nowhere among the Jews had He found any one willing to believe that He could heal without being present. It is natural that Lk. should express this preference for a Gentile more strongly than Mt., who has *παρ' οὐδενὶ τοσαύτην πίστιν ἐν τῷ Ἰσραὴλ εὗρον*. Lk. here omits the remarkable passage Mt. viii. 11, 12; but he gives it in quite a different connexion xiii. 28, 29. Such teaching, so necessary and so unwelcome to the Jews, may easily have been repeated.

10. ὑποστρέψαντες. See on i. 56 and iv. 14. Lk.'s **ὑγιαίνοντα** is stronger than the *ἰάθη* of Mt. The servant was not only cured, but "in good health." *Non modo sanum, sed sanitate utentem* (Beng.) Hobart remarks that Lk. "is the only N.T. writer who uses *ὑγιαίνειν* in this its primary sense, 'to be in sound health,' with the exception of S. John, 3 Ep. 2. For this meaning it is the regular word in the medical writers" (p. 10). See on v. 31 and comp. xv. 27. Here and v. 31 Vulg. has *sanus*; in xv. 27, *salvus*.

The identification of this miracle with that of the healing of the son of the royal official (*βασιλικός*) in Jn. iv. is not probable: it involves an amount of misinformation or carelessness on one side or the other which would be very startling. Irenæus *seems* to be in favour of it; but "centurion" with him may be a slip of memory or a misinterpretation of *βασιλικός*. Origen and Chrysostom contend against the identification. Is there any difficulty in supposing that on more than one occasion Jesus healed without being present? The difficulty is to explain one such instance, without admitting the possession of supernatural powers: this Strauss has shown, and the efforts of Keim and Schenkel to explain it by a combination of moral and psychical causes are not satisfying. There is no parallel to it in O.T., for (as Keim points out) the healing of Naaman is not really analogous.

11–17. § The Raising of the Widow's Son at Nain. Because Lk. alone records it, its historical character has been questioned. But there were multitudes of miracles wrought by Christ which have never been recorded in detail at all (iv. 23, 40, 41, vi. 18, 19; Jn. ii. 23, iv. 45, vii. 31, xii. 37, xx. 30, xxi. 25), and among these, as ver. 22 shows, were cases of raising the dead. We must not attribute to the Evangelists the modern way of regarding the raising of the dead as a miracle so amazing, *because so difficult to perform*, that every real instance would necessarily become widely known, and would certainly be recorded by every writer who had knowledge of it. To a Jew it would be hardly more marvellous than the healing of a leper; and to one who believes in miracles at all, distinctions as to difficulty are unmeaning. It is not unreasonable to suppose, either that this event never came to the knowledge of the other Evangelists, or that, although they knew of it, they did not see the necessity for recording it. It is worth noting that nearly all recorded instances of raising the dead were performed for women (1 Kings xvii. 23; 2 Kings iv. 36; Jn. xi. 22, 32; Acts ix. 41; Heb. xi. 35).

11. ἐν τῷ ἑξῆς. It is not easy to decide between the reading ἐν τῷ ἑξῆς, *sc.* χρόνῳ (A B R), and ἐν τῇ ἑξῆς, *sc.* ἡμέρᾳ (ℵ C D). On the one hand, Lk. elsewhere, when he writes ἐν τῷ, has καθεξῆς (viii. 1); on the other, when he writes τῇ ἑξῆς, he does not prefix ἐν (ix. 37; Acts xxi. 1, xxv. 17, xxvii. 18). The less definite would be more likely to be changed to the more definite than *vice versâ*. Thus the balance both of external and internal evidence is in favour of ἐν τῷ ἑξῆς, and we must not limit the interval between the miracles to a single day. In N.T. ἑξῆς is peculiar to Lk. (ix. 37; Acts xxi. 1, xxv. 17, xxvii. 18). So also is ὡς ἤγγισεν (*v.* 12, xv. 25, xix. 29, 41).

Ναΐν. The place is not mentioned elsewhere in Scripture; and the village of that name in Josephus (*B. J.* iv. 9. 4) is on the other side of the Jordan, and cannot be the same. *D. C. G.* art. "Nain."

A hamlet called *Nein* was found by Robinson about two miles west of Endor, on the north slope of Little Hermon, which is where Eusebius and Jerome place it; and it would be about a day's journey from Capernaum. "One entrance alone it could have had, that which opens on the rough hillside in its downward slope to the plain" (Stanley, *Sin. & Pal.* p. 357); so that the very path on which the two companies met can be identified. About ten minutes' walk on the road to Endor is a burying-place which is still used, and there are many tombs cut in the rock. Robinson, *Pal.* iii. p. 469; *Bibl. Res.* ii. 361; Thomson, *Land & Book*, p. 445; Tristram, *Land of Israel*, p. 127. The expression, πόλιν καλουμένην Ναΐν, looks as if Lk. were writing for those who were not familiar with the country; comp. i. 26, 39, iv. 31. See on vi. 15.

οἱ μαθηταὶ αὐτοῦ. Including more than the Twelve; vi. 13. See on xi. 29.

12. καὶ ἰδοὺ ἐξεκομίζετο τεθνηκώς. "Behold there was being carried out a dead man." Or, "there was being carried out dead the only son," etc. The καί introduces the apodosis of ὡς δὲ ἤγγισε, and must be omitted in translation: "then" would be too strong. See on v. 12. The compound verb occurs here only in N.T. and nowhere in LXX. It is equivalent to ἐκφέρειν (Acts v. 6, 9, 10) and *efferre*, and is used of carrying out to burial, Polyb. xxxv. 6. 2; Plut. *Agis*, xxi.; *Cic.* xlii. In later Gk. ἐκκομιδή is used for ἐκφορά of burial. With τεθνηκώς comp. Jn. xi. 44.

μονογενὴς υἱὸς τῇ μητρὶ αὐτοῦ. Comp. viii. 42, ix. 38; Heb. xi. 17; Judg. xi. 34; Tobit iii. 15, viii. 17. Only in Jn. is μονογενής used of the Divine Sonship (i. 14, 18, iii. 16, 18; 1 Jn. iv. 9).

καὶ αὐτὴ ἦν χήρα. The ἦν may safely be pronounced to be certainly genuine (ℵ B C L S V Ξ and most Versions). For αὐτή some editors write αὕτη, and a few authorities have καὶ αὐτῇ χήρᾳ. The mourning of a widow for an only son is typical for the extremity of grief: *orba cum flet unicum* *mater* (Catull. xxxix. 5). Comp. Jer. vi. 26; Amos viii. 10; Zech. xii. 10; Prov. iv. 3.

ὄχλος τῆς πόλεως ἱκανός. Some of this multitude would be hired mourners, and musicians with flutes and cymbals. The mother would walk in front of the bier, and Jesus would naturally address her before touching it. This use of ἱκανός for "enough and to spare, much," is specially freq. in Lk. (viii. 27, 32, xx. 9, xxii. 38, xxiii. 8, 9; Acts viii. 11, ix. 23, 43, xi. 24, 26, etc.). It is possibly colloquial: it occurs in Aristoph. *Pax* 354. See Kennedy, *Sources of N.T. Grk.* p. 79. D here has πολύς.

13. καὶ ἰδὼν αὐτὴν ὁ Κύριος ἐσπλαγχνίσθη ἐπ' αὐτῇ. The introduction of ὁ Κύριος has special point here: it is the Lord of Life meeting sorrow and death. The expression is characteristic of Lk. Comp. xxiv. 34, and see on v. 17. Compassion is elsewhere mentioned as a moving cause in Christ's miracles (Mt. xiv. 14, xv. 32, xx. 34; Mk. i. 41, viii. 2). The verb is peculiar to the Synoptists; and, excepting in parables (Lk. x. 33, xv. 20; Mt. xviii. 27), is used of no one but Christ. It is followed, as here, by ἐπί *c. dat.* Mt. xiv. 14; and by περί *c. gen.* Mt. ix. 36; but generally by ἐπί *c. acc.* (Mt. xv. 32; Mk. vi. 34, viii. 2, ix. 22).

Μὴ κλαῖε. "Do not go on weeping, cease to weep": comp. ver. 6. He is absolutely sure of the result; otherwise the command would have been unnatural. *Quis matrem, nisi mentis inops, in funere nati Flere vetat?*

14. ἥψατο τῆς σοροῦ, οἱ δὲ βαστάζοντες ἔστησαν. Lk. clearly intimates that the purpose of the touching was to make the bearers stand still. At such solemn times words are avoided, and this quiet sign sufficed. Perhaps it also meant that Jesus claimed as His own what Death had seized as his prey. Lk. equally clearly intimates that the resurrection was caused by Christ's command. This is the case in all three instances of raising the dead (viii. 54; Jn. xi. 43). The σορός may be either the bier on which the body was carried, or the open coffin (probably wicker) in which it was laid (Gen. l. 26; Hdt. i. 68. 3, ii. 78. 1).

It is worth noting that βαστάζειν, which occurs twenty-seven times in N.T. (x. 4, xi. 27, xiv. 27, xxii. 10, etc.), is found only thrice in LXX.

σοὶ λέγω. "To *thee* I say, Arise." To the *mother* He had said, "Weep not." The σοί is emphatic. For this use of λέγω, almost in the sense of "I command," comp. xi. 9, xii. 4, xvi. 9.

15. ἀνεκάθισεν ὁ νεκρός. The verb occurs only here and Acts ix. 40 in N.T.; in both cases of persons restored to life and sitting up. Not in LXX. In this intrans. sense it is rare, excepting in medical writers, who often use it of sick persons sitting up in bed (Hobart, p. 11). The speaking proved complete restoration.

To suggest that the young man was in a trance does not get rid of the miracle. How did Jesus know that he was in a trance, and know exactly how to rouse him? And can we suppose that this happened on *three* different occasions, even if we could reconcile Christ's action with a character for truthfulness? Here and in the case of Jairus' daughter it is the Evangelist who tells us that the person was dead; but Jesus Himself declared that Lazarus was dead (Jn. xi. 14). We are told that the symmetry of the three instances is suspicious; raised from the death-bed, raised from the bier, raised from the tomb. But no Evangelist gives us the triplet. Lk. is the only writer who records more than one, and the two which he records he places in unsymmetrical order, the raising from the bier coming before the raising from the death-bed. Strauss has shown how unsatisfactory the trance theory is (*Leben Jesu*, ed. 1864, p. 469).

ἔδωκεν αὐτὸν τῇ μητρί. The sudden change of nominative causes no obscurity. Comp. xiv. 5, xv. 15, xvii. 2, xix. 4; Acts vi. 6, x. 4. Jesus might have claimed the life which He has restored, *nam juvenis jam desierat esse matris suæ*; but compassion for the mother again influences Him. Comp. viii. 55; Acts ix. 41; 1 Mac. x. 9; 1 Kings xvii. 23; 2 Kings iv. 36.

16. Ἔλαβεν δὲ φόβος πάντας. It is natural that this should be the first feeling on seeing a corpse reanimated. But a writer of fiction would rather have given us the frantic joy of the mother and of those who sympathized with her. Comp. i. 65, v. 8, 26, viii. 37; Acts ii. 43, xix. 17. See on i. 12, and also Schanz, *ad loc.*

λέγοντες ὅτι . . . καὶ ὅτι. It is very forced to make ὅτι in both cases argumentative: "Saying, (We praise God) because . . . and because." It is possible to take the second ὅτι in this way; but the common method of making both to be recitative is preferable. Both, therefore, are to be omitted in translation, the words quoted being in the *oratio recta* (Tyn. Cran. Cov. RV.). Cases in which ὅτι may be taken either way are freq. in N.T. (i. 45, ii. 11, iv. 36, vii. 39, ix. 22, x. 21, xi. 38, xxii. 70; 1 Jn. ii. 12–14, etc.).

Ἐπεσκέψατο ὁ Θεὸς τὸν λαὸν αὐτοῦ. Comp. i. 68, 78; Acts xv. 14; Heb. ii. 6. The verb was specially used of the "visits" of a physician. Comp. Mt. xxv. 36, 43; Jas. i. 27; Acts vi. 3, vii. 23, xv. 36, the only other passages in N.T. in which the word occurs. In the sense of visiting with judgment or punishment it is never used in N.T. and but seldom in LXX (Ps. lxxxviii. 33; Jer. ix. 9, 25, xi. 22, li. 29). After the weary centuries during which no Prophet had appeared, it was indeed a proof of Jehovah's visiting His people that one who excelled the greatest Prophets was among them. No one in O.T. raised the dead with a word.

17. ἐξῆλθεν ὁ λόγος οὗτος ἐν ὅλῃ τῇ Ἰουδαίᾳ περὶ αὐτοῦ. The λόγος is the one just mentioned,—that God had visited His people in sending a mighty Prophet. The statement does not imply that Lk. supposed Nain to be in Judæa. Ἰουδαία here probably means Palestine: see on iv. 44 and xxiii. 5. But even if we take it in the narrower sense of Judæa as distinct from Galilee, Samaria, and Peræa, there is no need to attribute to Lk. any geographical inaccuracy. "This saying went forth (from Nain and circulated) in Judæa"; *i.e.* it reached the headquarters of Christ's opponents. For **περὶ αὐτοῦ** comp. v. 15. Syr-Sin. omits **ὁ λόγος**.

This pregnant use of a prep. of rest after a verb of motion is perhaps found only in late Grk., for in Thuc. iv. 42. 3 and Xen. *Hellen.* vii. 5. 10 the readings vary between *ἀπῄεσαν* and *ἀπῆσαν*. Comp. viii. 7, and see Win. l. 4. a, p. 514; Blass, *Gr.* p. 127.

καὶ πάσῃ τῇ περιχώρῳ. Note the position of this clause, which is added after *περὶ αὐτοῦ* with augmented force: "and (what is more) in all the region round about"; *i.e.* round about Ἰουδαία, not Nain. Comp. Acts xiv. 6. The verse prepares the way for the next incident by showing how the Baptist's disciples came to hear about "all these things."

The evidence that *Jesus raised the dead* is that of all four Gospels and of primitive tradition. The fact seems to have been universally believed in the early Church (Justin, *Apol.* i. 22. 48; *Try.* lxix.; Orig. *c. Cels.* ii. 48). Quadratus, one of the earliest apologists, who addressed a defence of Christianity to Hadrian A.D. 125, says in the only fragment of it which is extant, "But the works of our Saviour were always present, for they were true; those that were healed and those that were raised from the dead, who were seen not only when they were healed and when they were raised, but were also always present; and not merely while the Saviour was on earth, but also after His departure, they were there for a considerable time, so that some of them lived even to our own times" (Eus. *H. E.* iv. 3. 2). This does not mean that Quadratus had seen any of them, but that there was abundance of opportunity, long after the event, to inquire into the reality of these miracles. S. Paul uses the same kind of argument respecting the resurrection of Christ (1 Cor. xv. 5–8). Weiss points out how unsatisfactory are all the attempts to explain the evidence on any other hypothesis than the historical fact that Jesus raised the dead (*Leben Jesu*, i. pp. 557–565, Eng. tr. ii. 178–186). He concludes thus: "In no other miracle did the grace of God, which appeared in His Messiah, manifest itself so gloriously, by overcoming the consequences of sin and thereby giving a pledge for the highest consummation of salvation." See Aug. *In Joh. Trac.* xlix. 2.

18–35. The message from the Baptist to the Christ. Peculiar to Lk. and Mt., who place it in different connexions, but assign to it the same occasion, viz. that John had "heard in his prison the works of the Christ" (Mt. xi. 2). Lk.'s narrative, as usual, is the more full. He does not mention that John is in prison, having already stated the fact by anticipation (iii. 20). The *περὶ πάντων τούτων* shows that the works reported to the Baptist include the healing of the centurion's servant and the raising of the widow's son

πρὸς τὸν κύριον. This is probably the true reading (B L R X, a ff$_2$ Vulg.) rather than *πρὸς τὸν Ἰησοῦν* (ℵ A X Γ, b c f). See on ver. 13.

19. Σὺ εἶ ὁ ἐρχόμενος; "Art *Thou* (in emphatic contrast to ἕτερον) He that cometh," *i.e.* whose coming is a matter of quite notorious certainty (iii. 16, xiii. 35, xix. 38; Heb. x. 37).

ἢ ἕτερον προσδοκῶμεν; "Or must we look for another, different in kind?" whereas ἄλλον might be another of the same kind (Lft. on Gal. i. 6, 7). The reading ἕτερον (ℵ B L R X Ξ) is right, and is not taken from Mt. It is ἄλλον (A D) that is the corruption. For the delib. subj. comp. iii. 10, 12, 14. See on iii. 15.

The meaning of the question thus sent to Christ has been much discussed. 1. Chrysostom and other Fathers have suggested that the question was asked for the sake of John's *disciples*, who needed strengthening or correcting in their beliefs. See Oxford *Library of the Fathers*, x. p. 267, note e. Luther, Calvin, Beza, Grotius, Bengel, and others adopt this view. But the whole context is against it. Christ's reply is addressed to John, not to the disciples; and it is not clear that the disciples even understood the message which they carried. 2. Weiss and other critics follow Tertullian (*Marcion.* iv. 18) in contending that *John's own faith* was failing, because the career of Jesus did not seem to correspond with what he and the people had expected, and with what he had foretold (iii. 17). There is nothing incredible in this view; but the Baptist had had such a long and stern preparation for his work, and had received such convincing evidence that Jesus was the Messiah, that a failure in his faith is surprising. 3. Hase and others suggest that he was not failing in faith, but in *patience*. John was disappointed that Jesus did not make more progress, and he wished to urge Him on to take a more prominent and indisputable position. "If Thou do these things, manifest Thyself unto the world." Perhaps John was also perplexed by the fact that one who could work such miracles did not set His forerunner free, nor "cleanse His threshing-floor" of such refuse as Antipas and Herodias. This view suits the context better than the second. John's sending to Jesus is strong evidence that he was not seriously in doubt as to His Messiahship. For a false Christ would not have confessed that he was false; and what proof could the true Christ give more convincing than the voice from heaven and the visible descent of the Spirit? 4. The view of Strauss, that John had just begun to conjecture that Jesus is the Messiah, and that therefore this narrative is fatal to the story of his having baptized Jesus and proclaimed Him as the Messiah, is answered by Hase (*Gesch. Jesu*, § 39, p. 388, ed. 1891). See also Hahn, i. p. 475.

21. θεραπεύειν ἀπό. See on v. 15: it is peculiar to Lk.

μαστίγων. "*Distressing* bodily diseases"; Mk. iii. 10, v. 29, 34. In LXX it is used of any grievous trouble, but not specially of disease: Ps. xxxv. 15, lxxxviii. 32; Ecclus. xl. 9?; 2 Mac. vii. 37: comp. Hom. *Il.* xii. 37, xiii. 812; Aesch. *Sept.* 607; *Ag.* 642 The notion that troubles are Divine chastisements is implied in the word. It is used literally Acts xxii. 24 and Heb. xi. 36.

ἐχαρίσατο. "He graciously bestowed, made a free present of"; *magnificum verbum* (Beng.); comp. 2 Mac. iii. 31.

22. ἀπαγγείλατε Ἰωάνει. See on viii. 20. The answer is expressly sent to John: there is no intimation that it is for the instruction of his disciples, who are sent back, "like the messenger from Gabii to Sextus Tarquinius," to relate a symbolical narrative, which their master is to interpret. That *they* can understand it is neither stated nor implied.

τυφλοὶ ἀναβλέπουσιν, κ.τ.λ. There is probably a direct reference to Is. xxxv. 5, 6, lxi. 1. It is clear, not only that Lk. and Mt. understand Jesus to refer to bodily and not spiritual healings, but that they are right in doing so. John's messengers had not "seen and heard" Christ healing the spiritually blind and the morally leprous. Moreover, what need to add *πτωχοὶ εὐαγγελίζονται*, if all that precedes refers to the preaching of the good tidings? It is unnatural to express the same fact, first by a series of metaphors, and then literally. All the clauses should be taken literally. They seem to be arranged in two groups, which are connected by *καί*, and in each group there is a climax, the strongest item of evidence being placed last.

πτωχοὶ εὐαγγελίζονται. This was the clearest sign of His being the Christ (Is. lxi. 1), as He Himself had declared at Nazareth (iv. 18–21). His miracles need not mean more than that He was "a great Prophet"; moreover, the Baptist had already heard of them. But it was a new thing that the poor, whom the Greek despised and the Roman trampled on, and whom the priest and the Levite left on one side, should be invited into the Kingdom of God (vi. 20). For the passive sense of *εὐαγγελίζεσθαι* comp. Heb. iv. 2, 6, and see Win. xxxix. 1. a, p. 326, and Fritzsche on Mt. vi. 4. For *εὐαγγέλλιον* see on Rom. i. 1.

23. μακάριος. Not *μακάριοι*, as it would have been if the direct reference were to the disciples of John. It implies that the Baptist had in some way found an occasion of stumbling in Jesus (*i.e.* he had been wanting in faith, or in trust, or in patience); and it also encourages him to overcome this temptation.

σκανδαλισθῇ. Only here and xvii. 2 in Lk., but frequent in Mt. and Mk. The verb combines the notions of "trip up" and "entrap," and in N.T. is always used in the figurative sense of "causing to sin." See on xvii. 1. This record of a rebuke to the Baptist is one of many instances of the candour of the Evangelists. For **ὃς ἐάν** see Greg. *Proleg.* p. 96, and Win. xli. 6, p. 390; this use of *ἐάν* for *ἄν* is common in LXX and N.T. (xvii. 33?; Mt. v. 19, 32, xii. 32, xviii. 5; Jas. iv. 4).

24. περὶ Ἰωάνου. This is further evidence that the question and answer just recorded concerned John himself. The people had heard Jesus send a rebuke to the Baptist. But He forthwith guards them from supposing that John has ceased to be worthy of reverence. He waits till his disciples are gone; because if they had heard and reported Christ's praise of John to their master, it might have cancelled the effect of the rebuke. This panegyric is almost the funeral oration of the Baptist; for soon after this he was put to death. For ἤρξατο see on iv. 21.

Τί ἐξήλθατε. In each of the three questions it is possible to put the note of interrogation *before* the infinitive, and render, "Why went ye out? to behold?" etc. But the order of the words favours the usual punctuation. Perhaps *θεάσασθαι* implies "behold" with wonder and admiration.

κάλαμον . . . σαλευόμενον. The literal meaning makes excellent sense: "Did you go out into the wilderness to admire what you would certainly find there, but which would have no interest or attraction? Or did you go out to see what would no doubt have been interesting and attractive, but which you were not likely to find there?" But it also makes good sense to interpret, "Had John been a weak and fickle person, you would not have made a pilgrimage to see him."

25. ἄνθρωπον ἐν μαλακοῖς. Such a person would not be found in the wilderness; although he might have attracted them. This seems to show that the *κάλαμον* is not metaphorical, for this is obviously literal. Hastings, *D.C.G.* art. "Reed."

οἱ ἐν ἱματισμῷ ἐνδόξῳ καὶ τρυφῇ ὑπάρχοντες. "Those who live in gorgeous apparel and luxury." The word *ἱματισμός* is of late origin, and is seldom used excepting of costly vesture (ix. 29; Acts xx. 33; Jn. xix. 24; 1 Tim. ii. 9; Gen. xxiv. 53; Exod. iii. 22, xii 35; 1 Kings x. 5). See Trench, *Syn.* l. For ἐνδόξῳ comp. xiii. 17, and for ὑπάρχοντες see on viii. 41. In N.T. *τρυφή* occurs only here and 2 Pet. ii. 13; in LXX only as *v.l.* Lam. iv. 5. But it is freq. in class. Grk. It means an enervating mode of life (*θρύπτομαι*, "I am broken up and enfeebled").

26. περισσότερον προφήτου. This completes the climax: *κάλαμον, ἄνθρωπον, προφήτην, περισσότερον προφήτου.* In *περισσότερον* we have a late equivalent of *πλέον.* It may be masc. or neut., but is probably neut., like *πλεῖον* in xi. 32. Comp. xii. 4, xx. 47. They went out to see something more than a Prophet, and they did see it.

27. This quotation from Malachi (iii. 1) is given by Mk. at the opening of his Gospel coupled with φωνὴ βοῶντος, κ.τ.λ., and attributed as a whole to Isaiah. Neither Heb. nor LXX has πρὸ προσώπου σου, which Mt. Mk. and Lk. all insert in the first clause. See on ix. 52. Moreover, they all three have *ἀποστέλλω* and κατασκευάσει instead of the *ἐξαποστέλλω* and *ἐπιβλέψεται* of LXX. See on iv. 18. The passage was one of the common-places of Messianic prophecy, and had been stereotyped in an independent Greek form before the Evangelists made use of it.

28. ἐν γεννητοῖς γυναικῶν. A solemn periphrasis for the whole human race; that it implies weakness and frailty is not evident: in Job xiv. 1 these qualities are *expressed.* It is human generation as distinct from heavenly regeneration that is meant. John's superiority lay, not in his personal character, but in his office and mission: the glory of being the immediate forerunner of the Messiah was unique. He was a Prophet, like Moses and Elijah; yet he not only prophesied, but saw and pointed out to others Him of whom he prophesied. Lk. omits the Hebrew ἀμήν.

The word προφήτης is an interpolation. The external evidence against it is immense (ℵ B K L M X Ξ and most Versions), and it is improbable that the possibility of Prophets outside Israel would be indicated.

ὁ δὲ μικρότερος. There is no need to make this a superlative, as AV. alone among English Versions: better, "he that is inferior," *i.e.* less than other members of the Kingdom, less than any among the more insignificant. It is most unnatural to explain ὁ μικρότερος of Christ. Chrysostom says, περὶ ἑαυτοῦ λέγων εἰκότως κρύπτει τὸ πρόσωπον διὰ τὴν ἔτι κρατοῦσαν ὑπόνοιαν καὶ διὰ τὸ μὴ δόξαι περὶ ἑαυτοῦ μέγα τι λέγειν (*Hom.* xxxvii. p. 417), and above he explains μικρότερος as κατὰ τὴν ἡλικίαν καὶ κατὰ τὴν τῶν πολλῶν δόξαν (p. 416). Much the same view is taken by Hilary, Theophylact, Erasmus, Luther, Fritzsche, and others. In that case ἐν τῇ βασιλείᾳ τοῦ Θεοῦ must be taken after μείζων, which is awkward; and we can hardly suppose that Jesus would have so perplexed the people as to affirm that He was inferior to the Baptist, who in all his teaching had enthusiastically maintained the contrary (iii. 16; Mt. iii. 11; Mk. i. 7; Jn. i. 15, 20, 27, 30, iii. 28–30). By his office John belonged to the old dispensation; he was its last and highest product (*major prophetâ, quia finis prophetarum*), but he belonged to the era of preparation. In spiritual privileges, in grace, and in knowledge any even of the humbler members of the Kingdom are superior to him. He is a servant, they are sons; he is the friend of the Bridegroom, they are His spouse. It is possible to understand Ἰωάνου after μικρότερος, but it is unnecessary: more probably the comparative refers to others in the Kingdom. The paradox, "He that is less than John is greater than John," is capable of interpretation; but the principle that the lower members of a higher class are above the highest member of a lower class is simpler. The superlative of μικρός does not occur in N.T.

29, 30. Many have supposed that these two verses are a parenthetical remark of the Evangelist. But a comment inserted in the middle of Christ's words, and with no indication that it is a comment, is without a parallel and improbable. Jn. iii. 16–21 and 31–36 are not parallel. There the question is whether comment is *added.* In both passages it is probable that there is no comment. But, assuming that the Evangelist is in both cases commenting, he *appends* his comment: he does not *insert* it into the utterances of others. Here *vv.* 29 and 30 are part of Christ's address, who contrasts the effect which John's preaching had upon the people and upon the hierarchy (see Schanz). The connexion between ver. 30 and ver. 31 is close, as is shown by the οὖν.

29. πᾶς ὁ λαὸς ἀκούσας. "All the people, when they heard" the preaching of the Baptist. Note the πᾶς, and see small print on i. 66.

ἐδικαίωσαν τὸν Θεόν, βαπτισθέντες. "Admitted the righteousness of God (in making these claims upon them and granting them these opportunities) *by* being baptized." Their accepting baptism was an acknowledgment of His justice. See on ver. 35, and the detached note on *the word* δίκαιος *and its cognates*, Rom. i. 17.

30. οἱ νομικοί. Lk. often uses this expression instead of οἱ γραμματεῖς, which might be misleading to Gentile readers (x. 25, xi. 45, 46, 52, xiv. 3). Elsewhere in N.T. the word occurs only Mt. xxii. 35; Tit. iii. 9, 13. Comp. 4 Mac. v. 4; *Corp. Inscr.* 2787, 8. Hastings, *D.C.G.* art. "Lawyer."

τὴν βουλὴν τοῦ Θεοῦ ἠθέτησαν εἰς ἑαυτούς. "They frustrated the counsel of God *concerning* themselves": comp. εἰς ὑμᾶς in 1 Thes. v. 18. The rendering, "*for* themselves, so far as *they* were concerned, they rendered the counsel of God effectless," would require τὸ εἰς ἑαυτούς. The verb is a strong one: "render ἄθετον, placeless, inefficacious" (Gal. ii. 21, iii. 15; Jn. xii. 48; Lk. x. 16). Free will enables each man to annul God's purpose for his salvation. The phrase τὴν βουλὴν τοῦ Θεοῦ is peculiar to Lk. in N.T. (Acts xiii. 36, xx. 27; comp. ii. 23, iv. 28). It occurs Wisd. vi. 4; comp. Ps. xxxii. 11, cvi. 11; Prov. xix. 21. With μὴ βαπτισθέντες comp. the case of Nicodemus (Jn. iii. 4, 5).

31. The spurious reading εἶπε δὲ ὁ Κύριος was interpolated at the beginning of this verse to mark *vv.* 29, 30 as a parenthetical remark of the Evangelist. Owing to the influence of the Vulgate the interpolation was followed by all English Versions prior to RV. Almost all MSS. and ancient versions omit the words. But their spuriousness must not be quoted as evidence against the view which they support. Many false readings are correct glosses upon the true text, although that is probably not the case here.

Τίνι οὖν ὁμοιώσω. The οὖν would not be very intelligible if *vv.* 29, 30 were omitted; but after ver. 30 it is quite in place. "Seeing that the rulers and teachers have rejected the Divine invitation given by John, and that ye (λέγετε, ver. 34) follow them in refusing to follow Me, to what, then, shall I liken the people of this generation?" So comprehensive a phrase as **τοὺς ἀνθρώπους τῆς γενεᾶς ταύτης** may include the Baptist and the Christ: and to assume that it does include them frees the true interpretation of the parable from seeming to be somewhat at variance with the opening words. With the double question comp. xiii. 18; Mk. iv. 30.

32. There are two parties of children. This is more clearly marked by τοῖς ἑτέροις in Mt. than by ἀλλήλοις here. Which of the two groups is blamed? It has been taken both ways. (1) The children who invite the second group to play, first at dances and then at dirges, represent Jesus and the Baptist with their respective followers. The children who waywardly refuse to join in any kind of game are the Jews as represented by the hierarchy and the majority of the people. These rejected both the asceticism of John and the joyous freedom of the Gospel. Godet infers from ἀλλήλοις that the two groups of children change sides and take turns in proposing the form of play. But it is not necessary to give so much meaning to ἀλλήλοις. Yet such a change would not be difficult to interpret. The Jews may have proposed to the Baptist to become less stern. They certainly tried to force fasting on Jesus. And hence (2) the possibility of the other interpretation, which is preferred by Euthymius, Stier, and Alford, and is ably defended by Trench (*Studies in the Gospels*, pp. 150–153). The children sitting in the market-place and finding fault with their fellows are the Jews. John comes to them in his severity, and they want him to play at festivals. When he retains his strict mode of life, they complain and say, "We piped to you, and you did not dance." Then Christ comes to them as the bringer of joy, and they want Him to play at funerals. When He retains His own methods, they say, "We wailed, and you did not weep." This interpretation has two advantages. It makes the men of this generation, viz. the Jews, to be like the children who cry, "We piped," etc. And it gives the two complaints a chronological order. "We piped," etc., is a complaint against the Baptist, who came first; "We wailed," etc., is a complaint against the Christ, who came afterwards.

With **καθημένοις** comp. v. 27; with **ἀγορᾷ**, Mk. vi. 56; with **προσφωνοῦσιν ἀλλήλοις**, Acts xxii. 2; with **ηὐλήσαμεν**, 1 Cor. xiv. 7; with **ὠρχήσασθε**, 2 Sam. vi. 21; with **ἐθρηνήσαμεν**, Jn. xvi. 20. Of these προσφωνεῖν is a favourite word: see on vi. 13. Both **θρηνεῖν** and **κλαίειν** refer to the outward manifestation of grief as distinct from the feeling; and here the outward expression only is needed.

33. μὴ ἔσθων ἄρτον μήτε πίνων οἶνον. "Without eating bread or drinking wine"; spoken from the point of view of those who objected to John. He did not take the ordinary food of mankind; and so Mt. says, "neither eating nor drinking." For the poetic form ἔσθω see on x. 7. Syr-Sin. omits ἄρτον and οἶνον.

Δαιμόνιον ἔχει. They afterwards said the same of Jesus (Jn. vii. 20, viii. 48, x. 20); and δαιμόνιον ἔχεις shows that δαιμόνιον is acc. and not nom. Renan compares the Arabic *Medjnoun entè* as showing that Orientals consider all madness to be possession by a demon (*V. de J.* p. 263). See on iv. 33. One regrets that the American Revisers did not carry their point in getting "demon" substituted for "devil" as the rendering of δαιμόνιον. Tyn. Cov. and Cran. make great confusion by translating "hath *the* devil." Wic. is better with "hath a fende." The λέγετε in *vv.* 33 and 34 shows that some of those censured are present. Comp. xi. 15, where Jesus is accused of casting out demons with the help of Beelzebub.

34. φάγος. Like οἰνοπότης, this is a subst. and therefore paroxytone: φαγός, which L. and S. give, would be an adj. See Chandler, *Greek Accentuation*, § 215. Latin Versions vary between *devorator* (Vulg.), *vorator* (q), *vorax* (c e), *manducator* (d). English Versions vary between "devourer" (Wic.), "glutton" (Tyn. Cov.), "gurmander" (Rhem.), and "gluttonous man" (Cran. AV. RV.). The ref. is to v. 33 and similar occasions. For φίλος τελωνῶν see v. 27, 29, 30.

35. καὶ ἐδικαιώθη ἡ σοφία. "And yet wisdom was justified." In N.T. καί often introduces a contrast, which is placed side by side with that with which it is contrasted: "and (instead of what might be expected), and yet." This is specially common in Jn. (i. 5, 10, iii. 11, 32, v. 39, 40, vi. 36, 43, 70, vii. 28, etc.). *Atque* sometimes has the same force; Cic. *De Off.* iii. 11. 48. Although the Jews as a nation rejected the methods both of John and of Christ, yet there were some who could believe that in both these methods the Divine wisdom was doing what was right.

ἐδικαιώθη. This looks back to ἐδικαίωσαν in ver. 29, and ἡ σοφία looks back to τὴν βουλὴν τοῦ Θεοῦ in ver. 30. Here, as in Rom. iii. 4 (Ps. li. 6), δικαιόω means "Show or pronounce to be righteous, declare or admit to be just." The analogy of verbs in -όω is often wrongly urged. An important distinction is sometimes overlooked. In the case of *external* qualities, such verbs do mean to "*make* or *render*," whatever the noun from which they are derived signifies (ἐρημόω, τυφλόω, χρυσόω, κ.τ.λ.). But in the case of *moral* qualities this is scarcely possible, and it may be doubted whether there is a passage in which δικαιόω clearly means "I *make* righteous." Similarly, ἀξιόω never means "I make worthy," but "I consider worthy, treat as worthy." In the case of words which might apply to either external or moral qualities both meanings are possible acc. to the context: thus ὁμοιόω may mean either "make like," *e.g.* make an image like a man (Eur. *Hel.* 33, comp. Acts xiv. 11; Rom. ix. 29), or "consider like, compare" (ver. 31, xiii. 18, 20).

In ἐδικαιώθη we perhaps have an example of what is sometimes called the gnomic aorist. Comp. Jn. xv. 6; Jas. i. 11, 24; 1 Pet. i. 24. Burton, § 43. But see Win. xl. b. 1, p. 346, where the existence of this aorist in N.T. is denied.

ἀπὸ πάντων τῶν τέκνων αὐτῆς. "At the hands of all her children": the justification comes *from* them. It is certainly incorrect to interpret ἀπό as implying rescuing or protecting "from the attacks of all her children," viz. from the Jews. The children of the Divine Wisdom are the faithful minority who have welcomed the Baptist and the Christ, not the unbelieving majority who rejected them. In Mt. xi. 19 there is no πάντων, and D L M X omit it here. But it is certainly genuine: see on vi. 30. In A P Ξ πάντων is placed last with emphasis: there are no exceptions. But the order of ℵ B is to be preferred. Mt. has ἔργων for τέκνων, and ℵ has ἔργων here. For the personification of the Wisdom of God comp. Prov. viii., ix.; Ecclus. xxiv.; Wisd. vi. 22–ix. 18.

36–50. § The Anointing by the Woman that was a Sinner. Without note of time or express connexion. The connexion apparently is that she is an illustration of ver. 35. The proposal to identify this anointing with that by Mary of Bethany just before the Passion (Mt. xxvi. 6; Mk. xiv. 3; Jn. xii. 3) is ancient, for Origen on Mt. xxvi. 6 contends against it; and it still has supporters. Thus Holtzmann is of opinion that the act of a "clean" person in the house of "an unclean" (Simon the leper) has been changed by Lk. into the act of an "unclean" person in the house of a "clean" (Simon the Pharisee), in order to exhibit the way in which Christ welcomed outcasts, a subject which Lk. often makes prominent. But the confusion of Mary of Bethany with a notorious ἁμαρτωλός by Lk., who knows the character of Mary (x. 39, 42), is scarcely credible. And there is nothing improbable in two such incidents. Indeed the first might easily suggest the second. Simon is one of the commonest of names (there are ten or eleven Simons in N.T. and about twenty in Josephus), and therefore the identity of name proves nothing. Moreover, there are differences of detail, which, if not conclusive, are against the identification. The chief objection is the irreconcilable difference between Mary of Bethany and the ἁμαρτωλός. Strauss and Baur suggest a confusion with the woman taken in adultery. But the narrative betrays no confusion: everything is clear and harmonious. The conduct both of Jesus and of the woman is unlike either fiction or clumsily distorted fact. His gentle severity towards Simon and tender reception of the sinner, are as much beyond the reach of invention as the eloquence of her speechless affection.

On the traditional, but baseless, identification of the woman with Mary of Magdala see on viii. 2. The identification of this woman with *both* Mary of Magdala and Mary of Bethany is advocated by Hengstenberg. His elaborate argument is considered a *tour de force*, but it has not carried conviction with it. The *potest non eadem esse* of Ambrose is altogether an understatement. It is probably from considerations of delicacy that Luke does not name her: or his source may have omitted to do so.

The leading thought in the narrative is the contrast between Pharisees and sinners in their behaviour to Christ.

36. Ἠρώτα δέ τις αὐτὸν τῶν Φαρισαίων ἵνα φάγῃ μετ' αὐτοῦ. There is nothing to show that the Pharisee had any sinister motive in asking Him, although he was evidently not very friendly. As the Pharisees were generally hostile to Christ, it may have been a courageous thing. He is inclined to believe that Jesus may be a Prophet (ver. 39); and Jesus rebukes him as one who loved little, not as a secret enemy. But, like Herod Antipas, he may simply have been curious. Lk. records two other instances of Christ being the guest of a Pharisee (xi. 37, xiv. 1). For ἵνα see on iv. 3, and comp. vi. 31, vii. 6; and for κατεκλίθη (א B D L X Ξ) see on ix. 14.

37. Καὶ ἰδοὺ γυνὴ ἥτις ἦν. The opening words imply that her presence created surprise. The ἥτις is stronger than ἥ and has point here: "who was of such a character as to be": comp. viii. 3. This is the right order, and ἐν τῇ πόλει follows, not precedes, ἥτις ἦν (א B L Ξ and most Versions). The exact meaning is not quite clear: either, "which was a sinner in the city," *i.e.* was known as such in the place itself; or possibly, "which was in the city, a sinner." The city is probably Capernaum.

ἁμαρτωλός. A person of notoriously bad character, and probably a prostitute: comp. Mt. xxi. 32. For instances of this use of ἁμαρτωλός see Wetst. To the Jews all Gentiles were in a special sense ἁμαρτωλοί (vi. 32, 33, xxiv. 7; Gal. ii. 15; 1 Mac. ii. 44); but something more than this is evidently meant here. The ἦν need not be pressed to mean, "She was even up to this time" (Alf.); nor does *accessit ad Dominum immunda, ut rediret munda* (Aug.) imply this. The ἦν expresses her public character: ἦν ἐν τῇ πόλει. She had repented (perhaps quite recently, and in consequence of Christ's teaching); but the general opinion of her remained unchanged. Her venturing to enter a Pharisee's house in spite of this shows great courage. In the East at the present day the intrusion of uninvited persons is not uncommon (Trench, *Parables*, p. 302 n.; Tristram, *Eastern Customs in Bible Lands*, p. 36). Mary of Bethany was not an intruder. Note the idiomatic pres. κατακεῖται: just equivalent to our "He is dining with me to-day," meaning that he will do so.

ἀλάβαστρον μύρου. Unguent-boxes or phials were called ἀλάβαστρα even when not made of alabaster. But *unguenta optime servantur in alabastris* (Plin. *N. H.* xiii. 3, xxxvi. 12; comp. Hdt. iii. 20. 1). See Wetst. on Mt. xxvi. 6.

The word is of all three genders in different writers; but in class. Grk. the sing. is ἀλάβαστρος, either masc. or fem. The origin of μύρον is unknown, μύρω, μύρρα, σμύρνα, μύρτος being conjectures. In N.T. certainly, and probably in LXX also, μύρον, "ointment," is distinguished from ἔλαιον, "oil." Trench, *Syn.* xxxviii.

38. στᾶσα ὀπίσω παρὰ τοὺς πόδας αὐτοῦ. The sandals were removed at meals, and people reclined with their feet behind them; she could therefore easily approach the feet. While Lk. writes παρὰ τοὺς πόδας (viii. 35, 41, x. 39?, xvii. 16; Acts iv. 35, 37, v. 2, vii. 58, xxii. 3), Mk. has πρὸς τοὺς πόδας (v. 22, vii. 25), and Jn. πρὸς τοὺς πόδας (xi. 32). Mt. has παρὰ τοὺς πόδας (xv. 30).

τοῖς δάκρυσιν ἤρξατο βρέχειν τοὺς πόδας αὐτοῦ καὶ ταῖς θριξίν, κ.τ.λ. This was no part of her original plan. She came to anoint His feet, and was overcome by her feelings; hence the ἤρξατο. The βρέχειν led to the ἐξέμασσεν, which was also unpremeditated. Among the Jews it was a shameful thing for a woman to let down her hair in public; but she makes this sacrifice. For **βρέχειν** comp. Ps. vi. 7: it is probably a vernacular word (Kennedy, *Sources of N.T. Grk.* p. 39).

καὶ κατεφίλει. Note the compound verb and the change of tense: "She continued to kiss affectionately." The word is used of the kiss of the traitor (Mt. xxvi. 49; Mk. xiv. 45), which was demonstrative, of the prodigal's father (Lk. xv. 20), and of the Ephesian elders in their last farewell (Acts xx. 37), and nowhere else in N.T. Comp. Xen. *Mem.* ii. 6. 33. Kissing the feet was a common mark of deep reverence, especially to leading Rabbis (Xen. *Cyr.* vii. 5. 32; Polyb. xv. 1. 7; Aristoph. *Vesp.* 608).

39. προφήτης. Referring to the popular estimate of Jesus (*vv.* 16, 17). The **οὗτος** is contemptuous. No true Prophet would knowingly allow himself to be rendered unclean by contact with such a person. The reading ὁ προφήτης (B Ξ) would mean "the great Prophet" of Deut. xviii. 15 (comp. Jn. i. 25, vii. 40), or possibly "the Prophet that He professes to be." The art. is accepted by Weiss, bracketed by WH., put in the margin by Treg., and rejected by Tisch.

τίς καὶ ποταπὴ ἡ γυνὴ ἥτις ἅπτεται αὐτοῦ. "Who and of what character is the woman who is clinging to Him." She was notorious both in person and in life. See on i. 29. The **ἅπτεται** implies more than mere touching, and is the pres. of continued action. Trench, *Syn.* xvii.; Lft. on Col. ii. 21. *Imo si tu, Simon, scires, qualis hæc jam esset femina, aliter judicares* (Beng.). The **ὅτι** comes after **ἐγίνωσκεν**: "*that* she is," not "*because* she is." See on ver. 16, and comp. Is. lxv. 5.

40. ἀποκριθεὶς ὁ Ἰησοῦς. *Audivit Pharisæum cogitantem* (Aug. *Serm.* xcix.). Jesus not only answered but confuted his doubts. Simon questioned the mission of Jesus because He seemed to be unable to read the woman's character. Jesus shows Simon that He can read *his* inmost thoughts: He knows τίς καὶ ποταπός ἐστι. For **ἔχω σοί τι εἰπεῖν** see on xii. 4. Christ asks permission of His host to speak. As Godet remarks, there is a tone of Socratic irony in the address. The historic present (φησίν) is very rare in Lk

41. Δύο χρεοφιλέται ἦσαν δανιστῇ τινί. For the orthography of the two substantives see WH. ii. App. p. 154; Greg. *Proleg.* p. 89. In N.T. χρεοφιλέτης occurs only here and xvi. 5; in LXX Job xxxi. 37; Prov. xxix. 13. The word is of late origin. All English Versions, except Rhem. and AV., rightly have "lender" and not "creditor" for δανιστής: Vulg. *fœnerator*, Luth. *Wucherer*. In weight of silver the *denarius* was considerably less than a shilling; in purchasing power it was above two shillings, the wage of a day-labourer (Mt. xx. 2) and of a Roman soldier (Tac. *Ann.* i. 17. 8, where see Furneaux). The two debts were about £50 and £5.

42. μὴ ἐχόντων αὐτῶν ἀποδοῦναι. "Because they had not wherewith to pay"; *non habentibus illis unde redderent* (Vulg.). Comp. xii. 4, xiv. 14; Acts iv. 14. Others render ἔχειν in these passages "to be able," like *habeo quod* with the subjunctive. In ἐχαρίσατο, "he made them a present" of what they owed, we trace the Pauline doctrine of free grace and salvation for all. Comp. ver. 21.

τίς οὖν αὐτῶν πλεῖον ἀγαπήσει; This is the point of the parable, and perhaps the only point. The love and gratitude of those who have had debts remitted to them depends upon *their estimate* of the amount which has been remitted to them rather than upon the actual amount.

43. Ὑπολαμβάνω. "I suppose," "I presume," with an air of supercilious indifference. Comp. Acts ii. 15; Job xxv. 3; Tobit vi. 18; Wisd. xvii. 2. It is very improbable that ὑπολαμβάνω here means "I reply," as in x. 30; Job ii. 4, iv. 1, vi. 1, ix. 1, xxv. 1. In N.T. it is almost peculiar to Lk. The **Ὀρθῶς ἔκρινας** may be compared with the πάνυ ὀρθῶς of Socrates, when he has led the disputant into an admission which is fatal. In N.T. ὀρθῶς occurs only here, x. 28, xx. 21; Mk. vii. 35. Freq. in LXX. Comp. οὐκ ἐκρίνατε ὀρθῶς (Wisd. vi. 4).

44. στραφεὶς πρὸς τὴν γυναῖκα. She was behind Him. His turning to her while He spoke to Simon was in itself half a rebuke. Up to this He seems to have treated her as He treated the Syrophenician woman, as if paying no attention. The series of contrasts produces a parallelism akin to Hebrew poetry, and in translating a rhythm comes almost spontaneously.

Βλέπεις ταύτην τὴν γυναῖκα; This is probably a question: Simon had ignored her presence. The **σου** being placed before **εἰς τὴν οἰκίαν** gives point to the rebuke, but it hardly makes the σου emphatic. An enclitic cannot be emphatic, and σου here is enclitic. The meaning is not "I entered into *thine* house," in preference to others; but rather, "I came to thee in thy house," and not merely in the public street; "I was thy invited guest."

ὕδωρ μοι ἐπὶ πόδας. Comp. Gen. xviii. 4; Judg. xix. 21; 1 Sam. xxv. 41; Jn. xiii. 5; 1 Tim. v. 10. The reading is somewhat uncertain, and there are many variations between μοι and μου, πόδας and τοὺς πόδας, and also of order: μου ἐπὶ τοὺς πόδας (ℵ L Ξ) may be right.

45. **φίλημα.** Comp. Gen. xxxiii. 4; Exod. xviii. 7; 2 Sam. xv. 5, xix. 39, xx. 9. The traitor's choosing it as a sign seems to mark it as usual.

ἀφ' ἧς εἰσῆλθον. The reading *εἰσῆλθεν* (L[1] Vulg.) is an attempt to avoid the apparent exaggeration in "since the time I came in." But there need be no exaggeration, or difference of meaning, between the two readings. The woman very likely entered *with* Christ and His disciples in order to escape expulsion. Fear of it would make her begin to execute her errand directly the guests were placed. The compound **καταφιλοῦσα** makes the contrast with *φίλημα* more marked, and *τοὺς πόδας* makes it still more so. The *φίλημα* would have been on the cheek, or possibly (if Simon had wished to be very respectful) on the hand.

46. **ἐλαίῳ.** Very cheap in Palestine, where olives abound, and very commonly used (Ps. xxiii. 5, cxli. 5; Mt. vi. 17). The *μύρον* would be more valuable, and possibly very costly (Jn. xii. 3, 5). This woman, whom Simon so despised in his heart, had really done the honours of the house to his guest. This fact would be all the more prominent if she entered close after Jesus, and thus at once supplied Simon's lack of courtesy. See Hastings, *D.B.* i. p. 101.

47. This is a verse which has been the subject of much controversy. What is the meaning of the first half of it? We have to choose between two possible interpretations. 1. "For which reason, I say to thee, her many sins have been forgiven, because she loved much"; *i.e.* **οὗ χάριν** anticipates **ὅτι**, and **λέγω σοι** is parenthetical. Her sins have been forgiven for the reason that her love was great; or her love won forgiveness. This is the interpretation of Roman Catholic commentators (see Schanz), and the doctrine of *contritio caritate formata* is built upon it. But it is quite at variance (*a*) with the parable which precedes; (*b*) with the second half of the verse, which ought in that case to run, "but he who loveth little, wins little forgiveness"; (*c*) with ver. 50, which states that it was *faith*, not love, which had been the means of salvation; a doctrine which runs through the whole of the N.T. This cannot be correct. 2. "For which reason I say to thee, her many sins have been forgiven (and I say this to thee), because she loved much"; *i.e.* *λέγω σοι* is not parenthetical, but is the main sentence. This statement, that her many sins have been forgiven, is rightly made to Simon, because he knew of her great sinfulness, he had witnessed her loving reverence, and he had admitted the principle that the forgiveness of much produces much love. This interpretation is quite in harmony with the parable, with the second half of the verse, and with ver. 50. There were two things evident,—the past sin and the present love,—both of them great. A third might be known, because (according to the principle just admitted) it explained how great love could follow great sin,—the forgiveness of the sin. *Remissio peccatorum, Simoni non cogitata, probata a fructu, qui est evidens, quum illa sit occulta* (Beng).

αἱ ἁμαρτίαι αὐτῆς αἱ πολλαί. The second art. refers to v. 39: "The many sins of which thou thinkest." "Her sins, yes (according to thy estimate), her many sins."

ᾧ δὲ ὀλίγον ἀφίεται. "But he to whom little is forgiven," *i.e.* who thinks that he has committed little which could need forgiveness. It is said with evident reference to Simon. *O Pharisæe, parum diligis, quia parum tibi dimitti suspicaris; non quia parum dimittitur, sed quia parum putas quod dimittitur* (Aug. *Serm.* xcix.). For this use of the dat. comp. Soph. *Ant.* 904.

48. εἶπεν δὲ αὐτῇ. What He had to say to Simon (ver. 40) is finished: it is His true entertainer (44–46) who now occupies His attention.

ἀφέωνται. "Have been and remain forgiven": see on v. 20. There is nothing either in the word or in the context to show that her sins were not forgiven until this moment: the context implies the opposite, and this is confirmed by the use of the perf. Augustine's *accessit ad Dominum immunda, ut rediret munda* is in this respect misleading. The teaching of Christ had brought her to repentance and to assurance of forgiveness, and this assurance had inspired her with love and gratitude. Jesus now confirms her assurance and publicly declares her forgiveness. He thus lends His authority to rehabilitate her with society.

49. λέγειν ἐν ἑαυτοῖς. "To say within themselves" rather than among themselves; so that Jesus answered their thoughts, as He had already answered Simon's. The οὗτος is slightly contemptuous, as often (v. 21; Mt. xiii. 55; Jn. vi. 42, 52, etc.). The καί in ὃς καὶ ἁμαρτίας ἀφίησιν is "even" rather than "also." But "also" might mean "besides other outrages."

50. εἶπεν δὲ πρὸς τὴν γυναῖκα. "*But* He said unto the woman." He ignored their objection, and yet indirectly answered it, by telling her that it was her faith that had delivered her from her sins.

πορεύου εἰς εἰρήνην. "Depart into peace," *i.e.* into a lasting condition of peace: a Hebrew formula of blessing and of goodwill, with special fulness of meaning. Comp. viii. 48; Mk. v. 34; 1 Sam. i. 17, xx. 42. In Acts xvi. 36 and Jas. ii. 16 we have *ἐν εἰρήνῃ*, which is less strong, the peace being joined to the moment of departure rather than to the subsequent life: comp. Judg. xviii. 6. In Acts xv. 33 we have *μετ' εἰρήνης*.

Among the various points which distinguish this anointing from that by Mary of Bethany should be noted that *here* we have no grumbling at the waste of the ointment and no prediction of Christ's death, while *there* no absolution is pronounced and Mary is not addressed. See Hase, *Gesch. J.* § 91, p. 651, ed. 1891; also Schanz, p. 250, at the end of this section.

VIII. 1–3. § The ministering Women. This section is

evidence of the excellence of Lk.'s sources. The information contained in it is exact and minute. The names and other details are utterly unlike fiction. An inventor would avoid such things as likely to be refuted: moreover, no motive for invention can be discerned. The passage tells us—what no other Evangelist makes known—how Jesus and His disciples lived when they were not being entertained by hospitable persons. The common purse (Jn. xiii. 29; comp. xii. 6) was kept supplied by the generosity of pious women. This form of piety was not rare. Women sometimes contributed largely towards the support of Rabbis, whose rapacity in accepting what could ill be spared was rebuked by Christ (xx. 47; [Mt. xxiii. 14;] Mk. xii. 40) with great severity.

1. Καὶ ἐγένετο ἐν τῷ καθεξῆς καὶ αὐτὸς διώδευεν. See detached note p. 45, and comp. v. 1, 12, 14: for ἐν τῷ καθεξῆς see small print on vii. 11. The *αὐτός* anticipates *καὶ οἱ δώδεκα*, "He Himself and the Twelve." But the *καί* before *αὐτός* comes after *ἐγένετο* and must not be coupled with the *καί* before *οἱ δώδεκα*. In N.T. διοδεύω occurs only here and Acts xvii. 1, but it is freq. in LXX (Gen. xii. 6, xiii. 17, etc.); also in Polyb. Plut. etc. Comp. ix. 6, xiii. 22.

κατὰ πόλιν καὶ κώμην κηρ. *Ne quis Judæus præteritum se queri posset* (Grotius), Jesus preached city by city (Acts xv. 21) and village by village. The clause is amphibolous. It probably is meant to go with διώδευε, but may be taken with *κηρύσσων καὶ εὐαγγ.* The incidental way in which the severity of Christ's labours is mentioned is remarkable. Comp. ix. 58, xiii. 22; Mt. ix. 35; Mk. vi. 31. For εὐαγγελιζόμενος see on ii. 10. We are not to understand that the Twelve preached in His presence, if at all. Note the *σύν* (not *μετά*), and see on *vv.* 38, 51, and i. 56.

2. πνευμάτων πονηρῶν. See on iv. 33. We cannot tell how many of these women had been freed from demons: perhaps only Mary Magdalen, the others having been cured *ἀπὸ ἀσθενειῶν*. For the ἀπό comp. v. 15, vii. 21.

ἡ καλουμένη Μαγδαληνή. See on vi. 15. The adj. probably means "of Magdala," a town which is not named in N.T.; for the true reading in Mt. xv. 39 is "Magadan." "Magdala is only the Greek form of *Migdol*, or watch-tower, one of the many places of the name in Palestine" (Tristram, *Bible Places*, p. 260); and it is probably represented by the squalid group of hovels which now bear the name of *Mejdel*, near the centre of the western shore of the lake. Magdala was probably near to Magadan, and being much better known through *ἡ Μαγδαληνή*, at last it drove the latter name out of the common text. See Stanley, *Sin. & Pal.* p. 382. Mary being a common name, the addition of something distinctive was convenient; and possibly a distinction from Mary of Bethany was specially designed by the Evangelists. Mary Magdalen is commonly placed first when she is mentioned with other women (Mt. xxvii. 56, 61, xxviii. 1; Mk. xv. 40, 47, xvi. 1; Lk. xxiv. 10). Jn. xix. 25 is an exception. See on **i. 36.**

ἀφ' ἧς δαιμόνια ἑπτὰ ἐξεληλύθει. This fact is mentioned in the disputed verses at the end of Mk. (xvi. 9). It indicates a possession of extraordinary malignity (Mk. v. 9). We need not give any mystical interpretation to the number seven: comp. xi. 26; Mt. xii. 45. There is nothing to show that demoniacs generally, or Mary in particular, had lived specially vicious lives: and the fact that no name is given to the ἁμαρτωλός in the preceding section, while Mary Magdalen is introduced here as an entirely new person, is against the traditional identification of the two. Moreover, such an affliction as virulent demoniacal possession would be almost incompatible with the miserable trade of prostitution. If Lk. had wished to intimate that the ἁμαρτωλός is Mary Magdalen, he could have done it much more clearly. Had he wished to conceal the fact, he would not have placed these two sections in juxtaposition. Had he wished to withhold the name of the ἁμαρτωλός, who may possibly be included among the ἕτεραι πολλαί, he would have done as he has done. The ἁμαρτωλός and Mary Magdalen and Mary of Bethany are three distinct persons.

3. Ἰωάνα. She is mentioned with Mary Magdalen again xxiv. 10: all that we know about her is contained in these two passages. Godet conjectures that Chuza is the βασιλικός, who "believed and his whole house" (Jn. iv. 46–53). In that case her husband would be likely to let her go and minister to Christ. The Herod meant is probably Antipas, and his **ἐπίτροπος** would be the manager of his household and estates: comp. Mt. xx. 8. Blunt finds here a coincidence with Mt. xiv. 2; Herod "said to his *servants*, This is John the Baptist." If Herod's steward's wife was Christ's disciple, He would often be spoken of among the servants at the court; and Herod addresses them, because they were familiar with the subject. Comp. the case of Manaen (Acts xiii. 1), Herod's σύντροφος (*Undesigned Coincidences*, Pt. IV. xi. p. 263, 8th ed.). Of Susanna nothing else is known, nor of the other women, unless Mary, the mother of James and Joses, and Salome (Mk. xv. 40) may be assumed to be among them.

αἵτινες διηκόνουν αὐτοῖς. "Who were of such a character as to minister to them"; *i.e.* they were persons of substance. For **ἥτις** see on vii. 37, and for **διακονεῖν** comp. Rom. xv. 25. The αὐτοῖς means Jesus and the Twelve, the reading αὐτῷ (A L M X) being probably a correction from Mt. xxvii. 55; Mk. xv. 41. But αὐτοῖς has special point. It was precisely because Jesus now had twelve disciples who always accompanied Him, that there was need of much support from other disciples.

ἐκ τῶν ὑπαρχόντων αὐταῖς. It is this which distinguishes this passage from Mt. xxvii. 55 and Mk. xv. 41. There the διακονεῖν might refer to mere attendance on Him. We learn from this that neither Jesus nor the Twelve wrought miracles for their own support.

Here, as in xii. 15 and Acts iv. 32, τὰ ὑπάρχοντα has the dat. Everywhere else in Lk. (xi. 21, xii. 33, 44, xiv. 33, xvi. 1, xix. 8) and elsewhere in N.T. (five times) it has the gen. So also in LXX the gen. is the rule, the dat. the exception, if it is the true reading anywhere. Both τὰ ὑπάρχοντα and ὑπάρχειν are favourite expressions with Lk. See on ver. 41.

4–18. The Parable of the Sower. Mt. xiii. 1–23; Mk. iv. 1–20. We have already had several instances of teaching by means of parables (v. 36–39, vi. 39, 41–44, 47–49, vii. 41, 42); but they are brief and incidental. Parables seem now to become more common in Christ's teaching, and also more elaborate. This is intelligible, when we remember the characteristics of parables. They have the double property of revealing and concealing. They open the truth, and impress it upon the minds of those who are ready to receive it: but they do not instruct, though they may impress, the careless (ver. 10). As Bacon says of a parable, "it tends to vail, and it tends to illustrate a truth." As the hostility to His teaching increased, Jesus would be likely to make more use of parables, which would benefit disciples without giving opportunity to His enemies. The parable of the Sower is in some respects chief among the parables, as Christ Himself seems to indicate (Mk. iv. 13). It is one of the three which all three record, the others being the Mustard Seed and the Wicked Husbandmen: and it is one of which we have Christ's own interpretation.

4. Συνιόντος δὲ ὄχλου πολλοῦ καὶ τῶν κατὰ πόλιν ἐπιπορευομένων π. αὐτ. The constr. is uncertain, and we have choice of two ways, according as the καί is regarded as simply co-ordinating, or as epexegetic. 1. "And when a great multitude was coming together, *and* they of every city were resorting to Him." 2. "And when a great multitude was coming together, *namely*, of those who city by city were resorting to Him." According to 2, the multitude consisted wholly of those who were following from different towns (ver. 1). As no town is named, there was perhaps no crowd from the place itself. In any case the imperf. part. should be preserved in translation. It was the growing multitude which caused Him to enter into a boat (Mt. xiii. 2; Mk. iv. 1).

See on xi. 29. Except Tit. i. 5, κατὰ πόλιν is peculiar to Lk.

The Latin Versions vary greatly: *conveniente autem turba magna et eorum qui ex civitatibus adveniebant dixit parabolam* (a); *conveniente autem turba multa et qui de singulis civitatibus exibant dixit p.* (*c*); *congregato autem populo multo et ad civitatem iter faciebant ad eum dixit parabolam talem ad eos* (d); *cum autem turba plurima conveniret et de civitatibus pro-*

perarent ad eum dixit per similitudinem (Vulg.); *cum autem turba plurima convenisset* (συνελθόντος, D) *et de civitatibus advenirent multi dixit per similitudinem* (Cod. Brix.).

εἶπεν διὰ παραβολῆς. The expression occurs nowhere else. Mt. and Mk. write ἐν παραβολαῖς λέγειν or λαλεῖν, while Lk. has παραβολὴν εἰπεῖν or λέγειν. See on iv. 23, v. 36, and vi. 39; and on the parable itself see Gould on Mk. iv. 1 ff.

5. ἐξῆλθεν ὁ σπείρων. So in all three accounts: "*The* sower went forth." The force of the article is "he whose business it is to sow": he is the representative of a class who habitually have these experiences. Rhem. has "*the* sower" in all three places, Cran. in Mt. and Mk., Cov. in Mt. For the pres. part. with the article used as a substantive comp. iii. 11, v. 31, vi. 29, 30, 32, ix. 11, x. 16, etc. There is solemnity in the repetition, ὁ σπείρων τοῦ σπεῖραι τὸν σπόρον. The comparison of teaching with sowing is frequent in all literature; but it is possible that Jesus here applies what was going on before their eyes. See the vivid description of a startling coincidence with the parable in Stanley, *Sin. & Pal.* p. 425.

ἐν τῷ σπείρειν αὐτόν. "During his sowing, while he sowed": αὐτόν is subj., not obj., and refers to ὁ σπείρων, not τὸν σπόρον. See on iii. 21. Note the graphic change of prepositions: παρὰ τὴν ὁδόν (ver. 5), ἐπὶ τὴν πέτραν (ver. 6), ἐν μέσῳ (ver. 7), εἰς τὴν γῆν (ver. 8). In this verse Lk. has three features which are wanting in Mt. and Mk.: τὸν σπόρον, καὶ κατεπατήθη, and τοῦ οὐρανοῦ.

παρὰ τὴν ὁδόν. Not "along the way," but "by the side of the way." It fell on the field, but so close to the road that it was trampled on.

Both Lk. and Mk. here have μέν followed by καί: ὃ μὲν . . . καὶ ἕτερον, Comp. Mk. ix. 12. The absence of δέ after μέν is freq. in Acts, Pauline Epp., and Heb. See Blass, *Gr.* p. 261.

6. ἐπὶ τὴν πέτραν. The rock had a slight covering of soil; and hence is called τὸ πετρῶδες (Mk.) and τὰ πετρώδη (Mt.), which does not mean "stony ground," *i.e.* full of stones, but "rocky ground," *i.e.* with rock appearing at intervals and with "no depth of earth." The thinness of the soil would cause rapid germination and rapid withering; but Lk omits the *rapid* growth. With φυέν comp. Prov. xxvi. 9; Exod. x. 5; and (for the constr.) Lk. ii. 4. For ἰκμάδα, "moisture," Mt. and Mk. have ῥίζαν. The word occurs Jer. xvii. 8; Job xxvi. 14; Jos. *Ant.* iii. 1. 3; but nowhere else in N.T.

7. ἐν μέσῳ τῶν ἀκανθῶν. The result of the falling was that it was in the midst of the thorns: prep. of rest after a verb of motion: comp. vii. 17. Lk is fond of ἐν μέσῳ (ii. 46, x. 3, xxi

21, xxii. 27, 55, xxiv. 36; Acts i. 15, etc.). Elsewhere it is rare, except in Rev. Neither Mt. nor Mk. have it here.

συνφυεῖσαι. Here only in N.T. In LXX only Wisd. xiii. 13. In Plato and Aristotle it is transitive: "cause to grow together." We are to understand that the good seed fell into ground where young thorns were growing; otherwise the growing *together* would hardly be possible. Indeed the ἀνέβησαν αἱ ἄκανθαι of Mt. and Mk. almost implies that the thorns were not yet visible, when the good seed was sown in the midst of them. The ἀπέπνιξαν means "choked it *off*," so as to exterminate it: comp. the ἀπό in ἀποκτείνω. Wic. has "strangliden it"; but that, though sufficient for *suffocaverunt* (Vulg.), does not express the ἀπό. The verb occurs only here and ver. 33 in N.T., and in LXX only in Nah. ii. 12 and Tobit iii. 8. Mt. xiii. 7 is doubtful.

8. εἰς τὴν γῆν τὴν ἀγαθήν. Not merely upon, but into the soil. The double article in all three accounts presents the soil and its goodness as two separate ideas: "the ground (that was intended for it), the good (ground)." Mt. and Mk. have καλήν. This repetition of the article is specially frequent in Jn. Lk. omits the sixty- and thirtyfold. Isaac is said to have reaped a hundredfold (Gen. xxvi. 12). Hdt. (i. 193. 4) states that in the plain of Babylon returns of two hundred- and even three hundredfold, were obtained. Strabo (xvi. p. 1054) says much the same, but is perhaps only following Hdt. See Wetst. on Mt. xiii. 8 for abundant evidence of very large returns.

ὁ ἔχων ὦτα ἀκούειν ἀκουέτω. This formula occurs in all three. Comp. xiv. 35; Mt. xi. 15, xiii. 43. In Rev. we have the sing., ὁ ἔχων οὖς ἀκουσάτω (ii. 7, 11, 17, 29, iii. 6, 13, 22). The introductory ἐφώνει, "He cried aloud," indicates a raising of the voice, and gives a solemnity to this concluding charge. The imperf. perhaps means that the charge was repeated. Comp. Ezek. iii. 27; Hom. *Il.* xv. 129.

9. τίς αὕτη εἴη ἡ παραβολή. "What this parable might be in meaning." See small print on i. 29. Mt. says that the disciples asked why He spoke to the multitude in parables. Christ answers both questions. For ἐπηρώτων see on iii. 10.

10. τοῖς δὲ λοιποῖς. "Those who are outside the circle of Christ's disciples"; ἐκείνοις τοῖς ἔξω, as Mk. has it. This implies that it is disciples generally, and not the Twelve only, who are being addressed. Mt. is here the fullest of the three, giving the passage from Is. vi. 9, 10 in full. Lk. is very brief.

ἵνα βλέποντες μὴ βλέπωσιν. At first sight it might seem as if the ἵνα of Lk. and Mk. was very different from the ὅτι of Mt. But the principle that he who hath shall receive more, while he who hath not shall be deprived of what he seemeth to have, explains both the ἵνα and the ὅτι. Jesus speaks in parables, *because* the multitude see without seeing and hear without hearing. But He also speaks in parables *in order that* they may see without seeing and hear without hearing. They "have not" a mind to welcome instruction, and therefore they are taught in a way which deprives them of instruction, although it is full of meaning to those who desire to understand and do understand. But what the unsympathetic "hear without understanding" they remember, because of its impressive form; and whenever their minds become fitted for it, its meaning will become manifest to them.

WH. write συνίωσιν, from the unused συνίω, while other editors prefer συνιῶσιν, from συνίημι or the unused συνιέω. Similarly WH. have συνίουσιν (Mt. xiii. 13), where others give συνιοῦσιν. II. App. p. 167. Here some authorities have συνῶσιν, as in LXX.

11. Having answered the question διατί ἐν παραβολαῖς λέγεις; Jesus now answers τίς ἐστιν αὕτη ἡ παραβολή; To the disciples "who have" the one thing needful "more is given." The similarity between the seed and the word lies specially in the vital power which it secretly contains. Comp. "Behold I sow My law in you, and it shall bring fruit in you, and ye shall be glorified in it for ever. But our fathers, which received the law, kept it not, and observed not the statutes: and the fruit of the law did not perish, neither could it, for it was Thine; yet they that received it perished, because they kept not the thing that was sown in them" (2 Esdr. ix. 31–33).

ὁ λόγος τοῦ Θεοῦ. Mt. never (? xv. 6) has this phrase; it occurs only once in Mk. (vii. 13) and once in Jn. (x. 35). Lk. has it four times in the Gospel (v. 1, viii. 11, 21, xi. 28) and twelve times in the Acts. Here Mk. has τὸν λόγον (iv. 15) and Mt. has nothing (xiii. 18). So in ver. 21, where Lk. has τὸν λ. τοῦ Θ., Mk. has τὸ θέλημα τοῦ Θ. (iii. 35) and Mt. τὸ θέλημα τοῦ πατρός (xii. 50). Does it mean "the word which comes from God" or "the word which tells of God"? Probably the former. Comp. the O.T. formula "The word of the Lord came to." The gen. is subjective. Lft. *Epp. of S. Paul*, p. 15.

12. οἱ δὲ παρὰ τὴν ὁδόν. There is no need to understand σπαρέντες, as is clear from Mk. iv. 15. "Those by the wayside" is just as intelligible as "Those who received seed by the wayside."

εἶτα ἔρχεται ὁ διάβολος. Much more vivid than "And the birds are the devil." This is Christ's own interpretation of the birds, and it is strong evidence for the existence of a personal devil. Why did not Jesus explain the birds as meaning impersonal temptations? He seems pointedly to insist upon a personal adversary. See on x. 18. Mt. has ὁ πονηρός, Mk. ὁ σατανᾶς. The concluding words are peculiar to Lk.: "in order that they may not by believing be saved." Perhaps a sign of Pauline influence.

13. The constr. is ambiguous. In *vv.* 12, 14, 15 εἰσὶν is expressed, and it is usually understood here: "And those on the rock *are* they which, when they have heard, receive the word with joy; *and* these have no root." But it is not necessary to insert the εἰσίν. We may continue the protasis to τὸν λόγον and make καί mean also: "And those on the rock, which, when they have heard, receive the word with joy,—these also (as well as those by the wayside) have no root." Thus οὗτοι ἔχουσιν exactly corresponds to οὗτοί εἰσιν in *vv.* 14, 15. But the usual arrangement is better. The οἳ πρὸς καιρὸν πιστεύουσιν is a further explanation of οὗτοι. Neither Mt. nor Mk. has δέχονται, of which Lk. is fond (ii. 28, ix. 5, 48, 53, x. 8, 10, xvi. 4, 6, 7, 9, etc.). It implies the internal acceptance; whereas λαμβάνειν implies no more than the external reception.

ἐν καιρῷ πειρασμοῦ ἀφίστανται. Mt. and Mk. have θλίψεως ἢ διωγμοῦ, which shows that the temptation of persecution and external suffering is specially meant: comp. Jas. i. 2. In all times of moral and spiritual revival persons who are won easily at first, but apostatize under pressure, are likely to form a large portion: comp. Heb. iii. 12. The verb does not occur in Mt. Mk. or Jn. The repetition of καιρός is impressive. As *opportunity* commonly lasts only for a short time, καιρός may mean "a short time."

14. τὸ δὲ εἰς τὰς ἀκάνθας πεσόν. It is not probable that this is an acc. abs.: "Now as regards that which fell among the thorns." The attraction of οὗτοι (for τοῦτο) to οἱ ἀκούσαντες is quite intelligible.

ὑπὸ μεριμνῶν καὶ πλούτου καὶ ἡδονῶν τοῦ βίου. It is usual to take this after συμπνίγονται; and this is probably correct: yet Weiss would follow Luther and others and join it with πορευόμενοι, "going on their way under the influence of cares," etc. But ver. 7 is against this: the cares, etc., are the thorns, and it is the thorns which *choke*. This does not reduce πορευόμενοι to a *gehaltloser Zusatz*. The choking is not a sudden process, like the trampling and devouring; nor a rapid process, like the withering: it takes time. It is as they go on their way through life, and before they have reached the goal, that the choking of the good growth takes place. Therefore they never do reach the goal. The transfer of what is true of the growing seed to those in whose heart it is sown is not difficult; and συμπνίγονται is clearly passive, not middle and transitive. The thorns choke the seed (ver. 7); these hearers are choked by the cares, etc. (ver. 14). Here only in N.T. does τελεσφορεῖν occur. It is used of animals as well as of plants (4 Mac. xiii. 20; Ps. lxiv. 10, Sym.).

15. τὸ δὲ ἐν τῇ καλῇ γῇ, κ.τ.λ. It fell *into* the good ground (ver. 8), and it is *in* the right ground. Perhaps οἵτινες has its full meaning: "who are of such a character as to," etc. The two epithets used of the ground, ἀγαθή in ver. 8 and καλή in ver. 15, are combined for καρδίᾳ: "in a right and good heart." We must take ἐν καρδίᾳ with κατέχουσι rather than with ἀκούσαντες. Even if ἀκούειν be interpreted to mean "hearing gladly, welcoming," it is not the same as κατέχειν, which means "hold fast" (1 Cor. xi. 2). It is reasonable to suppose that ἀκούειν means the same in all four cases (12, 13, 14, 15). But κατέχουσιν (Lk.), παραδέχονται (Mk. iv. 20), and συνιών (Mt. xiii. 23) may all be equivalents of the same Aramaic verb, meaning "to take in": see footnote on v. 21. Comp. 1 Cor. xv. 2; 1 Thes. v. 21.

ἐν ὑπομονῇ. "With endurance, perseverance," rather than "patience," which would be μακροθυμία: *in patientia* (Vulg.), *in tolerantia* (c), *in sufferentia* (d), *per patientiam* (b f ff_2). See Lft. on Col. i. 11; Trench, *Syn.* liii. This ὑπομονή is the opposite of ἀφίστανται (ver. 13), and is not in Mt. or Mk. Thus Lk. gives the opposite of all three of the bad classes: κατέχουσιν, *non ut in via*; καρποφοροῦσιν, *non ut in spinis*; ἐν ὑπομονῇ, *non ut in petroso* (Beng.). Neither here nor in ver. 8 does Lk. give the degrees of fruitfulness. Mt. and Mk. do so both in the parable and in the interpretation. The suggestion that Lk. has mistaken three numerals for a word which he translates ἐν ὑπομονῇ seems to be a little too ingenious (*Expositor*, Nov. 1891, p. 381). That Jesus knew that all four of the classes noticed in the parable were to be found in the audience before Him, is probable enough; but we have no means of knowing it. We may safely identify the Eleven and the ministering women with the fourth class. Judas is an instance of the third. But all are warned that the mere receiving of the word is not decisive. Everything depends upon *how* it is received and how it is *retained*. Grotius quotes from the *Magna Moralia*: ᾧ τὰ ἀγαθὰ πάντα ὄντα ἀγαθά ἐστιν, καὶ ὑπὸ τούτων μὴ διαφθείρεται, οἷον ὑπὸ πλούτου καὶ ἀρχῆς, ὁ τοιοῦτος καλὸς καὶ ἀγαθός.

16–18. Practical Inference. The connexion with what precedes need not be doubted. By answering the question of the disciples (ver. 9) and explaining the parable to them, Jesus had kindled a light within them. They must not hide it, but must see that it spreads to others. Here we have the opposite of what was noticed in the Sermon on the Mount. Here Lk. has, gathered into one, sayings which Mt. has, scattered in three different places (v. 15, x. 26, xiii. 12: comp. xiii. 12, xxv. 29). Mk. and Lk. are here very similar and consecutive. Comp. xi. 33–36.

16. **λύχνον ἅψας καλύπτει αὐτὸν σκεύει.** "Having lighted a lamp," rather than "a candle." Trench, *Syn.* xlvi.; Becker, *Charicles*, iii. 86, Eng. tr. p. 130; *Gallus*, ii. 398, Eng. tr. p. 308. For ἅψας see on xv. 8: it occurs again xi. 33, but not in the parallels Mt. v. 15; Mk. iv. 21. Instead of σκεύει Mt. and Mk. have the more definite ὑπὸ τὸν μόδιον, which Lk. has xi. 33. As λύχνος is a "lamp," λυχνία is a "lamp-stand," on which several λύχνοι might be placed or hung: for, whereas the λαμπτήρ was fixed, the λύχνος was portable. Other forms of λυχνία are λυχνίον and λυχνεῖον (Kennedy, *Sources of N.T. Grk.* p. 40). Comp. the very similar passage xi. 33. In both passages οἱ εἰσπορευόμενοι, the Gentiles, are mentioned instead of οἱ ἐν τῇ οἰκίᾳ, the Jews (Mt. v. 15).

17. The poetic rhythm and parallelism should be noticed. Somewhat similar sayings are found in profane writers: ἄγει δὲ πρὸς φῶς τὴν ἀλήθειαν χρόνος (Menander); comp. Soph. *Ajax*, 646, and Wetst. on Mt. x. 26. For **φανερὸν γενήσεται** see on iv. 36; Mt has ἀποκαλυφθήσεται, Mk. φανερωθῇ. For **ἀπόκρυφον**, "hidden *away*" from the public eye, see Lft. on Col. ii. 3. It was a favourite word with the Gnostics to indicate their esoteric books, which might not be published. Comp. the very similar passage xii. 2; and see S. Cox in the *Expositor*, 2nd series, i. pp. 186, 372, and Schanz, *ad loc.*

18. βλέπετε οὖν πῶς ἀκούετε. Because the doctrine received must be handed on and made known to all, therefore it is all-important that it should be rightly heard, viz. with intelligence and a "good heart" (ver. 15). Whoever gives a welcome to the word and appropriates it, becomes worthy and capable of receiving more. But by not appropriating truth when we recognize it, we lose our hold of it, and have less power of recognizing it in the future. There is little doubt that **ὃ δοκεῖ ἔχειν** means "that which he *thinketh* he hath." Wic. has "weneth"; Tyn. and Cran. "supposeth"; Cov. and Rhem. "thinketh." "Seemeth" comes from Beza's *videtur*. It is *self*-deception that is meant. Those who received the seed by the wayside were in this condition; they failed to appropriate it, and lost it. Comp. xix. 26.

Mk. here inserts (iv. 24) the ᾧ μέτρῳ μετρεῖτε, κ.τ.λ., which Lk. has already given in the sermon (vi. 38): and both Mt. and Mk. here add other parables, two of which Lk. gives later (xiii. 18–21).

19–21. The Visit of His Mother and His Brethren. Christ's true Relations. Mt. (xii. 46–50) and Mk. (iii. 31–35) place this incident before the parable of the Sower; but none of the three state which preceded in order of time. Comp. xi. 27, 28, and see on xi. 29. On the "Brethren of the Lord" see Lange, *Leben Jesu*, ii. 2, § 13, Eng. tr. i. p. 329; Lft. *Galatians*, pp. 253–291, in his *Dissertations on the Apostolic Age*, pp. 3–45, Macmillan, 1892; J. B. Mayor, *Epistle of S. James*, pp. v–xxxvi, Macmillan, 1892.[1] *D.B.*[2] artt. "Brother"; "James"; "Judas, the Lord's Brother."

[1] The work as a whole, and the dissertation on this question in particular, deserve special commendation.

19. Παρεγένετο δὲ πρὸς αὐτὸν ἡ μήτηρ καὶ οἱ ἀδελφοὶ αὐτοῦ For the verb, which is a favourite with Lk., see on vii. 4. Here Mk. has *ἔρχονται* and Mt. *ἰδού.* In writing the sing. Lk. is thinking only of *ἡ μήτηρ.* Such constructions are common, and do not imply that the first in the series of nominatives was emphatic or specially prominent, except in the writer's thoughts. Comp. Jn. xviii. 15, xx. 3; Acts xxvi. 30; Philem. 23.

The precise relationship to be understood from the expression **οἱ ἀδελφοὶ αὐτοῦ** will probably never be determined or cease to be discussed. There is nothing in Scripture to warn us from what is the antecedently natural view that they are the children of Joseph and Mary, unless "I know not a man" (i. 34) is interpreted as implying a vow of perpetual virginity. The "*first*born" in ii. 7 and the *imperfect* followed by "till" in Mt. i. 25, seem to imply that Joseph and Mary *had* children; which is confirmed by contemporary belief (Mk. vi. 3; Mt. xiii. 55) and by the constant attendance of the *ἀδελφοί* on the Mother of the Lord (Mt. xii. 46; Mk. iii. 32; Jn. ii. 12). The Epiphanian theory, which gives Joseph children older than Jesus by a former wife, deprives Him of His rights as the heir of Joseph and of the house of David. It seems to be of apocryphal origin (*Gospel according to Peter*, or *Book of James*); and, like Jerome's theory of cousinship, to have been invented in the interests of asceticism and of *à priori* convictions respecting the perpetual virginity of Mary. Tertullian, in dealing with this passage, seems to assume as a matter of course that the *ἀδελφοί* are the children of Mary, and that she and they were here *censured* by Christ (*Marcion.* iv. 19; *De Carne Christi*, vii.). He knows nothing of the doctrine of a sinless Virgin. Renan conjectures that James, Joses, Simon, and Judas were the cousins of Jesus, but that the brethren who refused to believe in Him were His real brethren (*V. de J.* p. 23). This solution remains entirely his own, for it creates more difficulties than it solves. See *Expositor's Bible*, *James and Jude*, ch. iii., Hodder, 1891.

συντυχεῖν. Elsewhere in bibl. Grk. 2 Mac. viii. 14 only.

20. ἀπηγγέλη. A favourite word (*vv.* 34, 36, 47, vii. 18, 22, ix. 36, xiii. 1, etc.). Here [Mt.] has *εἶπεν δέ τις* and Mk. has *λέγουσιν.* The **λεγόντων** is certainly spurious: om. ℵ B D L Δ Ξ, Latt. Goth. etc.

21. μήτηρ μου καὶ ἀδελφοί μου. Note the absence of the article in all three accounts. This is the predicate, and *οὗτοι, κ.τ.λ.*, is the subject. And the meaning is not are "My actual mother or brethren," which would be *ἡ μήτηρ μου καὶ οἱ ἀδελφοί μου*, but "Mother to Me and brethren to Me," *i.e.* equal to such, equally dear. Mt. and Mk. have the singular here: *οὗτος* or *αὐτός μου ἀδελφὸς καὶ ἀδελφὴ καὶ μήτηρ ἐστίν.* We cannot infer from *καὶ* ἀδελφή that His sisters were present: they had settled at Nazareth (Mt. xiii. 56; Mk. vi. 3). The texts of Mk. iii. 32, which represent the multitude as telling Jesus that His sisters are with His Mother and brethren, are probably the result of this inference. A D and some Latin authorities insert "and Thy sisters"; ℵ B C G K L and most Versions omit the words. Christ's reply is not a denial of the claims of family ties, nor does it necessarily imply any censure on His Mother and brethren. It asserts that there are far stronger and higher claims. Family ties at the best are temporal; spiritual ties are eternal. Moreover, the closest blood-relationship to the Messiah constitutes no claim to admission into the Kingdom of God. No one becomes a child of God in virtue of human parentage (Jn. i. 13). Jesus does not say πατήρ μου, not merely because Joseph was not present, but because in the spiritual sense that relationship to Christ is filled by God alone. See on ver. 11.

22–25. The Stilling of the Tempest on the Lake of Gennesaret. This is the first of a pair of miracles which appear in the same order in all three Gospels (Mt. viii. 23 ff.; Mk. iv. 35 ff.), the second being the healing of the demoniacs in the country of the Gadarenes. To these two Mk. and Lk. add the healing of the woman with the issue and the raising of the daughter of Jairus, which Mt. places somewhat later. The full series gives us a group of representative miracles exhibiting Christ's power over the forces of nature and the powers of hell, over disease and over death.

22. Ἐγένετο δὲ ἐν μιᾷ τῶν ἡμερῶν καὶ αὐτός. All these expressions are characteristic, and exhibit Aramaic influence. See note at the end of ch. i., and comp. v. 1, 12, 17, vi. 12. There is nothing like them in Mk. iv. 35 or Mt. viii. 23, and ἐν μιᾷ τῶν ἡμερῶν is peculiar to Lk. (v. 17, xx. 1). Comp. ἐν μιᾷ τῶν πόλεων (v. 12) and ἐν μιᾷ τῶν συναγωγῶν (xiii. 10). Mt. tells us that it was the sight of the multitudes around Him that moved Jesus to order a departure to the other side of the lake; and Mk. says that the disciples "leaving the multitude, take Him with them, even as He was in the boat." This seems to imply that He was utterly tired, overcome by the demands which the multitude made upon Him. For διέλθωμεν see on ii. 15. The nautical expression ἀνάγεσθαι is freq. in Lk. and peculiar to him (Acts xiii. 13, xvi. 11, xviii. 21, xx. 3, 13, xxi. 2, xxvii. 2, 4, 12, 21, xxviii. 10, 11). Syr-Sin. omits καὶ ἀνήχθησαν.

23. πλεόντων δὲ αὐτῶν ἀφύπνωσεν. Excepting Rev. xviii. 17, πλεῖν is peculiar to Lk. (Acts xxi. 3, xxvii. 2, 6, 24). In *Anth. Pal.* 9. 517, ἀφυπνόω means "awaken *from* sleep." Here it means "fall *off* to sleep," a use which seems to be somewhat late (Heliod. ix. 12). In class. Grk. we should rather have καθυπνόω

(Lob. *Phryn.* p. 224). This is the only passage in which we read of Jesus sleeping.

κατέβη λαῖλαψ ἀνέμου. "There came down a violent squall of wind," from the heights which surround the lake. These are furrowed with ravines like funnels, down which winds rush with great velocity. See Thomson, *Land & Book*, p. 375; Keim, iv. p. 179, who quotes Rusegger, *Reisen*, iii. p. 136. For **λαῖλαψ** comp. Job xxi. 18, xxxviii. 1; Wisd. v. 14, 23; Ecclus. xlviii. 9; Hom. *Il.* xii. 375, xvii. 57. Mt. gives the effect of it as *σεισμὸς μέγας ἐν τῇ θαλάσσῃ*. For the accent comp. *καλαῦροψ*, *κλῖμαξ*, *κ.τ.λ.*, and see Chandler, § 668.

συνεπληροῦντο. The verb occurs only here, ix. 51, and Acts ii. 1. Note the imperf. in contrast to *κατέβη*. The squall came down with a single rush; the filling of the boat continued and was not completed. What was true of the boat is stated of the crew. In class. Grk. the act. is used of manning ships thoroughly (Thuc. vi. 50. 2).

24. Ἐπιστάτα, ἐπιστάτα. See on v. 5. The doubling of the name is here peculiar to Lk. Comp. x. 41, xxii. 31; Acts ix. 4, xxii. 7, xxvi. 14. Mt. has *Κύριε*, Mk. *Διδάσκαλε*. Augustine has some good remarks as to the differences between the exclamations attributed to the disciples in the three narratives. "There is no need to inquire which of these exclamations was really uttered. For whether they uttered some one of these three, or other words which no one of the Evangelists has recorded, yet conveying the same sense, what does it matter?" (*De Cons. Evang.* ii. 24, 25).

ἐπετίμησεν τῷ ἀνέμῳ καὶ τῷ κλύδωνι. This does not prove that Lk. regarded the storm as a personal agent: both the wind and its effect are "rebuked," a word which represents the disciples' view of the action. See on iv. 39. A **κλύδων** (*κλύζειν*, "wash against") is larger than a *κῦμα* (Jas. i. 6; Jon. i. 4, 12; Wisd. xiv. 5; 1 Mac. vi. 11; 4 Mac. vii. 5, xv. 31).

γαλήνη. Mt. and Mk. add *μεγάλη*: the word is common elsewhere, but in N.T. occurs only in this narrative. The sudden calm in the sea showed the reality of the miracle. Wind may cease suddenly, but the water which it has agitated continues to work for a long time afterwards. In Mk., as here, the stilling of the tempest precedes the rebuke: Mt. transposes the order of the two incidents. In both the rebuke is sharper than in Lk., who "ever spares the Twelve" (Schanz). See on vi. 13 and xxii. 45.

25. Ποῦ ἡ πίστις ὑμῶν; They might have been sure that the Messiah would not perish, and that their prayer for help would be answered. It is not their praying for succour that is blamed, but their want of faith in the result of their prayer: they feared that their prayer would be vain. Comp. His parents' anguish, and see on ii. 48.

τίς ἄρα οὗτός ἐστιν; Mt. has **ποταπός.** There is nothing incredible in the question. Their ideas of the Christ and His powers were very imperfect; and this was probably the first time that they had seen Him controlling the forces of nature. Their experience as fishermen told them how impossible it was in the natural course that such a storm should be followed immediately by a great calm. The fear which accompanies this question or exclamation is not that which the storm produced, but that which was caused by a sudden recognition of the presence of supernatural power of a kind that was new to them. Comp. v. 26, vii. 16. For the ἄρα comp. xxii. 23; Acts xii. 18.

One conjectures that the framer of a legend would have made the disciples accept the miracle as a matter of course: comp. v. 8, 9. Keim opposes Strauss for rejecting the whole as a myth, although he himself by no means accepts the whole as historical. "Unquestionably there rests upon this brief and pregnant narrative a rare majesty, such as does not reappear in the other nature-miracles. With a few masterly strokes there is here sketched a most sublime picture from the life of Jesus, and a picture full of truth. . . . Even His rising up against weather and sea is told by Mt. and Lk. quite simply, without any ostentation; and the tentative query of the disciples, after their deliverance was accomplished, Who is this? is the slightest possible, the only too modest and yet the true utterance of the impression which they must at that time have received" (*Jes. of Naz.* iv. p. 180). See Gould on Mk. iv. 41.

26–39. The Healing of the Demoniac in the Country of the Gerasenes.

Gerasenes seems to be the true reading both here and Mk. v. 1, while Gadarenes is best attested Mt. viii. 28; but in all three places the authorities vary between Gerasenes, Gadarenes, and Gergesenes. The evidence here is thus summarized—

Γαδαρηνῶν, A R Γ Δ Λ Π etc., Syrr. (Cur-Pesh-Sin-Harcl *txt*) Goth.
Γερασηνῶν, B C* (ver. 37, *hiat* ver. 26) D, Latt. Syr-Harcl *mg.*
Γεργεσηνῶν, ℵ L X Ξ *minusc. sex*, Syr-Hier. Boh. Arm. Aeth. See WH. ii. *App.* p. 11. If Lk. viii. 26 stood alone, one might adopt Γεργεσηνῶν as possibly correct there; but the evidence in ver. 37 is conclusive against it.

These Gerasenes are probably not the people of the Gerasa which lay on the extreme eastern frontier of Peræa, over thirty miles from the lake: even in a loose description to foreigners Lk. would not be likely to speak of the shore of the lake as in the country of these Gerasenes. Rather we may understand the town which Thomson rediscovered (*Land & Book*, ii. 34–38) under the name of *Gersa* or *Kersa* on the steep eastern bank. Gergesa is merely a conjecture of Origen, adopted upon topographical grounds and not upon textual evidence. It may be rejected in all three narratives. There is no real difficulty of topography, whichever reading be adopted. The expression τὴν χώραν τῶν Γ. gives considerable latitude, and may include a great deal more than the immediate vicinity of the town. Nor is there any difficulty in the fact that Mt. knows of two demoniacs, whereas Lk. and Mk. mention only one. The real difficulties in the miracle, for those who believe in the fact of demoniacal possession, are connected with the swine. 1. Can beings which are purely spiritual enter and influence beings which are purely animal? 2. How can we justify the destruction of the swine, which were innocent creatures, and which belonged to persons who do not seem to have merited such a heavy loss?

On the first of these two questions our ignorance is so great that we do not even know whether there is a difficulty. Who can explain how mind acts upon matter, or matter upon mind? Yet the fact is as certain, as that mind acts upon mind or that matter acts upon matter. There is nothing in experience to forbid us from believing that evil spirits could act upon brute beasts; and science admits that it has "no *à priori* objection to offer" to such an hypothesis. And if there is no scientific objection to demoniacal possession of brutes, *à fortiori* there is none to that of men, seeing that men have both bodies and spirits to be influenced. The influence may have been analogous to that of mesmerism or hypnotism. The real difficulty is the moral one. As Huxley puts it, "the wanton destruction of other people's property is a misdemeanour of evil example." The answers are very various. 1. The whole story is a myth. 2. The healing of the demoniacs and the repulse of the Healer by the inhabitants are historical, but the incident of the swine is a later figment. 3. The demoniacs frightened the swine, and the transfer of demons from them to the swine was imagined. 4. The drowning of the swine was an accident, possibly simultaneous with the healing, and report mixed up the two incidents. 5. The demoniacs were mere maniacs, whom Jesus cured by humouring their fancies; and His giving leave to imaginary demons to enter into the swine, produced the story of the disaster to the herd.—All these explanations assume that the Gospel narratives are wholly or in part unhistorical. But there are other explanations.—6. Like earthquakes, shipwrecks, pestilences, and the like, the destruction of the swine is part of the mystery of evil, and insoluble. 7. As the Creator of the universe, the incarnate Word had the right to do what He pleased with His own. 8. A visible effect of the departure of the demons was necessary to convince the demoniacs and their neighbours of the completeness of the cure. Brutes and private property may be sacrificed, where the sanity and lives of persons are concerned. 9. The keepers of the swine were Jews, who were breaking the Jewish law, which was binding on them, and perhaps on the whole district. "In the enforcement of a law which bound the conscience, our Lord had an authority such as does not belong to the private individual" (W. E. Gladstone, *Nineteenth Century*, Feb. 1891, p. 357). Against this it is contended that the swineherds were probably pagans, and that the district was not under Jewish law (*N. C.* Dec. 1890, p. 967; March 1891, p. 455). Certainty is not attainable, but it is probable that one of the last two reasons is the true explanation. See *Expositor*, 3rd series, 1889, ix. 303. Godet's conclusion seems to be sound, that it is one of those cases in which the power to execute the sentence guarantees the right of the judge.[1] Contrast the healing of a demoniac woman as recorded in the *Gospel of the Infancy*, xiv.

26. κατέπλευσαν εἰς τὴν χώραν τῶν Γερασηνῶν ἥτις ἐστὶν ἀντίπερα. "They landed at the country of the Gerasenes, which is in such a position as to be opposite Galilee." The verb is quite class. of coming to land from the high seas, but is found here only in N.T. Not in LXX. See Smith, *Voyage and Shipwreck of S. Paul*, p. 28, and reff. in Wetst. The statement tells us nothing as to the position of the country of the Gerasenes, for "opposite" would apply to the whole of the east shore. Lk. alone mentions its being "opposite Galilee"; perhaps to justify its inclusion in the Galilean ministry. *D.C.G.* artt. "Gadara," "Gerasenes."

Some texts have πέραν from Mt. or Mk., while others have ἀντιπέραν, of which ἀντιπέρα is a later form. Another form is ἀντιπέρας. For the accent see Chandler, § 867.

27. ὑπήντησεν ἀνήρ τις ἐκ τῆς πόλεως. The man belonged to the city, but he came out of the tombs to meet Jesus: ἐκ τῆς πόλεως belongs to ἀνήρ τις, not to ὑπήντησεν. For this force of ὑπό in composition comp. ὑποκρίνομαι, "answer *back*"; ὑπολογίζομαι, "reckon *per contra*"; ὑποστρέφω, "turn *back*." For ἱκανῷ see on vii. 12; and for ἐνεδύσατο see Burton, § 48. Lk. alone mentions that the demoniac wore no clothes; but Mk. implies it by stating that he was clothed after he was cured. All three mention the tombs; and near the ruins of Khersa there are many tombs hewn in the rocks. Excepting Mk. v. 3, 5 and Rev. xi. 9, μνῆμα is peculiar to Lk. (xxiii. 53, xxiv. 1; Acts ii. 29, vii. 16); but he more often uses μνημεῖον. With ἔμενεν comp. xix. 5, xxiv. 29.

28. Τί ἐμοὶ καὶ σοί; See on iv. 34.

Ἰησοῦ υἱὲ τοῦ Θεοῦ τοῦ ὑψίστου. This expression rather indicates that the man is not a Jew, and therefore is some evidence that the owners of the swine were not Jews. "The Most High" (*Elyon*) is a name for Jehovah which seems to be usual among heathen nations It is employed by Melchisedek, the Canaanite priest and king (Gen. xiv. 20, 22). Balaam uses it (Num. xxiv. 16). Micah puts it into the mouth of Balaam (vi. 6); Isaiah, into the mouth of the king of Babylon (xiv. 14). It is used repeatedly in the Babylonian proclamations in Daniel (iii. 26, iv. 24, 32, v. 18, 21,

[1] See some valuable remarks by Sanday in the *Contemp. Rev.* Sept. 1892, p. 348. He inclines to the second explanation, but with reserve.

vii. 18, 22, 25, 27). The girl with a spirit of divination at Philippi employs it (Acts xvi. 17). It is found in Phœnician inscriptions also. See Chadwick, *St. Mark*, p. 144, and Wsctt. on Heb. vii. 1. For φωνῇ μεγάλῃ see on i. 42, and for δέομαι see on v. 12: with ἀνακράξας of demoniac cries comp. iv. 41; Acts viii. 7.

μή με βασανίσῃς. Neither the verb nor its cognate substantive is ever used in N.T. of testing metals, or of obtaining evidence by torture, but simply of pain or torment. The demoniac identifies himself with the demon which controls him, and the torment which is feared is manifest from ver. 31.

29. παρήγγελλεν γὰρ τῷ πνεύματι. Authorities are very evenly divided between the imperf. and the aor. If παρήγγειλεν be right, it almost means "He had ordered." Burton, § 29, 48. We should have expected τοῖς πνεύμασιν, for both in ver. 27 and ver. 30 we have δαιμόνια. But the interchange of personality between the man and the demons is so rapid, that it becomes natural to speak of the demons in the sing. Note that while Lk. has his characteristic ἐξελθεῖν ἀπό (*vv.* 33, 38, iv. 35, 41, v. 8, etc.), Mk. has the more usual ἐξελθεῖν ἐκ.

πολλοῖς γὰρ χρόνοις συνηρπάκει αὐτόν. "Many times," *i.e.* on many occasions, *multis temporibus* (Vulg.), "it had seized him," or "carried him away": comp. Acts xxvii. 15. Mk. has πόλλακις. Others explain "within a long time." See Win. xxxi. 9, p. 273. The verb is quite class., but in N.T. peculiar to Lk. (Acts vi. 12, xix. 29, xxvii. 15). Hobart counts it as medical (p. 244). In LXX, Prov. vi. 25; 2 Mac. iii. 27, iv. 41.

ἁλύσεσιν καὶ πέδαις. Both Lk. and Mk. use these two words to distinguish the "handcuffs and fetters," *manicæ et pedicæ*, with which he was bound. See Lft. *Phil.* p. 8. The former is used of the chain by which the hand of a prisoner was fastened to the soldier who had charge of him. Like "chains," ἁλύσεις are of metal, whereas πέδαι might be ropes or withes. Both ἁλύσεις and πέδαι are included in τὰ δεσμά. The imperfects tell of what usually took place. During the calmer intervals precautions were taken to prevent the demons "carrying him away with" them; but these precautions always proved futile.

εἰς τὰς ἐρήμους. In order to take the man away from humane influences. But the wilderness is regarded as the home of evil spirits. See on xi. 24; and for the plural see on i. 80.

30. Τί σοι ὄνομά ἐστιν; In order to recall the man to a sense of his own independent personality, Jesus asks him his name. It was a primary condition of his cure that he should realize that he is not identical with the evil powers which control his actions. Perhaps also Christ wished the disciples to know the magnitude of the evil, that the cure might increase their faith (ver. 25): and this purpose may have influenced Him in allowing the destruction of the swine. The peculiar word Λεγιών,[1] which is preserved in Mk.

[1] That the man had ever seen a Roman legion, "at once one and many, cruel and inexorable and strong," is perhaps not probable. But see Trench. *Miracles*, p. 171, 8th ed. For other Latin words comp. x. 35, xi. 33, xix. 20.

v. 9 also, is a mark of authenticity. As Sanday points out, it is more probable that this strange introduction of a Latin word should represent something which really took place, than that it should be pure invention (*Contemp. Rev.* Sept. 1892, p. 349). The words **ὅτι εἰσῆλθεν δαιμόνια πολλὰ εἰς αὐτόν** are the remark of the Evangelist: comp. ii. 50, iii. 15, xxiii. 12.

31. παρεκάλουν αὐτόν. "They kept beseeching Him." The plurality of those who ask is emphatically marked: with *δαιμόνια* we might have expected *παρεκάλει*, as in Mk. The plur. would have been less noticeable in Mk., because the masc. plur., *πολλοί ἐσμεν*, precedes.

That *παρεκάλουν* (ℵ B C D F L S, Latt. Goth.) and not *παρεκάλει* is right here, need not be doubted.

εἰς τὴν ἄβυσσον. In class. Grk. *ἄβυσσος* is always an adj., "bottomless, boundless," and is mostly poetical. In LXX *ἡ ἄβυσσος* is used of the sea (Gen. i. 2, vii. 11; Job xli. 22, 23); without the art. (Job xxviii. 14, xxxvi. 16; Ecclus. 1 3, xvi. 18); of the depths of the earth (Ps. lxxi. 20; Deut. viii. 7); but perhaps nowhere of Hades. In N.T. it means Hades (Rom. x. 7), and esp. the penal part of it which is the abode of demons (Rev. ix. 1–11, xi. 7, xvii. 8, xx. 1, 3). The latter is the meaning here. The demons dread being sent to their place of punishment. See Cremer, *Lex. sub v.* In Mk. the petition is "that He will not send them *out of the country*"; but the verb is sing. and the man is the petitioner. He still confuses himself with the demons, and desires to stay where he feels at home. This is their wish and his also. The persistent confusion of personality renders it necessary that the man should have some decisive evidence of the departure of the evil spirits from him. In this way his cure will be effected with least suffering, Prof. Marshall thinks that *εἰς τὴν ἄβυσσον* and *ἔξω τῆς χώρας* may represent Aramaic expressions so nearly alike as readily to be confounded by copyist or translator (*Expositor*, Nov. 1891, p. 377). See footnote on v. 31.

32. ἀγέλη χοίρων ἱκανῶν. This illustrates the fondness of Lk. for *ἱκανός* in this sense: Mt. has *ἀγ. χοίρων πολλῶν* and Mk. *ἀγ. χοίρων μεγάλη*. With characteristic love of detail Mk. gives the number as *ὡς δισχίλιοι*, which may be an exaggeration of the swineherds or of the owners, who wished to make the most of their loss. Had the number been an invention of the narrator, we should have had 4000 or 5000 to correspond with the legion. It is futile to ask whether each animal was possessed. If some of them were set in motion, the rest would follow mechanically. For the *ἐπέτρεψεν αὐτοῖς* of Lk. and Mk. we have the direct *ὑπάγετε* in Mt., which need mean no more than "depart, be gone." But the distinction between commanding and allowing what He might have forbidden is not very helpful. Whatever the motive of the demons may have been, Jesus uses it for a good end, and secures the easy and effectual cure of their victim.

33. ὥρμησεν ἡ ἀγέλη κατὰ τοῦ κρημνοῦ. These words also are in all three. The word *κρημνός* need not mean an abrupt precipice: a steep and rocky slope suffices. MacGregor, Stanley, Tristram, Wilson, and others believe that the spot which suits the description can be identified. The art. implies that it was well known. Comp. 2 Chron. xxv. 12. The use of **ἀπεπνίγη** for suffocation by drowning is classical (Dem. p. 883).

34. τὸ γεγονός. Chiefly the destruction of the swine. In ver. 36 *οἱ ἰδόντες* means the disciples and others near to Jesus, not the swineherds.

35–39. Note how the characteristics of Lk.'s diction stand out in these verses. For *τὸν ἄνθρωπον ἀφ' οὗ τ. δ. ἐξῆλθεν* (see on ver. 29) Mk. has *τὸν δαιμονιζόμενον*, and *παρὰ τοὺς πόδας* (see on vii. 38) has no equivalent in Mk. For *ἀπήγγειλαν* (see on ver. 20) Mk. has *διηγήσαντο*, while *ἅπαν* (see on iii. 21), *τὸ πλῆθος* (see on i. 10), *φόβῳ μεγάλῳ* (see on i. 42, vii. 16), *συνείχοντο* (see on iv. 38), and *ὑπέστρεψεν* (see on i. 56) have no equivalents. For *ἐδεῖτο* (see on v. 12) Mk. has *παρεκάλει*; for *ὁ ἀνὴρ ἀφ' οὗ ἐξελήλύθει* (see on ver. 29) Mk. has the less accurate *ὁ δαιμονισθείς*; for *σύν* (see on i. 56) Mk. has *μετά*; and for *ὑπόστρεφε* (see on i. 56) Mk. has *ὕπαγε*.

35. ἱματισμένον. Some of the bystanders may have given him clothing; but there would have been time to fetch it. The verb is found neither in LXX nor in profane writers, but only here and Mk. v. 15. The **παρὰ τοὺς πόδας** implies an attitude of thankfulness rather than that he has become a disciple. It is the last of the four changes that have taken place in the man. He is *καθήμενον* instead of restless, *ἱματισμένον* instead of naked, *σωφρονοῦντα* instead of raging, and *παρὰ τοὺς πόδας τοῦ* 'I. instead of shunning human society. Baur would have it that he is meant to represent the conversion of the Gentiles. We are not sure that he was a Gentile; and this would have been made clear if he was intended as a representative. For *παρά* with the acc. after a verb of rest comp. Acts x. 6; Mt. xiii. 1, xx. 30; Mk. v. 21, x. 46.

36. ἀπήγγειλαν δὲ αὐτοῖς. This is not a repetition of ver. 34, but a statement of additional information which was given to the townspeople after they arrived on the scene.

37. ἅπαν τὸ πλῆθος. The desire that He should depart was universal, and all three narratives mention it. The people feared that His miraculous power might lead to further losses: and this feeling was not confined to the inhabitants of the *πόλις* close at hand (ver. 34); it was shared by the whole district. Comp. iv. 29, ix. 53, and contrast iv. 42; Jn. iv. 40. Although Keim rejects the incident of the swine, yet he rightly contends that this request that Jesus should leave the place gives the impression of a sober historical fact. There is nothing like it elsewhere in the history of Jesus; and neither it nor the locality is likely to have been invented. Why should a myth take Jesus across to Gerasa? Some historical connexion with the locality is much more probable. Here, as in *vv.* 30, 36, Syr-Sin. abbreviates.

38. ἐδεῖτο δὲ αὐτοῦ ὁ ἀνήρ. The δέ marks the contrast between Him and the rest. Mk. says that the request was made as Jesus was stepping into the boat. Mt. omits the whole incident. The man fears the unfriendly populace, and clings to his preserver.

39. διηγοῦ ὅσα σοι ἐποίησεν ὁ Θεός. In Galilee and Judæa, where Jesus and His disciples preached, He commonly told those who were healed to be silent about their cures. In this half-heathen Peræa there were no other missionaries, and the man was not fitted for permanent work with Christ elsewhere. Moreover, here there was no danger of the miracle being used for political purposes. Lastly, it might be beneficial to a healed demoniac to have free converse with all after his gloomy isolation. The **ὁ Θεός** is last with emphasis. Jesus shows the man that he must attribute his deliverance to *God.* Both Lk. and Mk. preserve the highly natural touch that, in spite of this command, the man proclaimed what *Jesus* had done for him. Note also that *καθ' ὅλην τὴν πόλιν* is much in excess of *εἰς τὸν οἶκόν σου*, and *κηρύσσων* of *διηγοῦ*. See on ix. 10.

καθ' ὅλην τὴν πόλιν. With *κηρύσσων*, not with *ἀπῆλθεν*: Win. xlix. d. a, p. 499. Mk. has *ἐν τῇ Δεκαπόλει*. Nowhere else in N.T. does *καθ ὅλην* occur: Lk. commonly writes *καθ' ὅλης* (iv. 14, xxiii. 5; Acts ix. 31, 42, x. 37). He nowhere mentions Decapolis.

40–56. The Healing of the Woman with the Issue and the Raising of the Daughter of Jairus. Mt. ix. 18–26; Mk. v. 21–43. The name of Bernice (Veronica) for this woman first appears in the *Acts of Pilate*, *Gospel of Nicodemus*, Pt. I. ch. vii. Respecting the statues, which Eusebius saw at Cæsarea, and which he believed to represent Christ and this woman, see *H. E.* vii. 18. 1–3. Sozomen says that Julian removed the statue of Christ and substituted one of himself, which was broken by a thunderbolt (v. 21). Philostorgius says the same (vii. 3). Malalas gives the petition in which the woman asked Herod Antipas to be allowed to erect the memorial (*Chrongr.* x. 306–8). That the statues existed, and that Christians thus misinterpreted their meaning, need not be doubted Pseudo-Ambrosius would have it that the woman was Martha the sister of Lazarus.

40–48. In these verses also the marks of Lk.'s style are very conspicuous (see above on *vv.* 35–39). In ver. 40 we have *ἐν δὲ τῷ c. infin.* (see on iii. 21), *ὑποστρέφειν* (see on i. 56), *ἀπεδέξατο* (see on ver. 40), *ἦσαν c. particip.* (see on i. 10), *πάντες* (see on ix. 43), and *προσδοκῶντες* (see on iii. 15). In ver. 41, *καὶ ἰδού* (see on i. 20), *καὶ οὗτος* (i. 36), *ὑπῆρχεν* (see on ver. 41), *παρὰ τοὺς πόδας* (see on vii. 38). In ver. 42, *καὶ αὐτή* (see on i. 17) and *ἐν δὲ τῷ c. infin.* In ver. 44, *παραχρῆμα* (see on v. 25). In ver. 45, *πάντων* (vi. 30, vii. 35) and *ἐπιστάτα* (v. 5). In ver. 46, *ἐξελθεῖν ἀπό* (see on iv. 35). In ver. 47, *ἀπήγγειλεν* (see on ver. 20), *ἐνώπιον* (see on i. 15), *παντός, τοῦ λαοῦ, ἰάθη*, and *παραχρῆμα*. Not one of these expressions is found in the parallel passages in Mt. and Mk. See on ix. 28–36.

40. ἀπεδέξατο. Peculiar to Lk. (ix. 11; Acts ii. 41, xviii. 27, xxi. 17, xxiv. 3, xxviii. 30, and possibly xv. 4). The meaning is they "received Him with pleasure, welcomed Him" (Euthym. Theophyl. Schanz). See on iv. 42 and on xi. 29. In class. Grk. the verb means "accept as a teacher, as an authority," or "admit arguments as valid": so in Xen. Plat. Arist. etc.

41. Ἰάειρος. The same name as Jair (Num. xxxii. 41; Judg. x. 3). It is strange that the name (= "he will give light") should be used as an argument against the historical character of the narrative. It is not very appropriate to the circumstances.

ὑπῆρχεν. Very freq. in Lk., esp. in Acts: not in Mt. Mk. or Jn. The use of this verb as almost equivalent to *εἶναι* is the beginning of the modern usage. But the classical meaning of a present state connected with a previous state still continues in N.T. (ix. 48, xi. 13, xvi. 14, 23, xxiii. 50). See *Sp. Comm.* on 1 Cor. vii. 26. Here also Christ does not refuse the homage (iv. 8), as Peter (Acts x. 26) and the Angel (Rev. xix. 10) do.

42. μονογενής. As in the cases of the widow's son and the lunatic boy (vii. 12, ix. 38), this fact may have influenced Christ. On all three occasions Lk. alone mentions the fact.

ἐτῶν δώδεκα. A critical time in a girl's life. Not only Lk., who frequently notes such things (ii. 36, 37, 42, iii. 23, xiii. 11), but Mk. also gives the age. All three mention that the woman with the issue had been suffering for twelve years. For **ἀπέθνησκεν** Mk. has *ἐσχάτως ἔχει* and Mt. *ἄρτι ἐτελεύτησεν*. The reason for the difference between Mt. and the others is plain. Lk. and Mk. give the arrivals, both of the father, who says, "She is dying," and of the messenger, who says, "She is dead." Mt. condenses the two into one.

συνέπνιγον. Mk. has *συνέθλιβον*, which is less strong: see on ver. 14. In both cases the *συν-* expresses the pressing together all round Him. The crowd which had been waiting for Him (ver. 40) now clings to Him in the hope of witnessing a miracle.

43. οὖσα ἐν ῥύσει. "Being in a condition of hemorrhage." The constr. is quite simple and intelligible; comp. *ἐν φθορᾷ, ἐν ἐκστάσει, ἐν δόξῃ, ἐν ἐκτενείᾳ, ἐν ἔχθρᾳ*. The form *ῥύσις* is from the unused *ῥύω*, from which come the late forms *ἔρρυσα* and *ἔρρυκα*, and *ῥεῦσις* is often a *v.l.* Win. xxix. 3. b, p. 230.

ἰατροῖς προσαναλώσασα ὅλον τὸν βίον. "Having, *in addition to all her sufferings*, spent all her resources on physicians," or "for physicians," or "in physicians." This use of βίος for "means of living" is freq. in N.T. (xv. 12, 30, xxi. 4; Mk. xii. 44; 1 Jn. iii. 17) and in class. Grk. In class. Grk. βίος is a higher word than ζωή, the former being that which is peculiar to man, the latter that which he shares with brutes and vegetables. In N.T. βίος retains its meaning, being either the "period of human life," as 1 Tim. ii. 2; 2 Tim. ii. 4, or "means of life," as here. But ζωή is raised above βίος, and means that vital principle which through Christ man shares with God. Hence βίος is comparatively rare in N.T., which is not much concerned with the duration of temporal life or the means of prolonging it; whereas ζωή occurs more than a hundred times. See Trench, *Syn.* xxvii.; Crem. *Lex.* p. 272; Lft. on *Ign. ad Rom.* vii. 3.

WH. follow B D., Arm. in omitting ἰατροῖς . . . βίον. Treg. and RV. indicate doubt in marg. Syr-Sin. omits.

οὐκ ἴσχυσεν. This use of ἰσχύω for "be able" is freq. in Lk. See on vi. 48. It is natural that "the physician" does not add, as Mk. does, that she had suffered much at the hands of the physicians, and was worse rather than better for their treatment. The remedies which they tried in such cases were sometimes very severe, and sometimes loathsome and absurd. See Lightfoot, p. 614; Tristram, *Eastern Customs in Bible Lands*, pp. 22, 23.

44. προσελθοῦσα ὄπισθεν ἥψατο. She came from behind that He might not see her. Her malady made her levitically unclean, and she did not wish to own this publicly. Her faith is tinged with superstition. She believes that Christ's garments heal magically, independently of His will. In other cases those who touched Him in faith seem to have done so openly. Comp. vi. 19; Mt. xiv. 36; Mk. iii. 10, vi. 56.

For ὄπισθεν a has *de retro*: comp. Baruch vi. 5, *visa itaque turba de retro* (Vulg.). Hence the French *derrière.*

τοῦ κρασπέδου τοῦ ἱματίου. "The tassel" rather than "the fringe" or "hem of His garment." The square overgarment or *Tallith* had tassels of three white threads with one of hyacinth at each of the four corners. Edersh. *L. & T.* i. p. 624 (but see *D.B.*[2] art. "Hem of Garment"). Of the four corners two hung in front, and two behind. It was easy to touch the latter without the wearer feeling the touch. *D.C.G.* art. "Border."

ἔστη ἡ ῥύσις. It "stood still, ceased to flow." Mk. has ἐξηράνθη. "This is the only passage in the N.T. in which ἱστάναι is used in this sense. It is the usual word in the medical writers to denote the stoppage of bodily discharges, and especially such as are mentioned here" (Hobart, p. 15). Both παραχρῆμα, for which Mk. has εὐθύς, and προσαναλώσασα, for which Mk. has δαπανήσασα, are also claimed as medical (pp. 16, 96).

45. There is no reason for supposing that the miracle was wrought *without the will of Jesus.* He knew that someone had been healed by touching His garment; and we may believe that He read the woman's heart as she approached Him in the belief that He could heal her. Lk. evidently dates the cure from her touching His garment; Mt. seems to place it in Christ's words to her; Mk. in *both* places.

τίς ὁ ἁψάμενός μου; This does not seem to be one of those cases in which Christ asked for *information*. He knew that He had been touched with a purpose, and He probably knew who had done it. Mk.'s περιεβλέπετο ἰδεῖν τὴν τοῦτο ποιήσασαν rather implies that He knew where to look. *For the woman's sake* she must be induced to avow her act. Note the masc., which makes the question all the more general: Mk. has τίς μου ἥψατο τῶν ἱματίων. The verb implies more than touching, "laying hold of." For other cases in which Jesus asked questions of which He knew the answer comp. xxiv. 17; Mk. ix. 33. See some good remarks in the *S. P. C. K. Comm.* on Lk. viii. 46.

ἀρνουμένων δὲ πάντων. This explains, and to some extent excuses, Peter's characteristic interference. Lk. alone tells us that Peter took the lead in this. See on ix. 20, and comp. Mk. i. 36. Note the πάντων, and see on ix. 43 and xi. 4. For ἐπιστάτα see on v. 5.

συνέχουσίν σε. "Hold Thee in, keep Thee a prisoner"; xix. 43, xxii. 63; comp. iv. 38. Here only in N.T. does ἀποθλίβειν occur: Lat. *affligere* (Vulg.), *comprimere* (f), *contribulare* (d); om. a b ff_2.

46. ἔγνων δύναμιν ἐξεληλυθυῖαν ἀπ' ἐμοῦ. For the constr. see Burton, § 458, and comp. Heb. xiii. 23; and for δύναμις see on iv. 36.

47. τρέμουσα ἦλθεν. The πάντων in ver. 45, if taken literally, implies that she had previously denied her action. The ἦλθεν, however, seems to show that she had gone a little way from Him after being healed. But she may also have been afraid that she had done wrong in touching His garment. Either or both would explain the τρέμουσα. She is afraid that the boon may be withdrawn. For the attraction δι' ἣν αἰτίαν see small print on iii. 19, and Burton, § 350: τοῦ λαοῦ is also characteristic.

48. ἡ πίστις σου σέσωκέν σε. All three record these words. It was the grasp of her faith, not of her hand, that wrought the cure. Thus her low view of the manner of Christ's healing is corrected.

49. ἔρχεταί τις παρὰ τοῦ ἀρχισυναγώγου. A member of his household arrives and tells Jairus that it is now too late. The delay caused by the incident with the woman must have been agonizing to him. But this trial is necessary for the development of his faith, as well as for that of the woman, and Jesus curtails no item in His work. The τέθνηκεν is placed first with emphasis. For σκύλλε see on vii. 6. See also Blass on Acts x. 44.

50. Μὴ φοβοῦ, μόνον πίστευσον. Change of tense. "Cease to fear; only make an act of faith." In Mk. v. 36 we have μόνον πίστευε, "only continue to believe." In either case the meaning is, "In the presence of this new difficulty let faith prevail, and all will be well." For μή φοβοῦ see on i. 13.

51. οὐκ ἀφῆκεν εἰσελθεῖν τινὰ σὺν αὐτῷ. "Did not allow anyone to enter with Him into the *room*." He and the disciples had already entered the house, and the parents had been there from the first. Here, as in ver. 38, Lk. has σύν where Mk. has μετά: see on i. 56.

Πέτρον καὶ Ἰωάνην καὶ Ἰάκωβον. The chosen three (ἐκλεκτῶν ἐκλεκτότεροι as Clem. Alex. calls them) are probably admitted for the sake of the Twelve, whose faith would be strengthened by the miracle. These three sufficed as witnesses. Moreover, they were in character most fitted to profit by the miracle. Here, as in ix. 28 and Acts i. 13, John is placed before James. Elsewhere the other order, which is almost certainly the order of age, prevails (v. 10, vi. 14, ix. 54), and always in Mt. (iv. 21, x. 2, xvii. 1) and Mk. (i. 19, 29, iii. 17, v. 37, ix. 2, x. 35, 41, xiii. 3, xiv. 33).

Irenæus had a text which omitted καὶ Ἰωάνην. *Quintus autem ingressus Dominus ad mortuam puellam suscitavit eam, nullum enim, inquit, permisit intrare nisi Petrum et Jacobum et patrem et matrem puellæ* (ii. 24. 4). No existing text makes this omission; but many authorities transpose James and John in order to have the usual order (ℵ A L S X L, Boh. Aeth. Arm. Goth.). But the evidence of B C D E F H K, a b c d e f ff_2 l q r Cod. Am. Cod. Brix. etc. is decisive. There is similar confusion in ix. 28 and Acts i. 13.

52. ἔκλαιον δὲ πάντες καὶ ἐκόπτοντο αὐτήν. The mourners (2 Chron. xxxv. 25; Jer. ix. 17) were not in the room with the corpse: Mt. and Mk. tell us that Christ turned them out of the house. The πάντες is again peculiar to Lk.'s account: comp. *vv.* 40, 45, 47. The acc. after κόπτομαι is class. (Eur. *Tro.* 623; Aristoph. *Lys.* 396): "they beat their breasts for her, bewailed her." Comp. xxiii. 27; Gen. xxiii. 2; 1 Sam. xxv. 1.

οὐ γὰρ ἀπέθανεν ἀλλὰ καθεύδει. This declaration is in all three narratives. Neander, Olshausen, Keim, and others understand it literally; and possibly Origen is to be understood as taking the same view. A miracle of power is thus turned into a miracle of knowledge. But the εἰδότες in ver. 53 is conclusive as to the Evangelist's meaning: not "supposing," but "*knowing* that she was dead." The καθεύδει is rather to be understood in the same sense as Λάζαρος κεκοίμηται (Jn. xi. 11). But the cases are not parallel, for there Jesus prevents all possibility of misunderstanding by adding Λάζαρος ἀπέθανεν. Yet the fact that Jesus has power to awaken explains in both cases why He speaks of sleep. We may, however, be content, with Hase, to admit that certainty is unattainable as to whether the maiden was dead or in a trance.

54. κρατήσας τῆς χειρὸς αὐτῆς. All three mention that He laid hold of her, although to touch a dead body was to incur ceremonial uncleanness. In like manner He touched the leper: see on v. 13

This laying hold of her hand and the raised voice (ἐφώνησεν) are consonant with waking one out of sleep, and the two may be regarded as the means of the miracle. Comp. and contrast throughout Acts ix. 36–42.

Ἡ παῖς, ἔγειρε. "Arise, get up," not "awake." Mt. omits the command; Mk. gives the exact words, *Talitha cumi.* For the nom. with the art. as voc. see on x. 21, xviii. 11, 13. For ἐφώνησεν comp. ver. 8, xvi. 24.

55. ἐπέστρεψεν τὸ πνεῦμα αὐτῆς. There can be no doubt that the Evangelist uses the phrase of the spirit returning to a dead body, which is the accurate use of the phrase. Only the beloved physician makes this statement. In LXX it is twice used of a living man's strength reviving; of the fainting Samson (Judg. xv. 19), and of the starving Egyptian (1 Sam. xxx. 12). Note that Lk. has his favourite παραχρῆμα, where Mk. has his favourite εὐθύς; and comp. ver. 44, v. 25, xviii. 43, xxii. 60.

διέταξεν αὐτῇ δοθῆναι φαγεῖν. This care of Jesus in commanding food after the child's long exhaustion would be of special interest to Lk. In their joy and excitement the parents might have forgotten it. The charge is somewhat parallel to ἔδωκεν αὐτὸν τῇ μητρὶ αὐτοῦ (vii. 15) of the widow's son at Nain. In each case He intimates that nature is to resume its usual course: the old ties and the old responsibilities are to begin again.

56. παρήγγειλεν αὐτοῖς μηδενὶ εἰπεῖν τὸ γεγονός. The command has been rejected as an unintelligible addition to the narrative. No such command was given at Nain or at Bethany. The object of it cannot have been to keep the miracle a secret. Many were outside expecting the funeral, and they would have to be told why no funeral was to take place. It can hardly have been Christ's intention in this way to prevent the multitude from making a bad use of the miracle. This command to the parents would not have attained such an object. It was given more probably for the parents' sake, to keep them from letting the effect of this great blessing evaporate in vainglorious gossip. To thank God for it at home would be far more profitable than talking about it abroad.

IX. 1–50. *To the Departure for Jerusalem.*

This is the last of the four sections into which the Ministry in Galilee (iv. 14–ix. 50) was divided. It contains the Mission of the Twelve (1–9), the Feeding of the Five Thousand (10–17), the Transfiguration (28–36), the Healing of the Demoniac Boy (37–43), and two Predictions of the Passion (18–27, 43–50).

1–9. The Mission of the Twelve and the Fears of Herod. Mt. x. 1–15; Mk. vi. 7–11. Mt. is the most full. Lk. gives no note of time or of connexion, and we may suppose that his sources gave him no information. See Weiss, *L. J.* ii. p. 119, Eng. tr. ii. p. 306. For mention of "the Twelve" see vi. 13, viii. 1, ix. 12, xviii. 31, xxii. 3, 47. All three mention this summons or invitation on the part of Jesus. Mt. and Mk. describe it by their usual προσκαλεῖσθαι, for which Lk. has συνκαλεῖσθαι, which he more commonly uses in his Gospel (ix. 1, xv. 6, 9, xxiii. 13), while in the Acts he generally uses προσκαλεῖσθαι (ii. 39, v. 40, vi. 2, xiii. 2, etc.).

1. δύναμιν καὶ ἐξουσίαν. Mt. and Mk. have ἐξουσίαν only (see on iv. 36): δύναμις is the power, ἐξουσία the authority to use it. The Jewish exorcists had neither δύναμις nor ἐξουσία, and made elaborate and painful efforts, which commonly failed. Elsewhere, when the two are combined, ἐξουσία precedes δύναμις (iv. 36; 1 Cor. xv. 24; Eph. i. 21; 1 Pet. iii. 22). The πάντα with δαιμόνια is peculiar to Lk. It covers all that would come under the head of possession.

The constr. is not really doubtful: νόσους θεραπεύειν depends on δύναμιν καὶ ἐξουσίαν, and is co-ordinate with ἐπὶ πάντα δαιμόνια. Others make ν. θερ. depend on ἔδωκεν and be co-ordinate with δύν. κ. ἐξ. The least satisfactory way is to couple νόσους with δαιμόνια, and make θεραπεύειν refer to both": "authority over all diseases and demons, to heal them." For this meaning Lk. would almost certainly have written τοῦ θεραπεύειν. He as usual mentions the curing of demoniacs separately from other healings (iv. 40, 41, vi. 17, 18, vii. 21, viii. 2, xiii. 32).

2. After ἰᾶσθαι C etc. ins. τοὺς ἀσθενοῦντας from Mt.; A D L Ξ ins. τοὺς ἀσθενεῖς: om. B, Syr-Cur. Syr-Sin.

2. κηρύσσειν τὴν βασιλείαν τοῦ Θεοῦ καὶ ἰᾶσθαι. These two verbs sum up the ministration to men's souls and bodies. See on v. 17. Mt. adds that they were to raise the dead (x. 8). Mk. tells us that they were sent out δύο, δύο. For ἀποστέλλω see on iv. 18, p. 121.

3. μήτε ῥάβδον. Mk. has εἰ μὴ ῥάβδον μόνον (vi. 8); and the attempts to explain away this discrepancy in a small matter of detail are not very happy. As between Mt. and Mk. it is possible to explain that both mean "Do not *procure* (κτήσεσθε) a staff for the journey, but *take* (αἴρωσιν) the one which you have." But both Mk. and Lk. use αἴρειν, and the one has "Take nothing except a staff," while the other has "Take nothing, neither a staff," etc. Yet in all three the meaning is substantially the same: "Make no special preparations; go as you are." From xxii. 35 we learn that the directions were obeyed, and with good results. Lk. says nothing about sandals, respecting which there is another discrepancy between Mt. and Mk., unless we are to suppose that ὑποδήματα are different from σανδάλια. *D.C.G.* art. "Staff."

μήτε ἀργύριον. Mk. has χαλκόν and Mt. has both, μηδὲ ἄργυρον μηδὲ χαλκόν. Thus Lk. is Greek, and Mk. is Roman, in choice of words. In LXX ἀργύριον is very common, ἄργυρος comparatively rare, while χαλκός is common as a metal, but not in the sense of money.

μήτε δύο χιτῶνας ἔχειν. As no πήρα was allowed, the second tunic, if taken, would have to be worn. Hence the form in Mk., "Put not on two tunics." Comp. Jos. *Ant.* xvii. 5. 7.

In ἔχειν we have an anacoluthon; change from direct to oblique oration. For it is scarcely admissible to take ἔχειν as infin. for imperat. The actual imperat. both precedes (αἴρετε) and follows (μένετε). Win. xliii. 5. d, p. 397. Mk. here is strangely abrupt in his mixture of constructions.

4. ἐκεῖ μένετε καὶ ἐκεῖθεν ἐξέρχεσθε. Vulg. has *et inde ne exeatis.* But only one cursive has μή (38). Cod. Brix. has *donec exeatis* fr. Mt. The meaning is "Go not from house to house," as He charges the Seventy in x. 7, a passage which should be compared with this. The mission both of the Twelve and of the Seventy was to be simple and quiet, working from fixed centres in each place. This is the germ of what we find in the apostolic age,—"the church that is in their house" (Rom. xvi. 5; 1 Cor. xvi. 19; Col. iv. 15; Philem. 2).

5. For **δέχωνται** see on viii. 13, and for **ἐξερχόμενοι ἀπό** see on iv. 35. In Acts xiii. 51 we find Paul and Barnabas performing this symbolical action of shaking off the dust. It signified that henceforth they had not the smallest thing in common with the place. It is said that Pharisees performed this action when re-entering Judæa from heathen lands. There and in Acts xviii. 6 Lk. uses **ἐκτινάσσ.**, which Mt. and Mk. have here. For **ἀποτινασσ.** comp. Acts xxviii. 5. The **ἐπ' αὐτούς** means lit. "upon them," and so "against them." Comp. 2 Cor. i. 23 and Acts xiii. 51, and contrast 2 Thes. i. 10. Mk. here has αὐτοῖς.

6. εὐαγγελιζόμενοι καὶ θεραπεύοντες. Comp. ver. 2. Union of care for men's bodies with care for their souls is characteristic of Christ and of Christian missions. The miraculous cures of the apostolic age have given place to the propagation of medical and sanitary knowledge, which is pursued most earnestly under Christian influences. For **διήρχοντο** see on ii. 15, and for **εὐαγγελιζόμενοι** see on ii. 10. Excepting Mk. i. 28, xvi. 20, 1 Cor. iv. 17, **πανταχοῦ** occurs only here and three or four times in Acts: here it goes with both participles.

7–9. The Fears of Herod. Mt. places this section much later (xiv. 1–13); but Mk. (vi. 14–16) agrees with Lk. in connecting it with the mission of the Twelve. It was their going in all directions up and down the villages (διήρχοντο κατὰ τὰς κώμας) that caused the *fame* of Christ's work to reach Herod φανερὸν γὰρ ἐγένετο τὸ ὄνομα αὐτοῦ (Mk. vi. 14), or, at anyrate, excite his fears.

7. Ἡρῴδης ὁ τετράρχης. So also Mt. But Mk. gives him his courtesy title of βασιλεύς. See on iii. 1, p. 83. The **τὰ γινόμενα πάντα**

means "all that was being done" by Jesus and His disciples. There is no πάντα in Mt. or Mk., either here or in the parallels to ver. 1. See on viii. 45. The thoroughly classical word διηπόρει does not occur in LXX, nor in N.T. excepting in Lk. (Acts ii. 12, v. 24, x. 17). Antipas was "utterly at a loss" as to what he was to think of Jesus. Note the change of tense: he heard once for all; he remained utterly at a loss. He had no doubt heard of Christ before. It was the startling theories about Him which perplexed Herod. *D.C.G.* i. p. 721; ii. p. 717.

Ἰωάνης ἠγέρθη ἐκ νεκρῶν. This is strong evidence of the effect of John's teaching. During his life he "did no sign," and yet they think it possible that so great a Prophet has risen from the dead and is working miracles. Comp. Mt. xvi. 14; Mk. viii. 28. For **ἐκ νεκρῶν** comp. xx. 35. For ἠγέρθη (א B C L Ξ 169) most MSS. have ἐγήγερται, which is not to be accepted because ἠγέρθη is found in Mt.

8. Ἠλείας ἐφάνη. The verb is changed from ἠγέρθη, because Elijah had not died. Mt. represents *Antipas* as saying that Jesus is the risen Baptist, and omits the suggestions about Elijah and other Prophets. The account of Lk. is intrinsically more exact. He would obtain good information at Cæsarea from Herod's steward (viii. 3), and at Antioch from Herod's foster-brother (Acts xiii. 1).

προφήτης τις τῶν ἀρχαίων. We know from Jn. vii. 40, 41 that some Jews distinguished the great Prophet of Deut. xviii. 15 from the Messiah. Comp. Jn. i. 21. And Mt. xvi. 14 seems to show that there was an expectation that Jeremiah or other Prophets would return at some future crisis. The τῶν ἀρχαίων is peculiar to Lk. (comp. ver. 19). It may be opposed either to a new Prophet (vii. 16), or to the later Prophets as compared with Moses and Samuel. The former is more probable.

9. Ἰωάνην ἐγὼ ἀπεκεφάλισα. "As for John, *I* beheaded him." Mt. and Mark represent Herod as saying of Christ, "This is John the Baptist; he is risen from the dead": and some interpret this remark as meaning much the same: "Seeing that I put him to death, he may have risen again." But this is very unnatural. Rather, "I thought that I had got rid of this kind of trouble when I beheaded John; and here I am having it all over again." Perhaps, as Bede suggests, Antipas afterwards came to the conclusion that the Baptist had risen from the dead, a view which to his guilty conscience was specially unwelcome. Lk. mentions the imprisonment of the Baptist by anticipation (iii. 20); but, excepting in this remark of Antipas, he does not record his death.

τοιαῦτα. This may refer either to the works of Christ or to the speculations of the multitude respecting Him. Although John had wrought no miracles during his ministry (John x. 41), yet, if he had risen from the dead, such things might be expected of him (Mt. xiv. 2).

The ἐγώ of TR. before ἀκούω is of very doubtful authority (A D X Γ etc.): Treg. brackets, Tisch. WH. RV. omit. It would have no point.

ἐζήτει ἰδεῖν αὐτόν. Not merely "he desired" (AV.), but "he *continued seeking* to see Him." He made various attempts to apply a test which would have settled the question. Herod knew the Baptist; and he could soon determine whether this was John or not, if only he could see Him. Comp. xxiii. 8, where the gratification of this desire is recorded. No doubt it was not merely the wish to settle the question of identity which led Antipas to try to see Jesus. That he was a Sadducee is a guess of Scholten.

10–17. The Feeding of the Five Thousand. This is the one miracle which is recorded by all four Evangelists (Mt. xiv. 13; Mk. vi. 30; Jn. vi. 1). In all four it is the climax of the ministry. Henceforward attention is directed more and more to the death which will bring Christ's work to a close. From S. John we learn that it took place shortly before the Passover. All four accounts should be compared. Each contributes some special features, and each appears to be to a large extent independent. The marks of Lk.'s style are abundant in his narrative.

10. ὑποστρέψαντες. See small print on i. 56. Lk. connects the miracle with the return of the Twelve; but he gives no hint as to the time of their absence. We may perhaps allow a few weeks. He does not often call the Twelve **οἱ ἀπόστολοι** (vi. 13, xvii. 5. xxii. 14, xxiv. 10).

διηγήσαντο αὐτῷ ὅσα ἐποίησαν. What this was has already been recorded in brief (ver. 6). It is strange that anyone should infer from Lk.'s not expressly mentioning, as Mk. does (vi. 12, 13), the casting out of demons, "that Lk. wishes us to believe that they had failed in this respect," and "had evidently been able to carry out only a part of their commission." Lk. records the success of the Seventy in exorcizing demons (x. 17): why should he wish to insinuate that the Twelve had failed? Excepting Mk. v. 16, ix. 9; Heb. xi. 32, *διηγεῖσθαι* occurs only in Lk. (viii. 39; Acts viii. 33, ix. 27, xii. 17). Comp. ver. 49. Lk. perhaps wishes us to understand that it was the report which the Apostles brought of their doings that led to Christ's taking them apart, as Mk. says, for rest. Mt. states that it was the news of the Baptist's death which led to the withdrawal. Jn. has only a vague *μετὰ ταῦτα.* All may be correct; but there can have been no borrowing.

παραλαβὼν αὐτούς. Comp. ver. 28, xviii. 31.

ὑπεχώρησεν κατ' ἰδίαν. The verb occurs only here and v. 16 in NT. Comp. Ecclus. xiii. 9 (12). Lk. does not seem to be aware that Christ and His disciples went by boat across the lake

(Mt. Mk. Jn.), while the multitude went round by land. Hence it is possible that he supposed that the miracle took place near Bethsaida on the west shore, and not at Bethsaida Julias on the Jordan near the north-east end of the lake. See *D.B.*[2] art. "Bethsaida." Mt. Mk. and Lk. all have κατ' ἰδίαν.

The common reading, εἰς τόπον ἔρημον πόλεως καλουμένης Βηθσαιδά (ACEGHKMSUV etc., Aeth. Arm. Goth.), seems to be an ingenious *conflation of the original text*, εἰς πόλιν καλουμένην Βηθσαιδά (BLXΞ 33, Boh. Sah.),—which is supported by D [only κώμην for πόλιν],—*with a correction of it*, εἰς τόπον ἔρημον (א*), or εἰς τόπον ἔρημον Βηθσαιδά (b c ff_2 l g Vulg. Syr.), or εἰς τόπον ἔρημον καλούμενον Βηθσαιδά (a e f). These corrections would be suggested by ver. 12 and Mt. and Mk. and the difficulty of associating the miracle with a πόλις. See WH. ii. Intr. p. 102, and also Wordsw. Vulg. *in loco*. For other apparent instances of conflation see xi. 54, xii. 18, xxiv. 53. Note Lk.'s favourite καλουμένην.

11. οἱ δὲ ὄχλοι γνόντες ἠκολούθησαν αὐτῷ. The Baptist was dead and the Twelve had returned to Jesus, so that there was no longer any counter-attraction. No Evangelist tells us how long Jesus and the disciples enjoyed their privacy before the multitudes arrived.

ἀποδεξάμενος αὐτούς. "He gave them a welcome," as they had given Him (see on viii. 40), although their arrival destroyed the retirement which He had sought. As Jn. states, it was His miracles of healing which attracted them rather than His teaching. For ἀποδεξάμενος (א BDLXΞ 1 33 69) AC etc. have δεξάμενος: the compound is peculiar to Lk. It corresponds to ἐσπλαγχνίσθη in Mt. and Mk.

ἐλάλει αὐτοῖς περὶ τῆς βασ. τ. Θ., κ.τ.λ. "He continued speaking to them about the kingdom of God; and those who had need of cure He healed." See on v. 17 and ix. 6. Neither Mt. nor Jn. say anything about His teaching the multitudes, or about His healing any of them.

12. ἡ δὲ ἡμέρα ἤρξατο κλίνειν. Comp. Jer. vi. 4; Judg. xix. 11, ix. 3; 1 Sam. iv. 2. In N.T. Lk. alone uses κλίνειν intransitively (xxiv. 29). Comp. ἐκκλίνετε ἀπ' αὐτῶν (Rom. xvi. 17). In Att. Grk. κλίνειν is generally trans., ἀποκλίνειν intrans. Win. xxxviii. 1, p. 315.

προσελθόντες δὲ οἱ δώδεκα. In the three it is the Twelve who take the initiative; in Jn. it is the Lord who does so.

εἰς τὰς κύκλῳ κώμας καὶ ἀγρούς. Being similar in meaning, the nouns have only one article, although they differ in gender: comp. i. 6 and xiv. 23, and contrast x. 21 and xiv. 26. See on i. 6.

ἐπισιτισμόν. Here only in N.T., but quite class. It is specially used of provisions for a journey: Gen. xlii. 25, xlv. 21; Josh. ix. 5, 11; Judith ii. 18, iv. 5; Xen. *Anab.* i. 5. 9, vii. 1. 9.

13. Both εἶπεν δέ and πρός are in Lk.'s style, and neither occurs in the parallels. The same is true of πάντα, and in ver.

14 of πρός and the second ὡσεί. Note the emphatic ὑμεῖς. "*Ye* are to find food for them, not they." There is no need to supply anything after εἰ μήτι ἡμεῖς ἀγοράσωμεν. "We have no more than five loaves," leads quite naturally to "unless we are to go and buy," etc.; and then the sentence is complete. The statement expresses perplexity (Weiss), not sarcasm (Schanz).

Οὐκ εἰσὶν ἡμῖν πλεῖον ἢ πέντε. The πλεῖον ἢ πέντε is virtually plur. and has a plur. verb. For the subjunct. after εἰ μή comp. 1 Cor. xiv. 5, and see Win. xli. 2. b, p. 368, and Burton, § 252, 253. The subjunct. after εἰ is not rare in late Grk. But this is rather a delib. subjunct.

Jn. tells us that it was Andrew who pointed out the lad with the loaves, and that they were of barley-bread. On the whole, his narrative is the most precise. The ἡμεῖς, like the preceding ὑμεῖς, is emphatic.

14. ὡσεὶ ἄνδρες πεντακισχίλιοι. They were roughly counted as about a hundred companies with about fifty men in each. Note the ἄνδρες: not ἄνθρωποι. The women and children, as Mt. tells us, were not included in the reckoning. They would be much less numerous than the men. Lk. says nothing about the grass, which all the others mention, and which made the companies in their Oriental costumes look like flower-beds (πρασιαί), as Mk. indicates.

Κατακλίνατε αὐτοὺς κλισίας. The verb is peculiar to Lk. in N.T. (vii. 36, xiv. 8, xxiv. 30); in LXX Num. xxiv. 9; Exod. xxi. 18; Judg. v. 27; Judith xii. 15. The κλισίας is cogn. acc. It occurs 3 Mac. vi. 31 and here only in bibl. Grk. Comp. Jos. *Ant.* xii. 2. 11; Plut. *Sertor.* xxvi.

ὡσεὶ ἀνὰ πεντήκοντα. In the spaces between the groups the Apostles would be able to move freely and distribute the food. That the arrangement (50, 5000) has any relation to the five loaves is not likely. The ἀνά is distributive: comp. x. 1; Mt. xx. 9; Jn. ii. 6; Rev. iv. 8.

16. Here Mt. Mk. and Lk. are almost *verbatim* the same. All three mention the taking the loaves and fishes, the looking up to heaven, the blessing, and the breaking, and the giving to the disciples. For εὐλόγησεν Jn. has εὐχαριστήσας. This blessing or thanksgiving is the usual grace before meat said by the host or the head of the house. The Talmud says that "he who enjoys aught without thanksgiving is as though he robbed God." We are probably to understand that this blessing is the *means* of the miracle. Comp. Jn. vi. 23; and of feeding the four thousand (Mt. xv. 36; Mk. viii. 6); and of the eucharist (Mt. xxvi. 26; Mk. xiv. 22; Lk. xxii. 17, 19; 1 Cor. xi. 24). The *manner* of the miracle cannot be discerned: it is a literal fulfilment of Mt. vi. 33. Lk. alone mentions that Jesus blessed *the loaves*, εὐλόγησεν αὐτούς. The preceding articles, τοὺς πέντε ἄρτους καὶ τοὺς δύο ἰχθύας, mean those which had been mentioned before in ver. 13, where the words have no article.

ἐδίδου τοῖς μαθηταῖς. "Continued giving them to the disciples." The imperf. in the midst of aorists is graphic. Comp. xxiv. 30; Mk. viii. 6, and contrast xxii. 19; Mk. xiv. 22.

17. The verbal resemblance between the three accounts continues. For ἐχορτάσθησαν see on vi. 21, and take κλασμάτων after τὸ περισσεῦσαν (De W. Hahn). All four mention the twelve κόφινοι, as also does Mt. in referring to this miracle (xvi. 9); whereas at the feeding of the four thousand (Mt. xv. 37; Mk. viii. 8), and in referring to it (Mt. xvi. 10), the word used for basket is σπυρίς. It is the more remarkable that Lk. and Jn. both have κόφινοι because they do not mention the other miracle. The σπυρίς was large, capable of holding a man (Acts ix. 25). The κόφινος was the wallet carried by every travelling Jew, to avoid buying food from Gentiles: *Judæis quorum cophinus fœnumque supellex* (Juv. *Sat.* iii. 14). Comp. *nupsisti, Gellia, cistifero*, "thou hast married a Jew" (Mart. *Epig.* v. 17. 4). These exact details would scarcely have been maintained so consistently in a deliberate fiction or in a myth. Still less would either fiction or myth have represented one who could multiply food at will as giving directions that the fragments should not be wasted (Jn. vi. 12). The possessor of an inexhaustible purse is never represented as being watchful against extravagance.

Note the climax in ver. 17. They not only ate, but were satisfied,—all of them; and not only so, but there was something over,—far more than the original supply.

Weiss well remarks that "the criticism which is afraid of miracles finds itself in no small difficulty in the presence of this narrative. It is guaranteed by all our sources which rest upon eye-witness; and these show the independence of their tradition by their deviations, which do not affect the kernel of the matter, and cannot be explained by any tendencies whatever. In the presence of this fact the possibility of myth or invention is utterly inadmissible. . . . Only this remains absolutely incontrovertible, that it is the intention of all our reports to narrate a miracle; and by this we must abide, if the origin of the tradition is not to abide an entirely inexplicable riddle" (*L. J.* ii. pp. 196–200, Eng. tr. ii. pp. 381–385). The explanation that Christ's generosity in giving away the food of His party induced others who had food to give it away, and that thus there was enough for all, is plainly not what the Evangelists mean, and it does not explain their statements. Would such generosity suggest that He was the Messiah, or induce them to try to make Him king? Still more inadequate is the suggestion of Renan: *Grace à une extrême frugalité, la troupe sainte y vécut; on crut naturellement voir en cela un miracle* (*V. de J.* p. 198, ed. 1863).

18–22. The Confession of Peter and First Announcement of the Passion. Mt. xvi. 13–21; Mk. viii. 27–31. No connexion with the miracle just related is either stated or implied. Lk. omits the sequel of the miracle, the peremptory dismissal of the disciples and gradual dismissal of the people, the storm, the walking on the sea, the discourse on the Bread of Life, the Syrophenician woman, the Ephphatha miracle, the feeding of the four thousand, the forgetting to take bread, and the healing of a blind man at Bethsaida Julias (Mt. xiv. 22–xvi. 12; Mk. vi. 45–viii. 26; Jn. vi. 14–71). Can he then have seen either Mt. or Mk.? So also here: both the others mention that the incident took place near Cæsarea Philippi, *on the confines of heathenism.* Lk. mentions no place. It is a desperate expedient to suppose with Reuss, that the copy of Mk. which Lk. knew chanced to omit these sections. From ver. 18 to ver. 50 Lk. is once more parallel in the main to the other two.

18. Καὶ ἐγένετο ἐν τῷ εἶναι αὐτὸν προσευχόμενον. See note at the end of ch. i. and on iii. 21. For the periphrastic infinitive comp. xi. 1, and Burton, § 97. *Jesus Patrem rogarat, ut discipulis se revelaret. Nam argumentum precum Jesu colligi potest ex sermonibus actionibusque insecutis*; vi. 12, 13 (Beng.).

κατὰ μόνας. Perhaps *χώρας* was originally understood. But the expression is used as a simple adv. and is sometimes written as one word, *καταμόνας*. In N.T. only here and Mk. iv. 10. In LXX Ps. iv. 9, xxxii. 15; Jer. xv. 17; Lam. iii. 28.

συνῆσαν αὐτῷ οἱ μαθηταί. This almost amounts to a contradiction of what precedes. "When He was alone praying, His disciples were with Him." "Alone" no doubt means "in private," or "in a solitary spot," and may be taken with *συνῆσαν*: so that the contradiction is only on the surface. Moreover we are perhaps to understand that His prayer was solitary: His disciples did not join in it. In either case *κατὰ μόνας* is quite intelligible, although the disciples may have been close to Him. But it is possible that the true reading is *συνήντησαν*, meaning, "His disciples met Him, fell in with Him," as He was engaged in prayer. This is the reading of B*, which a later scribe has corrected to *συνῆσαν*. And B* is here supported by the Old Latin f (*occurrerunt*) and one excellent cursive (157), besides two less important authorities. Nevertheless, it is on the whole more probable that *συνήντησαν* is an early attempt to get rid of the apparent contradiction involved in *κατὰ μόνας συνῆσαν*. See *Expositor*, 3rd series, iv. p. 159. Elsewhere in N.T. *συνεῖναι* occurs only Acts xxii. 11.

20. Ὑμεῖς δέ. With great emphasis: "But ye—who do ye say that I am?" The impulsiveness of Peter, and his position as spokesman for the Twelve, are here conspicuous. He is *στόμα τοῦ χοροῦ*: viii. 45, xii. 41, xviii. 28. *Licet cæteri apostoli sciant, Petrus tamen respondit præ cæteris* (Bede).

τὸν Χριστὸν τοῦ Θεοῦ. "Whom God hath anointed" and sent: see on ii. 26. Here Mk. has simply **ὁ Χριστός**, and Mt. **ὁ Χριστὸς**

ὁ υἱὸς τοῦ Θεοῦ τοῦ ζῶντος. See Keim on this confession, as "a solemn event of the very highest character" (*Jes. of Naz.* iv. p. 263). Lk. and Mk. omit the praise bestowed on Peter for this confession, and the much discussed promise made to him (Mt. xvi. 17–19).

21. μηδενὶ λέγειν τοῦτο. Because of the grossly erroneous views about the Messiah which prevailed among the people. Shortly before this they had wished to take Him by force and make Him king (Jn. vi. 15). Hence Jesus never proclaimed Himself openly to the multitude as the Messiah; and here, when He does to the Twelve, He explains the nature of His Kingdom, and strictly forbids them to make His Messiahship known. The nearest approach to exceptions to this practice are the Samaritan woman (Jn. iv. 26), and the outcast from the synagogue (Jn. ix. 37).

Others explain the command to keep silence as prompted by the fear lest the guilt of those who were about to put Jesus to death should be increased by the disciples proclaiming Him as the Messiah. Others again suggest the fear lest the people, if they knew that He was the Messiah, should attempt to rescue Him from the death which it was necessary that He should undergo. Neither of these appears to be satisfactory. In any case the **δέ** is adversative. What Peter said was quite true: "*but* He charged them, and commanded."

22. Lk. does not tell us, as Mk. does, and still more plainly Mt., that this was the *beginning* of Christ's predictions respecting His Passion: ἤρξατο διδάσκειν αὐτοὺς ὅτι Δεῖ, κ.τ.λ. (Mk. viii. 31); ἀπὸ τότε ἤρξατο δεικνύειν, κ.τ.λ. (Mt. xvi. 21). The first announcement of such things must have seemed overwhelming. Peter's protest perhaps expressed the feeling of most of them.

εἰπὼν ὅτι Δεῖ. The ὅτι is recitative, not argumentative. The Δεῖ is here in all three; but elsewhere Lk. uses it much more often than any other Evangelist. It expresses logical necessity rather than moral obligation (ὤφειλεν, Heb. ii. 17) or natural fitness (ἔπρεπεν, Heb. ii. 10). It is a Divine decree, a law of the Divine nature, that the Son of Man *must* suffer. Prophecy had repeatedly intimated this decree. Comp. xiii. 33, xvii. 25, xxii. 37, xxiv. 7, 26, 44; Jn. iii. 14, etc. For **τὸν υἱὸν τοῦ ἀνθρώπου**, the title which suggested, while it veiled, His Messiahship, see on v. 24.

ἀποδοκιμασθῆναι ἀπὸ τῶν, κ.τ.λ. "Be rejected after investigation at the hands of the," etc. The δοκιμασία was the scrutiny which an elected magistrate had to undergo at Athens, to see whether he was legally qualified to hold office. The hierarchy held such a scrutiny respecting the claims of Jesus to be the Christ, and rejected Him: xvii. 25, xx. 17; 1 Pet. ii. 4, 7. For the ἀπό, "at the hands of," comp. Ecclus. xx. 20; Lk. vii. 35; Acts ii. 22; Jas. i. 13; Rev. xii. 6.

τῶν πρεσβυτέρων καὶ ἀρχιερέων καὶ γραμματέων. The three nouns, as forming one body, have one article. So also in Mt.

xvi. 21. In Mk. xiv. 43, 53, where the Sanhedrin is spoken of with similar fulness, all three nouns have the article. The ἀρχιερεῖς are rarely placed second: comp. xx. 19; Mt. xvi. 21; Mk. viii. 31. The common formulæ are ἀρχ., γραμ., πρεσβ. or ἀρχ., πρεσβ., γραμ. and ἀρχ. πρεσβ. or ἀρχ., γραμ.

ἀποκτανθῆναι. The pass. of ἀποκτείνω is late Grk. Classical writers use θνήσκω or ἀποθνήσκω. For τῇ τρίτῃ ἡμέρᾳ Mk. has the less accurate μετὰ τρεῖς ἡμέρας. He also has ἀναστῆναι, while Mt. has ἐγερθῆναι, which is probably right here; but ἀναστῆναι (A C D, Just. Orig.) is well supported.

Lk. omits Peter's protest against the declaration that Christ must suffer, and the severe rebuke which he received. His omission of "Get thee behind Me, Satan," is sufficient answer to those who assert that it is out of ill-will to Peter that Lk. omits "Blessed art thou, Simon Bar-Jonah." See on v. 10 and xxii. 54–62.

23–27. The Self-Renouncement required in Christ's Followers. Mt. xvi. 24–28; Mk. viii. 34–ix. 1. Although the manner of introducing the words is different in all three, the similarity between the reports of the words is very close throughout, especially in the words quoted *vv.* 23, 24. Throughout the Gospels it is in the records of Christ's sayings that the closest resemblances are found. Comp. xviii. 16, 17, 25, 27.

23. πρὸς πάντας. Both words are characteristic: see on ver. 43 and i. 13. The πάντας represents Mk.'s τὸν ὄχλον σὺν τοῖς μαθηταῖς. The necessity of self-denial and self-sacrifice was made known to all, although for the present the supreme example of the necessity was a mystery revealed gradually to a very few.

ἀράτω τὸν σταυρὸν αὐτοῦ καθ' ἡμέραν. This is the first mention of the cross in Lk. and Mk. Its associations were such that this declaration must have been startling. The Jews, especially in Galilee, knew well what the cross meant. Hundreds of the followers of Judas and Simon had been crucified (Jos. *Ant.* xvii. 10. 10). It represents, therefore, not so much a burden as an instrument of death, and it was mentioned because of its familiar associations. Comp. xiv. 27; Mt. x. 38. The **καθ' ἡμέραν** here is peculiar to Lk.: comp. 1 Cor. xv. 31. We must distinguish between **ἀκολουθείτω μοι,** "follow Me loyally," and ὀπίσω μου ἔρχεσθαι, "become My disciple." There are three conditions of discipleship: self-denial, bearing one's cross, and obedience.

24. ὃς γὰρ ἂν θέλῃ. Here, as in ver. 23, "will" (AV.) is too weak as a translation of θέλειν, being too like the simple future: "desireth" or "willeth" is better: *si quis vult, qui enim voluerit.* Such inadequate renderings of θέλειν are common in AV. (xix. 14; Jn. vi. 67, vii. 17, viii. 44). See small print on **x. 22.** Comp. xvii. 33.

25. τί γὰρ ὠφελεῖται ἄνθρωπος. The same verb is used by all three; but AV. obliterates this by rendering "profit" in Mt. and

Mk., and "advantage" in Lk. Again, ζημιωθῆναι is common to all three: yet AV. has "lose" in Mt. and Mk., and "cast away" in Lk. The opposition between κέρδος and ζημία is common in Grk. See Lft. on Phil. iii. 7. In N.T. the act. ζημιόω does not occur, but only the pass. with either acc. of the thing confiscated (Phil. iii. 8), or dat. with ἐν (2 Cor. vii. 9), or absol. (1 Cor. iii. 15). The ἑαυτόν is equivalent to τὴν ψυχήν in ver. 24 and in Mt. and Mk. To be excluded from eternal life is death. Lk. omits "What should a man give in exchange for his life?" We must keep "life" for ψυχή throughout the passage: the context shows when it means life as men desire it on earth, and when life as the blessed enjoy it in the Kingdom. The Gospel has raised the meaning of ψυχή, as of ζωή, to a higher power. Comp. Rev. xii. 11. *Frumentum si servas perdis, si seminas renovas* (Bede)

For the combination of aor. part. with fut. indic. comp. 3 Jn. 6, and Burton, § 141.

26. ἐπαισχυνθῇ με καὶ τοὺς ἐμοὺς λόγους. Mt. omits. The ἐπί in comp. means "on account of": this is the *ground* of his shame: comp. xiii. 26, 27. For the constr. comp. Rom. i. 16; 2 Tim. i. 8, 16; Heb. xi. 16. The ἐν τῇ δόξῃ αὐτοῦ refers to the παρουσία, not to the Resurrection (xii. 36, xvii. 24, xviii. 8, xix. 15, xxi. 27), and is the first mention by Lk. of Christ's promising to return in glory. Lk. omits "in this adulterous generation" (Mk.).

27. ἀληθῶς. With λέγω, not with what follows. Mt. and Mk. have ἀμήν, which Lk. uses much less frequently than the others. In xii. 44 and xxi. 3 Lk. has ἀληθῶς, others have ἀμήν. For αὐτοῦ, "here," comp. Acts xviii. 19; Mt. xxvi. 36. Mt. and Mk. have ὧδε.

γεύσωνται θανάτου. The expression is found in the Talmud, but not in O.T. Comp. Mt. xvi. 28; Jn. viii. 52; Heb. ii. 9. It implies experience of the bitterness of death. Comp. ἰδεῖν θάνατον (ii. 26) and θάνατον θεωρεῖν (Jn. viii. 51). For γεύεσθαι in the sense of "experience" comp. Heb. vi. 4, 5; Ps. xxxiv. 9.

τὴν βασιλείαν τοῦ Θεοῦ. Mk. adds ἐληλυθυῖαν ἐν δυνάμει, and Mt. substitutes τ. υἱὸν τοῦ ἀνθρ. ἐρχόμενον ἐν τῇ βασιλείᾳ αὐτοῦ. The meaning is much disputed. The principal interpretations are:—1. *The Transfiguration*, which all three accounts closely connect with this prediction (most of the Fathers, Euthym. Theophyl. Maldon.); 2. *The Resurrection and Ascension* (Cajetan, Calvin, Beza); 3. *Pentecost* and the great signs which followed it (Godet, Hahn); 4. *The spread of Christianity* (Nösgen); 5. *The internal development of the Gospel* (Erasmus, Klostermann); 6. *The destruction of Jerusalem* (Wetstein, Alford, Morison, Plumptre, Mansel); 7. *The Second Advent* (Meyer, Weiss, Holtzmann). No interpretation can be correct that does not explain εἰσίν τινες, which implies *the exceptional privilege of some, as distinct from the common experience of all.* This test seems to exclude all but the first and the sixth of these interpretations; and, if we must choose between these two, the sixth must be right. "Shall not taste of death until" cannot refer *exclusively* to an event to take place the next week. But both may be right. The Transfiguration, witnessed by only three of those present, was a foretaste of Christ's glory both on earth and in heaven. The destruction of Jerusalem, witnessed by S. John and perhaps a few others of those present, swept away the remains of the Old Dispensation and left the Gospel in possession of the field. Only so far as the destruction of Jerusalem was a type of the end of the world is there a reference to the παρουσία (see on xxi. 32). A *direct* reference to the παρουσία is excluded by the fact that none of those present lived to witness it, except in the sense that all men will witness it. Jesus has told us that during His life on earth He was ignorant of the date of the day of judgment (Mk. xiii. 32): and we cannot suppose that in spite of that ignorance He predicted that it was near; still less that He uttered a prediction which has not been fulfilled. Moreover, the οὐ μὴ γεύσωνται θανάτου ἕως implies that the τινες *will* experience death *after* seeing the βασ. τ. Θεοῦ, which would not be true of those who live to see the παρουσία (1 Cor. xv. 51).

28–36. The Transfiguration. Mt. xvii. 1–13; Mk. ix. 2–13. Both Lk. (*vv.* 31, 32) and Mt. (xvii. 6, 7) give details which Mk. omits; but Mk. has very little (part of ix. 3) which is not in either of the others.

Here again (see on viii. 35–39, 40–48) the marks of Lk.'s diction are numerous: ἐγένετο, ὡσεί (ver. 28); ἐγένετο, ἐν τῷ with infin. (29); ἄνδρες (30); σύν, ἄνδρας (32); ἐγένετο, ἐν τῷ, εἶπεν πρός, ἐπιστάτα (33); ἐν τῷ (34); φωνὴ ἐγένετο (35); ἐν τῷ, καὶ αὐτοί, ἀπήγγειλαν, ἐν ἐκείναις ταῖς ἡμέραις, οὐδὲν ὧν (36).

For comment see Tert. *Adv. Marcion.* iv. 22; Trench, *Studies in the Gospels*, pp. 184–214; Herzog, *PRE.*[1] art. *Verklärung*, omitted in 2nd ed.; Schaff's *Herzog*, art. "Transfiguration."

28. ὡσεὶ ἡμέραι ὀκτώ. A nom. without construction of any kind. Comp. Acts v. 7; Mt. xv. 32; Mk. viii. 2, and πλεῖον in ver. 13. Win. lviii. 4, p. 648. The other two have "after six days," which agrees with "about eight days." We can hardly say that Lk. is "improving their chronology." It looks as if he had not seen their expression. For παραλαβών comp. ver. 10, and for the order of the names see on viii. 51. Note that Lk. changes the order of the names. He places John before James (viii. 51), which may be because he wrote after John had become the better known

εἰς τὸ ὄρος. The others have εἰς ὄρος ὑψηλόν. Both expressions would fit Hermon, which is about 9200 feet high, and would easily be reached in a week from Cæsarea Philippi. It is still called *Jebel esh Sheikh*, "the chief mountain." It is higher than Lebanon (8500) or Anti-Lebanon (8700), and its isolated white summit is visible from many eminences throughout Palestine (Conder, *Handbook of the Bible*, p. 205; *D.B.*[2] i. p. 1339; Tristram, *Bible Places*, p. 280). A tradition, which is first mentioned by Cyril of Jerusalem (*Catech.* xii. 16), places the scene of the Transfiguration on Tabor,[1] which at this time seems to have had a village or town on the top, which Josephus fortified against Vespasian (*B.J.* iv. 1. 8). In that case the solitude (κατ' ἰδίαν) which is required for the Transfiguration would be impossible. The **προσεύξασθαι** is peculiar to this account: see on iii. 21, a similar occasion.

29. ἐγένετο . . . ἕτερον. The Gentile Lk. writing for Gentiles avoids the word μετεμορφώθη (Mt. xvii. 2; Mk. ix. 2), which might be understood of the metamorphosis of heathen deities. Comp ἐν ἑτέρᾳ μορφῇ ([Mk.] xvi. 12). The **λευκός** need not be made adverbial. The asyndeton is not violent, if it be made co-ordinate with ἐξαστράπτων, a word which occurs Ezek. i. 4, 7; Nah. iii. 3.

30. Both **ἄνδρες** and **οἵτινες** are peculiar to Lk. here: see ii. 4. The three Apostles saw the forms of two men *who were such as to be* recognized as Moses and Elijah,—the representatives of the Law and the Prophets. The power to recognize them was granted with the power to see them; otherwise the sight would have been meaningless. In the same way S. Paul recognized Ananias in a vision, although he had not previously known him (Acts ix. 12). We might render the **οἵτινες** "who were no others than." That Moses was to reappear as well as Elijah at the beginning of the Messianic Kingdom, was a later dream of the Rabbis. See Lightfoot, *Hor. Heb. ad loc.* See small print on ii. 22 for the form Μωυσῆς.

31, 32. Peculiar to Lk. See on xxii. 43.

τὴν ἔξοδον αὐτοῦ. His departure from this world by means of the Passion, Resurrection, and Ascension. Comp. the use of εἴσοδος in Acts xiii. 24. For **ἔξοδος** in the sense of death see 2 Pet. i. 15; Wisd. iii. 2, vii. 6. That the Apostles heard this subject being discussed explains part of the meaning of the Transfiguration. It was to calm their minds, which had recently been disturbed by the prediction of Christ's sufferings and death.[2] The **ἤμελλεν** corresponds to δεῖ in ver. 22. It is all ordained by God, and is sure to take place; and when it takes place it may be regarded as a fulfilment (πληροῦν), and also as a filling full. There were types and prophecies shadowing forth the Divine purpose, every detail of which must be gone through.

[1] In the Greek Church the Feast of the Transfiguration, Aug. 6th, is called τὸ Θαβώριον. The combination in Ps. lxxxix. 12 may be noted.

[2] *In transfiguratione illud principaliter agebatur, ut de cordibus discipulorum scandalum crucis tolleretur* (Leo the Great, *Serm.* xliv., Migne, liv. 310).

It is perhaps to be regretted that RV. retains "accomplish," which is its freq. rendering of τελειόω (Jn. iv. 34, v. 36; Acts xx. 24; Jn. xvii. 4, etc.), instead of substituting "fulfil," which is its freq. rendering of πληρόω (xxi. 24, xxii. 16, xxiv. 44; Acts i. 16, etc.). And why not "exodus" here, and Heb. xi. 22, and 2 Pet. i. 15, for ἔξοδος?

βεβαρημένοι ὕπνῳ. In N.T. only the pass. of this verb is found, and the best writers do not use the pres. of either voice. In Mt. xxvi. 43 it is used of the eyes of these same three being heavy with sleep: comp. Lk. xxi. 34; 2 Cor. i. 8, v. 4; 1 Tim. v. 16.

διαγρηγορήσαντες δέ. "But having remained awake" in spite of this sleepiness would be the common meaning of the word;[1] but perhaps here it means "having become thoroughly awake." Syr-Sin. has "when they awoke." It is a late word, and occurs nowhere else in N.T. or LXX. Lk. is fond of compounds with διά:—διαγινώσκειν, διαδέχεσθαι, διαλείπειν, διαλύειν, διανέμειν, διανυκτερεύειν, διαπονεῖσθαι, διαπορεῖν, διαπραγματεύεσθαι, etc.

As the invention of a later hand these two verses (31, 32) do not explain themselves. What is the motive for the invention? As a narrative of facts they throw much light on the whole situation.

33. ἐν τῷ διαχωρίζεσθαι αὐτοὺς ἀπ' αὐτοῦ. "As they were parting from Him." This again is in Lk. only, and it explains Peter's remark. His first impulse is to prevent Moses and Elijah from going away. He wishes to make present glory and rapture permanent.

εἶπεν ὁ Πέτρος. Mt. and Mk. add ἀποκριθείς. It is his response to what he saw. For **Ἐπιστάτα** see on v. 5. He says that "it is *good* for us to be here," not "it is better." There is no comparison with any other condition. The **ἡμᾶς** probably means the Apostles, not all six persons. The Apostles are ready to help in erecting the σκηναί. If they were to remain there, they must have shelter.

μὴ εἰδὼς ὃ λέγει. We need not follow Tertullian in interpreting this of a state of ecstasy (*amentia*), as of one rapt into another world. Mk. tells us plainly why Peter "wist not what to answer," ἔκφοβοι γὰρ ἐγένοντο: and this he would have from Peter himself. In any case, neither Peter's strange proposal nor the comment upon it looks like invention.

34. ἐγένετο νεφέλη καὶ ἐπεσκίαζεν αὐτούς. Mt. calls it φωτεινή, a "luminous cloud." Here there is perhaps an association of ideas, suggested by similarity of sound, between ἐπεσκίαζεν and the Shechinah or δόξη mentioned in ver. 31. Comp. ἐπεσκίαζεν ἐπὶ τὴν σκηνὴν ἡ νεφέλη (Exod. xl. 29). Strictly speaking a luminous cloud cannot overshadow; but it may veil. Light may be as blinding as darkness. We cannot be sure whether the **αὐτούς** includes the three Apostles or not. It does not include them in

[1] Comp. πασῆς τῆς νυκτὸς . . . διαγρηγορήσαντες (Herodian, iii. 4. 8).

ver. 33, and probably does not include them here. The reading ἐκείνους εἰσελθεῖν (A D P R) is meant to exclude the Apostles; but εἰσελθεῖν αὐτούς (א B C L) is right. See *D.B.*[2] art. "Cloud."

35. For **φωνὴ ἐγένετο** see on iii. 22, and comp. Exod. xxxiii. 9. The reading ἀγαπητός (A C D P R) for **ἐκλελεγμένος** (א B L Ξ) comes from Mt. and Mk. The Versions are divided, and in many copies of the Aeth. the two readings are combined. Syr-Sin. has "the chosen."

36. ἐν τῷ γενέσθαι τὴν φωνήν. "*After* the voice had come", *i.e.* when it had ceased: see on iii. 21. Syr-Sin. has "when there was the voice." Peter had wished to make three tabernacles, as if Moses and Elijah were to be as abiding as Christ; but now the Law and the Prophets pass away, *ita dimissis, quasi jam et officio et honore dispunctis* (Tertul. *Adv. Marcion.* iv. 22), and εὑρέθη Ἰησοῦς μόνος.

καὶ αὐτοὶ ἐσίγησαν καὶ οὐδενὶ ἀπήγγειλαν ἐν ἐκείναις ταῖς ἡμέραις. See on v. 14, on viii. 20, and on i. 39. Lk. tells us that they kept silent; Mt. tells us that Jesus charged them to tell no one until the Son of Man was risen from the dead. Mk. relates both the command and their observance of it. The prohibition to speak of what they had seen is a strong confirmation of the incident as an historical fact. If the vision is an invention, how can we explain the invention of such a prohibition? The statement of all three, that the Transfiguration took place a week after the preceding incident, the characteristic impulsiveness of Peter, and the healing of the demoniac boy immediately afterwards, are marks of historical reality. *D.C.G.* art. "Transfiguration."

But, as in the case of other miracles, while we admit the fact, we must remain in ignorance as to the manner. Were Moses and Elijah, who were mysteriously removed from the earth, here present in the *body*? Or were their disembodied *spirits* made visible? Or was it a mere vision, in which they only *seemed* to be present? We cannot say: the third alternative is not excluded by the fact that all three saw it, whereas a mere vision is perceived by only one. As Weiss well remarks, "We are not here concerned with a vision produced by natural causes, but with one sent directly by God"; and he adds, "Our narrative presents no stumbling-block for those who believe in divine revelation" (*L. J.* ii. pp. 319, 320, Eng. tr. iii. p. 103). The silence of S. John respecting the whole incident is thoroughly intelligible. (1) It had already been recorded three times; (2) the glorification of Jesus as the Son of God, which is here set forth in a special incident, is set forth by him throughout his whole Gospel.

ἑώρακαν. With this form of the 3rd pers. plur. perf. comp. τετήρηκαν and ἔγνωκαν (Jn. xvii. 6, 7), εἴρηκαν (Rev. xix. 3), γέγοναν (Rev. xxi. 6), εἰσελήλυθαν (Jas. v. 4); also Rom. xvi. 7; Col. ii. 1; Rev. xviii. 3. Such forms are common in inscriptions and in the Byzantine writers. Win. xiii. 2. c, p. 90; Gregory, *Prolegom.* p. 124. In meaning the perfect seems here to be passing into the aorist; Burton, § 88, but see § 78.

37–43. The Healing of the Demoniac Boy. Mt. xvii. 14–18; Mk. ix. 14–29. In all three this incident is closely connected with the Transfiguration. The moral contrast between the peace and glory on the mount and the struggle and failure down below is intense, and is magnificently brought out by Raffaelle in the great picture of the Transfiguration, which was his last work. The combination of the two scenes is fatal to the unity of the subject, which is really two pictures in one frame; but it heightens the moral and dramatic effect. It is perhaps even more instructive to regard it as three pictures. Christ and the saints in glory; the chosen three blinded by the light; the remaining nine baffled by the powers of darkness.

The marks of Lk.'s style continue with considerable frequency: *ἐγένετο*, *ἑξῆς* (ver. 37); *καὶ ἰδού*, *ἐβόησεν*, *δέομαι*, *μονογενής* (38); *καὶ ἰδού* (39); *ἐδεήθην* (40); *ἰάσατο* (42); *πάντες* (43). None of these are in the parallel passages. See small print on viii. 35–39, 40–48.

37. τῇ ἑξῆς ἡμέρᾳ. See on vii. 11. The Transfiguration probably took place at night. Lk. alone tells us that the descent from the mountain did not take place until next day. Thus the three Apostles had time to think over what they had seen and heard, before receiving fresh experiences. Lk. omits the conversation about Elijah. Mk., who is here much more full than either Lk. or Mt., tells us that this ὄχλος πολύς was gathered round the other disciples, with whom scribes were disputing. The opportune arrival of Christ caused great amazement.

38. For **ἐβόησεν** comp. iii. 4, xviii. 7, 38, and for **δέομαι** see on v. 12.

ἐπιβλέψαι. 1 aor. inf. act.; not *ἐπίβλεψαι*, 1 aor. imper. mid., a tense which perhaps does not occur. It means "to regard with pity"; i. 48; 1 Sam. i. 11, ix. 16; Ps. xxiv. 16; Tobit iii. 3, 15; Judith xiii. 4.—For the third time Lk. is alone in mentioning that a child is *μονογενής*: vii. 12, viii. 42. Comp. Heb. xi. 17; Tobit iii. 15, viii. 17; Judg. xi. 34.

39. The three accounts differ in describing the symptoms. Mt. has *σεληνιάζεται καὶ κακῶς ἔχει*. Mk. has *ἀφρίζει καὶ τρίζει τοὺς ὀδόντας καὶ ξηραίνεται*. In Lk.'s description Hobart (pp. 17–20) claims **ἐξέφνης**, **μετὰ ἀφροῦ**, and **μόγις ἀποχωρεῖ** as medical expressions, together with the preceding **ἐπιβλέψαι**.[1] The *μόγις* occurs here only in N.T. Comp. 3 Mac. vii. 6. But *μόλις*, which is found Acts xiv. 18, xxvii. 7, 8, 16; Rom. v. 7; 1 Pet. iv. 18, may be the right reading here also (B R etc.). Both *μόγος* and *μόλος* mean "toil." The *ἀποχωρεῖν* means cessation of convulsions.

40. ἐδεήθην . . . ἵνα. See on iv. 3 and on x. 2. The disciples who failed here need not be the Apostles, who were charged to cast out demons (ver. 1). If they were, this one failure was exceptional (Mk. vi. 12, 13).

[1] Hobart adds, "It is worthy of note that Aretæus, a physician of about St. Luke's time, in treating of Epilepsy, admits the possibility of this disease being produced by diabolical agency (*Sign. Morb. Diuturn.* 27)."

41. ὦ γενεὰ ἄπιστος. This probably is neither addressed to the disciples, who had failed to cure the lad, nor includes them. It is addressed to the father, and includes the multitude. *Per unum hominem Judæos arguit infidelitatis* (Bede). As in the case of the paralytic (v. 20), the faith of those who had charge of the afflicted person is taken into account. This is more clearly brought out in Mk. It was a wish to see what the disciples could do, rather than faith in Divine power and goodness, which prompted the bringing of the boy to them. Possibly it was a wish to see what the disciples could *not* do that inspired some of them. The hierarchy sometimes attacked Jesus through His disciples (Mk. ii. 16, 18, 24, vii. 5; comp. Lk. xiii. 14). In xii. 46 ἄπιστος means "unfaithful," and in Acts xxvi. 8 "incredible."

καὶ διεστραμμένη. Not in Mk. It is a strong expression: "distorted, wrong-headed" (Acts xx. 30; Phil. ii. 15; Deut. xxxii. 5). Comp. ὁ θυμὸς ἄρχοντας διαστρέφει καὶ τοὺς ἀρίστους ἄνδρας (Arist. *Pol.* iii. 16. 5); εἰσὶ δ' αὐτῶν αἱ ψυχαὶ διεστραμμέναι [*a.l.* παρεστραμ.] τῆς κατὰ φύσιν ἕξεως (viii. 7. 7).

ἕως πότε ἔσομαι πρὸς ὑμᾶς; The notion is that of being turned towards a person for the sake of intercourse; and the question implies that Jesus is not of that generation, or that it is alienated from Him. Comp. Is. lxv. 2. For ἕως ποτε comp. Jn. x. 24; and for πρὸς ὑμᾶς, *apud vos*, comp. Mt. xiii. 56; Mk. vi. 3, xiv. 49; Jn. i. 1, etc. Mt. has μεθ' ὑμῶν. *Vita Jesu perpetua tolerantia* (Beng.).

In N.T. and LXX ἀνέχεσθαι has the gen. But in class. Grk., as sometimes in LXX, we have the acc. after ἀνέχεσθαι (Amos iv. 7; 4 Mac. xiii. 27).

42. προσερχομένου αὐτοῦ. This is to be understood of the lad's approach to Jesus, not of His approach to the lad. Jesus had just said, "Bring thy son hither."

ἔρρηξεν αὐτὸν τὸ δαιμόνιον. "The demon dashed him down." The word is used of boxers knocking down, and of wrestlers throwing, an opponent: and some distinguish ῥήσσω in this sense from ῥήγνυμι. Comp. Wisd. iv. 19; Herm. *Mand.* xi. 3; *Apost. Const.* vi. 1. There is also ῥάσσω, like ἀράσσω, in the sense of dashing to the ground (Is. ix. 10). The expulsion of the demon left the boy in a condition which still required healing. Lk. gives each act separately. Comp. Mk. ix. 27. For ἰάσατο see small print on v. 17; and with ἀπέδωκεν αὐτὸν τῷ πατρὶ αὐτοῦ, which Lk. alone mentions, comp. vii. 15 and viii. 55.

43. This also is peculiar to Lk., who omits the rebuke to the disciples, thus again sparing them. The division of the verses is unfortunate, half of ver. 43 belonging to one section and half to another. For μεγαλειότητι comp. Acts xix. 27; 2 Pet. i. 16: Latin texts have *magnitudo* (Vulg.), *magnificentia* (e), *magnalia* (d).

The πάντες in the first half of the verse, and the πάντων ἐπὶ πᾶσιν in the second half, strongly illustrate Lk.'s fondness for πᾶς: see on vii. 35 and xi. 4; and comp. Acts iv. 10, xvii. 30, xxi. 28, xxiv. 3.

43–45. The Second Announcement of the Passion. Mt. xvii. 23; Mk. ix. 31, 32.

Besides the πάντων and πᾶσιν, we have as marks of Lk.'s style, θαυμαζόντων ἐπί, the attraction in πᾶσιν οἷς, πρός after εἶπεν (ver. 43), and the analytical ἦν παρακεκαλυμμένον (ver. 45). See on ii. 33 and iii. 19.

43. θαυμαζόντων ἐπὶ πᾶσιν οἷς ἐποίει. See small print on ii. 33 and iii. 19. The imperfects include more than the preceding incident. It was because the people were so constantly in an attitude of empty admiration and wonder at His miracles, that Jesus again tells the disciples of the real nature of His Messiahship. He is not going to reign as an earthly king, but to suffer as a criminal.

Here d has one of several attempts to reproduce the gen. abs. in Latin: *omnium autem mirantium.* Comp. *et cogitantium omnium* (iii. 15); *audientium autem eorum* (xix. 11); *quorundam dicentium* (xxi. 5); *accipientium autem eorum* (xxiv. 31); *hæc autem eorum loquentium* (xxiv. 36).

44. Θέσθε ὑμεῖς εἰς τὰ ὦτα ὑμῶν. "Do *ye* lay up in your ears," in contrast to the gaping crowd. It perhaps means "Store My words in your memories, even if you do not understand them." Or again, "Do not let men's admiration of My miracles make you forget or doubt My declarations. It is into men's hands that I must be delivered." Comp. δὸς εἰς τὰ ὦτα Ἰησοῖ (Exod. xvii. 14). Cod Am. and other MSS. of Vulg. here have *in cordibus vestris.* All Grk. MSS. have εἰς τὰ ὦτα ὑμῶν. This is one of several places in which Jerome seems to have had a Grk. text which is no longer extant. Comp. *erat Petrus* (xxii. 55), *hic nos esse* (Mk. ix. 5), *Moses in quo vos speratis* (Jn. v. 45); also Jn. vi. 12, vii. 25, ix. 38, x. 16. The last (*ovile*, *ovile* for αὐλή, ποίμνη) is crucial.

ὁ γὰρ υἱὸς τοῦ ἀνθρώπου μέλλει. The γάρ is almost "namely": "For what you may believe without doubting is this, that the Son of Man," etc. The παραδίδοσθαι perhaps does not refer to the act of Judas, but to the Divine will. When His hour was come, the plots against Him were allowed to succeed.

45. ἦν παρακεκαλυμμένον ἀπ' αὐτῶν. A Hebraism, occurring here only in N.T. Comp. Ezek. xxii. 26, and the subst. Wisd. xvii. 3. More often we have ἀποκρύπτειν ἀπό: x. 21; Jer. xxxii. 17; or κρύπτειν ἀπό: Mt. xi. 25; Ps. xxxvii. 10. Lk. alone states that this ignorance of the disciples was specially ordered for them. The ἵνα here has its full telic force. They were not allowed to understand the saying then, in order that they might remember it afterwards, and see that Jesus had met His sufferings with full knowledge and free will. Comp. xviii. 34, xxiv. 16.

It is strange that this mention of their want of understanding should be attributed to a wish to abase the Twelve in the interests of S. Paul: for (1) it is plainly stated that they were prevented by God from understanding; and (2) Mk. mentions their ignorance no less than Lk. We saw above that Lk. omits the rebuke for want of faith addressed to the disciples who failed to heal the demoniac boy. See on ver. 43 and viii. 24.

46-50. The Close of the Galilean Ministry. Two Lessons in Humility. Mt. xviii. 1-7; Mk. ix. 33-39. We learn from the other two that this took place after the return from the neighbourhood of Cæsarea Philippi to Capernaum (Mt. xvii. 24; Mk. ix. 33). The dispute took place during the journey, the comment on it at Capernaum. See notes on xxii. 24-30.

46. Εἰσῆλθεν δὲ διαλογισμὸς ἐν αὐτοῖς. See small print on i. 17 and vii. 17. It is not necessary to confine the *διαλογισμός* to their thoughts (see on v. 22), and thus make a difference between Mk. and Lk. But the desire of each to be pronounced the superior was probably not expressed in the discussion; and this thought Jesus read and rebuked. Bede explains the occasion of the dispute to be *quia viderant Petrum, Jacobum, et Joannem seorsum ductos in montem, secretumque eis ibi aliquod esse creditum.* The **ἐν αὐτοῖς**, "among them," rather implies that the reasoning did not remain unexpressed.

τὸ τίς ἂν εἴη. "The question, who perchance might be," *wer wohl wäre*: see on iii. 15 and vi. 11; also Burton, § 179. For this use of *τό* see on i. 62, and comp. xix. 48, xxii. 2, 4, 23.

μείζων αὐτῶν. Although *αὐτῶν* does not here immediately follow *τίς* as it does xxii. 24 (see notes), yet doubtless *αὐτῶν* is the gen. after *τίς* and not after *μείζων*. Whether anyone outside their company was greater than they were, was not a question which interested them. The point in dispute was, who among themselves was greater than the rest of them; who stood nearest to the Christ, and had the highest place in the Kingdom (Mt.). The question illustrates the want of perception just mentioned (ver. 45).

47. τῆς καρδίας αὐτῶν. The discussion in words was, Who is the greatest? The thought in their hearts was, Am not I the greatest? Will the Master decide? Comp. v. 22, vi. 8.

ἐπιλαβόμενος παιδίον. The action indicates that the child belongs to Him, is one of His: it represents the humblest among His followers. For other instances of Christ's attitude towards children comp. x. 21, xvii. 2, xviii. 16; Mk. x. 15, etc.

In N.T. and LXX the mid. only of *ἐπιλαμβάνω* is used, sometimes with the acc. (Acts ix. 27, xvi. 19, xviii. 17), sometimes with the gen. (Acts xvii. 19, xxi. 30, 33; with gen. always in LXX). Here and xxiii. 26 the acc. is probably right (B C D, Orig.), but the reading is uncertain.

παρ' ἑαυτῷ. The place of honour. As Jesus was sitting with His disciples round Him (Mk. ix. 35), *παρ' ἑαυτῷ* would be the same as ἐν μέσῳ αὐτῶν (Mt. and Mk.). Syr-Sin. has "beside *them*"

The late tradition, that Ignatius was the child who was thus taken up by our Lord, probably arose from a misunderstanding of the name Θεοφόρος, which means "bearing God" in himself, and not "borne by God" (Θεόφορος). Even if Θεόφορος be the right accentuation, we must interpret "borne along and inspired by God" rather than "carried in the Divine arms." The identification was unknown to Eusebius, who does not mention it, and to Chrysostom, who states that Ignatius had not even seen Christ (*Hom. in Ign. Mart.* iv.). It cannot be found earlier than the ninth century (Anastasius Bibliothecarius, Migne, cxxix. 42; Nicephorus Callistus, *H. E.* ii. 35, Migne, cxliii. 848). See Lft. *Ignatius*, i. p. 27, ii. p. 22.

48. In this saying of Christ there is again (comp. *vv.* 23, 24) almost exact verbal agreement in the three reports.

τοῦτο τὸ παιδίον. Or any similar little one, ἓν π. τοιοῦτο (Mt.), ἓν τῶν τοιούτων π. (Mk.). The child is not the type of the honoured disciple; but the honoured disciple is he who welcomes little children, not because he is fond of children, but because they belong to Christ.

ἐπὶ τῷ ὀνόματί μου. "On the basis of My Name." He knows that he is dealing with something which concerns Christ and belongs to Him, and he welcomes it for Christ's sake. The phrase is specially common in Lk. (ver. 49, xxi. 8, xxiv. 47; Acts iv. 17, 18, v. 28, 40, xv. 14; comp. Lk. i. 59); not in Jn. or Paul.

ἐμὲ δέχεται . . . ἐμὲ δέξηται. The pronoun is emphatic.

ὁ γὰρ μικρότερος, κ.τ.λ. Not in Mk. or Mt. It explains how it is that to welcome a child for Christ's sake is to welcome the Father, for promotion in the Kingdom depends upon self-abasement. *Both* ὁ μικρότερος and μέγας are objective; really in a lowly position, really exalted. He who does the humble work of serving the insignificant is promoted by God. It is the chief proof of the Messiah's presence that the *poor* have the Gospel preached to them (vii. 22).

ἐν πᾶσιν ὑμῖν. "Among you all." The circle of the disciples is the sphere in which this holds good. For **ὑπάρχων** see on viii. 41 and xxiii. 50.

ἐστιν μέγας. Already *ipso facto* "is great"; not merely ἔσται (A D). Jesus does not say "is the greatest"; and He thus gives no encouragement to the desire to be above others. It is possible for all in the Kingdom to have this greatness, and there is no need for anyone to measure himself against others. The standard is Christ.

Syr-Sin. reads, "He that is small and is a child to you, that one is great."

49, 50. A Second Lesson in Humility, the Humility of Toleration. Mk. ix. 38–40. The ἀποκριθείς in ver. 49 shows that there is connexion with what precedes, but the precise link is not certain. The common explanation, that Christ's ἐπὶ τῷ ὀνόματί μου suggests to John's mind the case of the stranger who cast out demons ἐν τῷ ὀνόματι, is possible. But it is perhaps more likely that Christ's declaration about the blessedness of giving a welcome to the humblest of His followers has aroused misgivings in John's mind. His words are those of one who defends his conduct, or at least excuses it, and might be paraphrased, "But the principle just laid down must have limits, and would not apply to the case which I mention"; or, "But one who remains outside our body is not really a follower of Thee, and therefore ought not to receive a welcome." John does not mean that the man was not an Apostle, but that he was not a professed disciple. Jealousy for the credit of their Master, not jealousy for their own prerogatives, prompted the Apostles[1] to forbid this man from making use of the Name.

The reading ἐν τῷ ὀνόματί σου (ℵ B L X Δ Ξ 1 33 69) is to be preferred to ἐπὶ τ. ὀν. (A C D), and is not to be discarded because it is also found in Mk. ix. 38. On the expression see Deissmann, *Bible Studies*, p. 147.

49. Ἐπιστάτα, εἴδαμέν τινα. See on v. 5 and 26. Mk. has Διδάσκαλε. The exorcist was not pretending to be a disciple of Jesus when he was not one. But, in however faulty a way, he believed in the power of the name of Jesus, and tried to make use of it for good (Acts iii. 6, xvi. 18). Contrast the mere jugglery of the Jewish exorcists who tried to use the formula Ὁρκίζω ὑμᾶς τὸν Ἰησοῦν ὃν Παῦλος κηρύσσει as a charm (Acts xix. 13–16). Here the context shows that the exorcist was successful, and therefore sincere. The ἐκωλύομεν may mean either "we tried to forbid" or "we repeatedly forbade." The pres. ἀκολουθεῖ implies persistence in such conduct. For ἀκολουθεῖν μετά τινος comp. Rev. vi. 8, xiv. 13: the constr. is classical.

50. Μὴ κωλύετε. "Cease to forbid," not only the person in question, but any such. Comp. vii. 13 and the reply of Moses to the demand of Joshua, Κύριε Μωυσῆ, κώλυσον αὐτούς (Num. xi. 29).

ὃς γὰρ οὐκ ἔστιν καθ' ὑμῶν ὑπὲρ ὑμῶν ἐστίν. The reading ἡμῶν for ὑμῶν in one or both of these places comes from Mk. The saying, "He that is not with Me is against Me" (xi. 23, where see note; Mt. xii. 30) should be compared with this. There Christ gives a test by which His disciple is to try *himself*: if he cannot see that he is on Christ's side, he is against Him. Here He gives a test by which His disciple is to try *others*: if he

[1] It is possible that only John and one other were concerned in ἐκωλύομεν. The incident may have taken place while the Twelve were working two and two. John's companion was probably James, and this may be another illustration of the brothers' fiery temper (ver. 54).

cannot see that they are against Christ's cause, he is to consider them as for it. Renan hastily pronounces the two sayings to be *tout à fait opposées* (*V. de J.* p. 229, ed. 1863).

Here the fourth and last division (ix. 1–50) of the section which treats of the Ministry in Galilee (iv. 14–ix. 50) comes to an end, and with it the first main portion of the Third Gospel. The solemn maxim stated in ver. 50 makes a good conclusion to the Galilean ministry, and the narrative manifestly makes a new beginning in ver. 51.

IX. 51–XIX. 28. THE JOURNEYINGS TOWARDS JERUSALEM.

We may regard this as a narrative of the second main period of Christ's ministry. Galilee, with Capernaum as a centre, ceases to be the almost exclusive sphere of His teaching, and we may say that henceforward He has no centre. Although this period is only one-third as long as the preceding one, it is described with much greater minuteness, and the narrative of it is nearly one-third longer. It is manifest that Lk. is here employing material which was not used by Mk. or Mt., and we know neither its source nor its character. A great deal of it must have been either in writing or stereotyped in an oral form; and a great deal of it would seem to have had an Aramaic original, the translation of which abounds in marks of Lk.'s own style. From ix. 51 to xviii. 14 he is almost alone, and he gives us information which we obtain from no other source. Hence this large tract is sometimes called the "great interpolation" or "intercalation." It is also the "Peræan section" or "Samaritan section" (comp. ix. 51–56, x. 30–37, xvii. 11–19). An analysis, showing the parallels in Mt., is given in Birks, *Horæ Evang.* pp. 132 ff. Jn. gives us several important incidents belonging to the same period, viz. that which lies between the end of the Galilean ministry and the Passion; but we cannot be certain as to the way in which his narrative is to be fitted into that of Lk. See Hastings, *D.B.* i. p. 406.

If we had only Mt. and Mk., we might suppose that the journey from Capernaum to Jerusalem for the last Passover occupied at most one or two weeks. Few incidents are mentioned; and, where distances are indicated, not much time is required for traversing them. Lk. lets us see that the time occupied must have been several months. We are constantly reminded that Jesus is on His way to Jerusalem (ix. 51, 53, xiii. 22, 33, xvii. 11, xviii. 31, xix. 11, 28) but the progress is slow, because Jesus frequently stops to preach in different places. The direction of the journeying is only indirectly intimated, first eastwards along the southern part of Galilee, and then southwards through Peræa; but, however long the time, and however circuitous the route, it is a journey from Capernaum to Jerusalem. Jesus seems never to have returned to the neighbourhood of the lake until after His death. Jn. lets us know that during this interval Jesus was twice in Jerusalem; once at the latter part of the Feast of Tabernacles, after which He healed the man born blind; and again at the Feast of the Dedication; besides which there is the visit to Bethany for the raising of Lazarus; but, although there is room in Lk.'s narrative for what Jn. tells, we do not know where to place it. We cannot with any certainty show the correspondence between the two Gospels until Jerusalem is entered for the last Passover. It seems best, therefore, not to follow Wieseler (*Chron. Syn.* iv., Eng. tr. pp. 289–303), Ellicott (*Hulsean Lectures* for 1859, pp. 242–343), and in the main Caspari (*Chron. Einl.* § 126–143, Eng. tr. pp. 167–189), in making Lk. narrate three distinct journeys to Jerusalem, beginning respectively at ix. 51, xiii. 22, and xvii. 11, but to take his narrative with the indistinctness which he has left. That the journeyings which Jn. has so clearly given really took place, we need not doubt; and nothing in Lk. contradicts Jn.'s narrative; but all interweaving of the two Gospels must be taken as merely tentative arrangement. The thoroughness of Lk.'s investigation is once more shown by his giving us eight or nine long chapters of material which is given by no one else; while his honesty is conspicuous in the fact of his not attempting a precision which he did not find in his sources. The whole is largely didactic.

The proposal of Halcombe, to transfer the whole of Lk. xi. 14–xiii. 21 from the place which it occupies in *all* MSS. and Versions to the break between viii. 21 and 22, is too violent a method of arriving at harmony (*Gospel Difficulties, or the Displaced Section of S. Luke*, Camb. 1886). The amount of harmony obtained in this way is trifling (Lk. xi. 14–26 with Mt. xii. 22–30 and Mk. iii. 22–30, and perhaps Lk. xiii. 18, 19 with Mt. xiii. 31, 32 and Mk. iv. 30–32), and it is simpler to suppose that Lk. xi. 14–26 and xiii. 18, 19 are given out of their chronological order, or that the sayings of Christ there recorded were uttered more than once. Mackinlay's theory is no help.

The historical truth of this independent portion of Lk.'s Gospel is guaranteed (1) by the absence of discrepancy with the other Gospels, but chiefly (2) by the fact that it consists almost entirely of discourses which it would have been altogether beyond Lk.'s powers to invent. For convenience we may divide this long section into three parts: ix. 51–xiii. 35, xiv. 1–xvii. 10, xvii. 11–xix. 28. See Herzog, *PRE.*[2] art. *Jesus Christ*, p. 659.

IX. 51–XIII. 35. *The Departure from Galilee and First Period of the Journey.*

This section begins, as the previous one ends, with a lesson of toleration. In the one case the Apostles were taught that they were not to take upon themselves to hinder the work of an apparent outsider who seemed to be friendly. Here they are taught not to take upon themselves to punish professed outsiders who are manifestly unfriendly. Moreover, as the ministry in Galilee is made to begin with a typical rejection of Christ at

Nazareth (iv. 16–30), so this ministry outside Galilee begins with a rejection of Him by Samaritans.

The thoroughly Hebrew cast of the opening sentence seems to show that the source here used was either an Aramaic original which Lk. translated, or a translation from the Aramaic which he modified.

As marks of his style note *ἐγένετο, ἐν τῷ c. infin., συμπληροῦσθαι, τὰς ἡμέρας τῆς ἀναλήμψεως, καὶ αὐτός, τοῦ c. infin.* (ver. 51); *ἐδέξαντο, ἦν πορευόμενον* (ver. 53).

51–56. § Rejection by the Samaritans and Rebuke to the Disciples. Here we have what was perhaps a new departure in our Lord's method, viz. the sending messengers in advance to prepare for His arrival. The Baptist had prepared the way for Christ's work as a whole, but he had not gone beforehand to the places which Christ proposed to visit. The shortness of the time which still remained may have made a system of preparatory messengers necessary; and this is perhaps the meaning of the opening words.

51. ἐν τῷ συμπληροῦσθαι τὰς ἡμέρας. "When the days were being fulfilled"; *i.e.* when the number of days allotted to the interval was drawing to a close. The verb occurs in N.T. only viii. 23 and (exactly as here) Acts ii. 1, but with συνπλ. for συμπλ. See Gregory, *Prolegom.* p. 74. Comp. εἰς συμπλήρωσιν, 2 Chron. xxxvi. 21; Dan. ix. 2 (Theod.). For the constr. see on iii. 21; and for "the days of" see on i. 39. See also on i. 57.

τῆς ἀναλήμψεως αὐτοῦ. "Of His assumption," *i.e.* the Ascension.

The substantive ἀνάλημψις does not occur elsewhere in N.T. or LXX. But in *Test. XII. Patr.* Levi xviii. it is found, and in this sense, of the new Priest who is to be magnified in the world ἕως ἀναλήψεως αὐτοῦ. In *Ps. Sol.* iv. 20 it is used in a neutral sense of mere removal from the world. The wicked man is to have his old age in the solitude of childlessness until he be taken away (εἰς ἀνάλημψιν); which is perhaps the first appearance of the word in extant Greek literature. See Ryle and James, *ad loc.* They show that this neutral sense is exceptional, and that about the time when S. Luke wrote the word was probably becoming a sort of technical term for the "Assumption of the Blessed." *Erunt enim a morte et* receptione *mea usque ad adventum illius tempora c c l quæ fiunt* (*Assump. Mosis*, x. 12). Comp. *Et videbunt qui* recepti sunt *homines, qui mortem non gustaverunt a nativitate sua* (4 Esr. vi. 26); *Initium verborum Esdræ priusquam* assumeretur (Inscription at 4 Esr. viii. 20); *Et in eis* raptus est *Esras et* assumptus est *in locum similium ejus* (4 Esr. xiv. 49). See also the passage in which Enoch describes his own translation (lxx. 1, 2). The verb ἀνελήμφθη is freq. in N.T., and may be called the usual biblical expression for ascending to heaven: Mk. xvi. 19; Acts i. 2, 11, 22, x. 16; 1 Tim. iii. 16; comp. 1 Mac. ii. 58; Ecclus. xlviii. 9, xlix. 14; 2 Kings ii. 11.

The proposal of Wieseler and Lange to make ἀναλήμψις mean His "acceptance among men" (whether among the Galileans in particular or among Israel in general) is not worthy of much consideration. See Trench, *Studies in the Gospels*, p. 215; Suicer, *Thesaurus*, *s.v.*; Oosterzee, *ad loc.*

τὸ πρόσωπον ἐστήρισεν. A Hebraism: comp. Jer. xxi. 10; Ezek. vi. 2, xiii. 17, xv. 7, xx. 46, xxi. 2, xxv. 2, etc. See Gesenius, *Thes.* p. 1109, on the same form of expression in Syriac, Arabic, Turkish, and Persian. It implies fixedness of purpose, especially in the prospect of difficulty or danger: comp. Is. l. 7. The form ἐστήρισεν for ἐστήριξεν is late; for reff. see Veitch, *s.v.* For **τοῦ πορεύεσθαι** see on ii. 24.

52. ἀπέστειλεν ἀγγέλους. It is vain to speculate who these were. Probably it was a new measure; but perhaps was no more than a temporary precaution, owing to the probability of unfriendly treatment in Samaritan territory. See on ἀπέσταλκεν, iv. 18.

πρὸ προσώπου αὐτοῦ. Another Hebraism: comp. vii. 27, x. 1; Exod. xxxii. 34, xxxiii. 2, xxxiv. 6; Lev. xviii. 24; Num. xxxiii. 52; Deut. i. 21, etc.

Σαμαρειτῶν. Jesus is taking the direct route from Galilee to Judæa. This is the first mention of the Samaritans by Lk. Comp. x. 33, xvii. 16; Mt. x. 5; Jn. iv. 9, 39, viii. 48; Acts viii. 25. Mk. does not mention them. For the more important treatises in the copious literature on the subject see Schürer, *Jewish People*, ii. 1, p. 5; Herzog, *PRE.*[2] xiii. pp. 351–355; Schaff's *Herzog*,[3] iv. p. 2104; Hausrath, *N.T. Times*, i. pp. 14–27; Edersh. *L. & T.* i. pp. 394–403, *Hist. of J. N.* p. 249.

ὡς ἑτοιμάσαι αὐτῷ. This (א B), and not ὥστε, seems to be the true reading. Comp. Acts xx. 24, if ὡς τελειῶσαι is right there: also 3 Mac. i. 2; 4 Mac. xiv. 1. Purpose is implied. No case of ὡς *c. infin.* denoting result is found in N.T. Burton, § 372.

53. οὐκ ἐδέξαντο αὐτόν, ὅτι. The feeling was reciprocal. Some Jews taught that a Samaritan's bread was as defiling as swine's flesh: comp. Jn. iv. 9, 20. The fact that He was on His way to keep a feast at Jerusalem, thus repudiating the Samaritan temple on Mount Gerizim, increased the animosity of the Samaritans. Jos. *Ant.* xx. 6. 1; *B. J.* ii. 12. 3–7; *Vita*, 52; Wetst. on Jn. iv. 20.

τὸ πρόσωπον αὐτοῦ ἦν πορευόμενον. Another Hebraism: comp. 2 Sam. xvii. 11. Galileans in journeying to Jerusalem often went round by Peræa, in order to avoid the churlishness of the Samaritans: and this our Lord may possibly have done after this attempt to bring Jews and Samaritans together as guests and hosts had failed. The hospitality which He had received at Sychar many months before this (Jn. iv. 40) would not abolish the prejudices of *all* Samaritan towns and villages for *ever*.

54. ἰδόντες δέ. They saw the messengers returning from their fruitless errand. Their recent vision of Elijah on the mount may have suggested to them the calling down fire from heaven. The two brothers here, and perhaps also in ver. 49, show their fiery temper as "sons of thunder." Yet Lk., who alone gives this illustration of the title, does not give the title itself (Mk. iii. 17). *Quid mirum filios tonitrui fulgurare voluisse?* (Ambrose).

θέλεις εἴπωμεν. For the constr. comp. xviii. 41, xxii. 9; Mt. xx. 32; Mk. x. 51: Soph. *O.T.* 650. In class. Grk. this constr. is more common with βούλομαι; but in N.T. θέλω is about five times as frequent as βούλομαι, which in mod. Grk. has almost gone out of use. Note that ἵνα, which sometimes follows θέλω, is not inserted when the first verb is in the second person and the second verb in the first person. Win. xli. 4. b, p. 356; Burton, § 171. Syr-Sin. has "Our Lord" for Κύριε.

The words ὡς καὶ Ἠλίας ἐποίησεν (A C D X etc.) are probably a gloss. That they were omitted (ℵ B L Ξ) because some Gnostics used them to disparage the O.T., or because they seem to make Christ's rebuke to the disciples a condemnation of Elijah, is not probable. Rendel Harris thinks that the insertion is due to Marcionite influence both in this case and the next (*Study of Codex Bezæ*, p. 233, in *Texts and Studies*, ii. 1). There is less doubt about καὶ εἶπεν Οὐκ οἴδατε ποίου πνεύματός ἐστε (D F K M etc); and least of all about ὁ γὰρ υἱὸς τοῦ ἀνθρώπου οὐκ ἦλθεν ψυχὰς ἀνθρώπων ἀπολέσαι ἀλλὰ σῶσαι (F K M etc.). These two may safely be omitted as later additions to the text. In the last of them there are several variations in the witnesses which insert the words. Some omit γάρ, some omit ἀνθρώπων, and some have ἀποκτεῖναι for ἀπόλεσαι. WH. ii. App. pp. 59, 60; Sanday, *App. ad N.T.* pp. 118, 119.

It is quite possible that Οὐκ οἴδατε ποίου πνεύματός ἐστε is a genuine saying of Christ, although no part of this Gospel. The remainder, ὁ γὰρ υἱός, κ.τ.λ., may be an adaptation of Mt. v. 17 and [xviii. 11] (comp. Lk. xix. 10), and could more easily have been constructed out of familiar materials.

For other instances of what may be Marcionite influence upon the text see iv. 16 and xxiii. 2.

55. στραφεὶς δέ. "But (instead of assenting to their proposal) He turned." He was in front, and the disciples were following Him. Syr-Sin. omits στραφείς as well as the three clauses.

56. ἐπορεύθησαν εἰς ἑτέραν κώμην. Although ἑτέραν might very well mean a village of another *kind*, yet the probability is that it does not mean a non-Samaritan village. The difference lay in its being friendly and hospitable. There is no intimation that Jesus abandoned His plan of passing through Samaria and turned back to go round by Peræa. Moreover, to have gone away from all the Samaritans, because one Samaritan village had proved inhospitable, might have encouraged the intolerant spirit which He had just rebuked. With Hahn, Baur, Schenkel, and Wieseler we may assume that this other village was Samaritan also, although there is a strong consensus of opinion the other way.

57-62. Three Aspirants to Discipleship warned to count the cost. In part also in Mt. viii. 19-22. The section is well summarized in the chapter-heading in AV. "Divers would follow Him, but upon conditions." The first two instances are common to Lk. and Mt.; the third is given by Lk. alone. But Mt. has the first two in quite a different place, in connexion with the crossing to the country of the Gadarenes (viii. 19–22). Lk. connects the three instances with the final departure from Galilee and with the mission of the Seventy. That he understands these aspirants to be three of the Twelve is manifestly incorrect (vi. 13); and it is uncertain whether he regards all three incidents as having taken place at one and the same time. It is probable that they were grouped together because of their similarity, and that two were already so grouped in the source which both Mt. and Lk. seem to have used.

57. Καὶ πορευομένων αὐτῶν. The most natural, though not certain, reference is to the preceding ἐπορεύθησαν εἰς ἑτέραν κώμην. But it may almost equally well refer to πορεύεσθαι εἰς Ἰερουσαλήμ (ver. 51), and quite possibly to some journey otherwise unmentioned.

For the simple καὶ (ℵ B C L X Ξ) A Γ Δ Λ Π etc. have ἐγένετο δέ, and f Vulg. *factum est autem*; while D has καὶ ἐγένετο, and a c d e *et factum est*.

ἐν τῇ ὁδῷ. Like κλασμάτων (ver. 17) and κατὰ μόνας (ver. 18), these words can be taken either with what precedes or what follows. The Vulgate is as ambiguous as the Greek: *ambulantibus illis in via dixit quidam ad illum*. Beza has *quidam in via dixerit*; but Luther and all English Versions take the words with what precedes. Comp. iv. 1, v. 24, vi. 18, viii. 15, 39, x. 18, xi. 39, etc.

εἶπέν τις. Mt. has εἷς γραμματεὺς εἶπεν. The man had been a hearer, and now proposes to become a permanent disciple, no matter whither Jesus may lead him. To restrict the **ὅπου ἐὰν ἀπέρχῃ** to the journey then in progress, or to the different routes to Jerusalem (Schleierm.), is very inadequate. On the other hand, there is no sign that the man thinks that he is making a very magnificent offer. His peril lies in relying on his feelings at a moment of enthusiasm.

Here, as in Jn. viii. 21, 22, xiii. 33, 36, xviii. 20, xxi. 18, we have ὅπου for ὅποι, a word which does not occur in bibl. Grk.

WH. have ἐάν (A B C K L U Ξ 33 69) in their small ed., with Lach. Treg. In the large ed. they have ἄν (ℵ D), with Tisch. RV. "Predominantly ἄν is found after consonants, and ἐάν after vowels; but there are many exceptions" (ii. App. p. 173).

The κύριε after ἀπέρχῃ (A C Γ Δ Λ Π, f q δ Syr. Goth.) may safely be omitted (ℵ B D L Ξ, a c Vulg. Syr-Sin. Boh. Arm.).

58. Αἱ ἀλώπεκες φωλεοὺς ἔχουσιν. Jesus knows the measure of the scribe's enthusiasm. He also knows whither He Himself is going, viz. to suffering and to death. He warns him of privations which must be endured at once. The scribe was accustomed to a comfortable home; and that must be sacrificed: comp. xviii. 22; Mt. xx. 22. For other cases in which Jesus checked emotional impulsiveness see xi. 27 and xxii. 33. Foxes and birds are mentioned, not as representatives of the whole animal world, but as creatures which lead a vagabond life. Comp. Plut. *Tib. Grac.* ix.

Judg. xv. 4 the form ἀλώπηκας is well attested: φωλεός occurs nowhere else in bibl. Grk. excepting Mt. viii. 20, where see Wetst. for illustrations of the use of the word for lairs of animals. Syr-Sin. inserts "Verily" here.

κατασκηνώσεις. Lit. "encampings," and so "encampments, abodes." Therefore "roosts" would be better than "nests." Only for a short time in each year does a bird have a nest. Here Vulg. has *nidos*, in Mt. *tabernacula* (with *nidos* in many MSS.). Here d has *habitacula*. In both places many texts add to *nidos* the gloss *ubi requiescant*. In Ezek. xxxvii. 27 and Wisd. ix. 8 κατασκήνωσις (*tabernaculum*) is used of Jehovah encamping among His people: comp. Tob. i. 4 and *Ps. Sol.* vii. 5.

οὐκ ἔχει ποῦ τὴν κεφαλὴν κλίνῃ. Not because of His poverty, but because of the wandering life which His work involved, a life which was now more unsettled than ever. Nazareth had cast Him out; of His own choice He had left Capernaum; Samaritans had refused to receive Him: in the intervals of necessary rest He had no home.[1] For the constr. see xii. 17.

59. Εἶπεν δὲ πρὸς ἕτερον. Mt. tells us that this man was ἕτερος τῶν μαθητῶν, *i.e.* one of the casual disciples, who is now invited to become a permanent follower.

Quite without reason Clem. Alex. identifies him with Philip, probably meaning the Evangelist (*Strom.* iii. 4. 522, ed. Potter). So also Hilgenfeld, who identifies the scribe of ver. 57 with Bartholomew. Lange would make this second case to be the desponding Thomas, and the scribe to be Judas Iscariot (*L. J.* ii. p. 144, Eng. tr.). Keim more reasonably remarks that it is futile to attempt to discover the names by mere sagacity (*Jes. of Naz.* iii. p. 270).

Ἐπίτρεψόν μοι πρῶτον ἀπελθόντι θάψαι τὸν πατέρα μου. The most obvious meaning is the best. His father is *in extremis* or has just died, and the funeral will take place almost immediately (Acts v. 6, 10). Perhaps Jesus can wait; or he may be allowed to follow later, after he has performed the sacred duty of burial (Gen. xxv. 9; Tobit iv. 3). "I must first bury my father" is an almost brutal way of saying, "I cannot come so long as my father is alive": and to have put off following Jesus for so indefinite a period would have seemed like unworthy trifling. Yet Grotius and Hase (*Gesch. Jesu*, § 41) adopt this.

The κύριε before ἐπίτρεψον is of doubtful authority, and may come from Mt. viii. 21: om. B* D V, Syr-Sin. For the attraction in ἀπελθόντι see on

[1] Plutarch represents Tiberius Gracchus as saying: τὰ μὲν θηρία τὰ τὴν Ἰταλίαν νεμόμενα καὶ φωλεὸν ἔχει, καὶ κοιταῖον ἐστιν αὐτῶν ἑκάστῳ καὶ καταδύσεις· τοῖς δὲ ὑπὲρ τῆς Ἰταλίας μαχομένοις καὶ ἀποθνήσκουσιν ἀέρος καὶ φωτός, ἄλλου δὲ οὐδένος, μέτεστιν.

iii. 19. Mt. has ἀπελθεῖν καὶ θάψαι. In *vv.* 59 and 60 Lk. has his favourite εἶπεν δέ, which Mt. has in neither place.

60. Ἄφες τοὺς νεκροὺς θάψαι τοὺς ἑαυτῶν νεκρούς. Comp. viii. 51. The apparent harshness and obscurity of the saying is a guarantee for its authenticity. "Leave the spiritually dead to bury their own dead." There will always be plenty of people who have never received or have refused the call to a higher life; and these can perform the ordinary duties of the family and of society. These lower duties are suitable to them,—τοὺς ἑαυτῶν νεκρούς. For a similar change of meaning from the figurative to the literal comp. Jn. v. 21–29, where *vv.* 21–27 refer to spiritual resurrection from sin, *vv.* 28, 29 to actual resurrection from the grave; also Jn. xi. 25, 26, where "die" is used in a double manner. To take νεκρούς in both places as figurative, implies that the father is spiritually dead. To take νεκρούς in both places as literal, gives the harsh meaning, "Leave the dead to take care of themselves."

This disciple needs to be told, not of the privations of the calling, but of its lofty and imperative character. The opportunity must be embraced directly it comes, or it may be lost; and therefore even sacred duties must give way to it. Moreover, like the high priest (Lev. xxi. 11) and the Nazirite (Num. vi. 6, 7), his life will be a consecrated one, and he must not "make himself unclean for his father or for his mother." Comp. Mt. x. 37; Ezek. xxiv. 16. By the time that the funeral rites were over, and he cleansed from pollution, Jesus would be far away, and he might have become unwilling to follow Him.

σὺ δὲ ἀπελθὼν διάγγελλε τ. β. τ. Θ. Mt. omits this charge. Clem. Alex., quoting from memory, substitutes for it the preceding charge, σὺ δὲ ἀκολούθει μοι (*loc. cit.*). Word by word, it forms a contrast to the man's request; ἀπελθών to ἀπελθόντι, διάγγελλε to θάψαι, τὴν βασιλείαν to τὸν πατέρα, τοῦ Θεοῦ to μου. "Depart, not home, but away from it; not to bury, but to spread abroad; not a father, but the Kingdom; not thine own, but God's." The σύ is emphatic: "But *thou*, who art not a νεκρός." Jesus recognizes in him a true disciple, in spite of his hesitation; and the seeming sternness of the refusal is explained. For διάγγελλε, "publish everywhere," comp. Acts xxi. 26; Rom. ix. 17; Ps. ii. 7, lviii. 13; 2 Mac. iii. 34. Vulg. has *adnuntia*; **d**, *prædica: divulga* would be better than either.

61. εἶπεν δὲ καὶ ἕτερος. This third case is not given by Mt., and it probably comes from a different source. On account of its similarity it is grouped with the other two.

Godet regards it as combining the characteristics of the other two. *Cet homme s'offre de lui-même, comme le premier; mais il temporise, comme le second.* Lange takes the three as illustrations of the sanguine, melancholy, and phlegmatic temperaments, and thinks that this third may be Matthew.

ἀποτάξασθαι τοῖς εἰς τὸν οἶκόν μου. "To set myself apart from, bid farewell to, them that are at my house." The case of Elisha (1 Kings xix. 20) may have been in the man's mind. His heart is still with the past. He must enjoy it just once more before he gives it up. Levi had done what this man wished to do, but in a different spirit. He gave a farewell entertainment for his old associates, but in order to introduce them to Christ. The banquet was given to Him (v. 29). This man wants to leave Christ in order to take leave of his friends.

In N.T. ἀποτάσσειν occurs only in the middle: xiv. 33; Acts xviii. 18, 21; Mk. vi. 46; 2 Cor. ii. 13: *abrenunciare* (d), *renunciare* (Vulg.). Comp. ἀποταξάμενος τῷ βίῳ (Ign. *Philad.* xi.); οἱ ἀποταξάμενοι τῷ κόσμῳ τούτῳ (*Act. Paul. et Thec.* v.). The more classical expression would be ἀσπάζεσθαί τινα (Eur. *Tro.* 1276; Xen. *Cyr.* i. 3. 2). Comp. also the use of *renunciare* with a dative: *omnibus advocationibus renunciavi* (Plin. *Ep.* ii. 1. 8); *non multum abfuit quin vitæ renunciaret* (Suet. *Galb.* xi.). In eccles. Grk. ἀποταγή, ἀπόταξις, ἀποταξία are used of renunciation of the world. See Suicer, ἀποτάσσομαι.

τοῖς εἰς τὸν οἶκόν μου. The τοῖς is masc. with εἰς as a pregn. constr.: "to go to my house and bid farewell to those in it." Comp. Acts viii. 40; Esth. i. 5; and see Win. l. 4. b, p. 516. Many texts of Vulg. make τοῖς neut.; *renunciare his quæ domi sunt*; but Cod. Am. and Cod. Brix. have *qui*. He would have no need to go home to take leave of his possessions. But even if τοῖς be taken as neut. it is very doubtful whether ἀποτάξασθαι τοῖς, κ.τ.λ., can mean "to set in order the things," etc., as the Berlenburger Bible takes it. Tertullian has *tertium illum prius suis valedicere parentem prohibet retro respectare* (*Adv. Marcion.* iv. 23). Comp. *Clem. Hom.* xi. 36, xii. 23.

62. ἐπιβαλὼν τὴν χεῖρα ἐπ᾽ ἄροτρον καὶ βλέπων εἰς τὰ ὀπίσω. A proverb: ὃς ἔργου μελετῶν ἰθείην κ᾽ αὔλακ᾽ ἐλαύνοι μηκέτι παπταίνων μεθ᾽ ὁμήλικας, ἀλλ᾽ ἐπὶ ἔργῳ θυμὸν ἔχων (Hes. *Opp.* 443). Pliny says that a ploughman who does not bend attentively over his work goes crooked: *nisi incurvus prævaricatur; inde translatum hoc crimen in forum* (*N. H.* xviii. 19. 49). With βλέπων εἰς τὰ ὀπίσω comp. xvii. 31; Jn. vi. 66, xviii. 6; Phil. iii. 13; also μὴ περιβλέψῃς εἰς τὰ ὀπίσω and ἐπέβλεψεν ἡ γυνὴ αὐτοῦ εἰς τὰ ὀπίσω (Gen. xix. 17, 26).

D and some Lat. texts have εἰς τὰ ὀπίσω βλέπων καὶ ἐπιβάλλων τὴν χεῖρα αὐτοῦ ἐπ᾽ ἄροτρον. For a similar inversion see xxii. 42.

εὔθετός ἐστιν τῇ βασιλείᾳ τοῦ Θεοῦ. Literally, "is well-placed," and so, "useful, fit, for the Kingdom of God"; fit to work in it as a disciple of Christ, rather than fit to enter it and enjoy it. When used of time εὔθετος means "seasonable" (Ps. xxxi. 6; Susan. 15). It was a Pythagorean precept, Εἰς τὸ ἱερὸν ἐπερχόμενος μὴ ἐπιστρέφου, which Simplicius in his commentary on Epictetus explains as meaning that a man who aspires to God ought not to be of two minds, nor to cling to human interests. Jesus says to this man neither "Follow Me" (v. 27) nor "Return to thy house"

(viii. 39), but "I accept no lukewarm service" (Rev. iii. 16). For the constr. comp. Heb. vi. 7, and contrast xiv. 35.

Hahn thinks that this third follower, of whom Lk. alone tells us, may possibly be the Evangelist himself, and that this would account for his henceforward telling us so much which no one else records. He combines this conjecture with the hypothesis that Lk. was one of the Seventy, the difficulties of which have been discussed in the Introduction, § 2.

X. 1–16. § The Mission of the Seventy. The number was significant in more ways than one, and we have no means of determining which of its various associations had most to do with its use on this occasion. (1) *The Seventy Elders*, whom God commanded Moses to appoint, and who were endowed with the spirit of prophecy, to help Moses to bear the burden of the people in judging and instructing them: Num. xi. 16, 17, 24, 25. (2) *The number of the Nations of the Earth*, traditionally supposed to be seventy: Gen. x. (3) *The Sanhedrin*, which probably consisted of seventy members and a president, in imitation of Moses and the seventy Elders.[1] *D.C.G.* art. "Seventy."

That Jesus should have followed the number given to Moses, in order to suggest a comparison between the two cases, is probable enough. That He should have used the tradition about the number of Gentile nations, in order to point out the special character of this mission, viz. to others besides the Jews, is also not improbable.[2] So far as we can tell, the Seventy were sent out about the time of the Feast of Tabernacles. The number of bullocks offered during the Feast was seventy in all, decreasing from thirteen on the first day to seven on the last: and, according to the Talmud, "There were seventy bullocks to correspond to the number of the seventy nations of the world" (Edersh. *The Temple*, p. 240; Lightfoot, *Hor. Hebr.* on Jn. vii. 37). It was about this time that Jesus had declared, "Other sheep I have, which are not of this fold: them also I must lead, and they shall hear My voice" (Jn. x. 16). The connexion of the mission of the Seventy with this thought cannot be regarded as unlikely. It is much less probable that the number was meant "to suggest the thought that the seventy disciples were placed by Him in a position of direct contrast" with the Sanhedrin.

The account of the appointment of the Seventy to minister to all without distinction, like the account of the appointment of the Seven to minister to

---

[1] That the Jews regarded seventy as the normal number for a supreme court or council is shown by the conduct of Josephus, who in organizing Galilee "chose out seventy of the most prudent men, and those elders in age, and appointed them to be rulers of all Galilee" (*B. J.* ii. 20. 5; *Vita*, 14); and also of the Zealots at Jerusalem, who set up a tribunal of seventy chief men, to take the place of the courts which they had suppressed (*B. J.* iv. 5. 4). Comp. the legend of the Septuagint.

[2] See n. 74 in Migne, vol. i. p. 1267 (*Clem. Recog.* ii. 42).

the Hellenists (Acts vi. 1-7), is given by Lk. alone. This fact has led to the conjecture that he himself was one of the Seventy; a conjecture apparently sanctioned by those who selected this passage as the Gospel for S. Luke's Day, but implicitly contradicted by himself in his preface (i. 1-4), which indicates that he was not an eye-witness. His mention of the Seventy and the silence of Mt. and Mk. are very intelligible. The mission belongs to a period about which he had special information, and about which they tell us little. They omit many other matters connected with this part of Christ's ministry. Had they given us the other details and omitted just this one, there would have been some difficulty. Moreover, this incident would have special interest for the writer of the Universal Gospel, who sympathetically records both the sending of the Twelve to the tribes of Israel (ix. 1-6), and the sending of the Seventy to the nations of the earth. No mention of the Gentiles is made in the charge to the Seventy; but there is the significant omission of any such command as "Go not into any way of the Gentiles, and enter not into any city of the Samaritans: but go rather to the lost sheep of the house of Israel" (Mt. x. 5, 6). And in Peræa, which was to be the scene of their labours, the proportion of Gentiles would be larger than in the districts to the west of the Jordan. The silence of Jn. respecting the mission of the Seventy is no more surprising than his silence respecting the mission of the Twelve. He omits these, as he omits many things, because they have been sufficiently recorded, and because they are not required for the plan of his Gospel.

The proposals to treat the charge to the Seventy as a mere doublet of the charge to the Twelve, or as an invention of the Evangelist in the interest of Pauline ideas, will not bear criticism. In either case, why does Lk. also give us the charge to the Twelve (ix. 1-6), and in such close proximity? In the latter case, why does he not insert a special direction to go to the Gentiles? The difference and the similarity between the two charges are quite intelligible. The mission of the Seventy was not permanent, like that of the Twelve. Yet the object of it was not, like that of ix. 52, to prepare shelter and food, but, like that of the Twelve, to prepare for Christ's teaching.[1] The increased numbers were necessary because the time was short, and in many cases His first visit would also be His last. And when we examine the two charges in detail, we find that there is not only the prohibition noted above, which is given to the Twelve and not to the Seventy, but also several directions which are given to the Seventy and not to the Twelve. Neither in Mt. x. 5-15, nor in Mk. vi. 7-11, nor in Lk. ix. 1-5 is there any equivalent to Lk. x. 2, 8; while a good deal of what is similar in the two charges is differently worded or differently arranged. See Rushbrooke's *Synopticon*, pp. 35, 36. One may readily admit the possibility of some confusion between the traditional forms of the two charges; but no such hypothesis is required. The work of the Seventy was sufficiently similar to the work of the Twelve to make the directions given in each case similar. An address to candidates for ordination now would be largely the same, whether addressed to deacons or to priests. The uncritical character of the hypothesis that this section is an invention to promote Pauline doctrine is further shown by the fact that its authenticity is clearly recognized in a work of notoriously anti-Pauline tendency, viz. the *Clementine Recognitions*.[2] And whatever may be the worth of the traditions

---

[1] Renan has a remarkable passage, in which he shows how the customs of Oriental hospitality aided the preaching and spread of the Gospel (*V. de J.* p. 293).

[2] Peter is represented as saying: *Nos ergo primos elegit duodecim sibi credentes, quos apostolos nominavit, postmodum alios septuaginta duos probatissimos discipulos, ut vel hoc modo recognita imagine Moysis crederet multitudo, quia hic est, quem prædixit Moyses venturum prophetam* (i. 40). It is worth noting that in the *Recognitions* the number of the nations of the earth is given as seventy-two (ii. 42).

that this or that person was one of the Seventy, how could the traditions (some of which are as old as the second century) have arisen, if no such body as the Seventy ever existed?

As Eusebius remarks (*H. E.* i. 12. 1), "there exists no catalogue of the Seventy."[1] But he goes on to mention traditions as to a few of them, some of which come from the *Hypotyposes* of Clement of Alexandria. Barnabas (Acts iv. 36, etc.), Sosthenes (1 Cor. i. 1), Cephas (Gal. ii. 11), Matthias (Acts i. 26), Joseph called Barsabbas, who was surnamed Justus (Acts i. 23), and Thaddæus are mentioned as among the Seventy. Clement states definitely of Barnabas the Apostle that he was one of the Seventy (*Strom.* ii. 20, p. 489, ed. Potter), and in *Clem. Recog.* i. 7 he is called one of Christ's disciples. So far as we know, Clement was the first to separate the Cephas of Gal. ii. 11 from the Apostle. This second Cephas is an obvious invention to avoid a collision between two Apostles, and to free S. Peter from the condemnation of S. Paul. From Acts i. 21 we know that both Matthias and Barsabbas had been with Jesus during the whole of His ministry; and therefore the tradition that they were among the Seventy may be true. Thaddæus was one of the Twelve, and cannot have been one of the Seventy also. Eusebius gives the tradition as rumour (*φασί*). To these may be added an improbable tradition preserved by Origen, that Mark the Evangelist was one of the Seventy.

The early disappearance of the Seventy is sufficiently accounted for by (1) the temporary character of their mission; (2) the rise of the order of presbyters, which superseded them; (3) the fact that no eminent person was found among them. It is not improbable that the N.T. prophets were in some cases disciples who had belonged to this body.

The Fathers make the twelve springs of water at Elim represent the Apostles, and the threescore and ten palm trees represent the Seventy disciples (Exod. xv. 27; Num. xxxiii. 9). Thus Tertul. *Adv. Marcion.* iv. 24; Orig. *Hom.* vii. *in Exod.* and *Hom.* xxvii. *in Num.*; Hieron. *Ep.* lxix. 6.

1. Μετὰ δὲ ταῦτα. After the incidents just narrated (ix. 46–62). The historical connexion is clearly marked.

ἀνέδειξεν ὁ Κύριος. The verb is found in N.T. only here and Acts i. 24; freq. in LXX. Comp. *ἀνάδειξις* (i. 80). It means "show forth, display," and hence "make public, proclaim," especially a person's appointment to an office: *ἀναδέδειχα τὸν υἱόν μου Ἀντίοχον βασιλέα* (2 Mac. ix. 25; comp. x. 11, xiv. 12, 26; 1 Esdr. i. 34, viii. 23). This meaning of the word seems to be late (Polyb. Plut. etc.). But the use of an official word of this kind points to a more important preparation for Christ's coming than is indicated ix. 52. Therefore **ἑτέρους** points back to ix. 1–6, the mission of the Twelve. For **ὁ Κύριος** see on v. 17, and comp. vii. 13: *describitur hoc loco actus vere dominicus* (Beng.).

The *ἑτέρους* is in apposition, "others, viz. seventy." The *καί* before *ἑτέρους* (ℵ A C D) is of very doubtful authority, and is as likely to have been inserted in explanation as omitted because superfluous. Comp. xxiii. 32, where *καί* is certainly genuine; and see Win. lix. 7. d, p. 665.

ἑβδομήκοντα [**δύο**]. Both external and internal evidence are

[1] Steinhart in his ed. of the *Scholia on Luke*, by Abulfarağ Bar-Hebræus (p. 22, Berlin, 1895), questions the statement of Assemani (*B. O.* iii. ·. 320), that Bar-Hebræus gives a list of the Seventy. Such lists have been invented.

rather evenly balanced as to the addition or omission of *δύο*. The word might have been either inserted or omitted to make the number agree with the Seventy Elders, for with Eldad and Medad they were seventy-two. The nations of the earth also are sometimes reckoned as seventy, sometimes as seventy-two. The *δύο* might also be omitted to make a favourite number (Gen. xlvi. 27; Exod. i. 5, xv. 27; Judg. i. 7, ix. 2; 2 Kings x. 1; Ezra viii. 7, 14; Is. xxiii. 15; Jer. xxv. 11, etc.). See Ryle, *Canon of O.T.* p. 158.

ἑβδομήκοντα. ℵ A C L X Γ Δ Ξ Π etc., *bfq* Syrr. Goth. Aeth., Iren-Lat. Tert. Eus.

ἑβδομήκοντα δύο. B D M R, *ace* Vulg. Syr-Cur. Syr-Sin. Arm., Clem-Recogn. Epiph. Scrivener considers the evidence against *δύο* to be "overwhelming both in number and weight." So also Keim. WH. bracket, Treg. and Tisch. omit.

ἀνὰ δύο. For companionship, as in the case of the Twelve (Mk. vi. 7), of the Baptist's disciples (Lk. vii. 19), of Barnabas and Saul (Acts xiii. 2), of Judas and Silas (xv. 27), of Barnabas and Mark (xv. 39), of Paul and Silas (xv. 40), of Timothy and Silas (xvii. 14), of Timothy and Erastus (xix. 22). The testimony of two would be more weighty than that of one; and they had to bear witness to Christ's words and works. Comp. Eccles. iv. 9–12; Gen. ii. 18. The reading *ἀνὰ δύο δύο* (B K) seems to be a combination of *ἀνὰ δύο* and *δύο δύο* (Mk. vi. 7; Gen. vi. 19, 20).

ἤμελλεν αὐτὸς ἔρχεσθαι. "He Himself (as distinct from these forerunners) was about to come."

2. Ὁ μὲν θερισμὸς πολύς, . . . εἰς τὸν θερισμὸν αὐτοῦ. This saying is *verbatim* the same as that which Mt. ix. 37, 38 records as addressed to the disciples just before the mission of the Twelve. The Twelve and the Seventy were answers to the prayer thus prescribed; and both had the warning of the fewness of the labourers and the greatness of the work. The **ὀλίγοι** has no reference to the Seventy as being too few: the supply is always inadequate. We cannot conclude anything as to the time of year when the words were spoken from the mention of harvest. So common a metaphor might be used at any season. Com. Jn. iv. 35.

Why does RV. retain the "truly" of AV. in Mt. ix. 37 while abolishing it here? It has no authority in either place, and apparently comes from the *quidem* of Vulg., which represents *μέν*.

δεήθητε. The verb does not occur in Mk. or Jn., nor in Mt. excepting in this saying (ix. 38). It is a favourite with Lk. (v. 12, viii. 28, 38, ix. 38, 40, xxi. 36, xxii. 32; Acts iv. 31, viii. 22, etc.). Elsewhere rare in N.T., but very freq. in LXX. For the constr. see Burton, § 200.

ὅπως ἐργάτας ἐκβάλῃ. "Send forth with haste and urgency." The verb expresses either pressing need, or the directness with which they are sent to their destination. Comp. Mk. i. 12; Mt. xii. 20; Jas. ii. 25. There is always human unwillingness to be overcome: comp. Exod. iv. 10, 13; Judg. iv. 8; Jon. i. 3. For ἐργάτας of agricultural labourers comp. Mt. xx. 1, 8; Jas. v. 4; Ecclus. xix. 1; and of labourers in the cause of religion, 2 Cor. xi. 13; Phil. iii. 2; 2 Tim. ii. 15.

3. ἰδοὺ ἀποστέλλω ὑμᾶς, κ.τ.λ. The same is said to the Twelve, with *πρόβατα* for *ἄρνας* (Mt. x. 16).[1] For ἀποστέλλω see on iv. 18. In the ancient homily wrongly attributed to Clement of Rome (Lft., Clement, ii. p. 219) we have the following: *λέγει γὰρ ὁ Κύριος Ἔσεσθε ὡς ἀρνία ἐν μέσῳ λύκων· ἀποκριθεὶς δὲ ὁ Πέτρος αὐτῷ λέγει· Ἐὰν οὖν διασπαράξωσιν οἱ λύκοι τὰ ἀρνία; εἶπεν ὁ Ἰησοῦς τῷ Πέτρῳ· Μὴ φοβείσθωσαν τὰ ἀρνία τοὺς λύκους μετὰ τὸ ἀποθανεῖν αὐτά.* Then follows a loose quotation of Mt. x. 28 or Lk. xii. 4, 5. See A. Resch, *Agrapha*, *Texte u. Untersuch.* v. 4, p. 377, 1889.

4. μὴ βαστάζετε βαλλάντιον, μὴ πήραν, μὴ ὑποδήματα. The Talmud enjoins that no one is to go on the Temple Mount with staff, shoes, scrip, or money tied to him in his purse. Christ's messengers are to go out in the same spirit as they would go to the services of the temple, avoiding all distractions. Edersh. *The Temple*, p. 42. From *βαστάζετε* we infer that *ὑποδήματα* were not to be *carried* in addition to what were worn on the feet. Sandals were allowed in the temple. Comp. ix. 3, xxii. 35. The whole charge means, "Take with you none of the things which travellers commonly regard as indispensable. Your wants will be supplied." In N.T. βαλλάντιον occurs only in Lk. (xii. 33, xxii. 35, 36): in LXX Job xiv. 17. The word is quite classical: Kennedy, *Sources of N.T. Grk.* p. 42. See on ix. 3 and vii. 14.

μηδένα κατὰ τὴν ὁδὸν ἀσπάσησθε. They are to go straight to their destination, and not give their message of good tidings until they have reached it. It is not greetings, but greetings *κατὰ τὴν ὁδόν* that are forbidden.[2] *Omnia prætermittatis, dum quod injunctum est peragatis* (Aug.). Comp. 2 Kings iv. 29. Like the sayings in ix. 60, 62, this prohibition implies that entire devotion to the work in hand is necessary.

5. But directly they have reached a goal, and have obtained admission to a household, a greeting is to be given. Comp. ii. 14, *εἰρήνη ἐν ἀνθρώποις*; Jn. xx. 19, 21, 26, *εἰρήνη ὑμῖν*.

6. υἱὸς εἰρήνης. Another Hebraism: "one inclined to peace": *dignus qui illo voto potiatur.* Comp. *υἱὸς γεέννης* (Mt. xxiii. 15); *τῆς ἀπωλείας* (Jn. xvii. 12); *τῆς ἀπειθείας* (Eph. v. 6); *θανάτου* (2 Sam.

[1] Comp. *Non derelinquas nos sicut pastor gregem suum in manibus luporum malignorum* (4 Esr. v. 18). *Ovem lupo commisisti* (Ter. *Eunuch.* v. 1. 16). Other examples in Wetst. on Mt. x. 16. Here *ἄρνας ἐν μέσῳ λύκων* must be taken closely together: as certain of being attacked as lambs in the midst of wolves.

[2] See Tristram, *Eastern Customs in Bible Lands*, p. 57, for a graphic illustration of the value of the precept, "Salute no man by the way." *Pulchra est salutatio, sed pulchrior matura exsecutio* (Ambr. *in loco*).

xii. 5). Comp. τέκνα ὀργῆς (Eph. ii. 3). It was a saying of Hillel, "Be thou of Aaron's disciples, loving peace and seeking for peace."

ἐπαναπαήσεται. This is the reading of ℵ B for ἐπαναπαύσεται, like ἀναπαήσονται (Rev. xiv. 13). A 2 aor. pass. ἐπάην is given by Choeroboscus. Veitch, *sub.* παύω, p. 456. Comp. ἐπανεπαύσατο τὸ πνεῦμα ἐπ' αὐτούς (Num. xi. 25; 2 Kings ii. 15). Here ἐπ' αὐτόν probably refers to the son of peace, not to the house. For εἰ δὲ μήγε (which is freq. in Lk.) see small print on v. 36, and Burton, § 275.

ἐφ' ὑμᾶς ἀνακάμψει. "As if it had been unspoken"; or, "as if it had been spoken to you, instead of by you."[1] Comp. Mt. ii. 12; Acts xviii. 21; Heb. xi. 15; Exod. xxxii. 27; 2 Sam. i. 22, viii. 13, etc. But they have no discretion as to giving this salutation, however unworthy the recipient may seem to be.

7. ἐν αὐτῇ δὲ τῇ οἰκίᾳ μένετε. Not "in the *same* house" (as all English Versions, Vulg. and Luther), which would be ἐν τῇ αὐτῇ οἰκίᾳ, but "in that very house," viz. the one which has given a welcome. Comp. ii. 38, xii. 12, xiii. 1, 31, xx. 19, xxiii. 12, xxiv. 13, 33; in all which places RV. has rightly "that very." But here it has "that same," and ver. 21 it changes "that" (AV.) to "that same." Lk. prefers ἐν αὐτῇ τῇ ὥρᾳ, ἡμέρᾳ, κ.τ.λ. The other Evangelists prefer ἐν ἐκείνῃ τῇ ὥρᾳ, κ.τ.λ.

ἔσθοντες. The poetic form ἔσθω is very rare in prose: comp. vii. 33, xxii. 30; Mk. i. 6; Lev. xvii. 10; Is. ix. 20; Ecclus. xx. 18.

τὰ παρ' αὐτῶν. What their entertainers provide: they are to consider themselves as members of the family, not as intruders; for their food and shelter are salary and not alms. Comp. τὰ παρ' ὑμῶν, "the bounty which you provide" (Phil. iv. 18), and see Lft. on Gal. i. 12. The injunction is parallel to 1 Cor. ix. 7, not to 1 Cor. x. 27. Christ is freeing them from sensitiveness about accepting entertainment, not from scruples about eating food provided by heathen.

ἄξιος γὰρ ὁ ἐργάτης τοῦ μισθοῦ αὐτοῦ. Mt. x. 10 has τῆς τροφῆς αὐτοῦ. Epiphanius combines the two with Lk. iii. 14: ἄξιος γὰρ ὁ ἐργ. τ. μισθ. αὐτοῦ καὶ ἀρκετὸν τῷ ἐργαζομένῳ ἡ τροφὴ αὐτοῦ (*Hær.* lxxx. 5, p. 1072 A). Much more interesting is the quotation in 1 Tim. v. 18, which has been made an objection to the genuineness of the Epistle. But it is probable (1) that λέγει γὰρ ἡ γραφή applies only to Βοῦν ἀλοῶντα οὐ φιμώσεις, and (2) that Ἄξιος ὁ ἐργάτης τοῦ μισθοῦ αὐτοῦ is given as a well-known proverb or saying of Christ. See Introduction, § 6, i. a.

μὴ μεταβαίνετε ἐξ οἰκίας εἰς οἰκίαν. "Do not go on changing," *i.e.* μένετε. They were not to fear being burdensome to their first entertainers, nor to go back to those who had rejected them, still

[1] *Quod semel a dei opulentia exiit non frustra exiit, sed aliquem certe invenit, cui id obtingat. Solatium ministrorum, qui sibi videntur nil ædificare* (Beng.).
"Talk not of wasted affection; affection never is wasted" (Longfellow).

less to seek more pleasant quarters. Perhaps also this is a warning against accepting numerous invitations which would waste precious time. To this day in the East travellers who arrive at an Arab village are overwhelmed with a round of invitations (Lasserre, *Évangiles*, p. 324). Note the exact and original antithesis between ἐξ and εἰς, "out of" and "into *the interior* of."

8. καὶ εἰς ἣν ἂν πόλιν. Apparently *vv.* 5–7 apply to single dwellings, *vv.* 8–12 to towns. For **δέχωνται** see small print on viii 13. We might expect ἐὰν δέχωνται for καὶ δέχωνται.

τὰ παρατιθέμενα ὑμῖν. Just "what is offered," without demanding more or anything different. They must be neither greedy nor fastidious. Comp. ix. 16; Gen. xxiv. 33, xliii. 31; 1 Sam. xxviii. 22; 2 Sam. xii. 20; 2 Kings vi. 22; 4 Mac. vi. 15.

9. καὶ λέγετε αὐτοῖς. "And continue saying to them"; *i.e.* to the inhabitants generally, not merely to the sick.

Ἤγγικεν ἐφ' ὑμᾶς ἡ βασιλεία τοῦ Θεοῦ. So that the last preaching resembled the first: Mt. iii. 2, iv. 17; Mk. i. 15. The Kingdom of Heaven is naturally thought of as coming "*upon*" men, down from above. For ἐγγίζειν ἐπί τινα see Ps. xxvi. 2; 1 Mac. v. 40, 42. Comp. Mt. xii. 28. Note Lk.'s favourite ἐγγίζειν.

10. One house might receive them, but the town as a whole reject them. In that case they are to leave the house (ἐξελθόντες) and deliver a public warning before leaving the town.

εἰς τὰς πλατείας. "Into the open streets" (πλάξ, πλάτος): It is the fem. of πλατύς with ὁδός understood: xiii. 26, xiv. 21; Acts v. 15; Prov. vii. 6; Is. xv. 3; Ezek. vii. 19. Not in Mk. or Jn.

11. Καὶ τὸν κονιορτὸν τὸν κολληθέντα ἡμῖν. "*Even* the dust that cleaveth to us." "Not even the smallest thing of yours will we have." Hobart claims κολλάω as a medical word (pp. 128, 129). In N.T. it is used only in the passive with reflexive force. It occurs seven times in Lk. (xv. 15; Acts v. 13, viii. 29, ix. 26, x. 28, xvii. 34) and five times elsewhere (Mt. xix. 5; Rom. xii. 9; 1 Cor. vi. 16, 17; Rev. xviii. 5), two of which are quotations from LXX, where it is frequent; once in the active (Jer. xiii. 11). Neither in LXX (excepting Tobit vii. 16 ℵ) nor in N.T. does ἀπομάσσειν occur again: comp. ἐκμάσσειν (vii. 38, 44).

πλὴν τοῦτο γινώσκετε ὅτι. "But, although you reject us, the fact remains that you must perceive, that," etc. See on vi. 24, 35. Note that there is no ἐφ' ὑμᾶς (om. ℵ B D L Ξ) after ἤγγικεν. The message of mercy has become a sentence of judgment. "The Kingdom has come nigh, but not on you, because you have put it from you."

Lk. alone of the Evangelists uses τοῦτο . . . ὅτι (xii. 39; Acts xxiv. 14). Jn. has ὅτι after διὰ τοῦτο, but after τοῦτο has ἵνα.

12. ἐν τῇ ἡμέρᾳ ἐκείνῃ. The day of judgment following on the completion of the Kingdom, as is clear from ver. 14. Comp. xxi. 34; Mt. vii. 22; 2 Thes. i. 10; 2 Tim. i. 12, 18, iv. 8. Lk. vi. 23 is different. As in ver. 24, Lk. omits the introductory ἀμήν: he also omits καὶ Γομόρροις. The people in the cities of the plain had had no such opportunities as those to whom Christ's own disciples preached. Comp. Mt. xi. 23.

ἀνεκτότερον. *Remissius* (Vulg.); *tolerabilius* (Lat. Vet.). Only the comparative of ἀνεκτός (ἀνέχομαι) occurs in N.T., and always in this phrase: Mt. x. 15, xi. 22, 24. Not in LXX.

13–15. The Solemn Farewell to the Cities in which He had preached and manifested Himself in vain. The mention of the judgment which awaits the towns that shall reject His forerunners naturally leads to the mention of those places which have already rejected Him. It is plain from ver. 16 that this lamentation over the three cities is part of the address to the Seventy. The wording is almost the same as Mt. xi. 21–24, but there the comparison with Sodom is joined to the denunciation of Capernaum.

13. Χοραζείν. Excepting here and the similar Woe in Mt. xi. 21, Chorazin is not mentioned in N.T. This shows us how much of Christ's work is left unrecorded (Jn. xxi. 25). The name does not occur in O.T. nor in Josephus. It may be identified with the ruins now called *Kerâzeh*, about two miles N.E. of *Tell Hûm*, which is supposed to be Capernaum; and Jerome tells us that Chorazin was two miles from Capernaum: *est autem nunc desertum in secundo lapide a Capharnaum.* Some identify *Tell Hûm* with Chorazin; but Conder, who does not believe that *Tell Hûm* is Capernaum, nevertheless regards *Kerâzeh* as certainly Chorazin (*Handbook to the Bible*, pp. 324–326); and this is now the prevailing view. *D.B.*[2] *s.v.*; *D.C.G. s.v.*

ἐν σάκκῳ . . . καθήμενοι. *Constructio ad sensum*: comp. ver. 8. Χοραζείν and Βηθσαϊδά are feminine, and hence the reading καθήμεναι (D).

ἐν σάκκῳ. Our "sackcloth" gives a wrong idea of σάκκος, which was made of the hair of goats and other animals, and was used for clothing. But sacks were made of it (Gen. xlii. 25; Josh. ix. 4) as well as garments. Comp. Jon. iii. 6. The πάλαι points to a ministry of considerable duration in these cities.

μετενόησαν. Like μετάνοια (see on iii. 3), μετανοεῖν is much more frequent in Lk. (xi. 32, xiii. 3, 5, xv. 7, etc.) than in Mt. and Mk. Neither is found in Jn. See on v. 32.

14. πλὴν Τύρῳ καὶ Σιδῶνι. "But, guilty as Tyre and Sidon are, yet," etc. They were both of them heathen commercial towns, and are frequently denounced by the Prophets for their wickedness: Is. xxiii.; Jer. xxv. 22, xlvii. 4; Ezek. xxvi. 3–7, xxviii. 12–22. Of Chorazin and Bethsaida the paradox was true, that the Kingdom of God had come nigh to them, and yet they were far from the Kingdom of God.

15. **μὴ ἕως οὐρανοῦ ὑψωθήσῃ;** "Shalt thou be exalted as far as heaven? Thou shalt be thrust down as far as Hades." Both here and Mt. xi. 23 the reading ἡ . . . ὑψωθεῖσα is found in many authorities; but the evidence against it (א B D L Ξ) is conclusive. Godet supports it as being *parfaitement claire et simple*; which is the explanation of the corruption. There is less certainty as to whether καταβήσῃ, which is probably right in Mt., is right here (B D): καταβιβασθήσῃ is well supported. In Ezek. xxxi. 16, 17 we have both κατεβίβαζον εἰς ᾅδου and κατέβησαν εἰς ᾅδου. Heaven and Hades (not Gehenna) here stand for height of glory and depth of shame (Is. xiv. 13–15). The desolation of the whole neighbourhood, and the difficulty of identifying even the sites of these flourishing towns, is part of the fulfilment of this prophecy. See Jos. *B. J.* iii. 10. 9; Farrar, *Life of Christ*, ii. 101; Tristram, *Bible Places*, 267; Renan, *L'Antechrist*, p. 277.

16. **Ὁ ἀκούων ὑμῶν ἐμοῦ ἀκούει.** Note the *chiasmus*. This verse connects the work of Christ with the work of His disciples (Acts ix. 4), and forms a solemn conclusion to the address to the Seventy. Those who reject their message will share the lot of those who rejected Christ:[1] all alike have rejected God. Comp. Mt. x. 40; Jn. xiii. 20; 1 Thes. iv. 8; 1 Sam. viii. 7. The Seventy must do their utmost to avert so miserable a result of their labours. For ἀθετεῖ see on vii. 30. Syr-Sin. paraphrases.

17–24. The Return of the Seventy. They would not all return at once, and probably did not all return to the same place, but met Jesus at different points as He followed them. Contrast the very brief account of the return of the Twelve (ix. 10). Trench, *Studies in the Gospels*, p. 225.

17. **Ὑπέστρεψαν δὲ οἱ ἑβδομήκοντα.** Most of the authorities which add δύο in ver. 1 add it here also. By "returned" is meant that they came back to Jesus. He meanwhile had been moving. See on iv. 14 and i. 56.

καὶ τὰ δαιμόνια ὑποτάσσεται. "Even the demons are being subjected." This was more than they expected, for they had only been told to heal the *sick* (ver. 9); whereas the Twelve were expressly endowed with power to cast out demons (ix. 1). There is nothing to show that Lk. considers exorcizing evil spirits to be the highest of gifts; but the Seventy were specially elated at possessing this power. They think more of it than of their success in proclaiming the Kingdom; yet they recognize that it is derived from their Master. It is in His name that they can exorcize. His reply is partly (ver. 20) like the reply to the woman who pro-

[1] *Il cherchait de toute manière à établir en principe que ses apôtres c'était lui-même* (Renan, *V. de J.* p. 294).

nounced His Mother to be blessed (xi. 27, 28). They may admire this; but there is something much more admirable.

18. Ἐθεώρουν τὸν Σαταν̂αν. At the very time when His ministers were casting out Satan's ministers,—nay, even as He was sending them forth to their work, Jesus knew that Satan was being overcome. In the defeat of the demons He saw the downfall of their chief. This passage is again conclusive evidence as to Christ's teaching respecting the existence of a personal power of evil. See on viii. 12, and comp. xiii. 16, xxii. 31. In all these cases it would have been quite natural to speak of impersonal evil. See *D.B.*[1] art. "Satan"; Edersh. *L. & T.* ii. App. xiii. § ii.

In N.T. the form is Σατανᾶς (not excepting 2 Cor. xii. 7), which is declined, and almost invariably has the art.; but xxii. 3 and Mk. iii. 23 are exceptions. In LXX the word is rare. We have σατάν, indecl. and without art., 1 Kings xi. 14, [23, 25], in the sense of "adversary," a human enemy; and τὸν Σαταν̂αν, or τὸν Σατανά, Ecclus. xxi. 27.

For the imperf. comp. Acts xviii. 5, and see Win. xl. 3. d, p. 336.

ὡς ἀστραπήν. It was as visible and unmistakable: comp. xvii. 24; Mt. xxiv. 27. The words are amphibolous, but are better taken with ἐθεώρουν than with ἐκ τοῦ οὐρανοῦ, which is to be joined with πεσόντα: comp. ix. 17, 27, 57, xiii. 1, etc. In B 254 ἐκ τοῦ οὐρανοῦ precedes ὡς ἀστραπήν. As in ver. 15, heaven is here put for the height of prosperity and power: comp. Is. xiv. 12 and τὰ ἐπουράνια (Eph. vi. 12).[1]

πεσόντα. Last with emphasis. The "fallen" of RV. is no improvement on the "fall" of AV. "I beheld Satan fallen" means "saw him prostrate after his fall." The aor. indicates the coincidence between the success of the Seventy and Christ's vision of Satan's overthrow; and neither "fallen" nor "falling" (*cadentem*, Vulg.) express this so well as "fall" in English. See Burton, § 146, and T. S. Evans, *Expositor*, 2nd series, iii. p. 164. Some refer the fall to the original fall of the Angels (Jude 6), in which case ἐθεώρουν refers to the Son pre-existing with the Father. Others to the Incarnation, or the Temptation. Rather, it refers to the success of the disciples regarded as a symbol and earnest of the complete overthrow of Satan.[2] Jesus had been contemplating evil as a power overthrown. In any case there is no analogy between this passage and Rev. xii. 12: the point is not that the devil has come down to work mischief on the earth, but that his power to work mischief is broken.

This verse is sometimes quite otherwise explained. "You are elated at

---

[1] Comp. πρὸς οὐρανὸν βιβῶν (Soph. *O. C.* 381); *Cæsar fertur in cælum* (Cic. *Phil.* iv. 3), *collegam de cælo detraxisti* (*Phil.* ii. 42).

[2] *Cum vos nuper mitterem ad evangelizandum videbam dæmonem suâ potestate a me privatum quasi de cælo cadere, ac per vos magis casurum* (Corn. à Lap.).

your victory over the demons, and are proud of your spiritual powers. Beware of spiritual pride. There was a time when I beheld Satan himself fall even from heaven owing to this sin."[1] Others make it a rebuke to complacency and elation, but in another way. "You are overjoyed at finding that demons are subject to you. That is no very great thing. I once beheld their sovereign cast out of heaven itself; and their subjection was involved in his overthrow." Both these interpretations depend upon a misunderstanding of τοῦ οὐρανοῦ, which does not mean the abode of the Angels, but the summit of power (Lam. ii. 1). This is well expressed in the Clementine Liturgy, in the Collect at the dismissal of the *energumens*, ὁ ῥήξας αὐτὸν ὡς ἀστραπὴν ἐξ οὐρανοῦ εἰς γῆν, οὐ τοπικῷ ῥήγματι, ἀλλὰ ἀπὸ τιμῆς εἰς ἀτιμίαν, δι' ἑκούσιον αὐτοῦ κακόνοιαν. Hammond, *Liturgies Eastern and Western*, Oxford, 1878, p. 5.

19. δέδωκα ὑμῖν τὴν ἐξουσίαν. The powers which they have received are larger than they had supposed. They possessed during their mission, and still retain, *the* ἐξουσία to vanquish the powers of evil. Note the article, which is almost peculiar to this passage. Contrast v. 24, ix. 1, xii. 5, xix. 17; Acts ix. 14. The passage is possibly moulded on Ps. xci. 13: ἐπ' ἀσπίδα καὶ βασιλίσκον ἐπιβήσῃ, καὶ καταπατήσεις λέοντα καὶ δράκοντα; but comp. Deut. viii. 15: τοῦ ἀγαγόντος σε διὰ τῆς ἐρήμου τῆς μεγάλης καὶ τῆς φοβερᾶς ἐκείνης, οὗ ὄφις δάκνων καὶ σκορπίος. The meaning is that no fraud or treachery shall prevail against them.

καὶ ἐπὶ π. τὴν δύναμιν τοῦ ἐχθροῦ. Contrast the δύναμις of the enemy with the ἐξουσία given by Christ. Nor shall any hostile strength or ability succeed. The promise in both cases refers to victory over spiritual foes rather than to immunity from bodily injuries. "The enemy" means Satan: Mt. xiii. 25; Rom. xvi. 20; 1 Pet. v. 8. But protection from physical harm may be included (Acts xxviii. 3–5). The appendix to Mk. more clearly includes this (xvi. 18). Comp. the story of S. John being preserved from being harmed by boiling oil (Tertul. *Præscr. Hær.* xxxvi.), or by drinking hemlock (Lips. *Apokr. Apostelgesch.* i. pp. 426, 428, 432, 480, etc.). This latter story is unknown to the Fathers of the first six centuries.

ἐπὶ πᾶσαν τὴν δυν. This does not depend upon πατεῖν, as is shown by the change of prep. and case, but upon ἐξουσίαν. They have ἐξουσία over every δύναμις. Syr-Sin. omits πᾶσαν.

πατεῖν ἐπάνω. Not of trampling under foot as vanquished, but of walking upon without being hurt.

οὐδὲν ὑμᾶς οὐ μὴ ἀδικήσει. Strong negation: οὐδέν is probably the subject of ἀδικήσει. We might translate, "and the power of the enemy shall not in anywise hurt you." For ἀδικεῖν with double acc. comp. Acts xxv. 10; Gal. iv. 12; Philem. 18: and for ἀδικεῖν in the sense of "injure" comp. Rev. vii. 3, ix. 4. The reading ἀδικήσῃ (B C) looks like a grammatical correction.

---

[1] Thus Gregory the Great: *Mire Dominus, ut in discipulorum cordibus elationem premeret, mox judicium ruinæ retulit, quod ipse magister elationis accepit; ut in auctore superbiæ discerent, quid de elationis vitio formidarent* (*Moral.* xxiii. 6, Migne, lxxvi. 259).

This last clause sums up the other two. They have power over fraud and force; nothing shall harm them. Comp. Jn. x. 28, 29; Is. xi. 8, 9.[1]

20. πλὴν ἐν τούτῳ μὴ χαίρετε. "But (although you may well rejoice, yet) cease to rejoice in this, but continue to rejoice in something better." Pres. imperat. in both cases. *Ista lætitia periculo superbiæ subjacet: illa demissum gratumque animum Deo subjicit* (Grotius). The casting out of demons gives no security for the possession of eternal life. It is not one of *τὰ χαρίσματα τὰ μείζονα*: still less is it the *καθ' ὑπερβολὴν ὁδόν* (1 Cor. xii. 31). A Judas might cast out demons. Comp. "I will have mercy, and not sacrifice" (Hos. vi. 6), which does not mean that sacrifice is forbidden, but that mercy is greatly superior. See on **xxiii. 28** and comp. xiv. 12, 13. For *πλήν* comp. *vv.* 11, 14.

τὰ ὀνόματα ὑμῶν ἐνγέγραπται ἐν τοῖς οὐρανοῖς. "Your names have been written, and remain written, in heaven," as citizens possessing the full privileges of the heavenly commonwealth: *in cœlis unde Satanas decidit: etsi reclamavit Satanas: etiamsi in terra non sitis celebres* (Beng.). But there is probably no reference to *ἐν τῷ ὀνόματί σου* (ver. 17). "Do not rejoice because you exorcize demons in *My* name, but rejoice because *your* names are written in heaven," is a false antithesis.[2] There is no emphasis on *ὑμῶν*. Comp. Heb. xii. 23; Rev. iii. 5, xvii. 8, xx. 12, 15, xxi. 27, xxii. 19; Phil. iii. 20. The figure is one of many taken from O.T. and endued with a higher meaning: Is. iv. 3; Ezek. xiii. 9; Dan. xii. 1. Comp. Hermas, *Vis.* i. 3. 2; *Sim.* ii. 9. Contrast Jer. xvii. 13. For Rabbinical illustrations see Wetst. on Phil. iv. 3. Allusion to the Oriental custom of recording in the archives the names of benefactors (Esth. x. 2; Hdt. viii. 90. 6) is not probable. And it is clear from Rev. iii. 5, xxii. 19; Exod. xxxii. 32; Ps. lxix. 28 that absolute predestination is not included in the metaphor. For the Hebr. plur. *τοῖς οὐρανοῖς* comp. xii. 33, xxi. 26; Acts vii. 56.

21–24. The Exultation of Jesus over the Divine Preference shown to the Disciples. Mt. xi. 25–27. Nowhere else is anything of the kind recorded of Christ. Mt. connects it with the Woes on the three cities, and connects these with the message from the Baptist.

21. Ἐν αὐτῇ τῇ ὥρᾳ. "In that very hour" (see small print on ver. 7), making the connexion with the return of the Seventy close

[1] Justin Martyr says to the Roman Emperors, *ὑμεῖς δ' ἀποκτεῖναι μὲν δύνασθε, βλάψαι δ' οὔ* (*Apol.* i. 2). He is probably adapting Plat. *Apol.* 30 C.

[2] Augustine seems to suggest it *Enarr. in Ps.* xci. But *Enarr. in Ps.* cxxx. he says well: *Non omnes Christiani boni dæmonia ejiciunt; omnium tamen nomina scripta sunt in cœlo. Non eos voluit gaudere ex eo quod proprium habebant, sed ex eo quod cum ceteris salutem tenebant.*

and express. Both this and αὐτῇ τῇ ὥρᾳ (without ἐν) are peculiar to Lk. (vii. 21?, xii. 12, xx. 19: and ii. 38; Acts xvi. 18, xxii. 13). In the parallel passage we have ἐν ἐκείνῳ τῷ καιρῷ (Mt. xi. 25).

ἠγαλλιάσατο τῷ πνεύματι τῷ ἁγίῳ. "Exulted in the Holy Spirit," *i.e.* this holy joy is a Divine inspiration. The fact is analogous to His being "led by the Spirit in the wilderness" (iv. 1). Nowhere else is anything of the kind recorded of Christ. The verb is a strong one: comp. i. 47; Acts ii. 26, xvi. 34; 2 Sam. i. 20; 1 Chron. xvi. 31; Hab. iii. 18; Is. xii. 6, xxv. 9; Psalms *passim*. Mt. has merely ἀποκριθείς.

The strangeness of the expression "exulted in the Holy Spirit" has led to the omission of τῷ ἁγίῳ in A Syr-Sin. and some inferior authorities. There is no parallel in Scripture. Rom. i. 4; Heb. ix. 14; 1 Pet. iii. 18, are not analogous.

Ἐξομολογοῦμαί σοι, πάτερ κύριε τοῦ οὐρανοῦ καὶ τῆς γῆς. "I acknowledge openly to Thine honour, I give Thee praise"; Gen. xxix. 35; Ps. xxx. 4, cvi. 47, cxxii. 4; Rom. xiv. 11, xv. 9: Clem. Rom. lxi. 3. Satan is cast down from heaven, and vanquished on earth. God is Father and Lord of both; Father in respect of the love, and Lord in respect of the power, which this fact exhibits. For other public recognitions of God as His Father comp. Mt. xv. 13, xviii. 35; Jn. v. 17, xi. 41, xii. 27; Lk. xxiii. 34, 46. The genitives belong to κύριε only, not to πάτερ: comp. *Clem. Hom.* xvii. 5.

ἀπέκρυψας ταῦτα ἀπὸ σοφῶν καὶ συνετῶν, κ.τ.λ. The ταῦτα refers to the facts about the Kingdom made known by the Seventy. In sound as in sense there is a contrast between ἀπέκρυψας and ἀπεκάλυψας. The aristocracy of intellect, who prided themselves upon their superiority, are here the lowest of all. The statement is general, but has special reference to the scribes and Pharisees, who both in their own and in popular estimation were the wise and enlightened (Jn. vii. 49, ix. 40). The νήπιοι are the unlearned, and therefore free from the prejudices of those who had been trained in the Rabbinical schools. It is very arbitrary to confine the thanksgiving to ἀπεκάλυψας: it belongs to ἀπέκρυψας also. That God has proved His independence of human intellect is a matter for thankfulness. Intellectual gifts, so far from being necessary, are often a hindrance. S. Paul is fond of pointing out this law of the "Lord of heaven and earth": Rom. i. 22; 1 Cor. i. 19–31, 2 Cor. iv. 3, 4. Note the omission of the article before σοφῶν, συνετῶν, and νηπίοις. To be σοφός and συνετός is not fatal: such are not *ipso facto* excluded, although they often exclude themselves. Nor are the νήπιοι *ipso facto* accepted.

In *Clem. Hom.* viii. 6 the passage is quoted thus: ἐξομολογοῦμαί σοι, πάτερ τοῦ οὐρανοῦ καὶ τῆς γῆς, ὅτι ἀπέκρυψας ταῦτα ἀπὸ σοφῶν καὶ πρεσβυτέρων, καὶ ἀπεκάλυψας αὐτὰ νηπίοις θηλάζουσιν; and again, xviii. 15: ὅτι ἅπερ ἦν κρυπτὰ σοφοῖς, ἀπεκάλυψας αὐτὰ νηπίοις θηλάζουσιν. The latter form avoids the difficulty about thanking God for hiding from the wise. In application the νήπιοι are made to be the Gentiles. The Marcosians had the future,—ἐξομολογήσομαι (Iren. i. 20. 3).

The word νήπιος (νη, ἔπος) represents the Latin *infans*. Lat. Vet. and Vulg. have *parvulis* here and Mt. xi. 25; but *infantium*, Mt. xxi. 16. It is opposed to ἀνήρ, 1 Cor. xiii, 11; Eph. iv. 14; and to τέλειος, Heb. v. 13.

ναί. This resumes the expression of thanks; and hence the second ὅτι, like the first, depends upon ἐξομολογοῦμαί σοι: "I thank Thee that thus it was well-pleasing." Comp. Phil. iv. 3; Philem. 20; Rev. xvi. 7, xxii. 20.

ὁ πατήρ. The nom. with the art. often takes the place of the voc. in N.T., and generally without any difference in meaning. This is specially the case with imperatives (viii. 54, xii. 32; Mt. xxvii. 29?; Mk. v. 41, ix. 25; Col. iii. 18; Eph. vi. 1, etc.), and may often be due to Hebrew influence (2 Kings ix. 31; Jer. xlvii. 6). Here there is perhaps a slight difference between πάτερ and ὁ πατήρ, the latter meaning, "Thou who art the Father of all." The use of ὁ πατήρ for πάτερ may be due to liturgical influence. Comp. Mk. xiv. 36; Rom. viii. 15; and see Lft. on Gal. iv. 6 and Col. iii. 18; also Win. xxix. 2, p. 227; Simcox, *Lang. of N.T.* p. 76.

εὐδοκία ἐγένετο ἔμπροσθέν σου. A Hebraism, with εὐδοκία first for emphasis. See on ii. 14.

22. The importance of this verse, which is also in Mt. (xi. 27), has long been recognized. It is impossible upon any principles of criticism to question its genuineness, or its right to be regarded as among the earliest materials made use of by the Evangelists. And it contains the whole of the Christology of the Fourth Gospel. It is like "an aerolite from the Johannean heaven" (Hase, *Gesch. Jesu*, p. 527); and for that very reason causes perplexity to those who deny the solidarity between the Johannean heaven and the Synoptic earth. It should be compared with the following passages: Jn. iii. 35, vi. 46, viii. 19, x. 15, 30, xiv. 9, xvi. 15, xvii. 6, 10.[1]

The introductory insertion, καὶ στραφεὶς πρὸς τοὺς μαθητὰς εἶπεν (A C) is one of the few points in which the TR. (which with ℵ B D L M Ξ omits the words) differs from the third edition of Steph.

22. Πάντα μοι παρεδόθη. The πάντα seems primarily to refer to the revealing and concealing. Christ has full power in executing

[1] "This passage is one of the best authenticated in the Synoptic Gospels. It is found in exact parallelism both in Mt. and Lk., and is therefore known to have been part of that 'collection of discourses' (cf. Holtzmann, *Synopt. Evangelien*, p. 184; Ewald, *Evangelien*, pp. 20, 255; Weizsäcker, pp. 166–169), in all probability the composition of the Apostle St. Matthew, which many critics believe to be the oldest of all the Evangelical documents. And yet once grant the authenticity of this passage, and there is nothing in the Johannean Christology that it does not cover. Even the doctrine of pre-existence seems to be implicitly contained in it" (Sanday, *Fourth Gospel*, p. 109). Keim affirms that "There is no more violent criticism than that which Strauss has introduced" of repudiating a passage so strongly attested (*Jes. of Naz.* iv. p. 63).

the Divine decrees. But it is arbitrary to confine the πάντα to the *potestas revelandi*.

γινώσκει τίς ἐστιν ὁ υἱός. "Comes to know what His nature is, His counsel, His will." Mt. has ἐπιγινώσκει τὸν υἱόν, where the compound verb covers what is here expressed by the τίς. Both might be translations of the same Aramaic.

On purely subjective grounds Keim contends for the Marcionite reading ἔγνω, which is certainly as old as Justin (*Apol.* i. 63), although he has γινώσκει, *Try.* c. Even Meyer thinks that ἔγνω may be original. But the evidence against it is overwhelming.

Syr-Sin. makes the two clauses interrogative: "*Who* knoweth the Son, except the Father? and *who* knoweth the Father, except the Son?"

βούληται . . . ἀποκαλύψαι. "Willing to reveal" (RV.); "will reveal" (AV.), is the simple future. There is a similar weakening of βούλεσθαι in AV. Acts xviii. 15, and of θέλειν, xix. 14. See small print on ix. 24.

23, 24. In Mt. xiii. 16, 17 this saying, with some slight differences, occurs in quite another connexion, viz. after the explanation of the reason for Christ's speaking in parables. If the words were uttered only once, Lk. appears to give the actual position. The κατ' ἰδίαν seems to imply some interval between *vv.* 22 and 23. Christ's thanksgiving seems to have been uttered publicly, in the place where the returning Seventy met Him.

23. ἃ βλέπετε. The absence of ὑμεῖς is remarkable. Contrast ὑμῶν δὲ μακάριοι οἱ ὀφθαλμοί (Mt. xiii. 16). Lk. has no equivalent to καὶ τὰ ὦτα [ὑμῶν] ὅτι ἀκούουσιν. Comp. μακάριοι οἱ γινόμενοι ἐν ταῖς ἡμέραις ἐκείναις ἰδεῖν τὰ ἀγαθά (*Ps. Sol.* xvii. 50, xviii. 7).

24. πολλοὶ προφῆται καὶ βασιλεῖς. Balaam, Moses, Isaiah, and Micah; David, Solomon, and Hezekiah. For βασιλεῖς Mt. has δίκαιοι, and for ἠθέλησαν has ἐπεθύμησαν. Vulg. has *voluerunt* here and *cupierunt* in Mt. Neither AV. nor RV. distinguishes. Note that Lk. again omits the introductory ἀμήν, as in ver. 12. See on xii. 44. As to the Prophets comp. 1 Pet. i. 10, 11.

ἃ ὑμεῖς βλέπετε. Here Mt., who has given the emphatic contrast between "you" and the ancients at the outset, omits the ὑμεῖς. One suspects that his arrangement of the pronouns is the original one. Lk. has no ὑμεῖς with ἀκούετε. In 2 Cor. xi. 29 we have an emphatic pronoun with the second verb and not with the first.

25–29. The Lawyer's Questions. This incident forms the introduction to the Parable of the Good Samaritan. Comp. xii. 13–15, xiv. 15, xv. 1–3. The identification of this lawyer with the one who asked, "Which is the great commandment in the law?" (Mk. xii. 28–32; Mt. xxii. 35–40) is precarious, but perhaps ought not to be set aside as impossible. There the question is theological and speculative; here it is practical. Place, introduction, and issue are quite different; and the quotation from the Law which is common to the narratives is here uttered by the lawyer, there by Christ. An identification with the man who had great possessions, and who asked the very same question as the lawyer asks here, although in a very different spirit (Mk. x. 17–22; Mt. xix. 16–22), is impossible, because Lk. himself records that in full (xviii. 18–23). The opening words of this narrative point to an Aramaic source.

25. νομικός τις ἀνέστη ἐκπειράζων αὐτον. See on vii. 30. Excepting Mt. xxii. 35, which is possibly parallel to this, *νομικός* is used by no other Evangelist. The *ἀνέστη* implies a situation in which the company were seated. Neither this question nor the one respecting the great commandment was calculated to place Jesus in a difficulty, but rather to test His ability as a teacher: the *ἐκπειράζων* (see small print on iv. 12) does not imply a sinister attempt to entrap Him. This use of *τις* (*vv.* 30, 31, 33, 38) is freq. in Lk.

τί ποιήσας. The tense implies that by the performance of some one thing eternal life can be secured. What heroic act must be performed, or what great sacrifice made? The form of question involves an erroneous view of eternal life and its relation to this life. Contrast the Philippian gaoler (Acts xvi. 30).

ζωὴν αἰώνιον κληρονομήσω. The verb is freq. in LXX of the occupation of Canaan by the Israelites (Deut. iv. 22, 26, vi. 1, etc.), and thence is transferred to the perfect possession to be enjoyed in the Kingdom of the Messiah (Ps. xxiv. 13, xxxvi. 9, 11, 22, 29; Is. lx. 21); both uses being based upon the original promise to Abraham. See Wsctt. *Hebrews*, pp. 167–169. Lk. like Jn., never uses *αἰώνιος* of anything but eternal beatitude (xvi. 9, xviii. 18, 30). The notion of endlessness, although not necessarily expressed, is probably implied in the word. See Wsctt. *Epp. of St. John*, pp. 204–208; App. E, *Gosp. of S. John* in *Camb. Grk. Test.*; and the literature quoted in Zoeckler, *Handb. d. Theol. Wissft.* iii. pp. 199–201. With the whole expression comp. *οἱ δὲ ὅσιοι κυρίου κληρονομήσουσι ζωὴν ἐν εὐφροσύνῃ* (*Ps. Sol* xiv. 7), and *ὅσιοι κυρίου κληρονομήσαιεν ἐπαγγελίας κυρίου* (xii. 8).

26. Ἐν τῷ νόμῳ. First with emphasis. A *νομικός* ought to know that *ἐν τῷ νόμῳ* the answer to the question is plainly given: *ἐπὶ τὸν νόμον αὐτὸν παραπέμπει* (Euthym.).

πῶς ἀναγινώσκεις; Equivalent to the Rabbinical formula, when scriptural evidence was wanted, "What readest thou?" But perhaps the *πῶς* implies a little more, viz. "to what effect"? The form of question does not necessarily imply a rebuke. For **ἀναγινώσκειν** see iv. 16. That Jesus pointed to the man's phylactery and meant, "What have you got written there?" is conjecture. That he had "Thou shalt love thy neighbour as thyself" on his phylactery, is improbable. The *first* of the two laws *was* written on phylacteries, and the Jews recited it morning and evening, from Deut. vi. 5, xi. 13; hence it was the natural answer to Christ's question. That he adds the second law, from Lev. xix. 18, is remarkable, and it may be that he was desirous of leading up to the question, "And who is my neighbour?" See *D.B.*² art. "Frontlets"; Schaff's *Herzog*, art. "Phylactery."

27. Here, as in Mk. xii. 30, we have *four* powers with which God is to be loved. Mt. xxii. 37 follows Heb. and LXX in giving *three*. They cover man's physical, intellectual, and moral activity. Mk. and LXX have ἐξ throughout; Mt. has ἐν throughout; Lk. changes from ἐξ to ἐν. For the last words comp. Rom. xiii. 9.

28. Ὀρθῶς ἀπεκρίθης. Comp. ὀρθῶς ἔκρινας (vii. 43). In Mk xii. 32 it is the scribe who commends Jesus for His answer.

τοῦτο ποίει. Pres. imperat. "Continually do this," not merely do it once for all; with special reference to the form of the lawyer's question (ver. 25). See Rom. ii. 13, x. 5; Lev. xviii. 5.

29. θέλων δικαιῶσαι ἑαυτόν. Not merely "willing," but "*wishing* to justify himself." For what? Some say, for having omitted to perform this duty in the past. Others, for having asked such a question, the answer to which had been shown to be so simple. The latter is perhaps nearer the fact; but it almost involves the other. "Wishing to put himself in the right," he points out that the answer given is not adequate, because there is doubt as to the meaning of "one's neighbour." *Qui multa interrogant non multa facere gestiunt* (Beng.). For δικαιῶσαι see on vii. 35 and Rom. i. 17.

καὶ τίς ἐστίν μου πλησίον; The question was a very real one to a Jew of that age. Lightfoot, *ad loc.*, quotes from Maimonides, "he excepts all Gentiles when he saith, His neighbour. An Israelite killing a stranger inhabitant, he doth not die for it by the Sanhedrim; because he said, If any one lift up himself against his neighbour."

καὶ τίς ἐστίν μου πλησίον; The καί accepts what is said, and leads on to another question: comp. xviii. 26; Jn. ix. 36; 2 Cor. ii. 2. Win. liii. 3. a, p. 545. For the omission of the art. before πλησίον (μου perhaps taking its place) see Win. xix. 5. b, p. 163: but πλησίον may be an adverb.

30–37. § The Parable of the Good Samaritan. Entirely in harmony with the general character of this Gospel as teaching that righteousness and salvation are not the exclusive privilege of the Jew. The parable is not an answer to the original question (ver. 25), and therefore in no way implies that works of benevolence secure eternal life. It is an answer to the new question (ver. 29), and teaches that no one who is striving to love his neighbour as himself can be in doubt as to who is his neighbour. We may believe that the narrative is not fiction, but history. Jesus would not be likely to invent such behaviour, and attribute it to priest,

Levite, and Samaritan, if it had not actually occurred. Nowhere else does He speak against priests or Levites. Moreover, the parable would have far more point if taken from real life.[1]

30. ὑπολαβών. "Took him up" to reply to him. Here only in N.T. has *ὑπολαμβάνω* this meaning, which is quite classical and freq. in Job (ii. 4, iv. 1, vi. 1, ix. 1, xi. 1, xii. 1, xv. 1, xvi. 1, etc.). Contrast vii. 43; Acts ii. 15; Job xxv. 3, where it means "I suppose."

Here Vulg. has *suscipiens*, with *suspiciens* as *v.l.* in many MSS. Besides these two, Lat. Vet. has *subiciens* (e) and *respondens* (f); but not *excipiens*, which would be an equivalent. Syr-Sin. omits.

Ἄνθρωπός τις κατέβαινεν. The road is downhill; but besides this we commonly talk of "going down" from the capital. The narrative implies that the man is a Jew. Jericho is about twenty miles from Jerusalem; and the road still, as in Jerome's day, has a bad name for brigandage from "the Arabian in the wilderness" (Jer. iii. 2), *i.e.* the Bedawin robbers who infest the unfrequented roads. Sir F. Henniker was murdered here in 1820.[2] It is possible that Jesus was on this road at the time when He delivered the parable; for Bethany is on it, and the next event takes place there (*vv.* 38–42).

λῃσταῖς περιέπεσεν. Change from imperf. to aor. "Fell among robbers," so that they were all round him. Quite classical; comp. Jas. i. 2. Wetst. gives instances of this very phrase in profane authors, and it is in correct to classify *περιπίπτειν* as a medical word. For *λῃστής*, "robber" (xix. 46, xxii. 52; Jn. xviii. 40), as distinct from *κλέπτης*, "thief" (xii. 33, 39; Jn. xii. 6), see Trench, *Syn.* xliv.

οἳ καὶ ἐκδύσαντες αὐτόν. "Who, in addition to other violence, stripped him." Robbers naturally plunder their victims, but do

[1] "The spot indicated by our Lord as the scene of the parable is unmistakable. About half-way down the descent from Jerusalem to Jericho, close to the deep gorge of Wady Kelt, the sides of which are honeycombed by a labyrinth of caves, in olden times and to the present day the resort of freebooters and outlaws, is a heap of ruins, marking the site of an ancient khan. The Kahn el Ahmar, as the ruin is called, possessed a deep well, with a scanty supply of water. Not another building or trace of human habitation is to be found on any part of the road, which descends 3000 feet from the neighbourhood of Bethany to the entrance into the plain of Jordan. Irregular projecting masses of rock and frequent sharp turns of the road afford everywhere safe cover and retreat for robbers" (Tristram, *Eastern Customs*, p. 220).

[2] It was near Jericho that Pompey destroyed strongholds of brigands (Strabo, *Geogr.* xvi. 2. 41). Jerome explains "the Going up to Adummim" or "Ascent of the Red" (Josh. xv. 7, xviii. 17), which is identified with this road, as so called from the blood which is there shed by robbers. The explanation is probably wrong, but the evidence for the robbers holds good (*De Locis Heb.* *s.v.* Adummim). The Knights Templars protected pilgrims along this road. For a description of it see Stanley, *Sin. & Pal.* p. 424; Keim, *Jes. of Naz.* v. p. 71; Hastings, *D.C.G.* art. "Jericho."

not always strip them. Comp. Mt. xxvii. 28; with double accusative, Mt. xxvii. 31; Mk. xv. 20. It was because he tried to keep his clothes, and also to disable him, that they added blows to robbery. For the phrase **πληγὰς ἐπιθέντες** comp. Acts xvi. 23; Rev. xxii. 18: in class. Grk. *πλ. ἐμβάλλειν*. Cicero has *plagam alicui imponere* (*Pro Sest.* xix. 44); also *vulnera alicui imponere* (*De Fin.* iv. 24. 66). For ἡμιθανῆ comp. 4 Mac. iv. 11.

31. κατὰ συγκυρίαν. Not exactly "by chance," but "by way of coincidence, by concurrence." Vulg. has *accidit ut*; Lat. Vet. *fortuito* (a ff_2 q r), *forte* (d), *derepente* (e), while several omit (b c i l). The word occurs here only in N.T. and is rare elsewhere. In Hippocrates we have *δι' ἄλλην τινα συγκυρίαν* and *τὰ ἀπὸ συγκυρίας*. Neither *συντυχία* nor *τύχη* occurs in N.T.; and *τύχη* only once or twice, *συντυχία* not once, in LXX. *Multæ bonæ occasiones latent sub his quæ fortuita videantur. Scriptura nil describit temere ut fortuitum* (Beng.).

ἱερεύς τις κατέβαινεν. This implies that he also was on his way from Jerusalem. That he was going home after discharging his turn of service, and that Jericho was a priestly city, like Hebron, is conjecture.

ἀντιπαρῆλθεν. "Went by opposite to him." A rare word; here only in N.T. In Wisd. xvi. 10 it has the contrary meaning, "came by opposite to them" to help them; *τὸ ἔλεος γάρ σου ἀντιπαρῆλθεν καὶ ἰάσατο αὐτούς*. Comp. Mal. ii. 7–9.

32. The insertion of *γενόμενος* before *κατὰ τὸν τόπον* (A) makes *ἐλθών* belong to *ἰδών*, "came and saw": and thus the Levite is made to be more heartless than the priest, whom he seems to have been following. The priest saw and passed on; but the Levite came up to him quite close, saw, and passed on. But B L X Ξ omit *γενόμενος*, while D and other authorities omit *ἐλθών*; and it is not likely that both are genuine. Syr-Sin. omits one. Most editors now omit *γενόμενος*, but Field pleads for its retention, and would omit *ἐλθών* (*Otium Norvic.* iii. p. 43).

33. Σαμαρείτης δέ τις ὁδεύων. A despised schismatic, in marked contrast to the orthodox clergy who had shown no kindness.[1] Comp. ix. 52; Jn. iv. 39–42. He is not said to be *καταβαίνων*: he would not be coming from Jerusalem. See on xvii. 18.

ἦλθεν κατ' αὐτόν. "Came down upon him," or "where he was," or "towards him" (Acts viii. 26, xvi. 7; Phil. iii. 14). The fear of being himself overtaken by brigands, or of being suspected of the robbery, does not influence him. "Directly he saw him, forthwith (aor.) he was moved with compassion." See on vii. 13.

34. προσελθών. This neither of the others seems to have done:

[1] Blunt sees here a possible coincidence. Christ may have chosen a Samaritan for the benefactor, as a gentle rebuke to James and John for wishing just before this to call down fire on Samaritans (ix. 54). See *Undesigned Coincidences*, Pt. IV. xxxii. p. 300, 8th ed.

they avoided coming near him. He was half-unconscious, and they wished to get past without being asked to help.

κατέδησεν τὰ τραύματα αὐτοῦ ἐπιχέων ἔλαιον καὶ οἶνον. These medical details would be specially interesting to Lk. "Bound up, pouring on, as he bound, oil and wine." Neither compound occurs elsewhere in N.T. Comp. *τραῦμα ἔστιν καταδῆσαι* (Ecclus. xxvii. 21); and, for *ἐπιχέω*, Gen. xxviii. 18; Lev. v. 11. Oil and wine were recognized household remedies. The two were sometimes mixed and used as a salve for wounds. See evidence in Wetst. Both *τραῦμα* and *τραυματίζω* are pec. to Lk.

ἐπιβιβάσας δὲ αὐτὸν ἐπὶ τὸ ἴδιον κτῆνος. The verb is peculiar to Lk. in N.T. (xix. 35; Acts xxiii. 24), but classical and freq. in LXX. Comp. *ἐπιβιβάσατε τὸν υἱόν μου Σαλωμὼν ἐπὶ τὴν ἡμίονον τὴν ἐμήν* (1 Kings i. 33). **Κτῆνος** (*κτάομαι*) is lit. "property," and so "cattle," and especially a "beast of burden" (Acts xxiii. 24; 1 Cor. xv. 39; Rev. xviii. 13). The **πανδοχεῖον** was probably a more substantial place of entertainment than a *κατάλυμα*: see on ii. 7. The word occurs here only in bibl. Grk., and here only is *stabulum* used in the sense of "inn": comp. *stabularius* in ver. 35. It is perhaps a colloquial word (Kennedy, *Sources of N.T. Grk.* p. 74). Attic *πανδοκεῖον*.

35. ἐπὶ τὴν αὔριον. "Towards the morrow," as Acts iv. 5 and **ἐπὶ τὴν** *ὥραν τῆς προσευχῆς* (Acts iii. 1). Syr-Sin. has "at the dawn of the day." In Mk. xv. 1 some texts read *ἐπὶ τὸ πρωΐ*. This use of *ἐπί* is rare. Comp. *ἐπὶ τὴν ἕω* (Thuc. ii. 84. 2). The *ἐξελθών* after *αὔριον* (A C) is not likely to be genuine; but it would mean that he went outside before giving the money, to avoid being seen by the wounded man. ℵ B D L X Ξ and most Versions omit.

ἐκβαλὼν δύο δηνάρια. The verb does not necessarily imply any violence: "having put out, drawn out," from his girdle; not "flung out"; comp. vi. 42; Mt. xii. 35, xiii. 52. The two *denarii* would be more than four shillings, although in weight of silver much less than two shillings. See on vii. 41.

προσδαπανήσῃς. "Spend in addition" to the two *denarii*. Luc. *Ep. Saturn.* 39. From the Vulg. *supererogaveris* comes the technical expression *opera supererogationis*.

ἐγὼ ἐν τῷ ἐπανέρχεσθαί με. The *ἐγώ* is very emphatic: "I, and not the wounded man, am responsible for payment." Note the pres. infin. "While I am returning, in the course of my return journey": see on iii. 21. The verb occurs elsewhere in N.T. only xix. 15, but is classical and not rare in LXX.

36, 37. The Moral of the Parable. Christ not only forces the lawyer to answer his own question, but shows that it has been asked from the wrong point of view. For the question, "Who is my neighbour?" is substituted, "To whom am I neighbour? Whose claims on my neighbourly help do I recognize?" All the three were by proximity neighbours to the wounded man, and his claim was greater on the priest and Levite; but only the alien recognized any claim. The **γεγονέναι** is very significant, and implies this recognition: "*became* neighbour, *proved* neighbour": comp. xix. 17; Heb. xi. 6. "The neighbouring Jews became strangers, the stranger Samaritan became neighbour, to the wounded traveller. It is not place, but love, which makes neighbourhood" (Wordsworth). RV. is the only English Version which takes account of *γεγονέναι*: Vulg. Luth. and Beza all treat it as *εἶναι*.

37. Ὁ ποιήσας τὸ ἔλεος μετ᾽ αὐτοῦ. The lawyer goes back to his own question, *τί ποιήσας;* He thereby avoids using the hateful name Samaritan: "He that showed the act of mercy upon him," the *ἔλεος* related of him. Comp. *ποιῆσαι ἔλεος μετὰ τῶν πατέρων ἡμῶν* (i. 72), and *ἐμεγάλυνεν τὸ ἔλεος αὐτοῦ μετ᾽ αὐτῆς* (i. 58). The phrase is Hebraistic, and in N.T. peculiar to Lk. (Acts xiv. 27, xv. 4): freq. in LXX (Gen. xxiv. 12; Judg. i. 24, viii. 35, etc.).

Πορεύου καὶ σὺ ποίει ὁμοίως. Either, "Go; thou also do likewise"; or, "Go thou also; do likewise." Chrysostom seems to take it in the latter way: *πορεύου οὖν, φησί, καὶ σύ, καὶ ποίει ὁμοίως* (xi. p. 109, B). There is a rather awkward asyndeton in either case; but *καὶ σύ* must be taken together. Comp. Mt. xxvi. 69; 2 Sam. xv. 19; Obad. 11. "Go, and do *thou* likewise" would be *πορεύου καὶ ποίει σὺ ὁμοίως*. Field, *Otium Norvic.* iii. p. 44. Note the pres. imperat. "Thou also habitually do likewise." It is no single act, but lifelong conduct that is required. Also that *καὶ ζήσῃ* does not follow *ποίει*, as in ver. 28; perhaps because the parable says nothing about loving God, which does not come within its scope. It is an answer to the question, "Who is it that I ought to love as myself?" and we have no means of knowing that anything more than this is intended. **Comp. vi. 31.**

The Fathers delight in mystical interpretations of the parable. For references and examples see Wordsw. *Comm. in loco*; Trench, *Par.* xvii. notes. Such things are permissible so long as they are not put forward as the meaning which the Propounder of the Parable designed to teach. That Christ Himself was a unique realization of the Good Samaritan is unquestionable. That He intended the Good Samaritan to represent Himself, in His dealings with fallen humanity, is more than we know.[1]

38–42. § The Two Sisters of Bethany. That this incident took place at Bethany can hardly be doubted. If the sisters had not yet settled at Bethany, the place could hardly have been called *ἡ κώμη Μαρίας καὶ Μάρθας* (Jn. xi. 1). Jesus is on His way to

[1] Augustine's attempt to prove the latter point is almost grotesque. The Jews said to Christ, "Thou art a Samaritan, and hast a devil" (Jn. viii. 48). Jesus might have replied, "Neither am I a Samaritan, nor have I a devil": but He said only, "I have not a devil." Therefore He admitted that He was a Samaritan (*Serm* clxxi. 2).

or from a short visit to Jerusalem which Lk. does not mention. He perhaps inserts it here as a further answer to the question, "What must one do to inherit eternal life?" Mere benevolence, such as that of the Samaritan, is not enough. It must be united with, and be founded upon, habitual communion with the Divine. "The enthusiasm of humanity," if divorced from the love of God, is likely to degenerate into mere serving of tables. But the narrative may be here in its true chronological position. It is one of the most exquisite among the treasures which Lk. alone has preserved; and the coincidence between it and Jn. xi. with regard to the *characters* of the two sisters, the incidents being totally different, is strong evidence of the historical truth of both.[1] Comp. for both thought and language 1 Cor. vii. 34, 35.

38. Ἐν δὲ τῷ πορεύεσθαι αὐτούς. "Now during their journeyings": see on iii. 21. As Lk. does not name the village, we may conjecture that he did not know where this occurred. One does not see how the mention of Bethany would have put the sisters in danger of persecution from the Jerusalem Jews. If that danger existed, the names of the sisters ought to have been suppressed.

γυνὴ δέ τις ὀνόματι Μάρθα ὑπεδέξατο αὐτόν. She was evidently the mistress of the house, and probably the elder sister. That she was a widow, is pure conjecture. That she was the wife of Simon the leper, is an improbable conjecture (Jn. xii. 1, 2). The names Martha, Eleazar (Lazarus), and Simon have been found in an ancient cemetery at Bethany. The coincidence is curious, whatever may be the explanation. Martha was not an uncommon name. Marius used to take about with him a Syrian woman named Martha, who was said to have the gift of prophecy (Plut. *Mar.* 414). It means "lady" or "mistress": *κυρία*. For ὀνόματι see on v. 27, and for ὑποδέχομαι comp. xix. 6; Acts xvii. 7; Jas. ii. 25. The verb occurs nowhere else in N.T.

εἰς τὴν οἰκίαν. This is probably the right reading, of which *εἰς τὸν οἶκον αὐτῆς* is the interpretation. Even without *αὐτῆς* there can be little doubt that Martha's house is meant.

39. ᾗ καὶ παρακαθεσθεῖσα πρὸς τοὺς πόδας. The *καί* can hardly be "even," and the meaning "also" is not clear. Perhaps "Martha gave Him a welcome, and Mary also expressed her devotion in her own way," is the kind of thought; or, "Mary joined in the welcome, and also sat at His feet." The meal has

[1] "But the characteristics of the two sisters are brought out in a very subtle way. In St. Luke the contrast is summed up, as it were, in one definite incident; in St. John it is developed gradually in the course of a continuous narrative. In St. Luke the contrast is direct and trenchant, a contrast (one might almost say) of light and darkness. But in St. John the characters are shaded off, as it were, into one another" (Lft. *Biblical Essays*, p. 38).

not yet begun, for Martha is preparing it; and Mary is not sitting at table with Him, but at His feet as His disciple (Acts xxii 3). For τοῦ Κυρίου see on v. 17 and vii. 13. The verb is class., but the 1 aor. part. is late Greek (Jos. *Ant.* vi. 11. 9). Note the imperf. ἤκουεν: she continued to listen. Comp. 1 Cor. vii. 35.

40. περιεσπᾶτο. "Was drawn about in different directions, distracted." The word forms a marked contrast to *παρακαθεσθεῖσα*. Comp. Eccles. i. 13, iii. 10, v. 19; Ecclus. xli. 4.

ἐπιστᾶσα δὲ εἶπεν, Κύριε. "And she came up and said": see on ii. 38. Cov. has "stepte unto Him." Other Versions previous to AV. have "stood." The word perhaps indicates an impatient movement. Her temper is shown in her addressing the rebuke to Him rather than to her sister. Her saying ἡ ἀδελφή μου instead of Μαριάμ is *argumentum quasi ab iniquo* (Beng.), and μόνην is placed first for emphasis. The imperf. κατέλειπεν expresses the continuance of the neglect. The word does not imply that Mary began to help and then left off, but that she ought to have helped, and from the first abstained. *D.C.G.* art. "Martha."

For εἰπὸν . . . ἵνα comp. Mk. iii. 9, and for *ἀντιλαμβάνω* see on i. 54. Here the meaning of συναντ. is "take hold along with me, help me." Comp. Rom. viii. 26; Exod. xviii. 22; Ps. lxxxix. 22. See Field, *Otium Norvic.* iii. p. 44.

41. Μάρθα, Μάρθα, μεριμνᾷς. The repetition of the name conveys an expression of affection and concern: xxii. 31; Acts ix. 4; Mt. vii. 21. Comp. Mk. xiv. 36; Rom. viii. 15; Gal. iv. 6, and see on viii. 24.[1] The verb is a strong one, "thou art anxious," and implies division and distraction of mind (*μερίζω*), which believers ought to avoid: Mt. vi. 25, 28, 31, 34; Lk. xii. 11, 22, 26; Phil. iv. 26. Comp. *μέριμνα*, viii. 14, xxi. 34, and especially 1 Pet. v. 7, where human anxiety (*μέριμνα*) is set against Divine Providence (*μέλει*).

καὶ θορυβάζῃ. "And art in a tumult, bustle." The readings vary much, and certainty is not obtainable, respecting the central portion of Christ's rebuke. The form *θορυβάζομαι* seems to occur nowhere else: *τυρβάζω* is fairly common: *περὶ ταύτας τυρβάζεσθαι* (Aristoph. *Pax.* 1007). An unusual word would be likely to be changed into a familiar one. In any case *μεριμνᾷς* refers to the mental distraction, and the second verb to the external agitation. Martha complains of having no one to help her; but it was by her own choice that she had so much to do.

[1] *Repetitio nominis indicium est delectationis, aut movendæ intentionis ut audiret intentius* (Aug.). D doubles νεανίσκε in vii. 14. It is not serving, but excess in it, that is rebuked; and this is not rebuked until Martha begins to find fault with her sister. See Wordsw. It is characteristic of Mary that she makes no reply, but leaves all to the Master.

The difference between θορυβάζῃ (ℵ B C D L) and τυρβάζῃ (A P) is unimportant: the question is as to the words which ought to stand between Μάρθα and Μαριάμ. As regards the first part the decision is not difficult. Nearly all Greek MSS. have μεριμνᾷς καὶ θορυβάζῃ (or τυρβάζῃ) περὶ πόλλα after Μάρθα, and have γάρ or δέ after Μαριάμ or Μαρία. But on the evidence of certain Latin authorities (a b e ff_2 i Amb.) the Revisers and WH. give a place in the *margin* to θορυβάζῃ only after Μάρθα, with neither γάρ nor δέ after Μαριάμ: and these same authorities with D omit all that lies between θορυβάζῃ and Μαριάμ. This curt abrupt reading may be rejected. It is less easy to determine the second part. We may reject ὀλίγων δέ ἐστιν χρεία, which has very little support. Both this reading and ἑνὸς δέ ἐστιν χρεία ($A C^1 P Γ Δ Π$) are probably corruptions of ὀλίγων δέ ἐστιν χρεία ἢ ἑνός ($ℵ B C^2 L$). The last might be a conflate reading from the other two, if the evidence did not show that it is older than ὀλίγων δέ ἐστιν χρεία: it is found in Boh. and Aeth. and also in Origen. See Sanday, *App. ad N.T.* p. 119. Syr-Sin. has "Martha, Martha, Mary hath chosen for herself the good part, which," etc.

ὀλίγων δέ ἐστιν χρεία ἢ ἑνός. The ὀλίγων is opposed to περὶ πολλά, and ἑνός has a double meaning, partly opposed to περὶ πολλά, partly anticipatory of the ἀγαθὴ μερίς. There was no need of an elaborate meal; a few things, or one, would suffice.[1] Indeed only one portion was necessary;—that which Mary had chosen. Both χρεία and μερίς are used of food; τὰ πρὸς τὴν χρείαν being necessaries as distinct from τὰ πρὸς τὴν τρυφήν. For μερίς as a "portion" of food comp. Gen. xliii. 34; Deut. xviii. 8; 1 Sam. i. 4, ix. 23; Neh. viii. 12, xii. 47; Eccles. xi. 2. For μερίς in the higher sense comp. Κύριος ἡ μερὶς τῆς κληρονομίας μου (Ps. xv. 5). See also Ps. lxxiii. 26, cxix. 57, cxlii. 5; Lam. iii. 24; *Ps. Sol.* v. 6, xiv. 3.

Neither ὀλίγων nor ἑνός can be masc., because the opposition is to πολλά. And if the meaning were "Few *people* are wanted for serving, or only one," we should require μιᾶς, as only women are mentioned.

42. Μαριὰμ γάρ. Explanation of ἑνός, and hence the γάρ. Not many things are needed, but only one, as Mary's conduct shows.

The γάρ (ℵ B L Λ) would easily be smoothed into δέ (A C P), or omitted as difficult (D). Versions and Fathers support all three readings. WH. and RV. adopt γάρ.

τὴν ἀγαθὴν μερίδα. "The good part." No comparison is stated; but it is implied that Martha's choice is inferior. In comparison with Mary's it cannot be called "the good part," or "the one thing" necessary, although it is not condemned as bad. Her distracting anxiety was the outcome of affection. *Ecce pars Marthæ non reprehenditur, sed Mariæ laudatur* (Bede). ***Confirmata Mariæ immunitas*** (Beng.). Comp. Jn. vi. 27.

[1] Comp. Lucian, "But what if a guest at the same table neglects all that great variety of dishes, and chooses from those that are nearest to him one that suffices for his need, and is content with that alone, without even looking at all the rest, is not he the stronger and the better man?" (*Cynic.* 7).

ἥτις οὐκ ἀφαιρεθήσεται αὐτῆς. "Which is of such a character as not to be taken away from her." *Activa vita cum corpore deficit. Quis enim in æterna patria panem esurienti porrigat, ubi nemo sitit? quis mortuum sepeliat, ubi nemo moritur? Contemplativa autem hic incipitur, ut in cœlesti patria perficiatur* (Greg. Magn. *in Ezech.* ii. 34).

The omission of the prep. before the gen. (א B D L, *ei* a e, *illi* b i l q) is unusual. Hence A C P Γ Δ etc. insert ἀπ' before αὐτῆς (*ab ea* Vulg. f).

In this narrative of the two sisters in the unnamed village Lk. unconsciously supplies historical support to the Johannine account of the raising of Lazarus. If that miracle is to be successfully discredited, it is necessary to weaken the support which this narrative supplies. The Tübingen school propose to resolve it into a parable, in which Martha represents Judaic Christianity, with its trust in the works of the Law; while Mary represents Pauline Christianity, reposing simply upon faith. Or, still more definitely, Martha is the impulsive Peter, Mary the philosophic Paul. But this is quite incredible. Even Lk. has not the literary skill to invent so exquisite a story for any purpose whatever. And Martha was not occupied with legal ceremonial, but with service in honour of Christ. This service was not condemned: it was her excitement and fault-finding that were rebuked. The story, whether an invention or not, is ill adapted to the purpose which is assumed as the cause of its production.

XI. 1–13. § On Prayer. Lk. shows no knowledge of time or place, and it is possible that the paragraph ought to be placed earlier in the ministry. Mt. places the giving of the Lord's Prayer much earlier, in the Sermon on the Mount (vi. 5–15). Both arrangements may be right. Christ may have delivered the Prayer once spontaneously to a large number of disciples, and again at the request of a disciple to a smaller group, who were not present on the first occasion. But if the Prayer was delivered only once, then it is Lk. rather than Mt. who gives the historic occasion (Neander, De Wette, Holtzmann, Weiss, Godet, etc. See Page, *Expositor*, 3rd series, vii. p. 433). Mt. might insert it to exemplify Christ's teaching on prayer. Lk. would not invent this special incident.

The section has three divisions, of which the second and third belong to the same occasion: the Lord's Prayer (1–4); the Friend at Midnight (5–8); Exhortation to Perseverance in Prayer (9–13).

1–4. The Lord's Prayer. For abundant literature see Herzog, *PRE.*² iv. p. 772; Keim, *Jes. of Naz.* iii. p. 337. For the liturgical use of the Prayer see *D. Chr. Ant.* ii. p. 1056; Kraus, *Real-Enc. d. Chr. Alt.* i. p. 562.

Note the marks of Luke's style: ἐγένετο, ἐν τῷ εἶναι, εἶναι προσευχόμενον, εἶπεν πρός, εἶπεν δέ, τὸ καθ' ἡμέραν, αὐτοί, παντί. The last three, which are in the Prayer itself, point to the conclusion that at least some of the differences in wording between this form and that in Mt. are due to Lk., and that the form in Mt. better represents the original, which would be in Aramaic. The differences cannot be accounted for by independent translation The Greek of the two forms is too similar for that, especially in the use of the perplexing word ἐπιούσιος. Both Evangelists must have had the Prayer in Greek. F. H. Chase supposes that the disciples adapted the Prayer for use on special occasions, either by alterations or additions, and that *both* forms exhibit the Prayer as changed for liturgical purposes, ἐπιούσιος being one of these later features (*Texts & Studies*, vol. i. No. 3, Camb. 1891).

1. προσευχόμενον. See Introd. § 6. i. b. That this was at dawn, or at one of the usual hours of prayer, is conjecture. Nothing is known of a form of prayer taught by the Baptist; but Rabbis sometimes drew up such forms for their disciples.

2. εἶπεν δὲ αὐτοῖς. The disciple had said δίδαξον ἡμᾶς, and Jesus includes all in His reply.

After προσεύχησθε D inserts much from Mt. vi. 7, and in the Lat. has the form *multiloquentia* for *multiloquium : putant enim quidam quia in* multiloquentia *sua exandientur.*

Πάτερ. There is little doubt that the texts of Lk. which give the more full form of the Prayer have been assimilated to Mt. by inserting the three clauses which Lk. omits.[1] The temptation to supply supposed deficiencies would be very strong; for the copyists would be familiar with the liturgical use of the longer form, and would regard the abbreviation of such a prayer as intolerable. The widespread omission is inexplicable, if the three clauses are genuine; the widespread insertion is quite intelligible, if they are not. The express testimony of Origen, that in the texts of Lk. known to him the clauses were wanting, would in itself be almost conclusive; and about the second and third omitted clauses we have the express testimony of Augustine also (*Enchir.* cxvi.: see Wordsworth's Vulg. *in loco*). Syr-Sin. has "Father, hallowed be Thy name. *And* Thy Kingdom come. *And* give us *the continual bread of every day*. And forgive us our sins; *and* we also, we forgive everyone who is indebted to us. And lead us not into temptation." A few authorities, which omit the rest, add ἡμῶν to Πάτερ, and four have *sancte* for *noster* (a c ff_2 i). *D.C.G.* artt. "Prayer" and "Lord's Prayer."

In O.T. God is seldom spoken of as a Father, and then in reference to the nation (Deut. xxxii. 6; Is. lxiii. 16; Jer. iii. 4, 19, xxxi. 9; Mal. i. 6, ii. 10), not to the individual. In this, as in many things, the Apocrypha links O.T. with N.T. Individuals begin to speak of God as their Father (Wisd. ii. 16, xiv. 3; Ecclus. xxiii. i. 4, li. 10; Tobit xiii. 4; 3 Mac. vi. 3), but without showing

[1] For the details of the evidence see Sanday, *App. ad N.T.* p. 119. In general it is ℵ B L, Vulg. Arm., Orig. Tert., which omit the clauses in question; but ℵ is on the other side with regard to γενηθήτω τὸ θέλημά σου, κ.τ.λ. Other authorities omit one or more of the clauses. Those which contain the clauses vary as to the wording of the first two. "Neither accident nor intention can adequately account for such clear evidence as there is in favour of so large an omission, if S. Luke's Gospel had originally contained the clauses in question" (Hammond, *Textual Criticism applied to N.T.* p. 83, Oxford, 1890).

what right they have to consider themselves sons rather than servants. Christ gave His disciples ἐξουσίαν τέκνα Θεοῦ γενέσθαι (Jn. i. 12; comp. iii. 3; Rom. viii. 23; Gal. iv. 5). But we must notice how entirely free from Jewish elements the Prayer is. It is not addressed to the "Lord God of Israel," nor does it ask for blessings upon Israel. See Latham, *Pastor Pastorum*, p. 416.

ἁγιασθήτω. "Let it be acknowledged to be holy, treated as holy, venerated." Comp. 1 Pet. iii. 15; Is. xxix. 23; Ezek. xx. 41, xxxviii. 23; Ecclus. xxxiii. (xxxvi.) 4.

τὸ ὄνομά σου. A common expression in both O.T. and N.T. It is not a mere periphrasis for God. It suggests His revealed attributes and His relation to us. Comp. οἱ ἀγαπῶντες τὸ ὄνομά σου (Ps. v. 12); οἱ γιγνώσκοντες τὸ ὄνομά σου (Ps. ix. 11); οὐ βεβηλώσεις τὸ ὄνομα τὸ ἅγιον (Lev. xviii. 21). It is freq. in *Ps. Sol.* (v. 1, vii. 5, viii. 31, ix. 18, xv. 4, etc.). Codex D adds to this petition the words ἐφ' ἡμᾶς, *super nos*, which may be an independent addition, or a survival of the petition for the coming of the Spirit of which there are traces elsewhere.[1]

ἐλθάτω ἡ βασιλεία σου. It is asserted that in bibl. Grk. βασιλεία is the abstract noun, not of βασιλεύς, but of κύριος, and should therefore be rendered "dominion" rather than "kingdom." Had "kingdom" been meant, βασίλειον would have been more distinct, a word current then, and still the only designation in modern Greek. The petition therefore means, "Thy sway be extended from heaven to this world (now ruled by the adversary), so as to extirpate wickedness." See A. N. Jannaris in *Contemp. Rev.* Oct. 1894, p. 585. For Rabbinical parallels to these first two petitions see Wetst. on Mt. vi. 9, 10.

For such mixed forms as ἐλθάτω, which is specially common, see on i. 59.

3. From prayers for the glory of God and the highest good of all we pass on to personal needs.

τὸν ἐπιούσιον. We are still in ignorance as to the origin and exact meaning of this remarkable word. It appears here first in Greek literature, and is the only epithet in the whole Prayer. And it is possible that in the original Aramaic form there was nothing

[1] There is evidence from Tertullian (*Adv. Marc.* iv. 26), from Gregory Nyssen (*De Orat. Dom.* ed. Krabinger, p. 60), and from an important cursive (*Cod. Ev.* 604 = 700 Gregory), elaborately edited by Hoskier (1890), that the Lord's Prayer in Lk. sometimes contained a petition for the gift of the Spirit, instead either of "Thy kingdom come" or of "Hallowed be Thy name." In Gregory and *Cod. Ev.* 604 the petition runs thus: Ἐλθέτω τὸ πνεῦμά σου [τὸ ἅγιον] ἐφ' ἡμᾶς καὶ καθαρισάτω ἡμᾶς; but in Gregory τὸ ἅγιον is doubtful. This addition may have been made when the Prayer was used at the laying on of hands, and thus have got into some texts of Lk. Chase in *Texts & Studies*, i. 3, p. 28. The ἐφ' ἡμᾶς of D may have come from this addition. Comp. *Zu uns komme dein Reich.*

equivalent to it. The presence of the ι (ἐπιούσιος, not ἐπούσιος) makes the derivation from ἐπεῖναι, ἐπών, or ἐπί and οὐσία very doubtful. With Grotius, Scaliger, Wetstein, Fritzsche, Winer, Meyer, Bishop Lightfoot, and others, we may suppose that ἐπιούσιος comes from ἐπιών, perhaps with special reference to ἡ ἐπιοῦσα, "the coming day." The testimony of the most ancient Versions is strongly in favour of the derivation from ἐπιέναι and of a meaning having reference to *time*, whether "of to-morrow," or "that cometh," or "for the coming day," or "daily," "continual," or "for the day."

Jerome found *quotidianum* as the translation both in Mt. and Lk. He substituted *supersubstantialem* in Mt. and left *quotidianum* in Lk., thus producing a widespread impression that the Evangelists use different words. Cod. Gall. has *supersubstantialem* in Lk. See Lft. *On a Fresh Revision of the N.T.* App. i. pp. 218–260, 3rd ed. For the other views see McClellan, *The N.T.* pp. 632-647. Chase confirms Lft., and contends that (1) This petition refers to bodily needs; (2) The epithet is temporal, not qualitative; (3) The epithet is not part of the original form of the petition, and is due to liturgical use; (4) All the phenomena may be reasonably explained if we assume that the clause originally was "Give us our (*or* the) bread of the day" (*Texts & Studies*, i. 3, pp. 42–53). See Deissmann, *Bible Studies*, p. 214.

Jannaris contends that the word has nothing to do with time at all. He points to the use in LXX of περιούσιος in the sense of "constituting a property" (Exod. xix. 5; Deut. vii. 6, xiv. 2, xxvi. 18), as obviously coined from περιουσία, "wealth, abundance," for the translation of the Hebrew *segulla*. And he interprets, "Ask not for bread περιούσιον, to be treasured up as wealth (*segulla*, θησαυρός), but for bread ἐπιούσιον, mere bread." Accordingly the term ἐπιούσιος is a new formation coined for the purpose, on the analogy of, and as a direct allusion and contrast to, περιούσιος, that is, intended to imply the opposite meaning. He considers that the formation περιούσιος was apparently facilitated by the existence of such words as πλούσιος, ἑκούσιος, ἐθελούσιος, and that it was the existence of περιούσιος which produced the form ἐπιούσιος instead of ἐπούσιος. So also in the main Tholuck.

δίδου ἡμῖν. "Continually give to us," instead of δός in Mt. The change of tense brings with it a corresponding change of adverb: δίδου ἡμῖν τὸ καθ' ἡμέραν for δὸς ἡμῖν σήμερον: "continually give day by day" for "Give once for all to-day." In N.T. τὸ καθ' ἡμέραν is peculiar to Lk. (xix. 47; Acts xvii. 11). This fact and the insertion of his favourite παντί with ὀφείλοντι, and the substitution of his favourite καὶ αὐτοί for καὶ ἡμεῖς with ἀφίομεν, incline us to believe that some of the differences between this form of the Prayer and that in Mt. are due to Lk. himself. The petition in Lk. embraces more than the petition in Mt. In Mt. we pray, "Give us to-day our bread for the coming day," which in the morning would mean the bread for that day, and in the evening the bread for the next day. In Lk. we pray, "Continually give us day by day our bread for the coming day." One stage in advance is asked for, but no more: "one step enough for me."

D here has σήμερον, and most Latin texts have *hodie*. But Codd. Amiat. Gat. Turon. Germ. 2 support τὸ καθ' ἡμέραν with *cotidie* or *quotidie*.

4. τὰς ἁμαρτίας ἡμῶν. Mt. has τὰ ὀφειλήματα ἡμων, and there is reason for believing that Mt. is here closer to the Aramaic original. The ὀφείλοντι of Lk. points to this, and so does τὴν ὀφειλὴν ἡμῶν in the *Didaché* (viii. 2). Anyone accustomed to LXX would be likely to prefer the familiar ἄφες τὰς ἁμαρτίας (Ps. xxiv. 18; comp. Num. xiv. 19; Ex. xxxii. 32; Gen. l. 17), even if less literal. Moreover, ὀφειλήματα would be more likely to be misunderstood by Gentile readers.

καὶ γὰρ αὐτοὶ ἀφίομεν. For this Mt. has ὡς καὶ ἡμεῖς ἀφήκαμεν. The Old Syriac has the future in both Mt. and Lk., and in Lk. it has what may be the original form of the petition: "Remit to us, *and we also will* remit." Tertullian seems to have had the future in his mind when he wrote *Debitoribus denique dimissuros nos in oratione profitemur* (*De Pudic.* ii.). If this is correct, ἀφίομεν is closer to the original than ἀφήκαμεν is. But the connexion is the same, whether we ask for forgiveness because we *have* forgiven, or because we *do* forgive, or because we *will* forgive. It was a Jewish saying, *Dies expiationis non expiationis donec cum proximis in gratiam redieris.*

The form ἀφίω is found Mk. i. 34, xi. 16; Rev. xi. 9. Comp. συνίω, Mt. xiii. 13; WH. ii. App. p. 167.

παντὶ ὀφείλοντι ἡμῖν. Here the τοῖς ὀφειλέταις ἡμῶν of Mt. looks more like the original form, as being simpler. The introduction of παντί is in harmony with Lk.'s usage: see on vi. 30, vii. 35, ix. 43.

εἰσενέγκῃς. "Bring into." The verb occurs five times in Lk. (v. 18, 19, xii. 11; Acts xvii. 20) and thrice elsewhere (Mt. vi. 13; 1 Tim. vi. 7; Heb. xiii. 11); and everywhere, except in the Lord's Prayer, it is rendered in AV. by "bring," not "lead." In Lk. εἰσάγειν is also very common (ii. 27, xiv. 21, xxii. 54; Acts vii. 45, ix. 8, etc.). The latter word implies guidance more strongly than εἰσφέρειν does. For examples of the petition comp. xxii. 40, 46; Mk. xiv. 38; Mt. xxvi. 41. The inconsistency between this petition and Jas. i. 2 is only apparent, not real. This petition refers especially to the internal solicitations of the devil, as is shown by the second half of it, as given in Mt., "but deliver us from the evil one."[1] S. James refers chiefly to external trials, such as poverty of intellect (i. 5), or of substance (i. 9), or persecution (ii. 6, 7). Moreover, there is no inconsistency in rejoicing in temptations when God in His wisdom allows them to molest us, and yet praying to be preserved from such trials, because of our natural weakness. Aug. *Ep.* cxxi. 14, cxlv. 7, 8; Hooker, *Eccles. Pol.* v. 48. 13.

[1] Gregory Nyssen goes so far as to make ὁ πειρασμός a name for the devil: ἄρα ὁ πειρασμός τε καὶ ὁ πονηρὸς ἕν τι καὶ κατὰ τὴν σημασίαν ἐστί (*De Orat. Dom.* v., Migne, xliv. 1192). So also Nilus, the friend and pupil of Chrysostom: πειρασμὸς μὲν λέγεται καὶ αὐτὸς ὁ διάβολος (*Ep.* l., Migne, lxxix. 573).

There is a very early Latin gloss on *ne nos inducas* which found its way into the text of the Prayer itself. *Quis non* sinet *nos deduci in temptationem?* asks Tertullian (*Adv. Marcion.* iv. 26). *Ne* patiaris *nos induci*, or *ne* passus fueris *induci nos*, is Cyprian's form (*De Dom. Orat.* xxv.). Augustine says, *Multi precando ita dicunt*, *Ne nos* patiaris *induci in temptationem* (*De Serm. Dom.* ix. 30, Migne, xxxiv. 1282; *De Dono Persev.* Migne, xlv. 1000). And several MSS. of the Old Latin have these or similar readings (*Old Latin Biblical Texts*, No. ii. Oxford, 1886, p. 32). Dionysius of Alexandria explains the petition as meaning this: *καὶ δὴ καὶ μὴ εἰσενέγκῃς ἡμᾶς εἰς πειρασμόν, τοῦτ' ἔστι μὴ ἐάσῃς ἡμᾶς ἐμπεσεῖν εἰς πειρασμόν* (Migne, x. 1601). Evidently the idea of God's leading us into temptation was from early times felt to be a difficulty; and this gloss may have been used first in private prayer, then in the liturgies, and thence have found its way into Latin texts of the Gospels.

Jannaris contends that this is not a gloss, but a correct translation of the Greek. He holds that in the time of Christ the active of this verb was fast acquiring the force of the middle, and that *εἰσενεγκεῖν = εἰσενέγκασθαι*, "to have one brought into." The petition then means, "Have us not brought into temptation." And he suggests that the true reading may be the middle, *εἰσενέγκῃ*, to which **ς** has been added by a mistake. The evidence, however, is too uniform for that to be probable.

There is yet another gloss, which probably has the same origin, viz. the wish to avoid the difficulty of the thought that God leads us into temptation: *ne inducas nos in temptationem* quam ferre non possumus (Jerome *in Ezech.* xlviii. 16; comp. Hilary *in Ps.* cxviii.). Pseudo-Augustine combines the two: *ne patiaris nos induci in temptationem quam ferre non possumus* (*Serm.* lxxxiv.). "The fact that these glosses occur in writers who are separated from each other in time and circumstance, and that they are found in Liturgies belonging to different families, shows very clearly that they must be due to very early liturgical usage" (Chase, pp. 63-69). That Lk. omitted ἀλλὰ ῥῦσαι ἡμᾶς ἀπὸ τοῦ πονηροῦ because he saw that deliverance from the tempter is included in preservation from temptation, is less probable than that this clause was wanting (very possibly for this reason) in the liturgical form which he gives. All authorities here, and the best authorities in Mt., omit the doxology, which is no doubt a liturgical addition to the Prayer. See Treg. on Mt. vi. 13; Hastings, *D.C.G.* art. "Doxology."

5-8. § The Parable of the Friend at Midnight. This parable is parallel to that of the Unjust Judge (xviii. 1-8). Both of them are peculiar to Lk., whose Gospel is in a special sense the Gospel of Prayer; and they both teach that prayer must be importunate and persevering. So far as they differ, the one shows that prayer is never out of season, the other that it is sure to bring a blessing and not a curse.

5, 6. Τίς ἐξ ὑμῶν. The sentence is irregularly constructed: (1) the interrogative is lost in the prolongation of the sentence; (2) the future (ἕξει, πορεύσεται) drifts into the deliberative subjunctive (εἴπῃ), which in some texts has been corrected to the future (ἐρεῖ). Excepting Mt. vi. 27, τίς ἐξ ὑμῶν is peculiar to Lk. (xii. 25, xiv. 28, xv. 4, xvii. 7). Win. xli. 4. b, p. 357. Excepting Mk. xiii. 35, μεσονύκτιον is peculiar to Lk. (Acts xvi. 25, xx. 7). In the East it is common to travel by night to avoid the heat.

Φίλε, χρῆσόν μοι τρεῖς ἄρτους. As distinct from δανείζω ("I lend on interest" as a matter of business), κίχρημι, which occurs here only in N.T., is "I allow the use of" as a friendly act. There is no need to seek any meaning in the number three. For **παρατίθημι** of food comp. ix. 16; Mk. vi. 41, viii. 6.

7. Μή μοι κόπους πάρεχε. It is the trouble that he minds, not the parting with the bread. When he has once got up (ἀναστάς, ver. 8), he gives him as much as he wants. For **κόπους παρέχειν** comp. Mt. xxvi. 10; Mk. xiv. 6; Gal. vi. 17; and for κόπος see Lft. *Epp.* p. 26.

μετ' ἐμοῦ εἰς τὴν κοίτην εἰσίν. Prep. of motion after verb of rest; comp. Mk. [ii. 1], x. 10; Acts viii. 40: and plur. verb after neut. plur., the persons being animate; comp. Mt. x. 21; Mk. iii. 11, v. 13. Win. l. 4. b, pp. 516, 518, lviii. 3. β, p. 646.

8. εἰ καί. As distinct from καὶ εἰ, εἰ καὶ implies that the supposition is a fact, "although": xviii. 4; 2 Cor. xii. 11, vii. 8; 1 Pet. iii. 14. For εἰ καὶ . . . γε comp. xviii. 4, 5; Win. liii. 7. b, p. 554.

οὐ δώσει. "Will *refuse* to rise and give." The negative is part of the verb and is not affected by the εἰ. Otherwise we should have had μή: xvi. 31, xviii. 4; Rom. viii. 9; Mt. xxvi. 42; 1 Cor. vii. 9. The use is classical. Soph. *Aj.* 1131. Simcox, *Lang. of N.T.* p. 184; Win. lv. 2. c, p. 599.

διά γε. In N.T. γε is rare, except as strengthening other particles: xviii. 5; 1 Cor. iv. 8: "At least because of."

ἀναίδιαν. "Absence of αἰδώς, shamelessness"; Ecclus. xxv. 22; here only in N.T.

9–13. Exhortation to Perseverance in Prayer, based on the preceding parable and confirmed (11–13) by personal experience. Mt. has the same almost *verbatim* as part of the Sermon on the Mount (vii. 7–11).

9. Κἀγὼ ὑμῖν λέγω. "*I* also say to *you*": the ἐγώ is emphatic by being expressed, the ὑμῖν by position; contrast ver. 8, and see on xvi. 9. The parable teaches them; *Jesus* also teaches them. The parable shows how the urgent supplicant fared; the disciples may know how *they* will fare. The three commands are obviously taken from the parable, and they form a climax of increasing earnestness. They are all pres. imperat. "*Continue* asking, seeking, knocking." Comp. Jn. xvi. 24; Mt. xxi. 22; Mk. xi. 24.

10. λαμβάνει . . . εὑρίσκει. The parallel with ver. 9 would be more exact if these two verbs, as well as ἀνοιγήσεται, were futures. But here, as in Mt. vii. 8, ἀνοίγεται (B D) is possibly the true reading

11. τὸν πατέρα. "As being his father." Mt. has ἄνθρωπος, "as a human being," or (more simply) "person." The construction is broken, and can scarcely be rendered literally. "Of which of you as being his father will the son ask for a fish? Will he for a fish hand him a serpent?" The question ought to have continued, "and for a fish receive a serpent"; but the abrupt change to the father's side of the transaction is very emphatic.

For μή interrog. when a negative reply is expected comp. v. 34, x. 15, xvii. 9, xxii. 35. Syr-Sin. omits "father" and inserts "perhaps."

μὴ ἐπιδώσει. "Will he give over, hand to him": **xxiv. 30, 42**; Acts xv. 30.

The text is confused, and it is doubtful whether we ought to have two pairs, as in Mt., or three. If two, they are not the same two as in Mt. There we have the loaf and the stone with the fish and the serpent. Here we have the fish and the serpent with the egg and the scorpion. But perhaps before these we ought to have the loaf and the stone, although B and some other authorities omit. The insertion from Mt., however, is more intelligible than the omission.

12. σκορπίον. **x. 19**; Rev. ix. 3, 9, 10; Deut. viii. 15; Ezek. ii. 6. When its limbs are closed round it, it is egg-shaped. Bread, dried fish, and hardboiled eggs are ordinary food in the East. It is probable that some of these pairs, especially "a stone for a loaf," were proverbial expressions. "A scorpion for a fish," ἀντὶ πέρκης σκορπίον, seems to have been a Greek proverb. The meaning here is, that in answer to prayer God gives neither what is useless (a stone) nor what is harmful (a serpent or scorpion).

13. πονηροὶ ὑπάρχοντες. "Being evil from the first, evil already": much stronger than ὄντες (Mt.). *Illustre testimonium de peccato originali* (Beng.). See on viii. 41 and xxiii. 50.

δόματα. Mt. vii. 11; Eph. iv. 8; Phil. iv. 17. The word is very freq. in LXX, where it represents ten different Hebrew words.

ὁ ἐξ οὐρανοῦ. Pregnant construction for ὁ ἐν οὐράνῳ ἐξ οὐρανοῦ δώσει: comp. ix. 61; Col. iv. 16. Win. lxvi. 6, p. 784. With the assurance here given comp. αἰτείτω παρὰ τοῦ διδόντος Θεοῦ πᾶσιν ἁπλῶς καὶ μὴ ὀνειδίζοντος (Jas. i. 5). The change from ἐπιδώσει to δώσει in both Lk. and Mt. is noteworthy: the idea of "handing over" would here be out of place.

πνεῦμα ἅγιον. See on i. 15. Mt. has ἀγαθά: One of the latest maintainers of the theory that Lk. is strongly influenced by Ebionism, remarks on this difference between Mt. and Lk., "From this important deviation in Luke's version of this passage we learn that the course of thought is from the material to the spiritual: temporal mercies, even daily bread, are transcended altogether. . . . This is one of the most important passages in Luke that can be cited in support of an Ebionite source for much of his Gospel." This may well be correct: in which case the total amount of support is not strong.

D and some other authorities have ἀγαθὸν δόμα here. Hence various conflations: πνεῦμα ἀγαθόν (L 8), *bonum donum spiritus sancti* (Aeth.). From *bonum datum* (b c d ff_2 i l r), *bona data* (a_2), *spiritum bonum* (Vulg.), *spiritum bonum datum* (E), etc. Assimilation to the first half of the verse is the source of corruption. Syr-Sin. has "good things."

14–26. The Dumb Demoniac and the Blasphemy of the Pharisees. Mt. xii. 22–30; Mk. iii. 19–27 *may* be parallels.

14. δαιμόνιον κωφόν. The demon is called dumb because it made the man dumb: Mt. has *τυφλὸν καὶ κωφόν*. When the demon is cast out, it is the man who speaks, *ἐλάλησεν ὁ κωφός*. For ἐγένετο see p. 45.

ἐθαύμασαν. *Stupebant* (a_2 i l), *obstupebant* (b), *stupuerunt* (ff_2). Mt. has *ἐξίσταντο*. The combination of dumbness and blindness with possession made them suppose that no exorcist could succeed in such a case. Probably the man was deaf also, so that there seemed to be no avenue through which the exorcist could communicate with a victim who could neither see him, nor hear him, nor reply to his manipulations.

15. τινὲς δὲ ἐξ αὐτῶν εἶπαν. This is very vague. Mt. says οἱ Φαρισαῖοι, and Mk. still more definitely *οἱ γραμματεῖς οἱ ἀπὸ Ἱεροσολύμων καταβάντες*. They had probably come on purpose to watch Him and oppose Him. It was at Jerusalem about this time that they had said, "Thou art a Samaritan, and hast a devil," and, "He hath a devil, and is mad" (Jn. viii. 48, x. 20).

Ἐν Βεεζεβούλ. "In the power of B." The orthography, etymology, and application of the name are uncertain. Here, *vv.* 18, 19; Mt. x. 25, xii. 24, 27, ℵ B have Βεεζεβούλ, and B has this Mk. iii. 22. The word occurs nowhere else in N.T. and nowhere at all in O.T. With the form Βεελζεβούλ comp. Βάαλ *μυῖαν* (2 Kings i. 2, 3, 6) and Μυῖαν (Jos. *Ant.* ix. 2. 1) for Beelzebub = "Lord of flies." But Βεελζεβούβ is found in no Greek MS. of N.T., and the form *Beelzebub* owes its prevalence to the Vulgate; but even there some MSS. have *beelzebul.* With the termination -βουβ the connexion with the Ekronite god of flies must be abandoned. Βεελζεβούλ may mean either, "Lord of the dwelling," *i.e.* of the heavenly habitation, or, "Lord of dung," *i.e.* of idolatrous abomination. "Lord of idols," "Prince of false gods," comes close to "Prince of the demons." *D.B.*[2] art. "Beelzebub." It is uncertain whether the Jews identified Beelzebub with Satan, or believed him to be a subordinate evil power. Unless xiii. 32 refers to later instances, Lk. mentions no more instances of the casting out of demons after this charge of casting them out by diabolical assistance. See Deissmann, *Bible Studies*, p. 331.

16. πειράζοντες. The demand for a mere wonder to compel conviction was a renewal of the third temptation (iv. 9–12). Comp. Jn. ii. 18, vi. 30. See Martensen, *Chr. Dogm.* § 105.

17. τὰ διανοήματα. "Thoughts," not "machinations," a meaning which the word nowhere has. Here only in N.T., but freq in LXX and classical: Prov. xiv. 14, xv. 24; Is. lv. 9; Ezek. xiv. 3, 4; Plat. *Prot.* 348 D; *Sym.* 210 D.

οἶκος ἐπὶ οἶκον. Mt. xii. 25 and Mk. iii. 25 do not prove that διαμερισθείς is here to be understood. In that case we should expect ἐφ' ἑαυτόν or καθ' ἑαυτοῦ rather than ἐπὶ οἶκον. Comp. πίπτειν ἐπί τι, viii. 6, xiii. 4, xx. 18, xxiii. 30. It is better, with Vulg. (*domus supra domum cadet*) and Luth. (*ein Haus fället über das andere*), to keep closely to the Greek without reference to Mt. xii. 25 or Mk. iii. 25. We must therefore regard the clause as an enlargement of ἐρημοῦται: "house falleth on house"; or possibly "house after house falleth." Comp. ναῦς τε νηῒ προσέπιπτε (Thuc. ii. 84. 3). Wetst. quotes πύργοι δὲ πύργοις ἐνέπιπτον (Aristid. Rhodiac. p. 544). In this way Lk. gives one example, a divided *kingdom*; Mk. two, *kingdom* and *house*; Mt. three, *kingdom, city*, and *house*.

In class. Grk. ἐπί after verbs of falling, adding, and the like is commonly followed by the dat. In bibl. Greek the acc. is more common: λύπην ἐπὶ λύπην (Phil. ii. 27); λίθος ἐπὶ λίθον (Mt. xxiv. 2); ἀνομίαν ἐπὶ τὴν ἀνομίαν (Ps. lxviii. 28); ἀγγελία ἐπὶ ἀγγελίαν (Ezek. vii. 26). In Is. xxviii. 10 we have both acc. and dat., θλῖψιν ἐπὶ θλῖψιν, ἐλπίδα ἐπ' ἐλπίδι.

18. εἰ δὲ καὶ ὁ Σατανᾶς. Satan also is under the dominion of the same law, that division leads to destruction. The fondness of Lk. for δὲ καί is again manifest: see on iii. 9. Contrast εἰ καί in ver. 8. Here καί belongs to ὁ Σατ. and means "also." Burton, § 282. Mt. and Mk. here have simply καὶ εἰ.

ὅτι λέγετε. Elliptical: "*I use this language*, because ye say," etc. Comp. Mk. iii. 30, and see on vii. 47.

19. An *argumentum ad hominem.*

οἱ υἱοὶ ὑμῶν. First with emphasis. See Acts xix. 13 and Jos. *Ant.* viii. 2. 5 for instances of Jewish exorcisms; and comp. *Ant.* vi. 8. 2; *B. J.* vii. 6. 3; Tobit viii. 1-3; Justin M. *Try.* lxxxv.; *Apol.* ii. 6; 1 Sam. xvi. 14, 23.

20. εἰ δὲ ἐν δακτύλῳ Θεοῦ.[1] As distinct from the charms and incantations used by Jewish exorcists, who did not rely simply upon the power of God. Mt. has ἐν πνεύματι Θεοῦ. Lk. seems to be fond of Hebraistic anthropomorphisms: i. 51, 66, 73. But it is not likely that "the *finger* of God" indicates the *ease* with which it is done. Comp. Exod. viii. 19, xxxi. 18; Deut. ix. 10; Ps. viii. 4. See foot-note p. 473.

ἔφθασεν ἐφ' ὑμᾶς. In late Greek, φθάνω followed by a preposition commonly loses all notion of priority or surprise, and simply means "arrive at, attain to": Rom. ix. 31; Phil. iii. 16; 2 Cor. x. 14; 1 Thes. ii. 16; Dan. iv. 19. In 1 Thes. iv. 15 it is not followed by a preposition, and that is perhaps the only passage in N.T. in which the notion of anticipating survives. Here Vulg. and many Lat. texts have *prævenit*, while a_2 has *anticipavit*; but many others have *pervenit*, and d has *adpropinquavit.*

---

[1] The ἐγώ after εἰ δέ (D) or after Θεοῦ (B C L R) is of doubtful authority: in the one case it probably comes from ver. 19, in the other it may come from Mt. xii. 28.

21. ὅταν ὁ ἰσχυρὸς καθωπλισμένος. Here Lk. is very different from Mt. xii. 29 and Mk. iii. 27, while they resemble one another. "The strong one" is Satan, and the parable is very like Is. xlix. 24–26, which may be the source of it. Luther is certainly wrong in translating, *Wenn ein starker Gewapneter*: καθωπλισμένος is an epithet of ὁ ἰσχυρός. Coverdale is similar: "a stronge harnessed man." RV. restores the much ignored article: "*the* strong man fully armed."

τὴν ἑαυτοῦ αὐλήν. "His own homestead." Mt. and Mk. have οἰκίαν. Comp. Mt. xxvi. 3, 58; Mk. xiv. 54, xv. 16; Jn. xviii. 15. Meyer contends that in all these places αὐλή retains its meaning of "court, courtyard," as in Mt. xxvi. 69; Mk. xiv. 66; Lk. xxii. 55. But there is no hint here that "our Lord encountered Satan in the αὐλή of the High Priest." For **τὰ ὑπάρχοντα** see on viii. 3: *substantia ejus* (d), *facultates ejus* (a_2 c), *ea quæ possidet* (Vulg.). Mt. and Mk. have τὰ σκεύη.

22. ἐπὰν δέ. Note the change from ὅταν with pres. subj. to ἐπάν with aor. sub., and comp. χρὴ δέ, ὅταν μὲν τιθῆσθε τοὺς νόμους . . . σκόπειν, ἐπειδὰν δὲ θῆσθε, φυλάττειν (Dem. p. 525, 11); "*whenever* you *are* enacting . . . *after* you *have* enacted." So here: "*All the while that* the strong man is on guard . . . but *after* a stronger has come." In ver. 34 both ὅταν and ἐπάν have pres. subj.; in Mt. ii. 8 ἐπάν has aor. subj.; and ἐπάν occurs nowhere else in N.T.

ἰσχυρότερος αὐτοῦ ἐπελθών. This is Christ: ἀπεκδυσάμενος τὰς ἀρχὰς καὶ τὰς ἐξουσίας ἐδειγμάτισεν ἐν παρρησίᾳ θριαμβεύσας αὐτούς (Col. ii. 15). For ἐπέρχομαι in a hostile sense comp. 1 Sam. xxx. 23; Hom. *Il.* xii. 136, xx. 91. See on i. 35. Here Mt. and Mk. have εἰσελθών.

τὴν πανοπλίαν αὐτοῦ αἴρει ἐφ' ᾗ ἐπεποίθει. Because it had been so efficacious. Comp. Eph. vi. 11.

τὰ σκῦλα αὐτοῦ. Bengel explains, *quæ Satanas generi humano eripuerat*, identifying τὰ σκῦλα with τὰ ὑπάρχοντα (ver. 21: comp. Esth. iii. 13). But τὰ σκῦλα may be identified with τὴν πανοπλίαν. In either case Christ makes the powers of hell work together for the good of the faithful. Some who identify τὰ σκῦλα with τὰ ὑπάρχοντα interpret both of the souls which Satan has taken captive, and especially of demoniacs. Comp. τῶν ἰσχυρῶν μεριεῖ σκῦλα (Is. liii. 12).

23. ὁ μὴ ὢν μετ' ἐμοῦ κατ' ἐμοῦ ἐστίν. *Verbatim* as Mt. xii. 30. The connexion with what precedes seems to be that the contest between Christ and Satan is such that no one can be neutral. But that the warning is specially addressed to those who accused Him of having Beelzebub as an ally (ver. 15), or who demanded a sign (ver. 16), is less evident. See on ix. 50

συνάγων. Comp. iii. 17, xii. 17, 18. But the metaphor is perhaps not from gathering seed and fruit, but from collecting a flock of sheep, or a band of followers. Comp. συνάγει τοὺς ἐσκορπισμένους (Artem. *Oneir.* i. 56. 1). Hillel had said, "Whoso revileth the Name, his name perisheth; and whoso doth not increase it, diminisheth."

σκορπίζει. Ionic and Hellenistic for the more classical σκεδάννυμι; comp. Jn. x. 12, xvi. 32; 1 Mac. vi. 54; 2 Sam. xxii. 15.

24-26. Almost *verbatim* as Mt. xii. 43-45, where see Alford. It is not likely that there is any reference to the success of the Jewish exorcists, as being only temporary, and leading to an aggravation of the evil. The disastrous conclusion is the result, not of the imperfect methods of the exorcist, but of the misconduct of the exorcized. The case of a demoniac who is cured and then allows himself to become repossessed is made a parable to illustrate the case of a sinner who repents of his sins, but makes no effort to acquire holiness. Such an one proves the impossibility of being neutral. He flees from Satan without seeking Christ, and thus falls more hopelessly into the power of Satan again.

24. τοῦ ἀνθρώπου. "The man" who had been afflicted by it.

δι' ἀνύδρων τόπων. "Through *waterless* places" (Tyn. RV.). The wilderness is the reputed house of evil spirits; Tobit viii. 3, where Vulg. has *Angelus apprehendit dæmonium, et religavit illud in deserto superioris Aegypti.* Comp. Bar. iv. 35; Lev. xvi. 10; Is. xiii. 21; Rev. xviii. 2.[1] Martensen, *Chr. Dogm.* § 103.

ἀνάπαυσιν. "Cessation" from wandering (Gen. viii. 9): the demon seeks a soul to rest in. In LXX ἀνάπαυσις is common of the sabbath-rest: Exod. xvi. 23, xxiii. 12; Lev. xxiii. 3, etc. The punctuation is here uncertain. We may put no comma after ἀνάπαυσιν and make μὴ εὑρίσκον co-ordinate with ζητοῦν: "seeking rest and finding none." This necessitates a full stop at εὑρίσκον and the admission of τότε before λέγει as genuine. But τότε (ℵ^c B L Ξ) is probably an insertion from Mt. xii. 44 (om. A C D R, Vulg. Aeth. Arm.); and, if it be omitted, we must place a comma after ἀνάπαυσιν and take μὴ εὑρίσκον with λέγει. This is to be preferred.

μὴ εὑρίσκον [τότε] λέγει. "Because he doth not find it [then] he saith."

εἰς τὸν οἶκόν μου ὅθεν ἐξῆλθον. He still calls it "my house." No one else has taken it, and he was not driven out of it; he "went out." No mention is made of exorcism or expulsion.

25. [σχολάζοντα]. This also may be an insertion fr. Mt., but the evidence is stronger than for τότε (ℵ^c B C L R Γ Ξ, Aeth. f l r). Tisch. omits; WH. bracket the word. If it is genuine, it is placed first as the main evil. It is "standing idle," not occupied

[1] See Gregory Nazianzen's interpretation of "waterless places" as the unbaptized; "dry of the divine stream" (*Oration on Holy Baptism*, xxxv.; *Post-Nicene Library*, vii. p. 373). For the application of the parallel to the Jews, the Christian Church, and individuals, see Alford on Mt. xii. 44.

by any new tenant. The Holy Spirit has not been made a guest in place of the evil spirit.

σεσαρωμένον καὶ κεκοσμημένον. Ready to attract any passer-by, however undesirable. The three participles form a climax, and perhaps refer to the physical and mental improvement in the man. There is much for the demon to ruin once more, but there is no protection against his return. He brings companions to share the enjoyment of this new work of destruction, and to make it complete and final.

The verb σαρόω (σάρον = "a broom") is a later form of σαίρω, and occurs again xv. 8. For κεκοσμημένον comp. Rev. xxi. 2.

26. παραλαμβάνει. Comp. ix. 10, 28, xviii. 31; Acts xv. 39. Here again we have a climax. He brings additional spirits, more evil than himself, seven in number. Comp. the seven that went out from Mary of Magdala (viii. 2). Here in the best texts ἑπτά comes last, in Mt. first. In either case the word is emphatic. See Paschasius Radbertus on Mt. xii. 43, Migne, cxx. 478.

εἰσελθόντα κατοικεῖ. There is nothing to oppose them; "they enter in and settle there," taking up a *permanent* abode: xiii. 4; Acts i. 19, 20, ii. 9, 14, iv. 16, etc. The verb is freq. in bibl. Grk., esp. in Acts and Apocalypse. In the Catholic and Pauline Epp. it is used of the Divine indwelling (Jas. iv. 5; 2 Pet. iii. 13; Eph. iii. 17; Col. i. 19, ii. 9). Contrast παροικεῖν of a temporary sojourn (xxiv. 18; Heb. xi. 9; Gen. xxi. 23). In Gen. xxxvii. 1 both verbs occur.

χείρονα τῶν πρώτων. The expression is proverbial; Mt. xxvii. 64. Comp. 2 Pet. ii. 20; Heb. x. 29; Jn. v. 14. Lk. omits the words which show the primary application of the parable: Οὕτως ἔσται καὶ τῇ γενεᾷ ταύτῃ τῇ πονηρᾷ. The worship of idols had been exorcized, but that demon had returned as the worship of the letter, and with it the demons of covetousness, hypocrisy, spiritual pride, uncharitableness, faithlessness, formalism, and fanaticism.

27, 28. These two verses are peculiar to Lk., and illustrate his Gospel in its special character as the Gospel of Women. Christ's Mother is once more declared by a woman to be blessed (i. 42), and Mary's prophecy about herself begins to be fulfilled (i. 48). The originality of Christ's reply guarantees its historical character. Such a comment is beyond the reach of an inventor.

27. ταῦτα. Apparently this refers to the parable about the demons. Perhaps the woman, who doubtless was a mother, had had experience of a lapsed penitent in her own family. *Bene sentit, sed muliebriter loquitur* (Beng.). For a collection of similar sayings see Wetst.

ἐπάρασα φωνήν. The expression is classical (Dem. *De Cor.* § 369, p. 323: comp. *vocem tollit*, Hor. *A. P.* 93); in N.T. it is peculiar to Lk. (Acts

ii. 14, xiv. 11, xxii. 22). But it is not rare in LXX (Judg. ii. 4, ix. 7; Ruth i. 9, 14; 2 Sam. xiii. 36).

Μακαρία ἡ κοιλία. Mt. xii. 46 tells us that it was at this moment that His Mother and His brethren were announced. The sight of them may have suggested this woman's exclamation. Lk. records their arrival earlier (viii. 19–21), but he gives no connecting link. Edersheim quotes a Rabbinical passage, in which Israel is represented as breaking forth into these words on beholding the Messiah: "Blessed the hour in which the Messiah was created; blessed the womb whence He issued; blessed the generation that sees Him; blessed the eye that is worthy to behold Him" (*L. & T.* ii. p. 201). For κοιλία = "womb" comp. i. 15, 41, 42, 44, ii. 21, xxiii. 29; Acts iii. 2, xiv. 8.

28. Μενοῦν. This compound particle sometimes confirms what is stated, "yea, verily"; sometimes adds to what is said, with or without confirming it, but virtually correcting it: "yea rather," or "that may be true, but." Here Jesus does not deny the woman's statement, but He points out how inadequate it is. She has missed the main point. To be the Mother of Jesus implies no more than a share in His humanity. To hear and keep the word of God implies communion with what is Divine. The saying is similar to viii. 21. The relationship with Christ which brings blessedness is the spiritual one. For **τὸν λόγον τοῦ Θεοῦ** see on viii. 11.

Here and Phil. iii. 8 some authorities have *μενοῦνγε* (Rom. ix. 20, x. 18); but in N.T. *μὲν οὖν* is more common (Acts i. 18, v. 41, xiii. 4, xvii. 30, xxiii. 22, xxvi. 9). In class Grk. neither form ever comes first in a sentence. Of the Lat. text Wordsworth says, *Codices hic tantum variant quantum vix alibi in evangeliis in uno saltem vocabulo* (Vulg. p. 388). Among the renderings are *quippe enim*, *quippini*, *quinimmo*, *immo*, *manifestissime*, *etiam*. Many omit the word. See Blass, *Gr.* p. 264.

καὶ φυλάσσοντες. Comp. Jas. i. 22–25. S. James may have been present and heard this reply. *He* also says *μακάριος* is the man who hears and does *τὸν λόγον*.

29–36. The Rebuke to those who Demanded a Sign (ver. 16). A longer account of the first half of the rebuke is given Mt. xii. 39–42.

29. Τῶν δὲ ὄχλων ἐπαθροιζομένων. Lk. once more notes how the multitude was attracted by Christ's words and works: comp. ver. 27, iv. 42, v. 1, vi. 17, vii. 11, viii. 4, 19, 40, ix. 11, 37, xii. 1, 54, xiv. 25, xv. 1, xviii. 36, xix. 37, 48. The verb is a rare compound; here only in bibl. Grk. For **ἤρξατο λέγειν** see on iv 21 and iii. 8. To **πονηρά** Mt. adds *καὶ μοιχαλίς*.

εἰ μὴ τὸ σημεῖον Ἰωνᾶ. At first sight Lk. appears to make the parallel between Jonah and Christ to consist solely in their preaching repentance. He omits the explanation that Jonah was a type of the burial and resurrection of Christ. But *δοθήσεται* and *ἔσται* show that this explanation is implied. Christ had for long been preaching; yet He says, not that the sign has been given or is being given, but that it *shall* be given. The infallible sign is still in the future, viz. His resurrection. Nevertheless, even that ought not to be necessary; for His teaching ought to have sufficed. Note the emphatic repetition of *σημεῖον* thrice in one verse.[1]

Some have interpreted *σημεῖον οὐ δοθήσεται* as meaning, either that Jesus wrought no miracles, or that He refused to use them as credentials of His Divine mission. It is sufficient to point to ver. 20, where Jesus appeals to His healing of a dumb and blind demoniac as proof that He is bringing the kingdom of God to them. The demand for a sign and the refusal to give it are no evidence as to Christ's working miracles and employing them as credentials. What was demanded was something quite different from wonders such as Prophets and (as the Jews believed) magicians had wrought. These scribes and Pharisees wanted direct testimony from God Himself respecting Jesus and His mission, such as a voice from heaven or a pillar of fire. His miracles left them still able to doubt, and they ask to be miraculously convinced. This He refuses. See Neander, *L. J. C.* § 92, Eng. tr. p. 144.

31. βασίλισσα νότου. Lk. inserts this illustration between the two sayings about Jonah. Mt. keeps the two sayings about Jonah together. Lk. places the Ninevites after the Queen of Sheba either for chronology, or for effect, or both: their case was the stronger of the two. There is a threefold contrast in this illustration: (1) between a heathen queen and the Jews; (2) between the ends of the earth and here; (3) between Solomon and the Son of Man. There may possibly be a fourth contrast between that enterprising *woman* and the *men* of this generation implied in **τῶν ἀνδρῶν**, which is not in Mt.

νότου . . . ἐκ τῶν περάτων τῆς γῆς. Sheba was in the southern part of Arabia, the modern Yemen, near the southern limits of the world as then known. Comp. Ps. ii. 8.

πλεῖον Σολομῶνος. There is no need to understand *σημεῖον*: "a greater thing, something greater, than Solomon."

32. ἄνδρες Νινευεῖται. No article: "Men of Nineveh." RV. retains "*The* men of Nineveh."

εἰς τὸ κήρυγμα. "*In accordance with* the preaching" they repented; *i.e.* they turned towards it and *conformed to* it; comp. *ἐζωγρημένοι ὑπ' αὐτοῦ εἰς τὸ ἐκείνου θέλημα* (2 Tim. ii. 26); or else, "*out of regard to* it" they repented; comp. *οἵτινες ἐλάβετε τὸν*

[1] Sanday inclines to the view that Mt. xii. 40 "is a gloss which formed no part of the original saying, but was introduced, very naturally though erroneously, by the author of our present Gospel" (*Bampton Lectures*, 1893, p. 433). On the question whether Christ's appeal to Jonah requires us to believe that the story of the whale is historical see Sanday's *Bampton Lectures*, pp. 414-419; Gore's *Bampton Lectures*, 1891, pp. 195-200; with the literature there quoted.

νόμον εἰς διαταγὰς ἀγγέλων (Acts vii. 53); ὁ δεχόμενος δίκαιον εἰς ὄνομα δικαίου (Mt. x. 41). See on x. 13; and for κήρυγμα, as meaning the subject rather than the manner of preaching, see Lft. *Notes on Epp.* p. 161.

33–36. The Light of the inner Eye. There is no break in the discourse, and this should hardly be printed as a separate section: the connexion with what goes before is close. Christ is still continuing His reply to those who had demanded a sign. Those whose spiritual sight has not been darkened by indifference and impenitence have no need of a sign from heaven. Their whole soul is full of the light which is all around them, ready to be recognized and absorbed. This saying appears to have been part of Christ's habitual teaching. Lk. gives it in a rather different form after the parable of the Sower (viii. 16–18). Mt. has it as part of the Sermon on the Mount (v. 15, vi. 22, 23), but does not repeat it here. Mk. has a portion of it after the parable of the Sower (iv. 21). See S. Cox in the *Expositor*, 2nd series, i. p. 252.

33. λύχνον ἅψας. See on viii. 16.—**εἰς κρύπτην.** "Into a vault, crypt, cellar." But no ancient Version seems to give this rendering, although Euthym. has τὴν ἀπόκρυφον οἰκίαν. Win. xxxiv. 3. b, p. 298. For the word comp. Jos. *B. J.* v. 7. 4; Athen. v. (iv.) 205 A; and the Lat. *crypta*; Suet. *Cal.* lviii.; Juv. v. 106.

ὑπὸ τὸν μόδιον. "Under *the* bushel," *i.e.* the one in the room, or in the house; as we say "*the* sofa, *the* shovel." In capacity a *modius* is about a peck = 16 *sextarii* or $\frac{1}{6}$ μέδιμνος (comp. Nep. *Att.* ii.): elsewhere only Mt. v. 15; Mk. iv. 21. Syr-Sin. omits.

34. ὁ λύχνος τοῦ σώματος. "The *lamp* of the body." To translate λύχνος "candle" in ver. 33 and "light" in ver. 34 (Tyn. Cov. Cran. Gen. AV.) is disastrous. Vulg. has *lucerna* in both; Wic. has "lanterne" in both, and Rhem. "candel" in both; RV. still better, "lamp" in both. *D.C.G.* art. "Light."

ὅταν . . . ἐπάν. See on ver. 22. Here both are followed by the pres. subj., and there is no appreciable difference.

ἁπλοῦς. "Free from distortion, normal, sound."—**πονηρός.** "Diseased": πονηρία ὀφθαλμῶν occurs Plat. *Hip. min.* 374 D. Comp. πονηρὰ ἕξις σώματος (Plat. *Tim.* 86 D) and the common phrase πονηρῶς ἔχει. Faith, when diseased, becomes the darkness of superstition; just as the eye, when diseased, distorts and obscures. Comp. Mt. vi. 22, 23.

35. σκόπει οὖν. Here, and not in the middle of ver. 34, the meaning passes from the eye of the body to the eye of the soul.[1]

μὴ τὸ φῶς τὸ ἐν σοὶ σκότος ἐστίν. This happens when the eye of the soul is so diseased that it cannot receive any ray of Divine

[1] Comp. Seneca, *Effugisse tenebras, bono lucis frui, non tenui visu clara prospicere, sed totum diem admittere.*

truth. The μή is interrogative, and the indicative after it suggests that the case contemplated is an actual fact: "look whether it be not darkness"; *considera num*, *schaue ob wohl nicht*. The *vide ne* of Vulg. is not exact. Comp. Gal. iv. 11; Thuc. iii. 53. 2. Win. lvi. 2. a, p. 631; Simcox, *Lang. of N.T.* p. 109.

36. The tautology is only apparent. In the protasis the emphasis is on ὅλον, which is further explained by μὴ ἔχον μέρος τι σκοτινόν: in the apodosis the emphasis is on φωτινόν, which is further explained by ὡς ὅταν ὁ λύχνος, κ.τ.λ. "If thy *whole* body . . . it shall be wholly *full of light*." Complete illumination is illumination indeed, and those who possess it have no need of a sign from heaven in order to recognize the truth. Syr-Sin. condenses.

37–54. § The Invitation from a Pharisee. Christ's Denunciation of Pharisaic Formalism and Hypocrisy. A similar condemnation of the Pharisees is placed by Mt. somewhat later, and is given with great fulness (xxiii.). If these sayings were uttered only once, we have not much material for determining which arrangement is more in accordance with fact. See on ver. 54.

37. Ἐν δὲ τῷ λαλῆσαι. "Now after He had spoken" (aor.), rather than "As He spake" (AV. RV.). See on iii. 21. There is nothing to show that the invitation was the result of what Christ had just been saying. Indeed, there may have been a considerable interval between *vv.* 36 and 37. Syr-Sin. omits.

ὅπως ἀριστήσῃ. Here, as in Jn. xxi. 12, 15, the early meal of breakfast or lunch is meant rather than dinner or supper: comp. xiv. 12; Mt. xxii. 4. At this time the first meal of all was called ἀκράτισμα. Becker, *Charicles*, vi. excurs. i., Eng. tr. p. 240.

38. ἐθαύμασεν. We are not told that he expressed his surprise. Jesus read his thoughts and answered them. Jesus had just come from contact with the multitude, and, moreover, He had been casting out a demon; and the Pharisee took for granted that He would purify Himself from any possible pollution before coming to table. This was not enjoined by the Law but by tradition, which the Pharisees tried to make binding upon all (Mk. vii. 3). This man's wonder is evidence that his invitation was not a plot to obtain evidence against Jesus: he was not expecting any transgression.

ἐβαπτίσθη. This need not be taken literally of bathing. Probably no more than washing the hands is meant; and this often took place at table, the servants bringing water to each person. Edersh. *L. & T.* ii. pp. 204–207. We may understand Christ's omission to wash before coming to table, or refusal of the water offered to Him at table, as a protest against the attempt to "bind burdens" upon men, and to substitute trivialities for the weightier matters of the Law. Comp. Derenbourg, *Hist. de. la Pal.* p. 134.

39. εἶπεν δὲ ὁ Κύριος. The use of ὁ Κύριος here (see on v. 17

and vii. 13) perhaps has special point. The Pharisee might regard Him as an ordinary guest; but He has a message to deliver to him.

Νῦν. The meaning is not certain; but it probably refers to time, and is not merely concessive. "It was not so formerly, but this is the fact now." Comp. 2 Cor. vii. 9 and Col. i. 24, where see Lft. Or, "Here we have a case in point." Comp. 2 Kings vii. 6. Or, "This is what you as a matter of fact do," in contrast to what you ought to do—πλὴν τὰ ἐνόντα δότε. With the whole saying comp. Mt xxiii. 25. For **πίνακος** Mt. has *παροψίδος*: comp. Mk. vi. 25; Mt. xiv. 8.

τὸ δὲ ἔσωθεν ὑμῶν. Here the outside of the cup and platter is contrasted with the hearts of the Pharisees. In Mt. the point is that the outside of the vessels is kept clean, while the meat and drink in them are the proceeds of rapacity and the means of excess (ἀκρασίας). Comp. ἐν ποικιλίᾳ ἁμαρτιῶν καὶ ἀκρασίαις (*Ps. Sol.* iv. 3): *amantes convivia devoratores gulæ* (*Assump. Moys* vii. 4). Here some make τὸ ἔσωθεν mean the inside of the vessels, and take ὑμῶν with ἁρπαγῆς κ. πονηρίας. But the position of ὑμῶν is conclusive against this. Others make τὸ ἔσωθεν ὑμῶν mean "your inward parts" in the literal sense. "You can keep the vessels from polluting the food; but that will not prevent the food, which is already polluted by the way in which it was obtained, from filling you with uncleanness." But this is not probable. For Jewish trifling about clean and unclean vessels see Schoettg. and Wetst. on Mt. xxiii. 25, 26; and for the moral sterility of such teaching, Pressensé, *Le Siècle Apostolique*, p. 90.

40. ἄφρονες. A strong word: quite classical, but in N.T. almost confined to Lk (xii. 20) and Paul (Rom. ii. 20; 1 Cor. xv. 36; 2 Cor. xi. 16, 19, xii. 6, 11; Eph. v. 17. See on xxiv. 25).

οὐχ ὁ ποιήσας τὸ ἔξωθεν. This is almost certainly a question. "Not he who has done the outside has thereby done the inside," makes sense, but it is harsh and hardly adequate. It is better with most Versions to make οὐκ = *nonne*. "Did not God, who made the material universe, make men's souls also?"[1] It is folly to be scrupulous about keeping material objects clean, while the soul is polluted with wickedness.[2]

41. πλὴν τὰ ἐνόντα δότε ἐλεημοσύνην. The **πλήν** is here expans-

[1] We may get the same sense from the text of C D Γ and some cursives, which transpose ἔξωθεν and ἔσωθεν. So also from some Latin texts: *nonne qui fecit interiora et exteriora fecit* (a), *qui fecit quod intus est et quod foris est* (c e)

[2] *Ergo miser trepidas, ne stercore fœda canino*
Atria displiceant oculis venientis amici,
Ne perfusa luto sit porticus: et tamen uno
Semodio scobis hæc emundat servulus unus.
Illud non agitas, ut sanctam filius omni
Adspiciat sine labe domum vitioque carentem (Juv. xiv. 64).

ive and progressive, "only." See on vi. 24. The meaning of τὰ ἐνόντα is much disputed, and the renderings vary greatly: *quæ sunt* (b d g); *ex his quæ habetis* (f); *quod superest* (Vulg.); *ea quæ penes vos sunt* (Beza); *quantum potestis* (Grot.); *von dem, das da ist* (Luth.). *Quod superest* is impossible; and the others are not very probable. Nor is it satisfactory to follow Erasmus, Schleiermacher, and others, and make the saying ironical: "Give something to the poor out of your luxuries, and then (as you fancy) all your ἁρπαγή and πονηρία will be condoned." According to this τὰ ἐνόντα means either what is in the cups and platters, or what is in your purses. And this is perhaps right, but without irony. "The contents of your cup and platter give ye in alms, and, lo, all things are clean to you," *i.e.* benevolence is a better way of keeping meals free from defilement than scrupulous cleansing of vessels. We are told that this is "a peculiarly Ebionitic touch." But it is very good Christianity. Others make τὰ ἐνόντα = τὸ ἔσωθεν: "As for that which is within you, as for the care of your souls, give alms." See *Expositor*, 2nd series, v. p. 318. Or, "Give your souls as alms," *i.e.* give not merely food or money, but your heart. Comp. δῷς πεινῶντι τὸν ἄρτον ἐκ ψυχῆς σου (Is. lviii. 10). In any case, πάντα refers specially to the vessels used at meals. *They* will not defile where benevolence prevails. With the passage as a whole comp. Mk. vii. 18, 19 and the Baptist's commands (Lk. iii. 11).

42. ἀλλὰ οὐαὶ ὑμῖν. "But, far from acting thus and obtaining this blessing, a curse is upon you." Rue is mentioned in the Talmud as a herb for which no tithe need be paid.

παρέρχεσθε. "Ye pass by, neglect": comp. xv. 29; Deut. xvii. 2; Jer. xxxiv. 18; Judith xi. 10; 1 Mac. ii. 22. Elsewhere in N.T. it means "pass by" literally (xviii. 37; Acts xvi. 8), or "pass away, perish" (xvi. 17, xxi. 32, 33, etc.). Here Mt. has ἀφήκατε.

τὴν κρίσιν. "The distinction between right and wrong, rectitude, justice." This use of κρίσις is Hebraistic; comp. Gen. xviii. 19, 25; Is. v. 7, lvi. 1, lix. 8; Jer. xvii. 11; 1 Mac. vii. 18.

τὴν ἀγάπην τοῦ Θεοῦ. Here only does Lk. use the word ἀγάπη, which occurs once in Mt. (xxiv. 12), and not at all in Mk. It is fairly common in LXX, esp. in Cant. (ii. 4, 5, 7, etc.).

κἀκεῖνα μὴ παρεῖναι. Their carefulness about trifles is not condemned, but sanctioned. It is the neglect of essentials which is denounced as fatal. It is not correct to say that Christ abolished the ceremonial part of the Law while retaining the moral part: see Hort, *Judaistic Christianity*, pp. 30, 31.

43. ἀγαπᾶτε τὴν πρωτοκαθεδρίαν. "Ye highly value (Jn. xii. 43) the first seat." This was a semicircular bench round the ark, and facing the congregation. Edersh. *L. & T.* i. p. 436. Comp. xx. 46; Mt. xxiii. 6; Mk. xii. 39.

Some Latin texts agree with C D in adding to this verse *et primos discubitos in conviviis* (b l q r), or *et primos adcubitos in cenis* (d).

44. ἐστὲ ὡς τὰ μνημεῖα τὰ ἄδηλα. "Whosoever in the open field toucheth a grave shall be unclean seven days" (Num. xix. 16). Hence the Jews were accustomed to whitewash such graves to make them conspicuous. People mixed freely with Pharisees, believing them to be good men, and unconsciously became infected with their vices, just as they sometimes walked over a hidden grave and were polluted without knowing it. In Mt. xxiii. 27 the Pharisees are compared to the *whitewashed* graves, which look clean and are inwardly foul.

45. τῶν νομικῶν. See on vii. 30. Not all the Pharisees were professional students (νομικοί), or teachers of the Law (νομοδιδάσκαλοι).

καὶ ἡμᾶς ὑβρίζεις. "Thou insultest even us," the better instructed among the Pharisees. The verb implies outrageous treatment (xviii. 32; Acts xiv. 5; Mt. xxii. 6; 1 Thes. ii. 2), and "reproachest" is hardly strong enough. Comp. ἐνυβρίζειν (Heb. x. 29). In class. Gk. ὑβρίζειν is commonly followed by εἰς, esp. in prose. "Reproach" would be ὀνειδίζειν (Mt. xi. 20).

46. There is a triplet of Woes against the lawyers (*vv.* 46, 47, 52), as against the Pharisees (42, 43, 44). With this first Woe comp. Mt. xxiii. 4. In both passages φορτίον occurs; and, as distinct from βάρος and ὄγκος, it means that which a man is *expected* to bear (Mt. xi. 30). But Lk. shows his fondness for cognate words by writing φορτίζετε φορτία, while Mt. has δεσμεύουσιν φορτία. See on xxiii. 46, and comp. Gal. vi. 2.

δυσβάστακτα. Prov. xxvii. 3. The word probably occurs here only in N.T., and has been inserted Mt. xxiii. 4 from here. The reference is to the intolerably burdensome interpretations by which the scribes augmented the written Law. They made it far more severe than it was intended to be, explaining every doubtful point in favour of rigorous ritualism.

οὐ προσψαύετε. Touching with a view to *removing* seems to be meant; but it may indicate that, while they were rigorous to others, they were evasive themselves. They were scrupulous about their own traditions, but they did not keep the Law. It is not admissible, however, to interpret τοῖς φορτίοις in a different way from φορτία δυσβάστακτα, making the latter refer to traditions, and τοῖς φορτίοις to the Law. Both mean the same, the force of the article being "the φορτία just mentioned." Seeing that the νομικοί were not neglectful of traditions, τοῖς φορτιοις must mean the Law; and therefore φορτία δυσβάστακτα must have this meaning.

47. Comp. Mt. xxiii. 30; Acts. vii. 52.

οἰκοδομεῖτε τὰ μνημεῖα τῶν προφητῶν οἱ δὲ πατέρες ὑμῶν. "Ye build the tombs of the prophets, *while* your fathers." The "Tombs of the Prophets," near the top of the Mount of Olives, are still "an enigma to travellers and antiquarians." All that can safely be asserted is that they are not the "tombs of the prophets" mentioned here. Robinson, *Res. in Pal.* iii. p. 254.

48. μάρτυρές ἐστε καὶ συνευδοκεῖτε. "Ye are witnesses and consent to"; or, "Ye bear favourable witness to and approve": not, "Ye bear witness *that* ye approve."[1] Mt. has *μαρτυρεῖτε* only (xxiii. 31), which some texts introduce here (A C D). Comp. Saul, who was *συνευδοκῶν* to the murder of Stephen (Acts viii. 1). The ἄρα as first word is not classical: comp. Acts xi. 18.

τῶν πατέρων ὑμῶν. "Your fathers, morally as well as actually; for you carry on and complete their evil deeds." Externally the Pharisees seemed to honour the Prophets. Really they were dishonouring them as much as those did who slew them; for they neglected the duties which the Prophets enjoined, and ignored their testimony to Christ.

49. διὰ τοῦτο καί. "Because of your complicity with your fathers' murderous deeds, there is this confirmation of the Woe just pronounced." Comp. Mt. xxiii. 34.

ἡ σοφία τοῦ Θεοῦ εἶπεν Ἀποστελῶ. The words which are here ascribed to the "Wisdom of God" are in Mt. xxiii. 34 Christ's own words, spoken on a later occasion. It is improbable that Christ is here quoting what He said on some previous occasion. Nowhere does He style Himself "the Wisdom of God"; nor does any Evangelist give Him this title; nor does *Θεοῦ σοφίαν* or *σοφία ἀπὸ Θεοῦ* (1 Cor. i. 24, 30) warrant us in asserting that this was a common designation of Christ among the first Christians, so that tradition might have substituted this name for the *ἐγώ* used by Jesus. That He is quoting from a lost book called "The Wisdom of God" is still less probable.[2] Written words would be introduced with *λέγει* rather than *εἶπεν*, and the context seems to imply some Divine utterance. In the O.T. no such words are found; for Prov. i. 20–31; 2 Chron. xxiv. 20–22, xxxvi. 14–21 are quite inadequate. And we obtain nothing tangible when we make the passage "a general paraphrase of the *tenor* of several O.T. passages." Rather it is of the Divine Providence (Prov. viii. 22–31), sending Prophets to the Jewish Church and Apostles to the Christian Church, that Jesus here speaks: "God in His wisdom said." Comp. vii. 35. Jesus here speaks with confident knowledge of the Divine counsels: comp. x. 22, xv. 7, 10.

[1] Vulg. has *testificamini quod consentitis*, and a few cursives read *ὅτι συνευδοκεῖτε*. Lat. texts vary greatly: *quia consentitis* (r), *et consentitis* (CT), *consentitis* (E), *consentire* (cil), *consentientes* (f), *non consentientes* (abq), *non consentire* (d) following *μὴ συνευδοκεῖν* (D).

[2] See Ryle, *Canon of O.T.* p. 155; and for apparent quotations from Scripture which cannot be found in Scripture comp. Jn. vii. 38; 1 Cor. ii. 9; Eph. v. 14.

ἀποστόλους. Mt. has *σοφοὺς καὶ γραμματεῖς*, and mentions crucifixion and scourging along with death and persecution. By coupling the persecuted Apostles with the persecuted Prophets, Jesus once more indicates the solidarity of the Pharisees with their wicked forefathers: comp. Mt. v. 12. For **ἐξ αὐτῶν** (*τινας*) comp. Jn. xvi. 17; 2 Jn. 4; Rev. ii. 10. For **διώξουσιν** (א B C L X) in the sense of "persecute" comp. xxi. 12; Acts vii. 52, ix. 4, xxii. 4, 7, etc.

50. ἵνα ἐκζητηθῇ τὸ αἷμα. This is the Divinely ordered sequence. The verb is almost unknown in profane writings; and nowherse else in N.T. is it used of "demanding *back*, requiring as a *debt*." Comp. 2 Sam. iv. 11; Ezek. iii. 18, 20, xxxiii. 6, 8; Gen. ix. 5, xlii. 22.

τὸ ἐκκεχυμένον ἀπὸ καταβολῆς κόσμου. Comp. Mt. xxv. 34; Heb. iv. 3, ix. 26; Rev. xiii. 8, xvii. 8. The expression *καταβολὴ κόσμου* does not occur in LXX. Comp. *ἀπ' ἀρχῆς* (Ps. lxxviii. 2).

ἐκκεχυμένον. This is the reading of B and a few cursives; but almost all other authorities have *ἐκχυννόμενον*, which may easily have come from Mt. The grammarians condemn *ἐκχύνω* or *ἐκχύννω* (Aeolic) as a collateral form of *ἐκχέω*. It is used of bloodshed Acts xxii. 20, and the pres. part., if genuine here, is very expressive: "the blood which is perpetually being shed."

ἀπὸ τῆς γενεᾶς ταύτης. To be taken after *ἐκζητηθῇ*. The reference is specially to the destruction of Jerusalem (xxi. 32).

51. The murders of Abel and Zacharias are the first and last murders in the O.T., which in the Jewish Canon ends with Chronicles. In both cases the *ἐκζήτησις* is indicated: "The voice of the brother's blood crieth unto me from the ground" (Gen. iv. 10); "The Lord look upon it, and require it" (2 Chron. xxiv. 22). *Chronologically* the murder of Uriah by Jehoiakim (Jer. xxvi. 23) is later than that of Zachariah the son of Jehoiada. Zachariah *the son of Barachiah* was the Prophet, and there is no mention of his having been murdered: in Mt. xxiii. 35 "the son of Barachiah" is probably a mechanical slip. For **τοῦ οἴκου** Mt. has *τοῦ ναοῦ*, and the *ναός* is evidently the *οἶκος* meant here.

ναί, λέγω ὑμῖν. Comp. vii. 26, xii. 5. Not elsewhere in N.T.

52. τὴν κλεῖδα τῆς γνώσεως. "The key which opens the door to knowledge," not "which is knowledge": the gen. is not one of apposition. There is no reference to a supposed ceremony by which a "doctor of the law" was "symbolically admitted to his office by the delivery of a key." No such ceremony appears to have existed. The knowledge is that of the way of salvation, which can be obtained from Scripture. But the scribes had cut off all access to this knowledge, first, by their false interpretations; and, secondly, by their contempt for the people, whom they considered to be unworthy of instruction or incapable of enlightenment. Their false interpretations were fatal to themselves (*αὐτοὶ οὐκ* εἰσήλθατε) as well as to others. See Hort, *Judaistic Christianity* p. 141; *Recog. Clem.* i. 54, ii. 30, 46. Excepting in the Apocalypse (i. 18, iii. 7, ix. 1, xx. 1), κλείς occurs only Matt. xvi. 19. The reading ἐκρύψατε (D and some Versions) for ἤρατε is an interpretative gloss. Note that here Lk. has νομικοί where Mt. (xxiii. 14) has γραμματεῖς, and comp. xii. 44.

τοὺς εἰσερχομένους. "Those who were continually trying to enter" (imperf. part.). The aorists indicate what was done once for all and absolutely.

53. Κἀκεῖθεν ἐξελθόντος αὐτοῦ. In their vehemence they followed Him out of the Pharisee's house. But it by no means follows from what they did in their excitement that "the Pharisee's feast had been a base plot to entrap Jesus."

The text of this verse exhibits an extraordinary number of variations. The above is the reading of ℵ B C L 33, Boh. For it A D X, Latt. Syr-Cur. substitute Λέγοντος δὲ αὐτοῦ ταῦτα πρὸς αὐτούς or πρὸς τὸν λαόν: and to this D X Latt. Syr-Cur. add ἐνώπιον παντὸς τοῦ λαοῦ or τοῦ ὄχλου. For οἱ γραμματεῖς κ. οἱ Φαρ. D and various Lat. texts give οἱ Φαρ. κ. οἱ νομικοί, *legis periti* (Vulg. c d e f). For δεινῶς ἐνέχειν C has δεινῶς ἐπέχειν, H δ. συνέχειν, and D S with various Lat. texts δ. ἔχειν: *male habere* (b d q), *male se habere* (a), *graviter habere* (c e i), *graviter ferre* (l), and *moleste ferre* (r), representing δ. ἔχειν, while *graviter insistere* (Vulg.) is Jerome's correction to represent δ. ἐνέχειν. Again, for ἀποστοματίζειν αὐτόν D and most Lat. texts substitute συνβάλλειν αὐτῷ: *comminare illi* (a), *committere cum illo* (b i l q r), *committere illi* (d), *conferre cum eo* (c), *conferre illi* (e), *altercari cum illo* (f) representing συμβάλλειν αὐτῷ, while *os ejus opprimere* (Vulg.) represents ἐπιστομίζειν. Not one represents ἀποστοματίζειν.

ἐνέχειν. In Mk. vi. 19 and Gen. xlix. 23 (the only place in which the act. occurs in LXX) this verb is followed by a dat. It may be doubted whether χόλον, which is expressed Hdt. i. 118. 1, vi. 119. 2, viii. 27. 1, is here to be understood. If anything is to be understood, τὸν νοῦν is more probable, as in the analogous cases of ἐπέχειν (which C here reads) and προσέχειν. The meaning appears to be that they "watched Him intensely, were actively on the alert against Him"; which suits Gen. xlix. 23 (ἐνεῖχον αὐτῷ κύριοι τοξευμάτων) as well as the context here. But *external pressure* may be the meaning in both places, although in Mk. vi. 19 *internal feeling* suits the context better ("cherished a grudge against"). In the gloss of Hesychius, ἐνέχει· μνησικακεῖ, ἔγκειται (? ἐγκοτεῖ), it is possible that μνησικακεῖ refers to Mk. vi. 19 and ἔγκειται (or ἐγκοτεῖ) to Lk. xi. 53. See Field, *Otium Norvic.* iii. pp. 22, 45, and the note in Wordsworth's Vulgate.

ἀποστοματίζειν. Originally, "to dictate what is to be learned by heart and recited" (Plato, *Euthyd.* 276 C, 277 A); hence τὰ ἀποστοματιζόμενα, "the dictated lesson" (Arist. *Soph. El.* iv. 1). Thence it passed, either to the pupil's part, mere recitation, as of the Sibyl reciting verses (Plut. *Thes.* xxiv.); or to the teacher's part, the plying with questions "to provoke to answer," as here. See Wetst. *ad loc.*, and Hatch, *Bib. Grk.* p. 40.

54. Confusion in the text still continues; but the true reading is not doubtful. WH. give this as a good instance of conflation, the common reading being compounded of the original text and two early corruptions of it. Comp. ix. 10, xii. 18, xxiv. 53.

(α) ἐνεδρεύοντες αὐτὸν θηρεῦσαί τι ἐκ τοῦ στόματος αὐτοῦ. ℵ B L Boh. Aeth. Syr-Cur. (some omit αὐτόν).

(β) ζητοῦντες ἀφορμήν τινα λαβεῖν αὐτοῦ ἵνα εὕρωσιν κατηγορῆσαι αὐτοῦ D, d Syr-Sin.?

ζητοῦντες ἀφορμήν τινα λαβεῖν αὐτοῦ ἵνα κατηγορήσωσιν αὐτοῦ. Lat. Vet. (some omit αὐτοῦ).

(δ) ἐνεδρεύοντες αὐτόν, ζητοῦντες θηρεῦσαί τι ἐκ τοῦ στόματος αὐτοῦ, ἵνα κατηγορήσωσιν αὐτοῦ. A C E G H K M U V Γ Δ Λ Π, and with small variations X, all cursives, Vulg. etc. WH. ii. Introduction, p. 102.

ἐνεδρεύοντες. Elsewhere in N.T. only Acts xxiii. 21: comp. Deut. xix. 11; Prov. xxvi. 19; Wis. ii. 12; Ecclus. xxvii. 10, 28; Lam. iv. 19; Jos. *Ant.* v. 2. 12; in all which places it has, as here, the acc. instead of the usual dat.

θηρεῦσαι.[1] Here only in N.T. Comp. Ps. lviii. 4. Both this ord and ἐνεδρεύοντες are very graphic. Godet remarks that we have here *une scène de violence peut-être unique dans la vie de Jésus*: and *huic vehementiæ suberat fraudulentia* (Beng.). We infer from xii. 1 that now the disciples are present.

It is possible that in Mt. xxiii. what took place on this occasion is combined with what was said in the temple just before the Passion. Lk. gives only a very brief notice of the later denunciation (xx. 45–47; comp. Matt. xxiii. 1–7). But the fact that he gives two denunciations is against the theory that only one was uttered, which he assigns to one occasion and Mt. to another. It may, however, easily have happened that some of what was said on the first occasion has been transferred to the second, or *vice versâ*.

XII. The greater part of the utterances of Christ which Lk. records in this chapter are also recorded in different parts of Mt., for the most part either in the Sermon on the Mount (v.–vii.), or in the Charge to the Twelve (x. 5–42), or in the Prophecy of the Last Days (xxiv. 4–51). Here they are given in the main as a continuous discourse, but with marked breaks at *vv.* 13, 22, 54. Lk. evidently regards *vv.* 1–21 as spoken immediately after the commotion at the Pharisee's house; and there is little doubt that *vv.* 22–53 are assigned by him to the same occasion. How much break there is between *vv.* 53 and 54 is left undetermined. The fact that many of Christ's sayings were uttered more than

[1] Comp. Εἰπέ μοι, ὦ Σώκρατες, οὐκ αἰσχύνει, τηλικοῦτος ὤν, ὀνόματα θηρεύων καὶ ἐάν τις ῥήματι ἁμάρτῃ, ἕρμαιον τοῦτο ποιούμενος; (Plat. *Gorg.* 489 B).

once, and were differently arranged on different occasions, will partly explain the resemblances and differences between Lk. and Mt. here and elsewhere. But it is also probable that there has been some confusion in the traditions, and that words which one tradition placed in one connexion were by another tradition placed in another.

Lk. xii.	2–9 = Mt.	x. 26–33.	Lk. xii.	51–53 = Mt.	x. 34–36.
	22–32 =	vi. 25–34.		54–56 =	[xvi. 2, 3].
	33, 34 =	vi. 19–21.		57–59 =	v. 25, 26.
	39–46 =	xxiv. 43–51.			

1–12. Exhortation to Courageous Sincerity. This is closely connected with what precedes. The commotion inside and outside the Pharisee's house had attracted an immense crowd, which was divided in its sympathy, some siding with the Pharisees, others disposed to support Christ. His addressing His words to His disciples rather than to the multitude indicates that the latter were in the main not friendly. But the appeal made to Him by one of them (ver. 13) respecting a purely private matter shows that His authority is recognized by many. The man would not have asked Him to give a decision in the face of a wholly hostile assembly. But this warning to His followers of the necessity for courageous testimony to the truth in the face of bitter opposition implies present hostility. The connexion with the preceding scene is proved by the opening words, **Ἐν οἷς**, "In the midst of which, in the meantime."

1. τῶν μυριάδων τοῦ ὄχλου. Hyperbolical, as in Acts xxi. 20. The article points to what is usual; "the people in their myriads." Comp. *οὐ φοβηθήσομαι ἀπὸ μυριάδων λαοῦ τῶν κύκλῳ ἐπιτιθεμένων μοι* (Ps. iii. 7).

ἤρξατο λέγειν. The *ἤρξατο* gives a solemn emphasis to what follows: see on iv. 21, and comp. xiv. 18 and Acts ii. 4. It may possibly refer to *πρῶτον*; He began to address the disciples, and then turned to the people. The πρῶτον means that His words were addressed primarily to the disciples, although the people were meant to hear them. After the interruption He addresses the people directly (ver. 15). It makes poor sense to take *πρῶτον* with *προσέχετε*, "First of all beware" (Tyn. Cran. Gen.), for to beware of Pharisaic hypocrisy cannot be considered the first of all duties. For other amphibolous constructions see on ii. 22.

Προσέχετε ἑαυτοῖς ἀπό. "Take heed to yourselves and avoid; beware of." The warning phrase *προσέχετε ἑαυτοῖς* is peculiar to Lk. (xvii. 3, xxi. 34; Acts v. 35, xx. 28); but in LXX *πρόσεχε σεαυτῷ* is common (Gen. xxiv. 6; Exod. x. 28, xxxiv. 12; Deut. iv. 9, etc.). For the reflexive see on xxi. 30.

ἀπὸ τῆς ζύμης. This constr. is common after verbs of avoiding, ceasing from, guarding against, and the like; *παύω, κωλύω, φυλάσσομαι, κ.τ.λ.* Comp. *πρόσεχε σεαυτῷ ἀπὸ πάσης πορνείας* (Tobit iv. 12). The pronoun is often omitted, xx. 46; Mt. vii. 15, x. 17, xvi. 6, 11; Deut. iv. 23?.

This warning seems to have been given more than once (Mk. viii. 15). Leaven in Scripture is generally a type of *evil* which corrupts and spreads, disturbing, puffing up and souring that which it influences. The parable of the Leaven (xiii. 20, 21; Mt. xiii. 33) is almost the only exception. Ignatius (*Magnes.* x.) uses it in both a good and a bad sense. In profane literature its associations are commonly bad. The *Flamen Dialis* was not allowed to touch leaven or leaven bread (Aulus Gellius, x. 15): comp. Juv. iii. 188. The proverb *μικρὰ ζύμη ὅλον τὸ φύραμα ζυμοῖ*, is used of *pernicious* influence (1 Cor. v. 6; Gal. v. 9). Fermentation is corruption.

If *τῶν Φαρισαίων* is rightly placed last (B L), it is epexegetic. "Beware of the leaven which is hypocrisy,—I mean the Pharisees' leaven." In Mt. xvi. 12 "the leaven of the Pharisees and Sadducees" is interpreted as meaning their doctrine.

2. Οὐδὲν δὲ συγκεκαλυμμένον ἐστιν. "*But* there is nothing covered up, which shall not," etc. Hypocrisy is useless, for one day there will be a merciless exposure. It is not only wicked, but senseless.

3. ἀνθ' ὧν. This is commonly rendered "wherefore," like *ἀντὶ τούτου*, "for this cause" (Eph. v. 31). But in i. 20, xix. 44; Acts xii. 23 it = *ἀντὶ τούτων, ὅτι*; and it may have the same meaning here. "There is nothing hid, that shall not be known: *because* whatever ye have said in the darkness shall be heard in the light,"—*quoniam quæ in tenebris dixistis in lumine dicentur* (Vulg.). Christ is continuing to insist that hypocrisy is folly, for it is always unmasked at last. There was a saying of Hillel, "Think of nothing that it will not be easily heard, for in the end it must be heard." See small print on i. 20. It is in wording that this is parallel to Mt. x. 26, 27: the application is very different.

ἐν τοῖς ταμείοις . . . ἐπὶ τῶν δωμάτων. "Store chambers" are commonly "*inner* chambers, secret rooms," especially in the East, where outer walls are so easily dug through: comp. Mt. vi. 6, xxiv. 26; Gen. xliii. 30; Judg. xvi. 9; 1 Kings xxii. 25. To this day proclamations are often made from the housetops: comp. *ἐπὶ τῶν δωμάτων* (Is. xv. 3; Jer. xix. 13, xlviii. 38). See *D.B.*[2] i. p. 1407; Renan, *Les Évangiles*, p. 262 n.

The Latin Versions give a variety of renderings: *in cellariis* (i l r), *in promptalibus* (d), *in promptuariis* (e), *in cubilibus* (Vulg. (f); om. b q). Comp. ver. 24.

4. Λέγω δὲ ὑμῖν τοῖς φίλοις μου. "My friends are not likely to be hypocrites, although persecution will tempt them to become such": comp. Jn. xv. 15.

μὴ φοβηθῆτε ἀπὸ τῶν ἀποκτεινόντων. The use of ἀπό here is analogous to that in ver. 1, of that which one turns away from. It is Hebraistic (Lev. xix. 30, xxvi. 2; Deut. i. 29, iii. 22, xx. 1; Josh. xi. 6; 1 Sam. vii. 7; Jer. i. 8, 17; 1 Mac. ii. 62, viii. 12, etc.). It is not used of fearing God.

μετὰ ταῦτα. The plural may refer to the details of a cruel death, or to different kinds of death. Not in Mt. x. 28.

μὴ ἐχόντων. Lk. is fond of this classical use of ἔχειν: ver. 50, vii. 40, 42, xiv. 14; Acts iv. 14, xxiii. 17, 18, 19, xxv. 26, xxviii. 19 Here Mt. (x. 28) has *μὴ δυναμένων*.

5. φοβήθητε τὸν μετὰ τὸ ἀποκτεῖναι ἔχοντα ἐξουσίαν, κ.τ.λ. There is little doubt that this refers to God and not to the devil. The change of construction points to this. It is no longer *φοβήθητε ἀπὸ τούτου*, but *τοῦτον φοβήθητε*, "fear without trying to shun," which is the usual construction of fearing God. Moreover, we are not in Scripture told to fear Satan, but to resist him courageously (Jas. iv. 7; 1 Pet. v. 9); *τὸν θεὸν φοβήθητε, τῷ διαβόλῳ ἀντίστητε* is scriptural doctrine. Moreover, although the evil one tries to bring us to Gehenna, it is not he who has authority to send us thither. This passage (with Mt. x. 28), the king with twenty thousand (see on xiv. 33), and the Unjust Steward (see on xvi. 1), are perhaps the only passages in which the same words have been interpreted by some of Satan and by others of God.

ἐμβαλεῖν εἰς τὴν γέενναν. Excepting here and Jas. iii. 6, *γέεννα* occurs only in Mt. and Mk. in N.T. Not in LXX. The confusion caused in all English Versions prior to RV. by translating both *γέεννα* and *ᾅδης* "hell" has been often pointed out. Lft. *On Revision*, pp. 87, 88; Trench, *On the A V.* p. 21. Γέεννα is a transliteration of *Ge-Hinnom*, "Valley of Hinnom," where children were thrown into the red-hot arms of Molech. When these abominations were abolished by Josiah (2 Kings xxiii. 10), refuse of all kinds, including carcases of criminals, was thrown into this valley, and (according to late authorities) consumed by fire, which was ceaselessly burning. Hence it became a symbolical name for the place of punishment in the other world. *D.B.*[2] artt. "Gehenna," "Hinnom," and "Hell."

6. πέντε στρουθία . . . ἀσσαρίων δύο. Mt. has **δύο στρουθία ἀσσαρίου.** Both have **ἓν ἐξ αὐτῶν οὐ**, which is more expressive than *οὐδὲν ἐξ αὐτῶν*, throwing the emphasis on ἕν: "not even *one* of them," although five cost so little. Both *στρουθός* and *στρουθίον* commonly mean "sparrow," although sometimes used vaguely for "bird" or "fowl": *e.g.* Ps. xi. 1, lxxxiv. 4. The Heb. *tzippor*, which it often represents, is still more commonly generic, and was applied to any variety of small passerine birds, which are specially numerous in Palestine, and were all allowed as food. Tristram, *Nat. Hist. of B.* p. 201. It is unfortunate that ἀσσάριον and its fourth part κοδράντης (Mt. v. 26; Mk. xii. 42) should both be translated "farthing," while δηνάριον, which was ten to sixteen times as much as an ἀσσάριον, is translated "penny." "Shilling" for δηνάριον, "penny" for ἀσσάριον, and "farthing" for κοδράντης would give the ratios fairly correctly, although a shilling now will buy only a little of what a *denarius* would buy then.

ἐνώπιον τοῦ Θεοῦ. A Hebraism, very freq. in Lk. (i. 19, xvi. 15; Acts iv. 19, vii. 46: comp. Lk. i. 6, 15, 75; Acts viii. 21, x. 4). It implies that each bird is individually present to the mind of God. Belief in the minuteness of the Divine care was strong among the Jews: *Non est vel minima herbula in terra cui non præfectus sit aliquis in cœlo.*

7. ἀλλὰ καὶ αἱ τρίχες τῆς κεφαλῆς. "But (little as you might expect it) even the hairs of your head." Comp. xxi. 18; Acts xxvii. 34; 1 Sam. xiv. 45; 2 Sam. xiv. 11; 1 Kings i. 52; Dan. iii. 27.

μὴ φοβεῖσθε . . . διαφέρετε. "Cease to fear (pres. imper.) . . . ye are different from, *i.e.* are superior to": Mt. vi. 26, xii. 12; 1 Cor. xv. 41; Gal. iv. 1. This use of διαφέρω is classical.

8. Λέγω δὲ ὑμῖν. The "also" of AV. ("Also I say unto you") is impossible. The fear of men, which lies at the root of hypocrisy, as opposed to the fear of a loving God, appears to be the connecting thought.

πᾶς. *Nom pend.* placed first with much emphasis. For similar constructions comp. xxi. 6; Jn. vi. 39, vii. 38, xvii. 2.

ὁμολογήσει ἐν ἐμοί. The expression comes from the Syriac rather than the Hebrew, and occurs only here and Mt. x. 32. The phrase ὄμνυμι ἐν (Mt. v. 34–36) is not quite parallel. Here perhaps the second ὁμολογήσει requires ἐν, and this leads to its being used with the first. That Christ will confess His disciples is not true in the same sense that they will confess Him: but they will make a confession *in* His case, and He will make a confession *in* theirs; their confession being that He is the Messiah, and His that they are His loyal disciples. As early as the Gnostic teacher Heracleon (*c.* A.D. 170–180), the first commentator on the N.T. of whom we have knowledge, this ἐν after ὁμολογήσει attracted notice.[1]

9. ἀπαρνηθήσεται ἐνώπιον τῶν ἀγγέλων. This expressive compound verb is used of Peter's denial of Christ (xxii. 34, 61; Mt. xxvi. 34, 75, Mk. xiv. 30, 72). In Mt. we have ἀρνήσομαι κἀγὼ αὐτὸν ἔμπροσθεν τοῦ πατρός μου. Note that Lk. has his favourite ἐνώπιον for ἔμπροσθεν (see on i. 15), and that he has "the Angels of God" where Mt. has "My Father": comp. xv. 10.

[1] The fragment of Heracleon, preserved by Clem. Alex. *Strom.* iv. 9, is translated by Westcott, *Canon of N.T.* p. 275, 3rd ed. Syr-Sin. omits *v.* 9.

10. Comp. Mt. xii. 31, 32 and Mk. iii. 28, 29, in both which places this difficult saying is closely connected with the charge brought against our Lord of casting out demons through Beelzebub; a charge recorded by Lk. without this saying (xi. 15–20). We cannot doubt that Mt. and Mk. give the actual historical connexion, if these words were uttered only once.

πᾶς. Here again Lk. has a favourite word (see on vii. 35): Mt. has ὃς ἐάν, and Mk. has ὃς ἄν. Also for **εἰς τὸν υἱόν** Mt. has κατὰ τοῦ υἱοῦ. For this use of εἰς after βλασφημεῖν and the like comp. xxii. 65; Acts vi. 11; Heb. xii. 3. After ἁμαρτάνειν it is the regular construction, xv. 18, 21, xvii. 4; Acts xxv. 8, etc. The Jewish law was, "He that blasphemeth the name of the Lord, he shall surely be put to death: all the congregation shall certainly stone him" (Lev. xxiv. 16).

Τὸ ἅγιον πνεῦμα. See on i. 15.

οὐκ ἀφεθήσεται. Constant and consummate opposition to the influence of the Holy Spirit, because of a deliberate preference of darkness to light, renders repentance, and therefore forgiveness, morally impossible. Grace, like bodily food, may be rejected until the power to receive it perishes. See on 1 Jn. v. 16 in *Camb. Grk. Test.*, and comp. Heb. vi. 4–8, x. 26–31. The identity of the "blasphemy against the Holy Spirit" with the "sin unto death" is sometimes denied (*D.B.*[2] i. p. 442); but a sin which will never be forgiven must be a sin unto death. Schaff's *Herzog*, i. p. 302. In each case there is no question of the efficacy of the Divine grace. The state of him who is guilty of this sin is such as to exclude its application (Wsctt. on Heb. vi. 1–8, p. 165). Blasphemy, like lying, may be acted as well as uttered: and it cannot safely be argued that *blasphemy* against the Spirit must be a sin of *speech* (*Kurzg. Kom. N.T.* i. p. 75). See Aug. on Mt. xii. 31, 32; also Paschasius Radbertus, Migne, cxx. 470–472.

11, 12. Comp. xxi. 14, 15, which is parallel to both Mt. x. 19, 20 and Mk. xiii. 11, but not so close to them in wording as these verses are. The connexion here is evident. There is no need to be afraid of committing this unpardonable blasphemy by ill-advised language before a persecuting tribunal; for the Holy Spirit Himself will direct their words.

11. εἰσφέρωσιν ὑμᾶς ἐπὶ τὰς συναγωγάς. In all four passages their being brought before synagogues is mentioned. The elders of the synagogue were responsible for discipline. They held courts, and could sentence to excommunication (vi. 22; Jn. ix. 22, xii. 42, xvi. 2), or scourging (Mt. x. 17), which was inflicted by the ὑπηρέτης (see on iv. 20). Schürer, *Jewish People in the T. of J. C.* II. ii. pp. 59–67; Derenbourg, *Hist. de la Pal.* pp. 86 ff. The **ἀρχαί** and **ἐξουσίαι** would include the Sanhedrin and Gentile tribunals.

μὴ μεριμνήσητε πῶς ἢ τί ἀπολογήσησθε. Neither the form nor the matter of the defence is to cause great anxiety beforehand. See on ver. 22 and x. 41. Excepting Rom. ii. 15 and 2 Cor. xii. 19, ἀπολογεῖσθαι is peculiar to Lk. (xxi. 14 and six times in Acts). Here Mt. and Mk. have λαλήσητε.

D 157, a b c d e ff$_2$ i l q Syr-Cur. Syr-Sin. Aeth. omit ἢ τί, which may possibly come from Mt. x. 19. If so, this is a Western non-interpolation. See note at the end of ch. xxiv. WH. bracket.

12. **ἐν αὐτῇ τῇ ὥρᾳ.** "In that very hour": see small print on x. 7, and comp. Exod. iv. 12 and 2 Tim. iv. 17. Renan points out the correspondence between this passage and Jn. xiv. 26, xv. 26 (*V. de J.* p. 297, ed. 1863). Comp. Ex. iv. 11.

13–15. § The Avaricious Brother rebuked. This incident forms the historical introduction to the Parable of the Rich Fool (16–21), just as the lawyer's questions (x. 25–30) form the historical introduction to the Parable of the Good Samaritan. Comp. xiv. 15, xv. 1–3. We are not told whether the man was making an unjust claim on his brother or not; probably not: but he was certainly making an unjust claim on Jesus, whose work did not include settling disputes about property. The man grasped at any means of obtaining what he desired, invading Christ's time, and trying to impose upon his brother an extraneous authority. *Facile ii, qui doctorem spiritualem admirantur, eo delabuntur, ut velint eo abuti ad domestica componenda* (Beng.). Compare Christ's treatment of the questions respecting the payment of the *didrachma*, the woman taken in adultery, and payment of tribute to Cæsar.

13. **εἰπὲ τῷ ἀδελφῷ μου.** He does not ask Jesus to arbitrate between him and his brother, but to give a decision against his brother. There is no evidence that the brother consented to arbitration.

14. **Ἄνθρωπε.** A severe form of address, rather implying disapprobation or a desire to stand aloof, xxii. 58, 60; Rom. ii. 1, ix. 20. Comp. Soph. *Aj.* 791, 1154. As in the case of the lepers whom He healed (v. 14, xvii. 14), Jesus abstains from invading the office of constituted authorities. No one appointed Him (κατέστησεν) to any such office. Comp. Τίς σε κατέστησεν ἄρχοντα καὶ δικαστὴν ἐφ᾽ ἡμῶν; (Exod. ii. 14), words which may have been familiar to this intruder. Comp. Jn. xviii. 36.

μεριστήν. Here only in N.T. Not in LXX. There is no need to interpret it of the person who actually executes the sentence of partition pronounced by the κριτής. The κριτής who decides for partition is a μεριστής. Syr-Sin. omits.

15. **φυλάσσεσθε ἀπό.** The expression is classical (Xen. *Hell.* vii. 2. 10; *Cyr.* ii. 3. 9), but the only similar passage in N.T. is φυλάξατε ἑαυτὰ ἀπὸ τῶν εἰδώλων (1 Jn. v. 21): it is stronger than προσέχετε ἀπό.

πάσης πλεονεξίας. "Every form of covetousness": comp. *πάντα πειρασμόν*, "every kind of temptation" (iv. 13); *πᾶσα ἁμαρτία καὶ βλασφημία* (Mt. xii. 31). On *πλεονεξία*, "the greedy desire to have more," as a more comprehensive vice than *φιλαργυρία*, see Lft. *Epp.* p. 56 and on Col. iii. 5. He quotes *φυλάξασθε οὖν ἀπὸ τῆς πορνείας καὶ τῆς φιλαργυρίας* (*Test. XII. Patr.* Jud. xviii.), and somewhat differs from Trench, *Syn.* xxiv. Jesus, knowing what is at the root of the brother's unreasonable request, takes the opportunity of warning the whole multitude (*πρὸς αὐτούς*) against this prevalent and subtle sin.

οὐκ ἐν τῷ περισσεύειν τινι. "Not in the fact that a man has abundance is it the case that his life is the outcome of his possessions"; *i.e.* it does not follow, because a man has abundance, that his life consists in wealth. Some render, "For not because one has abundance, is his life part of his possessions," *i.e.* so that he can secure it. But the other is simpler. Life depends for its value upon the use which we make of *τὰ ὑπάρχοντα*, and for its prolongation upon the will of God. It is unlikely that ἡ ζωή here means or includes eternal life; but it includes the higher life as distinct from *βίος*. Comp. *οὐ γὰρ ἐν τῇ ὑπερβολῇ τὸ αὔταρκες οὐδ᾽ ἡ πρᾶξις, δυνατὸν δὲ καὶ μὴ ἄρχοντα γῆς καὶ θαλάττης πράττειν τὰ καλά· καὶ γὰρ ἀπὸ μετρίων δύναιτ᾽ ἄν τις πράττειν κατὰ τὴν ἀρετήν* (Arist. *Eth. Nic.* x. 8. 9).

For the dat. after *περισσεύειν* comp. xxi. 4 and Tobit iv. 16, and for that after *τὰ ὑπάρχοντα* see on viii. 3.

16–21. § The Parable of the Rich Fool, which illustrates both points;—that the life that is worth living does not depend upon wealth, which may be a trouble and anxiety; and that even mere existence cannot be secured by wealth.

16. Εἶπεν δὲ παραβολὴν πρός. Each separate combination is characteristic: *εἶπεν δέ, εἶπεν παραβολήν*, and *εἶπεν πρός*. See on vi. 39, and comp. xv. 3.

εὐφόρησεν. Here only in bibl. Grk. Josephus uses it of Galilee as productive of oil (*B. J.* ii. 21. 2); but elsewhere it occurs in this sense in medical writers only (Hobart, p. 144): comp. *τελεσφορεῖν* (viii. 14).

ἡ χώρα. Comp. xxi. 21; Jn. iv. 35; Jas. v. 4. There is no hint that the man's wealth was unjustly acquired; and this is some slight confirmation of the view that the brother's claim was not unjust (ver. 13). There is perhaps a reference to Ecclus. xi. 18, 19 or to Ps. xlix. 16–20.

17. Τί ποιήσω; Comp. Eccles. v. 10.

οὐκ ἔχω ποῦ συνάξω. *Quasi nusquam essent quibus pascendis possent impendi* (Grot.). *Inopum sinus, viduarum domus, ora infantum . . . istæ sunt apothecæ quæ maneant in æternum* (Ambr.)

Note the repetition of μου: "*my* fruits, *my* barns, *my* goods, *my* soul." It is just here that there is some resemblance to the story of Nabal: "Shall I take *my* bread, and *my* water, and *my* flesh that I have killed for *my* shearers and give it unto men of whom I know not whence they be?" (1 Sam. xxv. 11): but it is too much to say that there is an evident reference to Nabal.

18. καθελῶ. First with emphasis: he is eager to set to work. But *pauperum nulla mentio* (Beng.). Comp. ἀφελεῖ, which is the true reading, Rev. xxii. 19; and see Veitch, p. 25. Note the *chiasmus* between καθελῶ and οἰκοδομήσω.

The text of the words which follow καὶ συνάξω ἐκεῖ is much confused, but πάντα τὸν σῖτον καὶ τὰ ἀγαθά μου (ℵ[ac] B L T X, Syr-Harc. Boh. Sah. Aeth. Arm.) is probably correct, the μου after σῖτον (ℵ[ac] X, Syr-Harc. Boh. Sah. Aeth.) being rejected as an insertion.

WH. give the evidence in full (ii. p. 103), and regard it as a marked instance of conflation. Comp. ix. 10, xi. 54, xxiv. 53. The main facts are these. The expression τὰ γενήματα is very common in LXX for the fruits of the earth, and the phrase συνάγειν τὰ γενήματα occurs Exod. xxiii. 10; Lev. xxv. 20; Jer. viii. 13. The familiar τὰ γενήματά μου was substituted in some documents for the unusual combination τὸν σῖτον καὶ τὰ ἀγαθά (ℵ* D), in others for τὸν σῖτον (A Q E F G H etc.), in one for τὰ ἀγαθά μου (346); yet another variation is caused by the substitution of τοὺς καρπούς μου (from ver. 17) for the whole of the unusual combination (39), *omnes fructus meos* (a c d e). Thus we have—

(α) τὸν σῖτον [μου] καὶ τὰ ἀγαθά μου.
(β) 1. τὰ γενήματα μου.
 2. τοὺς καρπούς μου.
(δ) 1. τὰ γενήματά μου καὶ τὰ ἀγαθά μου.
 2. τὸν σῖτόν μου καὶ τὰ γενήματά μου.

The common reading (δ. 1) is a conflation of β. 1 and α.

19. ἐρῶ τῇ ψυχῇ μοῦ. There is probably no irony in making him address, not his body, but his soul: the ψυχή is here used as the seat of all joyous emotions. Comp. μὴ μεριμνᾶτε τῇ ψυχῇ τί φάγητε (ver. 22). Field quotes καρτέρησον, ψυχή, προθεσμίαν σύντομον, ἵνα τὸν πλείω χρόνον ἀπολαύσῃς ἀσφαλοῦς ἡδονῆς (Charit. *Aphrod.* iii. 2); and Wetst. quotes θαρρυνῶ ἐμαυτὸν καὶ πρὸς τὴν ἐμαυτοῦ ψυχὴν εἰπών· Ἀθηναῖος εἶμι (Libanius, D xvi. p. 463). See Stallbaum on Plat. *Repub.* ii. 8, p. 365 A.

κείμενα εἰς ἔτη πολλά· ἀναπαύου, φάγε, πίε. These words are omitted in D and some Latin authorities (a b c d e ff_2). With εἰς ἔτη πολλά comp. Jas. iv. 13–17; Prov. xxvii. 1; Ecclus. xxix. 12: and with φάγε, πίε comp. Tobit vii. 10 and the remarkable parallel Ecclus. xi. 19. The asyndeton marks the man's confidence and eagerness.

20. εἶπεν δὲ αὐτῷ ὁ Θεός. This is a parable, not history. It is futile to ask how God spoke to him. For Ἄφρων see on xi. 40 and xxiv. 25. The ταύτῃ τῇ νυκτί is placed first in emphatic contrast to the ἔτη πολλά. See Schanz, pp. 347, 348.

τὴν ψυχήν σου αἰτοῦσιν ἀπὸ σοῦ. "They are demanding thy

soul of thee": the present tense is very impressive. They do not demand it *for themselves*, and so we have act. and not mid. Comp. 2 Cor. xi. 20; and see the parallel lesson Wisd. xv. 8. For the impersonal plural comp. *vv.* 11, 48, vi. 38, xvi. 9, xxiii. 31. There is no need to think of ἄγγελοι θανατηφόροι (Job xxxiii. 23), or of λῃσταί (x. 30).

ἃ δὲ ἡτοίμασας, τίνι ἔσται; Vulg. Rhem. and RV. preserve the telling order: *quæ autem parasti cujus erunt?* "And the things which thou hast prepared, whose shall they be?" Comp. Ps. xxxix. 6, xlix. 6; Eccles. ii. 18–23; Job xxvii. 17–22. When not even his ψυχή is his own to dispose of, what will become of his ἀγαθά?

21. θησαυρίζων αὑτῷ. Comp. Mt. vi. 19; 2 Cor. xii. 14; and for the εἰς before Θεόν comp. xvi. 8. It is to be regretted that the εἰς is rendered differently in the two passages in both AV. ("in, towards") and RV. ("for, toward"). "Being rich toward God" means being rich in those things which are pleasing to Him. Amassing wealth without reference to the God who bestows it is πλεονεξία, and πλεονεξία is ἀφροσύνη.

The change from αὑτῷ to εἰς Θεόν, instead of Θεῷ, is intentional, and Juvenal's *dives tibi, pauper amicis* (v. 113) is not quite parallel; nor again Hecato in Cic. *De Off.* iii. 15. 63: *Neque enim solum nobis divites esse volumus, sed liberis, propinquis, amicis, maximeque rei publicæ.* The whole verse is omitted in D and a b d.

22–53. God's Providential Care and the Duty of Trust in Him (22–34) and of Watchfulness for the Kingdom (35–48) which Christ came to found (49–53). The address to the people (*vv.* 15–21) being ended, Jesus once more turns specially to the disciples; and it should be noticed that in doing so He no longer speaks in parables. That what follows was spoken on the same occasion as what precedes seems to be intended by Lk., but is not stated. The διὰ τοῦτο is included in the traditional report (see Mt. vi. 25), and proves nothing as to the original historical connexion. It is more to the point to notice that covetousness and hoarding are the result of want of trust in God (Heb. xiii. 5), and that an exhortation to trust in God's fatherly care follows naturally on a warning against covetousness. There is logical, but not necessarily chronological connexion. More convincing is the coincidence between details. The mention of sowing, reaping, store-chamber, and barn (ver. 24) may have direct reference to the abundant harvests and insufficient barns in the parable (*vv.* 17, 18). But it does not follow, because this lesson was given immediately after the parable of the Rich Fool, that therefore it was not part of the Sermon on the Mount; any more than that, because it was delivered there, it cannot have been repeated here.

22. Εἶπεν δὲ πρὸς τοὺς μαθητάς. Note both the δέ and the πρός, and comp. ver. 16, vii. 50, ix. 13, 14, 59, 62, etc. Assuming a connexion with what precedes, **Διὰ τοῦτο** will mean, "Because life does not depend on riches."

μὴ μεριμνᾶτε. "Be not anxious": comp. ver. 11 and x. 41. See Lft. *On Revision*, 2nd ed. p. 190; Trench, *On the A.V.* p. 39; T. L. O. Davies, *Bible English*, p. 100, for evidence that "thought" in the sixteenth and seventeenth centuries meant *distressing anxiety*. Comp. 1 Sam. ix. 5 with x. 2. S. Paul reiterates Christ's teaching (1 Cor. vii. 32; Phil. iv. 6).

τῇ ψυχῇ. Not, "*in* your soul," but, "*for* your soul." Here again the reference to the parable (ψυχή, φάγε) seems to be direct. If so, the necessity for translating ψυχή in the same way in both passages is all the stronger. The ψυχή is the source of physical life and physical enjoyment.

23. πλεῖόν ἐστιν τῆς τροφῆς. "Is something greater than the food" (comp. xi. 31, 32). Therefore He who gave the greater will not fail to provide the less.

24. κατανοήσατε. A favourite verb: see on ver. 27. Mt. has ἐμβλέψατε; and for **τοὺς κόρακας** he has τὰ πετεινὰ τοῦ οὐρανοῦ. Ravens are mentioned nowhere else in N.T., but often in O.T. See especially τίς δὲ ἡτοίμασεν κόρακι βοράν (Job xxxviii. 41), and καὶ διδόντι τοῖς κτήνεσι τροφὴν αὐτῶν καὶ τοῖς νοσσοῖς τῶν κοράκων τοῖς ἐπικαλουμένοις αὐτόν (Ps. cxlvii. 9). The name (Heb. *'oreb*) covers the whole of the crow tribe (including rooks and jackdaws) which is strongly represented in Palestine. Like the vulture, the raven acts as a scavenger: but it is a fable that it turns its young out of the nest, leaving them to feed themselves, and that this is the point of our Lord's mention of them. The raven is very careful of its young; and God feeds both old and young. Tristram, *Nat. Hist. of B.* pp. 198–201.

Here Vulg. b f l have *cellarium* for ταμεῖον, while d has *promptuarium.* See on ver. 3.

διαφέρετε τῶν πετεινῶν. See on ver. 7. "The birds are God's creatures; but *ye* are God's children": ὁ **πατὴρ** ὑμῶν (Mt.), not αὐτῶν.

25. Τίς δὲ ἐξ ὑμῶν. See on xi. 5.

μεριμνῶν δύναται ἐπὶ τὴν ἡλικίαν προσθεῖναι πῆχυν. "*By* being anxious can add a *span* to his *age*." That ἡλικία here means "age" (Heb. xi. 11; Jn. ix. 21, 23), and not "stature" (xix. 3), is clear from the context. It was prolongation of life that the anxiety of the rich fool failed to secure. Not many people give anxious thought to the problem of adding to their stature; and the addition of a πῆχυς (the length of the forearm) would be monstrous, and would not be spoken of as ἐλάχιστον. Many persons do give anxious thought to the prolongation of their allotted age, and that by any amount, great or small. Wetst. quotes Mimnermus, πηχυῖον ἐπὶ χρόνον ἄνθεσιν ἥβης τερπόμεθα. See on ii. 52, where ἡλικία probably means stature. For πῆχυς see *D.B.*[1] iii. pp. 1736 ff.; and for the literature on Hebrew Weights and Measures, Schaff's *Herzog*, iv. p. 2486; Hastings, *D.C.G.* ii. p. 818.

26. εἰ οὖν οὐδὲ ἐλάχιστον δύνασθε. These words have no equivalent in Mt. and are omitted in D, which for the whole verse has simply καὶ περὶ τῶν λοιπῶν τί μεριμνᾶτε. So also a b c d ff_2 i l r: *et de cæteris quid solliciti estis.* By **τῶν λοιπῶν** are meant clothing (Mt.), food, and other bodily necessities.

For οὐδέ we might have expected μηδέ. But εἰ = ἐπεί, and the sentence is conditional in form only. "If (as is certain) ye cannot" = "Since ye cannot." Comp. Jn. iii. 12, v. 47; 1 Cor. xi. 6; Heb. xii. 25. Win. lv. 2. a, p. 600. Or we may consider οὐδέ as belonging to δύνασθε, and not to the whole sentence: "If ye are unable." Simcox, *Lang. of N.T.* p. 183. But the former is better.

27. τὰ κρίνα. Mt. adds τοῦ ἀγροῦ. The word occurs nowhere else in N.T., but is freq. in LXX, esp. in Cant. (ii. 16, iv. 5, v. 13, vi. 2, 3, etc.): Heb. *shushan* or *shoshannah.* Some flower with a brilliant colour is evidently meant, and the colour is one to which human lips can be compared (Cant. v. 13). Either the scarlet Martagon (*Lilium Chalcedonicum*) or the scarlet anemone (*anemone coronaria*) may be the flower that is thus named. Like στρουθία, however (ver. 7), κρίνα may be generic; and to this day the Arabs call various kinds of flowers "lilies." See *D.B.* art. "Lily"; and comp. Stanley, *Sin. & Pal.* pp. 139, 430. Note that, while Mt. has καταμανθάνειν, Lk. has his favourite κατανοεῖν (ver. 24, vi. 41, xx. 23; Acts vii. 31, 32, xi. 6, xxvii. 39). For κοπιᾷ see on v. 5: it covers the works of men, νήθει that of women.

After τὰ κρίνα πῶς D has οὔτε νήθει οὔτε ὑφαίνει, while d has *quomodo neque neunt neque texunt*, and a has *quomodo non texunt neque neunt.* Several other Lat. texts have *texunt.* Thus, *quomodo crescunt non laborant neque neunt neque texunt* (b l r); *quomodo crescunt non nent neque texunt* (c); *quomodo crescunt non laborant non neunt neque texunt* (ff_2); and, by a curious slip, *quomodo* non *crescunt non laborant neque neunt neque texunt* (i).

28. εἰ δὲ ἐν ἀγρῷ. First with emphasis. "If in the field," where such care might seem to be superfluous. AV. wrongly takes ἐν ἀγρῷ with ὄντα σήμερον, following Vulg. *quod hodie in agro est.* Both here and in Mt. the right connexion is, "which to-day is, and to-morrow is cast into the oven." For κλίβανος, a portable oven, as distinct from ἰπνός, see *D.B.* The κλίβανος is often mentioned in LXX, generally as a simile for great heat (Ps. xx. 9; Hos. vii. 4–7, etc.); ἰπνός neither in LXX nor in N.T. Wood being scarce in Palestine, grass is commonly used as fuel. For ἀμφιάζει, which is a late word (Job xxix. 14, xxxi. 19), see Veitch.

29. **καὶ ὑμεῖς μὴ ζητεῖτε.** "And do *you* cease to seek": comp ver. 11, vi. 30, 37, vii. 13, viii. 49, 50, 52, etc. Mt. has the aor. μεριμνήσητε.

μὴ μετεωρίζεσθε. In class. Grk. and in LXX (Ps. cxxx. 1; 2 Mac. v. 17, vii. 34) this would probably mean, "Be not lifted up, do not exalt yourselves, seek not high things." So the Vulg. *nolite in sublime tolli.* Old Latin texts differ: *nolite solliciti esse; nec solliciti sitis* (c); *non abalienetis vos* (d): and many omit the passage. Luth. *fahret nicht hoch her.* Tyn. Cov. and Cran. "neither clyme ye up an high." But most commentators interpret it as a metaphor from ships tossing at sea: "Waver not anxiously, be not tossed about with cares." Comp. μετέωρον ἐν φόβῳ of a criminal expecting punishment (Jos. *B. J.* iv. 2. 5); and see S. Cox, who turns the word into a parable, *Expositor*, 1st series, i. p. 249, 1875. Edersheim contends for the LXX meaning, "be not uplifted" (*L. & T.* ii. p. 217). The verb is one of the rarer words which are common to N.T., Philo, and Plutarch.

30. **ταῦτα γὰρ πάντα.** This is the right combination; not πάντα τὰ ἔθνη: *hæc enim omnia gentes mundi quærunt.* The heathen seek anxiously after all these things, because they know nothing of God's providential care. The phrase τὰ ἔθνη τοῦ κόσμου occurs nowhere else in N.T. or LXX, but represents an Aramaic expression common in Rabbinical writings.

The plural verb shows that the different nations are considered distributively; and the compound expresses the anxiety with which they seek. Each nation seeks laboriously after the sum-total of these things. On the difference between ταῦτα πάντα here and πάντα ταῦτα, Mt. vi. 32, see Win. lxi. 2. b, p. 686. In both places ἐπιζητοῦσιν is the true reading, and ἐπιζητεῖ a grammatical correction.

ὑμῶν δὲ ὁ πατήρ. But *you*, who know that you have such a Father, have no need to be disturbed about these wants.

31. Lk. alone has his favourite πλήν. See on vi. 24. "But (dismissing all this useless anxiety) continue to seek," etc. Mt. adds πρῶτον to ζητεῖτε.

Origen quotes εἶπε γὰρ ὁ Ἰησοῦς τοῖς μαθηταῖς αὐτοῦ Αἰτεῖτε τὰ μεγάλα καὶ τὰ μικρὰ ὑμῖν προστεθήσεται, καὶ αἰτεῖτε τὰ ἐπουράνια καὶ τὰ ἐπίγεια προστεθήσεται ὑμῖν (*De Orat.* § 2). Comp. Clem. Alex. *Strom.* i. 24, p. 416, ed. Potter, and iv. 6, p. 579.

32. This verse has no parallel in Mt., and it is the only verse in this section which is entirely without equivalent in the Sermon on the Mount. The passage reads so well both with and without it, that it is difficult to see why it should have been either inserted or omitted without authority. In it the Good Shepherd assures His flock that, while the anxious seeking of the ὀλιγόπιστοι after food and raiment is vain, their seeking after the Kingdom of God will not be vain. He gives the Kingdom to those who seek it, and with it gives the necessaries of life. Whereas those who neglect the Kingdom that they may secure the necessaries, may lose both. *Κύριος ποιμαίνει με, καὶ οὐδέν με ὑστερήσει* (Ps. xxiii. 1). The *μικρὸν ποίμνιον* are the disciples as contrasted with the *μυριάδες τοῦ ὄχλου* (ver. 1).

ποίμνιον = ποιμένιον, which is not a diminutive, and therefore *μικρόν* is neither superfluous nor an epithet of affection, but an expression of fact. On the nom. with the art. for the voc. see on x. 21; and for *εὐδόκησεν* see Lft. on Col. i. 19, and comp. Rom. xv. 26.

33. The first half of this verse (to *παλαιούμενα*) has no parallel in Mt. As in vi. 29, 30, we have a rule given, not that it may be kept literally, but that it may illustrate a principle. So far as attachment to our possessions is concerned, we must be ready to part with them (1 Cor. vii. 30). Our fondness for them is not our justification for keeping them. But there is no Ebionism here, no condemnation of possessions as sinful.[1] As Bede points out, Christians are not commanded to retain nothing for their own use (for Christ Himself had a purse out of which He gave alms), but to take care that fear of poverty does not interfere with benevolence. Almsgiving is not to be a mere giving of what we can spare. Nor is it merely for the sake of the receiver. It is also for the good of the giver, that his heart may be freed from covetousness. The attempt to keep the letter of the rule here given (Acts ii. 44, 45) had disastrous effects on the Church of Jerusalem, which speedily became a Church of paupers, constantly in need of alms (Rom. xv. 25, 26; 1 Cor. xvi. 3; 2 Cor. viii. 4, ix. 1). For **τὰ ὑπάρχοντα** see on viii. 3; and for **βαλλάντια** see on x. 4.

ἀνέκλειπτον. Not elsewhere in N.T. or LXX. Comp. xvi. 9, xxii. 32; and, for the command, Mk. x. 41. Heaven is not to be bought with money; but, by almsgiving, what would be a hindrance is made a help.[2] In σής the reference perhaps is to costly garments, which are a favourite form of wealth in the East. The word occurs Is. l. 9, li. 8; Job iv. 19, xxvii. 18; Prov. xiv. 30; but in N.T. only here and Mt. vi. 19.

34. Almost *verbatim* as Mt. vi. 21. S. Paul states a similar

[1] On the alleged Ebionism of Lk. see Introd. § 3. b, and also Alexander, *Leading Ideas of the Gospels*, pp. 163–180, 2nd ed.

[2] Margoliouth quotes from El-Ghazzali's *Revival of the Religious Sciences* many striking sayings attributed to Christ by Mahometan writers: among them these. "He that seeks after this world is like one that drinks sea-water. The more he drinks the thirstier he becomes, until it slay him" (iii. 161). "There are three dangers in wealth. First, it may be taken from an unlawful source. And what if it be taken from a lawful source? they asked. He answered: It may be given to an unworthy person. They asked, And what if it be given to a worthy person? He answered, The handling of it may divert its owner from God" (iii. 178). See Hastings, *D.B.* i. p. 68.

principle 1 Cor. vii. 32–34. Wealth stored up in this world has many enemies; that which is stored in heaven is safe from them all. The γάρ is specially to be noted. The reason why treasure must be stored in heaven is that the hearts of those who bestow it may be drawn heavenwards.

35–48. The Duty of Loyal Vigilance. From ver. 35 to ver. 38 this section has no parallel in Mt. The interpellation of Peter (ver. 41) is also peculiar to Lk. But *vv.* 39, 40 and 42–46 are parallel to Mt. xxiv. 43–51. The discourse once more takes a parabolic turn, watchfulness being inculcated by the parables of the Master's Return (35–38, 42–48) and of the Thief's Attack (39, 40).

35. **Ἔστωσαν ὑμῶν αἱ ὀσφύες περιεζωσμέναι.** The long garments of the East are a fatal hindrance to activity. Comp. xvii. 8; Acts xii. 8; 1 Kings xviii. 46; 2 Kings iv. 29, ix. 1; Job xxxviii. 3, xl. 7; Jer. i. 17. Tristram, *Eastern Customs in Bible Lands*, p. 158. Note the emphatic position of ὑμῶν and ὑμεῖς. "Whatever others may do, this is to be *your* condition."

οἱ λύχνοι καιόμενοι, κ.τ.λ. This is the parable of the Ten Virgins condensed (Mt. xxv. 1).

36. **προσδεχομένοις.** *Expectantibus* (Vulg.) *cum desiderio et gaudio* (Beng.): comp. ii. 25, 38, xxiii. 51.

πότε ἀναλύσῃ ἐκ τῶν γάμων. If the rendering "when he shall return from," etc., is correct, this is the only place in N.T. in which the verb has this meaning: comp. 2 Mac. viii. 25, xiii. 7, xv. 28; 3 Mac. v. 21; Wisd. ii. 1. The more usual sense is "break up (a feast, camp, etc.), depart": comp. Phil. i. 23; Judith xiii. 1; 2 Mac. ix. 1: and this may be the meaning here. See instances in Wetst. So Luther, *wenn er aufbrechen wird.* The wedding is not his own, but that of a friend which he has been attending. In Esther (ii. 18, ix. 22) γάμοι is used of any banquet or festival: but the literal meaning is better here.[1]

For the plural of a single marriage feast comp. xiv. 8; Mt. xxii. 2, xxv. 10, and see Win. xxvii. 3, p. 219. For the constr. ἵνα ἐλθόντος . . . ἀνοίξωσιν αὐτῷ see Win. xxx. 11, p. 259, and comp. xv. 20.

37. **περιζώσεται καὶ ἀνακλινεῖ αὐτούς.** Comp. Rev. iii. 20, 21. Christ acted in this way when He washed the disciples' feet: not, however, in gratitude for their faithful vigilance, but to teach them humility. Nevertheless, that was a type of what is promised here: comp. Rev. xix. 9. References to the *Saturnalia*, when Roman masters and slaves changed places in sport, are here

[1] Kimchi on Is. lxv. mentions a saying of R. Johanan ben Zacchai, who invited his servants without fixing a time: *sapientes se ornarunt, stolidi abierunt ad opera sua.* Thus some went *ornati* and others *sordidi*, when the time came, and the latter were disgraced (Keim, *Jes. of Naz.* v. p. 256. Comp. Schoettgen, i. p. 216).

quite out of place. The parable xvii. 7–10 sets forth the usual course between master and man.

38. δευτέρᾳ. The first watch is not mentioned, because then the wedding-feast was going on. These are probably the two last of the *three* Jewish watches (Judg. vii. 19), not the two middle watches of the Roman *four* (Mk. xiii. 35; Acts xii. 4). See on xxii. 34 and *D.B.* art. "Watches of Night." In D, Marcion, Irenæus, and some other authorities, the first watch (τῇ ἑσπερινῇ φυλακῇ) is inserted: WH. ii. App. p. 61.

39. γινώσκετε. Probably indic. But Vulg. Luth. Beza, and all English Versions make it imperat. There is nothing strange in the sudden change of metaphor, especially in Oriental language. The "thief in the night" is a proverb for unexpected events (1 Thes. v. 2; 2 Pet. iii. 10; Rev. iii. 3, xvi. 15). Comp. the changes of metaphor in the parallel passage Mt. xxiv. 40–44.

ἀφῆκεν. "*Left* his house" (RV.). AV. makes no distinction between ἀφῆκεν here and εἴασεν in Mt. xxiv. 43, rendering both "suffered." But the RV. elsewhere renders ἀφίημι by "suffer" (viii. 51, xviii. 16); and ἀφῆκεν here cannot mean that he *went out* of the house, for "he would have kept awake" implies that he remained in it. If the distinction between εἴασεν and ἀφῆκεν is to be marked, the latter might be translated "allowed," a word which the Revisers nowhere use, except in the margin of Mk. iv. 29.

διορυχθῆναι. "To be dug through," the walls being made of mud. Wic. has "to be myned" here and "to be undermynyde" in Mt. for *perfodiri* of Vulg. Comp. διώρυξεν ἐν σκότει οἰκίας (Job xxiv. 16); ἐὰν δὲ ἐν τῷ διορύγματι εὑρεθῇ ὁ κλέπτης (Exod. xxii. 2); οὐκ ἐν διορύγμασιν εὗρον αὐτούς (Jer. ii. 34).

41. Εἶπεν δὲ ὁ Πέτρος. This interruption should be compared with that in ix. 33. Each of them connects the discourse in which it appears with a definite incident. It illustrates Peter's impulsiveness and his taking the lead among the Twelve. Perhaps it was the magnificence of the promise in ver. 37 which specially moved him. He wants to know whether this high privilege is reserved for the Apostles. For **παραβολὴν λέγεις** see on v. 36, and for **πρός** = "in reference to" comp. xviii. 1; Rom. x. 21; Heb. i. 7, 8, xi. 18, and possibly Lk. xix. 9 and xx. 19. Here πρὸς ἡμᾶς comes first with emphasis.

ἢ καὶ πρὸς πάντας. Peter is sure that it has reference to the Twelve: the question is whether others are included. The employment of parables would make him suppose that the multitude was being addressed, as in ver. 16; for Jesus did not commonly employ this kind of teaching with His permanent disciples. The spirit of the question resembles Jn. xxi. 21, and the answer resembles Jn. xxi. 22. In Mk. xiii. 37 we have what looks like a direct answer to the question here asked by S. Peter, "What I say to you I say to all, Watch."

42. Τίς ἄρα ἐστίν. Christ answers one question by another which does not tell the questioner exactly what he wishes to know, but what it concerns him to know. It is enough that each who hears recognizes that he is an οἰκονόμος with responsibilities. This was true in the highest sense of the Apostles. The οἰκονόμος here is a *dispensator* (Vulg.) or *villicus* (d), a superior slave left in charge of the household and estate (see on xvi. 1). Other names are *ordinarius*, *actor*, *procurator*, the meanings of which seem to have varied at different periods and on different estates. Becker, *Gallus*, Excursus iii. p. 204, Eng. tr. Hatch seems to assume that *dispensator* and *villicus* were terms of fixed and invariable meaning (*Bibl. Grk.* p. 62). With **πιστός** comp. Num. xii. 7; 1 Sam. xxii. 14; and with **φρόνιμος** comp. xvi. 8; Gen. xli. 39. With **θεραπείας** (abstr. for concr.) comp. ἐχάρη δὲ Φαραὼ καὶ ἡ θεραπεία αὐτοῦ (Gen. xlv. 16). Contrast Lk. ix. 11.

σιτομέτριον. "A measured portion of food, ration." These rations on Roman estates were served out daily, weekly, or monthly. The word occurs nowhere else, but σιτομετρεῖν is found (Gen. xlvii. 12, 14). Comp. Hor. *Ep.* i. 14. 40. See instances in Wetst., and in Deissmann, *Bible Studies*, p. 158.

44. ἀληθῶς λέγω ὑμῖν. Here, as in ix. 27 and xxi. 3, Lk. has ἀληθῶς, others have ἀμήν. See on x. 12. Comp. νομικοί (xi. 52) where Mt. has γραμματεῖς (xxiii. 14), and his never using Ῥαββεί.

ἐπὶ πᾶσιν τοῖς ὑπάρχουσιν αὐτοῦ. See on viii. 3. This passage and Mt. xxiv. 47 seem to be the only instances in N.T. of this use of ἐπί. Elsewhere we have the gen. (ver. 42) or acc. (ver. 14), the former being more common (Mt. xxiv. 45, xxv. 21, 23).

45. Χρονίζει ὁ κύριός μου. Comp. 2 Pet. iii. 3, 4; Eccles. viii. 11. The "But and if" of AV. is simply "But if" (RV.); "and if" being "an if," a double conditional, which was common in the sixteenth and seventeenth centuries.

ἄρξηται. He begins to do this, but the arrival of his lord puts a stop to it: comp. v. 21, xiii. 25; Acts xi. 15. This οἰκονόμος has a large *familia* of slaves under him. Perhaps he makes merry on what he ought to have given them. For παιδίσκη as a vernacular word for a female slave see Kennedy, *Sources of N.T. Grk.* p. 40. Μεθύσκεσθαι is "to get drunk," as distinct from μεθύειν "to be drunk" (Acts ii. 15).

46. For the attraction in ἐν ὥρᾳ ᾗ οὐ γινώσκει see on iii. 19.

διχοτομήσει. To be understood literally; for his having his portion with the unfaithful servants does not imply that he still lives: their portion is a violent death. For the word comp. Ex. xxix. 17; and for the punishment 2 Sam. xii. 31; 1 Chron. xx. 3; Susannah 59; Amos i. 3 (LXX); Heb. xi. 37. There is no example of the word being used of scourging or other severe treatment. There is a gradation of punishments: for vile misconduct and tyranny, death; for deliberate neglect, many stripes; for unintentional neglect, few stripes. Herodotus uses διατέμνειν: ii. 139. 2, vii. 39. 5. Comp. Suet. *Caligula*, xxvii.: *multos honesti ordinis . . . medios serra dissecuit.*

τὸ μέρος αὐτοῦ μετὰ τῶν ἀπίστων θήσει. "Will appoint his portion with the unfaithful servants," *i.e.* those guilty of a gross abuse of trust. "Unbelievers" here has no point. Mt. has τῶν ὑποκριτῶν, which means much the same as τῶν ἀπίστων. This unfaithful steward expected to be able to play the part of a trusty agent at the time of his lord's arrival. For τὸ μέρος we have ἡ μερίς in LXX, Is. xvii. 14; Jer. xiii. 25.

Here the parallel with Mt. xxiv. 43-51 ends. What follows is preserved by Lk. alone.

47. ἐκεῖνος δὲ ὁ δοῦλος. "*But* that servant," *Ille autem servus.* Both AV. and RV. have "and." The δέ marks the contrast between this transgressor and the οἰκονόμος, for μὴ ἑτοιμάσας ἢ ποιήσας πρὸς τὸ θέλημα αὐτοῦ is a less serious offence than the outrages which are described in *vv.* 45, 46, and one which *all* servants may commit.

δαρήσεται πολλάς. Understand πληγάς and comp. παίειν ὀλίγας (Xen. *Anab.* v. 8. 12). In N.T. δέρω is never "I flay," but always "I beat." Comp. the vulgar "hide, giving a hiding to." In LXX δέρω does not occur, except as *v.l.* in Lev. i. 6; 2 Chron. xxix. 34, xxxv 11; but in all three places the meaning is "flay," and the true reading possibly ἐκδέρω. Comp. Mic. ii. 8, iii. 3. The doctrine of degrees of punishment hereafter is taught here still more plainly than in x. 12, 14. See Aug. *De Civ. Dei*, xxi. 16.

There are two classes not mentioned here: ὁ γνοὺς καὶ ποιήσας and (so far as that is possible) ὁ μὴ γνοὺς καὶ ποιήσας: see on Rom. ii. 14.

48. ὁ μὴ γνούς. Seeing that he is a servant, he might have known his master's will, had he been anxious to find it out. Nevertheless it is true that even he, who, in ignorance for which he is not responsible, commits ἄξια πληγῶν, has to suffer. The natural consequences of excess or transgression must follow.

In the second half of the verse it is doubtful whether the two parallel statements mean exactly the same thing or not. Either, "He who receives much is expected to exhibit much gratitude, and also readiness to make return; and is expected to do more than *those who have received less*": or, "He who receives a *gift* (ἐδόθη), must make a proportionate return: and he who receives a *deposit* (παρέθεντο), must restore more than *he has received.*" In the latter case the second half states the principle of the parables of the Talents and the Pounds Note the impersonal plurals, and comp. ver. 20.

49-53. The discourse seems to return to its starting-point (*vv.* 1–2). Christ's teaching inevitably provokes opposition and a division between those who accept it and those who reject it. There is no parallel in Mt. or Mk. to *vv.* 49, 50.

49. Πῦρ. First for emphasis. "It is fire that I came to cast upon the earth." The context seems to show that the fire of division and strife is meant: or, comparing iii. 16, we may understand the fire of holiness, which excites hostility and controversy. *Ignis ille non est nativus terræ* (Beng.). Εἰς κρίμα ἐγὼ εἰς τὸν κόσμον τοῦτον ἦλθον (Jn. ix. 39: comp. iii. 19).

καὶ τί θέλω εἰ ἤδη ἀνήφθη; A passage of well-known difficulty, the translation of which remains doubtful. With this punctuation we may follow AV. and RV., "What will I, if it be (is) already kindled?" the meaning of which is not clear: comp. LXX of Josh. vii. 7. Or, with De Wette, Weiss, and many others, "How I wish that it were already kindled!" which does rather serious violence to the Greek. Or, with Origen, Meyer, etc., we may punctuate, καὶ τί θέλω; εἰ ἤδη ἀνήφθη. "And what will I? Would that it were already kindled!" (Win. liii. 8. c, p. 562); which is rather abrupt and harsh: but comp. xix. 42 and Jn. xii. 27. Perhaps the first is best, meaning, "What more have I to desire, if it be already kindled." The next verse does not imply that it is not kindled; and the history of Christ's ministry shows that it was kindled, although not to the full extent. Comp. Ps. lxxviii. 21. Christ came to set the world on fire, and the conflagration had already begun. Mal. iii. 2. Comp. the constr. in Ecclus. xxiii. 14.

50. βάπτισμα δὲ ἔχω βαπτισθῆναι. Having used the metaphor of fire, Christ now uses the metaphor of water. The one sets forth the result of His coming as it affects the world, the other as it affects Himself. The world is lit up with flames, and Christ is bathed in blood: Mk. x. 38. His passion is a flood in which He must be plunged. The metaphor is a common one in O.T. Ps. lxix. 2, 3, 14, 15, xlii. 7, cxxiv. 4, 5, cxliv. 7; Is. xliii. 2. Jordan in flood and mountain torrents in spate would suggest such figures. See on ix. 22.

πῶς συνέχομαι ἕως ὅτου τελεσθῇ. "How am I oppressed, afflicted, until it be finished": comp. viii. 37; Job iii. 24. The prospect of His sufferings was a perpetual Gethsemane: comp. Jn. xii. 27. While He longed to accomplish His Father's will, possibly His human will craved a shortening of the waiting. Comp. συνέχομαι δὲ ἐκ τῶν δύο (Phil. i. 23). With τελεσθῇ comp. τετέλεσται, Jn. xix. 28, 30.

51. With *vv.* 51 and 53 comp. Mt. x. 34, 35. It was the belief of the Jews that the Messiah would at once introduce a reign of peace and prosperity. Jesus does not wish His followers to live in a fool's paradise. He is no enthusiast making wild and delusive promises. In this world they must expect tribulation.

ἀλλ' ἤ. "Except, but." Although the ἀλλ' has no accent, it seems to represent ἄλλο rather than ἀλλά: "I came not to send *any other thing than* division." Or there may be a mixture of οὐδὲν ἄλλο ἤ and οὐδὲν ἄλλο, ἀλλά: comp. 2 Cor. i. 13; Job vi. 5; Ecclus. xxxvii. 12, xliv. 10. The expression is common in class. Grk.; and in Hdt. i. 49. 1, ix. 8. 3 the origin of it seems to be shown. See Stallbaum on *Phædo*, 81 B; Win. liii. 7. n. 5, p. 552.

διαμερισμός. Comp. Mic. vii. 12; Ezek. xlviii. 29; here only in N.T. Again Christ prepares them for disappointment.

52. This verse has no parallel in Mt. x. Comp. Mic. vii. 6, on which what follows seems to be based. Godet says that there are five persons here and six in ver. 53. There are five in both cases, the mother and mother-in-law being the same person. Excepting 2 Cor. v. 16, ἀπὸ τοῦ νῦν is peculiar to Lk. (i. 48, v. 10, xxii. 18, 69; Acts xviii. 6). It is not rare in LXX (Gen. xlvi. 30; Ps. cxii. 2, cxiii. 26, cxx. 8, cxxiv. 2, cxxx. 3, Is. ix. 7, etc.).

53. πατὴρ ἐπὶ υἱῷ . . . μήτηρ ἐπὶ θυγατέρα . . . πενθερὰ ἐπὶ τὴν νύμφην. The change from the dat. to the acc. *possibly* indicates that the hostility is more intense in the case of the women. But LXX of Mic. vii. 6 more probably was the cause of the change. There we have ἐπὶ τήν of the women, but υἱὸς ἀτιμάζει πατέρα of the men. In Mt. x. 35 we have *κατά c. gen.* in all three cases. Lk. omits "A man's foes shall be those of his own household." Comp. Mal. iv. 6.

For νύμφη = "daughter-in-law" comp. Mt. x. 35; Gen. xi. 31, xxxviii. 11; Lev. xviii. 15, etc.; Jos. *Ant.* v. 9. 1. In Jn. iii. 29; Rev. xviii. 23, etc., it has the classical meaning of "bride."

54–59. § Ignorance of the Signs of the Times. Christ once more addresses the multitude (ver. 15), apparently on the same occasion; but it is by no means certain that Lk. means this. If so, this is a last solemn word by way of conclusion. The parallel passage Mt. xvi. 2, 3 is of very doubtful authority. It can hardly be derived from Lk., from which it differs almost entirely in wording, but perhaps comes from some independent tradition.

54. Ἔλεγεν δὲ καί. The formula is suitable for introducing a final utterance of special point. Comp. v. 36, ix. 23, xvi. 1, xviii. 1. For τοῖς ὄχλοις see on xi. 29.

ἐπὶ δυσμῶν. In the West, and therefore from the Mediterranean Sea, which was a sign of rain (1 Kings xviii. 44). Robinson, *Res. in Pal.* i. p. 429; *D.B.* art. "Rain."

εὐθέως λέγετε ὅτι Ὄμβρος ἔρχεται. Both the εὐθέως and the pres. ἔρχεται point to the confidence with which the announcement is made: "at once ye say, Rain is coming." Comp. ἔρχεται ὥρα. Ὄμβρος is "heavy rain, a thunder-shower": Deut. xxxii. 2; Wisd. xvi. 16; Ecclus. xlix. 9; Jos. *Ant.* ii. 16. 3.

55. ὅταν νότον πνέοντα. Understand ἴδητε. One *sees* that it is a south wind by the objects which it moves. Lk. alone uses νότος of the south wind (Acts xxvii. 13, xxviii. 13). Elsewhere it means the South, as frequently in LXX (xi. 31, xiii. 29; Mt. xii. 42; Rev. xxi. 13; 1 Sam. xxvii. 10, xxx. 1, 14, 27; 2 Sam. xxiv. 7; 1 Kings vii. 25, 39 [13, 25], etc.).

καύσων. "Scorching heat": Mt. xx. 12; Jas. i. 11; Is. xlix. 10; Ecclus. xviii. 16, xliii. 22. Perhaps nowhere in N.T. does *καύσων* mean the burning *east wind* (Job xxvii. 21; Hos. xii. 1); but Jas. i. 11 is doubtful.

56. ὑποκριταί. Comp. Mt. xxiii. 14 ff. They professed to be unable to interpret signs, such as the birth, preaching, and death of the Baptist, the preaching and miracles of Jesus. But their weather-wisdom proved that they could be intelligent enough where their worldly interests were concerned.

δοκιμάζειν. "To test." In *τὸ πρόσωπον τοῦ οὐρανοῦ* and *καιρόν* we have almost the only words that are common to this passage and Mt. xvi. 2, 3. With *τὸν καιρόν* (*tempus Messiæ*) comp. xix. 44.

57. Τί δὲ καὶ ἀφ' ἑαυτῶν. "*But* why *even* of yourselves, out of your own hearts and consciences," without information from externals: comp. xxi. 30. Or possibly, "Of yourselves *also*," as readily (*εὐθέως*) as in the case of the weather. In either case *ἀφ' ἑαυτῶν* comes first for emphasis. For **δὲ** *καί* see small print on iii. 9.

58. ὡς γὰρ ὑπάγεις. *γὰρ sæpe ponitur, ubi propositionem excipit tractatio.* Here *ἐν τῇ ὁδῷ* stands first with emphasis; no time is to be lost. And the Latinism *δὸς ἐργασίαν*, *da operam*, occurs here only. Wetst. quotes Hermogenes, *De Inventione*, iii. 5. 7. Excepting Eph. iv. 19, *ἐργασία* in N.T. is peculiar to Lk. (Acts xvi. 16, 19, xix. 24, 25). Hobart regards it as medical (p. 243), but it is very freq. in LXX. Note *ὡς* = "when."

ἀπηλλάχθαι. "To be quit of him" by coming to terms with him. Christ is perhaps taking the case of the two brothers (*vv.* 13, 14) as an illustration. The *ἀπό* before the *αὐτοῦ* is omitted in B, but is certainly right Acts xix. 12. In class. Grk. both constructions are found, but the simple gen. is more common. Plat. *Leg.* 868 D; Xen. *Mem.* ii. 9. 6.

κατασύρῃ. Here only in N.T. and only once in LXX of ruining or demolishing: *ὅτι ἐγὼ κατέσυρα τὸν Ἡσαῦ* (Jer. xlix. 10). In Lat. *detraho* is used of dragging into court. For examples see Wetst. Mt. has *παραδῷ τῷ κριτῇ*.

παραδώσει τῷ πράκτορι καὶ ὁ πράκτωρ σε βαλεῖ εἰς φυλακήν. *Tradat te exactori et exactor mittat te in carcerem* (Vulg.). For *exactor* Cod. Palat. (e) has the strange word *pignerarius*. Nowhere else in bibl. Grk. does *πράκτωρ* occur. At Athens the magistrate who imposed a fine gave notice to the *πράκτορες*, who entered it as due from the person fined; but they did not enforce payment, if the fine was not paid. They merely kept the record. See *D. of Ant.*[2] art. *Practores*. For *πράκτορι* Mt. has *ὑπηρέτῃ*.

59. λέγω σοι. He addresses each individual. Mt. has *ἀμὴν λέγω σοί* (comp. ver. 44), and for **λεπτόν** has *κοδράντην*. The λεπτόν (λεπτός = "peeled, thin, small") was half a *quadrans* and the eighth of an *as*: see on ver. 6, and comp. xxi. 2; Mk. xii. 42. Can the payment be made ἐν φυλακῇ? The parable gives no answer to this question. But it teaches that the proper time for payment is before judgment is given, and that release is impossible until full payment is made. The Talmud says: "The offences between man and God the Day of Atonement doth atone for. The offences between man and his neighbour the Day of Atonement atoneth for, only when he hath agreed with his neighbour." There is no need to interpret the details in the parable, and make the ἀντίδικος mean the law of God, and the ἄρχων God Himself, and the κριτής the Son of God.

XIII. 1–9. § Three Exhortations to Repentance, of which two (1–3; 4, 5) are based upon recent occurrences, while the third (6–9) is a parable. All three seem to have been omitted by Marcion in his mutilated Gospel; but it is not easy to see what he disliked in them. They are peculiar to Lk., and both external and internal evidence guarantee their authenticity. Time and place are indefinite; but the connexion with what precedes is expressly stated, and the scene must have been away from Jerusalem.

1–3. The Moral of the Massacre of the Galilæan Pilgrims. There is no record of this massacre in any other source. But the turbulent character of the Galilæans, and the severity of Pilate and other Roman governors, make the incident more than credible. Horrible massacres are recorded by Josephus (*Ant.* xvii. 9. 3, xviii. 3. 1, xx. 5. 3; *B.J.* ii. 3. 3, 9. 4, v. 1. 5). The fact that such things were common accounts for the absence of other records; and possibly not very many were slain. But such an outrage on Galilæans may have been one of the causes of the enmity between Herod and Pilate (xxiii. 12); and Keim conjectures that it was on this occasion that Barabbas was imprisoned. So also Lewin, *Fasti Sacri*, 1407.

Others have conjectured the occasion to have been the insurrection under Judas of Galilee, the Gaulonite of Gamala (*Ant.* xviii. 1. 1; *B. J.* ii. 8. 1); but that was many years earlier (*c.* A.D. 6), and these new-comers evidently report some recent event. On the other hand, the insurrection of the Samaritans (*Ant.* xviii. 4. 1) took place later than this, being the immediate cause of the recall of Pilate (A.D. 36). And what had Samaritan rebellion to do with the massacre of Galilæans? Comp. Philo's summary of the enormities of Pilate: τὰς δωροδοκίας, τὰς ὕβρεις, τὰς ἁρπαγάς, τὰς αἰκίας, τὰς ἐπηρείας, τοὺς ἀκρίτους καὶ ἐπαλλήλους φόνους, τὴν ἀνήνυτον καὶ ἀργαλεωτάτην ὠμότητα (*Leg. ad Gaium*, xxxviii. p. 1034 c, ed. Galen.). Again he says of him: ἦν γὰρ τὴν φύσιν ἀκαμπὴς καὶ μετὰ τοῦ αὐθάδους ἀμείλικτος; and, οἷα οὖν ἐγκότως ἔχων καὶ βαρύμηνις ἄνθρωπος. See Lewin, 1493; Derenbourg, p. 198.

1. Παρῆσαν. Not, "there were present," as all English Versions render, but, "there came," *venerunt* (Cod. Brix.). These informants were not in the crowd which Jesus had been addressing, but brought the news afterwards. For this use of παρεῖναι comp. Acts

x. 21; Mt. xxvi. 50; Jn. xi. 28: sometimes followed by πρός (Acts xii. 20; Gal. iv. 18, 20), or by εἰς (Col. i. 6): comp. Lk. xi. 7. In Mt. xxvi. 50; Acts x. 21, xii. 20, Vulg. has *venio*; in Col. i. 6, *pervenio*. Wetst. quotes a close parallel: παρῆσάν τινες ἀπαγγέλλοντες πολλοὺς τῶν Ἑλλήνων νεωτερίζειν (Diod. Sic. xvii. 8)

ἐν αὐτῷ τῷ καιρῷ. "At that very opportunity," viz. just as He was speaking about the signs of the times. Possibly they had heard His last words, and thought that their story would be regarded as a sign: τῷ καιρῷ may look back to τὸν καιρόν (xii. 56: comp. i. 20, iv. 13).

ὧν τὸ αἷμα Πειλᾶτος ἔμιξεν μετὰ τῶν θυσιῶν αὐτῶν. These pilgrims from Galilee had come up to Jerusalem for one of the Feasts, probably Tabernacles, and had come into collision with the Romans, no doubt through some fanatical act of rebellion. The merciless *procurator*, himself in Jerusalem to keep order during the Feast, sent troops to attack them as they were sacrificing in the temple courts, and their blood was mingled with that of the slaughtered beasts. The expression, "mingling blood with blood," occurs elsewhere. Schoettgen quotes (of Israelites who were circumcised in Egypt at the Passover): *et circumcisi sunt, et commixtus est sanguis paschatis cum sanguine circumcisionis* (*Hor. Hebr.* p. 286). And again: David swore to Abishai, if he laid hands on Saul, "I will mingle thy blood with his blood" (*ibid.* p. 287; Lightfoot, *Hor. Hebr. ad loc.*).

2. We gather the object of these informants from Christ's answer. They did not want Him as a Galilæan to protest against Pilate's cruelty, perhaps by heading another Galilæan revolt. Rather, like Job's friends, they wanted to establish the view that this calamity was a judgment upon the sufferers for exceptional wickedness (Job iv. 7, viii. 4, 20, xxii. 5; comp. Jn. ix. 1, 2). Perhaps they had heard about the threatened "cutting asunder" (xii. 46), and thought that this was a case in point. There is no hint that they wished to entrap Him into strong language respecting Pilate.

παρὰ πάντας τ. Γ. ἐγένοντο. "*Showed themselves* to be (comp. x. 36) sinners *beyond* all the Galilæans." Comp. the use of παρά after comparatives, iii. 13.

3. πάντες ὁμοίως ἀπολεῖσθε. The suffering of a whole nation is more likely to be produced by the sin of the nation than the suffering of an individual by the sin of the individual. *Exempla sunt omnium tormenta paucorum.* Jesus condemns neither the Galilæans nor Pilate, but warns all present of what must befall *them* unless they free themselves from *their* guilt. It is this approach of judgment upon His whole people which seems to fill Christ's thought, and to oppress Him far more than the approach of His own suffer-

ings. Grotius points out how exact the ὁμοίως is. *Vide quam omnia congruerint. Paschatis enim die occisi sunt, magna pars in ipso templo pecudum ritu, ob eandam causam seditionis.* But it is unlikely that this massacre took place at the Passover. The rest is right. Πολλοὶ . . . πρὸ τῶν θυμάτων ἔπεσον αὐτοὶ καὶ τὸν Ἕλλησι πᾶσι καὶ βαρβάροις σεβάσμιον βωμὸν κατέσπεισαν ἰδίῳ φόνῳ (*B. J.* v. 1. 3). See Martensen, *Chr. Dogm.* § 110.

4, 5. The Moral of the Catastrophe at Siloam. This incident also is recorded here only. Jesus mentions it spontaneously as something fresh in their memories. "The tower" means the well-known tower.

4. ἐν τῷ Σιλωάμ. The ἐν perhaps indicates that it was surrounded by buildings.

The Greek form of the name varies. Σιλωάμ in LXX and Josephus; Σιλωάς in Josephus; Σιλωά in Aquila, Symmachus, and Theodotion. Note the article, which agrees with Jewish usage. In Jn. ix. 7 and in LXX the article occurs: comp. τὸν Σαρῶνα (Acts ix. 35). Few sites have been identified with more certainty than Siloam: Conder, *Handbk. of B.* p. 335; Stanley, *Sin. & Pal.* pp. 180, 428; Tristram, *Bible Places*, p. 162.

ὀφειλέται. vii. 41, xi. 4; Mt. vi. 12, xviii. 24–34. The change of word from ἁμαρτωλοί (ver. 2) ought to be marked in translation, as by Wic. Rhem. and RV.; and also the change from ὁμοίως (ver. 3) to ὡσαύτως (ver. 5), as by RV., although there is little change of meaning. If Ewald's guess is correct, that these eighteen were working at the aqueducts made by Pilate, to pay for which he had used τὸν ἱερὸν θησαυρόν (καλεῖται δὲ κορβανᾶς), then ὀφειλέται may be used in allusion to this, implying that it was held that these workmen ought to pay back their wages into the treasury (Jos. *B. J.* ii. 9. 4). Jesus reminds the people that they are all sinners, and that all sinners are debtors to Divine justice (xii. 58).

5. μετανοήσητε. The change of tense, if this be the right reading (א A D L M T U X), points to the need of *immediate* repentance, as distinct from a *state* or continued attitude of repentance, μετανοῆτε (ver. 3). Vulg. expresses the difference by *nisi pœnitentiam habueritis* (ver. 3) and *si pœnitentiam non egeritis* (ver. 5). See on iii. 3 and v. 32.

πάντες ὡσαύτως ἀπολεῖσθε. The ὡσαύτως is stronger than ὁμοίως, as "in the same manner" than "in like manner." In both verses the MSS. are divided, but with a balance in ver. 3 for ὁμοίως and for ὡσαύτως here. See Jos. *B. J.* vi. 5. 4, 7. 2, 8. 3, etc., for the similarity between the fate of these eighteen and that of the Jews at the fall of Jerusalem.

6–9. § The Parable of the Barren Fig tree. It sets forth the longsuffering and the severity of God. His visitation of sin, however long delayed in order to give opportunity of repentance, is sure. The fig tree, as in Mk. xi. 13, is the Jewish nation, but also any individual soul. Comp. Hos. ix. 10; Joel i. 7. It is arbitrary to assert that the withering of the barren fig tree in Mt. xxi. and Mk. xi. is a transformation of this parable into a fact, or that the supposed fact has here been wisely turned into a parable.

6. Ἔλεγεν δὲ ταύτην τὴν παραβολήν. See on v. 36. The parable is a continuation of the warning, "Except ye repent, ye shall all likewise perish." *D.C.G.* art. "Fig-tree."

Συκῆν . . . ἐν τῷ ἀμπελῶνι αὐτοῦ. The main subject of the parable is placed first. Deut. xxii. 9 forbids the sowing of corn in vineyards, but to plant other fruit trees there was not a violation of this. At the present day fruit trees of various kinds are common in vineyards and in cornfields in Palestine (Stanley, *Sin. & Pal.* p. 421). "The fig tree ripeneth her green figs, and the vines are in blossom" (*Cant.* ii. 13), perhaps implies this combination.

7. τρία ἔτη ἀφ' οὗ ἔρχομαι. Lit. "It is three years from the time when I continue coming": comp. Thuc. i. 18. 1. A fig tree is said to attain maturity in three years, and a tree that remained fruitless for so long would not be likely to bear afterwards. See quotations in Wetst. The three years of Christ's ministry cannot well be meant. The tree had been fruitless long before He began to preach, and it was not cut down until forty years after He ceased to do so. Cyril suggests Moses and Aaron, Joshua and the Judges, and the Prophets (Migne, vol. lxxii. 753). Ambrose proposes the annunciations to Abraham, Moses, and Mary (Migne, vol. xv. 1743). Other triplets equally good might be easily devised; but none are required. See Schanz, *ad loc.* p. 369.

ἵνα τί καὶ τὴν γῆν καταργεῖ; "Why, in addition to doing no good, does it sterilize the ground?" *Ut quid etiam terram occupat* (Vulg.). Excepting here and Heb. ii. 14, the verb is used in N.T. only by S. Paul. He has it often, and in all four groups of his Epistles. In LXX only in Ezra (iv. 21, 23, v. 5, vi. 8). Latin Versions vary between *occupat*, *evacuat*, *detinet*, and *intricat*; English Versions between "occupy," "keep barren," "cumber," and "hinder." All the latter, excepting Rhem. and RV., miss the *καί*: it not only gives no fruit, it also renders good soil useless (*ἀργόν*).[1]

8. κόπρια. Here only in N.T. In Jer. xxv. 33 (xxxii. 19) and Ecclus. xxii. 2 this plur. occurs as here without the art. The curious reading *κόφινον κοπρίων* is found in D, and is supported by *cofinum stercoris* or *cophinam stercoris* of various Latin texts, d having *qualum stercoris*.

9. εἰς τὸ μέλλον. In the true text (ℵ B L 33, Boh. Aeth.) this expression precedes *εἰ δὲ μήγε*, and we have an aposiopesis as in Acts xxiii. 9; Rom. ix. 22–24. Comp. Exod. xxxii. 32, where LXX supplies the apodosis. The ellipse of *καλῶς ἔχει* occurs in class. Gk. It is perhaps possible to make *εἰς τὸ*

---

[1] Both *ἀργός* (contr. from *ἀεργός*) and *ἀργία* are used of land that yields no return: Xen. *Cyr.* iii. 2. 19; Theophr. *H. Phys.* v. 9. 8. Comp. Rom. vi. 6, "that the body as an instrument of sin may be rendered unproductive, inactive" (*καταργηθῇ*); also 1 Cor. xv. 26; 2 Cor. iii. 14; 2 Tim. i. 10.

μέλλον the apodosis: "if it bear fruit, we may postpone the question; but if not," etc. That εἰς τὸ μέλλον may mean "against next year" is clear from Plutarch's use of it for magistrates designate: *e.g.* τὸν Πείσωνα κατέστησεν ὕπατον εἰς τὸ μέλλον (*Cæs.* xiv.); and perhaps it may mean "next year (Syr-Sin.)," the prep. being redundant, as in εἰς τὴν τρίτην: comp. Jos. *Ant.* i. 11. 2. But that ἔτος need not be understood, and that the prep. need not be redundant, is clear from 1 Tim. vi. 19, where εἰς τὸ μέλλον means "against the time to come." Only if the prep. be made redundant is the transfer of εἰς τὸ μέλλον to ἐκκόψεις (A D) possible; for "*against* next year thou shalt cut it down" would here make no sense; but the external evidence is conclusive against the transfer. Comp. Acts xiii. 42; Hom. *Od.* xiv. 384.

For the change from ἐάν to εἰ (κἂν . . . εἰ δὲ μήγε) comp. Acts v. 38, 39. It occurs in class. Grk.; and in most cases of this kind either conjunction might just as well have been used twice. Here it is possible that the first alternative is given as more problematical than the second.

ἐκκόψεις αὐτήν. "Thou shalt (have) it cut down," shalt give the order for it. The vine-dresser will not even then cut it down without express command. He does not say ἐκκόψω. Comp. the Baptist's warning, in which this same verb (ἐκκόπτεται) is used (iii. 9). Trench gives a striking parallel in an Arabian recipe for curing a barren palm tree (*Par.* p. 359, 10th ed.).

10–17. § Healing of a Woman on the Sabbath from a Spirit of Infirmity. The details are manifest tokens of historical truth. The pharisaic pomposity of the ruler of the Synagogue, with his hard and fast rules about propriety; Christ's triumphant refutation of his objections; and the delight of the people, who sympathize with the dictates of human nature against senseless restrictions;—all this is plainly drawn from life. See Keim, *Jes. of Naz.* iv. pp. 15, 162. Here, as in vi. 1–11, Christ claims no authority to abolish the sabbath. He restores it to its true meaning by rescuing it from traditions which violated it. See Hort, *Judaistic Christianity*, p. 32.

10. This is the last mention of His teaching in a synagogue, and the only instance of His doing so in the latter part of His ministry. In many places where He was known the elders would not have allowed Him to preach, seeing that the hierarchy had become so hostile to Him. It is evident that τοῖς σάββασιν is sing. in meaning, as always in the Gospels. See on iv. 31, where, as here, we have the periphrastic imperfect.

11. πνεῦμα ἔχουσα ἀσθενείας. "Who had a spirit that caused infirmity." See Sanday on Rom. viii. 15. Similarly a demon that caused dumbness is called a "dumb spirit" (xi. 14; Mk. ix. 17, 25). Weiss would have it that this expression is the Evangelist's own inference, and a wrong inference, from ἣν ἔδησεν ὁ Σατανᾶς (ver. 16), which probably means that Jesus knew her malady to be the consequence of her sinful life. Therefore Satan, who caused the sin, caused the malady. Weiss asserts that the laying on of hands never occurs in the case of demoniacs. And he appeals to θεραπεύεσθε (ver. 14), observing that exorcisms are not *healings* (*L. J.* ii. p. 53, Eng. tr. ii. p. 239). But we know too little to affirm that Jesus never laid His hands on demoniacs; and both θεραπεύειν (viii. 2; Mt. xvii. 16) and ἰᾶσθαι (ix. 42) are used of healing them. Jesus generally cured ordinary diseases with a touch or laying on of hands (iv. 40, v. 13, viii. 44, 54, xiv. 4, xxii. 51); but He sometimes healed such with a word (iv. 39, v. 24, vi. 10, vii. 10). Although He commonly healed demoniacs with a word (iv. 35, 41, viii. 29, ix. 42), He may sometimes have touched them. And it should be noted that ἀπολέλυσαι, which implies that she has already been freed from the πνεῦμα ἀσθενείας (comp. v. 20), precedes the laying on of hands. Therefore this act, like the laying hold of the demoniac boy (Mk. ix. 27), may have been added in order to complete the physical cure. There is nothing to show that the woman had come expecting to be healed by Jesus. For συνκύπτουσα see Ecclus. xii. 11, xix. 26.

ἔτη δέκα ὀκτώ. To suggest that this is a reminiscence of the eighteen on whom the tower fell, and that the twelve in viii. 43 is a reminiscence of the twelve in viii. 42, is hardly sober criticism. Do numbers never come a second time in real life? And he must be a poor inventor who is incapable of varying numbers. Syr-Sin. has "had a spirit eighteen years."

μὴ δυναμένη. As usual in N.T., we have μή with the participle, although it refers to a matter of fact. Comp. i. 20; Acts ix. 9; and see Simcox, *Lang. of N.T.* p. 188.

ἀνακύψαι εἰς τὸ παντελές. "Wholly to lift up herself, to straighten herself properly." Nearly all English Versions follow the Vulgate in taking εἰς τὸ παντελές with μὴ δυναμένη; *nec omnino poterat*, "could not in any wise, could not at all." But it may go with ἀνακύψαι, after which it is placed: "coulde not well loke up" (Cov.); *konnte nicht wohl aufsehen* (Luth.). Comp. σώζειν εἰς τὸ παντελὲς δύναται (Heb. vii. 25), the only other passage in N.T. in which it occurs. Not in LXX. Josephus always has it next to the word to which it belongs (*Ant.* i. 18. 5, iii. 11. 3, 12. 1, vi. 2. 3, vii. 13. 3).

12. ἀπολέλυσαι. "Thou hast been and remainest loosed"; an unasked for cure. Comp. ἀφέωνται (v. 20, vii. 48).

13. παραχρῆμα ἀνωρθώθη. See on v. 25. The verb occurs in N.T. only here, Acts xv. 16, and Heb. xii. 12; but is freq. in LXX. Hobart shows that it is used by medical writers of straightening abnormal or dislocated parts of the body (p. 22).

14. ἀποκριθεὶς δὲ ὁ ἀρχισυνάγωγος. Comp. viii. 41. No one had spoken to him, but he replies to what had been done. He indirectly censures the act of Jesus by addressing the people as represented by the woman.

15. Ὑποκριταί. All who sympathize with this faultfinder are addressed, especially οἱ ἀντικείμενοι αὐτῷ (ver. 17). There was hypocrisy in pretending to rebuke the people, when he was really censuring Jesus; and in professing to have a zeal for the Law, when his motive was *animus* against the Healer. There was no evidence that people had come in order to be healed. And, if they had done so, would they have broken the Law? Cyril has a very animated attack on this man, whom he addresses as *βασκανίας ἀνδράποδον*, rebuking him for not seeing that Jesus had not broken even the letter of the Law in keeping its spirit (Migne, vol. lxxii. 770; Payne Smith, p. 454). See also Iren. iv. 8. 2. For **ὁ Κύριος** see on v. 17 and vii. 13.

The sing. *ὑποκριτά* (D U X and some Versions) is an obvious correction. All English Versions prior to RV., even Wic. and Rhem., have the sing., in spite of *hypocritæ* in Vulg.

λύει τὸν βοῦν αὐτοῦ. Christ appeals from his perverted interpretation of the law to a traditional and reasonable interpretation. But here the Talmud makes the characteristic reservation that, although water may be drawn for the animal, it must not be carried to the animal in a vessel (Edersh. *L. & T.* ii. App. xvii.). For other arguments used by Christ respecting the Sabbath, see vi. 3, 5, 9; Mk. ii. 27, 28; Jn. v. 17. We may place them in an ascending scale. Jewish tradition; charity and common sense; the Sabbath is a blessing, not a burden; the Son of Man is Lord of it; Sabbaths have never hindered the Father's work, and must not hinder the Son's. Such appeals would be varied to suit the occasion and the audience.

16. An argument *à fortiori*. If an animal, how much more a daughter of Abraham; if one whom yourselves have bound for a few hours, how much more one whom Satan has bound for eighteen years. Comp. Job ii.; Acts x. 38; 1 Cor. v. 5; 2 Cor. xii. 7; 1 Tim. i. 20: and with *ἰδοὺ δέκα καὶ ὀκτὼ ἔτη* comp. *ἰδοὺ τεσσεράκοντα ἔτη* (Deut. viii. 4); also Acts ii. 7, xiii. 11.

ἔδει λυθῆναι. Not only she may be loosed, but she ought to be. The obligation was *for* the healing on the Sabbath. It was a marked fulfilment of the programme of the ministry as announced in the synagogue at Nazareth (iv. 18). There is no prescription against doing good; and a religion which would honour God by forbidding virtue is self-condemned.

17. λέγοντος αὐτοῦ. "As He said" (RV.), not "When He had said" (AV.).

κατῃσχύνοντο. "Were put to shame": comp. 2 Cor. vii. 14, ix. 4; 1 Pet. iii. 16; in all which passages RV. is more accurate than AV. See also LXX of Is. xlv. 16.

ἐπὶ πᾶσιν τοῖς ἐνδόξοις τοῖς γινομένοις ὑπ᾽ αὐτοῦ. "Over all the glorious things that were *being* done by Him." For *τοῖς ἐνδόξοις* comp. Exod. xxxiv. 10; Deut. x. 21; Job v. 9, ix. 10, xxxiv. 24;

and for the pres. part. Mk. vi. 2. It refers to much more than the healing of this woman: *quæ gloriose fiebant ab eo* (Vulg.).

Some would put a full stop at αὐτῷ, and make Καὶ πᾶς ὁ ὄχλος ἔχαιρεν the introduction to what follows. But this robs the statement of all point. As a revolt of the popular conscience against the censoriousness of the hierarchy it is full of meaning.

18–21. The Parables of the Mustard Seed and of the Leaven. The former is given by all three (Mt. xiii. 31, 32; Mk. iv. 30–32), the latter by two (Mt. xiii. 33). Thus Mt. as well as Lk. places them together. Both parables set forth the small beginning, gradual spread, and immense development of the Kingdom of God, the one from without, the other from within. Externally the Kingdom will at last embrace all nations; internally, it will transform the whole of human life. Often before this Jesus has mentioned the Kingdom of God (vi. 20, vii. 28, viii. 10, ix. 2, 27, 60, 62, x. 9, 11, xi. 20): here He explains some of its characteristics. Mk. places the Mustard Seed immediately after the parables of the Sower and of the Seed growing secretly; Mt. after those of the Sower and of the Tares. But neither gives any note of connexion. Whereas the οὖν of Lk. clearly connects this teaching with the preceding incident.[1]

18, 19. The Parable of the Mustard Seed.

18. Ἔλεγεν οὖν. It is a needlessly violent hypothesis to regard this as a fragment torn from its context, so that the οὖν refers to something not recorded. On the other hand, it is a little forced to connect the οὖν with the enthusiasm of the multitude for His teaching and miracles. This success is but an earnest of far greater triumphs. It is safer to refer it back to ver. 11. After the interruption caused by the hypocritical remonstrance He continued His teaching. With the double question which introduces the parable comp. τίνι ὡμοιώσατε κύριον, καὶ τίνι ὁμοιώματι ὡμοιώσατε αὐτόν; (Is. xl. 18). The parable itself is more condensed in Lk. than in Mk. and Mt.

19. κόκκῳ σινάπεως. It is the smallness of the seed in comparison with the largeness of the growth that is the point. Whether other properties of mustard need be taken into account, is doubtful.

It is not quite certain what plant is meant. Stanley is inclined to follow Royle and others in identifying it with the *Salvadora Persica*, called in the East *Khardel*, the very word used in the Syriac Version to translate σίναπι. It is said to grow round the lake of Gennesareth, and to attain the height of twenty-five feet in favourable circumstances. Its seeds are small and pungent,

---

[1] With this pair of Parables comp. the Garments and the Wine-skins (v. 36–39), the Rash Builder and the Rash King (xiv. 28–32), the Lost Sheep and the Lost Coin (xv. 3–10). Other pairs are not in immediate juxtaposition; *e.g.* the Friend at Midnight (xi. 5–8) and the Unjust Judge (xviii. 1–8).

and are used as mustard (*Sin. & Pal.* p. 427). Edersheim follows Tristram and others in contending for the *Sinapis nigra.* "Small as a mustard-seed" was a Jewish proverb to indicate the least drop of blood, the least defilement, etc. Even in Europe the *Sinapis* sometimes reaches twelve feet (*L. & T.* i. p. 593; *Nat. Hist. of B.* p. 472).

ἄνθρωπος. Comp. xx. 9. Lk. commonly writes *ἄνθρωπός τις*: x. 30, xii. 16, xiv. 16, xv. 11, xvi. 1, 19, xix. 12; comp. xviii. 2.

εἰς κῆπον ἑαυτοῦ. See Introd. § 6. i. f. Not merely "the earth" (Mk.) or "his field" (Mt.), but "his own garden," viz. Israel.

ἐγένετο εἰς δένδρον. All three use *γίνομαι*, Lk. alone adding *εἰς*; but *μέγα* before *δένδρον* is not genuine either here or in Mt. For *γίνομαι εἰς* comp. xx. 17; Acts iv. 11, and v. 36, etc. The expression is freq. in LXX, and is also classical.

τὰ πετεινὰ τοῦ οὐρανοῦ κατεσκήνωσεν, κ.τ.λ. All three have this expression. See on ix. 58, and comp. *ὑποκάτω αὐτοῦ κατεσκήνουν τὰ θηρία τὰ ἄγρια, καὶ ἐν τοῖς κλάδοις αὐτοῦ κατῴκουν τὰ ὄρνεα τοῦ οὐρανοῦ* (Dan. iv. 9, 18) and *ἐν ταῖς παραφυάσιν αὐτοῦ ἐνόσσευσαν πάντα τὰ πετεινὰ τοῦ οὐρανοῦ* (Ezek. xxxi. 6: comp. xvii. 23), passages which show that this was a recognized metaphor for a great empire giving protection to the nations.[1]

20, 21. The Parable of the Leaven. Mt. xiii. 33; comp. Lk xii. 1.

ἔκρυψεν εἰς ἀλεύρου σάτα τρία. The beginnings of the Kingdom were unseen, and Pagan ignorance of the nature of the Gospel was immense. But the leaven always conquers the dough. However deep it may be buried it will work through the whole mass and change its nature into its own nature. Josephus says that a *σάτον* was one and a half of a Roman *modius* (*Ant.* ix. 4. 5). It was a *seah*, or one third of an *ephah*; which was an ordinary baking (Gen. xviii. 6). There is no more reason for finding a meaning for the three measures than for the three years (ver. 7). But Lange is inclined to follow Olshausen in interpreting the three measures as the three powers in human nature, body, soul, and spirit; and he further suggests the material earth, the State, and the Church.

In class. Gk. we generally have the plur. *ἄλευρα* (*ἀλέω*). It means "wheaten meal" (Hdt. vii. 119. 2; Plat. *Rep.* ii. 372 B).

ἕως οὗ. Comp. Acts xxi. 26. In Lk. xxiv. 49 it is followed by the subj., as often.

22–30. The Danger of being excluded from the Kingdom of God. The warning grows out of the question as to the number of

[1] Wetst. quotes from the Talmud, "There was a stalk of mustard in Sichin from which sprang out three branches, of which one was broken off, and out of it they made a covering for a potter's hut, and there were formed on it three cabs of mustard. Rabbi Simeon, son of Calaphta, said, A stalk of mustard was in my field into which I was wont to climb, as men are wont to climb into a fig tree."

the saved, but no note is given of time or place. The introductory διεπορεύετο seems to point back to ix. 51, "He was continuing His journey" (see on vi. 1). In any case it is part of the last journeyings which ended in the Passion. For the substance of the discourse comp. Mt. vii. 13, 14, 22, 23, xix. 30; Mk. x. 31.

22. **κατὰ πόλεις καὶ κώμας.** Once more we have an amphibolous phrase: see on ver. 11, x. 18, xi. 39, xii. 1, etc. Either, "He went on His way, teaching through cities and villages"; or, "He went on His way through cities and villages, teaching."

23. **Εἶπεν δέ τις αὐτῷ.** We have no means of knowing whether he was a disciple or not, or what his motive was. The question has always been an attractive one to certain minds (2 Esdras viii.).

εἰ ὀλίγοι οἱ σωζόμενοι. The questioner perhaps supposes that, at any rate, none but Jews will be saved. Comp. Acts ii. 47; 1 Cor. i. 18; 2 Cor. ii. 15. In all these passages the pres. part. should be marked; "those who are being saved, who are in the way of salvation."

For εἰ introducing a *direct* interrogative comp. xxii. 49; Acts i. 6, xix. 2; Mt. xii. 10, etc. The constr. is not classical, and may be explained as arising from the omission of θαυμάζω, γινώσκειν θέλω, or the like. In German we might have, *Ob Wenige selig werden?*

εἶπεν πρὸς αὐτούς. Note the plur. As in xii. 15, 42, Jesus gives no answer to the question asked, but replies in a way that may benefit others as well as the interrogator far more than a direct answer would have done.

24. **Ἀγωνίζεσθε εἰσελθεῖν.** "Keep on striving to enter," or, "Strain every nerve." *Questio theoretica initio vertitur ad praxin* (Beng.). Comp. 1 Tim. vi. 12; 2 Tim. iv. 7; Ecclus. iv. 28; Dan. vi. 14 (Theod.). In Mt. vii. 13 we have εἰσέλθατε διὰ τῆς στενῆς πύλης. But the context is quite different; and there it is an outside *gate*, while here the *door* leads directly into the house, and is so narrow that only those who are thoroughly in earnest (βιασταί) can pass through it. Vulg. has *per angustam portam* in both places; but some Lat. texts have *januam* or *ostium* here.

ζητήσουσιν εἰσελθεῖν καὶ οὐκ ἰσχύσουσιν. The futures are most important, whether we place a comma or a full stop after the second. Jesus does not say that there *are* many who *strive* in vain to enter, but that there *will* be many who *will seek* in vain to enter, *after the time of salvation is past.* Those who continue to strive now, succeed. The change from "strive" to "seek" must also be noted. Mere ζητεῖν is very different from ἀγωνίζεσθαι (1 Tim. vi. 12). Comp. Jn. vii. 34.

οὐκ ἰσχύσουσιν. "Will not have strength to" (vi. 48, xvi. 3): appropriate to the attempt to force a closed door.

25. ἀφ' οὗ ἂν ἐγερθῇ. Connect this closely with what precedes. "Shall not be able, when once the master of the house shall have risen up," etc. With this arrangement a full stop is placed at πόθεν ἐστέ, and τότε begins a new sentence.

Those who place a full stop at ἰσχύσουσιν differ much as to the apodosis of ἀφ' οὗ. Some make it begin at καὶ ἄρξησθε, more at καὶ ἀποκριθεὶς, and others at τότε. Of these three the first is the worst, making ἄρξησθε = ἄρξεσθε, and the last is the best (AV. RV.).

26, 27. Comp. Mt. vii. 22, 23. When the attempt to force the door has failed, ye will begin to use this plea; but it will be cut short by the reply, Οὐκ οἶδα ὑμᾶς. The plea is almost grotesque in its insufficiency. To have known Christ after the flesh gives no claim to admission into the kingdom.

ἀπόστητε ἀπ' ἐμοῦ πάντες ἐργάται ἀδικίας. A quotation from Ps. vi. 9, where we have πάντες οἱ ἐργαζόμενοι τὴν ἀνομίαν. Aristotle says that as δικαιοσύνη sums up the whole of virtue, so ἀδικία sums up the whole of vice (*Eth. Nic.* v. 1. 19). Contrast the quotation of the same text in Mt. vii. 23. Vulg. preserves one difference by having *qui operamini* there and *operarii* here; but ignores another in using *iniquitas* for ἀνομία there and also for ἀδικία here. Similarly AV. and RV. have "iniquity" in both. With ἐργάται ἀδικίας comp. οἱ ἐργάται τῆς ἀνομίας (1 Mac. iii. 6); τῶν καλῶν καὶ σεμνῶν ἐργάτην (Xen. *Mem.* ii. 1. 27); τῶν πολεμικῶν (*Cyr.* iv. 1. 4).

28. Ἐκεῖ ἔσται ὁ κλαυθμός. There is no need to interpret ἐκεῖ of time, a use which is rare in class. Grk. and perhaps does not occur in N.T. Here the meaning is, "There in your exclusion, in your place of banishment." Note the articles with κλαυθμός and βρυγμός, "the weeping and the gnashing," which are indeed such. Elsewhere in N.T. βρυγμός occurs only in Mt. (viii. 12, xiii. 42, 50, xxii. 13, xxiv. 51, xxv. 30). In LXX Prov. xix. 12; Ecclus. li. 3; also Aq. Ps. xxxvii. 9. These two verses (28, 29) occur in Mt. (viii. 11, 12) in a different connexion and with some difference of wording.

Ἀβραὰμ καὶ Ἰσαὰκ καὶ Ἰακὼβ καὶ πάντας τ. προφήτας. For all this Marcion seems to have substituted πάντας τοὺς δικαίους, in order to avoid a direct reference to O.T. (Tert. *Adv. Marcion*, iv. 30). The evidence is wholly against the conjecture that Marcion's reading was the original one, which was altered in order to oppose him and agree with Mt. viii. 11. In Mt. πάντας τοὺς προφήτας is wanting. Some Lat. texts add *dei* to *prophetas*, and many add *introire*, or *intrare*, or *introeuntes* before *in regno* or *in regnum*.

ὑμᾶς δὲ ἐκβαλλομένους ἔξω. "But yourselves *being* cast forth without," in the attempt to enter. They never do enter; but, as they would have entered, but for their misconduct, their exclusion is spoken of as "casting out." Syr-Sin. omits the words.

29. ἥξουσιν ἀπὸ ἀνατολῶν, κ.τ.λ. A combination of Is. xlv. 6 and xlix. 12: comp. lix. 19; Jer. iii. 18; Mal. i. 11. In Mt. viii. 11, 12 the exclusion of the Jews and admission of the Gentiles is still more clearly expressed. This was the exact opposite of Jewish expectations. *In mundo futuro mensam ingentem vobis sternam, quod gentes videbunt et pudefient* (Schoettgen, *Hor. Heb.* p. 86); *i.e.* the Gentiles were to be put to shame at the sight of the Jews in bliss. Here it is the Jews who gnash their teeth, while the Gentiles are in bliss. There is no πολλοί with ἥξουσιν, so that the man's curiosity remains unanswered; but the context implies many rather than few. In Mt. πολλοί is expressed; and this also seems to have been against Jewish expectations. *Vidi filios cœnaculi qui numero admodum pauci sunt* (Schoettgen, p. 80). The Jews commonly spoke of the Messianic Kingdom as a banquet (xiv. 15; Rev. xix. 9). For the four quarters of the globe comp. Ps. cvii. 3; 1 Chron. ix. 24. Of the order in which they are given here Bengel remarks, *Hoc fere ordine ad fidem conversi sunt populi.* Mt. has only East and West. Comp. 2 Esdr. viii. 1.

Even if ὄψεσθε (B^1 D X) were the right reading for ὄψησθε (A B^2 R T, ἴδητε ℵ) in ver. 28, there would be no need to make ἥξουσιν depend upon ὅταν. There should in any case be a full stop at ἔξω.

30. εἰσὶν ἔσχατοι . . . εἰσὶν πρῶτοι. There are some of each class who will be transferred to the other. Mt. xx. 16 we have ἔσονται οἱ ἔσχατοι πρῶτοι καὶ οἱ πρῶτοι ἔσχατοι. From that passage coupled with Mt. xix. 30 = Mk. x. 31 we infer that this was a saying which Jesus uttered more than once. But here only is it introduced with καὶ ἰδού, of which Lk. is so fond (i. 20, 31, 36, v. 12, vii. 12, 37, etc.), and for which Mt. and Mk. have πολλοὶ δέ. The practical answer to the question in ver. 23 remains, "Whatever be the number of those who are in the way of salvation, that which concerns you is, that you should without delay secure a place among them."

31–35. § The Message to Herod Antipas and the Lament over Jerusalem. From ἐν αὐτῇ τῇ ὥρᾳ it is clear that the scene does not shift. It probably lies in Peræa, but we cannot be certain. Both Peræa and Galilee were under the jurisdiction of Antipas. The Pharisees wanted to frighten Jesus into Judæa, where He would be more in the power of the Sanhedrin; but that they did not invent this alarm about Antipas is clear from Christ's reply. He would have denounced *the Pharisees* for cunning and deceit, if they had brought Him a lying report; and it is very unnatural to make τῇ ἀλώπεκι ταύτῃ refer to the inventor of the report, or to the Pharisees as a body, or indeed to anyone but Herod. For the same reason we need not suppose that the Pharisees were in a plot with Herod. They reported his words without consulting him. Although the tetrarch wished to see Christ work a miracle, yet he probably regarded Him as a dangerous leader like the Baptist; and that he should openly threaten to put Him to death, in order to induce Him to leave his province, is probable enough. The wish to disturb Jesus in His work, and to create a panic among His followers, would make the Pharisees report this threat, even it they had no hope of driving Him into the power of the hierarchy. The incident is remarkably parallel to the attempt of Amaziah, priest of the golden calf at Bethel, who first denounced the Prophet Amos to Jeroboam II., and then tried to frighten Amos out of Israel into Judah, equally in vain (Amos vii. 10–17). See Trench, *Studies in the Gospels*, p. 238.

31. θέλει σε ἀποκτεῖναι. "Would fain kill Thee" (RV.). The "will" of all other English Versions is too like the simple future: comp. ix. 23. They do not say, "has determined to kill." Possibly Jesus was in the very district in which John had been captured by Antipas; and this may have suggested the threat or the report of it, or both.

32. εἴπατε τῇ ἀλώπεκι ταύτῃ. As *ἀλώπηξ* is usually fem. (ix. 58; Mt. viii. 20; Judg. i. 35; 1 Kings xxi. 10; and also in class. Grk.), we cannot infer that the fem. is here used in a contemptuous sense: but the masc. occurs Cant. ii. 15. Here, as usual, the fox is used as a symbol of craftiness, not of rapacity, as some maintain. Herod's craftiness lay in his trying to get rid of an influential leader and a disquieting preacher of righteousness by a threat which he had not the courage to execute. He did not wish to bring upon himself a second time the odium of having slain a Prophet.[1] In the Talmud the fox is called "the sliest of beasts." See examples in Keim, *Jes. of Naz.* iv. p. 344, and Wetst. Foxes of more than one species are very common in Palestine. *D.B.*[2] art. "Fox."

ἐκβάλλω δαιμόνια καὶ ἰάσεις ἀποτελῶ. As in the reply to the Baptist (vii. 22), Jesus gives the casting out of demons and the healing of the sick as signs of the Messiah's works. In N.T. *ἴασις* is peculiar to Lk. (Acts iv. 22, 30); in LXX Prov. iii. 8, iv. 22. See Hastings, *D.B.* i. p. 593.

The reading *ἐπιτελῶ* (A R) is a correction to a more familiar verb, for *ἀποτελῶ* occurs elsewhere in bibl. Grk. only Jas. i. 15; 1 Esdr. v. 73 (same *v.l.* as here); 2 Mac. xv. 39. It means, "I bring quite to an end."

σήμερον καὶ αὔριον καὶ τῇ τρίτῃ. The three days have been interpreted to mean (1) three actual days, (2) the three years of the ministry, (3) a long time, (4) a short time, (5) a definite time.

[1] Cyril argues that, because we have *ταύτῃ* and not *ἐκείνῃ* with *τῇ ἀλώπεκι*, the fox must be some one nearer the spot than Herod, viz. the Pharisees (Migne, vol. lxxii. p. 582). Theophylact uses the same argument. But it is the common use of *οὗτος* for that which is condemned or despised, *vulpi isti*; or still more simply, "that fox of yours," *i.e.* whom you put forward and make use of. Comp. *οὗτος*, v. 21, vii. 39, 49; Jn. vi. 42, vii. 15, 36, 49, ix. 16, xii. 34.

The last is probably right. The course of the Messiah is determined, and will not be abbreviated or changed because of the threats of a Herod.[1] For the same expression of three actual days comp. Ex. xix. 10, 11. See also Hos. vi. 2.

τελειοῦμαι. "I am perfected," *consummor* (Vulg.). Comp. Heb. ii. 10. In both cases the idea is that of "bringing Christ to the full moral perfection of His humanity, which carries with it the completeness of power and dignity" (Wsctt.). This is the only passage in N.T. outside the Epistle to the Hebrews in which this verb is used of Christ. In that Epistle it is thus used thrice (ii. 10, v. 9, vii. 28), and the idea which it represents is one of the main characteristics of the Epistle. It is doubtful whether there is here any reference to the special phrase τελειοῦν τὰς χεῖρας, which is used in LXX of the installation of *priests* in their office (Exod. xxix. 9, 29, 33, 35; Lev. viii. 33, xvi. 32; Num. iii. 3: comp. Lev. xxi. 10; Exod. xxviii. 37 (41); Jud. xvii. 5); although such a reference would be very appropriate on the approach of Christ's sacrifice of Himself. See Wsctt. on *The idea of* τελείωσις and on *The* τελείωσις *of Christ* (*Hebrews*, pp. 63–67).

τελειοῦμαι is probably pass. and not mid.; pres. and not Attic fut. Ellicott, *Hulsean Lectures*, 1859, p. 264, 4th ed.; Keim, iv. p. 344.

33. πλὴν δεῖ με σήμερον κ. αὔριον κ. τῇ ἐχομένῃ πορεύεσθαι. "Howbeit" (see on vi. 24, 35) "it is ordained by Divine decree (see on iv. 43, ix. 22) that I go on My way hence, as Herod desires; not, however, because you suggest it, but because My work at this time requires it." The same verb is used in both places: πορεύου ἐντεῦθεν and δεῖ με πορεύεσθαι. But, as ἐξελθεῖν is not repeated, the repetition of πορεύεσθαι (comp. πορευθέντες εἴπατε) may be accidental.[2] The expression τῇ ἐχομένῃ for "the next day" occurs elsewhere in bibl. Grk. only Acts xx. 15; 1 Chron. x. 8; 2 Mac. xii. 39: comp. Acts xiii. 44?, xxi. 26; 1 Mac. iv. 28?.

To understand χώρᾳ instead of ἡμέρᾳ and translate "I must go on My way to-day and to-morrow in the adjoining region also," is against the context: τῇ ἐχομένῃ plainly = τῇ τρίτῃ.

οὐκ ἐνδέχεται προφήτην ἀπολέσθαι ἔξω Ἰερουσαλήμ. "It cannot be allowed," *non convenit, non fieri potest:* 2 Mac. xi. 18; Plat. *Rep.* vi. 501 C. The saying is severely ironical, and that in two ways. (1) According to overwhelming precedent, Jerusalem is

[1] "The number three seems here, as in the three years (ver. 7), to denote a period of time as complete in itself, with a beginning, middle, and end" (Andrews, *L. of our Lord*, p. 396). *Universi temporis requisiti ad opus suum perfectio significatur* (Cajetan).

[2] Maldonatus, whom Trench approves, makes the πλήν signify, "Although I must die on the third day, yet threats will not interfere with My continuing My work until then." Rather, "Although I must go to Jerusalem, yet it is not threats which send Me thither."

the place in which a Prophet ought to be put to death. *Quæ urbi jus illud occidendi Prophetas quasi usu ceperat* (Grotius). Jewish usage has determined that Jerusalem is the right place for such crimes. (2) When the conditions of place and time have been fulfilled, it is not Herod that will be the murderer. "You profess to be anxious for My safety, if I remain in Herod's dominions. Do not be alarmed. I am in no danger here, nor from him. But I must go to your capital: and it is there, and at your hands, that I shall die." Jesus is not referring to the *Sanhedrin* as having the exclusive *right* to try a Prophet; nor does He mean that no Prophet had ever been slain outside Jerusalem. The Baptist had been murdered at Machærus.[1] But such cases were exceptional. By long prescription it had been established that Jerusalem was the proper scene for these tragedies.

προφήτην. Any Prophet. To make it equivalent to *τὸν προφήτην*, and interpret it of Christ in particular, does violence to the Greek.

34, 35. The Lament over Jerusalem. This lament is called forth by the thought of the previous verse. What sorrow that the Messiah should have to speak thus of the metropolis of His own people! The connexion is natural; all the more so if the Pharisees (ver. 31) came from Jerusalem. But the connexion in Mt. xxiii. 37 is not less natural; and there Christ is at Jerusalem. To decide between the two arrangements is not easy: and to suppose that such words were spoken on two different occasions is rather a violent hypothesis; which, however, is adopted by Alford, Andrews, Ellicott, and Stier. The wording is almost identical in both places, especially in the remarkable turn from the third sing. (*αὐτήν*) to the second sing. (*σου*), and thence to the second plur. (*ἠθελήσατε*). On the whole it seems to be more probable that the lament was uttered when Jerusalem was before His eyes, than when it and its inhabitants were far away. For the repetition of the name see on x. 41.

34. ἡ ἀποκτείνουσα τοὺς προφήτας. "The slayer of Prophets"; pres. part. This is her abiding character; she is a murderess, *laniena prophetarum*, *προφητοκτόνος*. Comp. Acts vii. 52.

λιθοβολοῦσα τοὺς ἀπεσταλμένους πρὸς αὐτήν. As the wicked husbandmen did (Mt. xxi. 35): comp. Heb. xii. 20. This is a repetition in a more definite form of the preceding clause. It is arbitrary to make *τοὺς ἀπεσταλμένους* refer to the Apostles and other messengers of the Gospel: they are the same class as *τοὺς προφήτας*. See Paschasius Radbertus on Mt. xxiii. 37, Migne, cxx. 789.

[1] But perhaps even in the case of the Baptist the hierarchy at Jerusalem had a hand. He was "delivered up" by some party. Comp. *παραδοθῆναι* (Mk. i. 14), *παρεδόθη* (Mt. iv. 12).

ποσάκις ἠθέλησα ἐπισυνάξαι τὰ τέκνα σου. These words, which are found in both Mt. and Lk., are evidence from the Synoptists themselves respecting much work of Christ in Jerusalem which they do not record. As S. John tells us, He ministered there at other times than just before His Passion. The context forbids us from taking τὰ τέκνα σου in any other sense than the inhabitants of Jerusalem. (Comp. xix. 44, and see Neander, *L. J. C.* § 110, Eng. tr. p. 165.) This is fully admitted by Strauss, if the words were really spoken by Christ.[1] He suggests therefore that they come from an apocryphal source, and probably the same from which he supposes xi. 49–51 to have been taken. In this he has been followed by Loman and Pfleiderer (see Hahn, ii. p. 255). But, like x. 22, this verse—so strongly confirming the Johannean tradition—is far too well attested to be got rid of by any suppositions. The prepositions in ἐπισυνάξαι mean "together to one place—to Myself." Comp. Ps. ci. 23 ?, cv. 47.

ὃν τρόπον ὄρνις τὴν ἑαυτῆς νοσσιάν. "Even as a hen her own brood." For ὃν τρόπον comp. Exod. ii. 14. Like "fowl" in English, ὄρνις is used specially of domesticated hens (Xen. *Anab.* iv. 5. 25; Aesch. *Eum.* 866). Mt. has τὰ νοσσία αὐτῆς, "her chickens." This similitude is not found in O.T., but is frequent in Rabbinical literature. Schoettgen, pp. 207–210. Comp. τὰ κείνου τέκν' ἔχων ὑπὸ πτεροῖς σώζω τάδε (Eur. *Heracl.* 10). Jerome quotes Deut. xxxii. 11 in illustration: "As an eagle that stirreth up her nest, that fluttereth over her young, He spread abroad His wings, He took them, He bare them on His pinions." With **ὑπὸ τὰς πτέρυγας** comp. Ruth ii. 12; Is. xxxi. 5; Mal. iv. 2; Ps. xvii. 8, xxxvi. 8, lvii. 2, lxi. 5, lxiii. 8.

καὶ οὐκ ἠθελήσατε. In tragic contrast with ποσάκις ἠθέλησα: comp. Jn. i. 5, 10, 11.

35. ἀφίεται ὑμῖν ὁ οἶκος ὑμῶν. Neither here (D E G H M U X Δ, Latt. Boh. Syr.) nor in Mt. xxiii. 38, where it is better attested, is ἔρημος more than a gloss. Comp. ὅτι εἰς ἐρήμωσιν ἔσται ὁ οἶκος οὗτος (Jer. xxii. 5), and ἐγκαταλέλοιπα τὸν οἶκόν μου, ἀφῆκα τὴν κληρονομίαν μου (Jer. xii. 7). "Is being left to you" means "You have it entirely to yourselves to possess and protect; for God no longer dwells in it and protects it." Comp. ἀφεθήσεται (xvii. 34, 35). By "your house" is meant the home of τὰ τέκνα σου, the city of Jerusalem. Note the repetition ὑμῖν . . . ὑμῶν. Syr-Sin. here has, "Your house is forsaken"; in Mt. it is defective.

λέγω δὲ ὑμῖν οὐ μὴ ἴδητέ με. With great solemnity and with strong assurance. Comp. Jn. vii. 34, viii. 21.

ἕως εἴπητε. Their seeing Him is dependent upon their repent-

[1] *Hier sind alle Ausflüchte vergebens, und man muss bekennen: sind diess wirkliche Worte Jesu, so muss er öfter und länger, als es den synoptischen Berichten nach scheint, in Jerusalem thätig gewesen sein* (*L. J.* 1864, p. 249).

ance; and this is left uncertain; for the ἥξει ὅτε or ἂν ἥξῃ ὅτε after ἕως (A D, Vulg.) is not genuine.[1] There are three interpretations of the point of time indicated by this declaration. (1) *The cries of the multitude on Palm Sunday* (xix. 38; Mt. xxi. 9; Mk. xi. 9). But this is quite inadequate. Christ would not have declared with this impressive solemnity the fact that He would not enter Jerusalem for some weeks, or possibly months. (2) *The Second Advent.* But where are we told that the unbelieving Jews will welcome the returning Christ with hymns of praise? (3) *The conversion of the Jews throughout all time.* This last no doubt is right. The quotation Εὐλογημένος, κ.τ.λ., is *verbatim* from LXX of Ps. cxviii. 26, and ἐν ὀνόματι Κυρίου means as the representative of Jehovah. Converted Israel will thus welcome the spiritual presence of the Messiah.

XIV. 1–XVII. 10. *The Second Period of the Journey.*

This forms a new division of the section which has been styled "the Journeyings towards Jerusalem": see on ix. 51. The first portion of it (xiv. 1–24) may be thus subdivided. A Sabbath-meal in the House of a Pharisee, including the Healing of a Dropsical Man on the Sabbath (1–6), a Discourse about taking the lowest seats (7–11) and inviting Lowly Guests (12–14), and the Parable of the Great Supper (15–24). The whole is peculiar to Lk., and probably comes from some source unknown to Mt. and Mk.

1–24. § A Sabbath-meal in the House of a Pharisee. Time and place are quite undetermined. The chief men among the Pharisees no doubt lived mostly at Jerusalem. Beyond that we have no clue.

1–6. The Cure of a Dropsical Man at the Sabbath-meal. The cure of the man with the withered hand (vi. 6–11; Mt. xii. 9–14; Mk. iii. 1-6) should be compared but not identified. Although Lk. records both cures, with very important differences of detail, Strauss and Keim maintain that this is a mere doublet of the other, and reject both. The style of the opening words indicates an Aramaic source.

Of the seven miracles of mercy on the sabbath, Lk. records five: the Demoniac at Capernaum (iv. 31), the Withered Hand (vi. 6), the Woman bowed down eighteen years (xiii. 14), Simon's wife's mother (iv. 38), and this. The others are: the Paralytic at Bethesda (Jn. v. 10), the Man born blind (Jn. ix. 14).

---

[1] Not only do ℵ B K L M R X, Syr. Boh. Arm. and some Lat. texts here omit ἥξει ὅτε, but no authorities insert the words Mt. xxiii. 39, which adds to the weight of the evidence against them here.

1. Καὶ ἐγένετο ἐν τῷ ἐλθεῖν αὐτόν. "And it came to pass after He had entered" (aor.), not "as He entered" (AV.) nor "when He entered" (RV.): *cum intrasset* or *introisset* (some MSS. of Vulg.) rather than *cum intraret* (Vulg.). See on iii. 21 and the note at the end of ch. i. p. 45.

τινος τῶν ἀρχόντων τῶν Φαρισαίων. "Of one of the chief men of the Pharisees." We have no knowledge of official rulers of the Pharisees; but of course they had their leading men. That the invitation of a leading Pharisee was accepted (ver. 12) after what is recorded xi. 37–54 might seem surprising, especially as Jesus knew the minds of those whom He was to meet (ver. 3). But there was still the possibility of influencing some of them for good. We know of no case in which Jesus refused an invitation.

σαββάτῳ φαγεῖν ἄρτον. Sabbath banqueting was common, and became proverbial for luxury. *Observa diem sabbati, non Judaicis deliciis*; and *Hodiernus dies sabbati est, hunc in præsenti tempore otio quodam corporaliter languido et fluxo et luxurioso celebrant Judæi* (Aug.). See Wetst. *ad loc.* and Polano, *The Talmud; Selections translated from the original*, p. 259.

καὶ αὐτοὶ ἦσαν παρατηρούμενοι αὐτόν. Lk.'s favourite construction. See on v. 14 and vi. 20. The καί introduces the apodosis of ἐγένετο: "it came to pass . . . that the Pharisees themselves were persistently watching Him." For παρατηρεῖσθαι of interested and sinister espionage see on vi. 7. Excepting Mk. iii. 2 and Gal. iv. 10, the verb occurs only in Lk. (xx. 20; Acts ix. 24).

The translation "were there, watching" is erroneous: ἦσαν παρατηρούμενοι is the periphrastic imperf. It is also an error to carry on the construction of ἐγένετο beyond ver. 1: *vv.* 1 and 2 are quite independent statements.

2. καὶ ἰδοὺ ἄνθρωπός τις. We are left in doubt whether the man was placed there as a trap, which the absence of γάρ does not disprove, or was there by accident, or had come in the hope of being healed. The last is probable: but the ἰδού seems to imply that his presence was unexpected by the company, and perhaps by the host. He was probably not an invited guest, as ἀπέλυσεν (ver. 4) appears to show. But in an Eastern house he would have no difficulty in obtaining admission (Tristram, *Eastern Customs*, pp. 36, 81): and, if he hoped to be healed, he would take care to appear ἔμπροσθεν αὐτοῦ. Note the τις *vv.* 2, 19, 20.

ὑδρωπικός. Not elsewhere in bibl. Grk., but freq. in medical writers. The disease seems to be indicated as a curse Num. v. 21, 22; comp. Ps. cix. 18. Comp. Hor. *Carm.* ii. 2. 13.

3. ἀποκριθεὶς . . . πρὸς τοὺς νομικοὺς καὶ Φαρισαίους. He answered their thoughts implied in ἦσαν παρατηρούμενοι. This watching had now a definite object owing to the presence of the dropsical man. Comp. v. 22, vii. 40. The νομικοί (see on

vii. 30) and Φαρισαῖοι are put as one class, and are a more definite description of the αὐτοί in ver. 1. Note the Hebraistic **εἶπεν λέγων.**

θεραπεῦσαι ἢ οὔ; Comp. ἀγαθοποιῆσαι ἢ κακοποιῆσαι (vi. 9); ἐξ οὐρανοῦ ἢ ἐξ ἀνθρώπων (xx. 4). The dilemma, if they had planned one against Him, is turned against themselves. These lawyers were bound to be able to answer such a question: and if rigorist Pharisees made no objection when consulted beforehand, they could not protest afterwards. They take refuge in silence; not in order to provoke Him to heal, but because they did not know what to say. They did not wish to say that healing on the sabbath was allowable, and they did not dare to say that it was not. For **ἡσυχάζω** in this sense comp. Acts xi. 18, xxi. 14; Job xxxii. 6; Neh. v. 8.

The εἰ before ἔξεστι (A, Syrr. Arm.) probably comes from Mt. xii. 10 (om. ℵ B D L 59, Latt. divided). If it is genuine, comp. xiii. 23. Most of the authorities which insert εἰ have θεραπεύειν for θεραπεῦσαι (also from Mt. xii. 10) and omit ἢ οὔ.

4. ἐπιλαβόμενος ἰάσατο. That the laying hold of him is to be regarded as the means of the cure is not certain. The touching in order to heal is more often expressed by ἅπτεσθαι (v. 13, xxii. 51; Mk. i. 41, vii. 33, viii. 22; Mt. viii. 3, 15, xvii. 7, xx. 34) or by ἐπιτιθέναι τὰς χεῖρας (iv. 40, xiii. 13; Mk. vi. 5, viii. 23, 25, etc.). Both ἰᾶσθαι (see small print on v. 17) and ἐπιλαβέσθαι (ix. 47, xx. 20, 26, xxiii. 26, etc.) are freq. in Lk. Christ read the man's faith, as He read the hostility of the Pharisees, and responded to it.

ἀπέλυσεν. This probably means something more than the letting go after the ἐπιλαβόμενος, viz. "dismissed him" from the company, to prevent interference with him.

5. Τίνος ὑμῶν υἱὸς ἢ βοῦς. The emphatic word is ὑμῶν. "How do *you* act, when *your* interests are concerned? When your son, or even your ox, falls into a well?"[1] Palestine abounds in unprotected cisterns, wells and pits. Wetst. quotes from the Mishna, *Si in puteum bos aut asinus . . . filius aut filia.* The argument is that what the Pharisees allowed themselves for their own benefit must be allowed to Christ for the benefit of others. Their sabbath help had an element of selfishness; His had none.

The reading ὄνος ἢ βοῦς probably comes from xiii. 15. The correction was doubly tempting: 1. because υἱός seemed rather to spoil the *à fortiori* argument; 2. because ὄνος is more naturally coupled with βοῦς. Comp. Deut. xxii. 4. The reading πρόβατον (D) for υἱός has a similar origin, while ὄϊς is a conjecture as the supposed original of both υἱός and ὄνος. The evidence is

[1] There is possibly a reference to the wording of the fourth commandment, in which son stands first among the rational creatures possessed, and ox first among the irrational (Deut. v. 14). But comp. Ex. xxi. 33.

thus divided: *υἱός* A B E G H M S U V Γ Δ Λ etc., e f g Syrr., Cyr-Alex.—*ὄνος* ℵ K L X Π, a b c i Syr-Sin. Vulg. Arm. Aeth. See WH. ii. App. p. 62; Sanday, *App. to Grk. T.* p. 120. The *ἀποκριθεὶς* before *πρὸς αὐτοὺς εἶπεν* (ℵ A, Vulg.) is probably an insertion.

Note the Hebraistic construction instead of *τίς ὑμῶν οὗ υἱὸς, κ.τ.λ., οὐκ εὐθέως ἀνασπάσει αὐτόν;*

6. οὐκ ἴσχυσαν ἀνταποκριθῆναι. Stronger than ἡσύχασαν (ver. 3): "They had no power to reply." Lk. is fond of noting that people are silenced or keep silence (xx. 26; Acts xi. 18, xii. 17, xv. 12, xxii. 2). For the compound verb comp. Rom. ix. 20; Judg. v. 29; Job xvi. 8, xxxii. 12.

7–11. Discourse on choosing the Lowest Seats at Entertainments. We may suppose that the healing of the dropsical man preceded the meal. This now begins; and, as they settle round the tables, there is a manœuvring on the part of some of the guests to secure the best places. To suggest a comparison between healing the dropsy and dealing with *duplicem animi hydropem, superbiæ tumorem et pecuniæ sitim* is almost as fanciful as supposing that "falling into a well" is meant to refer to the dropsy. The latter supposition (Aug. Bede) still finds favour.

7. Ἔλεγεν δὲ . . . παραβολήν. Comp. v. 36, xiii. 6, xviii. 1. The "parable" is not in the form of a narrative, but in that of advice, which is thus called because it is to be understood metaphorically. Christ is not giving counsels of worldly wisdom or of good manners, but teaching a lesson of humility. Every one before God ought to feel that the lowest place is the proper place for him. There is no need to suppose that this was originally a parable in the more usual sense, and that Lk. has turned it into an exhortation; still less that ver. 7 is a fictitious introduction to a saying of which the historical connexion had been lost.

ἐπέχων. *Sc. τὸν νοῦν*: comp. Acts iii. 5; 1 Tim. iv. 16; Ecclus. xxxi. 2. He directed His attention to this: not the same as its attracting or catching His attention. Syr-Sin. omits.

τὰς πρωτοκλισίας. In the mixture of Jewish, Roman, Greek, and Persian customs which prevailed in Palestine at this time, we cannot be sure which were the most honourable places at table. Josephus (*Ant.* xv. 2. 4) throws no light. But the Talmud says that, on a couch holding three, the middle place is for the worthiest, the left for the second, and the right for the third (Edersh. *L. & T.* ii. pp. 207, 494). Among the Greeks it was usual for each couch to have only two persons (Plat. *Sym.* 175 A, C), but both Greeks and Romans sometimes had as many as four on one couch. *D. of Grk. and Rom. Ant.* artt. *Cena, Symposium, Triclinium*; Becker, *Charicles*, Sc. vi. Exc. i.; *Gallus*, Sc. ix. Exc. i. ii. Comp. Lk. xx. 46; Mt. xxiii. 6; Mk. xii. 39.

ἐξελέγοντο. "They were choosing out for themselves; *eligebant* (b c d e f ff$_2$) rather than *eligerent* (Vulg.)." The same thing seems to have taken place at the Last Supper (xxii. 24), and the washing of the disciples' feet may have been intended as a rebuke for this.

8. εἰς γάμους. Probably sing. in meaning; "to a wedding-feast": see on xii. 36. The meal at which this was said was an ordinary one, as is shown by *φαγεῖν ἄρτον* (ver. 1), the common Hebrew phrase for a meal (ver. 15; Mt. xv. 2; Mk. iii. 20; Gen. xxxvii. 25, xliii. 16; Exod. ii. 20, etc.). Jesus singles out a marriage, not perhaps because such a feast is a better type of the Kingdom of God, but because on such occasions there is more formality, and notice must be taken of the rank of the guests.

κατακλιθῇς. Peculiar to Lk. in N.T. (vii. 36, ix. 14, xxiv. 30): see on ix. 14.

9. ὁ σὲ καὶ αὐτὸν καλέσας. It is misplaced ingenuity to render, "thee thyself also," *dich auch selbst*. "Thee and him," *te et illum* (Vulg.), is right. His inviting both gave him the right to arrange both guests as he pleased. Contrast ii. 35.

ἐρεῖ. For the change from subjunct. to fut. indic. comp. xii. 58. See also *ἐρεῖ* after *ἵνα*, ver. 10.

Δὸς τούτῳ τόπον . . . τὸν ἔσχατον τόπον. Here AV. is inferior to all previous versions. Vulg. has *locum* in both places. Luth. omits in both. Tyn. Cov. Cran. Gen. have "rowme" in both: Wic. and Rhem. "place" in both. "The lowest *room*" means "the lowest *place*"; but in that case "give this man room" should precede. Otherwise "lowest room" will seem to mean the bottom chamber. See Deissmann, *Bible Studies*, p. 267.

"Thou hast set my feet in a large *room*" (Ps. xxxi. 8), *i.e.* in abundant space (Ps. xviii. 19). Bishop Hall calls Pope Pius II. "as learned as hath sat in that roome this thousand yeeres" (*Letters*, Dec. ii. Ep. 3). Davies, *Bible English*, p. 152. Comp. Ter. *Heaut.* iii. 3. 25. Sy. *Jube hunc abire hinc aliquo.* Cl. *Quo ego hinc abeam?* Sy. *Quo? quo libet: da illis locum. Abi deambulatum.* Cl. *Deambulatum? Quo?* Sy. *Vah, quasi desit locus.*

ἄρξῃ . . . κατέχειν. The *ἄρξῃ* marks the contrast between the brief self-assumed promotion and the permanent merited humiliation. Comp. Prov. xxv. 6, 7, which Christ seemed to have had in His mind. The displaced guest goes from top to bottom, because the intermediate places have meanwhile been filled.

10. ἵνα . . . ἐρεῖ σοι. Perhaps *ἵνα* is here used ἐκβατικῶς, of the *result* rather than of the *purpose*: "so that he will say to thee." But if the idea of purpose be retained, it is Christ's purpose in giving the advice, not the purpose with which the hearer is to adopt the advice. There is no recommendation of "the pride that apes humility," going to a low place *in order to* be promoted. See small print on xx. 10.

The fut. indic. after ἵνα is common in late Greek: xx. 10; Mk. xv. 20; Jn. vii. 3, xvii. 2; Acts xxi. 24; Gal. ii. 4, etc. Win. xli. b. 1, p. 360; Simcox, *Lang. of N.T.* p. 109; Burton, § 199.

προσανάβηθι ἀνώτερον. Perhaps "*Come* up higher," *i.e.* to where the host is sitting: *accede* (a c f ff_2 i q r) rather than *ascende* (Vulg.). Comp. ἀνάβαινε πρός με (Prov. xxv. 7). The verb is classical and frequent in LXX, esp. in Joshua of geographical description (xi. 17, xv. 3, 6, 7, xviii. 12, xix. 11, 12; Exod. xix. 23, etc.). The adv. occurs elsewhere in bibl. Grk. only Heb. x. 8; comp. ἀνώτερος (Neh. iii. 25), ἀνώτατος (Tobit viii. 3), ἐσώτερος (Acts xvi. 24; Heb. vi. 19), κατώτερος (Eph. iv. 9).

ἐνώπιον πάντων. Both words are characteristic: see on i. 15 and vi. 30. The πάντων is unquestionably to be retained (א A B L X 1, 33 69, Syrr. Boh. Aeth.).

11. πᾶς ὁ ὑψῶν ἑαυτόν. One of our Lord's repeated utterances: xviii. 14; Mt. xxiii. 12. In all three places AV. spoils the antithesis by varying the translation of ταπεινόω, "abase," "humble." The saying here guards against the supposition that Christ is giving mere prudential rules of conduct or of good taste. Humility is the passport to promotion in the Kingdom of God. Comp. for the first half x. 15; and for the second half Jas. iv. 10; 1 Pet. v. 6. Note that while Lk. in both places has πᾶς with the participle (see on i. 66), Mt. has ὅστις.

12–14. The Duty of inviting Lowly Guests. The previous discourse was addressed to the guests (ver. 7): this is addressed to the host. It is a return for his hospitality. We cannot be sure that all the other guests were of the upper classes, and that this moved Jesus to utter a warning. Some of His disciples may have been with Him, and they were not wealthy. Still less may we assert that, if all the other guests were of the upper classes, this was wrong. All depends upon whether the motive for hospitality was selfish. But it is wrong to omit benevolence to the poor, in whose case the selfish motive is excluded. As before, we have a parable in a hortatory form; for Jesus is not merely giving rules for the exercise of social hospitality.

12. Ἔλεγεν δὲ καὶ τῷ κεκληκότι αὐτόν. "But He was saying to him also that had bidden Him"; *qui invitaverat eum* (d f), *invitanti eum* (δ), *invitatori* (a b c ff_2 i l q r): *convivatori suo benigne rependens*, πνευματικὰ ἀντὶ σαρκικῶν (Grotius). For **ἄριστον** see on xi. 37.

μὴ φώνει. Pres. imperat. "Do not *habitually* call." It is the *exclusive* invitation of rich neighbours, etc., that is forbidden.

As distinct from καλεῖν, φωνεῖν would specially apply to invitation by word of mouth: and the use of φωνεῖν for invitations is very rare. Neither Vulg. nor any English Version before RV. distinguishes between φώνει here and κάλει, ver. 13, although in *vv.* 7, 8, 12 καλεῖν is rendered *invitare* and ver. 12 φωνεῖν, *vocare*.

πλουσίους. With γείτονας only. It is pleasant to entertain one's friends, seemly to entertain one's relations, advantageous to entertain rich neighbours. But these are not high motives for hospitality; and we must not let our hospitality end there.

μή ποτε καὶ αὐτοὶ ἀντικαλέσωσίν σε. Godet remarks that this warning is playful. *Prends-y garde: la pareille à recevoir, c'est un malheur à éviter! Car, une fois la retribution reçue, c'en est fait de la remuneration future.* Comp. οὔτε μὲν ὡς ἀντικληθησόμενος καλεῖ με τις (Xen. *Symp.* i. 15).

13. δοχὴν ποιῇς. See on v. 29.

κάλει πτωχούς, ἀναπείρους. The former would not have the money, the latter would not have the strength, to give an entertainment. That ἀναπείρους is here generic, and that χωλούς and τυφλούς are species under it, is improbable: comp. ver. 21. The πτωχοί are one class,—those wanting in means; and all the rest belong to another class,—those wanting in physical strength. Beyond this we need not specify; but in Plato we have ἀνάπηροι[1] containing the other two classes, οἱ χωλοί τε καὶ τυφλοὶ καὶ οἱ ἄλλοι ἀνάπηροι (*Crito*, p. 53 A). The ἀνά is intensive: "very maimed." For the command comp. ver. 21 and Neh. viii. 10.

14. μακάριος ἔσῃ, ὅτι οὐκ ἔχουσιν ἀνταποδοῦναί σοι. The ὅτι is strictly logical. Good deeds are sure to be rewarded either in this world or in the world to come. Those persons are blessed whose good deeds cannot be requited here, for they are sure of a reward hereafter. For **οὐκ ἔχουσιν** see on xii. 4. For **ἀνταποδοῦναι** in a good sense comp. Rom. xi. 35; 1 Thes. iii. 9; in a bad sense, Rom. xii. 19; Heb. x. 30. The ἀντί expresses retaliation, exact repayment. Comp. Arist. *Eth. Nic.* ix. 2. 5, where we have δόσις, ἀποδοτέον, and ἀνταπόδοσις.

ἐν τῇ ἀναστάσει τῶν δικαίων. It is possible that there is here a reference to the doctrine of a double resurrection, first of the righteous, and then of all. Comp. 1 Cor. xv. 23; 1 Thes. iv. 16; Rev. xx. 5, 6. If so, this is the ἀνάστασις ἐκ νεκρῶν (xx. 35; Acts iv. 2; Phil. iii. 11; 1 Pet. i. 3: comp. Mk. ix. 9, xii. 25; Mt. xvii. 9; Gal. i. 1), which implies that some are for the present left unraised, as distinct from the ἀνάστασις νεκρῶν (Acts xvii. 32; 1 Cor. xv. 12, 21; Heb. vi. 2), which is the general resurrection. See Lft. on Phil. iii. 11. But τῶν δικαίων may be added merely to indicate the character of those who practise disinterested benevolence.

15–24. The Parable of the Great Supper. The identity of this with the Parable of the Marriage of the King's Son, often called the Parable of the Wedding Garment (Mt. xxii. 1–14), will continue to be discussed, for the points of similarity and of difference are both of them so numerous that a good case may be made for either view. But the context, as well as the points of difference, justifies

[1] The form ἀνάπειρος seems to be a mere misspelling of ἀνάπηρος (Tobit xiv. 2 ℵ; 2 Mac. viii. 24 A V); but it is well attested. WH. ii. App. p. 151.

a distinction. The parable in Mt. is a comment on an attempt to arrest Christ (xxi. 46), and tells of rebels put to death for insulting and killing their sovereign's messengers; this is a comment on a pious remark, perhaps ignorantly or hypocritically made, and tells of discourteous persons who, through indifference, lose the good things to which they were invited. It is much less severe in tone than the other; and even in those parts which are common to the two has very little similarity of wording.

15. τις τῶν συνανακειμένων. "The resurrection of the just" suggests the thought of the Kingdom, and this guest complacently assumes that he will be among those who will enjoy it. With this introductory incident comp. x. 25–30, xii. 13–15, xv. 1–3.

φάγεται ἄρτον. A Hebraism: comp. ver. 1; 2 Sam. ix. 7, 10; 2 Kings iv. 8, etc., and see on ver. 8. It points to the Jewish idea that the Messianic age will be inaugurated by a banquet and will be a prolonged festival (Is. xxv. 6). The reading *ἄριστον* (E H M S U V Γ) is a mere corruption of *ἄρτον*.

16. ὁ δὲ εἶπεν αὐτῷ. "*But* He said to him" (Rhem.). "And" (Wic.) and "Then" (Tyn. Gen. AV.) obscure the fact that Christ is opposing the comfortable self-complacency of the speaker. What he says is correct, but the spirit in which he says it is quite wrong. Only those who are detached from earthly things, and treat them as of small account in comparison with the Kingdom of God, will enter therein.

ἐποίει δεῖπνον μέγα. "Was about to make a great supper," similar to that at which Jesus was now sitting. One might expect the mid., but comp. ver. 12; Acts viii. 2; Xen. *Anab.* iv. 2. 23. The **πολλούς** are the Jews who observe the Law. In Mt. it is *ἄνθρωπος βασιλεύς* who made a marriage-feast for his son.

17. τὸν δοῦλον. The *vocator*, who was sent to remind them, according to custom, and not because they were suspected of unwillingness.[1] Comp. Esth. v. 8, vi. 14. This custom still prevails. To omit the second summons would be "a grievous breach of etiquette, equivalent to cancelling the previous more general notification. To refuse the second summons would be an insult, which is equivalent among the Arab tribes to a declaration of war" (Tristram, *Eastern Customs*, p. 82). The δοῦλος represents God's messengers to His people, and specially the Baptist and Jesus Christ. Comp. Mt. xi. 28–30.

Ἔρχεσθε, ὅτι ἤδη ἕτοιμά ἐστιν. The true reading may be *ἔρχεσθαι* (ℵ A D K L P R Δ) to follow *εἰπεῖν* (Syr-Sin.), *dicere invitatis ut venirent* (Vulg.). See small print note on xix. 13. But the *πάντα* after *ἐστιν* (A P, Syr-Sin. Vulg. f) or before *ἕτοιμα* (D, a e) comes from Mt. xxii. 4. ℵ* B L R, b c ff_2 i l q omit.

---

[1] *Vocatores suos ostendenti, ut diceret a quibus invitatus esset* (Plin. *N. H.* xxxv. 10. 36. 89). Comp. Suet. *Calig.* xxxix.; Sen. *De Ira*, iii. 37. 3.

18. ἤρξαντο ἀπὸ μιᾶς πάντες παραιτεῖσθαι. Every word is full of point. The very beginning of such conduct was unexpected and unreasonable, and it lasted some time. There was no variation; it was like a prearranged conspiracy: they all pleaded that they were at present too much occupied to come. And there was not a single exception. The παραιτεῖσθαι comes as a surprise at the end, there being no ἀλλά or δέ at the outset to prepare for a contrast. This absolute unanimity prepares us for a joyous *acceptance* of the courteously repeated invitation. On the contrary, they begin "to beg off," *deprecari* (Acts xxv. 11; 2 Mac. ii. 31). In Jos. *Ant.* vii. 8. 2 the verb is used, exactly as here, of excusing oneself from an invitation. They ought to have excused themselves when the first invitation came, if at all. Their begging off now was breaking their promise; and the excuses were transparently worthless. In Mt. there is no begging off. Those invited simply ἀμελήσαντες ἀπῆλθον; and some of them insulted, and even killed the *vocatores*. For ἄρχεσθαι of proceedings which last some time comp. vii. 38, xii. 45, xix. 37, 45, xxii. 23, xxiii. 2. Here the further idea of interruption is not present.

ἀπὸ μιᾶς. The expression is unique in Greek literature. Comp. ἀπ' εὐθείας, ἀπὸ τῆς ἴσης, ἐξ ὀρθῆς, διὰ πάσης. We are probably to supply γνώμης: ἀπὸ μιᾶς καὶ τῆς αὐτῆς γνώμης (Philo, *De Spec. Legg.* ii. p. 311). Both ἐκ μιᾶς γνώμης and ἐκ μιᾶς φωνῆς are also found. We might also supply ψυχῆς. Less probable suggestions are ὥρας, συνθήκης (Vulg. *simul*), αἰτίας, ὁδοῦ.

ἔχω ἀνάγκην. A manifest exaggeration. He had already bought it, probably after seeing it; and now inspection could wait. For the phrase, which is classical, comp. 1 Cor. vii. 37; Heb. vii. 27; Jude 3; and the insertion Lk. xxiii. 17. Not in LXX.

ἔχε με παρῃτημένον. It is doubtful whether this is a Latinism, *habe me excusatum*, *i.e.* "Consider me as one who has obtained indulgence."[1] But certainly με, which is enclitic, cannot be emphatic: "Whatever you do about others, *I* must be regarded as excused." This would require ἐμέ, and before rather than after ἔχε. Comp. οὐ θαρροῦντά με ἕξεις (Xen. *Cyr.* iii. 1. 35).

19. πορεύομαι. "I am on my way." He pleads no ἀνάγκη, and is too indifferent to care about the manifest weakness of his excuse. That he had bought the oxen "on approval" is not hinted. Both these two seem to imply that they may possibly come later, if the host likes to wait, or the feast lasts long enough. Hence the host's declaration ver. 24.

20. οὐ δύναμαι. He is confident that this is unanswerable. See on ver. 26. "When a man taketh a new wife, he shall not go

[1] *Invitas tunc me, cum scis, Nasica, vocasse.*
Excusatum habeas me rogo: cœno domi.
—(Mart. ii. 79.

out in the host, neither shall he be charged with any business: he shall be free at home one year" (Deut. xxiv. 5). Comp. Hdt. i. 36. 5.

21. The πάντες (ver. 18) probably means more than three. But three suffice as examples. Some said that they would not come now; others declared that they could not come at all. Comp. the parable of the Pounds, where three servants are samples of the whole ten, and represent two classes (xix. 16–21).

Ἔξελθε ταχέως. Not because his anger makes him impatient; but because he has no intention of putting off anything to please the discourteous persons who have insulted him. He goes on with his arrangements at once.

εἰς τὰς πλατείας καὶ ῥύμας. We have the same combination Is. xv. 3. This use of ῥύμη is late: Acts ix. 11, xii. 10; Ecclus. ix. 7; Tobit xiii. 18. A lane resembles a stream; and the original sense of ῥύμη is the rush or flow of what is in motion. See Kennedy, *Sources of N.T. Greek*, p. 16. The two words combined stand for the public places of the town, in which those who have no comfortable homes are likely to be found. Comp. 1 Cor. i. 26–28.

τοὺς πτωχοὺς καὶ ἀναπείρους, κ.τ.λ. The Jews who do not observe the Law; the *publicans and sinners*. These were not asked simply because the others refused, and in order to fill the vacant places. They would have been asked in any case; but the others were asked first. They both live in the city: *i.e.* both are Jews. But those who respected the Law had a prior claim to those who rebelled against it. The similarity of wording shows the connexion with the preceding discourse (ver. 13); and therefore Bengel's attractive distinction is probably not intended. He points out that the *poor* would get no other invitation; the *maimed* would not be likely to marry; the *blind* could not go to see farms; and the *lame* would not go to prove oxen. Contrast Mt. xxii. 9, 10.

εἰσάγαγε ὧδε. See on ii. 27. It is assumed that they can be "brought in" at once, without formal invitation. They are not likely to refuse. The mixture of guests of all classes is still seen at Oriental entertainments.

22. Κύριε, γέγονεν ὃ ἐπέταξας. He executes the order, and then makes this report. There is no ἤδη, and we are not to suppose that he had *anticipated* his master's order; which would have been audacious officiousness, and could hardly have been done without his master's knowledge.

ἔτι τόπος ἐστίν. Comp. ver. 9. No such expression is found in Mt. xxii. 10. It is added because the servant knows that his master is determined to fill all the places, and that the banquet cannot begin till this is done.

23. φραγμούς. "Hedges" (φράσσω = "I fence in"): Mt. xxi. 33; Mk. xii. 1. Just as πλατεῖαι καὶ ῥῦμαι represent the public roads inside the city, so ὁδοὶ καὶ φραγμοί the public roads outside the city; and this command is the invitation to the *heathen*.

ἀνάγκασον εἰσελθεῖν. By persuasion. A single servant could not use force, and those who refused were not dragged in. Comp. Mk. vi. 45 || and παρεβιάσαντο (xxiv. 29; Acts xvi. 15). The text gives no sanction to religious persecution. By showing that physical force was not used it rather condemns it.

ἵνα γεμισθῇ μου ὁ οἶκος. *Nec natura nec gratia patitur vacuum* (Beng.). We are not told the result of this third invitation; but we may conclude that the Gentiles fill the void which the unbelief of the Jews has left (Rom. xi. 25). In Mt. the result of the second invitation is ἐπλήσθη ὁ νυμφών, and there is no third. Augustine interprets this third summons as a call to heretics, which cannot be correct.

24. λέγω γὰρ ὑμῖν. Solemn introduction of the main point of the parable. The transition from sing. (ἔξελθε) to plur. (ὑμῖν) is variously explained. (1) That some of the πτωχοί (ver. 21) are present and are included in the address. (2) That there is a transition from the parable to its application, and Christ speaks half as the host to his servant and others, and half in His own person to the Pharisee and his guests. (3) That the host addresses, not only the servant, but all who may hear of what he has done. In favour of (2) we must not quote xi. 8, xv. 7, 10, xvi. 9, xviii. 14; Mt. xxi. 43. In all these places it is Jesus who is addressing the audience; not a person in the parable who sums up the result. Here the ἐκείνων and the μου show that the latter is the case. In Mt. the conclusion to the parable is πολλοὶ γάρ εἰσιν κλητοί, ὀλίγοι δὲ ἐκλεκτοί (xxii. 14), and these are the words of Christ, not of the βασιλεύς.

25–35. § Warnings against Precipitancy and Half-heartedness in Following Christ. The Parables of the Rash Builder, the Rash King, and the Savourless Salt. The section has been called "The Conditions of Discipleship." These are four. 1. The Cross to be borne (25–27; Mt. x. 37, 38). 2. The Cost to be counted (28–32). 3. All Possessions to be renounced (33). 4. The Spirit of Sacrifice to be maintained (34, 35; Mt. v. 13; Mk. ix. 49).

The journeying continues, but we are not told the direction; and a large multitude is following. They are disposed to believe that Jesus is the Messiah, and that the crisis of the Kingdom is at hand. They therefore keep close to Him, in order not to miss any of the expected glories and blessings. This fact is the occasion of the address. They must understand that following Him involves a great deal. Like the guest in the Pharisee's house (ver. 15), they have not realized what the invitation to enter the Kingdom implies.

25. Συνεπορεύοντο δὲ αὐτῷ. "Now there were going with Him," of what continued for some time. Comp. vii. 11, xxiv. 15. Elsewhere only Mk. x. 1 of people assembling, but often in LXX (Gen. xiii. 5, xiv. 24, xviii. 16, etc.).

26. οὐ μισεῖ τὸν πατέρα ἑαυτοῦ, κ.τ.λ. Does not hate them *so far as they are opposed to Christ.* The context and the parallel passages (Mt. vi. 24, x. 37) show that the case supposed is one in which choice must be made between natural affection and loyalty to Christ. In most cases these two are not incompatible; and to hate one's parents *as such* would be monstrous (Mt. xv. 4). But Christ's followers must be ready, if necessary, to act towards what is dearest to them as if it were an object of hatred. Comp. Jn. xii. 25. Jesus, as often, states a principle in a startling way, and leaves His hearers to find out the qualifications. Comp. vi. 29, 30; Mt. xix. 12. The **καὶ τὴν γυναῖκα** here is a comment, whether designed or not, on γυναῖκα ἔγημα in ver. 20. Comp. xviii. 29.

τὴν ψυχὴν ἑαυτοῦ. Not merely his carnal desires, but his life (ix. 24, xii. 23); all his worldly interests and affections, including life itself. *Nec tamen sufficit nostra relinquere, nisi relinquamus et nos* (Greg. Mag. *Hom.* xxxii.). So that μισεῖν τὴν ψυχὴν ἑαυτοῦ is ἀπαρνήσασθαι ἑαυτόν (ix. 23) carried to the uttermost.

εἶναί μου μαθητής. The emphasis is on μαθητής, not on μου, which is enclitic. "He may be following Me in some sense, but he is no *disciple* of Mine." Would any merely human teacher venture to make such claims? Syr-Sin. omits *v.* 27.

27. οὐ βαστάζει τὸν σταυρὸν ἑαυτοῦ. Comp. ix. 23; Mt. x. 38, xvi. 24; Mk. viii. 34. Only here and Jn. xix. 17 is βαστάζειν used of the cross; here figuratively, there literally. "Carrying his own cross" would be a familiar picture to many of Christ's hearers. Hundreds had been crucified in Galilee for rebellion under Judas the Gaulonite (A.D. 6). See Deissmann, *Bible Studies*, p. 102.

In late Gk. βαστάζειν seems to be more common than φέρειν, when the carrying is figurative: LXX of 2 Kings xviii. 14; Job xxi. 3. It is specially common in the later versions of Aq. Sym. and Theod. All three have it Is. xl. 11, lxvi. 12; Jer. x. 5: and both Sym. and Theod. have it Prov. ix. 12; Is. lxiii. 9. But in none of these places does it occur in LXX.

28–33. Two Parables upon Counting the Cost: the Rash Builder and the Rash King. Comp. Mt. xx. 22; Mk. x. 38. It is possible that in both parables Jesus was alluding to recent instances of such folly. It was an age of ostentatious building and reckless warfare. The connexion with what precedes (γάρ) seems to be that becoming a disciple of Christ is at least as serious a matter as any costly or dangerous undertaking.

28. τίς γὰρ ἐξ ὑμῶν θέλων. "For which of you (see on xi. 5), if he wishes."

καθίσας. In both parables (ver. 31) this represents long and serious consideration. The matter cannot be settled off-hand. Comp. Virg. *Aen.* x. 159.

ψηφίζει. "Calculates" (ψῆφος = *calculus*). In class. Gk. commonly in mid. of *voting.* Comp. Rev. xiii. 18: not in LXX. Neither ἀπαρτισμός nor δαπάνη occur again in N.T., but δαπάνη is fairly common in LXX, and ἀπαρτισμός is very rare in Greek literature.[1] In LXX ἀπαρτίζειν occurs (1 Kings ix. 25); also in Aq. and Sym. See Suicer, ἀπαρτίζω.

29. μὴ ἰσχύοντος ἐκτελέσαι. "Not having the means to finish." For ἐκτελεῖν comp. Deut. xxxii. 45; 1 Kings xiv. 15; 2 Chron. iv. 5; 2 Mac. xv. 9; Dan. iii. 40 (Theod.). Not elsewhere in N.T.

30. οὗτος. Contemptuous: v. 21, vii. 39, xiii. 32, where see reff. The lesson conveyed is not so much, "It is better not to begin, than to begin and fail," as, "It is folly to begin without much consideration."

31. συνβαλεῖν εἰς πόλεμον. To be taken together: "to engage with another king for the purpose of war." The verb. is intrans., as 1 Mac. iv. 34; 2 Mac. viii. 23, xiv. 17; and often in Polyb. The more common expression is συμβάλλειν εἰς μάχην (Jos. *Ant.* vi. 5. 3: so also in Polyb.). Comp. *confligere.*

ἐν δέκα χιλιάσιν. "*Equipped with* ten thousand," a meaning which readily flows from "clad in, invested with." Comp. i. 17; Rom. xv. 29; 1 Cor. iv. 21; Heb. ix. 25; Jude 14. The very phrase occurs 1 Mac. iv. 29.

32 εἰ δὲ μήγε. See small print on v. 36.

ἐρωτᾷ [τὰ] πρὸς εἰρήνην. "Asks for negociations with a view to peace." The τά is omitted in א B (? *homœotel.*), and the meaning will then be, "negociates for peace." B K Π have εἰς for πρός (perhaps from ver. 28). Comp. xix. 42 and examples in Wetst. There is a remarkable parallel to this second parable Xen. *Mem.* iii. 6. 8.

33. This verse shows the futility of asking what the tower means, and who the king with the twenty thousand is.[2] These details are part of the framework of the parables, and by themselves mean nothing. The parables as a whole teach that to become Christ's disciple involves something which ought to be well weighed beforehand. This something was explained before, and is shown in another form here, viz. complete self-renunciation.

[1] Dion. Hal. *De Comp. Verb.* xxiv., and Apoll. Dysc. *De Adv.* p. 532, 7, seem to be almost the only quotations. The Latin renderings here are *ad perficiendum* (f Vulg.), *ad consummandum* (a r), *ad consummationem* (e), *ad perfectum* (d).

[2] Those who insist on explaining the king with the twenty thousand commonly make him mean Satan. But would Christ suggest that we should come to terms with Satan? To avoid this difficulty others regard the king as representing God. But would Christ place the difference between the power of God and the power of man as the difference between twenty thousand and ten thousand? Contrast the ten thousand talents and the hundred pence (Mt. xviii. 24, 28). See on xii. 5 and xvi. 1.

ἀποτάσσεται πᾶσιν τοῖς ἑαυτοῦ ὑπάρχουσιν. "Renounceth all his own belongings," the chief of which were specified ver. 26. See on ix. 61 and viii. 3. All disciples must be *ready* to renounce their possessions. Many of the first disciples were called upon actually to do so. Comp. the sarcasm of Julian: "In order that they may enter more easily into the Kingdom of Heaven in the way which their wonderful law bids them, I have ordered all the money of the Church of Edessa to be seized" (*Ep.* xliii.). Note the characteristic *πᾶς* and *πᾶσιν*. Comp. v. 11, 28.

It is very forced to put a full stop at *πᾶς ἐξ ὑμῶν*, and make two independent sentences. "Such is the case therefore with all of you. Whoever renounceth not," etc.

MSS. vary much as to the order of the three words *εἶναί μου μαθητής*.

34, 35. The Spirit of Sacrifice. The similitude respecting salt was probably uttered more than once, and in more than one form. Comp. Mt. v. 13; Mk. ix. 50. The salt is the self-sacrifice spoken of *vv.* 26, 27, 33. The figure of salt is not found in O.T., but comp. Job. vi. 6.

34. Καλὸν οὖν τὸ ἅλας. The *οὖν* (א B L X 69, Boh.) perhaps refers to previous utterances: "Salt, therefore (as I have said before), is good." *Nihil utilius sale et sole* (Plin. *H. N.* xxxi. 9. 45. 102).

ἐὰν δὲ καὶ τὸ ἅλας. The *καί* (א B L X, Vulg. *codd.* Syr., Bede) must be preserved. "But if *even* the salt." In Mt. v. 13 there is no *καί*. Note the characteristic *δὲ καί*, and see small print on iii. 9.

In LXX and N.T. *ἅλας* is the common form, with *ἅλα* as *v.l.* in good MSS. In class. Gk. *ἅλς* prevails.

In class. Gk. *μωραίνω* is "I *am* foolish" (Eur. *Med.* 614); in bibl. Grk. *μωραίνομαι* has this meaning (Rom. i. 22; Mt. v. 13), *μωραίνω* being "I *make* foolish" (1 Cor. i. 20). Mk. has *ἄναλον γίνεσθαι*. Vulg. has *evanuerit*; **a d e** *infatuatum fuerit*.

ἐν τίνι ἀρτυθήσεται; Quite impossibly Tyn. and Cran. have "What shall be seasoned ther with?" From meaning simply "prepare," *ἀρτύω* came to be used of preparing and flavouring food (Col. iv. 6).

35. It is futile to discuss what meaning is to be given to "the land" and "the dunghill." They do not symbolize anything. Many things which have deteriorated or become corrupt are useful as manure, or to mix with manure. Savourless salt is not even of this much use: and disciples without the spirit of self-devotion are like it. That is the whole meaning.[1] If this saying was uttered only once, we may prefer the connexion here to that in the Sermon on the Mount. Mk. so far agrees with Lk. in placing it after the Transfiguration. But all three arrangements may be right.

---

[1] For this savourless salt in Palestine see Maundrell, *Journey from Aleppo to Jerusalem*, pp. 161 ff. (quoted by Morison on Mk. ix. 50); also Thomson, "I saw large quantities of it literally thrown into the street. to be trodden under foot of men and beasts" (*Land & Book*, p. 381).

κοπρίαν. The word is one of many which seem to be of a colloquial character, and are common to N.T. and the comic poets. See Kennedy, *Sources of N.T. Grk.* pp. 72–76. In N.T. only here. Comp. xiii. 8.

Ὁ ἔχων ὦτα ἀκούειν ἀκουέτω. A solemn indication that attention to what has been said is needed, and will be rewarded. It is another of Christ's repeated sayings. See on viii. 8.

XV. 1–32. Three Parables for the Encouragement of Penitent Sinners. The Love and Free Forgiveness of God. The Lost Sheep (3–7) and the Lost Coin (8–10) form a pair. Like the Mustard Seed and the Leaven (xiii. 18–21), and the Rash Builder and the Rash King (xiv. 28–32), they teach the same lesson, which the Prodigal Son (11–32) enforces and augments. In the first two Jesus justifies His own conduct against the criticisms of the Pharisees. In the third He rebukes their criticisms, but at the same time continues the lesson to a point far beyond that touched by the objectors. When we regard them as a triplet, each parable teaching a separate lesson, Bengel's classification will stand: 1. *Peccator stupidus*; 2. *sui plane nesciens*; 3. *sciens et voluntarius.* But the insertion of εἶπεν δέ (ver. 11) clearly marks off the third parable from the first two, whereas these are closely connected by ἤ, which almost implies that the second is little more than an alternative way of saying the same thing as the first.

1–3. The Murmuring of the Pharisees against Christ's Inter course with Publicans and Sinners. We have had several other cases in which Jesus has made a question, or an appeal, or a criticism, the occasion of a parable: ver. 15, x. 25–29, xii. 13–15, xiv. 15. There is once more no indication of time or place; but connexion with what precedes is perhaps intended. There a thoughtless multitude followed Him, intending to become His disciples, and He warns them to count the cost. Here a number of publicans and sinners congregate about Him, and He rebukes the suggestion that He ought to send them away. It was well to check heedless enthusiasts, that *they* might be saved from breaking down afterwards. It would have been a very different thing to have sent away penitents, that *He* might be saved from legal pollution.

1. Ἦσαν δὲ αὐτῷ ἐγγίζοντες πάντες οἱ τελῶναι καὶ οἱ ἁμαρτωλοί. The meaning of πάντες determines the meaning of the tense. We may regard it as hyperbolical for "very many,"—a common use of "all." Or it may mean all the tax-collectors and other outcasts of the place in which He then was. In either of these cases ἦσαν ἐγγίζοντες (see on i. 10) will mean "were drawing near" on some particular occasion. Or we may take πάντες literally of the whole class of publicans and sinners; and then the verb will mean "used to draw near," wherever He might be. This was constantly happening, and the Pharisees commonly cavilled (imperf.), and on one occasion He uttered these parables (aor.). It was likely that He would attract these outcasts more and more. Comp. vii. 29, 37, and see on xi. 29. For the characteristic πάντες see on i. 66, vi. 30, xii. 10, etc. Note the repeated article: the τελῶναι and the ἁμαρτωλοί are grouped together as *one* class by the Pharisees themselves (v. 30; Mt. ix. 11); not so here by the Evangelist.

2. διεγόγγυζον. "Murmured among themselves, throughout their whole company." In N.T. only here and xix. 7, which is very similar. Comp. Exod. xvi. 2, 7, 8; Num. xiv. 2; Josh. ix. 18. "The scribes" are usually placed before "the Pharisees" (v. 21, vi. 7, xi. 53; Mt. xii. 38, etc.). Here perhaps the Pharisees took the lead: comp. v. 30 (true text); Mk. vii. 1, 5.

προσδέχεται. "Allows them access, gives them a welcome": Rom. xvi. 2; Phil. ii. 29.

συνεσθίει. A much more marked breach of Pharisaic decorum than προσδέχεται. He accepted invitations from Levi and other tax-collectors, and in His outdoor teaching He took His meals with them.

3. εἶπεν δέ. "But (in answer to this cavilling) He said." Cov. and Cran. have "But"; Tyn. and Gen. "Then." Something stronger than "And" (AV. RV.) is needed. Note εἶπεν δέ, εἶπεν πρός, and εἶπεν τὴν παραβολήν as marks of Lk.'s style. None of them is found in Mt. xviii. 12.

4–7. The Parable of the Lost Sheep. Comp. Mt. xviii. 12–14, where this parable is given in a totally different connexion, and with some differences of detail. Comp. also Jn. x. 1–18. We have no means of knowing how often Jesus used the simile of the Good Shepherd in His teaching. No simile has taken more hold upon the mind of Christendom. See Tert. *De Pud.* vii. and x. Comp. Ezek. xxxiv.; Is. xl. 11; 1 Kings xxii. 17.

4. Τίς ἄνθρωπος ἐξ ὑμῶν. Once more He appeals to their personal experience. See on xi. 5, and comp. xii. 25, xiv. 5, 28. The ἄνθρωπος inserted here marks one difference between this parable and the next.

ἔχων ἑκατὸν πρόβατα. The point is, not that he possesses so much, but that the loss in comparison to what remains is so small.

ἀπολέσας ἐξ αὐτῶν ἕν. This is the point of the first two parables,—the particular love of God for each individual soul. In Mt. we have πλανηθῇ (Exod. xxiii. 4; Is. liii. 6; Jer. xxvii. 17) for ἀπολέσας.

καταλείπει τὰ ἐνενήκοντα ἐννέα. He is the owner, not the shepherd. His leaving them does not expose them to danger. The wilderness (in Mt. τὰ ὄρη) is not a specially perilous or desolate place, but their usual pasture, in which they are properly tended. He does not neglect them, but for the moment he is absorbed in the recovery of the lost. Cyril Alex. and Ambrose make the ninety and nine to be the Angels, and the one the human race. Ambrose adds, *Dives igitur pastor cujus omnes nos centesima portio sumus* Migne, xiv. xv. 1756; lxxii. 798; Payne Smith, p. 497.

πορεύεται ἐπὶ τὸ ἀπολωλός. For ἐπί of the goal comp. Acts viii. 26, ix. 11; Mt. xxii. 9; in each case after πορεύεσθαι. Mt. has here πορευθεὶς ζητεῖ τὸ πλανώμενον.

ἕως εὕρῃ αὐτό. Peculiar to Lk. There is no cessation of the seeking until the lost is found. See Lange, *L. of C.* i. p. 497.

5. ἐπιτίθησιν ἐπὶ τοὺς ὤμους αὐτοῦ. This also is peculiar to Lk. The owner does not drive it back, nor lead it back, nor have it carried: he carries it himself. Comp. Is. xl. 11, xlix. 22, lx. 4, lxvi. 12. In LXX ὦμος is common; in N.T. only here and Mt. xxiii. 4.

χαίρων. There is no upbraiding of the wandering sheep, nor murmuring at the trouble. Comp. the use of χαίρων, xix. 6; Acts viii. 39.

6. συνκαλεῖ τοὺς φίλους. See on ix. 1. In Mt. there is nothing about his calling others to rejoice with him. Only his own joy is mentioned. It is a mark of great joy that it seeks sympathy.

τὸ ἀπολωλός. Not ὃ ἀπώλεσα (ver. 9). The sheep went astray through its own ignorance and folly (Ps. cxix. 176): the coin was lost through the woman's want of care. This is another mark of difference between the first parable and the second.

7. λέγω ὑμῖν. Mt. has the characteristic ἀμὴν λέγω ὑμῖν.

ἢ ἐπί. For ἤ without a previous comparative see small print on xvii. 2, and comp. Mt. xviii. 8; Mk. ix. 43, 45, 47; 1 Cor. xiv. 19. Win. xxxv. 2. c, p. 302; Simcox, p. 92. Perhaps ἤ may be said to imply μᾶλλον by a usage which was originally colloquial. It is freq. in LXX; Gen. xlix. 12; Num. xxii. 6, etc. In Mt. xviii. 13 the μᾶλλον is expressed.

δικαίοις οἵτινες οὐ χρείαν ἔχουσιν μετανοίας. "Righteous who are of such a character as to have no need of repentance." The οἵτινες does not prove that δικαίοις means those who are really righteous. It will fit any explanation of δικαίοις and οὐ χρείαν ἔχουσιν. If both expressions be taken literally, the ninety-nine represent a hypothetical class, an ideal which since the Fall has not been reached. But as Jesus is answering Pharisaic objections to intercourse with flagrant sinners, both expressions may be ironical and refer to the external propriety of those whose care about legal observances prevents them from feeling any need of repentance. Comp. v. 31.

Mt. here has τοῖς μὴ πεπλανημένοις. In any case the χαίρων, ver. 5, and the χαρά here are anthropomorphic, and must not be pressed. *Insperata aut prope desperata magis nos afficiunt* (Grotius); but such *unlooked for* results are impossible to Omniscience. We must hold to the main lesson of the parable, and not insist on interpreting all the details.[1]

[1] In the Midrash there is a story that Moses, while tending Jethro's flocks, went after a lamb which had gone astray. As he thought that it must be weary,

Note the confidence with which Jesus speaks of what takes place in heaven, and compare it with the claims made upon His followers, xiv. 26, 33.

μετανοοῦντι . . . μετανοίας. Both verb and substantive are much more common in Lk. than in Mt. or Mk. Neither occurs in Mt. xviii. 14 or anywhere in Jn. See on v. 32 and iii. 3.

8–10. § The Parable of the Lost Coin. The main points of difference between this and the preceding parable are the changes from a *man* to a *woman*, and from a *sheep*, which could stray of its own accord, and feel the evil consequences, to a *coin*, which could do neither. From this it follows that, while the man might be moved by pity rather than by self-interest to bring back the sheep, the woman must be moved by self-interest alone to recover the coin; also that the woman can blame herself for the loss of the coin (ἣν ἀπώλεσα), which the man does not do with regard to the sheep (τὸ ἀπολωλός). Hence we may infer that the woman represents the Church rather than the Divine Wisdom, if she represents anything at all. The general result of the two parables is that each sinner is so precious that God and His Ministers regard no efforts too great to reclaim such.

8. τίς γυνή; No ἐξ ὑμῶν is added, perhaps because no women were present. Yet there may be something in the remark of Wetst. *Cum varios haberet auditores Christus, mares, feminas, juniores, iis parabolas accommodat: de pastore, de muliere frugi, de filio prodigo.* Women also may work for the recovery of sinners.

δραχμάς. The word occurs here only in N.T., but often in LXX (Gen. xxiv. 22; Ex. xxxix. 2; Josh. vii. 21, etc.). The Greek *drachma* was a silver coin of nearly the same value as a Roman *denarius*[1] (vii. 41, x. 35, xx. 24), which is not mentioned in LXX. It was the equivalent of a quarter of a Jewish shekel (Mt. xvii. 24). Ten drachmas in weight of silver would be about eight shillings, but in purchasing power above a pound. Wic. has "besant," Tyn. and others have "groat," Luth. has *Groschen.* That the ten coins formed an ornament for the head, and that the loss of one marred the whole, is a thought imported into the parable.

ἅπτει. The act. is peculiar to Lk. in N.T., and always in the sense of *kindling* (viii. 16, xi. 33; Acts xxviii. 2, and perhaps Lk. xxii. 55: comp. Ex. xxx. 8; Tob. viii. 13; Jud. xiii. 13). Oriental houses often have no windows, and a lamp would be necessary for a search even in the day.

he carried it back on his shoulders, Then God said, that, because he had shown pity to the sheep of a man, He would give him His own sheep, Israel, to feed (Edersh. *L. & T.* ii. p. 257; Wetst. on Lk. xv. 5).

[1] Nearly all Latin texts have *dragmas*, *dracmas*, or *drachmas* here; but Cod. Palat. and *Ad Novatianum* xv. (Hartel's Cypr. App. p. 65) have *denarios*.

σαροῖ.[1] *Non sine pulvere* (Beng.). It may be doubted whether there is any lesson intended in the coins being lost *in* the house, whereas the sheep strays *from* the fold; as showing that souls may be lost in the Church as well as by going out of it. In any case, the details are graphic, and express great and persevering activity. "The charge against the Gospel is still the same, that it turns the world upside down" (Trench, *Par.* p. 386).

9. τὰς φίλας καὶ γείτονας. "Her women friends and neighbours." No meaning is to be sought in the change of gender, which merely preserves the harmony of the picture. It is women who congratulate Naomi and Ruth (Ruth iv. 14, 17).

10. γίνεται χαρὰ ἐνώπιον. "There comes to be joy," etc. The γίνεται = ἔσται in ver. 7. Joy will arise in any case that may occur. "In the presence of" means "in the judgment of." The angelic estimate of the facts is very different from that of the Pharisees: comp. xii. 8, xvi. 22; Eph. i. 4-14.

ἐπὶ ἑνὶ ἁμαρτωλῷ. This is the moral throughout,—the value of a single sinner. The Pharisees condemned Jesus for trying to reclaim multitudes of sinners. They had a saying, "There is joy before God when those who provoke Him perish from the world."

11-32. § The Parable of the Prodigal Son. It completes the trilogy of these parables of grace, but we cannot be *sure* that it was uttered on the same occasion as the two other parables. The Evangelist separates it from them by making a fresh start: Εἶπεν δέ (comp. xxiv. 44). But this may mean no more than that Jesus, having justified Himself against the murmuring of the Pharisees, paused; and then began again with a parable which is a great deal more than a reply to objections. Even if it was delivered on some other occasion unknown to Lk., he could not have given it a more happy position than this. The first two parables give the Divine side of grace; the seeking love of God. The third gives the human side; the rise and growth of repentance in the heart of the sinner. It has been called *Evangelium in Evangelio*, because of the number of gracious truths which it illustrates.[2] It has two parts, both of which appear to have special reference to the circumstances in which Lk. places the parable. The younger son, who was lost and is found (11-24), resembles the publicans and sinners; and the elder son, who murmurs at the welcome given to the lost (25-32), resembles the Pharisees. In the wider application of the parable the younger son may represent the Gentiles, and the elder the Jews. Like the Lost Coin, it is peculiar to Lk., who would take

[1] MSS. of the Vulg. nearly all read *evertit*, which Wordsworth conjectures to be a slip for *everrit*. Lat. Vet. has *scopis mundavit* (b f ff_2 l), *scopis mundabit* (i q), *scopis commundat* (a), *scopis mundat* (c r), *mundat* (d), *emundat* (e).

[2] *Inter omnes Christi parabolas hæc sane eximia est, plena affectuum et pulcherrimis picta coloribus* (Grotius on ver. 20).

special delight in recording a discourse, which teaches so plainly that God's all-embracing love is independent of privileges of birth and legal observances. Its literary beauty would be a further attraction to the Evangelist, who would appreciate the delicacy, picturesqueness, and truth of this description of human circumstances and emotions. See Jerome, *Ep.* xxi., for a commentary.

11. Ἄνθρωπός τις εἶχεν. The appeal to the personal experience of each is no longer made; but the idea of *possession* still continues (ἔχων, ἔχουσα, εἶχεν). In each case it is the owner who exhibits the self-sacrificing care.

12. τὸ ἐπιβάλλον μέρος τῆς οὐσίας. According to Jewish law this would be half what the eldest received, *i.e.* one-third (Deut. xxi. 17): but had he any claim to it in his father's lifetime?

Very possibly he had. We have here perhaps a survival of that condition of society in which testaments "took effect immediately on execution, were not secret, and were not revocable" (Maine, *Ancient Law*, ch. vi. p. 174, ed. 1861), and in which it was customary for a father, when his powers were failing, to abdicate and surrender his property to his sons. In such cases the sons were bound to give the father maintenance; but the act of resignation was otherwise complete and irrevocable. Both in Semitic and in Aryan society this seems to have been the primitive method of succession, and the Mosaic Law makes no provision for the privileges of testatorship (*ibid.* p. 197). The son of Sirach warns his readers against being in a hurry to abdicate (Ecclus. xxxiii. 19–23), but he seems to assume that it will be done before death. We may say, then, that the younger son was not making an unheard-of claim. His father would abdicate some day in any case: he asks him to abdicate now. See *Expositor*, 3rd series, x. pp. 122–136, 1889; Edersh. *Hist. of J. N.* p. 367.

This intrans. use of ἐπιβάλλω occurs Tobit iii. 17, vi. 11; 1 Mac. x. 30. Comp. κτημάτων τὸ ἐπιβάλλον (Hdt. iv. 115. 1). Other examples in Suicer. For οὐσία comp. Tobit xiv. 13; 3 Mac. iii. 28.

διεῖλεν αὐτοῖς τὸν βίον. The verb occurs elsewhere in bibl. Grk. 1 Cor. xii. 11; Num. xxxi. 27; 1 Mac. i. 6, etc. For **τὸν βίον** see on viii. 43. Here it means the same as ἡ οὐσία: comp. ver. 31.

13. μετ' οὐ πολλὰς ἡμέρας. He allows no delay between the granting of his request and the realization of his freedom. On the fondness of Lk. for such expressions as **οὐ πολλοί, οὐ μακράν**, and the like, see on vii. 6.

συναγαγὼν πάντα. He leaves nothing behind that can minister to his desires; nothing to guarantee his return. The stronger form ἅπαντα is well attested (א A etc.).

εἰς χώραν μακράν. There is no reason for making μακράν an adv. (ver. 20) rather than an adj. either here or xix. 12: μακρός in the sense of "distant, remote" is quite classical.

ἐκεῖ. Away from his father's care and restraint, and from the observation of those who knew him.

διεσκόρπισεν τὴν οὐσίαν. The opposite of *συναγάγων πάντα*. It had cost him nothing to collect it together, and he squanders it as easily as he acquired it.

ζῶν ἀσώτως. The expression occurs Jos. *Ant.* xii. 4. 8; but *ἀσώτως* is not found again either in N.T. or LXX. The *ἄσωτος* is "one who does not save, a spendthrift, a prodigal": Prov. vii. 11; comp. Arist. *Eth. Nic.* ii. 8. 2, iv. 1. 5. For *ἀσωτία* see Eph. v. 18; Tit. i. 6; 1 Pet. iv. 4; Prov. xxviii. 7; 2 Mac. vi. 4. Sometimes *ἄσωτος* is taken in a passive sense, "one who cannot be saved, abandoned"; *perditus* rather than *prodigus*, as if for *ἄσωστος* (Clem. Alex. *Pæd.* ii. 1, p. 168, ii. p. 184, ed. Potter). But the active signification is appropriate here. Trench, *Syn.* xvi.; Suicer and Suidas *s. ἄσωτος*. Syr-Sin. adds "with harlots."

14. The working of Providence is manifested in coincidences. Just when he had spent everything, a famine, and a severe one, arose in precisely that land to which he had gone to enjoy himself, and throughout (*κατά*) the land. And he himself (*καὶ αὐτός*), as well as the country, began more and more to be in want.

λιμὸς ἰσχυρά. See small print on iv. 25. For **καὶ αὐτός** see on i. 17, v. 14, vi. 20. For **ὑστερεῖσθαι**, "to *feel* want" (mid.), comp. 2 Cor. xi. 9; Phil. iv. 12; Ecclus. xi. 11. Syr-Sin. omits the clause.

15. πορευθεὶς ἐκολλήθη ἑνὶ τῶν πολιτῶν. He has to leave his first luxurious abode and attach himself, in absolute dependence, to one of another nation, presumably a heathen. Evidently his prodigality has not gained him a friend in need. Godet sees in this young Jew, grovelling in the service of a stranger, an allusion to the *τελῶναι* in the service of Rome. Excepting the quotation from LXX in Heb. viii. 11, **πολίτης** in N.T. is peculiar to Lk. (xix. 14; Acts xxi. 39): in LXX Prov. xi. 9, 12, xxiv. 43, etc. For **ἐκολλήθη** see on x. 11. For the sudden change of subject in **ἔπεμψεν** comp. vii. 15, xiv. 5, xvii. 2, xix. 4; Acts vi. 6.

βόσκειν χοίρους. A degrading employment for anyone, and an abomination to a Jew. Comp. Hdt. ii. 47. 1. But the lowest degradation has still to be mentioned.

16. ἐπεθύμει χορτασθῆναι. Exactly as in xvi. 21, of the pangs of hunger. See on vi. 21. There is no doubt that *χορτασθῆναι* (א B D L R) is not a euphemism for *γεμίσαι τὴν κοιλίαν αὐτοῦ* (A P Q X Γ Δ), but the true reading: *cupiebat saturari* (d f), *concupiscebat saturari* (e). Syr-Sin. supports A.

ἐκ τῶν κερατίων ὧν ἤσθιον οἱ χοῖροι. The pods of the "carob tree," or "locust tree," or "John the Baptist's tree," or "S. John's Bread"; so called from the erroneous notion that its pods were the locusts which were the Baptist's food. The carob tree, *ceratonia siliqua*, is still common in Palestine and round the Mediterranean. It is sometimes called *Siliqua Græca*. But it is rash to assume that the *siliquæ* of Hor. *Ep.* ii. 1. 123; Pers. iii. 55; Juv. xi. 58, are carob pods (*D.B.*[2] i. p. 1412).[1] For the attraction in ὧν see on iii. 19.

οὐδεὶς ἐδίδου αὐτῷ. "No one used to give him" even this miserable food, so that the quantity which he got was small. The neighbours cared nothing about this half-starved foreigner, who even in this vile employment could not earn enough to eat.

17. εἰς ἑαυτὸν δὲ ἐλθών. Implies that hitherto he has been "beside himself": comp. ἐν ἑαυτῷ γενόμενος (Acts xii. 11). The expression is classical both in Greek (Diod. Sic. xiii. 95; Epictet. iii. 1. 15) and Latin, *redire ad se* (Hor. *Ep.* ii. 2. 138; Lucret. iv. 1020; Ter. *Adelph.* v. 3. 8). This "coming to himself" is manifested in the thought of home and the longing for it. Want rekindles what his revelry had extinguished. See Blass on Acts xii. 11.

Πόσοι μίσθιοι . . . περισσεύονται ἄρτων. There is no emphasis on ἄρτων in contrast to κερατίων: the contrast lies in their having plenty to eat. Godet sees the proselytes in these μίσθιοι. The word occurs in N.T. only here and ver. 19: in LXX Lev. xxv. 50; Job vii. 1; Tobit v. 11; Ecclus. vii. 20, xxxiv. 27, xxxvii. 11.

Only in late Greek is περισσεύω trans. In N.T. both act. (xii. 15, xxi. 4) and pass. (Mt. xiii. 12, xxv. 29) are used in much the same sense.

ἐγὼ δὲ λιμῷ ὧδε ἀπόλλυμαι. Comp. τῷ αἰσχίστῳ ὀλέθρῳ, λιμῷ τελευτῆσαι (Thuc. iii. 59. 4). The ὧδε is after λιμῷ in ℵ B L, before λιμῷ in D R U, *ego autem hic fame pereo* (Vulg.), while A E F etc. omit. The transfer to before λιμῷ caused it to be lost in ἐγὼ δέ.

18. ἀναστὰς πορεύσομαι. Not mere Oriental fulness of description (i. 39; Acts x. 20, xxii. 10). The ἀναστάς expresses his rousing himself from his lethargy and despair (Acts v. 17, ix. 6, 18).

εἰς τὸν οὐρανόν. "Against heaven." This is not a rare use of εἰς: comp. xvii. 4; Mt. xviii. 21; 1 Cor. vi. 18, viii. 12. It is common in LXX and is found also in class. Grk. Comp. Pharaoh's confession, Ἡμάρτηκα ἐναντίον Κυρίου τοῦ Θεοῦ ὑμῶν καὶ εἰς ὑμᾶς (Exod. x. 16); also Plat. *Rep.* iv. 396 A; *Phædr.* 242 C; Hdt. i. 138. 2; Soph. *O. C.* 968. Filial misconduct is a sin utterly displeasing to God. But the εἰς does not mean "crying to heaven for punishment," *himmelschreiend*, which is otherwise expressed (Gen. iv. 10, xviii. 21). For ἁμαρτάνω ἐνώπιόν τινος comp. 1 Sam.

[1] "These 'husks' are to be seen on the stalls in all Oriental towns, where they are sold for food, but are chiefly used for the feeding of cattle and horses, and especially for pigs" (Tristram, *Nat. Hist. of B.* p. 361).

vii. 6, xx. 1; Tobit iii. 3; Judith v. 17; Sus. 23. The sin is regarded as something to be *judged* by the person who regards it.

κληθῆναι υἱός σου. By the father himself. What other people may call him is not in question.

19. ὡς ἕνα τῶν μισθίων σου. This will be promotion from his present position. He asks it as a favour.

20. ἀναστὰς ἦλθεν. The repentance is as real and decided as the fall. He prepares full confession, but no excuse; and, having made a good resolution, he acts upon it without delay. Here the narrative respecting the younger son practically ends. What follows (20–24) is mainly his father's treatment of him; and it is here that this parable comes into closest contact with the two others. Every word in what follows is full of gracious meaning. Note especially ἑαυτοῦ, "his *own* father," αὐτοῦ μακρὰν ἀπέχοντος, ἐσπλαγχνίσθη, and δραμών. In spite of his changed and beggarly appearance, his father recognizes him even from a distance.

ἐπέπεσεν ἐπὶ τὸν τράχηλον αὐτοῦ καὶ κατεφίλησεν αὐτόν. The exact parallel in Acts xx. 37 should be compared. Excepting Mk. iii. 10 and the quotations Rom. xv. 3 and Rev. xi. 11, ἐπιπίπτειν is peculiar to Lk. in N.T. (i. 12; Acts viii. 16, x. 44, etc.), and he alone uses it in this sense: comp. Gen. xxxiii. 4, xlv. 14, xlvi. 29. Latin texts vary much in rendering ἐπέπεσεν: *cecidit* (Vulg.), *incubuit* (a d Hier. *ad Dam.*), *procidit* (r), *superjecit se* (e). None of them marks the κατα- in κατεφίλησεν, "kissed him tenderly," *deosculatus est*. See on vii. 38, and comp. Tobit vii. 6; 3 Mac. v. 49. As yet the son has said nothing, and the father does not know in what spirit he has returned; but it is enough that he *has* returned. The father has long been watching for this.

With the constr. αὐτοῦ ἀπέχοντος εἶδεν αὐτόν, for αὐτὸν ἀπέχοντα εἶδεν, comp. xii. 36.

21. He makes his confession exactly as he had planned it: but it is doubtful whether he makes his humiliating request. The words ποίησόν με ὡς κ.τ.λ., are here attested by ℵ B D U X; but almost all other MSS. and most Versions omit them. They may be taken from ver. 19, and internal evidence is against them. Augustine says, *Non addit quod in illa meditatione dixerat*, Fac me sicut unum de mercenariis tuis (*Quæst. Evang.* ii. 33). He had not counted on his father's love and forgiveness when he decided to make this request; and now emotion prevents him from meeting his father's generosity with such a proposal. But the servants are not present. They would not run out with the father. Not till the two had reached the house could the order to them be given.

22. Ταχὺ ἐξενέγκατε. "Bring forth quickly"; *cito proferte*

The father says nothing to his son; he continues to let his conduct speak for him.

The ταχύ must be retained with ℵ B L X, Syr-Sin. Vulg. Boh. Aeth. Arm. Goth. D and other MSS. have ταχέως.

στολὴν τὴν πρώτην. Not, "*his* best robe," still less "his *former* robe," which without αὐτοῦ is scarcely possible; but, "the best that we have, the finest in the house." Comp. Ezek. xxvii. 22. The στολή (στέλλω) was any long and stately robe, such as the scribes loved to promenade in (xx. 46), the *talar*: Mk. xii. 38, xvi. 5; Rev. vi. 11, vii. 9, 13; Esth. vi. 8, 11; 1 Mac. x. 21, xiv. 9. It is the common word for the liturgical vestments of Aaron: Exod. xxviii. 2, xxix. 21. Trench, *Syn.* l.; *D.B.*[2] i. p. 808.

The τήν before στολήν (D^2 R) has been inserted because of the τήν before πρώτην, for an epithet joined to an anarthrous noun is commonly itself anarthrous. But comp. Rom. ii. 14, ix. 30; Gal. iii. 21.

δακτύλιον. Here only in N.T., but freq. in LXX and in classical writers. Comp. ἀνὴρ χρυσοδακτύλιος (Jas. ii. 2). We are probably to understand a signet-ring, which would indicate that he was a person of standing and perhaps authority in the house (Esth. iii. 10, viii. 2; Gen. xli. 42). The **ὑποδήματα** were marks of a freeman, for slaves went barefoot. None of the three things ordered are necessaries. The father is not merely supplying the wants of his son, who has returned in miserable and scanty clothing. He is doing him honour. The attempts to make the robe and the ring and the sandals mean distinct spiritual gifts are misapplied labour.

23. θύσατε. Not "sacrifice" (Acts xiv. 13, 18; 1 Cor. x. 20), for the context shows that there is no thought of a thank-offering but "slay" for a meal (Acts x. 13, xi. 7; Jn. x. 10): it implies rather more ceremony than the simple "kill."

τὸν μόσχον τὸν σιτευτόν. There is only one, reserved for some special occasion. But there can be no occasion better than this. Comp. 1 Sam. xxviii. 24; Judg. vi. 25, 28 (A); Jer. xlvi. 21. With σιτευτός comp. ἀπαίδευτος, γνωστός, θεόπνευστος, χωνευτός.

εὐφρανθῶμεν. Excepting 2 Cor. ii. 2, this verb is always pass. in N.T., but with neut. meaning, "be glad, be merry" (xii. 19, xvi. 19; Acts vii. 41, etc.).

24. Note the rhythmical cadence of this refrain (24, 32), and comp. Exod. xv. 1, 21; Num. xxiii., xxiv.; 2 Sam. i. 19-27. *Carmine usi veteres in magno effectu* (Beng.). There is probably no difference in meaning between the two halves of the refrain; but νεκρός means "dead to me," and ἀπολωλώς "lost to me." Would the father speak to the servants of his son's being morally dead? Whereas he might well speak of one who had gone away, apparently for ever, as practically dead. And if we give a moral sense to νεκρός, why not to ἀπολωλώς (xix. 10; [Mt. xviii. 11])?

Here the first part of the parable ends. The welcome which Jesus gave to outcasts and sinners is justified. The words καὶ ἤρξαντο εὐφραίνεσθαι should be given to ver. 25 rather than to ver. 24. An interval elapses during which the father's command is executed; and then the banquet, which is the setting of the second part of the parable, begins.

25–32. In the episode of the elder son the murmuring of the Pharisees is rebuked, and that in the gentlest manner. They are reminded that they are sons, and that to them of right belongs the first place. God and His gifts have always been accessible to them (ver. 31), and if they reject them, it is their own fault. But self-righteousness and exclusiveness are sinful, and may be as fatal as extravagance and licentiousness.

25. ἐν ἀγρῷ. Doing his duty, but in no loving spirit. This explains why he was not present when his brother returned.

συμφωνίας καὶ χορῶν. Performed by attendants, not by those at the banquet. Comp. *Discumbens de die inter choros et symphonias* (Suet. *Calig.* xxxvii.). Neither word occurs again in N.T. In LXX χορός is freq. (Exod. xv. 20, xxxii. 19; Judg. xi. 34, etc.); συμφωνία (Dan. iii. 5, 10) is a musical instrument. *D.B.*[2] art. "Dulcimer"; Pusey, *Daniel*, p. 29. There were some who understood *symphonia* in this passage to mean a musical instrument, for Jerome (*Ep.* xxi.) protests against the idea. It almost certainly means a band of players or singers, and probably fluteplayers (Polyb. xxvi. 10. 5, xxxi. 4. 8). *D. of Ant.*[2] art. *Symphonia.*

26. τῶν παίδων. Perhaps not the same as the δοῦλοι (ver. 22), who are occupied with the banquet.

Vulg. has *servi* for both; Cod. Vercell. has *pueri* for both; Cod. Palat. has *pueri* for παῖδες and *servi* for δοῦλοι. No English Version distinguishes the two words, and RV. by a marginal note implies that the same Greek word is used. *D.C.G.* art. "Boy."

τί ἂν εἴη ταῦτα. "What all this might mean." Comp. Acts x. 17, and contrast Lk. xviii. 36, where there is no ἄν. Here ℵ A D omit ἄν. His not going in at once and taking for granted that what his father did was right, is *perhaps* an indication of a wrong temper. Yet to inquire was reasonable, and there is as yet no complaint or criticism. See second small print on i. 29.

27. ὅτι. Recitative, and to be omitted in translation: see on i. 45 and vii. 16. Not, "*Because* thy brother is come." There is no hint that the servant is ridiculing the father's conduct.

ὑγιαίνοντα. Not to be taken in a moral sense, about which the servant would give no opinion, but of bodily health. The house hold knew that the father had been anxious about his son's safety. See on vii. 10, and comp. Tob. v. 21. For ἀπέλαβεν of "receiving *back*" comp. vi. 34.

28. ὠργίσθη δὲ καὶ οὐκ ἤθελεν. Note the characteristic δὲ καί here and ver. 32 (see on iii. 9), and the change of tense: the unwillingness to go in was a state which continued. Hence the father's entreaties continue also (**παρεκάλει**). He treats both sons with equal tenderness: the ἐξελθών here is parallel to δραμών in ver. 20.

The reading ἠθέλησεν (A L P Q R X) arose from a wish to harmonize the tenses. The reading οὖν (P Q Γ Δ) instead of δέ (ℵ A B D L R X) is followed in Vulg. (*pater ergo illius*) and AV. ("therefore came his father out"): but it is a correction for the sake of smoothness. Lat. Vet. either *vero* or *autem*.

29. τοσαῦτα ἔτη δουλεύω σοι. His view of his relation to his father is a servile one. With **τοσαῦτα** comp. Jn. xii. 37, xxi. 11.

οὐδέποτε ἐντολήν σου παρῆλθον. The blind self-complacency of the Pharisee, trusting in his scrupulous observance of the letter of the Law, is here clearly expressed. This sentence alone is strong evidence that the elder brother represents the Pharisees rather than the Jewish nation as a whole, which could hardly be supposed to make so demonstrably false a claim. For **παρῆλθον** in the sense of "neglect, transgress," see on xi. 42.

ἐμοὶ οὐδέποτε ἔδωκας ἔριφον. The pronoun first with emphasis: "Thou never gavest *me* a kid,"—much less a fatted calf. He is jealous, and regards his father as utterly weak in his treatment of the prodigal; but what specially moves him is the injustice of it all. His own unflagging service and propriety have never been recognized in any way, while the spendthrift has only to show himself in order to receive a handsome recognition.

Both here and Mt. xxv. 32, B has ἐρίφιον for ἔριφος. Here the diminutive has point. In LXX ἔριφος prevails.

ἵνα μετὰ τῶν φίλων μου εὐφρανθῶ. He does not see that he is exhibiting much the same spirit as his brother. He wants to have his father's property in order that he may enjoy himself *apart from him*.

30. ὁ υἱός σου οὗτος. Contemptuous: "This precious son of yours." He will not say "my brother."

μετὰ πορνῶν. This is mere conjecture, thrown out partly in contrast to μετὰ τῶν φίλων μου (who of course would be respectable), partly to make the worst of his brother's conduct. That it shows how *he* would have found enjoyment, had he broken loose, is not so clear. But although there is contrast between πορνῶν and τῶν φίλων μου, and between τὸν σιτευτὸν μόσχον and ἔριφον, there is none between ἔθυσας and ἔδωκας, as if the one implied more exertion and trouble than the other, and therefore more esteem.

ἦλθεν. There is no bitterness in this, as if to imply that a stranger had *come* rather than a member of the family *returned.* Throughout the parable the prodigal is said to "come," not to "return" (*vv.* 20, 27; comp. 18). But there may be bitterness in σοῦ τὸν βίον. As the father had freely given the younger son his share, it would more fairly have been called τὸν βίον αὐτοῦ.

31. Τέκνον. More affectionate than υἱέ, although the son had not said, "Father." Comp. ii. 48, xvi. 25; Mt. xxi. 28; Mk. x. 24; 2 Tim. ii. 1.

σύ πάντοτε. In emphatic contrast to the one who has been so long absent, and perhaps in answer to his own emphatic ἐμοί (ver. 29). "What he is enjoying for this one day, *thou* hast *always* been able to command." But, like the Pharisees, this elder son had not understood or appreciated his own privileges. Moreover, like the first labourers in the vineyard, he supposed that he was being wronged because others were treated with generosity.

πάντα τὰ ἐμὰ σά ἐστιν. If he wanted entertainments he could always have them; the property had been apportioned: διεῖλεν αὐτοῖς τὸν βίον (ver. 12).

Thus the first reproach is gently rebutted. So far from the elder son's service never having met with recognition, the recognition has been constant; so constant that he had failed to take note of it. The father now passes to the second reproach,—the unfair recompense given to the prodigal. It is not a question of *recompense* at all; it is a question of *joy.* Can a family do otherwise than rejoice, when a lost member is restored to it?

32. εὐφρανθῆναι δὲ καὶ χαρῆναι ἔδει. Note the emphatic order. "To be merry and be glad was our bounden duty." The εὐφρανθῆναι of the external celebration, the χαρῆναι of the inward feeling. The imperf. perhaps contains a gentle reproof: it was a duty which the elder son had failed to recognize.

ὁ ἀδελφός σου οὗτος. The substitution of ὁ ἀδελφός σου for ὁ υἱός μου, and the repetition of οὗτος, clearly involve a rebuke: "this thy brother, of whom thou thinkest so severely. If I have gained a son, thou hast gained a brother."

Not the least skilful touch in this exquisite parable is that it ends here. We are not told whether the elder brother at last went in and rejoiced with the rest. And we are not told how the younger one behaved afterwards. Both those events were still in the future, and both agents were left free. One purpose of the parable was to induce the Pharisees to come in and claim their share of the Father's affection and of the heavenly joy. Another was to prove to the outcasts and sinners with what generous love they had been welcomed. Marcion omitted this parable.

XVI. 1–31. On the Use of Wealth. This is taught in two parables, the Unrighteous Steward (1–8) and the Rich Man and

Lazarus (19–31). The intermediate portion is partly supplementary to the first parable (9–13), partly introductory to the second (14–18). The first is addressed to the disciples (ver. 1), but is felt by the Pharisees who heard it to apply to them (ver. 14). The second appears to be addressed directly to the Pharisees. Both of them teach that riches involve, not sin, but responsibility and peril. They are a trust rather than a possession; and the use made of wealth in this world has great influence upon one's condition in the great Hereafter. The steward seems to illustrate the case of one who by a wise use of present opportunities secures a good condition in the future; while the rich man exhibits that of one who by misuse of his advantages here ruins his happiness hereafter.

Attempts have been made to connect these two parables with the three which precede, and also with the three which follow. A connexion in *fact* with what precedes cannot be established. There is no clear intimation of a break, but there is intimation of a fresh start, which may or may not be upon the same occasion. But in *thought* a connexion may be admitted. These two parables, like the previous three, are directed against special faults of the Pharisees. The former three combated their hard exclusiveness, self-righteousness, and contempt for others. These two combat their self-indulgence. It is still harder to establish a connexion in fact between these two and the three which follow; but Edersheim thinks that the thought which binds all five together is *righteousness*. The five run thus: the Unrighteous Steward, the Unrighteous Owner (Dives), and the Unrighteous Judge; the Self-righteous Pharisee and the Self-righteous Servant (*L. & T.* ii. p. 264). Milligan gives a somewhat similar grouping (*Expositor*, August, 1892, p. 114).

1–8. § The Parable of the Unrighteous Steward. The difficulty of this parable is well known, and the variety of interpretations is very great. A catalogue of even the chief suggestions would serve no useful purpose: it is sufficient to state that the steward has been supposed to mean the Jewish hierarchy, the tax-collectors, Pilate, Judas, Satan, penitents, S. Paul, Christ. Here again, therefore, we have absolutely contradictory interpretations (see on xiv. 33). But the difficulty and consequent diversity of interpretation are for the most part the result of mistaken attempts to make the details of the parable mean something definite. Our Lord Himself gives the key to the meaning (ver. 9), and we need not go beyond the point to which His words plainly carry us. The steward, however wanting in fidelity and care, *showed great prudence in the use which he made of present opportunities as a means of providing for the future.* The believer ought to exhibit similar prudence in using material advantages in this life as a means of providing for the life to come. If Christians were as sagacious and persevering in using wealth to promote their welfare in the next world, as worldly men are in using it to promote their interests here, the Kingdom of God would be more flourishing than it is. We may put aside all the details of the parable as mere setting. Every parable contains details which are not intended to convey any lesson, although necessary to complete the picture, or to impress it upon the memory. In this parable the proportion of such details is larger than in others. It should, however, be noticed that the steward provides for his future by means of goods which are not his own, but are merely entrusted to his care. The wealth out of which the Christian lays up treasure in heaven is in like manner not his own, but is held in trust. The method of the parable is very similar to that in the parable of the Unrighteous Judge (xviii. 2). In both we have an argument *à fortiori*. In that case the argument is, If an unrighteous judge will yield to the importunity of a stranger, how much more will a righteous and loving Father listen to the earnest prayers of His own children? Here the argument is, If an unrighteous steward was commended by his earthly master for his prudence in providing for his future by a fraudulent use of what had been committed to him, how much more will a righteous servant be commended by his heavenly Master for providing for eternity by a good use of what has been committed to him? But see the explanation given by Latham in *Pastor Pastorum*, pp. 386–398. The literature on the subject is voluminous and unrepaying. For all that is earlier than 1800 see Schreiber, *Historico-critica explanationum parabolæ de improbo œcon. descriptio*, Lips. 1803. For 1800–1879 see Meyer-Weiss, p. 515, or Meyer, Eng. tr. p. 209.

1. Ἔλεγεν δὲ καὶ πρὸς τοὺς μαθητάς. For ἔλεγεν δέ of a new start in the narrative see xviii. 1. The meaning of the καί is that at this time He also said what follows, and it was addressed to the disciples. The latter would include many more than the Twelve. Note both δὲ καί (xv. 28, 32) and πρός.

Ἄνθρωπός τις ἦν πλούσιος. The rich owner is almost as variously interpreted as the steward. The commonest explanation is God; but the Romans, Mammon, and Satan have also been suggested. Grave objections may be urged against all of these interpretations. It is more likely that the owner has no special meaning. We are probably to understand that he lived in the town while the steward managed the estate. Note the **τις**.

οἰκονόμον. Here he is a superior person to the one mentioned xii. 42. There the steward is a slave or freedman, left in charge of other slaves, corresponding on the whole to the Roman *dispensator* or *villicus*. Here he is a freeman, having the entire management of the estate, a *procurator*. Comp. *Si mandandum aliquid procuratori de agriculturâ aut imperandum villico est* (Cic.

De Orat. i. 58. 249). But the *procurator* was often a slave, and perhaps in some cases was not superior to the *dispensator* or the *villicus*. See *D. of Ant.*[3] ii. pp. 496, 957. Vulg. has *villicus* here and *dispensator* xii. 42 (where see note) and *arcarius* Rom. xvi. 23.

διεβλήθη αὐτῷ. This use of διαβάλλειν of hostile information presumably true is not common in class. Grk. It probably implies accusing *behind a person's back* (Dan. iii. 8, vi. 24 (Theod.); 2 Mac. iii. 11; 4 Mac. iv. 1; Hdt. viii. 110. 1; Thuc. iii. 4. 4); but ἐνδιαβάλλειν is used Num. xxii. 22 of mere hostility. Eusebius (perhaps quoting Papias) says of the woman, who may be identical with the woman taken in adultery, διαβληθείσης ἐπὶ τοῦ κυρίου (*H. E.* iii. 39. 16). Vulg. here has *diffamatus est*; Beza, *delatus est*; Luther, *der ward berüchtiget*. The ὡς by no means implies that the charge was false (Jas. ii. 9), but is in accordance with the best authors, who use it after κατηγορεῖν as well as after διαβάλλειν. The steward does not deny the charge.

ὡς διασκορπίζων. Not *quasi dissipasset* (Vulg.), "that he had wasted" (AV.); but "as wasting" or "as a waster of." For **τὰ ὑπάρχοντα αὐτοῦ** see on viii. 3. The epithet τὸν οἰκονόμον τῆς ἀδικίας (ver. 8) does not refer to this culpable neglect and extravagance, but to the fraudulent arrangement with the creditors. Nevertheless there is no hint that his fraud was a new departure.

2. φωνήσας αὐτόν. For φωνεῖν of summoning by a message comp. xix. 15; Jn. ix. 18, 24, xi. 28.

τί τοῦτο ἀκούω περὶ σοῦ; No emphasis on σοῦ, as if it meant "of *thee* among all people." The question is taken in three ways. "What? do I hear this of thee?" 2. "What is this that I hear of thee?" (RV.). 3. "Why do I hear this of thee?" Acts xiv. 15, where τί ταῦτα ποιεῖτε; means, "Why do ye these things?" is in favour of the last. See Blass on Acts xiv. 15.

ἀπόδος τὸν λόγον. "Render the (necessary) account." This is commonly understood of the final account, to prepare for the surrender of the stewardship. But it might mean the account to see whether the charge was true; and the use elsewhere in N.T. rather points to this (Mt. xii. 36; Acts xix. 40; Rom. xiv. 12; Heb. xiii. 17; 1 Pet. iv. 5). In that case the thought to be supplied is, "a steward who cannot disprove charges of this kind is an impossibility." The steward, knowing that he cannot disprove the charges, regards this demand for a reckoning as equivalent to dismissal.

With the originally Ionic form δύνῃ (ℵ B D P) contrast φάγεσαι and πίεσαι (xvii. 8).

3. εἶπεν ἐν ἑαυτῷ. Not then and there, but when he thought the matter over afterwards. Comp. vii. 39, xviii. 4; Mt. ix. 3

Note the pres. ἀφαιρεῖται, "is taking away," *i.e.* what he is doing amounts to that. He does not say, "has taken away."

σκάπτειν οὐκ ἰσχύω. "I have not strength to dig." Comp. σκάπτειν γὰρ οὐκ ἐπίσταμαι (Aristoph. *Aves*, 1432). Only here and xviii. 35 does ἐπαιτεῖν occur in N.T. Comp. Ps. cviii. 10; Ecclus. xl. 28. It means "to ask again and again, ask importunately," and so "to beg for alms." Soph. *O. C.* 1364. Comp. προσαιτεῖν, Jn. ix. 8.

4. ἔγνων. The asyndeton and the aor. express the suddenness of the idea: *subito consilium cepit* (Beng.). This aor. is sometimes called *aoristus tragicus*. Burton, § 45. The subject of δέξωνται is the debtors mentioned afterwards. See Blass on Acts xiii. 22.

5. χρεοφιλετῶν. Comp. vii. 41; Prov. xxix. 13; Job xxxi. 37. They paid in kind, and the steward had sometimes received more from them than he had put down in the accounts. This time he makes the amount paid agree with the amount entered by reducing the amount paid. He thus curries favour with the debtors, and to some extent lessens the number of his manifest defalcations. The covenants were kept by the steward; and he now hands to each debtor his written agreement,—Δέξαι σου τὰ γράμματα,—in order that the debtor may reduce the amount which he covenanted to pay. The debtor gained on this last payment. The steward gained on the previous payments.

6. βάτους. Here only in N.T. Comp. Aq. Sym. Theod. Is. v. 10 (where LXX has κεράμιον), and Jos. *Ant.* viii. 2. 9. The *bath* was for liquids what the *ephah* was for solids. It equalled about 8¾ gallons, being the μετρητής of Jn. ii. 6; and 100 *bath* of oil would probably be worth about £10. See Edersh. *Hist. of J. N.* p. 283, ed. 1896. For καθίσας see on xiv. 28.

7. κόρους. Here only in N. T. Comp. Lev. xxvii. 16; Num. xi. 32; Ezek. xlv. 13: Jos. *Ant.* xv. 9. 2. The *cor* or *homer* = 10 *ephahs* = 30 *seahs* or σάτα (xiii. 21; Mt. xiii. 33). It equalled about 10 bushels, and 100 *cor* of wheat would be worth £100 to £120. But there is very great uncertainty about the Hebrew measures, for *data* are vague and not always consistent. We are to understand that there were other debtors with whom the steward dealt in a similar manner; but these suffice as examples. The steward suits his terms to the individual in each case, and thus his arbitrary and unscrupulous dealing with his master's property is exhibited. See Schanz, *ad loc.* Syr-Sin. omits "Take thy bill."

Both βάτος and κόρος are instances of Hebrew words which have assumed regular Greek terminations. See Kennedy, *Sources of N. T. Grk.* p. 44.

8. τὸν οἰκονόμον τῆς ἀδικίας. These words are to be taken together, as τοῦ μαμωνᾶ τῆς ἀδικίας shows. In both cases we have a characterizing genitive. Comp. κριτὴς τῆς ἀδικίας (xviii. 6). Win. xxx. 9. b, p. 254, xxxiv. 3. b, p. 297; Green, p. 90.

It is grammatically possible to take τῆς ἀδικίας after ἐπῄνεσεν (4 Mac. i. 10, iv. 4); but in that case ὅτι φρονίμως ἐποίησεν would be very incongruous.

φρονίμως. "Prudently, intelligently," with a shrewd adjustment of means to ends. It is the man's prompt *savoir faire* that is praised. Wic. has "prudently" from *prudenter* (Vulg.); but all other English Versions have "wisely." Some have erroneously concluded from this that the scrutiny of the accounts ended favourably for the steward; others that, although he did not escape detection, yet he was allowed to remain steward for his shrewdness. The original charge was not disproved, and the steward was dismissed. His master saw that in spite of this he had found friends and a home, and for this commended him. Comp. Syr. *Eho, quæso, laudas qui heros fallunt?* Chr. *In loco ego vero laudo. Recte sane.* Ter. *Heaut.* iii. 2. 26. The adv. occurs here only in N.T., but φρόνιμος is common (xii. 42; Mt. vii. 24, x. 16, xxiv. 45, etc.).

ὅτι οἱ υἱοὶ τοῦ αἰῶνος τούτου. "He was justified in praising his shrewdness, because"; or, "I cite this example of shrewdness, because." This is the moral of the whole parable. Men of the world in their dealings with men like themselves are more prudent than the children of light are in their intercourse with one another. Worldly people are very farsighted and ready in their transactions with one another for temporal objects. The spiritually minded ought to be equally ready in making one another promote heavenly objects. "The *sons* of this world" occurs only here and xx. 34; but comp. Acts iv. 36; Mk. ii. 19.

φρονιμώτεροι ὑπέρ. For this use of ὑπέρ comp. Heb. iv. 12; Judg. xi. 25; 1 Kings xix. 4; Ecclus. xxx. 17; also παρά, iii. 13.

τοὺς υἱοὺς τοῦ φωτός. We have υἱοὶ φωτός, Jn. xii. 36; 1 Thes. v. 5; and τέκνα φωτός, Eph. v. 8; comp. 2 Thes. ii. 3. Is the expression found earlier than N.T.? Comp. i. 78, ii. 32; and see Lft. *Epp.* p. 74. Comp. also *Enoch* cviii. 11; Deissmann, *Bible Studies*, p. 163.

εἰς τὴν γενεὰν τὴν ἑαυτῶν. Not, "*in* their generation," but, "*towards* their *own* generation"; *erga idem sentientes; im Verkehr mit ihres Gleichen.* The clause belongs to both οἱ υἱοὶ τ. αἰῶνος τούτου and τοὺς υἱοὺς τ. φωτός, not to the former only. The steward knew the men with whom he had to deal: they would see that it was to their own interest to serve him. The sons of light ought to be equally on the alert to make use of opportunities.

Vulg. has *in generatione sua*; but Cod. Palat. reads *in sæculum istut*, which respects the εἰς, while it misrepresents ἑαυτῶν.

9–14. Comments respecting the Parable and its Application, which are still addressed to the disciples. To prevent possible misunderstanding owing to the commendation of a dishonest servant, Christ here insists upon the necessity of fidelity in dealing with worldly possessions. He shows clearly that it is not the dishonesty of the steward which is commended as an example, but his prudence in using present opportunities as a means of providing for the future.

9. Καὶ ἐγὼ ὑμῖν λέγω. "And *I* say to *you*," or "*I* also say to *you*"; balancing what the *master* said to the *steward*. The disciples ought to earn similar commendation in spiritual matters.

Here, as in ii. 48 and Acts x. 26, the correct reading seems to be καὶ ἐγώ: but almost everywhere else κἀγώ is right (xi. 9, xix. 23, xx. 3, xxii. 29, etc.). So also κἀμοί and κἀμέ rather than καὶ ἐμοί and καὶ ἐμέ. Greg. *Proleg.* p. 96.

ἑαυτοῖς ποιήσατε φίλους. The pronoun stands first with emphasis. "In your own interest make friends." The friends are those in need, who are succoured by the benevolent use of wealth, and show their gratitude by blessing their benefactors and praying for them. The poor are the representatives of Christ (Mt. xxv. 40), and it is well worth while having them as friends. Comp. 1 Tim. vi. 10. Mammon is not personified here as it is in ver. 13. Comp. μὴ ἔπεχε ἐπὶ χρήμασιν ἀδίκοις (Ecclus. v. 8).

The word appears to mean "that which is trusted in." *Lucrum Punice mammon dicitur* (Aug. *De Serm. Dom. in Monte*, ii. 14. 47). But although found in Punic it is of Syrian origin and was in use in the Targums. The expression occurs in the Book of Enoch: "Our souls are satisfied with *the mammon of unrighteousness*, but this does not prevent us from descending into the flame of the pain of Sheol" (lxiii. 10). There are rabbinical sayings which are akin to what Jesus here says: *e.g.* that "alms are the salt of riches," and that "the rich help the poor in this world, but the poor help the rich in the world to come." See Schœttg. i. p. 299; Herzog, *PRE.*[2] art. *Mammon*. The spelling μαμμωνᾶς, with double μ, is not correct.

ἵνα ὅταν ἐκλίπῃ δέξωνται ὑμᾶς. Here, as in xiv. 10, the ἵνα, if it expresses purpose and not result, refers to Christ's purpose in giving this advice rather than to that of the disciples in following it. "When it shall fail" means when the wealth shall have come to an end. The subject of ἐκλίπῃ is ὁ μαμωνᾶς. The reading ἐκλίπητε or ἐκλείπητε would mean "when ye die" (Gen. xxv. 8, xlix. 33; Ps. civ. 29; Jer. xlii. (xlix.) 17, 22; Tobit xiv. 11; Wisd. v. 13). In either case the verb is intrans. No acc. is to be understood. Comp. *Ps. Sol.* iii. 16, xvii. 5.

The evidence although somewhat confused, is quite decisive for the sing. ἐκλίπῃ or ἐκλείπῃ (א* A B* D L R X Π etc., Syr. Boh. Arm. Aeth.) as against the plur. ἐκλίπητε or ἐκλείπητε (F R U Γ Δ Λ etc. etc., Vulg. Goth.) Wordsw. is almost alone in defending ἐκλίπητε. Sadler represents the choice as between "ye fail" and "*they* fail."

δέξωνται. This may be impersonal, like αἰτοῦσιν in xii. 20.

But possibly the φίλοι are to be understood as *procuring* the reception: *qui eos introducant in tabernacula æterna, qui necessitatibus suis terrena bona communicaverint* (Aug. *Quæst. Evang.* ii. 34); or again, as *giving them a welcome* when they enter. Comp. the use of δέχεσθαι ix. 5, 48; Jn. iv. 45.

εἰς τὰς αἰωνίους σκηνάς. The emphasis is on **αἰωνίους**, "into the *eternal* tabernacles," in contrast to the uncertain and transitory houses of the debtors (ver. 4). The steward secured a home for a time; but a wise use of opportunities may secure a home for eternity. In 5 Esdras ii. 11 God is represented as promising to Israel, *dabo eis tabernacula æterna, quæ præparaveram illis* (Fritzsche, p. 643). Some such idea Peter seems to have had in his mind at the Transfiguration (ix. 33). The combination of "eternal" with "tabernacles" is remarkable, because σκηναί is commonly used of dwellings which are very temporary.

10. We have here a general principle which is capable of application in a variety of spheres. The reference to the parable is less direct than in ver. 9.

ἐν ἐλαχίστῳ. "In very little" rather than "in that which is least." Comp. xix. 17. We find in Irenæus, *Si in modico fideles non fuistis, quod magnum est quis dabit vobis* (ii. 34. 3), which is probably a loose quotation of Lk. made from memory. In the so-called 2 Ep. Clem. Rom. we have a similarly fused citation: εἰ τὸ μικρὸν οὐκ ἐτηρήσατε, τὸ μέγα τίς ὑμῖν δώσει; λέγω γὰρ ὑμῖν ὅτι ὁ πιστὸς ἐν ἐλαχίστῳ καὶ ἐν πολλῷ πιστός ἐστιν (viii.), which some suppose to have come from an apocryphal gospel, and others to be the source used by Irenæus. Comp. Hippol. *Hær.* x. 29, ἵνα ἐπὶ τῷ μικρῷ πιστὸς εὑρεθεὶς καὶ τὸ μέγα πιστευθῆναι δυνηθῇς. All three are probably reminiscences of Lk. Comp. Mt. xxv. 21, 23.

11. τῷ ἀδίκῳ μαμωνᾷ. Obviously this means the same as the μαμωνᾶ τῆς ἀδικίας, *i.e.* the wealth which is commonly a snare and tends to promote unrighteousness. Some, however, make τῷ ἀδίκῳ balance τὸ ἀληθινόν, and force ἄδικος to mean "deceitful," and so "false" wealth, which is impossible.

τὸ ἀληθινόν. That which is a real possession, genuine wealth. We are not to supply μαμωνᾶ, which is masc. Heavenly riches would not be called "mammon." It is clear that this is parallel to πολλῷ in ver. 10, as ἀδίκῳ μαμωνᾷ to ἐλαχίστῳ, and that this genuine wealth means much the same as the "ten cities" (xix. 17). The connexion between **πιστοί** and **πιστεύσει**, "trusty" and "entrust," is perhaps not accidental. Neither Latin nor English Versions preserve it. Cran. has the impossible rendering, "who wyll beleve you in that whych is true."

12. ἐν τῷ ἀλλοτρίῳ. Earthly wealth is not only trivial and unreal; it does not belong to us. It is ours only as a loan and a trust, which may be withdrawn at any moment. Heavenly possessions are immense, real, and eternally secure. With **οὐκ ἐγένεσθε**, "ye did not *prove* to be," comp. γεγονέναι (x. 36).

τὸ ὑμέτερον τίς δώσει ὑμῖν; "Who will give you (in the world to come) that which is entirely your own," your inheritance, "the kingdom prepared for you from the foundation of the world" (Mt. xxv. 34). The case sketched in these three verses (10–12) is that of a wealthy owner who educates his son for managing the estate to which he is heir, and proves his fitness for it by allowing him to have control of something that is of little value except as an instrument for forming and discerning character. If the son proves faithless in this insignificant charge, he is disinherited. *Il y a là une admirable conception du but de la vie terrestre et même de l'existence de la matière* (Godet).

It seems to be impossible to make satisfactory sense of the notable reading τὸ ἡμέτερον, attested by B L and Origen, and to some extent by Tertullian, who has *meum* (*Adv. Marc.* iv. 33): e i l also have *meum*, and 157 has ἐμόν. Almost all other witnesses (ℵ A D P R X Γ Δ Λ Π etc., Versions, Cypr. Cyr-Alex. etc.) have τὸ ὑμέτερον, which, however, would be an inevitable correction, if τὸ ἡμέτερον were genuine.

13. This verse forms a natural conclusion to the comments on the parable; and, if it was uttered only once, we may believe that this is its original position, rather than in the Sermon on the Mount, where it is placed by Mt. (vi. 24). So Schanz, Weiss.

Οὐδεὶς οἰκέτης δύναται δυσὶ κυρίοις δουλεύειν. "No domestic can *be a slave* to two masters": comp. Jas. iv. 4. To be a *servant* to two masters is possible, and is often done. But to be at the absolute disposal of two masters is not possible. The force of δουλεύειν must be preserved, and the special meaning of οἰκέτης is also worth noting.

ἢ ἑνὸς ἀνθέξεται. The omission of the article makes very little difference: "one or other of the two." As the second clause is less strong than the first, the ἤ may be understood in the sense of "*or at least* he will hold on to"—so as to stand by and support.

οὐ δύνασθε. It is morally impossible, for each claims undivided service. Mammon is here personified as a deity, devotion to whom is shown in "covetousness which is idolatry" (Col. iii. 5). No vice is more exacting than avarice. *D.C.G.* art. "Covetousness."

14–18. Introduction to the Parable of the Rich Man and Lazarus.

14. Ἤκουον δὲ ταῦτα πάντα. This shows that the occasion is the same; but the scoffs of the Pharisees diverted Christ's words from the disciples (ver. 1) to themselves. Note the πάντα.

φιλάργυροι ὑπάρχοντες. Avarice was their constant characteristic: for the verb see on viii. 41 and xxiii. 50. The adj. occurs 2 Tim. iii. 2 and nowhere else in bibl. Grk., but is quite classical. 2 Mac. x. 20 we have φιλαργυρεῖν. The covetousness of the Pharisees is independently attested, and they regarded their wealth as a special blessing for their carefulness in observing the Law. Hence their contempt for teaching which declared that there is danger in wealth, and that as a rule it promotes unrighteousness. They considered themselves an abiding proof of the connexion between riches and righteousness: moreover, they had their own explanation of the reason why a Rabbi who was poor declaimed against riches. Comp. xx. 47.

ἐξεμυκτήριζον. "Turned up the nose (μυκτήρ) at": xxiii. 35; Ps. ii. 4, xxxiv. 16. Here *deridebant* (f), *inridebant* (a), *subsannabant* (d). In class. Grk. μυκτηρίζειν is more usual: Gal. vi. 7; 2 Kings xix. 21; Pr. i. 30; Is. xxxvii. 22; Jer. xx. 7. In medical writers it means "bleed at the nose."

15. ἐνώπιον τῶν ἀνθρώπων. This is the emphatic part of the statement. The Pharisees succeeded in exhibiting themselves as righteous persons *in the judgment of men*; but God's judgment was very different. Comp. Mt. vi. 2, 5, 16, xxiii. 5, 6, 7, 25.

ὁ δὲ Θεὸς γινώσκει τὰς καρδίας. The use of γινώσκειν, which commonly implies the acquisition of knowledge, rather than εἰδέναι, is remarkable. We find the same word used of Christ, even where the knowledge must have been supernatural (Jn. ii. 24, 25, x. 14, 27, xvii. 25). The exact antithesis would have been, "but before God ye cannot justify yourselves." This, however, would have implied that there were no Pharisees who were not hypocrites: that God reads their hearts is true in all cases. Comp. ὁ δὲ Θεὸς ὄψεται εἰς καρδίαν (1 Sam. xvi. 7), and again, πάσας καρδίας ἐτάζει κύριος καὶ πᾶν ἐνθύμημα γινώσκει (1 Chron. xxviii. 9).

ὅτι τὸ ἐν ἀνθρώποις ὑψηλόν. We must understand something before ὅτι: "But God knoweth your hearts [and He seeth not as man seeth], because that which is exalted in the eyes of men," etc. For this use of ἐν comp. 1 Cor. xiv. 11, and perhaps Jude 1: it is clear that ἐν ἀνθρώποις = ἐνώπιον τῶν ἀνθρώπων above. Comp. Job x. 4; 1 Sam. xvi. 7.

βδέλυγμα. Here only in N.T. in the general sense of an abomination: comp. Gen. xliii. 31, xlvi. 34. Elsewhere (Mt. xxiv. 15; Mk. xiii. 14; Rev. xvii. 4, 5, xxi. 27) of the special abominations of idolatry: comp. 1 Kings xi. 5, 33, xx. 26; 2 Kings xvi. 3, xxi. 2. The word belongs to Hellenistic Greek, and is very freq. in LXX. It meant originally that which greatly offends the nostrils, and it is very much in excess of the usual antithesis to ὑψηλόν, viz. ταπεινόν. See Suicer, *s.v.*; *D.C.G.* "Abomination."

16–18. The discourse has been so greatly condensed that the connecting links have been lost. It is possible that the connexion is something of this kind. "To be justified before God is all the more necessary now when the Kingdom of God among men is being founded. The Law has been superseded. Its types have been fulfilled, and its exclusiveness is abolished: everyone now can force his way to salvation. But the *moral* principles of the Law are imperishable;

you cannot abolish them. And thus your frequent divorces violate the spirit of the Law." Others regard ver. 18 as symbolical. "You and those whom you instruct are wedded to the Divine revelation, and if you desert it for anything else you are guilty of spiritual adultery." But in that case what meaning can the second clause have? How can anyone commit spiritual adultery by accepting the revelation which the Jews rejected? See on ver. 18 for another attempt at a parabolic interpretation.

16. Ὁ νόμος καὶ οἱ προφῆται. A common expression for the O.T. Dispensation. It may point to a time when the Hebrew Canon consisted only of the Law and the Prophets (Mt. v. 17, vii. 12, xxii. 40; Acts xiii. 15, xxviii. 23). See Ryle, *Canon of O.T.* p. 118.

μέχρι Ἰωάνου. We supply ἦσαν: "they existed and had authority until John."

This is the only passage in which μέχρι is found preceding a vowel; elsewhere μέχρις is used (Mk. xiii. 30; Heb. xii. 4). See on ἄχρι, i. 20.

πᾶς εἰς αὐτὴν βιάζεται. "Every one forces his way into it,"—perhaps not always in the right spirit. See Hort, *Judaistic Christianity*, p. 26. The πᾶς is to be noticed: the Jew has no longer any exclusive rights. Here βιάζεται is mid. according to class. usage: in Mt. xi. 12 it is pass.—"the Kingdom of God is forced, taken by storm." Deissmann, *Bible Studies*, p. 258.

17. Εὐκοπώτερον. See on v. 23. The δέ which follows it is "But" (RV.), not "And" (AV.). Many English Versions omit the conjunction. *Facilius est autem* (Vulg.).

κερέαν. *Minimæ literæ minimus apex*, *i.e.* one of the little horns (κέρας) or minute projections which distinguish Hebrew letters, otherwise similar, from one another. There are several Jewish sayings which declare that anyone who is guilty of interchanging any of these similar letters in certain passages in O.T. will destroy the whole world. Wetst. on Mt. v. 18; Schoettg. i. p. 29; Edersh. *L. & T.* i. pp. 537, 538.

For the form κερέα = κεραία comp. ii. 13, and see WH. ii. App. p. 151. Marcion read τῶν λόγων μου, or τῶν λόγων τοῦ Κυρίου, instead of τοῦ νόμου. The reading has no support; and μίαν κεραίαν is more applicable to the written law than to the as yet unwritten words of Christ. See Tert. *Adv. Marcion.* iv. 33, and contrast Lk. xxi. 33.

πεσεῖν. "To fall to the ground" as devoid of authority: comp. Rom. ix. 6?; 1 Cor. xiii. 8. The moral elements in the Law are indestructible, and the Gospel confirms them by giving them a new sanction.

18. Perhaps this introduces an example of the durability of the moral law in spite of human evasions. Adultery remains adultery even when it has been legalized, and legalized by men who jealously guarded every fraction of the letter, while they flagrantly violated the spirit of the Law. "Because he hath found some unseemly thing in her" (Deut. xxiv. 1), was interpreted with such frivolity, that Hillel is said to have taught that a man might divorce his wife for spoiling the dinner. Comp. Mk. x. 11, 12 and Mt. v. 32 for other statements of Christ's doctrine. Mt. v. 32 states the one exception.

It is very forced to take the whole utterance as a parable. "It is spiritual adultery to cast off all the obligations of the Law; and it is also spiritual adultery to maintain all those obligations which have been rescinded by the Gospel." But this does not fit the wording; and, if it did, would it have been intelligible to those who heard it? According to this explanation the wife unlawfully put away = those elements in the Law which are eternal; and the divorced wife unlawfully married to another man = those elements of the Law which are obsolete. But in the parable (if it be a parable) we have not two women but one. It is better to take the words literally, and leave the connexion with what precedes undetermined.

19–31. § The Parable of the Rich Man and Lazarus; in two scenes, one on earth (19–22) and the other in Hades (23–31). It continues the lesson respecting the right employment of earthly possessions. The unjust steward showed what good results may follow from a wise use of present advantages. The rich man shows how disastrous are the consequences of omitting to make a wise use of such things. This second parable illustrates in a marked way some of the utterances which precede it. "That which is exalted among men" describes the rich man in his luxury on earth. "An abomination in the sight of God" describes him in his misery in Hades. "It is easier for heaven and earth to pass away, than for one tittle of the law to fail," shows that Moses and the Prophets still avail as the teachers of conduct that will lead a man to Abraham's bosom rather than to the place of torment. There is no taint of "Ebionitic heresy" in the narrative. It emphasizes the dangers of wealth; but it nowhere implies the unlawfulness of wealth. (See Milligan, *A Group of Parables*, in the *Expositor* for September 1892, p. 186.) It is not suggested that the rich man ought to have renounced his riches, but that he ought not to have found in riches his highest good. He ought to have made his earthly possessions a means of obtaining something much higher and more abiding. Out of this mammon, which in his case was unrighteous mammon, he might have made Lazarus and others his "friends," and have secured through them eternal tabernacles. His riches were "*his* good things," the only good things that he knew; and when he lost them he lost everything. "What doth it profit a man, to gain the whole world, and forfeit his life?" There is no reason for supposing that the second half of the parable is a later addition, or that it is the only part which has a meaning. It is when both are combined that we get the main lesson,—that to possess great wealth and use it solely for oneself, without laying up treasure in heaven, is fatal.

The parable is sometimes understood quite otherwise. Lazarus is the Jewish people, ill-treated by earthly powers, such as the Romans and their underlings; and Dives and his five brothers are the Herods: (1) Herod the Great,

(2) Archelaus, (3) Philip, (4) Antipas, (5) Agrippa I., (6) Agrippa II. Father, sons, and grandsons are thus all put together as brothers for simplification. It is a natural consequence of such an interpretation as this that the parable is assumed to be the invention of a later age, and to have been wrongly attributed to Christ. It is difficult to believe that He could have wished to suggest any such meaning.[1] Moreover, this interpretation destroys the connexion with the context.

19. Ἄνθρωπος δέ τις ἦν πλούσιος. "Now a certain man was rich" is less probable than "Now there was a certain rich man": comp. ver. 1, xiii. 11. Note the *τις*.

πορφύραν καὶ βύσσον. The former for the upper garment, the latter for the under. Both were very costly. The former means first the *murex*, secondly the dye made from it (1 Mac. iv. 23), and then the fabric dyed with it (Mk. xv. 17, 20). Similarly, *βύσσος* is first Egyptian flax, and then the fine linen made from it (Exod. xxvi. 1, 31, 36; Ezek. xvi. 10, xxvii. 7). The two words are combined Prov. xxxi. 22: comp. Rev. xviii. 12, 16. For εὐφραινόμενος comp. xii. 19, xv. 23, 29: λαμπρῶς occurs nowhere else in bibl. Grk.

20. ὀνόματι Λάζαρος. For *ὀνόματι* see on v. 27: the expression is freq. in Lk. Nowhere else does Christ give a name to any character in a parable. That this signifies that the name was "written in heaven," while that of the rich man was not, is far-fetched. Tertullian urges the name as proof that the narrative is not a parable but history, and that the scene in Hades involves his doctrine that the soul is corporeal (*De Animâ*, vii.).[2] It is possible that the name is a later addition to the parable, to connect it with Lazarus of Bethany. *He* was one who "went to them from the dead," and still they did not repent. As he was raised from the dead just about this time, so far as we can determine the chronology, there may be a reference to him. But it is more probable that the name suggests the helplessness of the beggar; and *some* name was needed (ver. 24). Tradition has given the name Nineuis to the rich man. The theory that the story of the raising of Lazarus has grown out of this parable is altogether arbitrary.

ἐβέβλητο πρὸς τὸν πυλῶνα αὐτοῦ. Not "had been flung at his gate," as if contemptuous roughness were implied. In late Greek *βάλλειν* often loses the notion of violence, and means simply "lay, place": v. 37; Jn. v. 7, xii. 6, xviii. 11, xx. 25, 27, xxi. 6; Jas. iii. 3; Num. xxii. 38. By *πυλῶνα* is meant a large gateway or portico, whether part of the house or not (Acts x. 17, xii. 14; Mt. xxvi. 71; 2 Chron. iii. 7; Zeph. ii. 14). It indicates the grandeur of the house.

[1] *Jésus se serait-il abaissé à de pareilles personalités?* asks Godet, with some reason.

[2] Ambrose also takes it as history: *Narratio magis quam parabola videtur, quando etiam nomen exprimitur* (Migne, xv. 1768).

εἱλκωμένος. The verb occurs here only in bibl. Grk., but is common in medical writers, especially in the pass., "be ulcerated."

The irregular augment, instead of the usual ἡλκωμένος, is well attested here, and perhaps arose from analogy with ἕλκω. Comp. κατειργάσατο (Rom. xv. 18). WH. ii. App. p. 161; Greg. *Proleg.* p. 121. Syr-Sin. omits.

21. ἐπιθυμῶν χορτασθῆναι. This does not imply (Iren. ii. 34. 1) that his desire was not gratified. His being allowed to remain there daily, and his caring to remain there daily, rather indicates that he did get the broken meat. He shared with the dogs (Mk vii. 28). But perhaps it *does* imply that what was given to him did not satisfy his hunger. Some authorities insert from xv. 16 *καὶ οὐδεὶς ἐδίδου αὐτῷ*, *et nemo illi dabat*, which even as a gloss seems to be false.

The silence of Lazarus throughout the parable is very impressive. He never murmurs against God's distribution of wealth, nor against the rich man's abuse of it, in this world. And in Hades he neither exults over the change of relations between himself and Dives, nor protests against being asked to wait upon him in the place of torment, or to go errands for him to the visible world.

ἀλλὰ καὶ οἱ κύνες. "Nay, even the dogs." This shows his want and his helplessness. Not only was his hunger unsatisfied, but even the dogs came and increased his misery. He was scantily clad, and his sores were not bound up; and he was unable to drive away the unclean dogs when they came to lick them. The suggestion that the dogs were kinder to him than the rich man was, is probably not intended; although the main point of *vv.* 20, 21 is to continue the description of Dives rather than to make a contrast to him. Here was a constant opportunity of making a good use of his wealth, and he did not avail himself of it.

ἐπέλειχον. "Licked the surface of." Here only in bibl. Greek. The reading ἀπέλειχον has very little authority. For ἀλλὰ καί comp. xii. 7, xxiv. 22.

22. This verse serves to connect the two scenes of the parable. The reversal of the positions of the two men is perhaps intimated in the fact that Lazarus dies first. The opportunity of doing good to him was lost before the rich man died, but the loss was not noticed.

ἀπενεχθῆναι αὐτόν. "His *soul* was carried," *a loco alieno in patriam.* Clearly we are not to understand that what never happened to anyone before happened to him, and that body and soul were both translated to Hades. In saying that he died (ἀποθανεῖν) the severance of soul and body is implied. And the fact that his burial is not mentioned is no proof that it is not to be understood

Jesus would scarcely have shocked Jewish feeling by the revolting idea that close to human habitations a corpse was left unburied In each case the feature which specially characterized the death is mentioned. See Aug. *De Civ. Dei*, xxi. 10. 2.

ὑπὸ τῶν ἀγγέλων. The transition was painless and happy. A Targum on Cantic. iv. 12 says that the souls of the righteous are carried to paradise by Angels. Comp. the λειτουργικὰ πνεύματα of Heb. i. 14 and the ἄγγελοι λειτουργοί of Philo. But *it is no purpose of the parable to give information about the unseen world.* The general principle is maintained that bliss and misery after death are determined by conduct previous to death; but the details of the picture are taken from Jewish beliefs as to the condition of souls in Sheol, and must not be understood as confirming those beliefs. The properties of bodies are attributed to souls in order to enable us to realize the picture.

εἰς τὸν κόλπον Ἀβραάμ. This is not the objective genitive, "the bosom which contained Abraham," but the subjective, "that in which Abraham received Lazarus." Comp. Mt. viii. 11. Lazarus in Sheol reposes with his head on Abraham's breast, as a child in his father's lap, and shares his happiness. Comp. Jn. i 18. The expression is not common in Jewish writings; but Abraham is sometimes represented as welcoming the penitent into paradise. Edersh. *L. & T.* ii. p. 280. Comp. οὕτω γὰρ παθόντας (*v.l.* θανόντας) ἡμᾶς Ἀβραὰμ καὶ Ἰσαὰκ καὶ Ἰακὼβ ὑποδέξονται (4 Mac. xiii. 17). Such expressions as "go to one's fathers" (Gen. xv. 15), "lie with one's fathers" (Gen. xlvii. 30), "be gathered to one's fathers" (Judg. ii. 10), and "sleep with one's fathers" (1 Kings i. 21), apply to death only, and contain no clue as to the bliss or misery of the departed. "Abraham's bosom" does contain this. It is not a synonym for paradise; but to repose on Abraham's bosom is to be in paradise, for Abraham is there (Jn. viii. 56: Diptychs of the Dead in the Liturgy of S. James).

καὶ ἐτάφη. It is not the contrast between the *magnificence* of his funeral (of which nothing is stated) and the *lack* of funeral for Lazarus (of which nothing is stated) that is to be marked, but the contrast between mere burial in the one case and the ministration of Angels in the other.

Some authorities seem to have omitted the καὶ before ἐν τῷ ᾅδῃ and to have joined these words with ἐτάφη. Vulg. has *et sepultus est in inferno: elevans autem oculos suos.* Aug. has both arrangements. Comp. Jn. xiii. 30, 31 for a similar improbable shifting of a full stop in some texts. Other examples Greg. *Proleg.* p. 181.

23. καὶ ἐν τῷ ᾅδῃ. "In Hades," the receptacle of *all* the departed until the time of final judgment, and including both paradise and Gehenna. That Hades does not mean "hell" as a place of punishment is manifest from Acts ii. 27, 31; Gen. xxxvii. 35, xlii. 38, xliv. 29; Job xiv. 13, xvii. 13, etc. That Hades includes a place of punishment is equally clear from this passage. In the *Psalms of Solomon* Hades is mentioned only in connexion with the idea of punishment (xiv. 6, xv. 11, xvi. 2). See Suicer, *s.v.* The distinction between Hades and Gehenna is one of the many great advantages of RV. Dives "lifts up his eyes," not to look for help, but to learn the nature of his changed condition.

ὑπάρχων ἐν βασάνοις. Torment is now his habitual condition: not *ὤν*, but *ὑπάρχων*. That he is punished for his heartless neglect of great opportunities of benevolence, and not simply for being rich, is clear from the position of Abraham, who was rich. Comp. *μέγας γὰρ ψυχῆς ἀγὼν καὶ κίνδυνος ἐν αἰωνίῳ βασάνῳ κείμενος τοῖς παραβᾶσι τὴν ἐντολὴν τοῦ Θεοῦ* (4 Mac. xiii. 15); and contrast *δικαίων δὲ ψυχαὶ ἐν χειρὶ Θεοῦ, καὶ οὐ μὴ ἅψηται αὐτῶν βάσανος* (Wisd. iii. 1). *Luxurioso carere deliciis poena est* (Ambr).

ὁρᾷ Ἀβραάμ. The Jews believed that Gehenna and paradise are close to one another: Edersh. *Hist. of Jewish Nation*, p. 432 ed. 1896. We need not suppose that the parable teaches *us* to believe this. The details of the picture cannot be insisted upon.

ἀπὸ μακρόθεν. The *ἀπό* is pleonastic, and marks a late use, when the force of the adverbial termination has become weakened: Mt. xxvii. 51; Mk. v. 6, xiv. 54, xv. 40, etc. In LXX we have *ἀπὸ ὄπισθεν* (freq. in 1 and 2 Sam.), *ἀπὸ ἐπάνωθεν, ἀπὸ πρωΐθεν*: and in Aq. *ἀπὸ ἀρχῆθεν* and *ἀπὸ κυκλόθεν*.

With *κόλποις* comp. *ἱμάτια* of a single garment (Acts xviii. 6; Jn. xiii. 4, xix. 23) and *γάμοι* of a single wedding (xii. 36). We have similar plurals in late class. Grk.

24. Πάτερ Ἀβραάμ. He appeals to their relationship, and to his fatherly compassion. Will not Abraham take pity on one of his own sons? Comp. Jn. viii. 53. Note the characteristic *καὶ αὐτός* (see on i. 17, v. 14). The **φωνήσας** implies raising his voice, in harmony with *ἀπὸ μακρόθεν*.

πέμψον Λάζαρον. Not that he assumes that Lazarus is at his beck and call, although Lange thinks that this is "the finest masterstroke of the parable" that Dives unconsciously retains his arrogant attitude towards Lazarus. See also his strange explanation of the finger-drop of water (*L. of C.* i. p. 507). On earth Dives was not arrogant; he did not drive Lazarus from his gate; but neglectful. In Hades he is so humbled by his pain that he is willing to receive alleviation from anyone, even Lazarus.

ἵνα βάψῃ τὸ ἄκρον τοῦ δακτύλου αὐτοῦ ὕδατος. The smallest alleviation will be welcome. On earth no enjoyment was too extravagant: now the most trifling is worth imploring.

With the part. gen. ὕδατος comp. βάψει τὸν δάκτυλον τὸν δεξιὸν ἀπὸ τοῦ ἐλαίου (Lev. xiv. 16). To understand τι and make ὕδατός τι nom. to βάψῃ is an improbable constr. See Win. xxx. 8. c, p. 252.

ὀδυνῶμαι ἐν τῇ φλογὶ ταύτῃ. "I am in anguish in this flame" of insatiable desires and of remorse: a prelude to the γέεννα τοῦ πυρός (Mt. v. 22). For ὀδυνῶμαι see on ii. 48.

25. Τέκνον. He does not resent the appeal to relationship: the refusal is as gentle as it is decided. The rich man cannot fail to see the reasonableness of what he experiences.

ἀπέλαβες. "Thou didst receive *in full*." This seems to be the meaning of the ἀπο-. Nothing was stored up for the future: comp. ἀπέχειν, vi. 24; Mt. vi. 2, 5, 16. Note the μνήσθητι. It is only in the mythological Hades that there is a river of Lethe, drowning the memory of the past. See second small print, p. 425.

τὰ ἀγαθά σου. Herein also was fatal error. He had no idea of any other good things, and he kept these to himself.

καὶ Λάζαρος ὁμοίως τὰ κακά. There is no αὐτοῦ. His evil things were not his own, but he accepted them as from God, while the rich man took his good things as possessions for which he had no account to render. Comp. *vv.* 11, 12.

νῦν δὲ ὧδε. Contrast of time and place: "But *now here.*" The ὅ δέ of TR. has scarcely any authority. The same corruption is found 1 Cor. iv. 2. Comp. οὐκ ἔστιν ἐν ᾅδου ζητῆσαι τρυφήν (Ecclus. xiv. 16). There is, however, no hint that during their lives Dives had been sufficiently rewarded for any good that he had done, and Lazarus sufficiently punished for any evil that he had done. And there is also no justification of the doctrine that to each man is allotted so much pleasure and so much pain; and that those who have their full allowance of pleasure in this world cannot have any in the world to come. Abraham's reply must be considered in close relation to the rich man's request. Dives had not asked to be freed from his punishment. He accepted that as just. He had asked for a slight alleviation, and in a way which involved an interruption of the bliss of Lazarus. Abraham replies that to interfere with the lot of either is both unreasonable and impossible. Dives had unbroken luxury, and Lazarus unbroken suffering, in the other world. There can be no break in the pangs of Dives, or in the bliss of Lazarus, now. *Apoc. Baruch*, lxxv. 9.

ὀδυνᾶσαι. An intermediate form between ὀδυνάεσαι and ὀδυνᾷ. Such things belong to the popular Greek of the time. Comp. καυχᾶσαι (Rom. ii. 17; 1 Cor. iv. 7), κατακαυχᾶσαι (Rom. xi. 18), and see on φάγεσαι and πίεσαι (Lk. xvii. 8). See *Expos. Times*, viii. p. 239.

26. ἐν πᾶσι τούτοις. *In his omnibus* (Vulg.). The ἐπί (A, etc.) for ἐν (ℵ B L) is a manifest correction. While ver. 25 shows that on equitable grounds no alleviation of the lot of Dives is admissible, ver. 26 shows that the particular kind of alleviation asked for is impossible. Can it mean, "In all these regions, from end to end"?

χάσμα μέγα ἐστήρικται. "Has been and remains fixed." Evidence is lacking to show that the Jews pictured the two parts of Hades as divided by a chasm. Here only in bibl. Grk. is χάσμα found: not Num. xvi. 30.

Chaos magnum firmatum est (Vulg. f), *chaus magnum confirmatus est* (d), *chaos magnus firmatus est* (l). For this use of *chaos* comp. *Posita est mihi regia cœlo: Possidet alter aquas, alter inane chaos* (Ovid, *Fast.* iv. 599). Bentley conjectured *chasma*, the *ma* having been lost in *magnum* and *chas* expanded into *chaos.* This conjecture finds support in two MSS. of Vulg., M having *chasma* and Y *chasmagnum.* Jerome would be likely to correct *chaos* into *chasma.*

ὅπως . . . μὴ δύνωνται. Not, "so that they cannot" (AV.); but, "in order that they may not be able."

μηδέ. "Nor yet": this would be still less permissible. The οἱ before ἐκεῖθεν is probably not genuine, but we may understand a new subject. Groups from each side are supposed to contemplate crossing; not one group to cross and recross.

27. But perhaps there is no χάσμα between paradise and the other world; and Dives makes another request, which, if less selfish than the first, is also less humble. It implies that he has scarcely had a fair chance. If God had warned him sufficiently, he would have escaped this place of torment.

28. διαμαρτύρηται αὐτοῖς. "May bear witness successfully," right through to a good issue. But the δια- need not mean more than "thoroughly, earnestly" (Acts ii. 40, viii. 25, x. 42, xviii. 5, xx. 21, 23, 24, xxiii. 11, xxviii. 23). Elsewhere in N.T. only five times, but freq. in LXX. That any five persons then living, whether Herods, or sons of Annas, or among the audience, are here alluded to, is most improbable. That the request is meant to illustrate the Pharisees' craving for signs is more possible: and the lesson that the desire to warn others from vicious courses may come too late is perhaps also included. But the simplest explanation of the request is that it prepares the way for the moral of the parable,—*the duty of making use of existing opportunities.*

29. ἀκουσάτωσαν αὐτῶν. *Nemo cogitur. Auditu fideli salvamur, non apparitionibus. Herodes, audire non cupiens, miraculum non cernit* (Beng.). Wonders may impress a worldly mind for the moment; but only a will freely submitting itself to moral control can avail to change the heart.

30. Οὐχί, πάτερ Ἀβραάμ. Not, "No, they will not repent for Moses and the Prophets," which Abraham has not asserted; but, "No, that is not enough." He speaks from his own experience.

It is better to take ἀπὸ νεκρῶν with πορευθῇ than with τις. Vulg. is as amphibolous as the Greek: *si quis ex mortuis ierit ad eos.* See on i. 8.

μετανοήσουσιν. "They will repent." Not, "they will give all to the poor," or "they will leave all and become as Lazarus." There is no hint that being rich is sinful, or that the poor are sure of salvation. In ver. 28 he did not say that wealth had ruined himself.

31. Εἰ . . . οὐκ ἀκούουσιν. "If, as matters now stand, they are refusing to hear." We go beyond the tenour of the reply when we make it mean that "a far mightier miracle than you demand would be ineffectual for producing a far slighter effect." Does *ἐκ νεκρῶν ἀναστῇ* imply "a far mightier miracle" than *ἀπὸ νεκρῶν πορευθῇ*? And does *πεισθήσονται* imply "a far slighter effect" than *μετανοήσουσιν*? "Persuaded" obviously means "persuaded to repent"; and one who "goes from the dead" to warn the living must "rise from the dead." By this conclusion Christ once more rebukes the demand for a sign. Those who ask for it have all that they need for the ascertainment of the truth; and the sign if granted would not produce conviction. Saul was not led to repentance when he saw Samuel at Endor, nor were the Pharisees when they saw Lazarus come forth from the tomb. The Pharisees tried to put Lazarus to death and to explain away the resurrection of Jesus. For allegorical interpretations of the parable see Trench, *Parables*, p. 470, 10th ed.[1]

In *οὐκ ἀκούουσιν* the negative belongs to the verb so as almost to form one word, and is not influenced by the *εἰ*: "If they disregard." Comp. xi. 8, xii. 26, xviii. 4. The pres. indic. represents the supposition as contemporaneous. Note the change from *εἰ* with pres. indic. to *ἐάν* with aor. subjunc. The latter is pure hypothesis.

The Idea of Hades or Sheol in the Old Testament.

It is surprising how very little advance there is in O.T., respecting conceptions of the unseen world, upon Greek mythology. It is scarcely an exaggeration to say that, until about B.C. 200, the Jewish Sheol is essentially the same in conception as the Hades of Greek poetry. There are no moral or spiritual distinctions in it. Good and bad alike are there, and are apparently much in the same condition. Moreover, there is no thought of either of them rising again. In some places, *possibly*, Sheol or Hades is merely a synonym for the grave or death, which receives good and bad alike, and retains them: *e.g.* Gen. xxxvii. 35, xlii. 38; 1 Sam. ii. 6. But in passages in which the unseen world of spirits is plainly meant, the absence of the religious element is remarkable. Nay, in one way the bad are better off than the good; for while the just have lost the joys which were the reward of their righteousness, the wicked have ceased to be troubled by the consequences of their iniquity. See Davidson on Job iii. 16–19. Sheol is a place of rest; but also of silence, gloom, and ignorance. In the only passage in which the word occurs in Ecclesiastes we are told that there is no work, nor device, nor knowledge, nor wisdom, in Sheol, whither thou goest" (ix. 10). Those who have gone thither return no more, and none escape it (Job vii. 9, 10, x. 21, 22, xx. 9). It is a land of forgetfulness, in which there

---

[1] Near the end of the Koran are two passages worth comparing. (Sale's *Koran*, chs. cii., civ.).

is no more remembrance of God or possibility of serving Him (Ps. vi. 5, xxx. 9, lxxxviii. 12; comp. Is. xxxviii. 11, 18). And it is insatiable (Prov. i. 12, xxvii. 20, xxx. 16; comp. Is. v. 14). In some Psalms there is some trace of hope for eternal life in God in the other world (xlix. 15), but not of hope for resurrection. In xvii. 15 "when I awake" probably does not mean awake from death, but from sleep. It is the *daily renewal* of communion with God that is desired. In Is. xxv. 8, and still more in Is. xxvi. 19, hope in a resurrection from Sheol is expressed; and in Dan. xii. 2 we reach the idea of resurrection with rewards and punishments. See Hastings, *D.B.* i. p. 740; *D.C.G.* ii. p. 514.

Side by side with the hope of a resurrection (2 Mac. xii. 43–45, xiv. 46) comes the belief that Sheol is only an intermediate state, at any rate for the righteous (2 Mac. vii. 9, 11, 14, 36, 37; *Enoch* li.): and along with the idea of a resurrection to rewards and punishments comes the idea that there is retribution in Sheol itself, and consequently a separation of the righteous from the wicked (*Enoch* xxii.). But the idea of rising again to be punished does not seem to have prevailed. The view rather was that only the righteous were raised, while the wicked remained for ever in Sheol (*Enoch* lxiii. 8–10, xcix. 11). In this way Hades becomes practically the same as Gehenna (*Ps. Sol.* xiv. 6, xv. 11, xvi. 2). In the parable of the Rich Man and Lazarus there is nothing to show whether Hades is intermediate or final: but the doctrine of its being a place of retribution, with a complete separation of the righteous from the wicked, could hardly be more clearly marked. In the Talmud, Sheol is identical with Gehenna, just as in popular English "hell" is always a place of punishment, and generally of final punishment. See *DB.*[2] art. "Hell"; Herzog, *PRE.*[2] art. *Hades*; Charles, *Book of Enoch*, p. 168.

XVII. 1–10. Four sayings of Christ. These are, The Sin of Causing Others to Sin (1, 2); The Duty of Forgiveness (3, 4); The Power of Faith (5, 6); and, The Insufficiency of Works (7–10). They have no connexion with the much longer utterances which precede them. Some of them are given by Mt. and Mk. in other positions. And the four sayings appear to be without connexion one with another. It is possible to make them into two pairs, as RV. does by its paragraphs. But the connexions between the first and second, and between the third and fourth, are too uncertain to be insisted upon.

1, 2. The Sin of Causing Others to Sin. These two verses are found in reverse order, and somewhat differently worded, Mt. xviii. 6, 7, and ver. 2 is found Mk. ix. 42.

1. Ἀνένδεκτον. Here only in bibl. Grk., and rare elsewhere, excepting in writers who knew this passage. In xiii. 33 we have ἐνδέχεται, from which this comes; and the intermediate ἔνδεκτόν ἐστι is found in Apollonius. The meaning is "it is unallowable, it cannot be," οὐκ ἐνδέχεται.

The gen. in τοῦ . . . μὴ ἐλθεῖν may be variously explained, but best as an expression of *design*, implied in what is not allowed, a construction of which Lk. is very fond: see on ii. 21. Win. xliv. 4. b, p. 408. Others refer it to the notion of hindering implied in ἀνένδεκτον (Burton, § 405); while Meyer makes ἀνέν. a substantive on which the gen. depends, "There is an impossibility of offences" not coming. Here only does σκάνδαλον occur in Lk. It is a late form of σκανδάληθρον (Aristoph. *Ach.* 687), the "bait-stick" in a trap, and combined the ideas of ensnaring and tripping up. It is a bibl. and eccles. word, freq. in LXX.

πλὴν οὐαὶ δι' οὗ ἔρχεται. See on vi. 24, and comp. xxii. 22.

2. λυσιτελεῖ αὐτῷ. "It is well for him, is worth his while": lit. "it pays the taxes (λύει τὰ τέλη), repays the outlay." Here only in N.T., but found Tobit iii. 6; Ecclus. xx. 10, 14, xxix. 14, and quite classical.

In Tertullian (*Adv. Marcion.* iv. 35) we have an insertion from Mt. xxvi. 24: *expedisse ei*, si natus non fuisset, aut *si molino saxo ad collum deligato*, etc. A similar mixture of texts is found in Clem. Rom. (*Cor.* xlvi.), who has ἕνα τῶν ἐκλεκτῶν for τῶν μικρῶν τούτων ἕνα.

λίθος μυλικός. "A stone fit for a mill" (μύλη). Mt. xviii. 6 and Mk. ix. 42 we have μύλος ὀνικός for λίθος μυλικός. Neither occurs in LXX.

καὶ ἔρριπται. Mk. has βέβληται. The change from pres. to perf. is graphic: "It is good for him if a millstone is hanged about his neck and he has been hurled." As to the double ρρ see Greg. *Proleg.* p. 121.

ἤ. "Rather than": see small print on xv. 7, and comp. λυσιτελεῖ μοι ἀποθανεῖν ἢ ζῆν (Tobit iii. 6). Such constructions are common in LXX (Gen. xlix. 12; Jon. iv. 3, 8; Tobit xii. 8; Ecclus. xx. 25, xxii. 15, etc.), but are found also in class. Grk. καλὸν τὸ μὴ ζῆν ἢ ζῆν ἀθλίως (Menander). Nothing is to be understood with ἵνα, such as "rather than (to remain alive) in order to." It is the late use of ἵνα with the telic force lost. Win. xliv. 8. c, p. 424; Burton, § 214. Comp. Mt. v. 29, 30; 1 Cor. iv. 3.

τῶν μικρῶν τούτων ἕνα. As the saying is addressed to the disciples (ver. 1), it is unlikely that the whole body of the disciples is included in "these little ones." It is more natural to understand it of the more insignificant among them (comp. vii. 28), or those who were young in the faith, or possibly children. The ἕνα comes last with emphasis. To lead even one astray is an awful responsibility.

προσέχετε ἑαυτοῖς. These words come better as a conclusion to the previous warning than as an introduction to the exhortation which follows. They are analogous to "He that hath ears to hear, let him hear." For the constr. see on xii. 1. For instances in which there is discrepancy as to the division of verses see Greg. *Proleg.* p. 175.

3, 4. § The Duty of Forgiveness. Those who connect this saying with the one which precedes it, make an unforgiving spirit to be set forth as a common way of causing others to stumble. Others regard it as an *à fortiori* argument. If we must avoid doing evil to others, much more must we forgive the evil which they do to us. A better link is found in the severity of *vv.* 1 and 2, "when thou sinnest against another," and the tenderness of *vv* 3 and 4, "when others sin against thee."

The δέ, which A etc. insert after ἐάν, is perhaps an attempt to mark a contrast between the two sayings and thus link them. Or it may come from

Mt. xviii. 15: om. ℵ B D L X, Latt. Boh. Aeth. Arm. Goth. Neither here nor Mt. xviii. 15 is the εἰς σέ, which D and some Latin authorities insert after ἁμάρτῃ, genuine: om. ℵ A B L X Δ, Cod. Am. Cod. Brix. Syr. Goth. Nevertheless, what follows shows that offences εἰς σέ are specially meant.

ἐπιτίμησον. The tenderness is not to be weakness. The fault is not to be passed over without notice (Lev. xix. 17).

4. ἑπτάκις τῆς ἡμέρας. In Peter's question (Mt. xviii. 21, 22) there is no τῆς ἡμέρας, which is genuine here after the first ἑπτακις only: and there is no μετανοῶ. See on xv. 7. The "seven times" is of course not to be taken literally. Comp. "Seven times a day do I praise thee" (Ps. cxix. 164). Unlimited forgiveness is prescribed. But too much meaning is put into λέγων, when it is explained to mean that the mere *expression* of repentance is to suffice. Professed repentance may be ostentatiously unreal.

5, 6. The Power of Faith. There is no sign of connexion with what precedes. The fact that we have τοὺς μαθητάς in ver. 1 and οἱ ἀπόστολοι here points to different occasions. Mt. connects this saying of Christ with the Apostles' question, "Why could not we cast it out?" (xvii. 19, 20). Mk. has a similar saying after the withering of the barren fig tree (xi. 23). Marcion omitted *vv.* 5–10.

5. τῷ κυρίῳ. See on v. 17 and vii. 13. The expression has point here. The Apostles ask the Lord who had given them their office to supply them with what was necessary for the discharge of that office.

Πρόσθες ἡμῖν πίστιν. "Give us faith in addition: add it to the gifts already bestowed." The "faith" here meant is faith in Christ's promises. It is very forced to make it refer to what precedes; the faith that enables one to forgive a brother seven times in a day. Power to fulfil that duty would have been otherwise expressed. See Sanday on Rom. i. 5 and additional note pp. 31–34.

6. Εἰ ἔχετε . . . ἐλέγετε ἄν. Irregular sequence, which has produced the reading εἰ εἴχετε (D E G H) as a correction. In the protasis the supposition is left open: in the apodosis it is implicitly denied. See Moulton's note 5. Win. p. 383. We have a further change of tense in ὑπήκουσεν ἄν, implying that the obedience would *at once* have followed the command. Comp. Xen. *Anab.* v. 8. 13.

ὡς κόκκον σινάπεως. It is not a question of *additional* faith. Is there genuine faith to any extent? See on xiii. 19.

τῇ συκαμίνῳ. At the present time both the white and the black mulberry are common in Palestine; and in Greece the latter is still called συκαμινέα. It is not certain that the συκάμινος here is a different tree from the συκομορέα (xix. 4).[1] But in any case

[1] "Two points may be urged in favour of those who identify the two trees: (1) In LXX every instance in which the Hebrew has *Shikmin* the Greek has συκάμινος, although the fig, and not the mulberry, is certainly intended. (2) As

both are different from the English sycomore, which is a maple. The *συκάμινος* is mentioned 1 Chron. xxvii. 28; 2 Chron. i. 15, ix. 27; Ps. lxxviii. 47; Is. ix. 10. In Mt. xvii. 20 we have *τῷ ὄρει τούτῳ* for *τῇ συκαμίνῳ ταύτῃ*, the saying being uttered just after the descent from the Mount of Transfiguration. Comp. Mt. xxi. 21||. Here Christ's reply seems to indicate that it is faith in His promise that they should work miracles that is desired by the Apostles.

To treat the saying as a parable, and make the tree mean the Kingdom of God and the sea the heathen world, is fanciful.

7–10. § The Insufficiency of Works, or, the Parable of the Unprofitable Servant. The attempts to find a connexion between this and the preceding saying are forced and unsatisfactory. Obviously these four verses are not concerned with miracles, which cannot be meant by *τὰ διαταχθέντα ὑμῖν* (ver. 10). It is the ordinary duties of the Christian life that are meant. See the illustration in Hermas (*Sim.* v. 2. 1–11), and comp. Seneca, *De Benef.* iii. 18.

7. Τίς δὲ ἐξ ὑμῶν. There is no need to seek for explanations as to why Jesus speaks to "the poor Apostles" as if they had slaves who ploughed for them, or to point out that Zebedee had had hired servants (Mk. i. 20). There is no evidence that these words were addressed to the Twelve; and the words almost necessarily imply that they were addressed to a mixed audience of well-to-do persons. For *τίς ἐξ ὑμῶν* see on xi. 5, 6.

Εὐθέως: belongs to *παρελθών* rather than to *ἐρεῖ*, as is shown by the *μετὰ ταῦτα* afterwards, which balances *εὐθέως*: "Come straightway and sit down to eat." Wic. Tyn. Cov. Cran. Rhem. RV. with Vulg. and Luth. adopt this arrangement. AV. follows Gen. with "say unto him by and by," where "by and by" has its original meaning of "immediately": AV. of xxi. 9; Mt. xiii. 21; Mk. vi. 25. Comp. "presently," Mt. xxvi. 53; 1 Sam. ii. 16 (T. L. O. Davies, *Bible English*, p. 109; Lft. *On Revision*, p. 196, 2nd ed.; Trench, *On the A.V. of N.T.* p. 48).

παρελθὼν ἀνάπεσε. "Come forward and sit down to meat." This use of *παρέρχομαι* is classical, but in N.T. is peculiar to Lk. (xii. 37). Comp. the insertion Acts xxiv. 7 and 2 Chron. xxv. 7 A.

8. Ἑτοίμασον τί δειπνήσω . . . διακόνει. Change from aor. to pres. "Prepare once for all . . . continue to serve." With *τί δειπνήσω* comp. Mt. x. 19: in class. Grk. we should have *ὅ τι*, as in Acts ix. 6.

The forms *φάγεσαι* and *πίεσαι* are analogous to *ὀδυνᾶσαι* (xvi. 25) and *δύνασαι* (Mt. v. 36). They belong to the popular Greek of the time, but are not quite constant; Mk. ix. 22 we have *δύνῃ*. See Veitch, *s.v.*; Win. xv.

---

to the mulberry it has yet to be shown that it was then known in Palestine; and further the mulberry is more easily plucked up by the roots than any other tree of the same size in the country, and the thing is oftener done" (Groser, *Trees and Plants in the Bible*, pp. 121, 123).

pp. 109, 110; WH. ii. p. 304. Both φάγεσαι and πίεσαι are found Ruth ii. 9, 14; Ezek. xii. 18.

With ἔχει χάριν comp. 1 Tim. i. 12; 2 Tim. i. 3; Heb. xii. 28: the expression is classical. The οὐ δοκῶ of A D, Vulg. etc. is an insertion.

10. οὕτως καὶ ὑμεῖς, ὅταν ποιήσητε πάντα. A purely hypothetical case. Nothing is gained by placing a full stop at ὑμεῖς. With τὰ διαταχθέντα ὑμῖν comp. τὸ διατεταγμένον ὑμῖν (iii. 13; Acts xxiii. 31).

ἀχρεῖοι. Not "vile" as in 2 Sam. vi. 22, nor "good for nothing" as in Ep. Jer. 15, the only places in which the word occurs in LXX; but "unprofitable," because nothing has been *gained* by them for their master. He has got no more than his due. Comp. Mt. xxv. 30, the only other passage in N.T. in which the word is found. That God does not need man's service is not the point. Nor are the rewards which He gives in return for man's service here brought into question. The point is that man can make no just *claim* for having done *more* than was due. *Miser est quem Dominus servum inutilem appellat* (Mt. xxv. 30); *beatus qui se ipse* (Beng.). Syr-Sin. omits ἀχρεῖοι.

XVII. 11–XIX. 28. *The Third Period of the Journey*

11–19. Here begins the last portion of the long section (ix. 51–xix. 28), for the most part peculiar to Lk., which we have called "the Journeyings towards Jerusalem": see on ix. 51. For the third time (ix. 51, 52, xiii. 22) Lk. tells us that Jerusalem is the goal, but we have no means of knowing whether this represents the beginning of a third journey distinct from two previous journeys. Marked breaks may be made at the end of xiii. 35 and xvii. 10. But we have no data for determining what the chronology of the different divisions is; and the geography is almost as indistinct as the chronology. This last portion, however, brings us once more (x. 38) to Bethany, and to the time which preceded the triumphal entry into Jerusalem.

11–19. §The Healing of the Ten Lepers. The gratitude of the Samaritan leper illustrates the special theme of this Gospel. The opening of the narrative indicates an Aramaic source: but that it is placed here "to contrast man's thanklessness to God with the sort of claim to thanks *from* God, which is asserted by spiritual pride," is not probable.

11. ἐν τῷ πορεύεσθαι. "As He was on His way." See on iii. 21 and comp. ix. 51, the beginning of this main portion, where the construction is similar. The *αὐτὸν* is probably a gloss (om. ℵ B L), but a correct gloss. As no one else is mentioned it is arbitrary to translate "as *they* were on their way." Latin texts all take it as singular: *dum iret*, *cum iret*, *dum vadit*, *dum iter faceret*. So also Syr-Sin., which omits *ἐγένετο*.

καὶ αὐτὸς διήρχετο. The apodosis of *ἐγένετο*: see on v. 12, 14, vi. 20; also on ii. 15. There is no emphasis on *αὐτός*.

διὰ μέσον. This is the reading of ℵ B D L, accepted by Tisch. Treg. WH. and RV. It means "through what lies between," *i.e.* along the frontier, or simply, "between." This is the only passage in N.T. in which *διά c. acc.* has its original local signification. Even if *διὰ μέσου* were the right reading, we ought to translate it "between" and not "through the midst of." This use is found in Xenophon: *διὰ μέσου δὲ ῥεῖ τούτων ποταμός* (*Anab.* i. 4. 4), of a river flowing between two walls; and in Plato: *ἢ τὸ τούτων δὴ διὰ μέσου φῶμεν* (*Leg.* vii. p. 805 D), of an intermediate course. "Through the midst of Samaria and Galilee" would imply that Jesus was moving *from* Jerusalem, whereas we are expressly told that He was journeying *towards* it. Samaria, as being on the right, would naturally be mentioned first if He was going eastward along the frontier between Samaria and Galilee possibly by the route which ends at Bethshean, near the Jordan. In order to avoid Samaritan territory (ix. 52–55), He seems to have been making for Peræa, as Jews often did in going from Galilee to Jerusalem. On the frontier He would be likely to meet with a mixed company of lepers, their dreadful malady having broken down the barrier between Jew and Samaritan. See Conder, *Handbk. of B.* p. 311; Tristram, *Bible Places*, p. 222; *Eastern Customs*, pp. 19, 21. In the leper-houses at Jerusalem Jews and Mahometans will live together at the present time.

There is no doubt that ver. 11 forms a complete sentence. To make from *καὶ αὐτός* to *Γαλιλαίας* a parenthesis, and take *ἀπήντησαν* as the apodosis of *ἐγένετο*, is quite gratuitous clumsiness.

12. δέκα λεπροὶ ἄνδρες. Elsewhere we read of four (2 Kings vii. 3), but so large a company as ten was perhaps at that time unusual. Now it would be common, especially in this central region. These ten may have collected on hearing that Jesus was approaching. No meaning is to be sought in the number.

ἔστησαν πόρρωθεν. In accordance with the law, which the leper of v. 12 possibly did *not* break: see notes there. The precise distance to be kept was not fixed by law, but by tradition, and the statements about it vary. See Lev. xiii. 45, 46; Num. v. 2, and the evidence collected in Wetst. The adv. occurs Heb. xi. 13 and often in LXX, esp. in Isaiah (x. 3, xiii. 5, xxxiii. 13, 17, xxxix. 3, etc.). On the authority of B F, WH. adopt *ἀνέστησαν* in the text, with *ἔστησαν* in the margin. Lk. is very fond of this compound.

13. **καὶ αὐτοὶ ἦραν φωνήν.** They took the initiative. Here ἦραν φωνήν agrees with πόρρωθεν, just as in xvi. 24 φωνήσας agrees with ἀπὸ μακρόθεν. Comp. ἐπαίρειν φωνήν (xi. 27) and ὑψοῦν φωνήν (Gen. xxxix. 15, 18). This phrase occurs Acts iv. 24; Judg. xxi. 2; 1 Sam. xi. 4. For ἐπιστάτα see on v. 5.

14. **καὶ ἰδών.** "And directly He saw": which seems to imply that, until they cried out, He had not perceived who they were. This previous supernatural knowledge was not necessary. But He knows, without seeing or hearing, that they all were cleansed (ver. 17). This knowledge *was* necessary.

ἐπιδείξατε ἑαυτοὺς τοῖς ἱερεῦσιν. "Show yourselves to the priests" appointed for this purpose. Each of the ten would go to the priest near his own home. In v. 14 we have τῷ ἱερεῖ, there being then only one leper. The Samaritan would go to a priest of the temple on Mount Gerizim.

ἐν τῷ ὑπάγειν. Their faith was shown in their obedience to Christ's command, and on their way the cure took place. As they were no longer companions in misery, the Jews would rejoice that the Samaritan turned back and left them.

15. **ὑπέστρεψεν.** See on iv. 14 and vii. 10. Even Hahn follows Schleiermacher in referring this to the Samaritan's return from the priest. In that case he would have *inevitably* returned without the others. It was because he *saw* (ἰδών) that he was *healed* (not after he had been *declared* to be *clean*) that he came back to give thanks. The **μετὰ φωνῆς μεγάλης** may mean that he still "stood afar off" (see on i. 42), as having not yet recovered the right to mix with others: for **παρὰ τοὺς πόδας** (see on vii. 38) need not imply close proximity. But if the loud voice be only an expression of great joy, a man in the jubilation of such a cure would not be punctilious about keeping the exact distance, especially when he knew that he was no longer a leper. It is most improbable that he did not *see* that he was cleansed till the priest told him that he was.

16. **καὶ αὐτὸς ἦν Σαμαρείτης.** Here the αὐτός has point: "and *he* was a S." The only one who exhibited gratitude was a despised schismatic. That *all* the others were Jews is not implied.

17. **ἀποκριθεὶς δὲ ὁ Ἰησοῦς.** See small print on i. 19, p. 16. Here first we learn that Jesus was not alone; for His "answer" is addressed to the bystanders, and is a comment on the whole incident rather than a reply to the Samaritan.

Οὐχ οἱ δέκα. "Were not *the* ten," etc.—all the ten who had asked Him to have mercy on them. The **ποῦ** with emphasis at the end, like σύ in ver. 8. These questions imply surprise, and surprise implies limitation of knowledge (vii. 9; Mt. viii. 10; Mk. vi. 6).

18. This sentence also may be interrogative: so WH. and RV.

text. The εὑρέθησαν is not a mere substitute for ἦσαν: it marks or implies the discovery or notice of the quality in question (1 Pet. ii. 22; Rev. xiv. 5).

ἀλλογενής. The classical word would be ἀλλόφυλος (Acts x. 28) or ἀλλοεθνής. But ἀλλογενής is very freq. in LXX, especially of the heathen (Exod. xii. 43, xxix. 33, xxx. 33; Lev. xxii. 10, etc.).

The Samaritans were a mixed people, both as regards race and religion. They were Israelites who had been almost overwhelmed by the heathen colonists planted among them by the Assyrians. Those from Cuthah (2 Kings xvii. 24, 30) were probably the most numerous, for the Jews called the Samaritans Cuthites or Cutheans (Jos. *Ant.* ix. 14. 3, xi. 4. 4, 7. 2, xiii. 9. 1). These heathen immigrants brought their idolatry with them, but gradually mixed with it the worship of Jehovah. Both as regards race and religion it was the Jewish element which grew stronger, while the heathen element declined. Refugees from Judæa settled among them from time to time; but we do not hear of fresh immigrants from Assyria. The religion at last became pure monotheism, with the Pentateuch as the law of worship and of life. But in race the foreign element no doubt predominated, although Christ's use of ἀλλογενής does not prove this. He may be speaking with a touch of irony: "this man, who is commonly regarded as little better than a heathen." See Schürer, *Jewish People in T. of J. C.* ii. 1, pp. 6–8; Edersh. *Hist. of Jewish Nation*, pp. 249, 486, 499, ed. 1896; Derenbourg, *Hist. de la Pal.* i. p. 43; Jos. *Ant.* xi. 8. 6, xii. 5. 5.

19. ἡ πίστις σου σέσωκέν σε. He did well to be thankful and publicly express his thankfulness; but he had contributed something himself, without which he would not have been cured. Comp. viii. 48, xviii. 42. Others refer the saying to some benefit which the Samaritan received and which the nine lost, and explain it of moral and spiritual salvation. Comp. vii. 50, viii. 48, 50.

20–37. The Coming of the Kingdom of God and of the Son of Man. The introductory verses (20–22) are peculiar to Lk. For the rest comp. Mt. xxiv. 23 ff.; Mk. xiii. 21 ff.

20. Ἐπερωτηθείς. There is no evidence that the question of the Pharisees was asked in contempt. Jesus had taught that the Kingdom was at hand, and they ask *when* it may be expected. Perhaps they wanted to test Him. If He fixed an early date, and at that time there were no signs of the Kingdom, they would know what to think. His reply corrects such an idea. There will be no such signs as would enable a watcher to date the arrival. A spiritual Kingdom is slow in producing conspicuous material effects; and it begins in ways that cannot be dated.

With this rather loose use of πότε for ὁπότε in an indirect question comp. xii. 36; Mk. xiii. 4, 33, 35; Mt. xxiv. 3. Nowhere in N.T. is ὁπότε found.

παρατηρήσεως. Here only in bibl. Grk. and not classical, although παρατηρεῖν is not rare either in N.T. or LXX, and occurs in medical writers of watching the symptoms of a disease (Hobart,

p. 153). It implies *close* rather than *sinister* watching, although the latter sense occurs. See on xiv. 1. The interpretation *cum multa pompa*, *cum regio splendore*, fits neither the word nor the context. The meaning is that no close observation will be able to note the moment of its arrival, which will not be marked by external sounds.

21. οὐδὲ ἐροῦσιν. "Neither will they say" (with any reason): *non erit quod dicatur* (Grot.). In ver. 23 they do say this; but it is a groundless statement. The ἰδού before ἐκεῖ (A D, Vulg.) is an insertion from ver. 23.

ἰδοὺ γάρ. See on i. 44. This ἰδού introduces the true statement in contrast to the previous ἰδού, which introduced a false one. The γάρ marks the reason why "Lo here" or "There" cannot be accepted. Note the solemn repetition of ἡ βασιλεία τοῦ Θεοῦ.

ἐντὸς ὑμῶν ἐστίν. Usage sanctions either translation: "within you, in your hearts" (Ps. xxxviii. 4, cviii. 22, ciii. 1; Is. xvi. 11; Dan. x. 16 (Theod.); Ecclus. xix. 23 [26]: comp. Mt. xxiii. 26); or, "among you, in your midst" (Xen. *Anab.* i. 10. 3; *Hellen.* ii. 3. 19; Plat. *Leg.* vii. 789 A). The latter seems to suit the context better; for the Kingdom of God was not in the hearts of the Pharisees, who are the persons addressed. The meaning will then be, "so far from coming with external signs which will attract attention, the Kingdom is already in the midst of you (in the person of Christ and of His disciples), and you do not perceive it." Note the contrast between ἐροῦσιν, the supposition that the Kingdom is still in the future, and ἐστίν, the fact that it is really present. But this rendering of ἐντός lacks confirmation in *Scripture*, and the context is not *decisive* against the other. If "within you" be adopted, the meaning will be, "Instead of being something externally visible, the Kingdom is essentially spiritual: it is in your hearts, *if* you possess it at all."

All Latin texts have *intra vos est*. But the interpretation of "within you" varies considerably. Gregory Nyssen explains it of the image of God bestowed upon all men at their birth (*De Virg.* xii.; comp. *De Beat.* i.), which cannot be right. Cyril of Alexandria makes it mean, "lies in your power to appropriate it," ἐν ἐξουσίᾳ κεῖται τὸ λαβεῖν αὐτήν (Migne, lxxii. 841). Similarly Maldonatus, *quia poterant, si vellent, Christum recipere*. But this is translating ἐντὸς ὑμῶν "within you," and interpreting "within you" as much the same as "among you." If they had *not* received Christ or the Kingdom, it was not yet within them. Against "in your hearts" Maldonatus points that not only does Lk. tell us that the words were addressed to the Pharisees, in whose hearts the Kingdom was not; but that he emphasizes this by stating that the *next* saying was addressed to the *disciples*. Among moderns, Godet argues ably for "within you" (see also McClellan): Weiss and Hahn for "among you." Syr-Sin. has "among." Comp. x. 9, xi. 20.

22. Εἶπεν δὲ πρὸς τοὺς μαθητάς. Apparently this is the same occasion (comp. xii. 22); and perhaps the Pharisees have retired. But we cannot be certain of either point. Christ takes up the subject which the Pharisees had introduced, and shows that it is the Second Advent that will be accompanied by visible signs. But with regard to these, discrimination must be used. Comp. Mt. xxiv. 23, 26 and Mk. xiii. 21, to which this is partly parallel.

Ἐλεύσονται ἡμέραι. No article: "Days will come": as in v. 35, xxi. 6; Mt. ix. 15; Mk. ii. 20. Even RV. has "*The* days will come." Comp. the Johannean phrase, ἔρχεται ὥρα, "There cometh *an* hour" (Jn. iv. 21, 23, v. 25, 28, xvi. 2, 25, 32). But it is erroneous to make this passage mean the same as v. 35; Mt. ix. 15; Mk. ii. 20:—"Days will come, when the bridegroom shall be taken away from them; then will they fast in those days." This means, not that hereafter there will be a time when the disciples will long in vain for one day of such intercourse with Christ as they are constantly enjoying now; but that there will be days in which they will yearn for a foretaste of the *coming* glory, a glory which must be waited for and cannot be anticipated. "Oh for one day of heaven in this time of trouble!" is a futile wish, but it will be framed by some. It is clear from ver. 26 what "the days of the Son of Man" must mean. But what does **μίαν τῶν ἡμερῶν, κ.τ.λ.**, mean? The common rendering, "*one* of the days," etc., makes good sense. But the possibility of taking the expression as a Hebraism, "one" being used for "first," as in *μιᾷ τῶν σαββάτων* (Mk. xvi. 2), is worth noting. Comp. xxiv. 1; Mt. xxviii. 1; Acts xx. 7; 1 Cor. xvi. 2; Jn. xx. 1. In this case the desire would be for "the *first* of the days of the Son of Man," the day of His return.

καὶ οὐκ ὄψεσθε. Not because it will never come; but because it will not come in those days of longing.

23. There is no contradiction between this and ver. 21. That refers to true signs of the First Advent; this to false signs of the Second. It covers all premature announcements of the approach of the Last Day. *All predictions of exact dates, and all statements as to local appearances, are to be mistrusted.*

μὴ ἀπέλθητε μηδὲ διώξητε. "Do not leave your ordinary occupation, still less go after those who offer to lead you to the place of the Son of Man's appearing."

24. ὥσπερ γὰρ ἡ ἀστραπή. As sudden, and as universally visible. None will foresee it, and all will see it at once; so that no *report* respecting it can have any value. *Non ejus ergo venturi tempus aut locus potest a mortalibus observari, qui fulguris instar omnibus coruscus videlicet et repentinus adveniet* (Bede). See on ii. 8, xi. 46, xxiii. 46 for Lk.'s fondness for cognate words. The wording here is almost identical with Mt. xxiv. 27.

The art. before ἀστράπτουσα is probably an insertion: om. ℵ B L X Γ. Without it translate, "when it lightens." For *fulgur* e has *choruscatio* and d has *scoruscus*. In what follows we again have an amphibolous expression (ix. 17, 18, 27, 57, x. 18, etc.); but ἐκ τῆς . . . ὑπ' οὐρανὸν should be taken with λάμπει rather than with ἀστράπτουσα. For the ellipse of χώρα after ἡ ὑπ' οὐρανὸν or ἡ ὑπὸ τὸν οὐρανόν comp. Deut. xxv. 19; Job i. 7, ii. 2, xviii. 4, xxxiv. 13, xxxviii. 18, xlii. 15. The words ἐν τῇ ἡμέρᾳ αὐτοῦ after ἀνθρώπου are of doubtful authority: om. B D, a b c d e i Aeth., while l has *in adventu suo* (comp. Mt. xxiv. 27): om. *filius hominis in die sua*, ff_2. Syr-Sin. has "so shall be the day of the Son of Man."

25. πρῶτον δὲ δεῖ αὐτὸν . . . ἀποδοκιμασθῆναι. "But there is no need to be expecting this now": the events immediately impending are very different. For δεῖ see on iv. 43, and for ἀποδοκιμασθῆναι see on ix. 22, and comp. xviii. 31. Just as the thought of impending suffering needs to be cheered by that of future glory, so the thought of future glory needs to be chastened by that of impending suffering. Comp. ix. 44.

26. Having told the disciples that the Son of Man will not come as soon as they wish (22), in what way He will not come (23), in what way He will come (24), and what will happen first (25), Christ now states in what condition the human race will be when He comes.

καὶ καθὼς ἐγένετο. Not ὥσπερ, as in ver. 24. There something *analogous* was introduced; here something *exactly similar* is cited. "Just as, even as." Comp. xi. 30; Jn. iii. 14; 2 Cor. i. 5, x. 7, etc. In Attic Greek we should rather have καθό (Rom. viii. 26), καθά (Mt. xxvii. 10), or καθάπερ (Rom. xii. 4).

27. ἤσθιον, ἔπινον, ἐγάμουν, ἐγαμίζοντο. The imperfects and the asyndeton are very vivid: "They were eating, they were drinking," etc. The point is not merely that they were living their ordinary lives, but that they were wholly given up to external things.

It is of no moment whether καὶ ἦλθεν ὁ κατακλυσμός is made to depend upon ἄχρι ἧς ἡμέρας or not: probably it is independent. But certainly ὁμοίως belongs to καθὼς ἐγένετο (*similiter sicut factum est*, Vulg.), and not to ἀπώλεσεν πάντας (*perdidit omnes pariter*), which is pointless. The ὁμοίως anticipates κατὰ τὰ αὐτά in ver. 30.

28, 29. There is no parallel to this in Mt. xxiv. It is a second instance of careless enjoyment suddenly overwhelmed. Comp. 2 Pet. ii. 5, 6.

29. ἔβρεξεν πῦρ καὶ θεῖον. The subject of ἔβρεξεν is Κύριος, which is expressed in Gen. xix. 24 (comp. Mt. v. 45) and must be supplied here, because of ἀπώλεσεν. The verb is not impers., as in Jas. v. 17. Grotius makes πῦρ καὶ θεῖον the nom. and compares ἵνα μὴ βρέχῃ ὑετός (Rev. xi. 6). Gen. xix. 24 and the sing. verb are against this. Comp. Hom. *Od.* xxii. 493.

30. ἀποκαλύπτεται. A technical expression in this connexion (1 Cor. i. 7; 2 Thes. i. 7; 1 Pet. i. 7, 13, iv. 13). The present indicates the certainty of the veil being withdrawn. Up to that day He is hidden from man's sight: then at once He is revealed.

31. In Mt. xxiv. 17, 18 and Mk. xiii. 15, 16 these words are spoken of *flight* before the destruction of Jerusalem. Here *flight* is neither expressed nor understood. The point is *absolute indifference to all worldly interests as the attitude of readiness for the Son of Man.* We need not discuss whether the words were spoken in a literal sense, as in Mk. and Mt., and Lk has applied them spiritually; or in a spiritual sense, and Mt. and Mk. have taken them literally. Christ may have used them in both senses. The warning about flight from Judæa is recorded by Lk. elsewhere (xxi. 21). On the *oratio variata* of the constr. see Win. lxiii. 2. 1, p. 722, 723.

32. μνημονεύετε τῆς γυναικὸς Λώτ. Lot's wife looked back with a wish to recover worldly possessions and enjoyments. She proved herself to be unworthy of the salvation that was offered her. In like manner the Christian, whose first thought at the Advent of the Son of Man was about the safety of his goods, would be unfit for the Kingdom of God.

Note that Christ says, "Remember," not "Behold." *Nothing that is in existence is appealed to, but only what has been told.* Attempts have been made to identify the Pillar of Salt. Josephus believed that he had seen it (*Ant.* i. 11. 4). Comp. Wisd. x. 7; Clem. Rom. *Cor.* xi.; Iren. iv. 31. 3; Cyr. Hier. *Catech.* xix. 8.

33. περιποιήσασθαι. "To preserve for himself": elsewhere "to gain for oneself" (Acts xx. 28; 1 Tim. iii. 13). The reading σῶσαι (A R) comes from ix. 24.

ζωογονήσει. "Shall preserve alive": Acts vii. 19; 1 Tim. vi. 13; Exod. i. 17; Judg. viii. 19; 1 Sam. ii. 6, xxvii. 9, 11; 1 Kings xxi. 31. The rendering "shall bring to a new birth" has been rightly abandoned by Godet. In bibl. Grk. it is not used of "bringing forth alive," "viviparous." From ix. 24; Mt. x. 39, xvi. 25; Mk. viii. 35; Jn. xii. 25 it appears that this solemn warning was often uttered: for most of these passages refer to different occasions. It is the one important saying which is in all four.

34, 35. The closest intimacy in this life is no guarantee of community of condition when the Son of Man comes. The strangest separations will take place between comrades, according as one is fit to enter the Kingdom and another not.

34. ταύτῃ τῇ νυκτί. This must not be pressed to mean anything, whether a time of great horror or actual night. Christ is not intimating that His return will take place in the night-time. "Night" is part of the picture, for it is then that people are in bed.

δύο ἐπὶ κλίνης μιᾶς. "Two on one bed." Not necessarily two *men*, although that is probably the meaning. AV. was the first English Version to insert "men," and RV. retains it. The "being taken" probably means "taken from destruction" (Jn. xiv. 3), ὡς ἀλλότριος τῆς ὀργῆς (Eus.), as Lot from Sodom; while "left" means "left to his fate" (xiii. 35). Or, "taken into the Kingdom" and "left outside" may be the meaning.

35. This image presupposes day rather than night, and refers to a fact which is still of everyday occurrence in the East. Whether people be sleeping or working when the Lord comes, those who still cling to things earthly will be left without share in the Messianic joy. And in this matter "no man may deliver his brother": ἔσται πλείστη καὶ ἀκριβὴς τῶν τρόπων ἡ δοκιμασία (Cyr.).

36. An ancient (D, Latt. Syrr.) insertion from Mt. xxiv. 40: om. ℵ A B Q R, Aeth. Copt. Goth.

37. Ποῦ, κύριε; The question is one of curiosity which Christ does not gratify. Moreover, it assumes, what He has just been denying, that the Second Advent will be local—limited to one quarter of the earth.

Ὅπου τὸ σῶμα, ἐκεῖ καὶ οἱ ἀετοί. This was perhaps a current proverb. The application is here quite general. "Where the conditions are fulfilled, there and there only will the revelation of the Son of Man take place." Or possibly, "Where the dead body of human nature, clinging to earthly things, is, there the judgments of God will come": *ubi peccatores, ibi Dei judicia.* Jesus thus sets aside all questions as to the *time* (ver. 20) or the *place* (ver. 37) of His return. One thing is certain; that *all* who are not ready will suffer (*vv.* 27, 29). Upon all who are dead to the claims of the Kingdom ruin will fall (37). The πτῶμα of Mt. xxiv. 28 expresses more definitely than σῶμα that the body is a dead one: comp. Mt. xiv. 12; Mk. vi. 29, xv. 45; Rev. xi. 8, 9. But σῶμα for a dead body is quite classical, and is always so used in Homer, a living body being δέμας: comp. Acts ix. 40.

οἱ ἀετοί. "The vultures." Here, as in Mic. i. 16, the griffon vulture (*Vultur fulvus*) is probably meant: comp. Job xxxix. 27–30; Hab. i. 8; Hos. viii. 1, and see Tristram, *Nat. Hist. of B.* p. 172; *D.B.*² art. "Eagle." Eagles neither fly in flocks nor feed on carrion. During the Crimean War, griffon vultures, which had previously been scarce round Sebastopol, collected in great numbers, "from the ends of the earth," as the Turks said. In the less general interpretation of this saying of Christ the ἀετοί are the ministers of judgment which overtake the ungodly. A reference to the eagles of the Roman standards is not in point here, although it is possible Mt. xxiv. 28. The patristic interpretation of the saints gathering round the glorified body of Christ is equally unsuitable to the context.[1] See Didon, *J. C.* ch. ix. p. 613, ed. 1891; also Hastings, *DB.* i. p. 632.

[1] Ὅταν ὁ υἱὸς τοῦ ἀνθρώπου παραγένηται, τότε δὴ πάντες οἱ ἀετοί, τουτέστιν οἱ τὰ ὑψηλὰ πετόμενοι, καὶ τῶν ἐπιγείων καὶ κοσμικῶν ἀνενηγμένοι πραγμάτων, ἐπ'

XVIII. 1-8. § The Parable of the Unrighteous Judge. Comp. xv. 8-10, 11-32, xvi. 1-9, 19-31, xvii. 7-10. The connexion with what precedes is close, and is implied in the opening clause; for αὐτοῖς naturally refers to the same audience as before. Had there been no connexion, αὐτοῖς would have been omitted: comp. xiii. 6. Godet appeals also to the formula ἔλεγεν δὲ καί; but here the καί is not genuine. The connexion is, that, although the time of Christ's return to deliver His people is hidden from them, yet they must not cease to pray for deliverance. Both here and xxi. 36 we have the command to be unremitting in prayer immediately after a declaration that the hour of Christ's coming is unknown; and the same connexion is found Mk. xiii. 33. See Resch, *Agrapha*, p. 297.

1. Ἔλεγεν δὲ παραβολήν. See on v. 36.

πρὸς τὸ δεῖν. Not merely the duty, but the necessity of perseverance in prayer is expressed; and prayer in general is meant, not merely prayer in reference to the Second Advent and the troubles which precede it. Only here and ver. 9 is the meaning of a parable put as the preface to it; and in each case it is given as the Evangelist's preface, not as Christ's.

πάντοτε προσεύχεσθαι. Comp. πάντοτε χαίρετε. ἀδιαλείπτως προσεύχεσθε (1 Thes. v. 17). Grotius quotes Proclus *ad Timæum*, χρὴ ἀδιαλείπτως εὔχεσθαι τῆς περὶ τὸ θεῖον θρησκείας. See Origen, περὶ εὐχῆς, xii.; Tert. *De Orat.* xxix.; Lft. *Epp.* p. 81. On the other hand, we have the Jewish doctrine that God must not be wearied with incessant prayer. *Tanchuma*, fol. 15. 3. A man ought not to pray more than three times a day. Hourly prayers are forbidden. *Si quis singulis horis ad te salutandum accedit, hunc dicis te contemtui habere: idem ergo quoque valet de Deo, quem nemo hominum singulis horis defatigare debet* (Schœttgen, i. 305).

The form ἐνκακεῖν is right here, and perhaps Gal. vi. 9; Eph. iii. 13; 2 Thes. iii. 13; ἐγκακεῖν, 2 Cor. iv. 1, 16; but in all six places some texts have ἐκκακεῖν. See Gregory, *Proleg.* p. 78. Ellicott makes ἐγκακεῖν mean "to lose heart *in* a course of action," and ἐκκακεῖν "to retire through fear *out* of it"; but authority for any such word as ἐκκακεῖν seems to be wanting. Perhaps ἐγκακεῖν is not found earlier than Polybius. See Suicer.

2. Κριτής τις ἦν ἔν τινι πόλει. We are probably to understand a Gentile official. He had no respect for either the *vox Dei* or the *vox populi*, consciously (ver. 4) defying Divine commands and public opinion. See numerous parallels in Wetst., and contrast 2 Cor. viii. 21. The Talmud speaks of frequent oppression and venality on the part of Gentile magistrates; and for a striking illustration of the parable witnessed by himself see Tristram, *Eastern Customs in Bible Lands*, p. 228. Note the τις.

αὐτὸν συνδραμοῦνται (Cyr. Alex., Migne, lxii. 848). *Justorum animæ aquilis comparantur, quod alta petant, humilia derelinquant, longævam ducere ferantur ætatem* (Ambr., Migne, xv. 1781). Comp. Paschasius Radbertus on Mt. xxiv. 28.

The idea of ἐντρέπομαι seems to be that of "turning towards" a person, and so "paying respect" (xx. 13; Mt. xxi. 37; Mk. xii. 6; 2 Thes. iii. 14; Heb. xii. 9). But as ἐντρέπω means "I put to shame" (1 Cor. iv. 14), ἐντρέπομαι may possibly have the notion of "being abashed, having a feeling of awe," before a person. In class. Grk. it is commonly followed by a gen.

3. χήρα δὲ ἦν. Typical of defencelessness: she had neither a protector to coerce, nor money to bribe the unrighteous magistrate. The O.T. abounds in denunciations of those who oppress widows: Exod. xxii. 22; Deut. x. 18, xxiv. 17, xxvii. 19; Job xxii. 9, xxiv. 3; Jer. xxii. 3; Ezek. xxii. 7, etc. Comp. *Non, ita me dii ament, auderet facere hæc viduæ mulieri, quæ in me facit* (Ter. *Heaut.* v. 1. 80).

ἤρχετο. "Continued coming, came often," *ventitabat.* The imperf. indicates her persistence.

Ἐκδίκησόν με ἀπό. "Give me a sentence of protection from; vindicate my right (and so protect me) from." *Assere me jure dicundo ab injuriâ adversarii mei* (Schleusn.). For the ἀπό comp. xii. 15, 58, xiii. 16, xx. 46: it does not express the *penalty exacted from* the adversary, but the *protection afforded from* him, as in ῥῦσαι ἡμᾶς ἀπὸ τοῦ πονηροῦ. The meaning is "preserve me against his attacks" rather than "deliver me out of his power," which would require ἐκ. For **ἀντίδικος** comp. xii. 58; Mt. v. 25.

As often, the ἀπό follows up the idea suggested by the ἐκ in the compound verb: see on ἐξέρχομαι ἀπό (iv. 35), and comp. also ἐκλέγομαι ἀπό (vi. 13), ἐκζητεῖν ἀπό (xi. 50, 51), ἐκδιώκω ἀπό (Joel ii. 20; Dan. iv. 22, 29, 30, Theod.), etc. Here d has *devindica me ab.*

4. οὐκ ἤθελεν. The imperf. (א A B D L Q R X Λ) has more point than the aor. (E etc.): he continued refusing, just as she continued coming. With **ἐπὶ χρόνον** comp. ἐπὶ πλείονα χρ. (Acts xviii. 20); ἐφ᾽ ὅσον χρ. (Rom. vii. 1; 1 Cor. vii. 39; Gal. iv. 1).

Εἰ καὶ τὸν Θεὸν οὐ φοβοῦμαι. "Although I fear not God," implying that this is the actual fact (2 Cor. xii. 11), whereas καὶ εἰ would have put it as an hypothesis (1 Cor. viii. 5; 1 Pet. iii. 1). Win. liii. 7. b, p. 554.

Perhaps its being given as a fact explains the use of οὐ rather than μή: or the οὐ coalesces with the verb, and thus escapes the influence of the εἰ: comp. xi. 8, xiv. 26, xvi. 11, 12, 31; 2 Cor. xii. 11. Burton, §§ 284, 469. But see Simcox, *Lang. of N.T.* p. 184.

οὐδέ. "Nor yet, nor even": a climax.

5. διά γε τὸ παρέχειν μοι κόπον. "Yet because she troubleth me." Comp. διά γε τὴν ἀναιδίαν αὐτοῦ (xi. 8), where, as here, εἰ καί is followed by οὐ and γε. Both κόπον and ὑπωπιάζῃ are strong words, and express the man's impatience.

On the reading τὴν χήρα ταύτην see Gregory, *Prolegom.* p. 58.

εἰς τέλος ἐρχομένη ὑπωπιάζῃ με. "Unto the end, to the uttermost" easily passed in meaning to either "continually" or "at last"; and either of these makes sense here, according as we join εἰς τέλος with the participle or the verb or both. Either, "by continually coming wear me out"; or, "at last by her coming wear me out"; or, "be for ever coming and plaguing me." The first is best: it was her *perpetual* coming that was so trying. Both τέλος and ἐς τέλος are frequent in class. Grk. In LXX εἰς τέλος is frequent.

ὑπωπιάζῃ. From ὑπώπιον, which means (1) the part of the face below the eyes; (2) a blow there, a black eye; (3) any blow. Hence ὑπωπιάζω means (1) hit under the eye, give a black eye; (2) beat black and blue; (3) mortify, annoy greatly (1 Cor. ix. 27). Comp. αἱ πόλεις ὑπωπιασμέναι (Aristoph. *Pax*, 541). There is no doubt that "annoy greatly" is the meaning here. Comp. *Qui me sequatur quoquo eam, rogitando obtundat, enecet* (Ter. *Eun.* iii. 5. 6). Meyer, Godet, Weiss and others advocate the literal meaning, and regard it as a *mauvaise plaisanterie* or an exaggeration on the part of the judge. But, as Field points out (*Otium Norvic.* iii. p. 52), the tenses are fatal to it. "Lest at last she come and black my eyes for me" would require ἐλθοῦσα ὑπωπιάσῃ. The judge was afraid of being annoyed continually, not of being assaulted once.

The Latin Versions vary much in their rendering both of εἰς τέλος and of ὑπωπιάζῃ: *in novissimo* (Vulg.), *in novissimo die* (q), *in tempus* (d), *usque ad finem* (e), *usque quaque* (l), *in finem* (r): *suggillet* (Vulg.), *constringat* (b ff_2 q), *molestior sit mihi* (e), *invidiam mihi faciat* (l).

Strauss has pointed out similarities of feature between the parables of the Rich Fool, the Friend at Midnight, and the Unrighteous Judge, especially with regard to the soliloquies in each case: διελογίζετο ἐν αὐτῷ λέγων Τί ποιήσω, ὅτι κ.τ.λ., τοῦτο ποιήσω (xii. 17, 18); εἶπεν δὲ ἐν ἑαυτῷ ὁ οἰκονόμος Τί ποιήσω, ὅτι κ.τ.λ., ἔγνων τί ποιήσω (xvi. 3, 4); εἶπεν ἐν ἑαυτῷ (xviii. 4), One may admit that these are "signs of a common origin," but that they are also "signs of a Jewish-Christian, or indeed of an Ebionite source," is not so evident. He says that this "mimic" repetition, "What shall I do? . . . This will I do," is thoroughly Jewish. But as Christ was a Jew, speaking to Jews, there is nothing surprising in that. He says also that the Ebionites laid great stress on prayer, and inculcated a contempt for riches; and that two of the three parables do the one, while the third does the other. But assuredly the Ebionites were not peculiar in advocating prayer, nor in despising riches, although in the latter point they went to fanatical excess. See Strauss, *L. J.* § 41, p. 257, ed. 1864.

6. Εἶπεν δὲ ὁ κύριος. The insertion indicates a pause, during which the audience consider the parable, after which Jesus makes a comment and draws the moral of the narrative. For **ὁ κύριος** of Christ see on v. 17 and vii. 13; and for **ὁ κριτὴς τῆς ἀδικίας** see on xvi. 8.

7. οὐ μὴ ποιήσῃ. This intensive form of the simple negative may be used in questions as well as in statements, and expresses the confidence with which an affirmative answer is expected: comp. Jn. xviii. 11. Rev. xv. 4 is not quite parallel. The argument here is *à fortiori*, or (as Augustine, *Quæst. Evang.* ii. 45) *ex dissimilitudine*, and has many points. If an *unjust judge* would *yield to the importunity* of an *unknown widow*, who came and *spoke* to him *at intervals*, how much more will a *just God* be ready to *reward the perseverance* of *His own elect*, who *cry* to Him *day and night?* Comp. the very similar passage Ecclus. xxxv. 13–18 [xxxii. 18–22], and the similar argument Lk. xi. 13. The treatment of the Syrophenician woman (Mt. xv. 22–28 ||) is an illustration of the text. With τῶν βοώντων αὐτῷ comp. the souls of the saints under the altar (Rev. vi. 9–11). In both cases it is deliverance from oppression that is prayed for.

καὶ μακροθυμεῖ ἐπ' αὐτοῖς. "And He is long-suffering over them" (RV.). This, and not μακροθυμῶν (E), is the reading of almost all uncials and of other important authorities: *et patiens est in illis* (d e), *et patientiam habebit in illis* (Vulg.).

The exact meaning of the different parts of the clause cannot be determined with certainty; but the general sense is clear enough, viz. that, however long the answer to prayer may *seem* to be delayed, constant faithful prayer always *is* answered.

The chief points of doubt are (1) the construction of καὶ μακροθυμεῖ, (2) the meaning of μακροθυμεῖ, (3) the meaning of ἐπ' αὐτοῖς. (1) We need not join καὶ μακροθυμεῖ to οὐ μὴ ποιήσῃ, but may take it with τῶν βοώντων, which is equivalent to οἱ βοῶσιν: the elect cry *and* He μακροθυμεῖ ἐπ' αὐτοῖς. (2) We need not give μακροθυμεῖ its very common meaning of "is slow *to anger*": it sometimes means "to be slow, be backward, tarry," and is almost synonymous with βραδύνω. Comp. Heb. vi. 15; James v. 7; Job vii. 16; Jer. xv. 15; and the remarkably parallel passage Ecclus. xxxv. [xxxii.] 22, καὶ ὁ Κύριος οὐ μὴ βραδύνῃ οὐδὲ μὴ μακροθυμήσει ἐπ' αὐτοῖς. So also μακροθυμία may mean "slow persistency" as well as "slowness to anger." Comp. 1 Mac. viii. 4, and see Trench, *Syn.* liii. (3) This being so, there is no need to make ἐπ' αὐτοῖς refer to *the enemies* of the elect, although such loose wording is not impossible, especially if Lk. had the passage in Ecclus. in his mind. The words naturally, and in strict grammar necessarily, refer to the elect, and indicate the persons in respect of whom the slowness of action takes place. Comp. μακροθυμῶν ἐπ' αὐτῷ (James v. 7). The meaning, then, seems to be, "And shall not God deliver His elect who cry day and night to Him, while He is slow to act for them?" That is, to them in their need the μακροθυμία of God *seems* to be βραδύτης (Rev. vi. 10), just as it does to the ungodly, when they see no judgment overtaking them (2 Pet. iii. 1–10). But it is possible that μακροθυμεῖ means "is not impatient." The unjust judge heard the widow's frequent request with impatience and dislike. God listens to the ceaseless crying of His saints with willingness and pleasure. In this sense μακροθυμεῖν is the opposite of ὀξυθυμεῖν, "to be quick-tempered."

8. ἐν τάχει. "Quickly, without delay"; *celeriter* (a), *confestim* (d), *cito* (Vulg.). Although He bears long, and to those who are suffering seems to delay, yet He really acts speedily. This interpretation is confirmed by Acts xii. 7, xxii. 18, xxv. 4; Rom. xvi. 20; 1 Tim. iii. 14; Rev. i. 1, xxii. 6. Others prefer *repente, inopinato.* Thus Godet says, that although God delays to act, yet when the moment comes, He acts swiftly, as at the Deluge and the destruction of Sodom. So Didon, *l'heure sonnée, la vengeance sera foudroyante* (*J. C.* ch. ix. p. 614). In any case, the ἐν τάχει is placed last with emphasis.

πλήν. "Howbeit (certain as the Messiah's deliverance of His people is, a sorrowful question arises) the Son of Man, when He is come, will He find faith on the earth?" The πλήν is not *im Uebrigen* (Weiss), nor *seulement* (Godet), but *doch* (Luther), *cependant* (Lasserre). Latin Versions have *verum* (d), *tamen* (b i l q), or *verumtamen* (Vulg.). Note the emphatic order, both ὁ υἱὸς τ. ἀνθρ. and ἐλθών being placed before the interrogative particle. Yet Syr-Sin. has, "Shall the Son of man come and find."

Only here and Gal. ii. 17 (where some prefer ἆρα) is ἄρα found in N.T. In LXX it is always followed by γε (Gen. xviii. 13, xxvi. 9, xxxvii. 10; Jer. iv. 10), but without γε it is freq. in Sym. Latin Versions have *numquid* (b c i l q) or *putas* (Vulg.). See Blass on Acts viii. 30.

τὴν πίστιν. "The necessary faith, the faith in question, faith in Jesus as the Messiah and Saviour." Others prefer "the faith which perseveres in prayer," or again "loyalty to Himself," which is much the same as faith in Christ. The answer to this desponding question, which seems, but only seems, "to call in question the success of our Lord's whole mediatorial work," has been given by anticipation xvii. 26: the majority, not only of mankind but of Christians, will be absorbed in worldly pursuits, and only a few will "endure to the end" (Mt. xxiv. 12, 13). No doubt is expressed or implied as to the coming of the Son of Man, but only as to what He will find.

There is therefore no reason for conjecturing that the parable received its present form at a time when belief in the Second Advent was waning. Still less reason is there for interpreting it of the Christian Church seeking help from pagan magistrates against Jewish persecutors, and then concluding that it must have been composed after the time of S. Luke (De Wette). On the other hand, Hilgenfeld sees in the thirst for vengeance, which (he thinks) inspires the parable, evidence of its being one of the oldest portions of the Third Gospel.

9–14. § The Parable of the Pharisee and the Publican. This has no connexion either with the parable which precedes it or with the narrative which follows it. The two parables were evidently spoken on different occasions and addressed to different audiences, the first to the disciples on a specified occasion, the second to the persons described in ver. 9 on some occasion not specified. They are placed in juxtaposition, probably because tradition assigned them to the same portion of Christ's ministry (Hahn); or *possibly* because they both (but in very different ways) treat of prayer (Keil). That Lk. brackets the two parables for some reason is shown by the καί. But note the δέ also, and see on iii. 9.

The καί is genuine (א B D L M Q R X Δ, Vulg.) although A etc. with several Versions omit.

9. As in ver. 1, this preface to the parable is the Evangelist's: εἶπεν δέ, δὲ καί, εἶπεν πρός, and εἶπεν παραβολήν are all marks of his style. It is possible to take **πρός** here as meaning "with a view to," as in ver. 1, or "against," as in xx. 19. But it is much more likely that it means "unto" after εἶπεν, because (1) this construction is specially common in Lk. and (2) we here have persons and not the substantial infinitive after πρός: *dixit autem et ad quosdam qui* (Vulg.). Syr-Sin. has "against."

τοὺς πεποιθότας ἐφ' ἑαυτοῖς ὅτι. They themselves were the foundation on which their confidence was built: xi. 22; 2 Cor. i. 9; Heb. ii. 13; Deut. xxviii. 52; 2 Sam. xxii. 3; Is. viii. 17, xii. 2, etc. The constructions ἔν τινι, ἐπί τινα, and εἴς τινα are less common. Grotius and others render ὅτι "because," making the righteousness a fact and the ground of their self-confidence; which is incredible. Comp. Prov. xxx. 12; Is. lxv. 5. The Talmud inveighs against the Pharisaism of those "who implore you to mention some more duties which they might perform."

ἐξουθενοῦντας. A strong word, common to Lk. and Paul: "utterly despised, treated as of no account," xxiii. 11; Acts iv. 11; Rom. xiv. 3, 10. Comp. *Ps. Sol.* ii. 5.

τοὺς λοιπούς. "The rest, *all* others" (RV.): comp. οἱ λοιποί (ver. 11). The "other" of AV. and most English Versions has been silently altered into "others" by the printers: "other" means "other folk," but τοὺς λοιπούς means "*all* other folk."

10. ἀνέβησαν. "They went *up*" from the lower city to Mount Moriah, the "Hill of the House," on which the temple stood. We are probably to understand one of the usual hours of prayer (i. 10; Acts ii. 15, iii. 1, x. 9).

11. σταθείς. This perhaps indicates the conscious adopting of an attitude or of a conspicuous place: *debout et la tête haute* (Lasserre); *après s'être placé en évidence* (Reuss); *in loco conspicuo instar statuæ stans erectus* (Valck.). Contrast ver. 13 and comp. ver. 40, xix. 8; Acts ii. 14, xvii. 22, xxvii. 21. The expression is peculiar to Lk. Standing was the common posture at prayer among the Jews (1 Sam. i. 26; 1 Kings viii. 14, 22; Mt. vi. 5; Mk. xi. 25). See Lightfoot on Mt. vi. 5.

πρὸς ἑαυτόν. These words probably follow ταῦτα (B L, Vulg. Boh. Arm. Orig.); but, even if they precede, they must be taken with προσηύχετο (comp. 2 Mac. xi. 13): *intra se precabatur* (e), *apud se orabat* (Vulg.). This use of πρὸς ἑαυτὸν is classical. "Standing by himself" would be καθ' ἑαυτόν, *seorsum*, which D here reads: comp. Acts xxviii. 16; Jas. ii. 17. The character of his prayer shows why he would not utter it so that others could hear.

εὐχαριστῶ σοι. There is no prayer, even in form; he asks God for nothing, being thoroughly satisfied with his present condition. And only in form is this utterance a thanksgiving; it is self-congratulation. He glances at God, but contemplates himself. Indeed he almost pities God, who but for himself would be destitute of faithful servants.

οἱ λοιποὶ τῶν ἀνθρώπων. "The rest of men" (RV.), "all other men," *ceteri hominum* (Vulg.). He is in a class by himself; every one else in a very inferior class. For other vainglorious thanksgivings used by Jews see Edersh. *L. & T.* ii. p. 291. Contrast S. Paul's declaration 1 Cor. xv. 9, 10, and see Schœttgen, i. p. 306. *Noli in precibus bona tua enumerare.*

ἅρπαγες, ἄδικοι, μοιχοί. *Gratias agit, non quia bonus, sed quia solus; non tam de bonis quæ habet, quam de malis quæ in aliis videt* (Bernard, *De Grad. Humil.* v. 17). But there is no hint that he was lying in acquitting himself of gross and flagrant crimes. Such falsehood in a silent address to God is scarcely intelligible. His error lay in supposing that all other men were guilty of these things, and that he himself was not guilty of sins that were as bad or worse. Hillel had taught, "Endeavour not to be better than the community, and trust not in thyself until the day of thy death." The **οὗτος** is contemptuous, as often. The τελώνης is pointed out to the Almighty as a specimen of οἱ λοιποὶ τ. ἀνθρώπων.

12. He cites these good works as instances of the ways in which he is still further superior to other men. He is superior not only in what he avoids, but in what he performs. Characteristically he names just those things on which Pharisees prided themselves (Mt. ix. 14, xxiii. 23).

δὶς τοῦ σαββάτου. Mondays and Thursdays. Moses was supposed to have ascended the mount on the fifth day, and to have come down on the second. For the sing. of **σάββατον** in the sense of "a week" comp. Mk. xvi. 9; 1 Cor. xvi. 2. It is amazing that any should have taken this as meaning "I fast twice on the sabbath," which would be unintelligible. The *jejuno bis in sabbato* of the Vulg. might mislead those who knew no Greek. The frequent statement that the Pharisees observed the second and fifth days as fasts all through the year (*D.B.*[2] i. 2. p. 1054), and held that this was enjoined by the oral Law, is without foundation: and those who make it are inconsistent in saying that this Pharisee boasts of works of supererogation. In that case he merely states that he keeps the Law in its entirety. The Mosaic Law enjoins only one fast in the year, the Day of Atonement. Other annual fasts were gradually established in memory of national calamities (Zech. viii. 19). Occasional fasts were from time to time ordered in seasons of drought and other public calamities, and these additional fasts were always held on Mondays and Thursdays. Thus, a five days' fast would not last from Monday to Friday inclusive, but would be held on all Mondays and Thursdays until the five days were made up (see the *Didache*, viii. 1; *Apost. Const.* vii. 23. 1). But many individuals imposed extra fasts on themselves, and there were *some* who fasted on Mondays and Thursdays *all the year round.* Such cases would be commonest among the Pharisees, and the Pharisee in the parable is one of them: but there is no evidence that all Pharisees adopted this practice or tried to make it a general obligation (Schürer, *Jewish People in the T. of J. C.* II. ii. p. 118; Edersh. *L. & T.* ii. p. 291; Wetstein and Lightfoot, *ad loc.*). The man, therefore, *is* boasting of a work of supererogation. What is told us about Jewish fasting in the N.T. (v. 33; Mt. vi. 16, ix. 14; Mk. ii. 18; Acts xxvii. 9) is confirmed by the Mishna. Note that the Pharisee has dropped even the form of thanksgiving.

With δὶς τοῦ σαββάτου comp. ἑπτάκις τῆς ἡμέρας (xvii. 4). The genitives in xxiv. 1; Mt. ii. 14, xxv. 6, xxviii. 13; Gal. vi. 17 are not parallel.

ἀποδεκατεύω πάντα. Here again, in paying tithe of *everything*, he seems to boast of doing more than the Law required. Tithe was due (Num. xviii. 21; Deut. xiv. 22), but not of small garden herbs (Mt. xxiii. 23). There is something for which God owes thanks to *him*.

The rare form ἀποδεκατεύω is found in B ℵ* here in place of the not very common ἀποδεκατόω or ἀποδεκατῶ. WH. ii. App. p. 171. The simple δεκατεύω is more usual.

ὅσα κτῶμαι. "All that I *get*" (RV.): *quæcunque adquiro* (i q), *quæ adquiro* (d). It was on what he *acquired*, not on what he possessed, that he paid tithe; on his income, not on his capital. All English Versions prior to RV. go wrong here with Vulg. (*quæ possideo*), Luth. (*das ich habe*), and Beza. "Possess" would be κέκτημαι. There is a similar error xxi. 19. Excepting Mt. x. 9 and 1 Thes. iv. 4, the verb is peculiar to Lk. in N.T. (Acts i. 18, viii. 20, xxii. 28): it is freq. in LXX.

13. μακρόθεν ἑστώς. Far from the *Pharisee*: nothing else is indicated. In his self-depreciation he thinks himself unworthy to come near in worship to one who must be a favoured servant of God. But we need not suppose that he remained in the Court of the Gentiles (Grot.), in which case the Pharisee in the Court of Israel would hardly have seen him. Comp. xxiii. 49. The change from σταθείς (ver. 11) to ἑστώς perhaps implies less of a set, prominent position in this case. Vulg. has *stans* in both places; but Cyprian has *cum stetisset* for σταθείς and *stabat et* for ἑστώς (*De Dom. Orat.* vi.). Comp. Tac. *Hist.* iv. 72. 4.

οὐκ ἤθελεν οὐδὲ τοὺς ὀφθαλμοὺς ἐπᾶραι. The common explanation, "would not lift up even his *eyes*," much less his hands and his face (1 Tim. ii. 8; 1 Kings viii. 22; Ps. xxviii. 2, lxiii. 4, cxxxiv. 2), does not seem to be satisfactory. The οὐδέ strengthens the previous οὐκ and need not be taken exclusively with τοὺς ὀφθαλμούς: "would not even *lift up his eyes to heaven*," much less adopt any confident or familiar attitude towards God. See Maldonatus, *ad loc.* Some Rabbis taught that it was necessary to keep the eyes down or to close them in praying (Schœttgen, i. p. 307).

ἔτυπτε. "He continued to smite"; *tundebat* (d), *percutiebat* (Vulg.). Comp. viii. 52, xxiii. 48. Om. εἰς after ἔτυπτε א B D.

ἱλάσθητί μοι τῷ ἁμαρτωλῷ. "Be merciful (Dan. ix. 19) to me *the* sinner." *He* also places himself in a class by himself; but he makes no comparisons. Consciousness of his own sin is supreme; *de nemine alio homine cogitat* (Beng.). For similar self-accusation comp. Ps. xxv. 11, xl. 12, li. 3; Ezra ix. 6; Dan. ix. 8; 1 Tim. i. 15. The verb occurs elsewhere in N.T. only Heb. ii. 17, with acc. of the sin. In LXX it is not common. Ps. lxiv. 3, with acc. of the sin. Ps. xxiv. 11, lxxvii. 38, lxxviii. 9, with dat. of the sin. 2 Kings v. 18, with dat. of the person, as here. The compound ἐξιλάσκομαι is the more usual word. The classical construction with acc. of the *person propitiated* is not found in bibl. Grk., because the idea of "propitiating God" is not to be encouraged. "The 'propitiation' acts on that which alienates God and not on God, whose love is unchanged throughout" (Wsctt. on Heb. ii. 17, and Additional Note on 1 Jn. ii. 2, *Epp. of S. John*, p. 83).

The Latin Versions have *propitiare* (c ff_2 l), *repropitiare* (b), *miserere* (d), *propitius esto* (Vulg.). See Deissmann, *Bible Studies*, p. 224.

14. λέγω ὑμῖν. As often, this formula introduces an important declaration uttered with authority (vii. 26, 28, ix. 27, x. 12, 24, xi. 9, 51, xii. 4, 5, 8, 27, 37, 44, 51, xiii. 3, etc.). Here Christ once more claims to know the secrets both of man's heart and of God's judgments.

κατέβη οὗτος δεδικαιωμένος. The pronoun perhaps looks back to the contemptuous οὗτος in ver. 11. "This despised man went down justified in the sight of God," *i.e.* "*accounted* as righteous, accepted." Comp. vii. 35, x. 29, xvi. 15; Is. l. 8, liii. 11; Job xxxiii. 32. The Talmud says, "So long as the temple stood, no Israelite was in distress; for as often as he came to it full of sin and offered sacrifice, then his sin was forgiven and he departed a just man" (Schœttgen, i. p. 308).

παρ' ἐκεῖνον. The expression is one of comparison, and *of itself* does not exclude the possibility of the Pharisee being justified in some smaller degree. Comp. xiii. 2, 4. But the context perhaps excludes it. Thus Tertullian (*Adv. Marcion.* iv. 36), *ideoque* *alterum reprobatum, alterum justificatum.* Also Euthym. (*ad loc.*), ὁ δικαιώσας μόνον ἑαυτὸν κατεδικάσθη παρὰ Θεοῦ, ὁ δὲ καταδικάσας μόνον ἑαυτὸν ἐδικαιώθη παρὰ Θεοῦ. Aug., however, points out that the Scripture does not say that the Pharisee was condemned (*Ep.* xxxvi. 4. 7).

The readings are various, but παρ' ἐκεῖνον (ℵ B L, Boh. Sah., Orig. Naz.) may be safely adopted: *ab illo* (Vulg.) is a misrepresentation of this, and μαλλον παρ' αικεινον τον φαρισειον (D) an amplification of it. The ἢ ἐκεῖνος (*min. pauc.*) of Elz. is a gloss; which, however, may have helped to produce the common reading ἢ γὰρ ἐκεῖνος (A E G H K M P Q etc.), ΠΑΡ being changed to ΓΑΡ. If ἢ γὰρ ἐκεῖνος (Tisch., Treg. *marg.*) be adopted, it must be interrogative: "I say to you, this man went down to his house justified—or did the other do so?" Other Latin variations are *præ illum pharisæum* (a), *magis quam ille pharisæus* (b c e), to which some add *qui se exaltabat* (f ff_2 i l q r). ἢ παρ' ἐκεῖνον (Hofm. Keil) and ἤπερ ἐκεῖνος (Hahn) are conjectures. See Blass, *Gr.* pp. 106, 139.

ὅτι πᾶς ὁ ὑψῶν, κ.τ.λ. *Verbatim* as xiv. 11 (where see note), which Weiss pronounces to be its original position, while its appearance here is due to Lk. Why is it assumed that Jesus did not repeat His sayings?

The suggestion (Aug. Bede) that the Pharisee represents the Jews and the publican the Gentiles cannot be accepted. Nor need we suppose (Godet) that Lk. is here showing that the Pauline doctrine of justification was based on the teaching of Christ. There is nothing specially Pauline here. We are not told that the publican was justified by faith in Christ, but by confession of sin and prayer. The meaning is simple. Christ takes a crucial case. One generally recognized as a saint fails in prayer, while one generally recognized as a sinner succeeds. Why? Because the latter's prayer is real, and the former's not. The one comes in the spirit of prayer,—self-humiliation; the other in the spirit of pride,—self-satisfaction.

15–17. Little Children brought to Christ. Mt. xix. 13–15; Mk. x. 13–16. The narrative of Lk., which has been proceeding independently since ix. 51, here rejoins Mt. and Mk. The three narratives are almost *verbatim* alike. Where Lk. differs either he has an expression peculiar to himself, as τὰ βρέφη (ver. 15) or προσεκαλέσατο (ver. 16); or he and Mk. agree against Mt., as in αὐτῶν ἅπτηται (ver. 15), ἔρχεσθαι and τοῦ Θεοῦ (ver. 16), ὃς ἂν μὴ δέξηται, κ.τ.λ. (ver. 17), where Mt. varies considerably in wording. Only in the καί before μὴ κωλύετε (ver. 16) does Lk. agree with Mt. against Mk.

15. Προσέφερον δὲ αὐτῷ καὶ τὰ βρέφη. The δέ and καὶ τὰ βρέφη are peculiar to Lk. For δέ Mk. has καί and Mt. τότε: for καὶ τὰ βρέφη both have simply παιδία. "Now people were bringing to Him even their babes," or "their babes also," as well as sick folk. In any case βρέφος must be rendered here as in ii. 12, 16: comp. i. 41, 44; Acts vii. 19; 1 Pet. ii. 2. AV. has "babe," "infant," and "young child." Vulg. has *infans* throughout.

ἅπτηται. Mt. says more distinctly, τὰς χεῖρας ἐπιθῇ αὐτοῖς καὶ προσεύξηται. Blessing them is meant: comp. Gen. xlviii. 14, 15.

The pres. subj. after imperf. indic. is a constr. that is freq. in LXX. It shows how the opt. is going out of use. But here it might be explained as expressing the thought of those who brought the babes, a thought put in a direct form for the sake of vividness: "that He may touch" for "that He might touch." Win. xli. b. 1. a, p. 360.

ἐπετίμων αὐτοῖς. Not because, as Chrysostom and Theophylact suggest, they thought that little children were unworthy to approach Him; but because they thought it a waste of His time and an abuse of His kindness; or, as Jerome, followed closely by Bede, puts it, *eum in similitudinem hominum offerentium importunitate lassari.* On the first anniversary of their birth Jewish children were sometimes brought to the Rabbi to be blest.

Lk. has the imperf. in both places, προσέφερον . . . ἐπετίμων: Mt. προσηνέχθησαν . . . ἐπετίμησαν: Mk. προσέφερον . . . ἐπετίμησαν.

16. προσεκαλέσατο. Even if with B we omit αὐτά, this would mean that He called the children (with their parents), and then addressed the disciples. Mk. has ἰδὼν . . . ἠγανάκτησεν, Mt. simply εἶπεν.

μὴ κωλύετε. "Cease to forbid." The wording is almost identical in all three narratives. Jerome and Euthym. (on Mt. xix. 14) point out that Christ does not say τούτων but τοιούτων, *ut ostenderet non ætatem regnare sed mores.* It is not these children, nor all children, but those who are childlike in character, especially in humility and trustfulness, who are best fitted for the Kingdom.

17. *Verbatim* as in Mk. x. 15. Mt. gives a similar saying on a different occasion (xviii. 3, 4). The δέξηται explains the τοιούτων: a child receives what is offered to it, in full trust that it is good for it, μηδὲν διακρινόμενος, μηδὲ ἀμφιβάλλων περὶ αὐτοῦ (Euthym.).

18–30. The Rich Young Ruler who preferred his Riches to the Service of Christ. Mt. xix. 16–30; Mk. x. 17–31. In all three narratives this section follows immediately upon the one about bringing children to Christ. This young ruler is humiliated by being told that there is still a great deal to be done before he is qualified for ζωὴ αἰώνιος. Thus the lessons supplement one another. The children, like the publican, are nearer the Kingdom than they could suppose themselves to be; the rich young man, like the Pharisee, is farther from it than he supposed himself to be. Those who can be benefited by being abased (9, 22), are abased; while those who cannot be harmed by being exalted (16), are exalted. Here again Lk. often agrees with Mk. in small details of wording against Mt., and only once (ἀκούσας in **ver.** 23) with Mt. against Mk.

18. ἄρχων. Lk. alone tells us this, and we are in doubt what he means by it. His being a νεανίσκος, as Mt. tells us (xix. 20, 22), is rather against his being a member of the Sanhedrin or a ruler of a synagogue. Weiss, Neander, and others conjecture that νεανίσκος is an error, perhaps an inference drawn by Mt. from Christ's charge, especially τίμα τὸν πατέρα σου, κ.τ.λ. Certainly ἐκ νεότητος (which is wanting in the best texts of Mt.) does not seem appropriate to a νεανίσκος. Yet Holtzmann supposes that νεανίσκος has been added through a misconception of ἐκ νεότητος. But the rich ruler's self-confidence might easily make him pose as an older man than he really was. Keim seems to be nearer the truth when he says that "the whole impression is that of an eager and immature young man" (*Jes. of Naz.* v. p. 36). The statement of Mk., that he ran to Jesus and kneeled to Him (x. 17), indicates youthful eagerness.

τί ποιήσας, κ.τ.λ. See on x. 25, where the same question is asked. In Mt. the "good is transferred from "Master" to "what," Διδάσκαλε, τί ἀγαθὸν ποιήσω; and hence Christ's reply is different, Τί με ἐρωτᾷς περὶ τοῦ ἀγαθοῦ; The ruler thought that by some one act, perhaps of benevolence, he could secure eternal life: he was prepared for great expenditure. Similar questions were discussed among the Rabbis: see Wetst. on Mt. xix. 16.

19. Τί με λέγεις ἀγαθόν; So also in Mk. In none of the three is there any emphasis on "Me," which is an enclitic. There is no instance in the whole Talmud of a Rabbi being addressed as "Good Master": the title was absolutely unknown among the Jews. This, therefore, was an extraordinary address, and perhaps a fulsome compliment. The Talmud says, "There is nothing else that is good but the Law." The explanation of some ancient and modern commentators, that Jesus is here speaking merely from the young man's standpoint, is not satisfactory. "You suppose Me to be a mere man, and you ought not to call any human being good. That title I cannot accept, unless I am recognized as God."[1] The young ruler could not understand this; and the reply *must* have had some meaning for *him*. His defect was that he trusted too much in himself, too little in God. Jesus reminds him that there is only one source of goodness whether in action (Mt.) or in character (Mk. Lk.), viz. God. He Himself is no exception. His goodness is the goodness of God working in Him. "The Son can do nothing of Himself, but what He seeth the Father doing. . . . For as the Father hath life in Himself, even so gave He to the Son also to have life in Him-

[1] So Cyril, *ad loc.*, Εἰ μὴ πεπίστευκας ὅτι Θεός εἰμι, πῶς τὰ μόνῃ πρέποντα τῇ ἀνωτάτω φύσει περιτέθεικάς μοι, καὶ ἀγαθὸν ἀποκαλεῖς, ὃν δὴ καὶ νενόμικας ἄνθρωπον εἶναι κατὰ σέ; and Ambrose, *Quid me dicis bonum, quem negas Deum? Non ergo se bonum negat, sed Deum designat.* See also Jerome, Basil, Epiphanius, etc. Maldonatus and Wordsworth follow.

self. . . . I can of Myself do nothing: as I hear, I judge: and My judgment is righteous, because I seek not My own will, but the will of Him that sent Me" (Jn. v. 19-30). *Non se magistrum non esse, sed magistrum absque Deo nullum bonum esse testatur* (Bede). There is no need to add to this the thought that the goodness of Jesus was the goodness of perfect development (see on ii. 52), whereas the goodness of God is that of absolute perfection (Weiss on Mk. x. 18).

οὐδεὶς ἀγαθὸς εἰ μὴ εἷς ὁ Θεός. So also Mk. Here the article is wanting in ℵ B. The saying appears in a variety of forms in quotations. Justin has two: *οὐδεὶς ἀγαθὸς εἰ μὴ μόνος ὁ Θεὸς ὁ ποιήσας τὰ πάντα* (*Apol.* i. 16), and *εἷς ἐστὶν ἀγαθός, ὁ πατήρ μου ὁ ἐν τοῖς οὐρανοῖς* (*Try.* ci.). Marcion seems to have read *εἷς ἐστὶν ἀγαθός, ὁ Θεὸς ὁ πατήρ*. In Hippol. *Philosoph.* v. 1 *εἷς ἐστὶν ἀγαθός, ὁ πατὴρ ἐν τοῖς οὐρανοῖς*, and a similar reading appears four times in *Clem. Hom.* See Zeller, *Apostelg.* pp. 32 ff., Eng. tr. pp. 105-119, and WH. ii. App. pp. 14, 15.

20. τὰς ἐντολὰς οἶδας. *Jesus securos ad Legem remittit; contritos Evangelice consolatur* (Beng.). This is, however, not the main point. Nothing extraordinary or not generally known is required for salvation: the observance of well-known commands will suffice.

Here again Lk. exactly agrees with Mk., except that he places the seventh before the sixth commandment, and omits, as Mt. does, *μὴ ἀποστερήσῃς*, which perhaps represents the tenth. In Rom. xiii. 9, Jas. ii. 11, and in Cod. B of Deut. v. 17 adultery is mentioned before murder. Philo says that in the second *πεντάς* of the decalogue adultery is placed first as *μέγιστον ἀδικημάτων* (*De decem orac.* xxiv., xxxii.). In all three of the Gospels the fifth commandment is placed last and none of the first four is quoted. In Mt. they are in the same form as in Exod. xx. and Deut. v., *Οὐ φονεύσεις, κ.τ.λ.* So also Rom. xiii. 9. In Mk. and Jas ii. 11, *Μὴ φονεύσῃς*.

21. ταῦτα πάντα ἐφύλαξα ἐκ νεότητος. Not so much a boast, as an expression of dissatisfaction. "I wanted to be told of something special and sublime; and I am reminded of duties which I have been performing all my life." The reply exhibits great ignorance of self and of duty, but is perfectly sincere.

That it was possible to keep the whole Law is an idea which is frequent in the Talmud. Abraham, Moses, and Aaron were held to have done so. R. Chanina says to the Angel of Death, "Bring me the book of the Law, and see whether there is anything written in it which I have not kept" (Schœttg. i. pp. 160, 161. See also Edersh. *L. & T.* i. p. 536).

Here, as in Mt. xix. 20; Gen. xxvi. 5; Exod. xii. 17, xx. 6, we have the act. of *φυλάττω*: Mk. x. 20; Lev. xviii. 4, xx. 8, 22, xxvi. 3, the mid. without difference of sense.

22. ἀκούσας δὲ ὁ Ἰησοῦς. Mk. has the striking *ἐμβλέψας αὐτῷ ἠγάπησεν αὐτόν*, which is strong evidence that behind Mk. is one who was intimate with Christ. From *ἠγάπησεν, πάντα* πώλησον, and ἀκολούθει μοι (v. 27, ix. 59) we may conjecture that this was a call to become an Apostle.

Ἔτι ἕν σοι λείπει. Mk. has ἕν σε ὑστερεῖ. Mt. transfers the words to the young man, τί ἔτι ὑστερῶ; Christ neither affirms nor denies the ruler's statement of his condition. Assuming it to be correct, there is still something lacking, viz. detachment from his wealth. In what follows we have two charges, one to sell and distribute; the other to follow Christ: and the first is preparatory to the second. But we may not separate them and make the first the one thing lacking and the second the answer to τί ποιήσας in ver. 18. In ἕξεις θησαυρὸν ἐν τοῖς οὐρανοῖς we have a clear reference to ζωὴν αἰώνιον, and this promise is attached to the first charge. The πάντα (comp. vi. 30, vii. 35, ix. 43, xi. 4) and the compound διάδος (xi. 22; Acts iv. 35; elsewhere only Jn. vi. 11) are here peculiar to Lk.

Mt., having transferred the words about "lacking something yet" to the rich young man, gives Christ's reply Εἰ θέλεις τέλειος εἶναι in place of Ἔτι ἕν σοι λείπει. These words cannot mean a perfection superior to the fulfilment of the Law, for no such perfection is possible (xvii. 10). A misconception of this point led to the distinction between the performance of duty and moral perfection, which has produced much error in moral theology. Clem. Alex. rightly says, ὅταν εἴπῃ Εἰ θέλεις τέλειος γενέσθαι (*sic*), πωλήσας τὰ ὑπάρχοντα δὸς πτωχοῖς, ἐλέγχει τὸν καυχώμενον ἐπὶ τῷ πάσας τὰς ἐντολὰς ἐκ νεότητος τετηρηκέναι· οὐ γὰρ πεπληρώκει τό, Ἀγαπήσεις τὸν πλησίον σου ὡς ἑαυτόν· τότε δέ, ὑπὸ τοῦ Κυρίου συντελειούμενος, ἐδιδάσκετο δι' ἀγάπην μεταδιδόναι (*Strom.* iii. 6, p. 537, ed. Potter). Neander, *L. J. C.* § 226, Eng. tr. p. 367.

In class. Grk. this use of λείπειν for ἐλλείπειν is mostly poetical.

For διάδος (B E F etc.) ℵ A D L M R Δ have δός from Mt. and Mk. And for ἐν τοῖς οὐρανοῖς (B D) ℵ A L R have ἐν οὐράνοις from Mt., and P, Vulg. Goth. have ἐν οὐρανῷ from Mk. The plur. is supported by *in cælis* (a d e), but the article is doubtful.

23. περίλυπος. Stronger than λυπούμενος (Mt. Mk.), to which Mk. adds the graphic στυγνάσας (Ezek. xxxii. 10; [Mt. xvi. 3]). For περίλυπος comp. Mk. vi. 26, xiv. 34; Mt. xxvi. 38. He wanted to follow Christ's injunctions, but at present the cost seemed to him to be too great.

πλούσιος σφόδρα. The statement explains, and perhaps in some measure excuses, his distress. He possessed a great deal more than a boat and nets; and Peter, James, and John were not told to sell their boats and nets and give the proceeds to the poor; because their hearts were not wedded to them.

24. Πῶς δυσκόλως. All three have this adv., which occurs nowhere else in bibl. Grk. Clem. Alex. seems to allude to the saying when he writes ὁ λόγος τοὺς τελώνας λέγει δυσκόλως σωθήσεται (*Strom.* v. 5. p. 662, ed. Potter). Lk. omits the departure of the ruler, which took place before these words were uttered. Mk. alone records (x. 24) the consternation which they excited in the disciples, and Christ's repetition of them. It was perhaps largely for the sake of Judas that these stern words about the perils of wealth were uttered to them.

25. In the Talmud an elephant passing through the eye of a needle is twice used of what is impossible; also a camel dancing in a very small corn measure. See Lightfoot, Schœttgen, and Wetstein, *ad loc.* For εὐκοπώτερον see small print on v. 23. The reading κάμιλον = "cable" here and Mt. xix. 24 is an attempt to tone down a strong statement. It is found only in a few late MSS. The word κάμιλος occurs only in Suidas and a scholiast on Aristoph. *Vesp.* 1030. Some would give the meaning of "cable" to κάμηλος (so Cyril on Mt. xix. 24), but no doubt the animal is meant. Others would make the "needle's eye" into a narrow gateway for foot-passengers; but this also is erroneous. See *Expositor*, 1st series, iii. p. 369, 1876; WH. ii. App. p. 151. For βελόνης, which occurs nowhere else in bibl. Grk., Mt. and Mk. have ῥαφίδος, and for τρήματος Mk. has τρυμαλιᾶς. Hobart claims both βελόνη and τρῆμα as medical, the former with good reason (p. 60).

Celsus said that this saying of Christ was borrowed along with others from Plato. But the passage which he quoted from the *Laws* (v. p. 742) merely says that a man cannot be at once very good and very rich. There is nothing about a camel or a needle. Orig. *Con. Cels.* vi. 16. 1. The saying in the Koran (vii. 38), "Neither shall they enter into paradise, until a camel pass through the eye of a needle," is probably taken from the Gospels (Sale, p. 108).

It is specially to be noted that this hard saying about the difficulty of those who have riches entering into the Kingdom of God is in all three Gospels and not merely in the one which is supposed to be Ebionite in tone. Comp. Mt. vi. 19–21; Mk. xii. 41, 42. Lk. omits the great amazement, ἐξεπλήσσοντο σφόδρα (Mt.), περισσῶς ἐξεπλήσσοντο (Mk.), which this second utterance on the impediments caused by wealth excited in the disciples.

The Latin translator of Origen's comm. on Mt. xix. has the following extract from "a certain Gospel which is called *According to the Hebrews.*" But neither this preface nor the extract are in the Greek text of Origen. *Dixit ad eum alter divitum, Magister, quid bonum faciens vivam? Dixit ei, Homo, legem et prophetas fac. Respondit ad eum, Feci. Dixit ei, Vade, vende omnia quæ possides et divide pauperibus et veni, sequere me. Coepit autem dives scalpere caput suum* (sic), *et non placuit ei. Et dixit ad eum Dominus, Quomodo dicis Legem feci et prophetas? quoniam scriptum est in lege Diliges proximum tuum sicut te ipsum, et ecce multi fratres tui, filii Abrahæ, amicti sunt stercore, morientes præ fame, et domus tua plena est multis bonis, et non egreditur omnino aliquid ex ea ad eos. Et conversus dixit Simoni discipulo suo, sedenti apud se, Simon, fili Johannæ, facilius est camelum intrare per foramen acus quam divitem in regnum cœlorum.* See also the fragment quoted from the narrative of the man with the withered hand (Lk. vi. 8). These specimens explain why the *Gospel according to the Hebrews* was allowed to pass into oblivion, and it is difficult to believe that this Nazarene Gospel was the original Hebrew of our Mt. If it was, "our Greek Evangelist must have been a most unfaithful translator" (Salmon, *Int. to N.T.* p. 166, 5th ed.). We may add that he must have been a person of very superior taste and ability.

26. Καὶ τίς δύναται σωθῆναι; Not "what *rich* man" (Weiss), but "what person of any description": Num. xxiv. 23. The whole world either possesses or aims at possessing wealth. If, then, what every one desires is fatal to salvation, who can be saved? The *καί* adds emphasis to the question, which arises out of what has just been said: comp. x. 29; Jn. ix. 36; 2 Cor. ii. 2.

27. Τὰ ἀδύνατα παρὰ ἀνθρώποις. This shows that ver. 25 means an impossibility, not merely something difficult or highly improbable. It is a miracle of grace when those who have wealth do not put their trust in it. Lk. omits the steadfast look (*ἐμβλέψας*) with which Mt. and Mk. say that this declaration was accompanied. He sympathizes with their perplexity and hastens to remove it.

Not only before proper names which begin with a vowel (Mt. xxviii. 15; Jn. i. 40), but also in other cases, *παρά* sometimes is found unelided; *παρὰ ἁμαρτωλῷ* (xix. 7). This is commonly the case before *ἄνθρωπος*: comp. Mt. xix. 26; Mk. x. 27; Jn. v. 34, 41; Gal. i. 12.

δυνατὰ παρὰ τῷ Θεῷ. Zacchæus proved this (xix. 1–10). Comp. Zech. viii. 6; Job xlii. 2. For parallels from profane writers see Grotius and Wetstein on Mt. xix. 26. But *παρὰ ἀνθρώποις* and *παρὰ τῷ Θεῷ* certainly do not mean *hominum judicio* and *Dei judicio* (Fri. Ew.): they refer to what each can do. Man cannot, but God can, break the spell which wealth exercises over the wealthy. Comp. i. 37; Gen. xviii. 14; Jer. xxxii. 17, 27; Zech. viii. 6.

28. εἶπεν δὲ ὁ Πέτρος. His being the one to speak is characteristic; but he does not speak in a spirit of boastfulness. Rather it is the reaction from their consternation which moves him to speak: *spe ex verbis Salvatoris concepta* (Beng.). He wants to be assured that God's omnipotence has been exerted on their behalf, and that they may hope to enter the Kingdom. Mt. adds *τί ἄρα ἔσται ἡμῖν;* Note the *εἶπεν δέ*, which neither Mt. nor Mk. has.

29. Ἀμὴν λέγω ὑμῖν. In all three: it is a declaration of great moment. Not only has God done this for the Twelve, but for many others: and every one who has had grace to surrender is sure of his reward. Lk. alone has *γυναῖκα*, and alone omits *ἀγρούς*, among the things surrendered. The omission is noteworthy in connexion with his supposed Ebionitism.

30. πολλαπλασίονα. Job's family was exactly restored; his goods were exactly doubled. The dramatic compensations of the

O.T. are far exceeded by the moral and spiritual compensations of the Gospel: and it is evident from this passage that material rewards are included also. What is lost in the family is replaced many times over in Christ and in the Church. This would apply in a special way to converts from heathen families, who found loving fathers and brethren to replace the cruel relations who cast them out. Lk. and Mt. omit (but for no imaginable dogmatic reasons) the important qualification μετὰ διωγμῶν. "He only is truly rich," said the Rabbi Meir, "who enjoys his riches." The Christian sacrifices what is not enjoyed for what brings real happiness.

Mk. has ἑκατονταπλασίονα. D supported by many Latin authorities (a b c d e ff_2 i l q r, Cypr. Ambr. Aug. Bede) here has ἑπταπλασίονα. Cyprian quotes the passage thrice, and each time has *septies tantum in isto tempore*. WH. conjectures "some extraneous source, written or oral." Vulg. and f have *multo plura in hoc tempore*.

Between λάβῃ (B D M, Arm.), which may come from Mk., and ἀπολάβῃ (ℵ A P R etc.) it is not easy to decide. With ἀπολάβῃ comp. xxiii. 41; Rom. i. 27; Col. iii. 24; 2 Jn. 8. It is often used with τ. μισθόν (Xen. *Anab.* vii. 7. 14; Her. viii. 137. 6). Vulg. has *et non recipiat*.

ἐν τῷ καιρῷ τούτῳ. Note the contrast with τῷ αἰῶνι: not merely in this world, but in this season. So also in Mk. Comp. ἐν τῷ νῦν καιρῷ (Rom. iii. 26, viii. 18), and τὸν καιρὸν τὸν ἐνεστηκότα (Heb. ix. 9), which means the same: see Wsctt.

ἐν τῷ αἰῶνι τῷ ἐρχομένῳ. "In the age which is in process of being realized." See on vii. 19, and comp. Eph. i. 21, ii. 7; Heb. vi. 5. Bengel remarks that Scripture in general is more explicit about temporal punishments than temporal rewards, but about eternal rewards than eternal punishments.

Millennarians made use of this promise as an argument for their views. It would be in the *millennium* that the faithful would receive literally a hundredfold of what they had given up for the Kingdom's sake: *non intelligentes quod si in cæteris digna sit repromissio, in uxoribus appareat turpitudo; ut qui unam pro Domino dimiserit, et centum recipiat in futuro* (Jerome on Mt. xix. 29).

Lk. omits the saying about last being first and first last, having already recorded it in a different connexion (xiii. 30).

31–34. The Third Announcement of the Passion. Mt. xx. 17–19; Mk. x. 32–34. For previous announcements (just before and just after the Transfiguration) see ix. 22, 44. The raising of Lazarus should probably be placed here. The decree of the Sanhedrin for the arrest of Jesus had very likely already been passed when our Lord made this new announcement of His death. *Apostolis sæpius dixit et indies expressius, ut in posterum testes essent præscientiæ ipsius* (Grotius).

The εἶπεν (ver. 31) is the one item which Lk. and Mt. have in common against Mk. In several expressions in *vv.* 32, 33 Lk. agrees with Mk.

against Mt. The εἶπεν πρός, the πάντα (see on vii. 35, ix. 43, xi. 4), τὰ γεγραμμένα (see on xxii. 37), and all of ver. 34 are peculiar to Lk.'s account.

31. Παραλαβών. "Took to Himself" (ix. 28, xi. 26; Acts xv. 39). The notion of taking *aside*, away from the multitude, is involved, but is not prominent. In class. Grk. it is freq. of taking a wife, a companion, an ally, or adopting a son. This announcement specially concerned the Twelve who were to accompany Him to Jerusalem. See the graphic account of their behaviour Mk. x. 32.

διὰ τῶν προφητῶν. This is the regular expression for the utterances of prophecy: they are spoken *by means of* the Prophets." The Prophet is not an originating agent, but an instrument. But this is the only place in which the phrase occurs in Lk., who says little to his Gentile readers about the fulfilment of prophecy. Comp. Mt. i. 22, ii. 5, 15, 23, iv. 14, viii. 17, xii. 17, xiii. 35, etc. In Mt. ii. 17 and iii. 3 ὑπό is a false reading. Comp. Hag. ii. 2.—See Gould on Mk. x. 33, 34.

τῷ υἱῷ τοῦ ἀνθρώπου. Once more an amphibolous expression. It can be taken with either τελεσθήσεται or τὰ γεγραμμένα. If with the former it may mean either "*by* the Son of Man" (which is not probable, for it is not what He does, but what others do to Him that is predicted), or "unto the Son of Man" (RV. Hahn, Nösgen). Comp. ἀναπληροῦται αὐτοῖς ἡ προφητεία (Mt. xiii. 14). But for this Lk. elsewhere has ἐν τῷ υἱῷ τ. ἀνθρ. (xxii. 37). It seems better to take the dat. with τὰ γεγραμμένα: "*for* the Son of Man," *i.e.* prescribed for Him as His course (Weiss, Godet), or "*of* the Son of Man" (Vulg. Wic. Tyn. Cov. Cran. Rhem. AV. Alf.). Hence the ancient gloss in the text of D, περὶ τοῦ υἱοῦ τ. ἀ. Win. xxxi. 4, p. 265. Green, p. 100.

32. παραδοθήσεται γὰρ τοῖς ἔθνεσιν. This is a new element of definiteness in the prophecy, and it almost carries with it, what Mt. xx. 19 distinctly expresses, that the mode of death will be crucifixion. It is said that this prediction has been made more definite by the Evangelist, who has worded it in accordance with accomplished facts. But, in that case, why were not ix. 22 and 44 made equally definite? That Christ should gradually reveal more details is in harmony with probability. Lk., however, omits the high priests and scribes, and their condemning Christ to death before handing Him over to the heathen, although both Mt. (xx. 18) and Mk. (x. 33) say that Jesus predicted these details on this occasion. Here Lk. alone has ὑβρισθήσεται (xi. 45; Acts xiv. 5; elsewhere twice).

33. τῇ ἡμέρᾳ τῇ τρίτῃ. Mk. has the less accurate μετὰ τρεῖς ἡμέρας, which can hardly have been invented to fit the facts. While the prediction of His death might shake the disciples' faith in His Messiahship, the prediction of His rising again was calculated to establish it.

34. Καὶ αὐτοὶ οὐδὲν τούτων συνῆκαν. Comp. ii. 50. Note the characteristic *καὶ αὐτοί* and *ἦν κεκρυμμένον.* Lk. alone mentions the appeal to prophecy (ver. 31), and he alone states—with threefold emphasis—that the Twelve did not at all understand. But Mt. and Mk. *illustrate* this dulness of apprehension by the request of the sons of Zebedee for the right and left hand places in the Kingdom, which Lk. omits. Their minds were too full of an earthly kingdom to be able to grasp the idea of a Messiah who was to suffer and to die: and without that they could not understand His rising again, and did not at first believe when they were told that He had risen. Their dulness was providential, and it became a security to the Church for the truth of the Resurrection. The theory that they believed, because they *expected* that He would rise again, is against all the evidence. Comp. ix. 45.

κεκρυμμένον ἀπ' αὐτῶν. This was changed when He *διήνοιξεν αὐτῶν τὸν νοῦν τοῦ συνιέναι τὰς γραφάς* (xxiv. 45). For **ἀπ' αὐτῶν** comp. ix. 45, x. 21, xix. 42; 2 Kings iv. 27; Ps. cxviii. 19?; Is. xl. 27; Jer. xxxix. 17. This statement is not identical with either of the other two. It explains the fact that they not only did not understand any of this at the time, but "did not get to know (*ἐγίνωσκον*) the things that were said."

35–43. The Healing of Blind Bartimæus at Jericho. Mt. xx. 29–34; Mk. x. 46–52. This miracle probably took place in the week preceding that of the Passion.

The three narratives have exercised the ingenuity of harmonizers. Lk. and Mk. have only one blind man; Mt. again mentions two (comp. Mt. ix. 27). Lk. represents the miracle as taking place when Jesus was approaching Jericho; Mt. and Mk. as taking place when He was leaving it. Lk. says that Jesus healed with a command, *ἀνάβλεψον*; Mk. with a word of comfort, *ὕπαγε, ἡ πίστις σου σέσωκέν σε*; Mt. with a touch, *ἥψατο τῶν ὀμμάτων αὐτῶν.* Only those who have a narrow view respecting inspiration and its effects will be concerned to reconcile these differences and make each of the three verbally exact. These make many suggestions. 1. There were *three* different healings (Euthym. on Mt. xx. 34). 2. As Christ entered Jericho, Bartimæus cried for help, and was *not* healed; he then joined a second blind man, and with him made an appeal as Jesus left Jericho, and then both were healed (Calvin and Maldon. followed by Wordsw.). 3. One blind man was healed as He entered, Bartimæus, and another as He left (Aug. *Quæst. Evang.* ii. 48). 4. One was healed as He entered and one as He left; and Mt. combines the first with the second (even Neander inclines to this, *L. J. C.* § 236, note). 5. There were two Jerichos, Old and New, and Lk. means that Jesus was approaching New Jericho, Mt. and Mk. that He was leaving Old Jericho (Macknight), although there is no evidence that Old Jericho was still inhabited, or that "Jericho" without epithet could at this time mean anything but the city which was given by Antony to Cleopatra, and afterwards redeemed by Herod the Great (Jos. *Ant.* xv. 4. 2, 4). See Stanley, *Sin. & Pal.* p. 310; also some good remarks by Sadler on Mk. x. 46, to the effect that "the inspiration of the Evangelists did not extend to minutiæ of this sort"; and by Harvey Goodwin against forced explanations (*Gosp. of S. Luke*, p. 311, Bell, 1865). 6. See below on ver. 35. The narrative of Mk., who gives the name Bartimæus and other details, is probably the most exact of the three. See Wsctt. *Intr. to the Gospels*, ch. vii. p. 367, 7th ed.

The attempts of Hitzig and Keim to use the name, which in Syriac may perhaps mean "son of the blind," to discredit the whole narrative, are rightly condemned by Weiss (*L. J.* ii. p. 439, Eng. tr. iii. p. 222). Strauss suggests that the name comes from ἐπετίμων (ver. 39; Mk. x. 48) and ἐπετίμησε (Mt. xx. 31) (*L. J.* §71, p. 429, 1864). For other possible meanings see Lightfoot, *Hor. Heb. ad loc.*

35. ἐν τῷ ἐγγίζειν αὐτὸν εἰς Ἰερειχώ. The translation, "When He was not far from Jericho," *i.e.* as He had just left it (Grotius, Nösgen), is perhaps the worst device for harmonizing Lk. with Mt. and Mk. The meaning of ἐγγίζειν is decisive; and there is the εἰς in addition. Both Herod the Great and Archelaus had beautified and enlarged Jericho, which at this time must have presented a glorious appearance (*D.B.*[2] art. "Jericho"). It was here that Herod had died his horrible death (Jos. *B. J.* i. 33. 6, 7). Note the characteristic ἐγένετο and ἐν τῷ *c. infin.* See on iii. 21, and comp. 2 Sam. xv. 5.

In class. Grk. ἐγγίζειν is not common, and usually has the dat. In bibl. Grk. it is very frequent; sometimes with dat., esp. in the phrase ἐγγίζειν τῷ Θεῷ (Jas. iv. 8; Exod. xix. 22; Lev. x. 3; Is. xxix, 13, etc.); sometimes with πρός (Gen. xlv. 4, xlviii. 10; Exod. xix. 21, etc.); and also with εἰς (xix. 29, xxiv. 28; Mt. xxi. 1; Mk. xi. 1; Tob. vi. 10 ℵ, xi. 1). In N.T. ἐγγίζειν is always intrans.

For ἐπαιτῶν (ℵ B D L, Orig.) A P Q R etc. have προσαιτῶν. Comp. xvi. 3.

36. ὄχλου διαπορευομένου. The caravan of pilgrims going up to the Passover. See on vi. 1 and on xi. 29; also Edersh. *Hist. of J. N.* p. 255, ed. 1896. Leaving His place of retirement (Jn. xi. 54, 55), Jesus had joined this caravan; and it is probable that He came to Jericho in order to do so. The crowd was there, according to all three narratives, *before* the miracle took place. This shows how untenable is the view of Keim, Holtzmann, and Weiss, that Lk. has purposely transferred the healing from the departure to the entry in order to account for the crowd at the meeting with Zacchæus (xix. 3): the miracle produced the crush of people. But according to Lk. himself the crowd was there before the miracle.

ἐπυνθάνετο τί εἴη τοῦτο. In N.T. πυνθάνομαι is almost peculiar to Lk. (xv. 26, where see note; Acts iv. 7, x. 18, 29, etc.). Omitting ἄν with ℵ A B P etc. against D K L M Q R X, "He enquired what this was," not "what this possibly might be." Mt. ii. 4; Jn. iv. 52.

37. For ἀπήγγειλαν see on viii. 20; for Ναζωραῖος see on iv. 34 (Mk. here has Ναζαρηνός, and Mt. omits the epithet); and for παρέρχεται see on xi. 42.

38. ἐβόησεν. Comp. ix. 38, xvii. 13.

υἱὲ Δαυείδ. This shows that he recognizes Jesus as the Messiah (Mt. ix. 27, xii. 23, xv. 22, xxi. 9, 15). It is not this which the multitude resent, but the interruption: comp. v. 15. They regard him as an ordinary beggar, asking for money. And Jesus was perhaps teaching as He went. Mk. tells us how the attitude of the people changed towards him, when they saw that Jesus had decided to listen to him. See Gould on Mk. x. 47.

39. σιγήσῃ. Excepting Rom. xvi. 25 and 1 Cor. xiv. 28, 30, 34, the verb is peculiar to Lk. in N.T. (ix. 36, xx. 26; Acts xii. 17, xv. 12, 13). Mt. and Mk. have σιωπᾷν, which א A Q R, Orig. read here.

ἔκραζεν. Note the change of verb and tense from ἐβόησεν. While βοάω is specially an intelligent cry for help, κράζω is often an instinctive cry or scream, a loud expression of strong emotion. In class. Grk. κράζω is often used of the cries of animals. The two words are sometimes joined (Dem. *De Cor.* p. 271; Aristoph. *Plut.* 722). Mt. and Mk. have κράζω in both places, and Mt. has the aor. in both. The man's persistency is evidence of his faith, which Christ recognizes.

40. σταθείς. See on ver. 11: the others have στάς. Excepting in Mt. and Acts, where the verb is common, κελεύω occurs here only in N.T. In LXX it is found only in the Apocrypha. Mk. here describes the man's casting away[1] his ἱμάτιον and leaping up to come to Jesus, when the people had passed on to him Christ's command. Christ's making those who had rebuked him to be the bearers of His invitation to him is to be noted.

With the constr., ἐγγίσαντος αὐτοῦ . . . αὐτόν instead of ἐγγίσαντα, comp. xii. 36, xv. 20, xvii. 12, xxii. 10, 53; Acts iv. 1, xxi. 17.

41. Τί σοι θέλεις ποιήσω; Not that Jesus gives him *carte blanche* (Godet) to have anything that he likes; but that He will make clear to the multitude that this is no ordinary beggar, but one who has faith to ask to be healed. For the constr. see on ix. 54. Both Mt. (xiv. 19, xx. 34) and Lk. (xix. 5) use ἀναβλέψω in both senses, "look up" and "recover sight."

42. ἡ πίστις σου. The multitude had called Jesus "the Nazarene," and had tried to silence the blind man. He had called Him the "Son of David," and had persevered all the more. Mt. says that Jesus touched the eyes, but omits these words. Comp. vii. 50, viii. 48, xvii. 19.

43. παραχρῆμα. Mk. has εὐθύς: comp. v. 25, viii. 44, 55, xxii. 60. Lk. alone records that the man glorified God, and that the people followed his example; comp. ix. 43. The poetical word **αἶνος** is not rare in LXX, but occurs in N.T. only here and in a

[1] In Syr-Sin. Timai Bar-Timai "rose and *took up* his garment, and came to Jesus." Comp. Jn. xxi. 7. In Diatess.-Tat. he asks for sight, "that I may see *Thee*."

quotation from Ps. viii. 2 in Mt. xxi. 16. With αἶνον διδόναι comp δόξαν διδόναι (xvii. 18; Rom. iv. 20; Rev. iv. 9).

It is worth while to collect together the characteristics of Lk.'s style which are very conspicuous in this section, especially when it is compared with Mt. and Mk. In ver. 35 we have ἐγένετο, ἐν τῷ c. infin., and ἐπαιτῶν (only here and xvi. 3); in ver. 36, διαπορευομένου (vi. 1, xiii. 22) and ἐπυνθάνετο (xv. 26); in ver. 37, ἀπήγγειλαν (viii. 20) and παρέρχεται (xi. 42); in ver. 38, ἐβόησεν (iii. 4, ix. 38, xviii. 38); in ver. 39, σιγήσῃ (ix. 36, xx. 26) and αὐτός; in ver. 43, παραχρῆμα (v. 25) and πᾶς (vii. 35, xi. 4). In all these cases, either other expressions are used by Mt. and Mk., or they omit the idea which Lk. thus expresses.

XIX. 1–10. § The Visit to Zacchæus, the Tax-collector of Jericho. The on other grounds improbable conjecture, that we have here a distorted variation of the Call of Matthew, the Tax-collector of Capernaum, is excluded by the fact that Lk. has recorded that event (v. 27–32). Even if the two narratives were far more similar than they are, there would be no good reason for doubting that two such incidents had taken place. The case of Zacchæus illustrates the special doctrine of this Gospel, that no one is excluded from the invitation to the Kingdom of God. The source from which Lk. obtained the narrative seems to have been Aramaic. In time it is closely connected with the preceding section.

1. διήρχετο τὴν Ἰερειχώ. "He was passing through Jericho," and the meeting took place inside the city. For the verb see on ii. 15, and for the constr. comp. ii. 35; Acts xii. 10, xiii. 6, xiv. 24, etc. Apparently the meeting with Zacchæus was what detained Him in Jericho: otherwise He would have gone through without staying: comp. xxiv. 28.

2. ὀνόματι καλούμενος Ζακχαῖος. For the dat. comp. i. 61. The name, which means "pure," shows him to have been a Jew: Ezra ii. 9; Neh. vii. 14. Tertullian says, *Zacchæus, etsi allophylus, fortasse tamen aliqua notitia scripturarum ex commercio Judaico afflatus* (*Adv. Marcion.* iv. 37. 1). But the Jews murmured because Jesus lodged with a man that was a *sinner*. They would have said a *heathen*, if it had been true. See below on ver. 9. The Clementines make Zacchæus a companion of Peter, who appoints him, much against his wish, to be bishop of Cæsarea (*Hom.* iii. 63; *Recog.* iii. 66); and the *Apost. Const.* say that he was succeeded by Cornelius (vii. 46). Clem. Alex. says he was identified with Matthias (*Strom.* iv. 6. p. 579). The Talmud mentions a Zacchæus who lived at Jericho and was father of the celebrated Rabbi Jochanan. He might be of the same family as this Zacchæus. The use of ἀνήρ here (comp. i. 27, viii. 41, xxiii. 50) rather than ἄνθρωπος (comp. ii. 25, vi. 6) perhaps is no mark of dignity: see ver. 7.

καὶ αὐτὸς ἦν ἀρχιτελώνης καὶ αὐτὸς πλούσιος. Note the double *καὶ αὐτός*, and see on v. 14 and vi. 20.

The second *καὶ αὐτός* (B K U Π, Vulg.) is doubtful: om. D, d e; *καὶ οὗτος ἦν* (A Q R); *καὶ ἦν* (ℵ L, Boh. Goth.). The last may be right.

ἀρχιτελώνης. This is evidently an official title, and means more than that Zacchæus was a very rich tax-collector (Didon). Had that been the meaning, we should have *ὅτι* or *γάρ* instead of *καί*. Perhaps we may render, "Commissioner of Taxes." The word occurs nowhere else, and the precise nature of the office cannot be ascertained. Probably he was intermediate between the *portitores* and the *publicani*, and by the Romans would have been called *magister*. Jericho, as a large frontier city, through which much of the carrying trade passed, and which had a large local trade in costly balsams, would be a likely place for a commissioner of taxes. This is the sixth notice of the tax-collectors, all favourable, in this Gospel (iii. 12, v. 27, vii. 29, xv. 1, xviii. 10).

3. ἐζήτει ἰδεῖν. Not like Herod (xxiii. 8), but like the Greeks (Jn. xii. 21). He had heard of Him, and perhaps as mixing freely with publicans and sinners. *Fama notum vultu noscere cupiebat* (Grotius). For the indic. after *τίς* dependent comp. Acts xxi. 33.

οὐκ ἠδύνατο ἀπὸ τοῦ ὄχλου. The multitude was the *source* of the hindrance. Comp. xxi. 26, xxiv. 41; Acts xii. 14, xxii. 11; Jn. xxi. 6; Heb. v. 7. His being unable to *free himself from* the throng is not the meaning of the *ἀπό*. In class. Grk. we should have *διά* with acc. For ἡλικίᾳ see on ii. 52.

4. εἰς τὸ ἔμπροσθεν. Strengthens the *προδραμών*. He ran on to that part of the city which was in front of Christ's route. There is nothing to show that he wished to *hide*, and that Christ's call to him was like His making the woman with the issue disclose her act (Trench). On the other hand, there is no evidence that he braved the derision of the crowd. We may say, however, that no thought of personal dignity or propriety deterred him from his purpose.

TR. omits *εἰς τό*, which is sufficiently attested by ℵ B L, *processit in priore et* (e), *antecedens ab ante* (d), D having *προλαβών* for *προδραμών*.

συκομορέαν. "A fig-mulberry," quite a different tree from the fig and the mulberry and the common sycomore. Its fruit is like the fig, and its leaf like the mulberry, and hence the name. The *συκάμινος* of xvii. 6 is commonly held to be the mulberry, but may be another name for the fig-mulberry, as Groser thinks. The fig-mulberry "recalls the English oak, and its shade is most pleasing. It is consequently a favourite wayside tree. . . . It is very easy to climb, with its short trunk, and its wide lateral branches forking out in all directions" (Tristram, *Nat. Hist. of B.* p. 398).

The MSS. vary much, but all early uncials except A have -*μορέα* and not -*μοραία*; and -*μορέα* is much better attested than -*μωρέα* or -*μωραία*. The common form is *συκόμορος*.

With *ἐκείνης sc.* *ὁδοῦ* comp. *ποίας*, v. 19.

For the sudden change of subject, *ἀνέβη . . . ἤμελλεν*, comp. xiv. 5, xv. 15, xvii. 2; and for the subjunctive after a past tense, *ἀνέβη . . . ἵνα ἴδῃ*, comp. vi. 7, xviii. 15, 39; Jn. iv. 8, vii. 32.

5. Ζακχαῖε. There is no need to assume that Jesus had supernatural knowledge of the name: Jn. iv. 17, 18 is not parallel. Jesus might hear the people calling to Zacchæus, or might enquire. And He seems not to use His miraculous power of knowledge when He could obtain information in the usual way (Mk. viii. 5; Jn. xi. 34). The explanation that He thereby showed Zacchæus that He knew all about him, is not adequate. Would Zacchæus have inferred this from being addressed by name?

σπεύσας κατάβηθι. He had made haste to see Christ: he must make haste to receive Him. *Accepit plus quam sperabat, qui, quod potuit, fecit* (Maldon.). As in the case of Nathanael (Jn. i. 47), Jesus knew the goodness of the man's heart. Here supernatural knowledge, necessary for Christ's work, is quite in place. For *σπεύδειν* see on ii. 16.

σήμερον γὰρ ἐν τῷ οἴκῳ σου. First, with emphasis. "This very day; in thy *house*." For δεῖ of the Divine counsels see on iv. 43. Taken in conjunction with *καταλῦσαι* (ver. 7), μεῖναι possibly means "to pass the night." But neither word necessarily means staying for more than a long rest.

7. πάντες διεγόγγυζον. Note the characteristic *πάντες*, and comp. v. 30, xv. 2. It was not jealousy, but a sense of outraged propriety, which made them all murmur.

Παρὰ ἁμαρτωλῷ. First, with emphasis. They allude, not to the personal character of Zacchæus, but to his calling. For *παρά* unelided before a vowel see small print on xviii. 27, and Gregory, *Prolegom.* p. 95.

καταλῦσαι. Only here and ix. 12 in N.T. has *καταλύω* the classical meaning of "loosing one's garments and resting from a journey": comp. Gen. xix. 2, xxiv. 23, 25; Ecclus. xiv. 25, 27, xxxvi. 31. Elsewhere in N.T. it means "throw down, destroy" (xxi. 6; Acts v. 38, vi. 14, etc.).

8. σταθείς. Perhaps indicates a set attitude: see on xviii. 11. It is a solemn act done with formality. The narrative represents this declaration as the immediate result of personal contact with the goodness of Christ. He is overwhelmed by Christ's condescension in coming to him, and is eager to make a worthy acknowledgment. That he was stung by the reproach *παρὰ ἁμαρτωλῷ ἀνδρί*, and wished to prove that he was not so great a sinner, is less probable. The *δέ* does not show that Zacchæus is answering his accusers, but that Lk. contrasts his conduct with theirs.

The solemn declaration is addressed πρὸς τὸν κύριον, not to them; and the Ἰδού with which it begins indicates a sudden resolution, rather than one which had been slowly reached.

τὰ ἡμίσια. "MSS. clearly certify to τὰ ἡμίσια (L alone has ἡμίσεια), apparently from a form ἡμίσιος, against τὰ ἥμισυ and still more against τὰ ἡμίση: this peculiar form occurs in an inscription from Selinus in Cilicia (*C.I.G.* 4428)." WH. ii. App. p. 158. But editors are much divided. Lach. ἡμίσεα, Treg. Tisch. and Weiss ἡμίσεια, TR. and RV. ἡμίση, WH. ἡμίσια. May not ἡμίσεια and ἡμίσια be mere mistakes for ἡμίσεα, and ἡμίση be a supposed improvement? The neut. plur. depends upon the neut. plur. of τῶν ὑπαρχόντων. Comp. τῶν νήσων τὰς ἡμίσεας (Hdt. ii. 10. 4); οἱ ἡμίσεις τῶν ἄρτων (Xen. *Cyr.* iv. 5. 4). For **τὰ ὑπάρχοντα** see on viii. 3.

τοῖς πτωχοῖς δίδωμι. "I hereby give to the poor": it is an act done there and then. The present tense might mean "I am in the habit of giving" (Godet); but this is not likely. For (1) this makes Zacchæus a boaster; (2) τῶν ὑπαρχόντων has to be interpreted "income," whereas its natural meaning is "that which one has possessed all along, capital"; (3) ἀποδίδωμι must follow δίδωμι, and it is improbable that Zacchæus was in the habit of making fourfold restitution for *inadvertent* acts of injustice; and a man so scrupulous as to restore fourfold would not often commit acts of *deliberate* injustice. Standing in Christ's presence, he solemnly makes over half his great wealth to the poor, and with the other half engages to make reparation to those whom he has defrauded. So Iren. Tertul. Ambr. Chrys. Euthym. Theoph. Maldon. etc. Aug. and Euthym. suggest that he kept one half, not to possess it, but to have the means of restitution. That he left all and became a follower of Christ (Ambr.) is not implied, but may eventually have taken place.

εἴ τινός τι ἐσυκοφάντησα. The indic. shows that he is not in doubt about past malpractices: "if, as I know is the case, I have," etc. Comp. Rom. v. 17; Col. ii. 20, iii. 1. For **συκοφαντεῖν** see on iii. 14, the only other place in N.T. in which the verb occurs: in LXX it is not rare. The constr. τινός τι is on the analogy of ἀποστερεῖν and similar verbs.

ἀποδίδωμι τετραπλοῦν. This was almost the extreme penalty imposed by the Law, when a man was *compelled* to make reparation for a deliberate act of destructive robbery (Exod. xxii. 1; 2 Sam. xii. 6). But sevenfold was sometimes exacted (Prov. vi. 31). If the stolen property had not been consumed, double was to be paid (Exod. xxii. 4, 7). When the defrauder confessed and made *voluntary* restitution, the whole amount stolen, with a fifth added, was sufficient (Lev. vi. 5; Num. v. 7). Samuel promises only simple restitution if anything is proved against him (1 Sam. xii. 3). Zacchæus is willing to treat his exactions as if they had been destructive robberies. In thus stripping himself of the chief part even of his honestly gained riches he illustrates xviii. 27. *Ecce enim camelus, deposita gibbi sarcina, per foramen acus transit, hoc est dives et publicanus, relicto onere divitiarum, contempto sensu fraudium, angustam portam arctamque viam quæ ad vitam ducit ascendit* (Bede).

9. πρὸς αὐτόν. Although Christ uses the third person, this probably means "unto him" (Mey. Hahn) rather than "in reference to him" (Grot. Nösg. Godet): see on xviii. 9. Ewald reads πρὸς αὑτόν, like πρὸς ἑαυτόν, xviii. 11, as if Jesus were thinking aloud. It is doubtful whether αὑτόν for ἑαυτόν occurs in N.T.

To avoid the difficulty some texts have the plur. πρὸς αὐτούς (R), *ad illos* (a b c ff_2 i l s), and some omit (d e, Cypr.). Some MSS. of Vulg. have *ad eos* or *ad illos* for *ad eum.*

ὅτι Σήμερον. The ὅτι is merely recitative and is not to be translated. The σήμερον confirms the view that δίδωμι and ἀποδίδωμι refer to a present resolve and not to a past practice.

σωτηρία . . . ἐγένετο. A favourite constr. with Lk. See on iv. 36. Only on this occasion did Jesus offer Himself as a guest, although He sometimes accepted invitations. Just as it was to a despised schismatic (Jn. iv. 26), and to a despised outcast from the synagogue (Jn. ix. 37), that He made a spontaneous revelation of His Messiahship, so it is a despised tax-collector that He selects for this spontaneous visit. In each case He knew that the recipient had a heart to welcome His gift: and it is in this welcome, and not in the mere visit, that the σωτηρία consisted.[1]

That **τῷ οἴκῳ τούτῳ** is said rather than τῷ ἀνδρὶ τούτῳ probably means that the blessing extends to the whole household; rather than that Jesus is alluding to the hospitality which He has received under this roof. In any case it is to be noted that it is the house which has suddenly lost half its wealth, and not the poor who have the promise of abundant alms, that Jesus declares to have received a blessing. To this occasion we may apply, and possibly to this occasion belongs, the one saying of Christ which is not recorded in the Gospels, and which we yet know to have been His, "It is more blessed to give than to receive" (Acts xx. 35).

καθότι καὶ αὐτὸς υἱὸς Ἀβραάμ. This is conclusive as to Z. being a Jew. The words cannot be understood exclusively in a spiritual sense, as Cyprian seems to take them (*Ep.* lxiii. 4, ed. Hartel). Chrysostom points out the moral sonship: Abraham offered his heir to the Lord, Zacchæus his inheritance. Comp. xiii. 16, and see Weiss, *L. J.* ii. p. 438, Eng. tr. iii. p. 221. For **καθότι**, which is peculiar to Lk., see small print on i. 7. The meaning is that he also, as much as any one else, is an Israelite.

[1] In the Roman Church this verse is part of the gospel in the service for the dedication of churches.

"His detested calling has not cancelled his birthright. My visit to him, and his receiving salvation, are entirely in harmony with the Divine Will" (ver. 5).

10. ἦλθεν. First with emphasis: "He *came* for this very purpose." The γάρ explains σωτηρία ἐγένετο: salvation to such as Z. is the object of His Epiphany. For the neut. of a collective whole, **τὸ ἀπολωλός**, comp. Jn. vi. 37, xvii. 2, 24; and for the thought, Lk. xv. 6, 9, 32; Ezek. xxxiv. 16. The expression is no evidence that Zacchæus was a heathen. Comp. τὰ ἀπολωλότα οἴκου Ἰσραήλ (Mt. x. 6, xv. 24).

11–28. § The Parable of the Pounds. It is probable that this is distinct from the Parable of the Talents (Mt. xxv. 14–30; comp. Mk. xiii. 34–36). It is more likely that Jesus should utter somewhat similar parables on different occasions than that Mt. or Lk. should have made very serious confusion as to the details of the parable as well as regards the time and place of its delivery.

Here Jesus is approaching Jerusalem, but has not yet entered it in triumph: apparently He is still in Jericho. In Mt. He is on the Mount of Olives a day or two after the triumphal entry. Here He addresses a mixed company publicly. In Mt. He is speaking privately to His disciples (xxiv. 3). Besides the difference in detail where the two narratives are parallel, there is a great deal in Lk. which is not represented in Mt. at all. The principal items are: (1) the introduction, ver. 11; (2) the high birth of the chief agent and his going into a far country to receive for himself a kingdom, ver. 12; (3) his citizens hating him and sending an ambassage after him to repudiate him, ver. 14; (4) the signal vengeance taken upon these enemies, ver. 27; (5) the conclusion, ver. 28. Strauss supposes that Lk. has mixed up two parables, the Parable of the Pounds, which is only another version of the Parable of the Talents in Mt., and another which might be called the Parable of the Rebellious Citizens, consisting of *vv.* 12, 14, 15, 27. Without denying the possibility of this hypothesis, one may assert that it is unnecessary. As regards the Talents and the Pounds, Chrysostom pronounces them to be distinct, while Augustine implies that they are so, for he makes no attempt to harmonize them in his *De Consensu Evangelistarum*. Even in the parts that are common to the two parables the differences are very considerable. (1) In the Talents we have a householder leaving home for a time, in the Pounds a nobleman going in quest of a crown; (2) the Talents are unequally distributed, the Pounds equally; (3) the sums entrusted differ enormously in amount; (4) in the Talents the rewards are the same, in the Pounds they differ and are proportionate to what has been gained; (5) in the Talents the unprofitable servant is severely punished, in the Pounds he is merely deprived of his pound. Out of about 302 words in Mt. and 286 in Lk., only about 66 words or parts of words are common to the two. An estimate of the probabilities on each side seems to be favourable to the view that we have accurate reports of two different parables, and not two reports of the same parable, one of which, if not both, must be very inaccurate. And, while both parables teach that we must make good use of the gifts entrusted to us, that in Mt. refers to those gifts which are unequally distributed, that in Lk. to those in which all share alike. See Wright, *Synopsis*, § 138, p. 127.

The lesson of the parable before us is twofold. To the *disciples* of all classes it teaches the necessity of patiently waiting and actively working for Christ until He comes again. To the *Jews* it gives a solemn warning respecting the deadly opposition which they are now exhibiting, and which will be continued even after His departure. There will be heavy retribution for those who persistently reject their lawfully appointed King. This portion of the parable is of special interest, because there is little doubt that it was suggested by contemporary history. Herod the Great, appointed procurator of Galilee by Julius Cæsar B.C. 47 and tetrarch by Antony B.C. 41, went to Rome B.C. 40 to oppose the claims of Antigonus, and was made king of Judæa by the senate (Jos. *Ant.* xiv. 7. 3, 9. 2, 13. 1, 14. 4; *B. J.* i. 14. 4). His son Archelaus in like manner went to Rome to obtain the kingdom which his father, by a change in his will, had left to him instead of to Antipas. The Jews revolted and sent an ambassage of fifty to oppose him at Rome. Augustus, after hearing them and the Jews on the spot, confirmed Herod's will, but did not allow Archelaus the title of king until he had proved his worthiness. This he never did; but he got his "kingdom" with the title of ethnarch (*Ant.* xvii. 8. 1, 9. 3, 11. 4; *B. J.* ii. 6. 1, 3). All this had taken place B.C. 4, in which year Antipas also went to Rome to urge his own claims against those of Archelaus. His more famous attempt to obtain the title of king did not take place until after this, and cannot be alluded to here. The remarkable feature of the opposing embassy makes the reference to Archelaus highly probable; and Jericho, which he had enriched with buildings, would suggest his case as an illustration. But the reference is by some held to be fictitious, by others is made a reason for suspecting that the author of this detail is not Christ but the Evangelist (Weiss).

11. Ἀκουόντων δὲ αὐτῶν ταῦτα. These words connect the parable closely with what precedes. The scene is still Jericho, in or near the house of Zacchæus; and, as **ταῦτα** seems to refer to the saying about *σωτηρία* (*vv.* 9, 10), **αὐτῶν** probably refers to the disciples and those with Zacchæus. The belief that the Kingdom was close at hand, and that Jesus was now going in triumph to Jerusalem, was probably general among those who accompanied Him, and the words just uttered might seem to confirm it. "*But because* they heard these things" (Mey.) is, however, not quite the meaning: rather, "*And as* they heard" (AV. RV.); *hæc illis audientibus* (Vulg.).

Here Cod. Bezae has one of its attempts to reproduce the gen. abs. in Latin: *audientium autem eorum*; comp. iii. 15, ix. 43, xxi. 5, 26, etc.

προσθεὶς εἶπεν παραβολήν. Not, "He spoke, and added a parable" to what He spoke; but, "He added and spoke a parable" in connexion with what had preceded. *Moris est Domino, præmissum sermonem parabolis adfirmare subjectis* (Bede). It is a Hebraistic construction: comp. Gen. xxxviii. 5; Job xxix. 1; Gen.

xxv. 1. In Lk. xx. 11, 12; Acts xii. 3; Gen. iv. 2, viii. 12 we have another form of the same idiom, προσέθετο πέμψαι, etc. See also on vi. 39 for εἶπεν παραβολήν.

The Latin equivalents are interesting: *addidit dicens* (a), *adjecit et dixit* (e), *addidit dicere* (s), *adjiciens dixit* (Vulg.). See also xx. 11.

διὰ τὸ ἐγγὺς εἶναι Ἰ. About six hours' march; 150 stades (Jos. *B. J.* iv. 8. 3), or about 18 miles. The goal was almost in sight the arrival could not be much longer delayed.

παραχρῆμα μέλλει . . . ἀναφαίνεσθαι. It is against this that the parable is specially directed. The Messiah was there Jerusalem was only a few hours distant; the inauguration of the Kingdom must be *imminent*: παραχρῆμα is placed first with emphasis. The μέλλει, "is sure to," and ἀναφαίνεσθαι, "come to view," are both appropriate: they believed that they were *certain* of a glorious *pageant.* Comp. Acts i. 6.

12. εὐγενής. In a literal sense here and 1 Cor. i. 26; comp Job i. 3: in a figurative sense Acts xvii. 11; comp. 4 Mac. vi. 5 ix. 23, 27. The μακράν, which is probably an adj. as in xv. 13 has obvious reference to παραχρῆμα: the distance would exclude an immediate return. Note the τις.

λαβεῖν ἑαυτῷ βασιλείαν. If we had not the illustrations from contemporary history, this would be a surprising feature in the parable. He is a vassal of high rank going to a distant suzerain to obtain royal authority over his fellow-vassals. For **ὑποστρέψαι** see small print on i. 56; it tells us that the desired βασιλεία is at the starting point, not at a distance.

13. He plans that, during his absence, servants of his private household shall be tested, with a view to their promotion when he is appointed to be king.

δέκα δούλους ἑαυτοῦ. "Ten bond-servants of his own." It does not follow, because we have not δέκα τῶν δ. αὑτοῦ, that he had only ten slaves. This would require τοὺς δ. δ., and would be very improbable; for an Oriental noble would have scores of slaves. The point of ἑαυτοῦ (? "his *household* slaves") is, that among them, if anywhere, he would be likely to find fidelity to his interests. As he merely wishes to test them, the sum committed to each is small,—about £4. In the Talents the householder divides the whole of his property (τὰ ὑπάρχοντα αὑτοῦ), and hence the sums entrusted to each slave are very large.

Πραγματεύσασθε. "Carry on business," especially as a banker or a trader: here only in N.T., and in LXX only Dan. viii. 27 and some texts of 1 Kings ix. 19. Vulg. has *negotiamini* (not *occupate*), which Wic. renders "chaffare." The "occupy" of Rhem. and AV. comes from Cov. and Cran., while Tyn. has "buy and sell." We have a similar use of "occupy" Ezek. xxvii. 9, 16, 19, 21, 22, where Vulg. has *negotiatio* and *negotiator*: comp. "occupy their business in great waters" (Ps. cvii. 23).

Latimer exhibits the same use of "occupy"; and in a letter of Thomas Cromwell to Michael Throgmorton, A.D. 1537, he calls Pole "a merchant and *occupier* of all deceits" (Froude, *His. of Eng.* ch. xiv.). "Occupy till I come" is now misunderstood to mean "keep possession till I come."

WH. are alone in reading *πραγματεύσασθαι* here. All other editors make the verb 2nd pers. plur. imper. not infin. WH. regard the decision difficult both here and xiv. 17, but prefer the infin. here as "justified by St. Luke's manner of passing from *oratio obliqua* to *oratio recta*" (ii. p. 309).

ἐν ᾧ ἔρχομαι. "During the time in which I am coming," *i.e.* the time until the return. For *ἔρχομαι* in the sense of "come back" comp. Jn. iv. 16 and esp. xxi. 22, 23. The meaning "to be on the journey" (Oosterz. Godet) is impossible for *ἔρχεσθαι*. The reading *ἕως* (TR. with E etc.) is an obvious correction of *ἐν ᾧ* (ℵ A B D K L R etc.).

14. While the δοῦλοι represent the disciples, the πολῖται represent the Jews. The Jews hated Jesus without cause, *ἐμίσησάν με δωρεάν* (Jn. xv. 25; Ps. lxviii. 5): but they had reason enough for hating Archelaus, who had massacred about 3000 of them at the first Passover after his accession (*Ant.* xvii. 9. 3; *B. J.* ii. 1. 3).

Οὐ θέλομεν τοῦτον. They state no reasons: *stat pro ratione voluntas.* The τοῦτον is contemptuous (*istum*), or at least expresses alienation: "he is no man of ours." So the Jews, of Christ.

15. For **Καὶ ἐγένετο . . . καὶ εἶπεν** see note p. 45, and for **ἐν τῷ ἐπανελθεῖν** see on iii. 21. The double compound occurs only here and x. 35 in N.T. Comp. *ἐπανάγειν* (v. 3, 4). Both verbs occur in LXX.

τοὺς δούλους τούτους οἷς. This implies that he had other slaves to whom nothing had been entrusted.

ἵνα γνοῖ. For this form comp. Mk. v. 43 and ix. 30. TR. with A etc. has *γνῷ* in all three places. The *τίς* after *γνοῖ* (A R, Syrr. Arm. Goth. Vulg.) is not genuine: om. ℵ B D L, Boh. Aeth. d e.

τί διεπραγματεύσαντο. "What business they had done": here only in bibl. Grk. In Dion. Hal. iii. 72, it means "attempt to execute." He wants to know the *result* of their trafficking. But the word does not assume that they have "*gained* by trading" (AV. RV.); and hence *negotiatus esset* (Vulg.) is better than *lucratus esset* (f).

16. ἡ μνᾶ σου προσηργάσατο. "Thy pound worked out in addition, won": *modeste lucrum acceptum fert herili pecuniæ, non industriæ suæ* (Grot.). Comp. *οὐκ ἐγὼ δὲ ἀλλὰ ἡ χάρις τοῦ Θεοῦ* [*ἡ*] *σὺν ἐμοί* (1 Cor. xv. 10): see also 1 Cor. iv. 7. The verb occurs here only in bibl. Grk. Comp. Mt. xxv. 16.

17. εὖγε. In replies approving what has been said this is classical; but the reading is doubtful: *εὖγε* (B D, Latt., Orig. Ambr.), *εὖ*, possibly from Mt. xxv. 21 (ℵ A R etc., Syrr.).

ἐν ἐλαχίστῳ πιστὸς ἐγένου. "Thou didst prove faithful in a very little": comp. xvi. 10. The management of £4 was a small matter.

ἴσθι ἐξουσίαν ἔχων. The periphrastic pres. imper. is not common in N.T. Comp. Gen. i. 6; Burton, § 97. Lk. is probably translating: Mt. is much more classical: ἐπὶ πολλῶν σε καταστήσω (xxv. 21). For ἐξουσίαν ἔχειν comp. Mt. vii. 29.

18. With ἐποίησεν πέντε μνᾶς comp. εἰ μή εἴ τις αὐτῶν ἀργύριον ποιεῖ (Plat *Rep.* ix. 581 C): *pecuniam facere* is fairly common.

19. ἐπάνω γίνου. "Come to be over, be promoted over." In both cases the efficient servants "receive as their reward,—not anything they can sit down to and enjoy,—but a wider sphere of activity" (Latham, *Pastor Pastorum*, p. 320). *Urbs pro minâ; minâ ne tugurium quidem emeretur. Magna rerum amplitudo ac varietas in regno Dei, quamvis nondum cognita nobis* (Beng.).

20. καὶ ὁ ἕτερος. The omission of the article in A and inferior MSS. is a manifest correction to avoid a difficulty. As there were ten servants, the third cannot rightly be spoken of as ὁ ἕτερος. Weiss takes this as evidence that in the original parable there were only three servants, as in the Talents; and therefore as evidence that the two narratives represent the same original. But it would have been tedious to have gone through all the ten, which is a round number, as in the Ten Virgins. The three mentioned are samples of the whole ten. Some gained immensely, some considerably, and some not at all. The two first classes having been described, the representative of the remaining class may be spoken of as ὁ ἕτερος, especially as he is of quite a different kind. They both belong to the profitable division, he to the unprofitable.

ἣν εἶχον ἀποκειμένην. "Which I was keeping stored up." He is not owning a fault, but professing a virtue: "I have not lost or spent any of it." In Col. i. 5; 2 Tim. iv. 8; Heb. ix. 27 the verb is used of what is "stored up" and awaits us in the future: here only in a literal sense.

σουδαρίῳ. A Latinism: *sudarium* (Acts xix. 12; Jn. xi. 44, xx. 7). Comp. ἀσσάριον (xii. 6), λεγιών (viii. 30), δηνάριον (x. 35), κεντυρίων (Mk. xv. 39), κοδράντης (Mt. v. 26), etc.

21. αὐστηρός. Here only in N.T. Comp. 2 Mac. xiv. 30, and see Trench, *Syn.* xiv. The word originally means "rough to the taste, stringent." It is in this servant's plea and in the reply to it that the resemblance between the two parables of the Pounds and of the Talents is closest.

αἴρεις ὃ οὐκ ἔθηκας. Perhaps a current proverbial expression for a grasping person. We need not decide whether he means, "If I had gained anything, you would have taken it," or, "If I had lost it, you would have held me responsible." The general sense is, "You are a strict man; and I have taken care that you should get back the exact deposit, neither more nor less."

22. κρίνω σε. "Do I judge thee"; *te judico* (f Vulg.), *condemno* (e). Most editors prefer κρινῶ, "will I judge" (AV. RV.); *judicabo* (a d). But Tyn. has "judge I thee" and Luth. *richte ich dich*. Hist. pres. (λέγει, xiii. 8, xvi. 7, 29) is very rare in Lk.

The Latin Versions vary greatly in rendering πονηρέ: *inique* (d), *infidelis* (e ff_2 i r), *crudelis* (b), *nequa et piger* (f), *infidelis et piger* (q), *infidelis et male* (a), *nequam* (Vulg.). Comp. Mt. xviii. 32. The *piger* comes from Mt. xxv. 26, πονηρὲ δοῦλε καὶ ὀκνηρέ.

23. ἐπὶ τράπεζαν. "On a banker's table." Here the interrogation ends, and κἀγώ begins a declaratory sentence. It would have been very little trouble to put it in a bank. There the money would have been as safe as in the napkin, and would have borne interest. See Hastings, *D.B.* i. p. 580.

The often quoted saying, "Show yourselves tried bankers," Γίνεσθε τραπεζῖται δόκιμοι, may easily be a genuine utterance of Christ. But if it is a mere adaptation, it comes from Mt. xxv. 27 rather than from Lk. See Resch, *Agrapha*, pp. 118, 234; Wsctt. *Int. to Gosp.* App. C.

τόκῳ. In N.T. the word occurs only in these parables; but is freq. in LXX; Deut. xxiii. 19; Lev. xxv. 36, 37; Exod. xxii. 25, etc. The notion that money, being a dead thing, ought not to *breed* (τεκεῖν, τόκος), augmented the prejudice of the ancients against interest Aristotle condemns it as παρὰ φύσιν (*Pol.* i. 10. 4; comp. *Eth. Nic.* iv. 1. 40). Cicero represents Cato as putting it on a level with murder (*De Off.* ii. 25. 89). "The breed of barren metal" (Shaks.).

ἂν αὐτὸ ἔπραξα. The protasis is readily understood from the previous question: comp. Heb. x. 2. For this use of πράσσειν see on iii. 13.

24. τοῖς παρεστῶσιν. His attendants, or body-guard, or courtiers: comp. 1 Kings x. 8; Esth. iv. 5. The man who had proved most efficient in service is rewarded with an additional sum with which to traffick for his sovereign.

25. The subject of εἶπαν and the meaning of αὐτῷ are uncertain. The common interpretation is that *the attendants* who have received this order here express their surprise to *the master* who gave it; *i.e.* the remonstrance is part of the parable. But it is possible that Lk. is here recording an interruption on the part of the audience, and thus lets us see with what keen interest they have listened to the narrative. It is the *audience* who remonstrate with *Christ* for giving the story such a turn. They think that He is spoiling the parable in assigning the unused pound to the servant who has most and therefore seems to need it least (see on xx. 15). But in any case the remonstrance serves to give point to the declaration which follows. Comp. Peter's interruption and Christ's apparent ignoring of it xii. 41, 42; and again xviii. 28, 29. In all the cases there is an indirect answer. A general principle is stated which covers the point in question.

Bleek rejects ver. 25 as an interpolation: om. D 69, b d e ff_2 q_2 Syr-Cur. Syr-Sin. The difficulty might cause the omission. The insertion of γάρ after λέγω in ver. 26 (A D R, Syrr. Goth.) is due to a similar cause. Both omission and insertion may be influenced by Mt. xxv. 28, 29.

26. λέγω ὑμῖν. Whose words are these? The answer will partly depend upon the view taken of ver. 25. If the interruption is made by the king's attendants, then ver. 26, like ver. 24 and ver. 27, gives the words of the king. But if the interruption comes from Christ's audience, then ver. 26 may be His reply to the audience; after which He finishes the parable with the king's words in ver. 27. The λέγω ὑμῖν does not prove that Christ is giving these words as His own: comp. xiv. 24. But in any case, either in His own person or in that of the king in the parable, Jesus is stating a principle which answers the objection in ver. 25. In Mt. xxv. 29 this principle is uttered by the householder in the parable without λέγω ὑμῖν.

ἀπὸ δὲ τοῦ μὴ ἔχοντος. With this apparent paradox comp. viii. 18, when an unused gift is spoken of, not as ὃ ἔχει, but as ὃ δοκεῖ ἔχειν. He alone possesses, who uses and enjoys his possessions.

27. πλὴν τοὺς ἐχθρούς μου τούτους. The τούτους represents the enemies as present to the thoughts of the audience: comp. τούτους in ver. 15. It is possible to take the pronoun with what follows, as in Syr-Sin.: "Bring hither mine enemies, those who would not," etc. And this makes one more witness for the reading ἐκείνους (A D R etc., Latt. Syrr. Goth.), which almost all editors reject as a correction of τούτους (ℵ B K L M Π, Aegyptt.). For πλήν comp. xviii. 8.

κατασφάξατε αὐτοὺς ἔμπροσθέν μου. Comp. ἔσφαξεν Σαμουὴλ τὸν Ἀγὰγ ἐνώπιον Κυρίου (1 Sam. xv. 33). The punishment of rebellious subjects and active opponents is far more severe than that of neglectful servants. The compound κατασφάζω occurs nowhere else in N.T., but is not rare in LXX. It means "hew them down, slay them utterly." The destruction of Jerusalem and the doom of all who deliberately rebel against Christ are here foreshadowed. Augustine more than once points to this sentence in answer to the objection that the severe God of the O.T. cannot be identical with the God of Love in the N.T. In the Gospels, as in the Law, the severity of God's judgments against wilful disobedience is plainly taught. Comp. *Con. Faust.* xxii. 14. 19.

The nobleman, who goes on a long journey and returns a

king, is Christ. He leaves behind Him servants of various degrees of merit, and enemies. When the King returns, each of these is rewarded or punished according to his deserts; and the rewards are larger opportunities of service. There is no special meaning in ten, which is a round number; nor in three, which gives a sufficiently representative classification. And it may be doubted whether there is any special meaning in the *transfer* of the pound from the unprofitable to the most profitable servant. The point is that *to neglect opportunities is to lose them*; and that *to make the most of opportunities is to gain others.* The main lesson of the parable is *the long period of Christ's absence*, during which there will be abundant time for both service and rebellion. There is not to be, as the disciples fancied, *immediate* triumph and joy for *all*; but, first a long time of probation, and then triumph and joy for those only who have earned them, and in exact proportion to their merits.

28. Historical conclusion, corresponding to the historical introduction in ver. 11.

ἐπορεύετο ἔμπροσθεν. "He went on before." Although the αὐτῶν is not expressed, this probably means "in front of the disciples": comp. Mk. x. 32. But ἔμπροσθεν may = εἰς τὸ ἔμπροσθεν (ver. 4), as ὀπίσω = εἰς τὰ ὀπίσω (Mt. xxiv. 18): in which case the meaning would be, "He went forwards" from Jericho towards Jerusalem. With **ἀναβαίνων** comp. **κατέβαινεν** (x. 30) of the opposite route.

D omits ἔμπροσθεν and a d have simply *ibat*; c ff$_2$ i l q r s *abiit*, while Vulg. has *præcedebat*. D inserts δέ after ἀναβαίνων. Syr-Sin. reads, "And when He had said these things, *they* went *out from there. And* as He was going up to Jerusalem, and had reached Bethphage," etc.

XIX. 29–XXI. 38. THE LAST DAYS OF PUBLIC TEACHING.

29–40. The Triumphal Procession to Jerusalem. Mt. xxi. 1–11; Mk. xi. 1–11. Comp. Jn. xii. 1–19. "The Journeyings towards Jerusalem" are over, and Lk. now permanently rejoins the other Gospels in describing the concluding scenes. As compared with them, he has both additions and omissions. He omits the supper at Bethany in the house of Simon the leper, which Mt. and Mk. place without date after the triumphal entry, but which Jn. states to have taken place before the entry. Lk. has already given a similar incident, a meal at which Jesus is a guest and a woman anoints Him (vii. 36–50), and perhaps for that reason omits the supper at Bethany. The chronology may be tentatively arranged thus. Jn. tells us that Jesus arrived at Bethany six days before the Passover, viz. Nisan 8, a day on which pilgrims often arrived at Jerusalem, as Josephus states. *Assuming* that the year is A.D. 30, Nisan 8 would be Friday, March 31. Jesus and His disciples reached Bethany that afternoon, either before the sabbath began, or after having done no more than "a sabbath day's journey" after it began. But the chronology of these last days, as of the whole of our Lord's life, is uncertain. At Bethany He would part from the large caravan of pilgrims in whose company He had been travelling. Most of these would press on to Jerusalem. See Wieseler, *Chron. Syn.* v. 2, Eng. tr. p. 358, and comp. Caspari, *Chron. Einl.* § 165, Eng. tr p. 217.

29. Βηθφαγή. Accent, derivation, and site are all doubtful. But Βηθφαγή is preferable to Βηθφαγῆ; the meaning is probably "House of unripe figs," and the situation must have been near Bethany. See Robinson, *Res. in Pal.* i. 433; Stanley, *Sin. & Pal.* p. 422; *D.B.*[2] *s.v.* Caspari, following Lightfoot, contends that Bethphage was not a village, but a whole district, including Bethany and all that lay between it and Jerusalem. The meaning in this case would be, that Jesus drew near to the district Bethphage and to the particular spot in it called Bethany (*Chron. Einl.* § 144, 145, Eng. tr. pp. 189–191). The passage is worthy of study. In N.T. Bethphage is mentioned in these three narratives only; in O.T. not at all. The Talmud says that it was east of the walls of Jerusalem. Origen, Eusebius, and Jerome knew it, but do not describe its position. Its being placed first points to its being more important than Bethany.

The derivation of *Bethany* is still more uncertain, but its site is well ascertained. The conjecture "House of dates" is confirmed by the adjacent "House of figs" and "Mount of olives." The names point to the ancient fertility of the neighbourhood.

τὸ καλούμενον Ἐλαιῶν. Here also there is doubt about the accent, which in this case, as in *κρίνω* (ver. 22), affects the meaning. In Mt. and Mk. the article, *τῶν* Ἐλαιῶν, shows that the word is gen. plur.; but here, with Lach. Tisch. Treg. and others, we may write Ἐλαιών, as nom. sing. In that case the name is treated as a sound and not declined. In xxi. 37 the same doubt arises. Acts i. 12 we have Ἐλαιῶνος, as in *Ant.* vii. 9. 2, from Ἐλαιών, *Olivetum*, "an olive-grove, Olivet." But ver. 37 and the parallels in Mt. and Mk. render Ἐλαιῶν the more probable here (WH. ii. App. p. 158: so also Hahn, Wittichen, and Wetzel). The fact that Ἐλαιῶν commonly has the article is not decisive (Field, *Otium Norvic.* iii. p. 53)

Jos. *B. J.* ii. 13. 5, v. 2. 3, vi. 2. 8 are all doubtful; but both Bekker and Dindorf edit Ἐλαιῶν in all three places. Deissmann, *Bible Studies*, p. 208.

In ver. 29 note the characteristic ἐγένετο and καλούμενον: In the latter we have an indication that Lk. is writing for those not familiar with Palestine: comp. xxi. 37, xxii. 1. Neither occurs in the parallels in Mt. and Mk. Note also ὡς = "when" and ἤγγισεν.

30. Ὑπάγετε. So also Mk., while Mt. has his favourite πορεύεσθε. The details which Mk. alone records render the conjecture that Peter was one of the two who were sent reasonable.

τὴν κατέναντι κώμην. Whether Bethany, or Bethphage, or an unnamed village, is quite uncertain. This compound preposition is not found in profane writers, but is common in bibl. Grk. (Mt. xxi. 2; Mk. xi. 2; Rom. iv. 17; 2 Cor. xii. 19; Exod. xix. 2, xxxii. 5, etc.). L. & S. *Lex.* quote *C. I.* 2905 D. 13.

ἐφ' ὃν οὐδεὶς πώποτε ἀνθρώπων ἐκάθισεν. This intimates to the disciples that it is no ordinary journey which He contemplates, but a royal progress: comp. Deut. xxi. 3; Num. xix. 2; 1 Sam. vi. 7. The birth of a virgin and the burial in a new tomb are facts of the same kind.

31. οὕτως ἐρεῖτε ὅτι. Vulg. and AV. make ὅτι the answer to Διὰ τί; So also Mey. and Hahn. But in Mt. xxi. 3 we have ὅτι and no διὰ τί; In both places the ὅτι is recitative. Comp. vii. 16, xxii. 70.

Ὁ κύριος. This rather implies that the owner has some knowledge of Jesus. Lk. omits the assurance that the owner will send the colt. That the whole had been previously arranged by Jesus is *possible*, for He gives no intimation that it was not so. But the impression produced by the narratives is that the knowledge is supernatural, which on so momentous an occasion would be in harmony with His purpose. Comp. Jn. xiv. 29, xvi. 32, xxi. 18, and see on Lk. xxii. 10, 13, 34. As Godet points out, this prophetic knowledge must not be confounded with omniscience.

32. καθὼς εἶπεν. "*Exactly* as He said." This καθώς, in slightly different connexions, is in all three narratives. Mt. has "they *did* even as He *appointed*"; Mk., "they *said* to them even He *said*"; Lk., "they *found* even as He *said*." They could not have done and said just what He had commanded, unless the facts had been such as He had foretold. Lk. and Mk., as writing for Gentiles, take no notice of the prophecy in Zech. ix. 9, which both Mt. and Jn. quote.

Justin, in order to make the incident a fulfilment of Gen. xlix. 11, "Binding his foal unto the vine," etc., says that the πῶλος was πρὸς ἄμπελον δεδεμένος (*Apol.* i. 32). Syr-Sin. omits most of *v.* 33.

33. οἱ κύριοι αὐτοῦ. The owner of the colt and those with him; τινες τῶν ἐκεῖ ἑστηκότων (Mk.). In all three narratives Jesus uses the singular. A fiction would have made exact correspondence by representing the remonstrance as coming from one person only Mt. omits the fulfilment of the predicted remonstrance.

35. αὐτῶν τὰ ἱμάτια. The pronoun stands first with emphasis: they did not spare their own chief garments. Comp. ἑαυτῶν in ver. 36.

In both verses readings vary: here TR. with A R etc. has ἑαυτῶν, while ℵ B D L, Orig. have αὐτῶν: there TR. with ℵ D has αὐτῶν, while A B K have ἑαυτῶν. The best editors are unanimous for αὐτῶν here.

ἐπεβίβασαν. Lk. alone tells us of their placing Him on the colt. The other three merely state that He sat on it.[1] Nowhere in O.T. do we find kings thus mounted. While there is much in this triumphal procession that tells of royalty, there is also something which adds, "My Kingdom is not of this world" (Godet). Against carnal chiliastic notions of the Kingdom this entry on "a colt the foal of an ass" is an *ironia realis* ordained by the Lord Himself (Nösgen, *Gesch. J. Chr.* p. 506). For ἐπιβιβάζω comp. x. 34; Acts xxiii. 24: it is not rare in LXX.

36. ὑπεστρώννυον τὰ ἱμάτια. Change of subject: it is the multitude that does this. Robinson tells how the people of Bethlehem spread their garments before the horses of the English consul and his suite (*Res. in Pal.* i. p. 473): other instances in Wetst. on Mt. xxi. 8. Lk. omits the branches strewn in the way. All three omit the multitude with palm branches coming *from* Jerusalem to meet the procession (Jn. xii. 13, 18).

37. Here every word differs from the wording of the others, although the substance is the same. As marks of style note ἅπαν, πλῆθος, φωνῇ μεγάλῃ, πασῶν ὧν. The ἤδη is amphibolous, and may be taken either with ἐγγίζοντος (AV.) or with πρὸς τῇ καταβάσει (RV.): see on xvii. 22 and xviii. 31. In either case πρὸς τῇ καταβάσει is epexegetic of ἐγγίζοντος, "When He was drawing nigh, viz. at the descent," etc. It is at the top of this descent that the S.E. corner of the "City of David" (but not the temple) comes in sight; and the view thus opening may have prompted (ἤρξαντο) this "earliest hymn of Christian devotion" (Stanley). Many of the pilgrims were from Galilee, where Jesus still had enthusiastic friends. Deissmann, *Bible Studies*, p. 232.

The reading πρὸς τὴν κατάβασιν (D) is an obvious correction. D M Γ with a d e Syrr. Aeth. omit ἤδη. In both readings D is supported by Syr-Sin., "When *they* came near to the descent," etc. With this plur. comp. that of Syr-Sin. in ver. 28.

---

[1] Mk. says ἐπ' αὐτόν (τὸν πῶλον), Jn. ἐπ' αὐτό (ὀνάριον). Mt. alone mentions both the colt and its mother and continues the plural throughout; ἐπέθηκαν ἐπ' αὐτῶν τὰ ἱμάτια, καὶ ἐπεκάθισεν ἐπάνω αὐτῶν: over which Strauss is sarcastically critical.

The Latin Versions are interesting in what follows. Nearly all MSS. of Vulg. have *omnes turbæ descendentium*, which is a mere slip for *discentium* (τῶν μαθητῶν), a reading preserved in G M of Vulg. as in Codd. Am. and Brix. *Discentes* was substituted for *discipuli* possibly to show that a larger body than the Twelve was meant. Cod. Bezae has *discentes* Jn. vi. 66, xxi. 2, while almost all have it Jn. xxi. 12, and c has it Lk. xxii. 45. Comp. Tert. *Præscr.* iii.

δυνάμεων. The healing of Bartimæus and the raising of Lazarus would be specially mentioned.

For δυνάμεων D has γεινομένων, *quæ fiebant* (d), *factis* (r); om. Syr-Cur. Syr-Sin.

38. Εὐλογημένος ὁ ἐρχόμενος . . . ἐν ὀνόματι Κυρίου. In these words all *four* agree. Lk. and Jn. add ὁ βασιλεύς, which in Mk. is represented by ἡ ἐρχομένη βασιλεία and in Mt. Ὡσαννὰ τῷ υἱῷ Δαυείδ. Lk. substitutes δόξα (more intelligible to Gentiles) for the Hosanna of the other three. See on ii. 14. "He that cometh in the name of the Lord" means God's representative, envoy, or agent. The words ἐν οὐρανῷ εἰρήνη are in Lk. alone, and are perhaps part of his paraphrase of Hosanna. Heaven is the abode of God, and there is peace there because man is reconciled to God, or perhaps because peace is now prepared for man in the heavenly Kingdom.

These cries (comp. iv. 34) clearly recognize Jesus as the Messiah. The Psalms from which they come were sung at the Passover and at the F. of Tabernacles, and hence were familiar to the people. Ps. cxviii. is said by some to have been written for the F. of Tabernacles after the Return, by others for the dedication of the second temple. The supposition that the Evangelists have confounded the Passover with the F. of Tabernacles, and have transferred to the former what was customary at the latter, is gratuitous. These responses from the Hallel were sung, not only at the Passover, but at other Feasts; and the waving of palm branches was not confined to the F. of Tabernacles (1 Mac. xiii. 51). See Edersh. *L. & T.* ii. p. 371.

Hase calls attention to the audacity of the whole transaction. Jesus and His disciples were under the ban of the hierarchy. The Sanhedrin had issued a decree that, if any one knew where He was, he should give information, that they might arrest Him (Jn. xi. 57). And yet here are His disciples bringing Him in triumph into Jerusalem, and the populace enthusiastically joining with them. Moreover, all this had been arranged by Jesus Himself, when He sent for the colt. What He had hitherto concealed, or obscurely indicated, or revealed only to a chosen few, He now, seeing that the fulness of time is come, makes known to the whole world. He publicly claims to be the Messiah. This triumphal procession is the Holy One of God making solemn entry into the Holy City. Hase is justly severe on Strauss for the way in which he changed his view from edition to edition: the truth being that the triumphal entry is an historical fact, too well attested to be discredited (*Gesch. Jesu*, § 94).

39, 40. Here Lk. is alone, not only in wording, but in substance. The remonstrance of these Pharisees is intrinsically probable. Having no power to check the multitude (Jn. xii. 19), and perhaps not daring to attempt it, they call on Jesus to do so. Possibly they wished to fasten the responsibility upon Him, and they may have been sent by the Sanhedrin to spy and report. This Messianic homage was offensive to them, and they feared a tumult which might cause trouble with Pilate.

39. **ἀπὸ τοῦ ὄχλου.** It matters very little whether we take these words with **τινες τῶν Φ.** (AV. RV.) or with **εἶπαν** (Weiss, Hahn). Perhaps **Διδάσκαλε** implies that He is no more than a teacher: it is the way in which His critics and enemies commonly address Him (vii. 40, xx. 21, 28; Mt. xii. 38, etc.). But comp. xxi. 7; Mk. iv. 38.

Syr-Sin. has, "Some of the *people* from amongst the crowd said unto **Him**, *Good* Teacher, rebuke Thy disciples, *that they shout not.*"

40. Christ's reply is of great sternness. It implies that their failure to appreciate the significance of the occasion is amazing in its fatuity. It is not likely that there is any reference to the crashing of the stones at the downfall of Jerusalem (Lange, Oosterzee). Perhaps **οἱ λίθοι κράξουσιν** was already a proverbial expression. Comp. λίθος ἐκ τοίχου βοήσεται (Hab. ii. 11): *Parietes, medius fidius, ut mihi videntur, tibi gratias agere gestiunt* (Cic. *Marcel.* iii.); and see other illustrations in Wetst. Nothing is gained by making οἱ λίθοι figurative: "men of stony hearts"; such an event "might rouse even the dullest to rejoice" (Neander). Comp. iii. 8.

ἐὰν . . . σιωπήσουσιν. This is the abundantly attested reading (ℵ A B L R Δ). With the exceptional constr. comp. ἐὰν μή τις ὁδηγήσει (Acts viii. 31); ἐὰν ὑμεῖς στήκετε (1 Thes. iii. 8); ἐὰν οἴδαμεν (1 Jn. v. 15); ἐὰν προσφέρει? (Lev. i. 14). In Jn. viii. 36 and Rom. xiv. 8 the indic. is probably a false reading. Win. xli. 2 (b), p. 369; Lft. *Epp.* p. 46; Simcox, *Lang. of N.T.* p. 110; Deissmann, *Neue Bibelstudien*, p. 29.

There is no authority for inserting *mox* (Beza), "shortely" (Genev.), or "immediately" (AV.) with "cry out."

The reading κεκράξονται (AR.) is a substitution of the form which is most common in LXX (Ps. lxiv. 14; Job xxxv. 9; Jer. xi. 11, 12, xlvii. 2, etc.). See Veitch, *s.v.* "The simple fut. perf. does not occur in N.T." Burton, § 93.

41–44. § The Predictive Lamentation of Jesus over Jerusalem. The spot where these words must have been uttered can be ascertained with certainty, although tradition, as in other cases (see on iv. 29), has fixed on an impossible site. See the famous description by Stanley, *Sin. & Pal.* pp. 190–193, together with that of Tristram (*Land of Israel*, p. 174), part of which is quoted in the Eng. tr. of Caspari's *Chron. Einl.* p. 188. See also Tristram, *Bible Places*, p. 125. This lamentation must not be confounded with the one recorded xiii. 34, 35; Mt. xxiii. 37.

41. **ἔκλαυσεν.** Stronger than ἐδάκρυσεν (Jn. xi. 35): it implies wailing and sobbing. It is used of the widow at Nain (vii. 13), the penitent in the Pharisee's house (vii. 38), and the mourners in the house of Jairus (viii. 52). It was the sight of the city and the thought of what might have been, which called forth the lamentation. The attitude of the Pharisees had just shown Him what the real condition of the city was. Christianity is sometimes accused of being opposed to the spirit of patriotism: but there is deep patriotism in this lamentation.

With ἐπ' αὐτήν comp. xxiii. 28; Rev. i. 7, xviii. 9. In class. Grk. we have ἐπ' αὐτῇ, but more often αὐτήν without a prep. Here TR. with E etc. has ἐπ' αὐτῇ.

42. Εἰ ἔγνως ἐν τῇ ἡμέρᾳ ταύτῃ καὶ σὺ τὰ πρὸς εἰρήνην—This is probably correct; but the text is somewhat uncertain. The aposiopesis is impressive. In the expression of strong emotion sentences are often broken: xxii. 42; Jn. vi. 62, xii. 27; Exod. xxxii. 32. Win. lxiv. 2, p. 749. The words imply that there have been various opportunities, of which this is the last. Thus once more (ποσάκις, xiii. 34) the synoptic narrative is found to imply the Judæan ministry recorded by Jn. The **καὶ σύ** perhaps implies no comparison: "even thou" (AV. RV.). But if "thou also" (Rhem.) be preferred, it probably means, "as well as My disciples." For the wish comp. Deut. xxxii. 29. The protasis, "If thou hadst known," does not imply any such definite apodosis as, "Thou wouldest weep as I do, for thy past blindness"; or, "Thou wouldest not perish"; or, "Thou wouldest hear Me and believe"; or, "I would rejoice like My disciples"; all of which have been suggested (Corn. à Lap. *ad loc.*). The expression is virtually a wish, "O that thou hadst known." Comp. εἰ εἶχον μάχαιραν ἐν τῇ χειρί μου (Num. xxii. 29); εἰ κατεμείναμεν καὶ κατῳκίσθημεν παρὰ τὸν Ἰορδάνην (Jos. vii. 7); εἰ ἤκουσας τῶν ἐντολῶν μου (Is. xlviii. 18). In all these places Vulg. has *utinam*, and RV. either "would that" or "O that." For **τὰ πρὸς εἰρήνην** see on xiv. 32. There is possibly an allusion to the name Jerusalem, which perhaps means "inheritance of peace."

The καί γε before ἐν τῇ ἡμέρᾳ (TR. with A R) can hardly be genuine; om. ℵ B D L, Boh. Aeth. Goth. Iren-lat. Orig. The σου after ἡμέρᾳ is still more certainly an insertion; om. ℵ A B D L, Boh. Aeth. Arm. Iren-lat. Orig. Eus. Bas. The σου after εἰρήνην has the support of Versions, but is just the kind of addition which is common in Versions; om. ℵ B L, Iren-lat. Orig. Epiph. Godet naively remarks, *Les deux mots* καίγε *et* σου *ont une grande valeur*; which explains the insertion. Elsewhere in N.T. καί γε occurs only Acts ii. 18 in a quotation.

νῦν δέ. "But now, as things are." The actual fact is the reverse of the possibility just intimated. Comp. Jn. viii. 40, ix. 41; 1 Cor. vii. 14, xii. 20.

ἐκρύβη. "Hidden once for all, by Divine decree": comp.

Jn. xii. 38–40. The nom. to ἐκρύβη is not "the fact that (ὅτι) days will come," etc. (Theoph.), but τὰ πρὸς εἰρήνην. For the form ἐκρύβη see Veitch, *s.v.*

43. ὅτι ἥξουσιν ἡμέραι. "Because days will come"; not "*the* days" (AV. RV.): see on v. 35 and xvii. 22. *Dies multi, quia unum diem non observas* (Beng.). The ὅτι probably depends upon εἰ ἔγνως: "Would that thou hadst known in time; because the consequences (now inevitable) of not knowing are terrible." Or ὅτι may introduce the explanation of νῦν δὲ ἐκρύβη: "They are hid from thine eyes, because the very reverse of peace will certainly come upon thee." But in any case ὅτι is "because, for," not "that." For the constr. see Blass, *Gr.* p. 256.

It is not easy to decide between παρεμβαλοῦσιν (א C* L), which Tisch. and WH. prefer, and περιβαλοῦσιν (TR. with A B etc.). D has καὶ βαλοῦσιν ἐπὶ σέ. In LXX παρεμβάλλειν is freq. for "to encamp": Num. i. 50, ii. 17, 27, iii. 38, xxxiii. 10, 11, 12, 13, etc. Here it would mean "cast up in front" or "plant in beside," rather than "surround." In Vulg., through carelessness on Jerome's part, *circumdabunt* is used to translate both περιβαλοῦσιν and περικυκλώσουσιν, although earlier Lat. texts distinguish. Similarly we have *pressura* for both ἀνάγκη (xxi. 23) and συνοχή (xxi. 25). For a converse inaccuracy see on xxiv. 14.

χάρακα. From meaning a single stake (*vallus*), χάραξ comes to mean, not only a "palisade" (*vallum*) but a "rampart" or "palisaded mound" (*vallum* and *agger* combined). This is its meaning here: comp. Is. xxxvii. 33; Ezek. iv. 2, xxvi. 8; Jos. *Vita*, xliii. In Ezek. iv. 2 we have περιβαλεῖς ἐπ' αὐτὴν χάρακα. "Pale" (Wic.), "rampars" (Gen.), and "bank" (Tyn. Cov. RV.) are all preferable to "trench" (Rhem. AV.). It is said that these details show that the prophecy has been re-worded to fit the event more precisely and that therefore this Gospel was written after A.D. 70. The argument is precarious, although the conclusion is probable. At any rate it is worthy of note that neither here nor elsewhere does Lk. call attention to the fulfilment of the prophecy, as he does in the case of Agabus (Acts xi. 28). To those who assume that Jesus was unable to foresee the siege of Jerusalem, the amount of detail in the prediction is not of much moment. But it is not logical to maintain that Jesus could foresee the siege, but could not have foreseen these details; or to maintain that He would make known the coming siege, but would not make known the details. What is there in these details which is not common to all sieges? Given the siege, any one might add them. *Il n'est pas nécessaire pour cela d'etre prophète* (Godet). Moreover it is possible that Jesus is freely reproducing Is. xxix. 3: καὶ κυκλώσω ἐπὶ σέ, καὶ βαλῶ ἐπὶ σὲ χάρακα, καὶ θήσω περὶ σὲ πύργους. In both cases note the solemn effect of the simple coordination of sentences with καί: here we have καί five times.

Note also the impressive repetition of the pronoun: we have σου, σοι, or σε ten times in two verses. For the fulfilment of this prophecy see Jos. *B. J.* v. 6. 2, 12. 2. The Jews burnt the palisade, and then Titus replaced it with a wall. See Hastings, *D.B.* i. p. 30.

συνέξουσίν σε πάντοθεν. One of Lk.'s favourite verbs: iv. 38, viii. 37, 45, xii. 50, xxii. 63; Acts vii. 57, xviii. 5, xxviii. 8. It is possibly medical (Hobart, p. 3). The adv. occurs elsewhere in N.T. in Mk. i. 45 and Heb. ix. 4 only: it is rare in LXX. This "keeping in on every side" was so severe that thousands died of famine (Jos. *B. J.* v. 12. 3, vi. 1. 1).

44. ἐδαφιοῦσίν σε καὶ τὰ τέκνα σου ἐν σοί. Not a case of zeugma, for ἐδαφίζειν may mean "*dash* to the ground" (RV.) quite as well as "*lay even* with the ground" (A.V.), and the former will apply to both buildings and human beings. Comp. ἐδαφιεῖ τὰ νήπιά σου πρὸς τὴν πέτραν (Ps. cxxxvii. 9); καὶ τὰ ὑποτίτθια αὐτῶν ἐδαφισθήσονται (Hos. xiv. 1). In Amos ix. 14 ἠδαφισμένας is a false reading for ἠφανισμένας, and therefore the passage gives no support to the rendering, "raze, level to the ground." Field, *Otium Norvic.* iii. p. 53. Add in confirmation, τὰ νήπια αὐτῆς ἐδαφιοῦσιν (Nah. iii. 10). The AV. translation, "lay thee even with the ground," makes this tautological with "not leave in thee one stone upon another." The **τέκνα** are all the inhabitants, not the young only.

The Latin Versions are interesting: *ad terram prosternent* (f Vulg.); *ad terram consternent* (some MSS. of Vulg.); *ad terram sternent* (E); *ad solum deponent* (e); *ad nihilum deducent* (d); *pavimentabunt* (a). In class. Lat. *pavimentare* means "to cover with a pavement" (Cic. *Q. Fr.* iii. 1. 1). Comp. the double meaning of "to floor."

οὐκ ἀφήσουσιν λίθον ἐπὶ λίθον. Comp. ὅπως μὴ καταλειφθῇ ἐκεῖ μηδὲ λίθος (2 Sam. xvii. 13); κατασπάσω εἰς χάος τοὺς λίθους αὐτῆς (Mic. i. 6). For ἀνθ' ὧν see on i. 20 and xii. 3.

οὐκ ἔγνως τὸν καιρὸν τῆς ἐπισκοπῆς σου. "Thou didst not recognize the time in which God visited thee"—ἐπεσκέψατό σε. The whole of this period of opportunity, which culminated ἐν τῇ ἡμέρᾳ ταύτῃ, was unnoted and unused. Like ἐπισκέπτομαι (see on i. 68), ἐπισκοπή is a neutral term, and may imply either blessing or punishment. Here and 1 Pet. ii. 12 (not v. 6) in the former sense, as in Gen. l. 24; Job xxix. 4; Ecclus. xviii. 20; and perhaps Wisd. iii. 7. In the sense of visiting with punishment it does not occur in N.T., but in LXX of Jer. x. 15; Is. x. 3, xxix. 6; Wisd. xiv. 11, xix. 15. It is not found in class. Grk. For τὸν καιρόν Syr-Sin. has "the day."

Here Lk. rather abruptly ends his account of the triumphal procession. The actual entry into the city is not recorded by him. The proposal of Schleiermacher and others to distinguish two triumphal entries, one unexpected and unannounced, recorded by the three, and one expected and arranged, recorded by S. John, is no real help. Does the hypothesis make either record more intelligible? What good purpose would a second triumphal procession serve? Would the Romans have allowed this popular Teacher to enter the city a second time with a tumultuous crowd hailing Him as King?

45, 46. The Second Cleansing of the Temple. Mt. xxi. 12, 13; Mk. xi. 15–17. Both Mt. and Mk. record the entry into Jerusalem. The latter tells us how He entered the city and the temple, and having "looked round about upon all things," went back in the evening to Bethany with the Twelve (ver. 11). It was the day following that He returned to Jerusalem and cleansed the temple, the cursing of the barren fig-tree taking place on the way. Lk. omits the latter, and records the former very briefly. He groups the cleansing and the subsequent teaching in the temple with the triumphal procession as a series of Messianic acts. They are all parts of the last great scene in which Jesus publicly assumed the position of the Christ.

That this is a second cleansing, and not identical with Jn. ii. 14–22, may be regarded as reasonably certain. What is gained by the identification, which involves a gross chronological blunder on the part of either Jn., who places it at the beginning of Christ's ministry, or of the others, who place it at the very end? Could any of those who were present, John or Peter, transfer so remarkable an event from one end of their experiences to the other? Such confusion in memory is not probable, especially when we consider the immense changes which distinguish the last Passover in the ministry from the first. That the three should omit the first cleansing is only natural, for they omit the whole of the early Judæan ministry. Jn. omits the second, as he omits the institution of the Eucharist and many other things, because it has been recorded already, and is not necessary for the plan of his Gospel. On the other hand, there is no difficulty in the supposition that the temple was twice cleansed by Jesus. He was not so reverenced in Jerusalem that one such act would put an end to the scandal for ever. The hierarchy would be glad of this opportunity for publicly treating His authority with contempt; and this would be the more easy, as Jesus does not seem to have kept the next Passover at Jerusalem (Jn. vi. 4). If a year or two later He found that the evil had returned, and perhaps increased, would He not be likely to act as He did before? There are differences in the details as given by Jn. and by the others, which confirm the view that he and they are recording different events. *D.C.G.* ii. p. 712.

45. εἰσελθὼν εἰς τὸ ἱερόν. If we had no other account, we should suppose that this took place on the same day as the triumphal entry. But as Lk. gives no note of time, there is no discrepancy between him and Mk. The Court of the Gentiles is meant. The traffic would be great as the Passover drew near; and, as the hierarchy profited by it, we may be sure that they would try to make the attempt to stop it fail.

ἤρξατο ἐκβάλλειν. So also in Mk., whose account is specially graphic, as that of an eye-witness. In this respect the narrative in Jn. ii. 14 ff. is similar. Here perhaps *ἤρξατο ἐκβ.* is merely the Hebraistic paraphrase for *ἐξέβαλεν* (Mt. xxi. 12) or *ἐξέβαλλεν*. See on iii. 8 and xii. 45, and comp. LXX of Gen. ii. 3; Deut. i. 5;

Judg. i. 27, 35; 1 Esdr. iv. 1, 13, 33. Lk. omits the buyers, the money-changers, and the dove-sellers (Mt. Mk.); also His allowing no vessel to be carried through the temple (Mk.).

46. Here the three narratives are almost *verbatim* the same, and very different from Jn. ii. 15, 16. On the first occasion, He charged them not to make His Father's house a *house of traffic* (οἶκον ἐμπορίου): now He charges them with having made it a *robbers' den* (σπήλαιον λῃστῶν). The scandal is worse than before. For a detailed description see Edersh. *L. & T.* i. pp. 364–374; also a remarkable passage in Renan, *V. de J.* p. 215, in which he points out how "antichristian" the traditions of the temple have always been. In the passage from Is. lvi. 7 Lk. substitutes ἔσται for κληθήσεται, and with Mt. omits πᾶσιν τοῖς ἔθνεσιν, which one would have expected Lk. to preserve. Would he have omitted this, if he had had Mk., who preserves it, before him? See on xx. 17. Comp. μὴ σπήλαιον λῃστῶν ὁ οἶκός μου οὗ ἐπικέκληται τὸ ὄνομά μου ἐπ' αὐτῷ ἐκεῖ ἐνώπιον ὑμῶν; (Jer. vii. 11).

That καὶ ἔσται before ὁ οἶκος, and not ἐστιν after προσευχῆς is the right reading is sufficiently attested by ℵ²BLR, Arm., Orig. But it is very unnatural to take καὶ ἔσται with γέγραπται: "It stands written and shall be so."

47, 48. The Publicity and Popularity of Christ's Final Teaching. Mk. xi. 19. These two verses form a link between the sections before and after them, introducing the public work which followed the public entry. Comp. the similar notice with which the record of this brief period of public work closes, xxi. 37, 38.

47. ἦν διδάσκων. Periphrastic imperfect expressing continued action: iv. 31, v. 17, xiii. 10. For τὸ καθ' ἡμέραν comp. xi. 3. Mt. says that He healed the blind and the lame who came to Him in the temple.

οἱ ἀρχιερεῖς καὶ οἱ γραμματεῖς. So in all three. The activity of the hierarchy is in marked contrast to His: while He teaches and heals, they seek to destroy. Lk. alone mentions οἱ πρῶτοι τοῦ λαοῦ. The difference of designation is against their being identical with οἱ πρεσβύτεροι. Comp. Acts xiii. 50, xxv. 2, xxviii. 7, 17; Mk. vi. 21.

Jésus restait ainsi à Jérusalem un provincial admiré des provinciaux comme lui, mais repoussé par toute l'aristocratie de la nation. . . . Sa voix eut à Jérusalem peu d'éclat. Les préjugés de race et de secte, les ennemis directs de l'esprit de l'évangile, y étaient trop enracinés (Renan, *V. de J.* p. 344).

48. τὸ τί ποιήσωσιν. For this use of τό see on i. 62, and comp. vi. 11.

ὁ λαὸς γὰρ ἅπας. Not ὄχλος, not the mere crowd, but the whole nation, which was numerously represented. A mixed multitude of

Jews from all parts of the world was gathering there for the Passover. These would sympathize with His cleansing of the temple; and His miracles of healing would add to the attractiveness of His teaching. This representative multitude "hung on His lips, listening." Comp. *pendet narrantis ab ore* (*Aen.* iv. 79); *narrantis conjux pendet ab ore viri* (Ov. *Her.* i. 30). Other examples in Wetst. and McClellan. See on xi. 29.

The form ἐξεκρέμετο (ℵ B, Orig.) is preferred by Tisch. and WH. It implies a pres. κρέμομαι. But ἐξεκρέματο, if genuine, is imperf. also. Veitch, *s.* κρέμαμαι.

XX. 1-8. The Question of the Sanhedrin respecting the authority of Jesus. Mt. xxi. 23-27; Mk. xi. 27-33. Having given a general description of the activity of Jesus and of His enemies during these last days, Lk. now gives some illustrations of both. It was fear of the people which kept His opponents from proceeding against Him: and therefore their first object was to discredit Him with His protectors. Then they could adopt more summary measures.

None of the Evangelists enables us to answer with certainty the question whether the hierarchy had at first any idea of employing the *sicarii* to assassinate Jesus. Mt. xxvi. 4 might mean this. But more probably this and other notices of plots against the life of Jesus refer to the intention of getting Him out of the way by some legal process, either as a blasphemer or as a rebel against the Roman government. Of course, if a mob could be goaded into a fury and provoked to put Him to death (iv. 29; Jn. viii. 59, x. 31), this would suit their purpose equally well. The intrinsic probability of the controversies reported by the Evangelists as taking place after the triumphal entry is admitted even by Strauss.

If the tentative chronology suggested above be accepted, this conversation about authority took place probably two days after the entry, and on Tuesday, April 4, Nisan 12. This day is sometimes called the "Day of Questions." We have (1) the Sanhedrin asking about Authority, and (2) Christ's counter-question about the Baptist; (3) the Pharisees and Herodians asking about the Tribute; (4) the Sadducees asking about the Woman with Seven Husbands; (5) the Scribe asking which is the First Commandment; (6) Christ's question about Ps. cx. It is *possible* that on this day the question was asked about the Woman taken in Adultery; but that is too precarious to be worth more than a passing mention, although Renan places it here without doubt, and makes it the proximate cause of the arrest and death of Jesus (*V. de J.* p. 346). If it were included, we might group the questions pressed upon Christ thus: (i.) a personal question; (ii.) a political question; (iii.) a doctrinal question; (iv.) an ethical question; (v.) a question of discipline. Of hardly any day in our Lord's life have we so full a report. With Lk. xx. and xxi. comp. Mt. xxi. 18-xxvi. 5; Mk. xi. 20-xiv. 2; Jn. xii. 20-43. It includes at least four parables: the Two Sons (Mt. xxi. 28-32), the Wicked Husbandmen (Mt. xxi. 33-44; Mk. xii. 1-11; Lk. xx. 9-18), the Ten Virgins (Mt. xxv. 1-13), and the Talents (Mt. xxv. 14-30). The day may be considered the last working-day of Christ's ministry, the last of His public teaching, the last of activity in the temple, the last of instruction to the people and of warning to their leaders. "It is a picture with genuine Oriental local colouring. . . . We see Jesus sitting, surrounded by a multitude awed into silence. They are all devoutly meditating on the great Messianic question. From time to time an emissary from His opponents steps up to Him, with Eastern solemnity and ceremoniousness, to propose some well-considered question. Anxiously do the multitude listen for Jesus' answer. Then again follows a meditative silence as before, until at last Jesus Himself delivers a connected discourse" (Hausrath, *N.T. Times*, ii. p. 250).

1. ἐν μιᾷ τῶν ἡμερῶν. Lk. alone uses this expression (v. 17, viii. 22; comp. v. 12, xiii. 10). He is still indefinite in his chronology. Mt. is a little more clear. It is Mk. who enables us to distinguish three days; presumably Sunday, Monday, and Tuesday. "*The* days" perhaps refers to the "daily teaching in the temple" (xix. 47); and this deputation from the Sanhedrin is the result of their "seeking to destroy Him." We have a similar deputation to the Baptist Jn. i. 19. See fourth note on Lk. ix. 22. For **εὐαγγελιζομένου**, which defines the character of His teaching more clearly than *διδάσκοντος*, see on ii. 10.

ἐπέστησαν. One of Lk.'s favourite words (see on ii. 38): "there came upon Him." So also **σὺν τοῖς πρ.** and **πρὸς αὐτόν** illustrate his fondness for these prepositions. Mt. and Mk. here have *καί* for *σύν* (see on i. 56), and neither of them has *πρός* after **λέγειν.**

The introduction of the *oratio recta* by λέγοντες or λέγων after εἰπεῖν is rare (Mk. xii. 26): but either is common after λαλεῖν (Acts viii. 26, xxvi. 31, xxviii. 25, etc.).

2. ἐν ποίᾳ . . . ποιεῖς; So in all three. The two questions are not identical; nor is the second a mere explanation of the first. It anticipates the reply, "By the Messiah's authority," with another question, "Who made Thee Messiah?" They ask by what *kind* of authority, human or Divine, ecclesiastical or civil, assumed or conferred, He acts. They refer not merely to His teaching, but also to His cleansing the temple, as *ποιεῖς* shows. On the first occasion they had asked for a *σημεῖον* as a guarantee for the lawfulness of His *ποιεῖν* (Jn. ii. 18). They do not venture to do more than question Him, for they know that the feeling and conscience of the people are with Him for putting down their extortionate and profane traffic, for His teaching, and for His works of healing. This was the one point where He seemed to be vulnerable. "For there was no principle more firmly established by universal consent than that *authoritative* teaching required previous authorization," because all such teaching was traditional (Edersh. *L. & T.* ii. p. 381). For *ἐν ἐξουσίᾳ* see on iv. 32.

3. εἶπεν πρὸς αὐτούς. Both Mt. and Mk. have *αὐτοῖς*.

Ἐρωτήσω ὑμᾶς κἀγὼ λόγον. The *λόγον* refers to their answer rather than His question, as is shown by *ὃν ἐὰν εἴπητέ μοι* (Mt. xxi. 24). "You ask Me to state My authority. I also will ask you for a *statement*"; not, "ask you a question" (RV.), nor, "ask you one thing" (AV.). As teachers they must speak first.

The ἕνα (A C D) is an insertion from Mt. and Mk. om. ℵ B L R, Syr-Sin. Latin texts are divided.

4. *Verbatim* as Mt. and Mk., except that Mt. inserts *πόθεν*, and Mk. adds *ἀποκρίθητέ μοι.* "Baptism of repentance" was the special characteristic of John's teaching (iii. 3). The question as to its origin is not a mere escape from their attack by placing them in a difficulty: the answer to it would lead to the answer to their question. John had testified to the Divine authority of Jesus, and his baptism was a preparation for the Messianic Kingdom. What had been their view of John's position? That was a question to which the official guides of the nation were bound, and had long been bound, to furnish an answer. For the alternative *ἐξ οὐρανοῦ* or *ἐξ ἀνθρώπων* comp. Acts v. 38, 39.

5. **συνελογίσαντο.** Here only in N.T., but classical. ℵ C D have *συνελογίζοντο.* Comp. ver. 14.

6. **καταλιθάσει.** Here only: but *λιθάζειν* is found Jn. x. 31–33, xi. 8; Acts v. 26, xiv. 19. In LXX *λιθάζειν* occurs twice (2 Sam. xvi. 6, 13), but *λιθοβολεῖν* is the common verb: comp. xiii. 34; Acts vii. 58. The *κατα-* expresses "stoning *down*, overwhelming with stones": comp. *καταλιθοβολεῖν* Exod. xvii. 4, and *καταλιθοῦν* in Josephus. Here Mt. and Mk. have the less definite expression, "fear the multitude."

προφήτην εἶναι. Their intense joy at the reappearance of a Prophet after three centuries of silence (p. 80) would be the measure of their fury against a hierarchy which should declare that John had not been a Prophet at all. Comp. vii. 29, 30. With ὁ λαὸς ἅπας comp. xix. 48. Nowhere else does **πεπεισμένος ἐστιν** occur.

7. **μὴ εἰδέναι πόθεν.** This shameful and dishonest avowal is excelled a few days later by their answer to Pilate, "We have no king but Cæsar" (Jn. xix. 15). *Timentes lapidationem, sed magis timentes veritatis confessionem* (Bede), these professed "Teachers of Israel" (Jn. iii. 10), who so scorned the ignorant multitude (Jn. vii. 49), confessed that they had not yet decided whether one, who for years had been recognized by the nation as a Prophet, had any Divine commission. If they were not competent to judge of the Baptist, still less were they competent to judge of the Christ. Nösgen, *Gesch. J. C.* i. p. 514.

8. **Οὐδὲ ἐγώ.** *Verbatim* as in Mt. and Mk. Their refusal to answer His question cancels their claim to an answer from Him. This they admit by ceasing to press it. See Gould on Mk. xi. 33.

9–19. The Parable of the Wicked Husbandmen. Mt. xxi 33–46; Mk. xii. 1–12. Mt. here gives a trilogy of parables, placing this one between the Two Sons and the Marriage of the King's Son. Godet thinks that the Two Sons cannot have been uttered where Mt. places it. But it fits the preceding discussion about the Baptist very well; and Mk., who records one parable only, says ἤρξατο αὐτοῖς ἐν παραβολαῖς λαλεῖν, which agrees well with the fact that more than one parable was spoken. The idea of "work in the vineyard" is common to both parables. In this parable Christ lets His enemies know that He is aware of their murderous plans against Himself; an in it He warns both them and the people generally of the fatal results to themselves, if their plans are carried out.[1] It is the special characteristic of this parable that *it does not teach general and permanent truths for the guidance of Christians, but refers to past, present, and future events.* From the conduct of His traditional enemies, especially at that very time, He predicts His own end and theirs. The parable is capable of spiritual application as to God's dealings with churches and individuals, but its primary reference is to the treatment which He is receiving from the Jewish hierarchy. The parable contains the answer to the question which they had raised. He is acting in the authority of His Father who sent Him to them. The imagery is taken from the O.T. and would be readily understood by the audience. The main source is the similar parable Is. v. 1–7; but comp. Jer. ii. 21; Ezek. xv. 1–6, xix. 10–14; Hos. x. 1; Deut. xxxii. 32, 33, and the many other passages in which Israel is spoken of as a vineyard or a vine; Ps. lxxx. 8 ff.; Joel i. 7, etc.

It has been said that the main difference between this parable and Is. v. or other O.T. figures is, that there the husbandmen or leaders and teachers of the people are not mentioned: it is *the nation as a whole* that fails in its duty to Jehovah. Here it is *those who have charge of the nation* that are condemned: the vineyard itself is not destroyed for its unfruitfulness, but is transferred to more faithful stewards. And, in support of this view, it has been pointed out that in the first times of the Kingdom the nation went voluntarily into idolatry; it was not led into it by the priests and other teachers: but now it was mainly the official teachers who prevented the people from accepting Jesus as the Messiah. This, however, does not fit *vv.* 15, 16, which show that the tenants are the Jewish nation, and not merely the leaders, and that the vineyard is not the nation, but its spiritual privileges. The nation was not to be transferred to other rulers, but its privileges were to be transferred to other nations.

9. Ἤρξατο δὲ πρὸς τὸν λαὸν λέγειν. There is a pause after the discomfiture of the deputation from the Sanhedrin; and then Jesus "begins" to address a different company. But while He speaks to the people He also speaks *at* the hierarchy, who are still present, though silenced. Mt. and Mk. regard the parable as addressed to the latter. Syr-Sin. has "to speak to *them*." D, a d e omit πρὸς τὸν λαόν. Comp. v. 36.

Ἄνθρωπος. Lk. commonly adds **τις**: see small print note on xiii. 19. TR. follows A in adding τις here.

---

[1] Keim speaks with severity of the "destructive criticism" which "again miserably fails to see anything but an invention of the dogmatic artist" in "this grand self-revelation of Jesus," which is attested by all three Gospels (v. p. 142).

ἐφύτευσεν ἀμπελῶνα. The phrase is freq. in O.T. (Gen. ix. 20; Deut. xx. 6, xxviii. 30, 39; Ps. cvi. 37, etc.). Lk. omits the fence, the winepress, and the tower.

ἐξέδετο. In all three narratives in this place, but nowhere else in N.T. In LXX it is used of giving a daughter in marriage; Exod. ii. 21; Ecclus. vii. 25; 1 Mac. x. 58: but the sense of letting out for hire is classical; Plat. *Leg.* vii. 806 D, γεωργίαι δὲ ἐκδεδομέναι δούλοις ἀπαρχὴν τῶν ἐκ τῆς γῆς ἀποτελοῦσιν ἱκανήν. Among the Jews rent was sometimes paid in money, but generally in kind. If in kind, it was either a fixed amount of produce, whether the harvest was good or bad; or a certain proportion, *e.g.* a third or fourth, of each harvest. This latter system led to much disputing and dishonesty, and does so still wherever it is adopted. The tenants in the parable have a long lease and pay in kind; but it is not clear whether they pay a fixed or a proportionate amount.

The same form (-ετο, not -οτο) is found in the best MSS. in all three. Comp. διεδίδετο (Acts iv. 35) and παρεδίδετο (1 Cor. xi. 23). Gregory, *Proleg.* p. 124.

χρόνους ἱκανούς. This addition is peculiar to Lk. See on vii. 12. We may understand several years.

10. καιρῷ. No doubt ὁ καιρὸς τῶν καρπῶν (Mt.) is meant. Syr-Sin. has "at one of the seasons."

ἀπέστειλεν . . . δοῦλον. So also Mk., while Mt. has τοὺς δούλους αὐτοῦ. In Lk. it is always a single slave who is sent, and the treatment becomes worse each time, culminating in the slaying of the heir, before whom no one is killed. In Mt. and Mk. there is no such dramatic climax, and several are killed before the son is sent: all which is more in accordance with facts in Jewish history. See 1 Kings xviii. 13, xxii. 24–27; 2 Kings vi. 31, xxi. 16; 2 Chron. xxiv. 19–22, xxxvi. 15, 16; Neh. ix. 26; Jer. xxxvii. 15, xliv. 4; Acts vii. 52.

ἵνα ἀπὸ τοῦ καρποῦ. Keim says that this means the O.T. tenth; but it does not necessarily imply a proportionate amount at all. A fixed amount, independent of the yield, would be paid ἀπὸ τοῦ καρποῦ.

ἵνα . . . δώσουσιν. The fut. indic. is found in class. Grk. after ὅπως, but not after ἵνα. In bibl. Grk. it is found most often in the *last* of a series of verbs following ἵνα: but cases in which the verb depends immediately upon ἵνα occur: 1 Cor. ix. 18; 1 Pet. iii. 1, Rev. vi. 4, viii. 3, ix. 20, xii. 12, xiv. 13, and other passages in which the reading is somewhat doubtful. See on xiv. 10. Burton, § 198, 199.

ἐξαπέστειλαν . . . κενόν. They probably told him, and perhaps tried to persuade themselves that his master's demand was unjust. Excepting Gal. iv. 4, 6, the verb is peculiar in N.T. to

Lk. (Acts vii. 12, ix. 30, xi. 22, xii. 11, xiii. 26, xvii. 14, xxii. 21); but it is freq. in LXX. For the phrase "send empty away" comp i. 53; Gen. xxxi. 42; Deut. xv. 13; 1 Sam. vi. 3; Job xxii. 9. For δείραντες see on xii. 47.

11. προσέθετο πέμψαι. A Hebraism: see on xix. 11. Whether this is a second messenger sent that same vintage, or the messenger sent at another vintage, is not stated. The important point is that chastisement does not follow upon the first outrage. The husbandmen have several opportunities; and these are brought by different persons. If one messenger's manner of delivering his message was unpleasing, another's would be the opposite. But this time they add insult (ἀτιμάσαντες) to violence. Comp. the use of ἀτιμάζειν in Jn. viii. 49; Acts v. 41; Rom. i. 24, ii. 23; Jas. ii. 6. The verb is freq. in LXX.

12. τραυματίσαντες. Worse than δείραντες κ. ἀτιμάσαντες, as ἐξέβαλον is worse than ἐξαπέστειλαν. Comp. Heb. xi. 36–38; Acts vii. 52.

13. Τί ποιήσω; Peculiar to this account; as also is the qualifying ἴσως, which occurs nowhere else in N.T., and only once in LXX (1 Sam. xxv. 21), where English Versions have "surely." Godet contends for such a meaning here: *pourtant*, *en tout cas*, *certainement*. But comp. ΚΛ. Ἴσως. ΑΘ. Οὐκ ἴσως, ἀλλ' ὄντως ὦ δαιμόνιε (Plat. *Laws*, xii. 965).

We must remember that it is the ἄνθρωπος of ver. 9 who deliberates as to what he shall do, says ἴσως, and expects that his son will be well received. All this is the setting of the parable, and must not be pressed as referring to God. This man represents God, not by his perplexity, but by his long-suffering and mercy.

ἐντραπήσονται. In all three: for the meaning see on xviii. 2. This form of the fut. is late. In Polyb. and Plut. the verb sometimes has an acc., but in class. Grk. a gen., when it means "reverence." Comp. Exod. x. 3; Wisd. ii. 10.

The ἰδόντες of TR. with A R, Vulg. Goth. comes from ver. 14; om. ℵ B C D L Q, a c d e ff_2 i l q r, Boh. Arm. The Syriac Versions are divided. Syr-Sin. is defective here.

14. διελογίζοντο πρὸς ἀλλήλους. This touch also is peculiar to Lk. It perhaps looks back to xix. 47, 48. Nothing is gained by taking πρὸς ἀλλήλους with λέγοντες: comp. πρὸς ἑαυτούς, which is equally amphibolous, ver. 5.

A K and Latt. have διελογίσαντο, *cogitaverunt*; and A C Q, Vulg. have πρὸς ἑαυτούς from Mk. xii. 7 for πρὸς ἀλλήλους (ℵ B D L R, Boh. Arm.). For ὁ κληρονόμος see Wsctt. on Heb. i. 2 and his detached note on Heb. vi. 12, p. 167.

15. ἐκβαλόντες ἀπέκτειναν. This perhaps was intended to represent their turning him out of his inheritance. It may be doubted whether it refers to Jesus "suffering without the gate." Outside the vineyard would be outside Israel rather than outside Jerusalem. Moreover in Mk. the heir is killed *before* he is cast out of his inheritance. It is possible that they regard the vineyard as already made over to the heir, as was often the case in ancient law: see on xv. 12. Comp. the case of Naboth: ἐξήγαγον αὐτὸν ἔξω τῆς πόλεως καὶ ἐλιθοβόλησαν αὐτὸν λίθοις, καὶ ἀπέθανεν (1 Kings xx. 13). No doubt ἔξω τ. ἀμπελῶνος goes with ἐκβαλόντες (iv. 29; Acts vii. 58, which is closely parallel), not with ἀπέκτειναν.

τί οὖν ποιήσει αὐτοῖς; Not, τί οὖν ἐποίησεν; Our Lord indicates that the parable is not a mere fiction: it is a key to a future which depends upon present action. Assuming that the heir is killed, what will happen? In Mt. some of the bystanders answer the question. They are so interested, and enter so fully into the spirit of the narrative, that, without seeing the application to themselves, they reply κακοὺς κακῶς ἀπολέσει αὐτούς. See on xix. 25, and comp. David's reply to Nathan's parable (2 Sam. xii. 5, 6).

16. ἐλεύσεται καὶ ἀπολέσει . . . καὶ δώσει. Three points: He will no longer send but come; will punish the wrong-doers; will transfer their privileges to others. The Jews were familiar with the idea of the Gentiles being gathered into the Messianic Kingdom (Is. ii. 2; lx. *passim*; Jer. iii. 17). Yet this was restricted to those Gentiles who had taken no part in oppressing Israel, but had submitted to Israel; and later Judaism as a rule denied even this to the heathen (Charles, *Enoch*, xc. 30). Here the Jews are to lose what the Gentiles gain. In *vv.* 16–19 Syr-Sin. is confused.

ἀκούσαντες δὲ εἶπαν Μὴ γένοιτο. We need not confine this to the *people* and conclude that "the Pharisees had too much wariness and self command to have allowed such an exclamation to escape from their lips." The exclamation may not mean more than "That is incredible," or "Away with the thought." See Lft. on Gal. ii. 17 and Sanday on Rom. iii. 4. This is the only instance of μὴ γένοιτο in N.T. outside the Pauline Epp., where it generally is used to scout a false inference which might be drawn. Burton, § 176, 177. Here it probably refers to the punishment rather than to the sin which brings it,—to ἀπολέσει καὶ δώσει rather than to ἀπέκτειναν.

The expression is rare in the Pauline Epp. except in Rom., where it occurs ten times: twice in Gal. and once in 1 Cor. In LXX it is rare, and never stands as an independent sentence: Gen. xliv. 7, 17; Josh. xxii. 29, xxiv. 16; 1 Kings xx. [xxi.] 3.

17. ἐμβλέψας αὐτοῖς. Lk. alone has this touch. Comp. xxii. 61 and Elisha's fixed look on Hazael (2 Kings viii. 11).

Τί οὖν ἐστίν. "If the destruction which I have just foretold is not to come (*μὴ γένοιτο*), how *then* do you explain this text?" The passage is once more (see on ver. 9) from the Hallel Psalms (cxviii. 22, 23), where see Perowne. The Rabbis recognized it as Messianic: see Schoettg. i. p. 173. In all three Gospels the quotation is *verbatim* as in LXX. For **τὸ γεγραμμένον** see on xxii. 37, and for **ἀπεδοκίμασαν** see on ix. 22. Perhaps **λίθον** is "*a* stone" rather than "*the* stone": the builders may have rejected many stones, one of which became *κεφαλὴ γωνίας*. But, if the Jews used *Λίθος* as a name for the Messiah, as seems to be probable, "*the* stone" is better. In Justin Martyr we have *Λίθος* as a name for Christ (*Try.* xxxiv. xxxvi.): see on Rom. ix. 33.

For the attraction of **λίθον** to *ὃν* see on iii. 19, and for *ἐγενήθη εἰς* see on xiii. 19.

κεφαλὴ γωνίας. Not the key-stone of the arch, but a corner stone uniting two walls; but whether a foundation-stone at the base of the corner, or a completing stone at the top of it, is uncertain. Comp. Acts iv. 11 and 1 Pet. ii. 7; also *ἀκρογωνιαῖος* in Eph. ii. 20 and Is. xxviii. 16. Mt. and Mk. quote ver. 23 of Ps. cxviii. as well as ver. 22, and Mt. adds the explanation that the Kingdom shall be transferred to a nation bringing forth the fruits thereof. Would Lk. have omitted this reference to the believing and loyal Gentiles if he had known it? We conclude that he was not familiar with Mt.'s account. See on xix. 46.

18. πᾶς ὁ πεσὼν . . . αὐτόν. These words are not in Mk. and are of somewhat doubtful authority in Mt. xxi. 44, where they are omitted by D 33, or b d e ff_{12} Syr-Sin., Orig. But the characteristic *πᾶς* is in any case peculiar to Lk. The first half of the saying seems to be an adaptation of Is. viii. 14, and the second half an adaptation of Dan. ii. 34, 35, 44. Christ is a stumbling-block to some (ii. 34), and they suffer heavily for their short-sightedness. They not only lose the blessing which is offered, but what they reject works their overthrow.

συνθλασθήσεται. "Shall be shattered"; *confringetur* (Lat. Vet., Beza), *conquassabitur* (Vulg.), *wird zerschellen* (Luth.). But in Mt. xxi. 44 Vulg. has *confringetur.* The verb occurs nowhere else in N.T., but the act. is found in LXX (Ps. lvii. 7; Mic. iii. 3), and several times as *v.l.*

ἐφ᾽ ὃν δ᾽ ἂν πέσῃ. Note the impressive change of construction. In the first case the man is the chief agent; in the second the stone. And the main thought now is simply *λίθος*: the metaphor of *κεφαλὴ γωνίας* is dropped. A chief corner-stone would not be likely either to trip up a person or to fall on him.

λικμήσει αὐτόν. The rendering "grind to powder," which all English Versions from Tyn. to AV. give (Rhem. "breake to pouder"), follows the *comminuet* of Vulg. (in Mt. *conteret*), but is without authority. Not only in classical authors (Hom. Xen. Plut. Lucian.), but also in LXX, it means "to winnow chaff from grain," from λικμός, "a winnowing fan." In Ruth iii. 2, λικμᾷ τὸν ἅλωνα τῶν κριθῶν, and Ecclus. v. 9, μὴ λίκμα ἐν παντὶ ἀνέμῳ, the meaning is indisputable. Hence "to blow away like chaff, sweep out of sight or out of existence": ἀναλήμψεται δὲ αὐτὸν καύσων καὶ ἀπελεύσεται, καὶ λικμήσει αὐτὸν ἐκ τοῦ τόπου αὐτοῦ (Job xxvii. 21); καὶ πόῤῥω αὐτὸν διώξεται ὡς χνοῦν ἀχύρου λικμώντων ἀπέναντι ἀνέμου (Is. xvii. 13); ὁ λικμήσας τὸν Ἰσραὴλ συνάξει αὐτόν (Jer. xxxi. 10); καὶ λικμήσω ἐν πᾶσιν τοῖς ἔθνεσιν τὸν οἶκον τοῦ Ἰσραήλ, ὃν τρόπον λικμᾶται ἐν τῷ λικμῷ (Amos ix. 9). Dan. ii. 44 is important, as being the probable source of the saying: there, while in LXX we read πατάξει καὶ ἀφανίσει, Theodotion has λεπτυνεῖ καὶ λικμήσει, showing that λικμήσει = ἀφανίσει. Comp. Theod. ἐγένετο ὡσεὶ κονιορτὸς ἀπὸ ἅλωνος θερινῆς, καὶ ἐξῆρεν τὸ πλῆθος τοῦ πνεύματος, καὶ τόπος οὐχ εὑρέθη αὐτοῖς (Dan. ii. 35). "Scatter him as chaff," therefore, is the meaning. When a heavy mass falls, what is pulverized by the blow is scattered by the rush of air. The *Commovet illum* of Cod. Palat. (e) looks like an attempt to preserve the right idea. Deissmann, *Bible Studies*, p. 225.

19. **ἐν αὐτῇ τῇ ὥρᾳ.** "In that very hour": Lk.'s usual expression: see on x. 7, 21. There is no equivalent to it here in Mt. or Mk.

ἔγνωσαν γὰρ ὅτι πρὸς αὐτούς. So also in Mk. xii. 12, while Mt. has περὶ αὐτῶν. Vulg. has *ad ipsos* here and *ad eos* in Mk. But πρός may be either "with a view to, in reference to" (see on xii. 41, xviii. 1, 9, xix. 9), or "against" (AV. RV.): comp. Acts xxiii. 30. Here, as in Heb. i. 7, 8, Wsctt. prefers the meaning "in reference to": comp. Rom. x. 21; Heb. xi. 18. The nom. to ἔγνωσαν is οἱ γραμματεῖς, not ὁ λαός, which would require ἔγνω, to be unambiguous. In Mt. the nom. to ἔγνωσαν must be the hierarchy. And γάρ gives the reason, not for ἐζήτησαν, but for ἐφοβήθησαν, as the order of the sentences shows: and this is still more clear in Mk. by the change of tense from ἐζήτουν (see Gould). The hierarchy recognize that the parable was directed against themselves; and this made them fear the people, who had heard the parable also. Syr-Sin. transfers this to *v.* 16.

In class. Grk. **πρός τινα** often means "in reply to," and hence "against," being less strong than κατά τινος, as *adversus* than *in*. Here Beza has *adversus ipsos* and Luther *auf sie*.

20–26. The Question about the Tribute. Mt. xxii. 15–22; Mk. xii. 13–17. There is no evidence that a night intervened between the previous question and this one. The connexion between *vv.* 19 and 20 is close; and ver. 19 took place ἐν αὐτῇ τῇ ὥρᾳ with what precedes. The previous question about authority had emanated from the Sanhedrin as a whole. The different parties represented in it now act separately and devise independent attacks. This one comes from the Pharisees (Mt. xxii. 15), who send a group composed of Pharisees and Herodians (Mt. xxii. 16; Mk. xii. 13). Neither Lk. nor Jn. mentions the Herodians. Their alliance with Pharisees is remarkable, for the Pharisees detested the Herodian dynasty; and this is not the first instance of such an alliance (Mk. iii. 6). But opponents often combine to attack those who are obnoxious to both.

20. παρατηρήσαντες. See on xiv. 1. Both AV. and RV. follow Tyn. Cran. Cov. and Gen. in translating "watched *him*"; but neither indicates by italics that "him" is not in the Greek. Wic. and Rhem. have no pronoun, in accordance with Vulg. *observantes miserunt.* It is doubtful whether the pronoun ought to be supplied, for παρατηρεῖν without case may mean "to watch an opportunity." See Field and Alford, *ad loc.* Mt. has his favourite πορευθέντες.

D and some Versions here have ἀποχωρήσαντες: so Goth. Aeth. *cum recessissent* (f i l), *cum discessissent* (a), *recedentes* (d), *secesserunt et* (e).

ἐνκαθέτους. "Suborned to lie in wait"; lit. "sent down into." In N.T. here only, and in LXX Job xix. 12, xxxi. 9: but classical. Comp. Jos. *B. J.* vi. 5. 2. The **ὑποκρινομένους** shows for what purpose they were suborned: they posed as scrupulous persons with a difficulty of conscience. In different ways all three accounts call attention to their hypocrisy. Meyer quotes, *Qui tum, cum maxime fallunt, id agunt ut viri boni videantur* (Cic. *De Off.* i. 13. 41).

ἐπιλάβωνται αὐτοῦ λόγου. "Take Him in His speech"; αὐτοῦ depending upon ἐπιλαβ. and λόγου being epexegetic (De W. Mey. Go.): rather than "take hold of His speech," αὐτοῦ depending upon λόγου (Holtz. Hahn). Vulg. has *eum in sermone.* So also Tyn. Cov. Cran. Gen. Rhem. Luth. Comp. ἐπελάβετό μου τῆς στολῆς (Job xxx. 18) and ἐπιλαμβάνεται αὐτοῦ τῆς ἴτυος (Xen. *Anab.* iv. 7. 12). Mt. has ὅπως αὐτὸν παγιδεύσωσιν ἐν λόγῳ, Mk. ἵνα αὐτὸν ἀγρεύσωσιν λόγῳ. Jesus had baffled them with a dilemma (ver. 4), and they now prepare a dilemma for Him. Comp. the constr. in xix. 4.

ὥστε παραδοῦναι . . . τοῦ ἡγεμόνος. Peculiar to Lk. *Quod per se non poterant, præsidis manibus efficere tentabant, ut veluti ipsi a morte ejus viderentur immunes* (Bede). For ὥστε comp iv. 29; Mt. xxiv. 24.

τῇ ἀρχῇ καὶ τῇ ἐξουσίᾳ τ. ἡγεμ. It is an improbable refinement to press the double article and separate τῇ ἀρχῇ from τοῦ ἡγεμόνος: "so as to deliver Him to the Government, and (in particular) to the authority of the governor" (Mey. Weiss); or, "so as to deliver Him to the rule (of the Sanhedrin) and to t authority of the governor" (Nösg. Hahn). For the combination of ἀρχή with ἐξουσία comp. xii. 11; 1 Cor. xv. 24; Eph. iii. 10, Col. i. 16, ii. 15; Tit. iii. 1. See Lft. on Col. i. 16.

The generic term ἡγεμών may be used of the emperor (comp. ἡγεμονία iii. 1) or any of his subordinates. In N.T. it is often used of the ἐπίτροπος or *procurator* (Mt. xxvii. 2, 11, 14, etc.; Acts xxiii. 24, 26, 33, xxiv. 1, 10, etc.) and less definitely of any governor (xxi. 12; 1 Pet. ii. 14). Comp. Jos. *Ant.* xviii. 3. 1; and ἡγεμονεύω ii. 2, iii. 1.

21. ὀρθῶς λέγεις καὶ διδάσκεις. The falseness of these fulsome compliments in their mouths (οἴδαμεν ὅτι) stamps this as one of the most dastardly of the attacks on Christ. They go on to emphasize their flattery by denying the opposite.

οὐ λαμβάνεις πρόσωπον. *Affreux barbarisme pour des lecteurs grecs* (Godet). The expression is a Hebraism, which originally meant "raise the face," *i.e.* make the countenance rise by favourable address, rather than "accept the face." Hence it came to mean "regard with favour," but not necessarily with *undue* favour: comp. Ps. lxxxi. 2; Mal. i. 8, 9. But the bad sense gradually prevailed; and both here and in Gal. ii. 6 (see Lft.) partiality is implied, as in Lev. xix. 15 and Mal. ii. 9. In LXX the common phrase is θαυμάζειν πρόσωπον: comp. Jude 16. The compounds προσωπολήμπτης, προσωπολημψία, etc., always imply favouritism.

Both Syr-Cur. and Syr-Sin. for "way of God" read "word of God."

22. The **φόρος** (classical and in LXX) or capitation-tax must be distinguished from τέλη, which are indirect taxes. Mt. and Mk. here have κῆνσον, but in Mk. ἐπικεφάλαιον is a notable *v.l.*

For **ἡμᾶς** (ℵ A B L) TR. has ἡμῖν (C D P Γ Δ Λ Π). Only here and vi. 4 does ἔξεστιν *c. acc. et infin.* occur in N.T. **Καίσαρι** stands first with emphasis. Usually both dat. and acc. *follow* δοῦναι: i. 74, 77, xii. 32, xvii. 18; Acts v. 31, vii. 5; Mt. xiv. 7, xx. 4, etc.

23. κατανοήσας . . . πανουργίαν. Mt. has γνοὺς . . . πονηρίαν, Mk. εἰδὼς . . . ὑπόκρισιν. See on xii. 27 for Lk.'s fondness for κατανοέω. In N.T., as in class. Grk., πανουργία always has a bad meaning (1 Cor. iii. 19; 2 Cor. iv. 2, xi. 3; Eph. iv. 14). In LXX it may mean "versatility, skill" (Prov. i. 4, viii. 5).

24. Δείξατέ μοι δηνάριον. Mk. has φέρετε, which implies that they had to fetch it. They would not have heathen money on their persons. Mt. has προσήνεγκαν αὐτῷ, which implies the same thing; and he calls it τὸ νόμισμα τοῦ κήνσου, because this poll-tax had to be paid in *denarii.*

Τί με πειράζετε (A C D P) is an insertion here from Mt. and Mk. ℵ B L omit. See Wright, *Synopsis*, § 80, p. 73.

Καίσαρος. Probably that of Tiberius. There was no royal effigy on Jewish coins: and Roman copper coins, if for circulation in

Palestine, had no image on them. It was a base piece of flattery on the part of Herod Philip that he placed on his coins the head of the emperor, and the *denarius* used on this occasion may have been one of his. It is possible but not probable that it was a foreign coin, such as circulated outside Palestine.[1] "Judas of Galilee" (Acts v. 37; Jos. *Ant.* xviii. 1. 6, xx. 5. 2) or the Gaulonite (*Ant.* xviii. 1. 1) had denounced the payment of tribute to Cæsar as treason against Jehovah, the only Lord that Israel could acknowledge (A.D. 6): and probably the Galileans who were listening to Jesus on this occasion were thoroughly in sympathy. But His adversaries had conceded the whole point when they admitted that the coinage was Cæsar's: for even Judaism admitted that coinage implies the right of taxation, and is evidence of the government to which submission is due. *Ubicunque numisma alicujus regis obtinet, illic incolæ regem istum pro domino agnoscunt* (Maimon.). See Edersh. *L. & T.* ii. p. 385; *Hist. of J. N.* p. 257. Grotius quotes Τίνα ἔχει χαρακτῆρα τοῦτο τὸ τετρασσάριον; Τραιανοῦ (Arrian. *Epict.* iv. 5. 17).

25. Τοίνυν ἀπόδοτε. This is the right order (ℵ B L, Boh. Goth. Arm.), contrary to the best usage; and hence the correction ἀπόδοτε τοίνυν (A C P Δ Λ Π). D, Syr-Sin. and Lat. Vet. omit τοίνυν. For τοίνυν first in the sentence comp. Heb. xiii. 13; Is. iii. 10, v. 13, and contrast 1 Cor. ix. 26; Wisd. i. 11, viii. 9. The τοίνυν (Mt. οὖν) marks the sayings as a conclusion drawn from the previous admission: "Then render to Cæsar," etc.

τὰ Καίσαρος Καίσαρι. This is the answer to the Pharisaic portion of His questioners, as τὰ τοῦ Θεοῦ τῷ Θεῷ to the Herodian. The error lay in supposing that Cæsar and God were mutually exclusive alternatives. Duty to Cæsar was part of their duty to God, because for purposes of order and government Cæsar was God's vicegerent. In Rom. xii. 1, 2 S. Paul insists on the second of these principles, in xiii. 1–7 on the first. See detached note at the end of Rom. xiii. As Judæa was an imperial province, its taxes would go to the *fiscus* of the emperor, not to the *ærarium* of the senate.

τὰ τοῦ Θεοῦ. No one duty is to be understood to the exclusion of others, whether offerings in the temple, or penitence, etc. All duties owed by man to God are included.[2] For ἀποδίδωμι of paying what is *due* comp. vii. 42, x. 35, xii. 59; and see Wsctt. on Heb.

[1] Some "heretic" sent R. Juda an imperial *denarius*, and he was deciding not to accept it, when another Rabbi advised him to accept it and throw it into a well before the donor's feet (*Avoda Sara* f. 6 quoted by Wetst. on Mt. xxii. 21). But see Schürer, *J.P. in T. of J.C.* p. 77.

[2] It may be doubted whether the idea that man bears the image of God just as the coin bears the image of Cæsar is to be supplied: "Render then the coin to Cæsar, and give the whole man up to God" (Latham, *A Service of Angels*, p. 50).

xii. 11. They had said φόρον δοῦναι, as if the tribute was a *gift*. By substituting ἀπόδοτε He indicates that it is a *due*.

26. οὐκ ἴσχυσαν . . . ἐναντίον τοῦ λαοῦ. Peculiar to Lk., who draws special attention to this further victory of Jesus. All three record the wonder of His adversaries.

For the constr. of **αὐτοῦ** see on ver. 20. This use of **ἐναντίον** is common in LXX, but in N.T. is found only here, xxiv. 19; Acts vii. 10, viii. 32: comp. ἔναντι i. 8; Acts viii. 21.

For **θαυμάζειν ἐπί** see on ii. 33, and for **σιγᾶν** see on xviii. 39.

27–38. The Question of the Sadducees respecting a Woman with Seven Husbands. Mt. xxii. 23–33; Mk. xii. 18–27. Mt. tells us expressly that this took place ἐν ἐκείνῃ τῇ ἡμέρᾳ. Lk. mentions the Sadducees several times in the Acts (iv. 1, v. 17, xxiii. 6–8) but here only in his Gospel. Mk. also here only. This question was less dangerous than the previous one. It concerned a matter of exegesis and speculation, not of politics, and was doctrinal rather than practical. Like the first two questions, it aimed at destroying Christ's influence with the multitude. While the first aimed at inspiring them with distrust, and the second at rousing their indignation against Him, this one is calculated to excite their ridicule. If Jesus failed to answer it, He and His supporters would be placed in a grotesque position. The Sadducees were not popular, for the doctrine of the resurrection is precious to the majority of mankind, and they would be glad of this opportunity of publicly exhibiting the popular doctrine as productive of ludicrous results. Josephus says that when Sadducees became magistrates, they conformed to the views of the Pharisees, for otherwise the people would not tolerate them (*Ant.* xviii. 1. 4). *D.C.G.* art. "Sadducees."

But the doctrine of the resurrection and of invisible powers (Acts xxiii. 8; Jos. *B. J.* ii. 8. 14) was not the main point in dispute between Sadducees and Pharisees, but a deduction from the main point. The crucial question was whether the oral tradition was binding (*Ant.* xiii. 10. 6). The Pharisees contended that it was equal in authority to the written Law, while the Sadducees maintained that everything not written was an open question and might be rejected. Apparently the Pharisees were willing to concede that the doctrine of the resurrection is not to be found in the written Law; and indeed outside the Book of Daniel it is not clearly taught in O.T. What is said in favour of it (Job xix. 26; Ps. xvi. 9, 11; Is. xxvi. 19) seems to be balanced by statements equally strong on the other side (Ps. vi. 5, lxxxviii. 10, 11, cxv. 17; Eccles. ix. 4–10; Is. xxxviii. 18, 19). Hence it followed, on Sadducean principles, that the doctrine was without authority, and was simply a pious opinion. That the Sadducees rejected the O.T., with the exception of the Pentateuch, is a mistake of Tertullian, Origen, Hippolytus, Jerome, and others; and perhaps arises from confusion with the Samaritans. But no Jew regarded the other books as equal in authority to the Books of Moses; and hence Jesus, in answering the Sadducees, takes His argument from Exodus (Bleek, *Int. to O.T.* § 305, Eng. tr. ii. p. 310). The name Σαδδουκαῖος probably comes from Zadok, the best attested form of which in many passages of LXX is Σαδδούκ (2 Sam. viii. 17;

Neh. iii. 29, x. 21, xi. 11, xiii. 13; Ezek. xl. 46, xliii. 19, xliv. 15, xlviii. 11): but *which* Zadok gave the name to the sect, remains doubtful (Schürer, *Jewish People in the T. of J. C.* II. ii. pp. 29–43; Hausrath, *N.T. Times*, i. pp. 136–150; Pressensé, *Le Siècle Apostolique*, pp. 87, 88, ed. 1888. For minor points of difference between Sadducees and Pharisees, see Kuenen, *Religion of Israel*, iii. pp. 234–238; Derenbourg, pp. 132–144).

27. τινες τῶν Σαδδουκαίων οἱ λέγοντες. The *οἱ λεγ.* may agree with *τινες*, or be an irregular description of *τῶν Σαδδ.* In the latter case comp. Mk. xii. 40; but the former is better. All Sadducees held that the resurrection was not an article of faith, but some may have believed that it was true. One might render *οἱ λέγοντες* "who were saying" at that moment.

λέγοντες is the reading of ℵ B C D L 1 33 etc., d e Syr-Sin. Syr-Cur. Aegypt. Goth. Aeth., which is not discredited because it is also in Mt. But Tisch. follows A P Γ Δ Λ Π etc. in reading *ἀντιλέγοντες*.

Ἐάν τινος ἀδελφός. The quotation gives the substance rather than the wording of Deut. xxv. 5; comp. Gen. xxxviii. 8. The levirate law is said still to prevail among the Kalmucks and other nations in the East. See Morison on Mk. xii. 19.

29. ἑπτὰ οὖν ἀδελφοί. The *οὖν* appears to indicate that what is about to be narrated was a *consequence* of this levirate law. But the *οὖν* may be a mere particle of transition. Mt. inserts *παρ' ἡμῖν*, as if they professed to describe what had actually taken place. It is said to have been a well-known problem, the recognized answer to which was, that at the resurrection the woman would be the wife of the first brother. This answer Christ might have given; but, while it would have avoided the ridicule to which the Sadducees wished to expose Him, it would not have refuted their doctrine. D, Syr-Sin. c d ff_2 l q ins. *παρ' ἡμῖν* here.

ἄτεκνος. "Childless" as in ver. 28: comp. ver. 31. All three imply that there was neither son nor daughter. And this is laid down in the Talmud,—that the deceased brother must have no child at all, although Deut. xxv. 5 says simply "have no son" (RV.). Some maintained that the levirate law, which to a large extent had gone out of use, did not apply to a wedded wife, but only to a betrothed woman. The Mishna recommends that the levirate law be not observed.

30. καὶ ὁ δεύτερος. This is the reading of ℵ B D L 157, e, omitting *ἔλαβεν* after *καί* and *τὴν γυναῖκα καὶ οὗτος ἀπέθανεν ἄτεκνος* after *ὁ δεύτερος*. These insertions are found in A P Γ Δ Λ Π, Syr-Sin. Syr-Cur. Vulg.

31. οὐ κατέλιπον τέκνα καὶ ἀπέθανον. The main point is placed first, although their death logically precedes.

33. τίνος αὐτῶν γίνεται γυνή; The question is a plausible appeal to the rough common sense of the multitude, and is based upon the coarse materialistic views of the resurrection which then prevailed.

34. Jesus begins by removing this erroneous basis and shows that the question is futile. The words οἱ υἱοὶ τοῦ αἰῶνος . . . τυχεῖν are peculiar to Lk., who omits "Ye do err, not knowing the Scriptures, nor the power of God." Comp. Eph. i. 21.

35. οἱ δὲ καταξιωθέντες τοῦ αἰῶνος ἐκείνου. One might have expected simply οἱ υἱοὶ τ. αἰῶνος ἐκ. But the substitution of καταξιωθέντες corrects the assumption that all the sons ot this world will enter the Kingdom which begins with the resurrection. Comp. Acts v. 41; 2 Thes. i. 5. Nowhere else does ὁ αἰὼν ἐκεῖνος occur in N.T. It means the age beyond the grave regarded as an age of bliss and glory. See on Rom. xii. 2. In itself it implies resurrection; but, inasmuch as this is the doctrine in dispute, the resurrection is specially mentioned. The word ἀνάστασις occurs Zeph. iii. 8; Lam. iii. 63; Dan. xi. 20; title of Ps. lxv. But not until 2 Mac. vii. 14, xii. 43 is it used of resurrection after death.

τῆς ἐκ νεκρῶν. This must be distinguished from [ἡ] ἀνάστασις [τῶν] νεκρῶν. The latter is the more comprehensive term and implies that *all* the dead are raised (Mt. xxii. 31; Acts xvii. 32, xxiii. 6, xxiv. 21, xxvi. 23; Rom. i. 4; 1 Cor. xv. 12, 13, 42; Heb. vi. 2). Whereas ἀνάστασις ἐκ νεκρῶν rather implies that *some* from among the dead are raised, while others as yet are not. Hence it is used of the resurrection of Christ and of the righteous, and is equivalent to the ἀνάστασις ζωῆς (Acts iv. 2; 1 Pet. i. 3: comp. Col. i. 18). The ἀνάστασις νεκρῶν includes the ἀνάστασις κρίσεως as well as the ἀν. ζωῆς (Jn. v. 29). Comp. xiv. 14; 1 Thes. iv. 16; Rev. xx. 5, 6; and see Lft. on Phil. iii. 11 and Mey. on Rom. i. 4. With the construction comp. τούτου τυχεῖν οὐκ ἠξιώθην αὐτός (Aesch. *P. V.* 239).

γαμίζονται. Identical in meaning with γαμίσκονται (ver. 34).

In both verses the simple verb is the right reading. In both places TR. follows inferior authorities in reading ἐκγαμ.

36. οὐδὲ γὰρ ἀποθανεῖν. The γάρ means that the abolition of death involves the abolition of marriage, the purpose of which is to preserve the human race from extinction.

For οὐδέ (A B D L P 106 157) Tisch. has οὔτε (ℵ Q R Γ Δ Λ Π). It looks like a correction.

ἰσάγγελοι γάρ εἰσιν. The adj. occurs here only in bibl. Grk. and was probably coined by Lk. on the analogy of ἰσάστερος (4 Mac. xvii. 5), ἰσάδελφος, ἰσόθεος, κ.τ.λ. Mt. and Mk. have ὡς ἄγγελοι. Grotius quotes from Hierocles τοὺς ἰσοδαίμονας καὶ ἰσαγγέλους καὶ τοῖς ἀγανοῖς ἥρωσιν ὁμοίους. "They do not marry, because they cannot die; and they cannot die, because they are like angels; and they are sons of God, being sons of the resurrection." In correcting the error of the Sadducees about the resurrection Jesus incidentally corrects their scepticism respecting Angels (Acts xxiii. 8). See Latham, *A Service of Angels*, pp. 52–60; Charles, *Apoc. of Baruch*, pp. lxxvii, 84.

The connexion of *καὶ υἱοί εἰσιν Θεοῦ* is uncertain. The repetition of *εἰσιν* is rather against the clause being taken with *ἰσάγγελοι γάρ εἰσιν*. More probably it is co-ordinate with *οὐδὲ ἀποθανεῖν δύνανται*. It is worth noting that both in Job i. 6, ii. 1, and Gen. vi. 2 LXX has not *υἱοί* but *ἄγγελοι τοῦ Θεοῦ*. Comp. 1 Cor. xv. 52; Rev. xxi. 4. But in any case it is the *immortality* of the Angels, not their sexlessness or immateriality, that is the point of the argument. For **τῆς ἀν. υἱοὶ ὄντες** see on **xvi. 8.**

37. Having shown that their question ought not to have been asked, being based upon a gross misconception of the conditions of the future state, Jesus proceeds to answer the objection which their question implied, viz. that the doctrine of the resurrection is inconsistent with the Mosaic Law. On the contrary, Moses implies the doctrine. The levirate law is no argument against a resurrection; and the passage here quoted is a strong argument in favour of it. See Martensen, *Chr. Dogm.* § 290, 274.

καὶ Μωυσῆς. "Even Moses," who was supposed to be against the doctrine (Mey. Weiss, Holtzm.). Less well, *etiam Moses, non modo prophetæ* (Beng.). Jesus quotes Moses because they had done so (ver. 28), not because the Sadducees accepted only the Pentateuch (Tert. Orig. Hieron.), which was not the case.

ἐμήνυσεν. Not, "hinted," but "disclosed, intimated, revealed." Both in class. and bibl. Grk. *μηνύω* is specially used of making known what was secret (Acts xxiii. 30; 1 Cor. x. 28; Jn. xi. 57; Soph. *O. R.* 102).

ἐπὶ τῆς βάτου. "In the Bush," *i.e.* in the portion of Scripture known as "the Bush." In Mk. we have *ἐν τῇ βίβλῳ Μωυσέως ἐπὶ τοῦ βάτου*, where AV. violently transposes *ἐπὶ τ. β.*,—"how in the bush God spake unto him." Comp. 2 Sam. i. 18 and Rom. xi. 2. The O.T. was divided into sections, which were named after something prominent in the contents. Examples are quoted from the Talmud. The rhapsodists divided Homer into sections and named them on a similar principle. In the Koran the chapters are named in this way. But the possibility of the simple local meaning here must not be excluded.

The gender of *βάτος* varies. Here and Acts vii. 35 it is fem. In Mk. and in LXX it is masc. (Exod. iii. 2, 3, 4; Deut. xxxiii. 16). So also in Polyb. and Theophr. Several Old Latin texts here read *sicut dixit vidi in rubo* (c f ff_2 i l q), which seems to imply a Greek text *ὡς λέγει εἶδον ἐν τῇ β.*

38. The Sadducees based their denial of the resurrection on the alleged silence of Scripture and on the incredibility of existence after the death of the body (Jos. *B. J.* ii. 8. 14). Christ demolishes their premises by showing that Scripture is not silent, but teaches the reality of existence after death.[1] His argument has less force against those who admit existence after death, but hold that this existence of the soul apart from the body will continue for ever. This, however, was not the error which He was combating, and perhaps was not a common view. Yet even against this error the argument has force, as Bengel points out. *Deus non est non entis deus: ipse est deus vivens; ergo ii qui deum habent, vivere debent, et qua parte vivere intermiserant, reviviscere in perpetuum.* But perhaps this is more than is intended. What is obvious is this:—Dead things may have a Creator, a Possessor, a Ruler: only living beings can have a God. If Abraham or any of the patriarchs had ceased to exist when he died, God would have ceased to be his God. "I *am* the God of Abraham" implies that Abraham still lives. Comp. οἱ διὰ τὸν Θεὸν ἀποθανόντες ζῶσιν τῷ Θεῷ, ὥσπερ Ἀβραὰμ κ. Ἰσαὰκ κ. Ἰακώβ (4 Mac. xvi. 25).[2] It is in reference to us that they seem to die: in reference to Him πάντες ζῶσιν. The πάντες need not be restricted to the three patriarchs: it includes all who are mentioned in *vv.* 35, 36. Mk. adds πολὺ πλανᾶσθε, but the condemnation of this doctrinal error is less severe than of the Pharisaic hypocrisy.

39, 40. The Testimony of the Scribes. Some of the Pharisees could not refrain from expressing their admiration of the manner in which Jesus had vanquished their opponents. That proof of the doctrine of the resurrection, which Sadducees had defied the Pharisees to find in the Pentateuch, Jesus had produced, and in the most convincing manner. The scribes were now persuaded that it was useless to ply Jesus with hard questions. Such attempts merely gave Him the opportunity of winning victories. But we learn from Mt. and Mk. that one of them came forward to try Him once more (πειράζων αὐτόν) with a question that was much debated, as to which commandment was chief. There is nothing to show, however, that there was any snare in the question: the scribe may have wished to try His sagacity on a point which was very interesting. That a similar inquiry has been narrated elsewhere (x. 25), may be Lk.'s reason for omitting the incident here.

40. γάρ. The fact that this was not understood caused it to be altered in many texts into δέ. Godet maintains that it "has absolutely no sense," and

[1] Gamaliel is said to have silenced Sadducees by quoting such promises as Deut. i. 8, xi. 9. God's promises must be fulfilled, and these were not fulfilled to the patriarchs during their lifetime. Again, if God quickened buried seed, how much more His own people (Edersh. *Hist. of J. N.* p. 316).

[2] The Fourth Book of Maccabees, although written before the destruction of Jerusalem, was probably written not very long before Christian interpolations, or conscious imitations of Christian phraseology, are possible (Schürer, *Jewish People in the T. of J. C.* II. iii. p. 244).

erroneously states that WH. have abandoned it. It is attested by ℵ B L, 33, Aegyptt., and gives excellent sense. Some of His opponents praised Him, *for* they saw that He was always victorious, and that they must risk no more defeats.

41–44 Jesus in turn asks a Question about David and the Messiah. Mt. xxii. 41–46; Mk. xii. 35–37, where see Gould. It is yet another opportunity of instructing them, not of vanquishing and humiliating them, that is sought. The approbation recorded in ver. 39 (comp. Mk. xii. 32) gave signs that some of His opponents were open to conviction, and might even now recognize the Christ.

41. πρὸς αὐτούς. The scribes who had expressed admiration are perhaps chiefly meant. In any case, "unto them" and not "in reference to them" is the meaning.

Πῶς λέγουσιν. Mk. gives *οἱ γραμματεῖς* as the subject of *λέγουσιν*, which does not imply that the scribes had gone away. "With what right do teachers say?" This is the usual doctrine; but do people consider what it involves in reference to other statements?

42. αὐτὸς γάρ. This is the reading of ℵ B L R 1 33, l, Aegyptt., and may be safely preferred to *καὶ αὐτός* (A D P, Syrr. Vulg. Goth.). Q has *καὶ αὐτὸς γάρ*.

ἐν Βίβλῳ Ψαλμῶν. See on iii. 4. Mt. has *πνεύματι* and Mk. *τῷ πν. τῷ ἁγίῳ* for *βίβλῳ Ψαλμῶν*. The quotation is *verbatim* the same in all three, excepting that Mt. and Mk. have *ὑποκάτω* for the *ὑποπόδιον* of LXX. and Lk. All three omit the *ὁ* before *Κύριος*. In the Hebrew we have different words for Lord: "Jehovah saith to Adonai." Ps. cx. was always believed to be Messianic, and to have been written by David. That it is Messianic is a matter of *spiritual interpretation*; and, as Jesus here gives this doctrine the sanction of His authority, no loyal Christian will consider that he is free to question it. The authorship of the Psalm is a question of *criticism*; and nothing in the method of Christ's teaching, or in the contents of Scripture generally, warrants us in believing that He here frees us from the duty of investigating a problem which is capable of being solved by our own industry and acuteness. We have no right to expect that Scripture will save us from the discipline of patient research by supplying us with infallible answers to questions of history, chronology, geology, and the like.

The last word has not yet been spoken as to the authorship of Ps. cx.; but it is a mistake to maintain that Jesus has decided the question. There is nothing antecedently incredible in the hypothesis that in such matters, as in other details of human information, He condescended not to know more than His contemporaries, and that He therefore believed what He had been taught in the school and in the synagogue (see footnote, p. 124). Nor ought we summarily to dismiss the suggestion that, although He knew that the Psalm was not written by David, He yet abstained from challenging beliefs respecting matters of fact, because the premature and violent correction of such beliefs would have been more harmful to His work than their undisturbed continuance would be. In this, as in many things, the correction of erroneous opinion might well be left to time. But this suggestion is less satisfactory than the other hypothesis. It should be noticed that, while Jesus affirms both the inspiration (Mt. Mk.) and the Messianic character (Mt. Mk. Lk.) of Ps. cx., yet the argumentative question with which He concludes need not be understood as asserting that David is the author of it, although it *seems* to imply this. It may mean no more than that the scribes have not fairly faced what their own principles involve. Here is a problem, with which they ought to be quite familiar, and of which they ought to be able to give a solution. It is their position, and not His, that is open to criticism. The question, "Why callest thou Me good?" appears to serve a similar purpose. It *seems* to imply that Christ is not to be called good in the sense that God is called good (Mk. x. 18). But it need mean no more than that the young man who addressed Jesus as "Good Master" ought to reflect as to the significance of such language before making use of it.[1]

44. **καὶ πῶς αὐτοῦ υἱός ἐστιν;** De Wette and Strauss both point out that this question must imply either (1) that the Messiah is *not* the Son of David, or (2) that the inspired Psalmist teaches that the Messiah is no mere political deliverer. Strauss, with Schenkel and Volkmar, prefers the former alternative.[2] But it is incredible that, even if Jesus were a mere human teacher, He would thus gratuitously have contradicted the express utterances of Scripture (2 Sam. vii. 8–29; Is. ix. 5–7, xi. 1–10; Jer. xxiii. 5–8; Mic. v. 2) and the popular belief which was built upon them; especially as this belief was a valuable help to His own work (xviii. 38; Mt. xv. 22, xii. 23, xxi. 9). Whereas, those who believe in His Divinity need have no difficulty in admitting, that, on a point which was no part of His teaching, Jesus might go all His human life without even raising the question as to the truth of what was authoritatively taught about the authorship of this or that portion of Scripture.

45–47. The Condemnation of the Scribes. Like Mk. xii. 38–40, this seems to be a summary of the terrible indictment of

[1] "If I by Beelzebub cast out devils, by whom do your sons cast them out?" (Lk. xi. 19) is possibly a similar case. It need not imply that Jewish exorcists had succeeded in casting out demons, but only that they were credited with no diabolical witchcraft in making the attempt. The question may mean no more than "Judge Me on the same principles as you judge your own exorcists." See Wright *ad loc.* and xvi. 19.

On Ps. cx. see Gore, *Bampton Lectures*, 1891, Lect. vii. *sub fin.* and note 55; Driver, *Int. to Lit. of O.T.* p. 362 and note; Perowne, *Psalms*, ii. p. 302, with the remarks of Thirlwall there quoted; Meyer on Mt. xxii. 43; Weiss on Mt. xxii. 43 with note; Bishop Mylne, *Indian Ch. Quar. Rev.* Oct. 1892, p. 486; Schwartzkopff, *Konnte Jesus irren?* 1896, pp. 21–36.

[2] Latham is of the same opinion from a different point of view. He thinks that Jesus repudiated the title "Son of David," as implying that the Redeemer of the world was a *Jewish* Messiah, with a title based on legitimacy and genealogy (*Pastor Pastorum*, p. 415).

the hierarchy given at length in Mt. xxiii. Lk. perhaps did not know the longer report preserved by Mt. As he had already given an account of a similar discourse (xi. 39–52), there was the less need to give a full report here.

45. Ἀκούοντος δὲ παντὸς τοῦ λαοῦ. It is in the hearing of the multitude who had just been witnesses of the contest, in which the scribes had been so signally defeated, that Jesus utters His final condemnation of them. Comp. the similar condemnation xii. 1, where as here we have *προσέχετε ἀπό*, and see notes there. Comp. also the somewhat parallel passage in Ezek. xxii. 25: *ἁρπάζοντες ἁρπάγματα, ψυχὰς κατεσθίοντες ἐν δυναστείᾳ, καὶ τιμὰς λαμβάνοντες· καὶ αἱ χῆραί σου ἐπληθύνθησαν ἐν μέσῳ σου.*

46. περιπατεῖν ἐν στολαῖς. Mk. also has this Hellenized expression for *πλατύνουσιν τὰ φυλακτήρια αὐτῶν* (Mt. xxiii. 5). The saying from *ἀσπασμοὺς ἐν ταῖς ἀγοραῖς* to *τοῖς δείπνοις* is in all three accounts. Comp. xiv. 7, and see Wetst. on Mt. xxiii. 6, 7.

Salmon quotes AV. of this and of Mk. xii. 38 in illustration of the variety which independent translation is sure to produce. There, "*love* to *go* in long *clothing*, and love *salutations* in the *market places* and the *chief* seats in the synagogues, and the *uppermost* rooms at feasts, which for a *pretence* make long prayers." Here, "desire, walk, robes, greetings, markets, highest, chief, show" for the words in italics, the Greek in all cases being the same.

τῶν θελόντων περιπατεῖν. This constr. of *θέλω* = "like, love" *c. infin.* occurs only here and Mk. xii. 38. It is perhaps an extension of the Hebraistic *θέλω τινα* or *τι* = "take delight in," and in Mk. xii. 38 an acc. is coupled with the infin. Comp. Mt. xxvii. 43, ix. 13, xii. 7; Heb. x. 5, 8. But Lk. separates the acc. from *θελόντων* by inserting the more usual *φιλούντων*, Win. liv. 4, p. 587. What follows is common to all three accounts. See on xi. 43 and xiv. 7.

47. οἳ κατεσθίουσιν τὰς οἰκίας τῶν χηρῶν. Comp. Mk. xii. 40; but this item in the condemnation is not found in the true text of Mt. xxiii. Probably wealthy widows are chiefly meant. They devoured widows' houses by accepting hospitality and rich presents from pious and weak women. *Sexus muliebris ut ad superstitionem pronior ita magis patet ad eas fraudes* (Grot.). They would find widows a specially easy prey, and their taking advantage of the defenceless aggravated their guilt. *C'étaient les Tartuffes de l'époque* (Godet). Josephus says of the Pharisees *οἷς ὑπῆκτο ἡ γυναικωνῖτις* (*Ant.* xvii. 2. 4). Comp. the cases of Fulvia (xviii. 3. 5) and of Helene (xx. 2. 5) as instances of devout and benevolent women. The wife of Pheroras, brother of Herod the Great, paid the fines of thousands of Pharisees who had been fined for refusing to swear loyalty to Cæsar (xvii. 2. 4). The Talmud gives evidence of the plundering of widows. *Inter plagas quæ a Pharisæis proveniunt hæc etiam est. Est qui consultat cum orphanis, ut alimenta viduæ eripiat* (*Sota Hieros.* f. 20. 1, Schoettg. i. 199). Of a plundered widow R. Eleazar says, *Plaga Pharisæorum tetigit illam.*

λήμψονται περισσότερον κρίμα. The "more abundant" may be understood in two ways: (1) in proportion to the high estimation in which they were held in this world; or (2) in proportion to the hypocrisy which makes a trade of religion (Gould). *Qui male agit, judicatur. Qui bono abutitur ad malum ornandum, magis judicatur* (Beng.). For **λήμψομαι κρίμα** comp. Rom. xiii. 2; Jas. iii. 1; and for **περισσότερον** see on vii. 26.

XXI. 1–4. The Widow's Mites. Mk. xii. 41–44. The incident is not recorded by Mt. The saying respecting "widows' houses" might lead to the preservation of this narrative. Mk. and Lk. give both, Mt. neither.

1. Ἀναβλέψας. Mk. has *καθίσας*. The long discussions had wearied Him, and He had been sitting with downcast or closed eyes.

εἶδεν τοὺς βάλλοντας . . . πλουσίους. Either, "He saw the rich who were casting," etc. Or, "He saw those who were casting . . rich people." The former is better. In either case the imperf. part. expresses what was continually going on: *vidit eos qui mittebant munera sua in gazophylacium divites* (Vulg.).

τὸ γαζοφυλάκιον. We are not sure that there was a separate building called the Treasury. But the thirteen trumpet-mouthed boxes which stood in the spacious Court of the Women appear to have been known as the Treasury. These *Shoparoth* or "trumpets" were each of them inscribed with the purpose to which the money put into them was to be devoted. See Edersh. *The Temple*, p. 26. Besides these there was the strong-room whither their contents were taken from time to time. This, however, cannot be meant here. Comp. Jn. viii. 20.

Both in LXX and in Josephus we find sometimes *τὰ γαζοφυλάκια* (Neh. x. 38, xiii. 9; *B. J.* v. 5. 2, vi. 5. 2), sometimes *τὸ γαζοφυλάκιον* (2 Kings xxiii. 11; 1 Mac. xiv. 49; *Ant.* xix. 6. 1): and we cannot say that there is any difference of meaning.

2. πενιχράν. Exod. xxii. 25; Prov. xxviii. 15, xxix. 7; but nowhere else in N.T. Vulg. and l have *pauperculam*: see also Vulg. of Is. lxvi. 2. Note the *τινα*.

λεπτὰ δύο. See on xii. 59. The exact amount would not be visible from a distance. Jesus knew this, as He knew that it was all that she had, supernaturally. It was not lawful to offer less than two *perutahs* or mites. This was therefore the smallest offering ever made by anyone; so that Bengel's remark on the two mites is out of place: *quorum unum vidua retinere potuit.* She could have kept *both.*

3. Ἀληθῶς λέγω ὑμῖν. Introduces something contrary to the usual view. Here, as in ix. 27 and xii. 44, Lk. has *ἀληθῶς*, where Mk. or Mt. has *ἀμήν*.

πλεῖον πάντων. *Non modo proportione geometrica, sed animo, quem spectabat Dominus* (Beng.).

For πλεῖον (A B Γ Δ Λ Π), which is supported by πλεον (א), Tisch. prefers πλείω (D Q X), which is supported by πλείονα (L). Orig. has πλεῖον several times.

4. πάντες γὰρ οὗτοι. Pointing to those of them who were still in sight.

εἰς τὰ δῶρα. "Unto the gifts," which were already in the boxes.

ἐκ τοῦ ὑστερήματος. Comp. 2 Cor. viii. 14, xi. 9; Judg. xix. 20; Ps. xxxiii. 10. Whereas they had more than they needed for their wants, she had less: they had a surplus, and she a *deficit*. Yet out of this deficient store she gave,—gave all she had.

The Latin Versions vary much in rendering both expressions: *de exuperantia* (s), *de eo quod superfuit illis* (e), *de quo super illis fuit* (a), *ex eo quod abundavit illis* (f), *ex abundanti* (Vulg.): *de exiguitate sua* (a), *de inopia sua* (e r), *de minimo suo* (d), *ex eo quod deest illi* (f Vulg.).

πάντα τὸν βίον. All that she had to support her at that time: comp. viii. 43, xv. 12, 30; Cant. viii. 7; Soph. *Phil.* 933, 1283.

5–36. The destruction of the Temple and of Jerusalem foretold. Mt. xxiv. 1–36; Mk. xiii. 1–32. The section falls into three divisions: the Occasion of the Prophecy (5–7), the Prophecy (8–28), the Exhortation to Vigilance based on the Parable of the Fig Tree (29–36). Edersheim has shown in detail how different contemporary Jewish opinion respecting the end of the world was from what is contained in this prediction, and therefore how untenable is the hypothesis that we have here only a reflexion of ordinary Jewish tradition (*L. & T.* ii. pp. 434–445).

5–7. Lk. gives no indication of time or place. Mk. and Mt. tell us that it was as Jesus was leaving the precincts that the remark of the disciples was made. The discourse as to the comparative merits of the offerings made in the Temple would easily lead on to thoughts respecting the magnificence of the temple itself and of the votive gifts which it received.

5. τινων λεγόντων. Mt. and Mk. tell us that these were disciples.

Here again Cod. Bezae has a reproduction of the gen. abs. in Latin, *quorundam dicentium*: comp. ver. 26.

λίθοις καλοῖς. Some of the stones of the substructure were enormous. The columns of the cloister or portico were monoliths of marble over forty feet high. See Josephus, whose account should be read in full (*B. J.* v. 5), Tacitus (*Hist.* v. 12), Milman (*Hist. of the Jews*, ii. bk. xvi. p. 332), Edersheim (*Temple*, p. 21), Renan (*V. de J.* p. 210). "It is almost impossible to realise the effect which would be produced by a building longer and higher than York Cathedral, standing on a solid mass of masonry almost equal in height to the tallest of our church spires" (Wilson, *Recovery of Jerusalem*, p. 9).

ἀναθήμασιν. Mt. and Mk. say nothing about the rich offerings, which were many and various, from princes and private individuals (2 Mac. iii. 2–7): *e.g.* the golden vine of Herod, with bunches as tall as a man (Jos. *B. J.* v. 5. 4; *Ant.* xv. 11. 3: comp. xvii. 6. 3; xviii. 3. 5, xix. 6. 1). *Illic immensæ opulentiæ templum* (Tac. *Hist.* v. 8. 1). For *ἀνάθημα* comp. 2 Mac. ix. 16; 3 Mac. iii. 17; Hdt. i. 183. 6. Here only in N.T.

On the relation between *ἀνάθημα* and *ἀνάθεμα* see Ellicott and Lft. on Gal. i. 8; Trench, *Syn.* v.; Cremer, *Lex.* p. 547. In MSS. the two words are often confounded. Here ℵ A D X have *ἀναθέμασιν*, which Tisch. adopts.

6. ταῦτα ἃ θεωρεῖτε. *Nom. pendens*: comp. Mt. x. 14, xii. 36; Jn. vi. 39, vii. 38, xv. 2, xvii. 2; Acts vii. 40.

ἐλεύσονται ἡμέραι. "Days will come": no article. Comp. v. 35, xvii. 22, xix. 43, xxiii. 29.

οὐκ ἀφεθήσεται λίθος ἐπὶ λίθῳ. A strange prediction to those who had been expecting that the Messianic Kingdom would immediately begin, and that Jerusalem would be the centre of it. Respecting the completeness of the fulfilment of this prediction see Stanley, *Sin. & Pal.* p. 183; Robinson, *Res. in Pal.* i. p. 295.

7. Just as Lk. omits the fact that the remark about the glorious buildings was made as Jesus was leaving the temple (ver. 5), so he omits the fact that this question was asked while Jesus was sitting on the Mount of Olives. Mt. knows that it was "the disciples" who asked; but the interpreter of Peter knows that Peter, James, John, and Andrew were the enquirers. Both state that the question was asked *κατ' ἰδίαν*.

πότε οὖν ταῦτα ἔσται; They accept the prediction without question, and ask as to the date, respecting which Christ gives them no answer: comp. xiii. 23, 24, xvii. 20. Perhaps they considered that this temple was to be destroyed to make room for one more worthy of the Kingdom. Their second question, *τί τὸ σημεῖον*, shows that they expect to live to see the preparatory catastrophe.

8–28. The Prophecy. The Troubles which will follow the Departure of Christ—False Christs, Wars, Persecutions (8–19). The Destruction of Jerusalem (20–24). The Signs of the Return of the Son of Man (25–28). The record of the prediction in Mt. and Mk. is similarly arranged. But in all three records the outlines of the two main events, with their signs, cannot always be disentangled. Some of the utterances clearly point to the Destruction of Jerusalem; others equally clearly to the Return of the Christ. But there are some which might apply to either or both;

and we, who stand between the two, cannot be sure which one, if only one, is intended. In its application to the lives of the hearers each event taught a similar truth, and conveyed a similar warning; and therefore a clearly cut distinction between them was as little needed as an exact statement of date. Some of the early commentators held that the whole of the prophecy refers to the end of the world without including the fall of Jerusalem.

8. πλανηθῆτε. "Be led astray." The verb is used nowhere else in Lk. It implies no mere mistake, but fundamental departure from the truth: Jn. vii. 47; 1 Jn. i. 8, ii. 26, iii. 7; Rev. ii. 20, xii. 9, xx. 3–10, etc. "Deceive" (AV.) would rather be ἀπατᾷν (Jas. i. 26: comp. 1 Cor. iii. 18; Gal. vi. 3).

ἐπὶ τῷ ὀνόματί μου. Christ's name will be the *basis* of their claim. We know of no false Messiahs between the Ascension and the fall of Jerusalem. Theudas (Acts v. 36), Simon Magus (Acts viii. 9), the Egyptian (Acts xxi. 38) do not seem to have come forward as Messiahs. Dositheus, Simon Magus, and Menander might be counted among the "many antichrists" of 1 Jn. ii. 18, but not as false Christs. We seem, therefore, at the outset to have a sign which refers rather to Christ's return than to the destruction of Jerusalem.

9. ἀκαταστασίας. Comp. 1 Cor. xiv. 33; 2 Cor. vi. 5, xii. 20; Jas. iii. 16; Prov. xxvi. 28; Tob. iv. 13. In Josephus we have abundant evidence of such things. Tacitus says of this period—*opimum casibus, atrox prœliis, discors seditionibus, ipsâ etiam pace sævum. Quatuor Principes ferro interempti. Trina bella civilia, plura externa ac plerumque permixta* (*Hist.* i. 2. 1).—**πτοηθῆτε.** Only here and xxiv. 37: Mt. and Mk. have θροεῖσθε.

δεῖ. It is so ordered by God: comp. xiii. 33, xvii. 25, xix. 5, xxiv. 7, 26, 44.

οὐκ εὐθέως. First, with emphasis: "Not immediately is the end." For "by-and-by" as a translation of εὐθέως see on xvii. 7. By τὸ τέλος is not meant τὸ τέλος ὠδίνων (comp. Mt. xxiv. 8), but πάντων τὸ τέλος (1 Pet. iv. 7), the end of the world and the coming of the Son of Man.

10. Τότε ἔλεγεν αὐτοῖς. A new introduction to mark a solemn utterance. The τότε with ἔλεγεν is unusual; but that does not make the combination of τότε with ἐγερθήσεται (Beza, Casaubon, Hahn) probable.

D, Syr-Cur. Syr-Sin. a d e ff_2 i l r omit the words.

ἐγερθήσεται ἔθνος ἐπ' ἔθνος. Only here and in the parallels is this use of ἐγείρεσθαι ἐπί τινα found in N.T. Comp. ἐπεγερθήσονται Αἰγύπτιοι ἐπ' Αἰγυπτίους . . . [ἐπεγερθήσεται] πόλις ἐπὶ πόλιν καὶ νομὸς ἐπὶ νομόν (Is. xix. 2).

11. After describing the general political disturbances which shall precede the end, Jesus mentions four disturbances of nature which shall also form a prelude: earthquakes, famines, pestilences, and terrible phenomena in the heaven. Lk. alone mentions the λοιμοί (elsewhere in a metaphorical sense: Acts xxiv. 5; Prov. xxi. 24; Ps. i. 1; 1 Mac. xv. 21). Lk. alone also mentions the *φόβηθρά τε καὶ σημεῖα.* On the prodigies which preceded the capture of Jerusalem see Jos. *B. J.* vi. 5. 3; Tac. *Hist.* v. 13.

According to the better text (ℵ B L, Aegyptt. Arm. Aeth.) *κατὰ τόπους* belongs to *λοιμοὶ καὶ λιμοί*, not (as in Mk.) to *σεισμοὶ μεγάλοι* (A D, Latt.). Syr-Sin. has "in divers places" with both. Many authorities (ℵ A D L, d e Boh.) have *λιμοὶ κ. λοιμοί.* For the *paronomasia* comp. *ζωὴν καὶ πνοήν* (Acts xvii. 25); *γινώσκεις ἃ ἀναγινώσκεις* (Acts viii. 30); *ἔμαθεν ἀφ' ὧν ἔπαθεν* (Heb. v. 8); *ὀναίμην* in *'Ονήσιμος* (Philem. 20); *τινὲς τῶν κλάδων ἐξεκλάσθησαν* (Rom. xi. 17). Some Latin, Syriac, and Aethiopic authorities here insert *et hiemes* (*tempestates*), "probably from an extraneous source written or oral" (WH. ii. App. p. 63). Comp. the addition of *καὶ ταραχαί* in Mk. xiii. 8. And as regards the terrors generally comp. 4 Esdr. v. 4–10.

12–19. Calamities specially affecting the Disciples; Persecution and Treachery. While Lk. and Mk. emphasize the persecution that will come from the Jews, Mt. seems almost to confine it to the Gentiles (but see Mt. x. 17–19). Jn. also records that Christ foretold persecution (xv. 18–21), and in particular from the Jews (xvi. 2, 3). The Acts may supply abundant illustrations. Note that Lk. has nothing about "the Gospel being preached *to all the nations*" (Mk. xiii. 10; Mt. xxiv. 14). Would he have omitted this, if either of those documents was before him?

12. πρὸ δὲ τούτων. The prep. is certainly used of time, and not of superiority in magnitude. Persecutions are among the first things to be expected. The tendency of Mt. to slur the misdeeds of the Jews is conspicuous here. While Lk. mentions *τὰς συναγωγάς* and Mk. adds *συνέδρια*, Mt. has the vague term *θλίψιν.*

13. ἀποβήσεται ὑμῖν εἰς μαρτύριον. "The result to you will be that your sufferings will be for a testimony." A testimony to what? Not to the *innocence of the persecuted*, which is not the point: and they were commonly condemned as guilty. Possibly to *their loyalty*: comp. Phil. i. 19. More probably to *the truth of the Gospel.* For the verb comp. Job xiii. 16; 2 Mac. ix. 24.

14. προμελετᾶν. The regular word for conning over a speech: here only in N.T. Mk. has the less classical *προμεριμνᾶν.* Comp. Mt. x. 20, and see on xii. 11. Hahn would make the word mean anxiety about the *result* of the defence.

15. ἐγὼ γάρ. With emphasis: "all of that will be *My* care." In the parallel assurances in Mt. x. 20 and Mk. xiii. 11 it is the help of the *Holy Spirit* that is promised. In form this verse is peculiar to Lk. By *στόμα* is meant the power of speech; by *σοφία* the choice of matter and form. Comp. *ἐγὼ ἀνοίξω τὸ στόμα σου*

(Exod. iv. 12), and δέδωκα .οὺς λόγους μου εἰς τὸ στόμα σου (Jer. i. 9).

ἀντιστῆναι. This refers to σοφία (Acts vi. 10) as ἀντειπεῖν to στόμα. Their opponents will find no words in which to answer, and will be unable to refute what the disciples have advanced. *Vos ad certamen acceditis, sed ego prælior. Vos verba editis, sed ego sum qui loquor* (Bede). *Quid sapientius et incontradicibilius confessione simplici et exserta in martyris nomine cum Deo invalescentis* (Tert. *Adv. Marc.* iv. 39. 20). Holtzmann would have it that these verses (12–15) are the composition of the Evangelist with definite reference to the sufferings of S. Paul and S. Stephen.

16. **καὶ ὑπὸ γονέων.** "*Even* by parents" (RV.) rather than "*both* by parents" (AV.). Cov. also has "even." Comp. xii. 52, 53; Mt. x. 35 for similar predictions of discord in families to be produced by the Gospel.

θανατώσουσιν. This verb is in all three accounts. It cannot be watered down to mean "put in danger of death" (Volkmar): ver. 18 does not require this evasion. Comp. ἐξ αὐτῶν ἀποκτενεῖτε καὶ σταυρώσετε (Mt. xxiii. 34) and ἐξ αὐτῶν ἀποκτενοῦσιν (Lk. xi. 49). Here ἐξ ὑμῶν naturally means "some of you Apostles." Three of the four who heard these words—James, Peter, and Andrew—suffered a martyr's death.

17. **καὶ ἔσεσθε μισούμενοι.** This verse is found in the same form in all three, excepting that Mt. inserts τῶν ἐθνῶν after πάντων, which is in harmony with his omitting synagogues as centres of persecution (xxiv. 9). For the paraphrastic future see on i. 20.

18. **καὶ θρὶξ . . . οὐ μὴ ἀπόληται.** Peculiar to Lk. This proverbial expression of great security must here be understood spiritually; for it has just been declared (ver. 16) that some *will* be put to death. "Your souls will be absolutely safe; your eternal welfare shall in nowise suffer" (Mey. Weiss, Nösg.). Jn. x. 28 is in substance closely parallel. This is more satisfactory than to take it literally and supply *sine præmio, ante tempus* (Beng.); or supply from Mt. x. 29 ἄνευ τοῦ πατρὸς ὑμῶν (Hahn). The proverb is used of physical preservation, Acts xxvii. 34; 1 Sam. xiv. 45; 2 Sam. xiv. 11; 1 Kings i. 52.

19. **ἐν τῇ ὑπομονῇ ὑμῶν.** "In your endurance" of suffering without giving way; whereas μακροθυμία is patience of injuries without paying back. See Trench, *Syn.* liii.; Lft. on Col. i. 11, iii. 12; Wsctt. on Heb. vi. 12. The Latin Versions often confuse the two words.

Here we have *patientia* (e f ff_2 i q r s Vulg.), *tolerantia* (a), *sufferentia* (d). These three translations are found also viii. 15. In no other Gospel does ὑπομονή occur; and in no Gospel does μακροθυμία occur.

κτήσεσθε τὰς ψυχὰς ὑμῶν. "Ye shall *win* your souls," or "your lives." This confirms the interpretation given above of ver. 18. There the loss of eternal salvation is spoken of as death. Here the gaining of it is called winning one's life. See on ix. 25 and xvii. 33. In Mt. (xxiv. 13, x. 22) and Mk. (xiii. 13) this saying is represented by "He that endureth (ὑπομείνας) to the end, the same shall be saved." Neither Lk. nor Jn. use ὑπομένειν in this sense.

The reading is uncertain as regards the verb. A B some cursives, Latt. Syrr. Arm. Aeth. and best MSS. of Boh., Tert. Orig. support κτήσεσθε, which is adopted by Treg. WH. RV. and Weiss; while ℵ D L R X Γ Δ etc., some MSS. of Boh., Const-Apost. Bas. support κτήσασθε, which is adopted by Tisch. Neither reading justifies "*possess* your souls," a meaning confined to the perf. Cov. has "holde fast"; but nearly all others have "possess," following in verb, though not in tense, the *possidebitis* of Vulg. Other Lat. texts have *adquiretis* (c ff_2 l) or *adquirite* (d i). See last note on xviii. 12.

20–24. The Destruction of Jerusalem.

20. **κυκλουμένην.** "*Being* compassed": when the process was completed it would be too late; comp. Heb. xi. 30. No English Version preserves this distinction: but Vulg. has *videritis circumdari*, not *circumdatam* (a e). Instead of this Mt. and Mk. have "the abomination of desolation," etc.

ἡ ἐρήμωσις. The word is freq. in LXX, but in N.T. occurs only here and the parallels. The disciples had been expecting an immediate glorification of Jerusalem as the seat of the Messianic Kingdom. It is the desolation of Jerusalem that is really near at hand.

21. **τότε . . . τὰ ὄρη.** *Verbatim* the same in all three. What follows, to the end of ver. 22, is peculiar to Lk. By "the mountains" is meant the mountainous parts of Judæa: but **ἐν μέσῳ αὐτῆς** (see on viii. 7) refers, like **εἰς αὐτήν**, not to Judæa, but to Jerusalem.

χώραις. "Land-estates" (xii. 16), "country" as opposed to the town. See Blass on Acts viii. 1. The Jews who fled from the country into Jerusalem for safety greatly increased the miseries of the siege. It is probably to this prophecy that Eusebius refers when he speaks of "the people of the Church in Jerusalem being commanded to leave and dwell in a city of Peræa called Pella, in accordance with a certain oracle which was uttered before the war to the approved men there by way of revelation" (*H. E.* iii. 5. 3). The flight to Pella *illustrates* the prophecy; but we need not confine so general a warning to a single incident. It is important to note that the wording of the warning as recorded here has not been altered to suit this incident. Marcion omitted *vv.* 18, **21, 22.**

Vulg. and Lat. Vet. are misleading in translating ἐν ταῖς χώραις *in regionibus*. The Frag. Ambrosiana (s) give more rightly *in agris*. See *Old-Latin Biblical Texts*, ii. p. 88.

22. ἡμέραι ἐκδικήσεως. Comp. LXX of Deut. xxxii. 35; Hos ix. 7; Ecclus. v. 9. In what follows note the characteristic construction, and verb, and adjective. There is an abundance of such utterances throughout the O.T. Lev. xxvi. 31–33; Deut. xxviii. 49–57; 1 Kings ix. 6–9; Mic. iii. 12; Zech. xi. 6; Dan. ix. 26, 27. The famous passage in Eus. *H. E.* ii. 23. 20 should be compared, in which (like Origen before him) he quotes as from Josephus words which are in no MS. of Josephus which is extant: "These things happened to the Jews to avenge (κατ' ἐκδίκησιν) James the Just, who was a brother of Jesus, that is called the Christ. For the Jews slew him, although he was a very just man."

23. οὐαὶ . . . ἡμέραις. *Verbatim* the same in all three. For ἀνάγκη Mt. and Mk. have θλίψις. In Job xv. 24 we have ἀνάγκη καὶ θλίψις: comp. Job vii. 11, xviii. 14, xx. 22. In class. Grk. ἀνάγκη rarely means "distress," a meaning common in bibl. Grk. (1 Cor. vii. 26; 1 Thes. iii. 7; 2 Cor. vi. 4, xii. 10; Ps. cvi. 6, 13, 19, 28; *Ps. Sol.* v. 8). See small print on ver. 25. The meaning of ἐπὶ τῆς γῆς is determined by τῷ λαῷ τούτῳ. The latter means the Jews, and therefore the former means Palestine (AV. RV.) and not the earth (Weiss). For the Divine ὀργή comp. 1 Mac. i. 64, ii. 49; 2 Mac. v. 20; *Ps. Sol.* ii. 26, xvii. 14. The ὀργή is provoked by the people *qui tantam gratiam cœlestem spreverit* (Beng.).

24. καὶ πεσοῦνται στόματι μαχαίρης. This verse and the last words of ver. 23 are peculiar to Lk. Note the characteristic πάντα, periphrastic future, and ἄχρι. The often repeated assertion of Josephus, that 1,100,000 perished in the siege and 97,000 were carried into captivity (*B. J.* vi. 9. 3) is quite incredible: they could not have found standing-ground within the walls. The *sexcenta millia* of Tacitus (*Hist.* v. 13. 4), if taken literally, is far too many for the number of those besieged: but *sexcenti* need not mean more than "very many." Perhaps 70,000 is an ample estimate.

The phrase ἐν στόματι μαχαίρας occurs Gen. xxxiv. 26; Jos. x. 28; ἐν στόματι ῥομφαίας, Jos. vi. 21, viii. 24; ἐν στόματι ξίφους, Jos. x. 30, 32, 35, 37, 39. The plur. στόματα μαχαίρης is found Heb. xi. 34. In the best MSS. substantives in -ρα form gen. and dat. in -ρης and -ρῃ (WH. ii. App. p. 156)

ἔσται πατουμένη. See on i. 20, and see also Burton, § 71. *Plus sonat quam* πατηθήσεται (Beng.): it expresses the permanent condition, *la domination écrasante* (Godet). Comp. the LXX of Zech. xii. 3, θήσομαι τὴν Ἰερουσαλὴμ λίθον καταπατούμενον πᾶσιν τοῖς ἔθνεσιν.[1] Jerusalem has more often been under the feet of

[1] This use of πατέω, "I tread," as = καταπατέω, "I trample on," is classical: Plat. *Phædr.* 248 A; Soph. *Aj.* 1146; *Ant.* 745; Aristoph. *Vesp.* 377. The meaning is certainly not "shall be inhabited by" (Hahn), as in Is. xlii. 5 Comp. Rev. xi. 2; *Ps. Sol.* vii. 2, ii. 2.

Gentiles than in the hands of Christians. Romans, Saracens, Persians, and Turks have all trampled upon her in turn.

The Latin Versions vary much: *erit calcata* (d δ), *erit incalcata* (e), *erit in concalcationem* (a), *concalcabitur* (r), *calcabitur* (Vulg.).

ἄχρι οὗ. See on i. 20: ἄχρις οὗ is possibly correct Rom. xi. 25; Heb. iii. 13.

καιροὶ ἐθνῶν. As stated already, the whole of this verse is peculiar to Lk., and some have supposed that the last part of it is an addition made by him. It is not necessary to charge him with any such licence; although it is possible that oral tradition has here, as elsewhere, paraphrased and condensed what was said. The "seasons of the Gentiles" or "opportunities of the Gentiles" cannot be interpreted with certainty. Either (1) *Seasons* for executing the Divine judgments; or (2) for lording it over Israel; or (3) for existing as Gentiles; or (4) for themselves becoming subject to Divine judgments; or (5) *Opportunities* of turning to God; or (6) of possessing the privileges which the Jews had forfeited. The first and last are best, and they are not mutually exclusive. Comp. ἄχρι οὗ τὸ πλήρωμα τῶν ἐθνῶν εἰσέλθῃ (Rom. xi. 25), where the whole section is a comment on the promise that the punishment of Israel has a limit. The plur. καιροί corresponds with the plur. ἔθνη: each nation has its καιρός: but comp. ἕως πληρωθῶσιν καιροὶ τοῦ αἰῶνος (Tob. xiv. 5), where the whole passage should be compared with this.

25–28. The Signs of the Second Advent. Lk. here omits what is said about shortening the days and the appearance of impostors (Mt. xxiv. 22–26; Mk. xiii. 20–23). On the latter subject he has already recorded a warning (xvii. 23, 24).

25. ἐν ἡλίῳ κ. σελήνῃ κ. ἄστροις. "In sun and moon and stars." In Mt. and Mk. the three words have the article. All English Versions prior to RV. wrongly insert the article here, Cov. with "sun," the rest with all three words. Similar language is common in the Prophets: Is. xiii. 10; Ezek. xxxii. 7; Joel ii. 10, iii. 15: comp. Is. xxxiv. 4; Hag. ii. 6, 21, etc. Such expressions indicate the perplexity and distress caused by violent changes: the very sources of light are cut off. To what extent they are to be understood literally cannot be determined: but it is quite out of place to introduce here the thought of Christ as the sun and the Church as the moon, as do Ambr. and Wordsw. *ad loc.* (Migne, xv. 1813). The remainder of this verse and most of the next are peculiar to Lk.

συνοχή occurs only here and 2 Cor. ii. 4 in N.T.; but comp. viii. 45, xix. 43, xii. 50. In LXX it is found Judg. ii. 3; Job xxx. 3; Jer. lii. 5; Mic. v. 1. In Vulg. Jerome carelessly uses *pressura* both for συνοχή here and for ἀνάγκη in ver. 23; although Lat. Vet. distinguishes, with *conpressio* (a), *conflictio* (d), *conclusio* (e), or *occursus* (f) for *συνοχή*, and *necessitas* (a d e r) or *pressura* (f) for *ἀνάγκη*. See small print on xix. 43.

ἐν ἀπορίᾳ ἤχους. All English Versions prior to RV. go astray here, but Wic. and Rhem. less than the rest, owing to the Vulgate: *in terris pressura gentium præ confusione sonitus maris et fluctuum.* Tertullian is better: *in terra angustias nationum obstupescentium velut a sonitu maris fluctuantis* (*Adv. Marc.* iv. 39). It is the nations who are "*in* perplexity *at* the resounding of sea and surge." Figurative language of this kind is common in the Prophets: Is. xxviii. 2, xxix. 6, xxx. 30; Ezek. xxxviii. 22; Ps. xlii. 7, lxv. 7, lxxxviii. 7. See Stanley, *Jewish Church*, i. p. 130.

It is uncertain whether ἠχους is to be accented ἠχοῦς as from ἠχώ, or ἦχους as from ἦχος (iv. 37; Heb. xii. 19; Acts ii. 2). See WH. ii. App. p. 158. The reading ἠχούσης (D Γ Δ Λ Π etc.) is a manifest correction: the evidence against it (ℵ A B C L M R X and Versions) is overwhelming. For the gen. after ἀπορίᾳ, "perplexity *because of*," comp. καταλέγων τῶν Σκυθέων τὴν ἀπορίην (Hdt. iv. 83. 1). The conjecture ἐν ἀπειρίᾳ is baseless, and gives an inferior meaning.

26. ἀποψυχόντων. "Fainting, swooning," as Hom. *Od.* xxiv. 348, rather than "expiring," as Thuc. i. 134. 3; Soph. *Aj.* 1031.

The *arescentibus* of Lat. Vet. and Vulg. is remarkable; but a has *a refrigescentibus* and d has *deficientium.*[1] Of these three words *refrigescere* best represents ἀποψύχειν. But in LXX ψύχειν is used of *drying* in the sun or air: Num. xi. 32; 2 Sam. xvii. 19. Comp. τοὶ δ' ἱδρῶ ἀπεψύχοντο χιτώνων, στάντε ποτὶ πνοιήν (Hom. *Il.* xi. 621): "They dried the sweat off their tunics." Rhem. renders *arescentibus* "withering away." Hobart claims both ἀποψύχειν and προσδοκία as medical (pp. 161, 166). But medical writers use ἀποψύχειν of *being chilled*, not of swooning or expiring. He gives many instances from Galen of προσδοκία (which occurs here and Acts xii. 11 only in N.T.) as denoting the expectation of an unfavourable result. For this use of ἀπό see on xxiv. 41.

τῇ οἰκουμένῃ. See on iv. 5.

αἱ δυνάμεις τῶν οὐρανῶν σαλευθήσονται. Comp. τακήσονται πᾶσαι αἱ δυνάμεις τῶν οὐρανῶν (Is. xxxiv. 4). The verb which Lk. substitutes is one of which he is fond (vi. 38, 48, vii. 24; Acts ii. 25, iv. 31, xvi. 26, xvii. 13). By αἱ δυνάμεις τ. οὐρ. is meant, not the Angels (Euthym.), nor the cosmic powers which uphold the heavens (Mey. Oosterz.), but the heavenly bodies, the stars (De W. Holtz. Weiss, Hahn): comp. Is. xl. 26; Ps. xxxiii. 6. Evidently *physical* existences are meant.

27. καὶ τότε ὄψονται. "Not *till* then shall *they* see." Not ὄψεσθε: there is perhaps a hint that those present will not live to see this. This verse is in all three: comp. 1 Thes. iv. 16; 2 Thes. i. 7, ii. 8; Rev. i. 8, xix. 11-16.

28. This word of comfort is given by Lk. alone. Only here in

[1] *Deficientium hominum a timore*: another reproduction of gen. abs. in Latin. Comp. iii. 15, ix. 43, xix. 11, xxi. 5, xxiv. 36, 41.

N.T. is ἀνακύπτειν used of being elated after sorrow. Comp. Job x. 15, and contrast Lk. xiii. 11; [Jn.] viii. 7, 10. The disciples present are regarded as representatives of believers generally. Only those who witness the signs can actually fulfil this injunction.

ἀπολύτρωσις. At the Second Advent. Here the word means little more than "release" or "deliverance," without any idea of "ransom" (λύτρον). See Sanday on Rom. iii. 24, Abbott on Eph. i. 7, and Wsctt. *Heb.* pp. 295–297. Comp. *Enoch*, li. 2.

29–33. The Parable of the Fig Tree. Mt. xxiv. 32–35; Mk. xiii. 28–32.

29. Καὶ εἶπεν. This marks the resumption of the discourse after a pause: comp. xi. 5. More often Lk. uses εἶπεν δέ or ἔλεγεν δέ: xiv. 12, xx. 41, etc. For **εἶπεν παραβολήν** see on vi. 39. Lk. alone makes the addition *καὶ πάντα τὰ δένδρα*: see on vi. 30 and vii. 35. Writing for Gentiles, Lk. preserves words which cover those to whom fig trees are unknown.

30. προβάλωσιν. Here only without acc. We must understand τὰ φύλλα. In Jos. *Ant.* iv. 8. 19 καρπόν is added: comp. Acts xix. 33.

ἀφ' ἑαυτῶν γινώσκετε. "Of your own selves ye recognize:" *i.e.* without being told. For ἑαυτοῦ, -ῶν, of the 2nd pers. comp. xii. 1, 33, xvi. 9, 15, xvii. 3, 14, xxii. 17, xxiii. 28. It occurs in class. Grk. where no ambiguity is involved.

There is no justification for rendering θέρος "harvest," which would be θερισμός (x. 2). In N.T. θέρος occurs only in this parable.

32. ἡ γενεὰ αὕτη. This cannot well mean anything but *the generation living when these words were spoken*: vii. 31, xi. 29–32, 50, 51, xvii. 25; Mt. xi. 16, etc. The reference, therefore, is to *the destruction of Jerusalem* regarded as *the type of the end of the world.* To make ἡ γενεὰ αὕτη mean the Jewish race, or the generation contemporaneous with the beginning of the signs, is not satisfactory. See on ix. 27, where, as here, the coming of the Kingdom of God seems to refer to the destruction of Jerusalem.

33. ὁ οὐρανὸς καὶ ἡ γῆ. Comp. 2 Pet. iii. 10; Heb. i. 11, 12; Rev. xx. 11, xxi. 1; Ps. cii. 26; Is. li. 6. A time will come when everything material will cease to exist; but Christ's words will ever hold good. The prophecy just uttered is specially meant; but all His sayings are included. Comp. οὐδὲ γὰρ παρῆλθεν ἀπ' αὐτῶν λόγος (Addit. Esth. x. 5).

οὐ μὴ παρελεύσονται. So also in Mk. xiii. 31; but in Mt. xxiv. 35 παρέλθωσιν, which A R X etc. read here and A C D X etc. read in Mk. As the subj. is the usual constr. in N.T. after οὐ μή, copyists often corrected the fut. indic. to aor. subj. Comp. Mk. xiv. 31; Mt. xv. 5; Gal. iv. 30; Heb. x. 17, etc. The Old Latin MSS. used by Jerome seem here to have read *transient . . . transient.* Our best MSS. of the Vulgate read *transibunt . . . transient.* Jerome may have forgotten to correct the second *transient* into *transibunt*: or he may have wished to mark the difference between παρελεύσονται and παρέλθωσιν. Cod. Brix. with the Book of Dimma and some other authorities has *transibunt* . . . *præteribunt*. See *Hermathena*, No. xix. p. 386.

34–36. Concluding Warning as to the Necessity of Ceaseless Vigilance. Comp. Mt. xxv. 13–15; Mk. xiii. 33–37. The form of this warning differs considerably in the three Gospels. Not many words are common to any two of them; and very few are common to all three. It should be noted that here as elsewhere (x. 7 = 1 Tim. v. 18, xxiv. 34 = 1 Cor. xv. 5), Lk. in differing from Mt. and Mk. agrees with S. Paul. Comp. with this 1 Thes. v. 3. See Lft. *Epp.* p. 72.

34. For **προσέχετε δὲ ἑαυτοῖς** see on ver. 30 and xii. 1; and for **βαρηθῶσιν** see on ix. 32.

κρεπάλῃ. Not "surfeiting," but the nausea which follows a debauch: *crapula.* Here only in bibl. Grk. For this and μέθῃ (Rom. xiii. 13; Gal. v. 21) see Trench, *Syn.* lxi.; and for the orthography see WH. ii. App. p. 151.

μερίμναις βιωτικαῖς. The adj. occurs 1 Cor. vi. 3, 4: but is not found in LXX, nor earlier than Aristotle. Comp. *πρὸς τὰς βιωτικὰς χρείας ὑπηρετεῖν* (Philo, *Vit. Mo.* iii. 18).

The remarkable rendering *soniis* for *μερίμναις* in Cod. Bezae has long attracted attention, and has been regarded by some as a manifest Gallicism. It is confidently connected with the French *soins*. But the connexion is not certain. The word may be a form of *somniis*, and the transition from "disturbing dreams" to "perplexities" and "cares" would not be difficult. The word occurs once in the St. Gall MS. of the *Sortes*, and *soniari* occurs four times. It was therefore a word which was established in use early in the sixth century. Whether it is original in the text of D, or is a later substitution, is much debated. Here other renderings are *sollicitudinibus* (a e), *cogitationibus* (b f), *curis* (Tert. Vulg.). The prevalent Old Latin rendering was *sollicitudines* (a b d f) both in viii. 14 and Mt. xiii. 22 (comp. Mk. iv. 19); and the translator of Irenæus has *sollicitudinibus* here. See Scrivener, *Codex Bezae*, pp. xliv, xlv. Rendel Harris, p. 26; and an excellent review in the *Guardian*, May 18, 1892, p. 743.

ἐφνίδιος. Here, but not 1 Thes. v. 3 or Wisd. xvii. 14, this form is best attested: WH. Intr. 309, App. 151. The Latin renderings are *repentaneus* (a), *subitaneus* (d e), *repentina* (f Vulg.).

ἡ ἡμέρα ἐκείνη. This is the one expression which in this section is common to all three accounts. Comp. x. 12, xvii. 31. The day of the Messiah's return is meant.

ὡς παγίς. According to the best authorities (ℵ B D L, a b c e ff_2 i Boh., Tert.) these words belong to what precedes, and the *γάρ* follows *ἐπεισελεύσεται*, not *παγίς*. The whole recalls *φόβος καὶ βόθυνος καὶ παγὶς ἐφ' ἡμᾶς τοὺς ἐνοικοῦντας ἐπὶ τῆς γῆς* (Is. xxiv. 17). The resemblance between the passages, and the fact that *ἐπεισελεύσεται* suits the notion of a *παγίς* ("noose" or "lasso"), accounts for the transposition of the *γάρ*. Originally a *παγίς* (*πήγνυμι*) is that which *holds fast*: Ps. xci. 3; Prov. vii. 23; Eccles. ix. 12. Here most Latin texts have *laqueus*, but Cod. Palat. has *muscipula*.

35–36. Note the characteristic repetition of **πᾶς**.

35. πάσης τῆς γῆς. Not the land of the Jews only. Possibly **καθημένους** indicates that, as at the flood, and at Belshazzar's feast, people are sitting at ease, eating and drinking, etc. (xvii. 27): but it need not mean more than inhabiting. Comp. *μάχαιραν ἐγὼ καλῶ ἐπὶ πάντας τοὺς καθημένους ἐπὶ τῆς γῆς* (Jer. xxv. 29). For *ἐπὶ προσ. π. τ. γῆς* comp. 2 Sam. xviii. 8. The phrase is Hebraistic.

36. ἀγρυπνεῖτε δέ. Comp. Eph. vi. 18; Heb. xiii. 17; 2 Sam. xii. 21; Ps. cxxvi. 1; Prov. viii. 34.

The **οὖν** (A C R, b c ff_2, Syrr. Aeth. Arm.) for *δέ* (ℵ B D, a d e) probably comes from Mt. xxv. 13 and Mk. xiii. 35.

ἐν παντὶ καιρῷ. xviii. 1 and 1 Thes. v. 17 are in favour of taking these words with *δεόμενοι* (Wic. Gen. Rhem. AV.) rather than with *ἀγρυπνεῖτε* (Tyn. Cov. Cran. RV.). For similar questions comp. ix. 17, 18, 57, x. 18, xi. 39, etc.

κατισχύσητε. This is the reading of ℵ B L X 33, Aegyptt. Aeth. and is adopted by the best editors. It properly means "prevail against" (Mt. xvi. 18; Jer. xv. 18; 2 Chron. viii. 3; comp. Lk. xxiii. 23; Is. xxii. 4; Wisd. xvii. 5). The *καταξιωθῆτε* of A C D R, Latt. Syrr. Arm., Tert. perhaps comes from xx. 35.

σταθῆναι. "To hold your place," comp. *Τότε στήσεται ἐν παρρησίᾳ πολλῇ ὁ δίκαιος* (Wisd. v. 1). It is clear from xi. 18, xviii. 11, 40, xix. 8; Acts ii. 14, v. 20, xi. 13, xvii. 22, xxv. 18, xxvii. 21, etc., that *σταθῆναι* is not to be taken passively of *being placed by the Angels* (Mt. xxiv. 31). Comp. *τίς δύναται σταθῆναι*; (Rev. vi. 17). For the opposite of *σταθῆναι* see xxiii. 30; Rev. vi. 16: comp. 1 Jn. ii. 28.

The Apocalypse of Jesus.

Hase (*Gesch. Jesu*, § 97), Colani (*J. C. et les croyances messianiques de son temps*), and others think that Jesus had penetration enough to foresee and predict the destruction of Jerusalem, but they cannot believe that He was such a fanatic as to foretell that He would return in glory and judge the world. Hence they conclude that these predictions about the *Parusia* were never uttered by Him. Keim sees that Mk. xiii. 32 cannot be an invention (*Jes. of Naz.* v. p. 241): in some shape or other Jesus must have foretold His glorious Return. Therefore this eschatological discourse is based upon some genuine utterances of Jesus; but has been expanded into an apocalyptic poem with the help of other material. Both Keim and some of those who deny the authenticity of any prediction of Christ's Return assume the existence of an apocalypse by some Jewish Christian as the source from which large portions of this discourse are taken. Weizsäcker holds that the apocalypse was Jewish, and was taken from a lost section of the Book of Enoch. Weiffenbach, followed by Wendt and Vischer, upholds the theory of a Jewish-Christian original.

But did this spurious apocalypse, the existence of which is pure conjecture, also supply Lk. with what he has recorded xi. 49–51, xiii. 23–27, 35, xvii. 23, 37, xviii. 8, xix. 15, 43, xx. 16? Did it supply Mt. with what he has recorded vii. 22, x. 23, xix. 28, xxi. 44, xxii. 7, xxv. 31, xxvi. 64? Mk. also with the parallels to these passages? That all three derived these utterances from Apostolic tradition is credible. Is it credible that a writing otherwise unknown and by an unknown author should have had such enormous influence? And its influence does not end with the three Evangelists. It has contributed largely to the Epistles of S. Paul, especially to the very earliest of them. Comp. 1 Thes. ii. 16, iv. 16, 17, v. 1–3; 2 Thes. ii. 1–12. And it would seem to have influenced much of the imagery in Revelation, which foretells wars, famine, pestilence, and persecution (vi. 4, 5, 8, 9), and the Return of the Saviour accompanied by the armies of heaven (xix. 11–16). This supposed fictitious apocalypse is assigned to A.D. 68, or thereabouts; and therefore long after the Pauline Epistles were written. Apostolic tradition, which is known to have existed, is a far safer hypothesis. See Godet, *ad loc.* (ii. pp. 430 ff.), whose remarks have been freely used in this note. See also Briggs, *The Messiah of the Gospels*, T. &. T. Clark, 1894, ch. iv. where this "Apocalypse of Jesus" is critically discussed, with special reference to the theory of Weiffenbach and others that the assumed Jewish-Christian apocalypse consisted of these three portions:—(α) the ἀρχὴ ὠδίνων, Mk. xiii. 7, 8=Mt. xxiv. 6–8=Lk. xxi. 9–11; (β) the θλίψις, Mk. xiii. 14–20=Mt. xxiv. 15–22; (γ) the παρουσία, Mk. xiii. 24–27=Mt. xxiv. 29–31=Lk. xxi. 25–27.[1] Briggs points out the insignificance of the fact that ideas such as these are found in Jewish *pseudepigrapha.* These ideas were by them derived from the O.T., which was the common source of both canonical and uncanonical apocalypses, whether Jewish or Christian. Jesus uses this source on other occasions, and there is nothing unreasonable in the belief that He uses it here. The cosmical disturbances foretold (*vv.* 25–27) "belong not only to the theophanies and the Christophanies of prophecy, but also to the theophanies and Christophanies of history in both the Old Testament and the New. They represent the response of the creature to the presence of the Creator" (p. 155). Both Briggs and Nösgen (*Gesch. J. C.* Kap. ix.) give abundant references to the literature of the subject in Beyschlag (*L. J.*), Hilgenfeld (*Einl. i. N.T.*), Holsten (*die Syn. Ev.*), Immer (*Ntl. Theol.*), Mangold in Bleek (*Einl. i. N.T.*), Pfleiderer (*Urchristen.*), Pressensé (*J. C.*), Spitta (*die Offbg. des Joh.*) and Wendt (*Lehre Jesu*). See also especially D. E. Haupt (*Eschatolog. Aussagen Jesu in d. Syn. Evang.*, Berlin, 1895).

37, 38. General Description of the Last Days of Christ's Public Ministry.

37. τὰς ἡμέρας. "During the days." From the other narratives we infer that this covers the day of the triumphal entry and the next two days. It is, therefore, retrospective, and is a repetition, with additional detail, of xix. 47. The contrast with τὰς δὲ νύκτας, "but during the nights," is obvious. It is not clear whether ἦν belongs to ἐν τῷ ἱερῷ or to διδάσκων, which probably ought to follow (ℵ A C D L R X Γ Δ Λ Π) and not precede (B K) ἐν τῷ ἱερῷ.

ἐξερχόμενος ηὐλίζετο εἰς. "Leaving (the temple) He used to go and bivouac on" (iv. 23, vii. 1, ix. 61, xi. 7). Comp. μηκέτι αὐλισθῆτε εἰς Νινευή (Tobit xiv. 10), ὑπὸ τοὺς κλάδους αὐτῆς αὐλισθήσεται (Ecclus. xiv. 26). On the M. of Olives He would be undisturbed (xxii. 39). For καλούμενον see on vi. 15, and for Ἐλαιων see on xix. 29. It is not probable that εἰς τὸ ὄρος is to be taken with ἐξερχόμενος, but the participle of motion has influenced the choice of preposition.

38. ὤρθριζε πρὸς αὐτόν. Another condensed expression: "rose early and came to Him." The verb occurs here only in N.T., but

[1] Holtzmann (*Handcomm.* on Mt. xxiv. 4–34, Eng. tr. p. 112) makes the divisions thus: (α) Mt. xxiv. 4–14; (β) 15–28; (γ) 29–34.

is freq. in LXX. Twice we have the two verbs combined, αὐλίσθητι ὧδε . . . καὶ ὀρθριεῖτε αὔριον εἰς ὁδὸν ὑμῶν (Judg. xix. 9) αὐλισθῶμεν ἐν κώμαις· ὀρθρίσωμεν εἰς ἀμπελῶνας (Cant. vii. 11, 12). The literal meaning is the right one here, although ὀρθρίζω may mean "seek *eagerly*" (Ps. lxxvii. 34; Ecclus. iv. 12, vi. 36; Wisd. vi. 14). Contrast Ps. cxxvii. 2; 1 Mac. iv. 52, vi. 33, xi. 67; Gospel of Nicodemus xv. The classical form ὀρθρεύω is always used in the literal sense.

Most MSS. of Vulg. here have the strange rendering *manicabat ad eum*, which is also the rendering in Cod. Brix. (f), the best representative of the Old Latin text on which Jerome worked. But G has *mane ibat*, which may possibly be Jerome's correction of *manicabat*, a word of which Augustine says *mihi non occurrit*. See Rönsch, *It. und Vulg.* p. 174. Other renderings are—*vigilabat ad eum* (d), *de luce vigilabant ad eum* (a), *ante lucem veniebat ad eum* (e r), *diluculo conveniendum erat* (Tert.). See on xvi. 26.

Five cursives (13, 69, 124, 346, 556), which are closely related, here insert the pericope of the Woman taken in Adultery, an arrangement which was perhaps suggested by ὤρθριζε here and ὄρθρου Jn. viii. 2. The common origin of 13, 69, 124, 346 is regarded as certain. See Scrivener, *Int. to Crit. of N.T.* i. pp. 192, 202, 231; T. K. Abbott, *Collation of Four Important MSS. of the Gospels*, Dublin, 1877. "The Section was probably known to the scribe exclusively as a church lesson, recently come into use; and placed by him here on account of the close resemblance between *vv.* 37, 38 and [Jo] vii. 53, viii. 1, 2. Had he known it as part of a continuous text of St. John's Gospel, he was not likely to transpose it" (WH. ii. App. p. 63).

XXII.–XXIV. THE PASSION AND THE RESURRECTION.

We now enter upon the last main division of the Gospel (xxii.–xxiv.), containing the narratives of the Passion, Resurrection, and Ascension. The first of these three subjects falls into three parts:—The Preparation (xxii. 1–38); the Passion (xxii. 39–xxiii. 49); and the Burial (xxiii. 50–56). In the first of these parts we may distinguish the following sections:—The Approach of the Passover and the Malice of the Hierarchy (xxii. 1, 2); the Treachery of Judas (3–6); the Preparation for the Paschal Supper (7–13); the Institution of the Eucharist (14–23); the Strife about Priority (24–34); the New Conditions (35–38). In this part of the narrative the particulars which are wholly or mainly peculiar to Lk. are those contained in *vv.* 8, 15, 24, 28–30, 35–38.

XXII. 1–38. The Preparation for the Passion. Comp. Mt. xxvi. 1–29; Mk. xiv. 1–25. For date see Hastings, *D.B.* i. p. 410.

1. Ἤγγιζεν. "Was drawing nigh." Mt. and Mk. say more definitely μετὰ δύο ἡμέρας. Keim calls attention to the fidelity of this introductory section, *vv.* 1–13 (v. p. 305, n.).

ἡ ἑορτὴ τῶν ἀζύμων. The phrase is freq. in LXX (Exod.

xxiii. 15, xxxiv. 18; Deut. xvi. 16; 2 Chron. viii. 13, etc.), but occurs nowhere else in N.T. Comp. ii. 41. Lk. is fond of these Hebraistic circumlocutions: *ἡ ἡμέρα τ. ἀζ.* (ver. 7), *ἡ ἡμέρα τῶν σαββάτων* (iv. 16; Acts xiii. 14, xvi. 13), *ἡμέραι τ. ἀζ.* (Acts xii. 3, xx. 6); *Βίβλος ψαλμῶν* (xx. 42; Acts i. 20), *Βίβλος τῶν προφητῶν* (Acts vii. 42), etc. See small print on iv. 16.

ἡ λεγομένη Πάσχα. Strictly speaking the Passover on Nisan 14th was distinct from the F. of Unleavened Bread, which lasted from the 15th to the 21st (Lev. xxiii. 5, 6; Num. xxviii. 16, 17; 2 Chron. xxx. 15, 21; Ezra vi. 19, 22; 1 Esdr. i. 10–19; comp. Mk. xiv. 1). But they were so closely connected, that it was common to treat them as one festival. Not only Lk. as "writing mainly for Gentiles" does so, but Mt. (xxvi. 17); and Josephus goes beyond either in saying *ἑορτὴν ἄγομεν ἐφ' ἡμέρας ὀκτὼ, τὴν τῶν Ἀζύμων λεγομένην* (*Ant.* ii. 15. 1). Comp. *κατὰ τὸν καιρὸν τῆς τῶν Ἀζύμων ἑορτῆς ἣν Φάσκα λέγομεν* (xiv. 2. 1). Elsewhere he distinguishes them (*Ant.* iii. 10. 5, ix. 13. 3).

2. ἐζήτουν . . . τὸ πῶς. "They continued seeking as to the method": comp. xix. 47, 48, and for the *τό* see on i. 62. Mt. tells us that they held a meeting in the house of Caiaphas.

ἀνέλωσιν. Another of Lk.'s favourite words. Here, xxiii. 32, and eighteen times in the Acts it has the special meaning of "remove, *slay*": so also 2 Thes. ii. 8, where the reading is doubtful. This meaning is common in LXX (Gen. iv. 15; Exod. ii. 14, 15, xxi. 29, etc.) and in class. Grk. Except Mt. ii. 16; 2 Thes. ii. 8, and Heb. x. 9 (where see Wsctt.), it occurs only in Lk. With **ἐφοβοῦντο** comp. xx. 19, xix. 48, xxi. 38.

3. Εἰσῆλθεν δὲ Σατανᾶς. Comp. Jn. xiii. 2, where this stage is represented as the devil making suggestions to Judas, while his entering and taking possession of the traitor is reserved for the moment before he left the upper room to carry out his treachery (xiii. 27). See on x. 18 and comp. iv. 13, to which this perhaps looks back. Satan is renewing the attack. Neither Mt. nor Mk. mentions Satan here. But there is no hint that Judas is now like a demoniac, unable to control his own actions (Hahn). Judas opened the door to Satan. He did not resist him, and Satan did not flee from him. Jesus must suffer, but Judas need not become the traitor.

τὸν καλούμενον Ἰσκαριώτην. All three give this distinctive surname (see on vi. 16), and also the tragic fact that he was *τῶν δώδεκα* Comp. i. 36, vi. 15, vii. 11, viii. 2, ix. 10, x. 39, xix. 2, 29.

For *καλούμενον* (ℵ B D L X) TR. has *ἐπικαλούμενον* (A C P R Γ Δ Λ Π), a form commonly used in Acts (i. 23, iv. 36, x. 5, 32, xii. 25). In Acts i. 23 we have both verbs.

4. στρατηγοῖς. Lk. alone mentions these officials. They are the leaders of the corps of Levites, which kept guard in and about the temple. The full title is στρατηγοὶ τοῦ ἱεροῦ (ver. 52). See Edersh. *The Temple*, p. 119; Jos. *B. J.* vi. 5. 3. These officers would be consulted, because they had to take part in carrying out the arrest. The chief of them was called ὁ στρατηγὸς τοῦ ἱεροῦ (Acts iv. 1, v. 24, 26), or "the man of the temple mount" or "the man of the mount of the house." Comp. 2 Mac. iii. 4. Here and ver. 52 the plur. has no art.

D, a b c d e ff$_2$ i l q Syr-Cur. Aeth. omit καὶ στρατηγοῖς, but all these, excepting D d, substitute καὶ τοῖς γραμματεῦσιν. C P retain both, adding τοῦ ἱεροῦ to στρατηγοῖς.

παραδῷ. In vi. 16 Judas is called προδότης, but elsewhere παραδιδόναι, not προδιδόναι, is the word used to describe his crime.

5. ἐχάρησαν. It was wholly unexpected, and it simplified matters enormously.

συνέθεντο. Acts xxiii. 20; Jn. ix. 22; and quite classical. Mk. has ἐπηγγείλαντο. The ἔστησαν of Mt. refers to the actual paying of the money. He alone states the amount,—thirty shekels.

6. ἄτερ ὄχλου. Either "without a crowd" or "without tumult." Comp. Mt. xxvi. 5. Contrast μετὰ ὄχλου, Acts xxiv. 18. In bibl. Grk. the poetical word ἀτέρ occurs only here, ver. 35, and 2 Mac. xii. 15. Very possibly the priests had intended to wait until the feast was over before arresting Jesus. The offer of Judas induced them to make the attempt before the feast began.

Keim rightly rejects with decision the theory that the betrayal by Judas is not history, but a Christian fiction personifying in Judas the Jewish people. That Christians should invent so appalling a crime for an Apostle is quite beyond belief. The crime of Judas is in all four Gospels and in the Acts, and is emphasized by Christ's foreknowledge of it. Speculations as to other causes of it besides the craving for money are not very helpful: but the motives may easily have been complex.

The well-known difficulty as to the time of the Last Supper and of our Lord's death cannot be conclusively solved with our present knowledge. But the difficulty is confined to the day of the *month*. All four accounts agree with the generally accepted belief that Jesus was crucified on a Friday. In the Synoptists this Friday seems to be the 15th Nisan. Jn. (xiii. 1, 29, xviii. 28, xix. 14, 31) clearly intimates that it was the 14th, and we shall probably do rightly in abiding by his statements and seeing whether the others can be brought into harmony with it. This is perhaps most easily done by regarding, in accordance with Jewish reckoning, the evening of the 13th as the beginning of the 14th. All, therefore, that is said to have taken place "on the first day of unleavened bread" may have taken place after sunset on what we should call the 13th. It seems improbable that the priests and their officials would go to arrest Jesus at the very time when the whole nation was celebrating the Paschal meal. It is more easy to believe that Jesus celebrated the Paschal meal before the usual time, viz. on the Jewish 14th, but before midnight and some twenty hours before the usual time for slaughtering the lambs, at which time He was dying or dead upon the cross.

Professor D. Chwolson of Petersburg has made a new attempt at a solution in a recently published essay, *Das letzte Passamahl Christi und der Tag seines Todes; Mémoire de l'Académie Impériale des Sciences*, viie Serie, tome xli. No. 1. A criticism in the *Guardian*, June 28, 1893, tends to show that it leaves the crucial question just where it was. A later contribution is that of G. M. Semeria, *Le Jour de la Mort de Jésus; Rev. bibl.* 1, 1896.

7. Ἦλθεν δὲ ἡ ἡμ. τ. ἀζ. The day itself *arrived*, as distinct from "was approaching" (ver. 1). This arriving would take place at sunset on the 13th. See Schanz, *ad loc.* Mt. and Mk. have *τῇ πρώτῃ τῶν ἀζύμων.*

ἔδει θύεσθαι. This in no way proves that the 14th, according to *our* reckoning, is intended. The day on which the lambs had to be killed began at sunset on the 13th, and ended at sunset on the 14th; and the lambs were killed about 2.30–5.30 P.M. on the 14th in the Court of the Priests. Each head of the company sharing the lamb slew the animal, whose blood was caught in a bowl by a priest and poured at the foot of the altar of burnt-offering (Edersh. *The Temple*, p. 190). It was on the evening of the 13th that the houses were carefully searched for leaven, in silence, and with a light: comp. 1 Cor. v. 7; Zeph. i. 12. The ἔδει refers to legal necessity: it was so prescribed.

8. ἀπέστειλεν. Both Mt. and Mk. omit this preliminary order and begin with the disciples' question: and Lk. alone gives the names of the two who were sent. As this does not harmonize with the theory that Lk. shows *animus* against Peter, we are told that Peter and John are named by Lk. as the representatives of the old Judaism. The treason of Judas might lead Jesus to select two of His most trusted Apostles.

10. The care with which Jesus avoids an open statement to all the disciples as to the place ordained for the supper may be explained in the same way. Until His hour is come Judas must be prevented from executing his project: and no miracle is wrought, where ordinary precautions suffice. In what follows Lk. and Mk. are almost identical: Mt. is more brief.

Evidently the ἄνθρωπος is not the head of the household, but a servant or slave: the carrying of water was specially the work of slaves or of women (Deut. xxix. 11; Josh. ix. 21–27; Gen. xxiv. 11; Jn. iv. 7). The head of the house is *in* the house (*vv.* 10, 11). The suggestion, therefore, that this is *the master of the house drawing the water for making the bread, according to custom, on the 13th of Nisan*, falls to the ground. This incident gives no help in deciding between the 13th and the 14th. The water was more probably for washing the hands before the evening meal. With κεράμιον ὕδατος comp. ἀλάβαστρον μύρου (vii. 37). As in the case of the colt (xix. 30), we are uncertain whether this is a case of supernatural knowledge, or of previous arrangement; but in both cases prophetic prescience seems to be implied.

For *amphoram aquæ portans* (Vulg.) *bajulans bascellum* (*vascellum*) *aquæ* (d).

11. ἐρεῖτε. Fut. for imperat. This is more common in prohibitions than in commands (iv. 12; Acts xxiii. 5; Mt. vi. 5). In the Decalogue, only the positive *τίμα τὸν πατέρα* has the imperative: the negative commandments have *οὐ* with the fut. indic. Win. xliii. 5. c, p. 396.

τῷ οἰκοδεσπότῃ τῆς οἰκίας. A pleonasm marking a late stage in the language, in which the meaning of *οἰκοδεσπότης* has become indefinite: comp. *ὑποπόδιον τῶν ποδῶν* (xx. 43), *συῶν συβόσια*, *στρατηγὸν τῆς στρατιῆς*, the *Daily Journal*, etc. The cogn. accus. (*πόλεμον πολεμεῖν*, *οἰκοδομεῖν οἶκον*) is different.

ὁ διδάσκαλος. Like *ὁ κύριος* (xix. 31), this implies that the man knows Jesus, and is perhaps in some degree a disciple.

τὸ κατάλυμα. Not necessarily the same as the *ἀνάγαιον* (ver. 12). It is possible that Jesus only asked for the large general room on the ground floor (comp. ii. 7), but that the man gave Him the best room, reserved for more private uses, above the *κατάλυμα*. It was a common thing for the inhabitants of Jerusalem to lend a room to pilgrims for the passover, the usual payment being the skin of the paschal lamb and the vessels used at the meal. Mt. alone gives the words *ὁ καιρός μου ἐγγύς ἐστιν*, which perhaps explains why Jesus is having the paschal meal before the time. Neither here, nor at the supper, is any mention of a lamb: and perhaps there was none. The time for slaughtering had not yet come; and, as Jesus was excommunicated, it is not likely that the priests would have helped His disciples to observe the ritual respecting it. Moreover, there would hardly be time for all this and for the roasting of the lamb. The Last Supper was the inauguration of a new order rather than the completion of an old one; and its significance is enhanced if the central symbol of the old dispensation was absent, when He whom it symbolized was instituting the commemoration of that which the old symbol prefigured. It was on the last great day of the F. of Tabernacles, when the water from Siloam was probably *not* poured out beside the altar, that Jesus cried, "If any man thirst, let him come unto Me, and drink" (Jn. vii. 37); and it was when the great lamps were *not* lit in the Court of the Women, that He said, "I am the Light of the World" (Jn. viii. 12). From *vv.* 15–19 it appears that **τὸ πάσχα** and **φάγω** refer to the eucharistic bread and wine.

12. ἀναγαιον. "Anything raised above the ground (*ἀνά* or *ἄνω* and *γαῖα* or *γῆ*), upper floor (Xen. *Anab.* v. 4. 29), upper room." Only here and Mk. xiv. 15. The MSS. vary between *ἀνάγαιον*, *ἀνόγαιον*, *ἀνώγεων*, *ἀνώγεως*, *ἀνώγαιον*, and *ἀνώγεον*. Most, including the best, have *ἀνάγαιον*. That this room is identical with the *ὑπερῷον*, Acts i. 13, is pure conjecture: the change of word is against it.

In both passages Vulg. has *cœnaculum*, for which Old Latin texts have here *medianum* (a), *pede plano locum* (b), *superiorum locum* (q), *in superioribus locum* (c e), and *superiorem domum* (d).

ἐστρωμένον. "Spread, furnished"—with *what*, depends upon the context, which here suggests couches or cushions: comp. Acts ix. 34. Luther erroneously has *gepflastert*. Mk. adds ἕτοιμον, which some insert here.

13. καθώς. "Even as": the correspondence was exact; comp. xix. 32. The Evangelists seem to intimate that Christ's knowledge was supernatural rather than the result of previous arrangement. But in any case the remaining ten, including Judas, were left in ignorance as to where the meal was to take place.

14–23. The Last Supper, with the Institution of the Eucharist as a new Passover: comp. Mt. xxvi. 20–29; Mk. xiv. 17–25. The declaration that one of them is a traitor is placed by Mt. and Mk. at the beginning of the section, by Lk. at the end (ver. 21): comp. Jn. xiii. 21, where the wording of the declaration agrees with Mt. and Mk. Lk. seems to have used an independent source: comp. 1 Cor. xi. 24, 25.

14. Lk.'s independence appears at once: nearly every word in the verse differs from Mt. and Mk.

ἀνέπεσεν. Mt. has ἀνέκειτο: the practice of standing (Exod. xii. 11) had long been abandoned; first for sitting, and then for reclining. *Mos servorum est, ut edant stantes; at nunc comedunt recumbentes, ut dignoscatur, exisse eos e servitute in libertatem*, was the explanation given by the Rabbins. The choosing of the lamb ten days in advance had also been given up. Here, as elsewhere, ἀναπίπτω implies a *change* of position (xi. 37, xiv. 10, xvii. 7; Jn. xiii. 12, 25, etc.). Lft. *On a Fresh Revision of N.T.* p. 80.

οἱ ἀπόστολοι. This is the true reading. In some texts δώδεκα has been inserted (A C P R) or substituted (L X) from Mt. and Mk. Ten to thirty was the number for a passover. Note that Lk. once more has σύν, where others have μετά or καί: comp. viii. 38, 51, xx. 1, xxii. 56.

15. The whole of this verse and most of the next are peculiar to Lk. The combination of ἐπιθυμίᾳ ἐπεθύμησα with τοῦ με παθεῖν is remarkable. The knowledge of the intensity of the suffering does not cancel the intensity of the desire.

Ἐπιθυμίᾳ ἐπεθύμησα. A Hebraism common in LXX. Comp. Acts v. 28, xxiii. 14; Jn. iii. 29; Mt. xiii. 14, xv. 4; James v. 17; Gen. xxxi. 30; Exod. xxi. 20; Deut. vii. 26, etc.

16. οὐ μὴ φάγω αὐτό. After this present occasion. The αὐτο must refer to τοῦτο τὸ πάσχα (ver. 15), and shows that this need not imply a lamb. The Passover of which Christ will partake, after having fulfilled the type, is the Christian Eucharist, in which He joins with the faithful in the Kingdom of God on earth. Others suppose the reference to be to the spiritual banquet in the world to come. But if αὐτό means the paschal lamb, in what sense could Jesus partake of that in the future? The Mishna itself contemplates the possibility of a passover without a lamb, and rules that unleavened bread is the only essential thing. With an influx of many thousands of pilgrims, to provide a lamb might be in some cases impossible.

17. δεξάμενος. It was handed to Him: contrast λαβών, ver. 19 (Schanz). It is usual to consider this as the first or second of the four cups that were handed round during the paschal meal; the eucharistic cup being identified with the third or fourth. But we are in doubt (1) as to what the paschal ritual was at this time; (2) as to the extent to which Jesus followed the paschal ritual in this highly exceptional celebration; (3) as to the text of this passage, especially as to whether Lk. records two cups or only one: so that identifications of this kind are very precarious. In any case, Lk. mentions a cup *before* the breaking of the bread, whether this be the eucharistic cup or not: and S. Paul twice mentions the cup first (1 Cor. x. 16, 21), although in his account of the institution he follows the usual order (1 Cor. xi. 23). In the Διδαχή the cup is placed first (ix. 2: see Schaff's 3rd ed. pp. 58-61, 191).

εὐχαριστήσας. This seems to imply the eucharistic cup. All three have εὐχαριστήσας of the cup. Lk. repeats it of the bread, where Mt. and Mk. have εὐλογήσας.

In the Jewish ritual the person who presided began by asking a blessing on the feast; then blessed, drank, and passed the first cup. Then Ps. cxiii. and cxiv. were sung and the bitter herbs eaten, followed by the second cup. After which the president explained the meaning of the feast: and some think that for this explanation of the old rite Jesus substituted the institution of the new one. After the eating of the lamb and unleavened cakes came the thanksgiving for the meal and the blessing and drinking of the third cup. Lastly, the singing of Ps. cxv.-cxviii. followed by the fourth cup: and there was sometimes a fifth.

διαμερίσατε. Comp. Acts ii. 45; Judg. v. 30. Followed by **εἰς ἑαυτούς**, it expresses more strongly than the mid. (xxiii. 34; Mt. xxvii. 35) the fact of mutual distribution. In some texts (A D etc.) εἰς ἑαυτούς has been altered into the more usual dat. (Jn. xix. 24; Acts ii. 45). The distribution would be made by each drinking in turn, rather than by each pouring some into a cup of his own. The εἰς ἑαυτούς perhaps corresponds to the πάντες of Mt. and Mk. Πίετε (ἔπιον) ἐξ αὐτοῦ πάντες.

18. ἀπὸ τοῦ νῦν. This at first sight appears to mean that Jesus did not partake of the cup. "I say, Divide it among *yourselves*, because henceforth I shall *not* drink," etc. But this would be strange; for (1) according to Jewish practice it would be monstrous for the presiding person to abstain from partaking; (2) Jesus had just said that He earnestly desired to partake of this paschal meal;

and (3) *vv.* 17, 18 seem to be parallel to 15, 16: He eats the paschal food, and then says that it is for the last time under these conditions; and He drinks of the paschal cup, and then says that it is for the last time under these conditions. There is nothing in any of the accounts to prevent us from supposing that Jesus drank before handing the cup to the others. The γάρ explains why they are to consume it among *themselves*, and not expect Him to take more than was ceremonially necessary; and the ἀπὸ τοῦ νῦν will then be quite exact. "I have just drunk; but from this moment onwards I will drink no more": comp. οὐκέτι οὐ μὴ πίω. It was possibly because ἀπὸ τοῦ νῦν seemed to mean that Jesus refused to drink that some texts (A C etc.) omitted the words.

τοῦ γενήματος τῆς ἀμπέλου. Some regard this as a reference to the Jewish benediction at the first cup: "Blessed be Thou, O Lord our God, the King of the world, who hast created the fruit of the vine." It is quite uncertain that this form was in use at the time. For γένημα see Deissmann, *Bible Studies*, pp. 109, 184.

Latin variations in rendering are of interest: *generatione vitis* (Vulg.), *fructu vineæ* (a), *creatura vineæ* (d), *genimine vitis* (δ). Comp. iii. 7. Syr-Sin. omits "of the vine." See Pasch. Radb. on Mt. xxvi. 29, Migne, cxx. 895.

19, 20. In connexion with what follows we have these points to consider. (1) Are the words from τὸ ὑπὲρ ὑμῶν διδόμενον to τὸ ὑπὲρ ὑμῶν ἐκχυννόμενον part of the original text? (2) If they are, is τὸ ποτήριον in ver. 20 the same as ποτήριον in ver. 17?

Assuming provisionally that the overwhelming external evidence of almost all MSS. and Versions in favour of the words in question is to be accepted, we may discuss the second point. As in the other case, neither view is free from serious difficulty. If the cup of ver. 20 is not the same as that of ver. 17, then Lk. not only states that Jesus did not drink of the eucharistic cup (for οὐ μὴ πίω ἀπὸ τοῦ νῦν excludes the partaking of any subsequent cup), but he also records that Jesus charged the Apostles to partake of the earlier cup, while he is silent as to any charge to partake of the eucharistic cup. So far as this report of the Institution goes, therefore, we are expressly told that the Celebrant refused the cup Himself, and we are not told that He handed it to the disciples. If, on the other hand, we identify the two cups, and regard *vv.* 17, 18 as the premature mention of what should have been given in one piece at ver. 20, then its severance into two portions, and the insertion of the distribution of the bread between the two portions, are inexplicable. Of the two difficulties, this seems to be the greater, and it is better not to identify the two cups. It is some confirmation of this that in ver. 17 ποτήριον is without the article, "*a* cup," while in ver. 20 it is "*the* cup." But τὸ ποτήριον *need* not mean more than "the cup just mentioned." In Mt. and Mk. ποτήριον has no article: and in all three ἄρτον has no article: so that its absence in ver. 17 and presence in ver. 20 is not of much weight in deciding between the two difficulties. The only way to avoid both these difficulties is to surrender the passage as an interpolation.

D a d ff_2 i l omit from τὸ ὑπὲρ ὑμῶν to ἐκχυννόμενον, and Syr-Cur. omits ver. 20, while b e Syr-Cur. and Syr-Sin. place ver. 19 before ver. 17, an arrangement which has been elaborately advocated by Dean Blakesley (*Prælectio in Scholis Cantab.* Feb. 14, 1850). The possibility of the whole being an importation from 1 Cor. xi. 24, 25 may be admitted on the evidence; but the probability of ver. 19, either to τὸ σῶμά μου (b e Syr-Cur.), or to the end (Syr-Sin.), having stood originally before ver. 17 is almost infinitesimal. In what way can we account for so simple an arrangement (harmonizing with Mt. and Mk.) becoming almost universally disturbed? "These difficulties, added to the suspicious coincidence with 1 Cor. xi. 24 f., and the Transcriptional evidence given above, leave no moral doubt (see *Introd.* § 240) that the words in question were absent from the original text of Lc, notwithstanding the purely Western ancestry of the documents which omit them" (WH. ii. App. p. 64). For the other view see Scrivener; also R. A. Hoffmann, *Abendmahlsgedanken Jesu Christi*, 1896, pp. 5–25.

19. λαβὼν ἄρτον εὐχαριστήσας ἔκλασεν. The taking bread (or a loaf), breaking, giving thanks, and the declaration, "This is My Body," are in all four accounts. But for *εὐχαριστήσας* here and 1 Cor. xi. 24 Mt. and Mk. have *εὐλογήσας*, and both here and 1 Cor. Λάβετε is omitted. Mt. alone has *φάγετε* with Λάβετε of the bread, and Lk. alone has Λάβετε of the cup (ver. 17); but perhaps this is not the eucharistic cup (see above).

Τοῦτό ἐστιν τὸ σῶμά μου. Not much is gained by pointing out that the *ἐστιν* would not be expressed in Aramaic. It *must* be understood; and the meaning of *τοῦτο*, and its relation to *τὸ σῶμά μου* must be discussed. The *τοῦτο* cannot mean the act of breaking and eating, nor anything else excepting "this bread." For the meaning of *ἐστι* see ver. 20, where the *ποτήριον* is identified with *ἡ καινὴ διαθήκη*, and comp. *εἰμι* in Jn. viii. 12, ix. 5, xiv. 6, xv. 1, 5. In taking this bread they in some real sense take His Body. See Thirlwall's *Charges*, vol. i. Charges v. and vi.; vol. ii. Charge x. and esp. p. 251, ed. Perowne, 1877; also Gould on Mk. xiv. 22.

τὸ ὑπὲρ ὑμῶν διδόμενον. Peculiar to this account: "which is *being given* for your advantage." The *κλώμενον*, which many texts add to *τὸ ὑπὲρ ὑμῶν* in 1 Cor. xi. 24, is not genuine.

τοῦτο ποιεῖτε. The proposal to give these words a sacrificial meaning, and translate them "Offer this, Sacrifice this, Offer this sacrifice," cannot be maintained. It has against it (1) the *ordinary meaning of ποιεῖν* in N.T., in LXX, and in Greek literature generally; (2) the authority of all the *Greek Fathers*,[1] who knew their own language, knew the N.T. and the LXX, and understood the words as having the ordinary meaning, "Perform this action"; (3) the authority of the *Early Liturgies*, which do not use *ποιεῖν* or *facere* when the bread and wine are offered, but *προσφέρειν* or *offerre*, although the words of institution precede the oblation, and thus suggest *ποιεῖν* or *facere*; (4) the authority of a *large majority of commentators*, ancient and modern, of the most various schools, who either make no comment, as if the ordinary meaning were too

[1] It has been asserted that Justin Martyr (*Try.* xli. and lxx.) is an exception. But this is a mistake. That Justin himself sometimes uses *ποιεῖν* in a sacrificial sense is possible; that he understood *τοῦτο ποιεῖτε* in this sense is not credible. No subsequent Father notes that Justin gives this interpretation, an interpretation so remarkable that it must have attracted attention.

obvious to need stating: or give the ordinary meaning without mentioning any other as worthy of consideration; or expressly reject the sacrificial meaning; (5) the testimony of the *Septuagint*, in which the various and frequent Hebrew words which mean "offer" or "sacrifice" are translated, not by ποιεῖν, but by προσφέρειν or ἀναφέρειν or the like; (6) the fact that here and in 1 Cor. xi. 24 *the writer might easily have made the sacrificial meaning clear* by using προσφέρειν or ἀναφέρειν. He has not even suggested such a meaning, as he might have done by writing ποιεῖτε τοῦτόν, *i.e.* τοῦτον τὸν ἄρτον. He has given as a translation of Christ's words neither "Offer this bread," nor "Offer this," nor "Do this bread" (which might have suggested "Offer this bread"), but "Do this thing." See *Expositor*, 3rd series, vii. 441; T. K. Abbott, *Essays on the Original Texts of O. & N.T.*, Longmans, 1891, p. 110; *A Reply to Mr. Supple's and other Criticisms*, Longmans, 1893; Mason, *Faith of the Gospel*, Rivingtons, 1888, p. 309.

εἰς τὴν ἐμὴν ἀνάμνησιν. "With a view to a calling to mind, a recollection, of Me." The word means more than a mere record or memorial, and is in harmony with the pres. imperat. ποιεῖτε: "Continually do this in order to bring Me to mind," *i.e.* "to remind yourselves and others of the redemption which I have won by My death." The eucharist is to be a continual calling to mind of Him who redeemed men from the bondage of sin, as the Passover was an annual calling to mind of redemption from the bondage of Egypt (Exod. xii. 24–27, xiii. 8, 14). In N.T. ἀνάμνησιν occurs only here, 1 Cor. xi. 24, 25, and Heb. x. 3, where see Wsctt. Comp. 1 Cor. iv. 17; 2 Tim. i. 6. In LXX it occurs Lev. xxiv. 7; Num. x. 10; Wisd. xvi. 6; the titles of Ps. xxxvii. and lxix. T K. Abbott has shown that a sacrificial meaning cannot be obtained from ἀνάμνησιν any more than from ποιεῖτε (*Essays*, etc. p. 122; *A Reply*, etc. p. 34).

The εἰς corresponds to ἵνα rather than to ὡς, and indicates the purport of the new institution. For the possessive pronoun used objectively comp. Rom. xi. 31; 1 Cor. xv. 31, xvi. 17.

The omission of this charge, τοῦτο ποιεῖτε, κ.τ.λ., in Mt. and Mk. has attracted attention. Dr. C. A. Briggs says, "Jülicher (*Zur Gesch. der Abendmahlsfeier in der ältesten Kirche*, in the *Theolog. Abhandlungen Weizsäcker gewidmet*, 1892, s. 238 *seq.*) and Spitta (*Urchristenthum*, i. s. 238 *seq.*) are doubtless correct in their opinion that the earliest Christian tradition, represented by Mark and Matthew, knew nothing of an institution of the Lord's Supper by Jesus on the night of His betrayal, as a sacrament to be observed continuously in the future. But they admit that Paul and Luke are sustained by the earliest Christian usage in representing it as a permanent institution. It is easier to suppose that the risen Lord in connection with these manifestations commanded the perpetual observance of the holy supper, just as He gave the Apostles their commission to preach and baptize, and explained the mystery of His life and death (Luke xxiv. 25–49). Paul and Luke would then combine the words of Jesus on two different occasions" (*The Messiah of the Gospels*, T. & T. Clark, 1894, p. 123). See Schaefer, *Das Herrenmahl nach Ursprung und Bedeutung*, Gütersloh, 1897.

20. τὸ ποτήριον. The τό may mean the cup which all Christians know as part of the eucharist, or (if this passage be genuine) the cup mentioned before (ver. 17). Paul also has the article, Mt. and Mk. not. The other portions of this verse which are in 1 Cor., but not in Mt. and Mk., are ὡσαύτως μετὰ τὸ δειπνῆσαι . . . τὸ ποτήριον . . . καινὴ . . ἐν τῷ. On the other hand, Paul and Lk. omit Πίετε ἐξ αὐτοῦ πάντες (Mt.) or ἔπιον ἐξ αὐτοῦ πάντες (Mk.). The **ὡσαύτως** means that He took it, gave thanks, and gave it to them. For **καινή**, which is opposed to παλαιά (2 Cor. iii. 6; comp. Rom. xi. 27), see on v. 38.

διαθήκη ἐν τῷ αἵματί μου. Mt. and Mk. have τὸ αἷμα μου τῆς **διαθήκης**, which is closer to LXX of Exod. xxiv. 8, τὸ αἷμα **τῆς** διαθήκης. Comp. **ἐν** αἵματι διαθήκης (Zech. ix. 11). **The** ***testamentum sanguine suo obsignatum*** of Tertullian (*Adv. Marcion.* iv. 40) gives the sense fairly well. The ratification of a covenant was commonly associated with the shedding of blood; and what was written in blood was believed to be indelible. For **διαθήκη** see Wsctt. on Heb. ix. 15, 16, with the additional note, p. 298.

τὸ ὑπὲρ ὑμῶν ἐκχυννόμενον. The ὑμῶν is peculiar to this passage. Mk. has ὑπὲρ πολλῶν, Mt. περὶ πολλῶν, and Paul omits. The ὑμῶν both here and in ver. 19 means the Apostles as representatives of all.

The part. is the Æolic form of the pres. part. pass. of ἐκχύνω = ἐκχέω (comp. Acts xxii. 20); "being poured out," like διδόμενον (ver. 19). In sense τὸ ἐκχ. agrees with αἵματι, but in grammar with ποτήριον: in Mt. and Mk., both in sense and grammar, with αἷμα. But see Win. lxvii. 3, p. 791.

21–23. The Declaration about the Traitor. Comp. Mt xxvi. 21–25; Mk. xiv. 18–21; Jn. xiii. 21–30.

If Lk. places this incident in its proper place, Judas did partake of the eucharist. But the question cannot be decided. See Schanz, *ad loc.* pp. 509, 510.

21. πλὴν ἰδοὺ ἡ χεὶρ . . . ἐπὶ τῆς τραπέζης. The expression is peculiar to Lk. The πλήν here indicates a transition; an expansion or change of subject. From the meaning of His death He passes to the manner of it. Others take it as a restriction of ὑπὲρ ὑμῶν; others again as marking a contrast between Christ's conduct and that of the traitor. See on vi. 24, 35, x. 11, 14. The verse may be understood literally, but probably means no more than that the traitor was sharing the same meal with Him: comp. Mt. xxvi. 23.

22. It is here that Lk. is almost *verbatim* the same as Mt. and Mk. Such solemn words would be likely to be remembered in one and the same form. Keim draws attention to their conspicuous originality. They are not adaptations of anything in O.T., although Obad. 7 and Mic. vii. 6 might appropriately have been used (v. p. 309). He regards Lk. as most exact. In any case πορεύεται, for which Mt. and Mk. have ὑπάγει, is to be noticed. It is probably used in the LXX sense of "depart, die": comp. Ps. lxxviii. 39.

ὅτι ὁ υἱὸς μέν. The "because" explains how such an amazing thing has come to pass. Failure to see the meaning of ὅτι (א B D L T, Sah. Boh.) has caused the substitution in many texts of καί (A X Γ Δ Λ Π, b c e f ff_2 Vulg. Syr-Sin. Arm. Aeth.), while others omit (a d, Orig.).

κατὰ τὸ ὡρισμένον. It is part of the Divine decree that the death of the Christ should be accompanied by betrayal: Mt. and Mk. have καθὼς γέγραπται περὶ αὐτοῦ: comp. Acts ii. 23. Excepting Rom. i. 4; Heb. iv. 7, ὁρίζειν is peculiar to Lk. (Acts ii. 23, x. 42, xi. 29, xvii. 26, 31).

πλὴν οὐαί. Mt. and Mk. have οὐαὶ δέ; but Lk. is fond of πλήν (ver. 21). Although God knows from all eternity that Judas is the betrayer of the Christ, *yet* this does not destroy the freedom or responsibility of Judas. The ἐκείνῳ marks him off as an alien: comp. Jn. xiii. 26, 27, 30. Mt. and Mk. add καλὸν αὐτῷ εἰ οὐκ ἐγεννήθη ὁ ἄνθρωπος ἐκεῖνος.

23. Here ἤρξαντο is the one word which is common to all three. Mt. and Mk. say that they each asked Jesus (and Mt. adds that Judas in particular asked) "Is it I?" No one seems to have suspected Judas; and perhaps Christ's Σὺ εἶπας was heard by Judas alone. Jesus may have had Judas next to Him on one side, S. John being on the other. For πράσσειν of doing evil comp. Jn. iii. 20, 21; Rom. vii. 19; Thuc. iv. 89. 2.

24–30. The Strife as to Precedence.

Disputes of this kind had taken place before, and the frequent records of them are among the abundant proofs of the candour of the Evangelists. But a comparison of the records seems to indicate that the tradition respecting them had become somewhat confused; and it is possible that what was said on one occasion has in part been transferred to another. Comp. Mt. xviii. 1–5; Mk. ix. 33–37; Lk. ix. 46–48; Jn. xiii. 14: also Mt. xx. 24–28; Mk. x. 41–45; Lk. xxii. 24–27. Of these last three passages, Mt. and Mk. clearly refer to the same incident, which took place considerably before the Last Supper. If Lk. merely knew what Jesus said on that occasion, but did not know the occasion, he would hardly have selected the Last Supper as a suitable place for the incident. He probably had good reason for believing that a dispute of this kind took place at the supper. Jesus may have repeated some of what He had said on a similar occasion; or Lk. may have transferred what was said then to the present occasion. But there is no note of time or sequence in ver. 24, where δὲ καί simply indicates that something of a different character (δέ) from what precedes also (καί) took place: and it is scarcely credible that this strife occurred after Jesus had washed their feet and instituted the eucharist. More probably the dispute arose respecting the places at the paschal meal—who was to be nearest to the Master; and the feet-washing was a symbolical rebuke to this contention. Here ver. 27 appears to have direct reference to His having washed their feet.

24. Ἐγένετο δὲ καί. "But there arose also": see small print on

iii. 9. The δέ perhaps contrasts this discussion with that as to which of them was the traitor. But we are not sure that the one discussion came closely after the other.

φιλονεικία. "Contentiousness." Here only in N.T., but quite classical. It is sometimes coupled with *βασκανία* (4 Mac. i. 26; M. Antonin. iii. 4), and easily comes to mean "contention" (2 Mac. iv. 4; Jos. *Ant.* vii. 8. 4).

δοκεῖ εἶναι. "Is accounted, allowed to be"—*omnium suffragiis*; implying who *ought* to be so accounted. See Lft. on Gal. ii. 6.

μείζων. Not quite equivalent to the superlative, which would have indicated several gradations from lowest to highest. The comparative implies only two,—a superior and all the rest as equals: ix. 46; Mk. ix. 34. Win. xxxv. 4, p. 305.

25. Almost *verbatim* as the account of the earlier strife provoked by James and John (Mt. xx. 25; Mk. x. 42). For **κυριεύουσιν** comp. Rom. xiv. 9; 2 Cor. i. 24; 1 Tim. vi. 15. Mt. and Mk. use the compounds, *κατακυρ.* and *κατεξουσιαζ.*

εὐεργέται καλοῦνται Peculiar to Lk. The phrase *εὐεργέτης βασιλέος ἀνεγράφη* (Hdt. viii. 85. 4: comp. Thuc. i. 129. 2; Esth. ii. 23, vi. 1) is not parallel. There persons who have done special service to the sovereign are formally credited with it. Here it is the sovereign who receives the title of Benefactor (*i.e.* of his country, or of mankind) as a perpetual epithet; *e.g.* some of the Greek kings of Egypt. Comp. Σωτήρ, *Pater patriæ*, *Servus servorum.* For less formal instances of the title see McClellan and Wetstein.

It is better to take **καλοῦνται** as middle: "claim the title," *hunc titulum sibi vindicant* (Beng.). This is what the disciples were doing.

26. ὁ μείζων. He who is really above the rest. True greatness involves service to others: *noblesse oblige.* For **γινέσθω**, "let him prove himself to be," comp. x. 36, xii. 40, xvi. 11, xix. 17. We have an echo of this 1 Pet. v. 3. For **νεώτερος** as **διακονῶν** comp. Acts v. 6, 10: *νεώτερον δὲ λέγει τὸν ἔσχατον* (Euthym.), the lowest in rank.

The Latin Versions have *junior* (e f Vulg.), *minor* (a c ff_2 i), *minus* (d, μεικρότερος D), *juvenis* (r), *adulescentior* (b q).

For *ὁ ἡγούμενος* we have *qui præest* (a b f q), *qui princeps est* (r), *qui primus est* (l), *qui præsens est* (e), *qui ducatum agit* (d), *qui præcessor est* (Vulg.). In N.T. *ἡγέομαι* means "lead" only in pres. part., and most often in Lk. It is used of any leader, ecclesiastical or civil (Acts vii. 10, xiv. 12, xv. 22; Mt. ii. 6; Heb. xiii. 7, 17, 24). In LXX it is freq.

27. ἐγὼ δὲ ἐν μέσῳ ὑμῶν. This need not be confined to the feet-washing (Euthym. De W. Godet, Hahn), nor to the fact that the person who presided at the paschal meal served the others (Hofm.): and the reference to either is uncertain. The whole of

Christ's ministry was one of service to His disciples (Nösg. Weiss). For ἐν μέσῳ see on viii. 7.

Strauss, Keim, and others regard the feet-washing recorded in Jn. as a mere fictitious illustration of Lk. xii. 37 and xxii. 27 (*L. J.* § 86, p. 542, ed. 1864; *Jes. of Naz.* v. p. 341 n).

28–30. Nearly the whole of this is peculiar to Lk. But comp. Mt. xix. 28. Having rebuked them for raising the question of precedence among themselves, Jesus shows them wherein the privileges which they *all* enjoy consist, viz. in their standing by Him in His service to others. He gives preference to none.

28. οἱ διαμεμενηκότες μετ' ἐμοῦ. The idea of *persistent loyalty* is enforced by the compound verb, by the perfect tense, and by the preposition (Lft. on Gal. ii. 5): "who have perseveringly remained with Me and continue to do so" (i. 22; Heb. i. 11; 2 Pet iii. 4).

ἐν τοῖς πειρασμοῖς μου. The trials to which He had been subjected during His ministry, and especially the latter portion of it. These, even to Him, were temptations to abandon His work. Comp. ἄχρι καιροῦ (iv. 13).

κἀγὼ διατίθεμαι ὑμῖν. "And *I* on My part, in return for your loyalty, hereby appoint to you dominion, even as My Father appointed to Me dominion." As in i. 33, βασιλεία is here "dominion" rather than "a kingdom": comp. xxiii. 42; Rev. xvii. 12; 1 Thes. ii. 12. See on xi. 2. Comp. τὴν βασιλείαν εἰς τὴν 'Αλεξάνδραν διέθετο (Jos. *Ant.* xiii. 16. 1).

A connexion with διαθήκη (ver. 20) is doubtful. The καινὴ διαθήκη is with all the faithful; this διατίθεμαι seems to be confined to the Apostles. The verb does not necessarily mean "covenant to give" or "assign by bequest," which would not fit διέθετο here, but may be used of any formal arrangement or disposition (Hdt. i. 194. 6; Xen. *Anab.* vii. 3. 10; *Mem.* i. 6. 13; *Cyr.* v. 2. 7, 9).

30. ἵνα ἔσθητε καὶ πίνητε. This is the purpose of conferring regal power upon them. Some make from καθώς to βασιλείαν a parenthesis and render, "I also (even as My Father appointed to Me dominion) appoint to you that ye may eat and drink," etc. So Theophyl. Nösg. Hahn. But βασιλείαν belongs to both διατίθεμαι and διέθετο. So Euthym. De W. Mey. Weiss, Schanz, Godet.

ἐπὶ τῆς τραπέζης μου. The Jews commonly regarded the Messianic Kingdom as a banquet: comp. xiii. 29, xiv. 15. *Cibus potusque, ille de quo alias dicitur. Beati qui esuriunt et sitiunt justitiam* (Bede).

καθῆσθε ἐπὶ θρόνων. The meaning of the promise is parallel to what precedes. As they have shared the trials, so they shall share the joy; and as they have proclaimed the Kingdom to Israel, so they shall exercise royal power over Israel, judging them according as they have accepted or rejected what was proclaimed. Comp. 1 Cor. vi. 2, 3; Rev. xx. 4.

As to the verb, the readings are very various: *καθίζεσθε* (E F K M S U V X Γ Δ), *καθίσησθε* (H), *καθέζησθε* (D). But the choice lies between *καθῆσθε* (B* T Δ), which must depend upon *ἵνα*, and *καθήσεσθε* (ℵ A B³ G L Q), which rather gives this as an independent promise. In Mt. xix. 28 *καθήσεσθε* is right, and may have been transferred to this passage, as *δώδεκα* has been in some authorities (ℵ D X, a b c d f l q) with *θρόνων*.

31–34. The Prediction of Peter's Denial.

Both the prediction and the fulfilment are given in all four Gospels. A comparison of them shows that Lk. and Jn. are quite independent of one another and of the other two. We have three separate narratives. Lk. agrees with Jn. (xiii. 36–38) in placing the prediction in the supper-room. Mt. (xxvi. 30–35) and Mk. (xiv. 26–30) place it on the way from the room to Gethsemane. It is not likely that it was repeated; and the arrangement of Lk. and Jn. is to be preferred. But some make three predictions; two in the room (Lk. being different from Jn.), and one during the walk to Gethsemane. Godet regards a repetition of such a prophecy *impossible de supposer* (ii. p. 476).

31. Lk. makes no break in Christ's words, but it is possible that a remark of Peter's, such as Jn. records, is omitted. The apparent want of connexion between *vv.* 30 and 31 has led to the insertion *εἶπε δὲ ὁ κύριος* (ℵ A D Q X, Latt.), as if to mark the beginning of a new subject. B L T, Sah. Boh. Syr-Sin. omit. Bede suggests by way of connexion, *Ne gloriarentur undecim apostoli, suisve viribus tribuerent, quod soli pæne inter tot millia Judæorum dicerentur in tentationibus permansisse cum Domino, ostendit et eos si non juvantis se Domini essent opitulatione protecti, eadem procella cum cæteris potuisse conteri.*

Σίμων Σίμων. The repetition of the name is impressive: see on x. 41. Contrast Πέτρε ver. 34. The whole of this address (31, 32) is peculiar to Lk. It tends to mitigate Peter's guilt, by showing how sorely he was tried. Lk. "ever spares the Twelve." See pp. 146, 172, 511.

ὁ Σατανᾶς ἐξῃτήσατο ὑμᾶς. "Satan *obtained* you by asking" (RV. *marg.*); "procured your being surrendered to him," as in the case of Job (i. 12, ii. 6): *exoravit vos.* Neither *postulavit* (Tert. Cypr.), nor *quæsivit* (c), nor *expetivit* (f Vulg.) is adequate. The aorist of the compound verb necessarily implies *success* in the petition. In class. Grk. the mid. would generally have a good sense: "obtained your release by entreaty." See instances in Wetst. and Field. As in x. 18 Jesus is here communicating a portion of His divine knowledge. See notes there and on viii. 12. Note the plur. ὑμᾶς, which covers both σύ and τοὺς ἀδελφούς σου. Satan was allowed to try them all (Mt. xxvi. 31, 56; Mk. xiv. 27, 50); *Judâ non contentus* (Beng.). Comp. *Apost. Const* vi. 5. 4: *Test. XII. Patr.* Benj. iii.

τοῦ σινιάσαι. See on i. 74: "in order to sift." Neither verb nor substantive (σινίον, "a sieve, winnowing riddle") is classical. They are probably colloquial for κόσκινον and κοσκινεύειν, which survives in modern Greek. In Amos ix. 9 we have **λικμᾶν.** See Suicer, *s.v.*

Ut ventilet (e f ff_2 i l q r, Ambr.), *ut vexaret* (Cypr. Aug.). *ut cerneret* (d, Tert. Hil.), *ad cernendum* (c), *ut cribraret* (Vulg.).

32. ἐγὼ δὲ ἐδεήθην. See on v. 12. The ἐγὼ δέ and the aor. are in marked contrast to Satan and his request. We may regard ἐξῃτήσατο and ἐδεήθην as contemporaneous.

περὶ σοῦ. As being the leader on whom so much depended, and as being in special need of help, as his fall proved. Jesus prayed for all (Jn. xvii. 2, 9, 15, 17). The interpolator of Ignatius understands this as a prayer for all: ὁ δεηθεὶς μὴ ἐκλείπειν τὴν πίστιν τῶν ἀποστόλων (*Smyrn.* vii.) For ἵνα after δέομαι comp. ix. 40, xxi. 36.

μὴ ἐκλίπῃ. "Fail not utterly, once for all." *Defecit in Petro* ἡ ἐνέργεια τῆς πίστεως *ad tempus: at* ἕξιν *labefactavit, non extinxit* (Grotius).

καὶ σύ. Answering to ἐγὼ δέ. Christ has helped him: he must do what he can for others.

ποτε ἐπιστρέψας στήρισον. "When once thou hast turned again, stablish" (RV.). It is unnatural to take ποτε with στήρισον (Mey. Weiss); and it is a mistake to make ἐπιστρέψας a sort of Hebraism (Ps. lxxxv. 7, ἐπιστρέψας ζωώσεις ἡμᾶς), meaning "in turn" (Grot. Maldon. Beng.), a use which perhaps does not occur in N.T. See Schanz. On the other hand, "when thou art converted" is too strong. It means turning again after a temporary aberration. Yet it is not turning *to the brethren*, but turning *from the fault* that is meant. It is not likely that the transitive sense is meant: "convert thy brethren and strengthen them": comp. i. 16, 17; Jas. v. 19, and contrast Acts iii. 19, xxviii. 27; Mt. xiii. 15; Mk. iv. 12. See *Expos. Times*, Oct. 1899, p. 6.

This metaphorical sense of στηρίζειν is not classical: comp. Acts xviii. 23; Rom. i. 11, xvi. 25; Jas. v. 8, etc. The form στήρισον for στήριξον is late.

Some Latin texts add, without any Greek authority, *et rogate ne intretis in temptationem* (a b c e ff_2 i q).

33. μετὰ σοῦ. First, with enthusiastic emphasis: "With *Thee* I am ready." The impulsive reply is thoroughly characteristic. As at the feet-washing (Jn. xiii. 6, 8) he has more confidence in his own feelings than in Christ's word; but this version of the utterance is less boastful than that in Mt. xxvi. 33 and Mk. xiv. 29.

34. Λέγω σοι, Πέτρε. For the first and last time in the Gospels Jesus addresses him by the significant name which He had given him. Rock-like strength is not to be found in self-confidence, but in humble trust in Him. Mt. and Mk. have Ἀμὴν λέγω σοι: Jn. Ἀμὴν ἀμὴν λ. σοι. The solemn earnestness with which this definite prediction was uttered made a deep impression upon all.

σήμερον. Mt. has ταύτῃ τῇ νυκτί. Mk. has both. The new day began after sunset. See iv. 40, v. 13, and xxiii. 38 for similar cases in which Mt. and Lk. have different parts of an expression, of which Mk. has the whole.

οὐ φωνήσει . . . ἀλέκτωρ. The third of the four Roman watches was called ἀλεκτοροφωνία, *gallicinium* (Mk. xiii. 35; *Apost. Const.* viii. 34. 1; Strabo, vii. 35; *Geopon.* 1153). The expression here is equivalent to "Before this night is past." Mk. alone mentions the double cock-crowing, and the fact that Peter, so far from being silenced, kept on protesting with increased vehemence.

ἕως τρίς με ἀπαρνήσῃ εἰδέναι. This is the true reading (ℵ B L M Q X T), The τρίς is in all four Gospels: the εἰδέναι in Lk. alone.

35–38. § The New Conditions; the Saying about the Sword. The opening words mark the beginning of a new subject; and there is no indication of any connexion with what precedes. It is one more proof of His care for them. Precautions and equipments, which would have hindered them in more peaceful times, have become necessary now. What He formerly forbade, He now enjoins. *Dominus non eâdem vivendi regulâ persecutionis quam pacis tempore discipulos informat* (Bede).

35. Ὅτε ἀπέστειλα ὑμᾶς ἄτερ β. The wording suggests a direct reference to x. 4, which is addressed to the *Seventy*. In ix. 3, where similar directions are given to the *Twelve*, the wording is different. In the source which Lk. is here using the words given in x. 4 would seem to have been addressed to the Apostles. There may have been some confusion in the tradition respecting two similar incidents, or in the use which Lk. makes of it.

This use of ὑστερεῖν τινος occurs here only in N.T. Comp. Jos. *Ant.* ii. 2. 1. The pass. is thus used xv. 14; Rom. iii. 23; Heb. xi. 37.

36. ὁ μὴ ἔχων. This is ambiguous. It may look back to ὁ ἔχων βαλλάντιον: "He that hath no *purse*, let him sell his garment and buy a sword" (Cov. Gen. Rhem. RV.). Or it may anticipate μάχαιραν: "He that hath no *sword*, let him sell his garment and buy one" (Tyn. Cran. AV.). The former is far the more probable. Only he who has no money or wallet, would sell the most necessary of garments (ἱμάτιον, vi. 29), to buy anything. But even the ἱμάτιον is less indispensable than a sword; so dangerous are their surroundings. "For henceforth the question with all those who continue in the land will not be whether they possess anything or not, but whether they can exist and preserve their lives" (Cyril Alex. *Syr. Com. ad loc.*, Payne Smith, p. 680)

Christ implies that His Apostles will have to rely upon their own resources and to confront deadly hostility. Comp. Jn. xv. 18–21. Christ does not mean that they are to repel force by force; still less that they are to use force in spreading the Gospel. But in a figure likely to be remembered He warns them of the changed circumstances for which they must now be prepared.

37. λέγω γὰρ ὑμῖν. The *γάρ* introduces the explanation of the change from *ὅτε ἀπέστειλα* to *νῦν*.

τὸ γεγραμμένον. Comp. xx. 17; 2 Cor. iv. 13. More often we have *τά γεγραμμένα*: xviii. 31, xxi. 22; Acts xiii. 29; Rev. xx. 12, xxii. 19.

The *ἔτι* before *τοῦτο* (Γ Δ Λ Π, Vulg. Arm.) is spurious. It is the kind of insertion which versions are apt to make for the sake of completeness: "must *yet* be fulfilled." For **δεῖ** see on iv. 43 and ix. 22.

ἐν ἐμοί. Therefore the disciples must expect no better treatment than the Master receives (Mt. x. 24; Jn. xv. 20, xiii. 16: see on vi. 40).

Καὶ μετὰ ἀνόμων. The *καί* is part of the quotation: *καὶ ἐν τοῖς ἀνόμοις ἐλογίσθη* (Is. liii. 12): "*even* with the transgressors" is incorrect. In AV. *ἄνομος* is translated in *five* different ways: "transgressor" (Mk. xv. 28); "wicked" (Acts ii. 23; 2 Thes. ii. 8), "without law" (1 Cor. ix. 21), "lawless" (1 Tim. i. 9), "unlawful" (2 Pet. ii. 8).

καὶ γάρ. An extension of the argument: "and what is more." This fulfilment is not only necessary,—it is reaching its conclusion, "is having an end" (Mk. iii. 26). The phrase *τέλος ἔχειν* is used of oracles and predictions being accomplished. See Field, *Ot. Norvic.* iii., and comp. *τετέλεσται* (Jn. xix. 30).

Om. *γάρ* D, a d e ff_2 i l Syr-Cur. Syr-Sin. Failure to see the point of the *γάρ* would cause the omission.

τὸ περὶ ἐμοῦ. This form of expression is found in no other Gospel; but the plur., *τὰ περὶ ἐμοῦ*, occurs xxiv. 19, 27 and is freq. in Acts (i. 3, xviii. 25, xxiii. 11, 15, xxiv. 10, 22, xxviii. 15, 31: in viii. 12, xix. 8, xxviii. 23 the *τά* is probably spurious). Some texts (A X Γ Δ etc.) have *τά* here for *τό*: *ea quæ sunt de me* (Vulg.); *ea quæ de me scribta sunt* (Cod. Brix.). But *τό* (ℵ B D L Q) has been altered to the more usual expression, perhaps to avoid the possible combination of *τὸ περὶ ἐμοῦ τέλος*. There is no need to understand *γεγραμμένον*. Much which concerned the Christ had never been written.

38. μάχαιραι. Chrysostom has supposed that these were two knives, prepared for the slaughtering (ver. 8) or carving of the paschal lamb. In itself this is not improbable: but nowhere else in N.T. does *μάχαιρα* mean a knife. Assuming that *swords* are meant, these weapons may have been provided against robbers on the journey to Jerusalem, or against attack in the city. Peter had one of them, and may have been the speaker here. It is one more instance of the Apostles' want of insight, and of the Evangelists' candour: comp. Mk. viii. 17. Schleiermacher points out that the obscurity of the passage is evidence of its genuineness and originality (p. 299, Eng. tr.).

Ἱκανόν ἐστιν. *Satis est* (c ff_2 q Vulg.), *sat est* (a i), *sufficit* (b d f l r), which last perhaps represents ἀρκεῖ (D). The reply is probably the equivalent for a Hebrew formula for dismissing the subject (Deut. iii. 26), not with impatience, but with satiety or sorrow. Comp. ἕως τοῦ νῦν [ἱκανόν] (1 Mac. ii. 33). But even if it means that two swords are a sufficient quantity ("They are enough for you," Syr-Sin.), it intimates that the subject is dismissed. Bede is hardly right in his view: *duo gladii sufficiunt ad testimonium sponte passi salvatoris, i.e.* to prove that he could have resisted, had He pleased. If the words apply to the swords, they are spoken with a sad irony (μονονυχὶ διαγελᾷ, Cyril Alex.), as meaning, not that the two weapons will be sufficient for the protection of the company, but that none at all are required: they have grievously misunderstood Him.[1] *Es gilt nicht mehr mit dem leiblichen Schwerdt fechten, sondern es gilt hinfort leiden um des Evangelii willen und Kreuz tragen: denn man kann wider den Teufel nicht mit Eisen fechten; darum ist Noth Alles dran zu setzen, und nur das geistliche Schwerdt, das Wort Gottes, zu fassen* (Luth.).

XXII. 39–XXIII. 49. The Passion. In this part of the narrative of the Passion proper, *i.e.* from the Agony to the Death, the particulars which are wholly or mainly peculiar to Lk. are xxii. 51, xxiii. 6–12, 27–32 [34], 40–43, 46: and these particulars are among the most precious details in the history of the Passion.

39–46. The Agony in the Garden. With regard to the omission of nearly the whole of the last discourses (Jn. xiv.–xvii.) Godet remarks that the oral tradition was not a suitable vehicle for transmitting such things: *c'étaient des trésors qu'un cœur d'élite pouvait seul garder et reproduire.* On the other hand Jn. omits

[1] The Bull *Unam Sanctam* of Boniface VIII., A.D. 1302, bases the double power of the Papacy on this text. The following are among the most remarkable passages: *Igitur Ecclesiæ, unius, et unicæ unum corpus, unum caput, non duo capita quasi monstrum, Christus scilicet et Christi vicarius, Petrus Petrique successor. . . . In hac ejusque potestate duos esse gladios, spiritualem videlicet et temporalem evangelicis dictis instruimur. Nam dicentibus Apostolis*: Ecce gladii duo hic; *in Ecclesia scilicet, cum Apostoli loquerentur; non respondit Dominus* nimis *esse, sed* satis. . . . *Uterque ergo in potestate Ecclesiæ, spiritualis scilicet gladius, et materialis: sed is quidem pro Ecclesia, ille vero ab Ecclesia exercendus; ille sacerdotis, is manu Regum et militum; sed ad nutum et patientiam sacerdotis. Oportet autem gladium esse sub gladio, et temporalem auctoritatem spirituali subjici potestati . . . sic de Ecclesia et ecclesiastica potestate verificatur vaticinium Jeremiæ* [i. 10]: Ecce constitui te hodie super gentes, et regna, etc. *quæ sequuntur. . . . Porro subesse Romano Pontifici omnem humanam creaturam declaramus, dicimus et definimus omnino esse de necessitate salutis* (Raynald. xxiii. p. 328; see Milman, *Lat. Chr.* Bk. xi. ch. ix.; Robertson, Bk. vii. ch. v.; Stubbs' *Mosheim*, ii. p. 261; Zoeckler, *Handb. d. Theol. Wiss.* ii. p. 167; Gregorovius, *Stadt Rom*, v. p. 562; Berchtold, *Die Bulle Unam Sanctam*. München, 1888).

the whole of this scene, although there is a clear reference to it xviii. 11. Lk.'s narrative once more differs considerably from that of Mt. (xxvi. 30–41) and of Mk. (xiv. 26–38), which are almost *verbatim* the same; and it is very much shorter. It is in *vv.* 39, 42, 46 that Lk. comes most closely to the other two.

39. ἐξελθών. From the house.

κατὰ τὸ ἔθος. Peculiar to Lk. (i. 9, ii. 42): comp. **πολλάκις** *συνήχθη Ἰησοῦς ἐκεῖ* (Jn. xviii. 2). It was no longer necessary to keep Judas ignorant of His movements; so He follows His usual practice. Lk. omits the *ὑμνήσαντες* which records the chanting of the second part of the Hallel. Jn. alone mentions the passing of the gloomy ravine of the Kidron (xviii. 1).

40. τοῦ τόπου. Lk. and Jn. call it "the place," Mt. and Mk. *χωρίον* and add the name *Γεθσημανεί* = "oil-press." The traditional Gethsemane is a questionable site. Both Robinson and Thomson would place the garden higher up the Mount of Olives. The tradition is continuous from the age of Constantine, but cannot be traced to any earlier source. Stanley inclines to accept it as correct (*Sin. & Pal.* p. 455). See *D.B.*[2] art. "Gethsemane."

Προσεύχεσθε. This first command to pray (comp. ver. 46) is recorded by Lk. alone. It is given to the eleven; the second is to the chosen three, whom Lk. does not notice particularly.

41. ἀπεσπάσθη. *Avulsus est* (Vulg.). "He was drawn away" by the violence of His emotion, which was too strong to tolerate the sympathy of even the closest friends: comp. Acts xxi. 1. It seems to be too strong a word to use of mere separation: but comp. 2 Mac. xii. 10, 17; 4 Mac. xiii. 18; Is. xxviii. 9.

ὡσεὶ λίθου βολήν. Mt. and Mk. have *μικρόν*. Comp. *ὡσεὶ τόξου βολήν* (Gen. xxi. 16): *λείπετο δουρὸς ἐρωήν* (Hom. *Il.* xxiii. 529). The acc. in Jn. vi. 19 is not quite parallel.

θεὶς τὰ γόνατα. Lk. alone mentions this. Standing was the more common attitude (xviii. 11; Mt. vi. 5; Mk. xi. 25; 1 Sam. i. 26): but on occasions of special earnestness or humiliation kneeling was more natural (1 Kings viii. 54; Ezra ix. 5; Dan. vi. 10). In N.T. kneeling is the only attitude mentioned; perhaps in imitation of Christ's example here: Acts vii. 60, ix. 40, xx. 36, xxi. 5; Eph. iii. 14. The phrase *τιθέναι τὰ γόνατα* is not classical, but comp. *genua ponere*. See on iii. 21: the imperf. **προσηύχετο** implies continued prayer.

42. Πάτερ, εἰ βούλει, παρένεγκε. We might have expected *εἰ θέλεις* (comp. *ἐὰν θέλῃς*, v. 12), because of *τὸ θέλημα* in the next sentence. But this is one of the passages which tend to show that in N.T. *θέλω* indicates mere choice, while *βούλομαι* implies deliberate selection (Mt. i. 19). The latter is far less common in N.T. In LXX there is not much difference.

This is the only passage in which the Attic βούλει for βούλῃ is well supported. Such forms are found in some texts Mt. xxvii. 4; Jn. xi. 40; Acts xvi. 31, xxiv. 8.

In D a c d e ff$_2$ μὴ τὸ θέλημα . . . γενέσθω precedes εἰ βούλει . . . ἐμοῦ, πλήν being omitted. Several of the same authorities have a similar inversion ix. 62.

The reading παρενεγκεῖν (A Q X Γ Δ Λ) turns the prayer into an unfinished pleading: "Father, if Thou be willing to remove this cup from Me."—Comp. Exod. xxxii. 32. B D T Versions, and Orig. support παρένεγκε. Vulg. *transfer calicem istum*; Tert. *transfer poculum istud*; but he may be quoting Mk. xiv. 36 (*De Orat.* iv.). Boh. Sah. Syr-Cur. Syr-Sin. have "let this cup pass."

παρένεγκε τοῦτο τὸ ποτήριον ἀπ' ἐμοῦ. "This cup" and the address "Father" are in all three accounts. In O.T. the metaphor of "cup" for a person's fortune, whether good or bad, is very common (Ps. xi. 6, xvi. 5, xxiii. 5, lxxv. 8, etc.). In N.T. specially of the sufferings of Christ (Mk. xiv. 36; Jn. xviii. 11; Mt. xx. 22, 23; Mk. x. 38, 39): comp. Rev. xiv. 10, xvi. 19, xviii. 6. In class. Grk. παραφέρειν ποτήριον would mean to place a cup at the side of a person, put it on the table near him (Hdt. i. 119. 5, 133. 3; Plat. *Rep.* i. p. 354). But in Plutarch παραφέρειν is used in the sense of "lay aside, remove" (*Camill.* xli.). Elsewhere in N.T. it is used of leading astray (Heb. xiii. 9; Jude 12).

τὸ θέλημά μου. Either βούλημα or βουλή might have been used of the Father's will, but less suitably of Christ's (Eph. i. 11). The γινέσθω is peculiar to Lk. It recalls γενηθήτω τὸ θέλημά σου (Mt. vi. 10), which Lk. omits (xi. 2). For πλήν comp. x. 11, 14, 20.

43, 44. As in the case of *vv.* 19, 20, we have to consider whether this passage is part of the original text. For the evidence see the additional note at the end of ch. xxiii. One thing is certain. "It would be *impossible to regard these verses as a product of the inventiveness of the scribes.* They can only be a fragment from the traditions, written or oral, which were, for a time at least, locally current beside the canonical Gospels, and which doubtless included matter of every degree of authenticity and intrinsic value. These verses and the first sentence of xxiii. 34 may be safely called *the most precious among the remains of this evangelic tradition which were rescued from oblivion* by the scribes of the second century" (WH. ii. App. p. 67). It matters little whether Lk. included them in his narrative, so long as their authenticity as evangelic tradition is acknowledged. In this respect the passage is like that respecting the Woman taken in Adultery.

43. ὤφθη. "Was visible" to the bodily eye is obviously meant. It is against the context and the use of the expression in other places to suppose that internal perception of an invisible spiritual presence is intended. Lk. is fond of the expression (i. 11, ix. 31, xxiv. 34; Acts ii. 3, vii. 2, 26, 30, 35, ix. 17, xiii. 31, xvi. 9, xxvi. 16; comp. 1 Cor. xv. 5–8), which Mt. and Mk. use once each (xvii. 3, ix. 4), and Jn. thrice (Rev. xi. 19, xii. 1, 3), but not in his Gospel. The ἀπ' οὐρανοῦ would not have been added if the presence of the Angel was invisible.

ἐνισχύων. Elsewhere in N.T. only Acts ix. 19, of *bodily* strengthening: comp. 2 Sam. xxii. 40; Ecclus. l. 4; and this may well be the meaning here, but without excluding the strengthening of soul and spirit. Either would tend to produce the other; and the sight of His Father's messenger would strengthen both body and spirit. Commentators have speculated as to what the Angel said (see Corn. à Lap. *ad l.*). There is nothing to indicate that he spoke. Hobart remarks of ἐνισχύειν that, outside the LXX "its use in the transitive sense, 'to strengthen,' is confined to Hippocrates and St. Luke" (p. 80). In Acts ix. 19 the true reading is probably ἐνισχύθη.[1]

ἐν ἀγωνίᾳ. Here only in N.T. Field contends that *fear* is the radical notion of the word. The passages in which it occurs in LXX confirm this view: 2 Mac. iii. 14, 16, xv. 19; comp. ἀγωνιᾶν Esth. xv. 8 [v. 1]; Dan. i. 10; 2 Mac. iii. 21. It is frequently coupled with such words as φόβος, δέος, φρίκη, etc. For examples see Field, *Ot. Norv.* iii. p. 56. It is, therefore, an agony of fear that is apparently to be understood. Mk. has ἀδημονεῖν with ἐκθαμβεῖσθαι, Mt. with λυπεῖσθαι.—ἐκτενέστερον. "More extendedly," and hence "more persistently." This seems to be parallel to the πίπτειν ἐπὶ πρόσωπον αὐτοῦ (Mt.) and ἐπὶ τῆς γῆς (Mk.). Heb. v. 7 probably refers specially to this. Comp. ἐκτενῶς of prayer, and ἐκτένεια of worship and service, Acts xii. 5, xxvi. 7.

44. ὡσεὶ θρόμβοι αἵματος καταβαίνοντες. Even if καταβαίνοντος (ℵ V X, Vulg. Boh.) be right, the words do not *necessarily* mean more than that the drops of sweat in some way resembled drops of blood, *e.g.* by their size and frequency. But it is not likely that no more than this is intended, or that the words are a metaphorical expression, like our "tears of blood." That Justin in referring to the statement omits αἵματος—ἱδρὼς ὡσεὶ θρόμβοι κατεχεῖτο (*Try.* ciii.)—does not prove that he did not understand actual blood to be meant. Rather it shows that he considered that θρόμβοι, "clots," sufficiently expressed "drops of blood."[2]

The expression "bloody sweat" is probably a correct interpretation: and the possibility of blood exuding through the pores seems to be established by examples. Comp. Arist. *Hist. Anim.* iii. 19. De Mezeray states of Charles IX.

---

[1] Even Meyer is disposed to admit that this strengthening by an Angel is legendary, because it is "singular" (*absonderlich*), and not mentioned by Mt. or Mk., who has Peter to rest upon. Let us admit that perhaps Lk. did not mention it either. That does not prove that it is legendary; unless we are prepared to admit that the ministry of Angels after the temptation, which is analogous to this, and which is attested by both Mt. (iv. 11) and Mk. (i. 13), is legendary also.

[2] In class. Grk. θρόμβος, both with and without αἵματος, may mean a drop of blood (Aesch. *Eum.* 184; *Choëph.* 533, 546; Plato, *Crit.* p. 120 A.).

of France that "During the last two weeks of his life (May 1574) his constitution made strange efforts . . . blood gushed from all the outlets of his body, even from the pores of his skin; so that on one occasion he was found bathed in a bloody sweat." See W. Stroud, *The Physical Cause of the Death of Christ*, 1847, pp. 85–88, 379–389. Schanz cites Lönarz, *De sudore sanguinis*, Bonn, 1850, and Langen, *Die letzten Lebenstage*, p. 214. Why is αἵματος added, if no αἷμα accompanied the ἱδρώς? It would be visible in the moonlight, when Jesus returned to the disciples: *ubi quidem non solis oculis, sed quasi membris omnibus flevisse videtur* (Bernard, *In Dom. Palm. Serm.* iii. 4). Diatess-Tat. has "like a *stream* of blood."

45. Lk. is much more brief than Mt. and Mk., but adds ἀναστὰς ἀπὸ τῆς προσευχῆς and also ἀπὸ τῆς λύπης. Prolonged sorrow produces sleep, and in mentioning this cause of their slumber Lk. once more "spares the Twelve." For ἀναστάς see on i. 39, and for ἀπό of the cause see on xix. 3, xxi. 26, xxiv. 41.

46. Τί καθεύδετε; The special address to Peter is omitted.

προσεύχεσθε ἵνα μή. All three assign this to the first return from prayer. No words are recorded of the second, and Lk. omits both it and the third. These movements are some evidence as to Christ's human knowledge. Would He have come to the disciples, without waking them (as seems on the second occasion to have been the case), had He known beforehand that they were asleep? And does not εὑρίσκειν, which is in all three, almost imply that until He came He did not know, as in the case of the barren fig tree (Mk. xi. 13)?

ἵνα μή. "That . . . not" (Wic. RV.) rather than "lest" (Tyn. Gen. Rhem. AV.). Comp. ver. 40, where the constr. is equivalent, although not identical. In both places we have the pres. imperat. of continuous prayer.

47–53. The Traitor's Kiss and the Arrest of Jesus. Mt. xxvi. 47–56; Mk. xiv. 43–52; Jn. xviii. 2–11. It would have been possible for Jesus to have evaded Judas by not going to the usual place (ver. 40) or by leaving it before he arrived. The sneer of Celsus, that Jesus went to the garden "to make His escape by disgracefully hiding Himself," is out of place. By going and remaining where Judas must find Him, He surrendered Himself voluntarily. As Origen says, "At the fitting time He did not prevent Himself from falling into the hands of men" (*Cels.* ii. 10).

47. Ἔτι αὐτοῦ λαλοῦντος . . . ὄχλος καὶ . . . Ἰούδας εἷς τῶν δώδεκα. These nine words are in all three accounts. He was still addressing the disciples when He was interrupted by a hostile multitude led by one of the Twelve. See Blass on Acts x. 44.

φιλῆσαι αὐτόν. Lk. omits that it was a prearranged sign; also the χαῖρε Ῥαββεί and the fact that an ostentatiously affectionate kiss (κατεφίλησεν) was given. Jn. does not mention the kiss.

His narrative shows how unnecessary the treacherous signal was, for Jesus came forward and declared Himself.[1]

48. φιλήματι. First, with great emphasis. "Is it with a kiss that thou betrayest?" *Osculo Filium hominis tradis? hoc est amoris pignore vulnus infligis, et caritatis officio sanguinem fundis, et pacis instrumento mortem irrogas, servus Dominum, discipulus prodis magistrum, electus Auctorem* (Bede). Jesus does not say, "betrayest thou Me?" but "betrayest thou the Son of Man?" He reminds Judas that it is the Messiah whom he is treating with this amazing form of treachery. Mt. words Christ's rebuke very differently: Ἑταῖρε, ἐφ᾽ ὃ πάρει. Mk. omits the rebuke.

49. Κύριε, εἰ πατάξομεν ἐν μαχαίρῃ; Lk. alone records this question. It is said that "since it was illegal to carry swords on a feast-day, we have here another sign that the Last Supper had not been the Passover." But if the μάχαιρα was a large knife used for killing the lamb, this would not hold: see on ver. 38.

For the constr. see on xiii. 23 and Burton, § 70, 169: and for the form μαχαίρῃ see on xxi. 24.

50. εἷς. All three use this indefinite expression: Jn. alone tells us that it was the impetuous Peter, who acted without waiting for Christ's reply. When Jn. wrote it was not dangerous to disclose the name of the Apostle who had attacked the high priest's servant. And John alone gives the servant's name. As a friend of the high priest (xviii. 15) he would be likely to know the name Malchus. Malchus was probably taking a prominent part in the arrest, and Peter aimed at his head.

τὸ οὖς αὐτοῦ τὸ δεξιόν. Mt. has ὠτίον, Mk. and Jn. ὠτάριον. Jn. also specifies the *right* ear. Mt. records the rebuke to Peter, "Put up again thy sword," etc.

51. Ἐᾶτε ἕως τούτου. The obscurity of the saying is evidence that it was uttered: an invented utterance would have been plainer. If addressed to the disciples (as ἀποκριθείς implies, for He is answering either their question or Peter's act), it probably means, "Suffer My assailants to proceed these lengths against Me." If addressed to those who had come to arrest Him, it might mean, "Tolerate thus much violence on the part of My followers,"—violence which He at once rectifies. It can hardly mean, "Allow Me just to touch the sufferer," for He is still free, as ver. 52 implies: the arrest takes place at ver. 54. Some even

[1] It was perhaps in memory of this treacherous act that the "kiss of peace" was omitted in public service on Good Friday. Tertullian blames those who omit it on fast-days which are less public and universal. But *die Paschæ, quo communis et quasi publica jejunii religio est, merito deponimus osculum* (*De Orat.* xviii.). At other times the omission would amount to a proclamation that one was fasting, contrary to Christ's command.

make ἕως τούτου masc. "to go as far as Malchus": but comp. Lev. xxvi. 18. In either of these last cases we should have had με after ἐᾶτε. For ἐάω see on iv. 41.

ἰάσατο αὐτόν. Lk. the physician alone records this solitary miracle of surgery. A complete restoration of the ear is meant and required. "He touched the *ear*," not the place where the ear had been. Peter's act had seemed to place Jesus in the wrong and to justify His enemies: He was shown to be the Leader of dangerous persons. To undo this result it was necessary to render Malchus uninjured, and to surrender without resistance. This confirms the interpretation given above of Ἐᾶτε ἕως τούτου: they are a public command to the disciples not to impede the arrest. Comp. Jn. xviii. 36. Marcion omitted *vv.* 49–51.

In the *Classical Review* of Dec. 1893 Dr. E. A. Abbott proposes to resolve this miracle into a misunderstanding of traditional language. The ingenuity is unconvincing. See Additional Note p. 545.

52. τοὺς παραγενομένους ἐπ' αὐτόν. These are not fresh arrivals, but portions of the ὄχλος of ver. 47 more particularly described. There is nothing improbable in the presence of ἀρχιερεῖς, who are mentioned by Lk. alone. Anxiety about the arrest, which might be frustrated by a miscalculation of time, or by the people, or by a miracle, would induce them to be present. For στρατηγοὺς τοῦ ἱεροῦ see on ver. 4. Jn. tells us that Roman soldiers with their chief officer were there also (xviii. 3, 12). Jesus addresses the Jewish authorities, who are responsible for the transaction.

The reading ἐπ' αὐτόν (A B D L T X Γ Λ Π), "against Him" (RV.), is to be preferred to πρὸς αὐτόν (ℵ G H R Δ), "to Him" (AV.); but Tisch., with his bias for ℵ, adopts the latter.

Ὡς ἐπὶ λῃστήν. First with emphasis. These words down to καθ' ἡμέραν are the same in all three accounts. Jesus is not a bandit (x. 30, xix. 46). The fact that they did not arrest Him publicly, nor without violence, nor in the light of day, is evidence that the arrest is unjustifiable. Perhaps ξύλων means "clubs," as Rhem. from *fustibus* (Vulg.): comp. Jos. *B. J.* ii. 9. 4.

53. Every point tells: "Every day there was abundant opportunity; you yourselves were there; the place was the most public in the city; and you made no attempt to touch Me." The sentence is certainly not a question (Hahn). Tisch. does not make even the first part, from ὡς to ξύλων, a question: so also Wic. and Cran.

ἀλλ' αὕτη ἐστίν. "But the explanation of such outrageous conduct is not difficult. This is your hour of success allowed by God; and it coincides with that allowed to the power of darkness." So Euthym. ὥρα ἐν ᾗ δύναμιν ἐλάβετε κατ' ἐμοῦ θεόθεν·

comp. Jn. viii. 44. Perhaps there is an intimation that the night is a fit season for such work: comp. Jn. xiii. 30, and see Schanz, p. 529.

ἡ ἐξουσία τοῦ σκότους. See Lft. on Col. i. 13, where the same phrase occurs. He points out that *ἐξουσία* is sometimes used of unrestrained and tyrannical power, as well as of delegated and constitutional power. But the latter may be the meaning here. It is by Divine permission that Satan is *ὁ ἄρχων τοῦ κόσμου τούτου* (Jn. xiv. 30).

Lk. omits the flight of *all* the disciples, which Mt. and Mk record. This is further evidence, if any be needed, that Lk. exhibits no *animus* against the Twelve. See on ver. 45 and vi. 13.

54–62. Peter's Denials are recorded in detail by all four Evangelists, who tell us that *three denials were predicted* (Mt. xxvi. 34; Mk. xiv. 30; Lk. xxii. 34; Jn. xiii. 38), and *record three denials* (Mt. xxvi. 70, 72, 74; Mk. xiv. 68, 70, 71; Lk. xxii. 57, 58, 60; Jn. xviii. 17, 25, 27). As already pointed out, Lk. and Jn. place the *prediction* during the supper, Mk. and Mt. on the road to the Mount of Olives, which is less likely to be correct, if (as is probable) the prediction was made only once.

As to the *three denials*, all four accounts are harmonious respecting the first, but differ greatly respecting the second and third. The first denial, provoked by the accusation of the maid, seems to have led to a series of attacks upon S. Peter, which were mainly in two groups; and these were separated from one another by an interval, during which he was not much noticed. Each of the four narratives notices some features in these groups of attacks and denials: but it is unreasonable to suppose that they profess to give the exact words that were spoken in each case. See on viii. 24 for Augustine's remarks on the different words recorded by the three Synoptists as uttered during the storm on the lake. Alford on Mt. xxvi. 69, and Westcott in an additional note on Jn. xviii., have tabulated the four narratives: see also Rushbrooke's *Synopticon*, p. 114. With these helps the four can readily be compared clause by clause; and the independence of at least three of them soon becomes apparent. This independence results from truthfulness, and the variations will be a difficulty to those only who hold views of verbal inspiration which are contradicted by abundant phenomena both in O.T. and N.T. "St. Luke adds force to the episode by placing all three denials together. With St. John, however, dramatic propriety is sacrificed to chronological accuracy" (Lft. *Biblical Essays*, p. 191).

54. Συλλαβόντες. All four use this verb in connexion with the arrest of Jesus. It is freq. in Lk., especially of the capture of prisoners: Acts i. 16, xii. 3, xxiii. 27, xxvi. 21. Jn. tells us that they bound Him and took Him *πρὸς Ἄνναν πρῶτον*, *i.e.* before His being examined by Caiaphas, as recorded Mt. xxvi. 57–68 and Mk. xiv. 53–65. Both these examinations were informal. They were held at night, and no sentence pronounced in a trial held at night was valid. Hence the necessity for a formal meeting of the Sanhedrin after daybreak, to confirm what had been previously decided. This third ecclesiastical trial is mentioned by all the

Synoptists (ver. 66; Mt. xxvii. 1; Mk. xv. 1); whereas Jn. gives only the first (xviii. 12), and shows that it was in connexion with it that Peter's denials took place. Lk. can hardly be said to give either of the first two hearings. He says that Jesus was taken to the high priest's house, and was there denied by Peter and ill-treated by His captors; and then he passes on to the formal assembly of the Sanhedrin; but there is no mention of any previous examination. With the help of the other narratives, however, we obtain an account of all three hearings. The space devoted by all four to these Jewish and Roman trials seems to be out of proportion to the brief accounts of the crucifixion. But they serve to bring out the meaning of the crucifixion by exhibiting the nature of the Messiahship of Jesus. Why was Jesus condemned to death by the Sanhedrin? Because He claimed to be the Son of God. Why was He condemned to death by Pilate? Because He claimed to be the King of the Jews.

ἤγαγον καὶ εἰσήγαγον. "They led Him (away) and brought Him." The latter verb is a favourite with Lk. See on ii. 27.

D Γ, Syr-Cur. Syr-Sin. some Old Lat. texts Vulg. Aeth. omit *καὶ εἰσήγαγον*.

εἰς τὴν οἰκίαν τοῦ ἀρχιερέως. It is impossible to determine whether this means of Annas or of Caiaphas (comp. iii. 2 and Acts iv. 6): but the narrative of Jn. (xviii. 12–24) renders it highly probable that Annas and his son-in-law Caiaphas shared the same palace, occupying different parts of it. As Lk. records no examination of Christ before either of them, we do not know whether he connects Peter's fall with the hearing before Annas (as Jn.), or with that before Caiaphas (as Mt. and Mk.). All that he tells us is that Jesus was kept a prisoner and insulted between the night arrest and the morning sitting of the Sanhedrin. Possibly his authorities told him no more. See Hastings, *D.B.* i. p. 100.

ἠκολούθει μακρόθεν. This following at a distance is noted by all three. *Quod sequitur, amoris est, quod e longo, timoris.*

55. περιαψάντων. Here only in N.T. Comp. 3 Mac. iii. 7. This would be April, at which time cold nights are not uncommon in Jerusalem, which stands high.

A D R X Γ Δ Λ Π have *ἁψάντων*, which is peculiar to Lk. in the sense of kindling: viii. 16, xi. 33, xv. 8; Acts xxviii. 2. For *ἐν μέσῳ* see on viii. 7.

ἐκάθητο ὁ Πέτρος μέσος αὐτῶν. Cod. Am. and other MSS. of Vulg. have *erat Petrus in medio eorum*. All Greek texts have *ἐκάθητο*. Where did Jerome find *ἦν*? See on ix. 44.

Here only in N.T. is *συνκαθίζω* intransitive: contrast Eph. ii. 6. D G, b c d e f ff_2 i l q Vulg. Arm. Syr-Sin. have *περικαθισάντων*. But a (*consedentibus*) supports ℵ A B L R X etc. (*συνκαθισάντων*): and this is doubtless right.

56. παιδίσκη. All four use this word of the person who began the attack on Peter. Jn. says that she was the doorkeeper. It was not Pilate, nor any of the Sanhedrin, nor a mob of soldiers, but a single waiting-maid, who frightened the self-confident Apostle into denying his Master. Note the **τις.**

πρὸς τὸ φῶς. Comp. Mk. xiv. 54. For **ἀτενίσασα,** which is a favourite word with Lk. (iv. 20 and often in Acts), Mk. has *ἐμβλέψασα.*

καὶ οὗτος σὺν αὐτῷ ἦν. The meaning of the *καί* is not obvious: as well as who? Possibly S. John, who was present and known to the household. With *σὺν αὐτῷ ἦν* comp. xxiv. 44; Acts xiii. 7. The fondness of Lk. for *σύν* here comes out. Mk. and Mt. have *μετά*, and Jn. has *ἐκ τῶν μαθητῶν.*

57. Οὐκ οἶδα αὐτόν. For *αὐτόν* Mk. and Mt. have the less explicitly false *τί λέγεις*. Lk. has *ὃ λέγεις* ver. 60, where they have *τὸν ἄνθρωπον.* Here Lk. again mitigates by omitting the oath which accompanied the second denial (Mt.), and the cursing and swearing which accompanied the third (Mt. Mk.). This first denial seems to have been specially public, *ἔμπροσθεν πάντων* (Mt.).

58. μετὰ βραχύ. Lk. alone states that a second denial followed close on the first. For *ἕτερος* Mt. has *ἄλλη*, Mk. *ἡ παιδίσκη*, Jn. *εἶπον.* For **ἄνθρωπε** see on xii. 14.

59. διαστάσης ὡσεὶ ὥρας μιᾶς. Mk. and Mt. say *μετὰ μικρόν.* The classical *διίστημι* is peculiar to Lk. (xxiv. 51; Acts xxvii. 28. In LXX Exod. xv. 8; Prov. xvii. 9, etc.).

ἄλλος τις. Jn. says a kinsman of Malchus; Mt. and Mk. say the bystanders. In this third attack all four call attention to the positiveness of the speaker; because he had seen Peter in the garden with Jesus (Jn.), and because of Peter's Galilean *λαλιά* (Mt.). The Galileans are said to have mixed the gutturals in pronunciation, and to have had in some respects a peculiar vocabulary.

διισχυρίζετο. Classical, but only here and Acts xii. 15 in bibl. Grk.

60. παραχρῆμα. All four note how quickly the crowing followed upon the third denial. Lk. has his favourite *παραχρῆμα* and Mk. his favourite *εὐθύς*: comp. v. 25, viii. 44, 55, xviii. 43. But the graphic **ἔτι λαλοῦντος αὐτοῦ** is given by Lk. alone.

ἐφώνησεν ἀλέκτωρ. No article: "a cock crew." A few cursives insert **ὁ**.

The objection which has been raised, that the Talmud pronounces fowls which scratch on dungheaps to be unclean, is futile. In this the Talmud is inconsistent with itself: and Sadducees would have no scruples about what was not forbidden by the written law. Certainly Romans would have no such scruples.

61. στραφείς. Lk. alone preserves this incident. Peter is probably still in the court, while Jesus is inside. It is improbable that Jesus was present when Peter denied Him. He may have been visible through door or window, but scarcely within hearing. The στραφεὶς ἐνέβλεψεν may have taken place as He was being led to or from the examination before Caiaphas.

σήμερον. Lk. alone repeats this word, as Mk. repeats his δίς: otherwise all three have the same words. Jn. omits Peter's recollection of the warning and also his bitter weeping.

The σήμερον is omitted in A D Γ Δ Λ and several Versions, but it is attested by ℵ B K L M T, Boh. Sah. Syr-Sin. Aeth. b ff_2 l.

62. WH. bracket this verse, which is wanting in a b e ff_2 i l* r. But ὁ Πέτρος (A Γ Δ Λ, Vulg.) is no doubt an addition both here and Mt. xxvi. 75.

63–65. The First Mocking. As Lk. omits the examination by Caiaphas, it is impossible to determine whether he places this mocking before or after it. He knows that Jesus, after being denied by His chief Apostle, was insulted by His captors, and then taken before the Sanhedrin. His omissions seem to show that he is making no use of Mt. or Mk. Comp. Mt. xxvi. 67, 68; Mk. xiv. 65.

63. οἱ συνέχοντες αὐτόν. Not members of the Sanhedrin, but the servants or soldiers in whose charge Jesus had been left. Here only is συνέχειν used of holding fast a prisoner. Comp. viii. 45; xix. 43. See Deissmann, *Bible Studies*, p. 160.

δέροντες. Comp. xii. 47, xx. 10. Of the five expressions which are used in describing these blows each Evangelist uses two: Lk. δέροντες and παίσας; Mt. ἐκολάφισαν and ἐράπισαν; Mk. κολαφίζειν and ῥαπίσμασιν ἔλαβον. Comp. the treatment of the Apostles, Acts v. 40; and of S. Paul, Acts xxi. 32, xxiii. 2. Lk. omits the spitting. All three have the **Προφήτευσον.**

65. ἕτερα πολλά. Comp. iii. 18. The statement here is made by Lk. only. On the combination of participle and verb, describing the same action from different points of view, see Burton, § 121.

66–71. The Third Jewish Trial. The Sanhedrin could hold no valid meeting before daybreak, and what had been irregularly done in the night had to be formally transacted after dawn.[1] Comp. Mt. xxvii. 1; Mk. xv. 1. But Lk. is quite independent; whereas Mt. and Mk. have much in common.

66. ὡς ἐγένετο ἡμέρα. All three note the early hour: εὐθὺς πρωΐ (Mk.), πρωΐας δὲ γενομένης (Mt.). The expression ἡμέρα γίνεται is characteristic of Lk. Comp. iv. 42, vi. 13; Acts xii. 18, xvi. 35, xxiii. 12, xxvii. 29, 33, 39.

τὸ πρεσβυτέριον τοῦ λαοῦ, ἀρχιερεῖς τε καὶ γραμματεῖς. The meaning is that the three component parts of the Sanhedrin met,

[1] *Synedrium magnum sedet a sacrificio jugi matutino ad sacrificium juge pomeridianum* (Maimonides, *Sanhed.* iii.); *sessiones judicii sunt instituendæ mane, non autem postquam homo edit et bibit* (*Synops. Soh.* p. 56 n. 2).

and that Jesus was brought before the whole assembly. Mt. and Mk. also give the parts as well as the whole; but the place of meeting is not given by any. That portions of what is recorded of one examination should resemble portions of what is recorded of another is natural. Before Annas, Caiaphas, and the Sanhedrin the same questions would be asked. At this last and only valid trial everything of importance would have to be repeated. It is probable that τὸ συνέδριον αὐτῶν is here used in a technical sense for the Great Council or Sanhedrin. Comp. Acts iv. 15, v. 21, 27, 34, 41, vi. 12, 15, xxii. 30, xxiii. 1, 6, 15, 20, 28, xxiv. 20. See Herzog, art. *Synedrium*; Keim, *Jes. of Naz.* vi. pp. 63–72; Edersh. *L. & T.* ii. pp. 553–557; *Hist. of J. N.* ch. v.; Farrar, *L. of C.* II. Excurs. xiii.; and above all Schürer, *J. P. in T. of J. C.* II. i. pp. 163–195, where the literature of the subject is given.

Note the τε καί, which neither Mt. nor Mk. has. In the Gospel Lk. never has τε without καί following: ii. 16, xii. 45, xxi. 11, etc.

67. Εἰ σὺ εἶ ὁ Χριστός, εἶπον ἡμῖν. *Si tu es Christus, dic nobis* (Vulg.). The εἰ is conditional, and the emphasis is on ὁ Χριστός, not on σύ. This is the simplest construction, and is adopted by Luth. Wic. Rhem. RV. De W. Schanz, Mey. Nösg. Go. Hahn, etc. Others prefer, "Art Thou the Christ? tell us": so Erasm. Tyn. Cran. Gen. AV. Or, "Tell us whether Thou art the Christ": Ewald and some others. The question was vital; and in the examination recorded by Mt. and Mk. it was coupled with "Art Thou the Son of God?" (ver. 70).

Ἐὰν ὑμῖν . . . ἀποκριθῆτε. This part of Christ's reply is peculiar to this occasion, whereas what follows (ver. 69) is almost *verbatim* as in Mt. and Mk. The meaning seems to be, "If I tell you that I am the Christ, ye will assuredly not believe; and if I try to discuss the question, ye will assuredly refuse to do so." Note that here the proceedings are conducted by the Sanhedrin as a body; not, as in the earlier trial, by the high priest alone (Mt. xxvi. 62, 63, 65; Mk. xiv. 60, 61, 63). For the addition ἢ ἀπολύσητε see additional note at the end of ch. xxiii.

69. ἀπὸ τοῦ νῦν δέ. His glorification has already begun: Jn. xii. 31. *Hoc ipsum erat iter ad gloriam* (Beng.) Comp. the parallel Acts vii. 56, where see Blass.

The δέ is thus placed because ἀπὸ τοῦ νῦν is virtually one word. TR. with Γ Δ Λ Π, Sah. omits δέ, and Syr-Cur. Syr-Sin. substitute γάρ. The Latin Versions are again interesting in their rendering of ἀπὸ τοῦ νῦν: *a modo* (acdr), *ex hoc* (f Vulg.): see on i. 48 and also on v. 10.

70. εἶπαν δὲ πάντες. The πάντες is again peculiar to Lk. (vii. 35, xix. 37, xx. 18): in Mt. and Mk. the high priest asks the question. In the allusion to Dan. vii. 13 they recognize a claim to Divinity, and they translate ὁ υἱὸς τοῦ ἀνθρώπου into ὁ υἱὸς τοῦ Θεοῦ. But it is not clear whether by the latter they mean the Messiah or something higher.

ὑμεῖς λέγετε ὅτι ἐγώ εἰμι. Both here and Jn. xviii. 37 "*that* I am" (English Versions, Godet) is more probable than "*because* I am" (Luth. Weiss, Hahn). A third possibility, to make the whole a question, is worth noting. For other cases of ambiguous ὅτι comp. i. 45, vii. 16, xix. 31.

71. ἠκούσαμεν. "We have heard" that He claims to be the Messiah and the Son of God. It is quite natural that in accusing Him to Pilate nothing is said about this charge of blasphemy,—one of great weight with the Sanhedrin, but which the heathen *procurator* would not appreciate.

XXIII. 1–7. The Civil Trial before Pilate. Comp. Mt. xxvii. 2, 11, 12; Mk. xv. 1–3; Jn. xviii. 28–37. Lk. assumes that his readers know that Jesus was condemned to death by the Sanhedrin. But it was necessary to have Him condemned by the Roman *procurator* also, in order that the sentence might be executed, and without delay, by him who possessed μέχρι τοῦ κτείνειν ἐξουσίαν (Jos. *B. J.* ii. 8. 1).[1] It is almost certain that at this time the Jews were deprived of the right of inflicting capital punishment. They sometimes did inflict it and risked the consequences, as in the case of S. Stephen: and the Romans sometimes found it expedient to ignore these transgressions (Jn. v. 18, vii. 1, 25, viii. [5,] 59; Acts v. 33, xxi. 31, xxvi. 10). A good deal would depend upon the character of the execution and the humour of the *procurator*. But besides Jn. xviii. 31 we have the express statement, *quadraginta annis ante vastatum templum ablata sunt judicia capitalia ab Israële* (*Bab. Sanh.* f. 24, 2). See Blass on Acts vii. 57.

But it is quite possible that in some of the cases in which the Jews are represented as trying to put persons to death, the meaning is that they wished to hand them over to the Romans for execution. See notes on Jn. xviii. 31 in *Camb. Grk. Test.* In the accounts of this Roman trial we have the attempts of the Jews to induce Pilate to condemn Jesus contrasted with Pilate's attempts to save Him from execution. The Sanhedrin hoped that Pilate would confirm their sentence of death; but Pilate insists on trying the case himself. This he does

---

[1] The expressions *jus gladii* and *potestas gladii* are of later date. Professor Chwolson argues that the Sadducees were dominant when Jesus was condemned to death. It was against the law as maintained by the Pharisees to sentence a criminal and execute him within a few hours. The law required an interval of forty days for the collection of evidence on his behalf. It was the Sadducees, the servile upholders of Roman authority, who took the lead against Christ. They were the wealthy class, who lived on the temple sacrifices and dues, and therefore were bitter antagonists of a Teacher whose doctrine tended to the reform of lucrative abuses (*Das letzte Passamahl Christi*, etc., Appendix).

in his πραιτώριον or palace (Mt. xxvii. 27; Mk. xv. 16; Jn. xviii. 28, 33, xix. 9). But we do not know where this was. A little later than this (Philo, *Leg. ad Gaium*, § 38, ed. Mangey, ii. 589) the Roman governor resided in "Herod's Prætorium," a large palace on the western hill of the city. But Pilate may have used part of the fortress Antonia, the site of which is supposed to be known; and some conjecture that a chamber with a column in it is the scene of the scourging. For the rather considerable literature concerning Pilate see Leyrer in Herzog, art. *Pilatus*, *sub fin.*, and Schürer, *Jewish People*, etc. I. ii. p. 82, who refers especially to G. A. Müller, *Pontius Pilatus*, Stuttgart, 1888.

1. **ἀναστὰν ἅπαν τὸ πλῆθος.** All three words are characteristic: see on i. 39, on iii. 21, and on i. 10. The whole body of the Sanhedrin (αὐτῶν) is meant, not including the populace, who at this point are not mentioned in any of the accounts.

ἐπὶ τὸν Πειλᾶτον. Neither in order to shift the responsibility on to him, nor to avoid disturbing the feast with a Jewish execution, nor to ensure death by crucifixion, but simply in order to get their own sentence of death confirmed.

2. Lk. is alone in giving clearly the three political charges, which could not fail to have weight with Pilate: (1) seditious agitation, (2) forbidding tribute to Tiberius, (3) assuming the title of king. The point of ἤρξαντο seems to be that they began to do all this, but Pilate interposed: comp. v. 21, xii. 45, xiii. 25, xix. 37. The τοῦτον is probably contemptuous: "this fellow" (Tyn. Cov. Cran. Gen. AV.). Whether εὕραμεν refers to "catching in the act" or to "discovering by investigation" is not certain.

The form εὕραμεν is well attested here (B* L T X) as ἀνεῦραν in ii. 16. In 2 Sam. xvii. 20 we have εὗραν with ἦλθαν and παρῆλθαν. See small print on i. 59.

διαστρέφοντα τὸ ἔθνος ἡμῶν. They imply that the perversion of the nation was seditious. The excitement caused by Christ's ministry was notorious, and it would not be easy to prove that it had no political significance. For the verb comp. ix. 41; Acts xiii. 10, xx. 30; Exod. v. 4; 1 Kings xviii. 17, 18.

κωλύοντα φόρους Καίσαρι διδόναι. Jesus had done the very opposite a day or two before (xx. 25). But this second charge seemed to be of one piece with the third. If He claimed to be a king, He of course would forbid tribute to a foreign power. Vulg. wrongly changes the *dare* of Lat. Vet. to *dari*.

Χριστὸν βασιλέα. "Messias, a king" (comp. ii. 11) is more probable than either "King Messias," or, "an anointed king" (Schegg). They add βασιλέα that Pilate may know the political significance of Χριστός (Schanz). It is here that the charge made before Pilate approximates to the charge on which they condemned Jesus (xxii. 69–71). But with them it was the theological significance of His claim that was so momentous: and this Pilate could not regard.

Epiphanius (*Marc.* 316, 317, 346) tells us that after διαστρέφοντα τὸ ἔθνος Marcion inserted καὶ καταλύοντα τὸν νόμον καὶ τοὺς προφήτας; and that after κωλύοντα . . . διδόναι he added καὶ ἀποστρέφοντα τὰς γυναῖκας καὶ τὰ τέκνα. The former of these interpolations is found in various MSS. of the Old Latin, *et solventem legem* [*nostram*] *et prophetas* (b c e ff_2 i l q), and in some MSS. of Vulg. (E Q R), while the latter is added to ver. 5 in some Old Latin texts: see below. Prof. Rendel Harris attributes these insertions to Marcion himself, who was himself accused of these things, *Texts & Studies*, ii. 1, p. 230. See small print note on xvi. 17.

3. Σὺ εἶ ὁ βασιλεὺς τῶν Ἰουδαίων; All four record this question, and in exactly these words. The pronoun is emphatic, implying that His appearance was very much against such a claim.

Σὺ λέγεις. Like the reply in xxii. 70, this is probably not interrogative. It condenses a conversation given at greater length by Jn., without whose narrative that of the three is scarcely intelligible. It would be extraordinary that Pilate should simply hear that Jesus admitted that He claimed to be King of the Jews, and at once declare, "I find no fault in this man." But a conversation with Jesus had convinced Pilate that He was a harmless enthusiast. He did not claim to be a king in the ordinary sense.

4. καὶ τοὺς ὄχλους. The first mention of them. The procession of the Sanhedrin would attract a crowd; and perhaps some had come to ask for the customary release of a prisoner (Mk. xv. 8).

αἴτιον = αἰτία is peculiar to Lk., and is always combined with a negative: *vv.* 14, 22; Acts xix. 40.

5. ἐπίσχυον. Intransitive, as in 1 Mac. vi. 6, so that nothing is to be understood: "they were the more urgent," *invalescebant* (Vulg.). They became more definite in their accusations, because Pilate took the matter too easily.

καθ᾽ ὅλης τῆς Ἰουδαίας. Comp. iv. 44. Whether this means the *whole of Palestine* (i. 5, vii. 17; Acts ii. 9, x. 37, xi. 1, 29) or *Judæa proper* (ii. 4; Acts i. 8, viii. 1), is uncertain. In either case we have allusion to an activity of Jesus in southern Palestine of which Lk. records very little.

ἀπὸ τῆς Γαλιλαίας. *Nutrix seditiosorum hominum* (Grot.). The ἕως ὧδε may have special reference to the triumphal entry into Jerusalem; but it may also refer to previous visits of Jesus to the city.

With the constr. ἀρξάμενος ἀπὸ . . . ἕως comp. Acts i. 22; Mt. xx. 8; [Jn. viii. 9]. The very words καθ᾽ ὅλης τῆς Ἰουδαίας, ἀρξάμενος ἀπὸ τῆς Γαλιλαίας occur Acts x. 37.

At the end of ver. 5 Cod. Colb. adds *et filios nostros et uxores avertit a nobis, non enim baptizatur sicut nos*; and Cod. Palat. has the same down to *nobis*, and continues *non enim baptizantur sicut et nos nec se mundant.*

The retention of "Jewry" in AV. here, Jn. vii. 1, and Dan. v. 13 (where the same word is translated "Jewry" and "Judah") was probably an oversight.

7. ἐπιγνούς. Freq. in Lk. in the sense of "thoroughly ascertain"; vii. 37; Acts xix. 34, xxii. 29, xxiv. 11, xxviii. 1, etc.

ἀνέπεμψεν αὐτόν. The verb may be used in the legal sense of "sending *up*" to a higher authority or "referring" to another jurisdiction, like *remitto*, which Vulg. has here and *vv.* 11, 15: comp. Acts xxv. 21; Jos. *B. J.* ii. 20. 5; Philo, *De Creat. Prin.* viii. But in *vv.* 11, 15 the meaning "send *back*" is more suitable, and may be retained here: comp. Philem. 12. If Jesus originally belonged to Herod's jurisdiction, sending Him to Herod was sending Him *back*; just as the man *born* blind is said to *recover* his sight (ἀναβλέπειν), because sight is natural to man (Jn. ix. 15, 18). It was perhaps chiefly in order to get rid of a difficult case, or to obtain official evidence from the tetrarch, that Pilate sent Jesus, rather than merely to conciliate Antipas. Justin says that Pilate χαριζόμενος δεδεμένον τὸν Ἰησοῦν ἔπεμψε (*Try.* ciii.); and comp. Vespasian allowing Agrippa to have the prisoners who came from the latter's kingdom (Jos. *B. J.* iii. 10. 10). Herod had come up to keep the feast, and probably occupied the palace of the Asamonæans (*B. J.* ii. 16. 3; *Ant.* xx. 8. 11).

8–12. § The Trial before Herod. It has been noticed by Schleiermacher that its omission by Jn. is no serious objection to its authenticity. "The transaction is too circumstantially detailed to admit a doubt, and our reporter seems to have had an acquaintance in the house of Herod who supplied him with this fact, as John seems to have had in the house of Annas" (*S. Luke*, p. 304, Eng. tr.). Joana, the wife of Chuza, Herod's steward (viii. 3), would be a likely source of information: see on viii. 3 and xxiv. 10.

8. ἦν θέλων, τὸ ἀκούειν, ἤλπιζεν. These expressions indicate the continuance of the wishing, hearing, and hoping: comp. ix. 9. Such curiosity is not gratified any more than the demand for signs from heaven (xi. 29). With **ἐξ ἱκανῶν χρόνων** comp. χρόνῳ ἱκανῷ (viii. 27; Acts viii. 11), χρόνους ἱκανούς (xx. 9).

TR. follows ΑRΓΔΛ in reading ἐξ ἱκανοῦ, to which HMXΠ add χρόνου. But ℵBDLT, Sah. Arm. give the plural.

9. αὐτὸς δὲ οὐδὲν ἀπεκρίνατο αὐτῷ. "But He on His part answered him nothing." The language and tone of Antipas showed that he was in no condition to profit by anything that Jesus might say: see on iii. 1. "He regarded Jesus as a *sight*." For **ἀπεκρίνατο** comp. iii. 16.

Cod. Colb. adds *quasi non audiens*: and Syr-Cur. has the more remarkable *quasi non ibi erat*. This may have suggested the possibly Docetic touch in the *Gospel of Peter*, "He held His peace *as in no wise feeling pain*." Both Syr-Cur. and Syr-Sin. for ἐν λόγοις ἱκανοῖς have "in cunning words." Syr-Sin. omits *vv.* 10, 11, 12.

10. ἱστήκεισαν. This, and not εἱστήκειν, is the pluperf. of ἵσταμαι. The evidence varies in the fourteen places; but ἱστήκειν is never a mere itacism, and is freq. in LXX. Even B, which often prefers ει to ι, supports ἱστήκει five times (WH. ii. App. p. 162).

εὐτόνως. "At full stretch, vehemently," in N.T. only here and Acts xviii. 28: comp. Josh. vi. 8; 2 Mac. xii. 23. In Latin texts we have *instanter* (c), *fortiter* (d), *vehementer* (a r), *constanter* (f Vulg.). Apparently they had kept silence while Herod was questioning Jesus; but His silence had exasperated them. Syr-Sin. omits *vv.* 10–12.

11. ἐξουθενήσας . . . ἐμπαίξας. These participles are put first in their clauses with emphasis. Herod's baffled curiosity takes this despicable revenge: comp. xviii. 9; Gal. iv. 14. We need not suppose that Antipas formally pronounced Him innocent, but that he did not condemn Him to death. He evaded the responsibility, as Pilate tried to do. In the *Gospel of Peter* Herod sentences the Lord; and when "Joseph, the friend of Pilate and of the Lord," asks Pilate *before* the crucifixion for the Lord's body, Pilate sends to ask Herod for it. The chief guilt throughout is transferred from Pilate to Herod and the Jews.

σὺν τοῖς στρατεύμασιν. Probably a guard of honour: *cum militibus suis* (f). It was one of these perhaps that he had sent to behead John in the prison (Mk. vi. 27; Mt. xiv. 10). It was fitting that the prince who had murdered the Baptist should mock the Christ.

ἐμπαίξας. He treats Him as a crazy enthusiast, and gives a mock assent to His claim to be a king, which the scribes no doubt reported. Latin texts have *irrisit* (c), *inludens* (d), *deludens* (r), *delusum* (a), *inlusit* (Vulg.).

ἐσθῆτα λαμπράν. "A bright robe," *splendidum* (c), rather than "a white robe," *candida* (a), *alba* (f Vulg.). That it was a *toga candida* to mark Him as a candidate for royalty, is not likely: it was to mark Him as already king. The epithet does not indicate its colour, but its "gorgeous" character: comp. Jas. ii. 2, 3. In Acts x. 30 it is used of angelic apparel. Elsewhere in N.T. ἐσθής occurs only xxiv. 4; Acts i. 10, xii. 21: comp. 2 Mac. viii. 35, xi. 8.

12. ἐγένοντο δὲ φίλοι. Although Pilate failed in the attempt to transfer the responsibility to Herod, yet something was gained by the transaction. In the *Gospel of Peter* Herod addresses him as Ἀδελφὲ Πειλᾶτε. The cause of enmity may easily have been some dispute about jurisdiction.

Ephrem conjectured that the enmity arose through Pilate sending soldiers to punish the chief men of Galilee who had been the guests of Herod when he put the Baptist to death, and that this was the occasion when the blood of Galileans was mingled with their sacrifices. For the importance of this strange idea as a link in the evidence respecting the *Diatessaron* see Rendel Harris in *Contemp. Review*, Aug. 1895, p. 279.

D transposes the clauses, and has ἀηδίᾳ for ἔχθρᾳ: ὄντες δὲ ἐν ἀηδίᾳ ὁ Π. κ. ὁ Ἡ. ἐγένοντο φίλοι ἐν αὐτῇ τ. ἡμ. So also Cod. Colb. *cum essent autem in dissensionem pil. et her. facti sunt amici in illa die.*

13–25. The vain Attempts of Pilate to avoid Sentencing Jesus to Death. Comp. Mt. xxvii. 15–26; Mk. xv. 6–15. Pilate's first two expedients had failed: (1) telling the Jews to deal with the case themselves; (2) sending it to Herod. He now tries two others: (3) to release Him in honour of the feast; (4) to scourge Him and let Him go. Roman dislike of a gross injustice to an innocent person possibly influenced him; but perhaps the chief motive was the superstitious fear, produced by his wife's dream and confirmed by Christ's bearing and words. Jn. states that he again and again declared Jesus to be innocent (xviii. 38, xix. 4, 6). In wording Lk. is not very similar to either Mt. xxvii. 15–26 or Mk. xv. 6–15; but the substance of all three is the same. Jn. is more full and quite independent; he distinguishes the conversation inside the *prætorium* with Jesus and outside with the Jews.

13. συνκαλεσάμενος. See on ix. 1. Pilate in taking the matter in hand again summons not only the hierarchy, whose bitterness against Jesus he knew, but the populace, whom he hoped to find more kindly disposed, and able to influence their rulers.

14. ἀποστρέφοντα τὸν λαόν. "Seducing the people from their allegiance." He condenses the three charges in ver. 2 into one. Note the emphatic ἐγώ and the ἐνώπιον ὑμῶν: the one anticipates Ἡρῴδης, and the other implies that they know with what thoroughness the case has been investigated.

ἀνακρίνας. In its forensic sense of a judicial investigation the word is peculiar to Lk. in N.T. (Acts iv. 9, xii. 19, xxiv. 8, xxviii. 18). But the classical use for a *preliminary* examination must not here be pressed. See *Dict. of Grk. and Rom. Ant.*, art. *Anakrisis*; Gardner and Jevons, pp. 574 ff. Pilate's οὐθὲν εὗρον is in direct contradiction to their εὕραμεν (ver. 2). For αἴτιον see on ver. 4.

15. ἀλλ᾽ οὐδὲ Ἡρῴδης. Therefore the friendship between Herod and Pilate is hardly "a type of Judaism and Heathenism leagued together to crush Christianity." Both were willing to set Jesus free. What we see here is, however, an anticipation of what not unfrequently happened during the first three centuries, viz. that Jewish mobs incited the heathen against the Christians.

ἀνέπεμψεν γὰρ αὐτὸν πρὸς ἡμᾶς. This reading agrees better with "No, nor yet Herod" than does "For I sent you to him," and the external evidence for it is decisive.

For the text, ℵ B K L M T Π and some cursives; for ἀνέπεμψα γὰρ ὑμᾶς πρὸς αὐτόν, A D X Γ Δ Λ. Versions are divided, Latt. against Ægyptt., while Syrr. including Syr-Sin. have the conflate, "For I sent Him to him." Wic. had a Lat. text such as Cod. Brix. *nam remisit eum ad nos*, for he renders "For he hath sent Him again to us," although Vulg. has *nam remisi vos ad illum*. Some Latin authorities combine both readings.

ἐστὶν πεπραγμένον αὐτῷ. "Is done *by* Him," or "hath been done *by* Him" (RV.). The former is perhaps better, as giving the result of the trial before Herod. The dat. indicates that what is done stands to the person's *credit*; Win. xxxi. 10, p. 274: xxiv. 35 is not parallel. "Nothing worthy of death is done unto Him" (AV.) is scarcely sense. Cov. has "There is brought upon Him nothing that is worthy of death." For the periphrastic perfect see Burton, § 84.

16. παιδεύσας. He uses a light word to express the terrible *flagellatio*, in order to excuse the injustice to his own conscience, and to hide his inconsistency from them. It is no punishment, but a chastisement to warn Him to be more circumspect in future. But the priests would see that a judge who was willing to inflict this on an innocent person could be induced by further pressure to inflict death. Scourging was sometimes fatal: Hor. *Sat.* i. 2. 41; comp. i. 3. 119. Comp. Deut. xxii. 18.

17. This verse is wanting in A B K L T Π, Sah. a, while D, Syr-Cur. Syr-Sin. Æth. insert it after ver. 19. It is a gloss based on Mt. xxvii. 15 and Mk. xv. 6. Alf. urges that ἀνάγκην εἶχεν is an idiom in Lk.'s manner. But Lk. uses it only once (xiv. 18), as do also S. Paul (1 Cor. vii. 37) and S. Jude (3). Homœoteleuton (ΑΝΑΓΚΗΝ, ΑΝΕΚΡΑΓΟΝ) might explain the omission in one family of witnesses; but against this is the widespread omission, and the fact that the gloss is inserted in two different places. The passage reads more naturally without the gloss than with it.

18. ἀνέκραγον. We have the 1 aorist iv. 33, viii. 28; Mk. i. 23, vi. 49: and in LXX both aorists are common. Here A D X Γ have ἀνέκραξαν, ℵ B L T ἀνέκραγον. Here only in bibl. Grk. does παμπληθεί occur.

Αἶρε τοῦτον. *E medio tolle istum*: Acts xxi. 36, xxii. 22; Mt. xxiv. 39; Jn. xix. 15: comp. Acts viii. 33. They are perhaps recalling such passages as Deut. xvii. 7, xix. 19.

ἀπόλυσον δὲ ἡμῖν. Nothing is known of this custom of releasing a prisoner at the Passover apart from the Gospels. Pilate says "*Ye* have a custom" (Jn. xviii. 39), which is against the hypothesis that he originated it. The Herods may have done so in imitation of Roman customs. At the first recorded *lectisternium* prisoners were released (Livy, v. 13. 7).

Βαραββᾶν. "Son of Abba" (father). Other instances of the name are given by Lightfoot: Samuel Bar-Abba, Nathan Bar-Abba (*Hor. Heb.* Mt. xxvii. 16). But evidence is wanting that Abba was a proper name. On the remarkable reading "Jesus Barabbas" Mt. xxvii. 16, 17 see WH. ii. App. 19.

19. διὰ στάσιν τινὰ γενομένην. Of Barabbas they might with some truth have said τοῦτον εὕραμεν διαστρέφοντα τὸ ἔθνος (ver. 2). Not that he had originated the στάσις, but that he had taken a conspicuous part in it. The στάσις was probably no popular movement, but some plundering disturbance. Jn. calls him simply "a robber," and he may have been connected with the other two robbers who were crucified with Jesus. The rather awkward order of the words in the verse is perhaps to intimate that while the *στάσις* took place in the city the murder did not.

On the rare form of periphrastic tense (*ἦν* with *aor.* part.), see Burton, § 20. *βληθεὶς* is the reading of B L T, for which ℵ[a] A D X Γ etc. have the more usual *βεβλημ(μ)ένος*: and while ℵ B L T X, f q have *ἐν τῇ φυλακῇ*, A D Γ Δ etc. have the obvious correction *εἰς τὴν φυλακήν*.

Excepting Mk. xv. 7 and Heb. ix. 8, *στάσις* in N.T. is peculiar to Lk. (ver. 25; Acts xv. 2, xix. 40, xxiii. 7, 10, xxiv. 5). In LXX it represents several Hebrew words of different meaning. Syr-Sin. here has "wicked deeds."

20. That we should read *δέ* (ℵ A B D T, Latt. Boh. Sah.) and not *οὖν* (X Γ Δ Λ etc.) after *πάλιν* is certain. That *αὐτοῖς* is to be added after *προσεφώνησεν* (ℵ B L T, Latt. Boh. Sah. Syr-Cur. Æth.) is also certain. But Lk. uses the verb absolutely, xiii. 12; Acts xxi. 40. Contrast vii. 32; Acts xxii. 2.

21. ἐπεφώνουν. "Kept shouting at him": *clamabant* (f), *proclamabant* (a), *succlamabant* (Vulg.). In N.T. the verb is peculiar to Lk. (Acts xii. 22, xxi. 34, xxii. 24); but it is classical. According to all four Gospels the demand for crucifixion was not made until Pilate had proposed to release Jesus on account of the feast. Lk. and Jn. give the double cry, "Crucify, crucify." Mt. has **σταυρωθήτω**, Mk. and Jn. **σταύρωσον**, Lk. **σταύρου**.

We must read *σταύρου*, 2 pers. imper. *act.*, and not *σταυροῦ*, *mid.* ℵ B D F[a] have *σταύρου* (*bis*), while A L P X Γ etc. have *σταύρωσον* (*bis*); but U 157, a b e f ff_2 l Arm. Aeth. omit the second "Crucify."

22. Τί γὰρ κακὸν ἐποίησεν; So in all three. The *γάρ* means "Impossible; *for* what evil hath this man done?" This is well represented by the idiomatic "Why," which we owe to the Vulg. *Quid enim*, through Rhem. Cov. has "What evil *then*," etc. The **τρίτον** refers to *vv.* 4 and 14.

οὐδὲν αἴτιον θανάτου. The *θανάτου* is a qualification added after the failure of the mission to Herod (ver. 15). Previously it was *οὐδὲν αἴτιον* without limitation (*vv.* 4, 14). In his weakness Pilate begins to admit, "Well, perhaps He may be guilty of something: but He is not guilty of a capital offence." He began by saying that Herod had not found Him worthy of death. Now he says the same himself. In each case the proposal is the same,—*παιδεύσας ἀπολύσω* (*vv.* 16, 22).

23. ἐπέκειντο φ. μ. αἰτούμενοι. Comp. *μᾶλλον ἐπέκειτο ἀξιῶν. μᾶλλον ἐπέκειντο βλασφημοῦντες* (Jos. *Ant.* xviii. 6. 6, xx. 5. 3). With *φωναῖς μεγάλαις* comp. i. 42, iv. 33, viii. 28, xvii. 15, etc.

κατίσχυον. Comp. xxi. 36: "they prevailed," but not until Pilate had tried whether the *παιδεύειν* would satisfy them (Jn. xix. 1). Mt. and Mk. connect the scourging with the crucifixion, because it usually preceded this punishment in Roman law.[1] It is extremely unlikely that Pilate allowed the scourging to be repeated. He merely separated it from the crucifixion in the hope that the latter would not be required. Note the impressive repetition of φωναί.

24. ἐπέκρινεν. "He gave sentence"; 2 Mac. iv. 47?; 3 Mac. iv. 2. Here only in N.T., but classical. For τὸ αἴτημα comp. Phil. iv. 6.

25. ἀπέλυσεν . . . παρέδωκεν. This tragic contrast is in all three; and all four use παρέδωκεν of the final surrender. Comp. Acts iii. 14, and note the contrast between these aorists and the imperfect ᾐτοῦντο, "kept demanding." Both the repetition of τὸν διὰ στάσιν, κ.τ.λ. and the addition of τῷ θελήματι αὐτῶν are peculiar to Lk. The writer thus emphasizes the enormity of the transaction. In the *Gospel of Peter* Herod is present at this point and gives the sentence. He does not wash his hands, and the blame is transferred to him and the Jews. So also in the *Acta Pilati* (B. x.) it is the Jews who hastily execute the sentence, as soon as Pilate has pronounced it. Comp. Justin (*Try.* cviii.) ὃν σταυρωσάντων ἡμῶν. See Hastings, *D.B.* i. p. 245.

26–32. § The Road to Calvary, Simon the Cyrenian, and the Daughters of Jerusalem. With the exception of ver. 26, the whole of this is peculiar to Lk. In ver. 26 his wording is closer to Mk. xv. 21 than to Mt. xxvii. 32.

26. Κυρηναῖον. Josephus tells of the origin of the Jewish colony in Cyrene (*Apion.* ii. 4), and quotes Strabo respecting it (*Ant.* xiv. 7. 2): this gives us important information respecting that branch of the Dispersion. Comp. *Ant.* xvi. 6. 1, 5; 1 Mac. xv. 23; 2 Mac. ii. 23. That Cyrene was the chief city of the district, which is the modern Tripoli, is shown by the name Cyrenaica and by Acts ii. 10. For the literature of the subject see *D.B.*[2] i. p. 688. This Simon may have been a member of the Cyrenian synagogue at Jerusalem (Acts vi. 9). It has been proposed to identify him with "Symeon that was called Niger," who is mentioned in company with "Lucius of Cyrene" (Acts xiii. 1). But Simon or Symeon was one of the commonest of names; and Lk. would probably have given the same designation in both books, if he had meant the same person. If the Rufus of Rom. xvi. 13 is the Rufus of Mk. xv. 21, then the wife of Simon of Cyrene was well known to S. Paul.

ἐρχόμενον ἀπ' ἀγροῦ. Mk. has the same. He might be taking "a sabbath day's journey"; so that this is no proof as to the date. But he would not be likely to be coming in from the country on such a sabbatical day as Nisan 15.

[1] Jos. *B.J.* ii. 14. 9, v. 11. 1; Livy, xxii. 13. 6, xxxiii. 36. 3; Cic. *In Verr.* v. 62. 162. Capital punishment of any kind was generally, according to Roman custom, preceded by beating.

The gen. of TR. following A P Γ Δ etc. (Σίμωνός τινος Κυρηναίου) is probably a grammatical correction.

ἐπέθηκαν αὐτῷ τὸν σταυρόν. His being a provincial may have made them more ready to make free with him. Perhaps it was only the cross-beam (*patibulum*) which he carried; and if he carried both pieces, they would not be fastened together as finally erected. On the shape of the cross see Justin, *Try.* xci.; 1 *Apol.* lv.; Iren. ii. 24. 4; Tert. *Adv. Jud.* x.; *Ad. Nat.* xii.; and Schaff's Herzog, art. "Cross"; Kraus, *Real-Enc. d. Chr. Alt.* ii. p. 225. At first Jesus carried it Himself (Jn. xix. 17), according to the usual custom, ἕκαστος τῶν κακούργων ἐκφέρει τὸν ἑαυτοῦ σταυρόν (Plutarch, *De Sera Num. Vind.* ix. p. 554 B), as indicated by the word *furcifer*: but He was physically unable to continue to do so. Indeed it has been inferred from φέρουσιν αὐτόν (Mk. xv. 22) that at length He was unable even to walk, and was therefore carried to Golgotha: but comp. Mk. i. 32, vii. 32, viii. 22, ix. 19. On the other hand Lange interprets φέρειν ὄπισθεν as meaning that Simon carried the lower end, while the top was still carried by Jesus. But this is not in harmony with ἵνα ἄρῃ τὸν σταυρὸν αὐτοῦ (Mt. Mk.). Syr-Sin. here has, "that he might bear the cross and follow Jesus." See Hastings, *D.B.* i. p. 529.

The Basilidian Gnostics taught that Simon was crucified in the place of Jesus, being transformed by Jesus to look like Him, while Jesus in the form of Simon stood by and laughed at His enemies: and it was for this reason that they disparaged martyrdom, as being an honour paid, not to Christ, but to Simon the Cyrenian. See Photius, *Bibl.* cxiv. 292. Irenæus (i. 24. 4) wrongly attributes this doctrine to Basilides himself, who was not docetic, but made the sufferings of Jesus an essential part of his system. Contrast Hippol. *Refut.* vii. 15. The Mahometans teach a similar doctrine; that God deceived the Jews and caused them to crucify a spy, or an emissary of Judas, or Judas himself, in mistake for Jesus. See Sale's *Koran*, pp. 38, 70, Chandos ed.

27. γυναικῶν αἳ ἐκόπτοντο. This incident is in place in the "Gospel of Womanhood" (i. 39–56, ii. 36–38, vii. 11–15, 37–50, viii. 1–3, x. 38–42, xi. 27, xiii. 11–16). These are probably not the women who had ministered to Him previously (viii. 1–3), but sympathizers from the city. Comp. Zech. xii. 10–14. In the Gospels there is no instance of a woman being hostile to Christ. For ἐκόπτοντο comp. viii. 52 and Mt. xi. 17.

The καί after αἵ—"which also bewailed" (AV.)—must be omitted upon decisive evidence: A B C* D L X, Boh. Sah. Vulg. etc.

28. στραφεὶς πρὸς αὐτάς. As they were following Him, this would hardly have been possible, if He was still carrying the cross: comp. vii. 9, 44, ix. 55, x. 23. For "daughter of" = "inhabitant of" comp. Is. xxxvii. 22; Zeph. iii. 14; Jer. xlvi. 19; Ezek. xvi. 46.

μὴ κλαίετε ἐπ' ἐμέ· πλὴν ἐφ' ἑαυτὰς κλαίετε. Comp. Judg.

xi. 37, 38. Note the *chiasmus*, making the contrast between ἐμέ and ἑαυτάς very emphatic. His sufferings will be short, and are the road to glory: theirs will be prolonged, and will end in shame and destruction. Christ is not rebuking mere sentimentality or sympathetic emotion, as if the meaning were that they ought to lament their own sins rather than His sufferings. The form of command is similar to that in x. 20. They are not wrong in weeping for Him: nevertheless there is something else for which they may weep with far greater reason. That for which He wept (xix. 41–44) may rightly move them to tears,—the thought that a judgment which might have been averted must now take its course. For the legend of Veronica see *D. of Chr. Biog.* iv. p. 1107.

Comp. an eloquent passage in a lecture on the relation of Art to Religion by Ruskin, in which he contrasts the barren emotion produced by realistic representations of the past agonies of Christ with sympathetic realization of the present miseries of mankind (*Lectures on Art*, Oxford, 1870, § 57, p. 54).

29. ἔρχονται ἡμέραι. "Days are coming": comp. Heb. viii. 8; Jer. vii. 32, ix. 25, xvi. 14, xix. 6, xxiii. 5, 7, etc. In all these cases ἰδού precedes ἔρχονται. In Lk. the fut. is more common: v. 35, xvii. 22, xix. 43, xxi. 6. Here the nom. to ἐροῦσιν is not τὰ τέκνα ὑμῶν, but "people, the world in general": *man wird sagen*.

Μακάριαι αἱ στεῖραι. As a rule childless women are commiserated or despised (i. 25, 36), but in these dreadful times they will be congratulated. Comp. Eur. *Androm.* 395; *Alc.* 882; Tac. *Ann.* ii. 75. 1. See on i. 24.

30. τότε ἄρξονται. The nom. is the same as to ἐροῦσιν,—the population generally, not the women only; and the τότε means simply ἐν ἐκείναις ταῖς ἡμέραις. The wish is that the mountains may fall on them and *kill* them, not hide and *protect* them. Death is preferable to such terror and misery. So also in the original passage Hos. x. 8; comp. Rev. vi. 6, and contrast Is. ii. 19.

31. ὅτι εἰ ἐν τῷ ὑγρῷ ξύλῳ. This is not a continuation of the cry of despair, but gives the reason for predicting such things. "These horrors will certainly come, *because*," etc. In Syr-Sin. the ὅτι is omitted: "Who do these things in the moist tree, what shall they do in the dry?" Proverbs of similar import are found in various languages, and are capable of many applications: comp. Prov. xi. 31; 1 Pet. iv. 17, 18. This saying is an argument *à fortiori*, and it may be easily applied in more than one sense here. (1) If the Romans treat Me, whom they admit to be innocent, in this manner, how will they treat those who are rebellious and guilty? (2) If the Jews deal thus with One who has come to save them, what treatment shall they receive themselves for destroying Him? (3) If they behave thus before their cup of wickedness is full, what will they commit when it overflows? The use of ξύλον, *lignum*, for a tree as well as for timber is late Greek (Gen. i. 29, ii. 9, iii. 1; Is. xiv. 8; Ps. i. 3). In Ezek. xxi. 3 [xx. 47] we have ξύλον χλωρόν and ξύλον ξηρόν combined; but otherwise there is no parallel.

For the delib. subjunct. γένηται comp. Mt. xxvi. 54, and Ὤμοι ἐγώ, τί πάθω; τί νύ μοι μήκιστα γένηται; (Hom. *Od.* v. 465). See Burton, § 169.

32. ἕτεροι κακοῦργοι δύο. This is the order of ℵ B and Aegyptt., which has been corrected to ἕτεροι δύο κακοῦργοι, to avoid the implication that Jesus was a κακοῦργος. With a similar object Syr-Sin. with Codd. Colb. and Palat. omits ἕτεροι, and perhaps the omission of καί before ἕτεροι (Syr-Cur. b) is due to the same cause. Yet the implication is not necessary. We may retain the order of ℵ B and translate, "others, viz. two malefactors"; or, "two very different malefactors." In the latter case κακοῦργος is used of Jesus with irony against those who treated Him as such: ἐν τοῖς ἀνόμοις ἐλογίσθη (Is. liii. 12). But it is perhaps best to regard it as what Field calls "a negligent construction" not likely to be misunderstood. In that case the AV. is courageously accurate with "two other malefactors": for the comma after "other" is a later insertion of the printers; it is not found in the edition of 1611. These two κακοῦργοι were bandits (Mt. xxvii. 38, 44; Mk. xv. 27). The hierarchy perhaps contrived that they should be crucified with Jesus in order to suggest similarity of crime. In the persecutions, Christians were sometimes treated in this way. Comp. πολλάκις ἅμα κακούργοις ἐμπομπεύσας τῷ σταδίῳ (Eus. *Mart. Pal.* vi. 3).

Note the characteristic σύν, and for **ἀναιρεθῆναι** see on xxii. 2.

The Latin Versions render κακοῦργοι *latrones* (a b e f ff_2 l), *maligni* (d), *rei* (c), *nequam* (Vulg.), to which are added the names of the robbers, *Ioathas et Maggatras* (l). Similarly in Mk. xv. 27 we have names added, *Zoathan et Chammatha* (c), and in Mt. xxvii. 38, *Zoathan et Camma.* See on ver. 39.

33–38. The Crucifixion. The narrative is substantially the same as Mt. xxvii. 33–44 and Mk. xv. 22–32; but it has independent features.

33. τόπον. This word is used by all three. The precise place is still a matter of controversy, and must remain so until excavation has determined the position of the old walls, outside which it certainly was. See MacColl, *Contemp. Rev.*, Feb. 1893, pp. 167–188; *D.B.*[2] i. pp. 1205, 1652–1657.

τὸν καλούμενον Κρανίον. See on vi. 15. It was so called on account of its shape, not because skulls were lying there unburied, which would have outraged Jewish feeling. Lk. omits the Hebrew name Golgotha (Mt. xxvii. 33; Mk. xv. 22; Jn. xix. 17), which would have conveyed no meaning to Greek readers, as he has already omitted (without Greek equivalent) Gethsemane and Gabbatha. It is from the Latin (*locum qui vocatur Calvariæ*) that the word "Calvary" has come into all English Versions prior to RV., which has, "the place which is called The Skull."

The ancient explanation that the place was thus called because of the skull of Adam, who was buried there by Noah after the Flood, is rejected by Jerome (on Mt. xxvii., Migne, xxvi. 209), as *interpretatio mulcens aurem populi, nec tamen vera.* But he wrongly adopts the view that it was a place in which *truncantur capita damnata*, a view which even Fritzsche (on Mt. xxvii. 33) has defended. No such place has ever existed in the East, least of all at Jerusalem: and such a place would be styled κρανίων τόπος not κρανίου. A rocky protrusion, resembling a skull in form, is no doubt the meaning. Thus Cyril of Jerusalem speaks of it as "rising on high and showing itself to this day, and displaying even yet how because of Christ the rocks were then riven" (*Catech. Lect.* xiii. 39).

For the attractive Adam legend compare Ambrose, *ad loc.*: *Congruebat quippe ut ibi vitæ nostræ primitia locarentur, ubi fuerant mortis exordia* (Migne, xv. 1852). Chrys. and Euthym. do not go beyond *tradition* (φασί τινες), which they do not expressly accept. See Tisch. *app. crit. ad* Jn. xix. 17.

ἐσταύρωσαν αὐτόν. It will always remain disputable whether our Lord's feet were nailed as well as His hands. Jn. xx. 25–27 proves that His hands were nailed: but it is not *certain* that Lk. xxiv. 39 has any reference to the nails. In the *Gospel of Peter*, before the burial, nails are taken from the hands only. Ewald refers to the *Zeitschrift für die Kunde des Morgenlandes*, i. 20, for evidence that in Palestine the mediæval tradition limited the nailing to the hands; but this is less probable.

ὃν μὲν . . . ὃν δέ . . . For this late use of the relative comp. Mt. xxi. 35, xxii. 5, xxv. 15; 1 Cor. xi. 21; 2 Tim. ii. 20; Rom. ix. 21.

34a. As in the cases of xxii. 19b, 20 and of 43, 44, we have to consider whether this passage is part of the original text. For the evidence see the additional note at the end of the chapter. "Few verses of the Gospels bear in themselves a surer witness to the truth of what they record than this first of the Words from the Cross: but it need not therefore have belonged originally to the book in which it is now included. We cannot doubt that it comes from an extraneous source. Nevertheless, like xxii. 43 f.; Mt. xvi. 2 f., it has exceptional claims to be permanently retained, with the necessary safeguards, in its accustomed place" (WH. ii. App. p. 68).

ὁ δὲ Ἰησοῦς ἔλεγεν. The δέ and the imperf. refer back to ἐσταύρωσαν αὐτόν: while they crucified Him, He in contrast to them was saying.

ἄφες αὐτοῖς. This cannot refer to the Roman soldiers, who were doing no more than their duty in executing a sentence which had been pronounced by competent authority. It was the Jews, and especially the Jewish hierarchy, who were responsible for what was being done: and but for the pressure which they had put upon him, even Pilate would have remained guiltless in this matter. What follows shows that the petition refers to the act of crucifixion, not to their sins generally. In this way He "made intercession for the transgressors" (Is. liii. 12); where, however, LXX has διὰ τὰς ἀνομίας αὐτῶν παρεδόθη.

οὐ γὰρ οἴδασιν τί ποιοῦσιν. This was true even of the rulers (Acts iii. 17), still more of the people, and most of all of Pilate. Their ignorance of what they were doing in crucifying the Christ mitigates their guilt. Comp. xii. 48, and ποιοῦσιν in ver. 31: also the use of the words attributed to James the Just at his martyrdom (Hegesip. *ap. Eus. H. E.* ii. 23. 16).

34b. Διαμεριζόμενοι . . . κλῆρον. The wording is very similar in all three, and is influenced by Ps. xxii. 19, which Jn. (xix. 24) quotes *verbatim* from LXX. Some texts wrongly insert the quotation Mt. xxvii. 35; but the Synoptists use the wording of the Psalm without directly quoting it. Jn. tells us that it was a quaternion of soldiers (comp. Acts xii. 4) who were carrying out the procurator's sentence, and thus came to share the clothes as their perquisite. And Jn. distinguishes, as does the Heb. of Ps. xxii. 19, although LXX and the Synoptists do not, between the upper and under garments. This dividing of the clothes is one more detail in the treatment of Christ as a criminal, and a criminal whose career was closed.

The sing. κλῆρον (א B C D L, b c d Aeth.) has been altered in some texts to κλήρους (A X, a e f ff_2 Vulg. *codd. plur.* Syr-Sin.) to harmonize with usage, *e.g.* 1 Chron. xxv. 8, xxvi. 13, 14; Neh. x. 34, xi. 1, etc.

35. θεωρῶν. ἐξεμυκτήριζον. Both words are from Ps. xxii. 8: πάντες οἱ θεωροῦντές με ἐξεμυκτήρισάν με. Mt. and Mk. use other words; but they add, what Lk. omits, the fulfilment of ἐκίνησαν κεφαλήν. Lk. marks clearly four kinds of ill-treatment which Jesus received. The people ἱστήκει θεωρῶν, the rulers ἐξεμυκτήριζον, the soldiers ἐνέπαιξαν, and the robber ἐβλασφήμει. They form a sort of climax. The θεωρῶν implies vulgar curiosity, staring as at a spectacle (comp. ver. 48): for ἐκμυκτηρίζω comp. xvi. 14, where, as here, Cod. Bezae has *subsannabant.* For the form ἱστήκει see on ver. 10.

Ἄλλους ἔσωσεν. This sarcasm is preserved in all three narratives, but Lk. alone gives the contemptuous οὗτος and ὁ ἐκλεκτός. Comp. ix. 35. Jesus was elected from all eternity to fulfil all these things. Comp. *Enoch*, xl. 5.

WH. and RV. put a comma after τοῦ Θεοῦ, which belongs to ὁ Χριστός, not to ὁ ἐκλεκτός. TR., following A C^3 Q X Γ etc., places ὁ before τοῦ Θεοῦ, while C*, ff_2 have ὁ ἐκλεκτός before τοῦ Θεοῦ. Syr-Sin. supports this combination. D has εἰ υἱὸς εἶ τοῦ Θεοῦ εἰ Χριστὸς εἶ ὁ ἐκλεκτός, *si filius es dei si christus es electus*; and the insertion of υἱός is found in other texts.

The σὺν αὐτοῖς after ἄρχοντες (A Γ Δ Π, f Vulg. Syr-Sin.) is an insertion to harmonize with Mt. and Mk.

36, 37. This mockery by the soldiers is peculiar to Lk.

Apparently it was the hierarchy who took the initiative. They told the King of Israel to come down from the cross; the soldiers told the King of the Jews to save Himself. Note the change of tense (ἐξεμυκτήριζον, ἐνέπαιξαν), which implies that the soldiers were less persistent in their derision than the rulers. The reading ἐνέπαιζον (A C D Q etc.) has all the look of a correction.

36. ὄξος προσφέροντες. Offering some of their sour wine or *posca*, which the Evangelists call ὄξος, perhaps in connexion with ἐπότισάν με ὄξος (Ps. lxviii. 22). Probably they could not have reached His lips with a vessel held in the hand; otherwise the sponge would not have been placed on a stalk, however short (Jn. xix. 29): but there is no reason for supposing that Christ's feet were on a level with the heads of the spectators, as pictures sometimes represent. Syr-Sin. omits the words.

Comp. the words which legend has put into the mouth of His Mother at the cross: κλῖνον σταυρέ, ἵνα περιλαβοῦσα τὸν υἱόν μου καταφιλήσω τὸν ἐμὸν υἱόν (*Acta Pilati*, B. x.).

38. ἦν δὲ καὶ ἐπιγραφὴ ἐπ᾽ αὐτῷ. For ἐπιγραφή Mt. has τ. αἰτίαν αὐτοῦ, Mk. ἡ ἐπιγραφὴ τῆς αἰτίας αὐτοῦ, Jn. τίτλον. Thus Mk. again has the whole expression of which Mt. and Lk. have each a part: comp. iv. 40, v. 13, xxii. 34. The name and crime of the person executed was sometimes hung round his neck as he went to the place of crucifixion and then fastened to the cross. The καί suggests that this inscription was an additional mockery.

The wording differs in all four Gospels, and perhaps it varied in the three languages. It was directed against the hierarchy rather than against Jesus. All four variations contain the offensive words "The King of the Jews" (Jn. xix. 21). But Lk. regards it as an insult to Jesus. In the *Gospel of Peter* the wording is "This is the King of *Israel*," just as at the mock homage the address is "Judge righteously, O King of *Israel*."

The words γράμμασιν Ἑλληνικοῖς καὶ Ῥωμαικοῖς καὶ Ἑβραικοῖς are almost certainly a gloss from Jn. xix. They are omitted in ℵ[ca] B C* L, Syr-Cur. Syr-Sin. Boh. Sah., and by the best editors. The authorities which insert the words differ as to the order of the languages and as to the introductory words γεγραμμένη or ἐπιγεγραμμένη, ἐπ᾽ αὐτῷ or ἐπ᾽ αὐτῷ γεγραμμένη. The omission of the statement, if it were genuine, would be unintelligible. Comp. Jos. *Ant.* xiv. 10. 2; *B. J.* vi. 2. 4, v. 5. 2. In the inscription itself the order of ℵ B L, ὁ βασ. τῶν Ἰ. οὗτος, is to be preferred. D has the same, adding ἐστιν after οὗτος, *rex Judæorum hic est*. Contrast Eus. *H.E.* v. 1. 44.

39–43. § The Two Robbers. Mt. (xxvii. 44) and Mk. (xv. 32) merely state that those who were crucified with Him reproached Him.

Harmonists suggest that during the first hour both robbers reviled Jesus, and that one of them (who may have heard Jesus preach in Galilee) afterwards changed his attitude and rebuked his comrade. So Origen, Chrysostom, Jerome, Theophylact, Euthymius, on Mt. xxvii. But Cyril of Jerusalem, Ambrose, and Augustine confine the reviling to one robber, who in Mt. and Mk. is spoken of in the plur. by *synecdoche*. See Maldonatus on Mt. xxvii. 44: with Suarez he adopts the latter view. Or they insist upon the difference between ὠνείδιζον, which Mt. and Mk. use of the two robbers, and ἐβλασφήμει, which Lk. uses of one of them. Both bandits *reproached* Jesus (perhaps for not having helped them in their revolt against existing conditions of society); but only one of them *railed upon* Him. It is much simpler to suppose that Mt. and Mk. regard the two λῃσταί as a class, to which the conduct of either of them may be attributed. Christ's conversation with the penitent robber would not be heard by many. The constant reviling (imperf.) of the other would be much more widely known. That ὀνειδίζω may mean much the same as βλασφημέω is seen from vi. 22; Rom. xv. 3; 1 Pet. iv. 14. The two verbs are combined 2 Kings xix. 22, and seem to be synonymous. Mt. and Mk. would hardly have omitted the incident of the penitent robber, if they had known it; but here Lk. once more has other sources of information. The incident would have special interest for him as illustrating the doctrine that salvation is open to all.

In the *Arabic Gospel of the Infancy* (xxiii.) the names of the two robbers are given as Titus and Dumachus. Titus bribes Dumachus to release the Holy Family, whom they had captured. In the Greek form of the *Gospel of Nicodemus* (*Acta Pilati* x.) the penitent malefactor is Dysmas, and the other is nameless. In the Latin form (*Gesta Pilati* x.) the two are Dismas and Gestas. See small print note on ver. 32.

39. Εἷς δὲ τῶν κρεμασθέντων. When used of hanging on a cross or gibbet ἐπὶ ξύλου is commonly added (Acts v. 30, x. 39; Gal. iii. 13; Gen. xl. 19, 22; Deut. xxi. 22, 23, etc.): but here the context is sufficient.

Οὐχὶ σὺ εἶ. This is the true reading (א B C* L and most Versions, including Syr-Sin.) rather than Εἰ σὺ εἶ (A Q R X etc. c f q Vulg.). "Art thou not" is a more bitter taunt than "If thou art."

D d e omit the utterance, and l substitutes *qui destruebas templum et in tribus diebus reædificabas illum, salvum te fac nunc et descende de cruce.*

40. Οὐδὲ φοβῇ σὺ τὸν Θεόν. The οὐδέ cannot be taken with either σύ (De W. Nösg.) or τὸν Θεόν (Pesh.), but only with φοβῇ. "Dost thou not even *fear*," to say nothing of penitent submission (Schanz). "Dost not even *thou* fear" would be οὐδὲ σὺ φοβῇ; Vulg. *Neque tu times*, Beza *Ne tu quidem times*, and Godet *Et toi non plus, tu ne crains donc point*, are all inaccurate. The meaning is, "You and He will soon have to appear before God. Does not even fear restrain you from adding to your sins; whereas He has nothing to answer for."

41. οὐδὲν ἄτοπον. A *meiosis*: "nothing unbecoming," still less anything criminal; Acts xxv. 5; Job xxvii. 6, xxxiv. 12, xxxv. 13; Prov. xxiv. 55; 2 Mac. xiv. 23.

D has οὐδὲν πονηρὸν ἔπραξεν and then adds a characteristic amplification: καὶ στραφεὶς πρὸς τὸν κύριον εἶπεν αὐτῷ Μνήσθητί μου ἐν τῇ ἡμέρᾳ τῆς ἐλεύσεώς σου. ἀποκριθεὶς δὲ ὁ Ἰησοῦς εἶπεν αὐτῷ τῷ επλησοντι (?) Θάρσει, σήμερον μετ' ἐμοῦ ἔσῃ ἐν τῷ παραδείσῳ. *Respondens autem Jesus dixit qui objurgabat animæquior esto, hodie mecum eris in paradiso.* See on ver. 53 and vi. 5.

42. Ἰησοῦ, μνήσθητί μου. "Jesus, remember me." The insertion of κύριε (A R X Γ Δ etc. and most Versions) was made because Ἰησοῦ was mistaken for the dat. after ἔλεγεν: *dicebat ad Jesum, Domine, memento mei* (Vulg.). So also Syr-Sin. Comp. ἀλλὰ μνήσθητί μου διὰ σεαυτοῦ ὅταν εὖ σοι γένηται (Gen. xl. 14). The robber knew that he had only a few hours to live, and therefore this prayer implies a belief in a future state in which Jesus is to receive him in His Kingdom. Possibly he believed that Christ would raise him from the dead. In any case his faith in one who is crucified with him is very remarkable. Some saw Jesus raise the dead, and did not believe. The robber sees Him being put to death, and yet believes. *Contempserunt Judæi mortuos suscitantem: non contempsit latro secum in cruce pendentem* (Aug. *Serm.* xxiii. 3). D again amplifies with στραφεὶς πρὸς τ. κύριον.

ἐν τῇ βασιλείᾳ σου. This is perhaps the best supported reading: comp. Mt. xvi. 28, xxv. 31. It means "when Thou comest *in* the glory and power of Thy Kingdom": whereas εἰς τὴν βασιλείαν σου (B L, Vulg., Hil. Ambr.) would mean "comest *into* Thy Kingdom." The former refers to Christ's return in glory, the latter to His return to the Father through death. The alteration of ἐν into εἰς as more appropriate to ἔλθῃς seems more probable than the converse. That the robber had heard what is recorded Jn. xviii. 36, 37 is possible, but not probable. He believes that Jesus is the Messiah, and he knows that the Messiah is to have a kingdom. It is all but certain that the robber was a Jew. This is antecedently probable; and to a heathen the word "paradise" would hardly have been intelligible.

There is no reason for supposing that the robber felt the need of obtaining forgiveness from the Messiah. To the Jew death is an expiation for sin. In the "Confession on a Death Bed" in the *Authorized Daily Prayer Book of the United Hebrew Congregations* we have, "O may my death be an atonement for all my sins, iniquities, and transgressions, of which I have been guilty against Thee" (p. 317).

43. Ἀμήν σοι λέγω. As usual, this introduces something of special importance, or beyond expectation: iv. 24, xii. 37, xviii. 17, 29, xxi. 32. B C* L have this order; others the common Ἀμὴν λέγω σοι.

σήμερον. To take this with λέγω robs it of almost all its force. When taken with what follows it is full of meaning. Jesus knows that both He and the robber will die that day, and He grants him more than he had asked or expected. *Uberior est gratia quam precatio. Ille enim rogabat ut memor esset sui Dominus cum venisset in regnum suum: Dominus autem ait illi: Amen, amen dico tibi: Hodie mecum eris in paradiso. Ubi Christus, ibi vita, ibi regnum* (Ambr. *ad loc.*).

μετ᾽ ἐμοῦ ἔσῃ. Not merely in My company (σὺν ἐμοί), but sharing with Me. The promise implies the continuance of consciousness after death. If the dead are unconscious, the assurance to the robber that he will be with Christ after death would be empty of consolation.

ἐν τῷ παραδείσῳ. The word, said to be of Persian origin, is used in various senses in Scripture: 1. "a park or pleasure-ground" (Neh. ii. 8; Cant. iv. 13; Eccl. ii. 5); 2. "the garden of Eden" (Gen. ii. 8–10, 15, 16, iii. 1–3, 8–10, etc.); 3. "Abraham's Bosom," *i.e.* the resting-place of the souls of the just until the resurrection (the meaning here); 4. "a region in heaven," perhaps identical with "the third heaven" (2 Cor. xii. 4). It is doubtful whether ὁ παράδεισος τοῦ Θεοῦ (Rev. ii. 7) is the same as 3 or 4, or is yet a fifth use. By His use of the word, Jesus neither confirms nor corrects Jewish beliefs on the subject. He assures the penitent that He will do far more than remember him at some unknown time in the future: this very day He will have him in His company in a place of security and bliss. See Wetst.

Epiphanius (317, 347) states that Marcion omitted this promise of Christ to the robber.

Origen sometimes adds τοῦ Θεοῦ to παραδείσῳ: e l r add *patris*. **Syr-Cur.** substitutes *in horto Eden*. See Deissmann, *Bible Studies*, p. 148.

44–49. The Death. In substance, and sometimes in wording, Lk. is the same as Mt. xxvii. 45–56 and Mk. xv. 33–41. But the words recorded in ver. 46 are peculiar to this Gospel, and once more (comp. *vv.* 27–32) are among the most precious details in the history of the Passion.

44. ἤδη ὡσεὶ ὥρα ἕκτη. This is Lk.'s first note as to the time of day (xxii. 66), and he qualifies it with his favourite ὡσεί (iii. 23, ix. 14, 28, xxii. 41, 59, xxiv. 11). In days in which there were no clocks, and on a day on which the darkness and the earthquake caused so much disturbance of the ordinary signs of the hour, very large margin for inaccuracy may be covered by ὡσεί. All three Synoptists give the sixth hour, *i.e.* about noon, as the time when the darkness began; while Mk. (xv. 25) gives the third hour as the time of the Crucifixion. On the apparent discrepancy between these statements and Jn. xix. 14 see Ramsay in the *Expositor* for March 1893 and June 1896. The ἤδη is in B C* L, Boh.

ἐφ' ὅλην τὴν γῆν. "Over the whole *land*" (Orig. Luth. Calv. Bez. Mald. Nösg. Schanz, Hahn, Tyn. Cov. Gen. RV.), rather than "over all the *earth*" (Euthym. Beng. De W. Mey. Godet, AV.). For "land" comp. iv. 25, xxi. 23: for "earth" xxi. 35; Acts i. 8. The *Gospel of Peter* has ἦν δὲ μεσημβρία καὶ σκότος κατέσχε πᾶσαν τὴν Ἰουδαίαν, where, as here, the time of day and the darkness are co-ordinate (καί, not ὅτε): Win. liii. 3, p. 543.

These exceptional phenomena, as Godet points out, may be attributed either to a supernatural cause or to a providential coincidence. *On ne peut méconnaitre une relation profonde, d'un côté, entre l'homme et la nature, de l'autre, entre l'humanité et Christ.* The sympathy of nature with the sufferings of the

Son of God is what seems to be indicated in all three accounts, which are here almost verbally the same; and possibly the Evangelists believed the darkness to have enveloped the whole earth.

45. τοῦ ἡλίου ἐκλείποντος. The reading is doubtful; but this is probably correct, although ἐκλιπόντος may possibly be correct. "The sun failing," or "the sun having failed," is the meaning: and we must leave it doubtful whether Lk. supposes that there was an *eclipse* (which is impossible at full moon), or uses ἐκλείπειν in its originally vague sense of "fail." The latter is probable. Neither in LXX nor elsewhere in N.T. is ἐκλείπω used of the sun. The fact that it might mean an eclipse, and that an eclipse was known to be impossible, would tempt copyists to substitute a phrase that would be free from objection; whereas no one would want to change ἐσκοτίσθη ὁ ἥλιος. The *Gospel of Peter* states that "many went about with lamps, supposing it is night," and that the darkness lasted until Jesus was taken from the cross, when the earthquake took place: "then the sun shone out, and it was found to be the ninth hour." See Charles, *Assump. of Moses*, 41, 87.

The evidence stands thus:—

τοῦ ἡλίου ἐκλείποντος (or *ἐκλιπόντος* ℵ L *al.*, Tisch.) ℵ B C* (?) L *codd. ap.* Orig. Aegyptt. Orig. "Cels." WH. RV. Weiss. *καὶ ἐσκοτίσθη ὁ ἥλιος* A C^3 D Q R X Γ etc., *codd. ap.* Orig-lat. Latt. Syr. Marcion *ap.* Epiph. Lach. Treg. D has *ἐσκ. δέ.* The Latin renderings are *intenebricatus est sol* (a), *tenebricavit sol* (c), *obscuratus est sol* (d e f Vulg.). See WH. ii. App. pp. 69–71 for a full discussion of the evidence.

Julius Africanus (*c.* A.D. 220) in his *Chronica* opposes the heathen historian Thallus for explaining this darkness as an eclipse, which at the Passover would be impossible (Routh, *Rel. Sacr.* ii. pp. 297, 476). In the *Acta Pilati*, A. xi. the Jews are represented as explaining away the darkness in a similar manner: *ἔκλειψις ἡλίου γέγονεν κατὰ τὸ εἰωθός*!

Origen (*Con. Cels.* ii. 33, 59; comp. 14) tells us that Phlegon (a freedman of Hadrian) recorded the earthquake and the darkness in his Chronicles. Eusebius in his Chronicle quotes the words of Phlegon, stating that in the 202nd Olympiad (4th year of the 203rd, Arm. Vers.) there was a very great eclipse; also that there was a great earthquake in Bithynia, which destroyed a great part of Nicæa (Eus. *Chron.* p. 148, ed. Schœne). It is impossible to determine whether the events recorded by Phlegon have any connexion with the phenomena which accompanied the death of Christ.

ἐσχίσθη δὲ τὸ καταπέτασμα. Between the Holy Place and the Holy of Holies (Exod. xxvi. 31; Lev. xxi. 23, xxiv. 3; Heb. vi. 19; comp. Heb. x. 20) there was a curtain called *τὸ δεύτερον καταπέτασμα* (Heb. ix. 3), to distinguish it from the curtain which separated the outer court from the Holy Place. The latter was more accurately, but not invariably, called *τὸ κάλυμμα* (Ex. xxvii. 16; Num. iii. 25). But Jewish traditions state that there were *two* curtains, one cubit apart, between the Holy Place and the Holy of Holies, the space between them being called *τάραξις* because of the perplexity which led to this arrangement (J. Lightfoot on Mt. xxvii. 51). It is not clear how many curtains are included in τὰ καταπετάσματα in 1 Mac. iv. 51. It is futile to speculate *how* the curtain was rent; but the fact would be well known to the priests, "a great company" of whom soon afterwards became "obedient to the faith" (Acts vi. 7). The μέσον of Lk. is more classical than the εἰς δύο of Mt. Mk. and the *Gospel of Peter*.[1]

46. φωνήσας φωνῇ μεγάλῃ. All three mention this loud voice, which seems to indicate that Jesus did not die of exhaustion. Comp. Stephen's cry (Acts vii. 60). But here the fondness of Lk. for cognate words is conspicuous. While he has φωνήσας φωνῇ, Mt. has κράξας φωνῇ, and Mk. ἀφεὶς φωνήν: comp. ii. 8 and 9, vii. 29, xii. 50, xvii. 24, xxii. 15: and see on xi. 46. The aorist does not prove that φωνήσας is not to be taken with εἶπεν, and we may suppose that what was uttered with a loud voice was the saying, "Father, into Thy hands," etc. Comp. the freq. ἀποκριθεὶς εἶπεν. But it is admissible to make the φωνήσας refer to "It is finished," or to some separate inarticulate cry. It is quite unnecessary to suppose that Lk. has here taken the words of Ps. xxxi. 6 and attributed them to Jesus, in order to express His submissive trust in God at the moment of death. Are we to suppose that Jesus did not know Ps. xxxi.? or that, if He did not, such a thought as this could not occur to Him?

εἰς χεῖράς σου παρατίθεμαι τ. πν. μ. The psalmist, thinking of a future death, has παραθήσομαι, which L and inferior MSS. read here. The *voluntary* character of Christ's death is very clearly expressed in this last utterance, as in ἀφῆκεν τὸ πνεῦμα (Mt.) and παρέδωκεν τὸ πνεῦμα (Jn.). None of the four says ἀπέθανεν, or ἐκοιμήθη, or ἐτελεύτησεν. *Quis ita dormit quando voluerit, sicut Jesus mortuus est quando voluit? Quis ita vestem ponit quando voluerit, sicut se carne exuit quando voluit? Quis ita cum voluerit abit quomodo cum voluit obiit?* (Aug. *Tr. in Joh.* xix. 30). To urge that this utterance is not consistent with ver. 43 is futile, unless we

[1] Jerome says, *In evangelio autem quod Hebraicis litteris scriptum est, legimus non velum templi scissum, sed superlimenare Templi miræ magnitudinis coruisse* (*Ad Hedyb.* viii.). Elsewhere he says, *superlimenare templi infinitæ magnitudinis fractum esse atque divisum legimus* (*Com. in Matt.* xxvii. 51). See Nicholson, *Gospel acc. to the Hebrews*, p. 62.

In the Gemara it is stated that some forty years before the destruction of Jerusalem, the heavy gates of the temple, which could with difficulty be moved by many men, and which were locked at the time, flew open about midnight at the Passover. Josephus (*B. J.* vi. 5. 3) reports an occurrence of this kind shortly before the capture of the city. As Neander remarks (*L. J. C.* § 293 n.), these accounts hint at *some* strange occurrence as being remembered in connexion with the time of the Crucifixion.

The rending of the veil perhaps symbolized the end of the temple and its services. In *Clem. Recogn.* i. 41 it is otherwise interpreted as a lamentation (comp. the rending of clothes) over the destruction which threatened the place. Better Theophylact: δεικνύντος τοῦ Κυρίου, ὅτι οὐκ ἔτι ἄβατα ἔσται τὰ Ἅγια τῶν ἁγίων, ἀλλὰ τοῖς Ῥωμαίοις παραδοθέντα, βάσιμα καὶ βέβηλα γενήσονται.

believe that God is excluded from paradise (Ps. xvi. 10, cxxxix. 8; Acts ii. 27).

Strauss, Renan, and others are unwilling to decide whether all the Seven Words from the Cross are to be rejected as unhistorical. Keim will commit himself to no more than "the two probable facts, that shortly before His death Jesus uttered a cry of lamentation, and when on the point of dying a death-cry" (vi. p. 162). One asks once more, Who was capable of inventing such words? Compare the inventions in the apocryphal gospels.

47. ὁ ἑκατοντάρχης. The one who was there to superintend the execution, *supplicio præpositus*: all three speak of him as "*the* centurion." Legend has invested him with the name Longinus (*Acta Pilati*, B. xi.), which perhaps originally meant the soldier with the λόγχη (Jn. xix. 34), and later writers make both him and the soldier with the spear die a martyr's death. See *D. of Chr. Ant.* p. 1041.

τὸ γενόμενον. Not merely the manner of Christ's death, but its extraordinary circumstances. Mt. has *τὸν σεισμὸν καὶ τὰ γινόμενα*, Mk. *ὅτι οὕτως ἐξέπνευσεν*. Mt. says that those with him joined in the exclamation, and that they "feared greatly."

ἐδόξαζεν τὸν Θεόν. He glorified God unconsciously by this public confession, by saying (λέγων) that Jesus was no criminal, but had died in accordance with God's will. The statement is the Evangelist's appreciation of this heathen's attitude towards the death of Christ. Some, however, suppose that the centurion was a proselyte, and that He first consciously praised God, and then added the remark which is recorded: comp. the use of the phrase ii. 20, v. 25, 26, vii. 16, xiii. 13, xvii. 15, xviii. 43; Acts iv. 21, xi. 18, xxi. 20. The good character of the centurions in N.T. confirms the statement of Polybius, that as a rule the best men in the army were promoted to this rank (vi. 24. 9). See small print on vii. 5. A C P Q X etc. have ἐδόξασε.

Ὄντως . . . δίκαιος ἦν. Mt. and Mk. have *ἀληθῶς Θεοῦ υἱὸς ἦν*. Harmonists suggest that the centurion said *δίκαιος* before the earthquake, and *Θεοῦ υἱός* after it. More probably the two expressions represent one and the same thought: "He was a good man, and quite right in calling God His Father" (*vv.* 34, 46). The centurion would not mean much by *υἱὸς Θεοῦ*. See Aug. *De Cons. Ev.* iii. 20.

48. συμπαραγενόμενοι . . . θεωρίαν. Neither word occurs elsewhere in N.T. For *θεωρία* comp. Dan. v. 7; 2 Mac. v. 26, xv. 12; 3 Mac. v. 24. Note the *πάντες* here and ver. 49. Neither Mt. nor Mk. has it: comp. xx. 18, 45, xxi. 29, xxiii. 1. The multitude would be very great, owing to the Passover, and thousands would see Jesus hanging dead upon the cross. They had looked on the whole tragedy as a sight, *spectaculum* (ver. 35).

τύπτοντες τὰ στήθη. Many of them had had no share in clamouring for Christ's death; and those who had taken part had been hounded on by the priests, and now felt remorse for what they had caused. In the *Gospel of Peter* they are made to say, "Woe to our sins, for the judgment and the end of Jerusalem is at hand!" One Latin MS. (G) here adds *dicentes væ nobis quæ facta sunt hodie propter peccata nostra, adpropinquavit enim desolatio hierusalem.* In Syr-Sin. the verse runs, "And all those who *had ventured there* and saw what happened, smote upon their breasts, saying, *Woe to us, what hath befallen us! woe to us for our sins!*" Syr-Cur. is similar. D adds καὶ τὰ μέτωπα to στήθη.

49. ἱστήκεισαν δὲ πάντες οἱ γνωστοὶ αὐτῷ. "*But* (not "And," as AV. RV.), in contrast to the crowds who ὑπέστρεφον (Lk.'s favourite word), the faithful few remained." Lk. alone mentions this fact: the Apostles perhaps are included. Comp. ἐμάκρυνας τοὺς γνωστούς μου ἀπ' ἐμοῦ (Ps. lxxxvii. 9); οἱ ἔγγιστά μου μακρόθεν ἔστησαν (xxxvii. 12).

For this use of γνωστός comp. ii. 44. In the common signification of "known," γνωστός is freq. in Acts: elsewhere in N.T. rare.

γυναῖκες. Mt. and Mk. name Mary Magdalen, Mary the mother of James and Joses, and Salome the mother of the sons of Zebedee.

ὁρῶσαι ταῦτα. These do *not* gaze as at a spectacle. The change of verb from θεωρήσαντες (ver. 48) is ignored in Vulg. Tyn. Gen. Rhem. AV., while Cov. Cran. RV. distinguish. Although feminine, because of the nearest substantive, ὁρῶσαι belongs to γνωστοί as well as to γυναῖκες.

50–56. The Burial. Comp. Mt. xxvii. 57–61; Mk. xv. 42–47. In this section the whole of *vv.* 54–56 and portions of the rest are peculiar to Lk. Mk. tells us of Pilate's surprise that Jesus was already dead, and of his sending for the centurion to be certified of the fact. Jn. xix. 38–42 is altogether independent. All four show how, even before the Resurrection, love and reverence for the Crucified was manifested.

50. Note the characteristic καὶ ἰδού (i. 20, 31, 36), ὀνόματι (see on v. 27), ὑπάρχων (see on viii. 3 and 41).

βουλευτής. A member of the Sanhedrin is meant; and ὑπάρχων is to be taken with βουλευτής. Another amphibolous expression: comp. *vv.* 35, 43.

The Latin Versions render βουλευτής by *decurio*, the technical word for a member of a municipal senate; but δ has *consiliarius.* Cod. Colb. after *Joseph* continues *de civitate arimathia cum esset decurio qui sperabat regnum dei et bonus homo **non** consentiens concilio et actui eorum hic accessit*, etc.—a free transposition.

ἀγαθὸς καὶ δίκαιος. Syr-Cur. and Syr-Sin. transpose the epithets, which refer to his life as a whole, and not merely to his conduct at this time (i. 6, ii. 25). Mt. says that Joseph was πλούσιος, Mk. that he was εὐσχήμων, Jn. that he was μαθητὴς τοῦ Ἰησοῦ κεκρυμμένος δὲ διὰ τὸν φόβον τῶν Ἰουδαίων.

51. οὐκ ἦν συνκατατεθειμένος. We do not know whether he had absented himself, or abstained from voting, or voted in opposition to the sentence: the verb occurs Exod. xxiii. 32. Apparently he was not present when the sentence recorded Mk. xiv. 64 was pronounced, for that was unanimous.

τῇ βουλῇ. Excepting 1 Cor. iv. 5; Eph. i. 11; Heb. vi. 17, *βουλή* is peculiar to Lk. in N.T. See on vii. 30. In LXX it is very common. Syr-Sin. has "to the accusers."

τῇ πράξει. When the word is used in a bad sense, the plur. is more common (Acts xix. 18; Rom. viii. 13; Col. iii. 9), as in our "practices": but Polybius uses the sing. in this sense. Here the method by which they compassed the death of Jesus is specially meant.

αὐτῶν. Who these are is suggested rather than stated by the preceding *βουλευτής*: *αὐτῶν* means "of the Sanhedrin." Win. xxii. 3 (2), p. 182.

ἀπὸ Ἀριμαθαίας πόλεως τ. Ἰ. The *ἀπό* probably means birthplace or former residence (Mt. xxi. 11): his having a burial-place at Jerusalem shows that he had settled there; and his being one of the Sanhedrin confirms this. Arimathæa is commonly identified with Ramah, the birthplace and home of Samuel. Its full name was Ramathaim-zophim = "Double Height of the Watchers." In LXX it is called Ἀρμαθαίμ (1 Sam. i. 19), and the identification of its site "is, without exception, the most complicated and disputed problem of sacred topography" (Stanley, *Sin. & Pal.* p. 224). The addition of *πόλεως τῶν Ἰουδαίων* points to Gentile readers.

προσεδέχετο τ. βασιλείαν τ. Θεοῦ. "He was waiting for the Messianic Kingdom": that he recognized Jesus as the Messiah is not implied. Comp. ii. 25, 38; Acts xxiii. 21, xxiv. 15. The verb is not found in Mt. or Jn., and only once in Mk., but occurs seven times in Lk. and Acts.

52. The wording of all three is very similar, and also of the *Gospel of Peter*, which represents Joseph as coming *before* Jesus was dead, and Pilate as sending to ask Herod for the body, who replies, "Brother Pilate, even if some one had not asked for Him, we were intending to bury Him . . . before the first day of the unleavened bread." Comp. the addition made in Cod. Colb.

53. ἐνετύλιξεν αὐτὸ σινδόνι. The verb occurs only here, Mt. xxvii. 59, and Jn. xx. 7. All three mention the *σινδών*, which was cut into strips (*ὀθόνια* or *κειρίαι*) for the burial. Mk. (xv. 46) tells us that it had been bought by Joseph for the purpose, and therefore on that day; which is another sign that the feast had not begun the previous evening. The *Gospel of Peter* says that Joseph washed the body before wrapping it in linen.

ἐν μνήματι λαξευτῷ. For **μνῆμα** see on xxiv. 1: the adjective is not classical; once in LXX (Deut. iv. 49) and four times in Aquila (Num.

xxi. 20, xxiii. 14; Deut. xxxiv. 1; Josh. xiii. 20). Comp. λαξεύω (Exod. xxxiv. 1, 4; Num. xxi. 19, xxiii. 14; Deut. iii. 27, x. 1, 3, etc.). Verb and adjective seem to belong to the important class of words which became current through having been needed to express Jewish ideas and customs. Kennedy, *Sources of N.T. Grk.* p. 116.

οὐκ ἦν οὐδεὶς οὔπω. Accumulation of negatives: comp. Heb. xiii. 5, and see Win. lv. 9. b, p. 626; Burton, § 489. Mt. has *καινῷ*. The fact is mentioned as a mark of special honour in contrast to the shameful death: comp. xix. 30.

Cod. Bezae has here one of its characteristic interpolations. After *κείμενος* it adds *καὶ θέντος αὐτοῦ ἐπέθηκε τῷ μνημείῳ λεῖθον ὃν μόγις εἴκοσι ἐκύλιον*: *et posito eo imposuit in monumento lapidem quem vix viginti movebant.* Scrivener (*Cod. Bezae*, p. lii) remarks that this "strange addition" is "conceived somewhat in the Homeric spirit." Comp. *Od.* ix. 241. Prof. Rendel Harris (*Cod. Bezae*, ch. vii.) finds a hexameter in the Latin: *imposuit . . . lapidem quem vix viginti movebant.* But against this (as an acute critic in the *Guardian* of May 25, 1892, p. 787, points out) are to be urged (1) the intrusive *in monumento*, (2) the shortening of the final syllable in *viginti*, which is improbable so early as the second century, (3) the fact that the same gloss, rather differently worded, is found not only in Cod. Colb., but in the Sahidic Version. Thus in one we have, *posuerunt lapidem quem vix viginti volvebant* (c); in the other, *posuit lapidem in porta sepulcri quem viginti homines volvere possent.* To assume a Greek gloss, which was differently translated in two Latin and one Egyptian text, is a simpler hypothesis than a Latin gloss translated into Greek and Egyptian, and then from the Greek into a different Latin. Moreover, the fact that the tone of the gloss is Homeric rather than Virgilian points to a Greek origin. That there were Homerizers and Virgilianizers at this early date may be inferred from Tertull. *De Præscr. Hær.* xxxix.

54. παρασκευῆς. The word may mean either the eve of the sabbath or the eve of the Passover: and on this occasion the sabbath probably coincided with Nisan 15, the first day of the Passover. This first day ranked as a sabbath (Exod. xii. 16; Lev. xxiii. 7), and therefore was doubly holy when it coincided with an ordinary sabbath. If the Passover had begun the previous evening, would Lk. and Mk. (xv. 42) speak of its first day as the eve of an ordinary sabbath? Just as we should hardly speak of "the first Sunday in April," if that Sunday was Easter Day. But, although the day was a *παρασκευή* to both sabbath and Passover, it is the former that is probably meant. Comp. Mk. xv. 42. Caspari (§ 157) would take it the other way.

For *παρασκευῆς* (ℵ B C* L 13 346, *cenæ puræ* a b c l *parasceues* Vulg.) A C² P X etc., f ff₂ have *παρασκευή*, Syr-Cur. *feria sexta.* For the whole verse D substitutes *ἦν δὲ ἡ ἡμέρα προσαββάτου, erat autem dies antesabbatum.*

σάββατον ἐπέφωσκεν. An inaccurate expression, because the sabbath began, not at dawn, but at sunset. But "it was dawning" easily comes to mean "it was beginning," and is transferred to things which cannot "dawn." In the *Gospel of Peter*, when Pilate before the Crucifixion asks Herod for the body of Jesus, Herod replies that in any case the body would have been buried that day, ἐπεὶ καὶ σάββατον ἐπιφώσκει, γέγραπται γὰρ ἐν τῷ νόμῳ, ἥλιον μὴ δῦναι ἐπὶ πεφονευμένῳ. The verb has nothing to do with lighting *lamps* at the beginning of the sabbath (J. Lightfoot, Wetst.), nor is the rising of the *stars* or the *glow* of sunset meant (Hahn).

55. Κατακολουθήσασαι. In N.T. here and Acts xvi. 17 only: in LXX Jer. xvii. 16; 1 Es. vii. 1; Judith xi. 6; Dan. ix. 10; 1 Mac. vi. 23. Their following from the Crucifixion (ver. 49) to Joseph's garden is meant, and the κατα- does not mean "*down* into the grave," but "*after* Joseph and his assistants." Syr-Sin. and Syr-Cur. have "And *the* women, who came with Him from Galilee, went to the sepulchre *in their footsteps*, and saw the body when they [had] brought it in there." The fact of the women beholding the tomb in which the body was laid is in all three Synoptic Gospels. It is part of the evidence for the Resurrection.

For αἱ γυναῖκες (B L P X, Boh. Sah.) D 29, a b e ff$_2$ q r have δύο γυναῖκες, while TR. follows certain cursives in reading καὶ γυναῖκες. ℵ A C Γ etc. have γυναῖκες without αἱ or δύο or καί, and this Tisch. adopts.

ὡς ἐτέθη. We might have expected πῶς: comp. vi. 4, viii. 47, xxiv. 35.

56. ἀρώματα. In N.T. only of these spices; freq. in LXX. For μύρα comp. vii. 37. Mk. says that when the sabbath was over, *i.e.* on Saturday evening, the women bought ἀρώματα that they might *anoint* Him, which shows that ἀρώματα are not to be confined to "sweet-smelling herbs" or to "*dry*" spices. The chapter ought to end at μύρα, for τὸ μὲν σάββατον plainly balances τῇ δὲ μιᾷ τῶν σαββάτων, and no more than a comma is needed after ἐντολήν. D omits κατὰ τὴν ἐντολήν.

ἡσύχασαν. The notice of this resting on the sabbath would be strange if they had been working on so sabbatical a day as Nisan 15; for it could not be urged that the preparation of spices and ointments was in any sense *necessary*. When a sabbath immediately preceded Nisan 15, it was lawful to work on the sabbath *at preparations for the feast*. But can we suppose that, if in this year Nisan 15 immediately preceded the sabbath, pious women would have worked merely to gratify affectionate feeling? Or, having thought themselves justified in working for this purpose on Nisan 15, that they would scrupulously have avoided continuing such work on the sabbath? If Nisan 15 coincided with the sabbath, all is explained: up to sunset on Friday it was lawful to work, and after sunset on Saturday it was lawful to work again. Of the interval Godet remarks, *On peut dire que ce sabbat était le dernier de l'ancienne alliance qui prenait fin avec la mort du Christ Il fut scrupuleusement respecté par tous ceux qui, sans le savoir allaient inaugurer la nouvelle.*

Additional Note on Readings in Chapters xxii. and xxiii.

(1) **xxii. 43, 44.** Ὤφθη δὲ . . . ἐπὶ τὴν γῆν.

Evidence for the passage:—

ℵ*c D F G H K L M Q U X Λ etc. and nearly all cursives. A has the Ammonian section of the passage marked in the margin, although it omits the passage in the text.

All MSS. of Lat. Vet. excepting f Vulg. some MSS. of Boh. of Sah. and of Arm. Syr-Cur. (omitting ἀπ' οὐρανοῦ) Syr-Pesh. Syr-Hier.

Just-M. Iren. Hippol. Dion-Alex. Eus. Greg-Naz. Epiph. Hil. Hieron. Aug.

Evidence against the passage:—

ℵa A B R T 124: 13 has ὤφθη δέ *prima manu*, the rest *secunda manu*. Cc 69 and all known Evangelistaria have the passage inserted after Mt. xxvi. 39. E S V Γ Δ Π and others, including nine cursives, have the passage marked with asterisks or obeli. *Et in Græcis et in Latinis codd. complur.* known to Hilary it was wanting, and it was found only *in quibusdam exemplaribus tam Græcis quam Latinis* known to Jerome.

f, most MSS. of Boh. including the best, some MSS. of Sah. and of Arm. (see Sanday, *App. ad N.T.* pp. 188, 191), Syr-Sin., Syr-Harcl. *marg.*

Cyr-Alex. omits in his Homilies on Lk. Ambr. likewise. The silence of Clem-Alex. Orig. Cyr-Hier. Ath. and Greg-Nys. can hardly be accidental in all cases, or even in most.

Excision for doctrinal reasons will not explain the omission. "There is no tangible evidence for the excision of a substantial portion of narrative for doctrinal reasons at any period of textual history" (WH. ii. App. p. 66).

Nor does "Lectionary practice" seem to be an adequate cause for such widespread omission. It is suggested that, because the passage was read after Mt. xxvi. 39 in the Lection for Holy Thursday, and omitted after Lk. xxii. 42 in the Lection for Tuesday after Sexagesima, therefore some MSS. came to omit in Lk. or both Gospels.

It will be observed that the early non-patristic evidence in favour of the words is ℵ* D, Latt. Syrr. "a frequent Western combination."

But, if we regard the passage as probably a Western insertion in the text of Lk., we need have no hesitation whatever in retaining it as a genuine portion of historical tradition. It is true, whoever wrote it.

(2) **xxii. 68.** After οὐ μὴ ἀποκριθῆτε the words μοι ἢ ἀπολύσητε.

Evidence for the words:—

A D X Γ Δ Λ Π etc., Latt. Syr-Cur. Syr-Sin.

Evidence against the words:—

ℵ B L T, Boh. one MS. of Vulg. (J), Cyr-Alex. Ambr.

A few authorities have μοι without ἢ ἀπολύσητε.

With Tisch. WH. RV. we may safely omit. Treg. brackets, Alf. the same, suggesting homœoteleuton as the cause of omission.

(3) **xxiii. 34 a.** ὁ δὲ Ἰησοῦς . . . ποιοῦσιν.

Evidence for the passage:—

ℵ*c A C D² L Q X Γ Δ Λ Π etc.

c e f ff₂ l r Vulg. most MSS. of Boh. Syrr. (Cur. Pesh. Harcl. Hier.) Aeth. Arm.

Iren-lat. Orig-lat. Hippol. Clem-Hom. Eus. Ath. Greg-Nys. Bas. Gest-Pilat. Chrys. Hil. Ambr. Hieron. Aug.

Evidence against the passage:—

ℵ[a] B D* 38 43 435. E has it marked with an asterisk.

a b d two best MSS. of Boh. Sah. Syr-Sin.

Cyr-Alex. is said by Arethas to have regarded it as spurious; and this is confirmed by the text prefixed to the Syriac Homily on Lk. xxiii. 32–43 (p. 718, ed. Payne Smith). This, however, exists in only one MS., which ends before ver. 34 is properly reached.

The omission in such witnesses would be very difficult to explain, if the passage had been part of the original text of Lk. But, even more strongly than in the case xxii. 43, 44, internal evidence warrants us in retaining the passage in its traditional place as a genuine portion of the evangelic narrative. That point being quite certain, it matters comparatively little whether we owe this precious fragment to Lk. or not.

Additional Note on xxiii. 45.

Dr. E. A. Abbott conjectures that both here and xxii. 51 we have instances of *substitution through misunderstanding*. In the *Classical Review* of Dec. 1893, p. 443, he writes: "Though these words (τοῦ ἡλίου ἐκλείποντος) might mean 'the sun failing (to give its light),' yet the natural meaning is 'the sun *being eclipsed*.' Now every one knew that an eclipse could not happen except at new moon, and every Jew knew that Passover was at full moon." Why, then, he goes on to ask, does Lk. give an explanation of the darkness, which neither Mt. nor Mk. give, and which involves a portentous miracle? To the imaginary reply, "Because Lk. wished to make it clear that it *was* a miracle and not a natural obscuration of the sun; for he is not afraid of being the only Evangelist to insert a miracle, as is shown by his account of the healing of Malchus' ear," Dr. Abbott rejoins that "the latter miracle is *substituted* rather than *inserted*. It is *substituted for a rebuke to Peter*, 'restore thy sword to its place.' Comp. Mt. xxvi. 52; Jn. xviii. 11, with ἀποκαταστάθητι in Jer. xxix. (Heb. xlvii.) 6, and it will appear that the miraculous narrative probably arose from a misunderstanding of some ambiguous word, such as ἀποκαταστάθητι ('be thou *restored*'), or ἀποκατασταθήτω ('let it be *restored*'), in the original tradition. 'It' (or 'thou') was interpreted by Mt. and Jn. (rightly) to be the 'sword,' and by Lk. (wrongly) to be 'the ear'; and the verb was interpreted by Mt. and Jn. (rightly) to mean 'restored *to its place*,' but by Lk. (wrongly, though more in conformity with the Synoptic vocabulary, Mt. xii. 13; Mk. iii. 5, viii. 25; Lk. vi. 10, where it is used of a withered hand, or of a blind man) to mean 'restored *to its original condition*.'"

Is it possible that the present, also, may be a case of *substitution through misunderstanding*? Let us turn to the parallel passage in Mt. (xxvii. 46–49) and Mk. (xv. 34–36). Here we find no mention of an eclipse, but of a saying of Jesus which was interpreted by the bystanders to mean that "*Elias*" had "*abandoned*" (ἐγκαταλείπειν) Jesus. *This Lk. omits altogether.* But the genitive case of "Elias" is the same as that of the "sun," viz. ἡλείου, or in MSS. ἡλίου: and ἐκλείπειν, although not often used of *persons* failing others in an emergency, *is* so used occasionally. Thus ἡλίου ἐκλείποντος might mean either "the *sun being eclipsed*," or "*Elias failing*, or *forsaking*."

But how could ἐγκαταλείποντος be changed into ἐκλείποντος? Curtailments of long compounds are not infrequent in MSS. of the N.T., and specially with κατά: comp. Mk. xiv. 40; Lk. vi. 36; Mt. xiii. 40; Jas. ii. 13, iii. 14. . . . If Lk., or others before him, concluded that ἡλίου must mean the sun, they would naturally infer that ἐγκαταλείποντος must be an error for ἐκλείποντος.

. . . It seems probable that Lk., finding obscure and divergent traditions about some utterance of Jesus, . . . considered that he was restoring the original meaning, and a meaning worthy of the subject, in retaining two or three words of the current tradition, but placing them in such a context as to show that it was the *sun*, and not *Elias*, that "failed."

XXIV. *The Resurrection and the Ascension.*

It is well known that the difficulty of harmonizing the different accounts of the Resurrection given by the Evangelists and by S. Paul is great; and this difficulty is perhaps at a maximum when the narrative of Lk. is compared with the others. Here, as so often in the Gospels, we have not sufficient knowledge to piece together the different fragments which have come down to us, and consequently the evidence for important facts is not what we might antecedently have expected or desired. But our expectations and wishes are not adequate criteria, and it is no paradox to say that the difficulty of harmonizing the various narratives is in itself a security for their general truthfulness. Dishonest witnesses would have made the evidence more harmonious. As it is, each witness fearlessly tells his own story according to the knowledge which he possesses, and is not careful as to whether it agrees with what may have been told elsewhere. Nevertheless there is agreement in the following important particulars:—

1. The Resurrection itself is not described. Like all beginnings, whether in nature or in history, it is hidden from view. (Contrast the attempt at description in the *Gospel of Peter.*)

2. The manifestations, while confined to disciples, were made to disciples who were wholly unexpectant of a Resurrection. The theory that they were visions or illusions, arising from intense and unreasoning expectation, is contrary to all the evidence that has come down to us. On the contrary,

3. They were received with doubt and hesitation at first, and mere reports on the subject were rejected.

4. The evidence begins with the visit of women to the tomb very early on the first day of the week, and the first sign was the removal of the stone from the door of the tomb.

5. Angels were seen before the Lord was seen.

6. He was seen on various occasions by various kinds of witnesses, both male and female, both individuals and companies, both sceptical and trusting.

7. The result was a conviction, which nothing ever shook, that "the Lord had risen indeed" and been present with them (see Wsctt. on Jn. xx. 1: he gives a tentative arrangement of the events of the first Easter Day, which at least shows that there is no serious discrepancy between the four narratives).

Sadler asserts, and Godet endeavours to show, that each narrative is determined by the purpose which each Evangelist had in view in writing; but in most cases the distinctions are not very convincing. Nearly the whole of Lk.'s narrative is peculiar to him, the partial exceptions being *vv.* 1–6 and 9, 10. The nucleus of the whole is the account of the walk to Emmaus (*vv.* 13–43); and the first part of the chapter is an introduction to this graphic account, with special reference to *vv.* 22, 23. See Loofs, *Die Aufstehungsberichte.*

An excellent opportunity of comparing six forms of the Old Latin (a b c d e f) with one another and with the Vulgate is given in Scrivener's edition of Codex Bezae in connexion with a large portion of this chapter. He prints the first twenty-four verses of this chapter as given in these authorities in seven parallel columns (pp. xxxvi, xxxvii). This passage is "rich in peculiar and idiomatic expressions, and little liable to be corrupted from the Synoptic Gospels." The result, he thinks, is to show that the Latin of Codex Bezae was made "immediately from its Greek text," which it generally servilely follows; but that occasionally the translator was led away by his recollection of the Old Latin, "sometimes for whole verses together," even when the Old Latin differed from the Greek text which he was translating. *Adhuc sub judice lis est.*

1–11. The Visit of the Women to the Tomb and the Vision of Angels. Comp. Mt. xxviii. 1–10; Mk. xvi. 1–8; Jn. xx. 1–10. Lk. and Jn. mention two Angels; Mt. and Mk. mention only one:

but we know too little about the manner of Angel appearances to be sure that Lk. and Jn. mention the same two Angels, or that Mt. and Mk. mention the same one. In the other two cases of similar difference (the Gerasene demoniacs and the blind men at Jericho) it is Mt. who mentions two, while Lk. gives only one. In all three cases Mk. mentions only one. Where, out of two or more, only one is spokesman, he is necessarily remembered. The other or others may easily be ignored or forgotten. It is an exaggeration to call such differences absolute discrepancies. Lk. records only those appearances of the risen Lord which took place in Judæa.

1. **τῇ δὲ μιᾷ τῶν σαββάτων.** "*But* on the first day of the week." The δέ corresponds to the previous μέν: they rested on the sabbath, but the next day they did not. Jn. has the same expression (xx. 1), which literally means "but on day one of the week," *una autem sabbati* (Vulg.). Cov. here translates "upon one of the Sabbathes," and in Jn. "upon one daye of the Sabbath." But here with Cran. he rightly has "But" (RV.) and not "And" (Rhem.) or "Now" (AV.).

Comp. Acts xx. 7; Mt. xxviii. 1; Mk. xvi. 2; Jn. xx. 19; Rev. ix. 12. This use of the cardinal for the ordinal is Hebraistic: Gen. i. 5; Esr. iii. 6; Ps. xxiii. *tit.* In class. Grk. it occurs only in combination with an ordinal: τῷ ἑνὶ καὶ τριηκοστῷ (Hdt. v. 89. 2).

ὄρθρου βαθέως. It is doubtful whether βαθέως is the Attic form of the gen. of βαθύς (De W. Nösg. Alf.) or an adv. (Mey. Weiss). The former is probable; for ὄρθρος βαθύς occurs (Aristoph. *Vesp.* 216; Plat. *Crit.* 43 A; see esp. *Prot.* 310 A; Philo, *De Vita Mosis*, i. 32), and 2 Cor. xi. 23 does not favour the latter. For ὄρθρου comp. [Jn.] viii. 2; Jer. xxv. 4, xxvi. 5.

τὸ μνῆμα. With the exception of Mk. v. 3, 5, xv. 46; Rev. xi. 9, the word is peculiar to Lk. in N.T. (viii. 27, xxiii. 53; Acts ii. 29, vii. 16). The common word is μνημεῖον (xi. 44, 47, xxiii. 55, xxiv. 2, 9, 12, 22, 24, etc.); but Mt. sometimes has τάφος (xxiii. 27, 29, xxvii. 61, 64, 66, xxviii. 1; comp. Rom. iii. 13). RV. has "tomb" for μνῆμα and μνημεῖον, and "sepulchre" for τάφος.

A C[3] D X Γ etc. d f q Syrr. (Cur. Sin. Pesh. Harcl. Hier.) Sah. Arm. Aeth. (most MSS.) add καί τινες σὺν αὐταῖς, and D c d Sah. add from Mk. xvi. 3 ἐλογίζοντο δὲ ἐν ἑαυταῖς, τίς ἄρα ἀποκυλίσει τὸν λίθον; ℵ B C* L 33 124 a b c e ff_2 l Vulg. Boh. Aeth. (some MSS.) omit. The insertion is a gloss from ver. 10 and Mk. xvi. 1, 3.

2. **εὗρον δὲ τὸν λίθον.** Lk. has not yet mentioned it, but he speaks of it as well known or as usual. All three use ἀποκυλίω of the stone, while Jn. has ἠρμένον ἐκ: the verb occurs nowhere else in N.T. Comp. Gen. xxix. 3, 8, 10; Judith xiii. 9.

3. **τοῦ κυρίου Ἰησοῦ.** The combination occurs nowhere else in the Gospels, although possibly right [Mk.] xvi. 19; but it is frequent in Acts (i. 21, iv. 33, viii. 16, etc.) and Epistles. Here the words are possibly a very early insertion. See note on Western Noninterpolations at the end of this chapter.

4. **καὶ ἐγένετο ἐν τῷ ἀπορεῖσθαι αὐτὰς περὶ τούτου, καὶ ἰδού.** Note

the strongly Hebraistic construction, so common in Lk., and see additional note, p. 45.

The Latin Versions differ greatly: *dum aporiarentur* (d), *hæsitarent* (f), *stuperent* (a c), *mente contristarentur* (ff_2), *mente consternatæ essent* (Vulg.). The last is wrong both in verb and tense. *Aporiari* occurs in Vulg. 2 Cor. iv. 8; Is. lix. 16; Ecclus. xviii. 6, and in Irenæus, ii. 7. 1, 2.

ἄνδρες δύο. The *plur.* agrees with ἀγγέλων in ver. 23. For ἀνήρ of an Angel in human form comp. Acts i. 10, x. 30; for ἐπέστησαν see on ii. 9; and for ἐσθής see on xxiii. 11. Only here and xvii. 24 in N.T. does ἀστράπτω occur.

Instead of ἐσθῆτι ἀστραπτούσῃ (ℵ B D, Latt. Orig. Eus.) TR. has ἐσθήσεσιν ἀστραπτούσαις with A C D Γ Δ etc., Sah. Boh. Arm. L has ἐσθήσεσιν λευκαῖς, Syr-Sin. "their garments were dazzling." ἔσθησις occurs Acts i. 10 only. See Deissmann, *Bible Studies*, p. 263.

The contrast between the *Gospel of Peter* and the Canonical Gospels is still more marked in the account of the Resurrection than in that of the Passion. There the watchers see δύο ἄνδρας come down from heaven; and ἀμφότεροι οἱ νεανίσκοι enter the tomb. But the watchers see τρεῖς ἄνδρας come out of the tomb. Then ἄνθρωπός τις comes down from heaven and enters the tomb; and the women find τινα νεανίσκον sitting in the tomb, and he addresses them.

5. ἐμφόβων δὲ γενομένων. In N.T. the use of ἔμφοβος (always with γίνεσθαι) is almost confined to Lk. (ver. 37; Acts x. 4, xxiv. 25; Rev. xi. 13): in LXX (without γίνεσθαι) Ecclus. xix. 24. The detail κλινουσῶν τὰ πρόσωπα εἰς τ. γῆν is peculiar to Lk Note πρὸς αὐτάς: Mt. and Mk. have the dat.

Τί ζητεῖτε τὸν ζῶντα μετὰ τῶν νεκρῶν; A rebuke: comp. ii. 49. There is possibly a reference to Is. viii. 19, τί ἐκζητοῦσιν περὶ τῶν ζώντων τοὺς νεκρούς; They ought to have remembered His assurance that on the third day He would rise again.

6. οὐκ ἔστιν ὧδε, ἀλλὰ ἠγέρθη. Like the doubtful words in ver. 3, this sentence is wanting in D and important Latin authorities. A reason for the omission is hard to find. A very early insertion from Mk. xvi. 6 = Mt. xxviii. 6 may be suspected: see note at the end of this chapter.

μνήσθητε. Angels "may be employed in endless ways of which we can form no idea, but we have Scripture warrant for supposing that they call things to remembrance, and it is not going much farther to suppose that they put thoughts into people's minds" (Latham, *A Service of Angels*, p. 162).

ὡς ἐλάλησεν ὑμῖν. The ὡς is not exactly ὅτι, but suggests the wording of the statement: in both ix. 22 and xviii. 32, 33 the important "on the third day" is predicted. The whole of this to the end of ver. 8 is peculiar to Lk. On the other hand Lk, who records no appearances in Galilee, omits προάγει ὑμᾶς εἰς τὴν Γαλιλαίαν, which refers back to Mk. xiv. 28; Mt. xxvi. 32.

7. δεῖ. See on iv. 43 and ix. 22.

9. ὑποστρέψασαι. Lk.'s favourite word: Mt. has ἀπελθοῦσαι and Mk. ἐξελθοῦσαι. Lk. omits the speed with which they returned in mingled fear and joy.

ἀπήγγειλαν. Mt. says the same (xxviii. 8), but Mk. says οὐδενὶ οὐδὲν εἶπαν, ἐφοβοῦντο γάρ. If we had the conclusion of Mk.'s Gospel we should know how this apparent contradiction is to be explained. Obviously they did not remain silent about it for the rest of their lives, but only so long as fear kept them silent. When the fear passed away, they told their tale to the disciples (not merely to the Apostles) in accordance with the angelic charge (Mt. xxviii. 7). But it is perhaps simpler to suppose that Mt. and Lk. here give, as Mt. and Mk. do in the case of the crucified robbers, the tradition which was generally current, and which attributed to all the women what was true of only one, viz. Mary Magdalen. She on her return told the Apostles, while the others kept silence through fear. A little later no doubt all told to all. Note the characteristic πάντα and πᾶσιν. Mt. has neither, and he sums up "the Eleven and all the rest" in τοῖς μαθηταῖς αὐτοῦ.

10. The other Evangelists give the names of the women at the beginning of the narrative. All four place Mary Magdalen first, and Jn. mentions no one else; but οὐκ οἴδαμεν (xx. 2) implies that others were with her. "Mary the [mother] of James" or "the other Mary" is mentioned by all three; Joana by Lk. alone, and Salome by Mk. alone. For Joana see on viii. 3: it is from her that Lk. may have got both these details, and also what he relates xxiii. 8–12. Here only does the order ἡ Μαγδ. Μαρία occur: elsewhere Μαρία ἡ Μαγδ. (so D here).

All English Versions previous to RV. follow a false reading, and make one sentence of this verse. There are two sentences. "Now they were Mary Magdalen, and Joana, and Mary the mother of James": these were the women specially referred to in ver. 9. "Also the other women with them told these things unto the Apostles." The evidence against the second *αἱ* (before ἔλεγον) is overwhelming (א* A B D E F G H etc. b d e ff_2 q Sah. Aeth.), and the reason for its insertion is obvious.

Syr-Cur. and Syr-Sin. interpret ἡ Ἰακώβου "the *daughter* of James." There is little doubt that "mother" is meant, and that James is not the Lord's brother, the first president of the Church of Jerusalem. She is called "the mother of James and Joses" (Mk. xv. 40), and "the mother of Joses" (Mk. xv. 47); and she is probably the same as "Mary the [wife] of Clopas" (Jn. xix. 25). See J. B. Mayor, *Ep. of St. James*, Macmillan, 1892, p. xv, perhaps the best discussion of the vexed question about the brethren of the Lord.

11. **ἐνώπιον αὐτῶν.** "In their sight," in the judgment of the Apostles and others; *apud illos* (c), *in conspectu eorum* (d), *coram illis* (f), *apostolis* (l). For ἐνώπιον see small print on i. 15, and for ὡσεί on i. 56.

λῆρος. "Nonsense"; the word "is applied in medical language to the wild talk of the sick in delirium" (Hobart): comp. 4 Mac. v. 11: here only in N.T. *derisus* (d), *delira* (a), *deliramentum* (f Vulg.). The incredulity with which mere reports were received is noted [Mk.] xvi. 11. Even S. John did not infer from the disappearance of the body that He had risen until he had examined the tomb himself (Jn. xx. 8). Apparently no one had understood Christ's predictions of His rising again. They were interpreted of His return in glory, either with a new body or as an incorporeal being. No Apostle had grasped the fact that He would be killed, buried, and raised again to life. They had seen Him dead, and women's talk about Angels who said that He was alive did not cancel that.

τὰ ῥήματα ταῦτα (ℵ B D L, a b c d e l q Vulg. Sah. Boh. Syr-Cur. Aeth.) is certainly to be preferred to τὰ ῥήματα αὐτῶν (A I X Γ Δ etc. f Arm.). Syr-Sin. has "They appeared in their eyes as if they had spoken *these* words *from their wonder*." For neut. plur. with plur. verb comp. Jn. xix. 31.

12. § The Visit of Peter to the Tomb.

The whole of this verse is of unknown and doubtful authority. It is absent from important Western documents, and has the look of an insertion. Its source is probably Jn. xx. 3–10, part of what is there said of "the other disciple" (ver. 5) being here transferred to S. Peter. The only words which are not found in Jn. xx. 3–10 are ἀναστάς, μόνα, θαυμάζων τὸ γεγονός: but of these ἀναστάς (not in Jn. and rare in Mt.) and τὸ γεγονός (not in Mt. or Jn. and once in Mk.) are specially frequent in Lk. And although Lk. more often writes θαυμάζειν ἐπὶ τῷ, yet he sometimes has θαυμάζειν τι (vii. 9; Acts vii. 31). Perhaps the hypothesis of an insertion made in a second edition is here admissible. See note on Western Noninterpolations at the end of this chapter.

The verse has probably no connexion with what precedes. Certainly it does not give the reason why the Apostles disbelieved, viz. because Peter had already been to the tomb and seen no Angels but only grave-cloths. That would require γάρ for δέ and the pluperf. The δέ would rather mark a contrast; although they disbelieved, yet Peter went to the grave to satisfy himself. Didon supposes *two* visits of Peter to the tomb, one with John when Mary Magdalen reported the tomb empty, and a second when she reported that she had seen Angels and the Lord Himself (*J. C.* ch. xii. p. 797). More probably this verse (whatever its source) is an imperfect account of the visit of Peter with John.

τὰ ὀθόνια μόνα. "The grave-cloths without the body."

This is the reading of ℵ^c^b B, Syr-Cur. Syr-Sin. Boh. Sah., omitting κείμενα, while ℵ* A K Π omit μόνα. L, c f Arm. have μόνα κείμενα, I X Γ Δ etc. κείμενα μόνα. Cod. Am. has *posita* only, but many MSS of Vulg. have *sola posita*.

πρὸς αὑτόν. So B L, the rest reading πρὸς ἑαυτόν. The words are amphibolous (comp. xxiii. 35, 43, 50), and may be taken either with ἀπῆλθεν, "he went away to his home," *i.e.* his lodging in the city (Syr-Sin. RV.[1] Hahn), or with θαυμάζων, "wondering with himself" (Vulg. Luth. AV. RV.[2]). But does αὑτόν for ἑαυτόν occur in N.T.?

13–32. The Manifestation to the Two Disciples at Emmaus

This narrative forms a counterpart to that of the manifestation to Mary Magdalen in Jn. There is a condensed allusion to the incident in the appendix to Mk. (xvi. 12, 13); but the narrative is peculiar to Lk., and is among the most beautiful of the treasures which he alone has preserved for us. He almost certainly obtained his information from one of the two disciples, and probably in writing. The account has all the effect of personal experience. If this is accepted, then Cleopas may be regarded as the narrator; for Lk. would know and be likely to name the person from whom he received the account.

The fact that Lk. was almost certainly a Gentile (Col. iv. 10–14), and that in the preface to his Gospel he indicates that he was not an eye-witness, renders the conjecture of Theophylact, that Lk. was the unnamed disciple who went with Cleopas to Emmaus, very improbable. This disciple was evidently a Jew (*vv.* 20, 27, 32) or a proselyte. Lk. *may* have been a proselyte before he was a Christian, and his preface *may* mean no more than that he was not one of those "which *from the beginning* were eye-witnesses": but nothing is gained by such conjectures. In the Acts he uses the first person plural, when he himself was present. Why does he not do the same here, if he was one of the two? It would have added greatly to "the certainty" which he wished to impart to Theophilus, if he had assured him that he himself had talked and eaten with Jesus on the very day of His Resurrection. But the hypothesis still finds supporters, *e.g.* Lange, Godet, Bp. Alexander. Origen twice gives Simon as the name of the unnamed disciple (*Cels.* ii. 62, 68). This may be an erroneous interpretation of ὤφθη Σίμωνι (ver. 34). Epiphanius conjectures Nathanael, which could hardly be right, if Nathanael is Bartholomew (ver. 33). But all such conjectures are worthless. Probably Lk. himself did not know who the other was.

13. Καὶ ἰδού. As often, introduces something new and unexpected: i. 20, 31, 36, ii. 25, v. 12, 18, vii. 12, etc.

δύο ἐξ αὐτῶν. Not of the Apostles (ver. 10), as is shown by ver. 33, but of the disciples generally. A direct reference to πᾶσιν τοῖς λοιποῖς (ver. 9) is not manifest. For ἐν αὐτῇ τῇ ἡμέρᾳ see small print on x. 7, and contrast AV. and RV.

ἑξήκοντα. The reading ἑκατὸν ἑξήκοντα (ℵ I K[1] N[1] Π and some other Gk. Lat. and Syr. authorities) is "an Alexandrian geographical correction, though not of the type of Γεργεσηνῶν or Βηθαβαρά; evidently arising from identification of this Emmaus with the better known Emmaus which was later called Nicopolis. The identification is distinctly laid down by Eus. Hier. Soz., though they do not refer to the distance" (WH. ii. App. p. 72). Syr-Sin. has "threescore."

Ἐμμαούς. The fortified town afterwards called Nicopolis cannot be meant, although all Christian writers from Eusebius to the twelfth century assume that it is meant. It is 176 stadia, or 20 English miles, from Jerusalem; and it is absurd to suppose that these two walked about 20 miles out, took their evening meal, walked 20 miles back, and arrived in time to find the disciples still gathered together and conversing (ver. 33). Yet Robinson contends for it (*Res. in Pal.* iii. pp. 147–151). *El Kubeibeh*, which is

63 stadia from Jerusalem, on the road to Lydda, is probably the place. It is about 7 miles N.W. of Jerusalem, in the beautiful Wady Beit Chanina, and the tradition in its favour dates from the crusades. Of other conjectures, *Kulonieh* and *Beit Mizzeh* are too near (36 to 40 stades), and *Khamasa* is not near enough (72 stades). But Caspari is very confident that *Kulonieh* is right (p. 242). See *D.B.*[2] and Schaff's *Herzog*, art. "Emmaus"; also Didon, *J. C.* App. U.

14. καὶ αὐτοὶ ὡμίλουν. If *αὐτοί* has any special force, it is "and *they* communed"—as well as those mentioned in ver. 10. Among the disciples this was the topic of conversation. The verb is peculiar to Lk. in N.T. (ver. 15; Acts xx. 11, xxiv. 26). The meaning of "converse, talk with" is classical, and survives in mod. Gk.

Vulg. leads the way in translating *ὁμιλεῖν* differently in ver. 14 (*loquebantur*, "talked" AV.) and ver. 15 (*fabularentur*, "communed" AV.). See footnote on ii. 9.

15. καὶ αὐτὸς Ἰησοῦς. B omits *καί*, which makes no difference to the sense, but is the common constr. after *ἐγένετο*: see note at the end of ch. i. "It came to pass . *that* Jesus *Himself*," about whom they were talking.

ἐγγίσας. He overtook them, for they assume that He comes from Jerusalem (ver. 18), from which they are walking.

16. ἐκρατοῦντο. There is no *need* to assume a special act of will on the part of Christ, "who would not be seen by them till the time when He saw fit." They were preoccupied and had no expectation of meeting Him, and there is good reason for believing that the risen Saviour had a glorified body which was not at once recognized. Comp. *ἐν ἑτέρᾳ μορφῇ* in the appendix to Mk. (xvi. 12), the terror of the disciples (ver. 37), the mistake of Mary Magdalen (Jn. xx. 14, 15), and the ignorance of the Apostles on the lake (Jn. xxi. 4). But it is quite possible that the Evangelist understands the non-recognition of Jesus here and the recognition of Him afterwards (ver. 31) to be the results of Divine volition. For **κρατεῖσθαι** comp. Acts ii. 24. See on xviii. 34.

τοῦ μή. This may mean either "in order that they might not" or "so that they did not." If the latter is adopted, the negative may be regarded as pleonastic. "Were holden from knowing" easily passes into "were holden so that they did not know," or "were holden that they might not know." Comp. *κατέπαυσαν τοῦ μὴ θύειν* (Acts xiv. 18); *κωλῦσαι τοῦ μὴ βαπτισθῆναι* (Acts x. 47); *οὐχ ὑπεστειλάμην τοῦ μὴ ἀναγγεῖλαι* (Acts xx. 27): see also Gen. xvi. 2; Ps. xxxiv. 14, etc.; Win. xliv. 4. b, p. 409. For *ἐπιγνῶναι* comp. Acts xii. 14, xxvii. 39.

17. ἀντιβάλλετε. Here only in N.T. and once only in LXX (2 Mac. xi. 3). It looks back to *συνζητεῖν* (ver. 15).

καὶ ἐστάθησαν σκυθρωποί. This is the reading of ℵ B, e Boh. Sah. It is supported by the *ἔστησαν* of L, and probably by the erasure in A. It is adopted by Tisch. Treg. WH. Weiss, RV., but contended against by Field, *Ot. Norv.* iii. p. 60. With this reading the question ends at *περιπατοῦντες*. For *σκυθρωποί* comp. Mt. vi. 16; Gen. xl. 7; Ecclus. xxv. 23.

18. ὀνόματι Κλεόπας. See on v. 27. The name is not to be identified with Κλωπᾶς (Jn. xix. 25), which is Aramaic, whereas Κλεόπας (= Κλεόπατρος) is Greek. The incorrect spelling *Cleophas* (AV.) comes from some Latin MSS. The mention of the name is a mark of reality.

Σὺ μόνος παροικεῖς Ἰερουσαλήμ. The pronoun is emphatic. The μόνος cannot mean "*only* a stranger" (AV.), but either "the only stranger" or "a lonely stranger," *i.e.* either "Dost thou alone sojourn at J.," or "Dost thou sojourn alone at J." The former is more probable: see Wetst. and Field for examples. The verb occurs only here and Heb. xi. 9 in N.T., but is common in LXX of being a stranger or sojourner (Gen. xxi. 23, 34, xxvi. 3, etc.). Comp. πάροικος (Acts vii. 6, 29) and παροικία (Acts xiii. 17). The usual construction would be ἐν Ἰερουσαλήμ: but we have γῆν ἣν παροικεῖς (Gen. xvii. 8; Exod. vi. 4).

19. Ποῖα; "What kind of things?" The question leads them on to open their hearts, and He is able to instruct them.

ὃς ἐγένετο ἀνὴρ προφήτης. "Who proved to be, showed Himself to be, a Prophet." The ἀνήρ is perhaps a mark of respect, as in addresses (Acts i. 16, ii. 29, 37, vii. 2, etc.); or mere amplification, προφήτης being a kind of adjective.

δυνατὸς ἐν ἔργῳ. Comp. Acts vii. 22, xviii. 24; Ecclus. xxi. 8; Judith xi. 8. In class. Grk. without ἐν. In *Ps. Sol.* xvii. 38, 42 we have both constructions, but in a sense different from this. With the order comp. 2 Thes. ii. 17: usually λόγος καὶ ἔργον.

ἐναντίον. He proved Himself to be all this before God and man; but no more than this. In thinking Him to be more they had made a mistake.

20. It is not out of any favour to the Romans (Renan) that Lk. does not mention their share in the crime. Lk. alone tells us that Roman soldiers mocked Jesus on the cross (xxiii. 36). And here their share (which was notorious and irrelevant) is implied in παρέδωκαν and ἐσταύρωσαν.

21. ἡμεῖς δὲ ἠλπίζομεν. "But *we* were hoping," until His death put an end to our expectation, "that precisely He," and no other, "was the one who should redeem Israel." Comp. the use of ὁ μέλλων in xxii. 23; Mt. xi. 14; Jn. xii. 4.

λυτροῦσθαι. "To cause to be released to oneself, set free for oneself the slave of another, redeem, ransom." Comp. Tit. ii. 14; Deut. xiii. 5; 2 Sam. vii. 23; Hos. xiii. 14.

The οἱ δὲ εἶπαν justifies us in concluding that *vv.* 19–24 were spoken partly by Cleopas and partly by his companion. But the attempt to assign definite portions to each (19, 20 to Cl., 21a to the other, 21b to Cl., and so on) is wasted ingenuity.

ἀλλά γε. The combination occurs elsewhere in N.T. 1 Cor. ix. 2. In class. Grk. another particle must immediately follow, and with this the γε coalesces, as ἀλλά γε δή or ἀλλά γε τοι. Otherwise a word or more must separate ἀλλά from γε. The force of the two is concessive. See Stallbaum on Plat. *Rep.* i. 331 B. The καί after ἀλλά γε is certainly genuine (B D L Δ 33, Arm.).

σὺν πᾶσιν τούτοις. *Super hæc omnia* (Vulg.): rather a lax use of σύν. Comp. Neh. v. 18; 3 Mac. i. 22. Syr-Sin. omits.

τρίτην ταύτην ἡμέραν ἄγει. The verb is probably impersonal: "one is keeping the third day, we are at the third day" (Grot. Beng. De W. Nösg. Wordsw. Hahn). Perhaps we may understand ὁ Ἰησοῦς (Mey. Godet, Weiss, Alf.): the speaker has an impression that there was a prediction about the third day. But it is not probable that either ὁ ἥλιος, or ὁ οὐρανός, or χρόνος, or Ἰσραήλ is to be supplied. Comp. περιέχει ἐν γραφῇ (1 Pet. ii. 6). The σήμερον after ἄγει (A P X Γ Δ etc. Syr-Pesh. Sah. Aeth. Vulg.) may be omitted (ℵ B L, Boh. Syr-Cur. Syr-Sin. Arm.) with Tisch. WH. RV.

22. ἀλλὰ καί. "*But*, in spite of this disappointment, there is *also* this favourable item."

ἐξ ἡμῶν: and therefore not wanton deceivers. With ἐξέστησαν comp. ἐξιστάνων Acts viii. 9: the trans. use is found nowhere else in N.T. There should perhaps be a colon at ἡμᾶς. To put a colon (AV.) or semicolon (RV.) at μνημεῖον implies that the being early at the tomb was the astonishing thing. Better "amazed us: having been early at the tomb and having failed to find His body, they came, saying," etc. ὀρθρινός is a later form of ὄρθριος.

23. ἦλθαν λέγουσαι . . . οἳ λέγουσιν. It is all hearsay evidence and unsatisfactory; but it is sufficiently disturbing. For the constr. see Burton, § 343.

24. ἀπῆλθάν τινες. If this refers to the visit of Peter and John, it confirms the view that ver. 12 was not part of the original narrative. The pleonastic καί before αἱ γυναῖκες ought probably to be omitted with B D and most Versions.

αὐτὸν δὲ οὐκ εἶδον. This was true of Peter and John: and perhaps Cleopas and his comrade had left Jerusalem without having heard that Mary Magdalen had said that she had seen Him. If they had heard it, like the rest, they had disbelieved it, and therefore do not think it worth mentioning.

25. ἀνόητοι. Four quite different Greek words are translated "fool" in AV.; ἀνόητος (elsewhere "foolish," Gal. iii. 1, 3; 1 Tim. vi. 9; Tit. iii. 3), ἄσοφος (Eph. v. 15), ἄφρων (xi. 40, xii. 20; 1 Cor. xv. 36, etc.), and μωρός Mt. v. 22, xxiii. 17, [19]; 1 Cor. iii. 18, iv. 10). The latter two are much stronger in meaning than the former two. Here the Latin translations vary between *insensati* (a c d e) and *stulti* (f Vulg.), as in xi. 40 between *insipientes* (c) and *stulti* (f Vulg.): xii. 20 and Mt. xxiii. 17 all have *stultus*, Mt. v. 22 all *fatuus*.

βραδεῖς . . . τοῦ πιστεύειν ἐπὶ πᾶσιν οἷς. The gen. is one of limitation depending upon βραδεῖς, which occurs here and Jas. i. 19 only. Comp. ἕτοιμοι τοῦ ἀνελεῖν (Acts xxiii. 15): ἕτοιμοι τοῦ ἐλθεῖν (1 Mac. v. 39). Elsewhere Lk. has the acc. after πιστεύειν ἐπί (Acts ix. 42, xi. 17, xvi. 31, xxii. 19), in all which cases the object of the belief is a *person*. The difference is between faith resting upon, and faith directed towards, an object. Note the characteristic attraction: see small print on iii. 19.

ἐπὶ πᾶσιν οἷς ἐλάλησαν οἱ προφῆται. There is special point in the *πᾶσιν*. Like most Jews, they remembered only the promises of the glories of the Messiah, and ignored the predictions of His sufferings. We cannot well separate *ἐπὶ πᾶσιν* from *πιστεύειν* and take *ἐπί* = "on the top of, after, in spite of": "slow of heart to believe, in spite of all that the Prophets have spoken" (Hahn). Still more unnatural is Hofmann's proposal to transfer these words to the next verse: "On the basis of all that the Prophets have spoken ought not Christ," etc.

26. οὐχὶ ταῦτα ἔδει. "Behoved it not the Christ to suffer these very things and thus enter into His glory?" According to the Divine decree respecting the Messiah as expressed in prophecy, precisely the things which these two had allowed to destroy their hopes were a confirmation of them. The *ταῦτα* stands first with emphasis: for *ἔδει* comp. ix. 22, xiii. 33, xvii. 25, etc. There is no need to understand *δεῖ* with *εἰσελθεῖν* in order to make it clear that He had not yet entered. Grammatically *ἔδει* belongs to both verbs, but it chiefly influences *παθεῖν*: the suffering comes first, and is the road to the glory. Comp. ver. 46. The same is said of Christ's followers Acts xiv. 22.

27. ἀπὸ Μωυσέως. For the form see on ii. 22. Such prophecies as Gen. iii. 15, xxii. 18; Num. xxiv. 17; Deut. xviii. 15, and such types as the scape-goat, the manna, the brazen serpent, and the sacrifices, are specially meant. Comp. Acts viii. 35.

καὶ ἀπὸ πάντων τῶν προφητῶν. This may be regarded as a lax construction not likely to be misunderstood: comp. *ἕτεροι κακοῦργοι δύο* (xxiii. 32). But this is not necessary, for with each Messianic passage there was a fresh start in the interpretation. It does not help much to say that Moses and the Prophets are here considered as one class in distinction from the rest of O.T., and that the meaning is that He began with these and thence passed to the Psalms (ver. 44) and other books (Hofm. Hahn). The repetition of the *ἀπό* shows that the Prophets are regarded as separate from the Pentateuch. The literal meaning of the characteristic *πάντων* and *πάσαις* may stand, but need not be pressed. There is nothing incredible in the supposition that He quoted from each one of the Prophets.

διερμήνευσεν (ℵ[c] B L U) supported by *διηρμήνευσεν* (M) is probably right, rather than *διερμήνευεν* (A G P X Γ Δ Λ) or *διηρμήνευεν* (E H K S V Π etc.). But instead of *ἀρξάμενος . . . διερμήνευσεν* we have in D *ἦν ἀρξάμενος ἀπὸ Μωυσέως καὶ π. τ. πρ. ἑρμηνεύειν*, *erat incipiens a mosen. et omnium propheetarum interpraetari* (d); also *erat incipiens . . . interpretans* (b ff_2 r), *fuit incipiens . . . interpretans* (c e). *erat inchoans . . . interpretans* (a). But f Vulg. have *et incipiens . . . interpretabatur*. The *καὶ διερμηνεύειν* of ℵ* points to some form of this Western reading.

διερμήνευσεν . . . τὰ περὶ ἑαυτοῦ. Comp. 1 Cor. xii. 30, xiv.

5, 13, 27. In Acts ix. 36 and 2 Mac. i. 36 the verb is used of interpreting a foreign language. Neither γεγραμμένα (De W. Mey Weiss) nor anything else is to be understood with τὰ περὶ ἑαυτοῦ: see small print on xxii. 37.

28. προσεποιήσατο. No unreal acting a part is implied. He began to take leave of them, and *would* have departed, had they not prayed Him to remain. Comp. His treatment of the disciples on the lake (Mk. vi. 48), and of the Syrophenician woman (Mk. vii. 27). Prayers are part of the chain of causation.

The Latin Versions suggest pretending what was not meant: *finxit se* (b c f ff_2), *dixit se* (l), *fecit se* (d), *simulavit se* (e), *adfectabat se* (a). But all of these, excepting the last, support προσεποιήσατο (א A B D L) against προσεποιεῖτο (P X Γ Δ Λ Π). The προσποιεῖσθαι did not continue. The verb does not occur elsewhere in N.T. Comp. Job xix. 14.

In this verse οὗ for οἷ or εἰς ἣν is genuine; not in xxii. 10.

29. παρεβιάσαντο. Moral pressure, especially by entreaty, is meant: Acts xvi. 15; Gen. xix. 9; 1 Sam. xxviii. 23; 2 Kings ii. 17, v. 16. In the last case the urgent entreaty is unsuccessful, and therefore the word does not imply compulsion. Comp. ἀνάγκασον εἰσελθεῖν (xiv. 23).

Μεῖνον μεθ' ἡμῶν. Combined with what follows, this implies a dwelling, which may have been the home of one of the two. Their allowing Him to preside does not prove that it was an inn. In their enthusiasm they naturally left the chief place to Him. On the other hand, μεθ' ἡμῶν is simply "in our company," not necessarily "at our house": comp. σὺν αὐτοῖς below.

πρὸς ἑσπέραν. Comp. Gen. viii. 11; Exod. xii. 6; Num. ix. 11; Zech. xiv. 7. The classical ἑσπέρα is very freq. in LXX, but in N.T. is peculiar to Lk. (Acts iv. 3, xxviii. 23). So also κλίνω of the declining day (ix. 12): comp. Jer. vi. 4.

The ἤδη after κέκλικεν (א B L 1 33, a b e f ff_2 Vulg. Boh.) is doubtless genuine. Syr-Cur. and Syr-Sin. paraphrase the sentence: "And they began to entreat Him that He would be (abide) with them, because it was nearly dark."

30. ἐν τῷ κατακλιθῆναι. "*After* He had sat down"; not "*as* He sat," etc. (AV.), nor *dum recumberet* (Vulg.): see on iii. 21. In N.T. the verb is peculiar to Lk. (vii. 36, ix. 14, 15, xiv. 8): see on ix. 14.

λαβὼν τὸν ἄρτον. "He took the bread" that was usual, or "the loaf" that was there. That this was a celebration of the eucharist (Theophylact), and a eucharist *sub unâ specie*, is an improbable hypothesis. To support it Maldonatus makes ἐν τῷ κατακλ. mean "after He had *supped*," as a parallel to μετὰ τὸ δειπνῆσαι (xxii. 20). But the imperf. ἐπεδίδου is against the theory of a eucharist. In the Last Supper there is no change from aor. to imperf. such as we have here and in the Miracles of the Five Thousand (κατέκλασεν καὶ ἐδίδου, ix. 16) and of the Four Thousand (ἔκλασεν καὶ ἐδίδου, Mk. viii. 6). In none of the Gospels is the imperf. used of the eucharist (xxii. 19; Mk. xiv. 22; Mt. xxvi. 26), nor in 1 Cor. xi. 23. Wordsworth, although he regards this as a eucharist, points out that "bread" was to the Jews a general name for food, including drink as well as meat; and that to "eat bread" and "break bread" are general terms for taking refreshment. That the bread was blessed in order that it might open the eyes of the disciples is also improbable: the εὐλόγησεν is the usual grace before meat. It was the breaking of the bread on the part of Jesus, rather than their own partaking of the bread, which helped them to see who He was: see ver. 35.

31. διηνοίχθησαν οἱ ὀφθαλμοί. This must be explained in harmony with ver. 16. If the one implies Divine interposition, so also does the other. These two had not been present at the Last Supper, but they had probably often seen Jesus preside at meals; and something in His manner of taking and breaking the bread, and of uttering the benediction, may have been the means employed to restore their power of recognizing Him. Wright's conjecture that the eucharist was instituted long before the Last Supper is unnecessary. Comp. Gen. xxi. 19; 2 Kings vi. 20; Gen. iii. 5, 7.

For the augment see WH. ii. App. p. 161. All three forms, ἠνοίχθην, ἀνεῴχθην, and ἠνεῴχθην, are found well attested in N.T. Gregory, *Prolegom.* p. 121. Syr-Cur. and Syr-Sin. add "immediately" to "were opened."

ἄφαντος ἐγένετο. "He vanished, became invisible": comp. ver. 37, vi. 36, xii. 40, xvi. 11, 12, xix. 17. It is very unnatural to take ἐγένετο with ἀπ' αὐτῶν and make ἄφαντος adverbial: "He departed from them without being seen." Something more than a sudden departure, or a departure which they did not notice until He was gone, is intended. We are to understand disappearance without physical locomotion: but we know too little about the properties of Christ's risen body to say whether this was supernatural or not. Nowhere else in bibl. Grk. does ἄφαντος occur: in class. Grk. it is poetical. In 2 Mac. iii. 34 ἀφανεῖς ἐγένοντο is used of Angels ceasing to be visible. The ἀπ' αὐτῶν implies no more than withdrawal from their sight: to what extent His presence was withdrawn we have no means of knowing. But His object was accomplished; viz. to convince them that He was the Messiah and still alive, and that their hopes had not been in vain. To abide with them in the old manner was not His object.

The Latin Versions vary much, but none of them suggest a mere quiet withdrawal: *nusquam comparuit ab eis* (c e ff_2) or *illis* (a), *non comparuit ab eis* (d r), *invisus factus est eis* (b f), *non apparens factus est ab eis* (δ), *evanuit ex oculis eorum* (Vulg.). Syr-Sin. has "He was lifted away from them": so also Syr-Cur. Respecting Jos. *Ant.* xx. 8. 6 see p. xxx.

32. καιομένη ἦν. The periphrastic tense emphasizes the continuance of the emotion. Common and natural as the metaphor is, it seems to have been misunderstood; and hence the reading κεκαλυμμένη (D), perhaps from 2 Cor. iii. 14–16; while *excæcatum* (c), and *optusum* (l) seem to imply πεπηρωμένη as another correction. Other variations are *exterminatum* (e) and *gravatum* (Syr-Cur. Syr-Sin. Sah. Arm.). They regard the glow in their hearts as further proof that it was indeed Jesus who was with them as they walked.

ὡς ἐλάλει . . . ὡς διήνοιγεν. "While He was speaking . . . while He was opening." Note the asyndeton and the use of the same verb for the opening of their eyes and the opening of the Scriptures.

33–43. § The Manifestation to the Eleven and the other Disciples at Jerusalem. We cannot determine whether this is the same appearance as Jn. xx. 19. If it is, then τοὺς ἕνδεκα is not exact, for on that occasion Thomas was absent; and in any case it is improbable that he was present. If he was, why was the incident which convinced him delayed for a week? Can we suppose that he withdrew between *vv.* 35, 36? It is much simpler to suppose that "the Eleven" is used inaccurately.

33. αὐτῇ τῇ ὥρᾳ. "That very hour": comp. x. 7. The lateness of the hour, which they had urged upon their guest (ver. 29), does not deter them. Note the characteristic **ἀναστάντες** (i. 39, iv. 29, etc.) and **ὑπέστρεψαν** (i. 56, ii. 20, 43, 45, iv. 1, etc.). It was in order that others might share their great joy that they returned at once to Jerusalem. Yet D c d e Sah. insert λυπούμενοι (*tristes*, *contristati*) after ἀναστάντες.

ἠθροισμένους. This is the reading of ℵ B D 33, adopted by all the best editors. The verb is not rare in LXX, but occurs here only in N.T. TR. has συνηθρ. with A L P X etc., a verb which is found in N.T. only in Acts xii. 12, xix. 25.

τοὺς σὺν αὐτοῖς. Much the same as πάντες οἱ λοιποί (ver. 9). Comp. Acts i. 14.

34. λέγοντας. This was the statement with which the assembled disciples greeted the two from Emmaus. The appendix to Mk. cannot be reconciled with this. There we are told that, so far from the two being met by news that the Lord was risen, their own story was not believed (xvi. 13).

ὤφθη Σίμωνι. There is no other mention of this manifestation in the Gospels; but S. Paul quotes it in the first rank as evidence of the Resurrection (1 Cor. xv. 5): and this coincidence between the Evangelist and the Apostle cannot well be accidental. It confirms the belief that this Gospel is the work of one who was intimate with S. Paul. For **ὤφθη** see on xxii. 43. This manifestation apparently took place after the two had started for Emmaus and before the disciples assembled at Jerusalem. The Apostle "most in need of comfort was the first to receive it." But Lange is fanciful when he adds, "We here learn that after his fall Peter named himself, and was named in the Church, Simon, not Peter" (*L. of C.* iii. p. 387). See on vi. 14.

35. καὶ αὐτοὶ ἐξηγοῦντο. "And they on their side rehearsed." Excepting Jn. i. 18, the verb occurs only here and Acts x. 8, xv. 12, 14, xxi. 19. Note that the Lord's breaking of the bread, and not their partaking of it, is spoken of as the occasion of their recognizing Him. Syr-Sin. has "as He brake bread."

36. ἔστη ἐν μέσῳ. A sudden appearance, analogous to the sudden disappearance (ver. 31), is intended. See on viii. 7. On the words *καὶ λέγει αὐτοῖς Εἰρήνη ὑμῖν*, which look like a very early insertion from Jn. xx. 19, see note at the end of the chapter. They express what is true in fact, but is probably not part of the original text of Lk.

37. πτοηθέντες δέ. There is some confusion of text here. This is the reading of A L P X Γ Δ etc. supported by *conturbatique* (b ff_2), *turbati autem* (c e), *et conturbati* (l), *conturbati vero* (f Vulg.). But D has *αὐτοὶ δὲ πτοηθέντες*, *ipsi autem paverunt* (d), ℵ *φοβηθέντες δέ*, *exterriti autem* (a), and B *θροηθέντες*. The last may possibly be right. Syr-Sin. has "shaken" both here and for *τεταραγμένοι* in ver. 38.

πνεῦμα. "The disembodied spirit of a dead person, a ghost." Comp. *φάντασμα* (Mt. xiv. 26), which D has here. Thomas would explain away their evidence by maintaining that this first impression respecting what they saw was the right one. For **ἔμφοβοι γενόμενοι** see on ver. 5; and for this use of *πνεῦμα* comp. 1 Pet. iii. 19. To introduce the notion of an *evil* spirit is altogether out of place.

38. τί . . . καὶ διὰ τί. So in ℵ A X Γ Δ Λ* Π, *quid . . . et quare*, a b c e f ff_2 l Syr-Cur. "Why . . . and wherefore" RV. But D L have *τί . . . ἵνα τί*, and B $Λ^2$ *τί . . . τί*, Syr-Sin. has Why . . . why, Tert. *quid . . . quid*. Vulg. inaccurately omits the second *quid*.

ἀναβαίνουσιν ἐν τῇ καρδίᾳ ὑμῶν. So A* (?) B D, *in corde vestro* (a b c e ff_2 l. Sah. Aeth.); for which *ἐν ταῖς καρδίαις ὑμῶν* (ℵ A^1 L X Γ Δ etc.), *in cordibus vestris* (f Syr-Sin.), is an obvious correction. Vulg. is again the least accurate with *in corda vestra*. Nowhere else does *ἀναβ. ἐν τῇ καρδίᾳ* occur: elsewhere *ἐπὶ τὴν κ.* (Acts vii. 23) or *ἐπὶ καρδίαν* (1 Cor. ii. 9; Jer. iii. 16).

39. ἴδετε τὰς χεῖράς μου καὶ τοὺς πόδας. This seems to imply that His feet as well as His hands had been nailed. Jesus first convinces them of His identity,—that He is the Master whom they supposed that they had lost; and secondly of the reality of His body,—that it is not merely the spirit of a dead Master that they see.

Tyn. Cov. Cran. Gen. AV. all have "Behold . . . see" for *ἴδετε . . . ἴδετε*. Wic. Rhem. RV. follow *videte . . . videte* of Vulg. with "See . . .

see." The first refers to the test of identity, the sight of the wound-prints, the second to the test of reality, the sense of touch.

ψηλαφήσατέ με. 1 Jn. i. 1 seems to be a direct reference to this passage: the same verb is used. The remarkable quotation in Ignatius (*Smyr.* iii. 1) should be compared: *ὅτε πρὸς τοὺς περὶ Πέτρον ἦλθεν, ἔφη αὐτοῖς· Λάβετε, ψηλαφήσατέ με, καὶ ἴδετε ὅτι οὐκ εἰμὶ δαιμόνιον ἀσώματον.* Eusebius (*H. E.* iii. 36. 11) does not know whence Ignatius got these words. Jerome more than once gives the *Gospel according to the Hebrews* as the source of the saying about the *incorporale dæmonium.* Origen says that it comes from the *Teaching of Peter.* As all three writers knew the *Gospel according to Hebrews* well, the testimony is perplexing. We may conjecture that Origen is right, that Eusebius had never seen the passage, and that Jerome's memory has failed him. That it is quite possible to forget much of a book that one has translated, every translator will admit. See Lft. on Ign. *Smyr.* iii.

ὅτι πνεῦμα. Once more an ambiguous ὅτι: comp. xix. 31, 43, xxii. 70, etc. But "because" or "for" (AV. RV. Nösg. Godet, Weiss) is much more probable than "that" (Mey. Hahn). Comp. *οὐ γὰρ ἔτι σάρκας τε καὶ ὀστέα ἶνες ἔχουσιν* (Hom. *Od.* xi. 219).

40. The evidence against this verse is exactly the same as against the doubtful words in ver. 36 with the addition of Syr-Cur. It may be regarded as an adaptation of Jn. xx. 20, *καὶ τὴν πλευράν* being changed into *καὶ τοὺς πόδας* to suit ver. 39. Apelles in Hipp. *Ref.* vii. 26 combines the two, *δείξαντα τοὺς τύπους τῶν ἥλων καὶ τῆς πλευρᾶς.* Tertullian uses ver. 40 to answer Marcion's perversion of ver. 39 (iv. 43). See note p. 568.

41. ἀπιστούντων αὐτῶν ἀπὸ τῆς χαρᾶς. A remark, "which, with many similar expressions, we owe to the most profound psychologist among the Evangelists." *Vix sibimet ipsi præ necopinato gaudio credentes* (Livy, xxxix. 49). For this use of *ἀπό* comp. xxi. 26, xxii. 45; Acts xii. 14; Mt. xiii. 44, xiv. 26, etc.

Ἔχετέ τι βρώσιμον ἐνθάδε; The objection that, if Jesus took food in order to convince them that He was no mere spirit, when food was not necessary for the resurrection-body, He was acting deceitfully, does not hold. The alternative—"either a ghost, or an ordinary body needing food"—is false. There is a third possibility: a glorified body, capable of receiving food. Is there any deceit in taking food, which one does not want, in order to place others, who are needing it, at their ease? With the double sign granted here, the handling and the seeing Him eat, comp. the double sign with Moses' rod and hand (Exod. iv. 1–8), and with Gideon's fleece (Judg. vi. 36–40). For **βρώσιμον** comp. Lev. xix. 23; Ezek. xlvii. 12; Neh. ix. 25: not elsewhere in N.T.

ἐνθάδε: rare in LXX, and in N.T., excepting Jn. iv. 15, 16 peculiar to Lk. (Acts x. 18, xvi. 28, xvii. 6, xxv. 17, 24).

42. καὶ ἀπὸ μελισσίου κηρίου. The evidence against these words is far stronger than against any of the other doubtful passages in this chapter (*vv.* 3, 6, 9, 12, 36, 40, 51, 52). Here ℵ A B D L, d e Boh. Syr-Sin. omit the whole, while a b omit *mellis*. Clem-Alex. Orig. Eus. Cyr-Alex. speak of the broiled fish in a way which makes it very improbable that they would have omitted the honey-comb, had it been contained in their copies of the Gospel. N X are the best uncials which contain the words, and of these X with E* has κηρίον for κηρίου. Even Godet admits that not only here, but in *vv.* 36 and 40, the disputed words are probably interpolations.

43. ἐνώπιον αὐτῶν ἔφαγεν. Comp. οἵτινες συνεφάγομεν καὶ συνεπίομεν αὐτῷ μετὰ τὸ ἀναστῆναι αὐτὸν ἐκ νεκρῶν (Acts x. 41). Nothing is said here or in the meal at Emmaus about drinking, but are we to infer that nothing was drunk?

K Π and some cursives with many Versions (Syr-Cur. Syr-Hier. Boh. Aeth. Arm. c Vulg.) after ἔφαγεν add καὶ [λαβὼν] τὰ ἐπίλοιπα ἔδωκεν αὐτοῖς, *sumens reliquias dedit eis*.

44–49. Christ's Farewell Instructions. This section seems to be a condensation of what was said by Christ to the Apostles between the Resurrection and the Ascension, partly on Easter Day and partly on other occasions. But we have no sure data by which to determine what was said that same evening, and what was spoken later. Thus Lange assigns only ver. 44 to Easter Day, Godet at least *vv.* 44, 45, Euthymius *vv.* 44–49, while Meyer and others assign all the remaining verses also (44–53) to this same evening. On the other hand Didon would give the whole of this section to a later occasion, after the manifestations in Galilee. It is evident that the command to remain ἐν τῇ πόλει (ver. 49) cannot have been given until after those manifestations, and was almost certainly given in Jerusalem.

44. Εἶπεν δὲ πρὸς αὐτούς. This new introduction points to a break of some kind between *vv.* 43 and 44; but whether of moments or of days we cannot be certain. It is probable that Lk. himself, when he wrote his Gospel, did not know what the interval was. This was one of several points about which he had obtained more exact information when he wrote the first chapter of the Acts.

Οὗτοι οἱ λόγοι. "These are My words, which I spake unto you formerly (and repeat now), viz. that all things," etc.

ἔτι ὢν σὺν ὑμῖν: refers to His intercourse with them before His death, a mode of intercourse which is entirely at an end: comp. Acts ix. 39. Not that the new intercourse will be less close or continuous, but it will be of a different kind. His being visible is now the exception and not the rule, and He is ceasing to share in the externals of their lives. That the words refer to what He said during the walk to Emmaus (ver. 26) is most improbable. Christ is addressing all the disciples present, not merely those who walked with Him to Emmaus. Such passages as xviii. 31–33 and ix. 22 are meant.

ἐν τῷ νόμῳ Μωυσέως καὶ [τοῖς] προφήταις καὶ ψαλμοῖς. This is the only place in N.T. in which the tripartite division of the Hebrew Canon of Scripture is clearly made. But it does not prove that the Canon was at this time fixed and closed; nor need we suppose that "Psalms" here means the whole of the *Kethubim* or Hagiographa. Of that division of the Jewish Scriptures the Psalter was the best known and most influential book; and, moreover, it contained very much about the Messiah. Hence it is naturally singled out as representative of the group. In the prologue to Ecclesiasticus we have the tripartite division in three slightly different forms (1) "the Law and the Prophets and others that have followed their steps"; (2) "the Law and the Prophets and other books of our fathers"; (3) "the Law and the Prophets and the rest of the books." Elsewhere we have "the Law and the Prophets" (xvi. 16; Mt. vii. 12); "Moses and the Prophets" (xvi. 29, 31, xxiv. 27); and "the Law of Moses and the Prophets" (Acts xxviii. 23); where the third division is not to be regarded as excluded because not specially mentioned. Ryle, *Canon of the O.T.* pp. 150, 191, 291.

Note that the prep. is not repeated with either προφήταις or ψαλμοῖς, and that the art. is not repeated with ψαλμοῖς and not quite certainly with προφήταις: the three divisions are regarded as one storehouse of Messianic prophecy. The evidence stands thus: καὶ προφήταις (A D N X Γ Δ Λ Π, *et prophetis* Latt.), καὶ τοῖς προφήταις (B, Boh.), ἐν τοῖς προφ. (ℵ), καὶ ἐν τοῖς προφ. (L).

45. This opening of their understanding is analogous to that in ver. 31. Comp. Acts xvi. 14, xxvi. 18; 2 Mac. i. 4. Godet regards this as parallel to "He breathed on them, and saith unto them, Receive ye the Holy Ghost" (Jn. xx. 22). It was by the gift of the Spirit that their minds were open to understand. Contrast xviii. 34. D has διήνυξεν (*sic*) αὐτῶν τὸν νοῦν, but d has *adaperti sunt eorum sensus*.

46. Godet would put a full stop at γραφάς and make καὶ εἶπεν αὐτοῖς introduce a fresh summary of what was said, possibly on another occasion. It is very unnatural to make ὅτι mean "because" or "for," and take it as the beginning of Christ's words. "He opened their minds and (in explanation of this act) said to them, Because thus it is written," etc. (Mey.). It is more doubtful whether ὅτι introduces the *oratio recta* (Weiss, Hahn), in which case it is left untranslated (AV. RV.), or the *oratio obliqua* (Rhem.).

οὕτως γέγραπται παθεῖν τὸν Χριστόν. Thus ℵ B C* L, Aeth. Syr-Harcl. So also D, a b c d e ff_2 l r Boh., but with τὸν Χριστὸν before παθεῖν. Syr-Sin. and Arm. substitute for γέγραπται the ἔδει of the similar ver. 26, while A C² N X Γ Δ Λ Π, f q Vulg. insert καὶ οὕτως ἔδει after γέγραπται, and c e Cypr. omit *οὕτως*. All are attempts to get rid of abruptness, and perhaps the reading of A C² etc. is a conflation of ℵ B etc. with Syr-Sin. and Arm. D omits *ἐκ νεκρῶν*.

For the aor. infin. referring to what is future in reference to the main verb see Burton, § 114.

47. ἐπὶ τῷ ὀνόματι αὐτοῦ. "On the basis of all that His name implies": it is His Messiahship which makes repentance effectual. Comp. the use of *ἐπὶ τῷ ὀν.* ix. 48, xxi. 8; Acts iv. 17, 18, v. 28, 40, etc.

μετάνοιαν εἰς ἄφεσιν ἁμαρτιῶν. The *εἰς* (ℵ B, Boh. Syr.) was corrected to *καί* (A C D N X etc.) on account of the second *εἰς*. The *εἰς* is confirmed by iii. 3; Mt. xxvi. 28; Mk. i. 4: comp. *τὴν μετάνοιαν εἰς ζωήν* (Acts xi. 18). Comp. also Mt. xxviii. 19.

ἀρξάμενοι. It is difficult to decide between taking this as a rather violent anacoluthon, as if "that ye should preach" had preceded, and making it the beginning of a new sentence, "Beginning from Jerusalem ye are witnesses of these things." The former is perhaps better. The correction *ἀρξάμενον* (A C³ etc.) is meant to agree with *τὸν Χριστόν*, or perhaps to be an impers. acc. abs. like *ἐξόν*, *παρόν*. Comp. *ἀπὸ δὲ Ποσειδηΐου πόλιος, ἀρξάμενον ἀπὸ ταύτης μέχρι Αἰγύπτου* (Hdt. iii. 91. 1). The priority of the Jewish nation in its right to the Gospel is still acknowledged, in spite of their rejection of the Messiah. D has *ἀρξαμένων*, d *incipientium*.

48. ὑμεῖς μάρτυρες τούτων. The omission of *ἐστέ* is against taking *ἀρξάμενοι ἀπὸ Ἰερ.* with this clause. That *ἐστέ* is rightly omitted (B D, Aeth. Aug.) is shown by its being inserted sometimes before (ℵ A C³ L etc.) sometimes after (C*) *μάρτυρες*. A C² X Γ etc. have *ὑμεῖς δέ*, D *καὶ ὑμεῖς δέ*. ℵ B C* L, Boh. Syr-Harcl. have *ὑμεῖς* alone. The omission of both conjunction and verb makes the sentence more forcible and *ὑμεῖς* more emphatic. That bearing testimony respecting the Passion and Resurrection was one of the main functions of an Apostle is manifest from Acts i. 8, 22, ii. 32, iii. 15, v. 32, x. 39, 41, etc.

49. καὶ ἰδοὺ ἐγώ. The *ἐγώ* balances the preceding *ὑμεῖς*. "I have told you your part: this is mine." The *ἰδού* is wanting in ℵ D L, Latt. Boh. Syr-Sin. The combination *ἰδοὺ ἐγώ* (xxiii. 14; Acts x. 21, xx. 22) is extraordinarily frequent in LXX.

ἐξαποστέλλω τὴν ἐπαγγελίαν. Present of what will come in the immediate and certain future. Here first in the Gospels have we *ἐπαγγελία* in the technical sense of the "promise of God to His people": see on Rom. i. 2. The gift of the Spirit is specially meant: comp. Is. xliv. 3; Ezek. xxxvi. 27; Joel ii. 28; Zech. xii. 10. "The promise" therefore means the thing promised. For *ἰδοὺ ἐγὼ ἐξαποστέλλω* comp. Jer. viii. 17; *ἰδοὺ ἐγὼ ἀποστέλλω*, vii. 27; Mt. x. 16; Mal. iv. 4 [iii. 23]: ℵ* A C D N Γ Λ Π have *ἀποστέλλω* here. In Jn. xv. 26 and xvi. 7, where, as here, Christ speaks of the Spirit as His gift, *πέμψω* is used: in Jn. xiv. 16 the Father *δώσει* at the petition of Christ.

ὑμεῖς δὲ καθίσατε ἐν τῇ πόλει. Once more an emphatic contrast between *ἐγώ* and *ὑμεῖς*. For *καθίζειν* of spending some time in a place comp. Acts xviii. 11; Exod. xvi. 29; Judg. xi. 17, xix. 4; Ruth iii. 1 [ii. 23]; 1 Sam. i. 23, etc. With the command here given comp. Acts i. 4. To suppose that it was spoken on Easter Day involves a contradiction with Mt. xxviii. 7, 10, 16; Mk. xvi. 7; Jn. xxi. 1. It implies patient waiting.

ἐνδύσησθε . . δύναμιν. The metaphor is common both in N.T. and LXX: Rom. xiii. 14; 1 Cor. xv. 53; Gal. iii. 27; Col. iii. 10; Eph. iv. 24; Job viii. 22, xxix. 14, xxxix. 19; Ps. xxxiv. 26, xcii. 1, etc. There is no need to discuss whether the Spirit is the δύναμις or confers it.

According to the best texts (ℵ B C* L 33, Eus. Syr-Hier.) ἐξ ὕψους precedes δύναμιν and immediately follows ἐνδύσησθε, to which it belongs. Comp. Is. xxxii. 15.

50–53. The Ascension and the Conclusion of the Gospel. It is not improbable that, at the time when he wrote his Gospel, Lk. did not know the exact amount of interval between the Resurrection and the Ascension. That was a piece of information which he may easily have gained between the publication of the Gospel and of the Acts. And while he does not state either here or ver. 44 that there was any interval at all, still less does he say that there was none: there is no ἐν αὐτῇ τῇ ἡμέρᾳ (ver. 13). Being without knowledge, or not considering the matter of importance, he says nothing about the interval. But it is incredible that he can mean that, late at night (*vv.* 29, 33), Jesus led them out to Bethany, and ascended in the dark. So remarkable a feature would hardly have escaped mention. Probably δέ both here and in ver. 44 introduces a new occasion.

50. ἕως πρὸς Βηθανίαν. It is doubtful whether this can mean "until they were *over against* Bethany." Field regards πρός after ἕως as a mere expletive and compares καὶ ἀφίκετο ἕως πρὸς ἄνθρωπόν τινα Ὀδολλαμίτην (Gen. xxxviii. 1). In LXX ἕως εἰς is common, and many texts (A C³ X Γ Δ Λ Π) substitute ἕως εἰς here for ἕως πρός (ℵ B C* L). D has πρός without ἕως. The ἔξω after αὐτούς (A C³ D X etc.) is omitted by ℵ B C* L 33, a c Boh. Syr. Arm.

The well-known passage in the *Epistle of Barnabas* (xv. 9) is probably only a clumsily expressed explanation for keeping Sunday as a day of joy; viz. because Jesus on that day rose from the dead, and (not to die again, as Lazarus and others,—on the contrary) manifested Himself and ascended into heaven. Διὸ καὶ ἄγομεν τὴν ἡμέραν τὴν ὀγδόην εἰς εὐφροσύνην, ἐν ᾗ καὶ ὁ Ἰησοῦς ἀνέστη ἐκ νεκρῶν, καὶ φανερωθεὶς ἀνέβη εἰς οὐρανούς. Grammatically ἐν ᾗ belongs to ἀνέβη as well as to ἀνέστη, and with Hefele we must admit the possibility that Barnabas believed that the Ascension took place on Sunday. But Funk is right in saying that ἐν ᾗ is perhaps not intended to go beyond ἀνέστη ἐκ νεκρῶν. Dressel's expedient, however, of putting a full stop at ἐκ νεκρῶν, is rather violent. Harmer does not place even a comma between the clauses.

51. διέστη ἀπ' αὐτῶν. "Parted, withdrew from them." The verb is peculiar to Lk. in N.T. (xxii. 59; Acts xxvii. 28). This refers to the Ascension, whatever view we take of the disputed words which follow. Weiss holds that, if the doubtful words are rejected, we must interpret διέστη of mere withdrawal, as after previous appearances; and that Lk. purposely reserves the narrative of the Ascension for the Acts. But at least a *final* departure is meant. It is evident that ver. 50 is preparatory to a final withdrawal, and that *vv.* 52, 53 are subsequent to such an event. And was there ever a time when Lk. could have known of Christ's final withdrawal without knowing of the Ascension? In the Acts (i. 1, 2) he expressly states that ὁ πρῶτος λόγος contained an account of the work of Jesus ἄχρι ἧς ἡμέρας . . . ἀνελήμφθη. He himself, therefore, considered that he had recorded the Ascension in his Gospel. See Hastings, *D.B.* i. p. 161; *D.C.G.* i. p. 124.

καὶ ἀνεφέρετο εἰς τὸν οὐρανόν. The important witnesses which omit the disputed words in *vv.* 3, 6, 9, 36, 40 are here joined by ℵ* and Aug. No motive for their omission, if they were in the original document, can be suggested. They look like a gloss on διέστη: but it is conceivable that Lk. himself (or Theophilus) may have added them in a second edition of the Gospel, in order to make it quite clear what διέστη ἀπ' αὐτῶν meant. See p. 569. Note the change from aor. to imperf.

52. προσκυνήσαντες αὐτόν. This again is either a very ancient gloss or an insertion made by the Evangelist in a second copy. See the note at the end of the chapter. Comp. Mt. xxviii. 17.

ὑπέστρεψαν εἰς Ἰερουσαλήμ: in obedience to καθίσατε ἐν τῇ πόλει (ver. 49).

μετὰ χαρᾶς μεγάλης. A writer of fiction would have made them lament the departure of their Master: comp. Jn. xiv. 28, xvi. 6, 7, 20, 22, 24.

Note how the marks of Lk.'s style continue to the end. In ver. 51 we have ἐγένετο, ἐν τῷ εὐλογεῖν, διέστη: in ver. 52 καὶ αὐτοί, ὑπέστρεψαν, and the addition of μέγας to an expression of emotion (ii. 9, 10, viii. 37; Acts v. 5, 11, xv. 3).

53. ἦσαν διὰ παντὸς ἐν τῷ ἱερῷ. These words are to be taken together: ἦσαν does not belong to the participle, and this is not an example of the periphrastic imperf. (Hahn). The continued attendance of the disciples in the temple is recorded in the Acts (ii. 46, iii. 1, v. 21, 42). It savours of childish captiousness to find a contradiction between διὰ παντός here and Acts i. 13, where it is stated, and ii. 44, where it is implied, that the Apostles were sometimes elsewhere than in the temple. No reasonable critic would suppose that διὰ παντός is meant with absolute strict ness. It is a popular expression, implying great frequency in their attendance both at the services and at other times. Comp. what is said of Anna, ii. 37, which is stronger in wording and may mean more.

Lachm. Treg. WH. Weiss write διὰ παντός, while Tisch. Wordsw. and the Revisers prefer διαπαντός. Comp. Acts ii. 25, x. 2, xxiv. 16; Mt. xviii. 10; Mk. v. 5, etc.

εὐλογοῦντες. The reading is uncertain. There is little doubt that αἰνοῦντες καὶ εὐλογοῦντες (A C² X Γ Δ Π, c f q Vulg. Syr-Pesh. Syr-Harcl. Arm.) and εὐλογοῦντες καὶ αἰνοῦντες (Aeth.) is a conflation. But is αἰνοῦντες (D, a b d ff$_2$ l Boh. Aug. Tisch.) or εὐλογοῦντες (ℵ B C* L, Syr-Sin. Syr-Hier. Weiss, WH. RV.) the original? The fact that αἰνοῦντες is a favourite word with Lk. does not turn the scale in its favour: εὐλογοῦντες might be corrected to αἰνοῦντες for this very reason. See WH. ii. p. 104, where the distribution of evidence in this and similar instances of conflation is tabulated. Comp. ix. 10, xi. 54, xii. 18. See Introduction, p. lxxiii.

The various conjectures as to why the disciples were so joyous and thankful may all be right: but they remain conjectures. Because of the promised gift of the Spirit (Euthym.); because of the Lord's teaching and blessing (Mey. Weiss); because of His glorious return to the Father, which was a pledge of the victory of His cause (Godet); because His Ascension confirmed all their beliefs and hopes (Maldon.); because His presence with God was a guarantee for the fulfilment of His promises and an earnest of their own success (Hahn).

Ἀμήν: probably not genuine, but a liturgical addition. It is absent from ℵ C* D L Π, several cursives, a b d e ff$_2$ l Syr-Sin. etc.

Western Non-interpolations.

Unless Mt. xxvii. 49 and Lk. xii. 11 (ἤ τί) are to be regarded as examples, all the instances of Western non-interpolations are found in the last three chapters of S. Luke. In ch. xxiv. they are surprisingly frequent. The opposite phenomenon of interpolation is among the most marked characteristics of the Western texts. And although omissions also are not uncommon, yet Western omissions for the most part explain themselves as attempts to make the sense more forcible.

But there are cases in which the absence of words or passages from Western authorities, and their presence in other texts, cannot be explained in this way. In these cases the more satisfactory explanation seems to be that it is the other texts which have been enlarged, while the Western documents, by escaping interpolation, have preserved the original reading in its simplicity.

It is evident that these insertions in the original text (if insertions they be) must have been made very early: otherwise they could not have become diffused in every text excepting the Western. Alexandrian corruptions which have spread widely are a common phenomenon. But these insertions have a different aspect; and neither internal nor external evidence favours such a theory of their origin. We must look elsewhere for an explanation. That the original readings should be preserved nowhere else but in a text which is wholly Western is so unusual a result that there is nothing extravagant in assuming an unusual cause for it.

It must sometimes have happened in ancient times that authors, having published their MS. and caused it to be multiplied, afterwards issued revised copies with corrections and insertions. In the cases before us "the purely documentary phenomena are compatible with the supposition that the Western and the Non-Western texts started respectively from a first and a second edition of the Gospels, *both conceivably apostolic* (WH. ii. p. 177)." This conjectural source of variations, viz. changes made in later copies by the authors themselves, is accepted by Scrivener as a general possibility (Scriv-Miller, i. p. 18), and is suggested as specially applicable to the latter part of S. Luke's Gospel (ii. pp. 298, 299 n.). Blass regards this as highly probable with regard to the Acts. Lk. made a rough copy first on cheap material, and then a better copy to give to Theophilus, who was a person of distinction. In this second copy he made alterations. But both remained in existence and became the parent of other copies, the Western text being derived from the rough draft, and the more widely diffused text from the presentation copy.[1] Salmon thinks that something of the same kind "took place with St. Luke's Gospel; and that in the case of the Gospel, as well as in that of the Acts, it was the first draft which went into circulation in the West." He supposes that the second edition of the Gospel was about contemporary with the Acts, and that between the two writings Luke had conversed with a witness able to give him additional information about the Lord's sayings and the Ascension. Having just written the full account of the latter in the Acts, he added a word or two to Lk. xxiv. 51, 52. "And since in Luke's account of the dying words of Stephen (Acts vii. 59, 60) we find an echo of two of the utterances which the common text of St. Luke's Gospel places in the mouth of the dying Saviour, I find it hard to regard the coincidence as fortuitous, and but the lucky hit of an unknown interpolator" (*App. to Hist. Int. to N.T.* 7th ed. p. 603). See also Rendel Harris, *Four Lectures on the Western Text*, Camb. 1894, p. 62. A theory such as this certainly is very welcome as an explanation of Lk. xxii. 43, 44 and xxiii. 34a, although neither of them can be called *Western* non-interpolations. But in other cases the apparent insertions are perhaps scarcely worthy of so high an origin: *e.g.* the non-Western insertions in xxiv. 3, 6, 9 seem to be about on a level with Western insertions. See WH. ii. pp. 175–177.

The question cannot be regarded as settled; but, assuming that there are such textual phenomena as Western non-interpolations, the more manifest examples are Lk. xxii. 19b, 20, xxiv. 3, 6, 9, 12, 36, 40, 51, 52. To which may be added as a possible instance in a secondary degree xxii. 62.

(1) xxii. 19b, 20. τὸ ὑπὲρ ὑμῶν διδόμενον . . . ἐκχυννόμενον.

Evidence for the passage:—

ℵ A B C E F G H K L M (P R defective here) S U X V Γ Δ Λ Π and all cursives.

Almost all Versions.

Marcion or Tertull. Cyr-Alex.

Evidence against the passage:—

D omits.

a d ff_2 i l omit.

b e Syr-Cur. omit and put *vv.* 17, 18 in the place of the omitted passage, so that the verses run—16, 19a [b], 17, 18, 21, 22, etc. Syr-Sin. has an elaborate transposition:—16, 19a b, 20a, 17, 20b, 18, 21, 22, etc. It also exhibits considerable changes in the wording.

But in order to appreciate these various attempts to get rid of the difficulty involved in the ordinary text, owing to the mention of two cups, it is necessary to see them in full in a tabular form.

Cod. Veron. (b).	*Cod. Palat.* (e).
[19] et accepto pane gratias egit et fregit et dedit illis dicens hoc est corpus meum [17] et accepto calice gratias egit et dixit accipite hoc et dividite inter vos [18] dico enim vobis . . . . . veniat. [21] veruntamen ecce, etc.	[19] et accepit panem et gratias egit et fregit et dedit eis dicens hoc est corpus meum [17] et accepit calicem et gratias egit et dixit accipite vivite inter vos [18] dico enim vobis . . . . . . veniat. [21] veruntamen ecce, etc.

[1] *Apostolorum Acta*, Fr. Blass, Gœttingen, 1895, § 13, p. 32.

It is obvious that these two Latin texts represent one and the same Greek original. There is much more difference between the two Syriac Versions, of which Syr-Cur. agrees more with the Latin texts than with its fellow.

Syr-Cur.

[19] And He took bread and when He had given thanks, He brake it, and gave to them, saying, This is My body, which (is given) for you: this do in remembrance of Me. [17] And He received a cup, and when He had given thanks, He said, Take this and divide it among yourselves: [18] for I say to you, I will . . . . come. [21] But behold, etc.

Syr-Sin.

[19] And He took bread and gave thanks over it, and brake, and gave unto them, saying, This is My body which I give for you: *thus* do in remembrance of Me. [20] And after they had supped, [17] He took the cup, and gave thanks over it, and said, Take this, share it among yourselves. [20] This is My blood, the new testament. [18] For I say unto you, that henceforth I will not drink of this fruit until the kingdom of God shall come. [21] But nevertheless behold, etc.

(2) xxiv. 3. After σῶμα the words τοῦ κυρίου Ἰησοῦ.
Evidence for the words:—
Almost all Greek MSS.
Most Versions.
Evidence against the words:—
D omits the whole, 42 omits κυρίου.
a b d e ff_2 l r omit the whole. Syr-Cur. Syr-Sin. Sah. omit κυρίου.

Nowhere else in the true text of the Gospels does ὁ κύριος Ἰησοῦς occur; but it may be right in the appendix to Mk. (xvi. 19).

In the remaining instances only the evidence *against* the passage need be stated.

(3) xxiv. 6. οὐκ ἔστιν ὧδε, ἀλλὰ ἠγέρθη.
D omits the whole. C* omits ἀλλά.
a b d e ff_2 l r* omit the whole. c substitutes *resurrexit a mortuis*, which perhaps is an independent insertion. Syr-Pesh. g_2 omit ἀλλά. Aeth. transposes, omitting ἀλλά: ἠγέρθη, οὐκ ἔστιν ὧδε, exactly as Mk. xvi. 6, which is the probable source of the insertion: comp. Mt. xxviii. 6.
Marcion *apud* Epiph. seems to have omitted all but ἠγέρθη.

(4) xxiv. 9. ἀπὸ τοῦ μνημείου.
D omits.
a b c d e ff_2 l r omit.

(5) xxiv. 12. Ὁ δὲ Πέτρος . . . γεγονός.
D omits.
a b d e l r omit. Syr-Harcl.* omits at the beginning of one lection, but perhaps accidentally.

(6) xxiv. 36. καὶ λέγει αὐτοῖς, Εἰρήνη ὑμῖν.
D omits.
a b d e ff_2 l r omit.
G P 88 127 130 after ὑμῖν add from Jn. vi. 20 ἐγώ εἰμι, μὴ φοβεῖσθε.
c f Vulg. Syrr. (Pesch. Harcl. Hier.) Arm. and some MSS. of Boh. after *vobis* add *ego sum nolite timere*. Aeth. adds *nolite timere, ego sum*.

Probably from Jn. xx. 19. Tisch. and Weiss omit. WH. place in double brackets.

(7) xxiv. 40. καὶ τοῦτο εἰπὼν . . . καὶ τοὺς πόδας.
D omits.

a b d e ff_2 l r Syr-Cur. omit. Syr-Sin. is here defective, but apparently contained the verse.

Probably an adaptation of Jn. xx. 20. Tisch. and Weiss omit. WH. place in double brackets.

(8) xxiv. 51. *καὶ ἀνεφέρετο εἰς τὸν οὐρανόν.*

ℵ* D omit.

a b d e ff_2 l* omit. Syr-Sin. condenses, omitting *διέστη* and *εἰς τὸν οὐρανόν*: "He was lifted up from them." Syr-Pesh. is defective.

Aug. omits once and inserts once.

Tisch. and Weiss omit. WH. place in double brackets.

(9) xxiv. 52. *προσκυνήσαντες αὐτόν.*

D omits the whole.

a b d e ff_2 l Syr-Sin. omit the whole.

Aug. omits the whole.

c Vulg. omit *eum*.

Tisch. and Weiss omit: WH. place in double brackets.

It will be observed that throughout these instances the adverse witnesses are very much the same. The combination D, a d e l prevails throughout; and in almost all cases these are supported by b and ff_2, and very often by r also. In xxii. 62, which was mentioned as a secondary instance of possible non-interpolation, D deserts its usual allies. The verse is found in all Greek MSS. and in all Versions, excepting a b e ff_2 i l* r.

Interpolations in the Sinaitic Syriac.

Some of these have been pointed out in the notes; *e.g.* pp. 53, 449, 468, 507, 540, 543, 556. But there are others which are of interest; and in some cases they are peculiar to this MS.

i. 3. to write of them *one by one carefully* unto thee.
6. blameless in *all their manner of life*.
12. was troubled *and shook*.
13. for *behold, God* has heard *the voice of* thy prayer.
49. name is *glorious and* holy.
64. *the string of* his tongue was loosened.

ii. 10. as they told them about *what they had seen and heard, wondered and* were astonished.
20. glorifying God, *and talking about* the things.
22. according *as it is written* in the law of Moses.
37. *the rest of her life* she was in widowhood.
39. Now *Joseph and Mary*, when they had fulfilled *in the temple on the first-born* all that is *written* in the law.
41. at the feast *of unleavened bread* of the passover.
44. supposed that He *had gone out* with their company . . . sought for *Jesus* among *the men of* their company.

iii. 4. make straight *in the plain* a path *for our God*.
6. the glory of the Lord *shall be revealed*, and all flesh shall see it *together*.

iv. 1. the *Holy* Spirit led Him *and took Him out* to the wilderness, *that He might be* tempted of Satan, *and He was there* forty days. And after *forty days that He had fasted*, He hungered.
6. *All these kingdoms* and their glory which are committed to me will I give Thee, all this power *and glory, because that to me He gave it.*
23. done in Capernaum, *ye will say to Me*, do also here.

v. 3. Jesus went up *and sat down in it*, and said, Take it from the *dry* land a little way *on the water*.
7. They were *nearly* sinking *from the weight of them*.
vi. 40. There is no disciple who is perfect as his master *in teaching*.
45. from the evil treasure *that is in his heart* (A C).
48. *when* the rivers *were full*, they beat upon that house.
vii. 15. that dead man *was raised and* sat up.
viii. 10. but to those without *it is not given to them to know*.
13. receive it *hastily* with joy (Cur.).
29. brake his bonds, *and cut them*, and was led.
44. *the fountain* of her issue of blood was stanched.
ix. 6. when *His apostles* had gone out they went about among the villages *and the cities*.
36. *in the sight of men* they told nothing.
40. they were not able *to deliver him* (comp. Cur.).
48. he that is small *and is a child to* you (comp. Cur.).
61. to them of my house, *and I will come* (Cur.).
x. 25. *while He said these things*, a certain (Cur. Lat. Vet.).
xi. 1. after He had ceased *from prayer* (Cur.).
29. no sign *from heaven* shall be given unto them, but the sign of Jona *the prophet* (A C, etc.).
36. thy body, *when there is in it no light that shines, is dark*.
53. And *as He said these things* (A) *against them in the sight of all the people* (D, Cur.).
xii. 7. the very hairs *of the hair* of your head are numbered (xxi. 18).
56. this time *and its signs* ye do not desire to prove (Cur.).
xiii. 13. immediately *her stature* was made straight.
23. a certain *man came, asking Him*, and said.
xiv. 1. they watched *what He would do* (Cur.).
13. call the poor, and the blind, and the lame, and the afflicted (order), *and the outcasts, and many others*.
21. *and the outcasts* (order changed).
22. yet there is room *at the feast* (Cur.).
xv. 13. because he was living wastefully *with harlots* (Cur.).
xvi. 23. And *being cast into* Sheol, he lifted up (Harcl.).
xviii. 24. when Jesus saw *that he was sorrowful*, He said (A D, Cur.).
32. spit *in His face*, and shall scourge Him (Cur.).
36. when he heard *the voice of* the multitude (Cur.).
xix. 39. *Good* Teacher, rebuke Thy disciples, *that they shout not* (Cur.).
xx. 9. planted a vineyard, *and surrounded it with a hedge*.
16. when they heard *these things, they knew certainly that He spake this parable about them* (from *v.* 19).
23. *Why tempt ye Me?* Show Me a penny (A C D, Cur., etc.).
24. And *they shewed it to Him*, saying, Cæsar's (C L, etc.).
29. There were seven brethren *amongst us* (D, Aeth.).
30. the second *took the woman, and he also died childless*.
34. The children of this world *beget and go on begetting, and* marry and are given in marriage (comp. D, Cur. Lat. Vet.).
37. Moses shewed, *when God spake with him from* the bush.
41. How say *the scribes concerning* the Christ (Cur.).
xxi. 11. great earthquakes *in divers places*, and pestilences in divers places, and famines.
18. one hair *of the hair* of your head (xii. 7).
25. distress upon the earth, and *weakness of the hands* of the nations (comp. Cur.).
30. shoot forth *and yield their fruit* (comp. D, Lat. Ver.).
34. by the eating *of flesh* and with the drunkenness *of wine*.

xxii. 58. *Let alone*, man, I know Him not.
68. answer, *nor even let Me go* (A D, Cur., etc.).
xxiii. 15. *nothing that is worthy of death did he find against Him*, nor has anything worthy of death been done by Him.
20. again Pilate called them, *and said unto them*, because he was willing to release Jesus, *Whom will ye that I release unto you?*
23. their voice prevailed, *and the chief priests were with them.*
37. Saying, *Hail to Thee!* If Thou be the King of the Jews, save Thyself. *And they placed also on His head a crown of thorns* (D, Cur.).
52. This man, *who had not consented to the accusers.*
xxiv. 5. bowed their heads *and looked* on the ground *for their fear. These men* said unto them (Cur.).
10. Mary the *daughter* of James.
19. *in power and* in deed and in word.
22. went to the sepulchre, *where He had been laid* (Cur.).
23. We have seen angels *there, and we were amazed*, and they said *about Him* that He was alive (Cur.).
33. *And He hath appeared.*

INDEX TO THE NOTES.

INDEX I. GENERAL.

INDEX II. WRITERS AND WRITINGS.

Quotations from Greek and Latin authors in illustration of Grammar and Diction are not included in this Index.[1]

[1] In the majority of cases the references given in this Index are to actual quotations. But, as one of its purposes is to supplement the list of commentaries given in the Introduction (pp. lxxx-lxxxv), by mention of other writers and writings which have been found helpful, bare references without quotation are often included.

INDEX III. GREEK WORDS.

INDEX IV. ENGLISH AND LATIN WORDS.